HOTOL: Britain's Spaceplane

HOTOL

Britain's Spaceplane

Dan Sharp

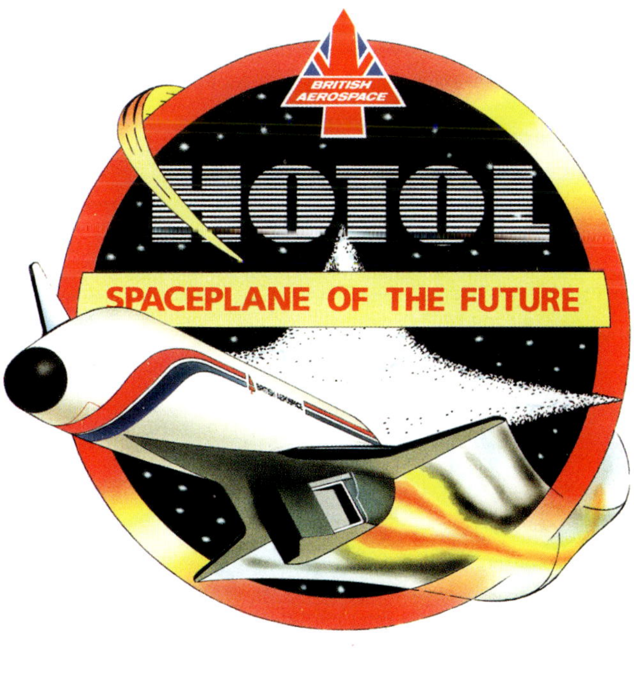

TEMPEST BOOKS

Published in Great Britain by Tempest Books
an imprint of Mortons Books Ltd.
Media Centre
Morton Way
Horncastle LN9 6JR
www.mortonsbooks.co.uk

ISBN 978-1-911704-29-4

Typeset by Jayne Clements (jayne@hinoki.co.uk), Hinoki Design and Typesetting

Original cover artwork by Piotr Forkasiewicz

Acknowledgements
My sincerest thanks to Joe Anselmo, David Baker, Richard Baker, Martin Bayer, Steve Blee, Alan Bond, JC Carbonel, Mark Daly, Calum Douglas, Andrew Fetherston, Ian Fisher, Steve Furniss, Mark Hempsell, Chris Hunter, Ian Lawrenson, Roger Longstaff, Scott Lowther, Andrew McDowell, Steve McDowell, Beth Neilson, Steve O'Hara, Grigory Omelchenko, Bob Parkinson, Chris Sandham-Bailey, Allan Seabridge, George Seyfang, Bill Sweetman, Alison Wake, Eric Webb, Gerald Wilson and Tony Wilson.

Hotol versus HOTOL
When the acronym was first applied to the system, Hotol was always written in all-caps as HOTOL. Indeed, the Hotol team were told to write it that way. However, it is evident that over time, in memos, letters and even in newspaper and magazine articles, the acronym gradually transitioned into an anacronym—a word in its own right. A similar process befell, for example, radar, which was originally an acronym standing for 'RAdio Detection And Ranging' but which has long since lost its caps. Around the time of Interim Hotol, the acronym came to be styled as HoToL. In choosing the style for this book, it was decided that simply 'Hotol', as it was commonly appearing towards the end of its existence as an ongoing project, would suffice.

About the author
Dan Sharp is a journalist, editor and researcher. His many previous works include British Secret Projects 5: Britain's Space Shuttle and Messerschmitt Me 262 Development & Politics. He lives in Nottinghamshire.

A note on sources
All sources are cited within the book text, rather than appearing separately with archival references—since the majority of sources used are not publicly accessible.

For Alan Bond and Gerald Wilson

CONTENTS

PREFACE

HOTOL WAS a British project to create a winged space vehicle able to take off from an ordinary runway, fly up into space, deliver a payload to orbit, then fly back down and land on an ordinary runway.

This operation depended on the use of a propulsion system which was airbreathing during the ascent through the Earth's atmosphere, before switching to onboard fuels for the second leg of the trip, through the airless upper atmosphere and into space.

The concept was devised in 1982 by Alan Bond, Dr Bob Parkinson and John Scott-Scott, with the airframe development being carried out by British Aerospace and the engine development being done by Rolls-Royce. These companies' involvement began in 1983 and continued into 1989, with British Aerospace then continuing to work on an air-launched all-rocket version from mid-1989 to 1993.

The aim of this book is to provide a detailed and accurate account of what happened during the course of the project and when—to tell Hotol's story from beginning to end.

The evolution of the vehicle and propulsion system through various iterations is described (such that I hope the reader will be able to tell one Hotol configuration from another), and the decisions made about the project's future and funding, both within the two companies and on the broader national and international stages, are noted.

Clearly, the Hotol project ended without the vehicle being built and an effort has been made, in the writing of this book, to avoid passing judgement on the decisions made by those involved in the Hotol story. It seems, where Hotol is concerned, that everyone familiar with the project has their own views on it one way or another.

Would the Hotol project have resulted in a viable vehicle if fully funded and given the development time asked for by the aerospace companies? It cannot be said for certain that it would. Neither can it be said with any certainty that it would not. Did the American National Aero-Space Plane (NASP) project, with vastly higher levels of funding, result in a viable vehicle? It seems that it did not.

Were the decisions made by company executives and directors with regard to the Hotol project correct? Were the decisions made by the politicians within whose remit the project fell correct? Some readers, I am sure, already have their own answers to these questions. Other readers are, I hope, provided with sufficient information and context to formulate their own views.

As to my own thoughts on Hotol, having been born towards the end of the 1970s and growing up during the 1980s, Hotol seemed very futuristic and spectacular but I had no idea at that time whether what I was reading about in various magazines would result in something that actually flew. Depictions of the vehicle were highly inconsistent—it was difficult to know at any given time what Hotol was even intended to look like—and there simply wasn't enough information available anywhere to form an opinion.

This book is primarily intended to supply that deficiency and at last offer a comprehensive account of the Hotol project.

***

Work on writing and researching Hotol: Britain's Spaceplane commenced in 2018, not long after the publication of my book on the British Aircraft Corporation's Mustard project (British Secret Projects 5: Britain's Space Shuttle, the initial part of that title being an addition of the publisher). I contacted Reaction Engines to see whether it was possible to get any information about Hotol and was put in touch with company founder Alan Bond. I told him that I wanted to write a book on Hotol—the first book on Hotol—and he invited me down to Culham to spend two days going through his personal archive with him. During the course of those two days, over seemingly endless cups of coffee, I was able to ask many questions about the project and Alan was very open in answering every one of them.

The next step was to contact Gerald Wilson, who had previously helped me with the Mustard book, and who I knew had been deputy technical manager of the Hotol project. Gerald too was very generous with his time and offered every assistance during the several days I spent up at Warton, photographing hundreds of documents from the BAE Systems archive.

Between my visits to Culham and Warton I photographed so many documents, in fact, that I ended up setting myself a truly daunting task in working out how I was going to arrange them all in such a way that they could become the basis for my book. Then the Covid pandemic hit in 2020 and other work, as well as personal circumstances, prevented me from following through on my Hotol project.

Nevertheless, I continued to work on transcribing my notes, ordering, reordering and reading through the documents I had photographed, gathering images from numerous sources and speaking to people who had been involved in the Hotol project. Finally, in early 2024, after discussing the book project again with Gerald, I realised that not only did I have sufficient material to complete the book in the form that I wanted—but I also now had, finally, a way of arranging the narrative that made sense and made it possible to actually write a viable manuscript.

I got back in touch with Alan, contacted Dr Bob Parkinson and Mark Hempsell, and set to work on writing the volume you now have in front of you. Both Gerald and Mark kindly reviewed the manuscript along the way and provided invaluable feedback and comments. So too did Steve Furniss, Eric Webb and Alison Wake—further enhancing the text with additional information.

During the course of my Hotol odyssey I corresponded with many people, both those who had been involved in the Hotol project and those who kindly provided assistance in other forms, and I am extremely grateful for the help and support of all concerned.

Preparing this book has been a longer journey than I had anticipated but also a richer and more fulfilling experience than I had expected too. I hope that you enjoy reading this book as much as I have enjoyed writing it.

Dan Sharp
November 2024

INTRODUCTION
HOrizontal Take Off and Landing

When ITN science correspondent Frank Miles revealed the existence of British Aerospace's (BAe's) formerly top-secret spaceplane project—Hotol—during the News at Ten on Thursday, August 23, 1984, it kindled a newfound sense of hope in some that Britain would finally take its rightful place at the leading edge of space science.

Others, particularly the international spaceflight community, were stunned. How could the British, who had seemingly been content to sit back and let others gain the upper hand when it came to launchers, have suddenly come up with a viable reusable single-stage satellite delivery system capable of operating from standard runways?

The chairman of Rolls-Royce, Sir Francis Tombs, was equally surprised, having not been told that his company was bankrolling early propulsion studies for it, and his project engineers had some explaining to do.

The British Aerospace Dynamics Group issued a press release on Friday, August 24, 1984, to hurriedly explain the Hotol concept in a little more detail than Miles had been able to manage using information, scant as it was, that he should not have had access to.

Under the headline 'HOTOL—A Horizontal Take-Off and Land [sic] Satellite Launcher Concept', it said: "British Aerospace is studying a new concept for the launch of payloads up to seven tonnes in mass into low earth orbit (LEO). The concept envisaged, called HOTOL, is an aircraft type vehicle, taking off and landing horizontally, using standard runways of Concorde length. The vehicle would achieve LEO using a combination of airbreathing and rocket engine propulsion. Rolls-Royce is contributing to the propulsion studies.

"The advent of the US Space Shuttle as a vehicle for launching satellites represents a change in launch vehicle concepts which are still evolving. The key features of Shuttle are reliability and reusability. However, the Orbiter design has been compromised by a need to turn it into a miniature space station that can remain in orbit for lengthy periods, and it needs a throwaway fuel tank plus boosters to augment the thrust of its own engines. As a result, expendable launch vehicles such as Ariane compete successfully against Shuttle, particularly for geosynchronous orbit applications.

"Ideally, a reusable launch vehicle should have no expendable parts and should be capable of repeated operations with a minimum turnaround, with minimum interfaces with its cargo. It should be designed to accommodate

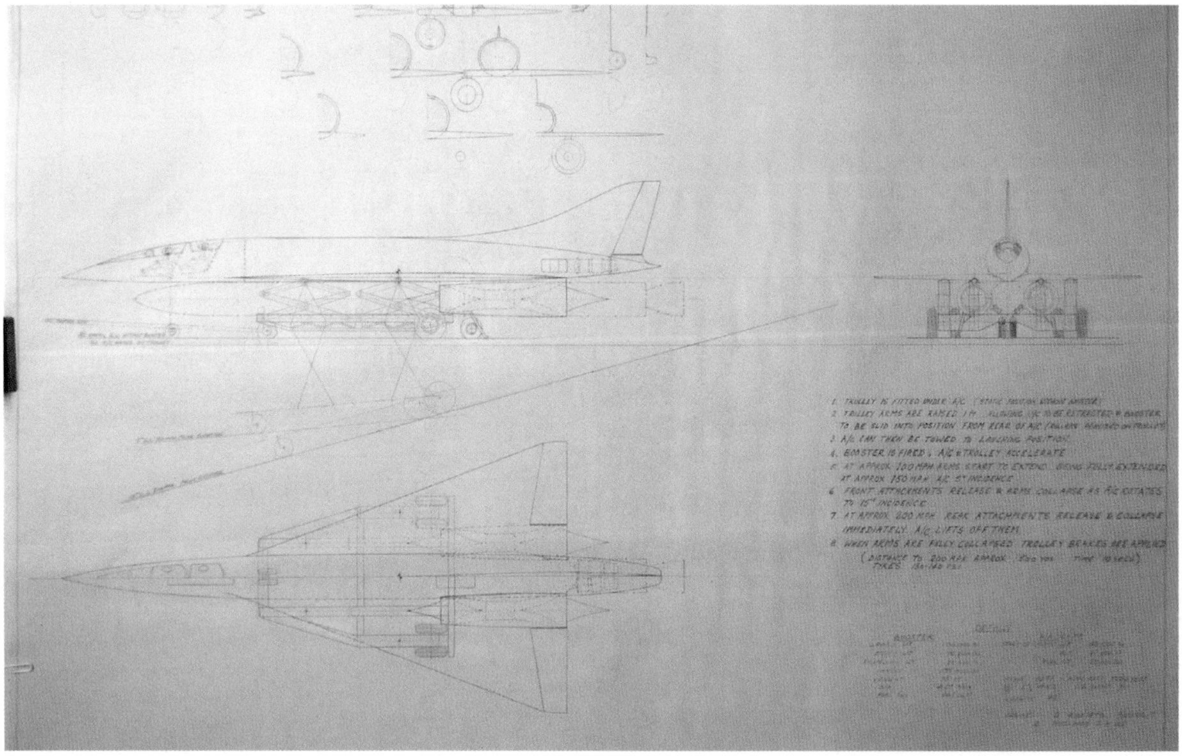

English Electric P.42 Scheme 7/1—a heavy hypersonic aircraft with a lightweight undercarriage, and massive booster rocket, designed to launch from a normal runway using a take-off trolley.

a typical single satellite cargo in the mass range of four to seven tonnes (or a pair of spacecraft of this total mass) to LEO, and it need not be manned. Automatic and remote piloting control systems are already capable of handling ascent, in-orbit manoeuvring, payload deployment, re-entry and landing.

"A vertical take-off version of such a vehicle will always suffer from the unfortunate fact that the Earth's gravitational field is about 10% too high to make a single-stage-to-orbit (SSTO) rocket practical, even with the highest performance fuels that can be expected in the foreseeable future. This means that vertical take-off will always need a two-stage lift, and many proposals exist for such systems, including fly-back boosters.

"In a liquid hydrogen/liquid oxygen rocket (the highest performance available today) 85% of the propellant mass is oxygen, which has to be lifted by the launcher to feed its engines. But the launcher is flying through a sea of free oxygen, and if airbreathing propulsion could be combined with rocket propulsion in the early phase of flight to gain that 10% advantage, a single stage to orbit could be achieved. Further, with such a system, vertical take-off would not be necessary.

"There is a trade-off between the mass of combined propulsion systems and the mass of wings to give lift, and the trade-off favours wings. It would then become feasible to design a launcher for which there is no payload mass penalty to be paid for the lower thrust/mass performance of combined air breathing and rocket propulsion. All that is needed is extra concrete to extend the length of the runway.

"HOTOL is a vehicle concept which is now under examination. It is envisaged that it could carry payloads of up to seven tonnes, within a cargo bay envelope of 9m x 4.5m diameter, in single stage burn to LEO."

The release then cited the development of the Blue Streak, Skylark and Black Knight rockets during the 1950s and 1960s as evidence of British Aerospace's experience with launch vehicles over the preceding two decades. In fact, BAe also had some experience of designing spaceplanes—just not actually building them. Back in 1963, the Ministry of Aviation had issued six-month research contracts to Hawker Siddeley Aviation and the British Aircraft Corporation to study hypersonic vehicles as recoverable launchers, boost glide vehicles, long-range high-speed cruise aircraft and spaceplanes.

The English Electric Aviation team at Warton, near Preston, in Lancashire were then chosen to fulfil BAC's contract and the project received the designation P.42. It would be carried out under the supervision of engineering director Ray Creasey and the head of the Advanced Projects department Tom Smith, with designer Gerald David 'Dave' Walley (pronounced war-lee) responsible for most of the necessary drawings.

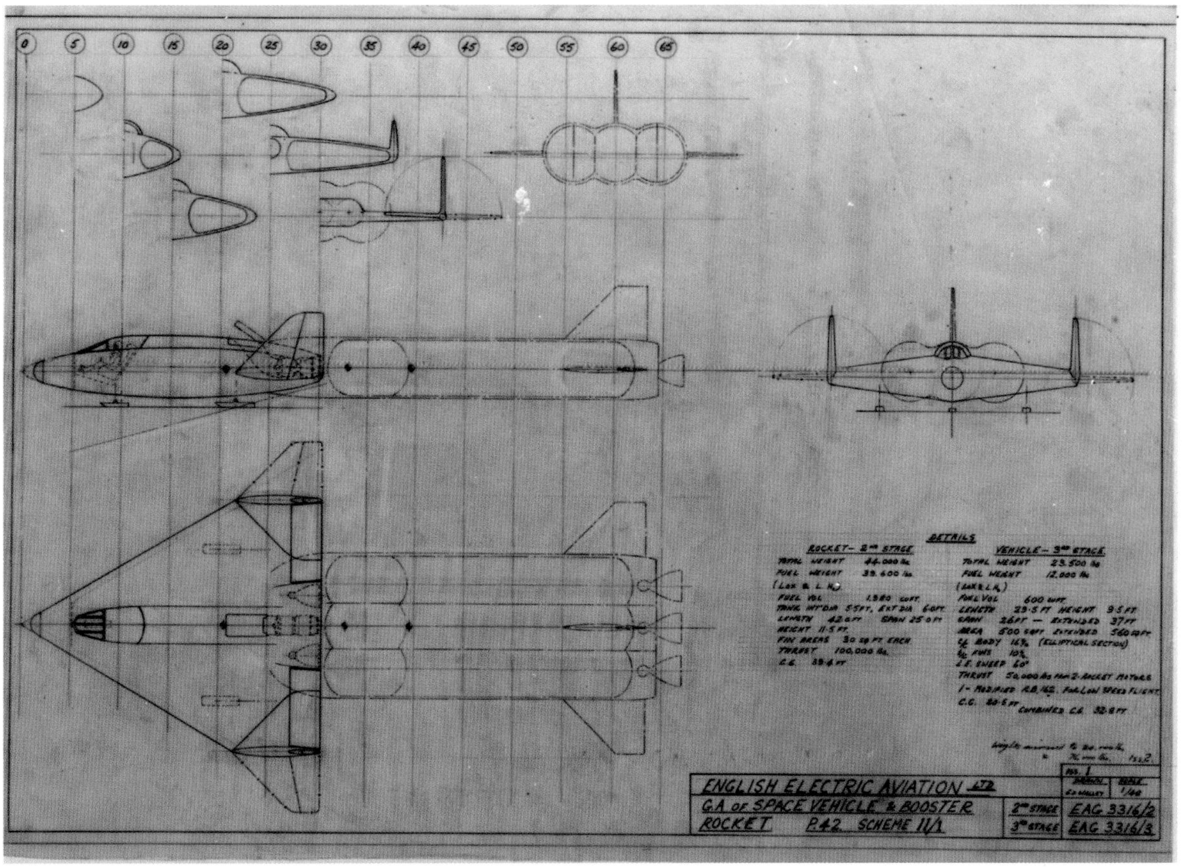

English Electric Aviation's earliest known orbiter, P. 42 Scheme 11/1.

LAUNCHERS AND SPACEPLANES

Early P.42 designs were for hypersonic research aircraft which would utilise unusual configurations and advanced turbojet and ramjet engines to reach speeds above Mach 5. Then came a series of fighter-like designs intended for use as high-altitude, high-speed launch platforms for small satellite-carrying rockets. These were quickly followed by designs for two-stage-to-orbit (TSTO) systems: large hypersonic carrier aircraft which would act as first-stage boosters for rocket-propelled, piloted, orbiter-type vehicles.

All told, more than 50 different layouts for hypersonic airbreathing aircraft were designed. This work had included particularly careful study of undercarriage requirements, since most of these aircraft were likely to be extremely heavy and would require correspondingly large landing gear as a result. Aircraft skin temperatures were also given close attention—leading to consideration of what structural materials might be used to absorb or reflect extreme heat.

With these particular difficulties in mind, English Electric also looked at the options for supersonic, as opposed to hypersonic launchers—whereby the upper stage would only be carried to speeds and altitudes which could be reached within the limits of existing technology prior to launch. It was thought that such a vehicle could even, theoretically, be created from an existing aircraft design such as an Avro Vulcan or Vickers VC10, but it was quickly found that the extensive modifications necessary would make this concept unworkable.

In parallel to these efforts, English Electric had come up with a smaller series of designs for spaceplanes. At this point, 1963, while the Americans and Soviets had successfully put manned capsules into space, winged, manoeuvrable, reusable space vehicles did not exist. The English Electric team had therefore applied what data was available on re-entry conditions as well as their knowledge of rocket engines and the aerodynamics of high-speed flight to formulate their designs.

The first English Electric orbiter, designated P.42 Scheme 11/1, was designed by Walley. This was a single-seater with an almost triangular shape and wingtips on either side that could be flipped up 90° to form fins for re-entry. It was to be a third stage, launched from the back of a first-stage hypersonic carrier aircraft with an expendable second-stage rocket booster at its rear to propel it into orbit.

More designs followed, with the orbiter being reimagined as a lifting body vehicle with options to mount it atop or beside a booster rocket for a vertical take-off—cutting out the hypersonic launcher stage. This

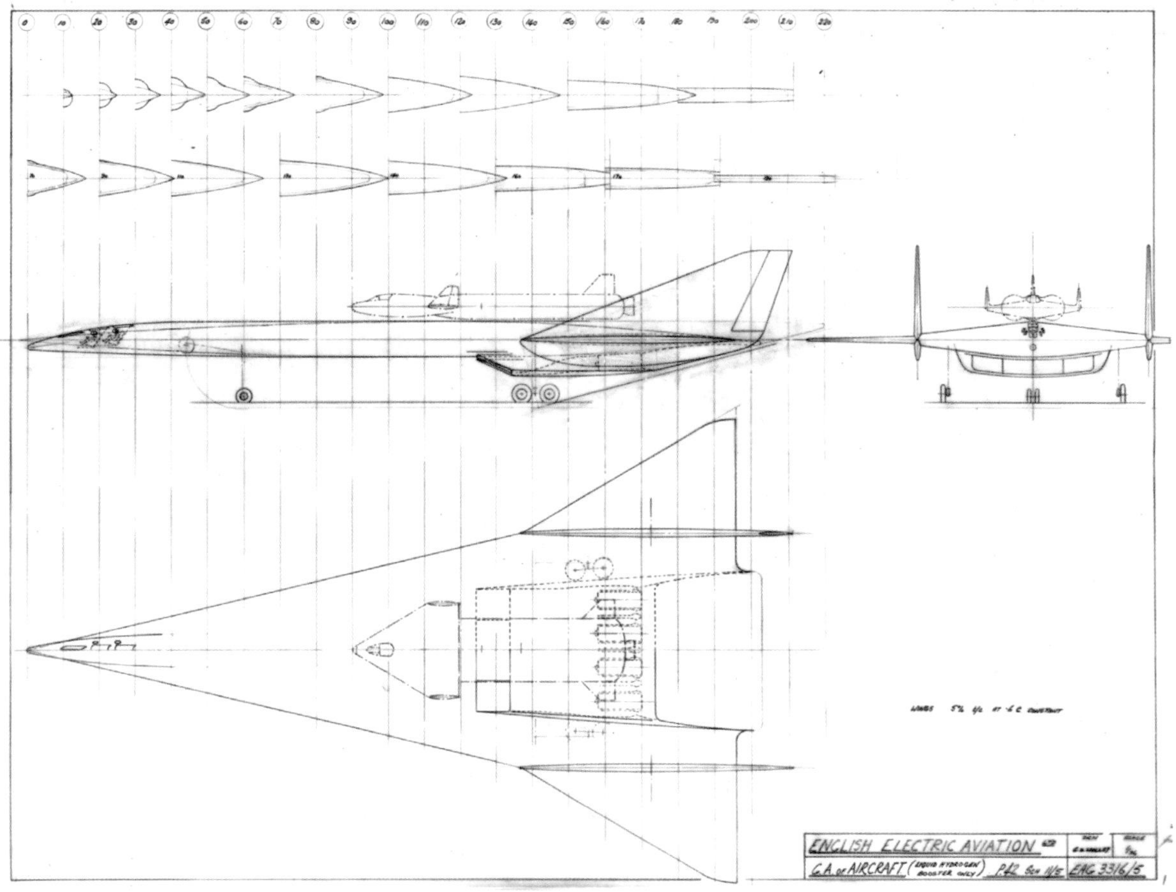

P.42 Scheme 11/5 was a hypersonic airbreathing booster aircraft, from the back of which the orbiter (with expendable rocket stage) could be launched into space.

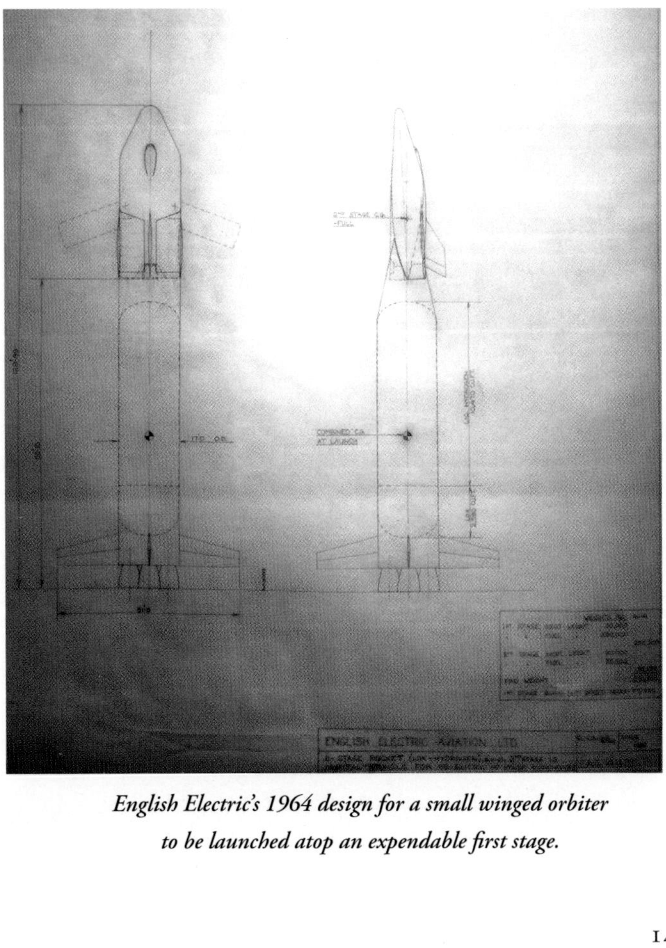

English Electric's 1964 design for a small winged orbiter to be launched atop an expendable first stage.

had the disadvantage of introducing a large and costly expendable component to the launch system, since the booster would not be reusable. Consequently, thoughts turned to the possibility of a winged and piloted booster which could return to earth and land once its mission of launching the upper stage or stages had been successfully completed.

Again, several such winged 'recoverable' booster rockets were designed and the study contract was then extended by nine months, up to September 1964. English Electric's Warton site, in the meantime, became fully absorbed into the British Aircraft Corporation as its Preston Division.

BAC MUSTARD

Before commencing the next phase of their study, the team undertook a review of the many launch systems being proposed by US aircraft companies at this time. Amid the bewildering variety of possible vehicle shapes, stages, engines and configurations, one particular design stood out: Douglas Astro.

This consisted of two similarly designed reusable lifting body vehicles—a large piloted rocket booster and a smaller piloted orbiter—positioned in tandem, with the latter

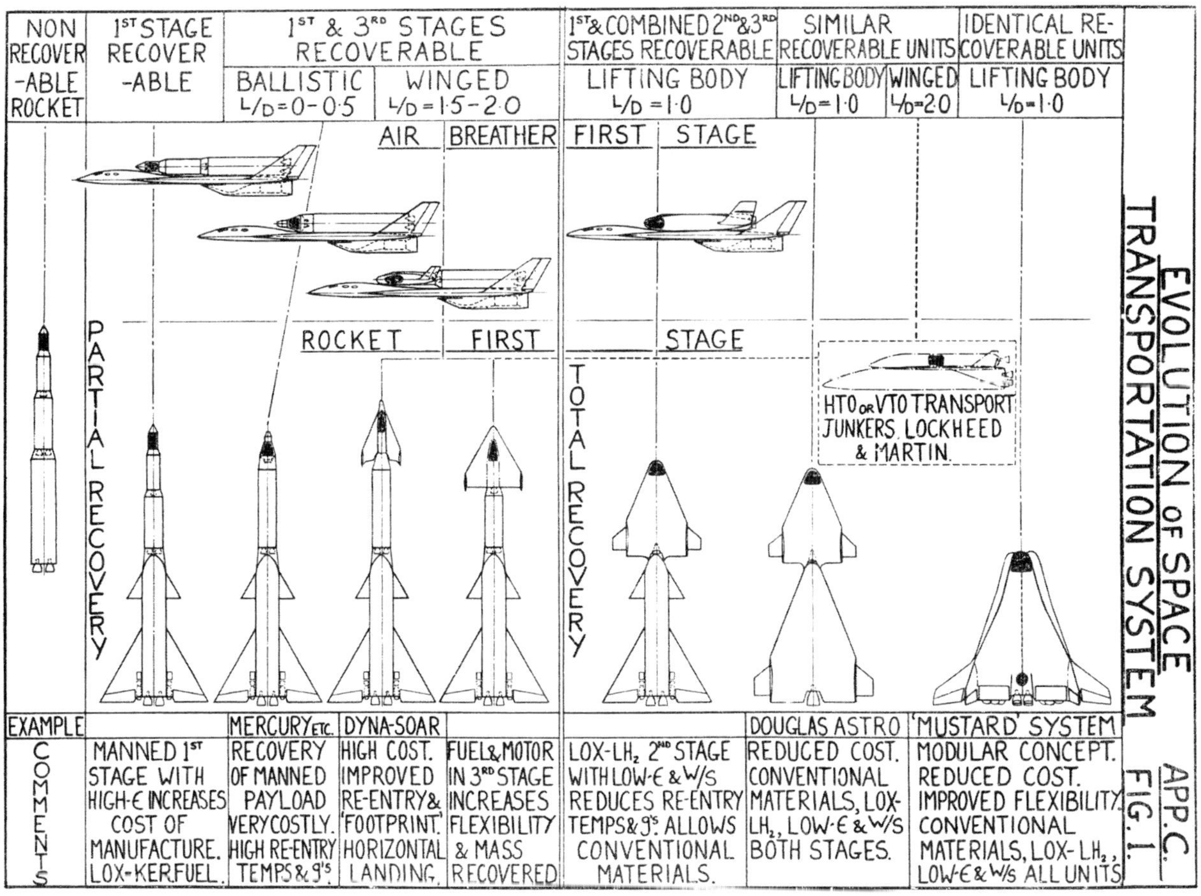

Launcher configurations studied by the BAC team at Warton—ranging from air-launched orbiters to tandem vertical launch systems and finally to the modular 'Mustard' concept.

atop the former for a vertical launch.

The Douglas concept made extensive use of existing technology and had been thoroughly and realistically costed, which appealed to the BAC team. What's more, part of the proposed Astro test programme involved creating an interim booster using the same airframe as the orbiter.

Basing both booster and orbiter on the same airframe was surely the ultimate economy measure. What if, the Warton team reasoned, the entire multi-vehicle system could be based on a single airframe design? It would be much cheaper if that same basic airframe could be fitted out as either a booster or an orbiter as required. One booster the same size as the spacecraft wouldn't be enough, but two or more would do the job. And positioning these vehicles side-by-side rather than one atop the other would reduce the loads placed on them during launch, which had been a concern for Astro.

It was a train of thought that resulted in a unique concept: the Multi-Unit Space Transport And Recovery Device or 'Mustard' of early 1964. The idea was to have the externally identical orbiter and boosters lifting off together, next to one another. The boosters would get the orbiter up to the edge of space before separating from it, their fuel expended, and flying back to base either as gliders or using built-in turbojets.

This promising system was studied in detail up to June 1964, with the BAC team convinced that they had hit upon a concept that was superior to any expendable launcher or, indeed, any other reusable launch system. At the end of September 1964, the 'hypersonics' contract was extended for a second time—up to March 31, 1965.

Engineering work focused on Mustard continued, with the airframe evolving through a variety of different configurations. Attention was paid to the engine, undercarriage, outer skin and fuel tank layout with a view to ensuring that the system was both practical and relatively affordable as well as being capable of carrying sufficient payload to make the effort worthwhile.

While the main intended purpose of Mustard was to launch satellites, limited study time was also given to other potential roles such as orbital reconnaissance, satellite inspection and satellite maintenance. It was even thought that the Mustard orbiter might be usable as a means of disabling 'hostile' enemy satellites.

When the third 'hypersonics' contract ended, the

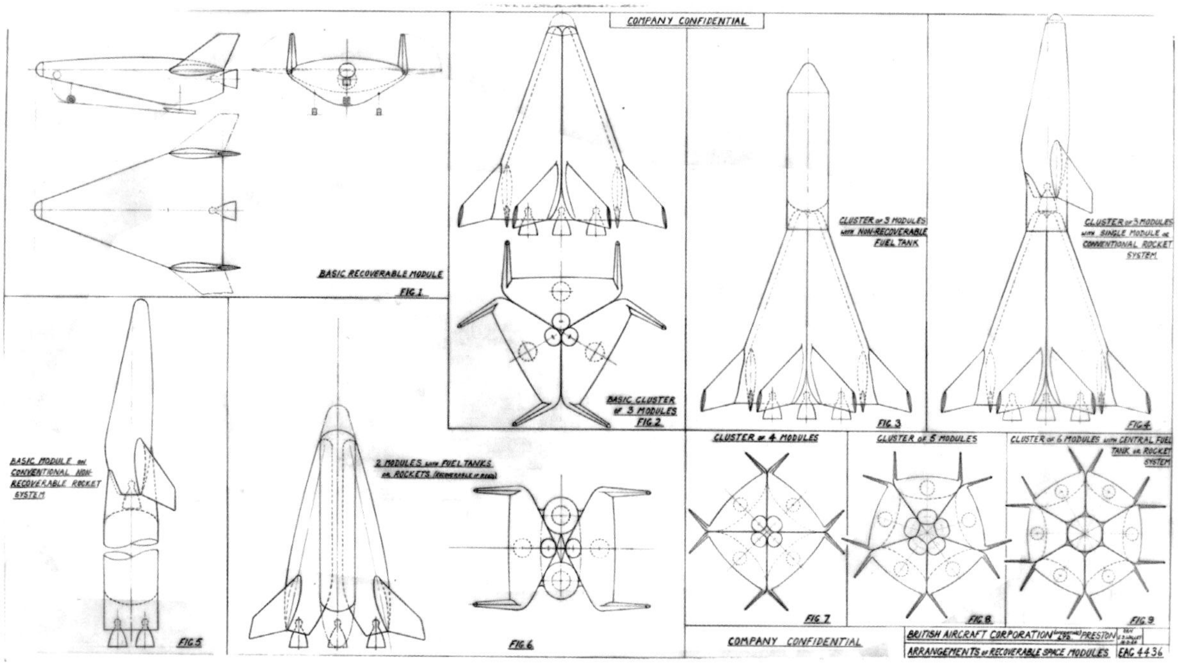

A wide variety of different potential arrangements were examined for Mustard's 'basic recoverable module'.

government money that had been financing the Mustard project ran out. However, BAC was aware that other European countries were studying their own launcher concepts—with a particular emphasis on the horizontal take-off TSTO designs that BAC had already dismissed—and therefore continued the project with its own money for several months.

The British government had required BAC to keep quiet about Mustard up to this point but the gagging order had been rescinded by March 2, 1966, when the project was finally revealed to the public by Robin Inskip, BAC's deputy managing director, during a lecture to the Royal Aeronautical Society's Bristol branch. Further lectures and magazine articles followed along with some further engineering work, albeit at a low level, which continued into 1967 before eventually petering out.

SPACE SHUTTLE

Over in the USA, on October 30, 1968, the Manned Spacecraft Center and Marshall Space Flight Center issued a joint request for proposals that could form the basis of an eight-month study of an Integral Launch and Re-entry Vehicle System. A few months later, in early 1969, NASA formed a Space Shuttle Task Group to evaluate potential requirements and missions for an orbiter—what would become the Space Shuttle. Preliminary analysis study contracts were issued to Lockheed, General Dynamics, McDonnell Douglas and North American Rockwell a month later.

Towards the end of 1969, the European aircraft companies were invited to give presentations on their launcher concepts at a Space Shuttle Symposium at the Museum of Natural History of the Smithsonian Institution in Washington, DC on October 16-17. Creasey and Smith went along to represent BAC, giving a joint presentation on Mustard.

Six months later, in April 1970, Smith wrote a report for the British government entitled A British View: The Place of Reusable Launch Vehicles in Western Europe's Future Space Posture, which assessed the options available for further space research and continued to press the case for a reusable launch system, though without mentioning any particular example.

Then, during mid to late 1970, the American administration asked the British government whether it would like to be involved in the NASA Post-Apollo Program—the Space Shuttle—for a price. The British government took this to both BAC and Hawker Siddeley and together the firms agreed to match-fund a government investment in joining Post-Apollo for a period of 12 months. The government paid 50% and the firms paid 25% each. New contracts were drawn up for the work and the Americans paired BAC up with Space Shuttle prime contractor North American Rockwell Corporation, while Hawker Siddeley was paired with McDonnell Douglas.

A team from BAC flew out to North American's Los Angeles facility in November 1970 and spent several weeks getting to know their American counterparts as well as getting up to speed with the Post-Apollo Program, which was in its Phase B period. At the same time, they were

The cover of BAC's final report on Space Shuttle work carried out in Britain up to the end of 1971.

encouraged to choose 'work packages'—the way in which work on the Shuttle was parcelled up so that different contractors could concentrate on different aspects of the build—that would be suitable for study in the UK.

The BAC effort was not directed by the firm's Warton offices however, but was under the direction of the Bristol Dynamics Group team. A final report on BAC's Space Shuttle work was published in January 1972 and noted that the British team had tackled successive work packages related to the orbiter's cargo bay doors, fin and avionics in that order. It was further pointed out that the work had been carried out in the full knowledge that the Shuttle configuration worked on was unlikely to be the one that ended up being built.

It was hoped that the British government would subsequently buy into the Shuttle programme but in the end the Americans themselves, specifically NASA, decided that working with non-US companies would make things too complicated and further offers of international involvement were withdrawn.

CHANGING FOCUS

The British Aerospace Dynamics Group press release of August 24, 1984, had mentioned three British rockets: Blue Streak, Skylark and Black Knight. It did not, however, mention Black Arrow—presumably because its manufacturers, Saunders-Roe and later Westland, had not been among the many precursors of BAe. Nevertheless, Black Arrow was a three-stage all-British launcher which had made four flights between 1969 and 1971. The last of these, on October 28, 1971, had successfully managed to get the British-made 102kg Prospero satellite into LEO.

Incredibly, the Black Arrow programme had by then already been cancelled by Ted Heath's Conservative government. The announcement came from the first Minister of State for Trade and Industry, Frederick Corfield, head of the newly formed Department of Trade and Industry (DTI) on July 29, 1971. This made the UK the only country in history to have successfully developed and then entirely abandoned its own satellite launch capability.

During the remainder of the 1970s, space activity across the UK as a whole shrank back from the heights it had attained during the previous decade. While the DTI had ministerial responsibility for space, the Science Research Council was responsible for administering the UK's space science programme and saw its funding dwindle significantly as the 70s wore on. By 1980 its spending on space science would be nearly two-thirds less than it had been in 1974. With hindsight this perhaps comes as no real surprise since the British economy had suffered through years of high inflation and economic turmoil by that point.

In 1975 the European Launcher Development Organisation (ELDO) and the European Space Research Organisation (ESRO) had merged to form the European Space Agency (ESA) with Britain as one of the ten founding member states alongside Belgium, Denmark, France, West Germany, Italy, the Netherlands, Spain, Sweden and Switzerland. As such, Britain became a junior partner in the primarily French-led Ariane launcher rocket programme.

BAC and Hawker Siddeley were merged and nationalised as of April 29, 1977, to form British Aerospace. The company's site in Stevenage, Hertfordshire, would increasingly focus on the design and manufacture of communications satellites—a field seen as a potential future money spinner for the company.

And so, while it was successfully designing and building satellites, Britain had no independent means by which to launch them. Mustard had promised to be cheap and reusable but its time had passed. Costly expendable launchers, particularly Ariane, were the only game in town and therefore came to dominate the landscape of space activity in Europe. Yet as the 1980s dawned, with Margaret Thatcher's Conservative government beginning to reshape British industry through a raft of tough reformist policies, there was a burgeoning sense of optimism within the British space science community. Perhaps, somehow, an alternative to Ariane was possible; perhaps the days of the cost-saving British-made launcher, far from being over, were just about to begin.

1

GENESIS: 1982 TO 1984

When the British Interplanetary Society's space technology committee organised a symposium on space transportation for June 11, 1980, aerospace engineers Alan Bond and Dr Bob Parkinson both made contributions.

Neither regarded expensive expendable rocket boosters and fuel tanks as an acceptable way forward and each considered a rocket-propelled multi-unit system, described in the minutes of the committee as "uprated versions of the Mustard concept", to be the most viable alternative. While the Mustard concept had ultimately settled upon a 'Triamese' cluster of three identical vehicles as the optimal approach, Parkinson was now considering a two-vehicle 'Siamese' variant.

Nearly two years later, on April 20, 1982, both men were among the attendees for another BIS-organised event in London on "space transportation systems for the 1990s and beyond".

Jean-Claude Bouillot of the French Centre National d'Études Spatiales (CNES) was giving a presentation on putting satellites and other payloads into space using the Ariane 5 heavy-lift space launch vehicle and the crewed Hermes spaceplane. Parkinson later recalled: "They showed pictures of the various concepts they had. The preferred concept was a core liquid stage with two big solids on either side and a little winged vehicle sitting on the top of it. And Alan and I looked at one another and said, we've seen this before—this is the Titan IV/Dyna-Soar that the Americans were doing in the 1950s that never came to fruition. And we're proposing to go into the 21st century by reinventing the 1950s. We said to one another, there ought to be a better way of doing it than that. This is not really the direction we ought to be going in."

The two men began to discuss the problem—and particularly the expense—of putting vehicles into LEO and within a short time had begun to conceptualise what a 'better way' might look like. Their thoughts coalesced around the notion of a single-stage vehicle that would reach space with the assistance of airbreathing engines rather than on pure rocket power alone.

According to Parkinson, a BIS Fellow who worked as a civil servant scientist with the Royal Armament Research and Development Establishment at Waltham Abbey: "Alan and I went our different ways and thought about slightly different things ... the ultimate ambition of the space launch vehicle was that you could build what we call a single stage to orbit reusable vehicle, that you could get a vehicle which didn't drop things into the Atlantic or wherever ... that would fly all the way up to orbit, get rid of its cargo and then return to Earth and be used again and again.

Aerospace engineer and Hotol vehicle inventor Dr Bob Parkinson.

Rocket scientist and Hotol propulsion system inventor Alan Bond. UKAEA

"My question that I was asking myself was, just how much assistance would you need to make that possible? Because it's at the bare edges of possibility and you wouldn't need an awful lot. I was kind of thinking about could you use jet engines or something to give you that extra bit of assistance to make it possible. Alan used to say that the world was about 10% too big, and if you could get that 10% advantage you could make it work. I did various sums and things which were a bit naïve at the time and thought [about it].

"Alan meanwhile had gone away in a different direction but was also thinking about the same problem. He started by thinking about rather exotic propellants that might be used but he also started thinking about engine cycles that you might use as well, that being more his line of territory.

"And in the late spring of 1982, he gave me a ring at Waltham Abbey, mainly because he'd been thinking about exotic propellants and he wanted to know my opinion about [them]. I knew that what he was proposing wasn't a very good idea, let's put it that way. While it looked attractive, anybody who'd done work on it had probably got cuts and bruises as a minimum from the results of it. But we talked on the phone and we talked about the other thing … about just how little you needed to do … and we

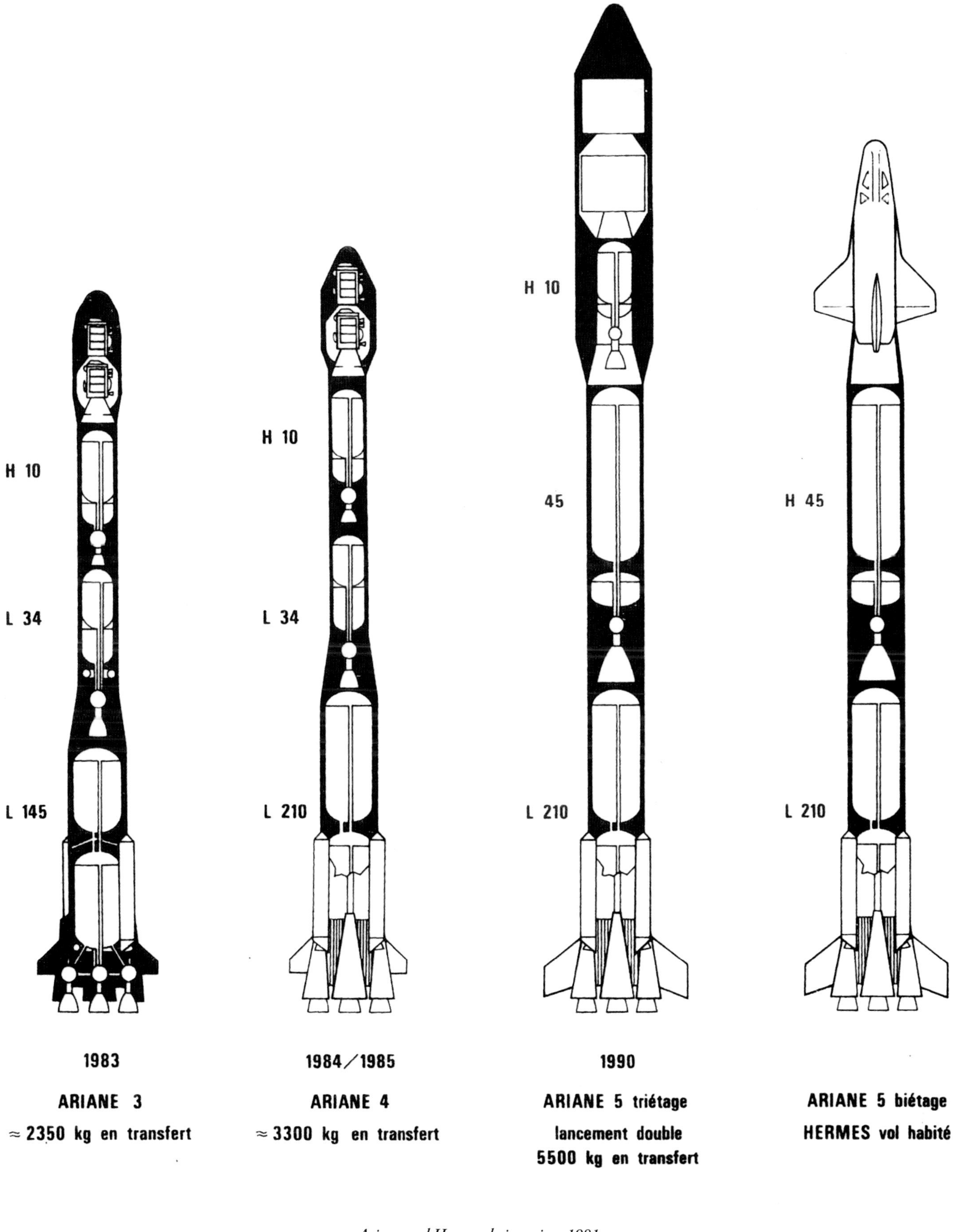

Ariane and Hermes designs circa 1981.

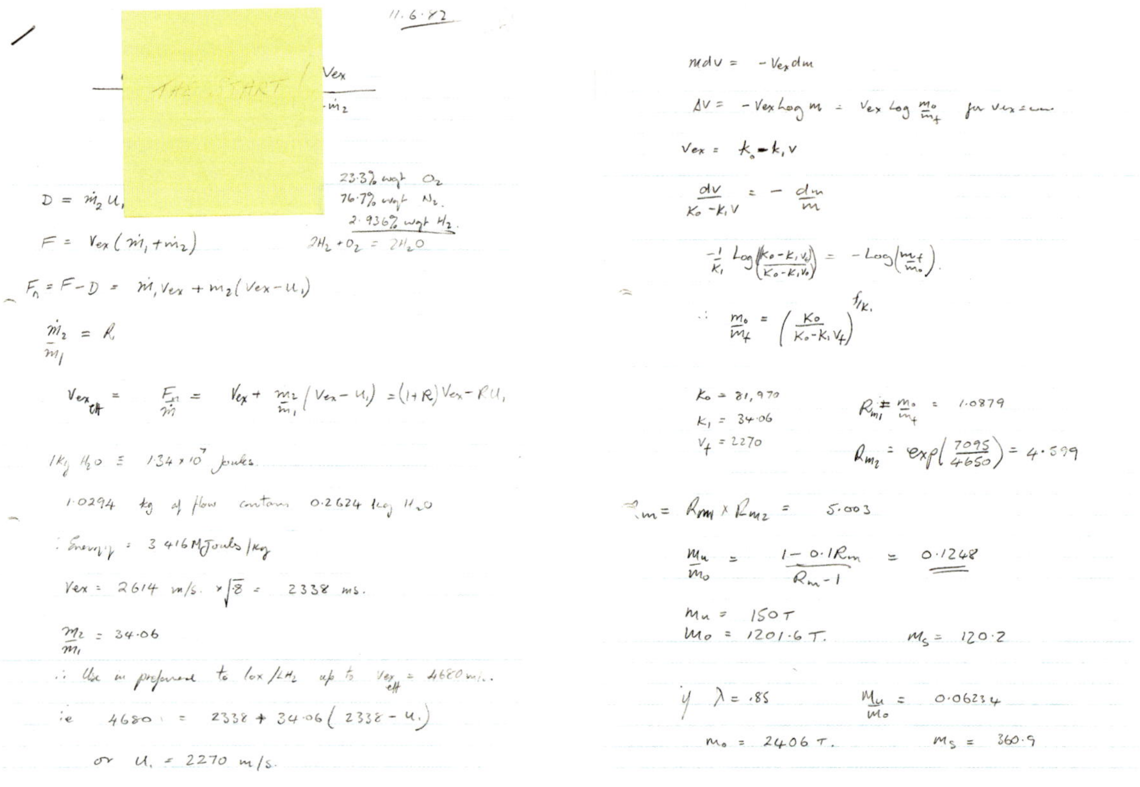

Bond's handwritten notes from June 11, 1982—the beginning of his work on a new propulsion system for spaceflight.

clearly were thinking along parallel lines."

Bond, who had worked under distinguished rocket engineer Val Cleaver at Rolls-Royce and had also worked for British Aerospace, put pencil to paper on June 11, 1982, and began making calculations for a new propulsion system that could use air from the Earth's atmosphere to help propel a reusable SSTO vehicle.

By September 16, he had produced a draft paper entitled A Combined Rocket and Air Cycle Engine for Single Stage to Orbit Launch Vehicles. This began: "It seems probable that during the mid-1990s Europe will be developing a launch vehicle to replace Ariane. The economics of satellite launching suggest that for the traffic expected for 1990-2010 a fully reusable single stage to orbit vehicle is desirable, if not essential."

He outlined the difficulties of designing a viable SSTO vehicle based purely on the use of rocket power—particularly the necessity of filling most of it with liquid hydrogen and liquid oxygen. To get a 15-tonne payload into orbit for example, a 31-tonne vehicle would be needed, carrying 45 tonnes of liquid hydrogen and 270 tonnes of liquid oxygen for a total launch mass of 361 tonnes.

He went on: "In order to improve on this performance using chemical propellants it is necessary to use in some manner the external atmosphere for the lower portions of the ascent trajectory. In general such schemes whilst attractive from the aesthetic point of view suffer from either severe performance limitations at high Mach numbers (for example if using conventional turbojets) or prohibitive development costs (for example using ramjets). For low extended trajectories at high Mach numbers, aerodynamic heating becomes a significant problem".

In other words, though they produced thrust using ordinary air, neither conventional turbojets nor ramjets were particularly attractive for the task at hand. But what about some of the unconventional turbojets that had been proposed by various parties up to this point? Bond went on: "A number of cycles for airbreathing engines have been proposed which offer borderline advantage, and so have remained interesting while not having been fully explored. We have in mind the Liquid Air Cycle Engine (LACE), the inverted turbojet, the pre-cooled turbojet and the turborocket. The first three cycles exploit the thermodynamic gains which are to be had by virtue of the low temperature and high thermal capacity of liquid hydrogen fuel.

"In this paper an engine cycle is presented which takes the thermodynamics concepts of these engine cycles and integrates them with a conventional preburner cycle rocket engine to give a potentially interesting mixed power plant.

"It exploits conventional rocket and gas turbine technology and is capable of normal test stand development. Whilst it makes some demands on heat exchanger technology (development of which is long overdue) these are

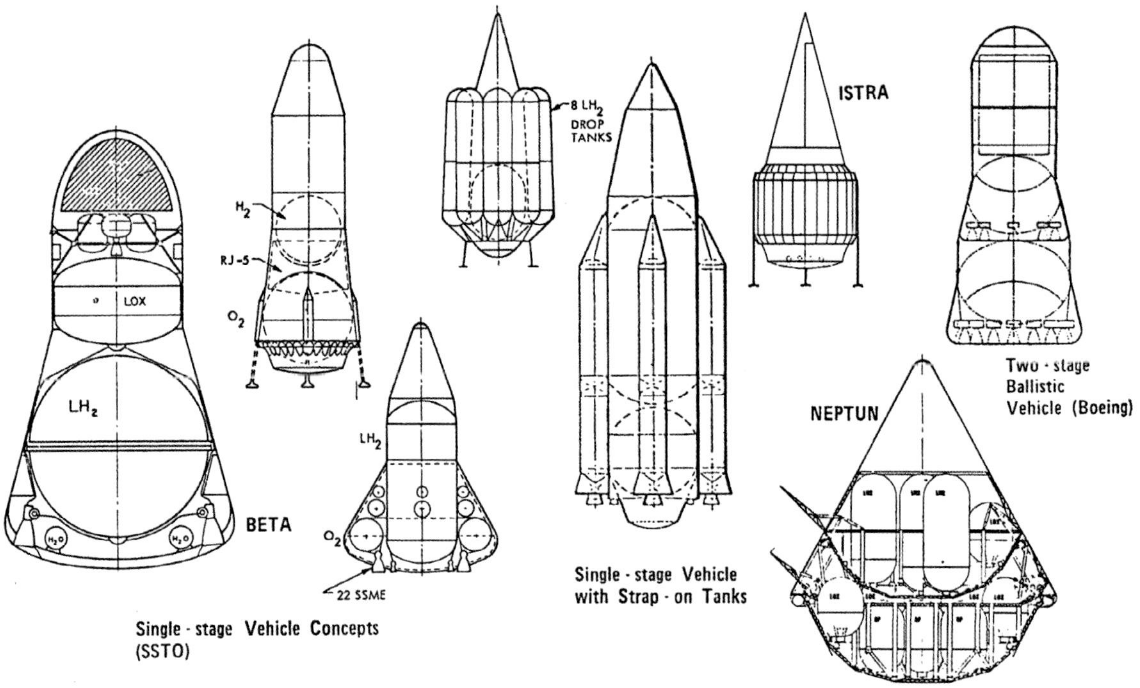

Up to 1982, practically every launcher—SSTO or multi-stage—was designed for ballistic take-off.

not considered extreme. Further, whilst it requires an air intake system, this has to have only nominal performance and is not a technologically demanding item.

"The cycle as portrayed here has been kept simple and not very demanding of component performance. Future developments could increase its overall effectiveness many-fold given better utilisation of the liquid hydrogen."

Bond's proposed engine cycle, dubbed 'CRACE' hence the 'Combined Rocket and Air Cycle Engine' of the paper's title, was essentially a rocket engine which could operate using liquid hydrogen and air at low altitude before switching to liquid hydrogen and liquid oxygen—from onboard tanks—at high altitude.

In airbreathing mode at low altitude, liquid hydrogen would be used to cool the air coming into the intake but only to the point of being saturated—rather than becoming a liquid—before it entered the engine's compressor. LACE engine designs up to this point took air through the latent heat of condensation to make it liquid, which required twice as much cooling and therefore double the hydrogen consumption. If the tricky balancing act inherent in CRACE could be achieved, an overly large heat exchanger and a high liquid hydrogen flow would be unnecessary.

Bond intended the switchover from air to liquid oxygen to occur at between Mach 6 and Mach 7.5 and an altitude of 28-32km.

He concluded that getting a 15-tonne payload into space using CRACE would require a vehicle weighing only 27.5 tonnes, carrying 57.7 tonnes of liquid hydrogen and 100 tonnes of liquid oxygen. While the vehicle itself was only 3.5 tonnes lighter, and the liquid hydrogen load had to be increased by 12.7 tonnes, the big saving came from the massively reduced liquid oxygen load. Using ordinary air to replace 170 tonnes of liquid oxygen cut the overall take-off mass by around 44% to just over 200 tonnes.

The CRACE vehicle, though Bond expected it to cost about the same as the pure rocket vehicle, would be smaller, more manageable and generally easier to handle.

Before long, Bond, then working for the Atomic Energy Authority at Culham in Oxfordshire, and Parkinson had recruited Rolls-Royce rocket engineer John Scott-Scott, based at the company's plant at Ansty on the edge of Coventry. Scott-Scott had previously worked with Bond at Rolls-Royce on nuclear engine concepts which used high performance heat exchangers. He remembered: "The whole thing ought to be blamed on Alan and Bob ... in our very early meetings ... Alan had proposed a completely ballistic vehicle. I said that'll never work".

Meanwhile, Parkinson had secured a new position with British Aerospace's Space and Communications Division at Stevenage—though he had yet to start. He said: "Alan and I had a phone conversation, realised we were on similar lines, and we organised a meeting in his office down at Culham [in October 1982] two days before I went to Stevenage and John Scott-Scott came to the meeting as well and I think David Andrews. And it looked as though we had something there that was worth studying further.

Aerospace systems business manager Peter Conchie.

That's actually the origin of Hotol.

"I went away from that meeting saying, I'm going to see whether somebody at British Aerospace would be interested. John Scott-Scott went away to see whether Rolls-Royce would be interested. And two days later I moved to Stevenage."

At this point, British Aerospace had only been a fully commercial concern for 20 months—the British Government having sold 51.57% of its shares in February 1981 to return the company to private ownership.

On November 3, 1982, an 'invitation only' BIS technical committee meeting was held in London where Bond outlined his engine concept before a small audience, including Peter Conchie. Conchie had worked on spacecraft and satellite designs with Hawker Siddeley Dynamics during the 1960s and 1970s before joining the infra-red division at British Aerospace Hatfield in 1978. He became director of air-to-air missiles there in 1982.

While Bond envisioned a vertical take-off vehicle at this point, Parkinson had a concept in mind that would be named Orbital Swallow. The inspiration for this moniker was a supersonic bomber designed by renowned inventor Barnes Wallis for Vickers-Armstrongs during the 1950s, which was simply named Swallow. Its key innovation was a mechanism which enabled its wings to be swept forward in flight, creating greater lift at low speeds for take-offs and landings, or swept back for reduced drag at high speed. Although Swallow was never built, the concept it pioneered had been widely adopted by 1982—notably in the General Dynamics F-111, the Grumman F-14 Tomcat and most recently at this time in the Panavia Tornado.

According to John Scott-Scott, "What we had done … is to dedicate the project to Barnes Wallis and it was known as the Swallow project. In fact, because it went up to the top, it was known as OS which was Orbital Swallow. Splendid project this was, and we thought it'll honour the man who used to fly all sorts of funny things down in Cornwall that we only found out about later—he was a very forward-looking chap."

Parkinson said later: "The configuration I was playing with was the swing-wing Orbital Swallow, mainly because I was concerned with simplifying the re-entry control by burying the actuation deep within the vehicle (this had been a problem with Shuttle) and because I was ignorant about aerodynamics."

As depicted in drawings dated January 1983, Parkinson's vehicle bore a fleeting resemblance to both its namesake and an English Electric Aviation design from 1963 designated EAG 4414—a re-entry vehicle which also featured swing-wing capability. It had a wide, flat fuselage tapering to a blunt nose and large triangular wings. Its low-profile forward-set cockpit canopy vaguely resembled that of the North American X-15 and its rectangular payload bay was positioned aft of the cockpit. The remainder of the vehicle's internal volume was largely filled with fuel tanks and two rocket engine nozzles were mounted at the extreme rear. A single nacelle on the underside of the fuselage contained four airbreathing engines. The undercarriage consisted of a tall nosewheel leg and two sets of mainwheels—though exactly where those were to be housed when retracted is unclear. Even at this stage, runway take-off in one form or another was being considered.

While Parkinson and Scott-Scott tried to drum up support for the new SSTO concept at their respective companies, Bond continued to refine his engine and drew up a new version of his CRACE paper on November 11, 1982.

This time the introduction steered clear of making predictions for the future and stuck to brass tacks: "This document describes preliminary proposals for a high performance (thrust/weight ratio, specific impulse) engine for use as a powerplant for a single stage, fully reusable earth to orbit space transportation vehicle.

"The objective of this particular design is to make use of atmospheric air as an oxidiser and working fluid up to a speed of about 1,800-2,200m/s (Mach no. 6-7.5) in order to reduce the gross lift-off weight (GLOW), but to especially reduce the sensitivity of vehicle payload to engine performance variations around the nominal levels and to mission velocity requirements relative to those for pure rocket concepts.

"The concept of using the atmosphere to assist the

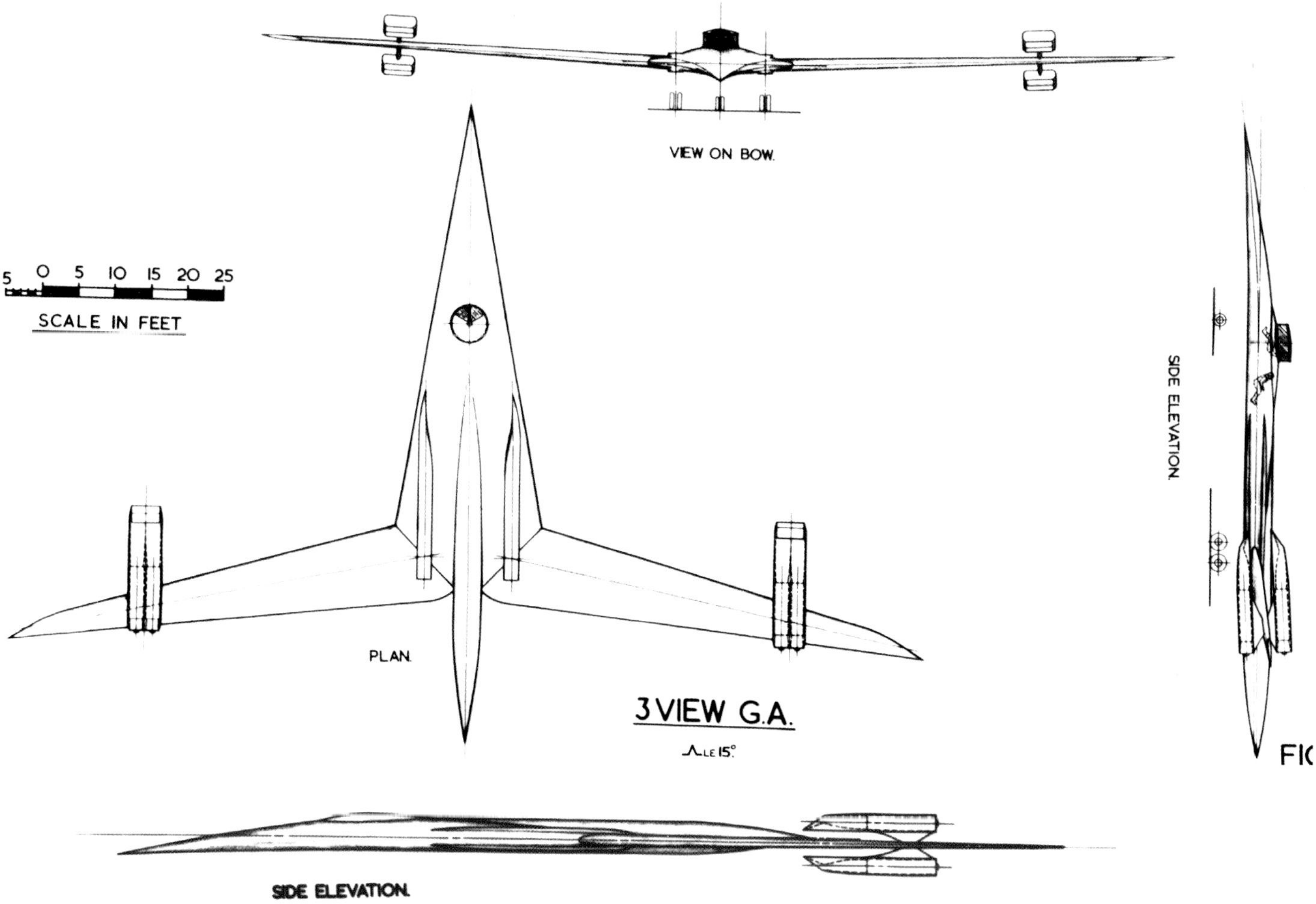

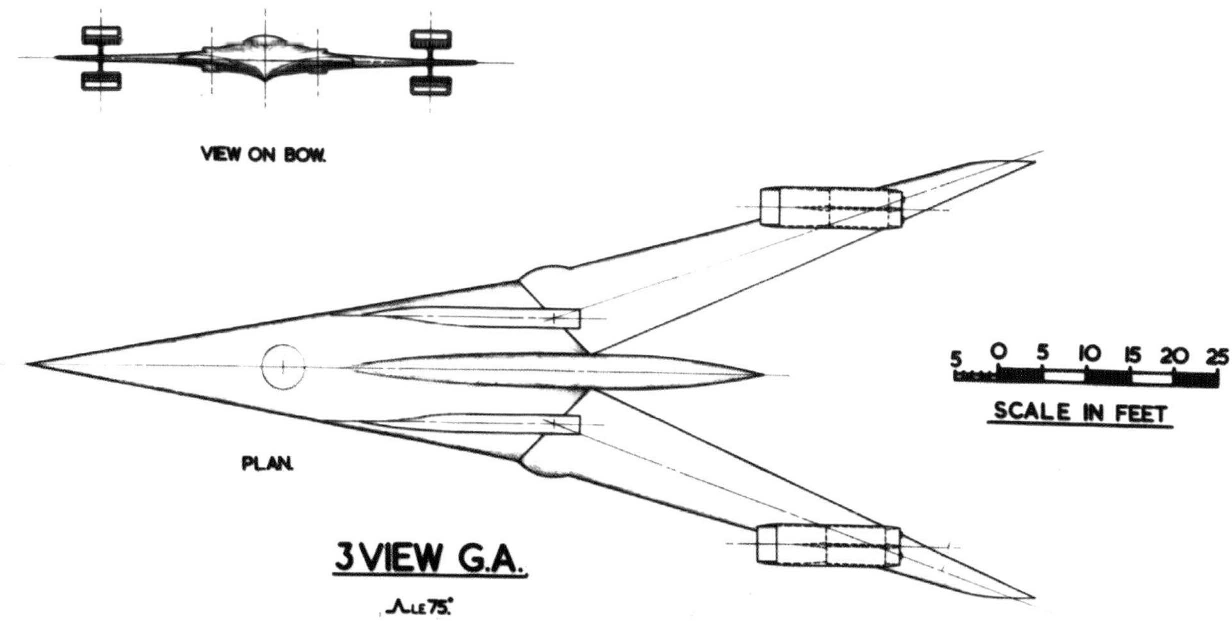

The Vickers-Armstrongs Swallow, designed by Barnes Wallis, as it appeared in a brochure produced by Vickers-Armstrongs (Aircraft) Department of Aeronautical Research and Development, Weybridge, in 1957. One view shows the aircraft in landing mode with 15-degree sweepback and with pop-up cockpit and landing gear extended, the other shows it in high-speed flight mode with 75-degree sweepback.

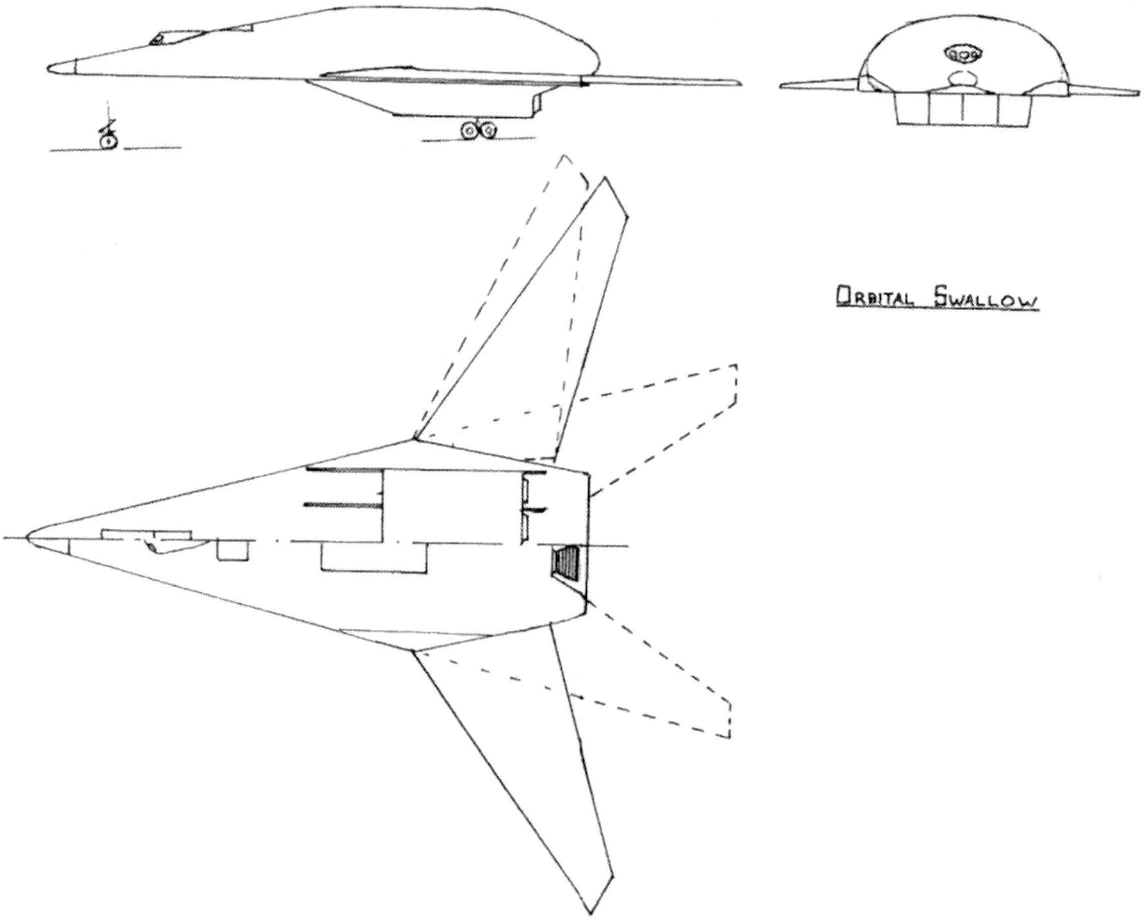

Rough three-view general arrangement sketch of Orbital Swallow circa January 1983, showcasing the type's variable geometry wings.

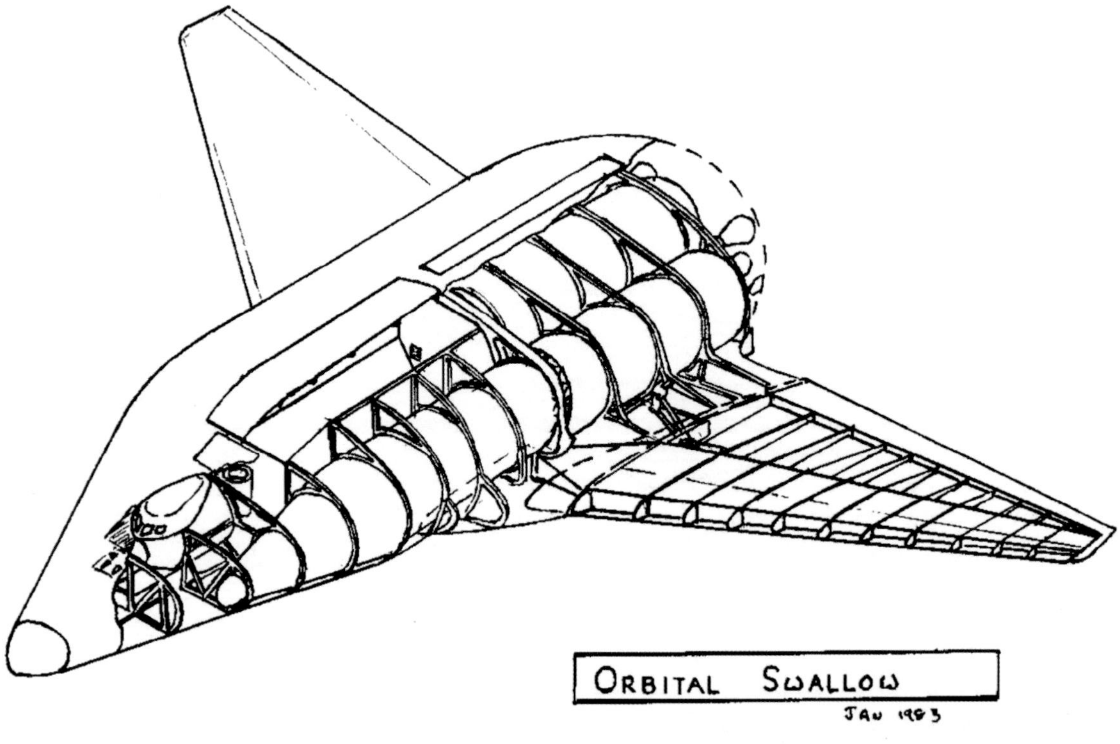

Cutaway sketch of Orbital Swallow, revealing the internal structure including the payload bay aft of the cockpit. No detail of the wing sweepback mechanism is depicted.

Artful contemporary depiction of Orbital Swallow in orbit, with payload bay doors open to reveal its satellite cargo.

Orbital Swallow shown ascending through Earth's atmosphere using the bank of four airbreathing engines on its underside.

lower part of the ascent trajectory is as old as considerations of spaceflight themselves. However, most study has surrounded ramjets and combined rocket/ramjet configurations. Whilst such concepts have an alluring simplicity they also have an enormous hidden development cost in terms of ground facilities. Further, they are in general low thrust/weight ratio devices."

He again cited the work done elsewhere on LACE, inverted turbojets and pre-cooled turbojets but "all of these in the final analysis have been found to have limitations due to component mass, inability to operate at low speeds or inadequate performance/cost benefit. The concept presented here has tried to navigate through the above deficiencies whilst attempting to avoid the ground facility penalty of the ramjet. Some of these attempts have apparently met with success although some technological development must be carried out before the engine proposed could be brought to fruition. In particular the heat exchangers required ahead of the engine air inlet would require extensive R and D effort."

LONG, THIN AND POINTY

Parkinson had persisted with his attempts to get British Aerospace support for the fledgling SSTO concept. He recalled: "When I went to Stevenage I tried it on ... it wasn't clear at all how that fitted in at Stevenage. While [assistant chief engineer] Charles Martin and Bill Childs who was the chief engineer at the time were, what you'd call sympathetic I guess, they didn't actually have a route forward either. If I did anything, I sort of played with it in my spare time."

But "getting somebody interested in the idea was solved when Peter Conchie (whom we already knew) returned to [British Aerospace's site at] Stevenage as director of sales and marketing."

Hatfield was in the process of shutting down and Conchie moved to Stevenage in early 1983, switching jobs to become business development director. Having been briefed on Bond's engine a few months earlier, he was clearly intrigued by Parkinson's SSTO.

Interviewed about his involvement in 1988, Conchie said: "I asked John Scott-Scott 'will it work?' In his bruff Derbyshire accent, John said 'I don't think it has much chance of working.' But then he came back and said, 'Much to my amazement, I think it will bloody well work.'"

But there was still the question of aerodynamics, since it was apparent that the original Orbital Swallow design was a non-starter. Parkinson: "What I don't remember is why Frank Crowfoot from [British Aerospace] Filton rang me. It was he who rang me and it wasn't about Hotol, I'm sure about that—it was probably in connection with something about my previous career at Westcott. However, after a telephone conversation it was apparent that he was the guy I needed to talk to about supersonic aerodynamics and I made arrangements to visit the team at Filton who were very enthusiastic about what we were trying to do and in no time had produced the long thin pointy configuration that you are all familiar with."

British Aerospace Filton had many key members of the Concorde aerodynamics team on staff—including Crowfoot and Concorde chief aerodynamicist Clive Leyman, who was the site's chief engineer. Leyman remembered: "If I'm horribly blunt about it ... it was the experience and personality of two people ... [It] was really done by a guy called Frank Crowfoot, ... and myself ... We were able to throw ideas around. Frank had this ability to turn it into a practical idea ... gut feelings, not done by clever sums ... backed up by rudimentary calculations, generally done after the event.

"It is experience, not expertise, and innovativeness I suppose. Actually, that's fairly typical of the way an aircraft comes about—doodles on the back of an envelope, takes it to the boss, who says 'don't be so bloody stupid!' It's easy if the boss has thought of it. It's a glamorous thing, engineers like me tend to get interested and say 'let's have a go at that'.

"If we had to get money for this hare-brained scheme, it wouldn't have happened. There wasn't any particular funding problem at that stage—only a few people were involved, they were all in one close-knit department. But if you've got to go out to other department heads and ask them to release men—then you've got to do some talking. The early stages were freelance. There is a critical sum of money beyond which it [has to be] formalised."

According to Scott-Scott: "Frank Crowfoot ... made the first model of Hotol. He made a little man, said 'don't forget this is a big machine'."

Crowfoot's design was radically different from the earlier Orbital Swallow concept. It was long, slender and vaguely Concorde-ish. The stubby wings had a compound delta form and twin tailfins were positioned to the extreme rear. On the vehicle's underside, also at the rear, was an enormous semi-circular intake with an equally enormous conical centrebody. At the other end of the vehicle, not quite at the nose tip, were a pair of canards. The forward part of the fuselage would house the liquid hydrogen tank, the payload bay was towards the rear and the liquid oxygen tank and engines were at the back.

There were no windows in evidence, indeed there was no cockpit and no space allocated for crew—since the

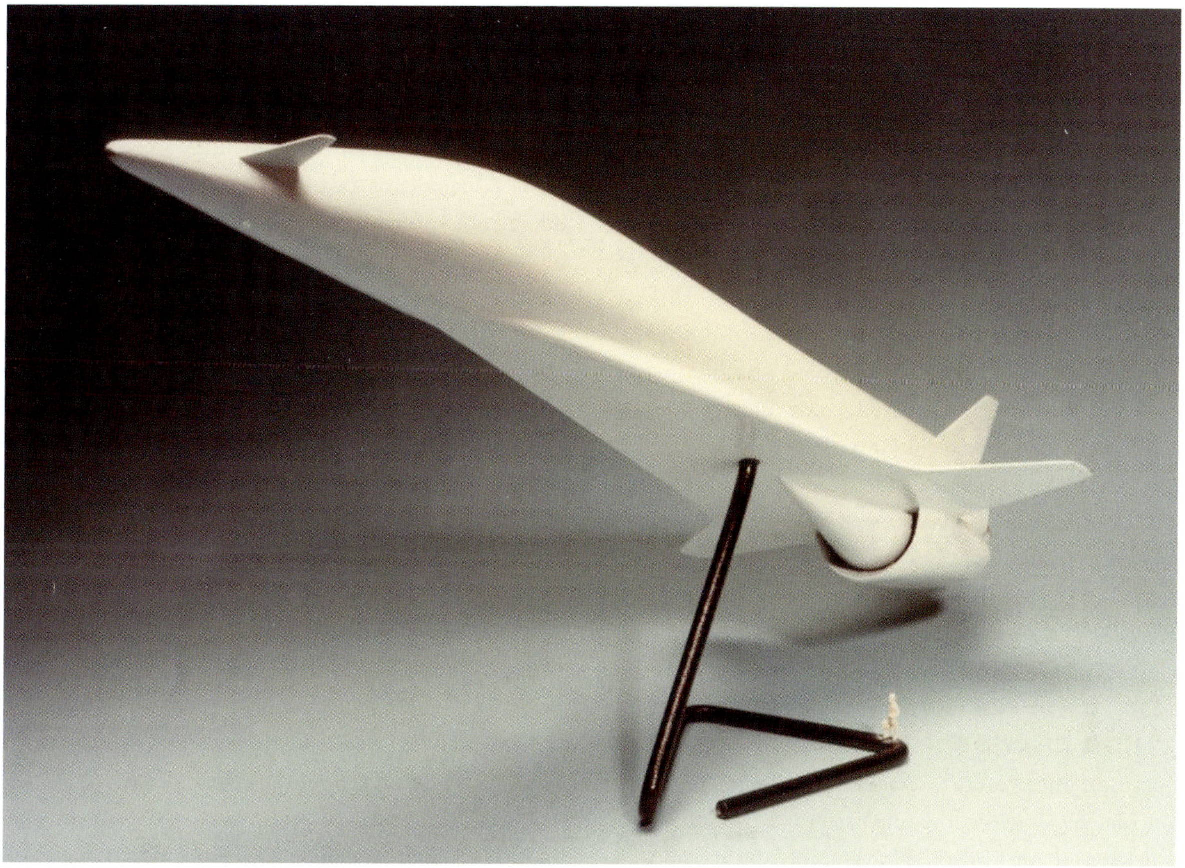

SSTO model made by aerodynamicist Frank Crowfoot—with a tiny human figure modelled onto the corner of the black metal stand for scale.

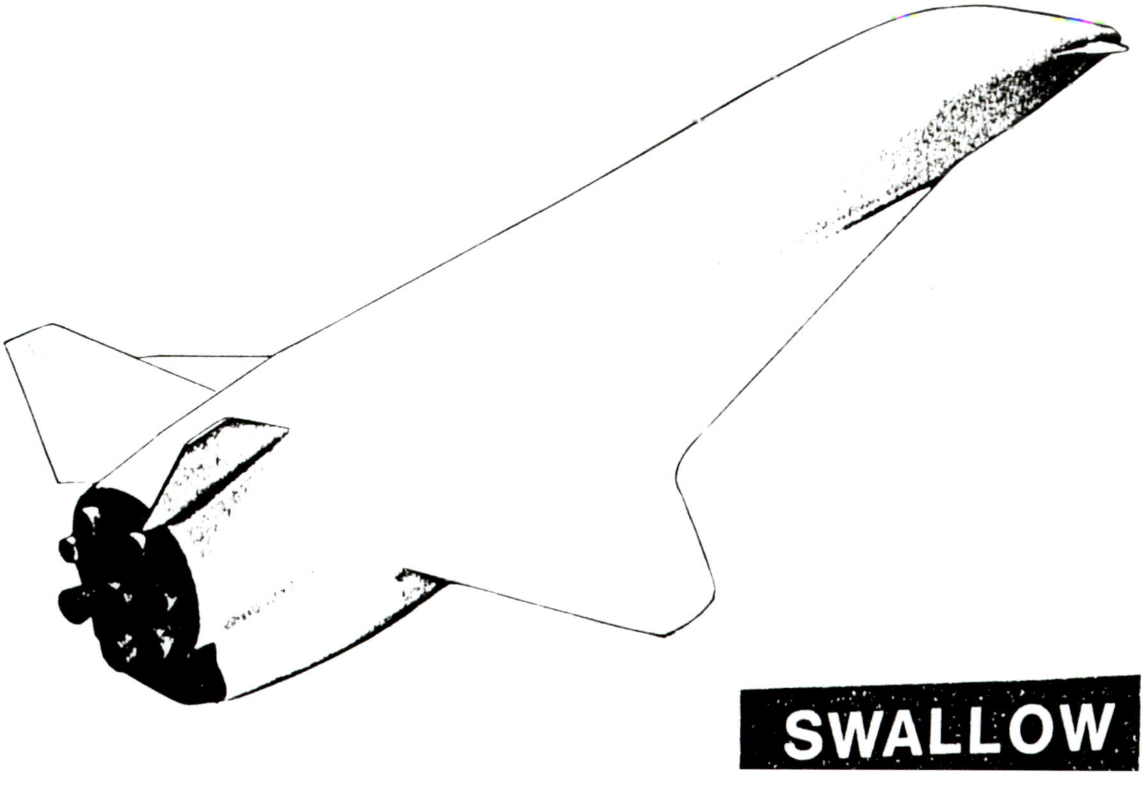

One of the earliest known artistic depictions of Hotol, from Bond's March 27, 1983, engine proposal. At this time it was still 'Swallow'.

vehicle would not only be unpiloted, it would operate autonomously using its own computer systems and sensors to fly the mission without the need for human intervention.

This enormous yet streamlined and supremely aerodynamic vehicle would be mounted on a sturdy wheeled trolley for take-off—enabling it to fly from a normal runway without having to then carry a heavy-duty undercarriage of its own up into space. Having thundered down the tarmac, at the point of rotation it would detach from the trolley and ascend. It did have its own undercarriage, a lightweight tricycle affair, but this would remain retracted until the vehicle, weighing far less having burned most of its fuel, came in to land at the end of its mission.

Detail changes aside, this was largely the configuration that would go forward to become Hotol. Initially however, Crowfoot's design appears to have retained part of the original name—Swallow.

THIRD CRACE PROPOSAL

Bond produced a third version of his engine proposal on March 27, 1983. The title page read: "A Combined Rocket and Air Cycle Engine for an Advanced Space Transportation System by Alan Bond" and the next page featured a full-page image of Crowfoot's model with the name 'SWALLOW' below it. The first section of text, the summary, was more business-focused than before: "Continued improvement in the economics of transportation into earth orbit can only be achieved by lower amortised hardware costs and reduced range activity in the launch and re-entry phases of system operation.

"At the present time propellant costs are not the dominant part of launch system operational costs although a reduction in vehicle launch mass by higher engine performance would have some impact on costs in terms of operational logistics and range safety. This report describes some preliminary studies carried out on an engine concept designed to have the capability of propelling a single stage vehicle to orbit, and of providing power for flyout and flyback trajectories of limited range. The engine has been termed a CRACE for ease of reference (Combined Rocket and Air Cycle Engine) and also to reflect its near relation to the Liquid Air Cycle Engine (LACE) studied in the early 1960s by Marquardt in the USA and the NGTE in the UK."

The CRACE cycle was briefly described, then: "It seems likely that the mission cost with such engines would . . . have propellant costs as a dominant factor. Although the engine described in this report was sized with a particular vehicle in mind, the report is intended to describe only the leading features of the engine and to highlight engine development problems. It is hoped that this report could form the basis for a more comprehensive investigation of the CRACE potential."

The remainder of the proposal outlined Bond's engine design in far greater detail than before, with descriptions of the individual components and diagrams showing the CRACE cycle and heat exchanger configurations. Handwritten at the back, was a section entitled: CRACE Heat Exchanger Development Programme. This read: "The CRACE depends on the viability of low pressure loss lightweight heat exchangers. The following programme is designed to increase confidence in the feasibility of these components by means of a very low-cost test programme. The major work areas to be addressed are a) The heat transfer correlations on the air side (Stanton number, passage geometry and effective friction factor). b) The technology of making the heat exchanger small diameter thin-walled tubes."

There then followed some technical specifications for a proposed heat transfer test rig as an appendix.

A working group was set up between BAe Stevenage and Roll-Royce "to explore the Hotol concept" in April 1983 and according to the official timeline presented in February 1986, "contact with Advanced Projects Group, BAe Aircraft Group, Bristol, introduces Concorde team to project" in June 1983—though it appears that Crowfoot and Leyman had been involved somewhat earlier.

According to Parkinson, "Peter Conchie . . . said money for a study may be possible. We went to the Department of Trade and Industry and after some considerable time, liberated forty thousand pounds." This was "not particularly about Hotol but looking at what was needed for future launchers."

The contract, and funding, awarded by the DTI in September 1983, took the form of a Future European Launch Vehicle concepts study which, according to the official timeline, established "[the] economic basis for pursuing [the] Hotol concept".

Discussing his own quest for funding at Rolls-Royce, which was a nationalised company at this point, Scott-Scott said: "Talked to our then head of engineering, was given a wandering brief to look around the company, found another old diehard. So with director's support I made contacts—'don't worry about the bookings'. That's how the job got started. Wrote up a feasibility report, routed round the ministry . . . got the first money."

The other 'old diehard' was company technical director Gordon Lewis, who had done much of the early design work on the Bristol Siddeley, later Rolls-Royce, Olympus engine and whose name was on the master patents for the Harrier's powerplant—the Pegasus.

Lewis, writing in 1989, remembered: "Work on the concept that became the proposed engine for Hotol started in the company at... Ansty, where a small team of engineers were examining advanced propulsion ideas for various applications. John Scott-Scott was a member of this team, and was in contact with Alan Bond as a result of their earlier association on rocket engines. I was in charge of new projects at Bristol and Derby at the time, and although aware of their activity in broad terms I was not in daily contact with progress. It is appropriate to encourage some new thinking with a reasonable degree of freedom to surface such new concepts."

Bond said: "John Scott-Scott had levered some local money out of Rolls-Royce—this was very important. The idea was not propagated into Rolls-Royce further than the line management. British Aerospace, however, talked at director level—they produced higher level money—we talked to the DTI."

Bond made an application to patent his engine on December 22, 1983. Crucially however, under an arrangement with Rolls-Royce, the company retained an option to purchase the rights. The application abstract read: "Improvements in Aerospace Propulsion. An engine for application to the propulsion of aerospace vehicles (terrestrial or orbital) capable of operating in two propulsive modes. The first mode employs liquid hydrogen to pre-cool the intake air of a turbo-compressor in order to deliver it at high pressure to a rocket type combustor/nozzle assembly. In this mode the external atmosphere is the source of oxidiser for the fuel. At a high Mach number in the hypersonic regime the engine changes to the second mode which is a conventional high-performance rocket engine using liquid oxygen carried on the vehicle to oxidise the liquid hydrogen fuel. Both modes of propulsion use common hardware, namely the liquid hydrogen pump and the combustor nozzle assembly." This was what would become Hotol's engine in a nutshell.

THE 'FATHER OF HOTOL'

With preliminary work on the SSTO concept now taking place at Stevenage and Filton and at Rolls-Royce in Ansty, word had begun to spread and before long the project had attracted the attention of Admiral Sir Raymond Lygo. Knighted in 1977 and retiring from the Navy in 1978, Lygo had then joined British Aerospace as director of its Dynamics Group, which included the Space and Communications Division at Stevenage. He quickly became chairman and chief executive of Dynamics before being appointed to the newly-created position of managing director of the whole company on January 1, 1983.

Sir Raymond Lygo, chief executive of British Aerospace for much of the 1980s.

Exactly when Lygo began to take an interest in what would become Hotol is unclear, but he wrote on July 24, 1987: "Sir George Cayley may be generally recognised as being the father of British aeronautics but I like to think of myself as the father of Hotol in that my original promotion [of the project] through both Norman Tebbit, then DTI, and Michael Heseltine, then Secretary of State for Defence, started nearly four years ago [i.e. late 1983] and its feature at the Farnborough Air Show [see Chapter 3] was only achieved by my direction!"

Nevertheless, no significant funding was forthcoming and going into 1984 the project remained a small-scale enterprise.

On April 11, 1984, Parkinson gave a presentation at the BIS Space Transportation & Space Station Symposium in London entitled The Cost of a Future European Launcher—presumably based on the DTI-funded study. His accompanying slideshow began with a quote from Jean Vandenkerckhove, assistant technical director of the European Space Agency dated January 1981: "For the present... there is no firm justification to embark on the development of a recoverable/reusable European transportation system unless advanced technology rather than mere scale permits a dramatic reduction of specific launch costs of geostationary satellites, say below 10 mAU (million accounting units) per ton."

This was followed by a list of key dates in the future: Final Shuttle First Flight: Oct. 1985. Ariane 4 First Flight 1986. Centaur G First Flight 1986 and so on. The last one was Second Generation Shuttle 2005. Next was a list of costs, with the Second Generation Shuttle coming in at 1.17 kAU (thousand accounting units) per kg of payload put into LEO, compared to 2.96 kAU for the original Space Shuttle and 7.9 kAU for Ariane 4.

Parkinson's paper continues by asking, 'Why are launchers expensive?' and gives a five-point answer: "Very high development costs; expensive hardware not reused; vehicle assembly and checkout extensive and occupies expensive facilities; launch vehicle failures politically sensitive; liquid hydrogen expensive."

Six different sample launch vehicles were then profiled—some of which might have been familiar to the audience, while others most likely were not. First up was Ariane 5 with Hermes mounted on top, total cost per flight: 32 mAU. Second was the ESA (European Space Agency)/Aérospatiale FLS (Future Launching System)—a winged recoverable rocket booster with a Gemini-type capsule or other second stage vehicle, total cost per flight: 12.4 mAU. And third was something with the title "Single Stage to Orbit".

The Single Stage to Orbit was a long slender vehicle with short stubby wings, shown by Parkinson in plan view only. Its cost per flight was just 10.6 mAU.

Each successive slide in the presentation had two black rectangular blocks at the top—one with "British Aerospace Dynamics Group" printed in it and the other solid black. But the black became less solid as the slides went on—and the word 'Swallow' is faintly visible within this block on later slides—having not been fully erased.

Parkinson's April 11 lecture appears to have been the last time 'Swallow' was applied to the new SSTO vehicle project as a whole, though his audience on that occasion can hardly have been expected to understand what the word meant in this context, and also the first of many presentations on what would become Hotol.

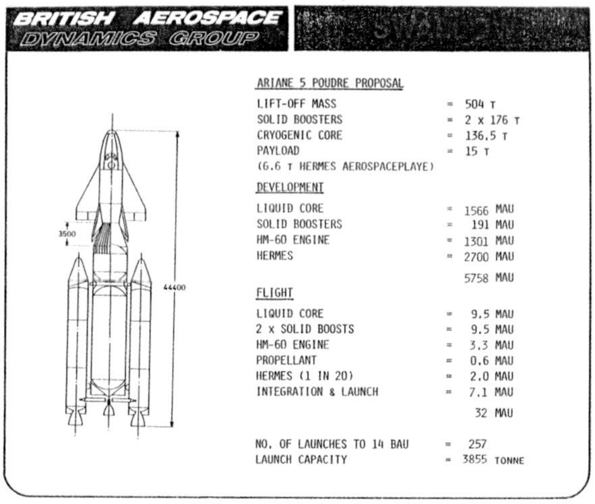

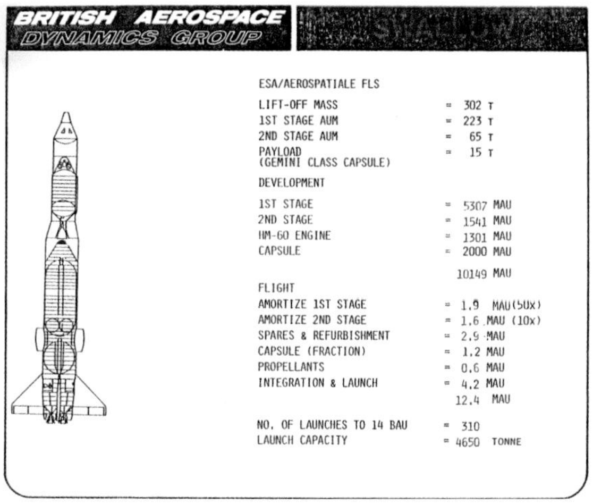

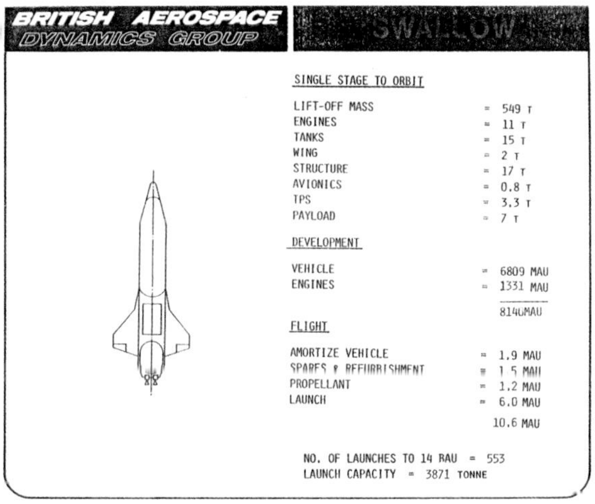

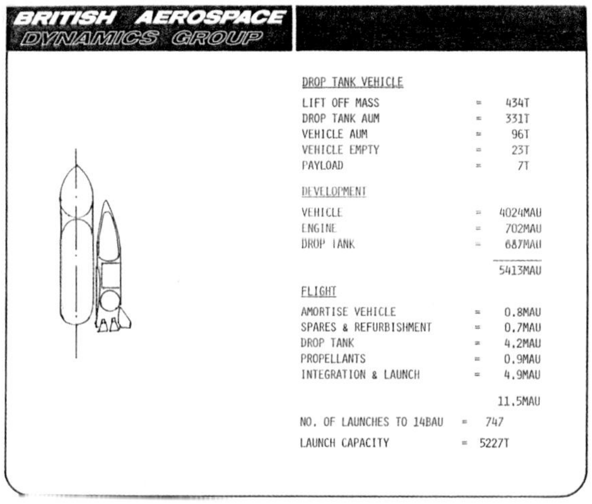

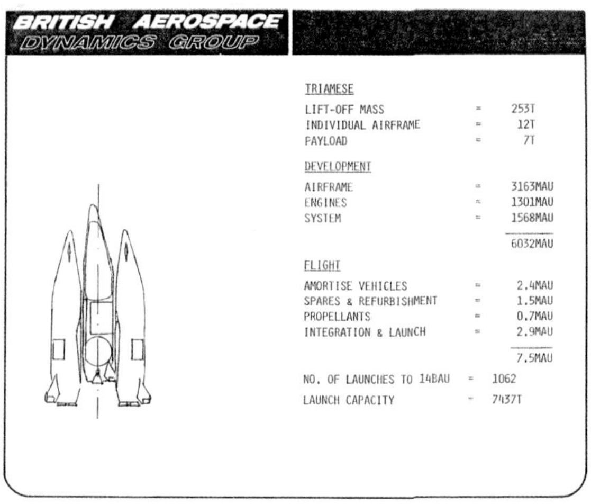

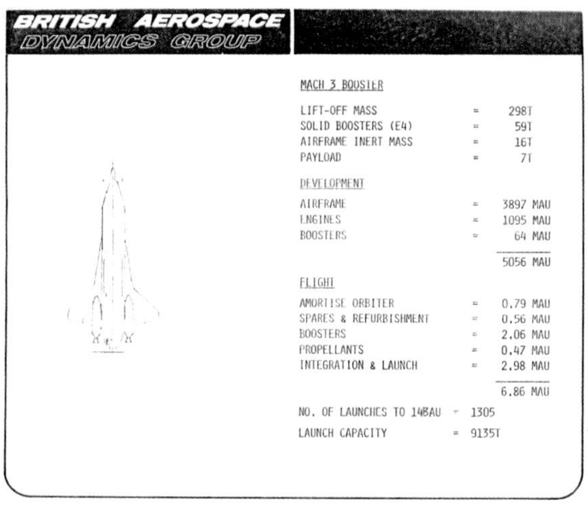

Slides used by Dr Bob Parkinson to illustrate his The Cost of a Future European Launcher presentation at the BIS Space Transportation & Space Station Symposium in London on April 11, 1984. The word 'Swallow' is faintly visible in the top right hand panel of at least three of them.

2

BREAKING NEWS: 1984 TO 1985

Having started out as Orbital Swallow, the SSTO vehicle conceptualised by Bond and Parkinson had become simply Swallow by the beginning of 1984 but Peter Conchie seems to have been unsatisfied with that name.

According to Alistair Scott, who joined the British Aerospace Space Systems Division in 1984: "When he [Conchie] returned to Stevenage Bob Parkinson, another BIS Fellow and Technical Committee member ... approached him with an idea he and Alan Bond ... had been working on, a winged launch vehicle with airbreathing engines! At a meeting a short while later Peter asked for a name for it. It is thought that Larry Blonstein came up with the name HOTOL (the HOrizontal Take-Off and Landing launcher)."

Blonstein had been project manager for UK3 aka Ariel 3, the first British satellite, during the early 1960s and by 1984 had been a sales manager at BAe Stevenage for five years. Naming Hotol would prove to be his only involvement with the project.

Scott-Scott later commented: "We didn't call it Hotol [originally], we thought this was a disgraceful horrible name. [It was called Hotol] because British Aerospace let some PR idiot loose once and they charged him with a duty of coming up with a snap off the tongue name ... anyway, we got lumbered with this wretched name."

HOTOL worked well from a PR perspective, however, because it neatly complemented VTOL—Vertical Take-Off and Landing—a term already lodged in the public consciousness thanks to BAe's most famous product of that time, the Harrier.

The other major event of early 1984, prompted by Bond's patent application, was the classification of his engine as secret by the Ministry of Defence (MoD). As Hotol deputy project team leader Gerald Wilson later recalled: "The secret classification put on the engine by MoD was a continual source of embarrassment to us because it meant we could not release information to the wider technical community to justify the claims made for Hotol."

Bond himself remembered: "It was agreed that I should apply for a patent for it and that started all sorts of problems with classification and I wish I'd never bothered."

Parkinson said: "Alan's engine concept got classified which meant that we couldn't actually tell anybody how the engine worked. And it took a long time to get it declassified and it was probably the security services adding two and making fifteen ... I don't know any of the details because whoever it is in the Ministry of Defence who decides these things didn't confide in me. But what it looks like is, Alan's engine concept depended on a trick with heat exchangers and to tell you the truth all Alan's tricks depended on... it's not quite true but we make a joke of

Hotol deputy project team leader Gerald Wilson.

it these days… every time I've known Alan I say that… I can tell it's his design 'cause it's got a heat exchanger in it.

"But it had a heat exchanger as a critical part of the deal… And it seems that about that same time, the Russians got interested, not because we were doing it but on their own account, in engines that had clever heat exchangers… So they classified the thing, which meant that if you wanted to talk with the European Space Agency for instance we couldn't, because the trick was classified so we couldn't tell them what the trick was."

By this time presentations had been made to both the DTI and the Royal Aircraft Establishment (RAE) Farnborough—the official BAe timeline has these taking place in March 1984.

According to Bond: "In the early DTI days there was an outline study… it was to equip ourselves with answers to get the strategy right. So Hotol was treated within that context, it had enough going for it for a view to form that you had to see what was there. The first step was for the rule to be run over it by RAE Farnborough, who came to the conclusion 'why not'. A quite sophisticated report was produced for Farnborough."

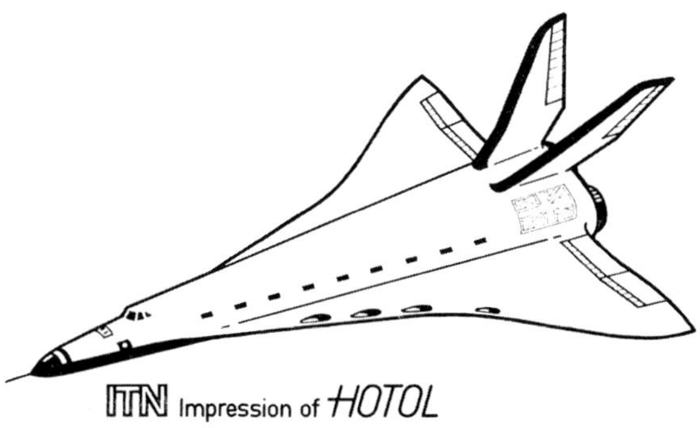

The 'artist's impression' of Hotol used by ITN. The original caption said: "ITN understands that the design of the craft bears a similarity to Concorde, and that British Aerospace will be applying many of the techniques learned in the testing of supersonic aircraft."

Scott-Scott noted that the National Gas Turbine Establishment at Pyestock, Farnborough, was also consulted: "Had to have the blessing of Pyestock—very old friends. It stopped them dead, floored them completely—how could this have grown up with two blokes at home? It generated a lot of resentment. There were a lot of battles fought to convince the powers-that-be, so they could… tell DTI."

The reaction from RAE Farnborough was positive according to Conchie: "The basic success was that Farnborough, when they saw it, thought it was something we as a nation had to do. A lot of people in the Ministry adopted a line that I was very happy with."

ITN NEWS AT TEN

The project was slowly gathering support by August 1984 when a British Aerospace facility was visited by Independent Television News science and technology editor Frank Miles. Bond recalled what happened: "In the run up to the Farnborough Air Show, Miles was visiting BAe and spotted some drawings and said 'what's that'. He was told it was classified. He took no notice and out it went on the News at Ten."

The veil of secrecy that had surrounded Hotol up to this point was abruptly yanked aside as a report went out on national television news at 10pm on Thursday, August 23, breathlessly revealing details of the new British space vehicle concept and its innovative Rolls-Royce engine. Miles had not asked for permission to tell the world about Hotol—he had simply elicited confirmation of the project from a well-informed third party before going ahead and breaking the story.

Those working on the project were stunned by the breach of security, none more so than John Scott-Scott, who suddenly found his career on the line. Neither the Rolls-Royce board, particularly chairman Sir Francis Tombs, nor the Rolls-Royce public relations department had even been aware of Hotol's existence up to this point.

According to Parkinson: "It was a summer evening. It was possibly the worst time that you could've done it. The following day I was going away with the family on holiday. John Scott-Scott was doing his gliding instruction somewhere over the Cotswolds, don't quite know where Peter was… all of a sudden various people within Rolls-Royce and British Aerospace became aware of this thing they felt they ought to have been aware of and weren't aware of and I had my deputy managing director on the phone here with us packing the car to go away on holiday.

"Various people remember this particular event fairly seriously, explaining what was going on and [there was] a sort of 'don't panic sir' going on. There were people at

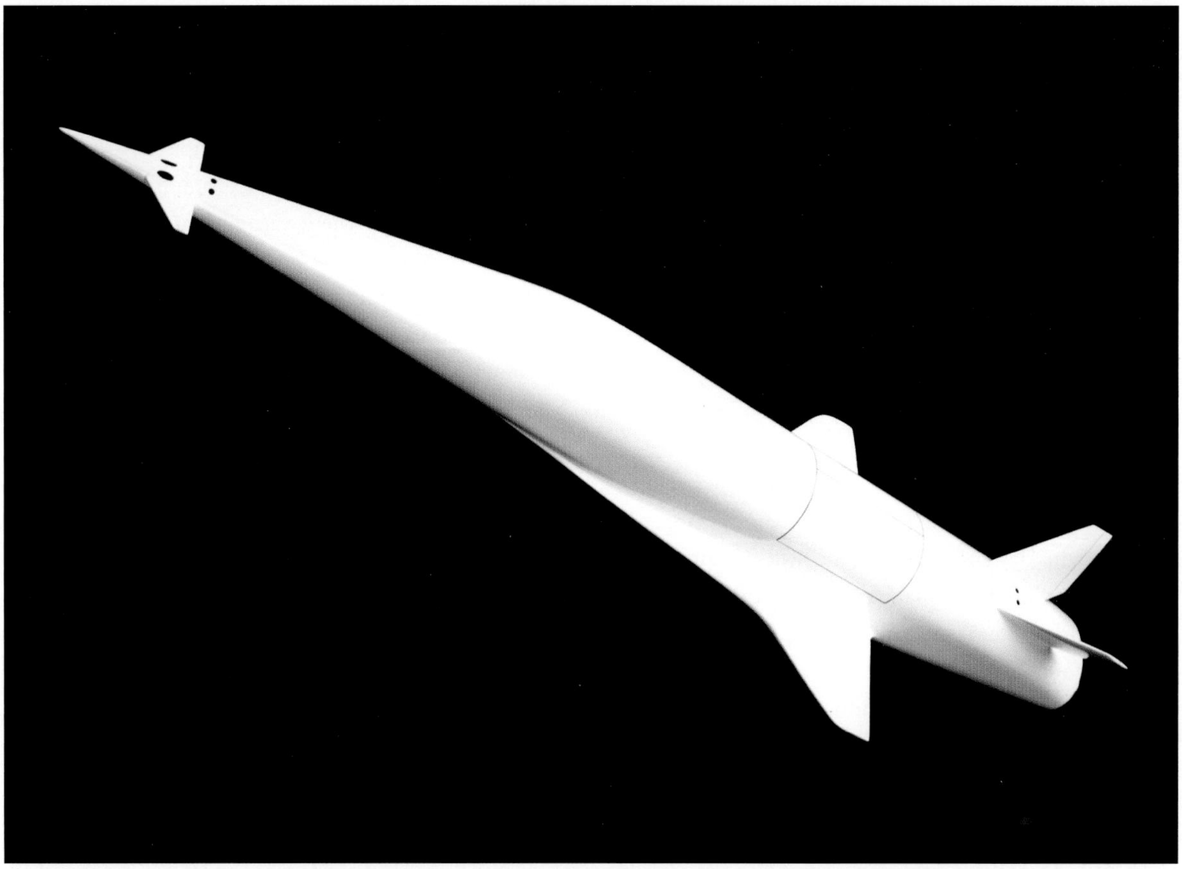

The Hotol model made available for public viewing—unlike Crowfoot's original model, this one featured a somewhat more pointed nose and the characteristic underside intake for the airbreathing engines was noticeably absent.

British Aerospace who suddenly wanted to know what it was about and so forth and nobody was there to explain anything—because we'd not been expecting this at all and all of a sudden it was out in public."

Scott-Scott recalled: "My wife and I were having a few days holiday on a deserted airfield down in the Cotswolds... And we decided we'd put the ten o'clock news on one night... And it said, you know, this is news breaking, dah de dah, stuff, you know, and whoever the technical bloke was, it's being shown today the start of a new type of space vehicle, dah da de dah, and so it went on.

"And I said—my wife said, 'What the hell, now what's happened?' I said, 'God only knows.' Some idiot in ITN. Well, I rang in the next morning, 'cause I couldn't get anybody at ten o'clock at night, and there was all hell to play, and the best thing to do was to sack Scottie [Scott-Scott himself] as far as I can make out... Anyway I managed to explain a few things to various people including people who would normally be on my side, but just could not believe that I would be so stupid as to divulge all this lot, because they blamed me ...

"In fact it wasn't [me], it turned out to be some British Aerospace bloke that had blabbed... And turned out he had filled in their—it's a sort of technical reporter, for want of a better word... And what I had to do is to come off holiday, catch the next train or two down to London, go and see him, and generally ball him out and this, that, and the other, for what he'd done... He vastly exceeded anything he should have done, and got it wrong at the same time, so there was all hell to play." Scott-Scott's story has never to date been independently verified.

FARNBOROUGH 1984

Miles' news report had revealed the existence of Hotol just days before it had been due to appear at the eight-day Farnborough Air Show, commencing on September 2, 1984. The British Aerospace stand, evidently at Lygo's behest, included a model of the Hotol vehicle and represented a more low-key follow-up to Miles' incendiary news story. It did, however, serve to put the project in front of leading members of the international aerospace community—who were unlikely to have seen the ITN broadcast.

The conversation surrounding Hotol suddenly became orders of magnitude wider and spiralled off in multiple directions. In particular, Hotol was thrust into competition with Ariane 5 itself, the launcher Bond and Parkinson had found so unappealing two and a half years earlier. Many commentators, now that they knew of its existence,

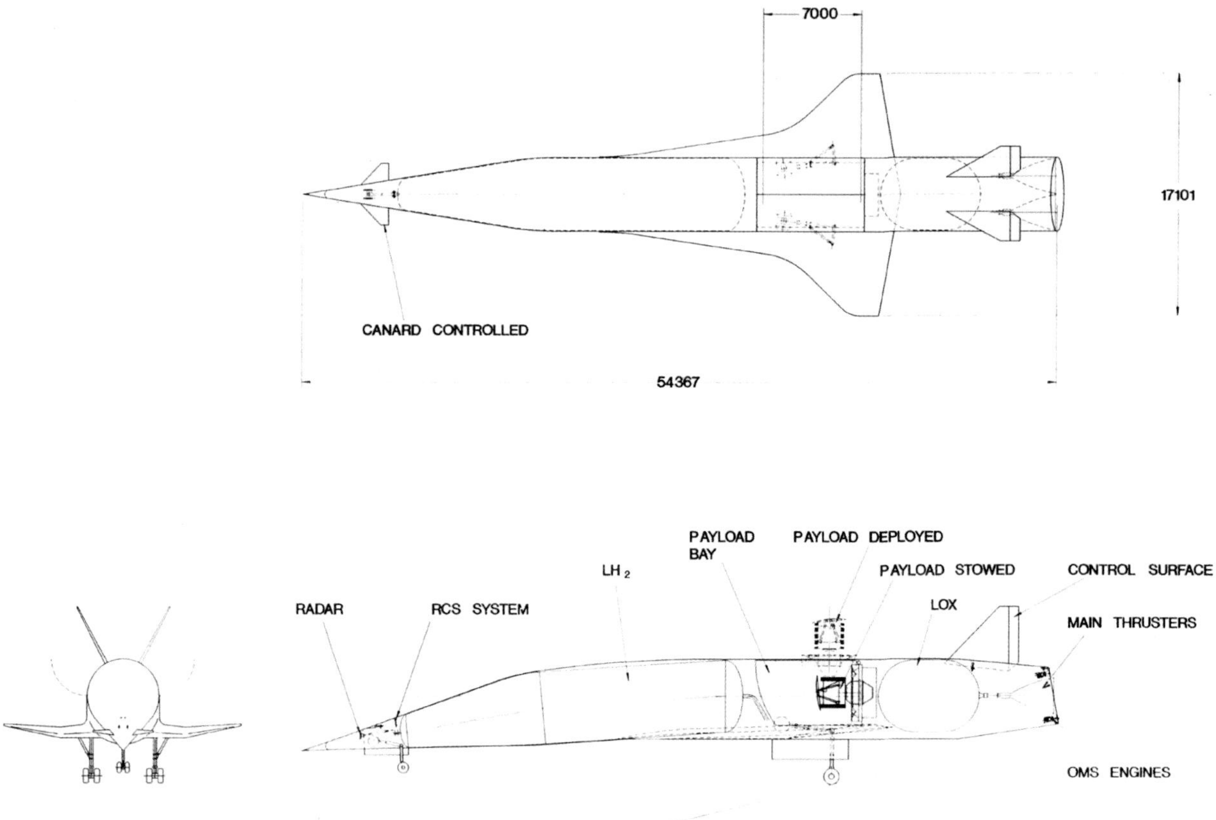

Hotol general arrangement drawing appended to the pre-Farnborough Air Show press release, giving an overall length of 54.367m and a wingspan of 17.101m. By way of comparison Concorde was 61.66m long with a wingspan of 25.6m. Again, the intake for the 'secret' engine is nowhere to be seen.

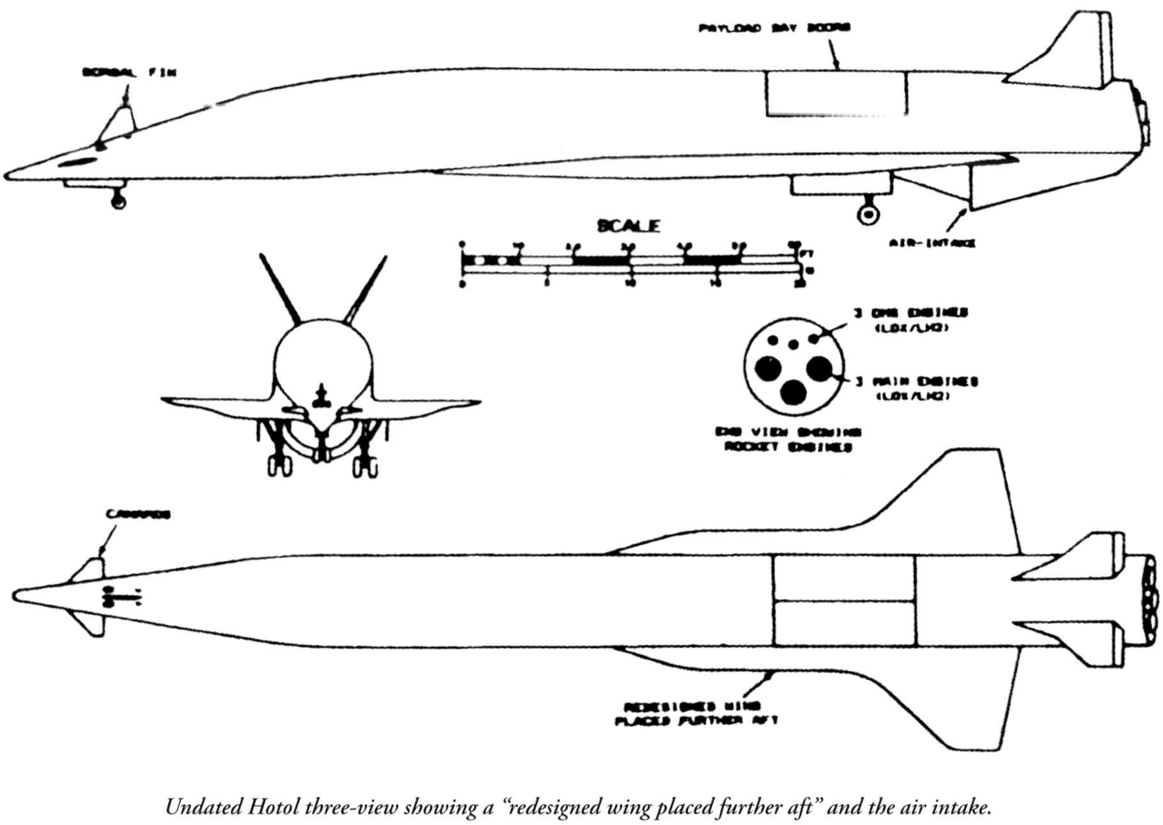

Undated Hotol three-view showing a "redesigned wing placed further aft" and the air intake. Note the modified, kinked, tailfins and the addition of a 'dorsal' or nose fin.

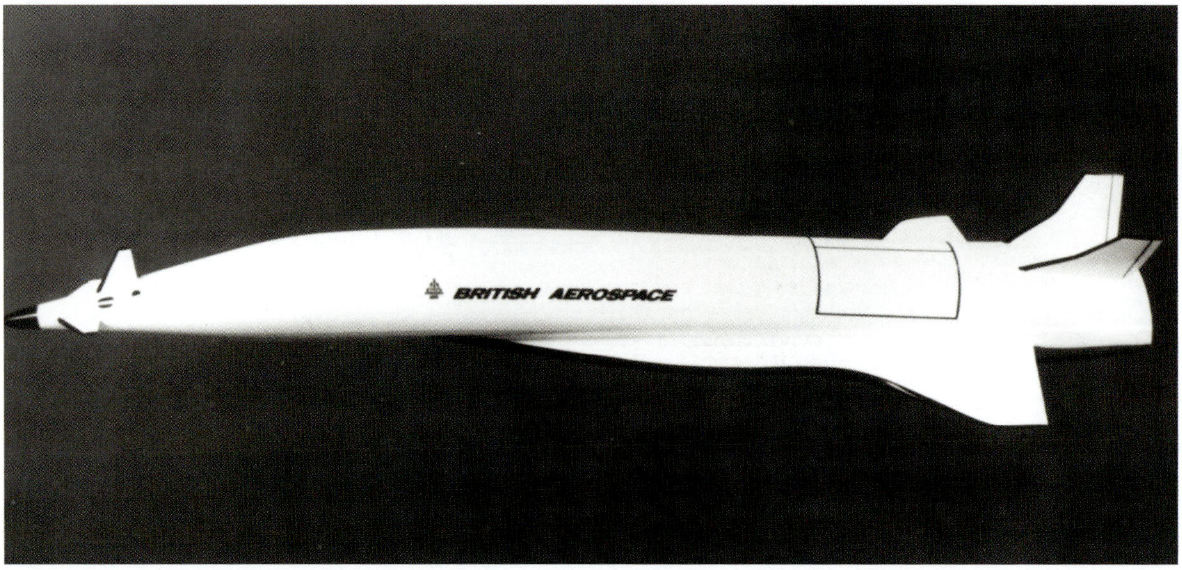

Modified version of the vehicle model—with new kinked tailfins and vertical nose fin. The underslung intake may also have been added by this point.

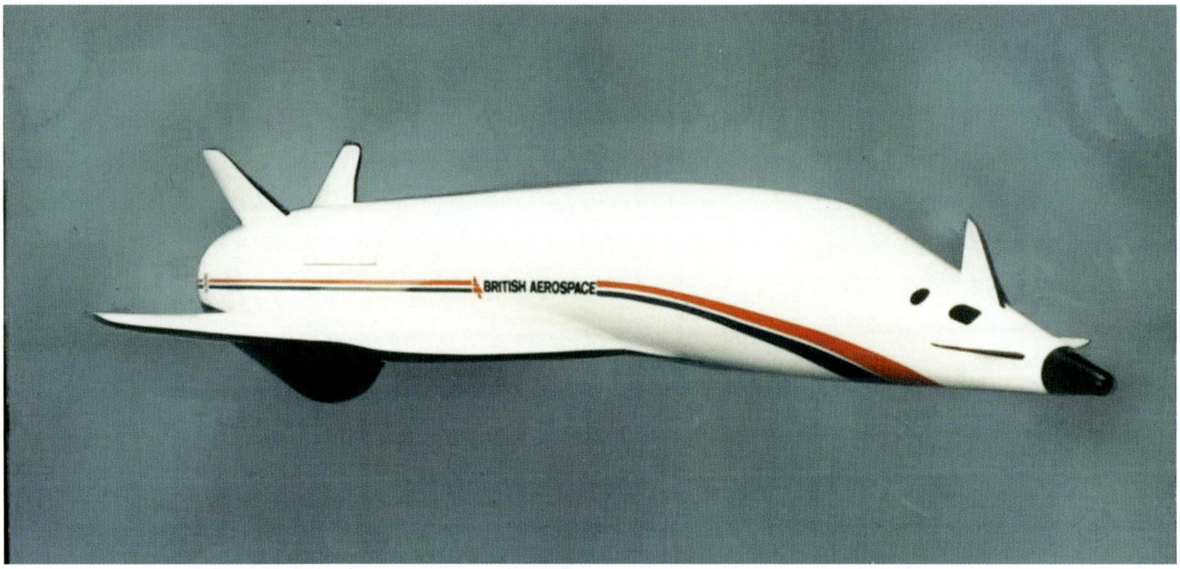

The modified vehicle model with a smart new decorative red, white and blue stripe. This image appeared across numerous magazines and newspapers of the time.

quickly concluded that securing financial and political support from abroad would be essential to Hotol's future viability.

Less than two weeks after the air show, on September 22, *Flight International* ran a story headlined 'Possible military role for BAe Hotol'. This said: "Potential military use of Britain's proposed horizontal take-off Space Shuttle offers perhaps the best hope of the project being adopted by the European Space Agency… Estimates of Hotol's development cost start at £500 million, effectively preventing Britain from 'going it alone'. As a vehicle for placing satellites in geostationary orbit, however, Hotol would inevitably conflict with ESA's Ariane launcher, effectively ruling out European backing for the project.

"One way forward is to promote Hotol's suitability for placing military payloads in low-Earth orbit. Reconnaissance and intelligence-gathering spacecraft are placed in non-geosynchronous orbits so that they cover all of the Earth's surface in successive orbits. Usually such satellites have limited lives, and are orbited when required.

"For this reason the US Air Force is seeking funds for ten expendable launchers to orbit military payloads when the Space Shuttle is unavailable. BAe sees Hotol offering NATO a unique rapid-reaction capability to orbit military satellites."

It was noted that Hotol was claimed to be more efficient than a conventional launcher due to its unique propulsion system and innate reusability.

Regarding the status of the project, "Hotol is currently the subject of paper studies funded by British Aerospace and Rolls-Royce, and by the UK Department of Industry to the tune of £300,000. A further DoI infusion of between £500,000 and £1 million is sought to fund wind tunnel studies. If pursued, Hotol could enter service by 2004."

HOTOL GOES TO ROME

Two months later, in November 1984, *New Scientist* magazine ran an article by Helen Gavaghan headlined 'Britain backs Hotol for Europe'. It stated that "a decision on which rocket Europe should develop [as a replacement for Ariane 4] will be considered by a Council of Ministers in Rome in January. Ariane 5 still looks the hot favourite". Gavaghan claimed "British engineers [say] the mainly French-built Ariane could come unstuck in the 1990s when Japanese launchers arrive on the scene, unless new plans are adopted now.

"This dispute over the future of Europe in space which comes to a head in January, lies behind the hasty unveiling this summer of British engineers' own bid for space stardom, the Anglo-shuttle known as the Hotol."

The 'hasty unveiling' of Hotol does not appear to have been prompted by the prospect of the ESA Council Meeting at Ministerial Level due to take place at Villa Madama in Rome on January 30-31, 1985. However, given that this meeting was being held to decide on financial priorities and spending for space research and technology over the next decade it made perfect sense that Hotol should be among the proposals put before decision-makers.

Britain had been a European Economic Community member state since January 1, 1973, and would therefore be sending along the British government's minister with responsibility for space research and technology—Geoffrey Pattie—to participate. Pattie, a former captain in the Queen's Royal Rifles and a director of advertising agency Collett Dickenson Pearce, had been Conservative MP for Chertsey and Walton since February 1974 and was appointed Minister of State, Industry and Information Technology (effectively putting him in charge of the DTI) by Prime Minister Margaret Thatcher in September 1983 following Conservative victory in the general election held on June 9, 1983.

Gavaghan's article went on to opine that even though Ariane 5's proposed HM60 cryogenic rocket engine was an "old-fashioned open-cycle motor" compared to Hotol's advanced propulsion system, ESA was still "expected to endorse the spending of £500 million" to develop it. Nevertheless, "Hotol [has] supporters outside Britain. Eric Quistgaard, the former director general of ESA, said this week: 'The BAe proposal is smart, it deserves to be given a fair try'."

BAe's Dynamics Group put together a new 'executive summary' style presentation on Hotol dated December 1984 and according to the official BAe Hotol timeline, this coincides with the "initial presentation of Hotol concept to ESA". It may also have been used to brief Pattie ahead of his trip to Italy.

The first slide posed four questions: "How does Ariane 4 compete now? Will Ariane 5 have the necessary performance (HM60)? Can the United States significantly reduce launch costs? Are there better technical solutions?" Next up were the advantages of Hotol: "Substantially reduce launch costs to remain competitive with improvements in US STS [Space Transportation System—the Space Shuttle] operations. Be sized for majority of payloads, not largest payload which can be envisaged. Retain effective access to geostationary orbit. Improve reliability to STS levels (98% launch success, 99.8% vehicle recovery). Achieve orbital recovery capability or man-in-space on an occasional basis."

Considerations and complications for vehicles such as Ariane and the Space Shuttle were "expendable hardware; vehicle size; number of stages; man on board; ground handling and launch preparations; utilisation; protection against re-entry heating (reusables)" whereas Hotol was characterised as "single stage to orbit; fully recoverable; of modest size; remotely controlled i.e. not permanently manned; easy to handle on ground (and have minimum interface with payload); capable of quick turnround".

Several slides were devoted to Hotol's proposed payload bay and exactly what it could and couldn't carry; there was a construction breakdown and an extremely basic mission profile diagram. The structural details are worthy of note, given what would come later: "Pressurised hydrogen tank as major structural member; payload bay on wing carry through structure; undersurface skin double skin Inconel plate TPS [Thermal Protection System] structure; topsurface titanium double skin structure (CFRP [Carbon Fibre-Reinforced Plastic] in places)."

There were also a number of slides on cost before the final conclusion: "A most cost-effective launch vehicle is required for LEO post-Ariane 4. An expendable vehicle of the required capacity would cost almost as much to develop as a reusable one and its recurring costs would be much higher.

"Two-stage reusable vehicles would still be costly and they would lack operational flexibility. The most economical vehicle would be a reusable SSTO. A pure rocket SSTO would not be practical. A reusable winged, hybrid

Promotional artwork based on the revised scheme—with kinked tailfins and nose fin.

airbreathing/rocket-engined SSTO as envisaged by BAe would be feasible and could be operational by 1998. It could deliver seven tonnes to low inclination LEO and smaller payloads to Molniya and polar orbit, and would have a substantial cross-range capability.

"Horizontal take-off from and landing on Concorde type runways would be possible. It would be compatible with the manned space station, an unmanned space platform and with the STS. Normal turnround time would be 14 days."

Pattie went to Rome, the meeting took place, and to no-one's great surprise the outcome was a commitment to go ahead with the Columbus programme—part of the International Space Station programme, including polar orbiting platforms—and the Ariane 5 launcher.

ESA director general Professor Reimar Lüst summarised the event in the February 1985 edition of *ESA Bulletin*: "The decision to endorse the development of the Ariane 5 launcher, equipped with the large cryogenic engine HM60, is a definite step in pursuit of one of the objectives that the ministers set for us, namely: 'to strengthen the European space-transportation capacity, meeting foreseeable future user requirements within as well as outside Europe, and remaining competitive with space transportation systems that exist or are planned elsewhere...'

"There can be no questioning that, with Ariane, Europe has a powerful voice in the forum of space-transportation systems... Beyond that, note has been taken of the UK studies of the future-generation Hotol project, and significantly other member States were invited to keep the Agency aware of studies in this area."

It was of some small consolation to the British that the French Hermes shuttle didn't get any money either. Lüst wrote: "The Resolution... looks further into the future to give due notice of our intention not to rest on our laurels, for there is the invitation to France to keep the Agency informed of progress on the Hermes manned spaceplane programme, with a view to its incorporation, as soon as feasible, into the optional programmes of the Agency."

'A MILLION OF MY MONEY'

Nearly a month after the conclusion of the meeting, on February 25, 1985, Pattie wrote to Treasury Chief Secretary Peter Rees to explain how the French had irritated other member states with their aggressive support for Hermes, the other states having then "welcomed the opportunity to express interest in [Hotol]". He further noted that if the UK were to take a leading role in the development of a new launcher, "it would be a major change in government policy".

Concept art showing Hotol's 'launch site'—effectively an ordinary airport. Note the take-off trolley between the hangars and the control tower.

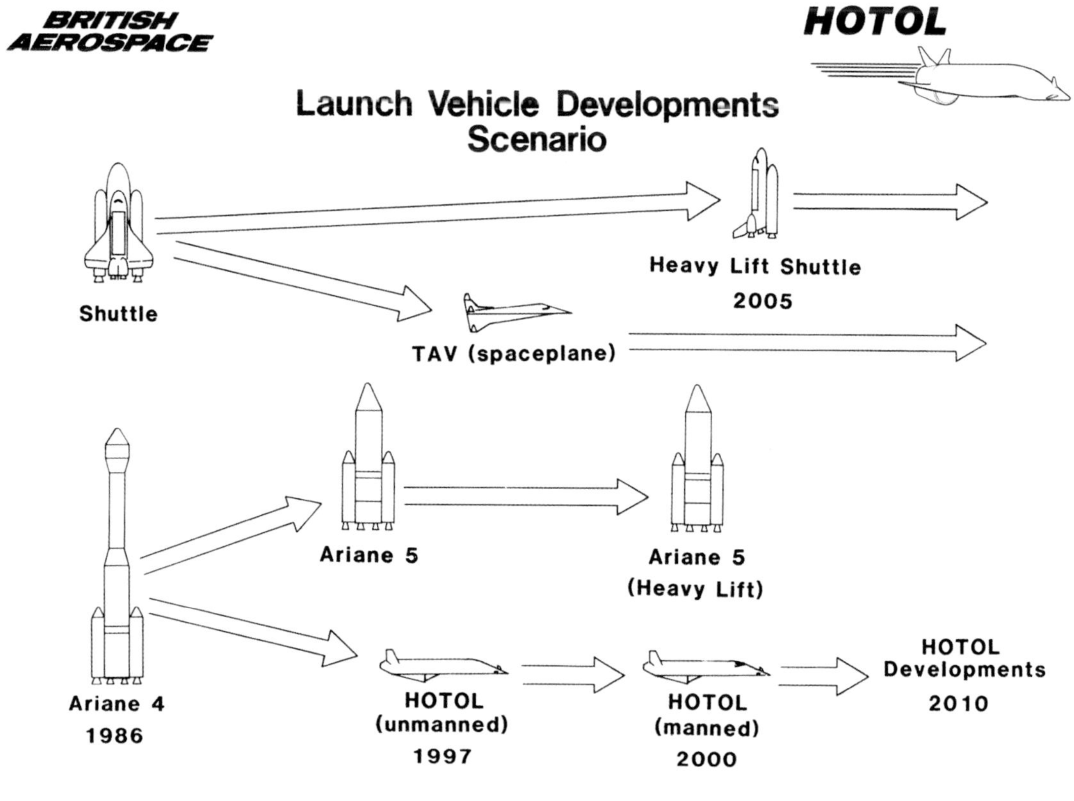

Diagram showing two paths leading from Ariane 4—towards Ariane 5 (Heavy Lift) or towards a future Hotol.

HOTOL and Concorde Comparison

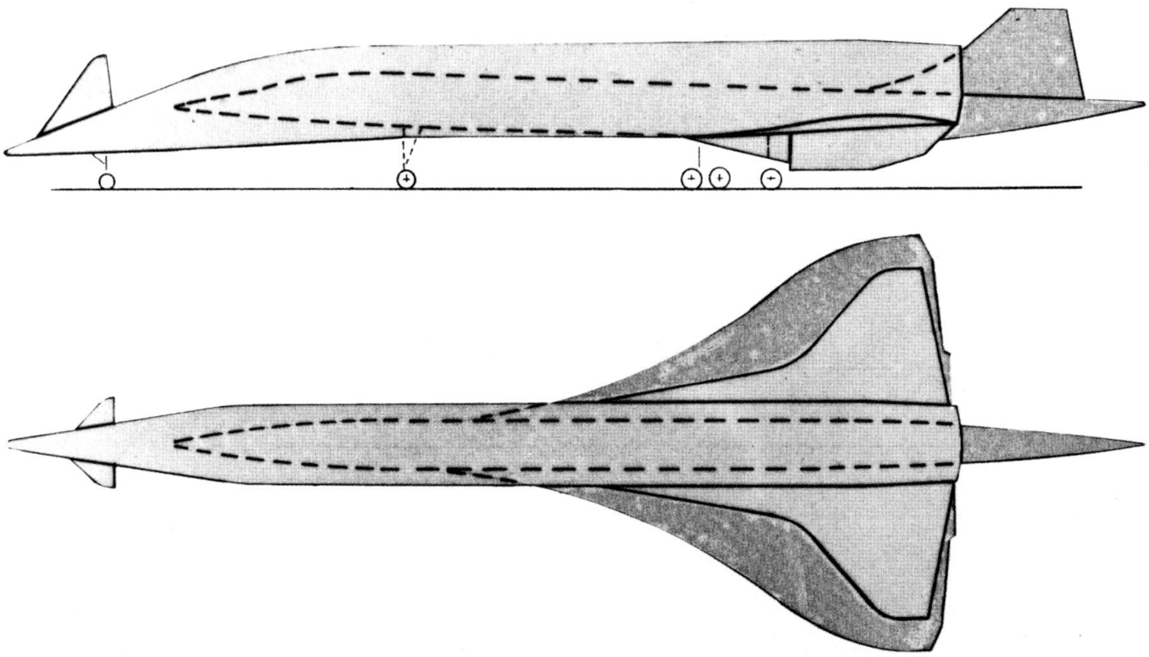

Size comparison between the earliest Hotol configuration—designed at Stevenage and Filton—and Concorde.

HOTOL and U.S. Orbiter Comparison

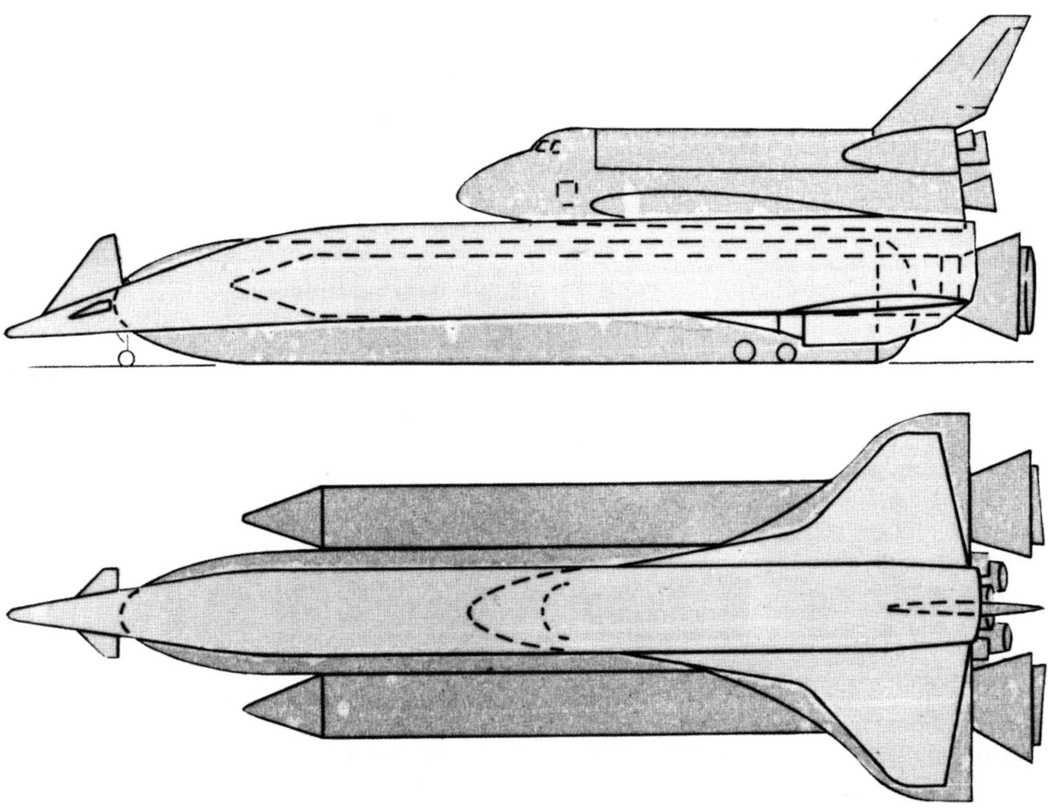

Hotol was not a small vehicle but its total mass was substantially lower than that of the complete American STS.

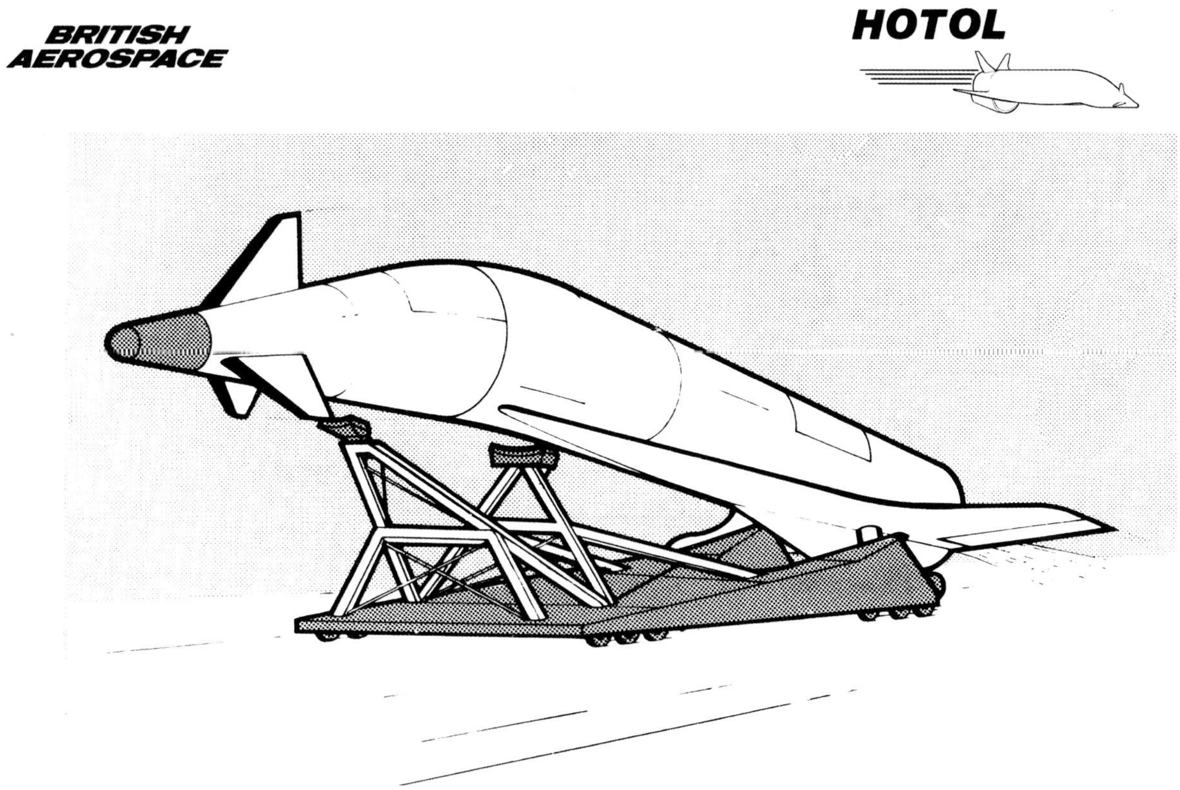

Early concept art showing Hotol aboard a trolley during take-off.

MoD support would be necessary for any future Hotol development due to the classification of its engine as 'secret'. However, MoD research and development department deputy controller James Barnes wrote to Cabinet Office chief scientific advisor Sir Robin Nicholson in April, stating that there was no defence requirement for Hotol.

Pattie saw space science as a worthwhile investment opportunity for Britain and seems increasingly to have become an ardent supporter of British space technology and those developing it. As such, he backed the establishment of a new British National Space Centre (BNSC) to oversee ongoing and future space projects. During a debate in the House of Commons on February 4, 1985, Spencer Batiste, the Conservative MP for Elmet and also Pattie's Parliamentary Private Secretary, had asked Pattie "what are the functions of the British National Space Centre; who will head it and from where it will be staffed; what its budget is and from where this will be provided".

Pattie responded: "The Government intend to establish a British National Space Centre in order to improve the development of space technology in the United Kingdom, and to strengthen the coordination of space policy. Detailed arrangements are being worked out and will be announced in due course."

The BNSC was a work in progress and it wasn't the only one. Concurrent with his work on Hotol, Parkinson had been involved in an ESA study group on the future International Space Station at the behest of Charles Martin—and the ESA meeting in January had already given the green light to European participation in space station plans.

Parkinson remembered: "I went off to look at the free-flying Polar Platform concept associated with the proposals for an International Space Station (which would eventually become Envisat). The ISS/Envisat story is important because that achieved some UK support and got us in front of Sir Raymond Lygo at BAe HQ, and the minister Geoffrey Pattie at DTI."

A meeting took place to discuss space station plans at around this time and according to Parkinson, "I was the least of the people present ... the Admiral [Lygo] was present, he turned to Pattie and said [of Hotol], 'This is important ... worth a million of my money, how much is it to you?' That is literally how it was done. But for the start of [a] proof of concept study, it is not as simple as that, the Admiral doesn't have any money, neither does Pattie."

But Lygo knew where to find the money within his organisation and Pattie was in a position to negotiate funding from other government departments.

It has been suggested but never confirmed that the timing of Hotol suited Lygo well because he had engineers on hold pending a decision on the Eurofighter project—and either had to pay them to do something else in the meantime or risk losing them. It has further

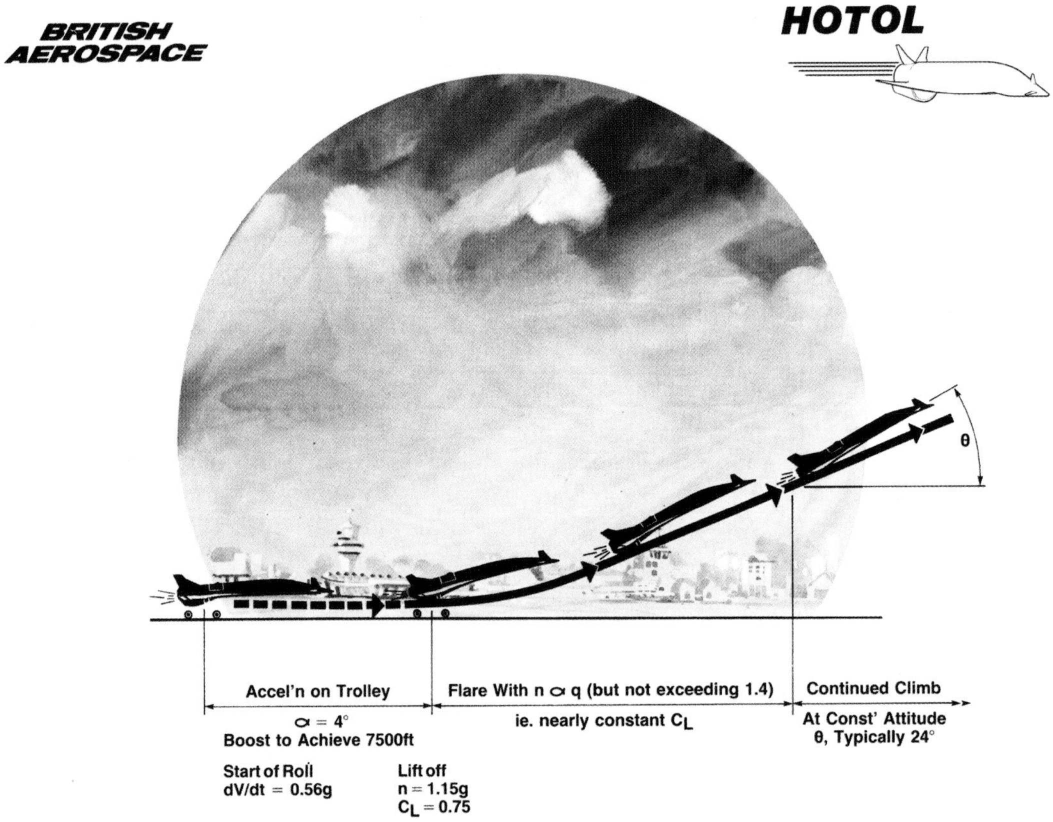

Illustrative diagram showing a Hotol take-off.

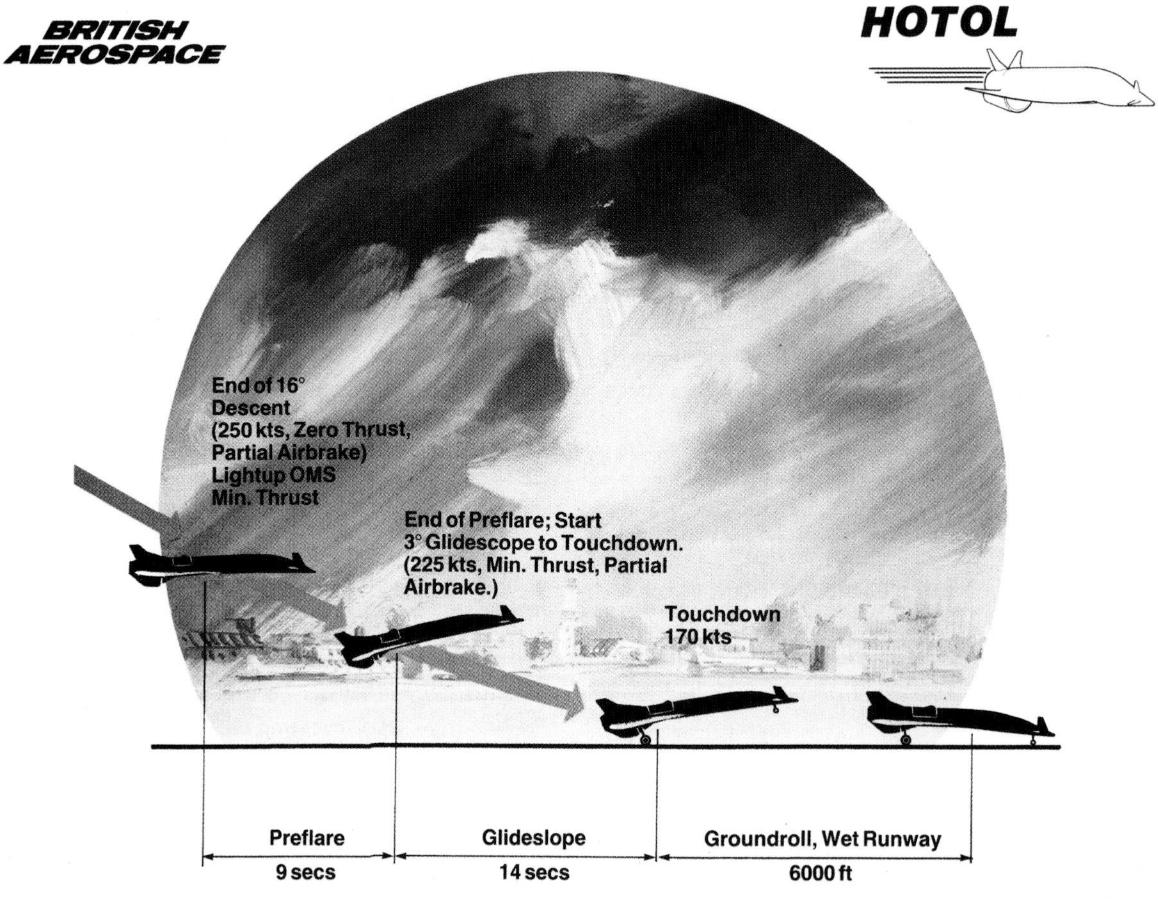

Hotol's landing procedure as shown in official concept art.

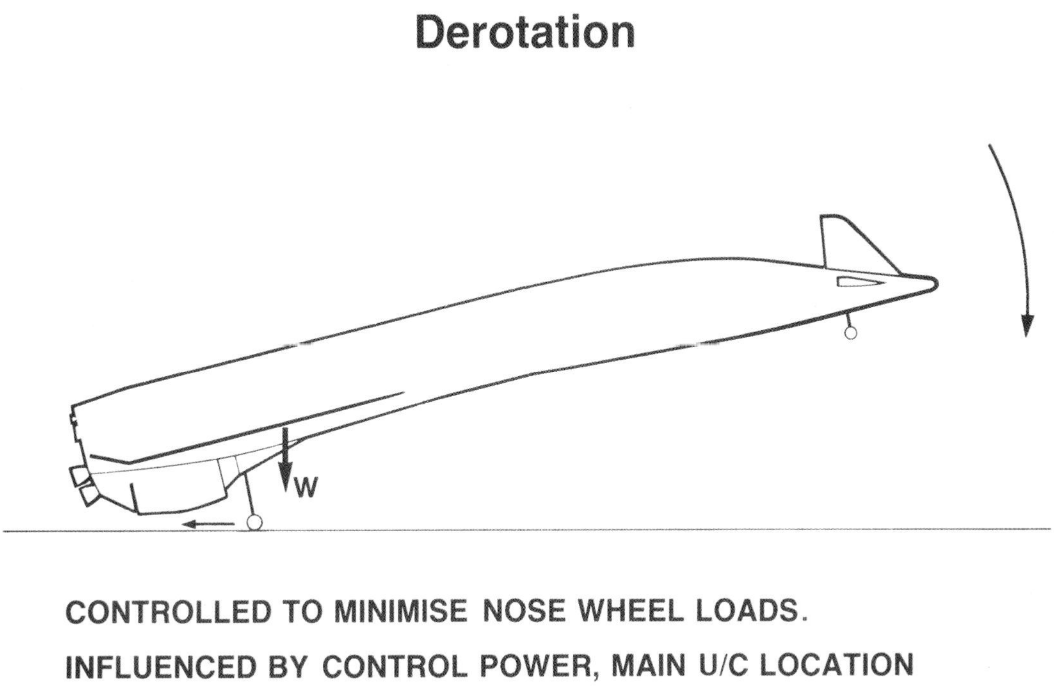

Diagram showing how nosewheel loads would be minimised on landing.

been suggested that Lygo was able to extract some of the required funding from BAe's publicity budget on the grounds that Hotol was already generating positive headlines for the company.

Later in April, Pattie wrote to Secretary of State for Defence Michael Heseltine outlining a plan to enter a public-private partnership with British Aerospace and Rolls-Royce for a two-year proof of concept study on Hotol. This would involve £1m in public money—MoD money—being match-funded by the other two for a total of £3m. Pattie told Heseltine that the expense was justifiable since it would enhance Britain's "strategic capability" and that the technology developed could result in international cooperation on this and other future projects.

Heseltine's feelings on the subject are unclear but one way or another Pattie was able to secure the necessary funding, or at least a commitment to provide it, and preparations commenced to put Hotol at the centre of a much larger-scale development process.

HOTOL GOES TO PARIS

Hotol was again on public display at the end of May 1985, this time in France as the 11-day Paris Air Show commenced. A different model was shown—featuring an extended undercarriage, a conical intake on its underside and taller fins to the rear—plus a cutaway drawing of the vehicle's engine. The British Aerospace team were able to supply some more accurate details of the vehicle's dimensions, with an overall length of 62m, fuselage diameter of 5.7m and cargo bay length of 7.5m being noted in *Aviation Week & Space Technology's* show report, published on June 17. The report also stated that the model "has three propulsion engines located at the rear of the spacecraft's long fuselage… three smaller engine bells are visible and there also are manoeuvring engines on the vehicle… underslung engine air intake is a semi-circular, two-cone external compression design. Location under the wing permits the intake to take advantage of the undersurface compression effect… the wings were developed from the Concorde design, but have been refined for increased lift. Wings are located aft to provide stability with the heavy, aft-mounted rocket motors".

Conchie had told the magazine: "I think we have to get the French to embrace the programme for it to go. The French spend more than any other European nation in this area and always have." Among other details, 'British Aerospace officials' had said that "a powered trolley for launch has not been studied as yet, but probably will be… the initial plan for the take-off system is to use an unpowered trolley and use the spacecraft's main engines for take-off thrust.

"The Hotol would climb to an altitude of 26km (16.12 miles) and reach a speed of Mach 5 nine minutes after take-off. The engine then would change from an airbreathing engine to a true rocket and accelerate the Hotol to orbital speed. Main engine cut-off would be at an altitude of 90km (55.8 miles) and a speed of 17,000mph and the Hotol would coast to orbit at 300km.

PARIS AIR SHOW

British Aerospace Defines Hotol Space Launcher

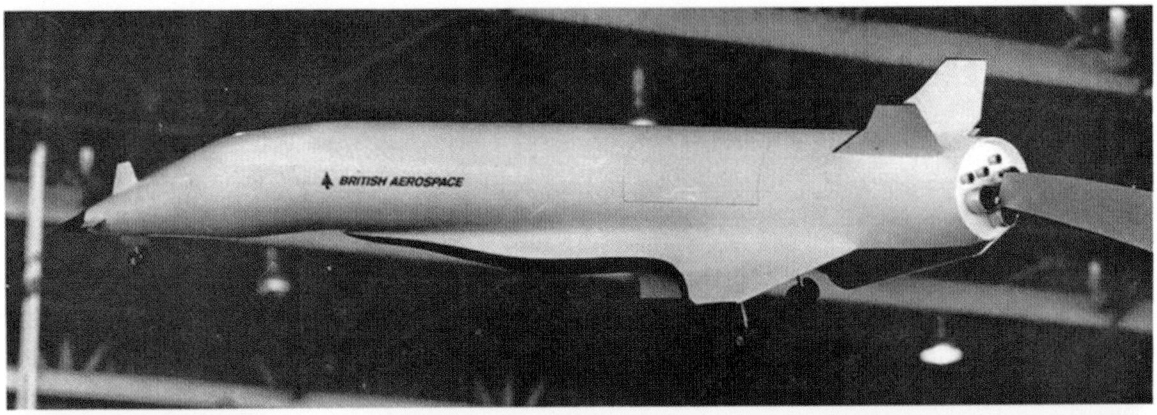

British Aerospace Hotol space launcher model, displayed at the Paris air show, has three propulsion engines located at the rear of the spacecraft's long fuselage (top). Three smaller engine bells are visible and there also are maneuvering engines on the vehicle. The spacecraft would be 62 meters from nose to engine bells, slightly longer than the present Concorde supersonic transport (AW&ST June 3, p. 356). Underslung engine air intake is a semi-circular, two-cone external compression design (photo directly above). Location under the wing permits the intake to take advantage of the undersurface compression effect. Note curvature of wing undersurface. The wings were developed from the Concorde design, but have been refined for increased lift. Wings are located aft to provide stability with the heavy, aft-mounted rocket motors. The cargo bay, approximately 24.6 ft. long, is located immediately forward of the engines and liquid oxygen tanks, and the vehicle's liquid hydrogen tanks are ahead of the cargo bay. View from under the forward portion of the Hotol fuselage (right) shows wing curvature and landing gear arrangement. This view makes the fuselage appear slightly longer in relation to the wingspan than it really is.

Images of the Hotol model displayed at the 1985 Paris Air Show, as they appeared in Aviation Week & Space Technology *magazine.* AW&ST

"Since the Hotol will be unmanned, a secure command link to the ground is required and British Aerospace currently is studying the possibility of control instructions being transmitted to the vehicle from a data relay satellite."

A more controversial aspect of the Hotol pitch was also outlined in the magazine—the idea that "British Aerospace is studying a transatmospheric transport version of Hotol, capable of carrying up to 60 passengers from London to Sydney, Australia, in approximately one hour.

"The concept envisages a pressurised module that would carry passengers and their baggage and that would be loaded into the Hotol spacecraft's cargo bay after the passengers were on board. British Aerospace has not yet determined if the vehicle would be manned by a human pilot, but believes that the automated control system planned for the non-man-rated Hotol satellite launcher could be successfully used."

A BAe official, evidently PR man John Humby, had explained that whether the Hotol airliner would have a human crew or not would "depend on whether people feel more confident with one human pilot or three computers by the year 2000".

Passengers boarding this theoretical version of Hotol—since little to no serious engineering work appears to have been carried out on it—would be subjected to 0.56g "or about twice that now experienced on the Concorde supersonic jet transport, and vertical acceleration during climb would be 1.15g. British Aerospace calculates flight time from overhead London to overhead Sydney at about 45 minutes and expects that the average wheels-off to wheels-on time would be about 67 minutes, due to air traffic control imposed delays".

Humby, who is widely credited with concocting the notion of Hotol as an airliner, correctly surmised that it would resonate with the public—but the Hotol team, knowing that this was never a realistic possibility, would find it something of an irritation as time went on.

PROOF-OF-CONCEPT

Less than a month later, on July 11, 1985, eight men sat down to map out the future of Hotol at BAe's offices in 100 Pall Mall, London: Conchie and Parkinson from Stevenage, Leyman from Filton plus British Aerospace deputy managing director (aircraft) Ivan Yates, divisional technical director Dr I. A. M. Hall and head of research and development John Arnall from head office along with technical director Brian Young and project/technical manager Bryan Robert Alexander 'Sandy' Burns from BAe's Military Aircraft Division at Warton in Lancashire. Warton was set to take the lead on the project since it had

Hotol project manager Sandy Burns.

experience in space vehicle design (see Introduction), the most suitable facilities for wind tunnel testing and the appropriate staffing availability.

According to the post-meeting summary, "The purpose of the meeting was to brief Mr Yates on the status of the Hotol project, including funding and work-sharing proposals for the 'Proof-of-Concept' study over two years. Proposals have already been submitted to DoT/RAE."

There would be three presentations—Conchie speaking on "justification/economics", Parkinson on "engineering description—overall" and Leyman on "aircraft and engine aspects". Conchie pointed out that satellite manufacture and operations were big business and that "forecasts suggest 1,000 tonnes per year in orbit by 2005" with a growth rate of 7% per year, "hence [the] urgent need for [an] economic launch vehicle". Shuttle was "too expensive to be a commercial proposition in the 1990s and beyond and turnround is too slow (two launches per month is probable maximum)". Ariane 5 would "be slightly cheaper for GEO [Geosynchronous Orbit] operations but not much different for LEO, probably not competitive with US post-1995 projects... Ariane propulsion is not hi-tech".

Hotol's objectives, he explained, were "fully reusable, quick turnaround" at half the cost of Shuttle into GEO and a fifth of the cost into LEO. Though, "Hotol payloads will need boosters to take them from LEO to GEO (established practice)". The success of Hotol "depends primarily on propulsion concept with airbreathing initial trajectory".

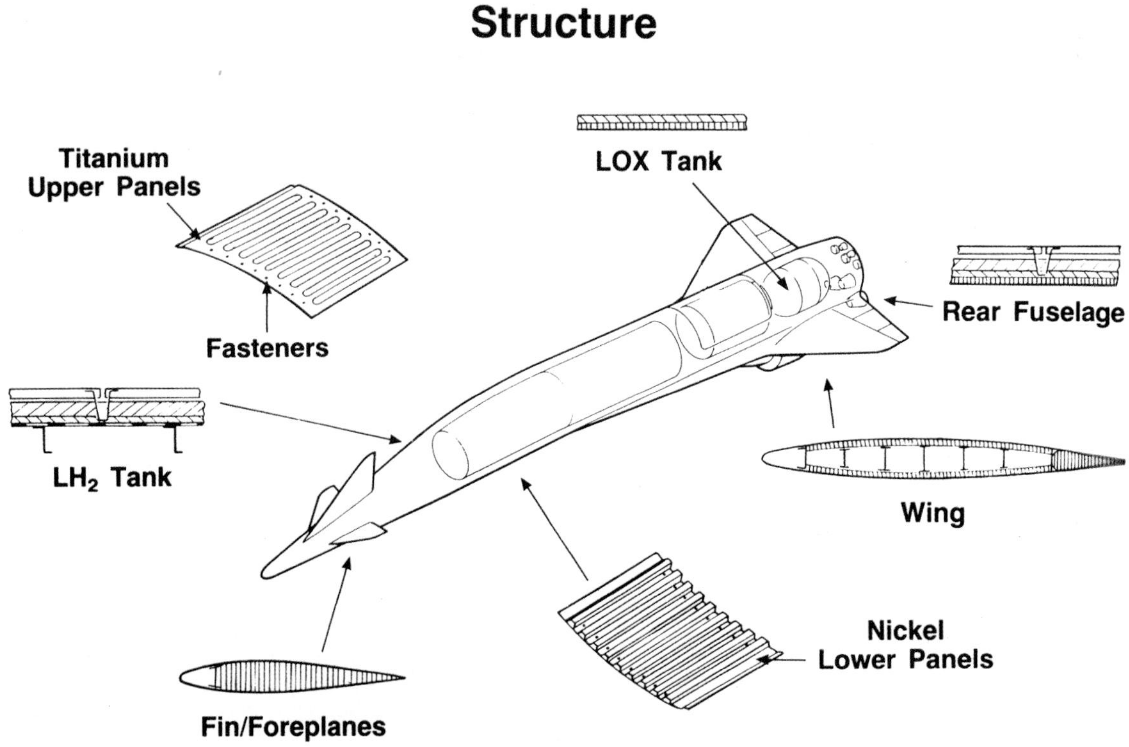

Structural layout of the earliest Hotol configuration.

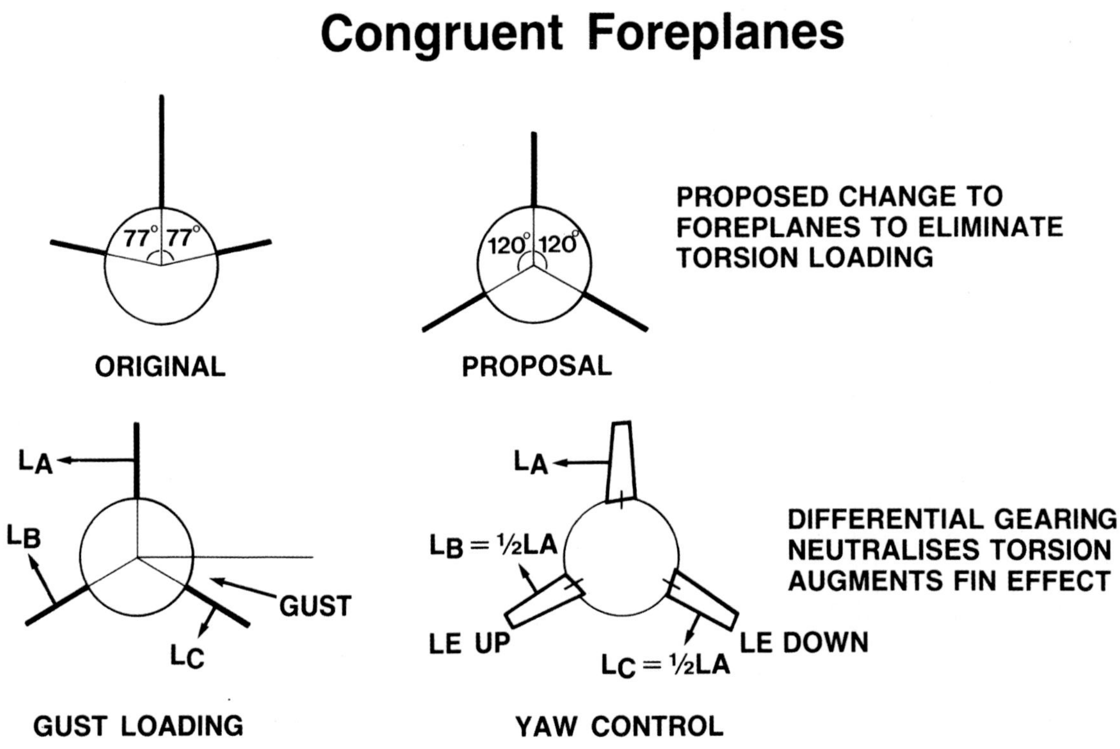

Some of the earliest work done on Hotol was intended to examine how it would deal with gusts—resulting in a proposed redesign of its foreplanes.

All-up weight would be 200 tonnes compared to American SSTO projects which were "all rocket" and typically around 500 tonnes.

The summary of his presentation wrapped up with, "Favourable response is expected following presentations (by Stevenage/Rolls-Royce) to Geoffrey Pattie et alia. Geoffrey Pope, director RAE, quoted 'Must spend £ to find out if it will work'."

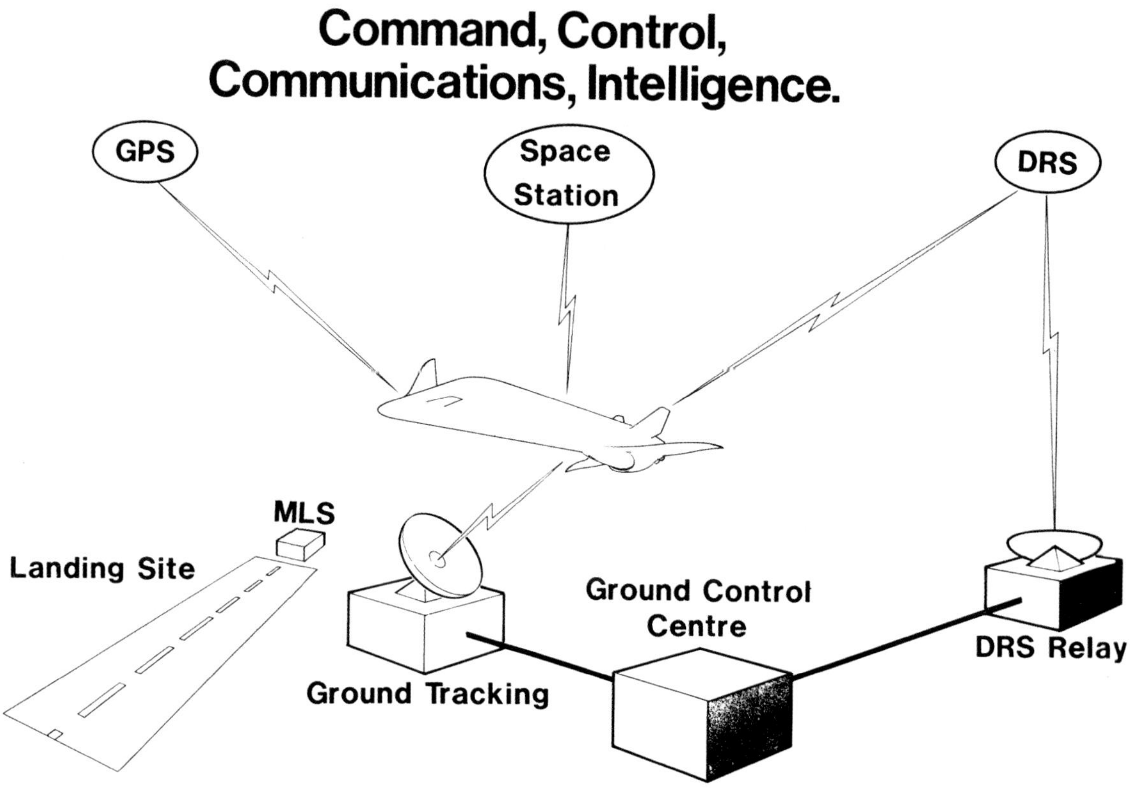

Hotol would rely on electronic systems and communications for command and control—rather than a human crew.

Parkinson's engineering description was short: "Key to propulsion is to compress air (unlimited free supplies) to pressure required for rocket motor (2,000psi), can't do with hot air (heated by stagnation); hence cool with cryogenic fuel (H2) in heat exchangers before compression. High drag/weight (low wing loading when empty) makes re-entry possible without lower skin temperatures exceeding limits for steel alloys, so no need for tiles or ablative coating. N.B. creep may limit structure life rather than fatigue. Titanium or CFRP okay for upper surfaces. Fuels H2 and air when air-breathing, H2+LOX rocket trajectory, Orbital Manoeuvring System (OMS) and retardation for re-entry. H2 direct for Reaction Control System (RCS)".

And Leyman's presentation was even shorter: "Wing area fixed by take-off—1.5g at 300 knots off trolley. Euro-engine rocket technology, current values compression ratio per stage, turbine efficiency etc. are assumed (i.e. not 'sometime-never' technology). Heat exchanger design/manufacture including avoidance of icing, is a key technology demonstration point in the 'proof-of-concept' study".

In other words, Hotol would get payloads into orbit at a fraction of the cost of the Space Shuttle or Ariane 5. The engine was its unique selling point, with other benefits such as reduced size and fuel load possible because of it. Trolley take-off was already presumed and much of the engine tech was off-the-shelf—a known quantity. The main area of concern was getting the novel heat exchanger right.

However, since the heat exchanger and the rest of the propulsion system fell within Rolls-Royce's remit, the post-presentation discussion naturally centred around BAe's study objectives. These included drag control and trajectory optimisation to minimise the quantity of fuel burned during the airbreathing part of the ascent; mass assessment; aeroelastic estimates and the compiling of data on heat transfer, suitable structures and the likely gust environment Hotol would encounter.

It was noted that "team manning [is] important—key men. No 'computer-bashers'. Structural design is a key area. Possibility of recruiting from the USA". There was also a need to determine what "enabling technologies" the RAE and NGTE could be working on to support the project. The budget was £2m and this would likely be split three ways. Warton would get £800,000 with 12 staff working on the vehicle structure, aerodynamics, systems and wind tunnel testing. Stevenage was allocated £300,000 to support five staff working on trajectory dynamics and operations while Filton would also get £300,000 to pay for 4.5 staff working on intake design, one wind tunnel model and liaison with Rolls-Royce.

Exactly where this money was coming from "was not clarified but Mr Yates instructed that this must not delay start of work". Furthermore, public relations work would need to be more than superficial and "good presentation of engineering is important. Warton need to keep in contact but 'raison d'etre' publicity is best kept at Stevenage". Management and communications structures for this new three-division team had yet to be defined but "Mr Yates requested a monthly progress report" and "Warton should assume lead division role with immediate effect".

AMERICA TAKES NOTE

Nearly two weeks after this meeting, on July 24, 1985, Congressman Tom Lewis, from Florida, was addressing a hearing on high-speed aeronautics before the US House of Representatives' subcommittee on transportation, aviation and materials. He said: "The shift in emphasis from subsonic aeronautics to high speed is a welcome change. We have neglected this important technology for too long. The competition is not waiting for us, and we simply cannot afford to drag our feet any longer … There … has been a growing awareness that we need to develop a more efficient means of space transportation and reduce the costs of putting payloads into orbit.

"An aerospace plane that can take off and land from conventional runways and reach orbital speeds promises to do that. A transatmospheric vehicle that can take off and land horizontally is an exciting concept. Apparently, others agree. The British are already working on this concept. They call it the Hotol … and they hope to have it flying by 1997. They estimate that they will be able to put a satellite into orbit for one-half to one-fifth the cost of our shuttle launches, and they predict they will have 75% of the commercial launch market by the year 2000.

"It is clear that if we don't want to play catch-up, we will have to move very fast. The competition is not waiting for us."

He said that building an SSTO aerospace plane was an ambitious goal but he believed it had "the support of the American people" and "it is a challenge we must accept. We cannot afford not to."

Further discussion followed and Congressman Harold Brubaker said that if US companies did not get involved in SSTO aerospace planes "we would lose our technological edge in the world aerospace business. As Mr Lewis points out, the British are already looking at horizontal take-off and landing, supersonic kind of aircraft and engine. They have closed, I understand, that engine to any outside look-see so they think they really have a breakthrough. We have to stay ahead in technology."

Hotol was now making waves around the world—with the classification of Bond's engine drawing serious attention from the heavy hitters of the aerospace industry. If the

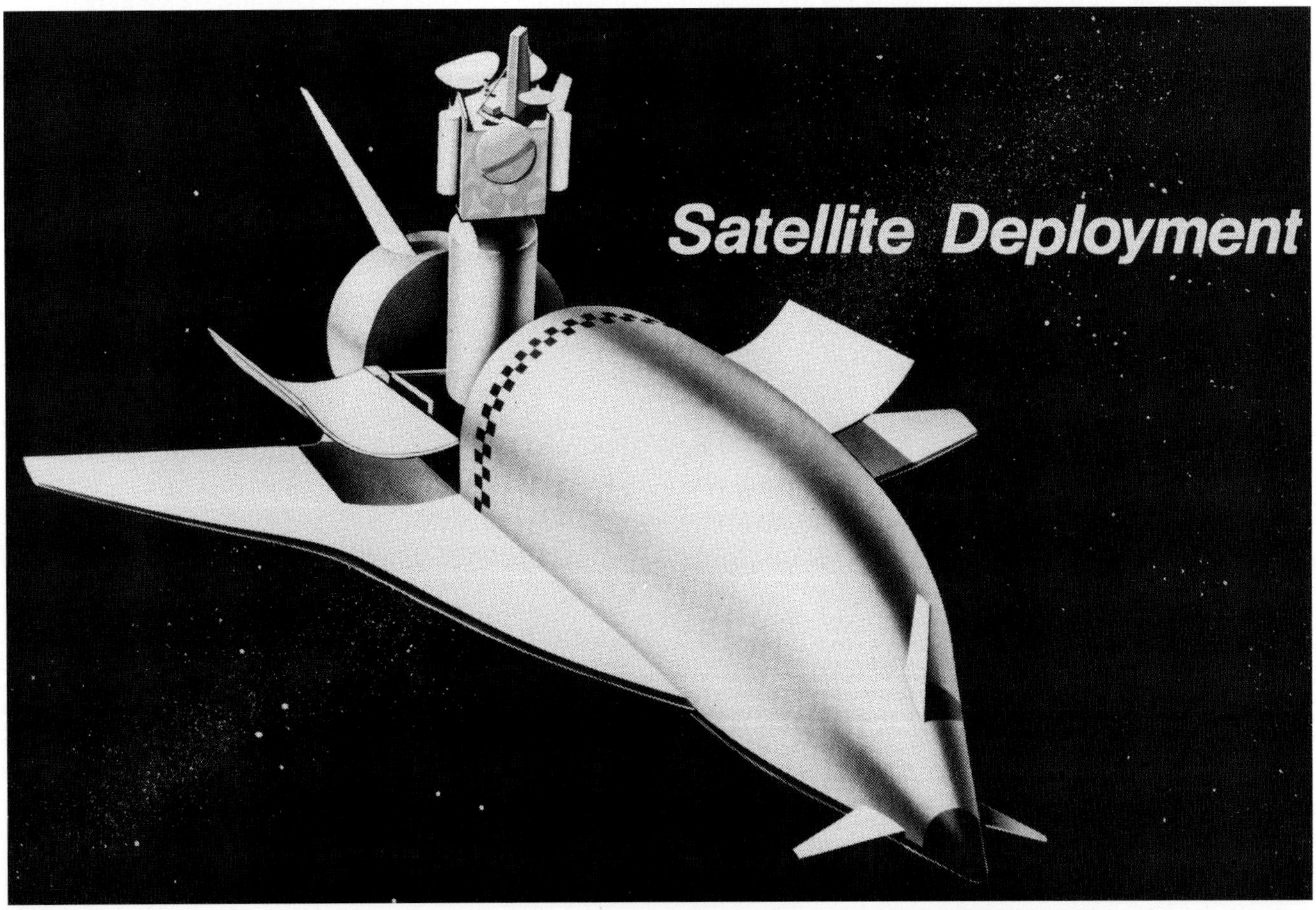

Launching satellites was big business and would have been Hotol's primary purpose.

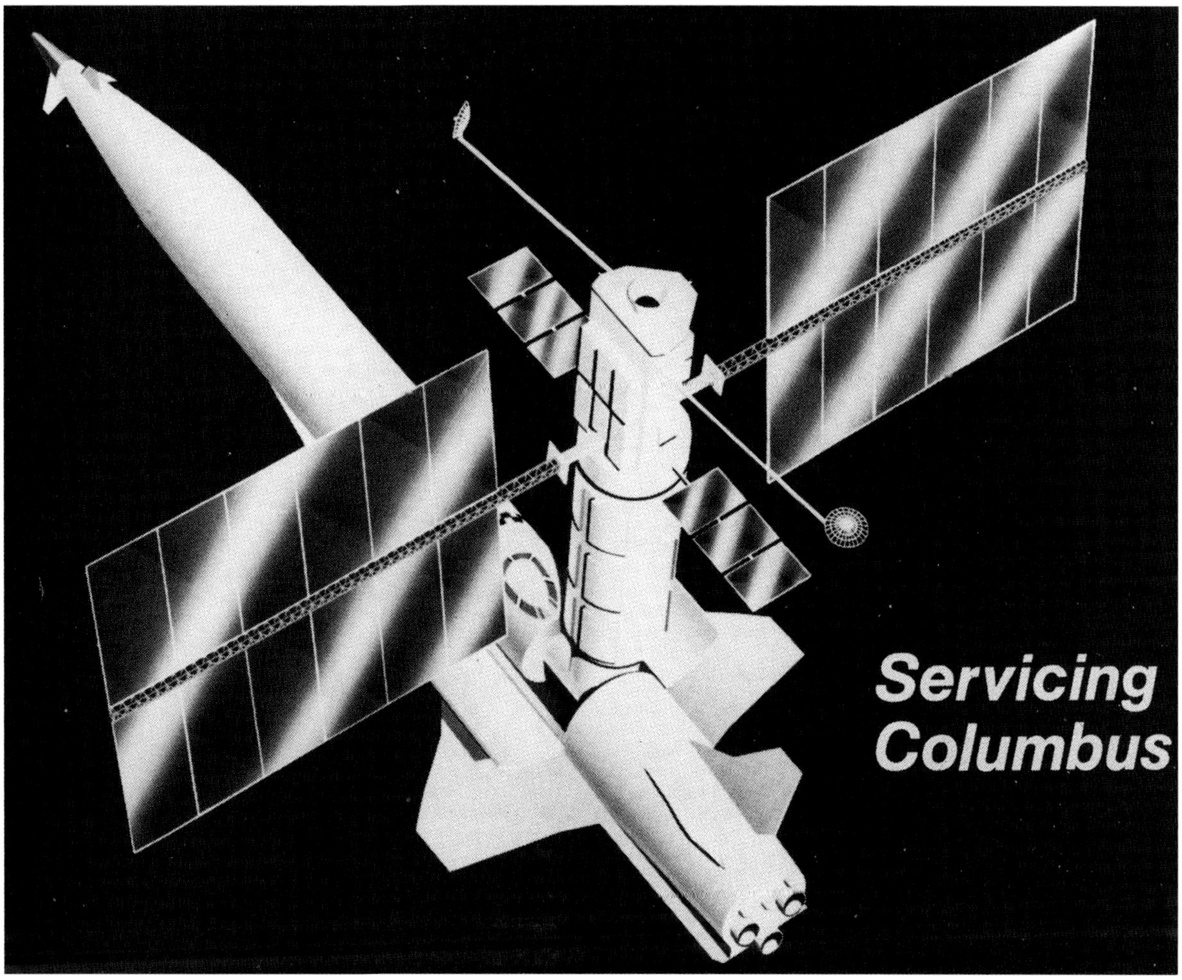

Another potential Hotol mission—servicing future space stations.

British had a 'breakthrough', how far would the Americans go to get hold of it for themselves? And how far would the British go to protect it?

BURNS GETS STARTED

On the same day that Congress was discussing Hotol, Sandy Burns, now charged with setting up and running the BAe side of the project at Warton, typed up a rough two-page summary of it with echoes of the Pall Mall presentations—perhaps as briefing notes for future team members.

He wrote: "The project was conceived by the Space and Communications Division at Stevenage. The main business of Stevenage Division is building satellites, primarily for communications, and these sell at a tremendous price and the technology per unit raw material is huge. In units people might understand, they sell at about £15,000 per pound in weight of material compared to aeroplanes, which are about £200 per pound weight and cars, which are about £5 per pound weight. For a country that imports most of its raw materials, satellites are tremendous business.

"Current satellites are put up into space by the American shuttle, or the French Ariane. The shuttle can cope with a maximum of 500 tons per year put into orbit at a maximum launch rate, so we will need something else beyond 1995.

"The shuttle, for one thing, could not carry the amount of stuff we expect to put into orbit at the beginning of the next century and its costs are far too great because they have to pay 5,000 men on the ground at the Kennedy Space Center. 42% of the cost of the shuttle is staffing, then there are the throwaway tanks that carry the fuel, a lot is spent on refurbishing the head rocket boosters and only 16% of the total cost is on reusable fuel and hardware.

"The Americans are putting all their space money into the manned space station over the next ten years, and they are not spending a great deal of money at the moment on a shuttle replacement. Space and Communications have looked at various types of vehicle to put satellites into orbit to replace the shuttle, and concluded that the Hotol type vehicle is the most economic proposition.

"The objective of the replacement vehicle is quick turnround. The shuttle fleet cannot do more than about two

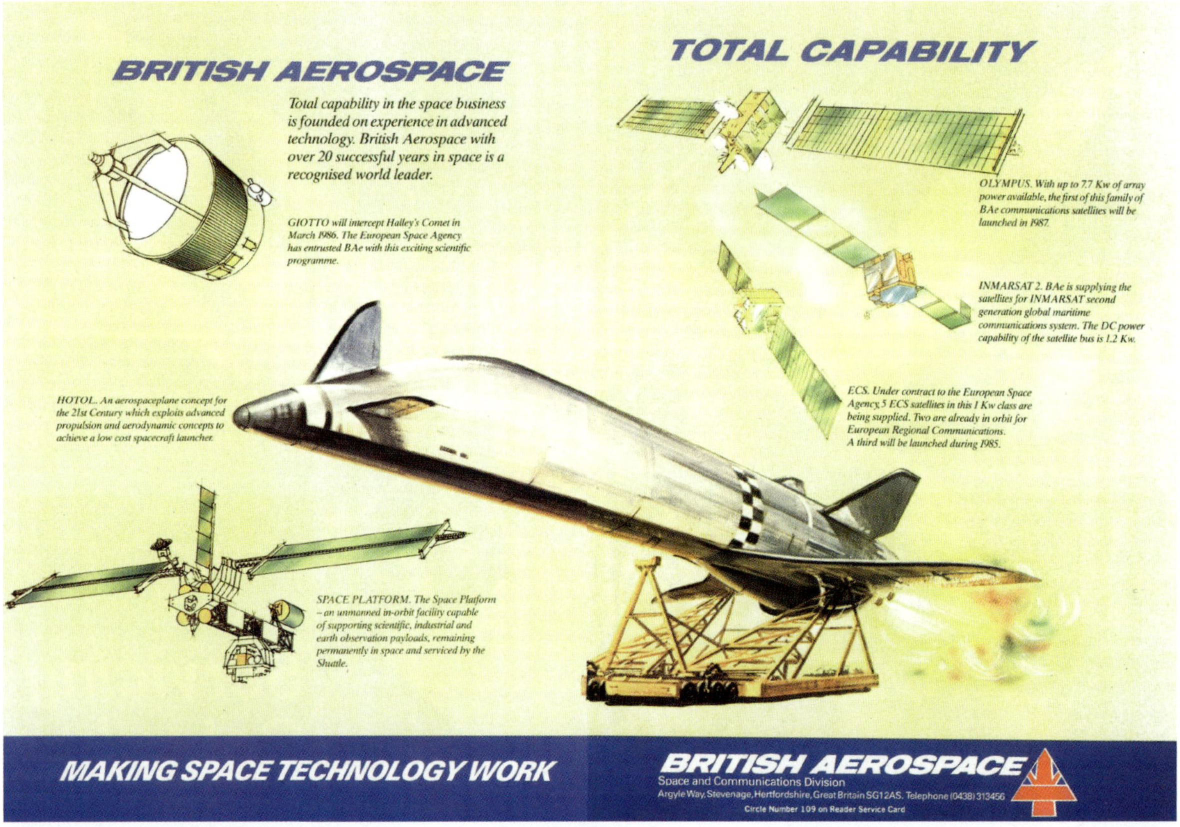

Early Hotol publicity advertisement.

launches per month, their limitation being the ground facility, proving for flight, etc.

"What is being sought is reduced cost for putting staff into orbit, quick turn-round and preferably unmanned because the safety factor isn't quite as critical if lives are not involved. The single-stage vehicles that have been studied in the past have been extremely large and heavy, typically 500 tons, which is more than a Jumbo.

"The breakthrough that will make this vehicle possible is that it has air-breathing propulsion on the first part of the trajectory. The propulsion concept is to use air (which is free), treated and compressed in a particular way and use the inner conventional rocket chamber with the liquid hydrogen and then when you get up to a certain height and speed you shut down the air intake and continue on liquid oxygen and hydrogen.

"This concept makes possible a vehicle of about 200 tons take-off weight to put 700 tons of payload into orbit. This is about the size of Concorde. The concept of horizontal take-off and landing means that you don't need any special gantry facilities, like you have at Kennedy Space Center, to sit it on its end. It can operate from relatively conventional runways.

"Initially, the project was conceived by Stevenage Space and Communications Division, and the Bristol site of the Civil Aircraft side have participated in the aircraft engineering parts of the project study: the first part of the climb and recovery of landing.

"They got it to a certain stage where it looked as if it would be possible for that size, weight and cost. The next stage, where Warton Division becomes involved, is the proof-of-concept study. Sir Raymond Lygo has decreed that Warton should be lead Division on this project from now, on the next phase of the study at least, which is the proof-of-concept stage, over two years, and that we would lead this study in conjunction with Space and Communications at Stevenage, Bristol site of Civil Aircraft side and Rolls-Royce, with whom we are doing the propulsion studies. It will be a joint study to put more depth into the studies already done. The scale of effort at Warton will be about 10-12 people, plus some wind tunnel testing. The scale of effort at Stevenage will be about six people and 4-5 at Bristol, over two years.

"Following the successful completion of this phase after two years, the Warton Division manpower on the job will increase significantly and there will be an overall programme of about ten years of detailed design, engineering and testing to bring it into being as an operational vehicle."

Sixteen days later, on August 9, 1985, he produced the first of 42 monthly reports he would make on the project to Yates. He noted that the work-share between the Military Aircraft Division at Warton, the Space and Communications Division at Stevenage and the Civil Division at Filton had now been finalised. Warton was responsible for the project as a whole with technical management and overall airframe engineering responsibility. Stevenage "retains major responsibility for operational aspects" and Filton "retains a share of the aerodynamic tasks, notably air intake design and the airframe/engine interface. Propulsion responsibilities are unchanged".

The core Hotol team at Warton would be nine-strong, with additional work being carried out by the division's specialist departments. Meanwhile, Parkinson had made contact with Maurice Deller at RAE Farnborough's Space Department and "three other RAE specialists, Dr Mowbray, Messrs. Dommett and Wade, have been nominated as having interest in the project". A meeting with them had been arranged for early September.

Parkinson had himself been contacted by Dr Peter Natenbruk of ERNO—a German company then engaged in building laboratory modules for the Space Shuttle known as Spacelab pallets—"who suggested the possibility of work packages on Hotol, concerned mainly with space operations, but also with aerodynamic heating".

Lastly, Burns stated that "no information has so far been received regarding the funding arrangements [for the project], from either DoT [DTI] or from BAe". Even by the time of his second monthly report, issued on September 12, 1985, this situation persisted and was having a negative impact on preparations to get the Proof-of-Concept study going.

Burns wrote: "The means of allocating BAe funding to the three divisions involved in this study has not yet been defined. A meeting had been arranged with the managing director, Sir Raymond Lygo, at Kingston on September 3, but this was postponed. Pending agreement on funding, Civil Aircraft Division are doing no work; Stevenage are carrying on with promotional activity and operational studies; Warton have begun to build up the technical team and have started investigations on aerodynamics and structural design."

RAE SPECIALISTS

The meeting with the RAE specialists took place in the Board Room at Warton over two days—September 16-17, 1985. For the first day, Deller was joined by his colleagues David Way from the Propulsion Department, T. A. Cook from aerodynamics and J. A. E. A. Cook from materials and structures. The BAe representatives were Burns, Young, Leyman, Parkinson and Conchie. It had been hoped that Scott-Scott would also be there but he was ill and Gordon Lewis had rung Burns personally to explain that there was "no suitable deputy and that he himself was currently fully occupied with EFA [European Fighter Aircraft—eventually to become the Eurofighter Typhoon] matters".

The RAE delegates were treated to a Hotol video—presumably specially prepared—followed by presentations from Conchie, Parkinson, Leyman and this time Burns too, on the Proof-of-Concept (PoC) study itself. During subsequent discussions the issue of a timescale for approaching prospective partners for international cooperation was addressed: "It is believed that [an] ... overture, to the French initially, should be made in about a year's time. The end of the PoC Study (two years) would be too late because the momentum of the Ariane 5 programme would be established by then. Note that the French attitude up to now has been 'must be after Ariane 5 because Hotol uses unproven technology'. We must make maximum progress during this first year to convince Europe and the USA of the soundness of the project ... the current work programme includes a mid-term report after a year's work but this date might have to be advanced to meet the above requirement".

Each RAE specialist, excluding Deller, then put forward their own comments. T. A. Cook raised concerns about air intake flow instability damaging the heat exchangers, discussed potential flow simulations and talked about measuring re-entry heat transfer using wind tunnel models. The other Mr Cook wanted reassurances that Hotol's proposed metallic thermal protection system, which lacked the familiar tiles as seen on Shuttle or ablative coating, would be sufficient for re-entry. "BAe replied that this question could not be answered at present but the accuracy of such predictions will become evident during the course of the study". Cook then proposed tests of structural samples during the PoC period to demonstrate the effectiveness of the TPS and it was agreed that a separate meeting would be held on this.

There was a brief discussion on acoustic loading but "it is believed that this is unlikely to be a major problem, effects being confined to the rear part of the fuselage during the early part of the take-off. Noise levels will be lower than those of the Space Shuttle due to the use of liquid fuel rocket propulsion rather than solid rocket boosters. It was noted that the size of the sliding outer skin panels may possibly be limited by panel flutter".

The RAE propulsion man, Way, was full of praise for Bond's engine: "RAE recognise the novelty and cleverness of the proposed hybrid propulsion cycle and strongly support the proposed study. RAE commented that there was a need for design, construction and test of a number

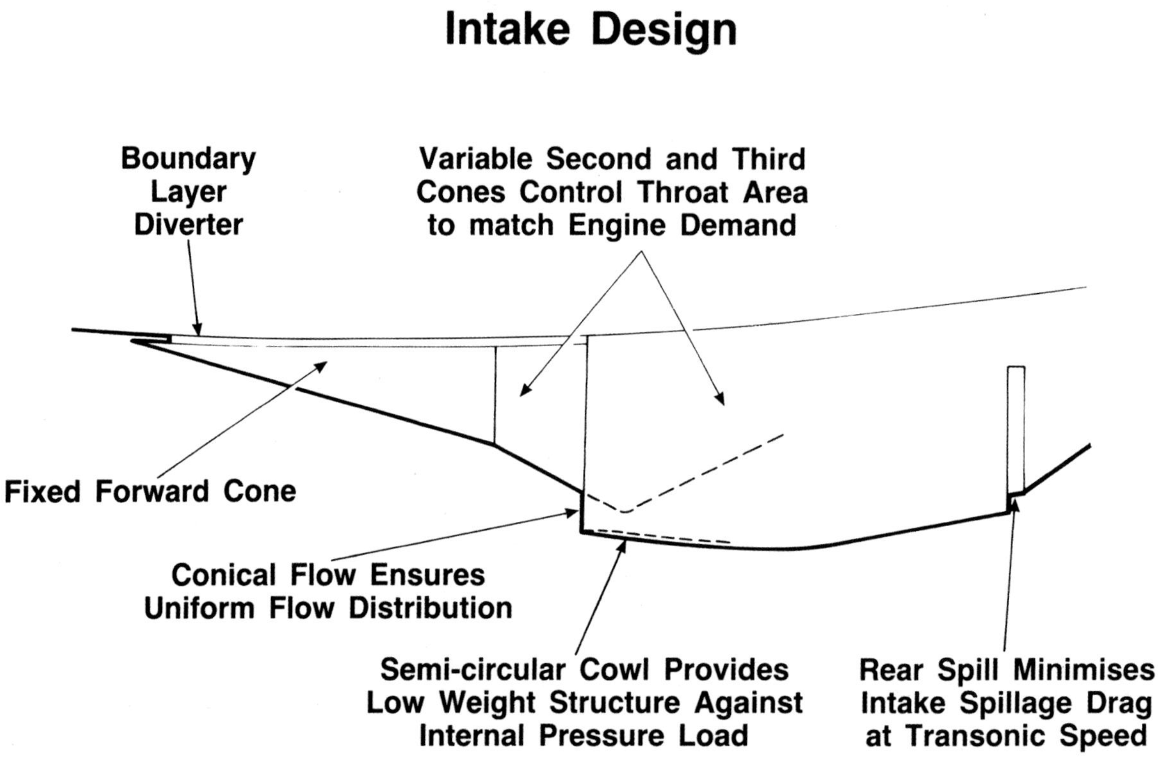

Hotol's early intake design was semi-circular with shock cones.

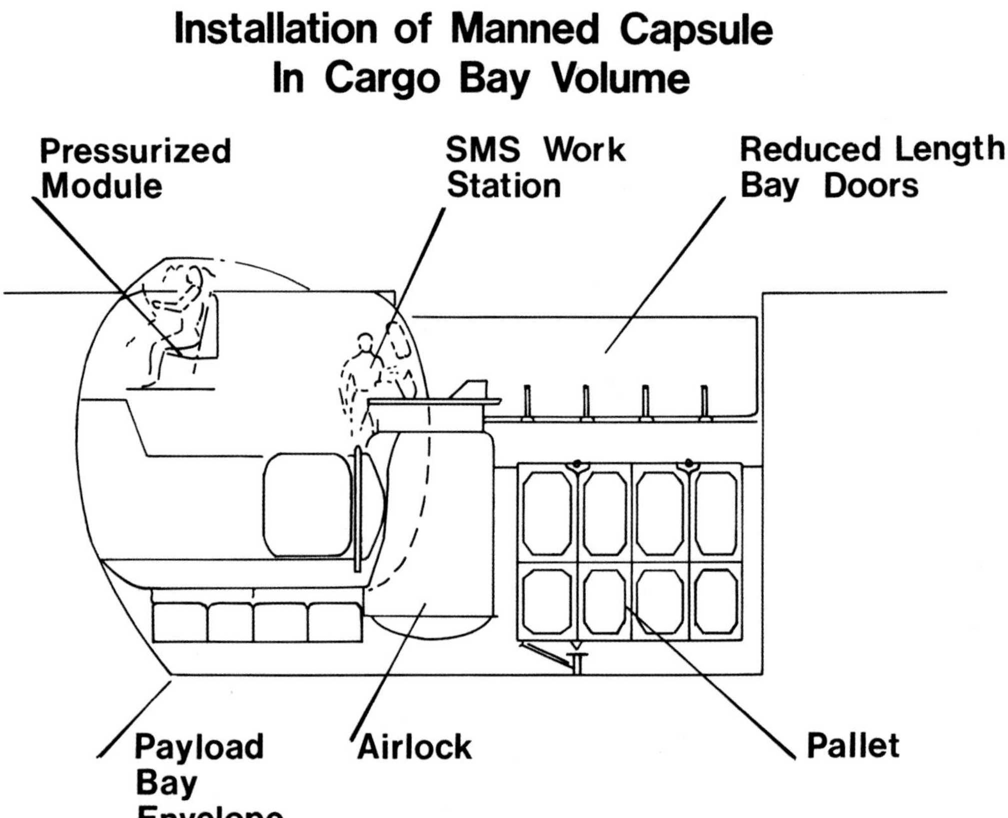

If it became necessary for Hotol to carry crew, they would have been housed within a capsule installed in the payload bay as shown here.

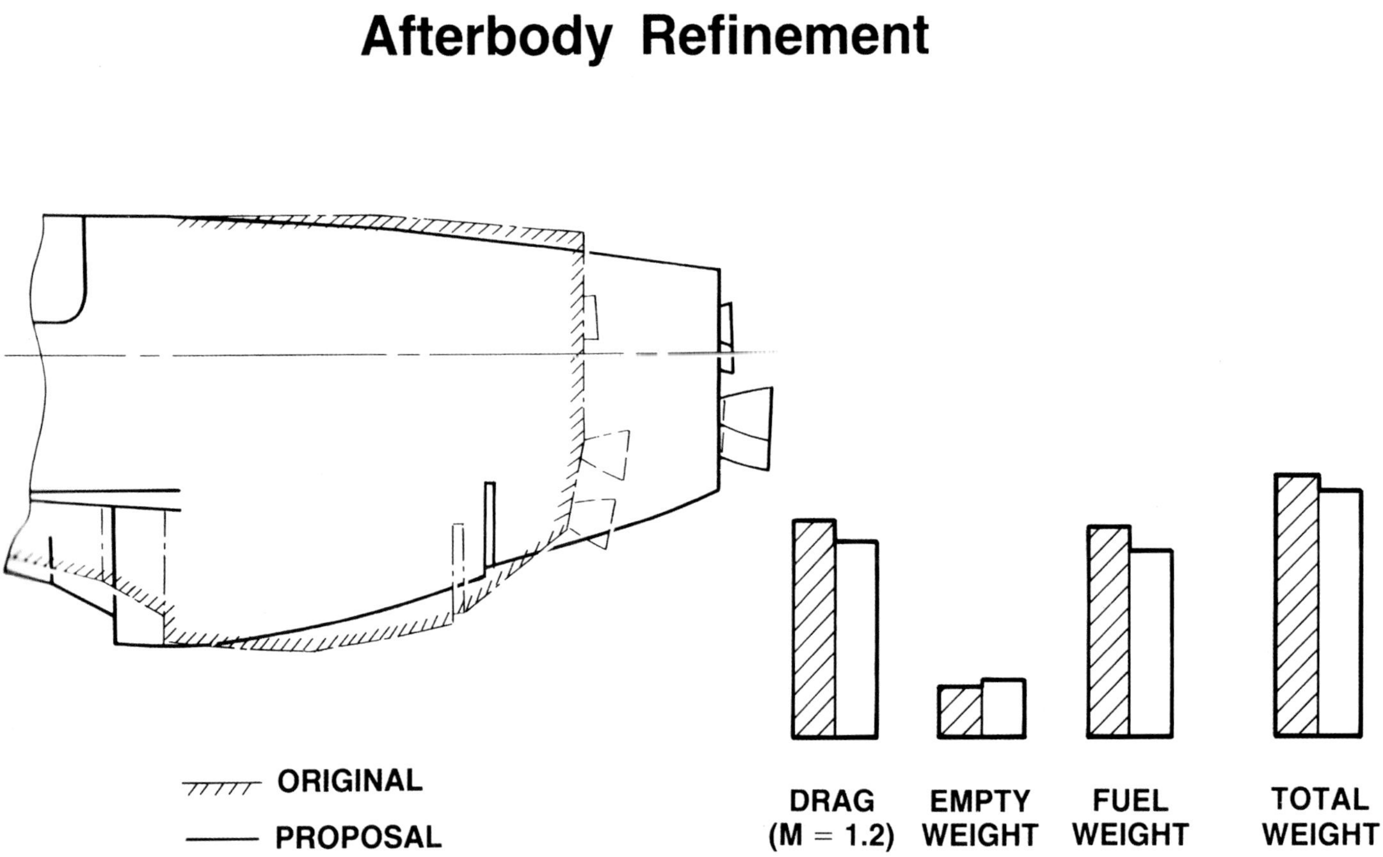

The design evolution of Hotol commenced in earnest as soon as BAe Warton took responsibility for development of the vehicle.

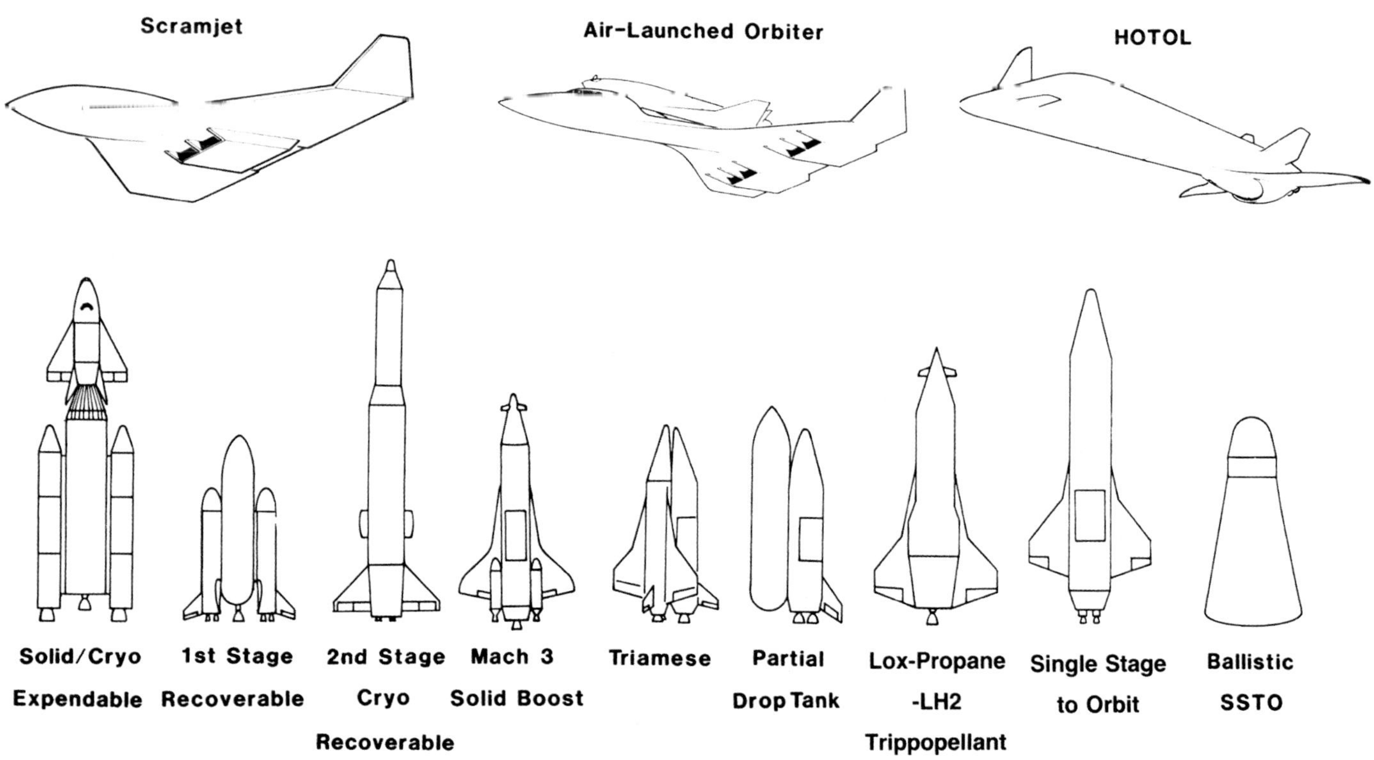

Launcher alternatives—an official BAe comparison reusing art from Parkinson's early 1984 presentation.

of propulsion components, other than the heat exchangers, at an early date. In the absence of RR, BAe replied that the design of the compressors and turbines did not rely on unproven technology and therefore would be undertaken in subsequent phases beyond the two-year PoC. Such work would commence in phase 2. It could be done earlier, but this would require significantly increased expenditure."

Way attempted to probe further on various aspects of the engine's design but the BAe representatives were forced to steer him in the direction of Rolls-Royce, being unable to provide ready answers. At one point he "queried whether a study of scramjet auxiliary propulsion, burning the hydrogen dumped overboard, would be included in phase 1. BAe replied that the mainstream design would be worked up without this, which will be a phase 2 item, unless a strong need for additional thrust emerges from initial studies".

HUMAN CREW? MILITARY USE?

The BAe team told the RAE men that providing support for a human crew "is considered to be an 'add-on package' on Hotol. The basic system integrity level will be high in any case, based on economic considerations. Any specialist missions requiring a human crew might require some additional back-up services (e.g. flight control), in the vehicle(s) assigned to such tasks".

When it came to any possible military use for Hotol, this fell outside the DTI-funded study but "if an approach to BAe is made by the Ministry of Defence, it will be considered by BAe who would require a separate contract".

Evidently the Americans had attempted to acquire information on Hotol via the RAE but as the BAe post-meeting report noted under the heading 'US approach to RAE on Hotol': "The US request for a briefing by RAE on the project will be blocked because it is believed that any such discussions would greatly increase the difficulty of maintaining secrecy on the power plant concept. It is BAe's and the UK government's stated view (Pattie, Heseltine), that an approach to the French should be made before any overture to the USA.

Finally, in summary of the first day's discussions, "RAE support the proposed PoC Study and will make suitable recommendations to the DTI".

The second day saw a somewhat pared back attendance, with Deller, Young and Conchie having left. Just three items remained on the table: fleet size, time on orbit and the overall programme. How many Hotol vehicles would be needed? "Based on non-military applications only, allowing for Ariane's continued programme and assuming 30% capture of the remaining market and a life of 100 flights, about eight vehicles would be required."

It had been determined that each vehicle could remain in orbit for up to 52 hours "based on the severe assumption of continuous sunlight and worst orientation. It is likely that this could be increased by a factor of two by rotation and taking account of partial darkness".

And as far as the overall programme was concerned, Burns would provide the RAE with an executive summary including a chart showing the development sequence and phases for both airframe and engine. A chart appended to the BAe/RAE meeting summary showed projected 'private venture' spending by BAe on Hotol: in 1985 Stevenage would spend £46,000, Filton £21,500 and Warton £67,500. For 1986, the only full year of the PoC, this rose to £86,000, £125,000 and £375,000 respectively, then declined in 1987 to £64,500, £29,500 and £187,000.

By the end of September 1985, everything seemed to be falling into place for Hotol. British Aerospace was fully committed to the PoC, with three divisions engaged in Hotol work and with chief executive Sir Raymond Lygo on board. The British government, with Geoffrey Pattie as political standard bearer, was also backing the project. Even the notoriously difficult to win over Royal Aircraft Establishment at Farnborough had given its seal of approval.

Pledges and commitments aside, the injection of hard cash necessary to get everything running smoothly remained absent, however, and Rolls-Royce's corporate enthusiasm for the project appears to have been lukewarm at best. Nevertheless, Hotol was on its way.

BRITISH AEROSPACE

HOTOL

An aerospace plane concept for the 21st century which exploits advanced propulsion and aerodynamic techniques to create a low cost spacecraft launcher.

The history of Europe in the Space Age is the history of British Aerospace. From the jet engine and the Blue Streak ballistic missile, through advanced scientific spacecraft, to a wide spectrum of communication satellites, the Company has been and remains Europe's innovative and technology pace-setting leader. The same inventiveness and search for technical excellence that led to the world's first jetliner and Concorde now offer the concept of an aerospace plane for the 21st Century.

It stems from our belief that Europe's space programme will remain viable only so long as she can field a launch vehicle to compete with the American Shuttle. The expendable Ariane rocket does so today. It is unlikely, however, that a launcher system which operates by throwing away its components in flight will compete successfully with a greatly improved, second-generation Shuttle.

Convinced that total reliance on expendable launchers can only be seriously detrimental to Europe's interests, British Aerospace has undertaken far-reaching studies to identify and design the optimum commercial launch vehicle. That is to say, one which will meet the requirements of the vast majority of payload sponsors by placing up to 7 tonnes in low earth orbit cheaply and safely. From these studies the HOTOL concept has evolved.

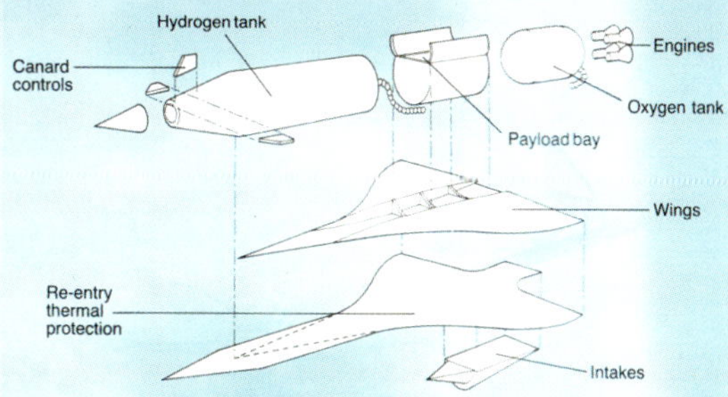

HOTOL is based on a remarkable new propulsion technique which allows the use of atmospheric oxygen to reduce on-board propellant mass and permits the use of wings to optimise the initial flight trajectory after take-off from a standard runway. This combination makes the long sought-after, single-stage-to-orbit launcher a practical proposition. The propulsive and aerodynamic characteristics result in a vehicle that is fully recoverable and totally and quickly reusable with minimum refurbishment, preparation and expense.

Most of the forward fuselage of HOTOL is occupied by a large pressurised liquid hydrogen fuel tank while at the rear is a liquid oxygen tank for flight outside the atmosphere where air breathing is not possible. The payload bay – of Shuttle diameter – is between the two tanks and the overall layout ensures minimum movement of the centre of gravity during flight. The engine – details of which are security classified – is conventionally rear mounted. The protection for re-entry heating is concentrated largely underneath the fuselage and wing. Small, forward-mounted canards provide positive aerodynamic control.
Since an undercarriage strong enough for take-off would be very heavy, HOTOL is launched off a simple trolley and a lightweight undercarriage is provided for landing, thus avoiding the carriage of dead weight into orbit.

ESSENTIAL DATA ON HOTOL

Take off mass	=	200T
Landing mass	=	42T
Payload mass (300km, equatorial orbit)	=	7T
Length	=	76m
Wingspan	=	20m
Fuselage diameter	=	5.7m
Runway length	=	3000m
Take-off acceleration	=	0.56g
Take-off speed	=	150 m/s (334 mph)
Landing speed	=	88 m/s (196 mph)
Lift-drag ratio	=	6.5:1 subsonic
	=	4.5:1 supersonic
Propellants	=	Liquid hydrogen Liquid oxygen

Take off
The take-off speed of 290 knots (150 metres per second) is achieved with an acceleration of 0.56g and a run of 7500 feet (2300 metres). Vertical acceleration at lift off is 1.15g, and the climb attitude is about 24 degrees. The vehicle goes supersonic after 2 minutes. It clears commercial air lanes (40,000 feet, 12 km) after 4.5 minutes and reaches 26 km/Mach 5 after 9 minutes. Thereafter, various problems preclude air-breathing and dictate a ballistic trajectory on main engine.

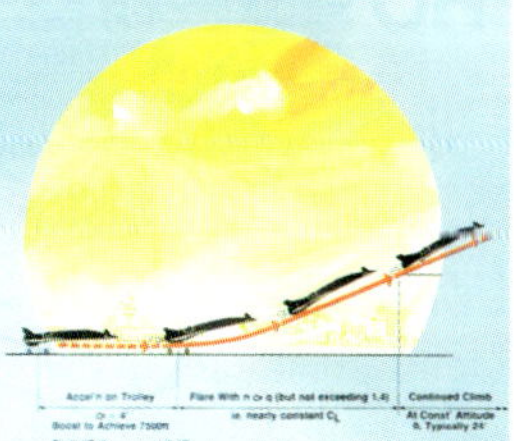

In orbit
Orbital velocity is achieved at 90 km, the main engine is cut off and HOTOL coasts to operating altitude of some 300 km. A typical mission duration is 50 hours, with position and altitude changes achieved by the orbital manoeuvring system (OMS). At the end of this time the OMS slows the vehicle and brings the perigee down to about 70 km altitude for re-entry.

HOTOL re-enters at very high incidence, about 80 degrees, which reduces as speed falls; a hypersonic glide commences at about 25 km altitude. Because of its large wing and low mass, the vehicle behaves much less like a projectile than Shuttle. Re-entry temperatures are therefore lower and a high temperature metal alloy skin will suffice for protection of the undersurface. Ordinary titanium is used on the upper surfaces. This all adds up to simple and economic construction and maintenance.

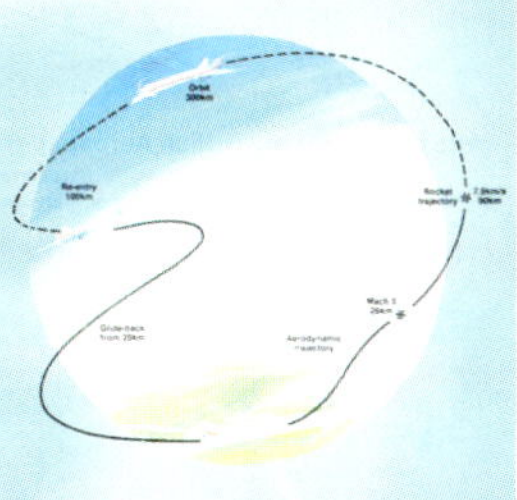

The high hypersonic lift-to-drag ratio of HOTOL during entry (more than twice that of Shuttle) gives it a high cross-range capability sufficient, say, for a landing in Europe from an Equatorial orbit. Indeed, the Kourou site need be used only as a re-fuelling stop on the way from Europe to orbit.

Landing technique
Final approach and landing techniques are similar to Shuttle but gentler: approach angle is 16 degrees, touchdown speed is 170 knots (88 mps) and the wet runway ground roll is 1800 m; the OMC can be relit for thrust control.

For simplicity and economy the first operational HOTOL will be remotely piloted by means of artificial intelligence and robotics systems. From the outset however provision will be made for manned operation.

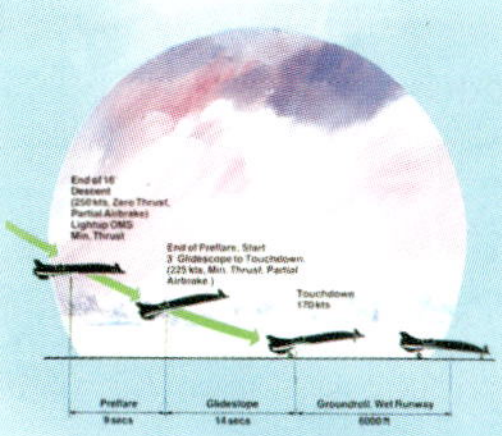

HOTOL will reduce costs to low earth orbit by a factor of five and, even with current perigee stages, will halve geosynchronous launch costs. This economy of operation, coupled with quick reaction and a rapid turnround capability will enable HOTOL to compete realistically for about 75% of the commercial market from the year 2000 onwards.

Above all, HOTOL technology is forward-looking with ample potential for development beyond the cheap and effective spacecraft launcher which it is presently planned to be. A one-hour passenger flight from Europe to Australia is a distinct possibility and little imagination is needed to identify other important uses for this remarkable aerospace plane of the future.

HOTOL - A Transatmospheric Skyliner for the 21st century

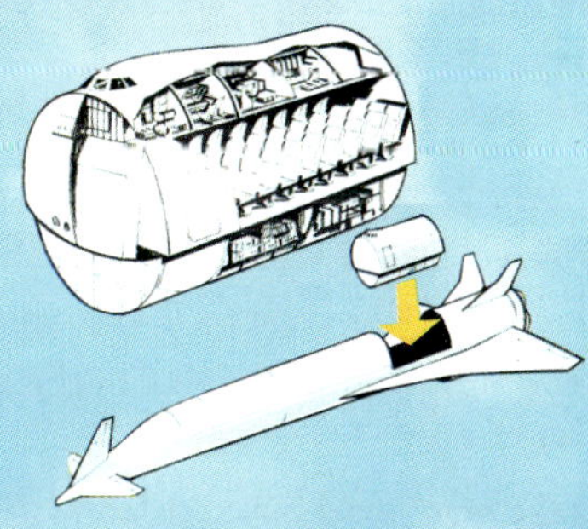

Into the future with British Aerospace from London to Sydney in 45 minutes
(overhead to overhead)
Elapsed time take-off to landing allowing for normal air traffic procedures is 67 minutes

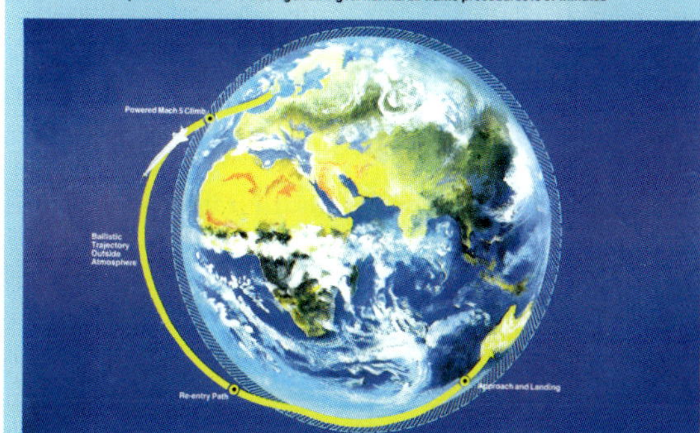

BRITISH AEROSPACE
Space & Communications Division
Argyle Way, Stevenage,
Hertfordshire SG1 2AS.
Telephone: National 0438–313456
International +44 438 313456
Telex: 82130 answerback BADSTE.G

3

PROOF OF CONCEPT: 1985 TO MAY 31, 1986

British aerospace reports cite the beginning of October 1985 as the starting point for the two-year Hotol PoC—but in reality ongoing uncertainty about the allocation of funds continued to hamper and delay its full commencement.

Reporting to Yates on October 17, Burns wrote: "A meeting has been arranged by the managing director, Sir R. Lygo, for November 19 when it is hoped that this matter will be clarified ... allocation of DTI funding is believed to be imminent as reported in Mr Conchie's memo dated October 14."

Stevenage was "working at a level of two to three men" and "Bristol are doing nothing at present, other than answering queries, pending allocation of funds". Warton, however, was pressing on with a team of six engineers and another due to start in November. Already, "a review of alternative structural design schemes has been completed and initial schemes for front fuselage, payload bay, rear fuselage and flying surfaces have been selected for study. A review of relevant materials is in progress".

Gust cases and undercarriage loads on touchdown were being investigated and "a low value design vertical velocity on landing (5.5ft/sec) has been selected based on Concorde statistics for auto-land".

A visit to Cranfield Institute of Technology (CIT) had been arranged for October 30 to discuss hypersonic estimation methods since "it is expected that a small sub-contract on CIT will be arranged to do initial calculations relevant to the re-entry manoeuvre which is likely to be critical for controllability/centre of gravity (cg) location".

BAe Warton's specialism was the design and manufacture of military aircraft, which had commenced with the Canberra bomber in the late 1940s, continuing with the Lightning fighter in the 1950s and 1960s, and the Jaguar and Tornado combat aircraft in the 1970s and 1980s. Initial design, the size and shape of the aircraft, utilised a system known as CAPS (Computer Aided Project Studies), which was developed by the Advanced Projects Department at Warton in the late 1960s following the series of hypersonic vehicle studies which led to Mustard.

For Hotol, CAPS was being updated to model Hotol's ascent trajectory by Eric Webb, a member of the original Mustard team in Advanced Projects and an original developer of the CAPS system. Work to look at flutter characteristics, drag estimation and flight control was also under way.

Warton's chief airworthiness engineer had also raised the issue of how would Hotol, once built, could be certified airworthy. Certainly, "there is no procedure in the UK, either in the civil or military fields, for certification of unmanned airborne vehicles ... it is believed that it can never be too early to raise this question".

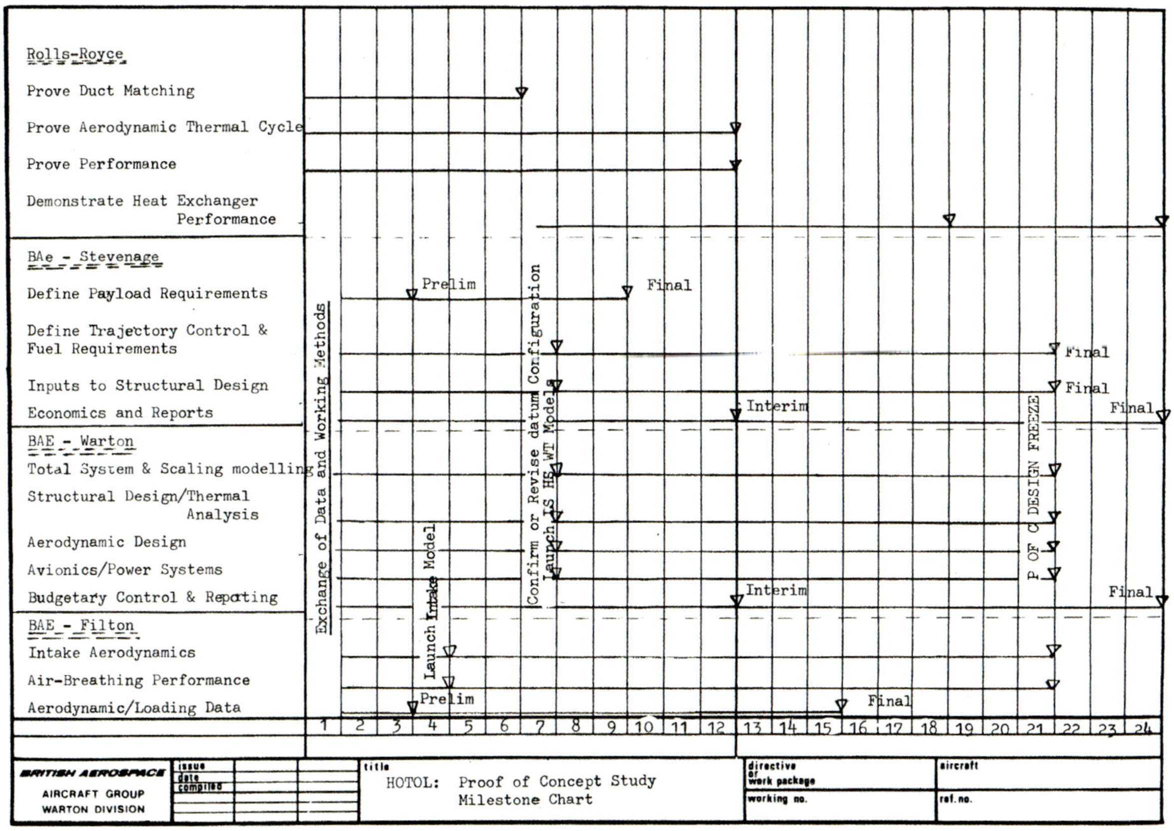

Proposed timeline for Hotol development, set out at the very beginning of Proof of Concept Study in 1985.

Early publicity image showing the three-engine Hotol design.

At the same time, the Americans were persisting in their attempts to gain intelligence on Hotol. Burns noted: "An invitation to visit US space research facilities was made by the American EOARD [European Office of Aerospace Research and Development] in London, to staff of S&C Division, Stevenage. A letter was also received at Bristol from NASA, Langley, inviting discussions and offering an independent assessment of the Hotol design. It has been agreed that these approaches will be blocked, for the present at least, to minimise the risk of leaks concerning the propulsion system and until we have a better feel for the engineering of the project."

Attached to Burns' report was a proposed timeline for Hotol's airframe development—the two-year PoC, followed by another two years of project definition (up to 1989), then two years of initial development (up to 1991) with a configuration freeze at the end, then four years of development and manufacture (up to 1995) with the first flight then taking place followed by two years of flight trials up to 1997. Commercial Hotol spaceflight operations would then begin.

In parallel, design, manufacturing and testing of a demonstration engine would take place from 1987 to 1991, with design, manufacturing and testing of development engines partly in parallel from 1989 up to 1995.

AMERICAN AMBITION

An article by Craig Covault in the American *Aviation Week & Space Technology* magazine of November 4, 1985, noted that "the US is building momentum toward possible development of a large new manned space transport that could take off from conventional aircraft runways, be operational by the early 21st century and eventually replace the current Space Shuttle. Studies on what new vehicle should be developed beyond the Shuttle have not settled upon a single candidate, but this SSTO concept is emerging as a stronger option than earlier envisioned, as a second-generation US space transport that could be test flown as early as 1995".

Hardly a week went by without publicity for Hotol appearing in the press. However, this image, taking its inspiration from the iconic image of Marilyn Monroe in the 1955 film The Seven Year Itch, went unused.

The USAF had said that "new propulsion developments will be a key to any SSTO space transport succeeding the Space Shuttle" and "the new propulsion technology focuses on using combined or mixed cycle hydrogen engine systems that consume outside air for large portions of their ascent, as opposed to carrying massive cryogenic oxygen supplies to use in connection with on-board fuel. Tons of weight and structure and extensive costs are saved by using the oxygen in the air, instead of using a tank".

Covault stated that Robert F. Cooper, a researcher from the USAF's Aero Propulsion Laboratory at Wright-Patterson Air Base, and William J. D. Escher from the Astronautics Corporation of America, had co-authored a paper looking at engine options for the new American vehicle and this had "revealed the combined cycle airbreathing/rocket propulsion system as the probable system of choice". And now "General Electric, Pratt & Whitney and Aerojet are examining engine concepts for such a vehicle while Boeing and McDonnell Douglas have been examining airframe issues".

This almost made it appear as though the Americans had somehow managed to lay hands on Bond's design, but Covault then reported that "Aerojet engineer Willard J. Green [said] the propulsion system for the concept would use a mixed cycle approach between launch and acceleration to Mach 6. During this period, outside air would be used to augment the primary propulsion then coming from the rocket system.

"At Mach 6, however, the vehicle's propulsion would convert primarily to an airbreathing system, augmented by the rockets. This propulsion mode would continue between Mach 6 and Mach 16 but at Mach 16 the airbreathing phase would cease entirely as the vehicle left the atmosphere. Pure rocket power would then be used for the final acceleration to orbital velocity of about Mach 25."

On the British side, there had never been any question of the airbreathing phase extending beyond Mach 7.5.

The day after Covault's article hit newsstands, a meeting was held at Rolls-Royce's Ansty facility, attended by Bond (as a consultant), the RAE's propulsion specialist, BAe Stevenage representatives and BAe Warton representatives Burns and Gerald Wilson, the latter having just joined the Hotol team.

Scott-Scott presented the engine-side programme for the two-year PoC, a key part of which would be the preparation of a heat exchanger icing demonstration. This was expected to show that ice crystals would only form upstream of the heat exchanger, laying to rest any fears of ice blocking the system. Manufactured sample heat exchangers were expected to be ready for testing before the two years were up. In addition, it was indicated that two further Rolls-Royce centres—Bristol and Derby—were also being brought on board to investigate compressor/turbine design and detailed engineering respectively.

HOTOL CONFIGURATIONS A AND B

Burns reported to Yates on November 15 that the Hotol funding situation as far as British Aerospace was concerned had now been clarified. Warton would take charge of the company's spending on the project, allocating money to the other divisions as required. Having spoken with Deller on the phone, Burns was also able to confirm that the RAE was recommending DTI funding for Hotol and reported that a presentation to government officials had been arranged to take place on November 20 at BAe's offices in Pall Mall.

During the preceding month, Warton had been hard at work assessing the Hotol vehicle design worked up by Stevenage and Filton. This had originally been known as 'ELV' but had now been designated Hotol Configuration A. While precise figures on every dimension of this initial version are unclear—particularly given that the design was subject to regular alterations—the layout which appeared in British Aerospace Advanced Projects Department Filton drawing SSV 30154 dated June 10, 1984, configuration 220/1850, was 62m long from the tip of its nose to the end of its main engine nozzles. Wingspan was 19.66m and wing area was 296.55sqm. That length, at least, was the same as that of the configuration shown to the public at the Paris Air Show a year later.

A vital consideration, which could make or break the design, was what materials to use when building it. According to Burns' report, "new proposals include the possible use of Columbium for leading edge 'hot spots'. This material offers better resistance to damage (e.g. bird strike), being less brittle than carbon-carbon [carbon fibre within a carbon matrix], but its availability and cost have yet to be investigated. The use of boron/epoxy for the hydrogen tank is being investigated; this offers better strength/weight than titanium and appears to be suitable for use at cryogenic temperatures. The use of polyimides in the rear fuselage is proposed; this material is usable at higher temperatures than CFC [carbon fibre composite] with similar strength/weight properties".

Thermal studies were getting under way to investigate trade-offs between insulation thicknesses and weight, structural materials and thickness, and fuel boil-off.

Assessment of Hotol's forward fuselage had shown that

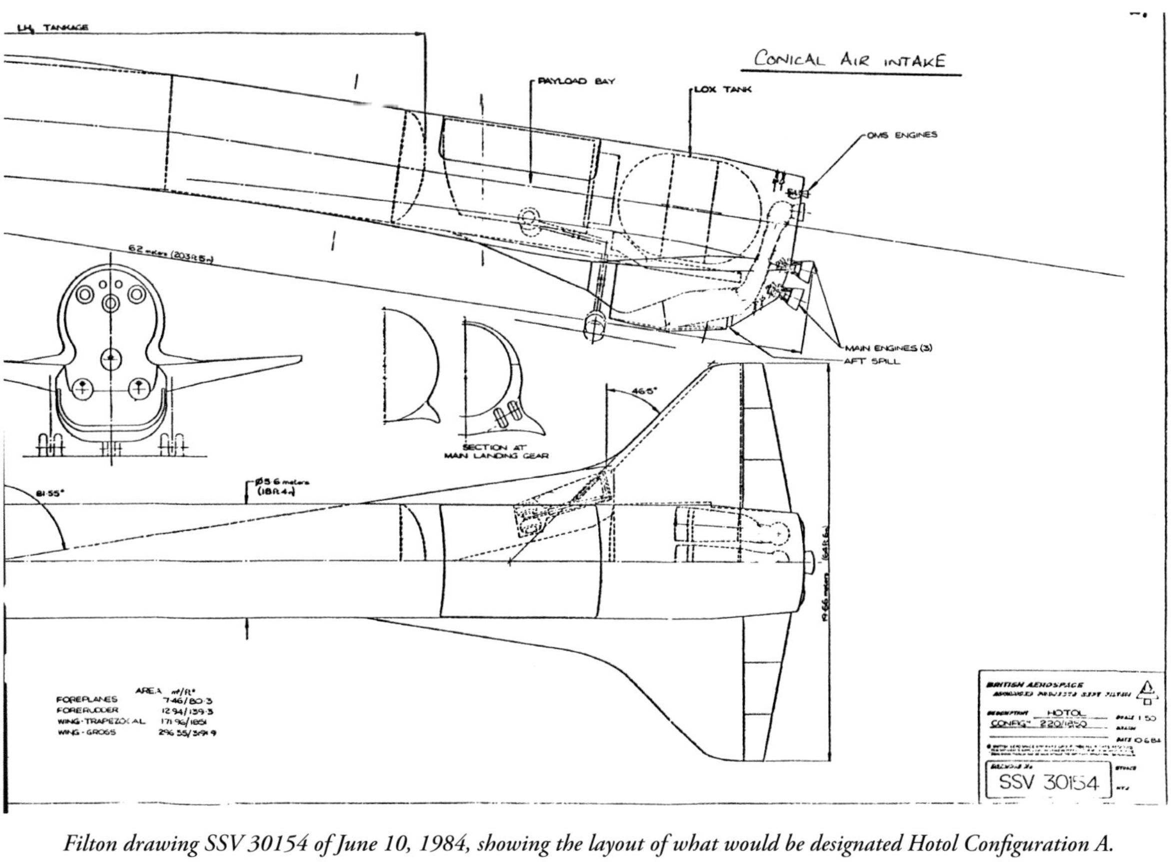

Filton drawing SSV 30154 of June 10, 1984, showing the layout of what would be designated Hotol Configuration A.

Hotol Configuration A. CHRIS SANDHAM-BAILEY

Hotol Configuration B. CHRIS SANDHAM-BAILEY

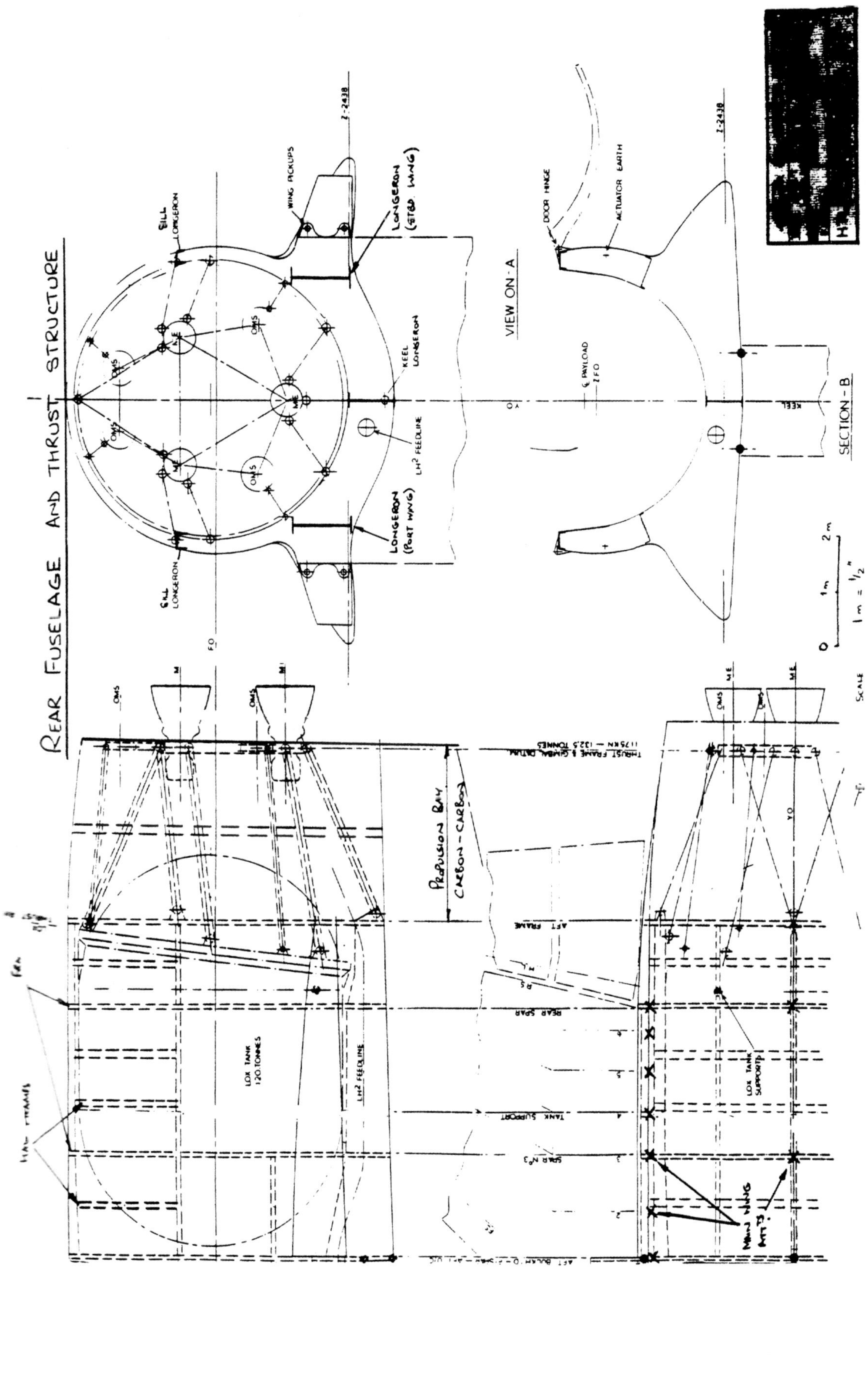

Rear fuselage and thrust structure for a three-engined Hotol variant—making this Configuration A, B or C.

An unusual Hotol display model with conical intake but without canards—making it unplaceable within the alphabetical configuration series.

its skin should not be subject to compression loads—therefore the hydrogen tank it contained would need to be pressurised to a point where it became a structural element, like a balloon. This had a knock-on effect for the take-off trolley, which would need to provide more support in Hotol's nosewheel and mid-tank area. And that would make the trolley heavier, which increased the likelihood that it would need its own rocket propulsion.

Warton's aerodynamicists were investigating a refinement of the rear fuselage shape intended to reduce drag and it was likely that the wing thickness/chord ratio would be increased from four to six percent.

Stevenage had also been hard at work. Burns reported that a new colour brochure for Hotol would be ready by the New Year, ascent and re-entry computer programmes had been evaluated and would be revised, and studies had shown that Hotol had "commercially viable market potential ... between Shuttle and Ariane 5/Hermes".

At a technical progress meeting between representatives of Stevenage, Filton and Warton on November 18, it was stressed to Filton chief future projects engineer Terry Brown, who had just replaced Leyman, that his team needed to get started immediately on Hotol's intake, including the drafting of specifications for a wind tunnel model. The Warton representatives also outlined further changes to Configuration A that were being reviewed, including the introduction of congruent foreplanes (making them the same size and shape as the nose fin—so that all three were identical), shifting the wings forward, reducing the wing dihedral and reducing the nose droop inherent in the Stevenage/Filton design.

The introduction of these four changes, plus reshaping and lengthening of Hotol's rear fuselage—resulted in a new variant that would be defined as the short-lived Hotol Configuration B.

Lastly, 53 different aspects of Hotol development work were allocated to named individuals across the three divisions.

THATCHER'S BLESSING

Meanwhile, Pattie had finally appointed a director for the new British National Space Centre (see Chapter 2): Roy Gibson. This was a popular choice because Gibson had been intimately involved in international space technology development since the early 1970s. Most notably, he had overseen the amalgamation of the ELDO and ESRO to form ESA in 1975—and had then become its first director-general, remaining in the role until 1980.

Interviewed in 2007, Gibson said that prior to his appointment, he had been "invited to Downing Street to meet the Chinese Prime Minister [along with Margaret Thatcher] and [we talked about] what we were going to do, our space programme. She [Thatcher] was full of enthusiasm. She seemed to have been sold at that time. There was, of course, always a strong opposition inside the DTI, they felt that the money could be much better spent on other things."

Explaining the BNSC's role to the House of Commons on November 26, Pattie said: "The BNSC will have two main elements: a technology directorate and a policy and programmes directorate. The technology directorate will be based on those parts of existing establishments which currently undertake space-related research, notably the RAE, Farnborough, and the Rutherford Appleton Laboratory, Chilton, involving the equivalent of some 100 and 140 full-time staff respectively.

"The policy and programmes directorate will consist of about 35 staff forming the headquarters unit at Millbank Tower, London ... One of the BNSC's principal aims will be to provide better coordination of Britain's £100 million a year space research and development effort ... to this end I have asked Mr Gibson to develop a longer-term space strategy taking into account scientific and industrial interests and the needs of both civil and defence users".

The BNSC would essentially draw together all the space-related work already being undertaken by the DTI, the MoD, the Science and Engineering Research Council and the Natural Environment Research Council.

Gibson recalled: "The DTI was very welcoming and made arrangements for us and we got support from industry... Science Research Council was a bit ambivalent. They wanted to control the new BNSC but keep their budget separate, this kind of thing. But eventually they came around and we didn't have any problems with them."

He said there was support for the BNSC at the highest levels of government at this time: "Geoffrey Howe [then Foreign Secretary] personally was very committed to it and really stuck his neck out a long way. Minister of Defence [Heseltine] was also very much for it. It was at the time when Thatcher was looking round for wets and Geoffrey Pattie—our Minister—if not a wet, was a bad case of rising damp. So we had the wrong support."

'Wets' was a term coined by Thatcher during the early days of her first government to describe people or policies which she considered 'weak'. The term's meaning was rapidly expanded to encompass anyone who opposed her hardline policies or who generally fell out of favour.

Concerns about political support aside, Gibson was now able to begin work on a fundamental requirement of his new office: the drafting of a 15-year space plan for the UK, due to be delivered in September 1986. This would make proposals and recommendations for which space projects Britain should be undertaking and how much money should be spent on them.

GETTING BEHIND HOTOL

A week prior to Pattie's Commons speech on the BNSC, on November 19, Lygo had been given a full personal presentation on Hotol engineering progress and the next day, November 20, he was joined by Pattie, Batiste, Gibson and Sir Robin Nicholson, the Government's chief scientist, for another one at BAe Pall Mall. Also present were MoD representatives, Deller from the RAE, Lewis from Rolls-Royce, Parkinson, Scott-Scott, Conchie and Burns. The latter four each gave a presentation before Conchie "then summarised the political scene making the point that UK and Europe should lead rather than follow USA". Lewis "made a brief statement to the effect that RR had been in the advanced propulsion game for many years and were currently bidding into US R&D programmes. Sir Raymond Lygo stated that he was impressed by the amount of work done and that he had made the right decision in moving project control to Warton; this released S&C Division to Space activities".

Apparently Pattie then "summarised a recent bilateral get-together with the French which culminated in a round table summary meeting with the Prime Minister [Laurent Fabius] and the French President [Francois Mitterrand]. He stated that his opposite number [Hubert Curien] unprompted, mentioned that he believed Hotol to be 'a very fine project'. He then questioned Mr Deller of the RAE regarding their assessment. Mr Deller replied that they had formed a consensus opinion on the risk areas and had reported favourably, backing the project. He was expecting to assign two staff in each department to support the project".

Nicholson said that "unless UK were fully behind this project and the radical propulsion system in particular, the US will probably invent it themselves and run ahead with it".

An informal discussion with Gibson over funding arrangements ensued and according to the post-meeting summary report written by Burns: "It is believed that an announcement will be made of a general UK move towards increased spending on space activities including Hotol. The following morning a telephone call was received from Mr T. Abrahams (Secretary to the Minister), requesting the spread of expected DTI funding over the three financial years. This was quoted as £0.18m up to March 1986, £0.58m in the next (full financial year) and £0.24m in the final part up to September 1987.

"A further telephone call was received from Mr L. J. Robinson of DTI (assistant director to Cliff Nicholas, head of Space Department), November 25, 1985. He reported that the Minister was enthusiastic about Hotol. He is clear about BAe's commitment to the project but needs convincing about RR's commitment because of their 'disclaimer' letter earlier this year. RR's presentation on November 20 helped to clear the air but they wish to see something on paper."

The precise nature of the 'disclaimer' sent by Rolls-Royce to the DTI is unclear—but while Scott-Scott and Lewis were clearly committed to Hotol, the rest of the company's senior personnel appear to have been significantly less enthusiastic.

ROLLS-ROYCE SWALLOW

Scott-Scott produced an official Rolls-Royce-branded report in December 1985, a revised version of an earlier one, which outlined a "Proposal for Swallow Engine Proof-of-Concept Study". The introduction began: "Rolls-Royce now contains the combined experience of several British rocket engine companies, all of which merged into a single operation about 1970. Thus the expertise of Bristol-Siddeley, De Havilland and Rolls-Royce was combined, covering a variety of propellant combinations. The main projects were Blue Streak, Black Knight, Black Arrow

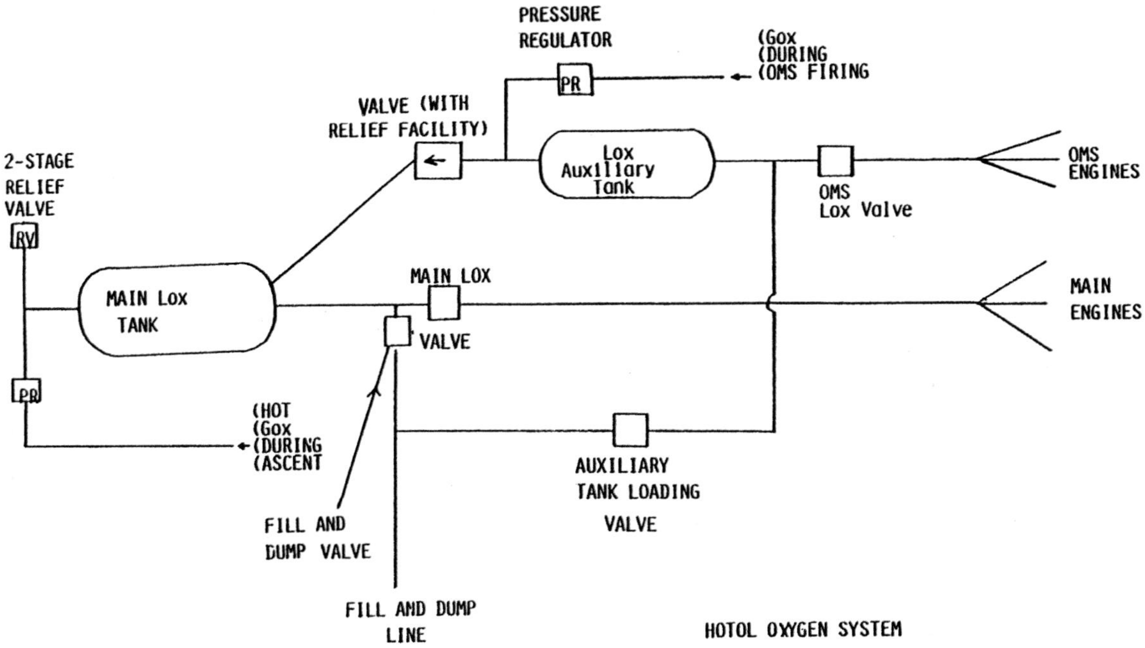

Diagram showing a basic outline of Hotol's liquid oxygen system.

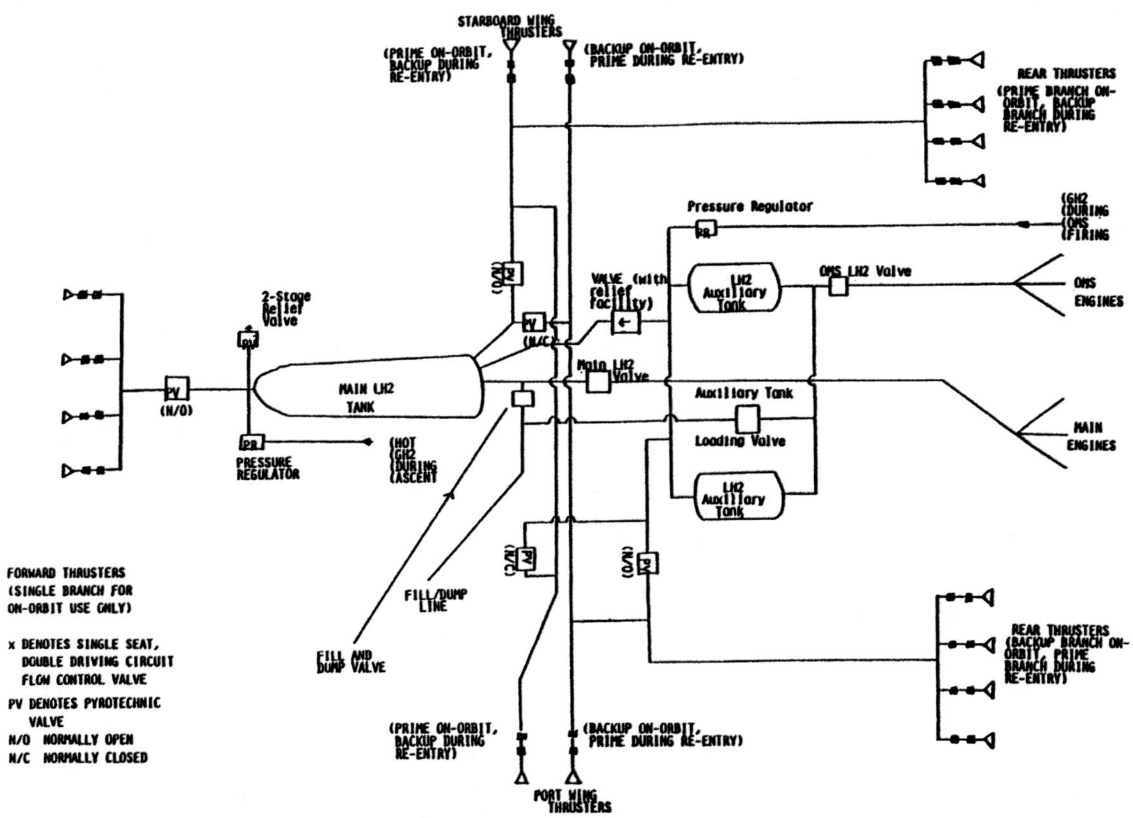

Hotol's liquid hydrogen system.

launchers and the Blue Steel stand off nuclear bomb... the industrial scene changed and the British rocket industry declined although the expertise remained with those enthusiasts who had worked on these launcher propulsors.

"When the scenario changed again and there surfaced a requirement for a cheap to operate, quick turnaround shuttle type vehicle, the single stage to orbit vehicle was considered as a first option. The problem was to design a propulsor specifically matched to the characteristics of the vehicle flight envelope to achieve the spacecraft designer's ultimate dream. Hence evolved the Swallow engine and the Hotol vehicle."

With the Orbital Swallow vehicle as a whole having become Hotol, the Barnes Wallis tribute Swallow monicker had evidently been retained for Bond's engine alone. The report went on: "Studies of a preliminary nature have been carried out by Rolls-Royce on this airbreathing rocket engine concept. These have been partly private-venture and partly DTI-funded, the latter as part of a joint BAe/RR contract." Practical trials were now needed to show that the engine could perform as claimed: "In order to be able to adopt a firmer approach to the range of vehicle applications now foreseen, it is necessary to obtain positive proof of certain fundamental aspects, which, whilst being theoretically possible using known materials and technology, have not actually been verified in practice under these conditions.

"At Rolls-Royce Limited, Ansty, several of the old rocket test beds are still available, some have recently been used for other company research programmes involving hazardous conditions. There are spaces to site freely ventilated gaseous hydrogen supplies and also existing blast-proof exclosures for liquid oxygen tanks. With some refurbishment and refitting these could be made fully serviceable for the testing of heat exchanger and turbopump components... More than any other aspect of the study, verification of the feasibility of the propulsion system is critical to the proof of concept."

Scott-Scott noted that "operational details of the [engine] cycle are still classified, but the controlling factor to the propellant flows is the use of the liquid hydrogen, not only as a propellant, but also as a heat sink for the high enthalpy intake air during the airbreathing phase. The use of hydrogen and oxygen as sole propellants was decided in the earlier study and the main engines, the OMS [Orbital Manoeuvring System] engines and the RCS [Reaction Control System thrusters] (hydrogen only) must achieve their required performance, using a common propellant source, during all phases of flight.

"In order to minimise the power plant weight, system components have to do more than one duty wherever possible. For example, the thrust chamber has to be capable of operation of either air-hydrogen or oxygen-hydrogen as required. This dual use of components is an important part of the concept as it is a characteristic of single stage to orbit vehicles that the final orbital payload is only a small percentage of the take-off weight."

During the PoC phase, Rolls-Royce would study seven 'key areas', three directly related to the heat exchanger, two to the dual-use combustion chamber and two concerning component weights.

Where the heat exchanger was concerned, firstly it would be vital to "investigate techniques to eliminate frosting of the inlet heat exchangers". It was critical to the engine's success that air entering the inlet and immediately being cooled by the liquid hydrogen kept moving through the system—rather than freezing solid and clogging it up. Scott-Scott proposed to set up an anti-frosting rig to test the process.

Secondly, the heat exchanger would largely consist of numerous small diameter tubes, the forming and brazing of which would potentially be very difficult. This was to be investigated. Thirdly, sample heat exchanger sections would be used to test whether the rates of heat transfer possible in theory could be achieved in practice.

For the dual-use combustion chamber, it would be necessary to work out the required injector geometry—for which computer programs would be used—and the design of the chamber's internal heat exchanger would also be worked out. Lastly, the weight of the heat exchangers, when they had been fully designed, would need to be checked and verified, as would the engine's turbo-compressor weights.

Work packages for these tasks were set out and some details of the anti-frosting test rig were outlined: "The rig selected obtains its air by compressor bleed from a slave Avon [jet] engine (ex-Scimitar aircraft, already having extensive bleed for slot-blowing), which is subsequently cooled and humidified.

"The first set of instrumentation will be arranged to verify these test conditions. Downstream of this 'bad weather machine' comes a section where other fluids can be injected (either as spray or other seeding) followed by the test section proper. This is about 8in square and 3ft long, having viewing windows on two adjacent sides and provision for holding a variety of representative sections or models of heat exchanger elements."

Simply turning an existing air flow rig into an anti-frosting rig would cost £33,000. Instrumentation, operating costs, manufacture of test section models and labour would then boost the overall cost to £163,000—about half a million pounds in today's money.

CONCERN OVER ROLLS-ROYCE

Aviation Week & Space Technology of December 16 ran an article by Brendan M. Greeley Jr. on the US Defense Department and NASA initiating "planning for a joint aerospace plane research programme to design an experimental aircraft, or X-vehicle, capable of operating in the atmosphere at hypersonic velocities or accelerating directly into orbit". Greeley stated that "definition of the aerospace plane concept took place during 1982-85 and involved exploratory efforts by DARPA [the Defense Advanced Research Projects Agency] and NASA with significant participation by industry and other government research centres.

"The present concept envisions a hydrogen-powered aircraft capable of horizontal take-off and landing from conventional runways, thus reducing the large support crews now required for shuttle launches. The aerospace plane would operate at Mach 12-25 and altitudes of 100,000-350,000ft. The next phase of the programme, which will start in 1986 under DARPA direction, will concentrate on further developing the technologies required for an experimental flight vehicle".

The American Hotol rival was well under way. But back in Britain the same could not be said for Rolls-Royce. Funding was again top of Burns' agenda when he provided Yates with his monthly Hotol briefing on December 18. He briefly recounted the November 20 presentation and efforts to "counteract [Rolls-Royce's] 'disclaimer' letter written earlier in the year". And "more recently ... Deller [of the RAE] ... called to say that £200,000 would be released for Hotol to cover the period to the end of March 1986, provided that BAe and RR would commit at least an equivalent spend of PV funds ... This is currently being negotiated. BAe's PV spend alone will exceed £200,000 by the end of 1985.

"It is understood that RR have written to Mr Pattie regarding Hotol and are submitting their proposal via the department of engineering at MoD, but the lack of RR's visible commitment of resources to Hotol continues to give cause for concern ... Rolls-Royce still have no formal 'go-ahead' and their late start (January 1, 1986?) is already causing slippage of some early milestones".

Engineering work on Hotol continued at Warton and "initial wing structural design is complete, with titanium upper skin, nickel alloy lower skin and spars and carbon-carbon leading edges" the six percent thickness/chord wing would "almost certainly be adopted, leading to a lighter structure than the project estimate. Further investigations include a titanium lower skin with a thermal protection shield and increase of thickness/chord to eight percent at the body side (highly swept), both to reduce mass". This would also allow a reduction in overall fuselage length of 2m.

Filton was busy mulling over Hotol's intake shape—"reconsidering three separate intakes in place of a single semi-circular one in the interests of easing stowage of heat exchangers, which are now somewhat larger than previously envisaged. Two-dimensional intake schemes are also being reconsidered for ease of actuation and closure, although rectangular lip structure is heavier than semi-circular".

The front fuselage/hydrogen tank had been defined and would be made from Kevlar/epoxy, boron/epoxy having been found unsuitable. Hotol's metallic TPS panels had also been defined—the hottest areas during re-entry would get panels made of nickel alloy, weighing 4.8kg per square metre, whereas cooler areas would get panels made of titanium, weighing 2.2kg/sqm. Due to panel flutter and deflection concerns, the maximum allowable size per panel would be about 90cm x 30cm.

NEW YEAR – NEW INTAKE

Burns' report of January 22, 1986, noted that now "a completely new intake configuration has been schemed at Filton. The previous semi-circular intake with conical pre-entry body is replaced by a vertical wedge centre-body with twin intakes feeding the three heat exchangers and turbo compressors. The central heat exchanger is staggered to avoid excessive width on the intake pod. The main wheels are housed within the intake pod and extend in a similar way to the BAe 146.

"This revised proposal offers the following clear advantages over the previous scheme: simpler closure of the intake by single hinged doors. Narrower intake pod with lower cross section area. Lighter undercarriage.

"The only obvious disadvantage would appear to be a sharp forward corner of the pre-entry wedge being a 'hot-spot' on re-entry. This could be avoided by use of a retractable shield on re-entry, or by alternative means of retraction of the sharp nose. Alternatives need to be considered".

Even Rolls-Royce had finally, grudgingly, agreed to put some of its own money into Hotol—but not out of any love for the project. Burns wrote: "Pending allocation of DTI funds, build-up of work at Rolls-Royce on a PV basis has commenced and, while this will undoubtedly be at a slower rate than BAe would like, there is clearly now a

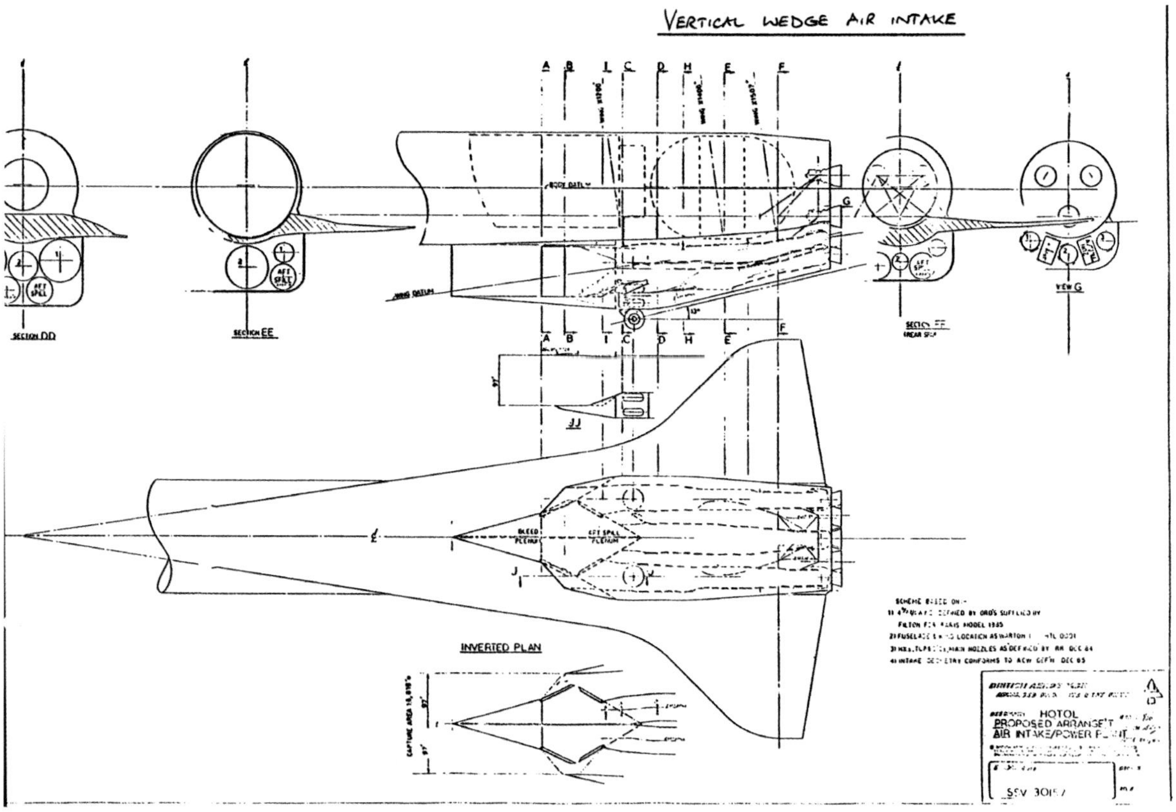

Initial proposal for a vertical wedge intake in early 1986 based on data "supplied by Filton for Paris model 1985" fuselage, wing position from Warton, main nozzles defined by Rolls-Royce in December 1984 and intake geometry definition from December 1985.

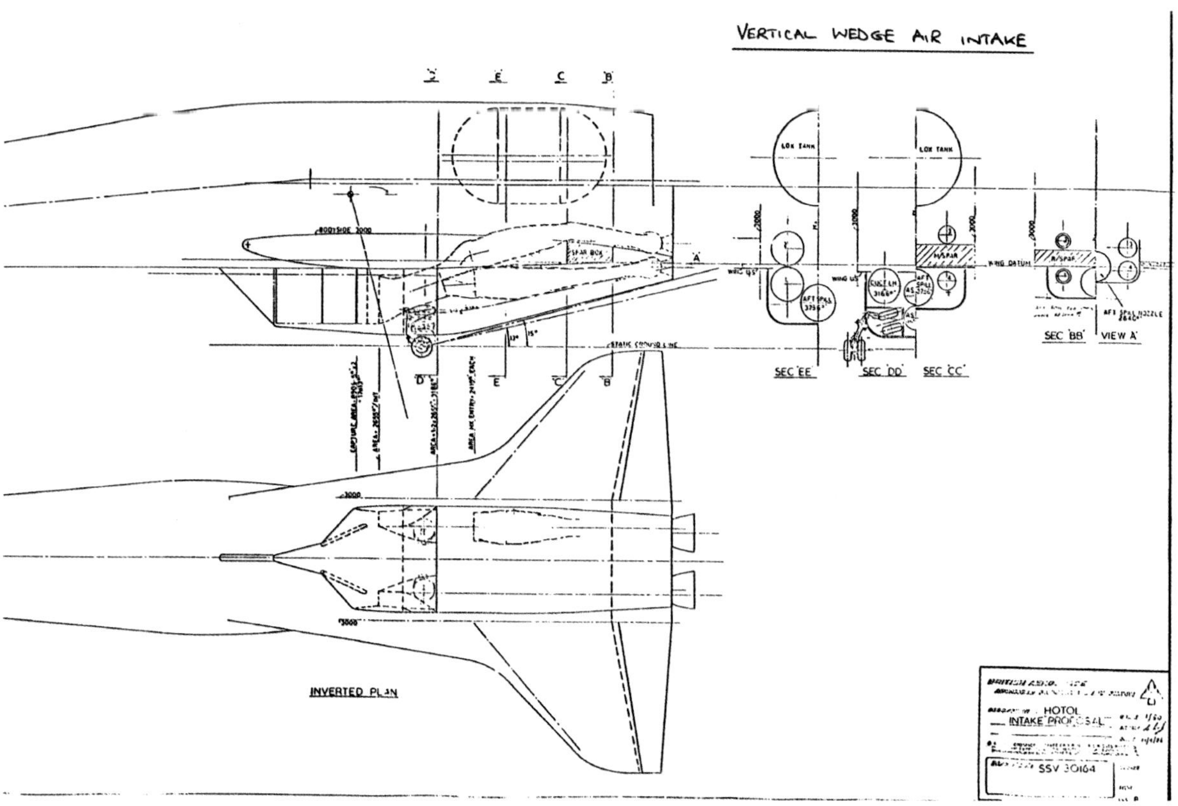

Refined vertical wedge intake design, dated April 1986, featuring recontoured rear fuselage and revised undercarriage bay.

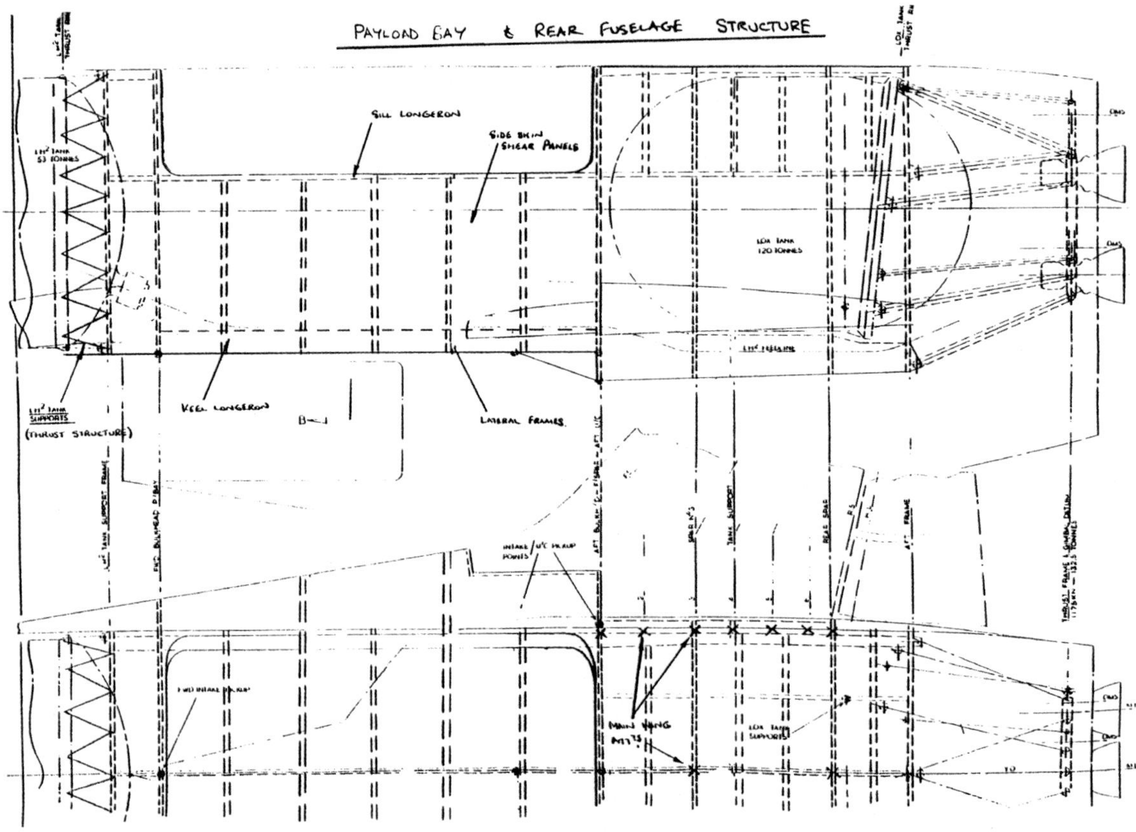

Payload bay and rear fuselage structure with wedge intake—making this Hotol Configuration D.

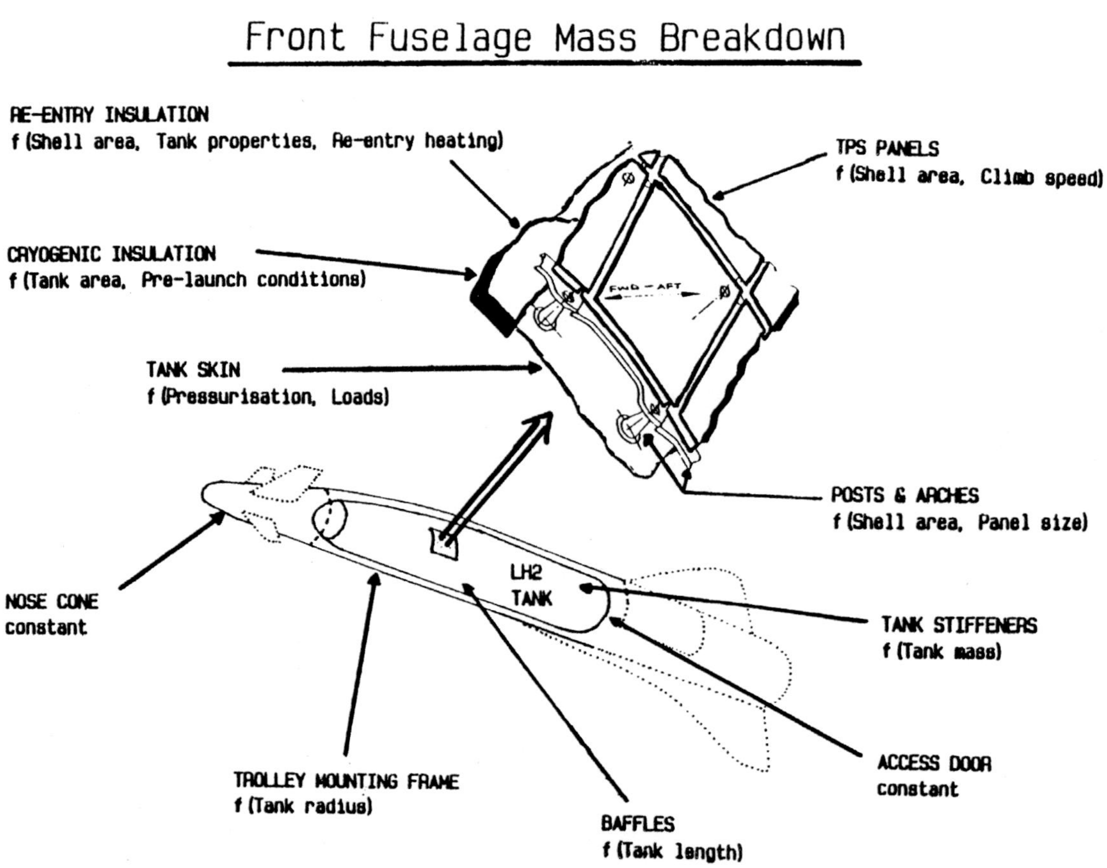

Hotol front fuselage structural details.

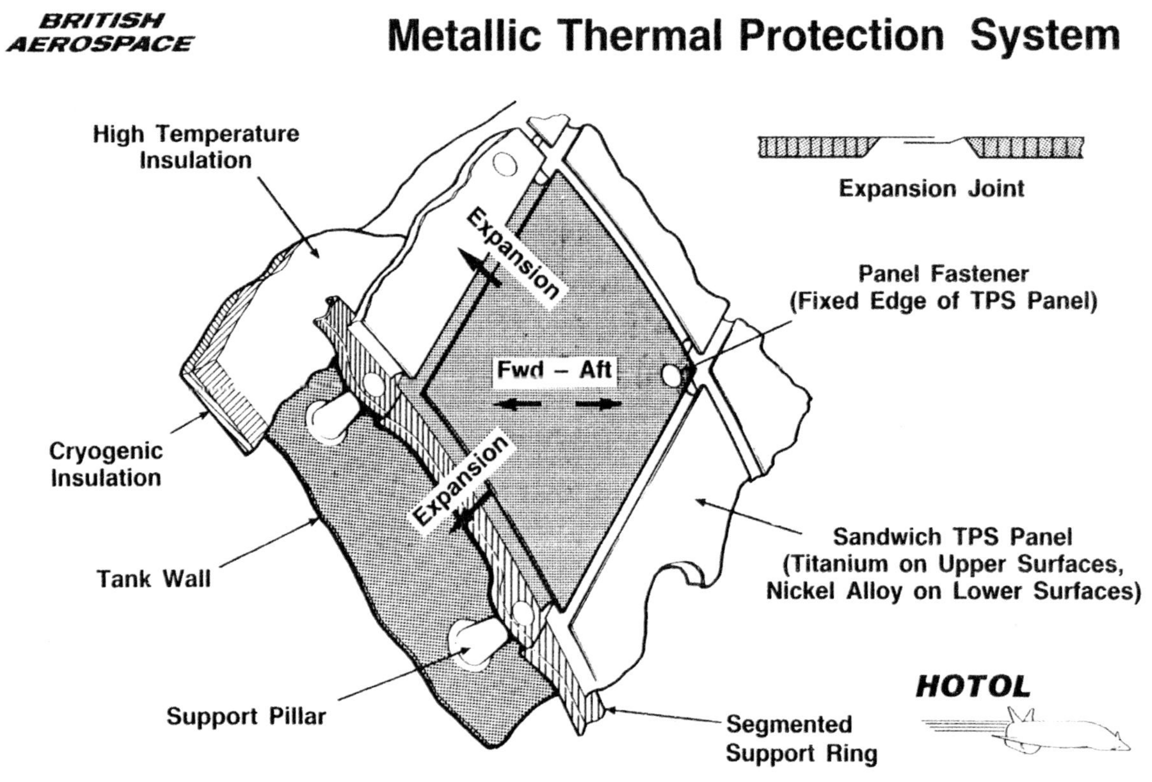

Detailed view of Hotol's intended metallic thermal protection system panels, which would be made of titanium for upper surfaces and nickel alloy for lower surfaces.

more positive attitude emerging. Some overlap of objectives with a one-year USAF contract [that] Rolls-Royce now have, to study high-speed propulsion for hypersonic transport, may have helped."

Stevenage's contribution for the month had been to define the required operating pressures in the hydrogen and oxygen tanks throughout the mission profile—critically important in working out tank mass and fuel reserve estimates for re-entry and recovery.

Stevenage had also met with Warton flight operations and flight test personnel to consider possible operating bases from which to carry out atmospheric and orbital test flights: "A notional test programme of 20 flights over a period of two years has been defined." In addition, "Stevenage have issued a report on abort contingency planning. It concludes that successful recoveries should be possible following system or partial engine failures at any point".

As for Warton, the earlier optimism about Kevlar/epoxy for the hydrogen tank had evaporated: "Further consideration... has raised doubts about the suitability of composite materials due to cracking or crazing at cryogenic temperatures. For the present titanium, which is slightly heavier, will be taken as the datum material and testing of proposed alternative composite material samples will be put in hand."

Re-entry temperature studies had shown that lightweight titanium TPS panels wouldn't do either—most of Hotol's underside, and up to the centreline of the fuselage for its whole length, would need the heavier nickel alloy panels. Hotol would be hotter than expected all across its underside on its way back to Earth.

Additionally, a 1:23 scale preliminary low speed wind tunnel model was being made and testing in Warton's 5.5m tunnel was expected to commence in February.

THE RACE IS ON

BAe gave a Hotol presentation to the MoD's director of Defence Concepts Staff, Air Commodore John Thomson plus around 15 MoD staff, on February 6, followed by a presentation to ESA director general Lüst and his senior staff on February 10.

The *Challenger* Shuttle disaster on January 28 had had the knock-on effect of further focusing media attention on Hotol, so BAe held a press conference on February 14 attended by correspondents from various newspapers, magazines, radio and television stations. Both BBC and ITV crews also visited BAe at Warton and filmed preliminary Hotol tests in the 5.5m low speed wind tunnel.

The *Flight International* of February 15, 1986, ran a two-part article: '[President Ronald] Reagan gives thumbs-up for hypersonic spaceplane' and 'UK space agency backs Hotol'. In the first part, the reporter noted

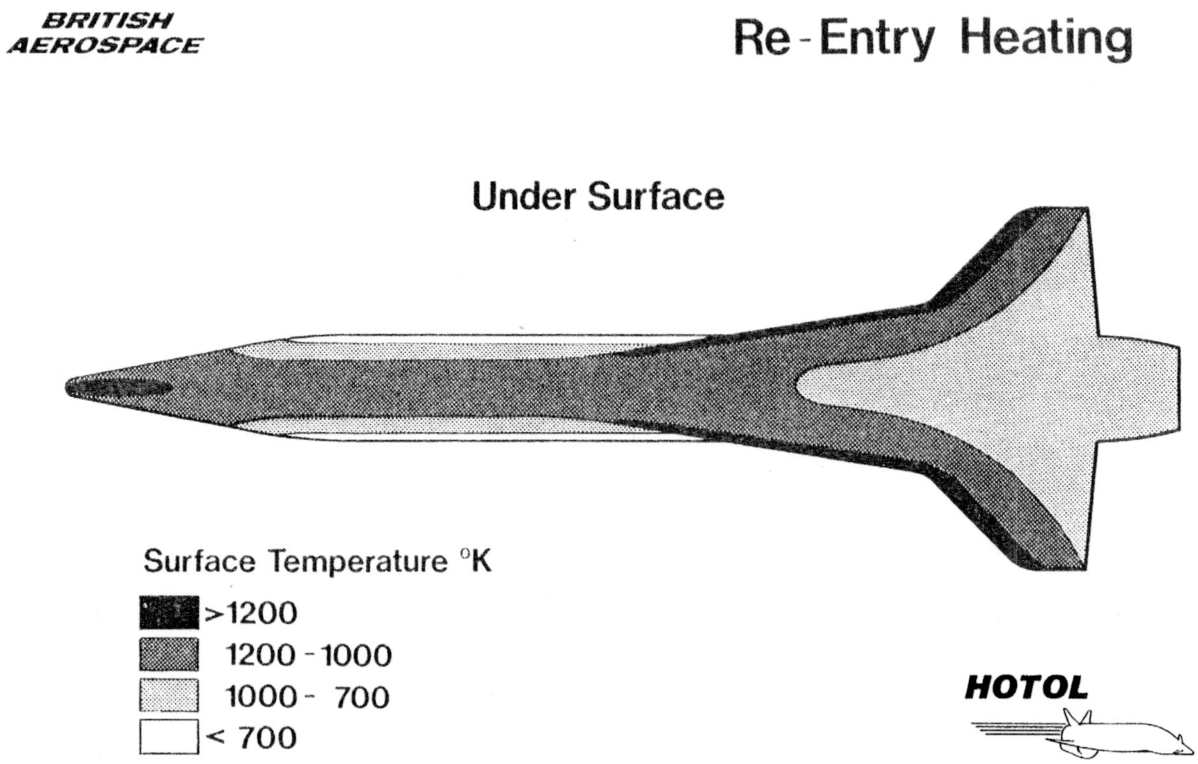

Illustration showing how hot different areas of Hotol's underside were expected to become during re-entry.

that "the US concept of a Mach 25 hypersonic spaceplane was given its preliminary go-ahead in President Reagan's State-of-the-Union address on February 4. A three-year, $600 million programme has been voted by Congress for validation of the necessary technologies. This could be followed by a $3,000 million programme leading to a pair of flight-test X-designated vehicles in 1993".

And in the UK, "the day after President Reagan unveiled [his] plans… the UK national space centre announced proof-of-concept funding for Hotol… the space centre is spending £3 million on continued work to validate the necessary technologies. Geoffrey Pattie, minister of state for industry and information technology, says that the studies 'will establish if there are any insuperable difficulties with the concept, and will provide credible design, performance, and cost data with which to explore the technology with our partners in the European Space Agency'".

The reporter further noted that "of the £3 million to be spent, £2 million goes to BAe, the rest to Rolls-Royce. The project will remain exclusively British until the end of the PoC phase. If Hotol's feasibility is proved it will almost certainly be submitted to [ESA] for a full-scale development programme that is expected to cost at least £4,000 million".

What Reagan had actually said in his address was: "… we are going forward with research on a new Orient Express that could, by the end of the next decade, take off from Dulles Airport, accelerate up to 25 times the speed of sound, attaining low Earth orbit or flying to Tokyo within two hours".

Frank Miles put out another broadcast on Hotol that evening on the News at Ten: "There's now a worldwide race to become the first to have such a spacecraft. President Reagan says America is to build one: the French and Japanese want one, too. But, with Britain well in the lead, ITN has discovered that the European Space Agency, of which Britain is a member, has now offered a substantial contract to any European aerospace company that can come up with something equal to Hotol's top-secret airbreathing engine.

"British Aerospace are standing firm. They've even turned down offers of cash from America because the engine—a wholly British design—is classified by the Ministry of Defence."

Burns' monthly report to Yates of February 25, 1986, ruefully observed: "It has been widely reported that BAe have been 'given' £3m for the PoC Study. The true picture is that the total cost of the study is estimated at £3m, BAe's share being £2m, but not more than 50% of the funding will be provided by the Government.

"Detailed contract negotiations are in progress with the MoD Contracts Branch for an initial package of £220,000

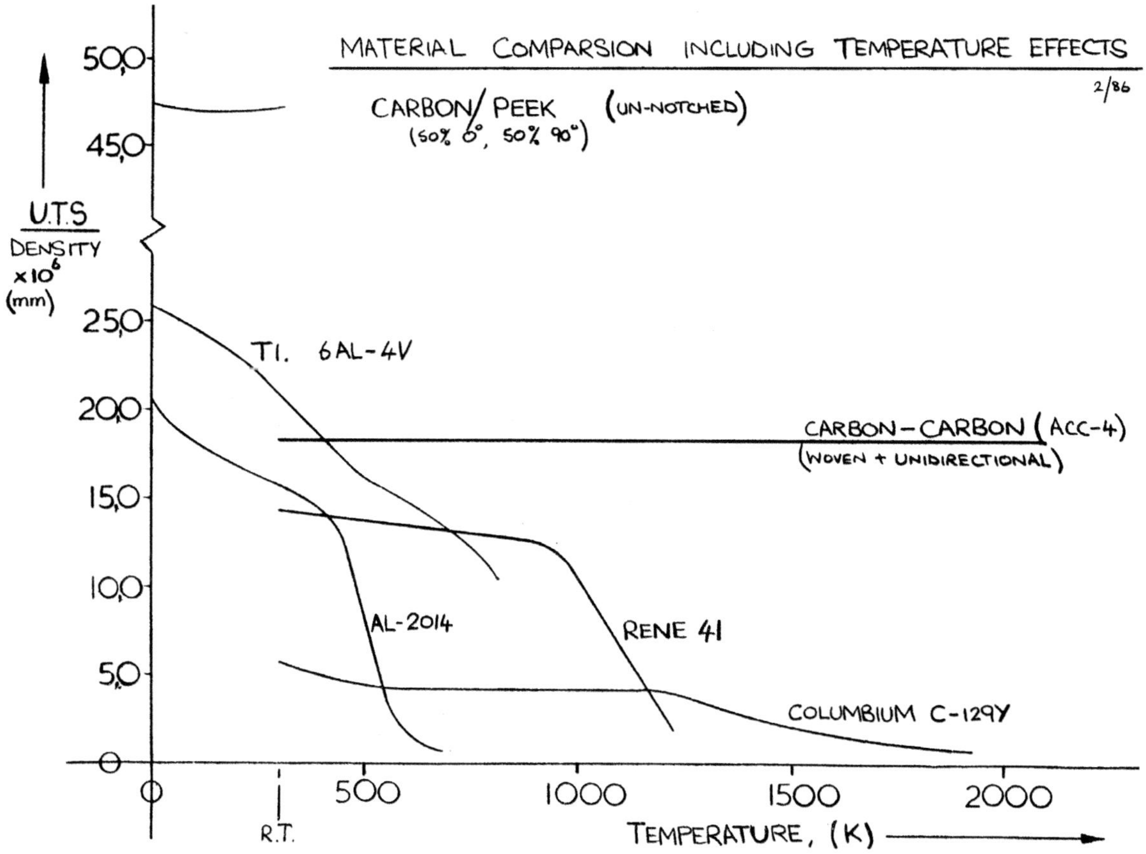

Comparison of temperature effects on carbon-PEEK, carbon-carbon, Rene 41 and other heat-resistant materials.

for part 1 of the study, ending April 30, 1986. Rolls-Royce are being funded separately. It is believed that their funds for part 1 will amount to £163,000 for preliminary heat exchanger icing tests plus 25% of their expected expenditure on theoretical studies, with the end of part 1 on June 30, 1986."

CONTROL SURFACE CONUNDRUMS

Low-speed wind tunnel testing of the 1:23 scale model was nearing completion at Warton by now and it had been found that "lift and stability measurements agree well with predictions generally; wing flap effectiveness is somewhat better". It wasn't all good news however: "A fairly severe pitch-up occurs at about 20-degrees incidence; this is probably acceptable, being about five degrees beyond the normal operating limit but further investigation of gust margins is necessary… more seriously, the forward fin control effectiveness is substantially lower than estimated due to adverse interference of the forebody at low incidence; it recovers at high incidence. Alternative controls are being investigated."

Planning work was now under way to prepare for high-speed, as opposed to low-speed, wind tunnel testing. The majority of this was to be done at Warton but nevertheless, a request had been made to the RAE to see whether its high-speed tunnels could be made available free of charge for detailed hypersonic tests. In particular, Burns hoped to examine a small nose-plus-foreplanes model to investigate local heating effects.

The RAE had meanwhile offered to lend the Filton team a Mach 4 wedge intake model that had been manufactured in 1967, known as Model 351. Burns reported that "its suitability and [the] cost of modifications as a Hotol intake model are being investigated by Filton staff". Up to this point, Hotol had been specified with three engines—this layout being "based on economic studies in the project stage" but Filton had pointed out that the wedge intake would work better with an even number of engines. Four, to be precise. Burns said that "this matter will be discussed with Rolls-Royce in the near future".

Furthermore, "following requests from BAe, RR have indicated that a slimmer design of heat exchangers is feasible which will make installation easier. However, progress of definition of propulsion items by RR is disappointingly slow; visits to obtain design information have twice been deferred".

Detailed work on Hotol's nosecone structure had concluded that it should be manufactured from 25mm thick carbon-carbon at the front for bird strike resistance, reducing to 7mm thick at the rear. The foreplanes were supposed to be made from nickel alloys but studies had shown that severe problems would then be caused by differential thermal expansion. In other words, the extreme heat would cause different components to change in size relative to one another if they were made of different materials—potentially leading to mechanical failure.

According to Burns, "a more attractive solution appears to be to manufacture the support frame, spigots and foreplane surfaces all from carbon-carbon. This will require some materials development, notably to introduce fibres in the third dimension and the use of ceramic bearings for the moving surfaces will also be investigated".

Further research on potential materials for the hydrogen tank had settled on PEEK (polyetheretherketone)—a semi-crystalline thermoplastic known for its exceptional thermal stability as a possible replacement for titanium. This would theoretically "not be susceptible to cracking or crazing at cryogenic temperatures but this will need to be proved by testing".

VENTILATED SKIRT

During the early stages of the Hotol project, Bond had established his own company, Reaction Engines, to act as a vehicle for his consultancy services—named in honour of Reaction Motors, the long-defunct firm behind the engine which propelled the Bell X-1 during its supersonic flight in 1947.

He travelled to the Cranfield Institute of Technology on March 12, 1986, for a meeting with Scott-Scott and CIT's professors Ian Smith and Barrie Moss. The post-meeting report appears to be the earliest mention of him in relation to Hotol as a Reaction Engines representative.

The goal of the meeting was to discuss potential collaboration on Swallow's combustion chamber and injector systems as well as ventilated high area-ratio nozzles. It was explained to the CIT men that the PoC study needed to demonstrate the engine injectors' functionality but "at the present time, Rolls-Royce do not have commissioned facilities where this type of rocket combustion experiment can be carried out... CIT are fortunate in having an existing small rocket test bed, where all aspects necessary for this injector proof programme can be investigated. It would need to be modified to cater for high pressure gaseous propellants but is otherwise adequate, and does not have a high degree of usage".

Bond "had prepared provisional designs for both injectors, details of which were given to Rolls-Royce. These were used as the basis for the discussion on possible practical programmes. The objects of the test programme are to establish the combustor stability and mixing processes resulting from this unusual combination of propellants. The best technique discussed appeared to entail the use of an uncooled copper combustion chamber, made in sections and furnished with an adequate array of thermocouples".

Where the nozzles were concerned, Scott-Scott wanted to investigate the possibility of switching individual nozzles between two different area ratios—lower and higher—while the engine was running. At startup, gas or air would be vented into the nozzle skirt "at a place where the normal separation line would be found in ground running" to retain a low area ratio. Then, "at a sufficiently high altitude, the gas/air supply is closed off, thus permitting the flow to reattach and 'fill' the nozzle to a larger area ratio".

This type of nozzle was "known as one with a 'ventilated skirt' or one with 'controlled separation'. Apart from a limited study made at Rolls-Royce many years ago (under the guidance of Professor Smith) little is known about the possibilities of the technique and so it was agreed that within the PoC programme, some limited, small-scale tests should be made in support of the concept".

CIT said they would quote for the injector work but couldn't help with the nozzles beyond some theoretical studies.

HOTOL'S WEIGHT PROBLEM

Burns' regular report for Yates on March 24, 1986, opened once again with the familiar refrain on funding—the MoD Contracts Branch were still haggling over funds for the first part of the PoC. Beyond that however, work on Hotol's structure was advancing rapidly.

The payload bay design investigation had concluded and work on the liquid oxygen tank and its surrounding structure was well advanced. Filton were also making good progress on designing the combined intake/mainwheel bay/engine support structure.

But again, there were dark clouds on the horizon: "From the first round of structural design, nearing completion, a serious structure mass growth, in the region of 20% above the project estimates, is evident". In short, having crunched the numbers and made some necessary changes to materials, Hotol was shaping up to be a lot heavier than expected.

Therefore, "an alternative layout, with a shorter, fatter, tapered front fuselage/hydrogen tank is being investigated. Scaling studies indicate that this offers a very substantial mass reduction... this revised layout is likely to be

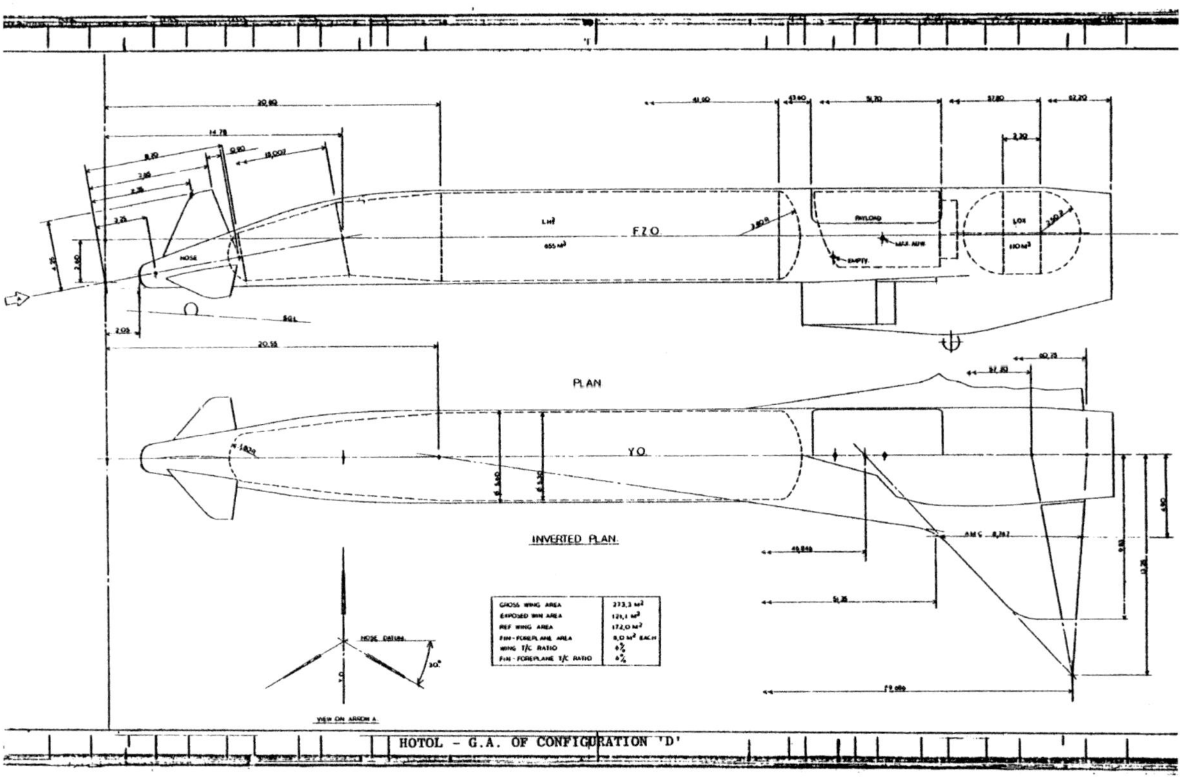

Hotol Configuration D. This was the project's baseline design from April to June 1986, when it was superseded by the contentious Configuration F.

adopted as the datum for the joint design activity planned at Warton in weeks 14 and 15. It may also be possible to dispense with the 'horizontal' foreplanes, leading to further reduction in structure and systems mass".

Earlier concerns about the potential for making components out of carbon-carbon had been somewhat allayed during a visit to Dunlop's manufacturing facilities in Coventry. This "has shown that they are more advanced in this field than had been expected. 3D carbon-carbon components are possible; it can be machined to a similar standard of surface finish as metal". Dunlop Aerospace had started out developing carbon-carbon for use in aircraft brake discs but by the mid-1980s was promoting it for use in a wide variety of applications.

Engine-wise, Rolls-Royce had agreed to dispense with the three-engine layout. The new configuration "more suited to the favoured vertical wedge intake... has two heat exchangers, two turbo-compressors and four main rocket chambers. Sizing the intake for a lower Mach number than 5, the nominal transition M [the speed at which Hotol would go from airbreathing to pure rocket], offers significant weight saving".

There was more ominous news from Stevenage arising from their studies on Hotol's operational possibilities: "Work at Stevenage indicates that the 7,000kg datum payload for equatorial launch is probably too light and results in insufficient payload for polar orbit missions. Also manned operations are gaining increased emphasis". Despite this the original plan for "an unmanned vehicle with 7,000kg payload in eastern equatorial orbit... will be maintained".

Rolls-Royce Bristol's Installation Aerodynamics Department held a Hotol review meeting on April 9, now led by Ralph Denning as Lewis's replacement, and it was confirmed that three months of heat exchanger icing tests were due to commence in July. In addition, the programme of work was now to be split between Rolls-Royce Ansty and Rolls-Royce Bristol. Ansty would handle the icing tests; the main heat exchanger design; the dual use combustion chamber; the nozzle design and the cryogenic pumps and associated systems. Bristol would tackle the calculations on system performance and weights; comparison with alternative systems; turbo-machinery including hydrogen turbines; air-intake and heat exchanger design/integration in liaison with BAe Filton and Ansty, and a survey of literature on cryogenic heat exchangers.

Under 'technical issues' it was emphasised that "the air intake must be properly understood by RR and required integration with the various heat exchangers. Installation aerodynamics will establish a close relationship with BAe Filton on this item". It was noted that "the stressing of

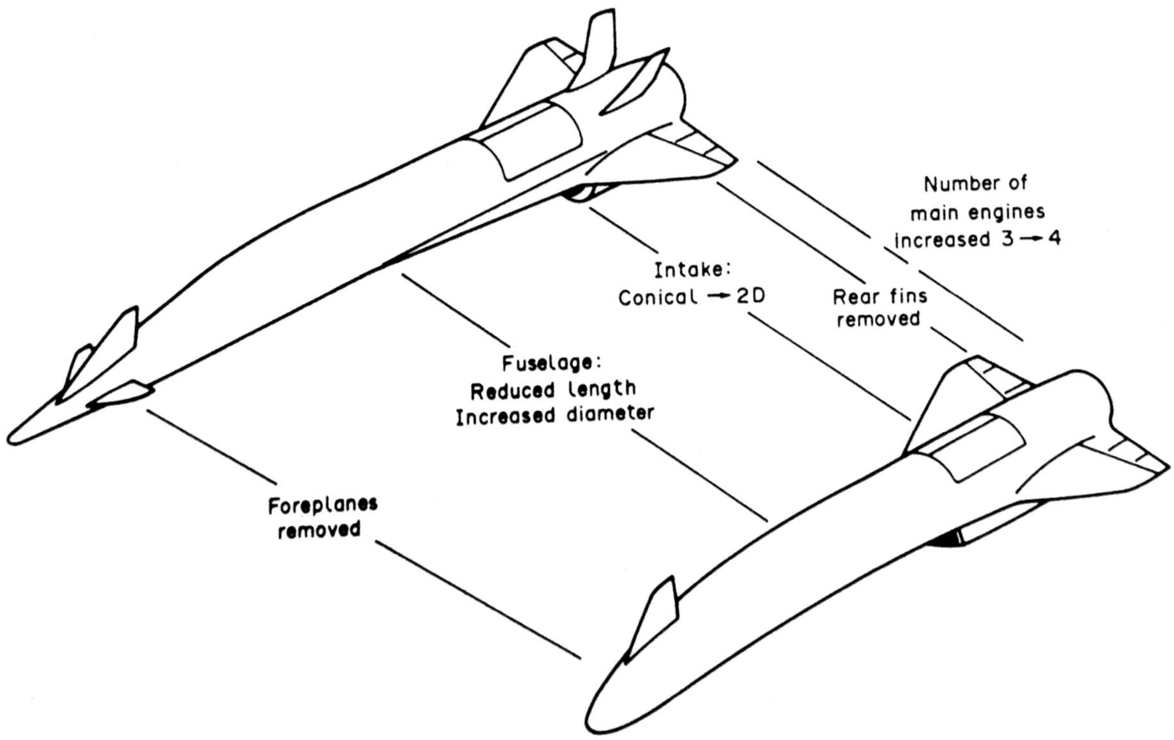

Diagram showing the major configuration changes between the Stevenage design and what was becoming Configuration F.

the very high absolute pressure compressor and turbine components needs to be looked at carefully since this is outside our normal experience" and that the aimed-for ventilated skirt nozzle "may be difficult to realise in practice".

$0.5BN FOR NASP

With BAe and Rolls-Royce yet to receive a penny of their £1.5m Hotol match-funding from the British government, *Aviation Week & Space Technology's* Herbert J. Coleman reported on April 14, 1986, that over in the US, the DoD and NASA had awarded seven contracts for what was now dubbed the National Aero-Space Plane Project (soon to be widely known as 'NASP')—worth around half a billion dollars over a 42-month period.

Two of these contracts, worth around $175m each, had gone to General Electric/Aerojet TechSystems and Pratt & Whitney for the design and development of "airbreathing (scramjet) engines ... [and testing] them in special ground facilities". The other five contracts, each worth around $32m, had been dished out to airframe manufacturers Boeing, General Dynamics, Lockheed, McDonnell Douglas and Rockwell International. It was expected that a design competition would see these whittled down to just two or three competitors during the first year.

The monumental disparity between the British government's miserly attitude towards Hotol and the American government's lavish and enthusiastic spending on NASP is clearly evident.

Even by April 28, 1986—nearly seven months after its official start date—Burns was reporting that the contract for funding Hotol's first stage PoC had yet to be finalised. He also stated that the first round of structural design analyses was almost complete, with mass now slightly improved at 18% greater than the original project estimates. Options for putting Hotol on a diet included, "alternative means of fuel supply with lower tank pressures; alternative intake schemes including semi-circular with translating cone and scoop intake [presumably reverting to something like the original design]; carbon-carbon lower TPS panels; deletion of upper surface TPS with 'hot' titanium tank skin; carbon-carbon sandwich construction in certain areas".

Work was also proceeding on the shorter, fatter, foreplane-less Hotol to see what mass reduction benefits this would offer. Preliminary investigation of all Hotol's systems had been completed and all masses had been defined. Some mass had been saved by switching from a microwave landing system to one which employed "dual GPS".

Investigation of Hotol's propulsion system "is being hampered by lack of new data from Rolls-Royce" but Stevenage had been busy. The site had issued reports on both ground processing of the Hotol vehicle—preparing it for a new mission—and design schemes for a manned capsule. In addition, "a full computerised cost model to

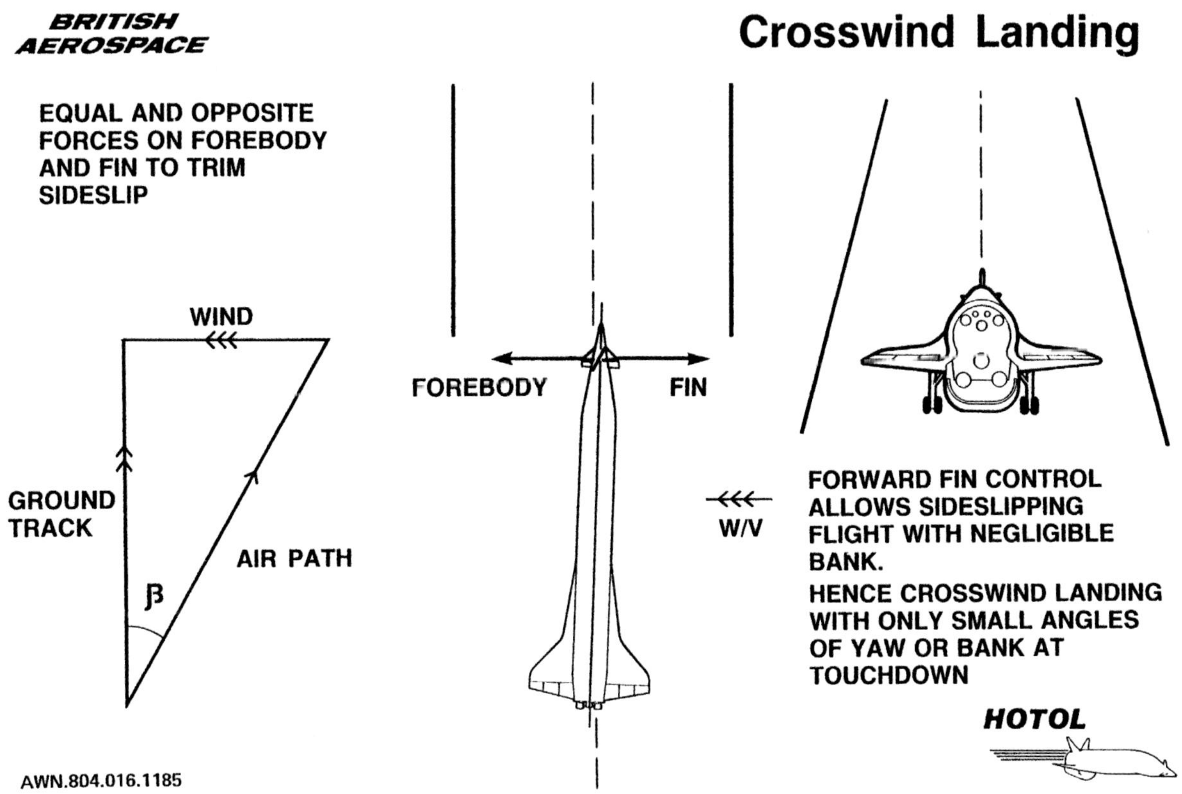

Using the fin to control the vehicle during a crosswind landing.

define development, prototype and production manufacturing costs has been developed at Stevenage and a draft report issued. This has been used also to define a [potential] geographical distribution of work sharing between possible European partners".

On April 25, a Hotol propulsion system meeting had been held to discuss data transfer between British Aerospace and Rolls-Royce. The former requested data on the ratio of liquid hydrogen to liquid oxygen during the pure rocket part of Hotol's ascent; the optimum rocket nozzle area ratio and heat exchanger weight variation relative to intake flow. The latter particularly wanted data on intake pressure recovery versus Mach number for the various intake designs being reviewed.

HOTOL GOES TO GENEVA

All of this work was now compiled into the first full Hotol engineering study paper, the content of which was presented to representatives of the RAE and BNSC on May 8. Burns then travelled to Geneva for a three-day conference on May 14-16—Space Tech 86. Six papers were presented: Boeing's James Jenkins on alternative concepts for a Space Shuttle replacement; Xie Guang Xuan on the Chinese Long March I, II and III rockets; Aérospatiale's Bernard Deloffre on Hermes; MBB's Wolfgang Kleinau on BETA—a reusable ballistic SSTO vehicle; Belgian consultant Jean Vandenkerckhove on vehicle sizing, and Burns/Parkinson on Hotol. The latter was presented by Burns alone since Parkinson was unable to attend and there was a closing session which featured a paper by the conference chairman—BNSC's Roy Gibson.

The Hotol paper was entitled Hotol—A Multi Role Space Transport for Europe and it kicked off with the usual explanation of Hotol's cost benefits compared to Shuttle and Ariane. The two-year PoC was outlined, the computerised scaling model was mentioned and mission requirements were listed. These included "delivery of payloads into low Earth, near-equatorial orbit (together with the possibility of retrieval and return); delivery of a satellite and perigee stage into LEO for transfer to geosynchronous orbit; delivery into (and possible retrieval from) a sun-synchronous polar orbit of automatic payloads" and lastly "manned operations in LEO".

Evidently, "in the early stages of the programme, manned operations were separated from unmanned (cargo) operations. A minimum manned 'capsule' would add perhaps 2.5 tonnes to the mass of the payload needing to be carried. In most cases the mission requirements are sufficiently simple to allow straightforward automatic operations, and it is felt that men should be exposed to the risks of launch only when the system has been proven, and then only when their presence is required in orbit".

VEHICLE ENGINEERING

In terms of vehicle design: "The wing of Hotol, of Shuttle-like planform, is sized by both airfield operations and re-entry considerations. The low planform loading on re-entry (about 100kg/sqm) results in early start of deceleration at high altitude, minimising peak velocity and surface temperatures. This enables the use of a metallic TPS over most of the structure instead of troublesome tiles or ablative coatings. The wing thickness/chord ratio is 6% outboard. With 45-degree leading edge sweep ... this yields satisfactory transonic stability and control—always a critical region for flight control system design."

Take-off speed/distance was given as 270 knots/1,800m and landing speed/distance was 150 knots/1,500m. Hotol's nose fin "provides sufficient control power to stabilise the vehicle over the full Mach range on ascent and to trim sideslip for crosswind landing. A notable virtue of the forward fin is that it allows a virtually 'uncrabbed' unbanked sideslipping approach in crosswind, avoiding the need for coordination of a 'kick-off drift' manoeuvre with the landing flare".

The latest thinking on structure was given in some detail: "The nose cone will be made of carbon-carbon, designed to withstand moderate bird strikes and aerodynamic pressures, combined with stagnation heating, up to 1,750°K locally. The major support frame for foreplanes and nosewheel will also be manufactured from carbon-carbon, as will the fin and foreplanes themselves, to avoid differential expansion problems, with close tolerances. UK expertise in the development of c-c components with multi-dimensional fibres gives a high level of confidence in this method of construction.

"All aerodynamic and inertia loads on the front fuselage will be carried by the liquid hydrogen tank skin. This tank will be pressurised to a level required to prevent fuel boiling and to remove compression loading in the thin skin. The tank skin will be made of carbon-PEEK, a UK development, which is resistant to cracking and crazing at cryogenic fuel temperatures (20°K).

"The metallic TPS will consist of panels, titanium sandwich on the upper (700°K) surface, nickel alloy on the lower (1,200°K) surface. The panels are sized, of the order of 1m side length, by avoidance of panel flutter, and designed to resist thermal, acoustic and pressure loadings. Thermal stresses are minimised by expansion gaps along all sides, with interlocking edges.

"Layers of cryogenic insulation on the outside of the tank and 'hot' lagging on the inside of the TPS minimise fuel boil off and protect local structures. The payload bay, with load-carrying doors, is of relatively conventional construction ... Hotol has been designed with thermal radiators as part of the outer skin, and the payload bay doors do not have to be kept open throughout the flight. This avoids the need for complex sun-shields for many deployed payloads.

"Leading edges of wings and intake structure will be manufactured from c-c. The wings will be largely of titanium construction with nickel sandwich TPS panels to protect the lower ('hot') surface."

A table was appended listing Hotol's systems without further explanation.

OPERATING HOTOL

It had been mentioned that the whole point of using Hotol as a launcher was to keep costs down, but "achieving low transport costs into LEO is not simply a matter of choosing the right reusable vehicle and payload size ... As hardware costs fall, operating costs become more and more important. In Hotol careful attention has been given to minimising operating and turn-round costs. All that will be needed at the operating base will be: cryogenic fuel storage, maintenance hangar, payload loading facilities, laser guidance equipment for the trolley and trolley servicing facilities".

Features of the take-off trolley were listed as "roll-on, fly-off operation; refuel on trolley; conventional runway operation; auxiliary propulsion; laser steering; shock-absorbing suspension; conventional tyres; braking parachute(s) [and] wheel brakes".

Recovery of Hotol was possible following "a failure at any stage of its mission". Apparently, "abort immediately after take-off demands dumping on-board propellants [and] using rocket pumps (as available) while circling to land. Rocket propulsion can be used if airbreathing has failed". For a down range abort, "at higher speeds, return to launch site will not be possible. Control then selects [a] down range field for landing. Sub-orbital ballistic flight possible. Vehicle can land at any 'Concorde-class' airfield". It was even possible to 'abort to orbit': "Late in ascent, loss of thrust in one engine still allows vehicle to achieve orbit. Some engine throttling will be required to limit maximum accelerations in any case".

Burns concluded: "The PoC Study of Hotol is progressing well; the prospect of engineering a vehicle with the characteristics described looks good. As we address the questions associated with operating such a vehicle, it becomes more and more apparent that a vehicle of this type is needed. The Shuttle represented the first step away from expendable 'fireworks', demonstrating a whole range of new capabilities which might be achieved in space.

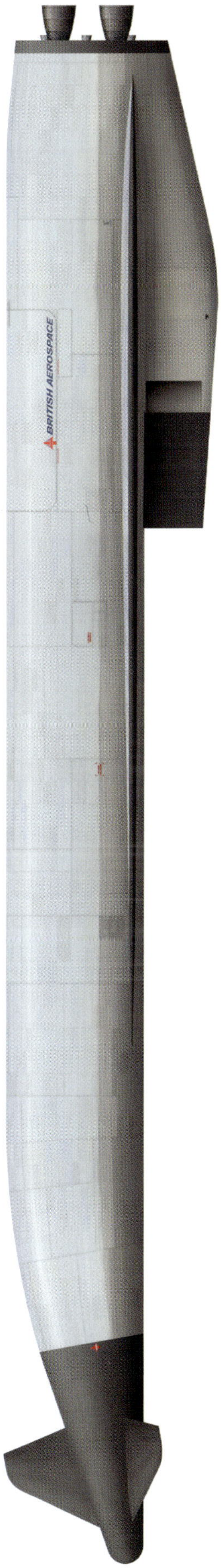

Hotol Configuration D. CHRIS SANDHAM-BAILEY

Hotol offers the possibility of versatile economic operations in space and a mature transportation system. It is up to Europe to grasp this opportunity."

Meanwhile, a tour of major European countries had been planned to drum up political support for Hotol. Shortly after Burns' return, on May 19, Pattie, Lygo, Yates and others received a further update briefing from Burns, Conchie, BNSC's Jack Leeming and Stewart Miller of Rolls-Royce—presumably incorporating everything Burns had discussed in Geneva.

Gibson recalled: "We went to the major countries and we induced Pattie to come and to make a pitch. So we did Germany, we did Italy and France, and we put on a kind of dog and pony show with industry to show what the concept was and to try and win support for it. It's difficult to judge in hindsight. I mean I think a lot of the stuff that was done then, a lot of the technology, has proved to be correct and is probably the way that people will go. But it was way ahead of its time. It was almost like a Concorde breakthrough at that time."

HOTOL F AND THE RB.545

The Stevenage/Filton Hotol had been the original 1984 Configuration A, with Configuration B then being an evolution of that design with revised foreplanes, a straightened fuselage and a lengthened rear fuselage—becoming the baseline design at the end of 1985. Configuration C replaced B in February 1986 but precisely how C differed from B is unclear. Configuration D became the new baseline as of April 1986 with the adoption of four engines, rather than three, and a new vertical wedge intake. Now it was time to skip a letter. Burns reported on May 29: "Scaling work based on refined mass models has led to definition of a revised datum design, Configuration F, which is taking shape on the drawing board. Main features of this design are: shorter, fatter front fuselage/liquid hydrogen tank; overall length reduced by 9.2m; maximum diameter increased from 5.6m to 7.7m; deletion of lifting foreplanes.

"A significant structural mass saving is calculated for this version compared with the previous datum. However, further significant mass reductions must be achieved to approach the target (project) figure of 200 tonnes take-off mass to put seven tonnes in orbit. The revised configuration, with an 'optimism factor' of 0.8 on structure mass would have a take-off mass of 230 tonnes.

"Without this 'optimism factor' it would scale to 320 tonnes at take-off. However, to put this in perspective, the previous Configuration D could not be scaled to reach orbit with a seven-tonne payload."

Essentially, no matter how it was tweaked, there was

The SA1 subsonic wind tunnel model was designed to test the shape of Hotol Configuration C. It is pictured in Warton's south side 18ft (5.5m) low-speed tunnel.

no way of making a design fundamentally based on the Stevenage/Filton model achieve the seven-tonnes-to-orbit objective. Hotol Configuration D, which would be the subject of Warton's PoC Study Part 1 report on May 31, simply couldn't do what was needed. Configuration E had gone unassigned (for reasons which are not entirely clear) and now the team were focused on the shorter, fatter Configuration F as Configuration D's successor. But even this would rely on a certain amount of 'optimism' in terms of exactly how much mass was required to build it.

On a slightly more positive note: "The contract for Part 1 of the Study is not yet finally agreed; BAe objections to the wording concerning industrial property rights remain to be settled. A payment of £200,000 has however been made."

Concerning high speed wind tunnel testing, a session to try out the borrowed 1960s RAE Mach 4 intake model in the RAE's own 3ft by 4ft tunnel at Bedford had been booked for July. It was hoped that, through negotiation between BAe Warton Technical Director Brian Young and

RAE Chief Superintendent Dr Geoffrey Pope, the standard £20,000 per day fee for using the tunnel could be waived. The same model was also to be tested in Warton's 18in high speed wind tunnel and a model of Hotol Configuration F was to be tested in Warton's 1.2m tunnel and its Guided Weapons tunnel.

Burns also noted that the 'Swallow' designation had now finally been dropped from the project altogether: "Meetings of the power plant steering group and at working level indicate that Rolls-Royce are putting effort into the propulsion system, now labelled RB.545. A request has been made for 'trade-off' figures to enable airframe and power plant to be scaled together to arrive at an optimum design."

Across the whole project however, "little [engineering] work has been done during [May], most effort being devoted to the presentation to RAE/BNSC on May 8 and the engineering report on Part 1, due on May 31.

POC STUDY PART 1

The first major report on design and engineering work carried out during the Proof-of-Concept Study, the content of which had already been presented to the RAE and BNSC 23 days earlier, was published on May 31 with the document reference number HPN 0001. It covered the first six months and encompassed all three BAe sites—Warton, Stevenage and Filton.

The introduction to this hefty multi-part tome stated that the objective of this period, from an engineering perspective, had been "to demonstrate that the proposed vehicle can be engineered at a size and mass that is economically attractive. To this end a structural analysis has been made of all major components, identifying critical loadings and extremes of temperature, choosing appropriate structural materials, defining a baseline structure, calculating material thicknesses and defining masses.

"Aerodynamic work has covered definition of critical design loads, sizing [of] control surfaces, defining centre of gravity limits, drag calculation, initial flutter calculations and assessment of critical stability and control features".

As mentioned, the design arrived at and already superseded was known as Configuration D. The key changes between Configurations B and D, encompassing Configuration C, were listed as: "Adoption of congruent foreplanes and fin, set at 120-degrees included angles, to minimise torsional loading due to gusts and to control inputs; deletion of kink in the fuselage lower surface, to reduce down-loading on the forebody; adoption of a 'curved triangular' nose section to improve foreplane 'cling' to the fuselage lines over a range of control angles; increase of wing thickness/chord ratio from 4% to 6% on the outer part, to save weight; wing planform modification with 10° sweep on the control hinge line, to ensure smooth variation of transonic control effectiveness; extension of afterbody lines to reduce base area and 'boat-tail' angles, to reduce transonic and supersonic drag; adoption of 'back to back' vertical wedge intakes in the interest of simpler variable geometry and intake closure; number of [engines] increased from three to four, fed in pairs from each intake. Main propulsion units mounted horizontally and shifted forward, to improve balance; adoption of 'BAe 146-style' main undercarriage, retracting into the intake pod".

Dimensionally, Hotol Configuration D was 62.2m long with a 19.66m wingspan. Gross wing area was 273.3sqm, though exposed wing area was only 121.1sqm. The forward fuselage was almost entirely filled by the 655 cubic metre capacity liquid hydrogen tank. The payload bay behind the tank was 8.1m long and behind that was the 110 cubic metre capacity liquid oxygen tank.

Structurally, it would be 25% carbon-carbon (nosecone, wing leading edge, foreplane and air intake), 25% carbon/PEEK (liquid hydrogen and liquid oxygen tanks), 40% titanium (wing, front fuselage upper aerodynamic shell aka aeroshell, payload bay structure, rocket support structure and rear fuselage aeroshell) and 10% nickel (wing and front fuselage lower surface).

NOSECONE

Being subject to the most extreme temperatures, aerodynamic pressures and the threat of birdstrike, Hotol's nosecone had to be tough. Since February, its thickness at the front had increased from 25mm to 27mm and at the rear from 7mm to 14mm. And in order to support the fin and foreplanes, it needed a strong frame which couldn't be made out of nickel owing to the thermal expansion problem.

Therefore, almost the entire nosecone inside and out, including the control surfaces, would be made from carbon-carbon. This was even less straightforward than it might have seemed since "the carbon-carbon is subjected to oxidation and catalysis and hence must be protected; doped silicon carbide is the proposed protective treatment. Any cracks in the silicon carbide are sealed by the impregnation of tetraethyl orthosilicate and MAP [propyl methacrylate]. Details of the doping and MAP have not been released by the USA and this research will have to be duplicated in the UK".

In addition, the nosecone had to house Hotol's nosewheel. According to the report: "The nosewheel is as short as possible but consistent with giving ground clearance

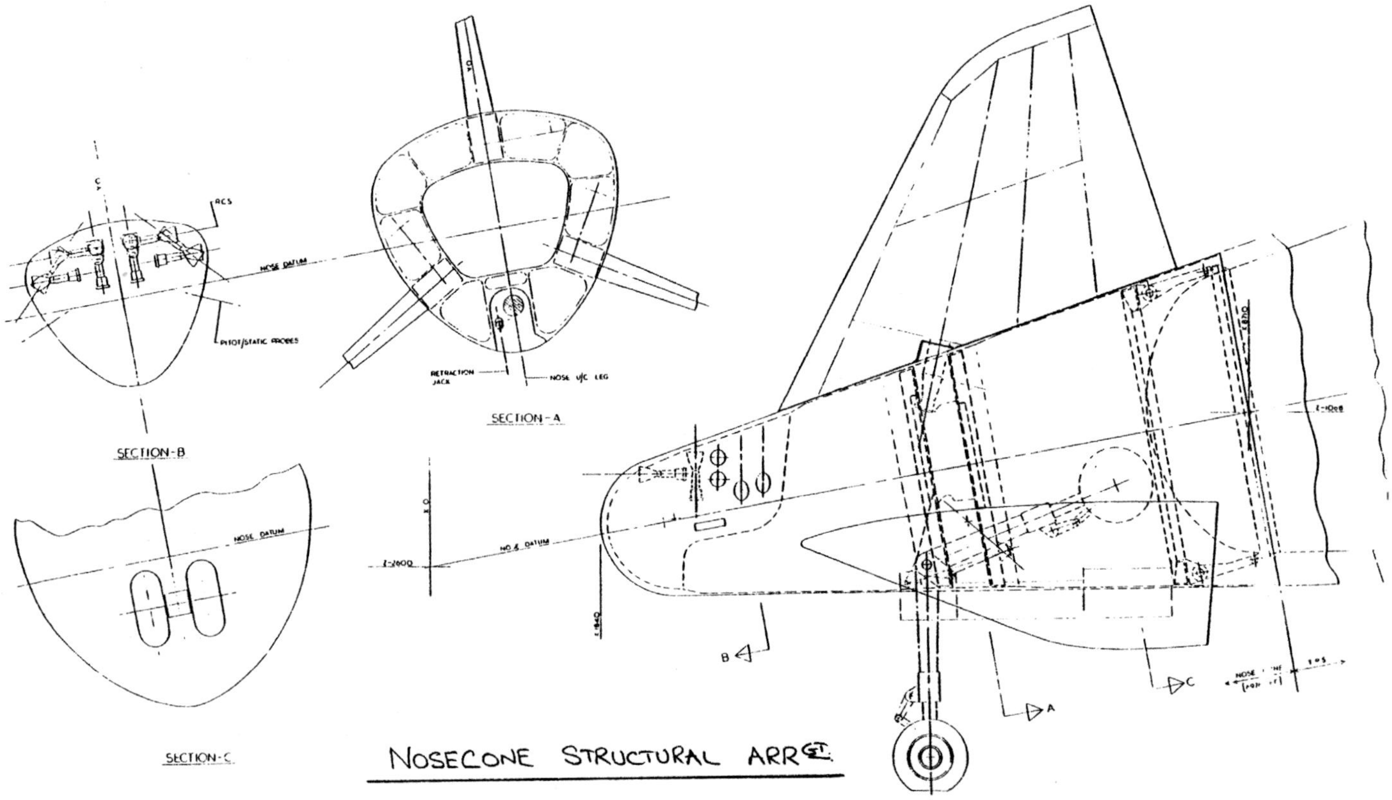

Hotol nosecone structural arrangement, including nosewheel housing, fin and foreplanes.

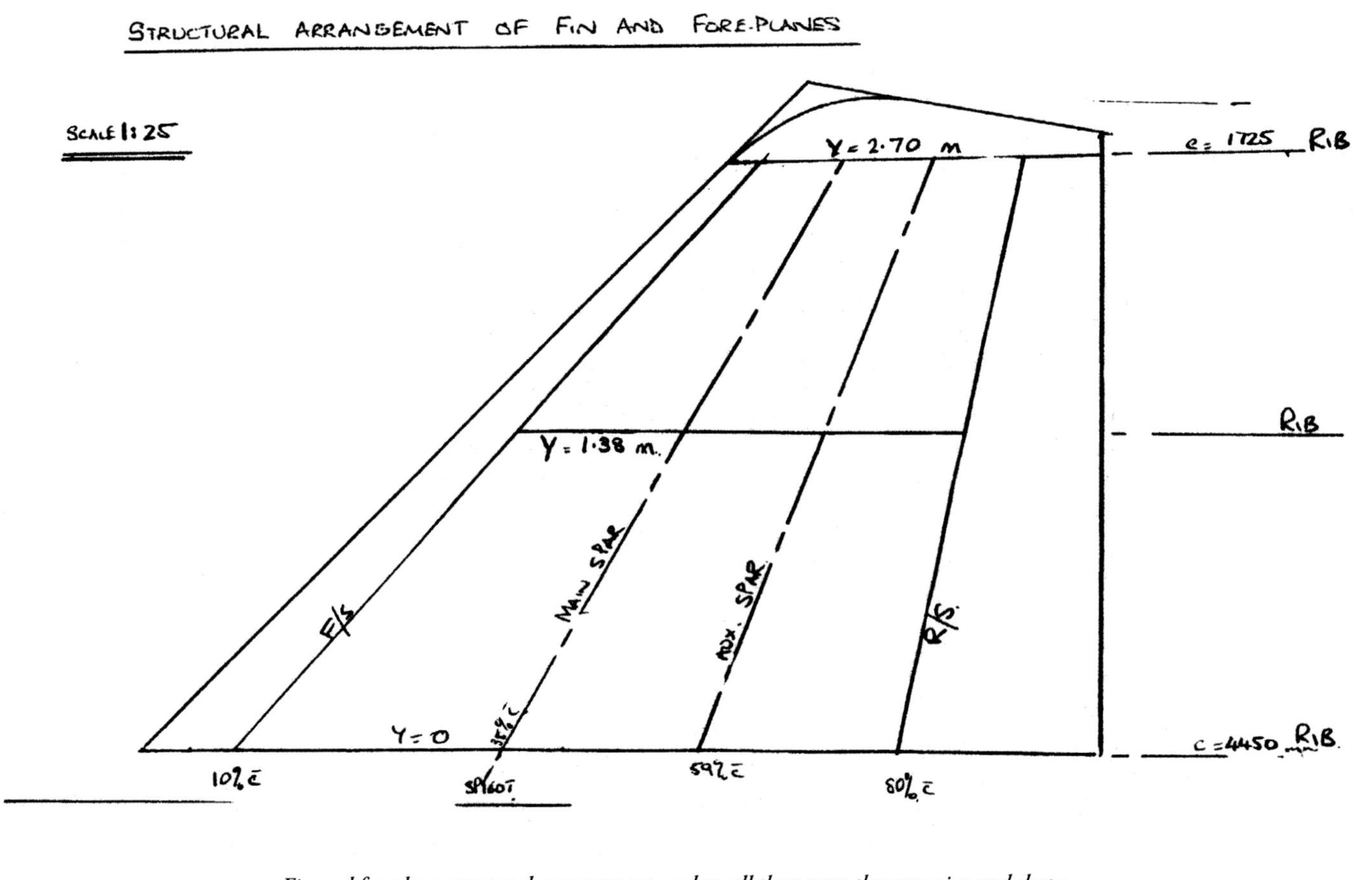

Fin and foreplane structural arrangement—when all three were the same size and shape.

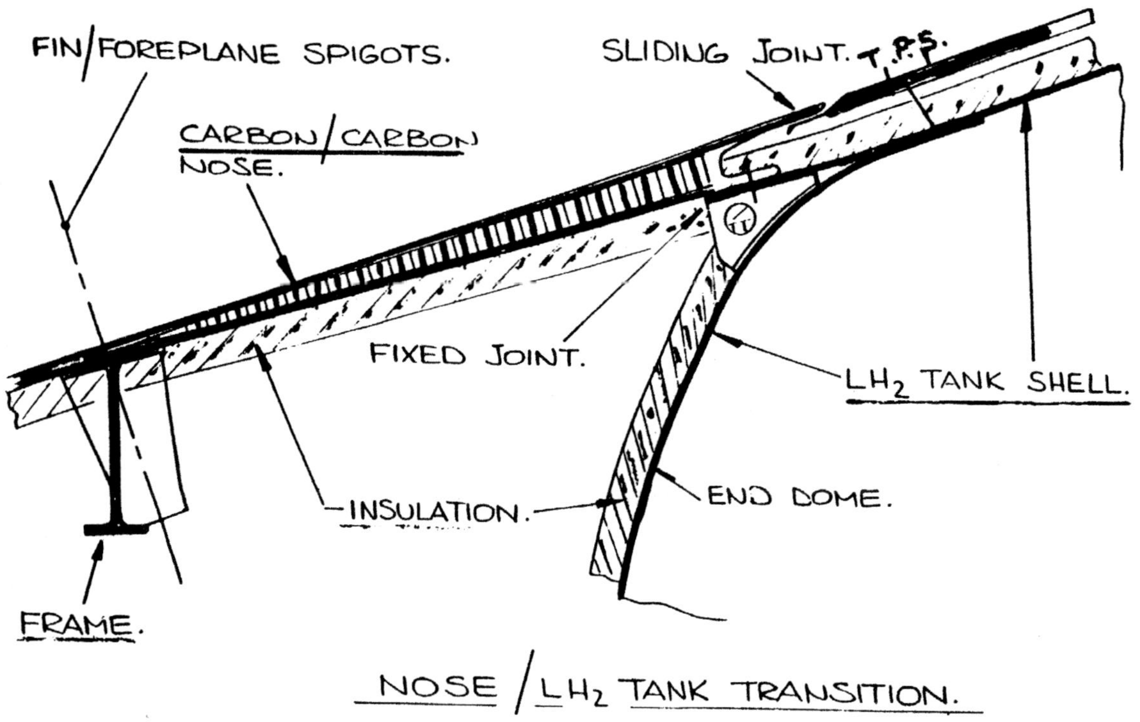

Structural transition point between the nosecone and the liquid hydrogen tank.

to the air intake which lies between the nose and main-wheels. The undercarriage retracts rearwards into the nosecone [and] it is supported from the same strong frame that supports the fin and foreplane and sits in a temperature-controlled bay in the nose. The tyres and hydraulic fluid are the components which require thermal protection. The nosewheel is steerable and has an oleo pneumatic design."

LIQUID HYDROGEN TANK

The pressurised liquid hydrogen tank basically formed Hotol's main fuselage structure, with the TPS panels being attached to it rather than forming a stress-resistant structure in their own right. A bulkhead was needed halfway along the tank at the point where Hotol would attach to its take-off trolley, to reduce fuselage bending. According to the report, "the tank pressurisation level required to stabilise the tank skins when full of fuel and standing on the trolley defines the minimum absolute pressure for the liquid hydrogen tank at altitude. Also a tank differential pressurisation of 0.12 atmospheres is required to stabilise the tank when empty and with Hotol supported on its own undercarriage in between missions".

In other words, it was essential to maintain the correct pressure within the liquid hydrogen tank at all times, in order to prevent Hotol's structure from collapsing.

FRONT FUSELAGE AEROSHELL

The shell of TPS panels surrounding the tank was in two parts—the upper part covered 60% of the forward fuselage circumference and the lower part the remaining 40%. The upper part panels would be made of titanium honeycomb sandwich construction and the lower part panels would be made of nickel-based alloy René 41 honeycomb sandwich.

The interlocking individual panels would be 10mm deep with a surface area of 1sqm each and they would be attached to the tank using posts and arches. Approximately 2,000 posts would be needed for this and each would be made of two materials—the part attaching to the tank would be fibreglass while the part attaching to the aeroshell panels would be titanium for the upper panels and nickel for the lower panels.

The upper panels were designed to deflect outwards by 25mm and the lower panels by 7mm. All panels would be subjected to an estimated noise level of 140 decibels, which required the panel edges to be thickened using a 'doubler'.

REAR FUSELAGE

This consisted of an aeroshell structure of frames and skinning enclosing the payload bay and liquid oxygen tank as well as housing the radiators. The underside of its forward section was protected from re-entry heat by the wings and

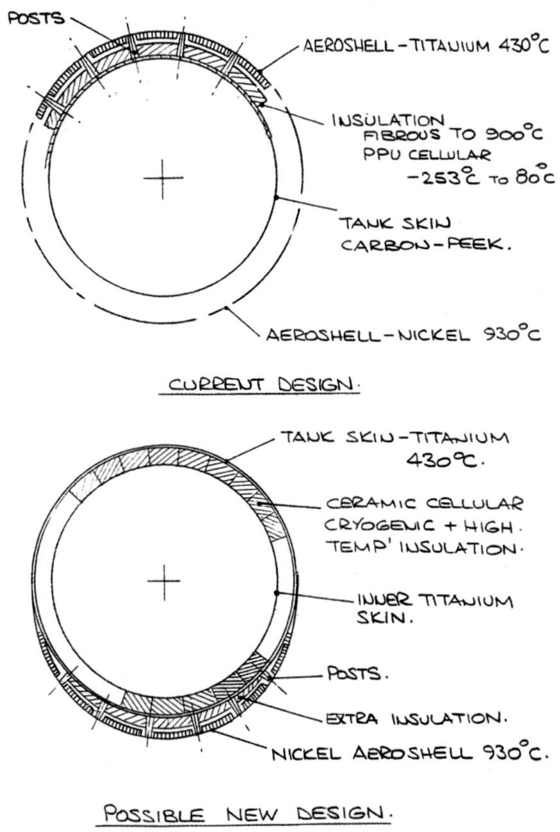

Internal structure of Hotol's front fuselage aeroshell—with proposed alternative.

intake nacelle and could therefore be made from titanium alloys. The lower rear section was exposed however, and would therefore need to be made from carbon-carbon.

The upper skin panels would be titanium alloy honeycomb but would be subjected to noise levels of up to 165 decibels, necessitating extra reinforcement at their edges.

The rear fuselage's four internal frames would be combined with the wing centre section to form a carry-through box structure capable of supporting the engines and the liquid oxygen tank.

PAYLOAD BAY

Positioned behind the hydrogen tank, the payload bay formed Hotol's centre fuselage and included the structure necessary to carry the intake and main undercarriage. The payload bay doors themselves were load-bearing during atmospheric flight, which would "ensure that the centre fuselage maintains an adequate stiffness compared to the front fuselage hydrogen tank (which was not required on the US Orbiter [Shuttle] design where the payload bay doors dominated the structure)".

Both the doors themselves and the area surrounding them could be made of titanium alloy since "the hotter lower surface is dominated by the carbon-carbon intake structure and the upper surface is shielded from the high

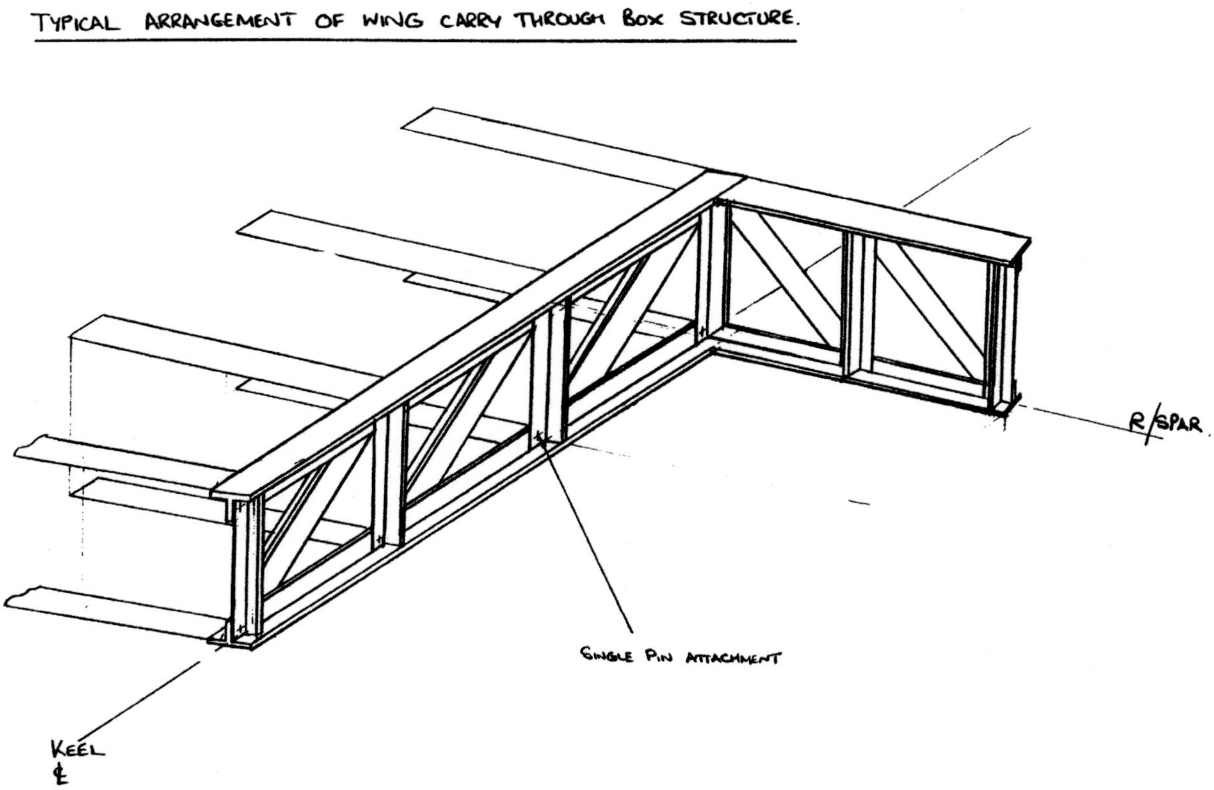

The wing centre section/carry-through box which was to support the engines and liquid oxygen tank.

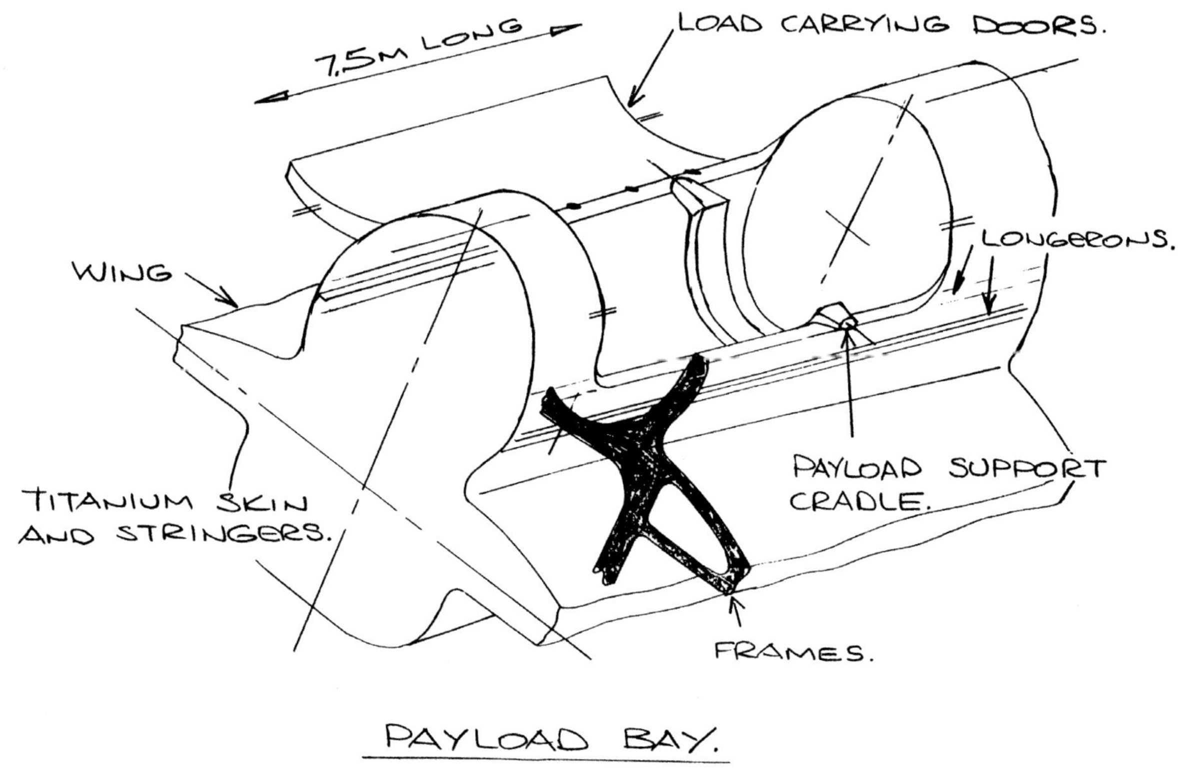

Structural details of the payload bay/centre fuselage.

temperatures by the wing strake". Given that the doors were load-bearing, "it is important to ensure that the doors close satisfactorily, which requires the lateral deflections of the bay to be minimised".

The temperature within the bay would need to be maintained at between 15°C and 40°C and the payload itself would be supported "by means of trunnions onto the sill and keel members, using additional bridging members between adjacent lateral frames".

LIQUID OXYGEN TANK

When filled, Hotol's liquid oxygen tank, behind the payload bay, would be the heaviest component of Hotol at take-off, accounting for more than 50% of the vehicle's total take-off mass. It would be made of 1.3mm thick carbon/PEEK and would sit on top of the wing centre section. Although it only needed to be pressurised to 0.3 atmospheres to maintain its form, it would have an operating pressure of 2.05 atmospheres.

The report noted that "for the take-off case, there should be a strong load path from the LOX tank via the wing root to the trolley aft supports".

ROCKET THRUSTERS

The four main rocket chambers would be supported by a mounting ring which in turn would be supported by 12 struts. Four of these would be attached to the rear fuselage structure and the remaining eight would be attached to the liquid oxygen tank. Each rocket chamber would therefore be supported by "a tripod of struts and the apex of each tripod is connected to two other tripods by beams".

The OMS rockets would be positioned between the four main rockets and would be supported by the mounting ring's vertical beams.

The pipes feeding the liquid oxygen and liquid hydrogen to the rocket chambers would be supported by the 12 struts.

The lower two rocket chambers could be pivoted through six degrees up and down, while the upper two could be moved two degrees from side to side.

WINGS

Hotol Configuration D was designed with empty wings—no internal fuel tanks or other complex systems. They would consist of seven spars with a corrugated construction and upper and lower torsion box skins of welded titanium honeycomb panel construction. Four ribs were assumed. The metallic TPS would be installed over the lower torsion box skin panels and the carbon-carbon leading edges and control surfaces were an auxiliary structure.

The outer wing thickness/chord was 6% outboard of the wing 'kink' and 8% for the inner wing. The report noted that "the thickness of the carbon-carbon leading

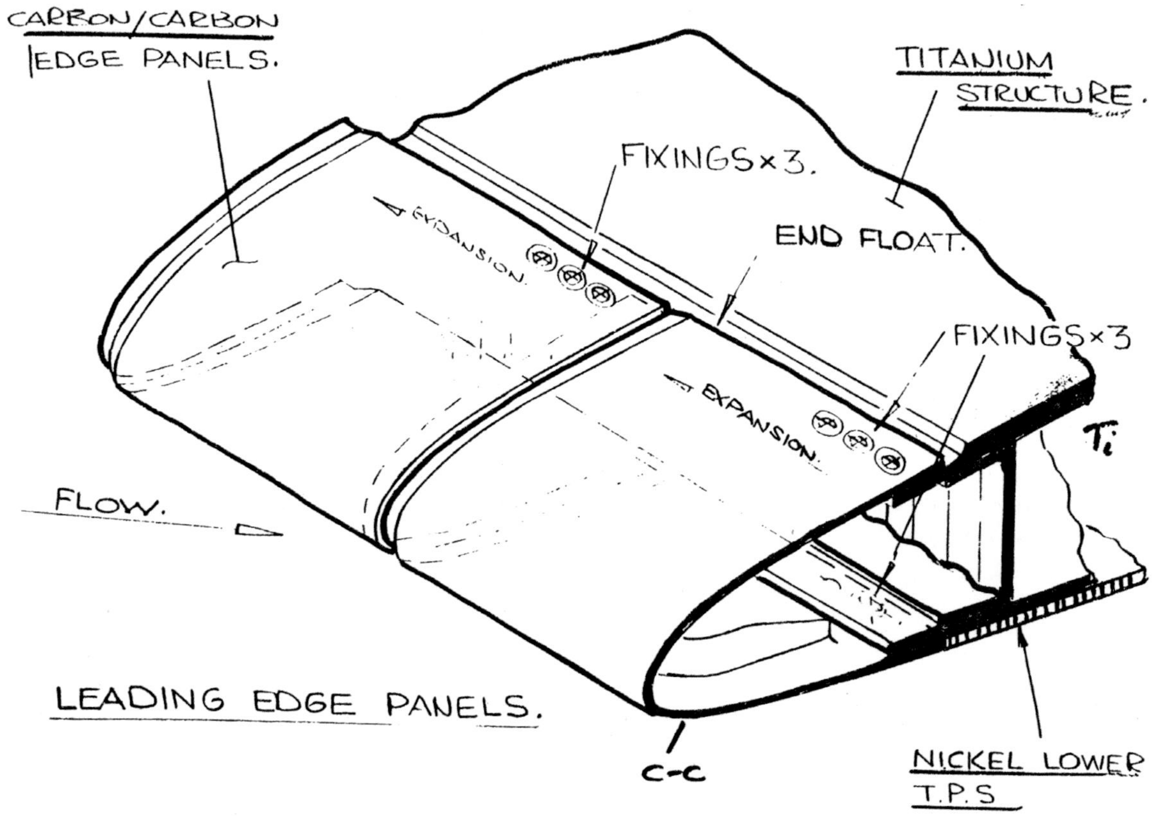

Hotol wings would have featured heat-resistant carbon-carbon leading edge panels fitted to the lightweight titanium wing structure.

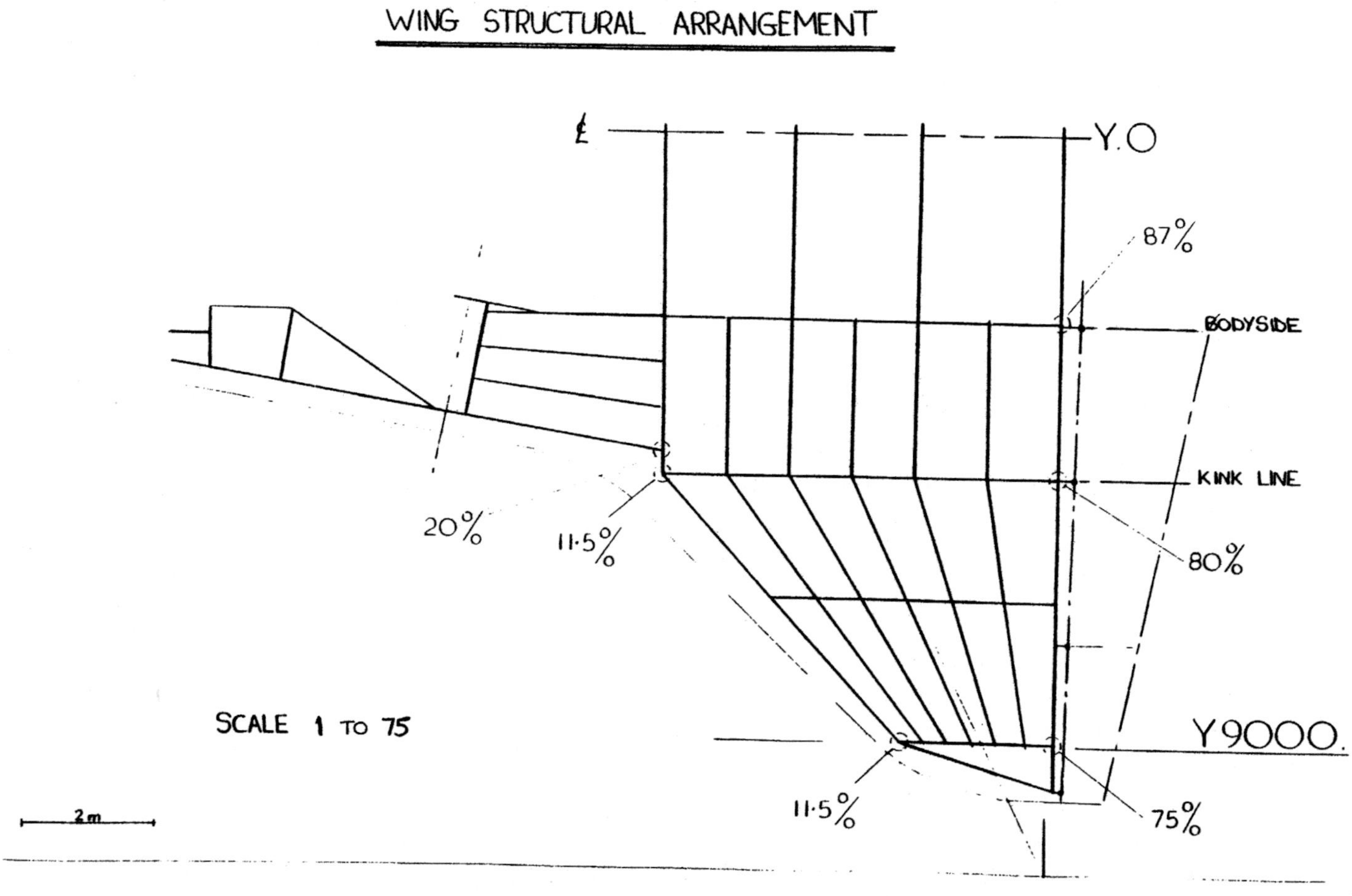

Numerous different wing designs were proposed for Hotol throughout its existence. This diagram shows one of the earlier variants.

edge is sufficient to resist the impact of a 1.8kg bird at 350 knots, but a detection method for a birdstrike during the ascent phase (pressure or discontinuity sensing) may be required, because a damaged leading edge TPS, due to a more severe bird strike, would allow the ingestion of hot gases during the re-entry phase, eventually leading to a structural failure".

MAIN LANDING GEAR

Hotol's main gear would effectively be lifted wholesale from the relatively new BAe 146 short-haul airliner, which had entered service three years earlier. According to the report: "For this phase of the PoC study, a landing mass of 40 tonnes has been assumed, which is substantially the same as the BAe 146 aircraft. The geometry of the main gear produced by Dowty Rotol Ltd for that aircraft has a very small retracted envelope and has therefore been adopted as a convenient well-defined datum... to minimise the mass and size (particularly height), it is housed in an environmentally controlled bay in the underslung air intake pod, the structure of the latter thus performing a dual purpose".

ENGINE BAY

Hotol's engines would be mounted directly to the internal box/fuselage structure at the undercarriage aft frame. The report stated: "Side trunnions are proposed at present with a tangential vertical link at the forward end... the external shrouding of this bay carries aerodynamic loading only. No high pressure leakage from the main ducts is considered.

"To minimise the weight no provision will be made for quick access (e.g. by folding out these panels). No conventional latches are provided. Expansion effects relative to the body structure may be covered by slotting the panel upper edges into steady grooves for lateral support with vertical links for vertical load reaction".

ENGINE AIR INTAKE

The report made no bones about the fact that Hotol's intake design had been extremely problematic and a source of significant mass increase during the course of the PoC.

The initial Stevenage/Filton intake—a Mach 5 expanding centrebody intake supplying three heat exchanger/engines—was depicted in drawing no. SSV 30154 (see p61). The report noted that "at the start of Proof of Concept, engineering advice was that this 20ft diameter intake design posed formidable, perhaps insuperable, problems and that a less speculative approach should be adopted.

"A second radical feature of this design was the way the powerplant was swept upwards aft of the oxygen tank to produce a very short installation. Further consideration suggested that this arrangement in which the ducts are 'threaded through' the nozzle support structure and supply pipes is impractical.

"Furthermore, the location of so much powerplant mass so far aft creates mass balance problems. Consequently, in all PoC designs a substantially 'streamwise' installation of powerplant components has been adopted."

The first promising Mach 5 replacement, shown in drawing number SSV 30157 (see p69), was a pair of vertical wedge intakes feeding three diffusers and therefore three engines. It featured a variable front ramp which could be completely closed for re-entry and its staggered duct arrangement resulted in "a relatively slim practical-looking installation".

However, "the principal criticism of this design was the fact that the effect of failure of any single engine would be transmitted to all intakes. While this did not infringe any rules, it was felt to be unwise. The other worry was the very large amount of testing needed to 'prove' the design".

Next had come another Mach 5 vertical wedge twin (drawing SSV 30159), scaled for three engines with two heat exchangers: "This simpler design retained all of the good features of the preceding design and overcame its deficiencies". Drawing SSV 30163 had seen the 30159 intake resized for Mach 4 and scaled up for four engines, retaining two ducts. SSV 30164 (see p69) was the same as 30163 but with a slimline quad duct, bifurcated arrangement. With this design "some burying of the powerplant components within the wing box/fuselage has been possible. This is the lightest arrangement for which mass estimates are currently available".

However, "the Hotol intake is in excess of two times larger than Concorde" and its mass, given its construction in carbon-carbon, was substantially greater. According to the report "such a mass is clearly unacceptable. Unconventional structures must be designed to reduce this figure".

The mass of the Concorde intake nacelle was 1,153kg and the original target for Hotol's intake was 1,310kg. However, "this figure derived from a mass estimate for the three-engined expanding centrebody intake (SSV 30154). The very low intake structure mass more directly reflects the low rear duct pressures assumed (3.0kPa) rather than any structural efficiency associated with an axisymmetric structure. This low pressure was itself appropriate to the two shock intake employed in early project design, the pressure recovery of which is now seen to be too low with the present heat exchanger design.

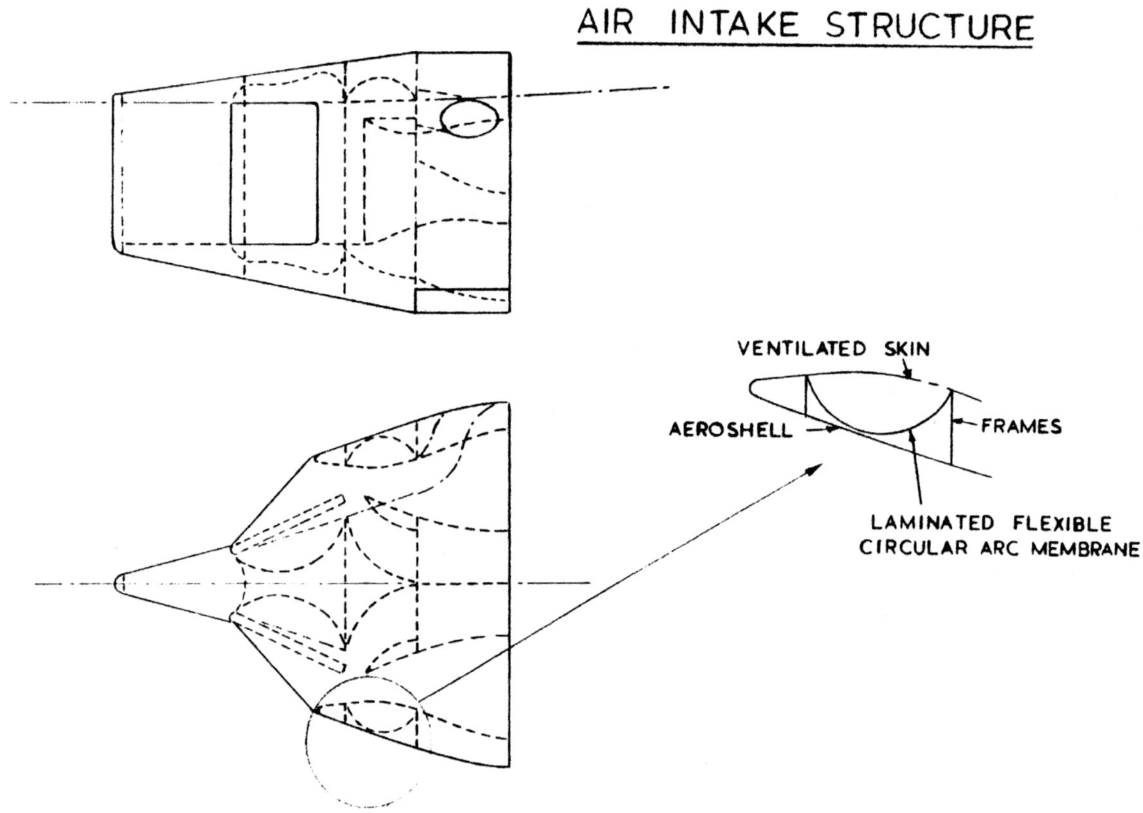

Air intake basic structural layout—side and top views.

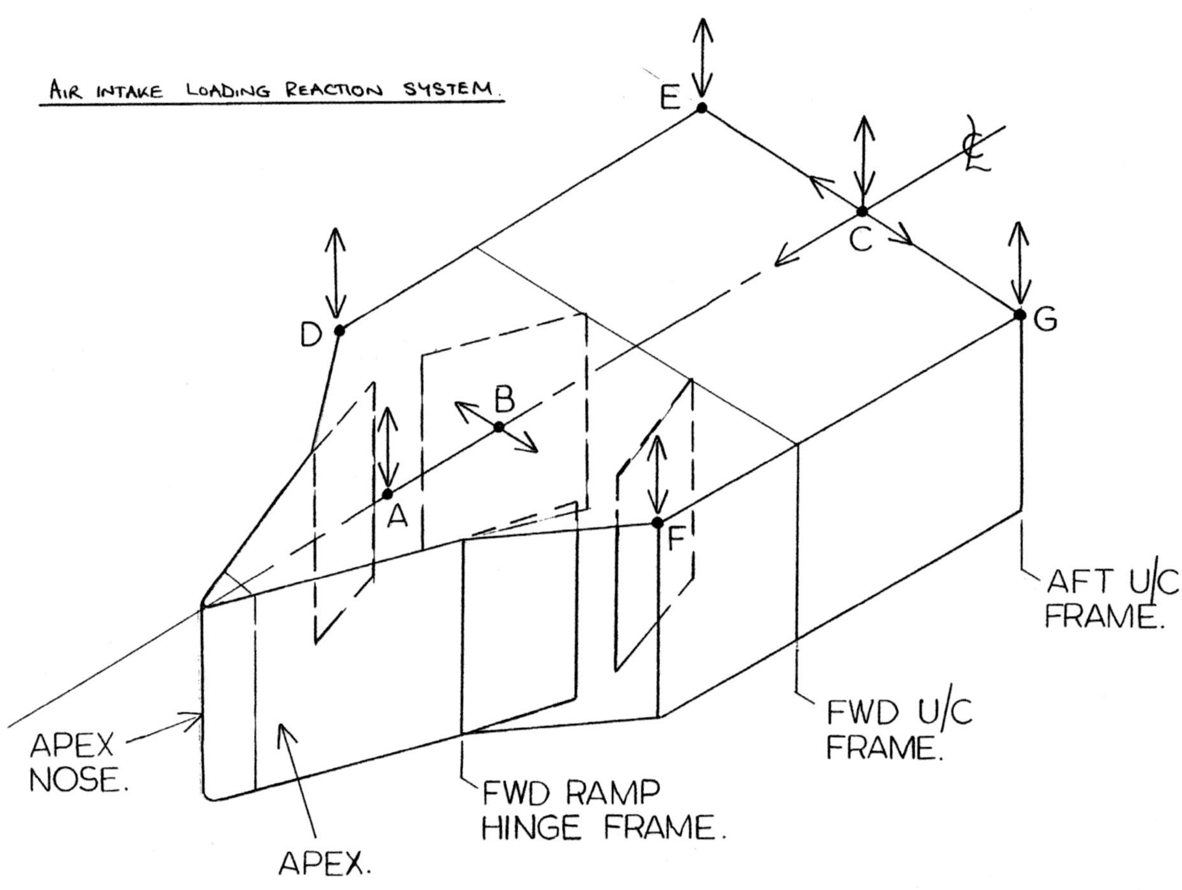

Ramps, hinges and undercarriage connection frames within the air intake pod.

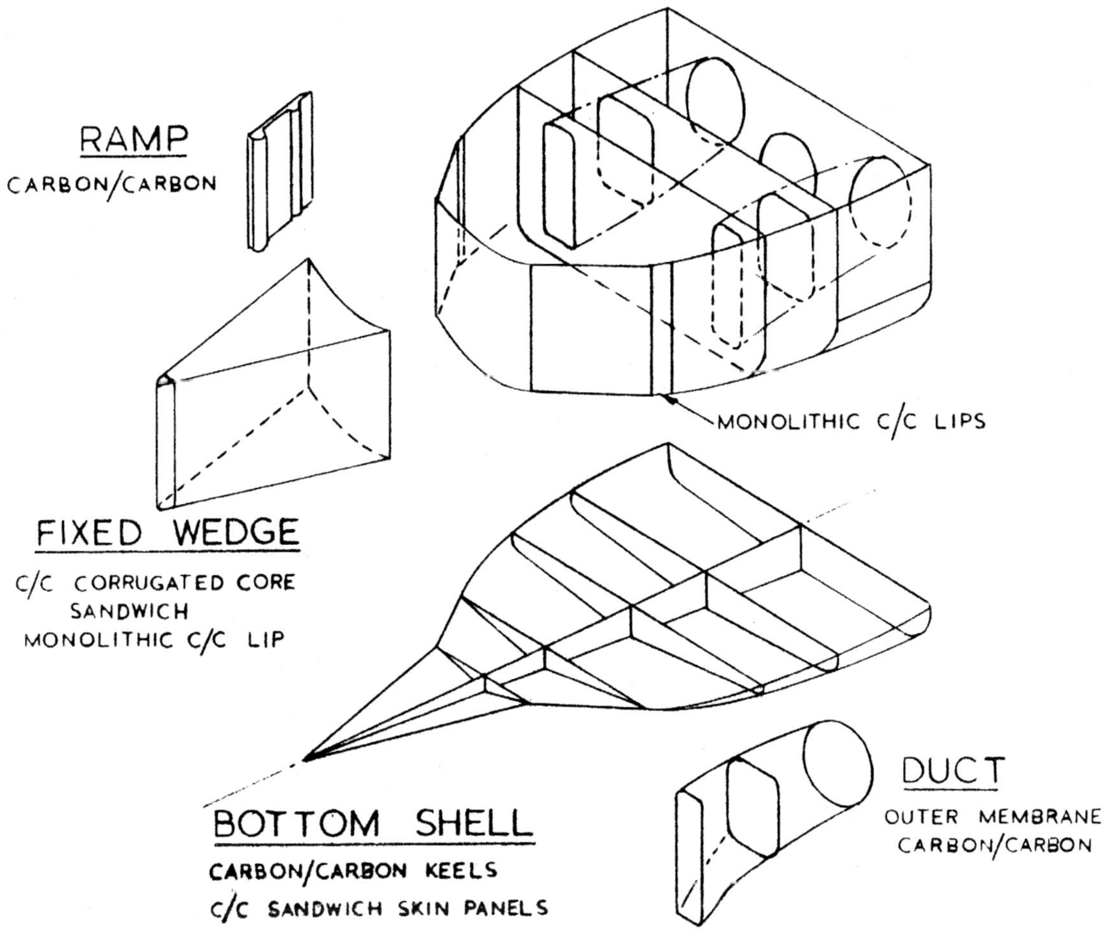

Selecting the best heat-resistant materials for each component part of the intake was crucial.

"The adoption of vertical wedge intakes designed to deliver 30% pressure recovery at Mach 5 and scaled for four engines, produced a solution with a mass of 5,300kg. The four times increase in the mass of the intake is not so surprising given the three times increase in duct pressure and the 4/3 increase in intake area.

"Mach 4 intakes are significantly smaller but in addition, with the intake operating supercritical at the design point, there is a substantial reduction in design pressure (9.0kPa becomes 6.5) and an overall 1,500kg reduction in intake mass results. Note, however, that the intake must not be allowed to go critical during shutdown.

"Further mass reductions are possible from the adoption of smaller slim duct units ... the end result is an installation weighing some 3,200kg ... Burying the engine bay installation also produces a mass reduction. Together these adjustments lead to a projected figure for a four-engine arrangement of 2,500kg. When scaled down for three engines, this corresponds to a mass of 1,660kg or 350kg more than the datum figure."

AERODYNAMICS

The report confidently stated that "flutter, flight control system and drag have been assessed with no significant problems found", although "some areas of concern have been identified. These are: sharp pitch-up; inadequate fin power; hypersonic trim ... [the first two] have possible solutions".

High-speed wind tunnel tests were "awaiting configuration freeze" and "further low speed tests will be necessary on the revised configuration [Hotol Configuration F], aimed at achieving adequate fin control power".

It was pointed out that "Warton experience with unstable aircraft flight control systems, using full time fly-by-wire, enables design to exploit the advantages of unstable configurations, e.g. increase in trimmed lift. Therefore Hotol can be controlled whether the configuration is stable or unstable, within limitations". The wing planform "has been modified to include a 10° sweep on control hinge line to give better transonic effectiveness, to smooth the transition between sub and supersonic speeds. Apart from this, no other changes are yet necessary to the wing planform".

Some more detail was provided on attempts to assess and cure the nose fin issues identified during low-speed wind tunnel testing: "The fin power was much lower than

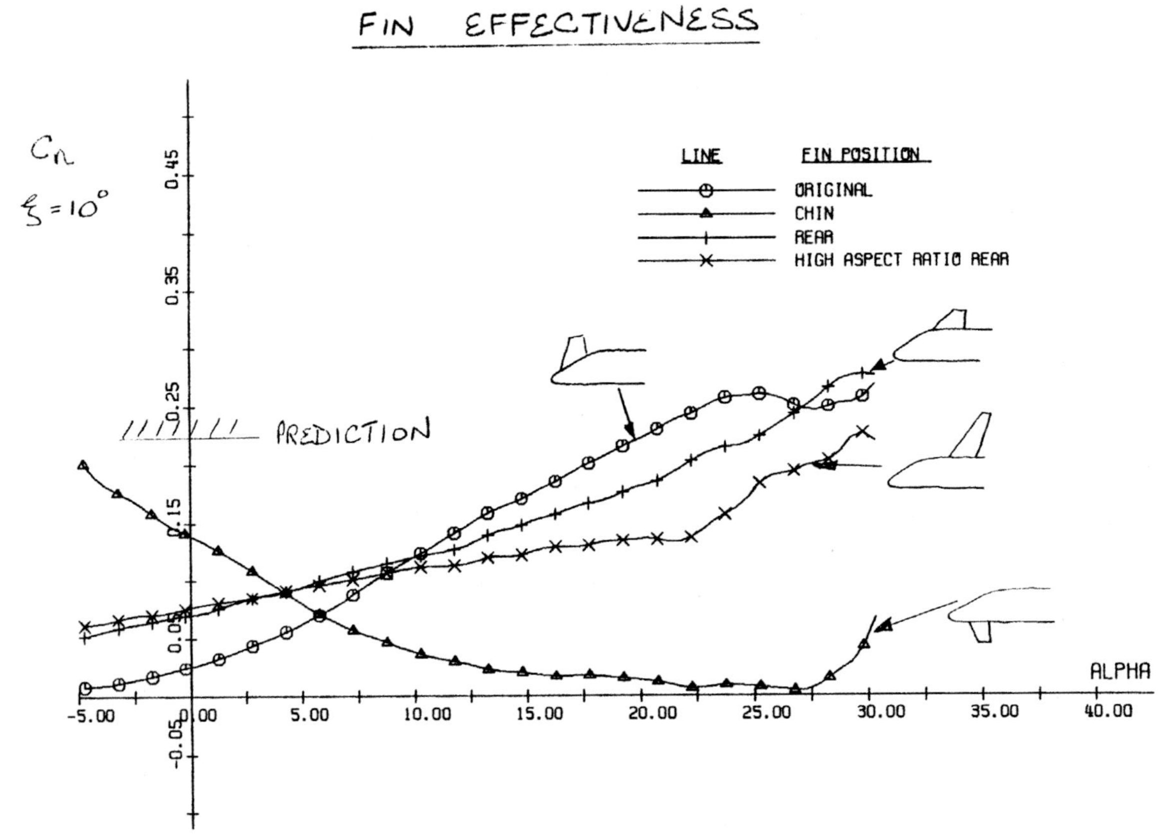

Graph showing the relative effectiveness of different fin positions on the vehicle—nose, chin, short rear and long rear.

predicted at low incidence. The predicted required level was only reached at an angle of 20°. Investigation with smoke and tufts showed crossflow on the sloping portion of the nose. Several solutions were tried in the tunnel to improve this, but no completely satisfactory configuration was tested."

This had involved testing a model with the fin further back, mounted on the flat area of fuselage above the hydrogen tank; trying out a thinner 'blade' fin to see whether a change in aspect ratio had any effect and putting the fin on Hotol's chin—"where results were compatible with other chin tests on non-Hotol configurations".

An assessment had found that during subsonic flight, Hotol had ample trimmable centre of gravity range—but this was not the case during hypersonic re-entry unless the RCS was used, and "there is a large fuel/weight penalty for trimming with RCS in aerodynamic flight". This was a problem to which no immediate solution had presented itself.

Landing performance had been assessed assuming a flight control system from the EAP (BAe's Eurofighter Typhoon technology demonstrator aircraft), EAP/BAe 146 undercarriage characteristics, various control inputs and a range of different landing masses with and without payload. These had shown that "the undercarriage must be positioned not further aft than 4m behind the most forward possible landing centre of gravity to respect the design pitch rate at nosewheel touchdown".

SYSTEMS

Around ten percent of Hotol's dry mass was taken up by its systems—guidance and control, navigation, communications, vehicle and systems management, mission equipment, hydraulics, electrics, active thermal control, propellant supply and auxiliary propulsion (OMS engines and RCS thrusters).

The report stated that "in a project as novel as Hotol there is very limited information available from which to establish equipment and component reliability and there is little understanding of the complex interactions between each of the vehicle's systems. Simplified assessments have been made of the integrity levels of individual systems. In general this leads to aircraft-like systems on the assumption of aircraft-like failure rates and aircraft-like interactions between different systems".

For guidance and control during aerodynamic and ballistic flight, four linked guidance computers were planned—which would allow Hotol to keep going even after two failures. These would be positioned at the front of the vehicle with four actuator and air data interface

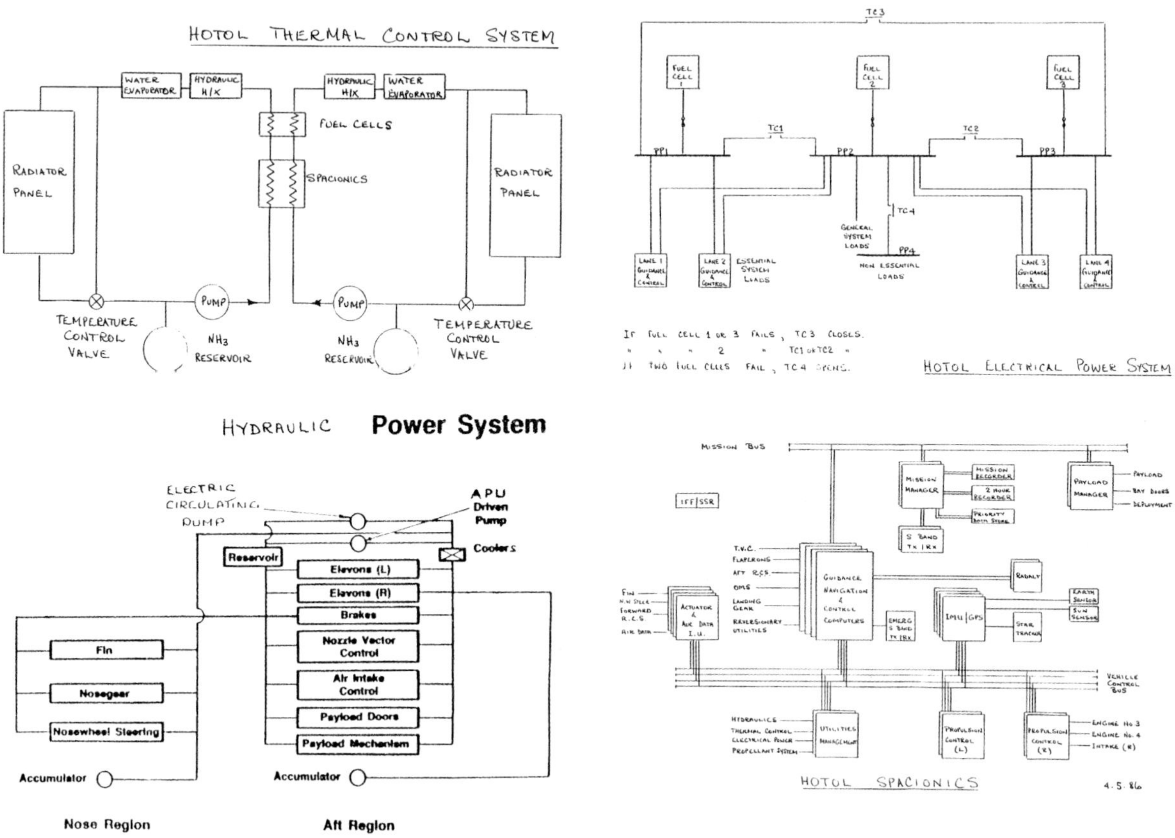

Charts illustrating the various systems planned for Hotol—internal thermal control, electrics, hydraulics and computers.

units. The RCS thrusters on the vehicle's rear end would be duplicated, so in the event of a computer failure affecting one set it would still be possible to manoeuvre for re-entry.

The guidance system proposed, including a laser gyro inertial measurement unit and GPS receiver, would also be quadruplex. There would be a single back-up system featuring a star sensor, sun sensor and infrared Earth sensor too. Navigating towards the airfield for landing would be accomplished using differential GPS based on the four GPS units already installed, with GPS error data being transmitted to the vehicle from a ground station which "therefore relies on a ground-to-vehicle radio link".

These systems would be linked to two mission computers and two payload managers, which naturally interfaced with the payload. The report explained that "the mission computers maintain the vehicle flight plan and manage communications with the executive authority on the ground. Since communication may be limited to a single five minute communications window per orbit, the mission computers have access to long term, medium term and short term memory devices.

"It is envisaged that the databuses will be high-speed, fibre optic systems which will give more than adequate data rates together with protection against electromagnetic interference".

Hotol's control surfaces would be hydraulically actuated, powered by auxiliary power units running on anhydrous hydrazine monopropellant—the same as those on the Space Shuttle. Indeed, "other features of the hydraulic system are state-of-the-art and include: water boilers for heat rejection, heat exchange with the thermal control system to keep the hydraulic fluid warm on orbit, and electric circulating pumps to circulate warm fluid on orbit".

The electrical power supply was also based on that of the Shuttle, with three 1,500W fuel cells feeding three electrical power buses. It had been calculated that Hotol would need less than 3kW for normal operations and around 1,500W for an emergency re-entry and landing.

The temperature of all these systems would be controlled using a double two-phase pumped ammonia loop, transferring heat to external skin radiators while in orbit and water boilers during ascent and descent since the radiators would be shut off and bypassed during these operations. This two-phase system "is a technological advance over the state-of-the-art single phase Freon system of Space Shuttle... BAe Stevenage are currently involved together with Dornier in an ESA contract into such systems".

When Hotol was originally designed, it had been assumed that the OMS engines would use hydrogen drawn straight from the main tank, which required a main tank pressure of 3 atm. But "subsequent analysis ... indicated that the OMS needed a pressure in excess of 3 atm and even then, satisfactory operation of the OMS from the main tank would have necessitated main tank insulation to minimise heat leak on orbit. It was therefore agreed that the OMS would be operated from separate auxiliary tanks". These would contain all the OMS propellant and some of the RCS propellant too—a total of 500kg of liquid hydrogen—and would operate at 12.5 bar pressure. The remainder of the RCS supply would come from the main tank. The liquid oxygen for the OMS, 1,900kg of it, would also be housed in an auxiliary tank.

HOT/COLD HOTOL

The requirement for Hotol to carry extremely cold fuel yet also endure extremes of external heat—common to many space vehicle designs—nevertheless posed a number of design challenges. According to the report, "thermal considerations affect virtually all aspects of Hotol design. Temperatures experienced range from 20K [-253°C], the temperature of liquid hydrogen, to over 1,700K [1,427°C] at certain leading edges during re-entry and this imposes the requirement for careful choice of materials ... and insulants to limit heat flow to other parts of the vehicle".

Thermal design tasks included "lagging of propellant tanks to limit pre-launch boil-off of propellants and prevent formation of ice; lagging of auxiliary propellant tank to limit pre-launch, ascent and on-orbit boil-off of propellants; design of thermal protection system to limit temperatures experienced by structure and equipment not designed for high temperatures (e.g. propellant tanks, titanium structure etc.) and design of a base heat shield to protect against plume radiation and fountain flow".

The lengthy forward fuselage in particular required two separate lagging systems—a cryogenic one around the cold hydrogen tank and a high-temperature one between that and the hot metallic aeroshell. For the former, the possible options were closed cell polyurethane foam, closed cell polyvinyl chloride foam, open cell polyphenylene oxide foam with separate vapour barrier or closed cell polymethacrylimide foam. For the latter, options including alumina/silica felt, amorphous silica/titanium oxide block and silicone-resin bonded fibrous felt were considered. An alternative to double lagging was "the application of a non-porous high temperature insulant (such as Microtherm) directly to the tank to fulfil both high temperature and cryogenic requirements". No firm decision had been made either way as of the report's publication.

The "certain leading edges" where temperatures could rise above 2,000K were those of the foreplanes. The report stated: "For the foreplanes ... a further complication of shock/shock interaction occurs and this is likely to raise temperature locally by some 1,000K ... Temperatures experienced on the foreplane leading edges are therefore predicted to be well in excess of current state-of-the-art. While materials data does suggest that advanced carbon-carbon retains its strength to temperatures in excess of 2,000K, the phenomena of oxidation and catalysis would be expected to be accelerated at such temperatures leading to the requirement for a highly sophisticated and expensive protective treatment.

"It is concluded therefore that the presence of canard foreplanes poses a very severe thermal/materials design problem. The intake wedge leading edge may also be subject to superheating on re-entry but since the intake is not active in these conditions, that part of the structure could be made from ablative material."

WARTON'S CAPS

As mentioned earlier, the CAPS system at Warton had been modified to suit the Hotol project—covering geometry, aerodynamics, mass estimation, performance and vehicle scaling (working out how big the vehicle needed to be to complete its mission).

According to the report, "the vehicle was scaled so that it was just capable of placing a seven-tonne payload into orbit. The wing area and engine scale factor were computed to maintain constant take-off wing loading and thrust/weight ratio". CAPS had been used to model the five phases of Hotol's operation: airbreathing ascent, rocket ascent, orbital manoeuvres, re-entry and airfield performance.

The airbreathing ascent calculations were based on a constant 600kts (690mph) following take-off, with sharp acceleration up to Mach 5 at 25km altitude. The report noted that "the longer and higher the airbreathing phase can be continued the greater the advantage from the airbreathing installation. However, a high initial climb angle (20°) is required at transition [to pure rocket power] to reduce drag losses during the rocket ascent. Hence considerable work is required to optimise the transition point and manoeuvre".

The transition to rocket power was expected to take place at 26km altitude with main engine cutoff at 90km altitude. Following the initial 20° climb, the ascent angle would "flatten off as orbital altitude is approached".

Following orbital manoeuvres "the re-entry phase is initiated by a retrograde OMS burn, which places the vehicle on a descent trajectory from mission orbit (typically 300km altitude) to interface with the Earth's atmosphere.

The first tenuous effects of drag are encountered at an altitude of around 100km, when the vehicle velocity is 7,900m/s inclined at -1° to the local horizontal. The vehicle is then required to execute a re-entry trajectory in such a way as to minimise... skin temperatures, and total heat loads".

As far as airfield performance was concerned, initial take-off speed was calculated to be 270kts (310mph) following a take-off run of 1,750m. Touchdown speed was expected to be a mere 120kts (138mph) with a landing roll distance of 1,400m before coming to a halt.

It was CAPS assessment of all relevant data which was now pointing towards a shorter, fatter, more optimised Hotol—Configuration F.

THE TAKE-OFF TROLLEY

Very little detail of Hotol's take-off trolley was given in the PoC Study part 1 report. It simply reported: "A datum concept for a launch trolley for Hotol has been established. The trolley is to allow roll on/fly off operation from conventional runways. The trolley will include auxiliary propulsion. Other launch concepts, including a rail-mounted system, may be evaluated if the datum solution is found to be unacceptably heavy or costly.

"The determination of Hotol/trolley dynamic characteristics is to be undertaken by BAe Bristol, Space and Communications Division. The task has been defined and will include the formulation of a dynamic model for the calculation of suitable trolley suspension system parameters... The Systems Engineering Department at Warton are to investigate the balance pre- and post-lift off and the required wheel geometry and tyre loading. In addition, an assessment of stopping devices is to be undertaken."

There was no trolley drawing appended and no further details given. It would have wheels, suspension, brakes and its own propulsion system but beyond that it remained somewhat ill-defined.

The report concluded: "The first six months of the PoC Study have established a coherent design. All areas of concern on structural design, aerodynamics, systems and thermal studies have been investigated and preliminary design solutions defined. A 'once-round' structural analysis has been completed on all items except the intake, material thicknesses defined and mass estimates made.

"The structure and systems mass of the datum design, Configuration D, is some 18% greater than the project design estimate. Mass growth has occurred primarily on the front fuselage/liquid hydrogen tank and on the intake. In addition, the following problems identified on the datum design give particular cause for concern: high temperature of foreplane leading edges on re-entry; foreplane root gaps, even with 'cling' to the fuselage lines over 30° rotation, restrict radiation and cause severe local heating; differential expansions due to severe temperature gradients over the foreplane roots, support frame, spigots and bearings prevent the use of dissimilar materials, enforcing all-carbon structures".

Hotol's design was rapidly evolving and effort would now be concentrated on Configuration F. Beyond British Aerospace, Scott-Scott and his team were forging ahead despite clear ongoing reluctance on the part of Rolls-Royce senior management. The Government's funding commitment remained extremely spartan but Pattie had emerged as a political champion for the project and Britain's interest in space technology generally, particularly with the establishment of the BNSC, was at its highest point since the 1970s. Hotol's future was uncertain, and the technical provenance of its revolutionary engine remained hidden behind the Official Secrets Act, yet there was curiosity bordering on avid interest from foreign powers both in Europe and around the world.

Going into the summer of 1986 there were certainly grounds for cautious optimism.

4

CONFIGURATION F: JUNE 1 TO DECEMBER 31, 1986

Hotol had gone from promising concept to fully-defined ground-breaking SSTO vehicle design in the space of a year—but there were still question marks over crucial elements of its propulsion system, it was overweight and a number of detail issues persisted.

May 1986 had largely been spent making presentations and preparing reports to meet contractual obligations, rather than concentrating on the essential engineering, and unavoidable extracurricular activity would continue to sap the small but enthusiastic and highly motivated team's time as the PoC Study progressed.

Burns embarked on another Hotol presentation trip, to the Winged Spacecraft Conference, at Hanover airport, Germany, on June 6. His paper from May was reiterated, with other speakers discussing the *Challenger* disaster, NASA's Shuttle 2 project, Hermes and turbo-ramjets.

According to Burns' post-meeting summary the latter paper, by Helmut Hopmann of MBB, "described advanced propulsion studies made in conjunction with Snecma and Rolls-Royce. He showed diagrams of a turbo-ramjet aimed at Mach 6, 35km and a hybrid propulsion system which had some similar features to the Hotol propulsion including a pre-cooler and compressors in tandem with air going into the rocket chamber... it seemed that the rocket chamber pressures were very much lower than the proposed Hotol figures".

There was no way Hopmann could have obtained classified information about the RB.545 but the general principles of its operation had been made publicly available and it was inevitable that other scientists and engineers would increasingly focus their efforts in the same area.

In summing up the conference the chairman, Professor Hsu Lo, had mentioned Hotol and "said the UK must 'open their books' if they wish [for] European support". Burns noted that this was now "a familiar comment. The conference was felt to be useful in that it gave us another opportunity to publicise Hotol in relation to Hermes and other contenders. It is becoming clear that ESA are regarding Hermes as a technology demonstrator and it cannot make a serious impact on the future orbital payload requirements in the next century. We must push Hotol as the workhorse rather than the research and technology aspect.

"In private conversation with Herr [Heinz] Pfeffer, of ESA, he stated that ESA are now taking Hotol seriously. A letter is being, or has been, written from Professor Lüst to Mr [Hugh] Metcalfe (Deputy Chief Executive (Operations)). He mentioned contacts [who had been] nominated to keep an eye on Hotol [such] as Herr Liebherr, concerned with propulsion and himself with airframe and systems. ESA wish to continue spending

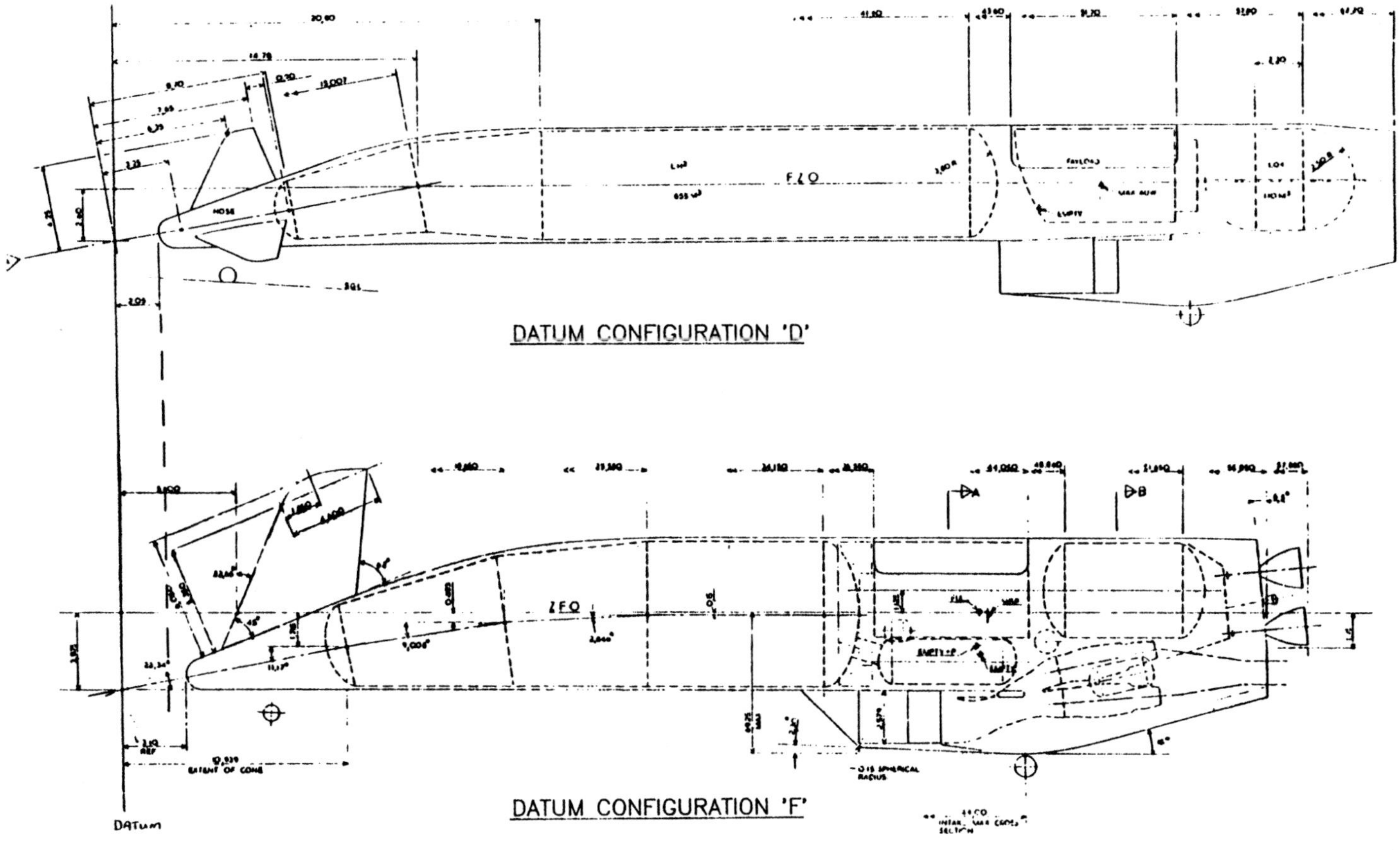

Comparison between the last long slender Hotol, Configuration D, and the new shorter, fatter, Configuration F.

on propulsion systems without a definite commitment to Hotol. He believed that Hermes as a technology project could coexist with Hotol. He queried whether Hotol had sufficient agility in orbit; we should consider this, possibly working it into our fundamental design requirements."

Conchie also travelled to Hanover on June 10 to give a general Hotol presentation to an audience of German engineers, alongside BNSC's Jack Leeming, who covered "the political aspects" and Lewis from Rolls-Royce who spoke about the RB.545.

He wrote to Burns on June 17 to describe what happened: "The audience was generally aggressive, even for Jack Leeming's part. I took a fairly bullish approach and following half an hour of presentation and half an hour of questions, had evened matters somewhat. However, it was clear that Gordon Lewis had to go as far as necessary to get them on our side. This he did very adequately, so that following some good support work by Maurice Deller (RAE) we had brought them to a standstill and had reversed the process!

"After the meeting broke up some of our German colleagues informed us that we had won their support and I gather this was repeated to Jack Leeming on the following day, much to his satisfaction. Last week the Spanish Minister Mejo, who we presented to on the Minister Pattie tour, called the representatives of Spanish industry to his Ministry to tell them Spain would support Hotol to between 10 and 20%, asking them to submit their suggestions for tasks together with financial estimates in this region.

"Spanish firms have been in contact with me. I shall have to play this very carefully in light of UK government view that we should not follow the French approach of dividing the cake prior to ESA adoption of the programme and then to follow the normal ESA approach to work distribution."

However, there was still strong momentum in the Hermes programme, since during the 74th meeting of the ESA Council, which took place shortly afterwards, from June 25-27, an enabling resolution was passed for a preparatory programme on Hermes. Taking place from autumn 1986 to June 1987, this was intended to give ESA member states the opportunity to declare an interest in participating in a future Hermes development programme—particularly in manufacturing parts of it. Once a plan had been worked out on who would build what and when, this would be taken back to the ESA Council in mid-1987 for a decision on whether to go ahead with it.

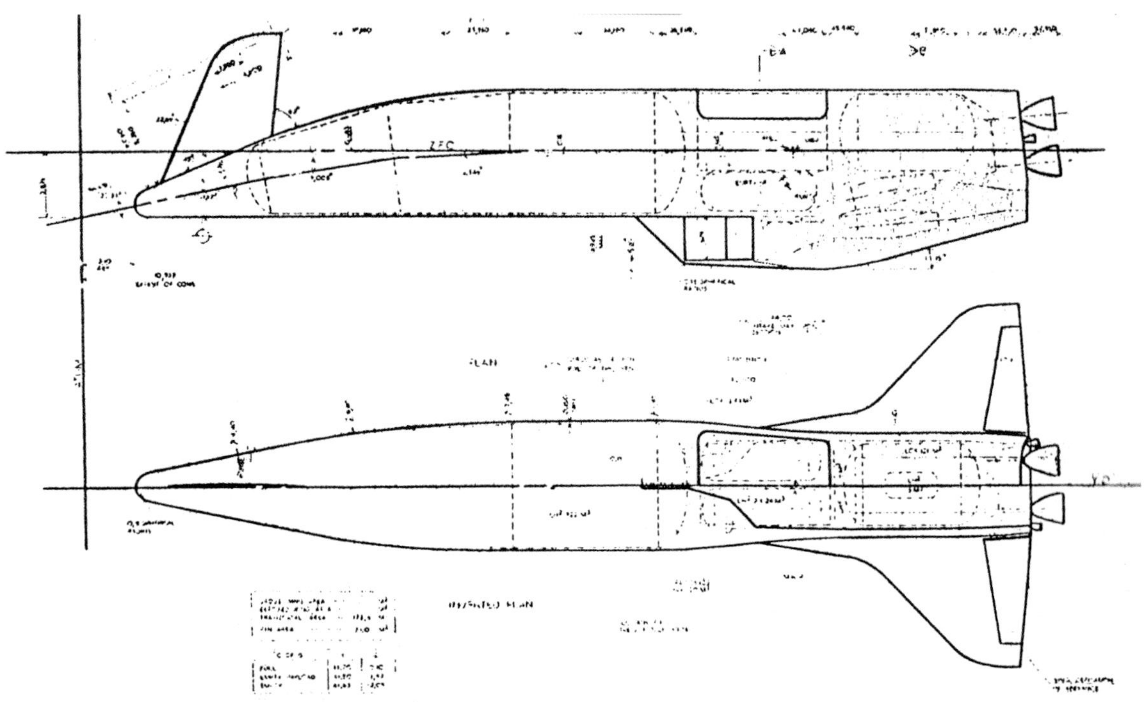

For all the impressive artworks that were created featuring Configuration F, very few general arrangement views appear to have survived. This cleaned up drawing, with mostly illegible annotations, is a rare exception.

BOND'S COMPUTERS

Meanwhile there had been an RB.545 propulsion working party meeting led by Scott-Scott at Rolls-Royce Patchway on June 12, attended by two of his personnel, six men from RR Bristol including Richard Varvill, Tranter from the DTI, Derek Gould from the RAE/BNSC, Gerald Wilson from Warton, Terry Brown and Tony Willmer from BAe Filton, Alan Bond and John Allen. The latter, acting as a consultant, was chief engineer of the Advanced Projects Group at BAe Kingston.

It was noted that RR Bristol had established a computer model of the engine which was "now giving stable results in the Mach number range 3 to 5. The low-speed end is now being addressed, but there are complications with heat exchanger questions that need to be resolved". In addition, "work has commenced on the preparation of individual component drawings to support general arrangement and installation drawings at Patchway [RR Bristol]. It was emphasised that because of the overlap of design work, particularly in the air intake area, an informal interchange of designers from the Patchway and Filton sites is to be encouraged".

It was hoped that two or three weeks of anti-frosting tests could take place by the end of July at Ansty and early design work on the heat exchangers was being consolidated ahead of more detailed drawings being made. A one-year contract was due to be signed with Cranfield for practical work on "injector geometries in a small, uncooled chamber".

Wilson provided Rolls-Royce with "several classified drawings of detailed engine installations" for study as well as a data pack on the design of Hotol Configuration F. Stan Lock, who wasn't listed as an attendee but who appears to have been part of Brown's Filton team, put forward "prints of several alternative intake/engine installation schemes... briefly, the differences were in the case of nose-mounted and over-wing intakes, which offered both weight savings and improved re-entry configurations". These were due to be assessed by both BAe and RR prior to further discussion at the next propulsion working party meeting.

As the meeting drew to a close, it was noted that the RAE 351 Mach 4 intake model was going to be tested at Mach 5, though this had yet to be arranged, and the BAe team wanted better data from RR about permissible temperatures in the engine bay. RR said it was too early to provide this, given the variety of different installation arrangements being studied.

The next day another, much smaller, meeting was held in Bristol on the RB.545 with just Bond and two Rolls-Royce Bristol engineers, Geoff Hodges and Keith George, present. It was stated that "the Bristol RB.545 simplified model was functioning at off-design conditions, with George providing initial results for discussion". Furthermore, "the more sophisticated model... was now working correctly at design conditions, but there were currently difficulties in producing off-design data". Bond then gave

Cover of Hotol brochure featuring Configuration F.

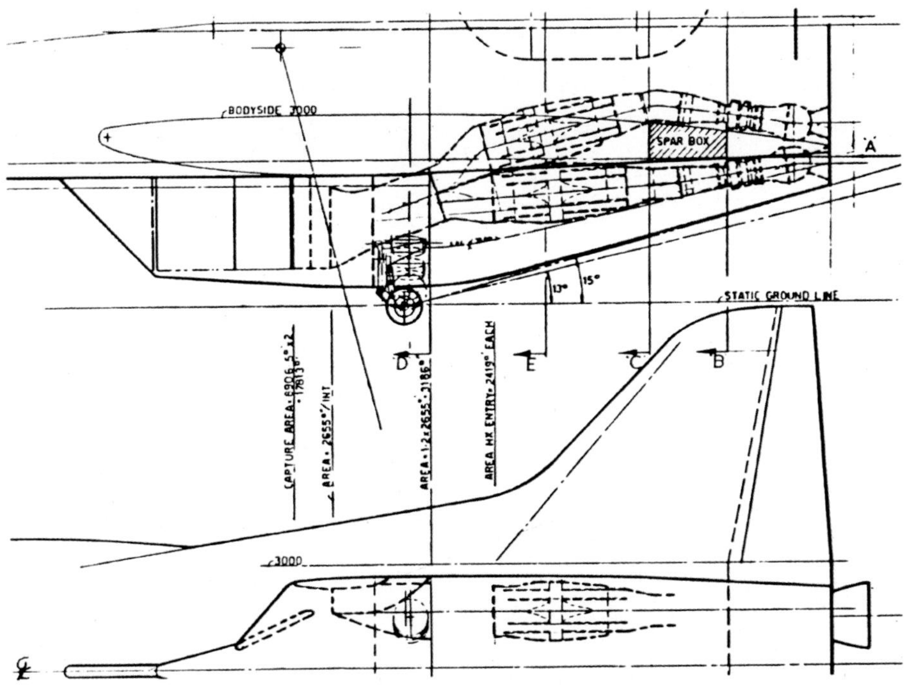

Engine installation for Hotol Configuration F, with minimal geometric variability, thick structures and blunt lips.

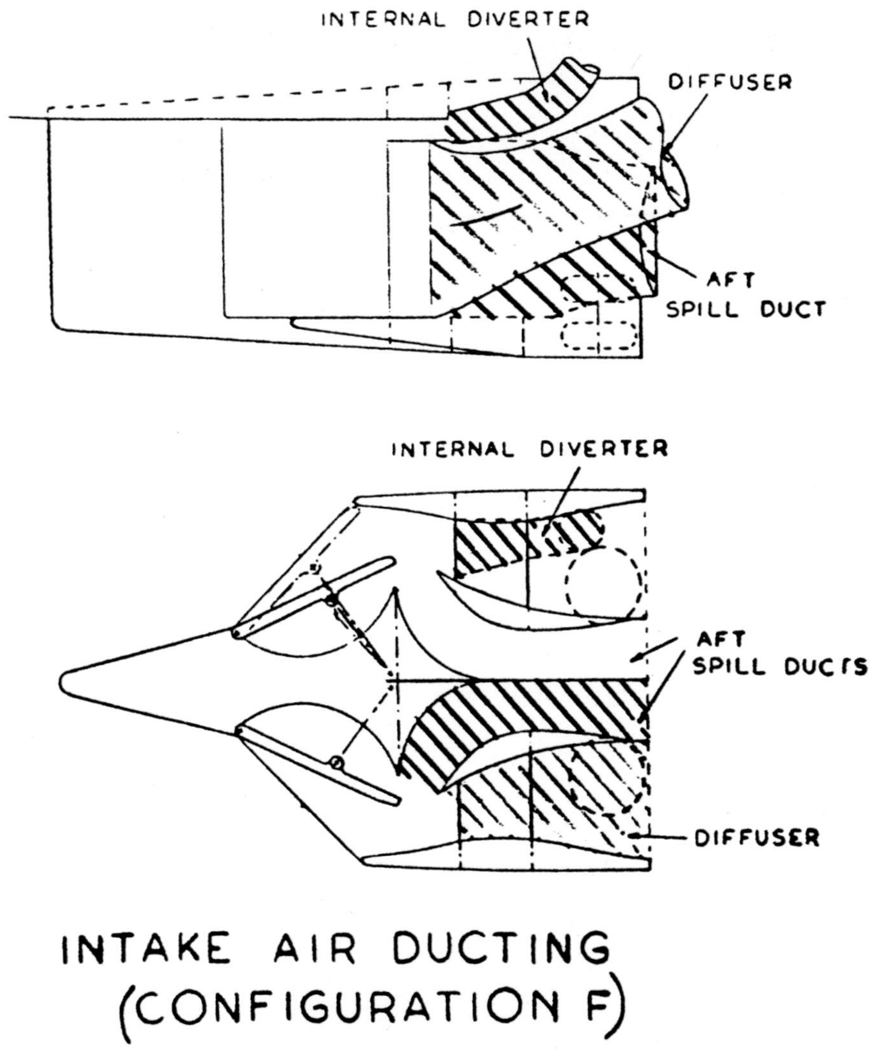

Configuration F intake air ducting.

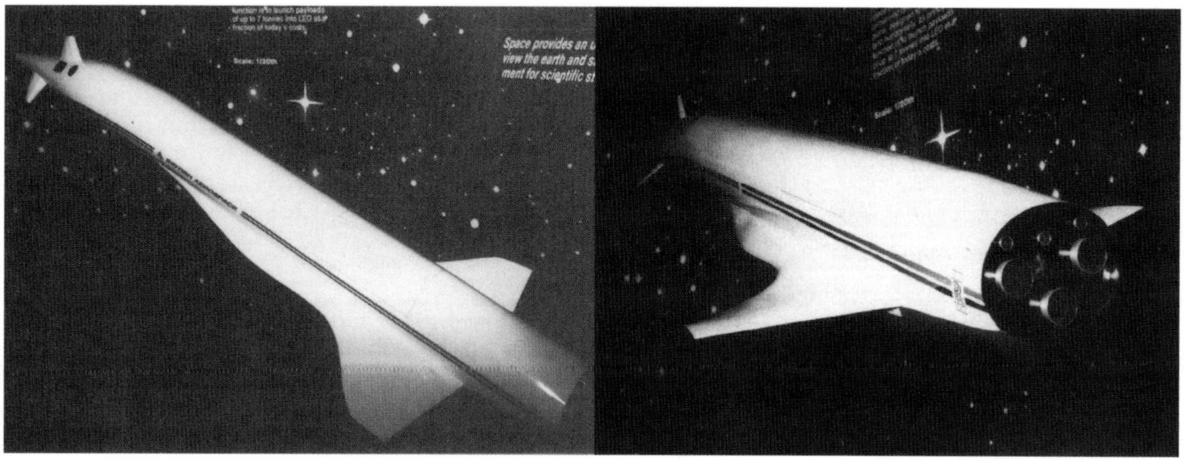

Outdated Hotol model, still with three engines, shown on the BAe stand at the Space Commerce '86 event in Montreux, Switzerland, from June 16-20, 1986.

the pair data on pump efficiency, peak pump pressure, compressor polytropic efficiencies and heat exchanger performance equations. Four required 'actions' were listed as arising from the meeting, all of them concerning the provision of further data and all of them were to be completed by Bond.

Scott-Scott, interviewed in 2010-2011, remembered: "Alan Bond [would] go home that night, say, and halfway through the next day he'd have a printout waiting of that particular step of engine performance. Because he'd got all these computers in his front room, and he'd feed them all and go to bed and put the alarm clock somewhere, I think it used to go off about three, something like that, and he could get a printout from it then, and he'd print out the prediction and bring it to the meeting the next day if we wanted it. I mean, he just showed that... he could shame the whole system, and get it right, and it was with his little [Sinclair] ZX... computers as well. Loads of them all coupled together somehow.

"I don't know how he coupled them up, I really don't. But... he had this thing like our kitchen table spread out across his bay window... I don't know whether he set them separate tasks or what he'd set them, but anyway they were all buzzing and clicking and doing. And then some of them were geared onto printers... he'd go down in the morning as though you were picking up the mail, clip this lot together and say, well, there's a prediction for a Mach four and a half, or something. And this is it, and it did, it predicted the whole engine, it simulated it".

SCOTTISH BASES

With negotiations over the Hotol PoC Study Part 1 funding evidently concluded, the negotiations over Part 2 had already got started according to Burns' monthly report of June 30, 1986. Bristol was now developing a computer program to optimise the rocket-powered part of Hotol's ascent and oxygen/hydrogen fuel ratios were being assessed.

Getting the necessary funding for the PoC itself from the MoD Contracts Branch seems to have been like getting blood from a stone but the BNSC was a little more forthcoming, agreeing to hand over £70,000 of additional funding for high-speed tests of RAE intake model 351 in the RAE's Bedford tunnel, now scheduled to begin in mid-August. Initial testing was expected to cost £25,000, of which BAe was expected to chip in £5,000. Both low- and high-speed wind tunnel models were now being manufactured at Warton and were expected to be ready for tests by September.

In addition, investigations into the best form of insulation for the hydrogen tank were ongoing and "the best alternative appears to be carbon-carbon TPS panels with internal insulation, with an air-gap between the inside of the panels and the cryogenic insulation bonded to the outside of the carbon-PEEK tank. This scheme offers a weight reduction on the front fuselage of about 12%".

A lot was now resting on the suitability and availability of carbon-carbon and carbon-PEEK. There had been discussions with both the Materials & Manufacturing Department and the Structural Test Department at Warton and "it is evident that significant work must be undertaken during the period of the PoC Study and this will require additional funding over and above what has already been allocated".

Filton had been busy working on the intake analysis and "two alternative layouts, a nose intake and wing-mounted intakes have also been proposed ... These are being assessed qualitatively with limited quantitative information to follow later".

With Configuration F as the new baseline design for

1 OBJECTIVES
Payload Requirements
Aim for most commercially attractive payload – not the largest payload that can be conceived.
Occasional very large payloads could still be launched by Ariane 5.
European Requirements
Retain independent launch capabilities into the 21st Century.
Reduce by a substantial factor the costs of launching payloads into low Earth orbit.
Service Platforms and permanent facilities in low Earth orbit, and recover experimental equipment to Earth.
Develop independent, European Man-in-Space operations.

- **7 – 10 tonnes in low Earth orbit can handle communications satellites, the Columbus Space Station requirements, and eventual Man-in-Space missions.**

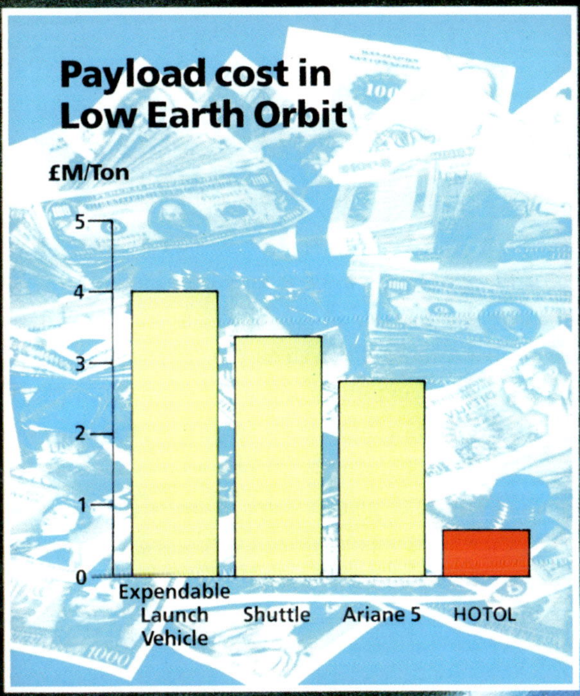

Estimated Market – Flights/Year

2000 – 2010 AD

	MIN		MAX
Communications Satellites	7	–	12
Earth Observation	3	–	5
Columbus Space Station	8	–	15
Science/Planetary Missions	2	–	4
Infrastructure Development	4	–	6
	24	–	42

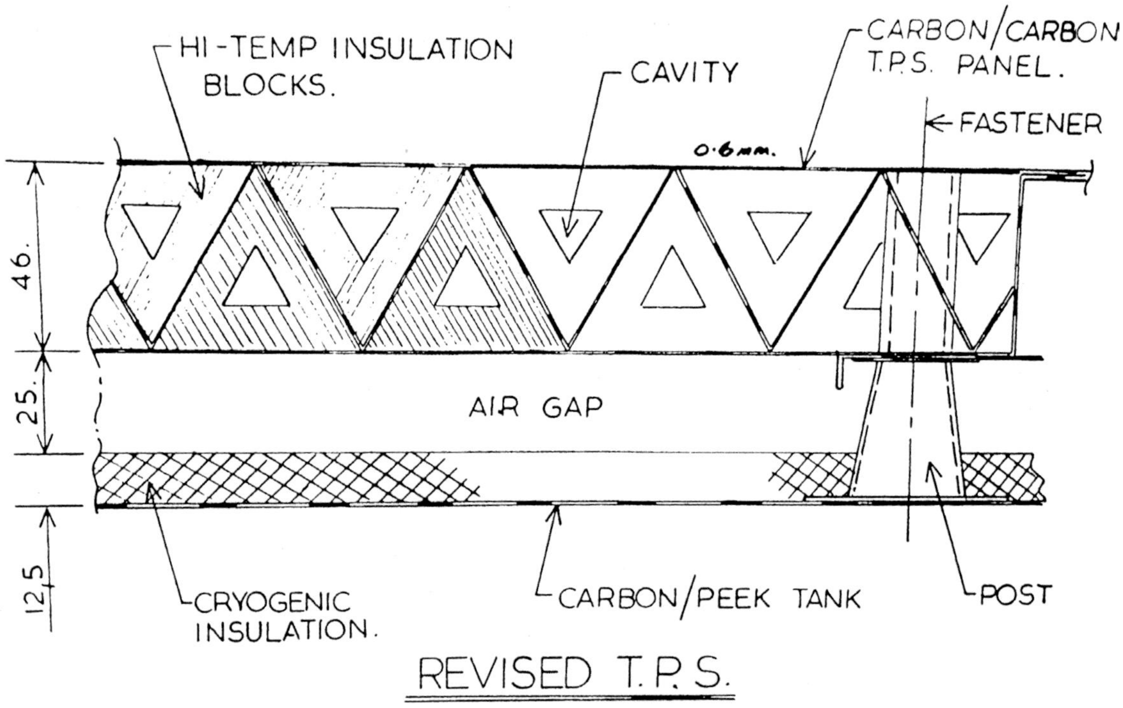

Design for carbon-carbon TPS panels.

future studies, "detailed design work on the engine installation has led to definition of all the pipework in the engine bay area. It is confirmed that all four engines need to be gimballed, rather than pivoted in pairs to safeguard failure cases and to minimise thrust losses due to centre of gravity tracking. It is evident also that flexible joints and universal joints in the high-pressure large diameter gas pipes in this region will require considerable development".

Hotol's pipework was extremely complex, with pipes being typically a foot in diameter. It became known as 'the spaghetti'.

Rolls-Royce continued to be a source of frustration. No progress had been made on the engine except where the icing test rig was concerned, though "Mr A. Bond, consultant, produced curves showing the variation of oxygen/hydrogen mixture ratio and nozzle expansion ratio on rocket performance. These are being used in the scaling studies... No trade-off information is available from Rolls-Royce nor is there any promise of when it will appear. Basic performance data is promised in July... basic mass estimates will not be available until the end of 1986".

The Warton Flight Test and Flight Operations Staff had been assessing European airfields as possible sites from which to conduct test flights "including a visit to the north of Scotland. A base in this area, if a suitable location could be found, has the prospect of offering a safe operational environment with possible development into a European site for polar orbital operations at a later date".

In his 2013 talk on space studies at Warton, Wilson remembered that "a European launch site was... desirable on political grounds and for polar orbit launches or for flight testing. Polar orbit launches need to launch in a north-north westerly direction, which led to a rather interesting day out for both Eric [Webb] and myself in a Cessna looking at sites on the west coast of Scotland. [We were] on Benbecula where the rocket test range on the adjacent island South Uist seemed to offer some potential". Alongside Wilson and Webb was "Derek Reeh ... he was the project pilot for Hotol despite the fact that it was an unmanned air vehicle".

On the same day that his monthly report was issued, Burns also wrote to Ralph Denning at Rolls-Royce to ask about Hotol/RB.545 flight testing: "We are considering the demonstrator programmes that are desirable to bridge the gap between the drawing board or computer and full-scale flight trials. Will you please consider this matter and advise us as to what test facilities are considered essential and desirable to prove the propulsion system?

"The following possibilities need to be considered: component tests in ground facilities; integrated propulsion system tests in ground facilities; subsonic tests of a complete propulsion system in a 'flying test-bed' (e.g. a modified TriStar tanker); supersonic wide envelope (M/h) trials in a single-engined test vehicle, probably unmanned; any other suggestions."

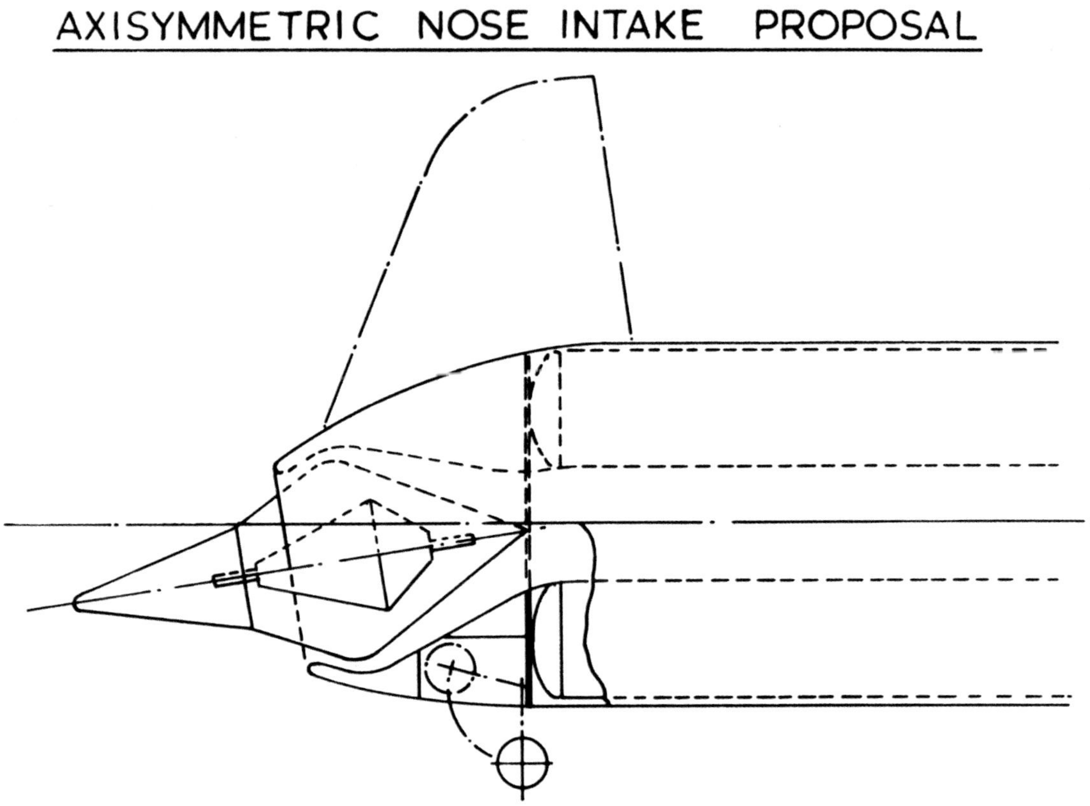

One alternative layout suggested for Hotol involved a nose intake.

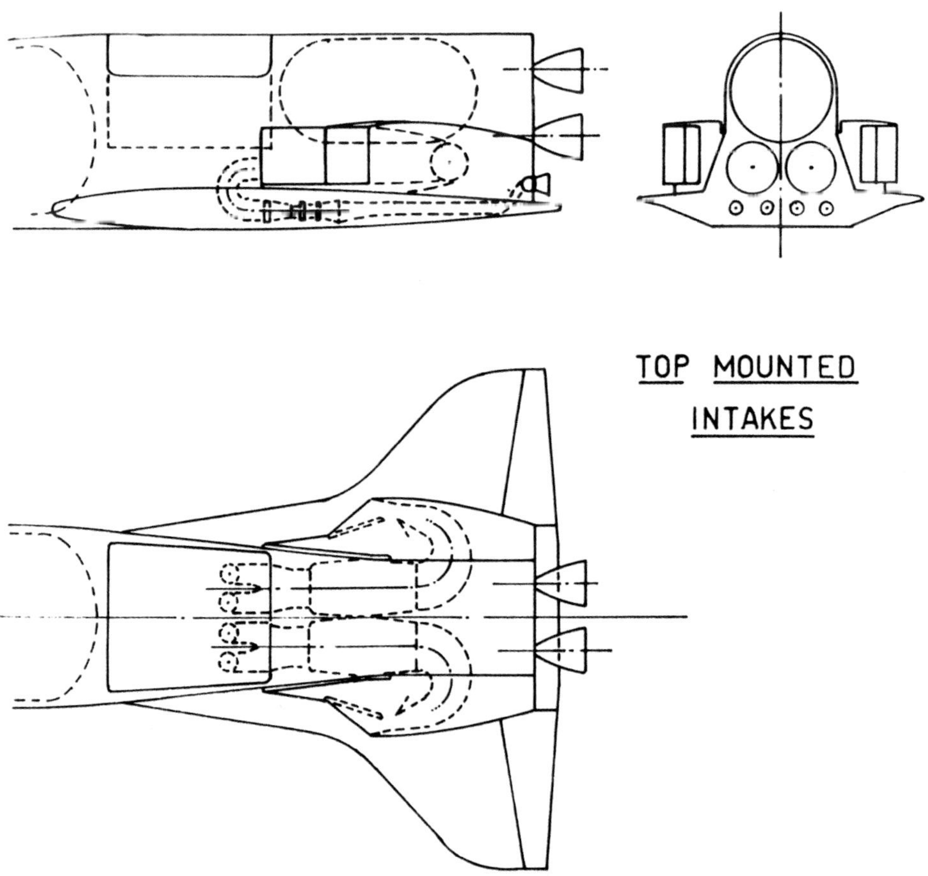

Another alternative was to position an intake above each wing, either side of the fuselage.

2 VEHICLE CHARACTERISTICS

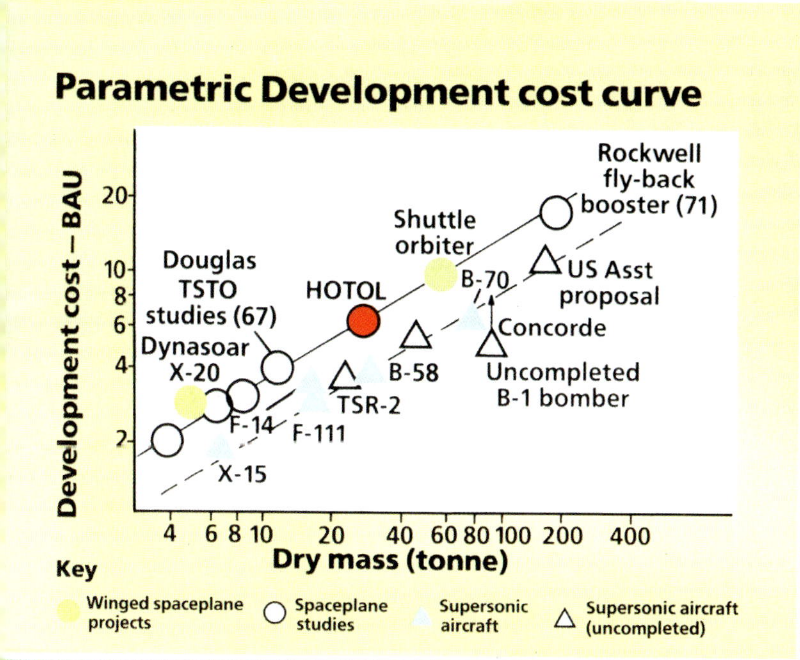

Why a Single Stage Aerospaceplane?

- No expensive throw-away hardware. The vehicle is fully recoverable and reusable.
- No vehicle/stage integration problems before each launch, reducing preparation costs.
- Quick turn-around with simple facilities, also reducing operational costs.
- The vehicle can be made simpler and hence cheaper to build and operate.

Looking out over Benbecula from the window of Cessna 401, G-AWWW, while searching for potential Hotol launch sites.

Hotol project test pilot Derek Reeh, centre, with Nobby Clark, left, and Frank Bevan, right, during the BAe visit to the north of Scotland.

CATCHING HERMES

The July 1986 issue of science journal *Nature* ran an article by Robert Walgate titled 'British HOTOL closes in on French Hermes'. It said: "A bid to make [Hotol] a European project will be made at the next (October) council meeting of ESA. Hotol, which was little more than a gleam in a British Aerospace designer's eye a couple of years ago, thus seems to be racing ahead.

"With its launch date brought forward, what once seemed almost science fiction is now in direct conflict with the more conventional French project Hermes." It was also noted that the American NASP programme was "pushing ahead" with supporting technological research. Parkinson, cited as British Aerospace launch vehicles project manager, told the magazine that "Hotol is a conceptual, not technological breakthrough ... we saw a way of doing the propulsion system that no-one else has spotted".

Evidently Gibson had "made progress" in getting Hotol's engine declassified and "we've been able to lift the veil enough to make a tour round Europe [seeking partners]".

In October, BAe would "present ESA members ... with a proposal for a four-year, $400m Hotol feasibility study; but this will clash, politically at least, with the simultaneous effort being made by the French to win participants in a cheaper, $48m study of their Hermes space shuttle. Hermes is ahead on the political timetable, as ESA passed an 'enabling resolution' approving the study in June (only the money is yet to be found); and it is also ahead on the engineering timetable (as the French space agency CNES has been working on Hermes far longer than the British on Hotol). But Germany has been hesitating to give full support to Hermes, and according to a Bonn research ministry spokesman, Hotol has already won the heart of his minister, Heinz Riesenhuber.

"France has said it will go it alone with Hermes if it cannot raise European support. Britain, however, is sounding equally bullish about Hotol. According to Gibson, whose first British space plan will go to ministers this week, participation of the French in the Hotol programme would not be essential.

"There is no French technology that cannot be found or developed elsewhere, according to Gibson, and even French money may not be essential. It is not inconceivable, therefore, that Hotol will go ahead like Concorde ... as a bi-national project, though this time the nations involved may be Britain and West Germany."

Burns wrote to Denning on July 4 concerning Hotol Configuration F: "We have agreed with Stevenage that we will not 'go public' on the new shape before Farnborough '86. We will be grateful if you would make this known to all those concerned with Hotol/RB.545 at Rolls-Royce."

Four days later, Denning wrote to one of his engineers, A. T. J. Morris, instructing him to "produce an outline development programme for qualification of [the RB.545] to the timescale and rules set out in the chart provided to you. A. Bond will be giving his views on the methods of testing, but in the meanwhile, you should assume that the methods will be: by major use of ground rigs and simulation for all components including segmental pre-cooler testing at Bristol/Ansty; system testing at SLS conditions at a remote site e.g. Spadeadam; the possible use of a testbed aircraft (type undefined).

"We should also examine the BAe suggestion of a single-engined test vehicle, although this seems to me to pose a large number of problems in its own right".

Bond then wrote to Denning on July 10 to say, "Ralph, I am sorry for these scrappy bits of paper but

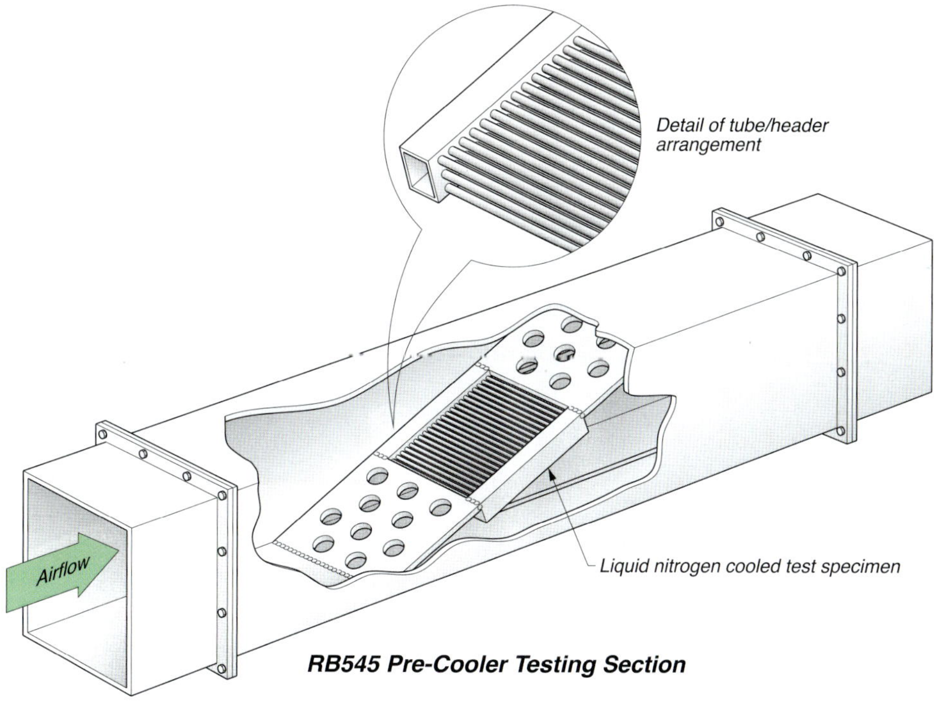

Artist's impression of the Hotol pre-cooler test section. GRAHAME CHAMBERS

hopefully they will serve their purpose. I hope you can get them prepared. There are three viewgraph suggestions: 1) RB.545 History—it is time it was realised that RR funded work on this project even before BAe, thanks to J. Scott-Scott. 2) Future European Space Transportation—push for a far-reaching integrated system, light [and] highly reusable, plus heavy, modular [and] expendable, with some common engine hardware (we must explore this amongst ourselves soon). 3) Performance of RB.545 vs other types".

Government funding for Hotol was finally, conclusively, agreed during a meeting on July 16 between BAe, the RAE, the BNSC and the MoD. The 'Part 2' cash would cover the remainder of the PoC period and would be paid in instalments, one every six months. If any more money was requested by BAe, this was to be considered separately.

Meanwhile, Pfeffer from ESA had travelled to Farnborough and on July 17 received personal Hotol presentations by both BAe and Rolls-Royce. According to Burns: "The meeting was attended by RAE specialists and BNSC representatives. Herr Pfeffer expressed satisfaction with the engineering detail presented. He summarised by stating that ESA were prepared to fund technology programmes which would be relevant to Hotol and other European launch vehicles to a level of about £15m per year and project studies to a level of about £3m.

"He commented also that he considered the Rolls-Royce programme to be very ambitious, being the same overall timescale as the HM60 rocket engine [for Ariane] but much more radical."

STRESS FRACTURES

By the end of July 1986, the Hotol project had been ongoing for nine months. While the intricacies of the RB.545 remained hidden beneath a blanket of secrecy, the airframe engineering, the economic case for the vehicle and above all the political wrangling necessary to draw in further funds from abroad had been subject to intense scrutiny both in Britain and around the world.

The 'competition' between Britain's Hotol and France's Hermes to win favour with ESA had become a regular talking point in respected scientific and aerospace publications the world over—while the cash-rich American NASP was threatening to overshadow both European projects.

The British Government, represented by the BNSC, the MoD and the RAE, was expecting results despite the incredibly meagre resources it had provided. And the BAe/RR team were being expected to make the case for Hotol themselves on the international stage—frequently facing scepticism and a barrage of questions from audiences composed of the world's most talented and knowledgeable aerospace engineers. They were answering individual personal letters on technical matters submitted by members of the public, providing articles on Hotol for magazines and journals, even responding to points raised in the letters pages of those publications. And thanks to ITN's Frank Miles, Hotol's progress was being regularly broadcast on national television.

With the selection of Configuration F as the new baseline design, differences of opinion on Hotol's development

3 THE VEHICLE

General Data

All Up Mass	= 250 t
Mass at Meco*	= 50 t
Payload	= 7 t
Overall Length	= 62 m
Maximum Diameter	= 7 m
Wingspan	= 28 m

(* MECO = Main Engine Cut-Off)

Mass Breakdown

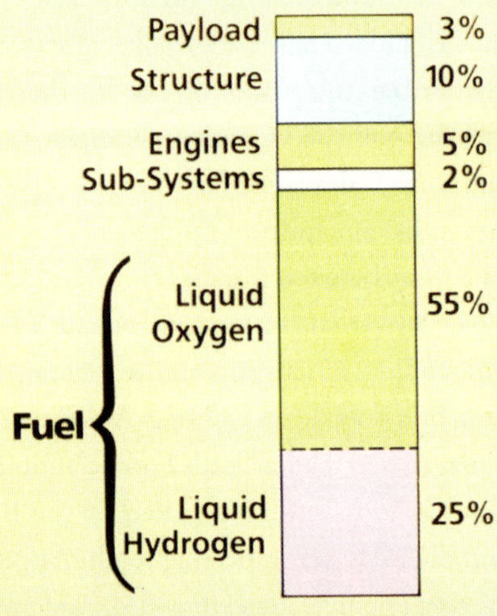

Propulsion System Comparison

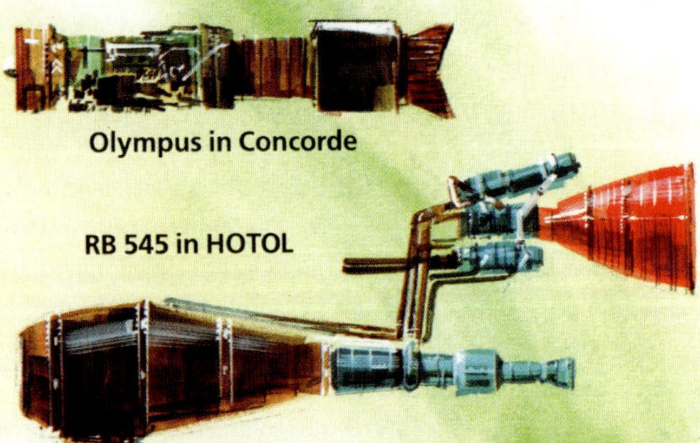

Olympus Power Plant Mass = 4080Kg

RB545 Power Plant Mass = 2840Kg

Comparison with Concorde
Concorde All Up Mass = 188 tonnes
HOTOL All Up Mass = 250 tonnes

path were beginning to come to a head. In particular, friction was particularly growing between the 'newcomers' of Warton and Hotol's original inventors—Bond, Parkinson and Scott-Scott.

Burns' report to Yates on July 29 noted that "a report has been issued at Stevenage on rocket performance of Configuration F, identifying optimum climb angle and orbital insertion point". Pencil markings next to this on the hard copy report state "sub optimal analysis" and, with an arrow pointing to "identifying", stating: "Not yet identified—work being conducted by Bristol".

Elsewhere in his update, under 'systems', Burns wrote: "A meeting is being held at Stevenage on July 29, 1986, with Hernandez engineering who have an ESA contract on the safety and reliability aspects of launch vehicles." Next to this, in pen, was written: "Hardly the high point of systems activity!"

Regarding the relationship between Stevenage and Warton, Conchie said in 1989: "The traditional engineers come to meetings with books, try to write it all down; I remember one from Warton in one of the early meetings, the poor guy got lost. The Warton guys took a long time to get up to speed ... now they are different from the other guys there."

Parkinson said: "Warton emphasise experts in disciplines to an extent that I wouldn't—you can't originate the thing without people who cross boundaries, you can't validate the thing without experts. You need a balance between the two.

"At several critical points it has been important that there was a major difference of opinion between Warton and Stevenage, otherwise we would not have got into the right area".

He explained: "One of the problems ... was having people who had not been there from the beginning ... who had not been through the positive phase of the programme. The first phase in a project is excitement, and feeling that you've solved the world's problem; then comes disillusion, or at least seeing over-optimism. The first drives you through this second phase to the third."

HERMES WORK PACKAGES

Nevertheless, Burns noted that Warton were pressing on with the airframe: "A 'second round' of structural design investigations is in progress, considering carbon-carbon sandwich construction, carbon-carbon TPS panels and application of fibre-reinforced titanium in the centre fuselage, rear fuselage and wings, all aimed at reducing weight".

The third meeting of the BAe/Rolls-Royce working party took place on August 7 and it was reported that preliminary work on the icing rig had started and that early results were "encouraging". In addition, BAe's representatives were handed a full performance definition of the baseline RB.545 engine.

Three weeks later, on August 28, 1986, Burns reported on the ongoing effort to find a solution for the overweight intake: "Brief investigations have been made of retractable, shielded and jettisonable intake pods. These alternatives appear to involve more penalties than benefits."

Attempts had also been made to solve the oxidation problem inherent in using carbon-carbon: "Consideration is being given to the use of silicon carbide matrix structural material with embedded fibres as an alternative to carbon-carbon for high temperature structures. It is somewhat inferior to carbon-carbon in strength/mass ratio but is inherently immune to oxidation and catalysis.

"The effects of advanced structural materials on mass estimates are being assessed and a mass update is targeted for the end of October. Structural design investigations have been delayed by staff changes and advisory support to the Hermes manufacturing proposal."

The Hermes project, now embedded in ESA's planning schedule thanks to the enabling resolution for a preparatory programme agreed in June, had reached the point of inviting bids for work under contract and BAe could not afford to be left out. As a result: "Proposals for work packages on the Hermes aerospace plane are being prepared at Stevenage and Warton. Stevenage are bidding for cargo bay doors, the Ariane 5 adaptor, fuel cells and flight control system. Warton are bidding for front fuselage, centre fuselage and wings."

At the next RB.545 working party meeting, at Filton on September 6, Bond put forward the first version of an engine mass model and "explained the longer-term possibilities that could improve engine-airframe optimisation". Additionally, "in order to make the most effective use of the Rolls-Royce engine model, the Reaction Engines program and the BAe CAPS program, it was decided unanimously to form a small, dedicated Performance Integration Group (PIG). This would meet separately and respond periodically to the main working party". One representative from each site would join the PIG—Steve Furniss from Warton, Graham Swinerd from Stevenage, Willmer from Filton, George from Rolls-Royce Bristol and Bond, representing Reaction Engines.

BAD WEATHER MACHINE

Scott-Scott gave an overview of the practical icing tests conducted so far using his Avon-powered rig. According to the post-meeting report, "it has achieved all its design

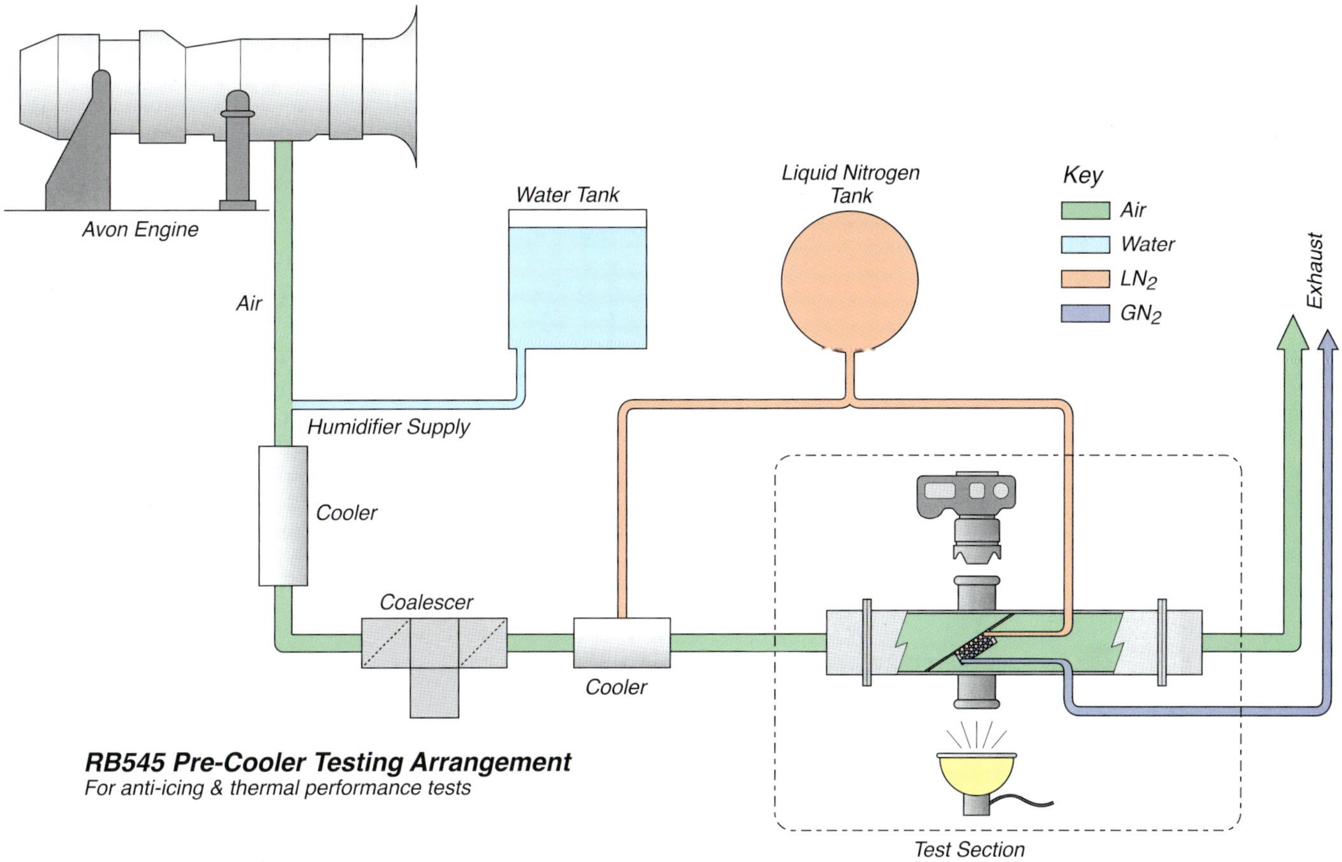

Diagram showing the layout of Scott-Scott's pre-cooler test rig. GRAHAME CHAMBERS

John Scott-Scott, wearing ear defenders, at the de-icing test rig.

parameters, and can therefore be regarded as a versatile tool for use in the anti-frosting programme. A list of interim findings from early precooler tests was also given ... the findings formed the basis of the ongoing programme, which addresses four main anti-frosting techniques, in combination with theoretical studies".

Interviewed in 2010-2011, Scott-Scott recalled: "We set up the test rig, and we were running it round about month five I suppose, well within the six months, and we found a way to go. I wouldn't say we solved the problem completely, but we found a way a go. And it amused quite a number of the people up in the test area at Ansty because we made it snow in the middle of June, snow was pouring down round that test rig.

"The air was coming out so cold that on a summer's day it took all the ... moisture that's in the atmosphere and froze it promptly and instantly, so on the downwind side of the test [rig] it was snowing quite cheerfully when we were running it, and that proved that we were doing the right thing ... there were chaps running round with clip-boards over their heads because it was snowing so much, couldn't believe it ... We could use something like ... seven tons of liquid nitrogen in a day, something like that. And the liquid nitrogen was what provided the cold part of it, and it reacted with anything it found then, and the first thing it finds is moisture in the atmosphere. Saying that this snow is quite ... positive ordinary snow ... but the air temperature coming out of the thing was something like ... minus 100 centigrade, maybe a little bit more ... a lot of things actually go solid at that temperature, things

4 ENGINE CONCEPT

Operates in Airbreathing and Pure Rocket Modes

- The RB545 combines gas turbine and rocket engine features. It uses atmospheric oxygen during initial climb and on-board liquid oxygen for final ascent to orbit.

Air Cooler

- Reduces temperature of incoming air which can be as high as 1000°C and minimises size and mass of turbomachinery.

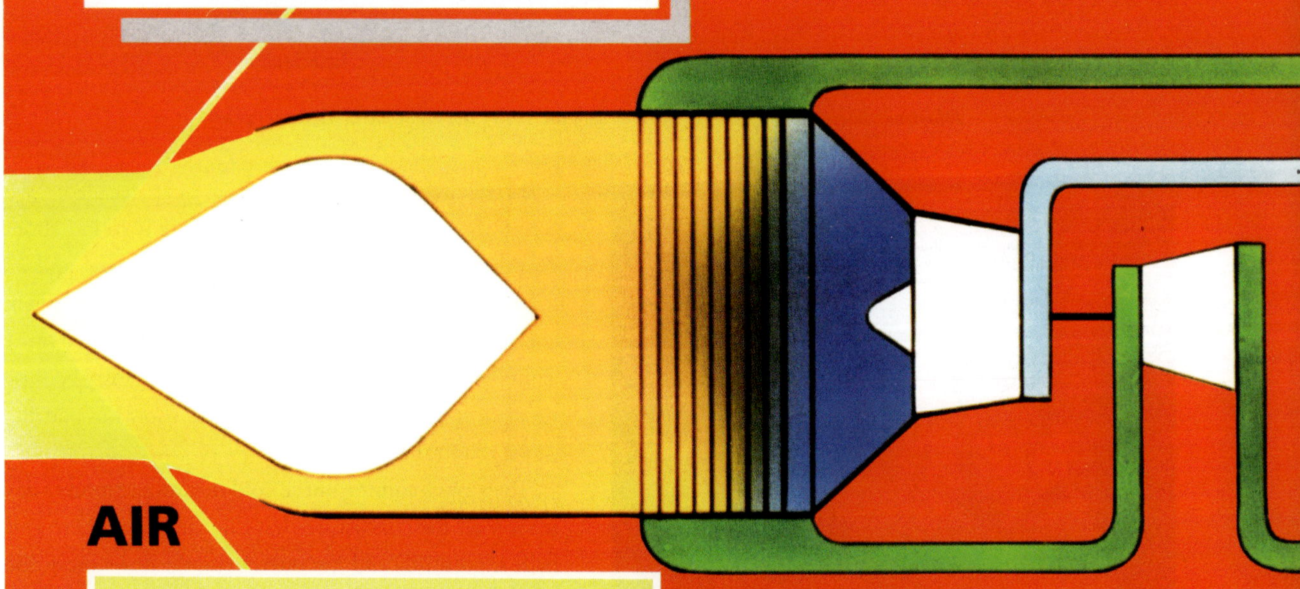

Turbomachinery

- Compressors to raise air pressure to rocket chamber requirement are driven by Turbines during airborne phase of flight.

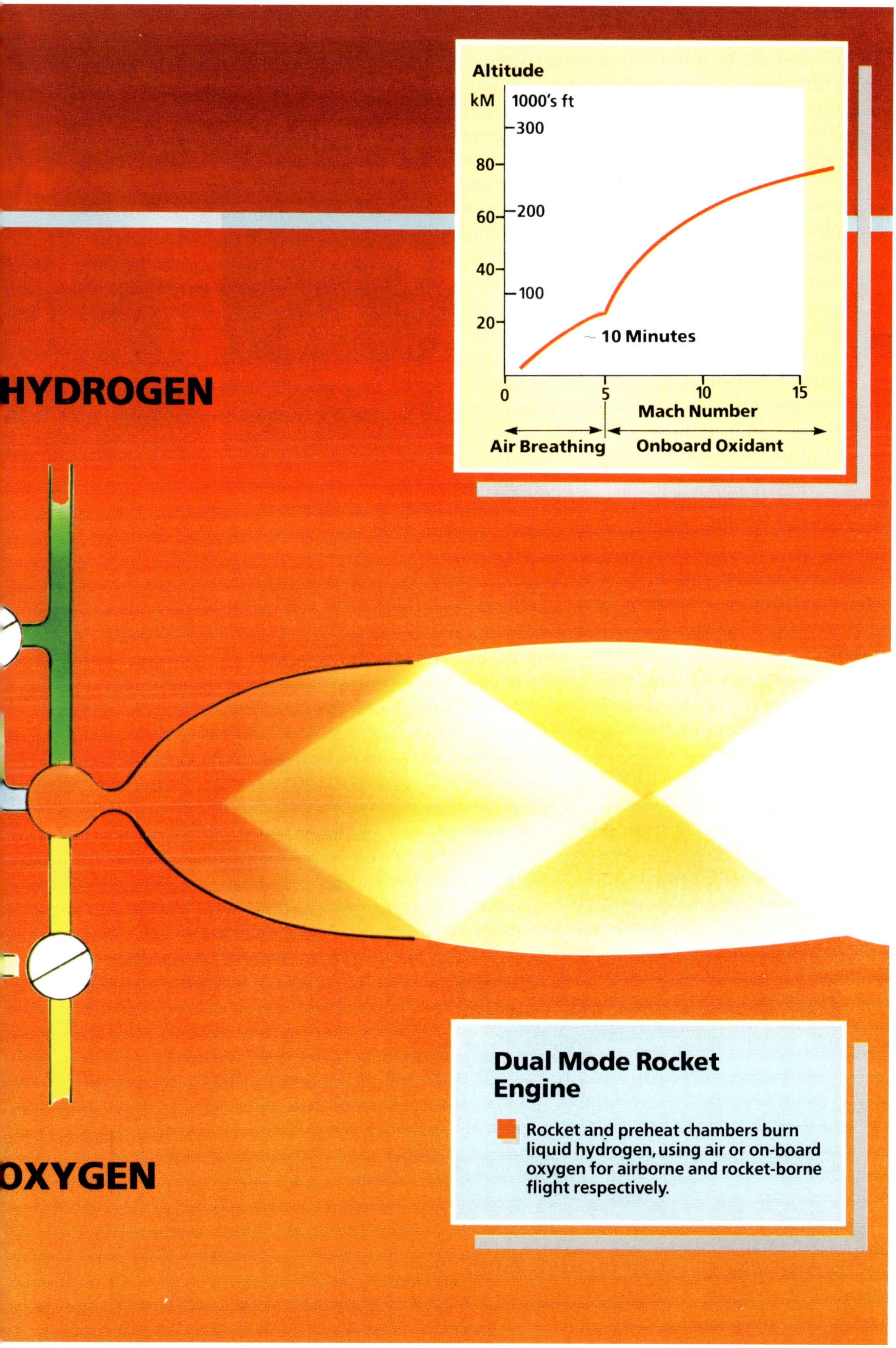

Dual Mode Rocket Engine

Rocket and preheat chambers burn liquid hydrogen, using air or on-board oxygen for airborne and rocket-borne flight respectively.

freeze up…But at least up the mighty exhaust pipe we'd got there, there was snow puttering away and people came from a long distance to see it, because it was the middle of June."

CREDIT WHERE IT'S DUE

The CAPS-derived shorter, fatter Hotol Configuration F had been the baseline design for around four months by late September 1986. However, some who had worked on the original Stevenage/Filton Hotol believed it was a big step in the wrong direction.

Burns wrote to Parkinson on September 25, 1986, ostensibly to express displeasure at the latter's publicity work: "Dear Bob, when Gerald Wilson or I have given presentations/lectures or written papers on Hotol (e.g. Geneva, Hanover, RAeS Preston, *Intercom* etc.) we have made a point of stating that credit for the conception of Hotol and its propulsion system is due to Space and Communication Division, yourself in particular, and to Alan Bond. Our job at Warton is to pick it up and show, we hope, that it can be done at something like the size/mass that was projected, cooperating with yourselves, Filton and Rolls-Royce.

"Having recently read the article 'Hotol Breathes Fire to Orbit' in the recent (Vol 2 No. 3) issue of *Space*, I feel bound to express my irritation (on behalf of the Warton team) that Warton gets only a passing mention, in the caption to the LSWT model photograph. As written, it appears that the whole design and development is being done at Stevenage and you are referred to as 'Project Manager'.

"The 'design revisions' referred to are entirely the result of work done here. While I recognise that, having given an interview, one can have little influence on the final product, one is in a position to insist that particular points are made and credit is given where due. I ask you to take note of this in future, on behalf of our colleagues at Filton as well as Warton, in the interests of goodwill, avoiding 'us and them' attitudes.

"With regard to your 'ding-dong' correspondence with [German aerospace engineer and student of Wernher von Braun] Harry Ruppe in *Spaceflight* [magazine], he is of course quite right in point 6 that 'Hotol's structure is impossible with present-day technology' (at 200-250t GLOW). You are on dangerous ground when you state, in your reply '… technology required is in fact no more than marginally improved over…EFA'. EFA [European Fighter Aircraft—later renamed the Eurofighter Typhoon] has to use today's technology; Hotol would not survive if it had to.

"It is worth reminding ourselves of what we are up against. A year ago, when we came into the act, the project mass statement (ex Filton) stood at 196t, with 5.5t payload. That omitted about 3t insulation and the

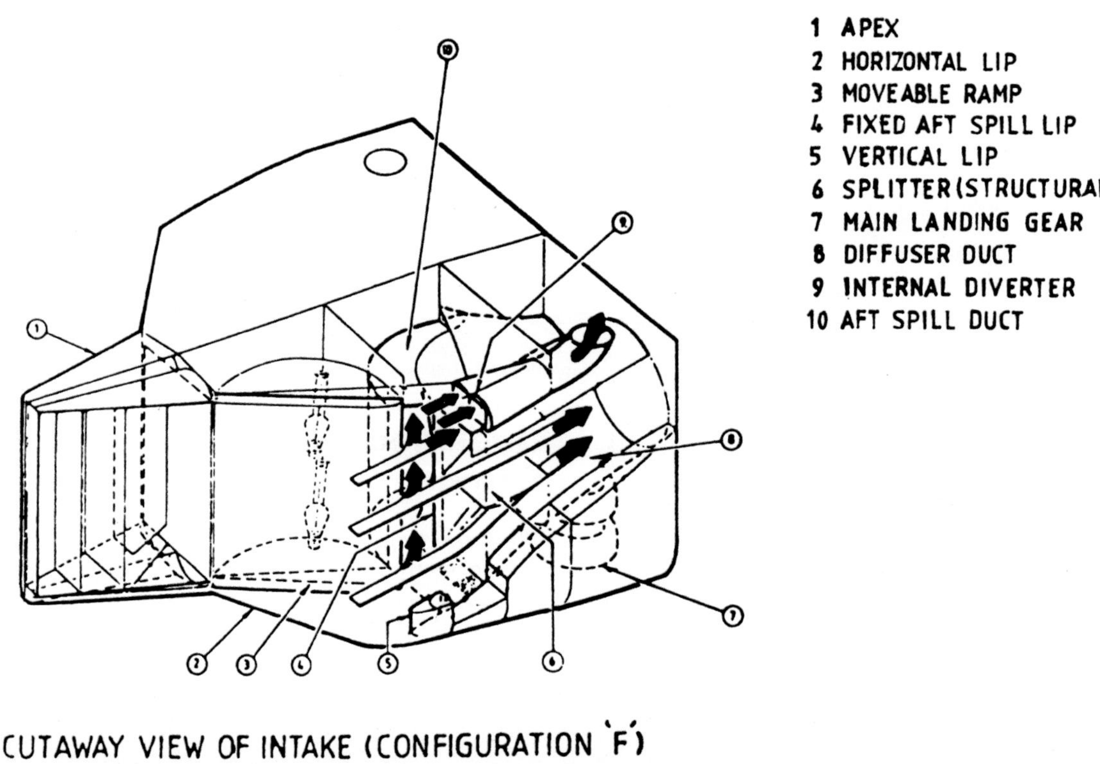

Hotol's intake was a continuous work in progress—this being the iteration planned for Configuration F.

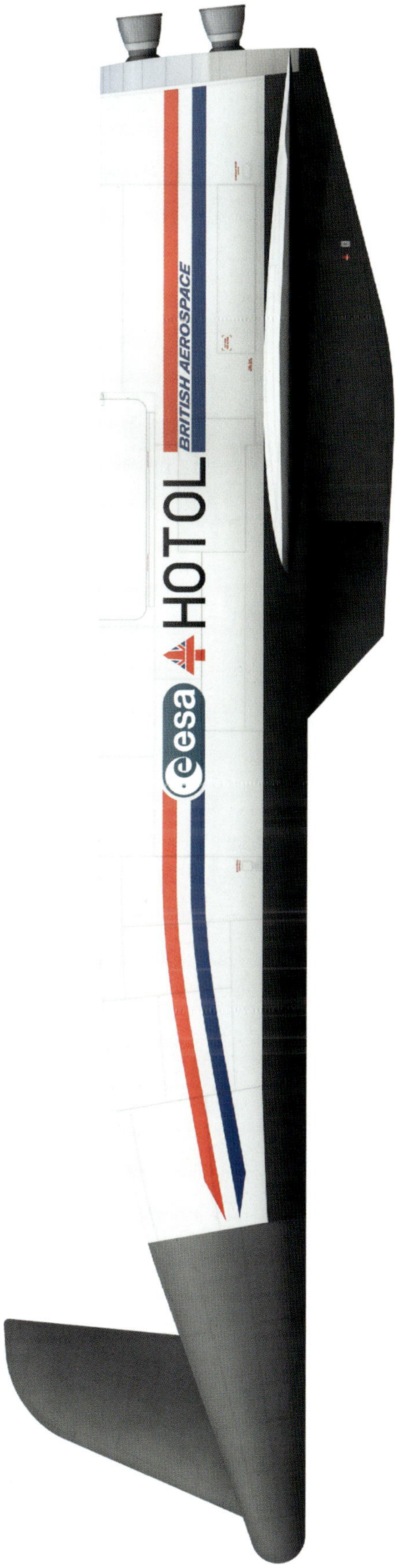

Hotol Configuration F. CHRIS SANDHAM-BAILEY

intake mass was based on a design pressure of less than half the correct figure; its mass went up from 1,310 to 3,426kg by April 1986. The payload vanished and with realistic mass estimates, Version 'D' could not be scaled to put even a Union Jack in orbit.

"Having a credible scaling model by then, Version 'F' emerged, but its true dry mass would be 53t, GLOW 327t without optimism factors. With structure x 0.8 the figures reduce to 34.6 and 230; we have drawn it that way. All this assumes project figures for propulsion mass and efficiency; we have been told on several occasions that those figures are optimistic.

"We have one year left to improve the situation. While we must put on a bold face to the public, we must not delude ourselves with fanciful project estimates. To enable Hotol to survive beyond PoC there are two major tasks: 1) To adopt structural materials and designs that bring about a saving of 15% in structure mass. 2) To define an airbreathing propulsion system of improved efficiency and lightness.

"We have the following four years of enabling technology testing to raise the level of confidence in these areas to get the backing of corporate management, BNSC and ESA to proceed into the development phase."

The latter part of this letter makes it clear that the underlying bone of contention was the changes Warton had made to the vehicle's design—switching from Configuration D, the ultimate derivation of the Stevenage/Filton Hotol, to the significantly different Configuration F. Warton stood firmly by this design, despite inherent and acknowledged issues, but Stevenage, with Parkinson in the lead, was having great difficulty in accepting it.

A BIG LUMP OF ICE

Burns reported on the establishment of the PIG in his monthly update for Yates on September 29, 1986. He also noted that the low-speed wind tunnel model of Hotol Configuration F was nearing completion but would not be tested immediately "due to urgent Tornado and EFA work". Similarly, tests on RAE intake model 351 had begun on September 26 "after some difficulties but have been interrupted by other work". Australian professor Ray Stalker had visited the UK and extolled the virtues of the hypersonic wind tunnel at Canberra for simulating re-entry conditions and consequently "a test programme has been prepared for formal costing".

Assessment of advanced materials was ongoing, a report on airworthiness clearance had been prepared, Filton had been hard at work on the intake design, a document on safety and reliability was nearly complete, work on

5 HOW IT OPERATES

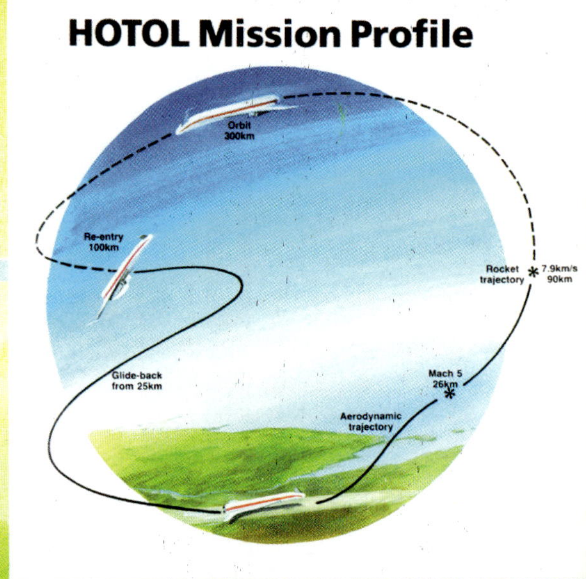

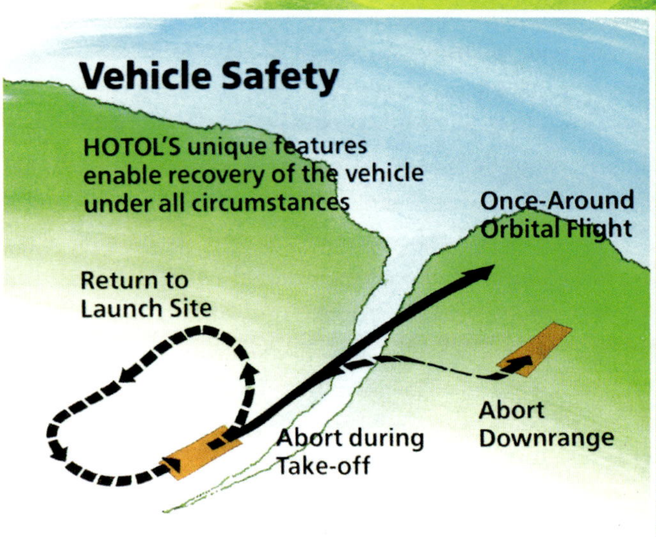

Operations

- Ground turn-around operations are designed for short handling times and minimum support facilities.
- Orbital flight operations will be carried out with a limited ground control staff supported by "expert system" computer software.
- The vehicle has sufficient on-board autonomy to survive one or more orbits without ground intervention.

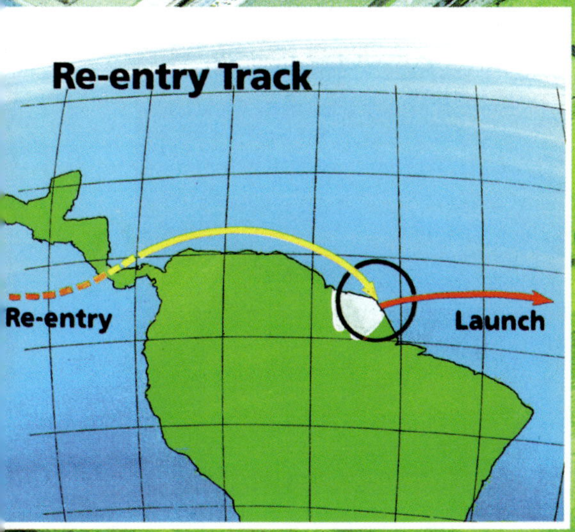

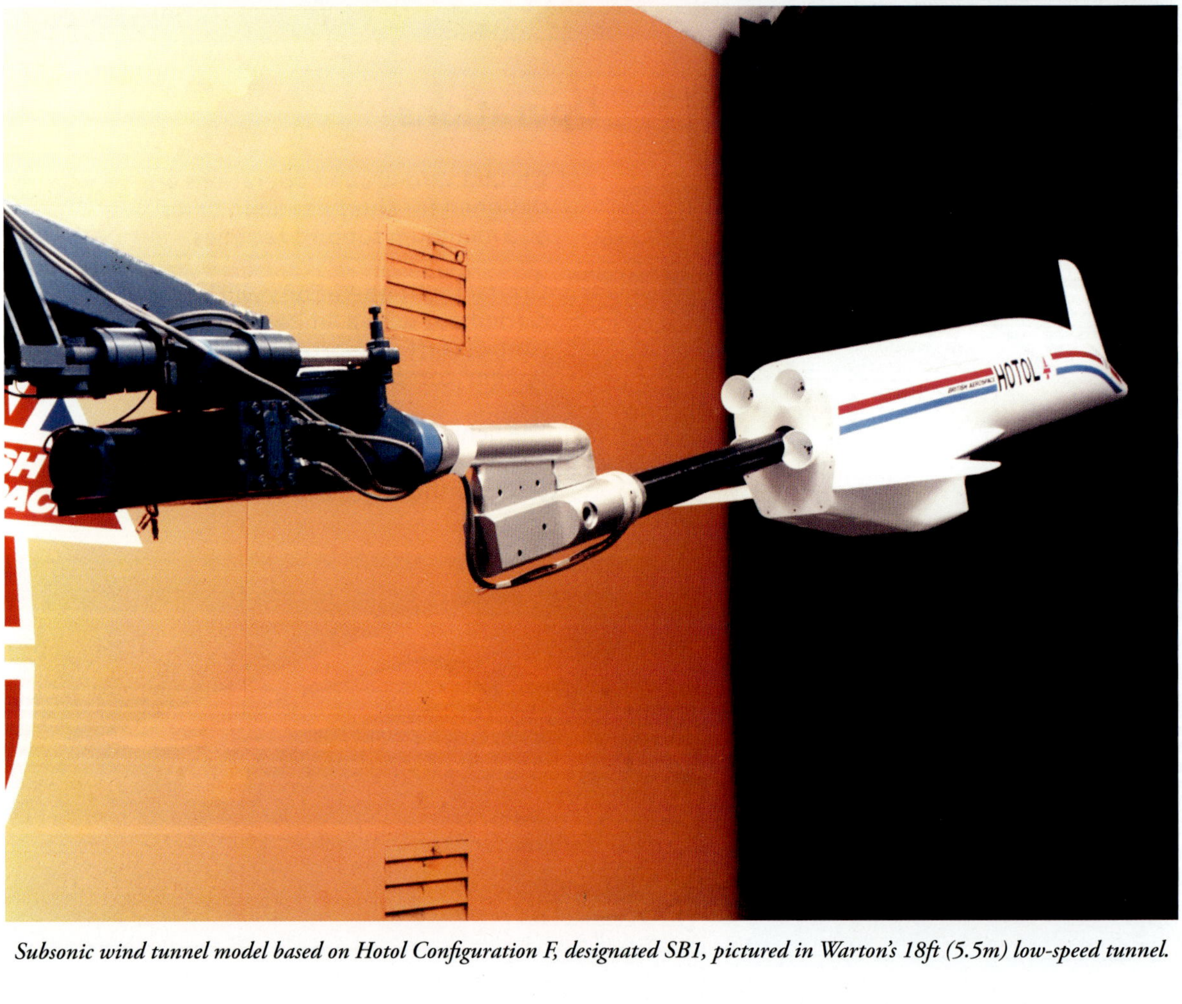

Subsonic wind tunnel model based on Hotol Configuration F, designated SB1, pictured in Warton's 18ft (5.5m) low-speed tunnel.

alternative TPS schemes went on, a total take-off trolley engineering report was to be prepared and "escape systems for manned operations are being assessed at Warton. Contact with Martin-Baker, who are also examining escape systems for Hermes and the Shuttle, suggest that ejection seats with protective screens are the best solution for Hotol, whose crew will be 'passengers' during critical mission phases".

But "detailed assessment of hydraulic systems has led to a mass growth of 400kg. This is serious and emphasises the need for comparative evaluation of all-electric actuation". On the original hard copy of the report, a pencil note had been added to make a new sentence: "This is serious and emphasises the need... *to get rid of forward fin!*"

Early results of the icing rig tests at Ansty had given "some cause for concern and a number of alternative de-icing measures are to be evaluated".

Interviewed in 2010-2011, Scott-Scott said the greatest difficulty he had had in developing the Hotol engine was "the big cooler, because it's not just a cooler, it cools so hard, such a long way down, that any moist air that's in it not only turns to snow but... to ice. And the one demonstration we used to be able to do at Ansty was just to run the rig, turn the liquid nitrogen on, and you get seven seconds before it's blocked up solid with a big lump of ice. So you can't fly that, can you?

"So we used to have to make devices and techniques that would allow you to run the rig continuously, and not just for seven seconds." He said a cloud physicist had been hired on from the Met Office to consider the problem of dealing with excessive moisture and icing. "And I remember saying to him once, 'Well I'll give you a rough outline of the problem... it's all to do with changing from moisture [like you get in clouds]... to ice.' 'Oh, well,' he says, 'how long do you want to fly it for?' And we said something about 20 minutes before it gets [up above it]. 'Oh,' he says, 'that's all right, it takes it a long, long time to form you see.' I said, 'How do you mean a long, long time to form?' 'Well,' he says, 'you know, clouds start to form there.' 'No, no, no,' I said. 'You misunderstood that completely, you've got one millisecond, one thousandth of a second in which to turn this into something else.' And he just couldn't understand this for a bit... I showed him, took him down to the test rig and showed him how we could do it in one millisecond, and we're in real trouble."

Burns' end of September report went on: "Following discussion with BNSC and MoD, RR are extending their programme to the end of 1987 and compressing the urgent test programme into the next few months, with additional funding. There is to be a review point at the end of February 1987. RR quote that they are 'not 100% confident of success'."

PLANNING AHEAD

Elsewhere, the BNSC had now completed its 15-year space plan—which called for the UK government to spend an additional £200 million on space technology over and above the £112 million already being spent annually.

Gibson remembered that it included "a low, middle, and upper option and you could mix and match a little bit between the areas and what we did was to make a plea for a national activity. Not really national satellites but a national technological activity, which was strong enough to improve our position both in ESA and... for British industry to make better bids into Inmarsat, Intelsat and other international organisations.

"So we were looking for a very strong British industry which would not be flogging satellites left, right and centre, but one that would be making use of the technology that was being developed and then going to ESA to get leverage out of their technology programme in areas that we thought would be interesting. We identified a number of areas that to us were the key: navigation from satellites was one of the first ones. I remember we pushed remote sensing in the sense of environmental control and planning, agricultural land use, town development and this kind of thing, to try to underpin... with a better informatics programme.

"We left manned space flight as an optional extra but highly recommended that we didn't close the door to it and we wanted the UK to go into the Ariane launcher in a modest way because we felt that not to do anything we would be excluded and the influence the UK would have would be very much reduced."

It went unpublished for the time being but Sir Robin Nicholson, formerly the Government's chief scientist, was asked to write a report on it for Thatcher's cabinet to discuss.

The BNSC now held the purse strings for Hotol—so the space plan's success would open the door to ongoing financial support. Conversely, its failure would likely condemn the project to, at best, a slow death unless another source of funding could be found.

HELPFUL SUGGESTIONS

Another Hotol presentation was required from Burns on October 8, 1986, this time at British Aerospace's corporate headquarters, which had moved from Pall Mall to 11 Strand, London. Accompanying him from Warton was BAe managing director of Military Aircraft Frank Roe,

6 FLYING HOTOL

HOTOL deploys its cargo during a 50 hr stay in orbit.

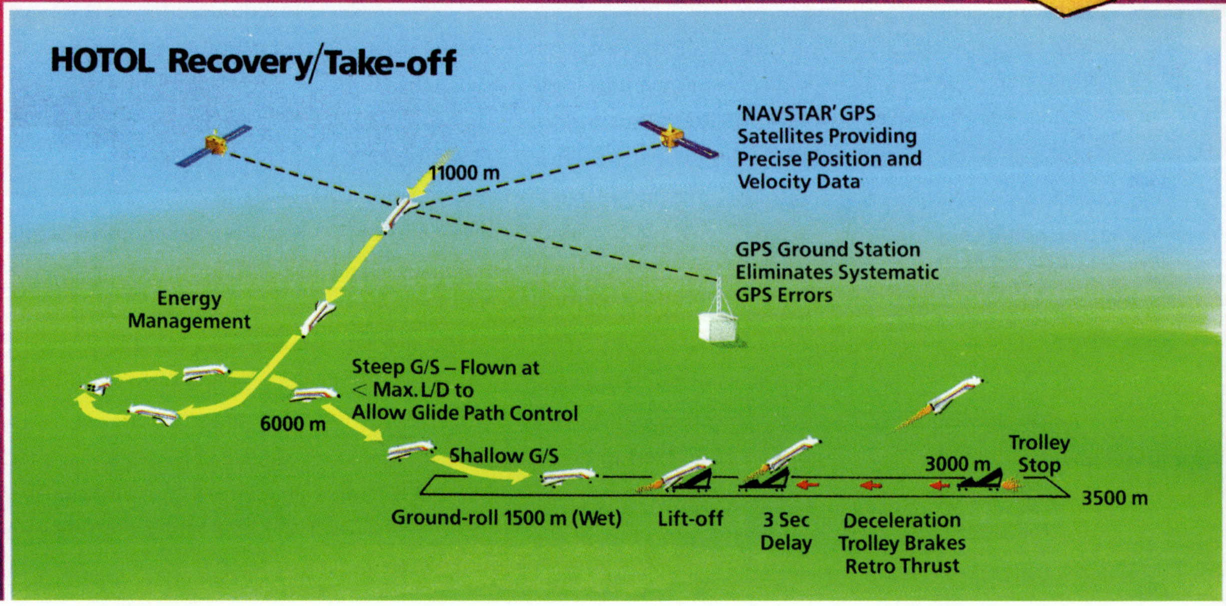

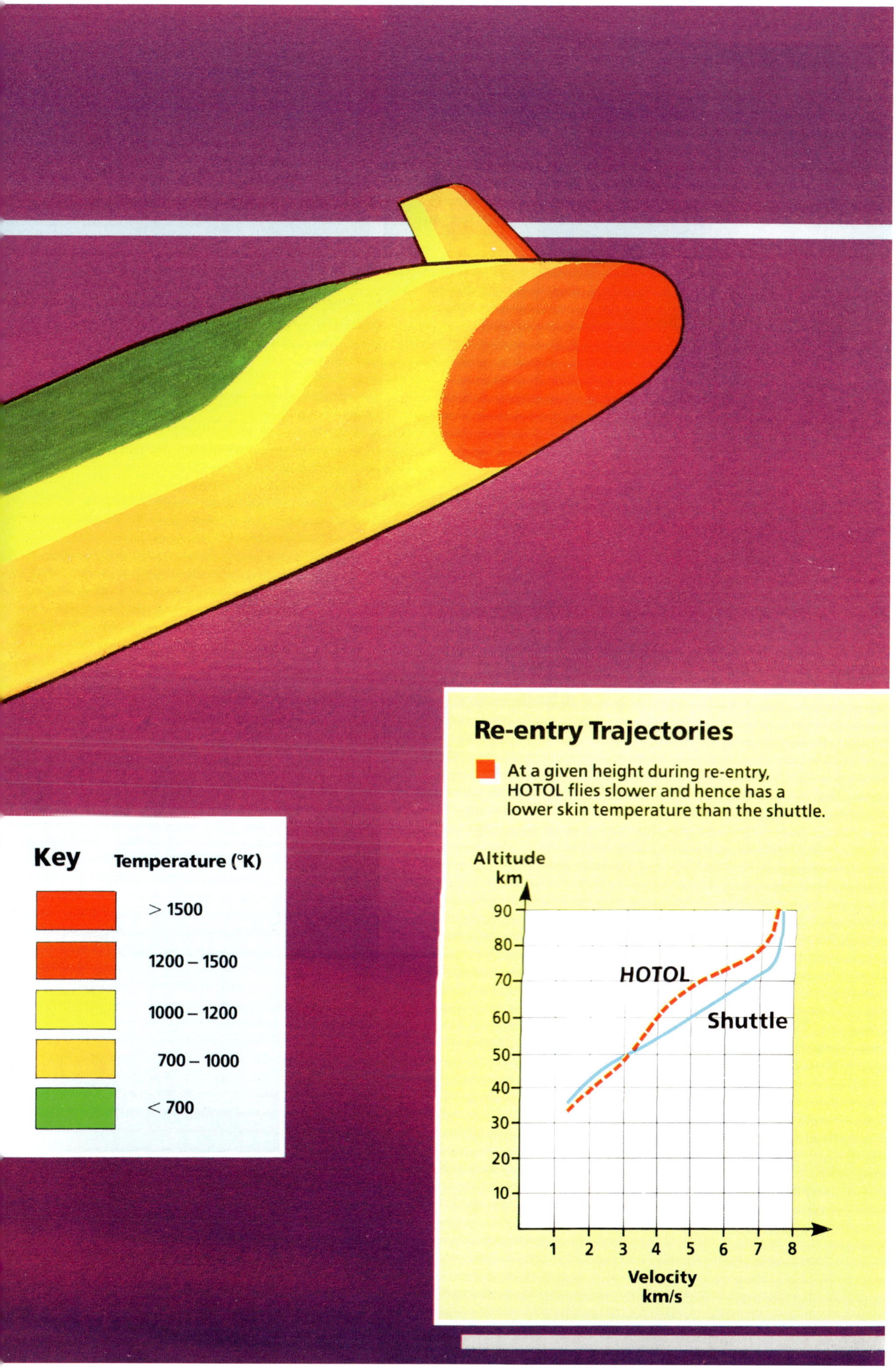
Key
Temperature (°K)
> 1500
1200 – 1500
1000 – 1200
700 – 1000
< 700
Re-entry Trajectories
At a given height during re-entry, HOTOL flies slower and hence has a lower skin temperature than the shuttle.
Altitude km
90
80
70
60
50
40
30
20
10
HOTOL
Shuttle
1 2 3 4 5 6 7 8
Velocity km/s

and attending for Stevenage were Parkinson, Conchie and managing director of Space Systems John Holt.

Burns had outlined progress on the PoC and evidently it was not good news, with the difficulties posed by Hotol's as-designed mass being laid bare. Consequently, the remainder of the meeting saw a wide range of suggestions aimed at lightening the vehicle being reviewed.

First up was a potential way to keep the size of Hotol's nose fin down, which in turn would reduce the weight of the hydraulics needed to power it: "The size of the front fin is set by cross-wind landing. Some alleviation appears possible by introducing a rear fin and this will be tested in the wind tunnel. If we ignore the landing case we need to know what sizes the front fin elsewhere, and whether we could get round the landing problem in another way". Parkinson recorded that Burns would investigate the front fin plus rear fin concept.

Assessments of the heating Hotol would undergo on re-entry had resulted in some heavier-than-expected materials being specified for its construction. Therefore, there was talk of sending a Warton representative on a tour of US companies to see what other advanced materials were available or likely to become available. Yates "proposed that a 'club' of advanced materials suppliers and users be formed ... with a view to focusing development programmes".

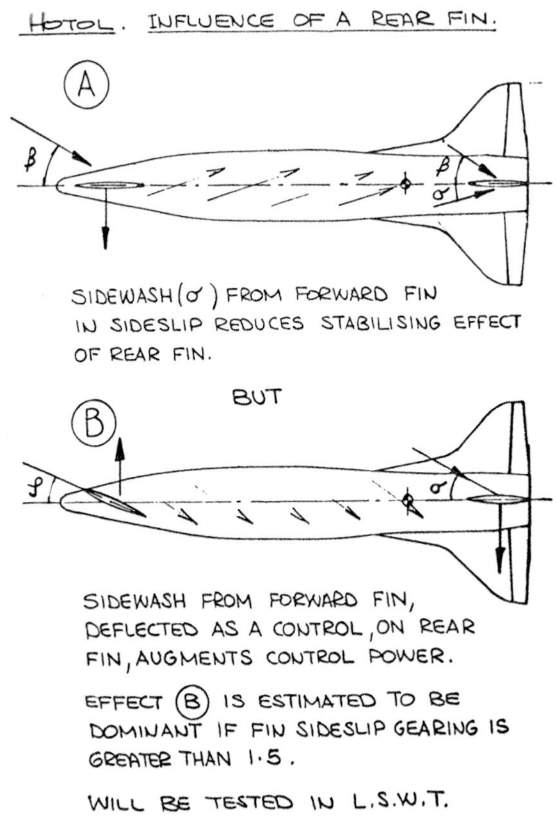

A Hotol design with both forward and rear fins was assessed to see how controllability would be affected.

Further discussion concerned the possibility of an alternative Hotol structure, with an "unbroken pressurised external skin and a minimal hydrogen propellant tank", and the effect that the payload bay length was having on Hotol's mass. According to Parkinson's summary: "The 9m payload bay length quoted in the Farnborough leaflet was introduced to cater for future manned operations and equipment. Warton need to consider ways in which a longer payload bay might change the organisation of the vehicle configuration. Stevenage need to consider constraints on the payload bay length as a continuing activity. It was noted that the Hermes payload bay is 8.8m long [an annotation in ballpoint pen here notes: "but smaller diameter"]. The datum payload bay length for Hotol of 7,000kg/7.5m remains unchanged."

There was also now uncertainty about the use of a trolley for take-off: "It is considered that the operational requirement for the trolley needs to be reviewed in depth as a consequence of a dialogue between Stevenage and Warton (including Flight Ops) and the rules governing alternative possibilities should be defined. It was noted that the Spanish (Sener [Aerospace & Defence, based in Getxo, Spain]) have offered to use their own money to look at this area and this should be encouraged."

Beyond Hotol's airframe design, it was recorded that "among the various demonstrator programmes tabled, the proposal for a flying test bed for the RB.545 appears as a major cost item. The need for a demonstrator programme needs to be discussed with RR, BAe Stevenage and others (e.g. BNSC). We need to consider whether a flying test bed is really required for the engine and which flight experience is actually required. I. Yates believed it might be possible to do engine testing on the prototype Hotol with one engine air-breathing and the remainder operating in rocket mode. Scenarios for a flight programme along these lines need to be identified".

In connection with this point, "concern was expressed about the lack of commitment by Rolls-Royce, at board level, to the RB.545 programme".

By this point the Germans, who had previously appeared supportive of Hotol as a project for Europe, had revealed their own two-stage horizontal take-off spaceplane concept: Sänger aka Sänger II. This system had reportedly been devised by MBB earlier in 1986 and consisted of a large delta-wing aircraft with a small Hermes-like orbiter mounted on its back. There was now a third European launch system in contention.

At BAe's October 1986 meeting, "in discussing the relative attractions of Hotol and Sänger the chart comparing different airbreathing power plants was discussed. It is

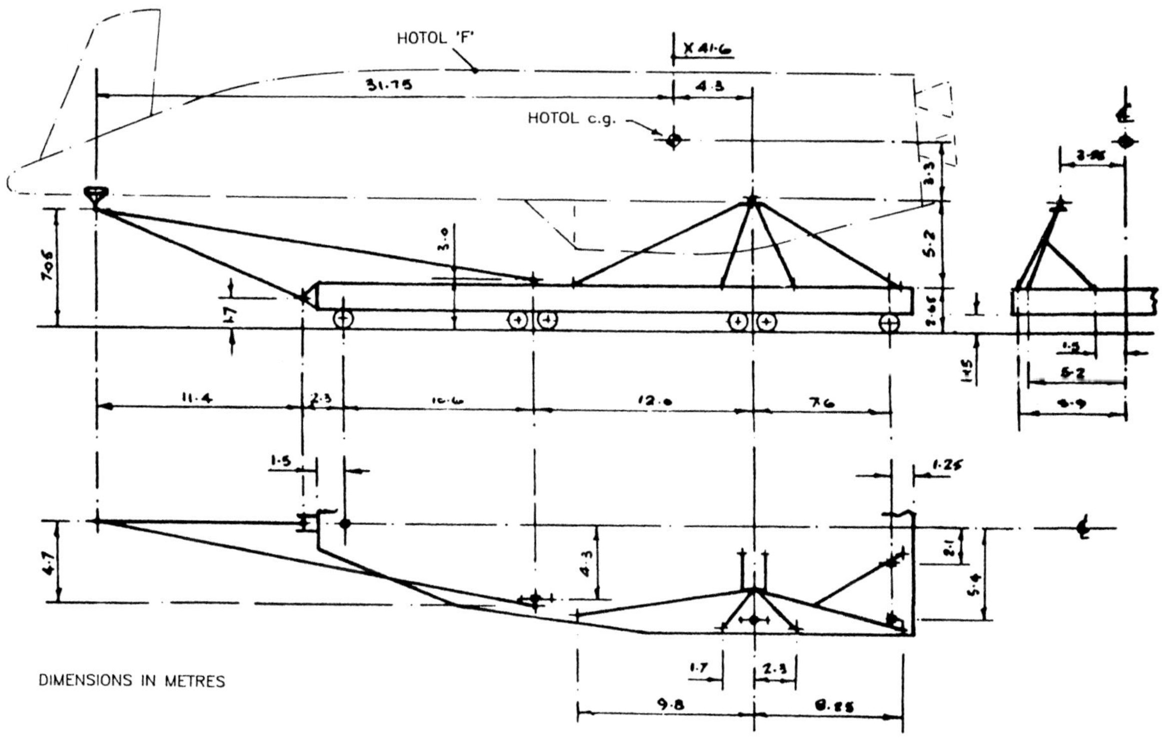

INITIAL THREE POINT TROLLEY LAYOUT – CONFIGURATION 'F'

Early trolley design with three attachment points.

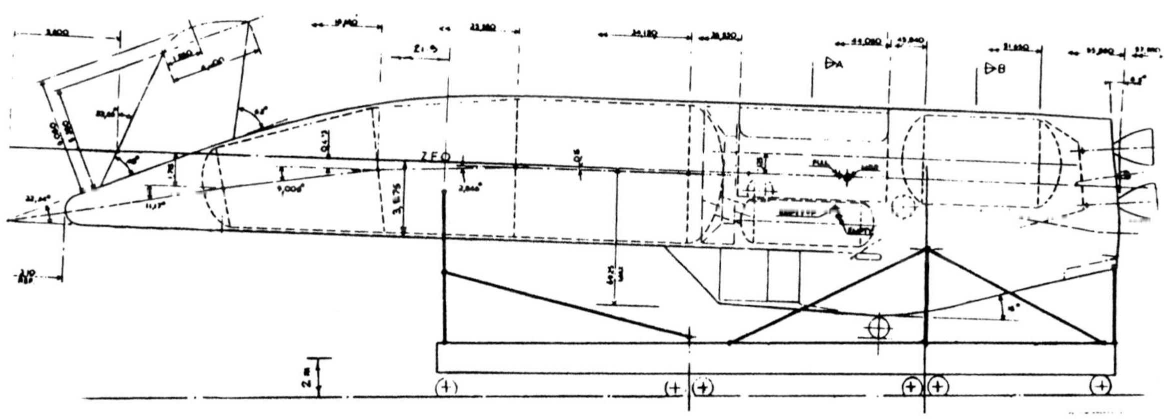

HOTOL 'F' ON TROLLEY, VERSION 4

Revised trolley design for Hotol Configuration F.

apparent that the requirement for Sänger is significantly different from that for Hotol... BNSC regard Sänger as the German 'me too' project... BNSC strategy with respect to Hermes is that Hotol is Ariane 6 and Hermes is a side alley... MBB have actively pursued the possibilities of a bi-lateral German collaboration on aerospaceplane technology. The feeling is that current collaboration should be directed towards discussing requirements and utilisation and should not include joint project studies since we appear to be significantly in advance of Germany in this area.

"It was felt that in any German collaboration Dornier would play an important part and might be more ready to adopt our position than MBB. We need to encourage Dornier to think about the enabling technology programme. Roy Gibson had suggested that he would talk to Dornier but I. Yates will talk to [Dornier president Johan] Schaeffer at high level to open direct contacts."

Even as all this was going on, BAe continued to press ahead with efforts to get a slice of the pie should Hermes end up actually getting built: "There was discussion on

7 ENGINE TECHNOLOGY

Sea Dart

Concorde

Intakes

- Rolls-Royce designed the intakes for the Sea Dart Missiles and with BAe, developed the Intake Engine matching in Concorde. The HOTOL vehicle is an extension of this technology.

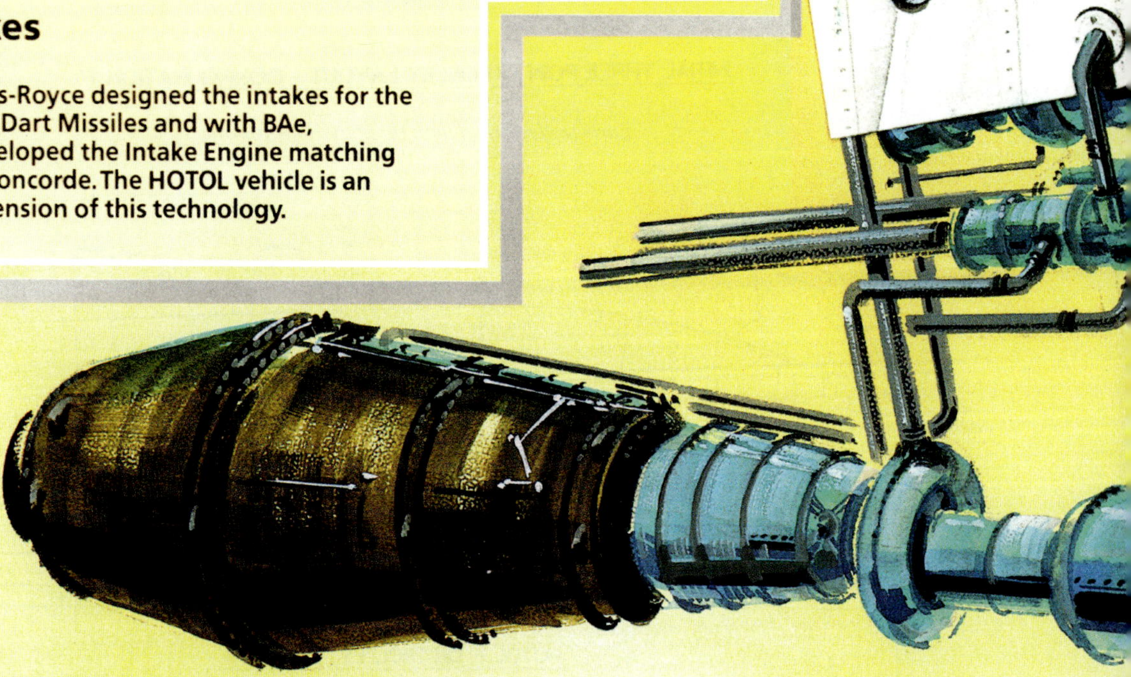

Heat Exchangers

- Basic concept defined. Design and Manufacturing technology being developed.

Blue Streak

Rockets

- Dual-mode rocket engine will be developed from existing European experience.

Ariane

Materials

- Existing Rolls-Royce materials research strategy largely meets RB545 requirements. Additional work is required to mitigate effects of Hydrogen environment on material properties.

RB 199

Turbomachinery

RB 211

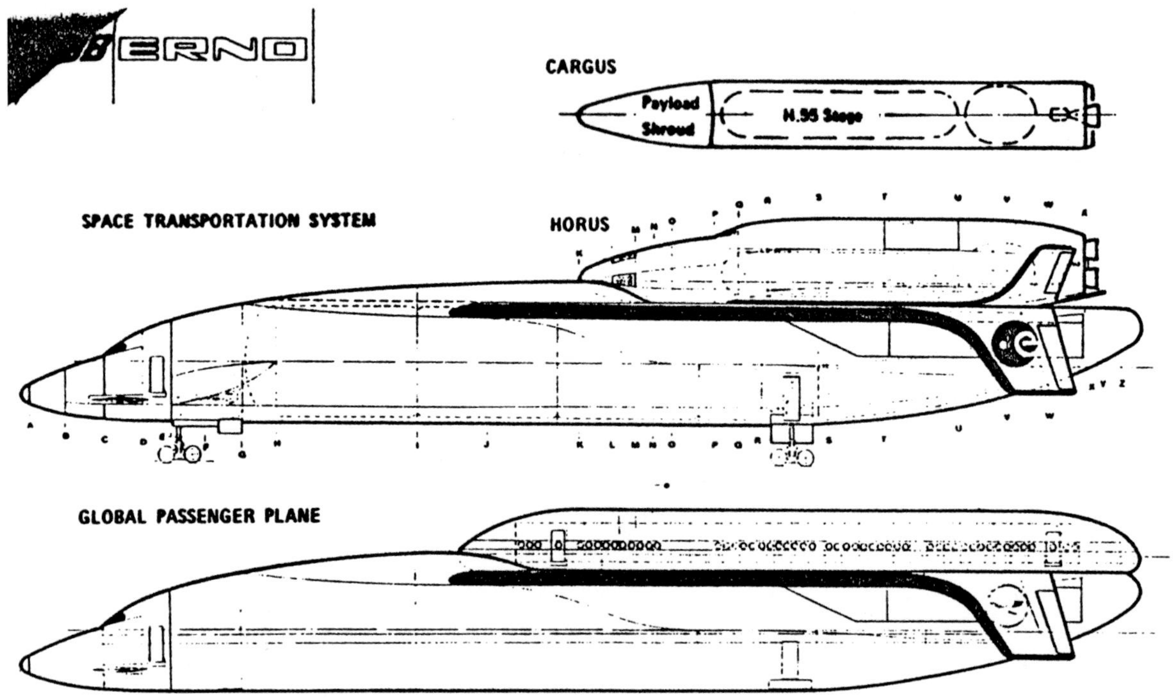

The two-stage-to-orbit Sänger system in its earliest form—either as a space transportation system with crewed (Horus) or autonomous (Cargus) upper stage, or as a "global passenger plane". AIRBUS

a proposal for a joint bid with Aeritalia on the Hermes wing. A joint letter of agreement has been drafted and it was agreed that the bid on the wing should be put forward in those terms."

Appended to Parkinson's summary was a chart showing overall spending on Hotol from the fourth quarter of 1985 to the end of the third quarter 1986 between the three BAe centres: £0.865m.

Also appended was an 'audit plan' for the project which would bring in another British Aerospace centre: Brough. Starting on November 1, 1986, a six-strong team at BAe Brough comprising Technical Director Stan Field, Chief Designer N. Jackson, Chief Stressman K. Broddle plus three other full-time staff would be asked to review the Hotol team's work to date. They would need to provide the answers to three questions: are the design schemes/mass estimates realistic? Are projections of benefits of advanced materials/structures realistic? Are assessments of risk areas and associated investigation programmes realistic? And their report was to be delivered in March 1987.

HOTOL CREW CAPSULE

Parkinson produced a report in October 1986 entitled 'Hotol—Minimum Size Manned Capsule' which, as this title suggested, considered "the size and mass that might be associated with a 'minimum size' four-man capsule, and potential crew escape systems which might be associated with the design".

Work previously carried out on this concept at Stevenage had identified four potential design considerations: the original crew capsule size, 5.56m long and 1.8m in diameter including allowances for an airlock, with a 2m berthing interface diameter, took up too much space; the original plan had allowed for just two crew but "it is now felt desirable to be able to carry up to four crew on polar missions"; crews could probably cope with a fairly restricted cabin area during short missions; and finally, crew safety and escape "are seen as important features in the overall design".

The original design was to be "faired into the Hotol surface so that forward windows can look over the residual payload bay". Its structural mass was 536kg, plus 719kg for internal systems, a 660kg allowance for the crew themselves and their suits, and 259kg for a manipulator arm.

Four different options had been considered for crew escape: full crew capsule ejection, simple ejection seats, a hybrid capsule with ejection seats and individual escape pods. Evidently, "the maximum dynamic pressure associated with crew ejection (600kts estimated air speed) is no worse than that already encountered on high-performance fighter aircraft. The principle new problems expected to be encountered with Hotol are associated with the heat pulse encountered while ejecting through an exhaust plume and partial 're-entries' encountered if ejection takes place at later stages of the launch".

The full crew capsule offered the best survivability

but at a significant mass penalty thanks to the necessary enhanced structural strength, explosive bolts, booster rockets, parachute system, flotation devices and more. Open ejection seats would be the cheapest and lightest option but "will not be effective throughout the vehicle's flight envelope". The hybrid system would involve a capsule capable of getting the crew clear of the vehicle, to a point where ordinary ejection seats would work—improving survivability and reducing mass.

The individual escape pods—a 'clamshell' enclosing each crew member prior to ejection—also saved mass and offered a better chance of survival but "the principal problem associated with 'pod' ejection seats appears to be integrating them with the other requirements of a life supporting cabin for use by the astronauts on orbit. This would either involve designing the pods to somehow fold away after launch, or connecting the pods by some sort of access device to a lower cabin. Neither approach appears free of mass implications".

In the 'recommendations' section of the report, Parkinson wrote: "A reduced size capsule, capable of carrying four men into orbit for a mass penalty in the region of 2.7 tonnes, including provision of a crew escape system [is possible]. The most promising crew escape system would appear to be a hybrid capsule/ejection seat system in which the crew capsule would be ejected from the vehicle for high speed or high-altitude escape, but where the crew would separate from the capsule before landing.

"Further work is required on potential re-entry loads on the vehicle in the case of a complete propulsion failure during ascent to establish the required escape envelope. To meet geometric constraints associated with providing additional volume for 'mid-deck' experiments, and berthing interfaces with orbital facilities, it may be necessary to offset the crew capsule position to one side of the vehicle centreline."

Following on from this, Wilson would write to ejection seat manufacturer Martin-Baker Aircraft to see what they systems they would recommend for helping a Hotol crew escape.

ALTERNATIVE CONCEPTS

BAe Filton and Warton called an informal meeting on October 13, 1986, to discuss "the management and organisation of Hotol propulsion integration activity". Just four representatives were present: Scott-Scott, Brown, Parkinson and Wilson.

Progress by the PIG was discussed and it was agreed that a complementary design integration group—DIG—led by BAe Filton would also be set up to work on component design and installation, pipework, valves, induction system integration, air pre-conditioning and intake studies.

Wilson outlined "the proposed Warton-based Alternative Concepts Team and its scope of activity" and there was an extensive discussion of rocket performance assumptions. Lastly, it was noted that 11 heat exchanger test piece models would be tried on the icing rig over the next three months.

The 'Alternative Concepts Team', established in January 1987 as the Alternative Launch Vehicles (ALV) team, would be led by Dave Walley, who would be returning to space vehicle design after two decades. Its goal would be to review a vast range of alternative launch vehicle designs, including radical reworkings of Hotol itself, to seek out the best possible configuration. Walley and his team would make extensive use of CAPS during this process—see Chapter 6.

On October 22, 1986, *The Times* ran a piece by Keith Hindley under the heading 'Off into space, economy class' which reviewed Hotol's progress in roundabout fashion, illustrated by John Grimwade—whose diagram presented a highly inaccurate view of the vehicle seemingly based on the model displayed in Paris more than a year earlier. A somewhat better-informed article by Martin Ince appeared in *The Engineer's* October 30 issue. Ince opined that "the competition to provide Europe's next generation of space launchers seems to have been won by Hermes… [it] has now become an ESA project, and a £35 million preparatory programme is now being started by ESA in Toulouse which should put Hermes on course for operational service in the late 1990s. The two main rivals to Hermes, the UK's Hotol and West Germany's Sänger spaceplanes, will now be developed at a slower pace.

"At the suggestion of Roy Gibson… ESA will now probably undertake a three-year study of European launcher requirements. This will involve a detailed look at the technology of Hotol, including its engines… Even if Hotol turns into a full ESA project, which will probably mean killing off Sänger, it is unlikely to fly until about 2005, perhaps eight years after Hermes. And even this timetable hinges on a decision by the full council of ESA, perhaps early next year, to go ahead with the study proposed by Gibson.

"The ESA commitment to Hermes will mean spending major sums on detailed engineering from summer 1987 onwards. A decision to do this will probably be endorsed by the technology ministers of the ESA member nations around May of next year. But the ministers will want reassurances that Hermes contracts will be spread across ESA member countries rather than being heavily concentrated

8 STRUCTURAL TECHNOLOGY

Characteristics of HOTOL structural materials

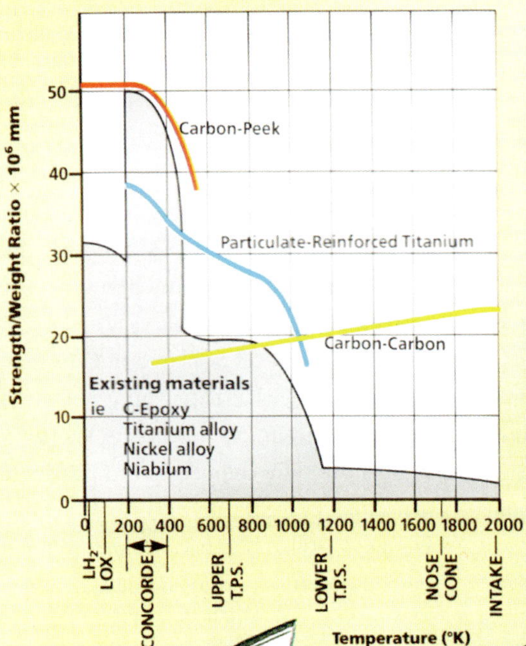

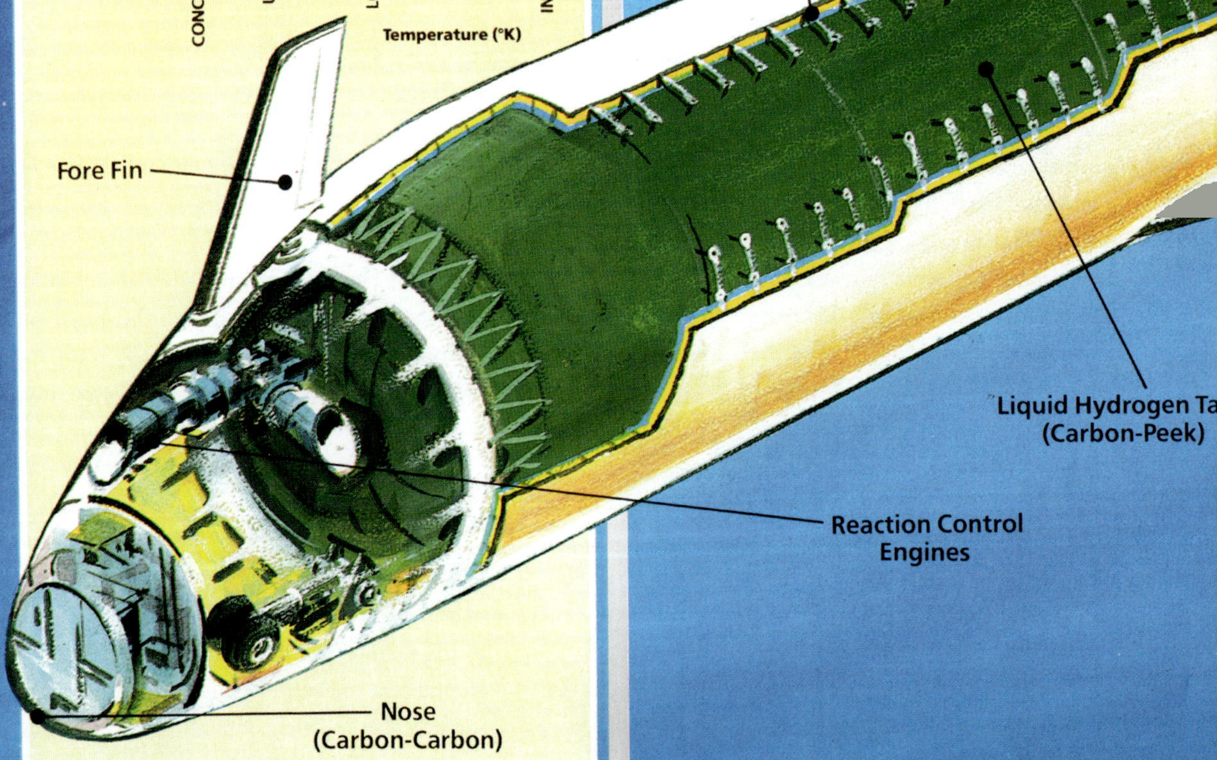

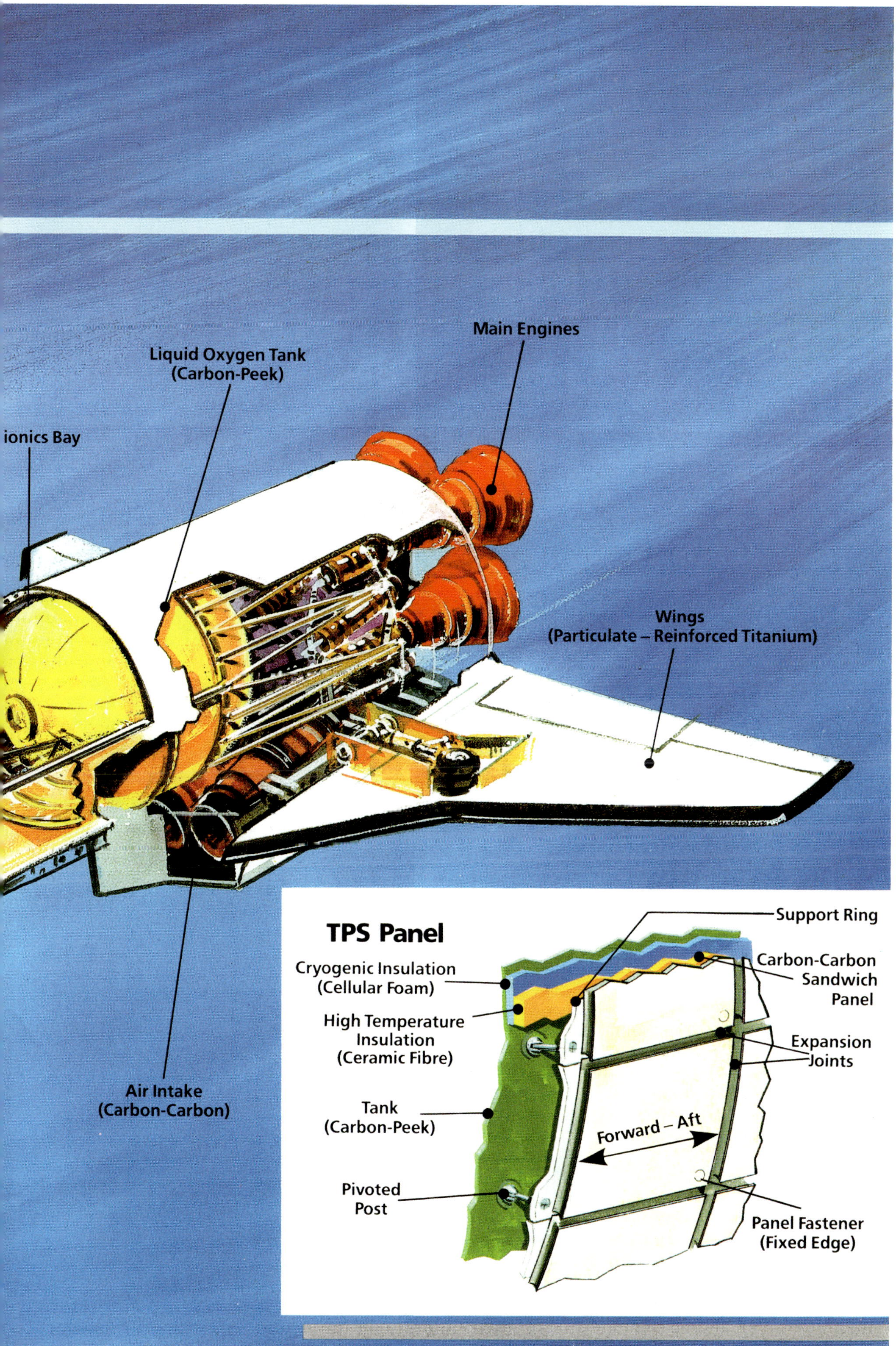
Main Engines
Liquid Oxygen Tank
(Carbon-Peek)
ionics Bay
Wings
(Particulate – Reinforced Titanium)
Air Intake
(Carbon-Carbon)
TPS Panel
Support Ring
Cryogenic Insulation
(Cellular Foam)
Carbon-Carbon
Sandwich
Panel
High Temperature
Insulation
(Ceramic Fibre)
Expansion
Joints
Tank
(Carbon-Peek)
Forward – Aft
Pivoted
Post
Panel Fastener
(Fixed Edge)

in France, as has happened so far with the Ariane launcher. All Hermes work so far has been done by the French space agency CNES.

"British Aerospace claims that Hotol will be able to place payloads in orbit for about $600 per kg. This is a fifth of the price of the most advanced version of Ariane now being planned and comfortably below the prices available with Hermes. This will make Hotol attractive even if it slips a few years behind Hermes in ESA planning."

JAPANESE DE-ICING

The low-speed model of Configuration F was finally undergoing tests in Warton's 5.5m wind tunnel by the time of Burns' monthly report of October 30, 1986. So far it had been discovered that lift had been reduced compared to Configuration D but the pitch-up problem was now delayed and when it came was milder than before. Fin effectiveness was also improved, albeit slightly, but this was offset by a greater destabilising effect from the fuselage. Burns noted that "alternative means of directional control are being investigated".

Preliminary testing of RAE intake model 351 had now been completed and plans had been laid to test a small Hotol model in the Australian hypersonic wind tunnel. This was going to cost around £15,000 plus the cost of building the model at Warton.

The intake mass situation had got even worse since "definitive figures... from Filton, including thermal protection, have added about 1,100kg". Not only that, "revised figures for the density of carbon-PEEK, used in the liquid oxygen and hydrogen tanks, have increased the mass of these items but this has been offset, to some extent, by the deletion of stiffeners in the hydrogen tank". Thankfully though, "revision of propellant budgets, following work at Stevenage and Warton, has led to a reduction of some 1,400kg, which more or less offsets the increases in basic structure mass noted above".

A saving of 800kg was also expected to come from using an alternative TPS design which featured carbon-carbon sandwich outer panels and bagged insulation between those panels and the cold tank below.

At a propulsion steering group meeting two weeks earlier, on October 14, "Rolls-Royce were concerned that funds would not be available to start technology programmes before 1988. BAe requested that RR should prepare plans for what they would wish to do irrespective of funding and resources limitations and present these to their board and to BNSC. RR agreed to consider this... it was agreed also to investigate the possibility of doing early flight trials with pure rocket propulsion and sub-standard airframe. It is clear that RR are not putting adequate manpower resources into RB.545 work although [Rolls-Royce director of advanced projects] Mr [Hugh] Hillier reported a more favourable attitude at board level.

"Work on the icing rig is being pursued although the budget for that work was cut by some 50%. In parallel with the rig tests, work has been put in hand at universities to produce physical explanations of observed results".

Evidently Bond had attended a conference at Innsbruck where "a Japanese engineer showed film demonstrating successful anti-icing of the heat exchanger of a liquid air cycle engine, proving that it can be done".

It was hoped that some ESA money might be secured to pay for enabling technology—work on developing new tech which could potentially benefit all European space projects, not just Hotol. And to that end, a preliminary meeting to discuss going to ESA for funds had been held between Conchie, Parkinson and Dr Ernst Högenauer, vice president of technical operations at MBB's space systems group. A list of possible areas of beneficial research "has been prepared with indications of international preferences, UK, Germany, Italy. It is believed that ESA require an early indication of the important topics and national preferences in this area".

GOING TO EUROSPACE

The European space industry consortium, Eurospace, held a Future Prospect Group meeting in Paris on October 15 to "prepare a revised version of the Eurospace proposals formulated in 1984 regarding the Long-Term Programmes of ESA". These would be arranged into six categories—sciences, communications, earth observation, microgravity, launcher systems and in-orbit infrastructures—and would be presented at a joint meeting with ESA in January 1987.

The meeting summary report recalled that there had been four original Eurospace proposals to ESA in 1984: completion of the Ariane IV programme, costing 210 MAU between 1985 and 2000; Kourou spaceport, costing 640 MAU; Ariane V and Hermes, costing 5,150 MAU and ancillary vehicles costing 450 MAU. It stated: "The completion of Ariane V (including man-rating) was proposed for the end of 1995. The recommended dates for maiden flight and the first operational flight of Hermes were respectively 1995 and 1996."

It was further recapped that, at Rome, the ESA Council of Ministers had not quite gone along with this. While they "had 'welcomed and endorsed' the Ariane V programme estimated at 2,600 MAU", they had only "taken note with interest" of the Hermes programme. In addition, "regarding the budget, the Rome Conference recommended, for the post-1988 period, a total ESA budget of 1,650 MAU per year, of which some 960 [would be] for the launchers and space infrastructure activities. In 1985 the ESA expenditure on Space Transportation systems [launchers] amounted to 280 MAU".

The meeting now heard that "the present situation is marked by a number of difficulties and cost increases that the group members did not want to discuss during this meeting. It is also marked by the advent of new ideas. The necessity was felt to arrange one or several meetings of a specialised group in which the recommendations to be made to ESA for the short and medium term and for the long term [are to be discussed].

"Regarding the long term in particular it was observed that it was already necessary to study the post Ariane V generation of launchers. It was agreed that this study of long-term ideas would have to be carried out in a way that would not lead to the re-examination of programmes that have already been adopted."

It was decided that a new launchers sub-group would be established to review ten specific topics: Ariane V, Hermes, Hotol, Sänger, Small Launchers (specifically a mini-Ariane derivative known as Marianne, being proposed by a Swedish team from Volvo), Ariane VI, in-orbit transfer vehicles, recovery capsules, estimation of demand and launch/test ground facilities.

The first meeting of the sub-group, under the snappy title Eurospace Future Prospect Group Meeting on Space Transport, took place on November 5, 1986, and was attended by Burns. He put together a slideshow for the occasion, "covering Hotol design aims, engineering, operations and programme plus six viewfoils [slides] of enabling technology headings (without costs or national preferences)". Gordon Lewis, presumably in his consultant role, was also present to talk about the RB.545.

Aérospatiale gave presentations on Ariane 5 and Hermes first, then it was Burns' turn. Three questions were posed afterwards by audience members: Is tyre development for the trolley critical? What would the enabling technology costs be? And what would the endurance limit be for manned operations? The answers were "Dunlop say OK", "Upwards of £5m per annum for five years" and "Not known, but can be extended as required" respectively.

Lewis then outlined the engine's features. In his summary, Burns listed just one question arising from this: "Lift the veil [of secrecy surrounding the RB.545] before February 1987?" to which there was apparently no answer.

MBB then gave a talk on Sänger, during which "nothing new [was] revealed... Aérospatiale commented 'Horus [the second stage] very expensive compared with Hermes' (it was originally conceived for vertical launch)". After this, another MBB representative discussed the BETA single-stage recoverable rocket.

A paper from Volvo describing Marianne was then distributed—though no one was there to present it—and an Italian team presented on an in-orbit transfer vehicle.

Finally, Aérospatiale wrapped up proceedings with another presentation in conjunction with Italian firm SNIA-BPD, this time on a recovery capsule. Burns reported: "Complementary to Hermes to recover hardware rather than men. (No pictures + difficult to follow in broken English, delivered in a 'we know best, being in this business longer than the rest of you' manner.) Evidently proposes to recover small payloads individually following multiple launch, not depending on US Shuttle for recovery. ('Space Courier')."

THE HOTOL SHOW

The British Interplanetary Society organised a Hotol Symposium for November 20, 1986, and were so overwhelmed by demand for tickets that it was necessary to change the venue from the society's own Conference Centre at 27/29 South Lambeth Road, London, to the Conference Theatre in Millbank Tower, Millbank, on the other side of the Thames, almost next to the Tate Gallery.

Those attending got a half-hour introduction from Roy Gibson, followed by 45 minutes on the 'Background to Hotol' by Conchie. Then, after coffee, F. A. Hewitt of Rolls-Royce spoke, presumably rather ambiguously, about 'Aerospaceplane Propulsion' for half an hour before Parkinson gave a half-hour chat on 'Why Hotol?', Wilson then matching that run-time to give a 'Hotol System Engineering Overview'. After lunch, Warton aerodynamicist Alison Wake explained Hotol's 'Aerodynamics & Re-entry', with Wilson then stepping back up to the podium to outline 'Hotol Structure Design & Systems'. Parkinson followed him to speak on 'Hotol Operations and Economics'. After tea, S. G. Andrews, from S. G. Andrews Consultants, finished up with 'An Alternative Computer Control Configuration for Hotol'.

The list of registered attendees included personnel from the California Space Institute, the RAF, Birmingham University, Dunlop, the Science Museum, Rutherford Appleton Laboratory, Logica, Mitsubishi Heavy Industries, the University of Tokyo, Bristol University, Cranfield, Fuji Heavy Industries, MBB/ERNO, the BNSC, the National Aerospace Laboratory, Kawasaki Heavy Industries, the University of Leicester, Marconi, Ishikawajima-Harima Heavy Industries, the National Space Development

9 COMMAND AND CONTROL

Automatic Control

- High-speed, safety-critical, high-reliability software.
- "Artificial intelligence" technology.
- To cope with:
  - unstable vehicle configuration.
  - rapid transition to abort flight modes in an emergency.
  - periods out of communication while on-orbit and during re-entry.
  - automatic landing.

Growth in Safety Critical Software

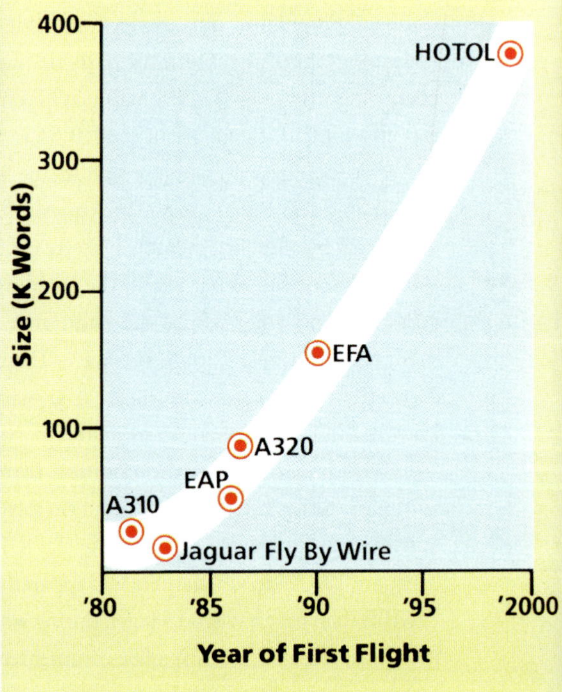

Engine Full Authority Digital Electronic Control

- Olympus 1976
- RB199 1986
- Pegasus 1987

EAP

- The British Aerospace EAP Programme has already demonstrated:
  - Unstable fly-by-wire flight control.
  - Completely digital control systems.
  - High-reliability software management.

Communications Satellite Control Electronics Unit

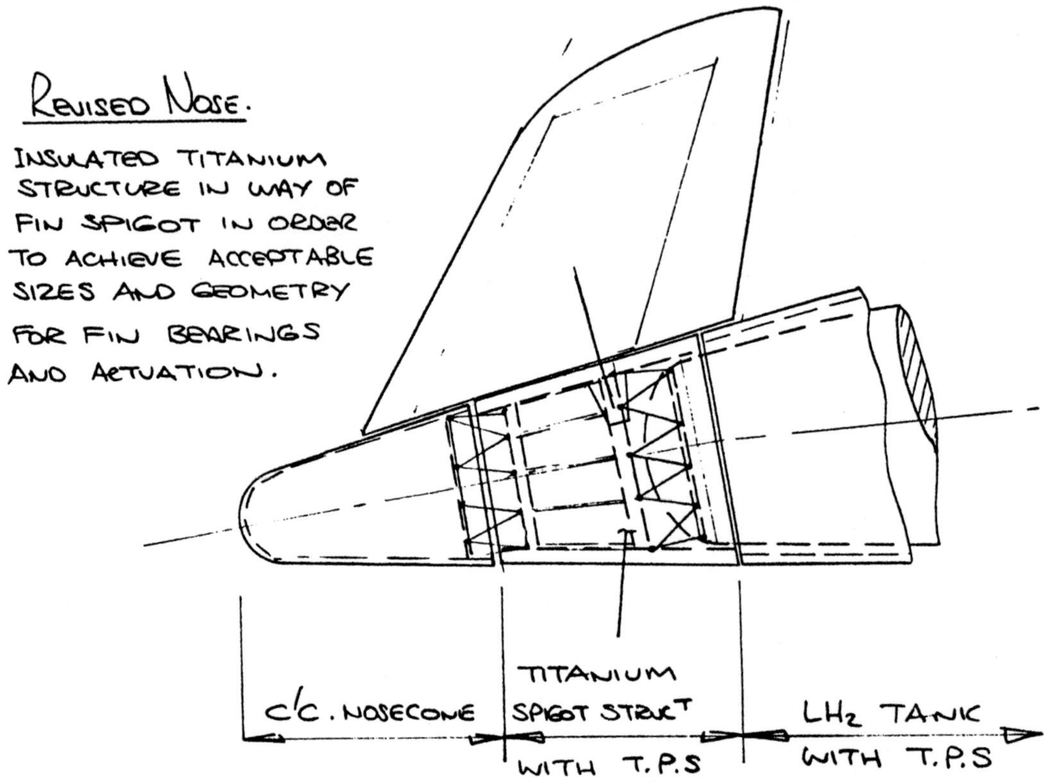

Working out how to actuate Hotol's forward fin proved tricky, given the extreme heat the mechanism would be subjected to during re-entry.

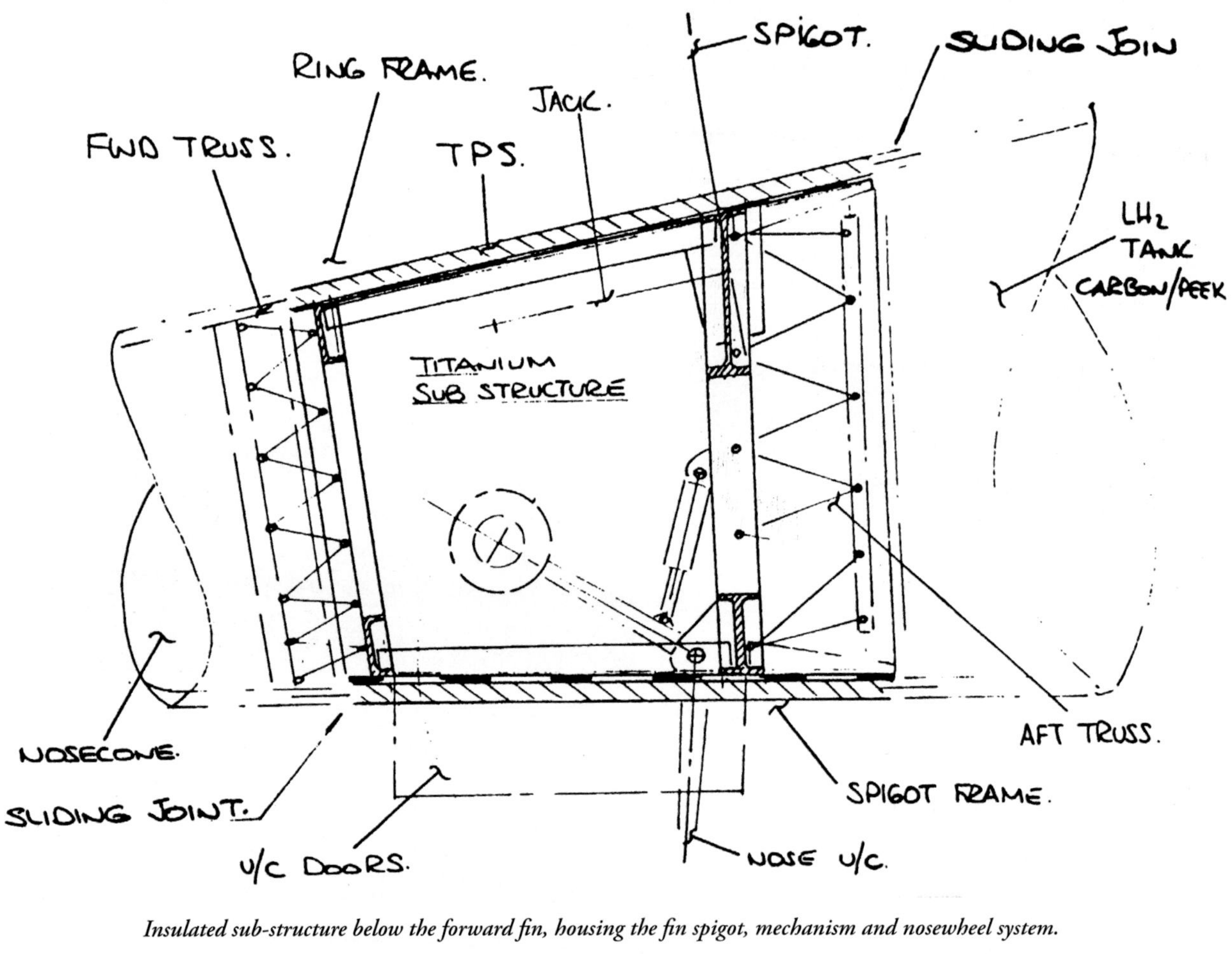

Insulated sub-structure below the forward fin, housing the fin spigot, mechanism and nosewheel system.

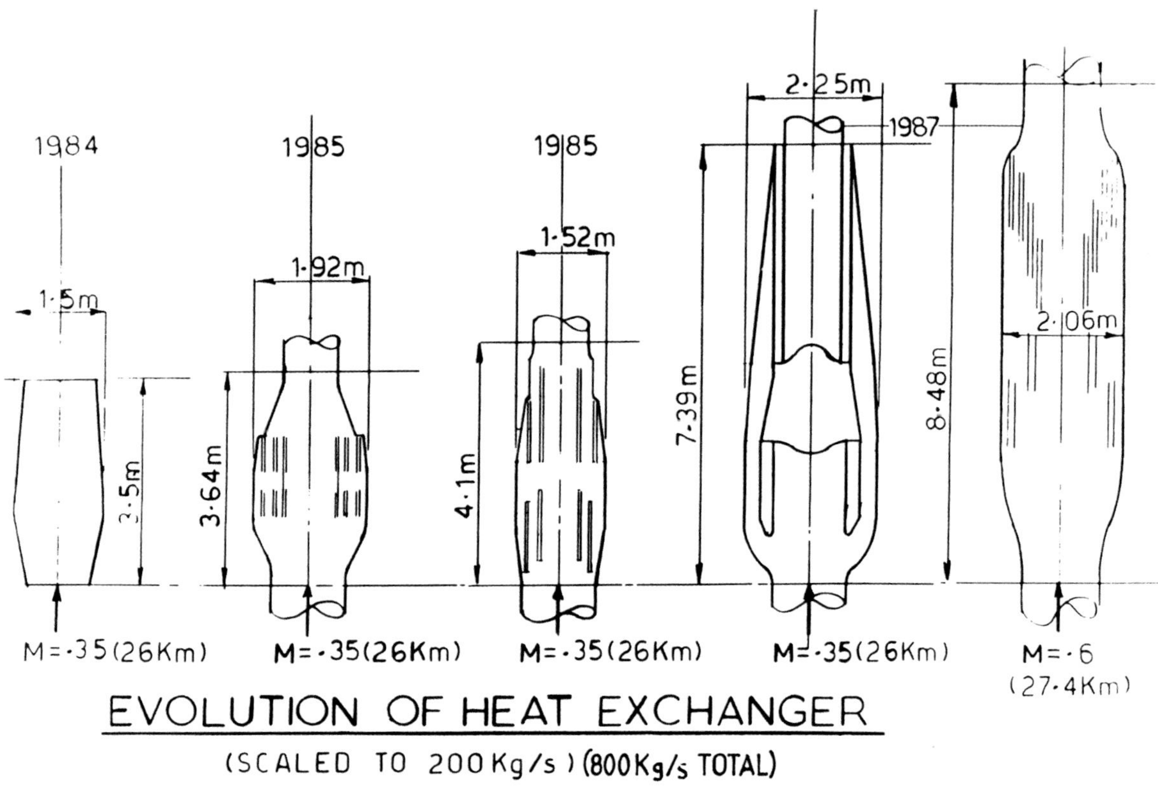

Evolution of the heat exchanger intended for Hotol's propulsion system.

Agency of Japan and ESA plus Frank Miles from ITN and Concorde's first test pilot André Turcat, yet more company and organisation representatives, BIS fellows and a limited number of ordinary BIS members.

The high number of Japanese delegates in attendance was a clear signal that, inspired by Hotol, Japan too was now waking up to the possibilities—and potential savings—offered by a SSTO vehicle.

Meanwhile, Warton and Stevenage had been hard at work on a statement of work (SOW) for Hotol's Project Definition Phase (PD1), the block of work which would follow the Proof-of-Concept Study when that came to an end in ten months' time—at the end of September 1987. Even as the company's engineers were giving their presentations in London, four representatives of each division were meeting at Stevenage to review cost estimates and the project's work breakdown structure (WBS), the division of work tasks across the firm.

In his monthly report of November 28, Burns noted that the PD1 SOW was now being circulated for comment within the Hotol team and once approved would need to be submitted to the MoD/BNSC by the end of June 1987.

Another report, an economic analysis of Hotol's future prospects, "including life cycle costs" was almost complete and once internally approved by BAe would be submitted to the MoD/BNSC by the end of January 1987.

On the aerodynamics front, testing of the low-speed Configuration F wind tunnel model was now complete and apparently "the most promising means of augmenting direction control tested was a trailing edge flap on the all moving [nose] fin which would be geared to main surface deflection at low speed. This would allow a 30-40% reduction in area, sized for the crosswind landing case. Design schemes for operation of a geared flap are now in progress of investigation; [but] hydraulic actuation is not suitable because of the temperature environment and mechanical means are being investigated".

While the possibility of a mechanically operated nose fin flap was being looked at, the trolley support points on Hotol's underside were also being reviewed with a view to preventing "excessive bending loads on the rear fuselage". A mathematical model to simulate the motion of the trolley itself and its suspension system had been formulated, taking account of potential runway gradients and roughness variations. No severe loads would be transmitted to the vehicle "provided that a tie down restraint at the tail is incorporated to prevent pitch-down loads in the aborted take-off case".

The first of the 11 heat exchanger test pieces was being tried out in the icing rig over at Ansty and another weight saving measure had been adopted: separate hydraulic systems for Hotol's nose section and rear end. Having two systems rather than a single unified one for the whole vehicle resulted in a 30% weight saving.

Stevenage had by now negotiated an enabling technology workshop proposal with MBB, which had been submitted to ESA but "Rolls-Royce have not yet produced their enabling technology plan, promised at the last steering group meeting".

DARK THOUGHTS AT RR

Gordon Lewis, having handed the reins over to Denning, was now working for Rolls-Royce as a consultant and gave a decidedly pessimistic talk to the Space Society's dinner at Café Royal, Regent Street, London, on the subject of 'Power for Hotol' on November 25.

Having outlined the project, and the company's involvement in it up to that point, he said: "The details of the engine design are classified but we have embarked on an engineering study to establish the feasibility of the key elements and to provide secure estimates of performance, weight and (above all) cost of development.

"We are looking at the test facilities needed to ensure that pre-flight testing is not a dominant part of R&D costs, and at the engineering resource that would be required to carry the programme through. We are also looking at alternatives. For example, what about using the pure rocket for take-off, followed by a ramjet, and returning to the rocket mode for entry into space? Is the two-stage vehicle a competing concept? What are the collaborative opportunities with European countries... What is the likely UK budget for such an enterprise? Is the timing such that a Hotol-like concept could compete with Ariane and Hermes?

"... From the standpoint of our company we have other questions to answer. What would be the stability of a decision to proceed, having regard to past experience in the UK in this respect? Would we build up an expert team, to the detriment no doubt of other activities, only to have the agony of disbanding it when the next government announces a rejection of 'technomania', to use a phrase from the 1960s, in favour of more immediate social services?

"In view of the scarcity in this country of highly capable engineers, would those that we have and can recruit be better devoted to defence needs and to the creation of commercial products that can earn profit in the world market place? Hotol is an exciting technical challenge, but what is the nature of the commercial business?

"Taking a sober view of the European collaborative scene there might be a need for five to eight SSTO vehicles to put in place the anticipated satellite business. This yields a requirement for 40-64 engines with spare units for a four-engined vehicle. The vehicle will require engine running times of eight to ten minutes per flight, and, to have a man-rated capability, must be assumed to survive for say 600 flights, i.e. about 100 hours per engine running time.

"The vehicle will, in effect, be subject to continuous development and improvement throughout its life since flight conditions cannot be adequately simulated on ground facilities without astronomic costs. This is not typical of the normal aero-engine business and is essentially an R&D operation, i.e. there is little production arising from the expenditure of very high-quality technological manpower.

"Rolls-Royce, as an autonomous company, would have to consider carefully how it achieved its return on investment with acceptable commercial risks. My personal view is that the main risk has to be borne by the European governments in collaboration."

Despite having helped the RB.545 get off the ground back in 1983, Lewis was perhaps echoing the view taken by Rolls-Royce's directors in late 1986—that Hotol and its engine would require a huge investment in time and manpower without actually making the company any money. Unless substantial quantities of European cash were there for the taking, corporate Rolls-Royce evidently felt it had better things to do.

RETURN TO EUROSPACE

Just two days later, Lewis was back in Paris to represent Rolls-Royce again at the Eurospace Future Prospect Group Meeting on Space Transport, this time with Wilson representing BAe.

Since Burns had already comprehensively described Hotol itself, Wilson instead provided details of the overall proposed development programme— particularly the enabling technology aspects—and the project's funding profile.

In his post-meeting summary, he reported: "In answer to questions such as why aren't hydrogen ramjets included in the propulsion technology programme, it was explained that the enabling technology programme was a basic level and had to be supported by a system study programme which ran alongside and examined the implications of the technology on the system concept, and vice-versa... Predictably, M. Villain [representing Aérospatiale] said that most of this work was already in hand for Hermes."

Lewis then presented the enabling technology programme as it applied to the RB.545 and Volvo's Ohlsen discussed Marianne. Wilson noted: "The choice of Kiruna in Sweden as a suitable polar launch site gave rise to some discussion. I mentioned that not only Marianne but also Hotol/Sänger required such a site and that in a European environment there were a number of places which could be suitable e.g. Norway, Scotland, North-West Spain."

At the end, "the chairman [Eurospace's Marcel Toussaint] summarised the proposed content of the Eurospace recommendations to ESA: support to AR5/Hermes, urgent start to future launcher enabling technology, full development of future launcher system to start in 1992 and support to Marianne proposal. Within the constraints of a committee of this sort, I felt BAe objectives had been fairly represented".

REDUCED STANDARD PROTOTYPE

Burns' next task was to provide yet another presentation—this time for the RAE and BNSC—on December 2, 1986. Various BAe staff gave talks, illustrated with overhead slide projections, "on all important subjects" and a variety of queries were fielded. The meeting summary presented these in a Q&A format:

Q. Are costs for alternative recovery sites included? A. Spare trolleys, yes, other facilities, no.

Q. Is BAe held up in any way by RR? A. Not now.

Q. Are hypersonic calculations reliable? A. CIT [Cranfield] have been very helpful and are continuing to be. Inaccuracies in calculation of forces and heating rates have to be covered by tolerances on control surface design and insulation. Improved methods are part of the proposed enabling technology plans to remove these tolerances.

Under a heading of 'manned systems', Burns noted: "Following R. W. [Roger] Longstaff's presentation on escape system operations it was mentioned that we were ahead of Hermes on this activity. (Many other adverse comments on Hermes were made in the course of the day)."

During the 'final discussion', the BAe team were asked: "What do we consider to be the most critical single aspect to be investigated in future years." The response was: "(Excluding the powerplant) materials structures manufacture and associated facilities."

Burns then had his own question for the BNSC: "How much finance can we expect to be available from BNSC for UK launch vehicle studies?" Cliff Nicholas of the BNSC had replied, with Burns recording: "BNSC are shaping a programme to suit. A figure of £120m over three years was mentioned. He confirmed that UK must be able to put in enough national effort, independent of ESA, to ensure our desired share of future activities."

Burns reported on December 4 that the proposal for a reduced standard prototype of Hotol had been raised at the steering group meeting on October 4, 1986. He wrote: "The objective is to minimise the risk in flying a full-scale prototype with four engines which have not previously flown in a novel structure and under automatic control.

"It has been discussed within the Hotol team and the following points noted: flight under rocket power would eliminate the risks associated with intake operation and malfunction of airbreathing engine components. Removal of airbreathing hardware would reduce weight provided that liquid hydrogen load is reduced to preserve centre of gravity location within limits.

"Substitution of TPS panels and hot lagging by a light alloy continuous, stressed skin structure could allow flight within a restricted envelope (say Mach 2/600 knots) if TPS panel and lagging become pacing items or to minimise risk areas.

"Nose cone, wing leading edges, intake lips and centre-body could be made in GRP or light alloy if carbon-carbon (or alternative) become pacing items.

"Take-off on landing undercarriage, probably with local reinforcement should be possible at light weight to divorce trolley risks from early flight risks.

"It is believed that the above approach would greatly reduce the number of new 'eggs in one basket' and enable aerodynamics, systems and autonomous control to be investigated with progressive expansion of the flight envelope. It is likely to extend the planned development programme by a year or so but might reduce it in reality by avoiding delays due to 'final hardware' development."

Following on from this, Wilson wrote to Burns on December 23 on the topic of 'X-Plane Rocket Demonstrator': "I think this should go in the bottom drawer, just in case the idea comes from elsewhere (actually, I have already seen it suggested in *The Times*).

"Configuration: The proposed vehicle would be a one-third scale vehicle powered either by four HM7 or two LE-5. The vehicle would be of similar length to Tornado and have an all-up-mass of 20 tonnes. Reallocation of the internal volume in the necessary proportions of a pure rocket operating with O/F of six would give 12 tonnes of propellant and a burn time of four minutes. Maximum Mach would be Mach 5+. Launch could be from an integral undercarriage, or by piggyback or underwing drop.

"Design standard: the demonstrator could go ahead on the basis of 60% Hotol technology i.e. after three years of the ET programme. It would demonstrate the structural production technology available at that time, e.g. composite cryogenic tanks, available insulations, unprotected carbon-carbon. The engines would be minimum change units modified for sea level operation: this would require the nozzle area ratio to be 'cropped' from 30 from 63 (HM7) or 140 (LE-5). Guestimated SI is 400s with a thrust of 42kN (HM7) or 70kN (LE-5).

"Rationale: The Hotol programme is different from traditional aircraft programmes in that amortised development costs make up over half the economic cost of a vehicle rather than the more usual few percent. It is important therefore not only to reduce the flight risks for the prototype but also to reduce programme risks.

"This can only be achieved by flying a demonstrator as early in the programme as possible so that lessons can be fed back as appropriate into the main programme. By starting on a demonstrator after three years of ET it should be possible to fly in 4-5 years giving several years advance on Hotol first flight. Cost could be around £500m.

"Technologies demonstrated would be: advanced materials manufacturing; unmanned and autonomous command and control; active directional control; Hotol configuration aerodynamics; autoland; horizontal propellant management; cryogenic ground operations; demonstration of these technologies would reduce both programme risk and physical risk to the Hotol prototype."

THE UNACCEPTABLE DRAFT

A full meeting of the Eurospace Future Prospect Group took place on December 10, 1986, at the headquarters of French company Air Liquide in Paris and Wilson went along with Mike Tayler from BAe Filton Space & Communications, minus a Rolls-Royce representative this time.

In his summary, Wilson wrote: "This meeting... was intended to be the final approval of the Eurospace proposal for the ESA long-term programme. The various chapters of this document should have been fully agreed at sub-group level beforehand, but this process had not been completed.

"This was particularly so in respect of the space transport chapter where the previous (and only second) sub-group meeting had been less than two weeks previously... The draft Eurospace recommendations on space transport included 'vigorous approval of present Ariane V/Hermes programme'...

"As instructed, I apologised for the unavoidable absence of Rolls-Royce and said that this recommendation was unacceptable to both BAe and RR, following up with the prepared statement from the Hotol Steering Group: 'BAe and Rolls-Royce's interest in the Ariane V and Hermes programmes is within the framework of an adequate study of the present alternatives and longer-term developments in launch vehicle technology.'

"This caused considerable furore a) because it appeared to run contrary to BNSC support to the Ariane V programme and b) because it appeared to contradict our current participation and tendering activity in the Hermes programme.

"In response and clarification, I made the following points:

i) BAe and RR are fully committed to participate in a European future launcher programme but only on the basis of a comparative and equal study of all the options.

ii) The impetus towards a new launcher was not on the basis of a natural next step from Ariane V, but arose from the urgent necessity to reduce launch costs and the shortfall in launch capacity predicted around 2000 with STS and Ariane.

iii) Hotol and Ariane V are complementary in terms of their payload capability, and their respective development programmes should not be considered as sequential, although in terms of initial operating capability Hotol is accepted to be 'post-Ariane V'."

This resulted in an "animated discussion" and it was proposed that the structure of the Eurospace proposal on space transport should be considerably changed. Tayler thought "that the matter should be referred back to the sub-group, but the chairman seemed against it, believing that the differences were fundamental and that such a meeting would not resolve them".

During the remainder of the discussion, which overran by almost three hours, it was agreed that the proposal to ESA on space transports "should highlight the urgent need for a future launcher system with economic operation and high capacity; the list of possible candidates should be on the basis of equal status; development programmes and funding profiles should show the various possibilities (i.e. 1992 or 1998 start to full development); enabling technology topics are to be couched in more generic terms and possibly identified as typical examples, e.g. for Hotol; an urgent start to enabling technology is necessary" and lastly, "BAe would propose a set of recommendations (action in hand)".

Wilson noted that there would be a final meeting of the Future Prospect Group in late January 1987 to agree the revised Eurospace proposal document and it would be finalised in February prior to an industry/ESA workshop on the latter's long-term plan in April. It was "unclear whether a further meeting of the space transport sub-group will be called".

Burns, Wilson, Webb, Furniss and Bill Dobie from BAe met F. A. Hewitt, M. Johnson and P. George from

Rolls-Royce at Warton on December 12, 1987, to discuss the RB.545's performance. It was noted that during "the early part of the PoC Study, when the definition of the powerplant performance data for the vehicle optimisation which resulted in Configuration F was defined, there was inadequate recognition and definition of engine pressure limitations.

"The installed engine performance assumed, therefore, was in excess (up to 45%) of more recent powerplant performance. Rolls-Royce stated that the level of thrust/weight used for Configuration F was quite impossible to achieve".

It was concluded that "Configuration F standard engine performance (take-off weight) cannot be achieved; the various engine performance programs/data are being correctly used; the PIG will be an official liaison group between RR and BAe". The PIG would now attempt to redefine Configuration F into something more viable.

At some point during December, a meeting was held at Rolls-Royce's corporate headquarters in 65 Buckingham Gate, Westminster, London, at which it was agreed that a joint BAe/RR report should be prepared for Pattie on the position of the project, now that two-thirds of the PoC had been completed.

Hotol had reached the end of 1986 as the increasingly contentious Configuration F—with wind tunnel models of that design being tested. The materials it would be manufactured from, however, remained unclear. Unhappy with the 'shorter, fatter' Hotol, Parkinson was becoming increasingly vocal in his opposition to Configuration F, while Rolls-Royce's board of directors could hardly have appeared less enthusiastic about the project, short of withdrawing their support all together. Nevertheless, BAe personnel continued press ahead with determination on all fronts.

5

POPULAR MYTHS: JANUARY 1 TO JUNE 10, 1987

Just nine months remained of the Hotol Proof-of-Concept Study at the beginning of 1987 and preparations continued for the next-step Project Definition Phase.

BAe's proposed wording for the Eurospace space transport proposal to ESA was sent to Toussaint by Wilson on January 9 and five days later Burns wrote to Parkinson, clearing up some technical queries the latter had raised.

Firstly, Parkinson wondered how, and how often, Hotol's fuel tanks would be checked for cracks given the aeroshell of interlocking TPS plates that completely covered them. Burns responded: "We envisage that during routine operation the tanks would be pressure tested between flights. If a crack is evident [due to a loss of pressure], then it would be necessary to remove the TPS, fit the external frame, depressurise and locate the cracks prior to repair, i.e. go inside only when essential."

Other queries concerned outgassing, noise levels in the rear fuselage, liquid oxygen tank support, the locking mechanism for the load-bearing payload bay doors, the use of carbon-PEEK for pipework, the use of aluminised Mylar for insulation, additional new materials, fin sizing, full-scale structural testing (only sections would be tested — not complete components) and bird strike ("I do not agree that it is important to define the numerical probability during the PoC Study").

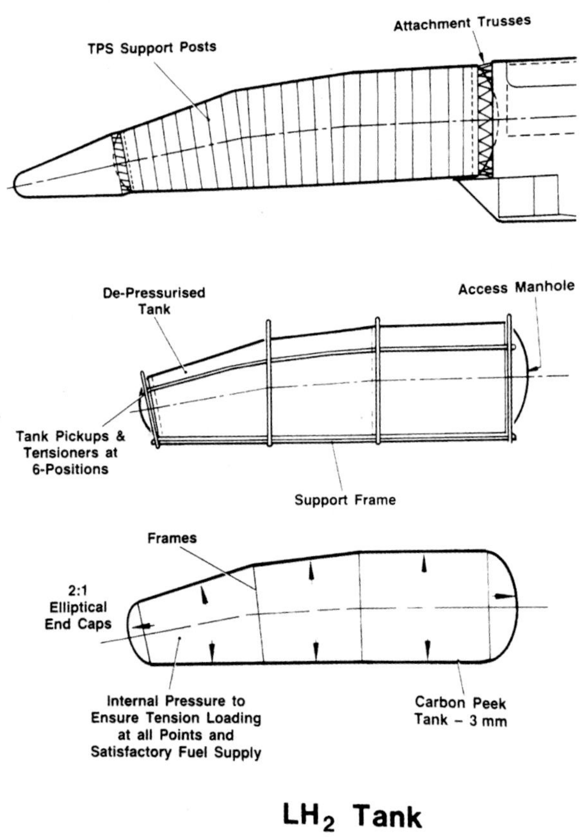

Detail of Hotol's liquid hydrogen tank with TPS panels removed. Depressurised, it would require a support frame to retain its shape.

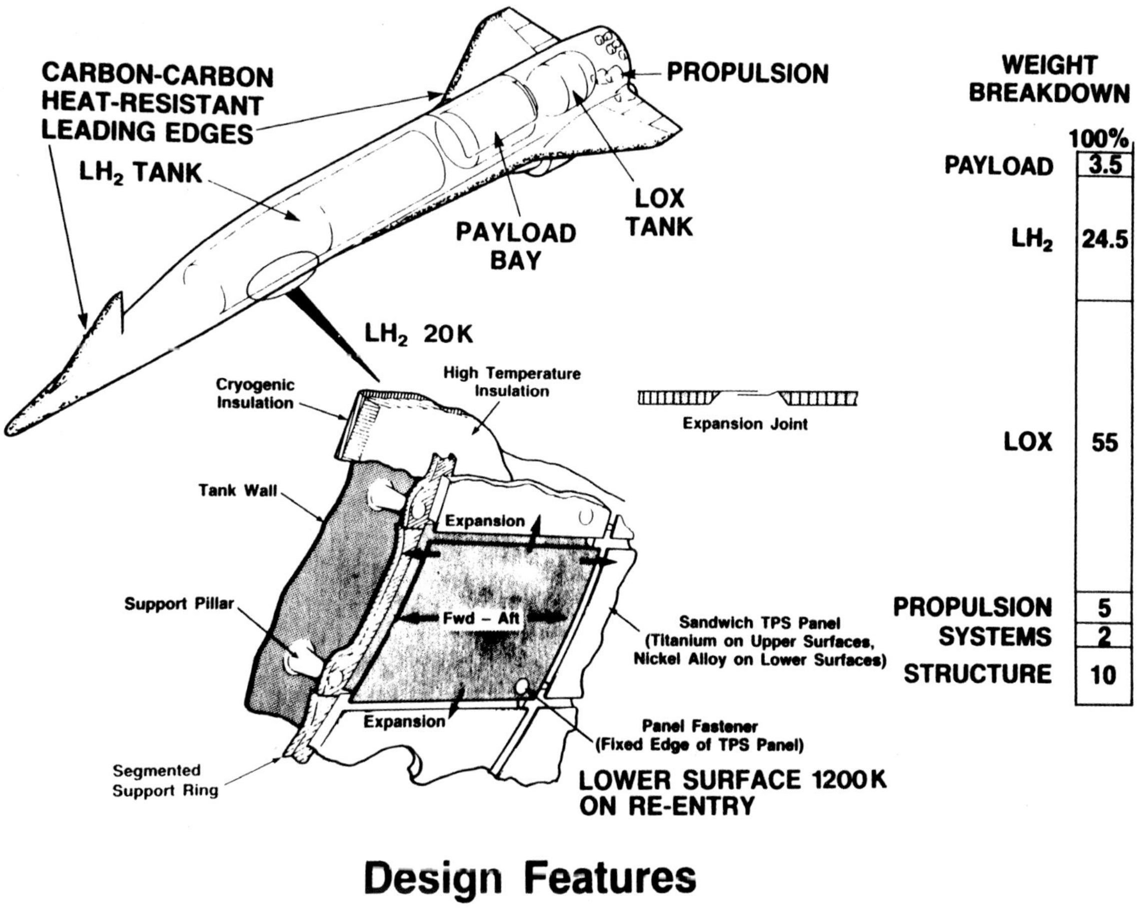

Diagram from an early 1987 report showing an even earlier version of Hotol, with the original annular intake design, and a payload cited as 3.5 tonnes.

Lygo wrote to Yates on the same day, instructing him to set up another personal Hotol presentation. This time though, "it would be useful if this could be done in conjunction with Rolls-Royce and a suitable date could be fixed when both [Rolls-Royce CEO] Ralph Robins and I could receive the presentation together. I believe it is important to be brought up to date before the Europeans begin to be brought into the picture, which I understand is later in March".

Brian Young was copied in on the letter and forwarded his copy to Burns with a handwritten note at the bottom: "I guess mid-Feb but I am sure the process will have to be: 1) Agreement of content with Rolls-Royce (Brian Young/Hugh Hillier). 2) Presentation rehearsal with Ivan Yates. 3) Presentation with Sir Raymond Lygo/Ralph Robins." A further handwritten note had also been added, addressed to Young: "Will RL [Raymond Lygo] want to see ALVs [Alternative Launch Vehicles]?"

Rapid progress was now being made on a host of CAPS-derived alternative launch vehicle configurations—some closely related to the baseline Hotol Configuration F, others being much more extreme concepts which had little in common with the original vehicle. See Chapter 6.

Lygo's reference to "the Europeans" was an acknowledgement of the enabling technology workshop that Stevenage and MBB had jointly arranged with ESA—which was due to take place in Rome on March 18-19.

HOTOL TEAM TALLY

Burns' monthly report, issued on January 29, 1987, noted that at the end of 1986 a total of 66 full-time equivalent personnel had been working on Hotol: 50 at Warton (that figure being artificially boosted by the ongoing wind tunnel work), 9.5 at Stevenage and 6.5 at Filton. The average staffing throughout the year had been 37.5.

A total of £586,000 had been received by BAe from the British government, which represented 12% under-funding up to the end of 1986 based on the 50/50 cost sharing that was supposed to be taking place. BAe had therefore spent £665,909 during the course of the project—the combined total spend, excluding RR's side of the project, being approximately £1.25m.

The PIG, assessing the propulsion system, had

Frontal view of the Configuration F-based model SB2 in Warton's guided weapons wind tunnel.

SB2 top and side views.

determined that the engine and intake would be two tonnes heavier than expected. In aerodynamics, testing of the Configuration F-based Hotol high-speed wind tunnel model, known as SB2, in the Warton 1.2m tunnel had begun ahead of schedule in the third week of 1987. At the end of the fifth week, a free-flow intake would be fitted to the model and further testing would commence both in the 1.2m and guided weapons tunnels over the full Mach range.

Each Hotol wind tunnel model had a three-character code, beginning with an 'S' for Space, then the configuration freeze (not directly related to the Hotol configuration sequence)—'A' was the first freeze, at Configuration C, then 'B' was the second freeze, at Configuration F. Then there was a number denoting the type of testing the model would be used for—1 for low Mach number tests, 2 for transonic and/or supersonic and 3 for hypersonic.

So the first model SA1 (pictured in Chapter 3) was 'Space/design freeze A/low Mach number tests'. SB1 (pictured in Chapter 4) was 'Space/design freeze B/low Mach number tests'. Therefore, SB2 was 'Space/design freeze B/transonic and/or supersonic tests'.

In terms of structure, investigations had indicated that using carbon-carbon for the wing structure would save 480kg of mass. Representatives of ICI and American firm Fiberite had visited Warton for a meeting on January 26

Schlieren photo from testing of SB2.

and the "US specialist on carbon-carbon offered the opinion that although carbon-carbon is not yet a proven structural material the chances of it becoming so in the next five years are 'excellent'. However, a chain of companies involved in the different stages of processing needs to be set up to ensure that this happens". Carbon-PEEK was now being investigated for use in the centre and rear fuselage.

Lastly came the trolley: "Preliminary structural design of the trolley has led to a projected mass of 35 tonnes, plus a further 27 tonnes for propulsion, systems and fuel." This was going to be one big trolley. Furthermore, "some deficiencies in the structural design, notably stiffness, were identified but further work is in abeyance due to concentration on airframe design matters".

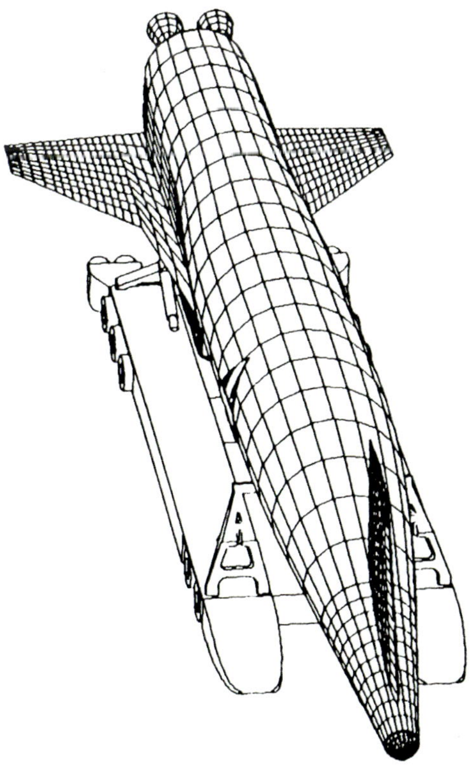

Digital model of Hotol Configuration F with launch trolley designed using Dassault's CATIA software.

At this time Australia had aspirations to build a spaceport on the Cape York peninsula in Far North Queensland and BAe Australia space systems manager Gordon Briggs had written to Burns to enquire about the runway length Hotol would need.

Burns responded, also on January 29: "Hotol runway safety distance for rejected take-off case is 3,500m. Normal landing is about half that but we have to assess Autoland scatter by simulation. Peter Conchie will be visiting Australia [on] February 10-12 and will discuss other requirements."

POTENTIAL EUROPEAN PARTNERS

The first draft of the BAe contribution to the joint BAe/RR report to Pattie, arising from the December meeting in Buckingham Gate, was sent to RR's Hugh Hillier by Burns on February 9. However, he told Hillier: "Although the action was nominally due to be completed by the end of January 1987, we now feel that it should not be submitted until after the review by Sir Raymond Lygo and Mr R. H. Robins on March 11, 1987."

Burns' joint report submission rattled through the project staffing, the state of the vehicle design and the economic case for Hotol in its completed form before getting to the benefits of the enabling technology research proposals that were about to be put to potential European partners: "Enabling technology—airframe: one of the objectives of the PoC Study is to identify areas of high technical risk and propose programmes to investigate these matters. In parallel with the proposed definition phase of Hotol, it is proposed that there should be a three-year programme of enabling technology studies forming a basis for future development work.

"Although BAe and MBB have rival projects (Hotol and Sänger), there is a high degree of agreement between the two companies regarding future technology requirements and Aeritalia are also in agreement with the proposals which come under the following major headings: Materials and structures—carbon-carbon for elevated temperatures; thermoplastic composites for reusable cryogenic fuel tanks; fibre-reinforced and rapid-solidifying alloys for high strength/weight ratio. Aerodynamics including heating effects: hypersonic computational methods; wind tunnel facilities and instrumentation. Command and control for unmanned flight including ground infrastructure: advanced systems architecture; intelligent knowledge-based systems; high order high integrity computer languages.

"An enabling technology programme was prepared by

BAe in August 1986 and has been distributed to RAE and BNSC. The subject has also been discussed with representatives of ESA with a favourable reaction. A 'workshop' meeting is planned to take place in Rome in March 1987. At this meeting representatives from BAe, Rolls-Royce, other UK suppliers, and continental companies, notably MBB, AIT [Aeritalia], Aerospatiale and AMDBA [Dassault-Breguet] offer papers on subjects for which funding will be sought from ESA. The scale of the ESA funding has not been confirmed but is believed to be in the region of 40 to 60 MAU per annum over the next few years.

"Concluding remarks: two third of the way through the PoC Study all major milestones have been achieved. There is a high degree of commitment by all personnel involved in the project. It is believed that refinement of the design during the remainder of the study period and the adoption of advanced technology features will place us in a commanding position vis a vis alternative projects and give us confidence to proceed with the definition phase in parallel with the enabling technology programmes.

"It is proposed that ESA should: 1. Propose and develop a requirement for a future European spaceplane programme fulfilling the following roles: satellite launch and recapture; satellite maintenance; space platform logistic support; microgravity and other research. 2. Manage industrial studies and assess the relative merits of alternative designs to meet the requirement. 3. Manage the enabling technology studies."

The prospect of establishing joint tech development projects with European aerospace companies, overseen by ESA, was very attractive and had manifold potential benefits. Besides developing actual technology that could be used as part of the Hotol programme, it would attract funding, raise Hotol's profile and encourage the other European nations to regard Hotol as something they wanted to be a part of.

HOW MUCH PER HOTOL?

Warton's chief cost estimator for new projects, Richard McNally, wrote to Burns on March 2 to provide a revised estimate on what each Hotol vehicle would actually cost to manufacture. His covering letter said: "Following receipt of some unofficial information from Rockwell on Shuttle manufacturing costs, both Stevenage and ourselves have revised our production costs for Hotol ... I thought you should be aware of the growth in the Warton estimate from £185m to £235m. This is almost entirely due to the cost information provided by Rockwell of the production costs of the Thermal Protection Tiles. We have related this cost to the Thermal Protection Tile mass of Hotol and this has largely influenced this increase. I have provided the detailed calculations to Stevenage ... in order to assist them in their estimates."

On the original copy of the letter, the £185m was circled with an associated note: "Airframe + engines (no trolley)?"

McNally's full statement on Hotol's per-unit cost said: "Warton have carried out a similar exercise to that conducted by Stevenage in appraising the Hotol vehicle production unit cost taking into account recently acquired Shuttle Orbiter data.

"The Warton analysis gives a good agreement with Stevenage for a direct read across the Shuttle Orbiter data and suggests that the cost of manufacturing Hotol in the USA using manufacturing technology appropriate to the late 60s is in the region of £500m, per unit.

"However, after adjusting for future enhancements in manufacturing technology, and product complexity, the average unit cost of manufacturing Hotol in the UK is estimated by Warton to be: £235m. This represents a 25% increase on our previous estimate and a realistic top figure taking into account the Shuttle data would appear to be £300m."

ORIGINATORS' ORIGIN

A meeting chaired by Ivan Yates evidently took place on March 3, 1987, at which, according to Parkinson, "a task was placed on the originators of the Hotol concept to compare the current design proposals with the original 'back of the envelope' studies, with the intention of establishing whether current problems in generating a viable design are the product of greater realism in the studies, or the loss of some critical feature in the design.

"The current situation on design presented by Warton as a consequence of CAPS modelling is generally accepted as unsatisfactory, with an all-up mass of 300t only achievable by assuming a high limit to rocket specific impulse and an 85% 'optimism' on structure masses as the limit believed achievable with advanced materials.

"As its part in the 'Originators' Group' investigation the BAe Space and Comms. Division Hotol team at Stevenage [was to carry] out the following investigations: i) Visit to Warton to understand the methodology of the CAPS approach to vehicle modelling. ii) Investigation of typical CAPS output provided by Warton to match the results to a qualitative understanding of the vehicle behaviour. iii) Correlation of CAPS performance estimates with a Stevenage performance assessment system. iv) Correlation of the original Stevenage mass model with the Configuration

F mass studies. v) A brief assessment of vehicle base drag/plume interactions. vi) An attempt to recalculate the original Filton 'ELV' configuration performance using recalculated drag data provided by Filton and a mass model correlated with Configuration F."

Parkinson now had official authorisation to investigate Configuration F and was determined to work out how it had come to exist, what its specific problems were and how these could be resolved.

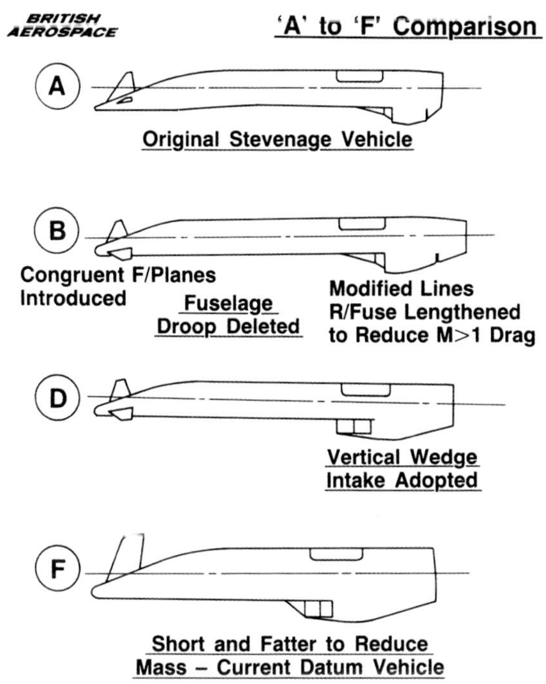

Comparison chart showing the evolution from Configuration A—the design presented to BAe Warton by BAe Stevenage at the beginning of the former's involvement—to Configuration F.

THE PIG'S INTAKE

Burns' March 5, 1987, monthly report to Yates noted that Deller of the RAE "has proposed that BAe apply to BNSC for a six-month extension to the PoC Study, to lead into the next phase". In addition, the enabling technology timetable had been stepped up—with the workshop in Rome now set for March 16-17. BAe Warton would present six Hotol-relevant papers, Stevenage another six and Filton one, out of a total of 67 papers.

He further reported that the PIG had produced an optimum engine cycle and intake, albeit associated with an ascent which terminated at a higher altitude. As such, "intake area is increased by 75% but design pressure reduced by 65%... Variable intake geometry and sharp lips are required to minimise intake drag. Compared with the previous propulsion model, which ignored certain important engine limits, 'target' dry mass is increased by about two tonnes (ungrown), for the same airbreathing fuel fraction... measures to recover performance include utilising the unburnt hydrogen turbine exhaust, a 'spill ramjet' and, more radically, liquid oxygen enrichment of airbreathing".

The joint BAe/RR tour of US advanced materials manufacturers first mooted in October 1986 had now taken place and this had "confirmed the view expressed by Fiberite... that protected carbon-carbon for major airframe structure would become available within five years. A meeting with Dunlop confirmed their intention to develop carbon-carbon for structural application in cooperation with BAe, subject to UK funding and protection for their intellectual property rights.

"Investigation of advanced materials has led to a preference for titanium reinforced with particulates for wing, centre and rear fuselage and fin structure, being lighter than carbon-carbon or insulated carbon-PEEK. Reinforced titanium, together with carbon-carbon TPS panels, smaller fin with geared flap, carbon-carbon sandwich nosecone and leading edges is predicted to result in a mass saving of about 15%."

Tests of the SB2 wind tunnel model up to Mach 3 with both blocked and free-flow 'intakes' attached had been completed and the results showed drag values in line with predictions but difficulties with pitch control, particularly at high Mach. Whether this degree of instability was acceptable was "to be checked".

'SIGNIFICANTLY WORSE' THAN BEFORE

Even as Burns was producing his update, Parkinson and Bond were holding an ad hoc 'Hotol—Originators Working Group' meeting.

According to Parkinson's summary of this get-together: "Our observation is that the Rolls-Royce engine cycle studies have shown that the initial predictions for engine performance (specific impulse) and mass have been confirmed or slightly improved upon, and that opportunities exist to further reduce mass and provide additional thrust in key flight regimes.

"Our assessment of the vehicle structural design is that Warton have improved the specific mass of all components over the initial assumptions (we believe even for the same shape of vehicle), but that additional mass has had to be added for the intake over the initial assumption. The forward fin has also grown, but it is not clear whether this will not shrink again if crosswind limits are reduced in line with conditions existing in the equatorial zone. In addition

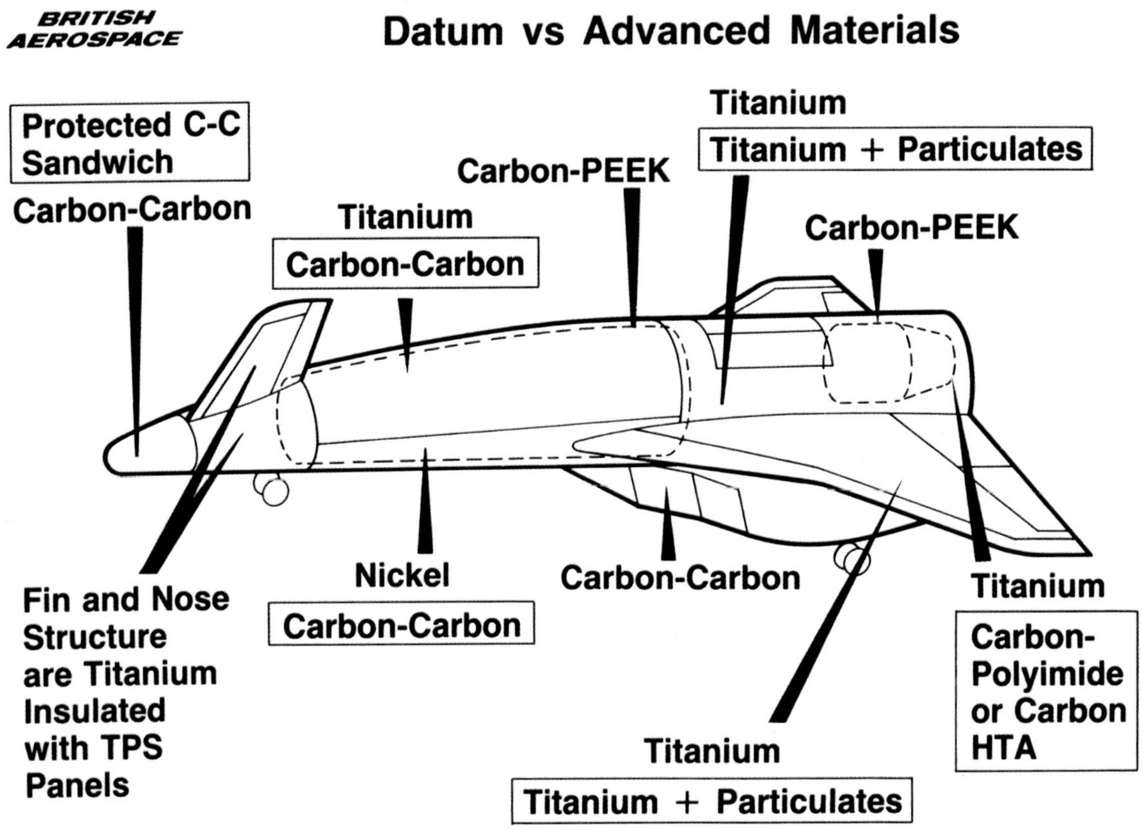

Diagram showing the advanced materials under consideration for Hotol circa March 1987—including titanium reinforced with particulates.

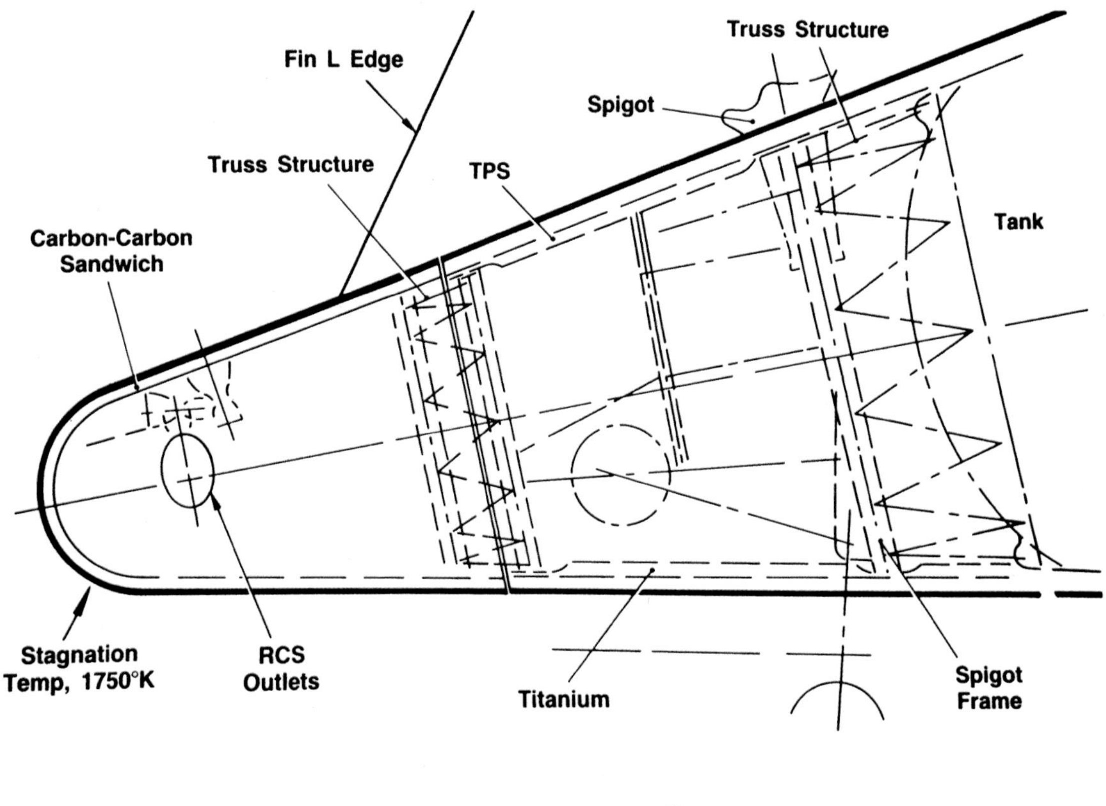

Hotol Configuration F nose cone arrangement.

to the structural mass reduction, propellant storage pressures and residuals have been reduced with significant mass saving. Despite the above, the predicted performance of the vehicle is significantly worse than originally."

Essentially, the originators believed that by switching from the original long, slender, Filton-derived Configuration D shape to the shorter, fatter, Configuration F, Warton had increased drag to a point where the vehicle could no longer perform as intended.

Parkinson went on: "Airbreathing propulsion was proposed for Hotol on the basis that the performance would be superior to a rocket, and unless the vehicle can operate at higher lift/drag values, no improvements in structure mass will give a case for airbreathing propulsion ... As a minor corollary to the above, we observe that wing body setting, body camber, wash out and other wing curvatures originally proposed by Filton have all been abandoned in the current design ... We also observe, without being able to interpret the consequences, that Warton appear to hold the wing size constant while varying the vehicle size in establishing optima, and this represents a change from the starting point."

Bond then wrote a pessimistic letter to Hillier at

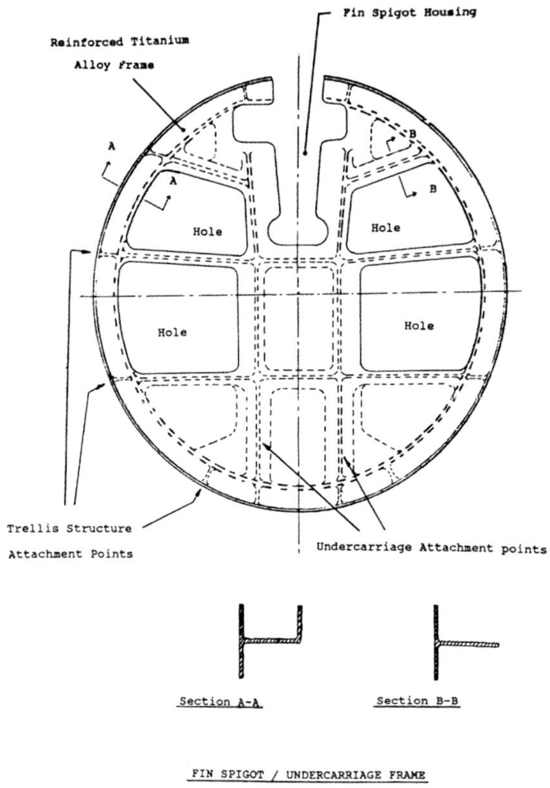

Cross-sectional view of the nose cone fin spigot/nosewheel housing frame.

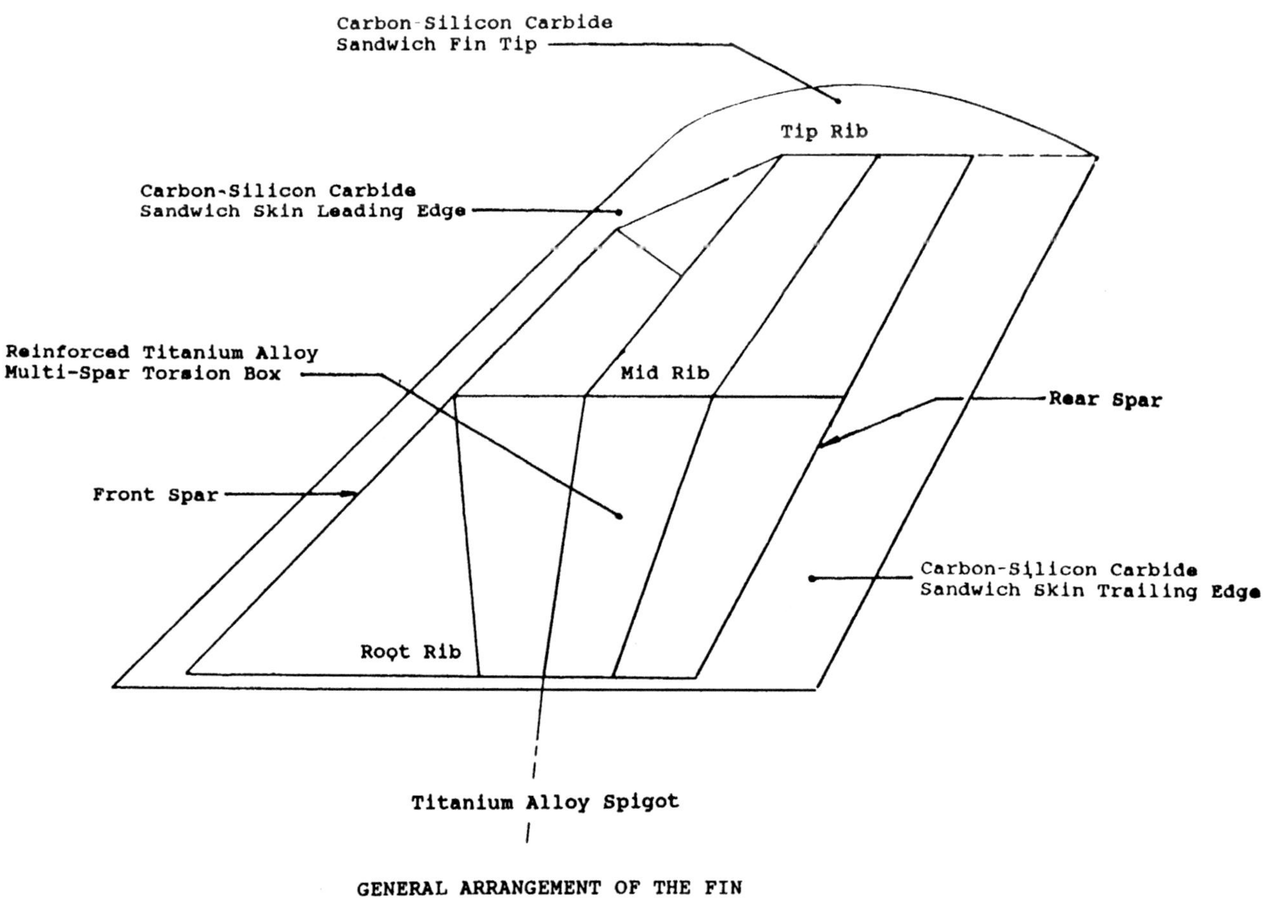

Structural detail of Configuration F's fin.

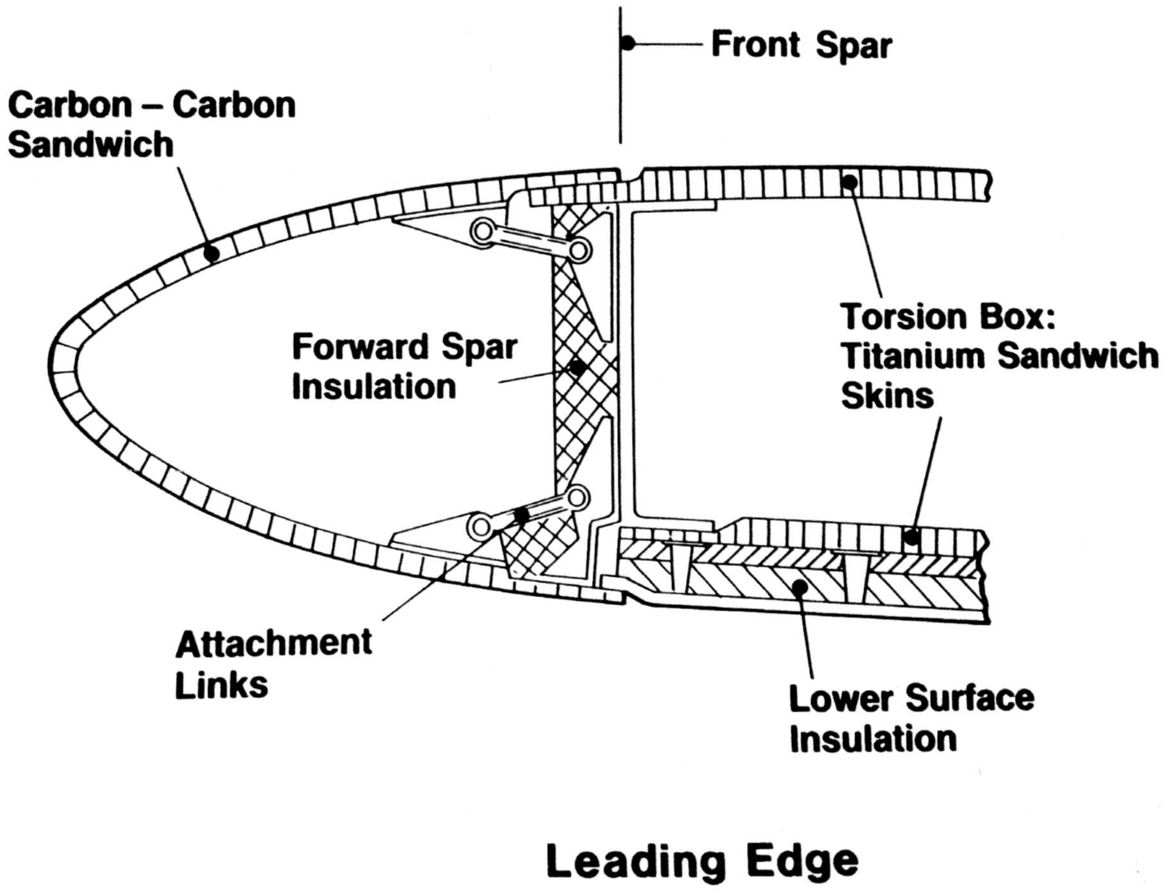

Wing leading edge internal structure.

Rolls-Royce on March 9, saying: "I have produced this note at the request of Ralph Denning in order that I should have on paper my view of the current situation on Hotol, namely that with the Warton design the project appears to be infeasible. This conclusion is, of course, at total variance to those which we reached at the pre-project phase and on which the approach to Government was made for funding to carry out a feasibility study.

"The difference between the two vehicle designs appears to lie in the estimation of drag and structural weight. In both vehicle studies, the performance characteristics of the engine in terms of total system mass per unit thrust and thrust per unit fuel flow have remained unchanged. However, airframe drag and airframe bare mass appear to have increased somewhat above those that were estimated in the original study.

"The reasons for this unfavourable change appear to be unclear at the present time and I am carefully studying all the contributing components to assess which estimate is correct. The Warton study surprisingly regards drag as relatively unimportant. This was not our conclusion during the pre-project study nor is it my conclusion at the present time. Drag has several effects. It increases the engine mass required to achieve a given acceleration and hence to minimise the losses on the trajectory. Further, it pushes up the altitude at which the vehicle must operate in order to keep the total of induced and basic drag to a minimum.

"The overall result of this is a larger hydrogen tank which in itself contributes to the increased drag and also a larger intake which contributes substantially to the increased mass, especially since the intake mass is one of the masses which was underestimated in the pre-project phase.

"A major factor which has contributed to the increased drag on the Warton Configuration F vehicle is the increase in body diameter and reduction in slenderness ratio with the fuselage. Their conclusion is that a high fineness ratio fuselage has a very substantial weight penalty associated with it due to the mass of the aeroshell and the thermal insulation system to protect the hydrogen tank during re-entry.

"This change to slenderness ratio has been the major change from the original pre-project study. I must confess that I have failed to find any such sensitivity and that the trade-off in engine mass greatly exceeds any trade-off due to variation in aeroshell mass when changing vehicle diameter. Thus, I would still conclude that a slender body was the correct shape to have."

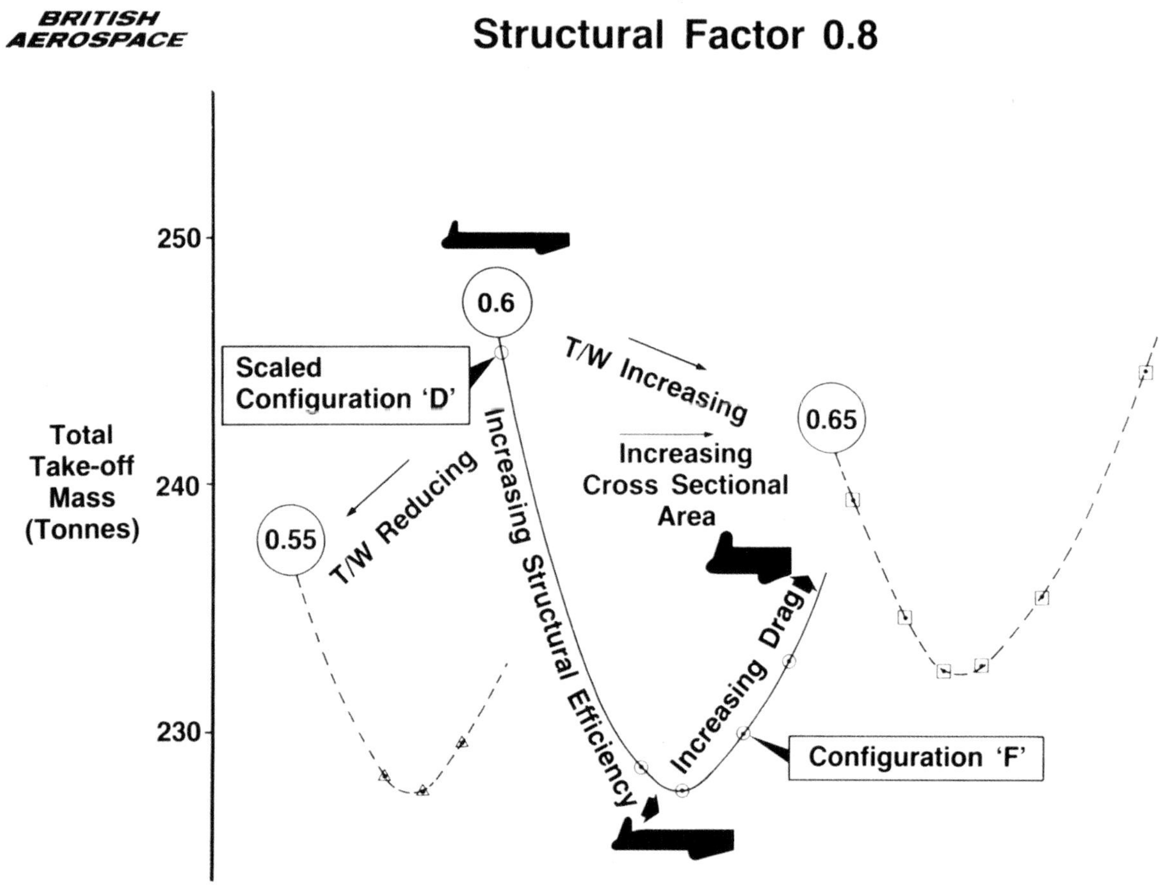

Chart showing the take-off weight and drag considerations which led to the evolution of the long slender Configuration D into the shorter, fatter, Configuration F design.

He acknowledged that the omission of thermal insulation for the hydrogen tank was a major oversight in the original pre-project study but thought that "the structural improvements that Warton have instigated would almost certainly have absorbed this", and the air intake mass was also "grossly underestimated by a factor of two or so".

Nevertheless, "a major question of course is where do we go from here. Warton are of the opinion that the answer to this problem is a higher thrust to weight ratio engine and I am sure that this would solve the problem. However, the sort of improvement in thrust to weight that they are asking for with no penalty in specific impulse I believe to be impractical. As I am sure you are aware, we have several improvements in weight in the pipeline. This, however, will not double the thrust to weight ratio of the engine.

"My own view is that the correct thing to do is to reduce the requirement for thrust in the first place and therefore install a lower engine mass. This comes about by reducing the basic vehicle drag and then re-optimising the trajectory to capitalise on that... The area in which the current vehicle is most primitive is in its aerodynamic design. The pre-project vehicle had a number of sophisticated innovations in the aerodynamics. These have all been discarded by Warton in an attempt to keep the vehicle mass to a minimum. The merit of these innovations needs re-examining."

In short, Bond also wanted the long, slender Hotol form back.

ESCAPING HOTOL

Brian A. Miller, head of marketing at Martin-Baker Aircraft, responded to Wilson's letter of the previous October on March 10, 1987, to outline a "concept for an encapsulated escape system suitable for Hotol". He went on: "In view of the very high Mach numbers involved, we do not believe that a conventional ejection seat will be suitable. In order to reduce stagnation temperatures it will be essential to have as streamlined a shape as possible and we have, therefore, fully enclosed the man for this purpose".

A set of diagrams were included with the letter, showing "an alternative shuttered clamshell and a single piece carapace. I feel the shuttered version is to be preferred because it is more easily operated and stowed. The single piece clamshell has better structural integrity and is, of course, simpler in design but introduces problems of stowage when not in use".

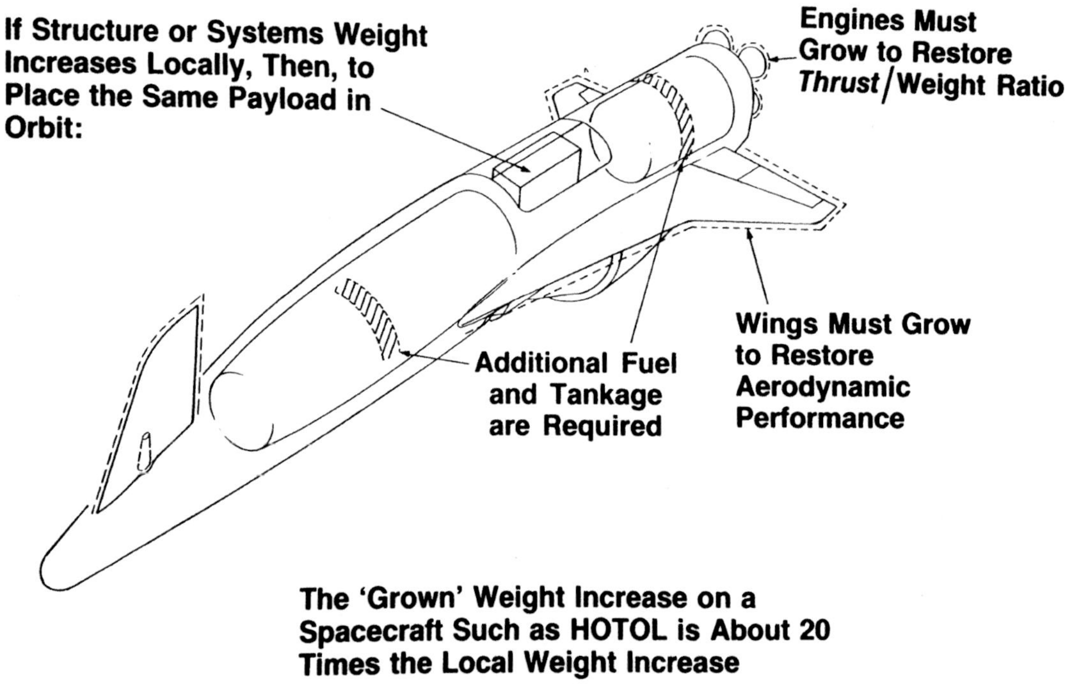

Weight Growth

Diagram, using an older picture of Hotol, illustrating the difficulties inherent in trying to keep the vehicle's weight down.

The first shuttered clamshell diagram showed a very compact pod design which wrapped neatly around a seated crew member wearing a full pressure suit with legs bent at the knee and arms down by their sides. The pod incorporated a segmented composite clamshell which dropped neatly downwards in front of the crew member, a rocket ejection system, life support package, aerodynamic heatshield, parachute container and parachute deployment rocket.

A second diagram showed the pod launch sequence at low speed, with the clamshell itself remaining undeployed. A third and fourth showed a high-speed, high-altitude launch—with the clamshell dropping immediately prior to launch. Just as Miller had said, in the diagram illustrating the single-piece 'carapace' design there was nowhere for the fairing to go when not in use.

CONCEPT VALIDATION

Deller's notion of a PoC Study extension gained further currency at a contracts meeting held on March 12, 1987. In an undated memo to Conchie, Burns said BAe had been "invited to propose a work programme to follow the PoC Study of six to nine months duration, provisionally titled Concept Validation (CV). To make a sensible proposal, we need to know the long-term planning assumptions for the phases which would follow the proposed CV Study."

Plans already agreed with Rolls-Royce at a steering group meeting on December 9 had made provision for a preliminary Hotol prototype first flight at the end of 1997 with the full standard production model vehicle being ready by the end of 1999. However, "there is apparently, as reported in *Air & Cosmos* of March 14, 1987, (copy attached) a 'FESTIP' programme which would imply later dates. Does that programme have any official status? We require your guidance on this matter prior to holding a meeting between the three sites involved and possibly RR to get our act together."

The Future European Space Transportation Investigations Programme (FESTIP) was a new ESA project intended to review the technical feasibility and commercial viability of launcher concepts. While its origin was in 1987, the actual programme would not formally commence for another seven years.

On March 16, Burns sent another memo, this time to Young, on the subject of 'divisional strategy input'. This began by reiterating the Hotol concept, its purpose and the basic terms of the PoC contract, then went on: "Latest indications from BNSC/RAE sources suggest a six to nine month 'bridging phase' between PoC and PD1. Commencing on October 1, 1987, this should allow time for: European (ESA) and National (BNSC) funding strategies to be determined; a greater level of confidence to

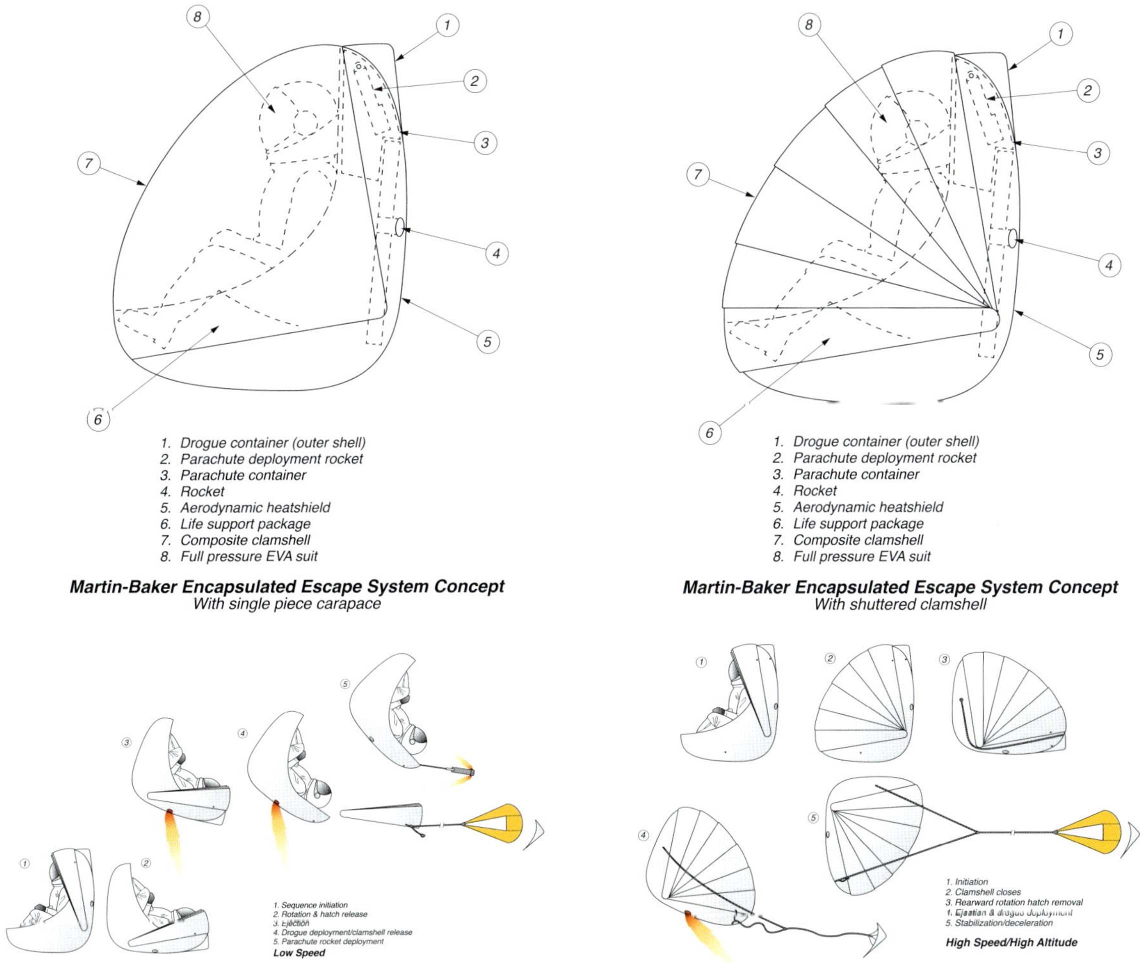

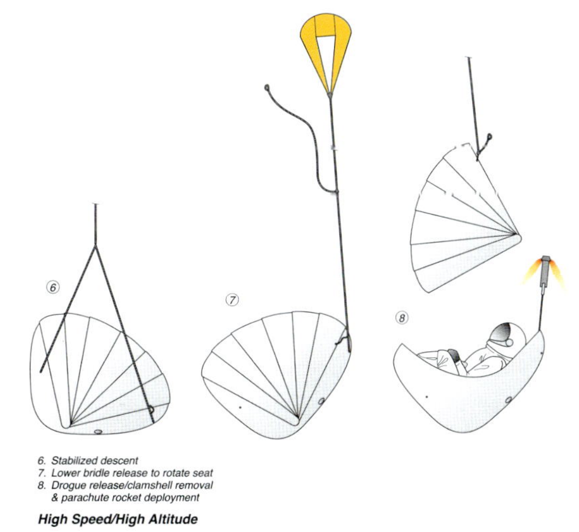

Diagrams showing the proposed Martin-Baker encapsulated escape system for Hotol. GRAHAME CHAMBERS

be achieved in respect of the propulsion system, before embarking on a full Project Definition (PD1) programme.

"For the airframe, the main task is to design a light structure, recognising the high growth factor in space vehicles and that cost is closely related to size/mass. For the engine the major hurdle is ensuring freedom from icing on the critical components. Market projections envisage a fleet size of four or five unmanned vehicles for satellite operations. Manned operations, with a habitable capsule in the payload bay, could follow, once vehicle integrity is established, for Space Platform transit operations and research activities. These might require a further two vehicles.

"The cost of the overall development programme is estimated to be in the region of £4 billion. It is envisaged as a European collaborative programme with UK leadership and a 25-30% share of the work. Overtures to possible European partner nations, Germany, Italy, France, Holland, Spain and Sweden have been made at Secretary of State/BAe director level during 1986. UK/BAe preferences are for: programme leadership, avionics/software control, a significant share of manufacturing. Location of the combined final assembly and flight test centre is bound to influence work-sharing and management decisions.

"It is also recognised that the scale of the Hotol project will exceed the management capability of the ESA and so an industrial management consortium will be required. The project was reviewed by the managing directors of BAe and Rolls-Royce on March 11, 1987, and a further review is planned for June 1987. A presentation to the Secretary of State is planned in the near future...a four-year

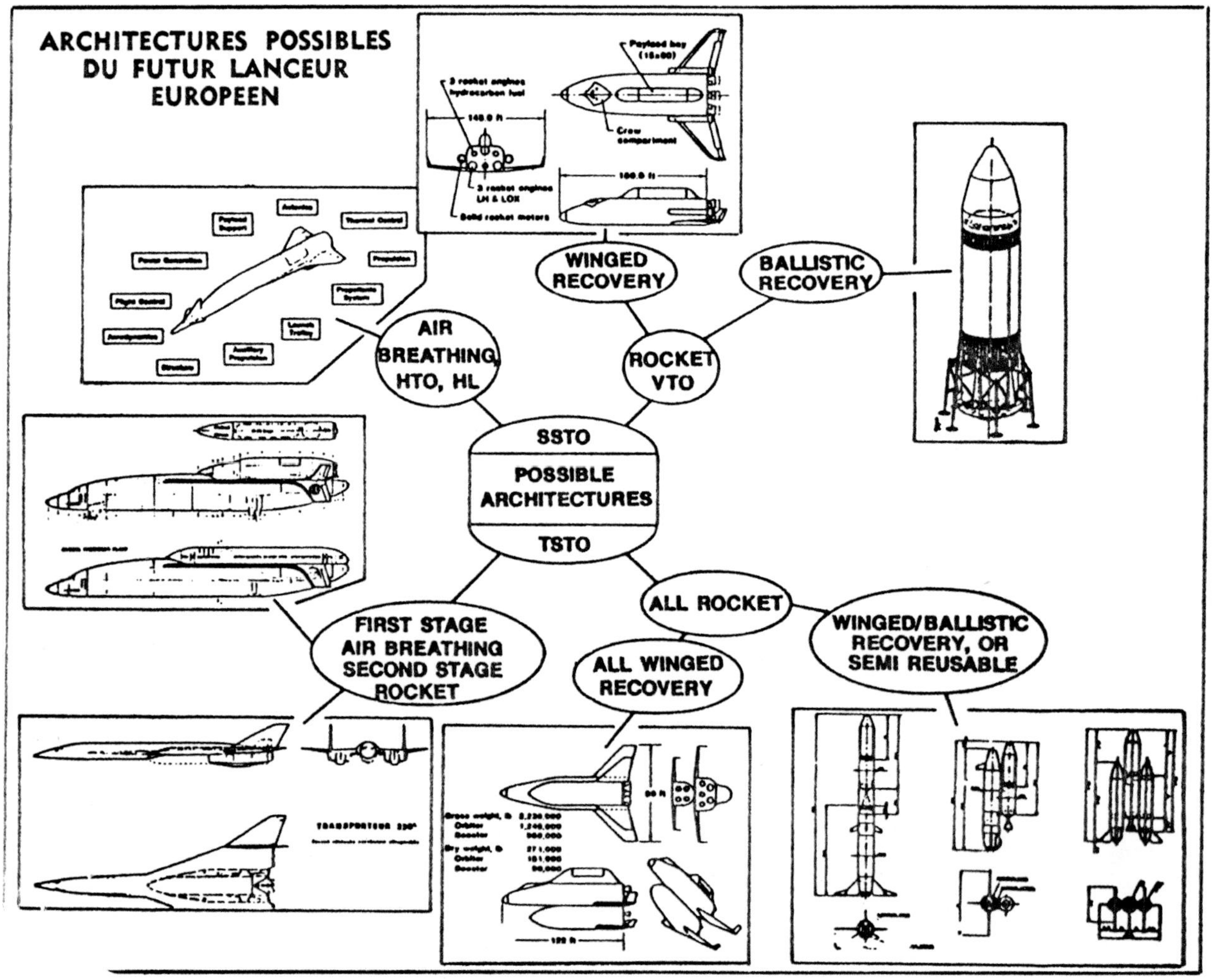

The graphic featured in French magazine Air & Cosmos *on March 14, 1987, showing the options for a Future European Space Transportation Investigations Programme.* AIR & COSMOS

Project Definition phase is planned to follow the PoC Study, leading into the Development phase for the next six years. Key dates are: first demonstration engine 1993; first prototype design freeze, end 1995; first flight (reduced standard), end 1997; first flight (full standard) end 1999; initial operating capability, 2002.

"These dates will be possible only with a full European commitment to funding each stage, without delays. They are consequently 'earliest possible' dates. In parallel with the Project Definition phases an Enabling Technology programme is envisaged to advance to maturity: a) Advanced materials and structures (necessary to enable a vehicle of competitive size/mass), b) Avionics, particularly development of onboard and ground station software to enable autonomous control of the unmanned vehicle. Software methodology must be advanced to reduce the task by a factor of ten compared with existing methods. A drone demonstrator is planned as a precursor to the Hotol prototype. c) Aerodynamics—notably computational fluid mechanics and wind tunnel investigations, to improve the accuracy of prediction of aerodynamic forces and heating during the critical re-entry phase. Autoland glide model precursor trials are also planned. d) Systems, notably actuation and power systems.

"The envisaged funding required for these programmes is £15-20 million per annum." The memo was signed on Burns' behalf by aerodynamicist Alison Wake.

THE CASE AGAINST CAPS

As part of his Yates-mandated 'investigation', Parkinson had visited Warton to see the CAPS computer modelling system for himself during early to mid-March. On March 20 he submitted a post-visit report, stating: "It is apparent that BAe Warton are very committed to the CAPS system to define the vehicle, and any eventual design solution will have to be made in terms that can be put through CAPS to give the right numbers. Since CAPS is a flexible and modular system it ought to be possible to do this, but the mechanics of CAPS may not encourage discovery of effective routes by itself."

He outlined the structure and operation of CAPS as he understood it then went on to reiterate his concern that while the engine was performing "as well as originally proposed", performance was being eroded by drag due to the vehicle's shape. He also identified issues with the way wing sizing was being modelled and the fact that Scott-Scott's variable nozzle area ratio had not been accounted for, concluding: "Warton promised copies of recent CAPS runs for us to analyse further and it may be necessary to make a further visit to discuss the specific trade-offs which have been made after that analysis has been carried out. No definite conclusion can yet be drawn about the source or reality of our current problems."

THE CASE FOR CAPS

The engineer behind the CAPS software, Eric Webb of Warton's Advanced Studies Department, had meanwhile written a memo entitled 'Hotol—The Part Played by CAPS', on March 18. This gave a blow-by-blow account of how CAPS had been used during the project's first 18 months.

Work had started in the autumn of 1985 with "various notes etc." being received from Filton and Stevenage which were used to begin developing a digital Hotol mass model. Aerodynamic drag was estimated and "all methods agreed that the rear fuselage drag of the original vehicle would be extremely high. A 'smoothed' rear fuselage shape was adopted for all further work. This resulted in CAPS computing overall drag levels of roughly the same order as estimated by Filton—provided an optimistic analysis of body wave drag was accepted".

Webb said that the only engine performance data available at this stage "was crude, being based on a small number of hand calculations by RR. Filton had expanded these to cover a range of heights and speeds by simple factoring to allow for different ambient pressures".

Mass modelling continued into the winter of 1985, with the first results being issued in December, but "the standard of the available engine performance data made any attempt at trajectory optimisation pointless".

Then, in January 1986, "a request was received from I. R. Yates to explore the possibility of launching Hotol from a subsonic transport. CAPS was used to rescale Hotol assuming various start points... Conclusion: a launch mass reduction of about 12% compared with ground take-off". This was the second round of CAPS work and the third began during the spring of 1986, with the Hotol mass model now ready for testing. Yet "still only crude engine performance data [was available] (despite repeated requests to Rolls-Royce)".

Early testing had revealed a low sensitivity to drag increases so, "as expected, the configuration optimisation resulted in a shorter fatter vehicle with low thrust-to-weight and the highest acceptable wing loading. The reasons were: a) the drag penalty associated with a fatter vehicle can be balanced against its lower mass per unit volume; b) the penalty of carrying extra engine mass to orbit cannot be offset by the lower fuel burns of a higher thrust-to-weight vehicle; c) the ascent performance benefits of a larger wing are more than cancelled by the extra wing mass. At this stage doubts about the original launch mass prediction (less than 200 tonnes) were confirmed".

At the beginning of the fourth round, circa mid-1986, "the revised Filton estimate of intake mass, a threefold increase, was incorporated in the mass model used by CAPS. Filton supplied revised installed performance data (still based on limited RR hand calculations). A significant feature was reduced thrust at Mach 5.

"Repeated CAPS scaling confirmed the choice of a shorter fatter vehicle (Configuration F) but also pointed to the need to reduce structure and intake masses by about 20% to achieve a 'respectable' launch mass. Doubts about transition performance grew. It had been assumed that the penalty due to low climb angle at transition could be reduced by pulling up during the final stages of the airbreathing ascent. A limited study using CAPS performance modules showed this to be unlikely".

During the summer of 1986, Hotol CAPS work had been bifurcated—the airbreathing/rocket vehicle now being tested in parallel with a single-stage pure rocket vehicle. According to Webb: "When it was apparent that there were serious doubts about the original Hotol predictions it was decided that alternatives should be re-examined. The first of these was a single-stage rocket-powered vehicle."

The mass model for this rocket-Hotol was based on the original Hotol model "with only minor adjustments to eliminate intakes and other airbreathing components. The vehicle geometry was modified to provide for the different ratio of liquid oxygen to liquid hydrogen.

"Ascent performance from take-off to MECO [Main Engine Cut-Off] was computed using a simple rocket-type trajectory. The resultant fuel fractions were checked against published American data and proved to be OK. The results... showed that a pure rocket vehicle had a lower empty mass than Hotol but higher take-off mass. This result cast doubt on the supposed cost advantage of Hotol".

While this was going on, during the second half of 1986, "new data from RR and intake studies at Filton [for the original airbreathing Hotol] confirmed the suspicions that the 600kt equivalent air speed trajectory was

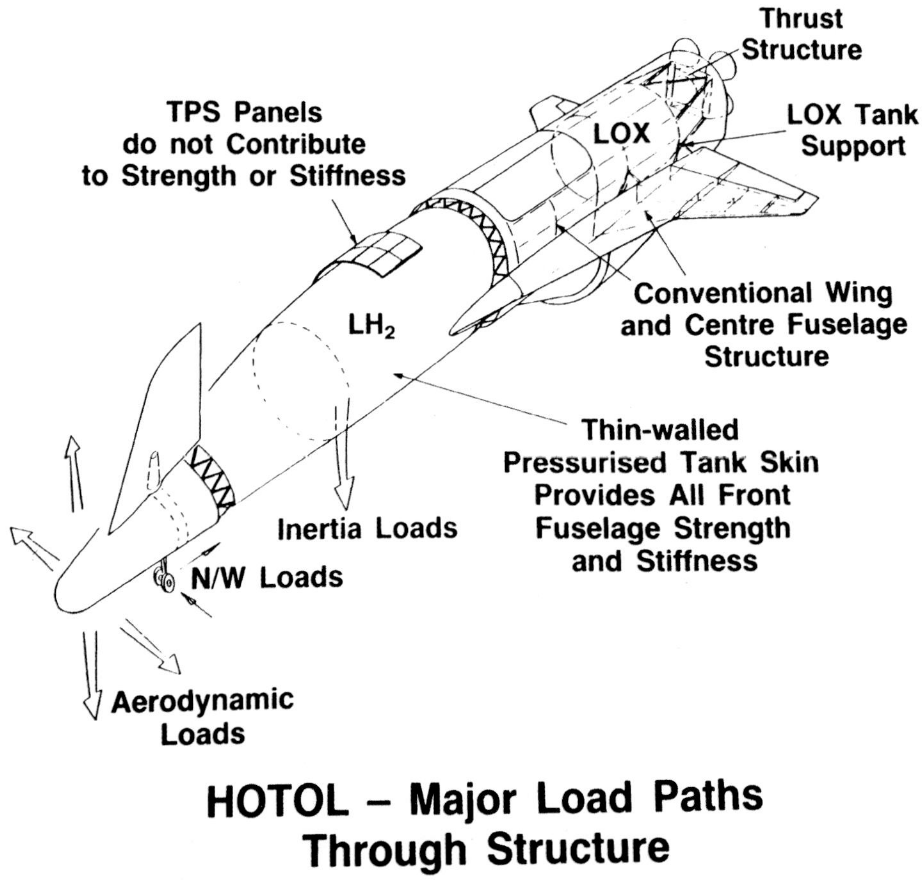

Load paths through Hotol's structure. Part of the justification for a 'rocket-Hotol' was potential weight savings derived from reduced ascent loads.

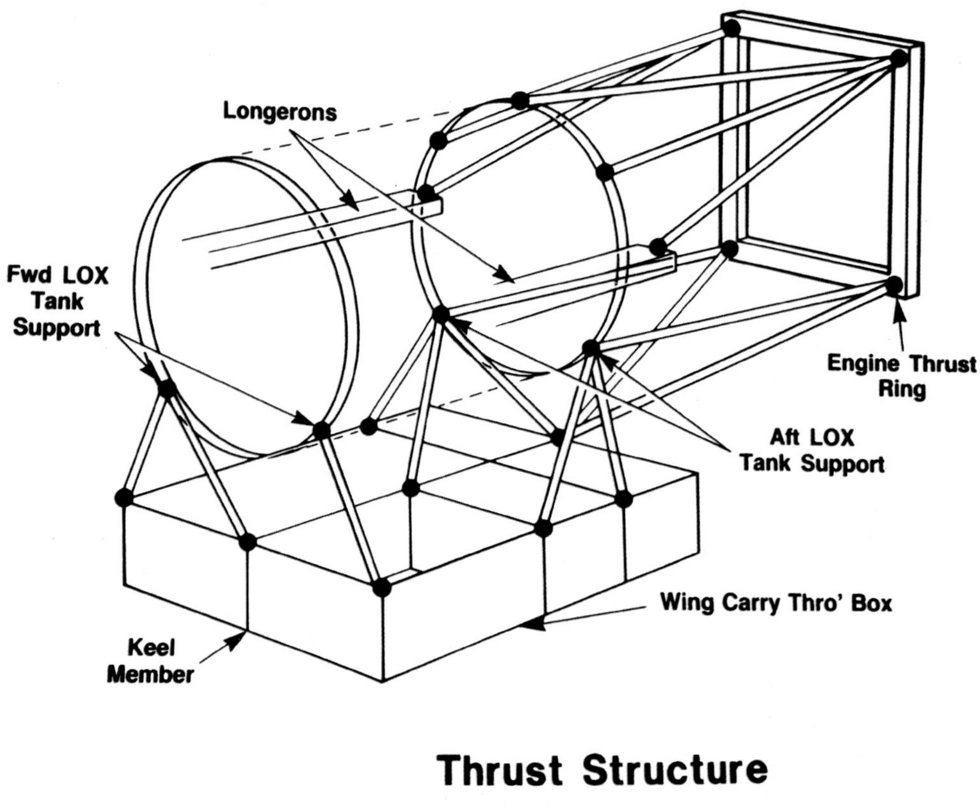

Thrust structure of Hotol's rear fuselage.

optimistic. If reasonable engine and intake masses were to be achieved, constraints would have to be imposed on the ascent trajectory. CAPS was used extensively to explore the interaction between engine/intake design and overall vehicle performance. Despite the difficulties airbreathing fuel burn was kept within a few percent of the original estimate".

During the spring of 1987, up to Parkinson's visit, the rocket-Hotol mass model was "modified to incorporate the latest Hotol data and methods". Consequently, Webb reported: "Results show that whereas the changes since last summer have resulted in a significant growth in [the original] Hotol's scaled mass (mainly due to engine/intake changes), rocket vehicle masses have reduced (mainly due to reduced wing size). Rocket vehicles now show a scaled empty mass about half that of Hotol. Launch mass is also lower." Not only that, the rocket-Hotol was now being considered for vertical launch and "vertical take-off vehicles are smaller because reduced ascent loads on the wing yield a wing mass saving". By now, the rocket-Hotol had been rolled into the ALV studies.

Back with airbreathing Hotol, the spring of 1987 had seen "scaling... repeated using the latest engine and mass data. Drag estimation has been modified to meet some of the aerodynamicists' objections that the CAPS estimate for Configuration F was too low. The new CAPS drag estimates still represent very optimistic targets. Spillage drag has been completely ignored. Fuel burn penalties due to the rapid pull up required at transition have been ignored. Even with these optimistic (unrealistic) assumptions and a 0.8 factor on structure masses the scaled Hotol launch mass approaches 300 tonnes".

'POPULAR MYTHS'

Webb also set out to debunk four 'popular myths' about the CAPS system. First up: "CAPS results are significantly worse than Stevenage/Filton predictions. NOT TRUE: As is now well known, the early publicity, i.e. a <200 tonne vehicle with a seven-tonne payload, was based on erroneous calculations. A proper summation of the Stevenage/Filton masses with the omitted items included and errors corrected left at best a payload of less than two tonnes; rocket ascent calculations at Stevenage resulted in a significant decrease from the A. Bond figure; CAPS drag and mass estimates are in broad agreement with the corrected Stevenage/Filton results... the main difference arises when CAPS is asked to optimise the configuration."

Secondly: "'Configuration F' was a retrograde step. NOT TRUE—Configuration F is an IMPROVEMENT: Structurally a shorter fatter vehicle is more efficient; the original long thin vehicle drag estimate (both CAPS and Filton) was so low that a significant increase could be tolerated in order to achieve lower structure mass; body fineness ratio is always going to be a compromise involving drag and mass; the best vehicle is the cheapest (smallest?) vehicle; this is not the same as the vehicle with lowest drag or lowest fuel burn."

And third: "High lift/drag during the ascent is a key to success. OVERSIMPLIFIED." A detailed explanation of why this was the case followed, and lastly: "A bigger wing would be better. FALSE—the smallest acceptable wing is best: If, as is currently the case for Hotol, a significant part of the trajectory is flown at incidences greater than that for maximum lift/drag, the usual procedure is to increase the wing area. This reduces induced drag; all the CAPS studies completed to date have shown that the extra mass of the bigger wing always more than cancels the benefits of drag reduction; the conclusion is that the smallest acceptable wing is best; re-entry requirements set the ultimate lower limit for wing size."

In conclusion, Webb wrote: "The problems being revealed by the CAPS studies are not due to faults or shortcomings in the CAPS methods of analysis. All that CAPS has done is to bring into the open problems that have always been inherent in the Hotol concept. CAPS is quite capable of handling vehicle configuration and trajectory optimisation; indeed, that is what it has been developed to do. We have almost 20 years' experience in its use in this mode.

"The fact that CAPS results may at first sight appear to be in conflict with expectations is nothing new. In the past this situation has almost always been shown to be due to the fact that the early expectations were based on an incomplete analysis of the many interactions which affect the optimisation of a vehicle's design. It would appear that Hotol studies are no exception."

FRENCH LEAD ON MATERIALS

Burns reported to Yates on March 31, 1987, that a costed plan for the new Concept Validation phase was being prepared.

The joint presentation to Lygo and Robins on Hotol's current status had taken place as planned on March 11 and at this point, Hotol had an empty mass of 50 tonnes or 300 tonnes when fully loaded. Studies planned for the immediate future were "aimed at propulsion improvements by means of hydrogen exhaust 'reheat', spill ramjet and liquid oxygen enrichment, used selectively. Alternative configurations under study are a delta wing and a flattened forebody".

The enabling technology workshop in Rome had also taken place and "was generally regarded as successful". Perhaps surprisingly, "only BAe made a strong case for large scale development of advanced structural materials. AMDBA and SEP [Société Européene de Propulsion] are clearly ahead in the field of high-temperature materials and showed data indicating carbon-silicon carbide to be superior to both silicon-carbide/silicon-carbide and carbon-carbon at elevated temperatures. MBB and AIT showed no evidence of advanced thinking in these fields".

On command and control systems, "the session chairman, Mr Deller of RAE, strongly supported the BAe line for a large-scale attack on the software problem and the need for a drone demonstrator". In aerodynamics, "AMDBA are clearly European leaders in advanced CFM [Carbon Fibre Matrix] applied to hypersonics. BAe papers pointed to the need for work on control powers and base-plume interaction, which were not mentioned elsewhere".

And in propulsion, "MBB are well advanced in the field of advanced airbreathing propulsion but requirements are somewhat confused by hypersonic transport considerations".

Burns and Sid Walmsley had travelled to Yorkshire on March 24 to receive the results of the Hotol project audit begun in November 1986 by BAe Brough (see Chapter 4). Burns considered that "generally the audit report is considered fair but some local points of disagreement are being investigated before issue of the report".

Back at Warton, testing of the Hotol high-speed wind tunnel model in the Mach 3-5.5 range had commenced in the division's guided weapons wind tunnel. In addition, a simulation of Hotol's autoland system was nearly ready and "a graphics representation of the approach and landing, as 'seen' by a chase aircraft, has been set up and will be filmed for display purposes".

Meanwhile, Miller at Martin-Baker had written to Wilson again to say, "I had a meeting last week with McDonnell Douglas to discuss their requirements for a very similar programme. This meeting, and those with other companies also investigating an aerospace plane, indicates to me that this form of transportation will have a definite escape system requirement for the future. Our basic concept of a podded ejection seat has been very favourably received and we are most encouraged to proceed with the feasibility study on such an escape system. I will endeavour to arrange an appointment with you when I next visit Warton to discuss the EFA programme".

Beyond this point, however, it appears that little further work was done on Hotol's proposed crew capsule.

THE OG'S FINDINGS

Parkinson wrote to Burns on April 8, 1987, with the results of his 'investigation' into Hotol Configuration F and CAPS, saying: "Dear Sandy, the Hotol 'Originators' Group' has come to some conclusions, and I attach a 'final statement'. Since you have seen Alan Bond's report and the data Terry Brown produced at the PLM [Propulsion Liaison Meeting] you will already have some prevision of what is coming. However, we at Stevenage performed our own review and a 'Technical Report' is attached.

"By its nature, an 'Originators' Group' must raise questions rather than produce complete and wholly 'tidied up' work. We are not really in the business of redesigning the vehicle. I hope therefore you will take the concerns contained herein as 'constructive criticism' and 'things we do not understand' rather than a frontal attack on Warton competence. However, I do believe that the conclusions reached by Alan, Filton and ourselves, with relatively little detailed interaction, raise serious questions as to whether the pessimistic view at Warton regarding finding a design point for Hotol are valid.

"I also believe that the attempt by Filton and ourselves to relate directly to what we know, and the directness of the 'extrapolation' means that the divergence between Warton and OG cannot be accounted for simply by the argument 'but we have a more detailed (and hence more exact) model than you'. I believe that you should take particular note of the argument presented in Section 2 of our report which gives an overview which allows for considerable 'decoupling' of the key factors in the argument.

"I hope that we can resolve these problems swiftly as they are key to the whole project."

The document ran to nearly 40 pages and reiterated many of the points previously raised in earlier documents albeit in much greater detail. There were a few choice statements which apparently caused consternation at Warton however. At one point Parkinson wrote: "One of the results coming from the Warton CAPS modelling is the suggestion that a pure rocket vehicle would be superior to Hotol. This is an indication of problems with the modelling." On the Warton copy of the report, the latter sentence is highlighted and a note in pen next to it says, "Unsubstantiated statement". Elsewhere, Parkinson opined that, "Warton's failure to see the problem appears to be a consequence of a reluctance to do 'back of the envelope' sums." The comment next to this says, "Oh God!"

BRIEFING PRINCE CHARLES

While Parkinson was making his 'final statement', Brian Young was dashing off a letter addressed to Buckingham

Palace—asking whether the Prince of Wales would be interested in a personal briefing on Hotol's progress. A response would be received from Prince Charles's deputy private secretary Humphrey Mews on April 22 to say: "His Royal Highness has asked me to thank you for this kind offer and would indeed like to be briefed at Kensington Palace at some convenient date in the autumn."

Meanwhile, Burns wrote to Denning on April 10 ahead of a meeting scheduled for May 12, reminding him that both BAe and RR were contractually obliged to give the government another Hotol update at the end of June 1987 and urging him to hurry up and provide data on the projected benefits of hydrogen exhaust reheat, the spill ramjet and liquid oxygen enrichment. He wrote: "These improvements have been discussed and actions placed by the Propulsion Liaison Meeting, but possibly with insufficient urgency... will you please give this work the necessary priority?"

In his briefing report to Yates on May 1, he noted that paying for "additional performance work, actioned by the Originators Working Group, publicity material for presentations and the audit by Brough" had resulted in a projected overspend compared to the Hotol project cost plan.

Efforts to refine the Hotol configuration were continuing and "studies of alternative tankage layouts are in progress. These are associated with increased liquid oxygen/liquid hydrogen ratios which will result from propulsion improvements; they are aimed also at reducing the centre of gravity travel, in order to increase the controllable incidence range at the top of airbreathing ascent, where the current configuration is highly unstable".

The radical flattened oval 'lifting body' forward fuselage for Hotol noted at the end of March had been studied but "the additional fuselage structure mass was found to be in the region of four tonnes, which completely negates any aerodynamic benefit". Wind tunnel testing of the high-speed model SB2 continued.

A briefing for the technical directors of advanced material supplier companies had been held at Warton on April 23 in advance of a managing director-level meeting due to be scheduled for July 1987.

Burns also noted that, "a report has been issued by Originators Working Group [Document No. HTL/S/Eng/3 Stevenage System Performance Analyses of Current Hotol Design], purporting to show that the original ELV configuration, with updated assumptions, would still be satisfactory. This report has been studied at Warton and a meeting chaired by Mr B. Young is due to be held on May 6, 1987, to discuss the matter".

HOTOL'S 'RED TEAM'

The May 6 meeting chaired by Young was attended by Parkinson, Bond, Longstaff, Brown, Burns, Wilson, Webb and Furniss.

The post-meeting report began: "A full day's meeting was held to allow Warton to respond to the OG reports and to agree a future course of action. The Warton team made a comprehensive viewfoil presentation which provoked extensive discussion."

Two lists were appended: 'agreements' and 'actions'. The first agreement was that "OG masses are an underestimate based on current structural concepts. ELV mass was agreed to be approximately 37 tonnes rather than 30 tonnes as estimated in 1984."

Secondly, "the relatively high rate of exchange of mass on the front fuselage with fineness ratio is valid for the current structural concept. The OG had used a simple area-based rule."

Warton, for their part, agreed that "an alternative structural concept for the front fuselage may give a significant reduction in mass particularly for vehicles of high fineness ratio. This will be studied." In addition, "CAPS drag was agreed to be optimistic particularly as fineness ratio is reduced. Base drag will be superseded by wind tunnel-based values" and "aerodynamic refinement was agreed to be a fundamental necessity with respect to any proposed configuration, particularly for achievement of target drag".

Warton and Filton agreed that "there is scope for significant improvement in the drag of Configuration F" and "the drag assumed by Reaction Engines for the proposed 287 tonne vehicle was lower than current Warton or Filton ELV estimates".

The payload capacity of the vehicle being proposed by the OG at 200 tonnes "was agreed to be probably around zero. Configuration F was agreed to be no longer the optimum shape based on current assumptions which would lead to a vehicle of a higher fineness ratio".

Once again, the intake design was acknowledged to be a source of difficulty: "It was agreed that incidence effects on the intake had not been fully accounted in CAPS trajectory optimisation. The existing line of propulsion integration activity was agreed: low drag intake design, integration of spill ramjet, possible use of liquid oxygen enrichment to improve transition, [and] re-optimisation of vehicle shape.

"This must take a realistic view of aerodynamic drag and any improved structural concepts and be developed to include proper optimisation of the compression system (intake, heat exchanger, and compressor)."

Further, "the OG estimation of acceleration had

omitted the climb angle term and was agreed to be wrong". On Alan Bond's personal copy of the meeting minutes written by Wilson, next to this point, he wrote in pencil: "Sadly true."

Lastly, "no agreement was reached on the comparison of Hotol and a pure rocket. It was agreed that the comparison was premature and that the issued reports should be withdrawn until the completion of the whole of the alternative study, by which time Hotol will be on a sounder basis".

The 'actions' section included six points:

"1. There is to be no further OG or 'red team' activity. All further activity will be on an integrated basis so that the OG members are fully informed and involved.
2. OG reports are to be corrected and reissued after agreement with the Project Manager.
3. Technical agreement is to be reached on drag levels and their rate of exchange with vehicle shape.
4. Technical agreement is to be reached on design concepts for hydrogen tanks and their mass scaling laws.
5. Technical agreement is to be reached on mass rules in general.
6. Performance improvements are to be embodied and a revised configuration to be defined based on a agreed standards of drag, mass, engine performance etc."

The outcome of this intensive debate, combined with Warton's already well-advanced work on revised aerodynamic and structural layouts, was a new design: Hotol Configuration G.

THE WAY AHEAD

Pattie had been on the campaign trail in his constituency of Chertsey and Walton in Surrey ahead of the 1987 General Election, due to take place on June 11, but took time out on May 18 to receive a fresh Hotol briefing. This

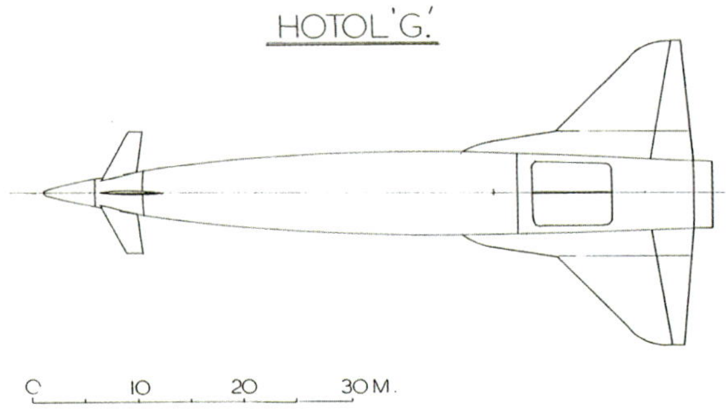

Early top view drawing of Hotol Configuration G.

apparently encompassed not only Configuration G but also the ALV studies being conducted in parallel.

Young sent Burns a post-meeting memo on May 19 to say that Yates, who had also been present, was "satisfied with the presentations and the response from the Minister" and wanted the Hotol team to proceed in six areas. The first five were: complete a definition of Configuration G; complete the ALV studies; contribute to a letter inviting materials company MDs to "consider wider market potential"; consider establishing a software and artificial intelligence 'club' for Hotol with major UK companies, and set up a joint intake/engine team to replace the PIG.

The sixth order of business Yates had for the team was: "Provide for discussion, June 10, an updated version of the final 'activities' viewgraph covering a) major milestones involving ministers, BNSC, ESA. b) BAe/RR engineering plan based on 'G'. c) UK industrial plan including enabling technology. d) European industrial plan including enabling technology, system evaluation, system studies etc. e) ESA plan covering small nations, FRG, France approach. All showing the major points of interaction."

Burns reported to Yates on June 1 that "the BAe funding requirement for the nine-month Concept Validation phase, to follow Proof-of-Concept, has been estimated to be £1.6m. At a meeting on May 13 at Warton with BNSC and RAE, BAe suggested that this phase be funded 100%

Hotol Configuration G. CHRIS SANDHAM-BAILEY

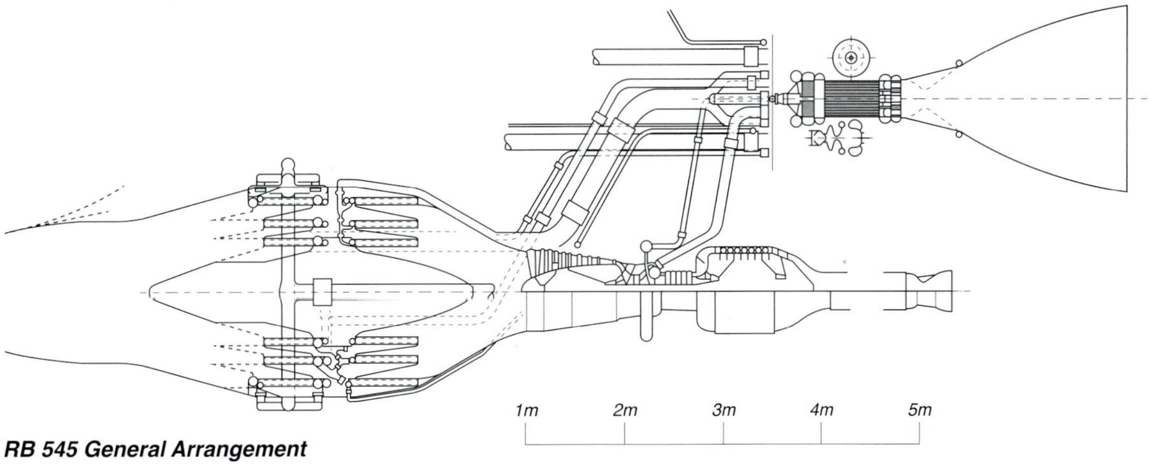

RB 545 General Arrangement

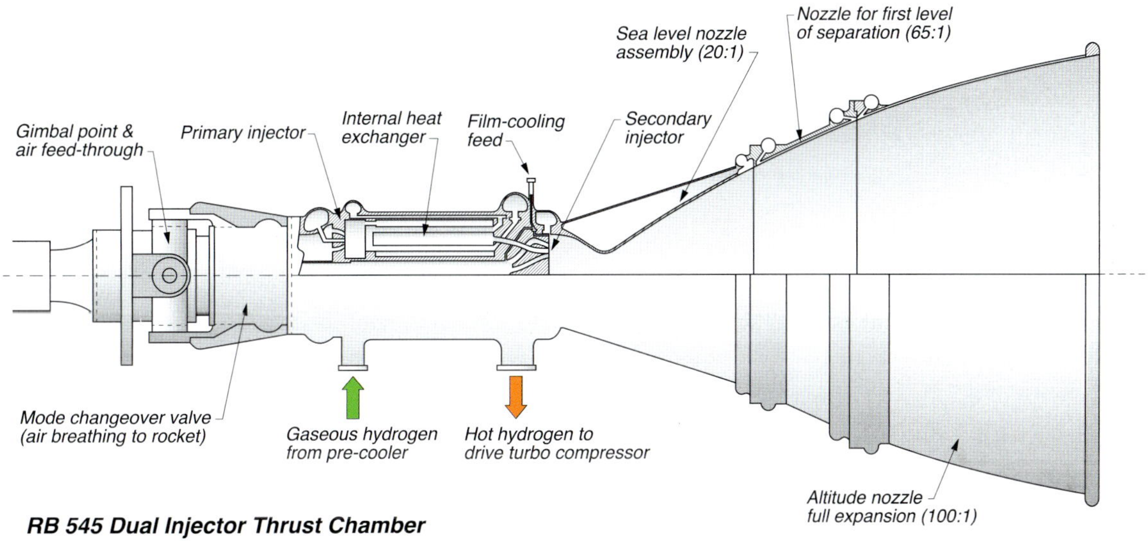

RB 545 Dual Injector Thrust Chamber

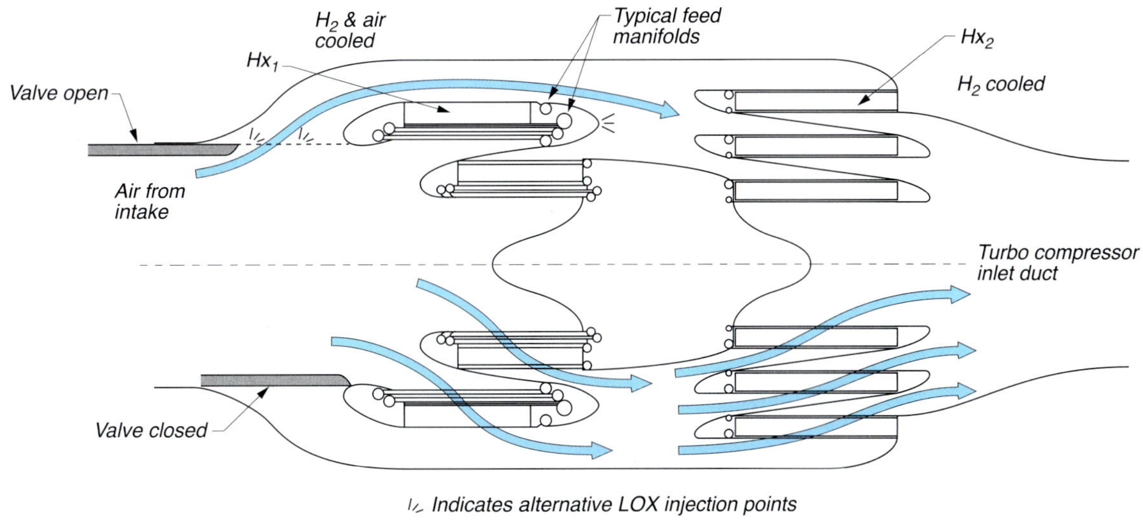

RB 545 Pre-Cooler System Bypass Operation Sequence

Basic diagrams showing the RB.545's workings were prepared in May 1987 for an anticipated presentation to Pattie. GRAHAME CHAMBERS

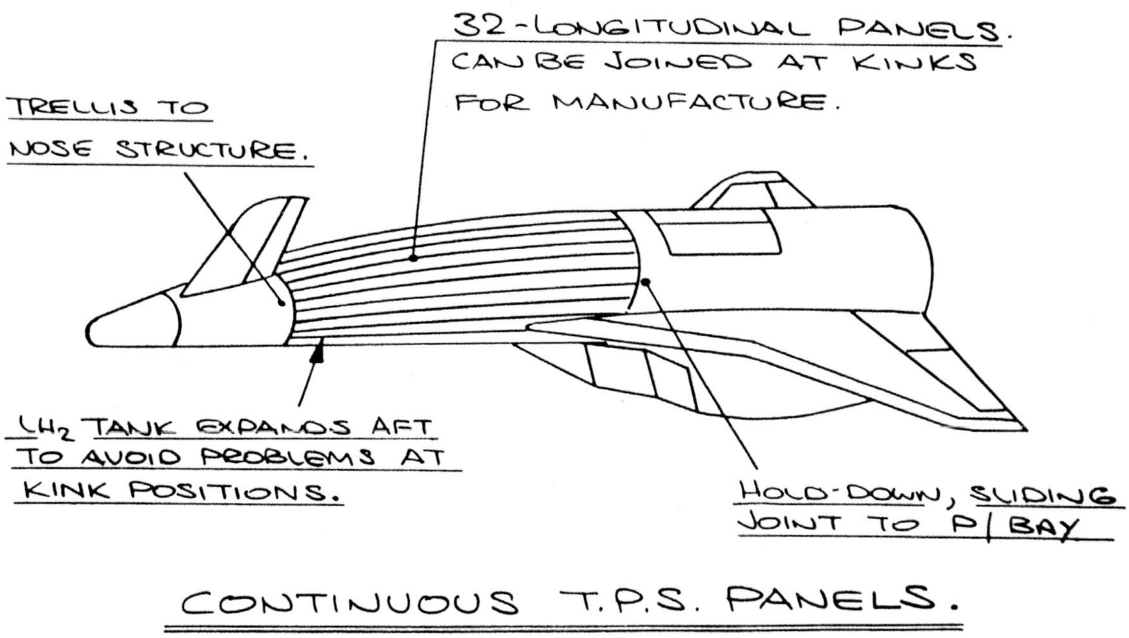

Revised TPS system considered for Hotol Configuration G, consisting of 32 very long carbon-carbon sandwich panels positioned around the forward fuselage.

by the government, in view of BAe's spend of £1.2m in 1987 (over and above 50% PoC) on enabling technology, plus additional spend on [the Brough] audit and Alternative Launch Vehicles".

In the wake of the May 6 Originators' Group Report meeting, "concerted effort will now be devoted to defining an optimum Configuration G based on agreed mass and drag relationships with fuselage dimensions. Alternative hydrogen tank schemes, including stiffened skin with lower pressurisation and a compartmented tank with differential pressurisation, are being studied.

"Aerodynamic refinements are being assessed. Rolls-Royce are due to communicate revised RB.545 data plus the effects of spill ramjet, hydrogen exhaust reheat and liquid oxygen enrichment at a meeting on June 1 at Ansty. The size and mass of the heat exchangers is a matter of concern to BAe. RR report that a preliminary solution to the icing problem has been found, but this requires 16t liquid oxygen for a temperate high humidity environment (more for tropical). The mass penalty will be offset, partially at least, by reducing airflow requirement which may result in engine/intake rescaling". Evidently, "a necessary step towards 'Europeanisation' [of Hotol] is declassification of the propulsion system, which demands more progress on solution of the icing problem".

A structural innovation being considered for Configuration G was "a revised TPS scheme consisting of longitudinally continuous carbon-carbon sandwich panels, with pin-jointed attachment posts. This scheme appears superior to the metallic multi-panel scheme, being lighter, having very low thermal expansion and [being] essentially 'fail-safe'. Testing of the SB2 up to Mach 5.5 had now been completed and "high apparent induced drag has been measured at Mach numbers of 3 and above with intake blocked. This appears as a steep increase in axial force with incidence, so it is not a true lift-induced effect. Investigation is being pursued urgently".

PARKINSON'S OLIVE BRANCH

In a memo to Burns on June 10, 1987, headed 'CAPS Analysis', Parkinson wrote: "I understand that implications that the Originators' Group asserted that there were 'errors in CAPS' have created problems at Warton in proposing the system for other projects. I understand that this may have been the cause for concern in a letter from P. W. [Peter] Liddell [head of advanced projects at Warton] to P. J. Conchie dated May 18. We shall, as requested, update HTL/S/Eng/3 in due course, but in the meantime I would hope that this memo would clear up the misunderstanding. Please use it in any way you feel necessary.

"We did not really believe that there were fundamental errors in CAPS per se, and the material from the May 6 meeting helped explain some apparent 'curiosities' we noted. Our reservations were two-fold: 1. The results of CAPS outputs occasionally need clarification to gain effective understanding of the system interactions to make progress towards a workable design for a system as interactive as Hotol. 2. A significant part of the CAPS model originates with the user, and if this is not realistic for any reason, unrealistic answers arise. (The reconsideration of forebody structural design currently in progress is therefore a positive move forward).

"If good mass models, geometry models and propulsion models are put in then I have no doubt that CAPS predicts the performance accurately within the limits of its aerodynamic model which as I understand it, refers specifically to an axisymmetric fuselage shape. As long as care is taken over inputs, and relating outputs back to input assumptions, I see no reason for doubting the accuracy of the CAPS analysis."

While it wasn't an apology, this memo did amount to a conciliatory gesture on Parkinson's part—a signal of willingness to end the disagreement over CAPS and move forward.

Unfortunately, it wasn't enough. Burns wrote back on June 12, apparently at the behest of Liddell, to say: "Your memo dated June 10, 1987, on this subject is not considered sufficient to undo the harm that has been done by your unjustified criticism of the system. While you are, of course, at liberty to comment on and criticise the input data as applied to Hotol, it is the criticism of the program itself that has to be removed entirely."

This was followed by a list of points within the memo that had been found to be objectionable. Conchie weighed in later in the month with a further memo to both Burns and Parkinson, saying: "I believe this continued correspondence is not helpful. We have to move forward and should encourage constructive criticism at all times." Burns then replied to this with a handwritten note, saying: "I agree with this, but a great deal of harm has been done by continued criticism of the CAPS system (I am not referring to input data, that is another matter). I believe that it is necessary to redress the balance by a simple memo to those whose professional reputations have been damaged by the earlier criticism."

Eventually, on July 2, Burns would write a memo to Young headed 'Hotol: Originators Working Group Report—Repercussions'. It said: "Eight weeks have passed since the meeting at which you ruled that the OG report should be corrected and reissued. In the interest of moving forward and satisfactory relations with Stevenage, I have not pressed them on this point.

"In the meantime, I received a memo from RCP [Parkinson] aimed at placating Mr P. W. Liddell and his staff with regard to criticism of CAPS. I considered that memo to be insufficient; see reply, which was polite but firm. PJC has replied. I find his reply unsatisfactory; OWG's criticism was largely unfounded and certainly not 'constructive'.

"I do not wish to prolong the agony, but staff involved in performance and scaling work were very upset by the OWG report and their current performance is, I believe, adversely affected by the lack of a withdrawal of criticisms by Stevenage. The results of the Alternative Launch Vehicles work are becoming known and although the Hotol team staff are dedicated to making the best of our particular project, I have heard phrases such as 'trying to keep a corpse alive' from other areas of Warton.

"I therefore ask for your personal intervention to persuade Stevenage to withdraw the CAPS (system) criticism and correct the OG report without further delay, in the interest of improving morale and productivity of those concerned."

Young seems to have sent this memo back with a pencilled note at the top addressed to Burns: "I have told PJC [Conchie] to drop it. I suggest you do the same."

This effectively put an end to the matter—nothing further could be done and Liddell would have to take Parkinson's criticisms on the chin. In the meantime, work on the Alternative Launch Vehicle studies had largely been completed and events were occurring on the national stage that would have a far more significant impact on the Hotol project.

6

A SOUND BASIS FOR COMPARISON: ALTERNATIVE LAUNCH VEHICLE STUDIES

When Ivan Yates asked the Warton CAPS team to explore the possibility of launching Hotol from a subsonic transport—negating the need for a launch trolley—in January 1986 it was the beginning of a lengthy period of investigation into alternative launch vehicle concepts.

Around six months after work in this vein began, with Configuration F firmly installed as the Hotol baseline design, it was decided that a more comprehensive and wide-ranging approach was required—leading to the establishment of the Alternative Launch Vehicle (ALV) Group in October 1986.

Burns produced a report that month entitled 'Hotol Assessment of Alternative Launch Vehicles. Task Description', which began: "At the half-time point in the two-year PoC Study of Hotol a reasonably sound basis of structural design, mass, aerodynamics and performance has been established. At this point it is considered prudent to review a range of alternative launch vehicle configurations using design assumptions consistent with the database established for Hotol.

"The objectives of this work are:

1) To confirm, or otherwise, the conclusion of earlier project work that the Hotol configuration with its hybrid airbreathing/rocket propulsion system is the most cost-effective solution.
2) To establish a sound basis for comparison with competitive European launch vehicle projects.

To this end, each of the candidate configurations will be designed, scaled to a common mission requirement and development and operating costs assessed."

The ground rules were: "All vehicles will be designed for the same primary mission, namely to place a 7,000kg payload in LEO from an Eastern equatorial launch, unmanned. All vehicles will be designed to similar design criteria, safety factors and allowable failure rates. The same range of structural materials will be considered for all vehicles and identical material properties used."

For each one, it would be necessary to "scheme a layout at preliminary scale; establish a database of aerodynamics, propulsion and structures; define limiting temperatures/zones; select materials; define design loadings; stress all major structural components; define systems/redundancy

BAE WARTON ALVS	
Scaled Hotol 'F'	Hotol 'F' scaled using CAPS for 7t payload to orbit
Hotol 'F' (DF+PN+LT)	Hotol Configuration F with dual fuel and plug nozzle
ALV 01	SSTO powered by rocket-ejector-ramjets
ALV 02	SSTO powered by turbo-ramjet-rockets
ALV 10	Two-stage Hotol powered by turbo-ramjet-rockets
ALV 20	Two-stage 'mini-Sänger' powered by turbo-ramjet-rockets/rockets
ALV 20A	Mach 5 booster for ALV 20B powered by turbo-ramjets
ALV 20A/2	As ALV 20A but with built-in rocket boosters
ALV 20 Modified	As ALV 20A but modified to accommodate ALV 60B orbiter
ALV 20B	Rocket powered orbiter carried by ALV 20A
ALV 30A	Rocket powered SSTO with trolley launch
ALV 30B	Rocket powered horizontal take-off booster for Hotol
ALV 30C	Vertical take-off rocket powered SSTO
ALV 30D	Vertical take-off rocket powered booster for Hotol
ALV 31C	Vertical take-off rocket powered SSTO with dual fuel and plug nozzle
ALV 32A	Reusable rocket powered booster for ALV 32B orbiter
ALV 32B	Rocket powered orbiter carried by ALV 32A
ALV 33A	Reusable rocket powered booster for ALV 33B orbiter
ALV 33B	Rocket powered orbiter carried by ALV 33A
ALV 34A	Reusable rocket powered booster for ALV 34B orbiter
ALV 34B	Rocket powered orbiter carried by 2 x ALV 34A
ALV 40A (issue 1)	Expendable cryogenic booster for ALV 40B (based on Ariane 5)
ALV 40A (issue 2)	Expendable cryogenic booster for ALV 40B (redesign)
ALV 40B (issue 1)	Rocket powered orbiter carried by ALV 40A (based on Hermes)
ALV 40B (issue 2)	Rocket powered orbiter carried by ALV 40A (redesign)
ALV 50	Single stage VTO based on MBB/ERNO BETA
ALV 60A	Reusable rocket powered booster for ALV 60B orbiter
ALV 60B	Rocket powered orbiter carried by ALV 20A, ALV 60A and/or ALV 70A
ALV 70A	Turbofan powered booster for ALV 60B, ALV 70B and/or ALV 70C
ALV 70B	RB.545 powered orbiter carried by ALV 70A
ALV 70C	Rocket powered orbiter carried by ALV 70A
ALV 70 Modified	As ALV 70A but modified to accommodate ALV 60B orbiter
ALV 80A	Triamese booster for ALV 80B (Mustard)
ALV 80B	Orbiter carried by 2 x ALV 80A (Mustard)
ALV 90	Elliptical bodied SSTO powered by rocket-ejector-ramjets
ALV 90 TJ	Elliptical bodied SSTO powered by rockets with flyback turbojets
ALV 91A	Elliptical bodied SSTO powered by rockets
ALV 100A	SSTO powered by rocket-ejector-oblique detonation wave ramjet-rocket
ALV 100B	SSTO powered by RB.545 with oblique detonation wave ramjet-rocket
ALV 100C/4	SSTO powered by 4 x RB.545
ALV 100C/8	SSTO powered by 8 x RB.545
ALV 100C/10	SSTO powered by 10 x RB.545
ALV 100D	SSTO powered by ducted wing-rocket-ejector-ramjet-rocket

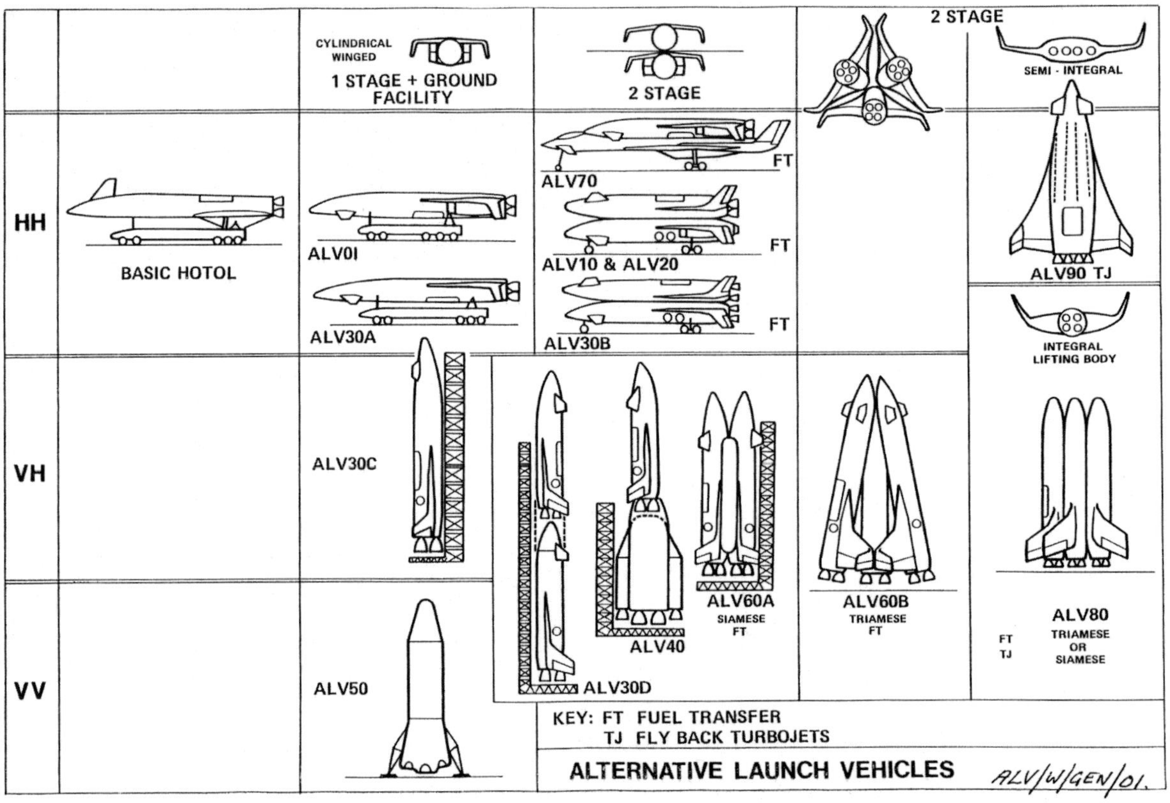

Early drawing from the Alternative Launch Vehicles project, comparing the 'basic Hotol' against a selection of alternative configurations and designs in three categories: HH—Horizontal take-off, Horizontal landing, VH—Vertical take-off, Horizontal landing, and VV—Vertical take-off, Vertical landing.

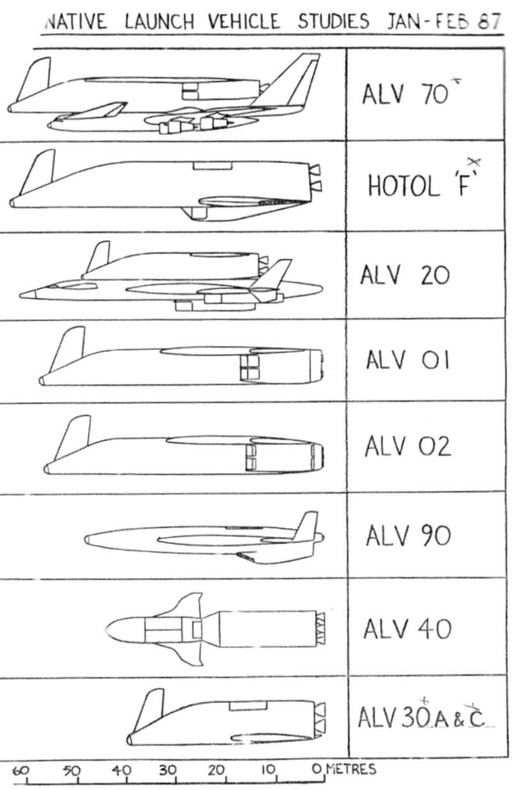

During January-February 1987, the most promising candidate designs were identified.

levels; estimate masses and calculate performance". Those working on the designs would then "confirm preliminary decisions, reiterate as necessary, establish sensitivity to design assumptions, 'freeze', define operating base facilities required to support development programme," and lastly "define geographical/political considerations influencing the programme (e.g. 'could use Kourou [France's spaceport in French Guiana] launch site, Ariane 5 boosters' etc.)".

A list of eight configurations was appended, including the 'basic' RB.545-powered Hotol; a two-stage Hotol; a turbo-ramjet-powered "mini-Sänger"; an all-rocket Hotol; the Hermes/Ariane 5 type configuration; an MBB/ERNO BETA type vertical launch SSTO; the Mustard type system and an air-launched Hotol.

The assessment team would be led by Dave Walley, responsible to Burns, with additional personnel seconded for the duration of the study—expected to be from four to six months. Burns wrote: "All vehicle design, stressing, aerodynamics and performance assessment will be carried out in the team, maintaining close liaison with the basic Hotol study team." Team members included Richard Baker, Mike Ingamells, Keith George and Bob Brown and they would be housed in a Portakabin on site.

George Seyfang of Warton's Future Defence Systems

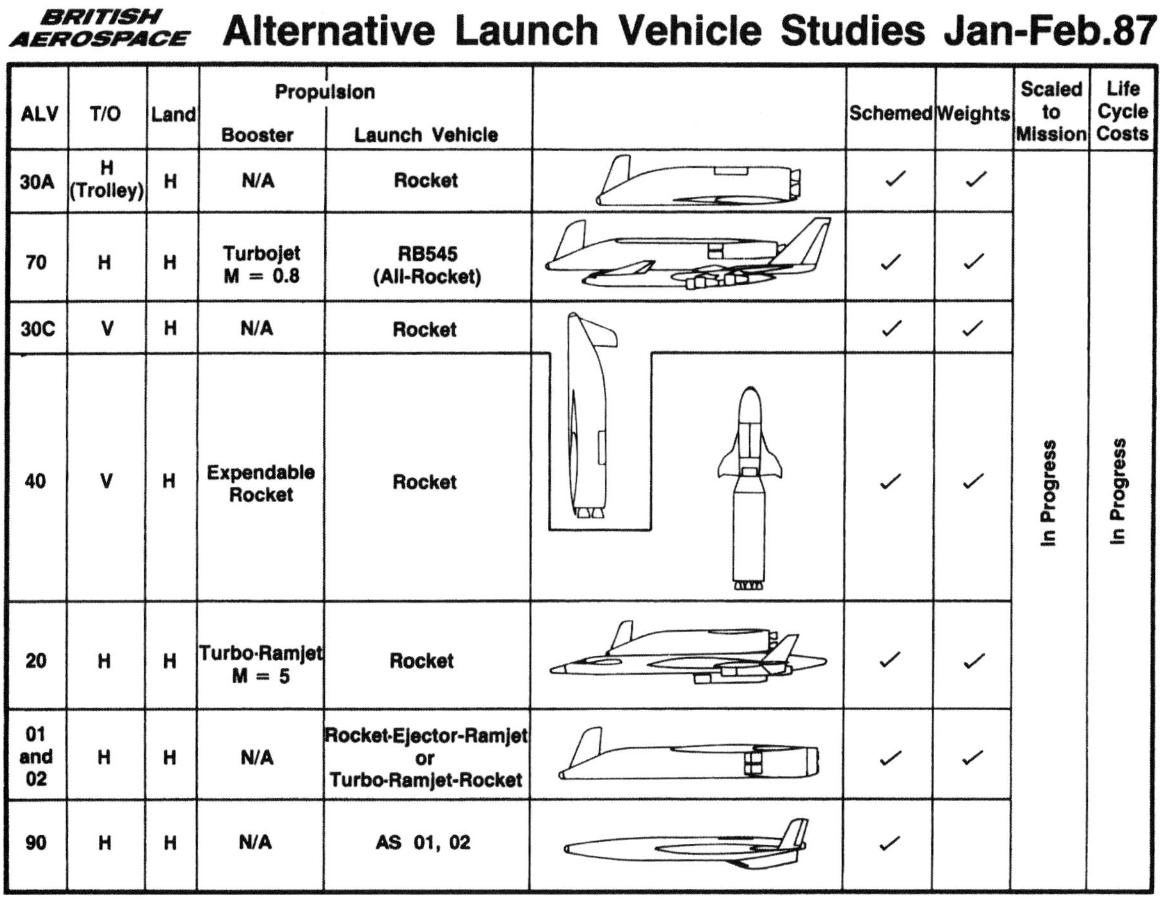

BRITISH AEROSPACE **Alternative Launch Vehicle Studies Jan-Feb.87**

ALV	T/O	Land	Propulsion: Booster	Propulsion: Launch Vehicle		Schemed	Weights	Scaled to Mission	Life Cycle Costs
30A	H (Trolley)	H	N/A	Rocket		✓	✓	In Progress	In Progress
70	H	H	Turbojet M = 0.8	RB545 (All-Rocket)		✓	✓		
30C	V	H	N/A	Rocket		✓	✓		
40	V	H	Expendable Rocket	Rocket		✓	✓		
20	H	H	Turbo-Ramjet M = 5	Rocket		✓	✓		
01 and 02	H	H	N/A	Rocket-Ejector-Ramjet or Turbo-Ramjet-Rocket		✓	✓		
90	H	H	N/A	AS 01, 02		✓			

Further detail from an ALV report on the January-February 1987 period.

Department would be "available in an advisory role" and Eric Webb would be seconded from the Advanced Projects Department to continue the service he had provided to the main Hotol team in developing digital scaling models for each configuration using the CAPS program suite.

Parkinson would give advice on economic models, Brown would provide intake design advice and data for alternative propulsion systems would be agreed with Denning from Rolls-Royce. The official start date was November 3, 1986, and by July 1987, Walley and his team had created a whole menagerie of designs—around 40 in total. Many were given their own designation, ranging from ALV 01 to ALV 100, while a few had a purely descriptive name such as 'Hotol (Scaled)' or 'Hotol 'F' (DF+PN+LT)'. Baker recalled: "An early version of the list was pinned upon the notice board in the Portakabin. In usual tongue-in-cheek fashion, ALV 99 was a frisbee!"

An executive summary of the group's work, covering January to June 1987, was issued by Walley on July 7. The introduction to this began: "A series of Alternative Launch Vehicles (ALVs) has been studied in sufficient depth to establish: the technical implications and costs of several competing ALVs; the effect of likely growth factors and risks involved; [and] a sound basis for comparison with other launch vehicle proposals including Hotol… Extensive use has been made of the Warton Computer Aided Project Study (CAPS) program.

"Although time and resources have been strictly limited, two alternative launch systems are proposed; also firm conclusions and recommendations are made. The main conclusions are: the Hotol system, as presently conceived will not be viable; even if Hotol can be improved there are more cost-effective launch systems; two-stage, rocket only, launch systems offer the lowest risks and lowest life-cycle costs.

"Recommendations: further studies, in greater depth, must be undertaken to establish more clearly: operational requirements, the viability of competing launch systems, prime candidate ALVs, enabling technology required, total costs and commercial viability of selected ALVs."

A no-holds-barred assessment of every conceivable option for meeting the necessary requirements was precisely what had occurred back in the 1960s—with English Electric's original concepts for a horizontal take-off two-stage system being rapidly superseded by the vertical take-off Mustard concept. But Hotol was not so easily set aside. And the notion that the Hotol vehicle was not viable in its existing form was not likely to be enthusiastically embraced by the main Hotol team nor indeed by Lygo who, as mentioned, regarded himself as 'the father of Hotol'.

Nevertheless, the ALV Group's work was not dismissed out of hand and it is worth considering their efforts and findings in more detail.

BACK TO THE FUTURE

When it came to the search for a low-cost space launcher concept Walley had, for the most part, seen it all before. Warton's project files already contained copious quantities of material on rocket-propelled launchers as well as launchers based on the use of an airbreathing booster. Therefore, in putting together the ALV studies he noted that "extensive reference has been made to the previous Warton studies, 1963-65. During that period many alternative configurations and airbreathing engines were considered. In addition, cost estimation methods were devised which, have to some extent, been used in current studies.

"The main conclusions from those studies, to quote, were: 'We believe that all concepts for space transportation must be judged by the criterion of minimum total cost. We have studied the use of a multi-module lifting-body vehicle as a way of reducing R&D costs, and having satisfied ourselves that it is feasible, we believe that it should be considered a serious proposition for the space transporter. Comparison with other systems on a manufactured-weight basis shows VTO [Vertical Take-Off] rocket-propelled systems with modular or tandem stages to be the best. This conclusion is equally true when total costs are compared in so far as we can truly estimate them by existing methods. Our thoughts on a development programme include a small manned glider, and a rocket launched re-entry test vehicle, which we feel should lead straight to a prototype'.

"The chosen lifting body module 'Mustard', was able to be 'stacked' or 'clustered'. Since those studies were completed little has occurred which changes the above conclusions other than: a) further advances in technology, b) changed requirements assumed for Hotol such as 7t payload to LEO, unmanned, and larger re-entry footprint. Previous Warton studies found airbreathing first stages were not competitive, however, there is currently renewed European interest in such systems, i.e. Sänger (MBB) and STS 2000 (Aérospatiale). The ALV studies have therefore included similar systems".

The ALV Group had also attempted to assimilate all existing Hotol data: "More recent Stevenage studies leading up to the Swallow concept and subsequently Hotol have been considered during the ALV studies. One of the more significant conclusions is that a triamese system, similar to Mustard, has the next lowest total system cost. In addition, a Mach 3 air launch is [only a] little greater at the proposed lifetime launch capability of 5,040 tonnes (six vehicles) or 3,360 (four vehicles)".

He stated that "all current Hotol studies have been used as the basis for much of the ALV work" and that the BAe Brough technical audit of Hotol Configuration F was also examined: "During the period when this report was being compiled this audit was issued. It is worthy of note that the ALV study team had reached similar conclusions and already embodied many of the recommendations/alternatives in the ALV studies."

While the ALV executive summary had been issued in July 1987, the full summary was not made available until September. This lengthy and highly detailed report divided most of the ALVs up into three groups: A, B and Reference. A number of ALVs do not appear in any group, being apparently considered the least interesting or the least viable.

Group A included "those ALVs which are evolved directly from Hotol… [these] have been scaled using CAPS and studied in sufficient detail for lifecycle cost estimates to be prepared". Group B included "those ALVs having novel or complex design features/unknowns, which make early CAPS analysis impractical. They have been studied in sufficient detail to establish their likely practicality and to provide data for mass estimates". The Reference group included alternative launcher concepts that were, effectively, unchanged pre-existing designs.

GROUP A: HOTOL EVOLUTIONS

The ALVs directly derived from Hotol were subdivided into four further categories: single-stage airbreathers (Hotol Scaled), single-stage rocket only (ALV 30), two-stage rocket only (ALV 32, ALV 33, ALV 34, ALV 40) and air-launched (ALV 20, ALV 70).

Scaled Hotol 'F'. Little detail was given on Scaled Hotol 'F', except to say that it was the same as Hotol Configuration F but bigger, particularly in length and engine size. The summary report stated: "For the purposes of this study, and following detailed CAPS analysis, it is assumed that Hotol 'F' can be scaled and a significantly larger vehicle results."

SINGLE-STAGE ROCKET ONLY

ALV 30A. This was effectively a rocket-only Hotol, with the RB.545s and their associated intakes and other systems deleted. It was based on Configuration F albeit "optimised and scaled". Other changes included: "Wing area modified to suit the reduced re-entry mass; wing carry-through

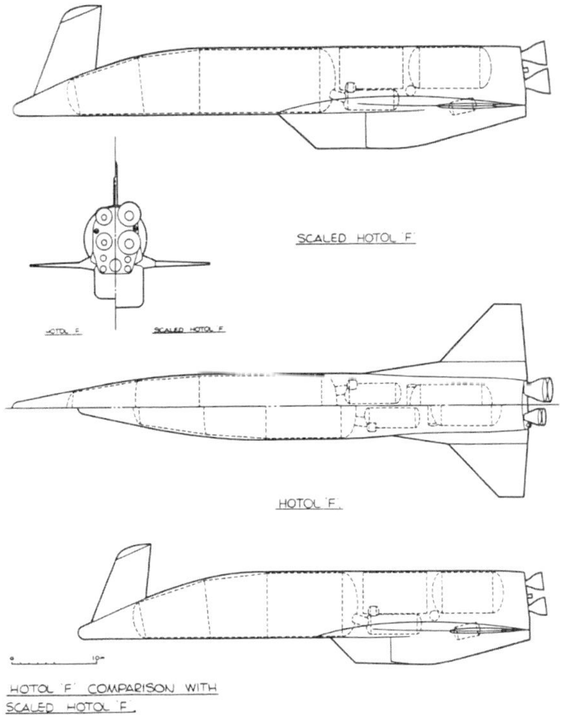

As part of the ALV study, Hotol Configuration F was reassessed using CAPS and the result was Scaled Hotol 'F'—a larger vehicle in practically every dimension.

structure improved; liquid oxygen tank enlarged to suit increased requirements; rocket motors scaled up to meet increased liquid oxygen requirements; wheeled undercarriage reconfigured".

ALV 30C. This was a VTO version of ALV 30A, with scaling making it somewhat smaller. It was "assumed that the vehicle will be prepared for launch in the horizontal position on a mobile ground preparation and erection vehicle".

TWO-STAGE ROCKET ONLY

ALV 32A + ALV 32B. It is rather difficult to see how this VTO two-stage tandem rocket-only launch system was evolved from Hotol—aside from the fact that it was (almost) fully reusable, with both the ALV 32A booster and ALV 32B orbiter able to fly back to base. The only expendable part was the interstage adaptor which would be jettisoned during separation. According to the report: "The vehicles shown are sized around the minimum fuselage diameter which will enclose the standard 7t payload bay. Every effort has been made to make the vehicles as near identical as possible since this has been shown to have a significant influence on costs. Both vehicles have a

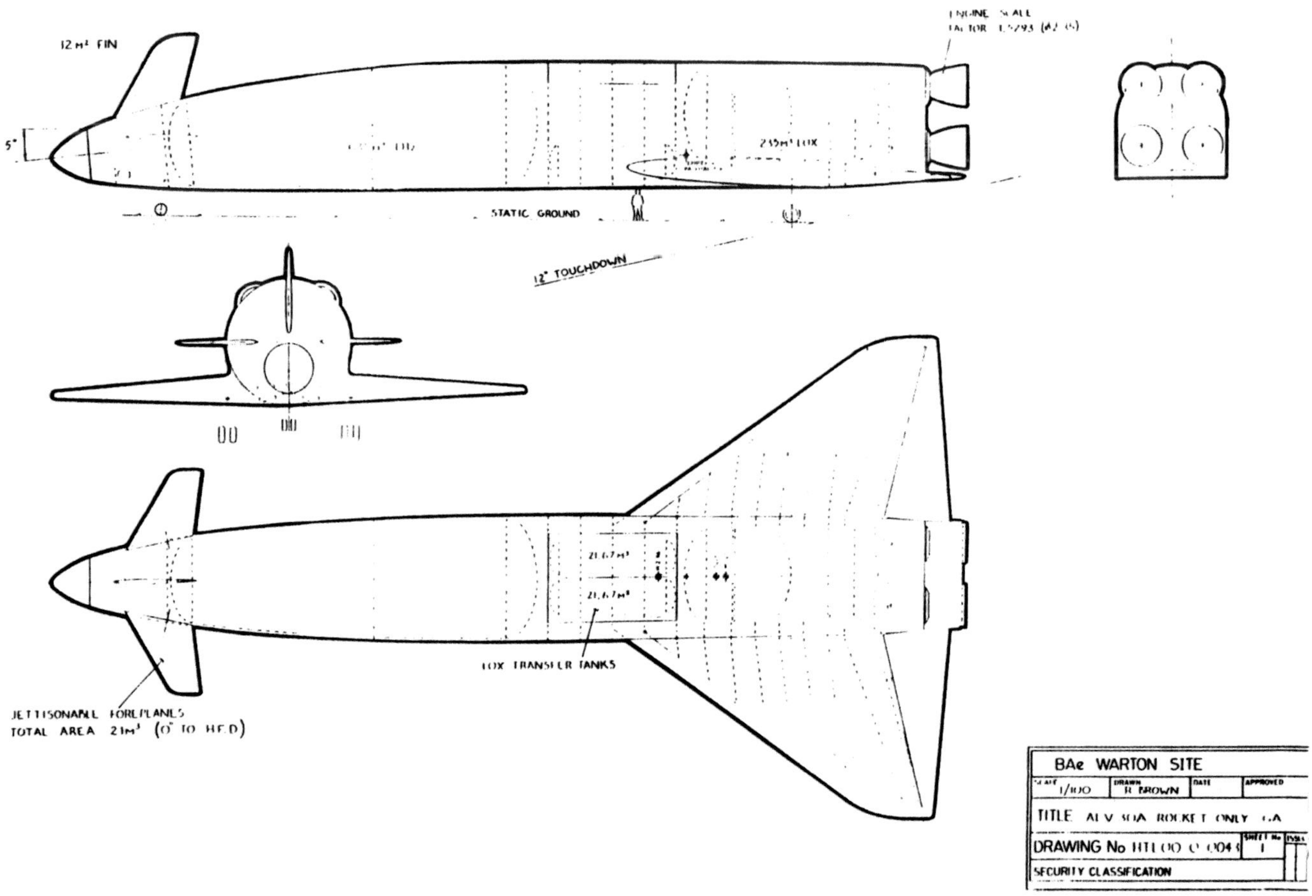

This oddity appears to be an early version of ALV 30A—looking more akin to ALV 01 and 02 than the design that would eventually be presented under the ALV 30A designation.

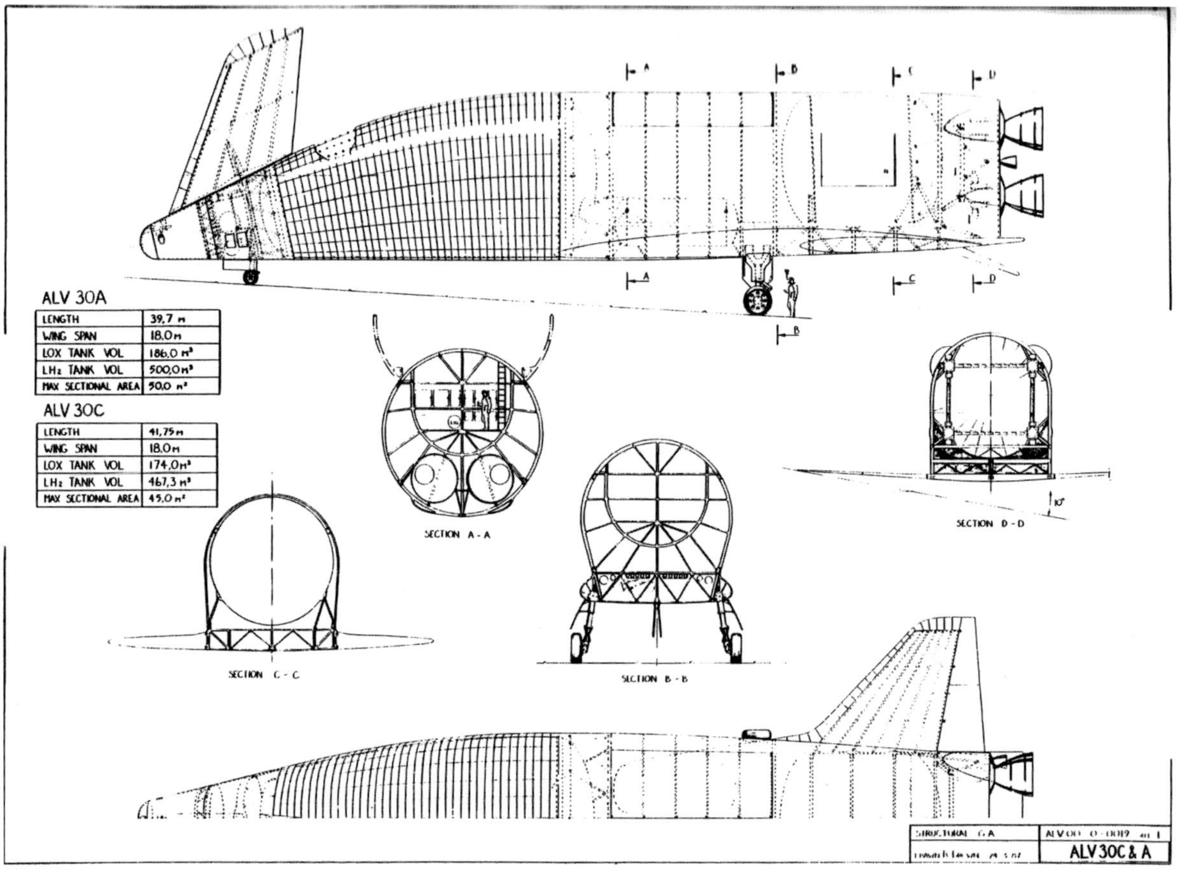

The pure rocket ALV 30A and C as presented in Walley's summary report. ALV 30A was the horizontal take-off version, while ALV 30C was little longer and was designed for vertical take-off.

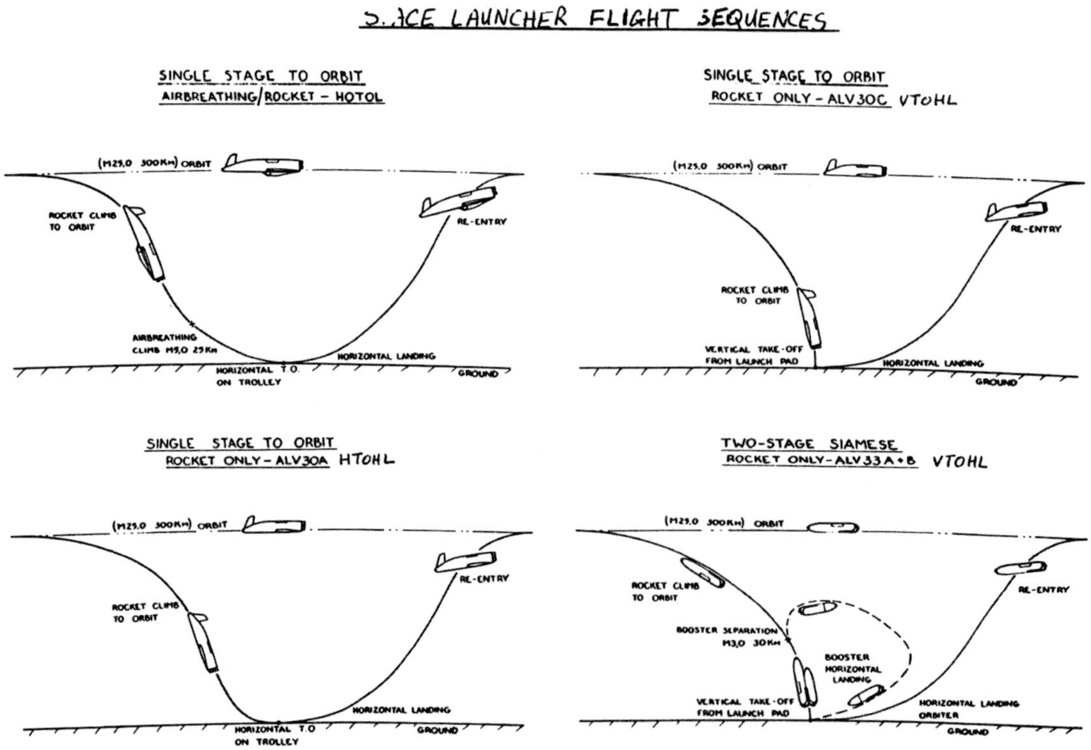

Comparison of Hotol's launch sequence against those of ALV 30C, ALV 30A and ALV 33A+B.

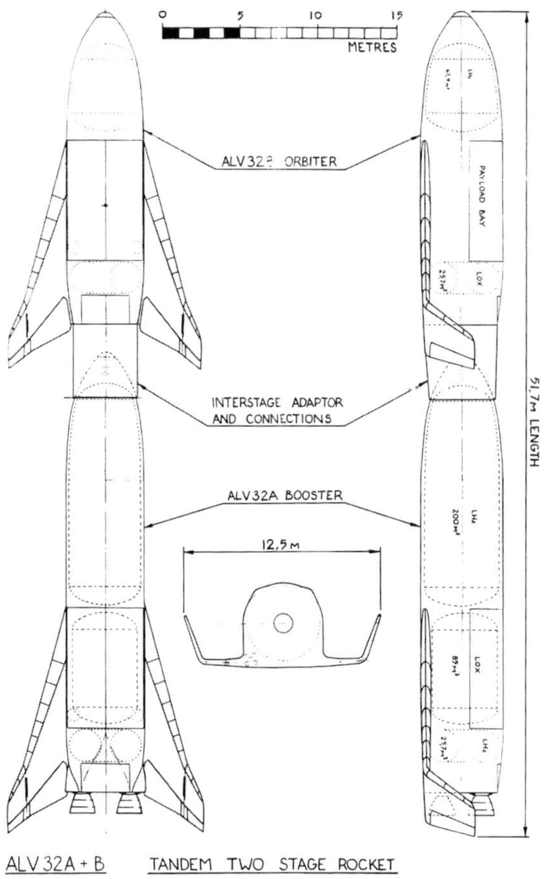

ALV 32A booster and ALV 32B orbiter in tandem.

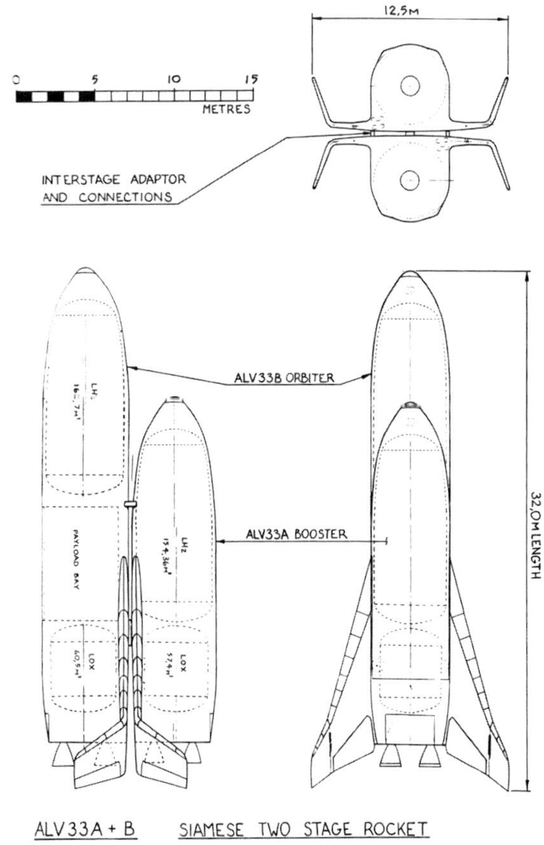

ALV 33A booster and ALV 33B orbiter in side by side 'siamese' configuration.

similar landing mass when the orbiter, ALV 32A, returns with a 7t payload.

"The geometric layout of both vehicles is therefore almost identical with [the only] major differences, from the orbiter to the booster, being increased liquid hydro gen and liquid oxygen volumes, thus increased fuselage length; liquid oxygen tank in cargo bay; four greater thrust rocket motors with lower nozzle area ratio; additional load-carrying structure for additional thrust and support of interstage adapter; attachment/release points for interstage adapter.

"Although the CAPS studies have been based on ALV 30C data, the vehicles drawn have been modified to show the 75° sweep (similar to Hermes) wing and tip fin controllers. Upper and lower body flaps are fitted. The need for retractable vortex generating foreplanes has not yet been proved, they are not fitted but could be if required."

ALV 33A + ALV 33B. Similar to ALV 32A/B but mated side by side rather than in tandem. Both vehicles were again fully reusable except for interstage fittings—though with this layout it was thought possible that these could be retracted and saved, rather than being unavoidably jettisoned.

Walley's report says: "It is assumed that all engines will be used during the ascent and up to separation when the booster breaks away and returns to base while the second stage continues into orbit. It is proposed to transfer fuel from the booster fuel system to the orbiter fuel system thereby keeping the orbiter fuel unused until after separation. Appropriate thrust vectoring will be necessary as the centre of gravity of the composite vehicle moves towards the orbiter as the booster tanks are emptied.

"CAPS studies have included a nominal allowance for shear loads between the vehicles, interstage adapters, fuel transfer pipes and valves, etc. In addition, an allowance has been made for additional, composite vehicle drag. There is evidence, from previous studies, that return-to-base propulsion will not be required."

ALV 34A x 2 + ALV 34B. Similar to ALV 33A/B but with two identical booster modules instead of one.

ALV 40A + ALV 40B (issue 1). This was a BAe analogue for Hermes in tandem with the expendable Ariane 5. According to the report: "At the outset of the design, before any significant CAPS work had been undertaken, initial studies were based on a three-stage system similar to Ariane 5/Hermes. At that time sufficient hand calculations were done to establish that, using design data consistent with Hotol 'F', a two-stage system would be practical.

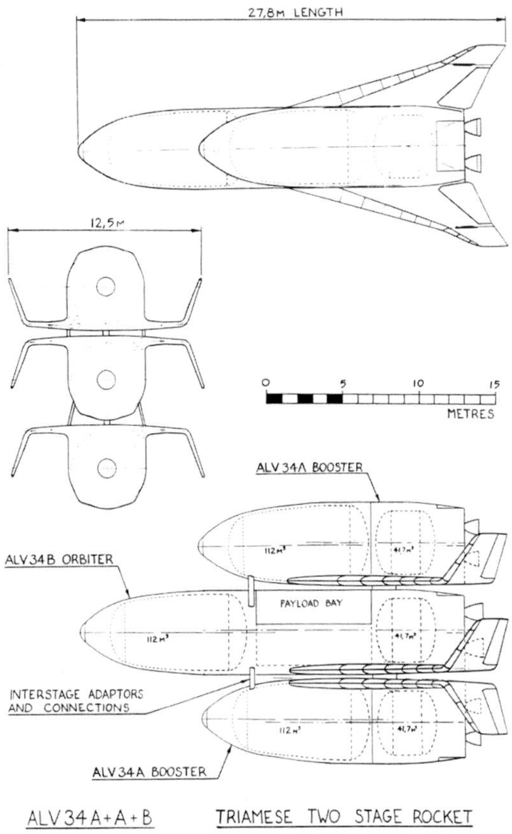

Two ALV 34A boosters and ALV 34B orbiter in 'triamese' stack configuration.

"From the outset of this design, the upper stage ALV 40B, was made as small as considered practical for comparison with Hermes. The 7t payload/bay determining the fuselage diameter and hence fuselage length, volume and mass were then established and from this the size of the first stage was derived... ALV 40A was made as simple... as possible to house the liquid oxygen and liquid hydrogen tanks [and] to support the interstage adapter and upper stage. It followed well-established design rules for similar expendable boosters and used 5 x HM60 Vulcain rocket engines currently being developed for Ariane 5. It was considered that advanced technology could offer very little further reduction in mass since booster design is already well optimised. In addition, it was unlikely to be cost effective on an expendable vehicle."

ALV 40A + ALV 40B (issue 2). Having designed the original ALV 40A/B and run it through CAPS, the ALV Group found that it was actually larger than necessary, so "some modest reduction in total lift-off and empty masses should be possible". ALV 40A/B (Issue 2)—a somewhat different design to the original, with reduced fuel volume—was therefore drawn.

AIR-LAUNCHED

ALV 70A + ALV 70C. Some of the earliest ALV work assessed an air-launched Hotol, with CAPS studies indicating "that by air launching Hotol at Mach 0.8 and 12.5km its mass could be reduced by ~13% but a special

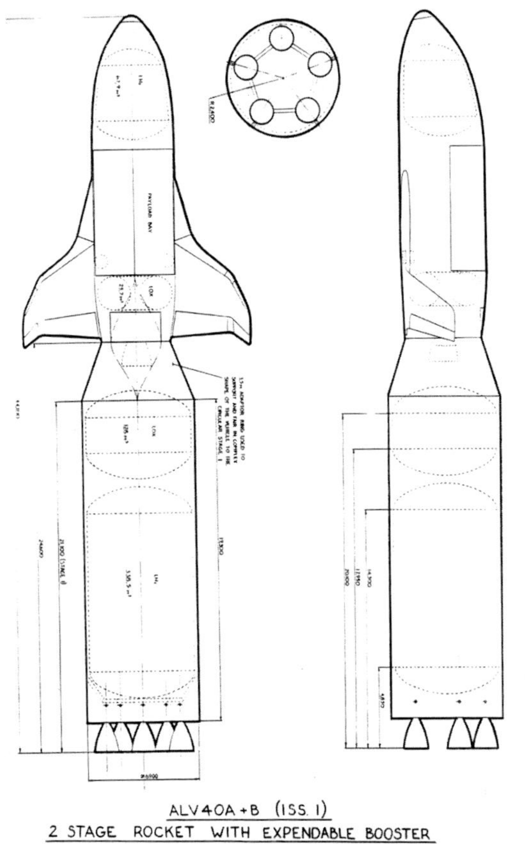

ALV 40A + ALV 40B—the BAe analogue of Hermes and Ariane 5, respectively. This is 'issue 1', the initial design.

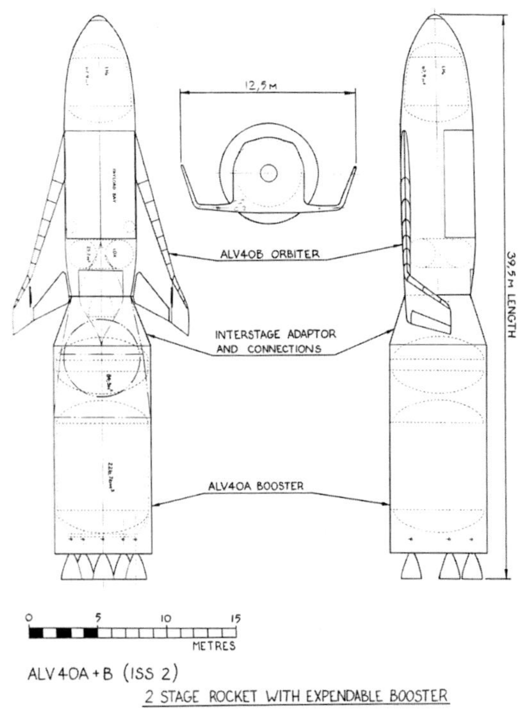

ALV 40A + ALV 40B (issue 2)—a revised and slightly smaller version of the design appearing in issue 1.

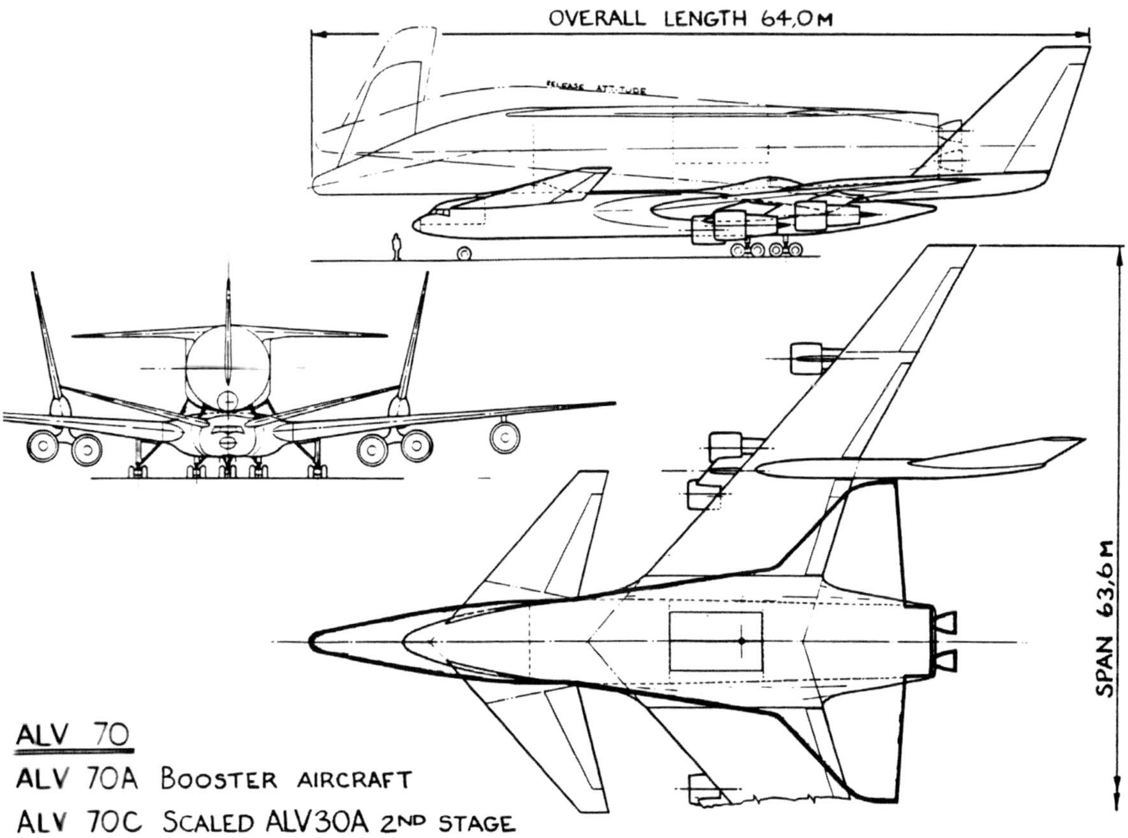

The monstrous ALV 70A booster aircraft—composed of repurposed Boeing 747 wing and tail parts married to a new fuselage—with the ALV 70C vehicle, which was a scaled version of ALV 30A.

launch aircraft would be necessary". The ALV Group looked at every existing large aircraft capable of Mach 0.8 and concluded that "even the heaviest Boeing 747 Freighter would be unsuitable for direct conversion," so "in order to minimise development and manufacturing costs for a completely new aircraft it was proposed that as many 747 Freighter components as practical be used".

The resulting aircraft was the rather spectacular ALV 70A—all the more spectacular for the fact that apart from the new wide/flat fuselage on which the orbiter sat, it was largely composed of Boeing 747 components. Walley wrote: "It provides a platform for the orbiter [and] its attachment/launch apparatus and contains accommodation for personnel monitoring the orbiter and its launch. In addition, it contains kerosene tanks, liquid oxygen and liquid hydrogen tanks for orbiter 'top-up' fuel and the main undercarriage bays.

"To facilitate loading of the orbiter, the main undercarriage legs are shortened and an air transportable ramp is attached to the lowered rear of the aircraft. The orbiter is then winched into place and locked to the attachment points. It will be necessary for all the orbiter's systems to be fully active, with the flying controls operating simultaneously to those of the launch aircraft, therefore power supplies and electrical/electronic connections must also be made."

The orbiter, ALV 70C, was based on the rocket-Hotol ALV 30A and designed to launch at Mach 0.8 and an altitude of 12.5km. It differed quite dramatically, however, in having a high wing position "to minimise interference with the launch aircraft".

The ALV 70A/C combination would need to reach 240kts in order to get airborne and Walley noted that further refinements to the concept might be necessary to achieve a reasonable take-off, such as expendable fairings over the rocket motors and "immediately prior to launch, the partial use of orbiter engines to assist in acceleration and pull up to release attitude of 20°". In addition to both vehicles reaching 20°, the orbiter itself would need to be raised 5°—which would pose its own difficulties.

Combined take-off mass would be around 420t, though "examination of existing aircraft and new projects suggests that 400t is likely to be a realistic maximum for major airfields". Aborted take-off on a wet runway would require 4,800m and ferry range with an empty orbiter was 2,300NM.

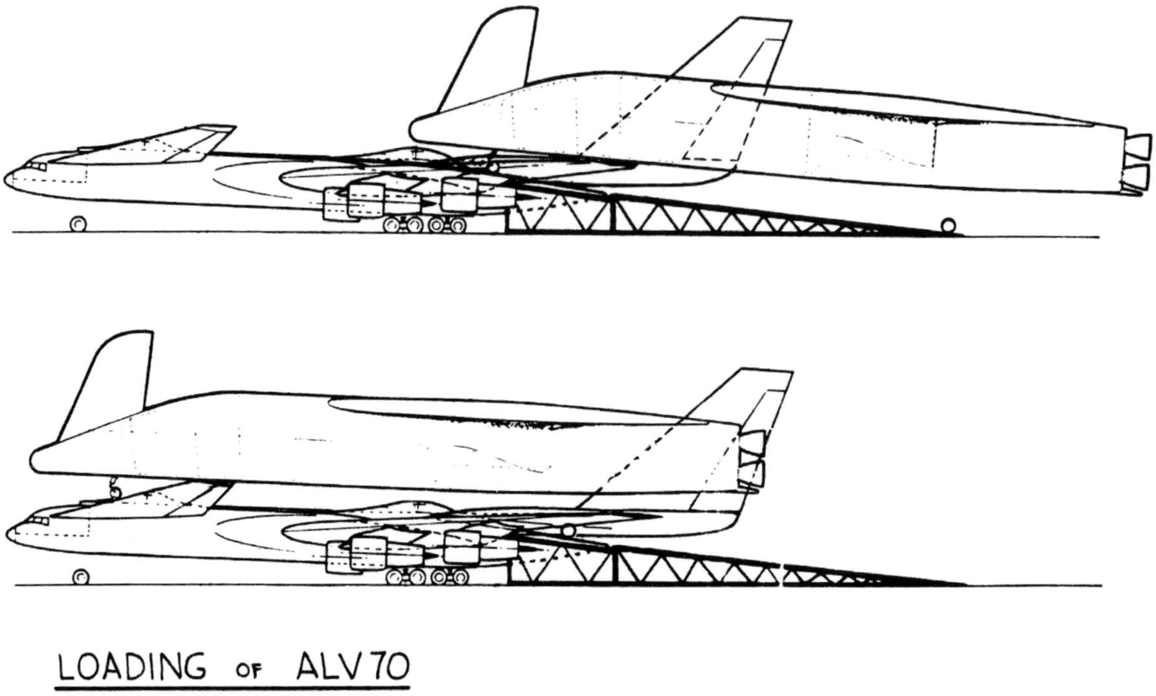

The process of loading the ALV 70C onto the ALV 70A booster.

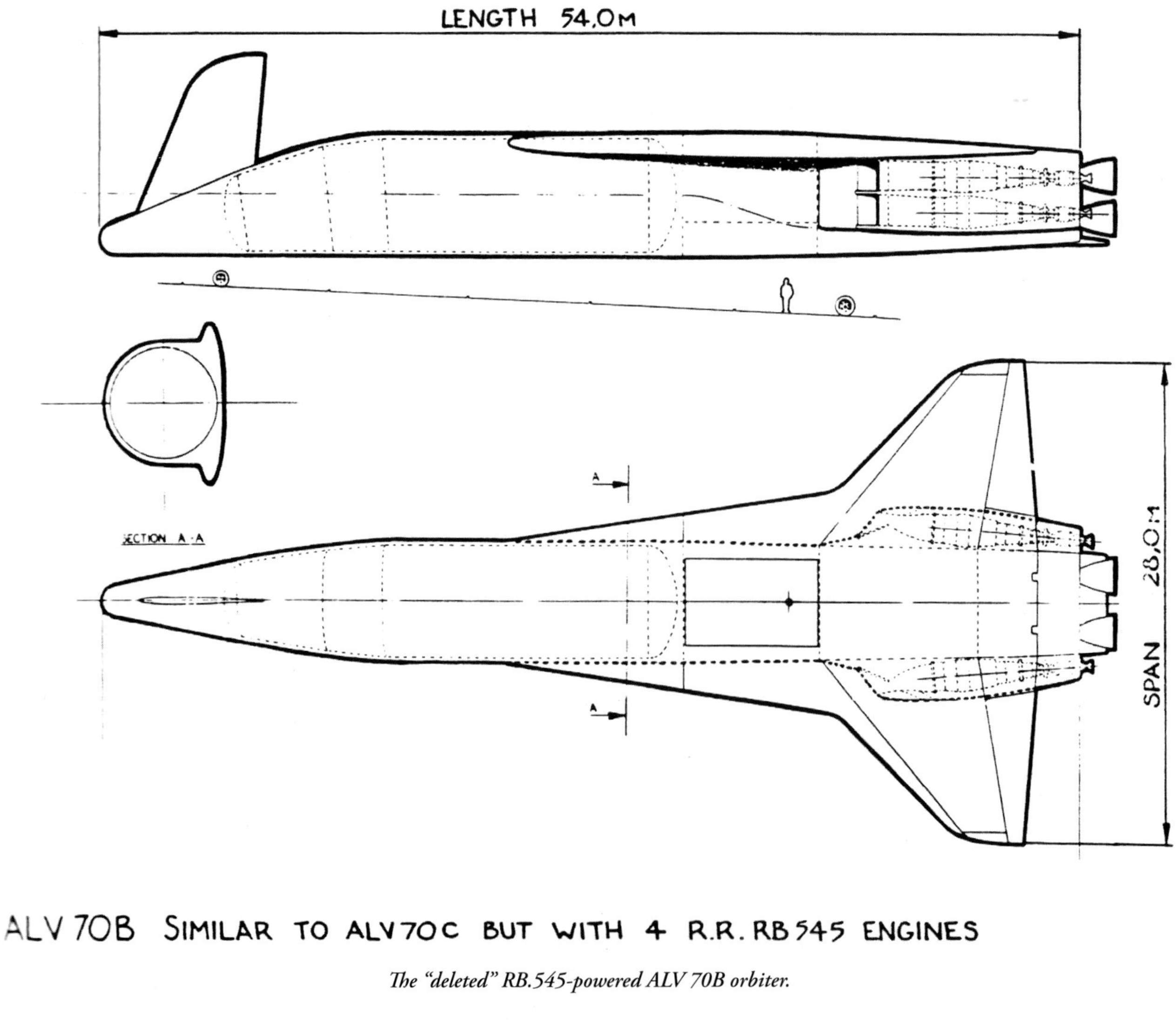

The "deleted" RB.545-powered ALV 70B orbiter.

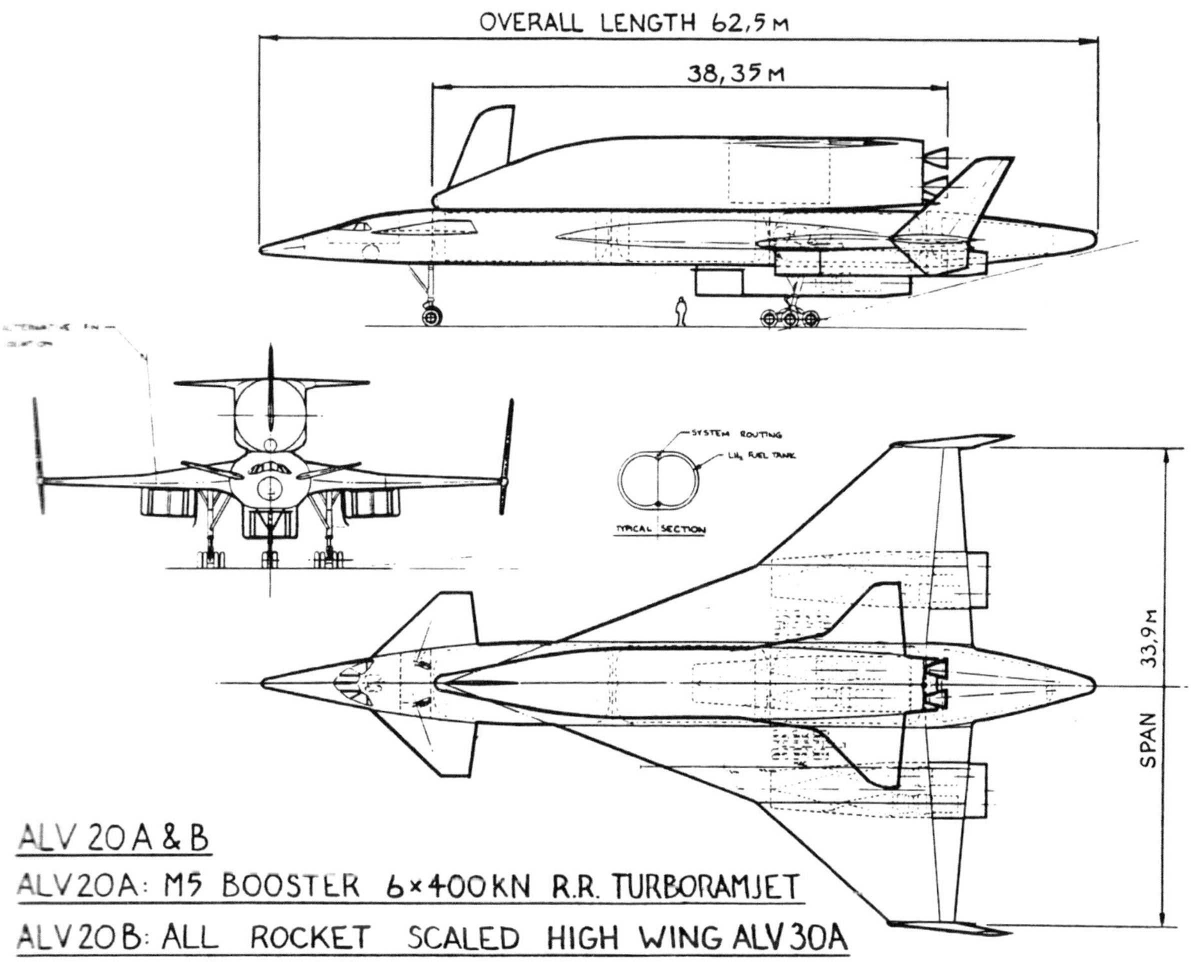

ALV 20A booster aircraft with ALV 20B orbiter, the latter being another scaled-up high-wing variant of ALV 30A — the all-rocket horizontal take-off Hotol.

ALV 70B. This was the originally-planned orbiter for the ALV 70 system, using four RB.545 engines mounted in nacelles on the rear fuselage sides, below the wing, but these apparently "offered little advantage and were deleted", resulting in ALV 70C.

ALV 20A + ALV 20B. A second boost aircraft (ALV 20A) and orbiter (ALV 20B) combination, with ALV 20B being another high-wing derivative of ALV 30A. It differed from ALV 70C in having a much shorter wingspan. ALV 20A differed from ALV 70A in being a completely new aircraft composed entirely of bespoke parts.

According to the report: "This system was studied for direct comparison with the MBB/ERNO Sänger project although previous BAe studies found it was not competitive. Initial configuration studies were based on the previous BAe work but were updated to include aircraft longitudinal instability, the use of all moving foreplanes and a more advanced wing. The six RR proposed turbo-ramjet engines, using LH2 fuel, are housed in three twin installation nacelles. The main undercarriage units retract into a thickened wing root section."

Unlike the subsonic ALV 70A, ALV 20A would carry its orbiter up to Mach 5 and launch it at an altitude of 26km, though take-off speed would be just 200kts. Take-off mass would be around 270t. Aborted take-off on a wet runway would need a quite reasonable 2,500m but ferry range with an empty orbiter was just 1,700NM.

ALV 20A/2. This was largely the same as the regular ALV 20A but with two liquid-fuelled rocket motors in the rear of the fuselage replacing the two centreline turboramjets. They would only be used during the final acceleration to Mach 5 and pull up to launch attitude.

GROUP B: COMPLEX DESIGNS

The second set of ALVs was for those which incorporated "novel or complex design features and many unknowns which have made early CAPS analysis impossible". The Group B designs were divided into four overlapping subcategories: single-stage airbreathers (ALV 01, ALV 02, ALV 90, ALV 100), single-stage rocket only (ALV 91A, ALV 60 with reduced payload), two-stage rocket only (ALV 60 x 2 or 3) and air-launched (ALV 70A/ALV 60B, ALV 20A/ALV 60B).

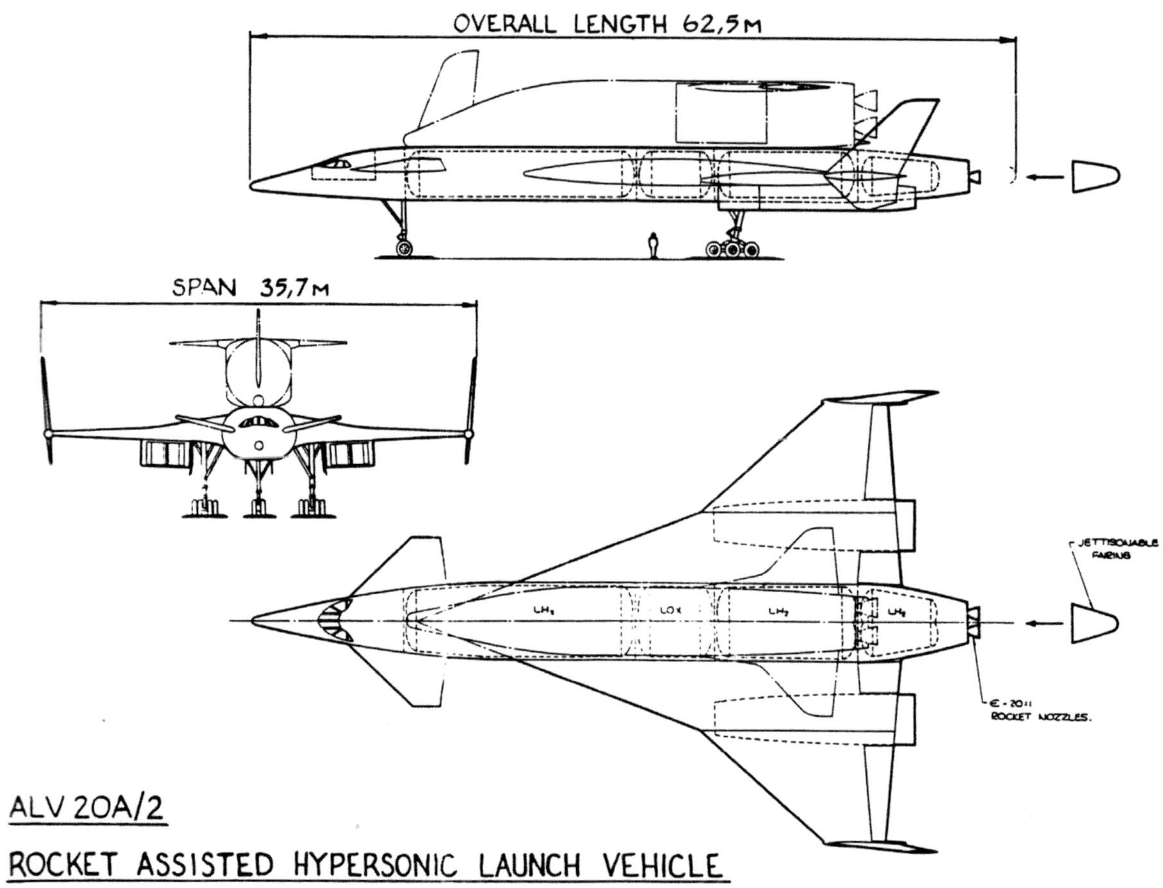

ALV 20A/2 booster aircraft with ALV 20B orbiter. The ALV 20A/2 featured a pair of liquid-fuelled rocket motors in its rear fuselage in place of the regular ALV 20A's two centreline turboramjets.

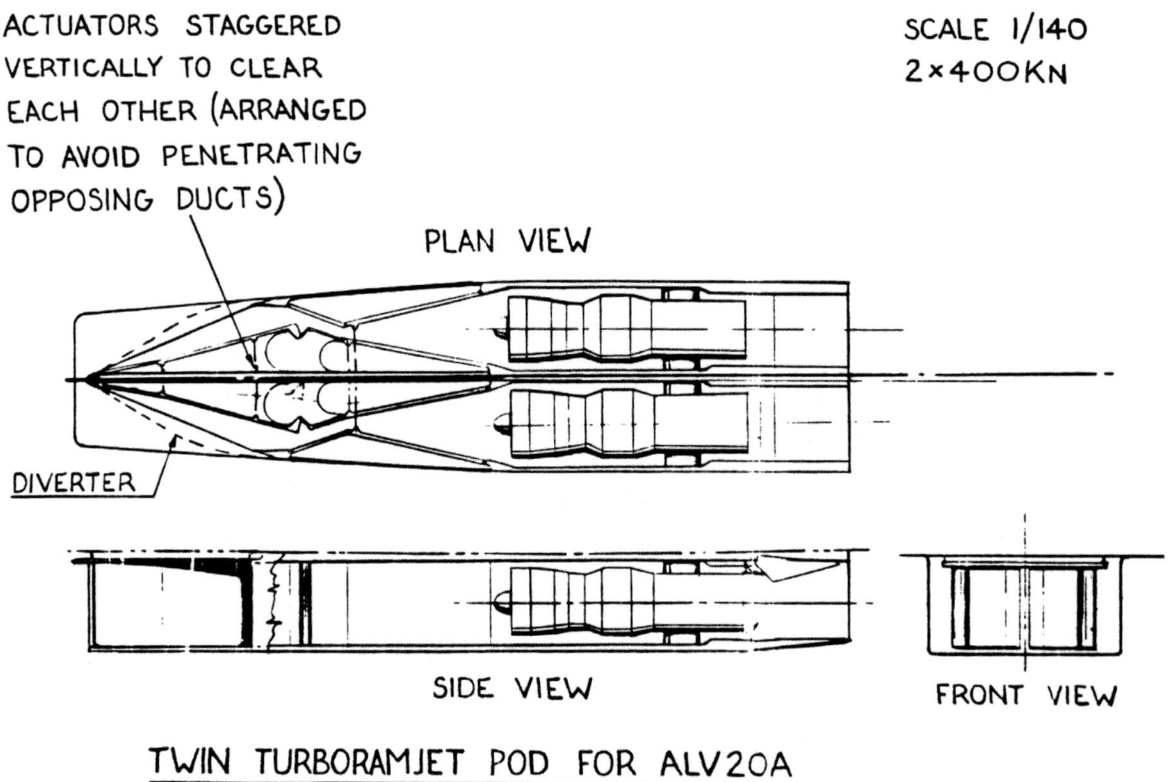

The standard ALV 20A would have three underslung pods, each containing a pair of turboramjets.

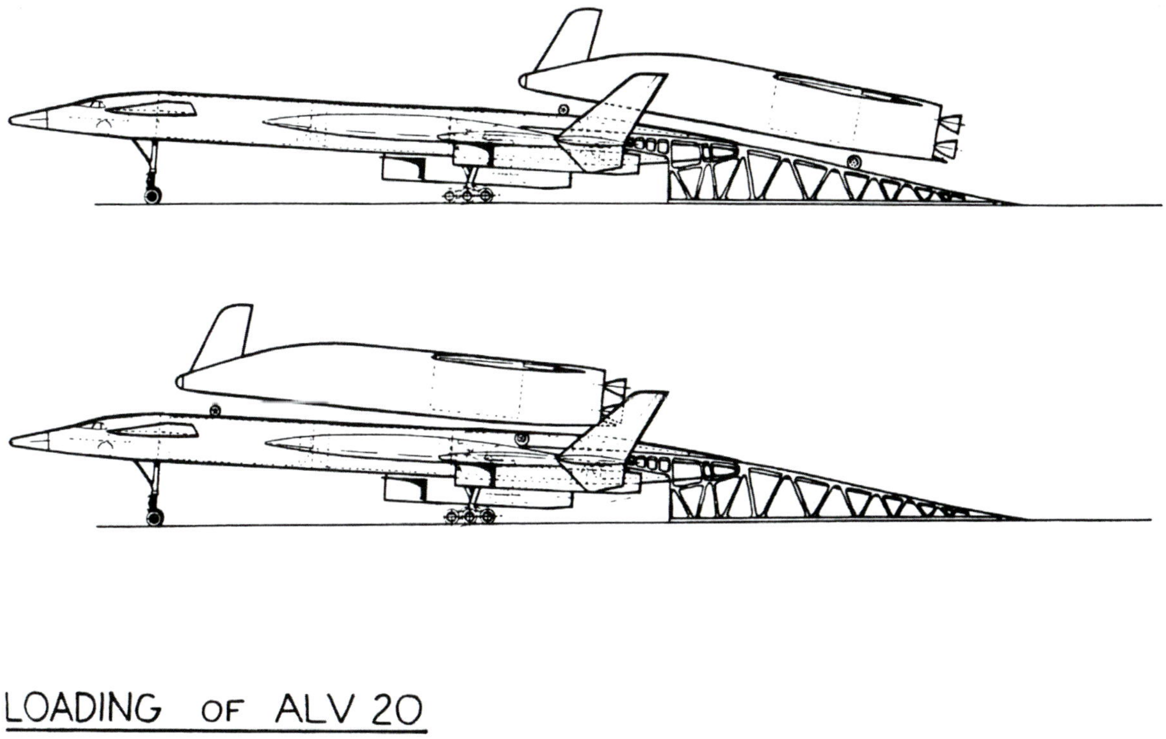

The ALV study group gave some consideration to how an ALV 20B could actually be loaded onto the first-stage ALV 20A aircraft—via a lowered rear end and a ramp.

ALV 01. CHRIS SANDHAM-BAILEY

ALV 01 and **ALV 02**. This pair of Hotol Configuration F derivatives were "adapted to suit alternative RR engine proposals which, unlike the RB.545 in Hotol, demanded an 'inline' installation. A high wing with large inboard strakes, which provided an 'armpit' engine installation was chosen. Either vehicle would be trolley-launched. A significant amount of work was done on these vehicles but this was abandoned following the results of the CAPS airbreathing engine versus rocket engine studies, which indicated that they were not competitive".

ALV 01 was to be powered by a quartet of Rolls-Royce rocket-ejector-ramjets, while ALV 02 was designed to accommodate four Rolls-Royce turbo-ramjet-rockets. Despite their designation, they appear to have been part of a trio which also included the aborted ALV 70B, which looked very similar but had four supplemental RB.545s.

ALV 100C/4. The ALV 100C concept was remarkably straightforward: put Hotol's RB.545s into its wings. This had manifold benefits, such as reducing the total mass of the intakes, engines, nozzles and even the wings themselves. The fuselage structure could be simplified and the fin and rudder could be positioned at the rear, with a more forward-set centre of gravity resulting in lower fuselage bending moments—allowing for further reduced mass.

Another significant benefit was a central payload bay directly above the wing carry-through structure. Another was the installation of a second liquid hydrogen tank in the rear of the vehicle, allowing for more even weight distribution and maintenance of the centre of gravity even as the fuel was drained. It was to have thrust deflectors for pitch/thrust vectoring, elevons for roll control, a central under-fuselage flap for pitch-down, the aft rudder for yaw control and retractable vortex-generating foreplanes for additional pitch-up, if required.

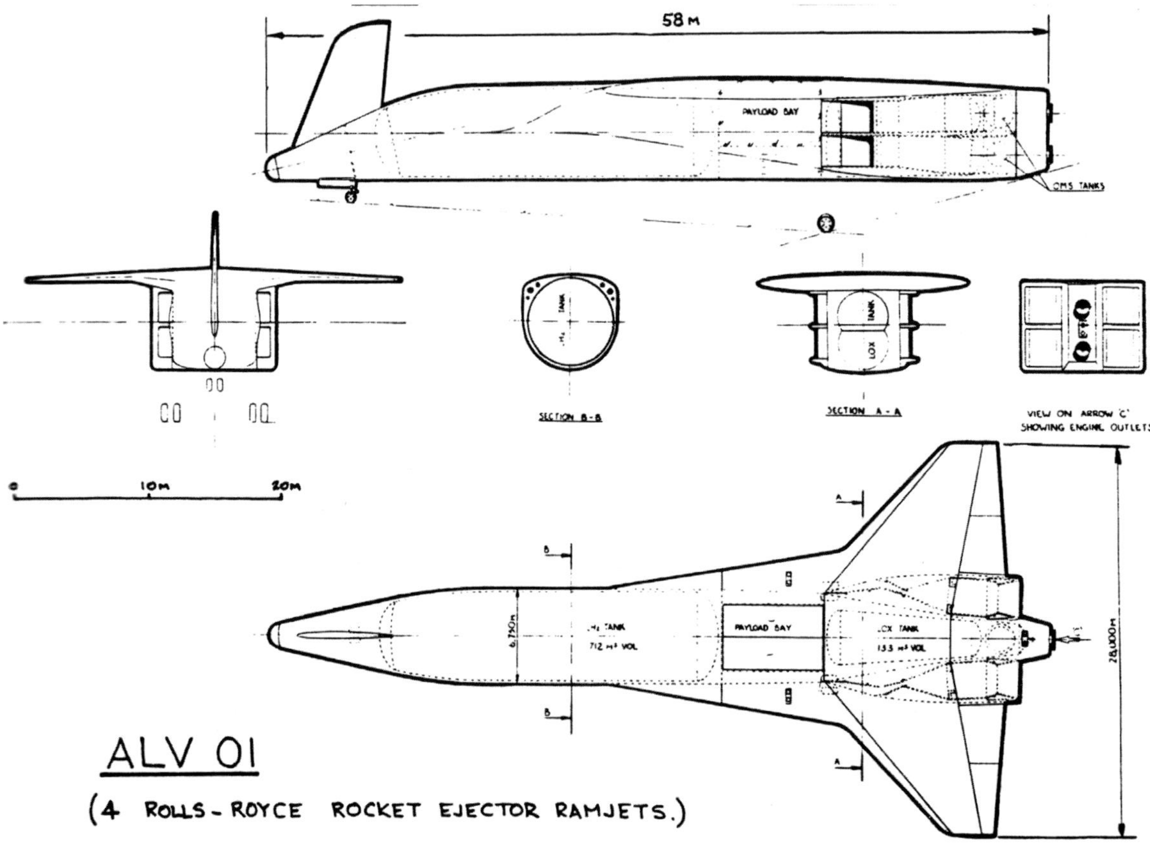

The high-wing ALV 01, powered by a quartet of Rolls-Royce rocket ejector ramjets with side-mounted intakes.

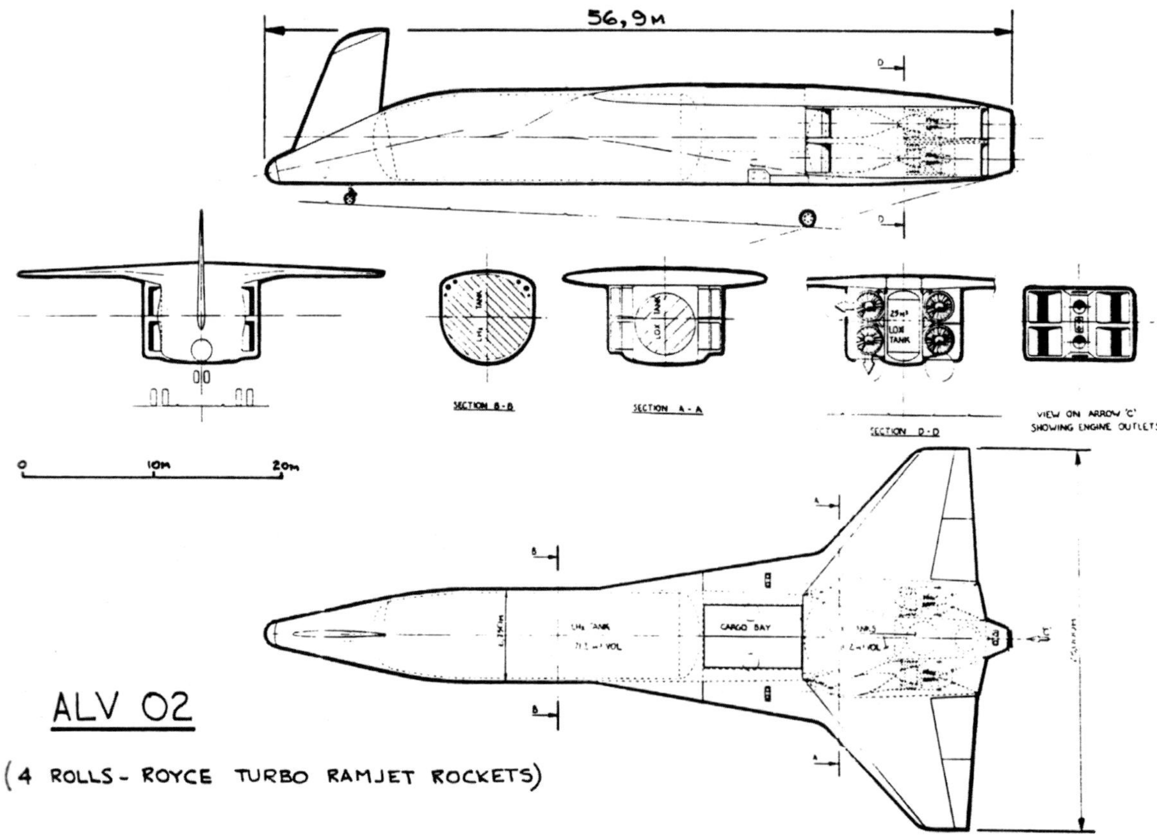

ALV 02 differed from ALV 01 in its propulsion system—four Rolls-Royce turbo ramjet rockets—and its overall size, being somewhat smaller.

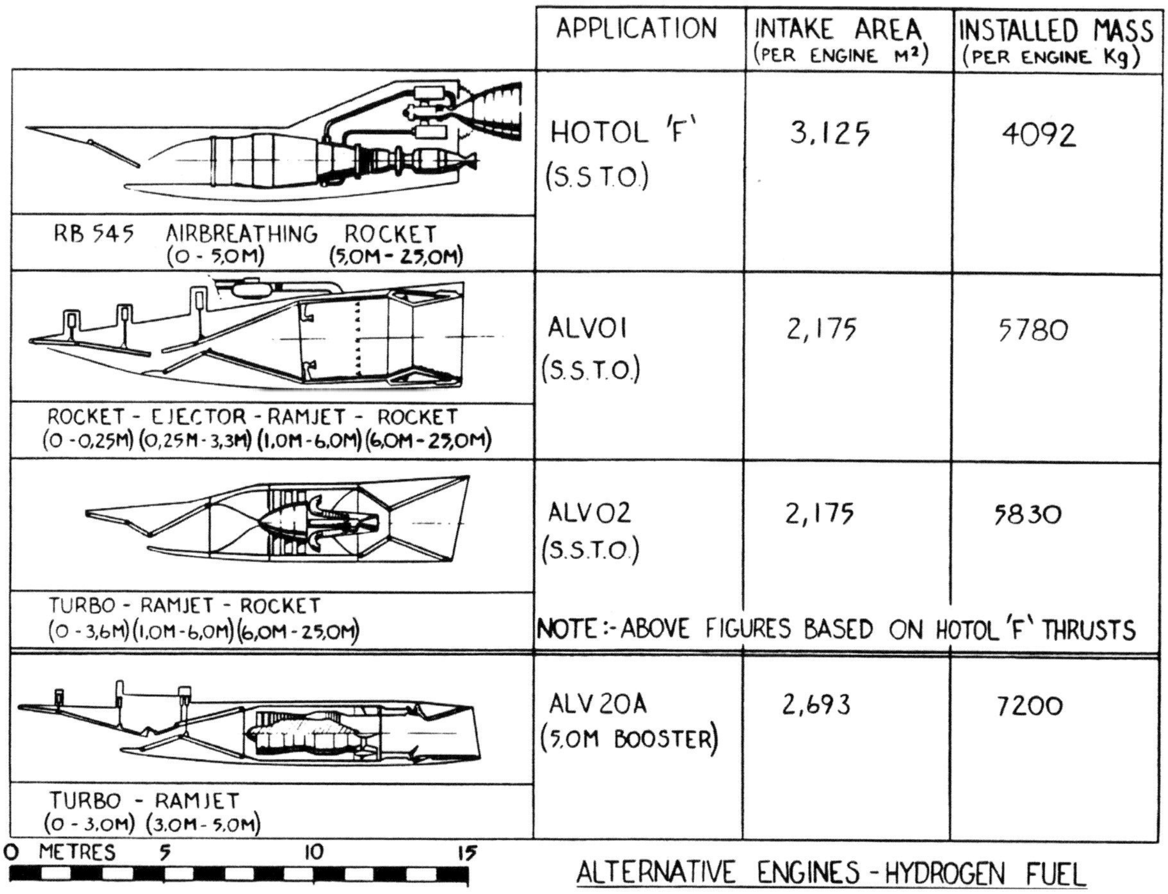

The RB.545 used by Hotol compared to the rocket ejector ramjet of ALV 01, the turbo ramjet rocket of ALV 02 and the turbo-ramjet of the ALV 20A Mach 5 booster aircraft.

A dual fuel variant was proposed but ALV 100C was the liquid hydrogen version. It had been "sized around the original Hotol 'D' which had a launch mass of 205t. It was considered that mass and drag (hence fuel savings) should be possible to enable this mass to be achieved. Initial mass estimates and a preliminary aerodynamic assessment are promising and indicate that the configuration is worthy of more detailed study".

Walley and his team seem to have thought they were really onto something with ALV 100. It offered a potential solution to some of Hotol's most intractable problems—such as the trim issue and foreplane overheating. The configuration also seemed to offer significant mass reductions.

As such, the ALV summary report went into a little more detail on ALV 100 than many of the other designs and iterated upon it considerably. To begin with, it outlined a possible 'development route': "An important feature of the ALV 100 concept is the more gradual development route and also the potential for significant future growth. For instance, a pair of engines could be developed slung beneath Concorde."

ALV 100C/8 and **ALV 100C/10**. Another part of the ALV 100C development path was that "initial airframe development and flight testing (also for smaller payloads) could use a four-engined vehicle; subsequent variants with eight or ten engines and a lengthened fuselage could launch larger heavier payloads". In other words, putting the RB.545s into the wings also made it a little easier to add engines without having to change the whole airframe.

Yet another advantage of the wing-mounted engines was in reference to the trolley take-off, since airflow to the intakes would remain unaffected throughout. And, "alternatively a jettisonable heavy-duty undercarriage, to which solid booster rockets (RATO) are attached, may be fitted. The undercarriage units would be jettisoned and parachuted into a recovery area after lift off. For aborted take-off, heavy duty brakes and an arrestor hook, for engagement with a conventional ground arrest system, are fitted".

The ALV Group had even gone so far as to consult Warton's Aerodynamics Department on the ALV 100 configuration. The noted structural advantages were listed as "simple fuselage structure, mid centre of gravity, lower bending moments hence small diameter and high fineness ratio; aft conventional fin and rudder, torsion box can be RP-1 [kerosene] fuel tank. Best location, loads

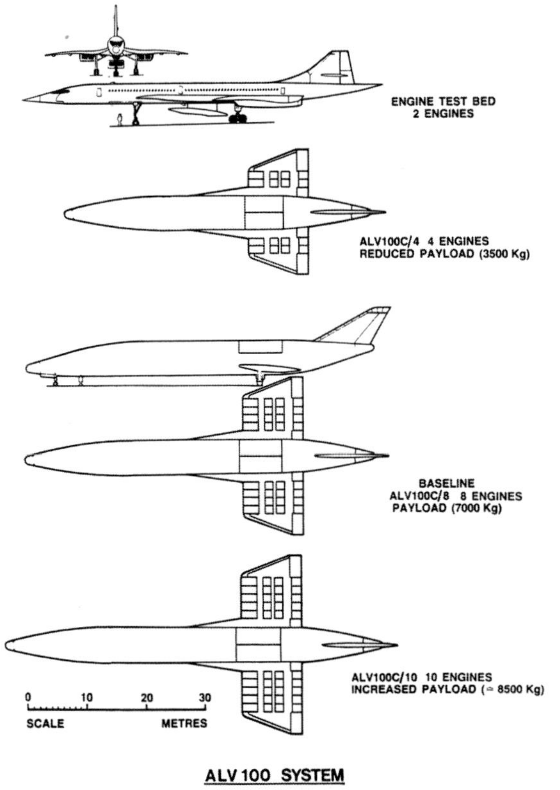

The ALV 100 'system' scaled for four, eight or ten engines.

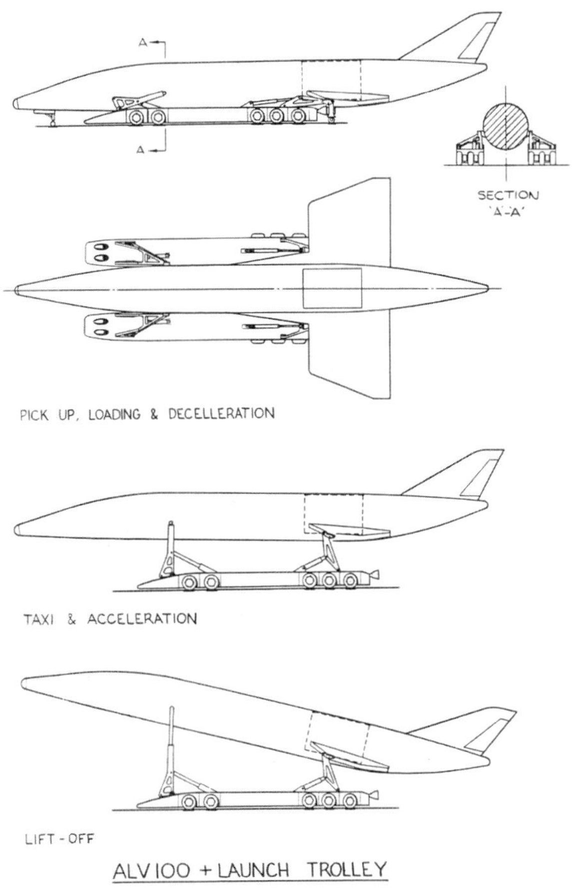

ALV 100 could take off using a launch trolley, like Hotol, or using jettisonable landing gear.

more easily carried, reduced actuation problems, shielded during re-entry; engines in wings provide bending relief; simple shortest possible undercarriage located in best position; structural arrangement permits ready attachment to a launch trolley or jettisonable heavy-duty undercarriage and arrestor hook".

In terms of aerodynamics, "engines in wings ... give lower induced and profile drags whilst airbreathing. Some airflow entrainment/lift augmentation expected from rocket exhaust; additional lifting area from intakes and nozzles; very slender fuselage and effectively a 3% thickness to chord wing give a lift/drag of 3.7 compared to Hotol 'F' of 2.3. One of the main terms is the absence of base drag; best centre of gravity—should avoid need for a retractable foreplane, especially on the dual fuel variant; conventional most effective fixed aft fin and rudder; minimum intake drags, minimum spill drag (if at all), since fully variable. Intake designed for best possible total pressure recovery; intakes well clear of any turbulent air from launch trolley or jettisonable undercarriage".

And in terms of general advantages, the "integrated engine units can be developed separately; vehicle could be progressively developed from small prototype, providing alternative payload capability and significant development potential; integrated engine units more readily serviced/replaced; manufacturing and assembly problems minimised".

There were also some disadvantages. Structurally, there would be a strong transfer of loads from the wings to the fuselage; the wing structure would be complex, with inconvenient upper surface access panels; acoustic effects on the rear fuselage and fin could be significant; and both intakes and nozzles would be subjected to very high temperatures which "may require cooling and/or the use of ceramics".

Also, an engine-out scenario on take-off could result in a tricky situation since it would "require uprating of remaining engines on the same side and throttling the opposite side. Critical for only a few seconds since fuel is being used rapidly". Lastly, as a general note of caution, there was "little historical data/information on integrated engine systems/aerodynamics".

ALV 100A, ALV 100B and **ALV 100D.** While the favoured ALV 100C was powered by RB.545s, three other variants were studied which derived somewhat from the ALV 100 concept's origin—some three decades earlier. In short, it was based on English Electric's P.10 reconnaissance aircraft design of the early 1950s. Walley included both a diagram of this and a photo of a wind tunnel model. The summary report explained: "The P.10 was

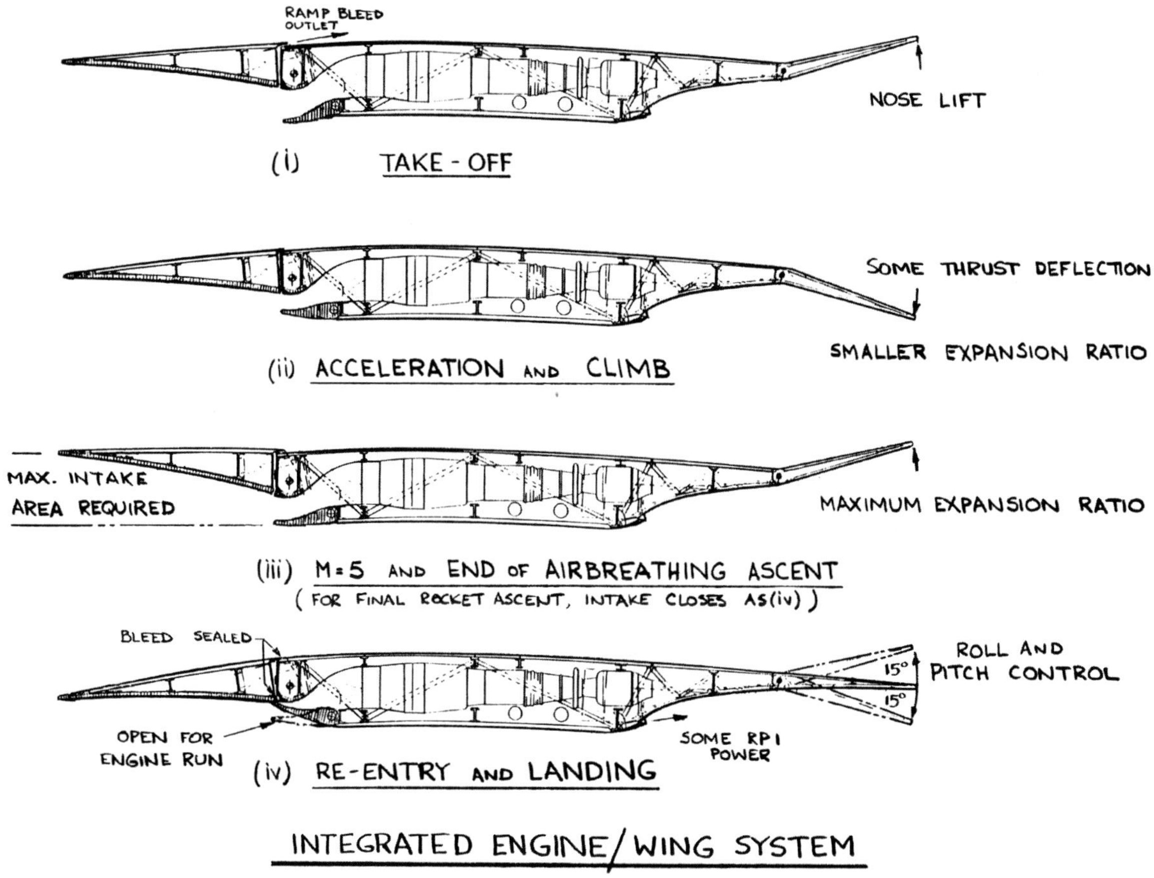

The RB.545 reimagined as a linear system for installation in the ALV 100C's wings.

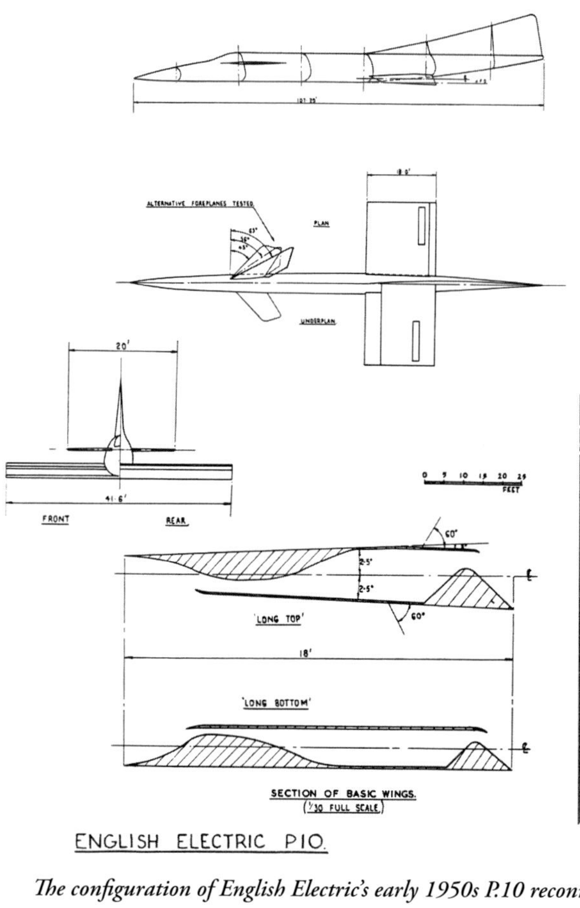

a project studied at Warton and RAE/NGTE Farnborough … conceived in response to a military requirement for a high altitude (70,000-100,000ft), high Mach No. (3-5) reconnaissance aircraft.

"Since this was well beyond the capability of turbojets, ramjets were to be used. One of the most novel features was the series of ramjets, together with two turbojets for take-off and acceleration, located/integrated into the unswept wings. Alternative arrangements of fixed

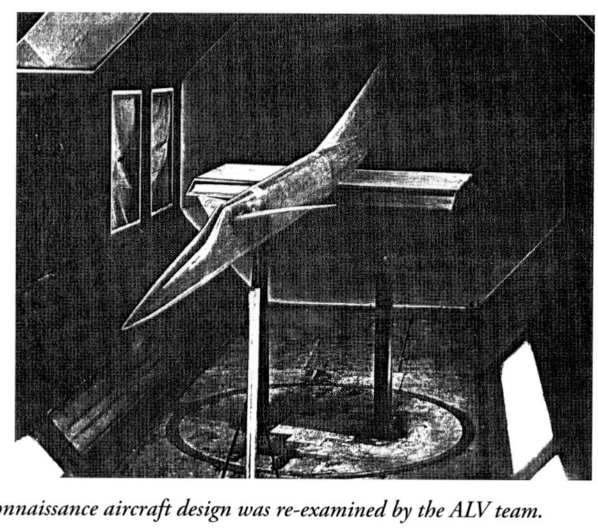

The configuration of English Electric's early 1950s P.10 reconnaissance aircraft design was re-examined by the ALV team.

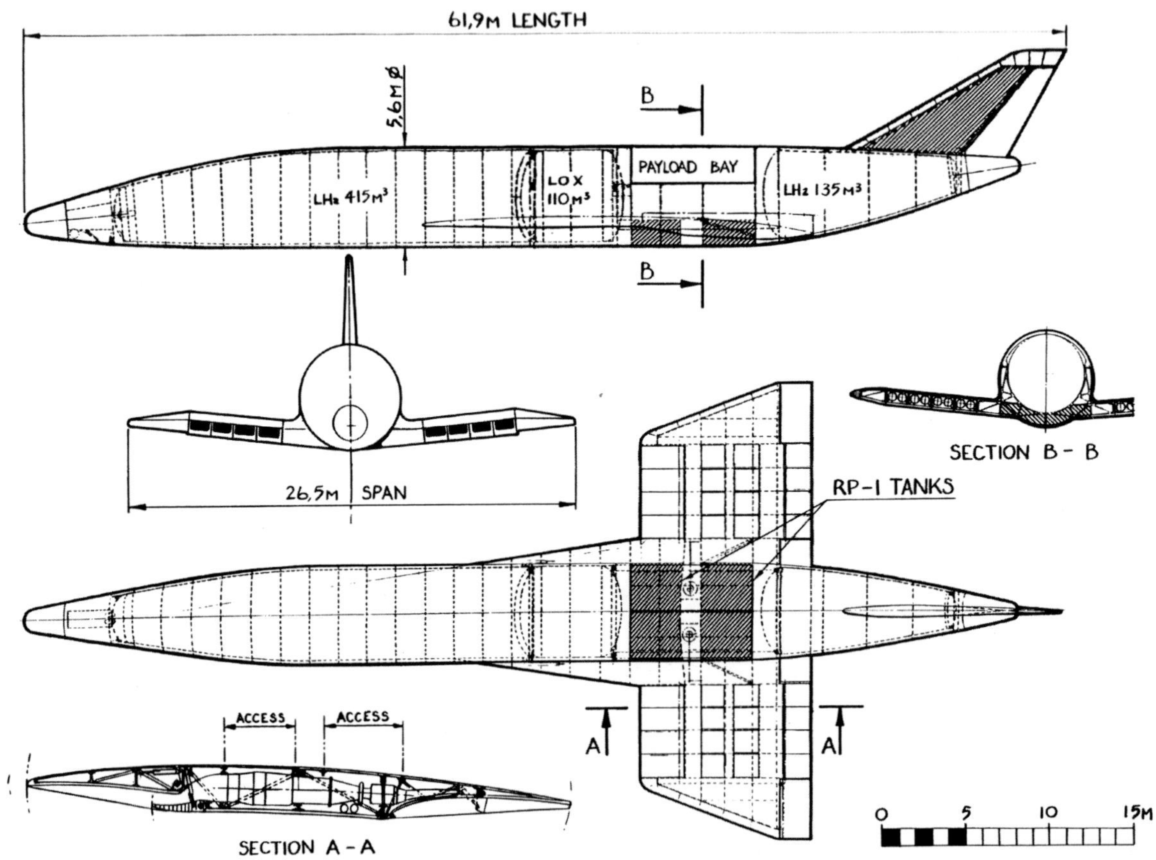

ALV 100, a vehicle design characterised by banks of engines installed in its wings "mouthorgan" style.

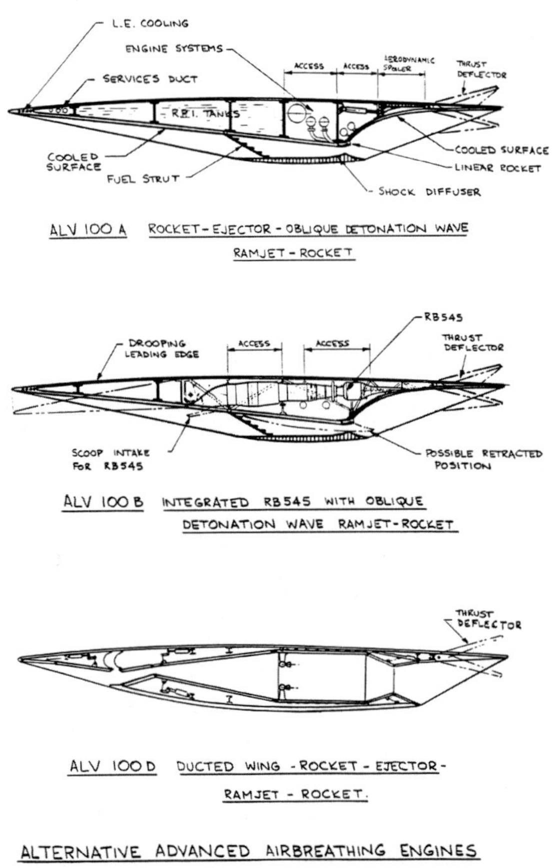

Engine installations for ALV 100A, 100B and 100D.

isentropic intakes and nozzles were proposed. Many detailed studies, together with high- and low-speed wind tunnel tests on the alternative configurations, were undertaken. In general, wind tunnel results were favourable, flow through the ducted wing was found to reduce both induced and profile drag increasing lift/drag significantly.

"Far more work would however have been essential to develop the concept, in particular the intakes and nozzles, to achieve the optimum configuration. The project was abandoned late in 1955 due to lack of government interest in the project. Sufficient work was however completed to suggest that such a configuration should be studied as an alternative to the Hotol 'F' system."

ALV 100A was to be powered by a rocket-ejector-oblique detonation wave (ODW) ramjet-rocket, ALV 100B was to have RB.545s with ODW ramjet-rocket and ALV 100D would have had ducted wing-rocket-ejector-ramjet-rockets.

LIFTING BODIES

ALV 90. Sandy Burns' monthly reports going into early 1987 included several mentions of flat, broad, lifting body-type fuselage concepts for Hotol and it seems likely that he was referring to designs being studied by the ALV Group.

Walley's summary report outlined this train of thought: "The use of lifting bodies for re-entry vehicles, missiles and

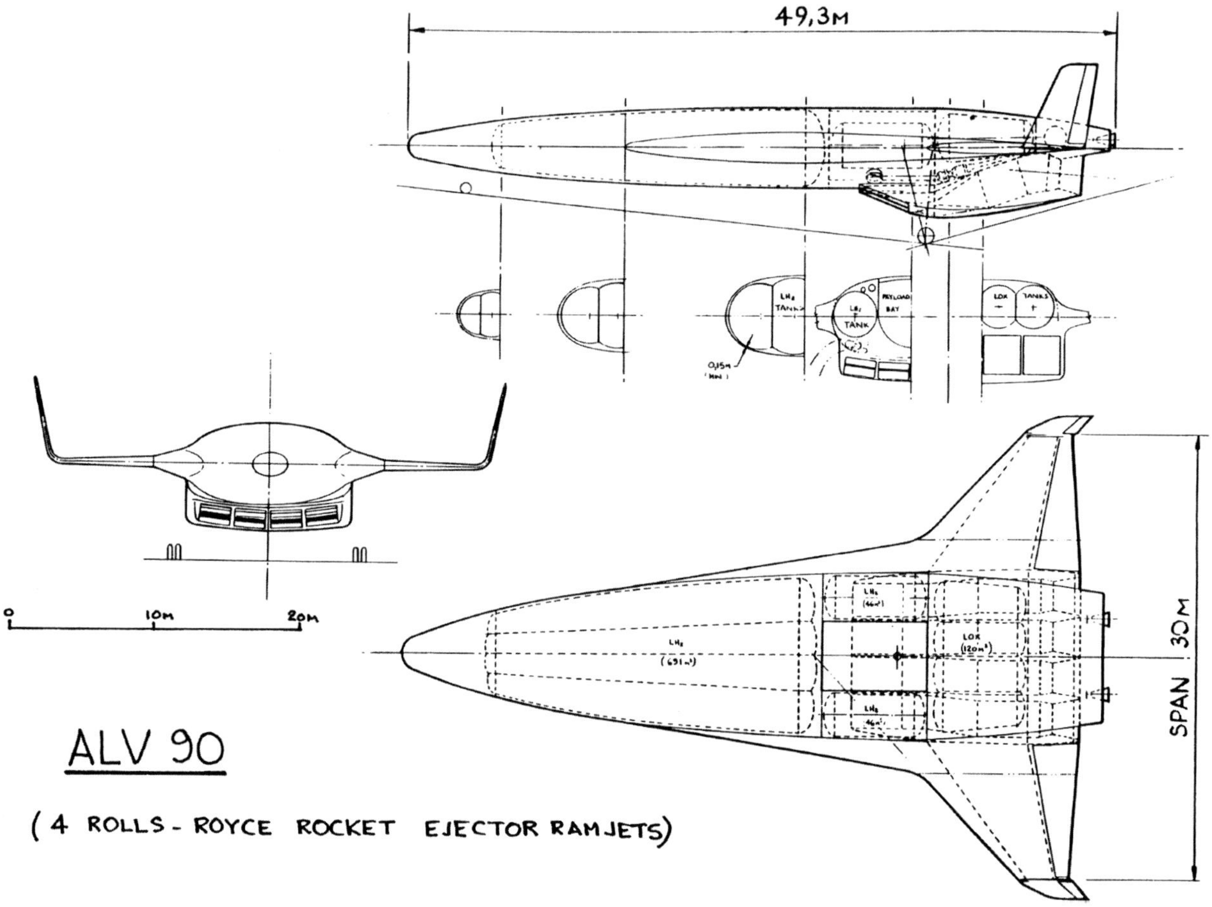

ALV 90 had a flattened lifting body-type fuselage and was powered by four Rolls-Royce rocket ejector ramjets.

hypersonic vehicles has been widely investigated, particularly in the USA where some experimental types have been built and flown. They also formed the basis for the BAe Mustard proposals. At that time a significant amount of detailed aerodynamic and structural work was done.

"[By] the time that contract ended, the model had evolved to [a form] ... for which some wind tunnel data is available. As part of the ALV studies the basic characteristics of lifting bodies have been re-examined and alternative configurations generated. A NASA Langley survey of bodies with non-circular cross-section indicated that elliptical bodies have significantly higher lift/drags than their circular equivalents and that mid-wings are generally best. A general analysis of vehicles with circular and elliptical fuselages has been made, and in general confirmed the NASA findings ... Current Aérospatiale proposals for a hypersonic transport are based on an elliptical fuselage with mid-wings and tip fins.

The ALV 90 configuration was specifically designed as an alternative to ALV 01, with the same propulsion system of four Rolls-Royce rocket-ejector-ramjets, but "whilst the configuration was considered feasible it was abandoned once the CAPS results indicated that airbreathing engines were not sufficiently competitive to rockets. A situation unlikely to be improved significantly by this configuration".

ALV 91A. Consequently, the ALV Group moved on to studying what amounted to a flattened version of rocket-Hotol, ALV 30A—designated ALV 91A. Walley noted that although "it did not originate from the current Hermes arrangement, a comparison can be made, in particular the 75° sweep wing, tip fins/rudders and overall centre of gravity/aerodynamic centre balance/trimming problems and solutions. It is considered suitable for horizontal or vertical launch, or when scaled down, air launch.

"The ALV 91 configuration has been studied in some depth and published data has been used for comparison purposes whilst other data has been generated internally. Preliminary centre of gravity/aerodynamic centre relationships have been checked and are considered acceptable. The basic layout lends itself to moving the payload bay further aft and liquid oxygen further forward if necessary.

"Pitch control is by use of elevons and the twin aft underbody flaps. Retractable vortex generating foreplanes may be installed if required. Yaw control is by use of tip fin controllers. Four conventional rocket motors are assumed and these can be gimballed/throttled sufficiently to avoid asymmetry should one of the outer motors fail. Alternative

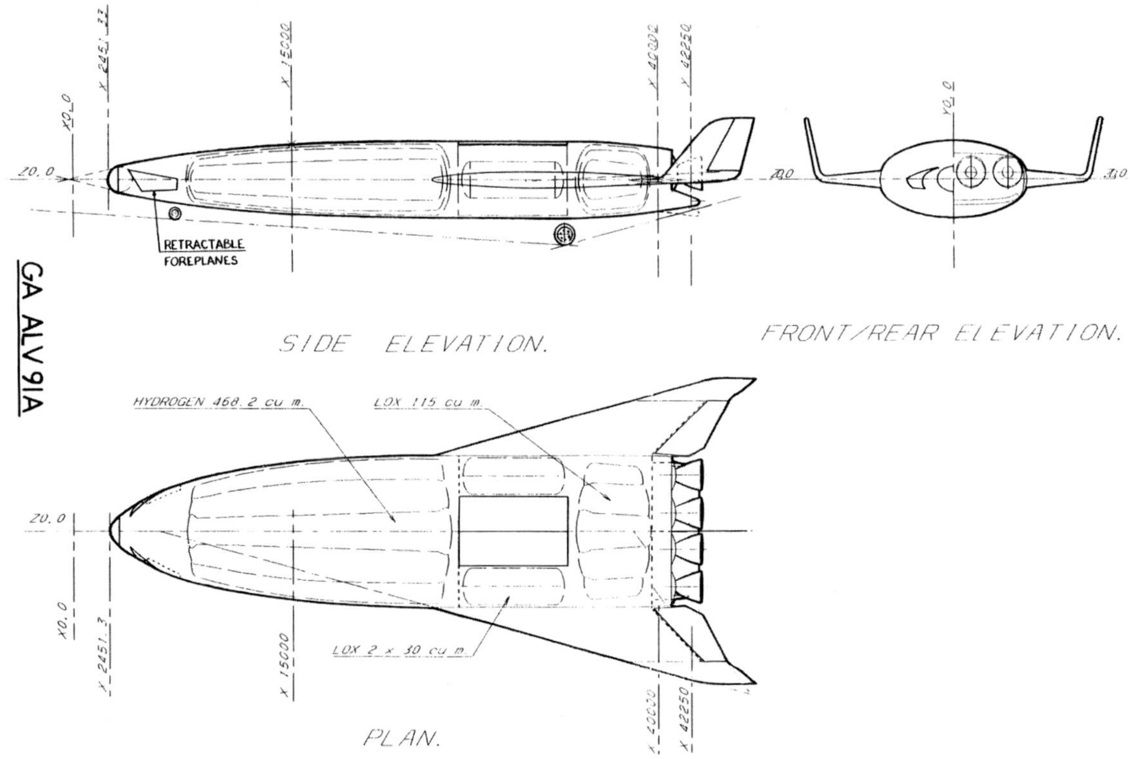

The 'flattened' pure rocket Hotol (ALV 30A), ALV 91A.

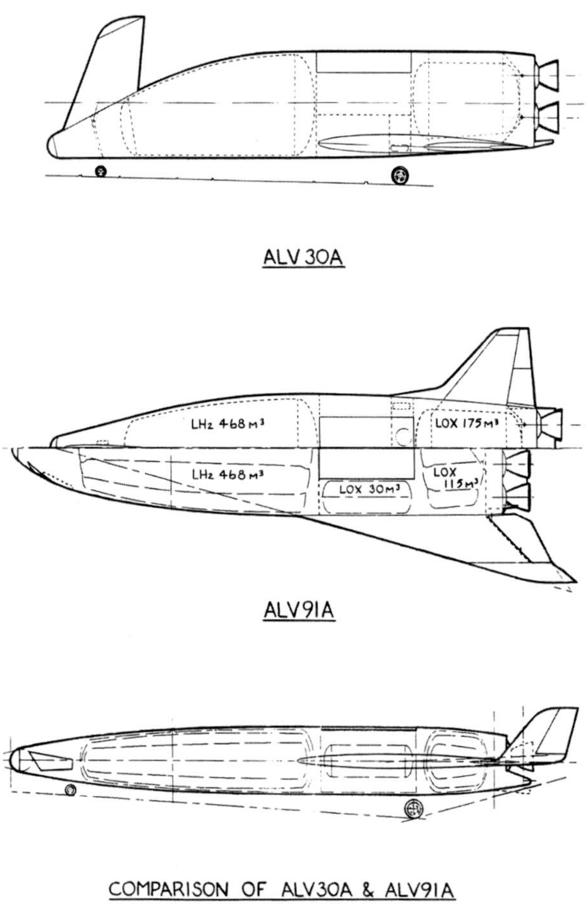

Comparison between the pure rocket ALV 30A and the 'flattened' version, ALV 91A.

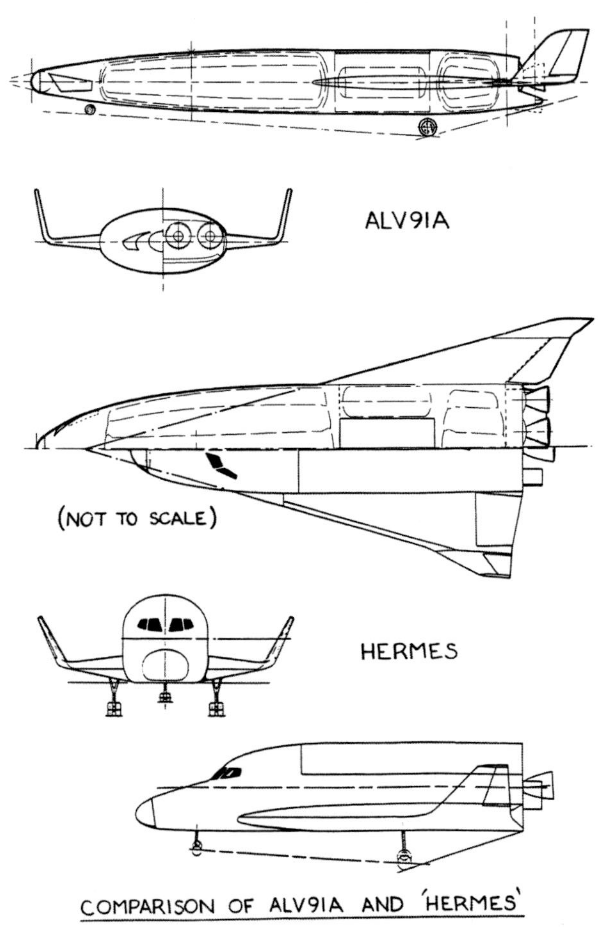

Comparison of ALV 91A and Hermes.

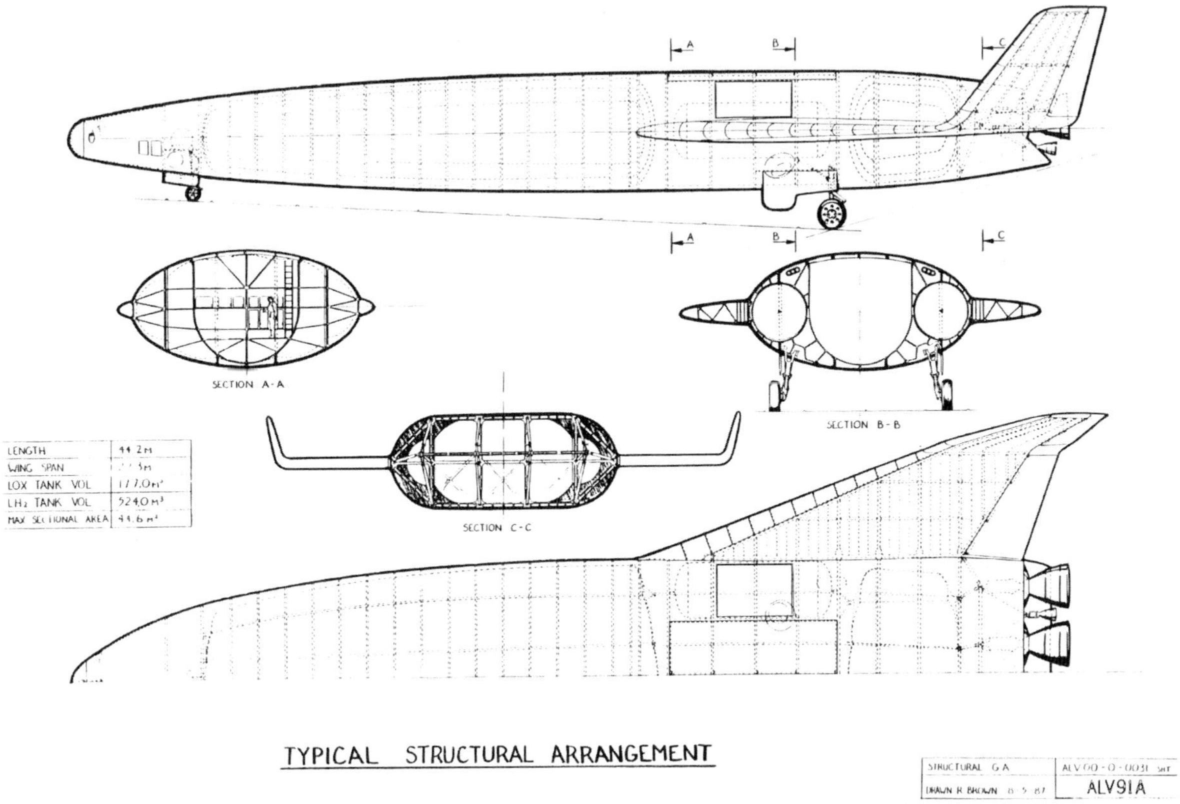

Structural detail of ALV 91A.

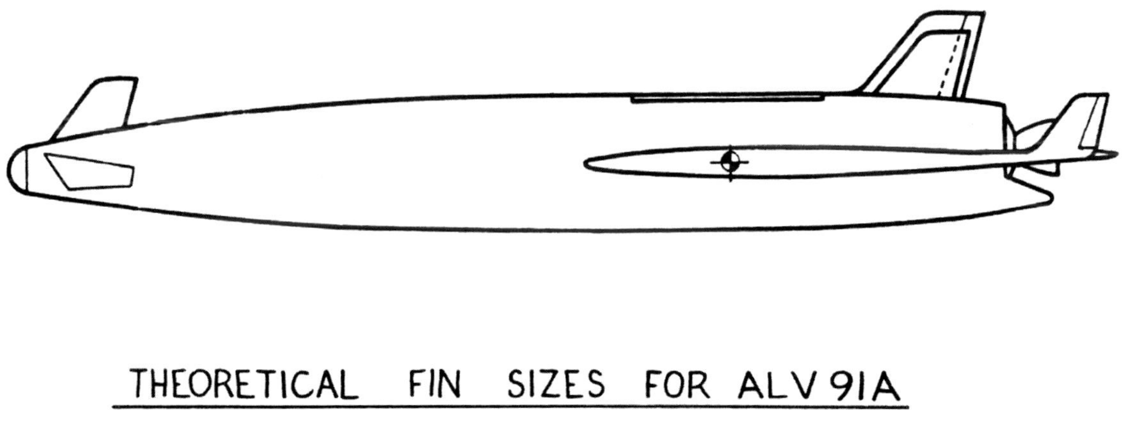

ALV 91A with fins fore and aft.

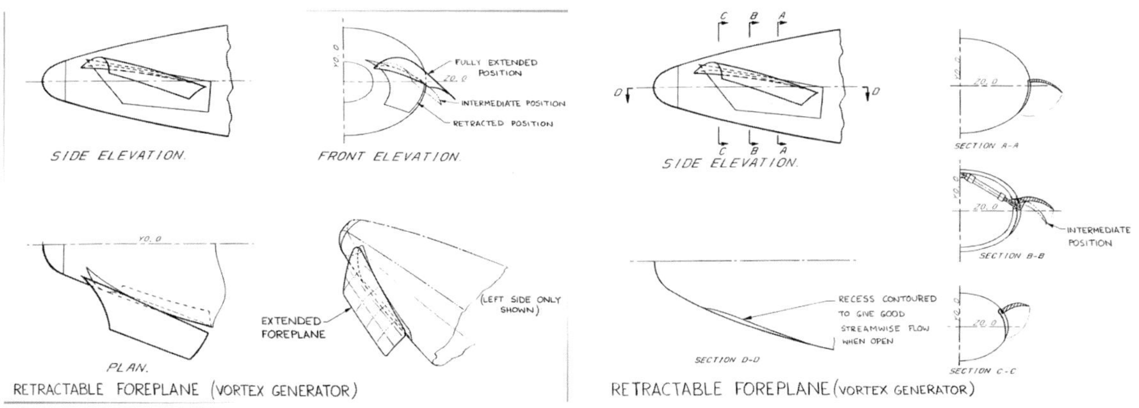

Retractable foreplanes of the type envisioned for ALV 91A.

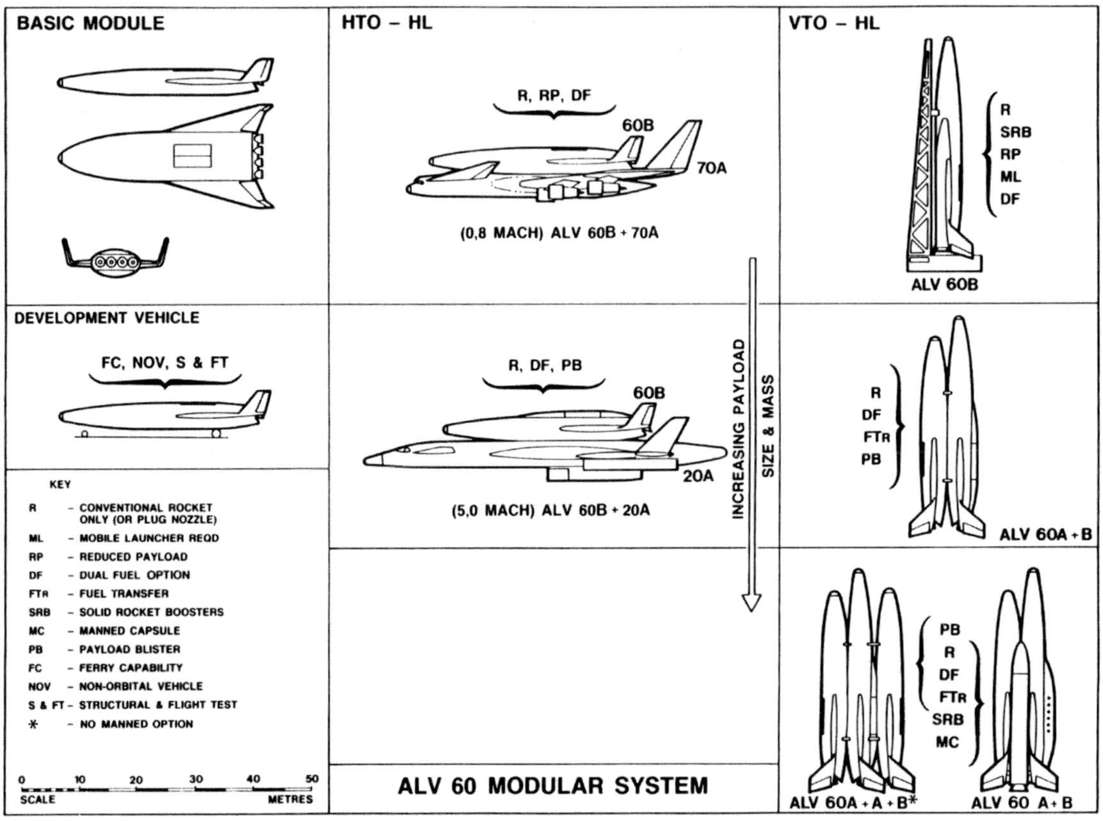

The modular ALV 60 could be adapted to a variety of different launch configurations.

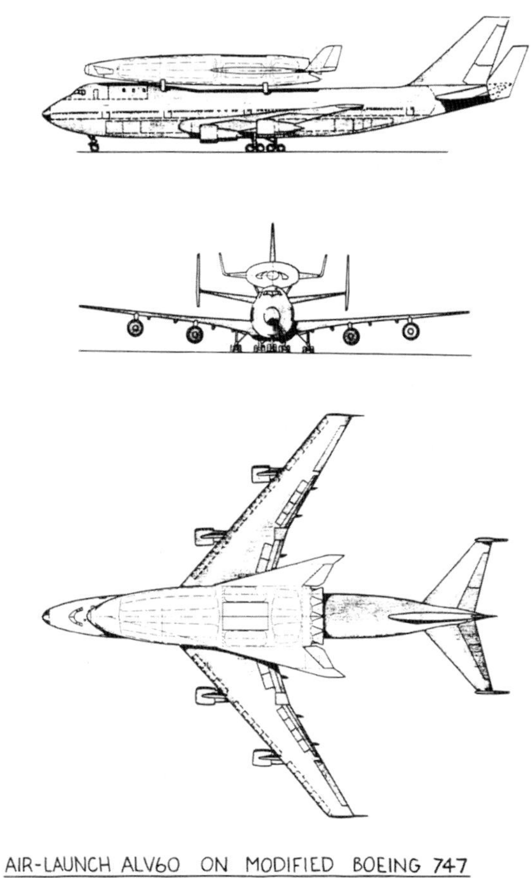

ALV 60 module atop a modified Boeing 747 for subsonic air launch.

plug nozzle arrangements and/or dual fuels may be fitted with advantage, if required. Alternative structural arrangements have been studied in depth and realistic proposals generated".

ALV 60A and **ALV 60B**. The last Group B design was a scaled down variant of ALV 91A (0.8 or 0.9 depending on whether it had a subsonic or supersonic air launch requirement). ALV 60, the report stated, could be used as a development vehicle; a single-stage vehicle for smaller payloads; a two-stage two-module Siamese system; a two-stage three-module triamese system; a three-stage system using two modules plus booster rockets or arrangements with more modules for even larger payloads.

In these configurations, ALV 60B was the module when used as the orbiter and ALV 60A was the module when used as a booster.

As the report pointed out, "this proposal, to use several recoverable lifting bodies is not new. It formed the basis of the original Mustard patent (No. 1,114,414-1968) and is still relevant today. In the previous Warton studies, the use of similar modules was most effective in reducing R&D and production costs".

The ALV 60 module, depending on how it was scaled, could be launched either subsonically from an ALV 70A booster—or supersonically from an ALV 20A. There was even the possibility that it could be air-launched from a

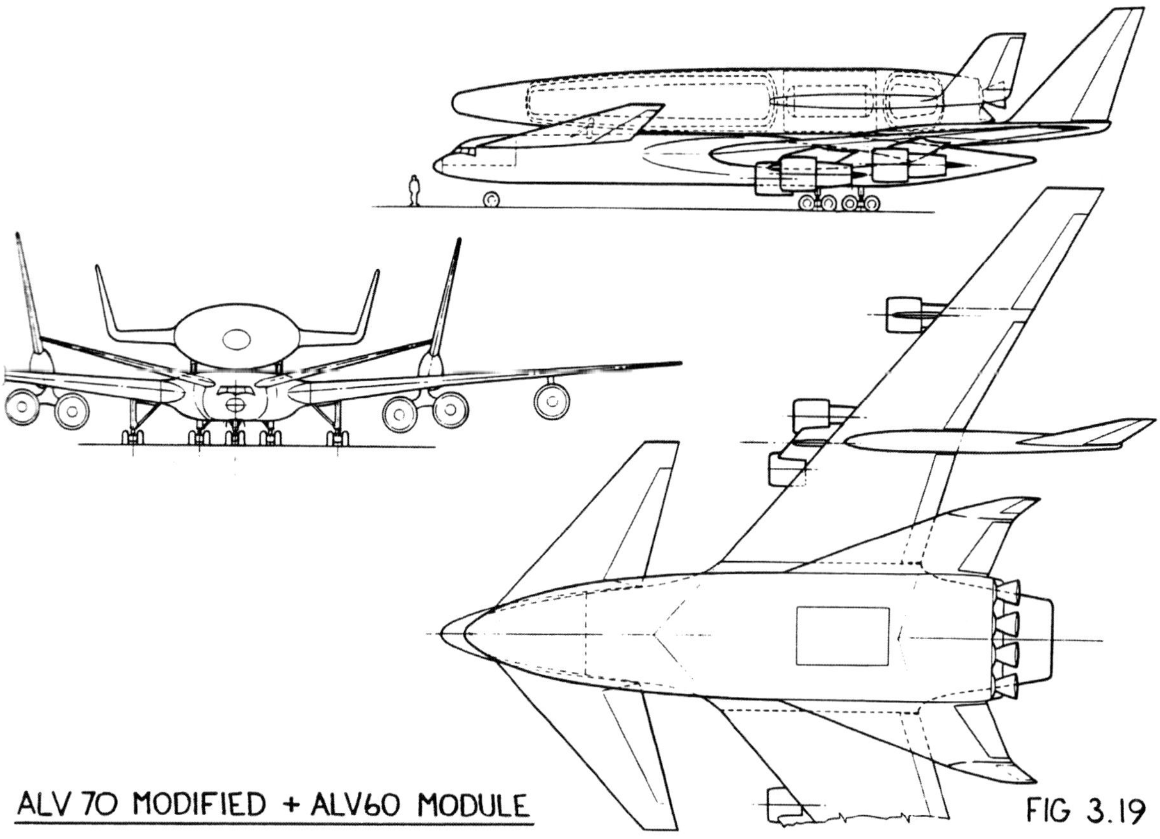

The Boeing 747-derived ALV 70A booster became the ALV 70 Modified when used to launch the ALV 60B module.

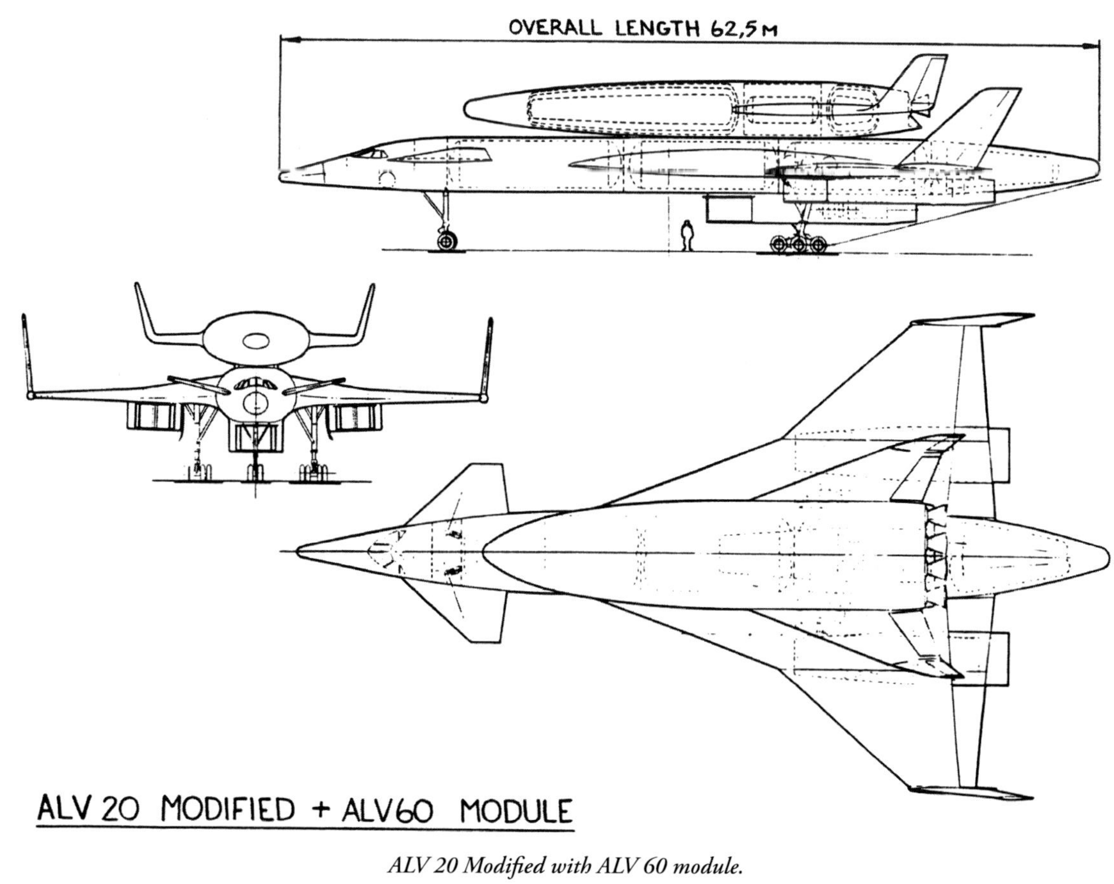

ALV 20 Modified with ALV 60 module.

Boeing 747 Freighter.

This was a particularly attractive design, given the difficulties being faced by the Hotol team in finding the right materials to make the system work, because "as proposed, currently available structural materials are assumed and preliminary work could start without delay".

The general advantages of a lifting body configuration compared to a tubular fuselage, according to Walley, were slightly better subsonic lift/drag, significantly better supersonic lift/drag; reduced heating rates and temperatures during re-entry; the 50% lower forebody destabilising moment in yaw; base drag reduction thanks to the four rocket motors being placed in row; reduced exposed wingspan reducing bending moment and therefore wing mass; smaller fins and smaller wings; low structural density; potential for stacked launch arrangements.

ALV 70 Modified and **ALV 20 Modified**. Used as a booster for an ALV 60B, the ALV 70A or ALV 20A would become the ALV 70 Modified and ALV 20 Modified respectively. The modifications would presumably have entailed relatively small detail changes to attachment points and other refinements.

DUAL FUEL AND PLUG NOZZLES

Hotol 'F' (DF+PN+LT). NASA's Langley Research Center had been ordered to begin looking at potential future launcher configurations under the umbrella title 'Shuttle II' in January 1985. A wide range of concepts had been assessed, including dual fuel arrangements.

In such a system, the launcher would carry liquid oxygen and liquid hydrogen as normal but also a second fuel such as kerosene (RP-1). The kerosene, with its high density impulse, would be used during the first half of the trajectory, while the hydrogen, a high specific impulse fuel, would be used during the second half of the trajectory. Swapping some of the hydrogen for kerosene would allow the vehicle to be smaller overall.

Walley's summary noted: "A dual fuel variant of Hotol 'F' (i.e. Hotol 'F' Dual Fuel+Plug Nozzle+Launch Trolley) could reduce vehicle size significantly and sufficient RP-1 fuel could, practically and to advantage, be located in the wings. Alternative RP-1 and liquid hydrogen rocket engines would need to be developed and may be combined, to advantage, with plug or linear nozzles. There appears to be no reason why dual fuels should not be used with the RB.545, or similar engine, and their use on Hotol or ALVs should be examined in much greater depth."

The use of plug nozzles for rocket motors, rather than variable geometry bell nozzles, was also seen as a concept worthy of further investigation. According to the report:

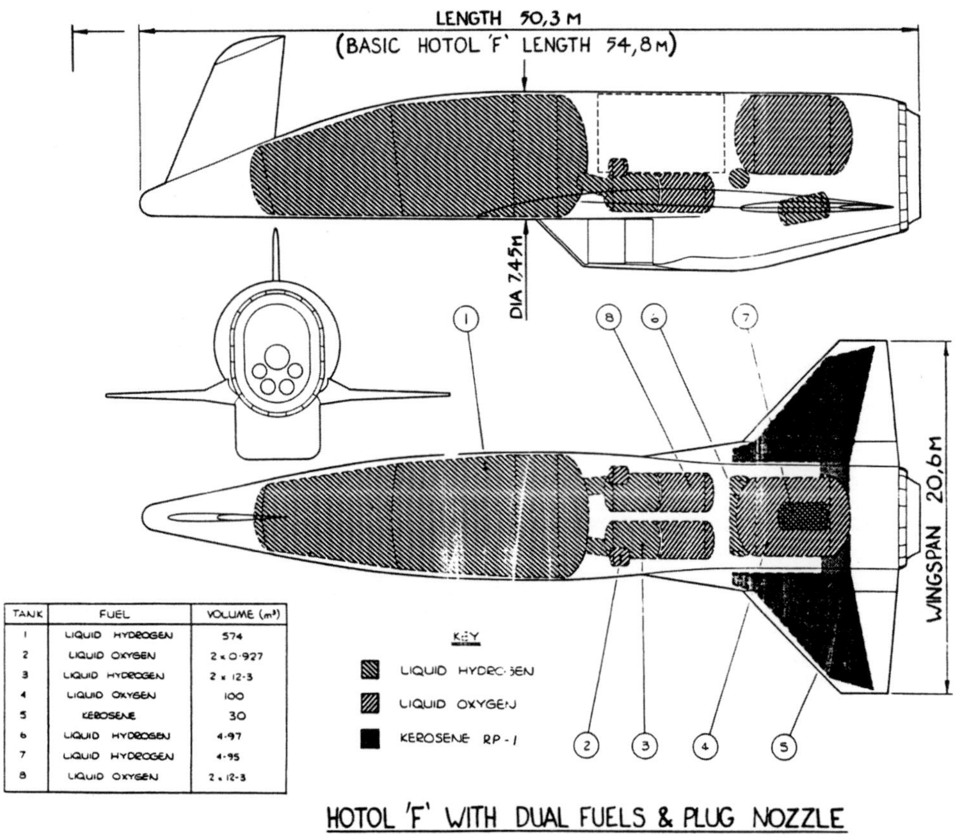

TANK	FUEL	VOLUME (m³)
1	LIQUID HYDROGEN	574
2	LIQUID OXYGEN	2 × 0·927
3	LIQUID HYDROGEN	2 × 12·3
4	LIQUID OXYGEN	100
5	KEROSENE	30
6	LIQUID HYDROGEN	4·97
7	LIQUID HYDROGEN	4·95
8	LIQUID OXYGEN	2 × 12·3

Hotol Configuration F with dual fuels (liquid hydrogen and kerosene) and plug nozzle.

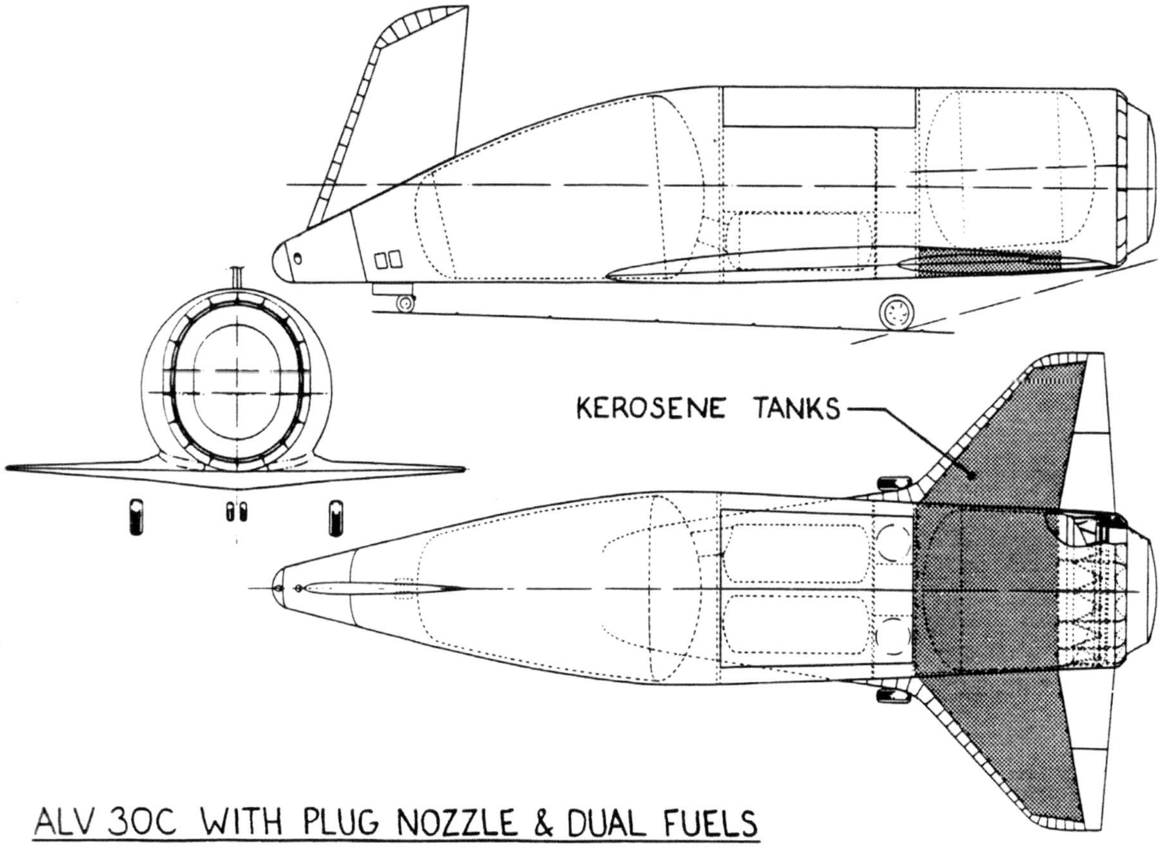

ALV 30C—the pure rocket, vertical take-off Hotol, with plug nozzle and dual fuels.

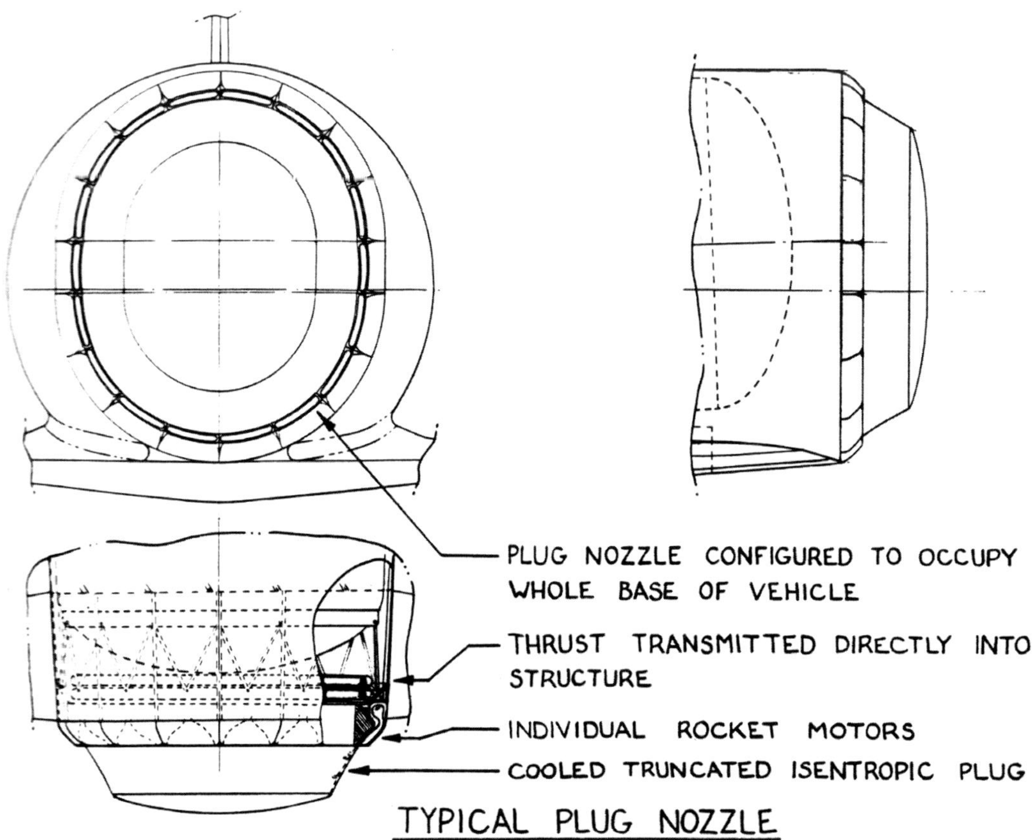

Detail of a typical plug nozzle.

"Plug nozzles comprise several small rocket motors located around the periphery of a central cooled plug... From the limited studies undertaken to date it is considered that plug nozzles warrant further more detailed assessment since they could be applicable to almost any rocket powered vehicle."

A long list of plug nozzle advantages was given, with the system's compact size compared to conventional bell nozzles being a particular favourite. The numerous small rocket motors, controlled individually, would create a thrust vectoring effect which negated the need for gimballing and they could even be used for the OMS. A big disadvantage was increased complexity, particularly in devising an effective means of keeping the central 'plug' cool. Also, putting so many rocket motors so close to one another would result in dynamic interactions which "may create problems".

REFERENCE ALVS

The final two alternative launch vehicles discussed in the summary report were essentially pre-existing designs assigned ALV numbers for reference purposes.

ALV 80. This was the last variant of Mustard drawn up during the 1960s. Walley said that "it was studied to examine the implications of fitting the large central payload bay. The basic vehicle shape was particularly attractive since it offered good volume utilisation and had low structural masses. In addition, re-entry heating problems were minimised by the use of very large surface radii in all exposed positions apart from the fin leading edges.

"Reference to the previous Warton studies and the wind tunnel tests on alternative lifting bodies was made. The results of these studies indicated the difficulty of introducing the payload bay whilst, at the same time, obtaining suitable fuel tank arrangements. In addition, it was considered that the [design's] lift/drag was inadequate for the current cross range requirements. It was therefore decided that an elliptical body and discrete highly swept wings offered the best solution despite some increase in leading edge heating problems".

ALV 50. MBB/ERNO had come up with a concept for a reusable single-stage-to-orbit vertical take-off, vertical-landing heavy launch vehicle known as BETA. It had 13 rocket engines clustered around a central heat shield with a plug nozzle arrangement. Evidently, "whilst it was recoverable, it did not have the ability to return payloads to earth".

BETA had been subjected to a detailed examination

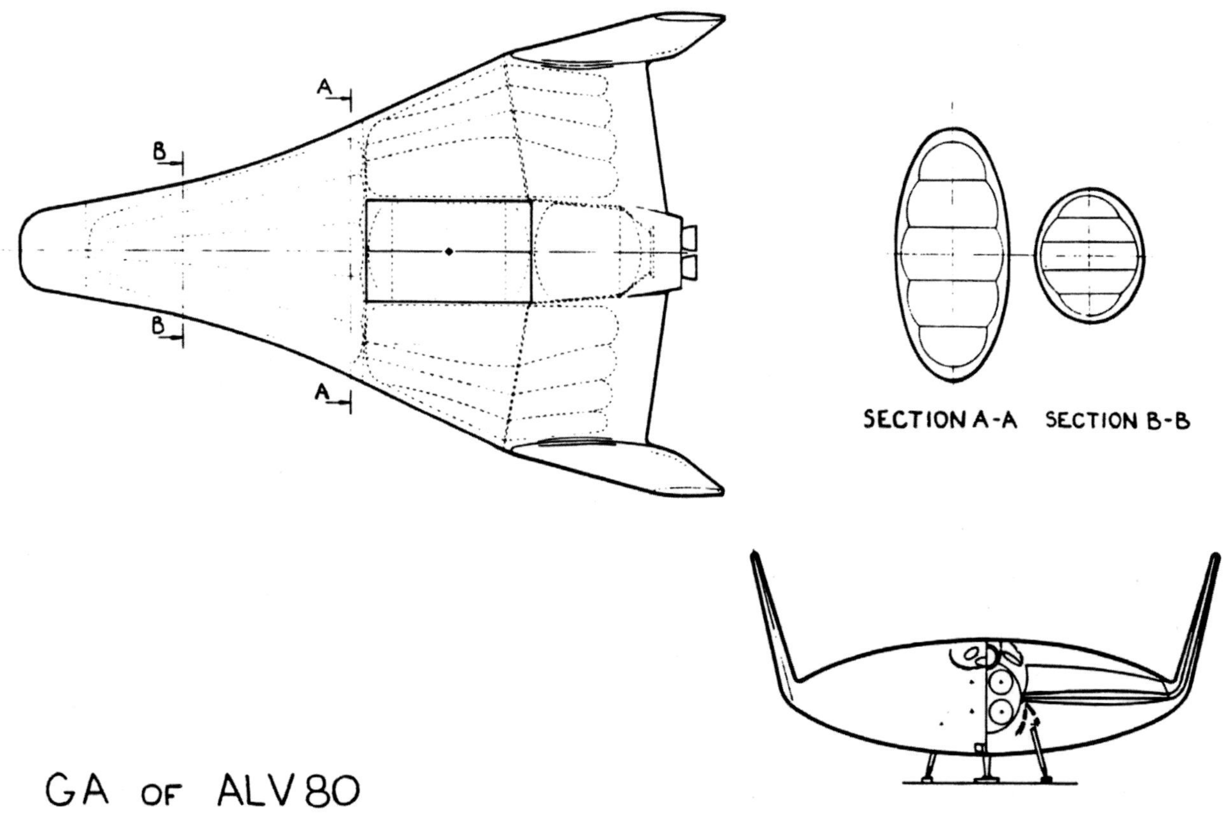

ALV 80 was the Mustard module—included in the ALV studies for reference purposes.

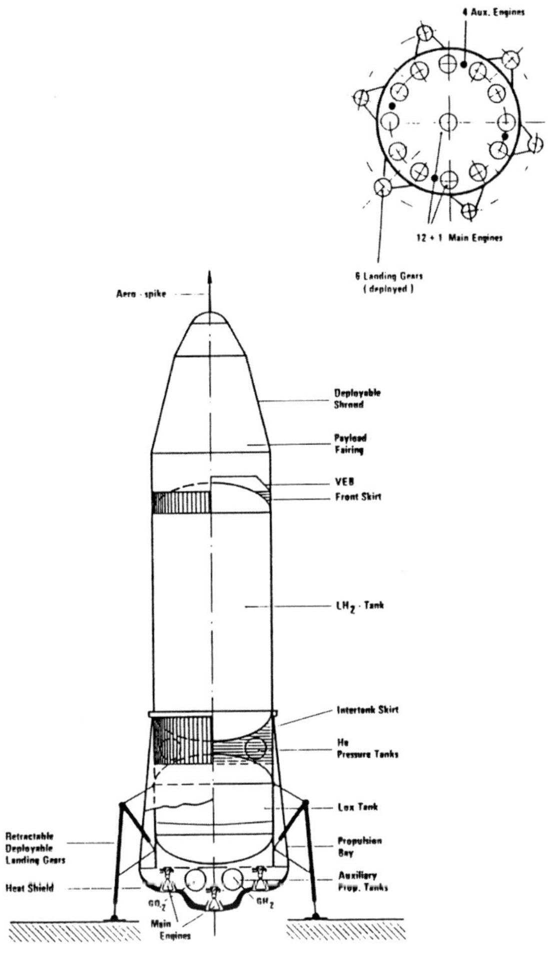

ALV 50
(MBB/ERNO BETA)

ALV 50 was MBB/ERNO's BETA vehicle, another reference design for the ALV studies.

but then abandoned due to "the payload bay being at the top of the vehicle. Payloads could not be returned since the overall centre of gravity would be too high, leading to almost impossible re-entry control problems; the ballistic re-entry, which relies on the lower heat shield for protection. It therefore has a very low lift/drag value which gives virtually zero cross range performance; centre of gravity location which is critical to the re-entry trajectory. This could be difficult to determine/control (due to residual fuel condition, etc.) and hence landing point inaccuracies; difficulties in manoeuvring as the vehicle makes its final rocket powered vertical descent onto the landing site. Further studies were therefore considered to be pointless".

MISSING ALVS

A handful of additional ALVs were mentioned in early reports by the group but apparently failed to make the final cut for Walley's summary report.

ALV 10. Burns had specifically asked for a two-stage Hotol to be among the configurations studied and the ALV Group obliged. ALV 10 was composed of two "basically similar vehicles"—a redesigned Hotol carrying another on its back during a runway take-off. By necessity, the nose fins of both vehicles were replaced by wingtip control surfaces. Both vehicles, following separation, would eventually return for a runway landing. ALV 10 was seemingly abandoned quite quickly.

ALV 30B. Where ALV 30A was a single-stage rocket-Hotol, ALV 30B was a two-stage rocket-Hotol. The arrangement was similar to that used for ALV 10, with two similar vehicles, one carrying the other on its back for a horizontal take-off followed by separate landings. And like ALV 10 it did not progress beyond the study's early stages.

ALV 30D. The VTO version of the single-stage ALV 30A was the single-stage ALV 30C, so the VTO version of the two-stage ALV 30B was the two-stage ALV 30D. But rather than the vehicles being positioned side by side, one rocket-Hotol was stood on the nose of the other beside a launch tower for a vertical take-off. Again, following separation the vehicles would land separately. And again, like ALV 10 and ALV 30B, ALV 30D was soon ditched.

ALV 90 TJ. This was broadly similar to the regular ALV 90 but would have been fitted with both supplemental turbojets, to help it fly back to base under its own power following re-entry, and foreplanes for enhanced controllability.

UNCOMPETITIVE AIRBREATHERS

While many of the ALV designs used pure rocket propulsion, there were also plenty which used either the RB.545 or another variety of airbreathing engine. Rocket-ejector-ramjet-rockets, turbo-ramjet-rockets and turbo-ramjets had apparently been proposed by Rolls-Royce as alternatives to the RB.545. However, the report stated that "CAPS has been used to establish the airbreathing engine specific impulses and thrust-to-weights necessary to be competitive with conventional rocket engines. There is little or no advantage to be gained for any airbreathing engine which does not result in a vehicle which is smaller than the equivalent rocket".

On this basis, the rocket-ejector-ramjet-rocket and turbo-ramjet-rocket had been found to be "not competitive and were not considered further" but "the turbo-ramjet was relevant to the ALV 20A studies". The ALV 20A booster aircraft would use "two of these, scaled to 400kN … installed into engine pods" to reach Mach 5.

CAPS had indicated that the RB.545 too was "not competitive" and "the other engines shown… have also been plotted and are somewhat worse than the RB.545". In fact, "studies at Rolls-Royce and Warton indicate that it is extremely difficult to conceive an airbreathing engine system which, when installed, can be at all competitive with the rocket engine for a SSTO vehicle".

Following on from these studies, "in an attempt to find an airbreathing engine system which would be superior to the RB.545," Walley's team looked at the ODW ramjet-rocket, the RB.545 integrated with ODW ramjet-rocket, and the ducted wing rocket-ejector-ramjet-rocket. The ODW ramjet-rocket, built into the ALV 100A's unswept wing, "could operate to much higher Mach numbers (Mach 16) and give much higher specific impulses than rocket motors. Very high stagnation temperatures, up to 1,925°K, were calculated for the nose cone and wing leading edges of such a vehicle". The RB.545/ODW ramjet-rocket would operate under RB.545 power up to Mach 5 before switching to the ODW ramjet-rocket and using that up to Mach 16. But "whilst both these engines seemed attractive and were discussed with Rolls-Royce, no further work was done since development costs were considered prohibitive".

Lastly, integration of the ducted wing, rocket-ejector-ramjet-rocket "into the wing [of the ALV 100] was considered but the large size of the combustion chamber made this impractical and further work was abandoned".

SHELLS AND BUBBLE TANKS

Hotol's pressurised liquid hydrogen tank was an essential part of its load-bearing structure—but Walley's team were determined to take a different approach with the ALVs. The report noted that "the risk of penetration of the structure by space debris and/or meteoroids is significant. Structural concepts must take account of this and the use of pressurised tanks as primary structure should be avoided. Possible detection and evasion techniques should also be investigated".

Therefore, "all ALV orbiters should have readily removeable monocoque fuselage shells with freely supported fuel tanks" and "metallic multi-bubble fuel tanks are considered practical".

It was considered that three monocoque outer shell sections would be necessary—front, centre and rear—and the non-load bearing tanks fitted inside them would be welded metal. Both shells and tanks would be made from "currently available metallic and composite materials (light alloy, titanium, René 41 etc.)" in order to "reduce the risk and therefore cost in acquiring and operating ALVs".

For the lifting body ALVs such as ALV 60B, ALV 90 and ALV 91A, "it is proposed that the front fuselage monocoque is fabricated from mechanically fastened skin and stringer panels and frames. Lower surface material is René 41 and upper surface material is conventional titanium. The liquid hydrogen tank is of welded light alloy construction and is simply supported at each end within the front fuselage monocoque".

Rather than a single regularly-shaped tank, the lifting body ALV would use 'multi-bubble' type tanks, because they "form an efficient method of containing fuel under pressure in lifting body type vehicles. Such tanks are formed from a series of intersecting cylinders with internal webs linking upper and lower intersection lines and are subject to both primary and secondary loads. The primary load is the internal pressurisation required either for structural stabilisation or fuel system purposes. The secondary loads are non-uniform in their action and derive from fuel head gradients, fuel sloshing, etc.

"This report shows that by following simple rules multi-bubble tanks can be designed to support internal pressure by means of pure membrane forces and that by adding transverse stiffening frames to the basic tank the secondary loads can also be carried, particularly when low density fuels, such as liquid hydrogen, are contained… Multi-bubble tanks are… shown to be structurally viable and competitive with cylindrical tanks. Consideration should now be given to manufacturing aspects".

FINS, FOREPLANES AND INTAKES

In addition to the ALV layout concepts themselves, the ALV Group also looked at the technologies and innovations that would be necessary to make them work in the real world. Hotol's nose fin and foreplanes were a source of difficulty—particularly given their exposure to extremely high temperatures during re-entry—so alternative solutions were assessed.

Simply deleting the nose fin and using wingtip fins instead was thought to "offer significant advantages". In particular, it had been calculated that two wingtip fins combined would still be significantly smaller than the equivalent central fin—saving mass. Foreplanes had already been deleted from Hotol Configuration F, but it would be desirable to reinstate them as a means of producing a nose-up pitching moment without resorting to overlarge flaps.

One potential solution was pop-out foreplanes. According to Walley's report: "The possibility of fitting foreplanes to the ALVs has been examined. Fixed foreplanes are expected to be severely damaged during re-entry therefore retractable surfaces are essential. The proposed retractable vortex generating foreplanes fold flush into the front fuselage when not in use. They are deployed by rotating outwards about a sloping hinge axis ... To enable them to fit neatly into the contoured fuselage recesses they are low aspect ratio and also contoured."

Another difficulty faced by the Hotol team was the RB.545's intake. While the ALV Group had no innovative solutions to offer for an under-fuselage intake, they did look carefully at how the ALV 100's wing intakes should be designed. It was proposed these should take a two-dimensional form with a variable incidence upper cowl similar to that of the McDonnell Douglas F-15 Eagle combined with a variable incidence lower cowl similar to that of the EAP. Together, these would "provide exact control of capture area required for a wide range of Mach numbers zero to 5 or 6, hence avoiding spill drag problems". In addition, they could be "drooped and closed when the airbreathing engine is inoperative and also during re-entry and power off landing".

The main disadvantage was, again, complexity. The intakes would need to be computer controlled—requiring substantial development—and they would need to incorporate actively cooled components, requiring even more development time. According to the report, "a preliminary assessment of the proposed intake has been made by [the] Aerodynamics Dept ... it is considered feasible but extensive theoretical analysis and wind tunnel tests will be necessary".

WALLEY'S TROLLEY

A whole section of Walley's report was devoted to the undercarriage studies and proposals. Firstly, he advocated for the use of an innovative, patent-pending, trolley he had designed in cooperation with Dr J. Reynolds at Filton and his ALV group colleague Brown.

According to the description: "The proposed system ... is designed to minimise the size, weight (and cost) of a trolley suitable for launching airborne vehicles from conventional runways. In addition, it can be readily dismantled and transported by air in a large transport plane such as [a] Lockheed C-5 Galaxy.

"This system assumes two identical self-powered, fully manoeuvrable, 'wheeled units' which have retractable airborne vehicle attachment beams fitted. They also have acceleration and deceleration rockets, fuel tanks and systems fitted. A laser guidance system is also fitted to each 'wheeled unit'.

"The wheeled units are manoeuvred into position on either side of the airborne vehicle which is standing on its undercarriage in the empty, unladen condition. Accurate alignment is essential and is made possible by suitable devices fitted to the wheeled units and the airborne vehicle. When the wheeled units are in the correct position the attachment beams are raised and located in/on the special fittings on the airborne vehicle and local stabilisation pads lowered to the ground.

"After this is complete, light weight quickly attachable crossbeams are fitted between the two-wheeled units and suitable decking panels bolted in position. These then make one trolley which is structurally complete. All system interconnections between the two wheeled units are then connected and checked.

"The attachment beams may now be raised slightly, lifting the airborne vehicle off the ground and allowing its undercarriage to be retracted and secured. The airborne vehicle may now be loaded and prepared for flight. The self-powered wheeled units, now interconnected, may be driven out onto the runway to a suitable take-off position. Any ground personnel involved leave the area and fully automatic control is established.

"Final pre-flight checks are made, all engines are started and airborne vehicle and trolley accelerate down the runway. The airborne vehicle being raised to the optimum position/incidence for this phase. Once airborne vehicle lift-off/rotation speed is reached the vehicle attachment points are raised still further. Due to the different beam length, the front ones longer than the rear ones, the correct incidence is applied and the airborne vehicle leaves the trolley. The trolley is now arrested, by retro-rockets and brakes, and may then be returned to the vehicle preparation area.

"If, during take-off, the abort signal is given then the attachment beams are lowered rapidly to give the airborne vehicle minimum or negative incidence and at the same time lowering its centre of gravity as far as possible and moving it aft. In this way the pitch forward moment is minimised and the tendency to lift the rear multi-wheeled bogies from the ground, with loss of braking efficiency, is kept as small as practical.

"The trolley assembly may be readily dismantled into its basic components and driven into a suitable transport aircraft or along conventional roads. As an alternative, once the trolley has been fully assembled the airborne vehicle could be attached to it as follows, a) ramps are added to the front and rear of the decking between the wheeled units. b) The front of the airborne vehicle, while empty and on its wheels, may then be drawn forward over the decking.

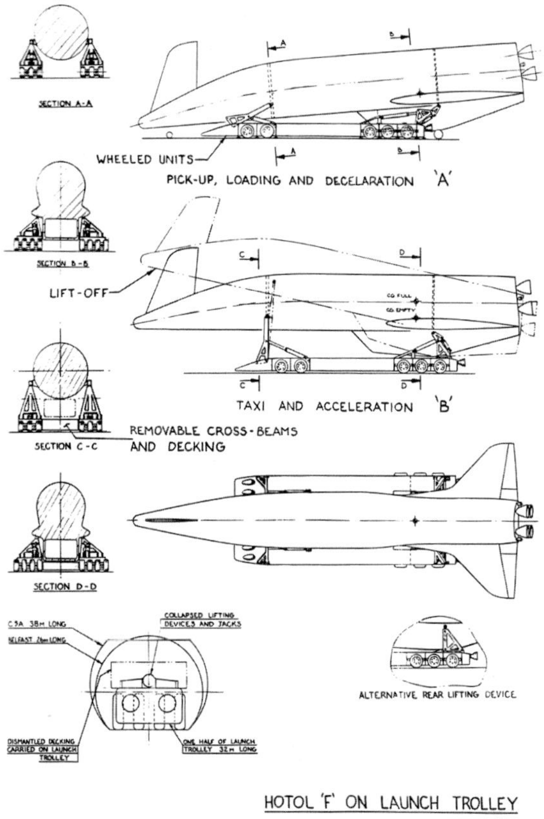

Modified Hotol launch trolley design by BAe Warton's Bob Brown, dated January 16, 1987. It was designed to be split in two for transportation by air. Each half would have fitted neatly inside a Lockheed C-5A Galaxy.

"A differential, adaptive suspension system will be used on each of the wheeled unit axles. This would ensure even wheel/tyre loading and provide the maximum tyre footprint minimising LCNs, improving braking efficiency and minimising tyre wear."

JETTISONABLE UNDERCARRIAGE

As an alternative to the trolley, a jettisonable undercarriage with integral RATO rockets was proposed. This system, mentioned earlier in connection with the ALV 100C, would see the vehicle fitted with two undercarriages at take-off: a pre-retracted lightweight post-mission landing set and a heavy-duty non-retractable set that would be jettisoned shortly after take-off. Once released, the two sets of mainwheels and the nose wheel would each deploy their own parachute for a safe descent to the ground, whereupon they would be recovered and subsequently reused.

For the mainwheels, "examination of tyre catalogues suggests that eight tyres, 56in x 16in at 315psi with a 3B ply rating should be satisfactory. These are arranged on two main leg modules ... They are mounted on a common axis, two either side of the central leg to avoid the complication of a bogie system. (alternative arrangements are possible if necessary). The main legs are mounted to the wing centre section using a four-point bracing system to that used for some jettisonable fuel tanks.

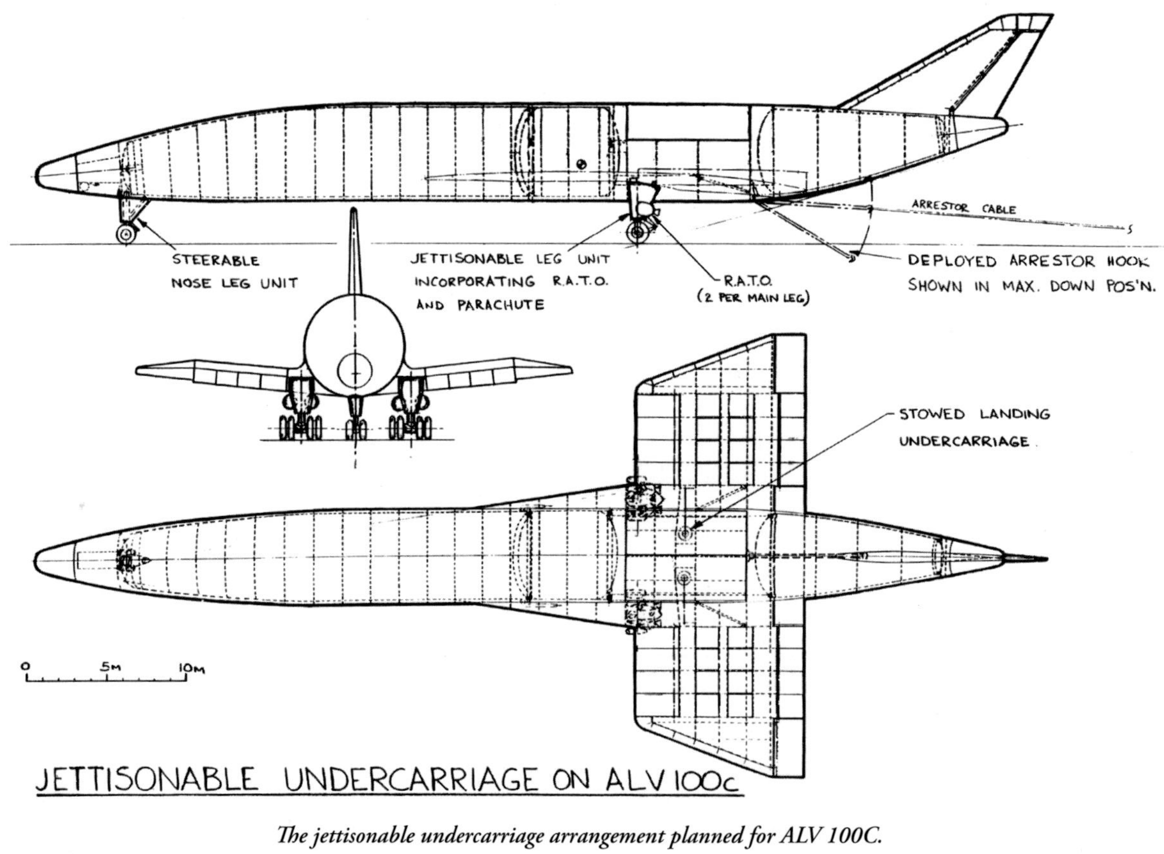

The jettisonable undercarriage arrangement planned for ALV 100C.

"A main forward attachment takes all major loads and incorporates a triplex release system, possibly explosive bolts, to ensure the undercarriage units are jettisoned. The use of a rear hook about which the module rotates to the point of release, also side support crutching pads, simplifies the release mechanism. Each main undercarriage unit is enclosed in a fairing which also contains the parachute pack.

"The use of four RATO rockets, two per main leg, is proposed. They are sized to give a combined total thrust of approx. 10% of the total vehicle thrust. Examination of suppliers' brochures has allowed a preliminary assessment to be made. The rockets are located/aligned to give the maximum pitch-up moment for nosewheel lifting whilst minimising exhaust plume effects on the vehicle or offset loads on the leg attachment." The rockets would be designed to burn out or be shut down before undercarriage release and would remain with the main legs as they floated to the ground.

The jettisonable nose leg would be "attached to the front fuselage in a similar manner to the main legs. In addition, the main attachment incorporates a splined linkage connecting the nosewheel steering to the basic on-board steering system. This disconnects when the nose undercarriage is released. As on the main undercarriage units, a parachute is fitted and also a fairing. The loads on the nosewheel will be greatest during aborted take-off but will depend on a number of factors not yet examined. A preliminary check suggests that two tyres approx. 49in x 17in at 200psi should be satisfactory".

The use of an arrestor hook was also proposed "for aborted take-off and possibly normal landings, especially for wet runways or brake failure cases ... This would be a permanent feature but could be relatively light mass which could be traded against basic undercarriage brake mass. The hook would be attached to suitable structure and located to minimise offset loads about the centre of gravity during deceleration to prevent excessive pitch-down loads on the nosewheel. It would be stowed, by hand, in a recess along the bottom of the rear fuselage and suitably protected. A retention/release mechanism also a release spring and damper would be necessary".

VERTICAL LAUNCH PREP

If the vertical take-off ALVs proved to be of interest, Walley's team had very briefly considered what sort of vehicles would be needed to move them into position and set them up for launch. Apparently, "it is known that USSR prepare VTO vehicles in the horizontal position, providing improved accessibility, only erecting them immediately prior to refuelling and launch". Drawings were included showing the not-very-snappily-named Mobile Ground Preparation and Erection Vehicle (MGPEV), which was designed to both transport a VTO ALV and get it into the correct launch position.

But if money was no object then why not construct a fixed launch pad? The ALV Group had enlisted the aid of Warton's Civil Engineering Department in working out what the construction of such a site might entail. An undeveloped 'greenfield' site was assumed and efforts were directed at the design of concrete exhaust deflectors and a water surface cooling system but "it was not possible, in the time available, to make any detailed estimates of the manning requirements for VTO launch sites or to establish if there are any significant difference between vertical and horizontal launch. This should be undertaken during future studies".

The task of loading an ALV orbiter onto an airbreathing launcher was as described for the ALV 70 vehicles.

MOST PAYLOADS ARE SMALL

While every ALV was designed to get a seven-tonne payload into low earth orbit, as per Burns' instructions, the ALV Group did some work on what would happen if vehicles were designed with a smaller or larger payload in mind.

Firstly, it was noted that payloads intended for geostationary orbit would need their own boost stage, so a 2.5 tonne satellite would become a seven-tonne payload when factoring in that booster—unless the 2.5 tonne satellite was to be mated with a separately-launched booster in orbit. LEO payloads didn't need a booster, so a 2.5 tonne satellite was a 2.5 tonne payload.

Secondly, 178 possible payloads had been listed during a February 1986 Hotol presentation and these had been assessed in more detail. Ninety of them, around 50%, were below 4.5 tonnes, 41 (23%) were between 4.5 and seven tonnes, and 47 were greater than seven tonnes—though there was no indication of exactly how physically large any of the payloads were.

According to the summary report: "Preliminary examination of this data indicates that a vehicle designed for smaller payloads, say five tonnes, would only lose 14% of the market ... it may be concluded that a launch system which is designed for smaller payloads but could be reconfigured for larger payloads should be chosen ... A survey of other existing or proposed launch systems indicates that 4-4.5 tonnes would be a reasonable size payload for the basic ALV 60 module. With this in mind the basic ALV 91, seven-tonne payload, has been scaled by 0.9 and

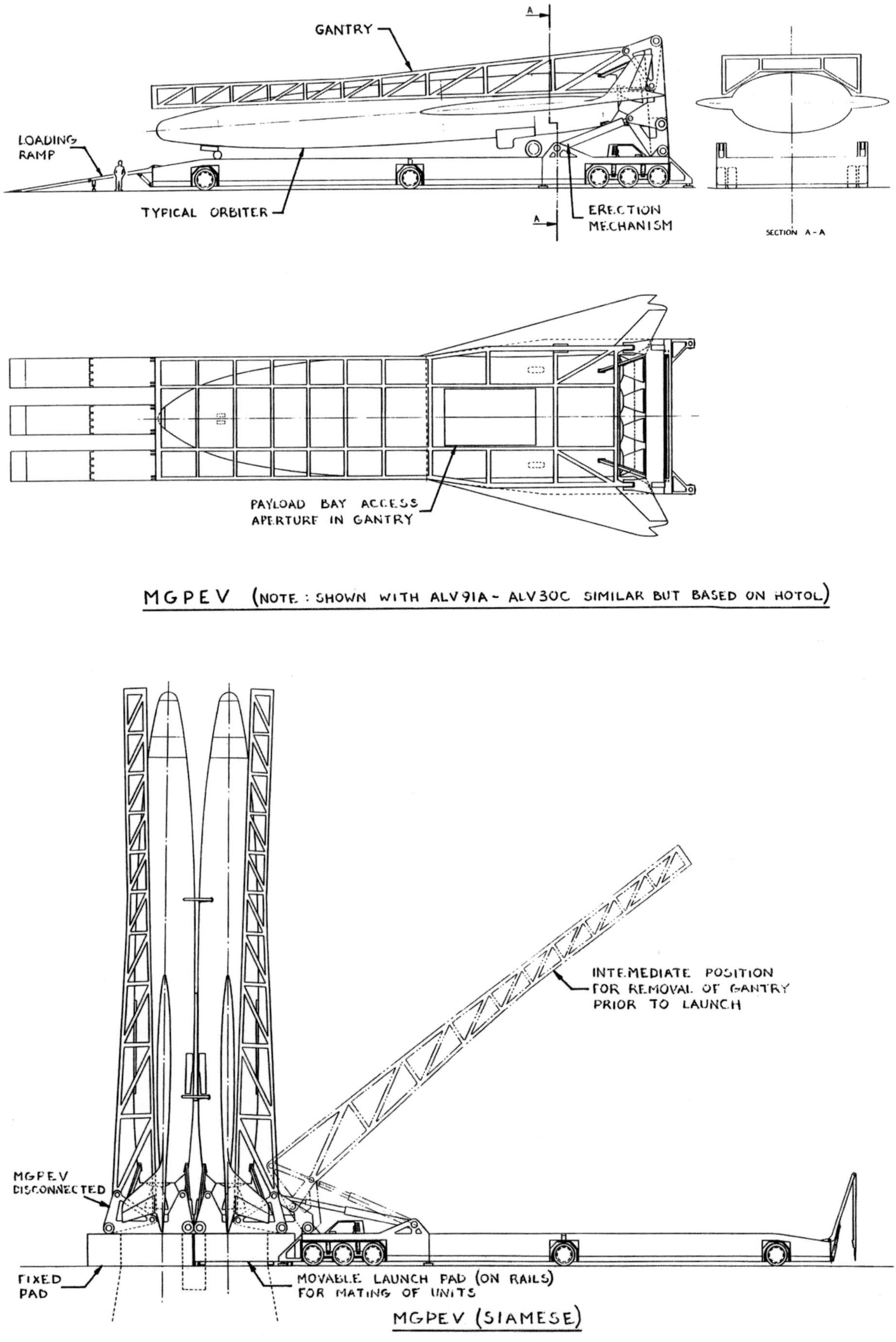

Mobile Ground Preparation and Erection Vehicle (MGPEV) with ALV 91A.

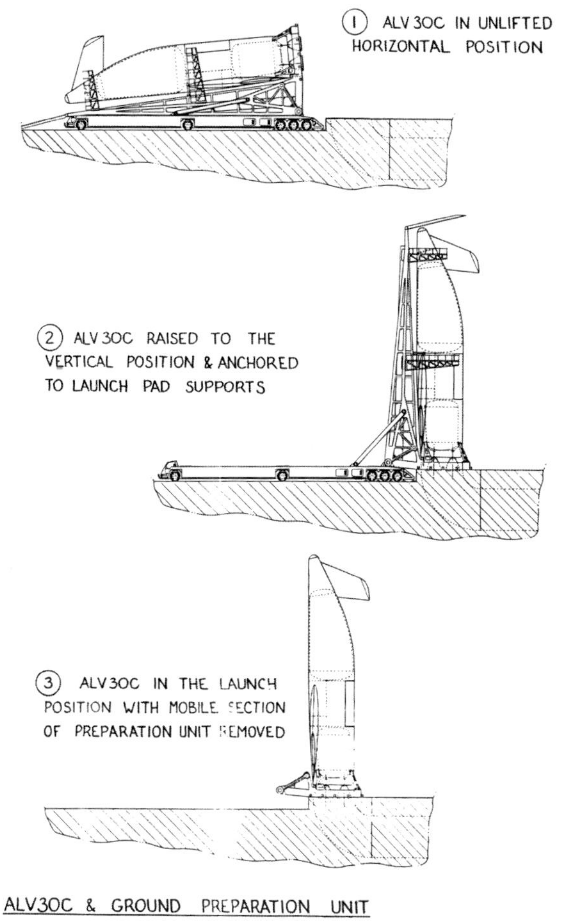

Setting up the ALV 30C for launch.

0.8 (linear factors) and the resulting payload bay sizes established. For larger payloads it should be possible to extend the payload bay outwards using modified doors and fairings".

SO WHICH ALV WON?

The ALV Group's preliminary investigations had been thorough and time-consuming. Baker said: "One thing that I can remember is taking an inordinate length of time, approximately a week, to solve the single integral equation that defines the hypersonic lift generated by the curved underside of a space vehicle. The problem turned out to be caused by the assumption that, as the vehicle would have a vertical axis of symmetry, it would be easier to use polar co-ordinates, as opposed to Cartesian co-ordinates, to define the curve of the body. This approach consistently failed because it always threw up a function, as a result of integration by parts, that could not be integrated. In the end I used the much more long-winded Cartesian co-ordinate approach, which resulted in a solvable equation."

The executive summary, as mentioned, had been completed by July 1987 and Walley felt able to draw some conclusions from around nine months of work: "It is considered that the current Hotol system is critically dependent for its viability on [the following:] the feasibility, successful development and integration into the

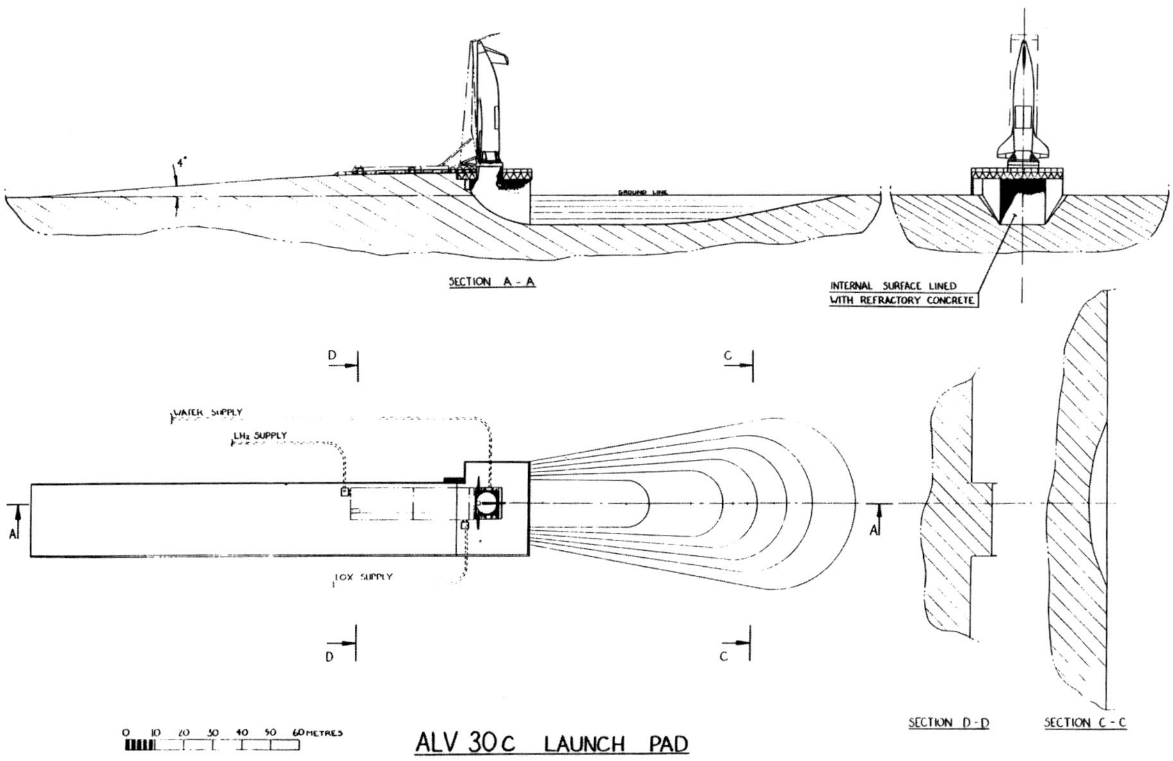

Launch pad for the ALV 30C.

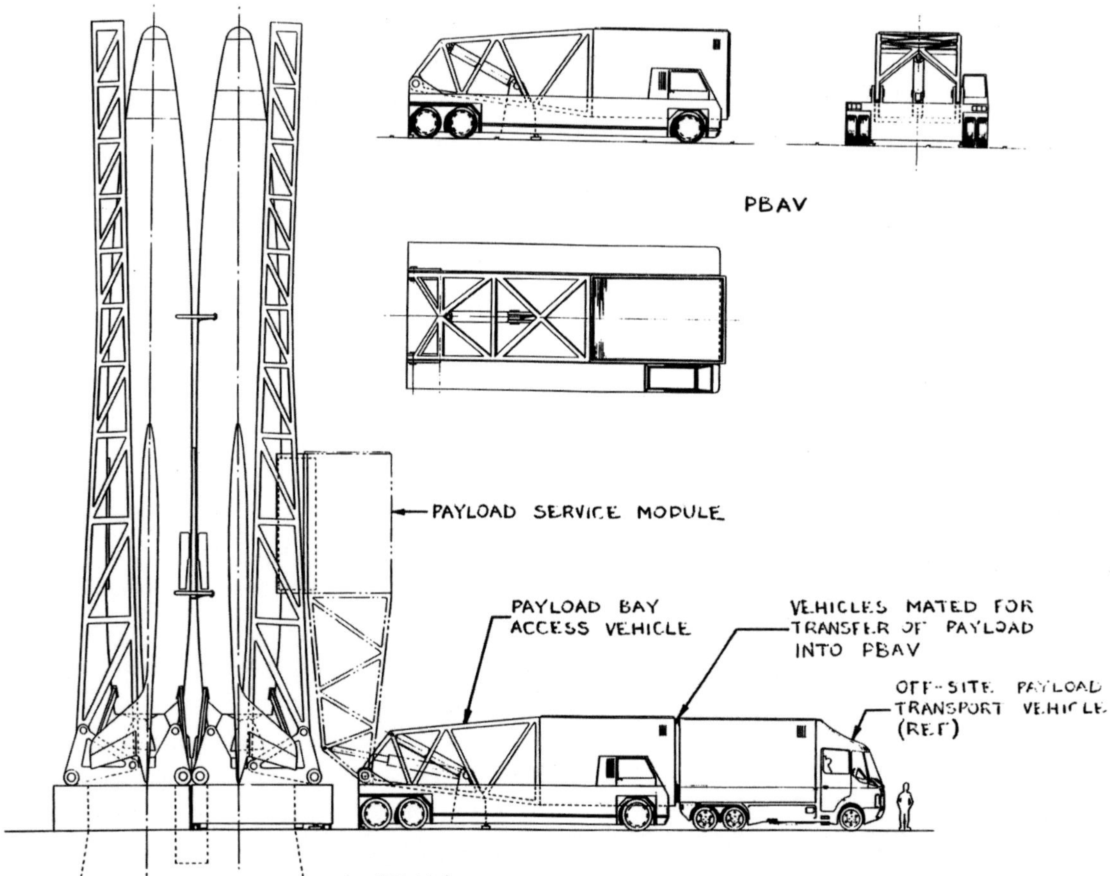

PBAV - VERTICAL LAUNCH APPLICATION

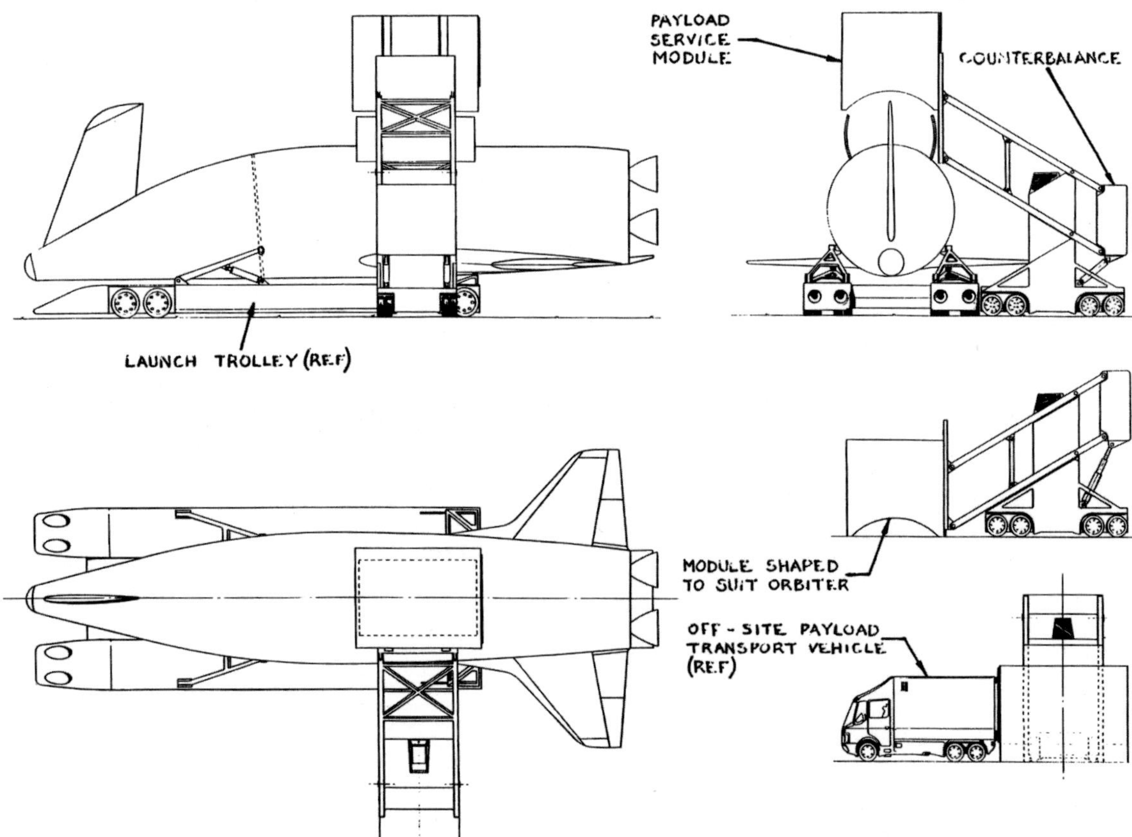

PBAV - TROLLEY LAUNCH APPLICATION

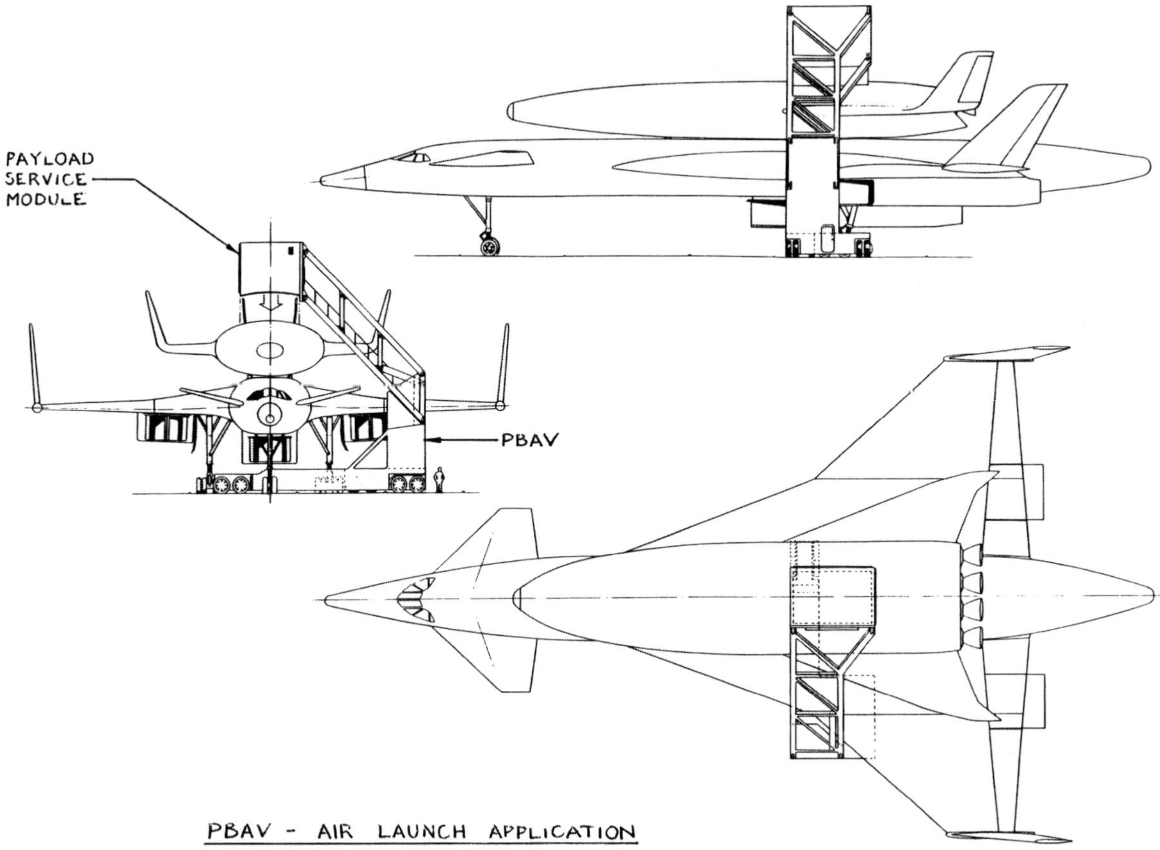

Left and above: ***Details for Payload Bay Access Vehicles (PBAVs) sketched out by the ALV team.***

airframe of a hybrid airbreathing/rocket engine such as the RB.545; achievement of high installed weight and specific impulse; achievement of exceptionally low vehicle mass; an extensive and very expensive materials and manufacturing development programme which must be well advanced before the vehicle design can be frozen; development, in very short timescales, of avionic and utility systems and software suitable for unmanned and mostly autonomous operation; development of a sophisticated ground based launch trolley with appropriate control and site facilities; appropriate airworthiness/flight certification clearances for the unmanned vehicle, in particular for operation to and from dedicated sites or major airfields".

Put that way, the Hotol programme certainly seemed like a steep mountain to climb. Indeed, Walley stated: "Realistic cost estimates of the Hotol system indicate that the true cost is likely to be prohibitive. Experience from previous high-risk prestige projects, such as Concorde, is that costs will escalate well beyond their original estimates."

Some of the ALVs studied suffered from similar issues but "two-stage, more conventional, rocket-only systems, such as ALVs 32, 33 and 34 offer the lowest risk, the greatest flexibility and possibly the lowest lifecycle costs. They could be improved upon by the ALV 60 system. [In addition,] should there be a paramount military (or civil) requirement for an airbreathing hypersonic aircraft then the ALV 100 system may offer sufficient advantages to make it viable and the very high costs and risks acceptable".

The best candidate launch systems, therefore, were considered to be the modular and decidedly Mustard-like ALV 60 and the ALV 100, which effectively reconfigured Hotol to put its engines into its wings and swapped its nose fin for a more conventional tail fin. Reflecting on this in 2024, Baker noted that "from the outset I had the feeling that, within the leadership of the ALV Group, the group was expected to come to that conclusion".

According to the 1987 report, the ALV 60 system "has been evolved around the use of a smaller basic module and a reduced basic payload. These modules can be used as: a two-stage, two-module siamese system, a two-stage, three-module triamese system, [or] a three-stage system, using two modules and booster rockets". And "further arrangements are possible for even larger, non-recoverable, payloads. Lifting body modules are favoured since they have significant aerodynamic and structural advantages, are less dependent on advanced materials/technology [and] offer greatest launcher arrangement flexibility and long-term development".

The ALV 100 system "has been studied in some depth and is included on the assumption that: there could be an

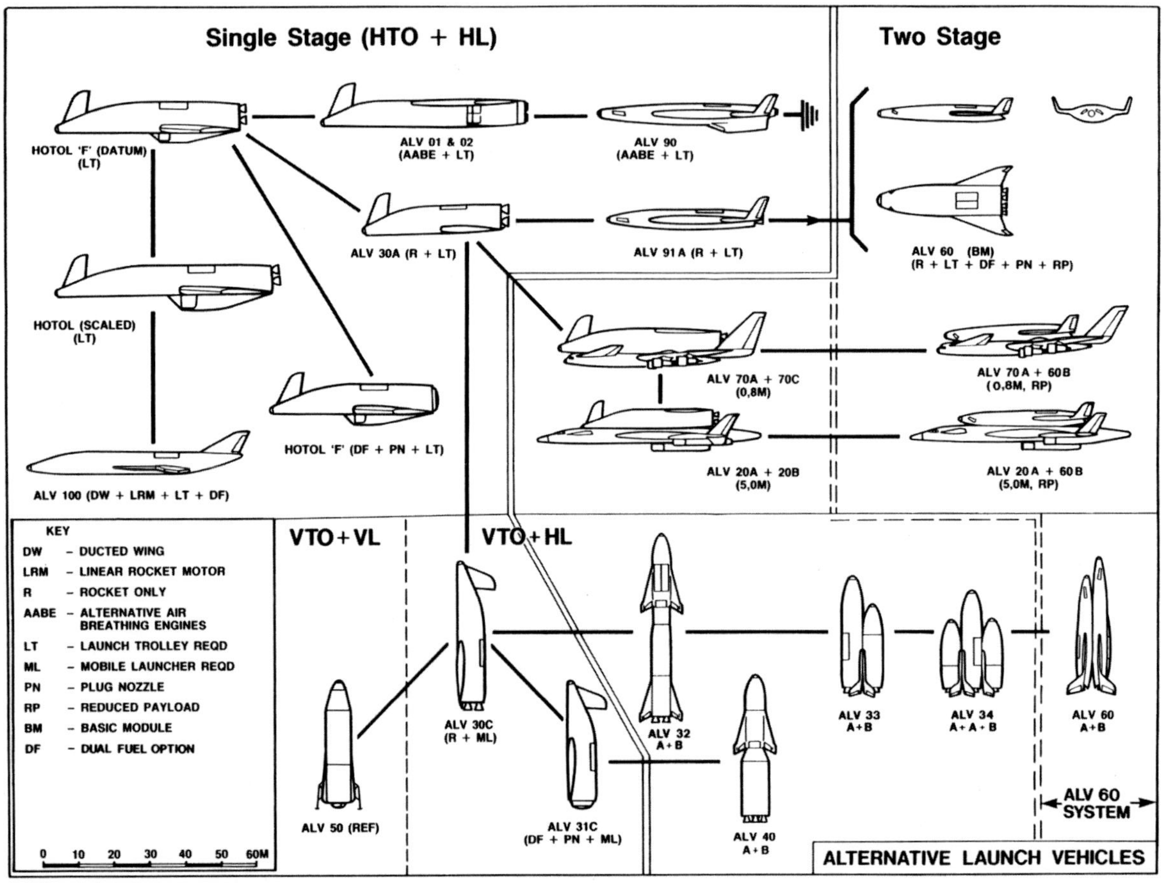

Alternative Launch Vehicles overview.

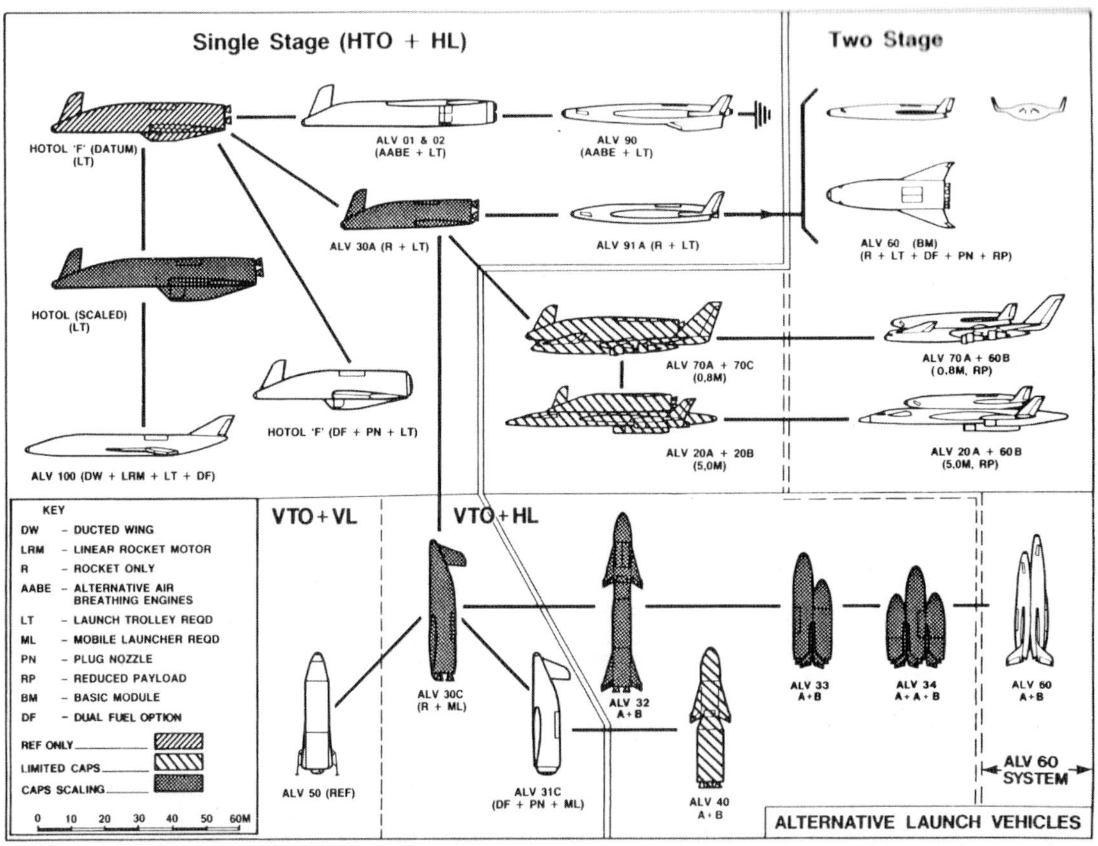

Overview with markings to show how much CAPS effort had been expended on certain designs.

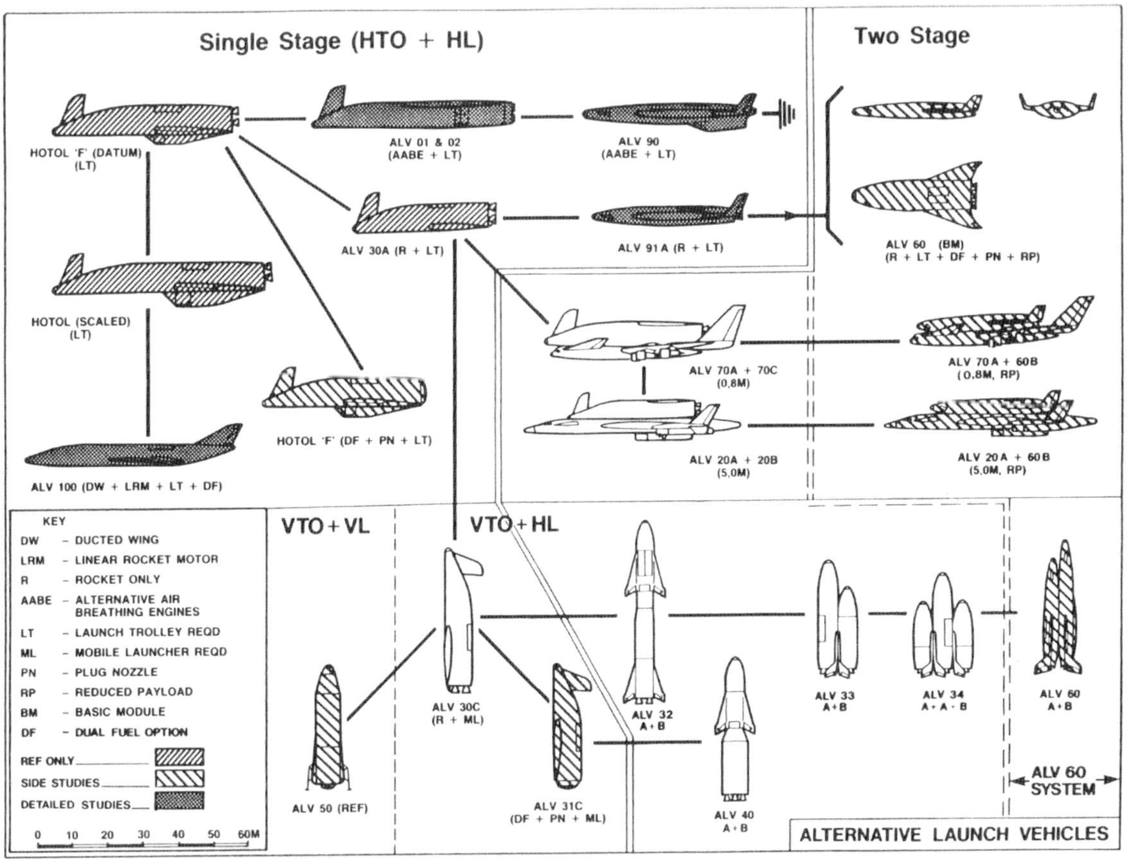

Overview showing which designs had been studied in detail and which were 'side studies'.

ALTENATIVE LAUNCH VEHICLES OPERATING COST 'BREAKDOWN.

VEHICLE TYPE / CATEGORY	H.TO + HL HOTOL	ROCKET H.T.O + HL ALV 30A	V.T.O H.L ALV 30C	V.T.O H.L ALV 32 A+B	V.TO H.L ALV 33 A+B	V.TO H.L ALV 34 A+A+B	V.T.O H.L ALV 40 A+B	H.TO + HL ALV 70A+70C	H.TO + HL ALV 20A+20B
1.0 LAUNCH SITE FACILITIES :-									
1.1 LAUNCH SITE ENHANCEMENTS	40 M	40M	92M				92M	40M	60M
1.2 LAUNCH SITE MAINTENANCE	500M	500M	578M				584M	500M	318M
2.0 LAUNCH EQUIPMENT MAINT:	216M	202M	3M				—	—	—
3.0 MAINTENANCE INCLUDING SPARES)									
3.1 VEHICLE MAINT:	1222M	830M	744M				408M	716M	464M
3.2 VEHICLE ENGINE MAINT:	578M	338M	351M				88M	308M	238M
3.3 BOOSTER MAINTENANCE.	—	—	—				} 63M	468M	954M
3.4 BOOSTER ENGINE MAINT:	—	—	—					108M	913M
5.0 PROPELLANT COST	293M	141 M	132M		IN PREPARATION		109M	113M	225M
6.0 GROUND SUPPORT EQUIPMENT:-									
6.1/2 ADDITIONAL OPERATIONAL EQUIPT	155M	108M	86M				48M	131M	145M
6.3 G.S.E MAINT:	248M	173M	138M				77M	210M	232M
7.0 SPARES :-									
7.1 ADDIT'L SPARE ENGINES	321M	188M	195M				49M	171M	132M
7.2 INTEREST ON SPARES	385M	262M	210M				108M	308M	476M
8.0 INSURANCE :-									
8.1 MISSION FAILURE	} 548M	387M	308M						
8.2 LAUNCH VEHICLE LOSS							323M	501M	975M
9.0 BASE OVERHEAD	228M	222M	212M				212M	238M	238M
TOTAL OPERATING COST	4734	3391	3049				2,161*	3,812	5.570

* NOTE. 720 PRODUCTION EXPENDITURE BOOSTER ARE EXCLUDED @ £7.M EACH (TOTAL £5040M)

Operating cost breakdown for Hotol compared to the ALV 30A, 30C, 40A+B, 70A+C and 20A+B, with costs for 32A+B, 33A+B, 34A+A+B still "in preparation".

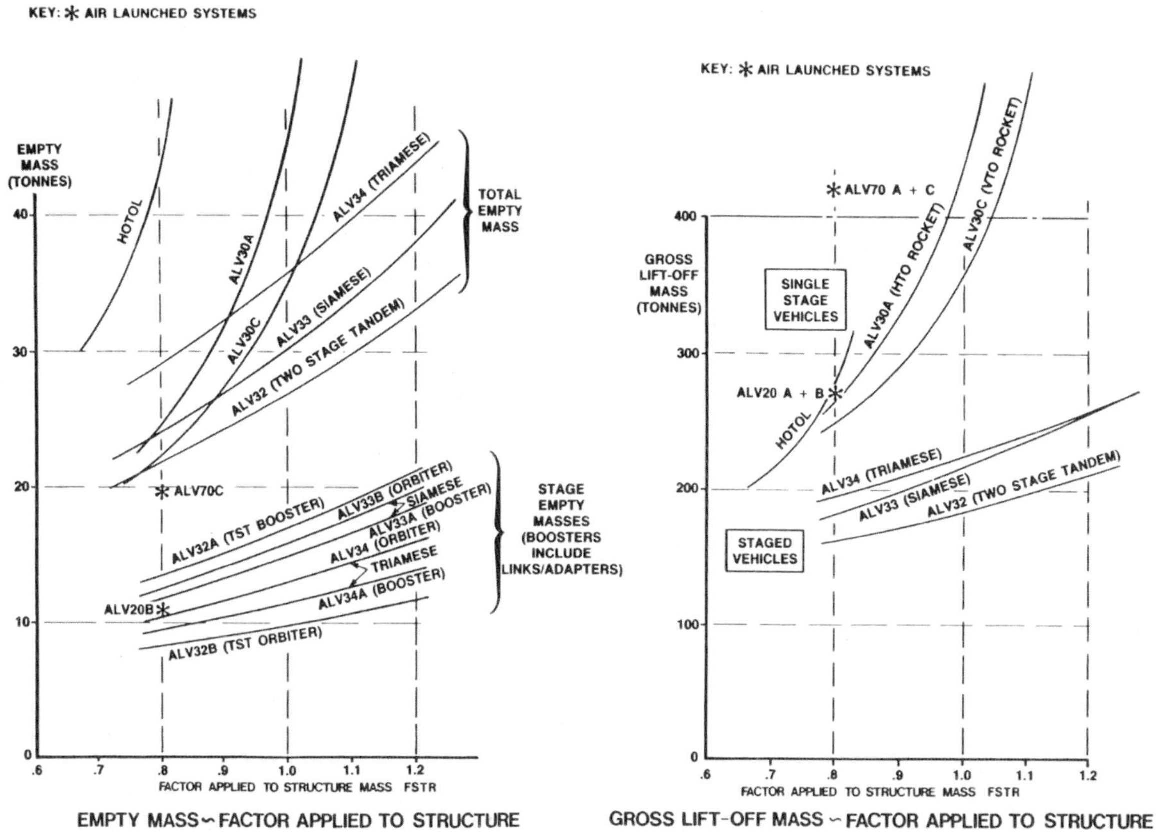

Alternative Launch Vehicles mass comparison.

overriding military or civil requirement for a hypersonic transatmospheric vehicle; a hybrid airbreathing engine, such as the RB.545, is practical and can be integrated into an unswept wing; it can be used as a satellite launch vehicle and lowest costs are not a paramount requirement".

It was pointed out that "whilst the costs and risks of such a system will not be much less than Hotol, it has significant advantages and may prove a better alternative. In addition, it can be progressively developed ... Initial airframe development and flight testing, (also for smaller payloads) could use a four engined vehicle [and] subsequent variants with eight or ten engines and a lengthened fuselage could launch larger heavier payloads".

WALLEY RECOMMENDS

There were four appended recommendations arising from the ALV Group's studies. Firstly, that "further studies, in greater depth, must be undertaken to establish more clearly: the likely operational requirements, manned or unmanned, payloads, orbits, frequencies of launch, etc. — including any possible military applications (outside ESA); the viability or otherwise of likely competing launch systems which may be proposed by USA, Japan and Europe".

Secondly, that "further studies must be undertaken on: prime candidate ALVs, manned or unmanned; alternative advanced rocket engines, nozzles and fuels; more advanced alternative airbreathing/integrated engines (although unlikely to be competitive unless required for other reasons); practical operational aspects throughout the whole mission envelope, including base operations for VTOHL and HTOHL vehicles; and all airworthiness aspects, including certification, flight clearance, reliability etc."

Thirdly, ALV enabling technologies needed more work and lastly more detailed and realistic cost estimates for selected ALVs were needed.

THE END FOR ALVS?

Following the publication of Walley's summary report in September 1987, the ALV Group did indeed continue to study its chosen concepts in greater depth. Walley appears to have moved on to other work before the end of the year but his remaining team members forged ahead into early March 1988 under the supervision of BAe Warton's head of future concepts Tom Smith.

Brian Young wrote to Burns, copying in Tom Smith, M. D. Parry and BAe Military Aircraft Division Technical Director Dave Gardner on March 7, 1988, to say: "I wish you to stop activity on Alternative Launch Vehicles,

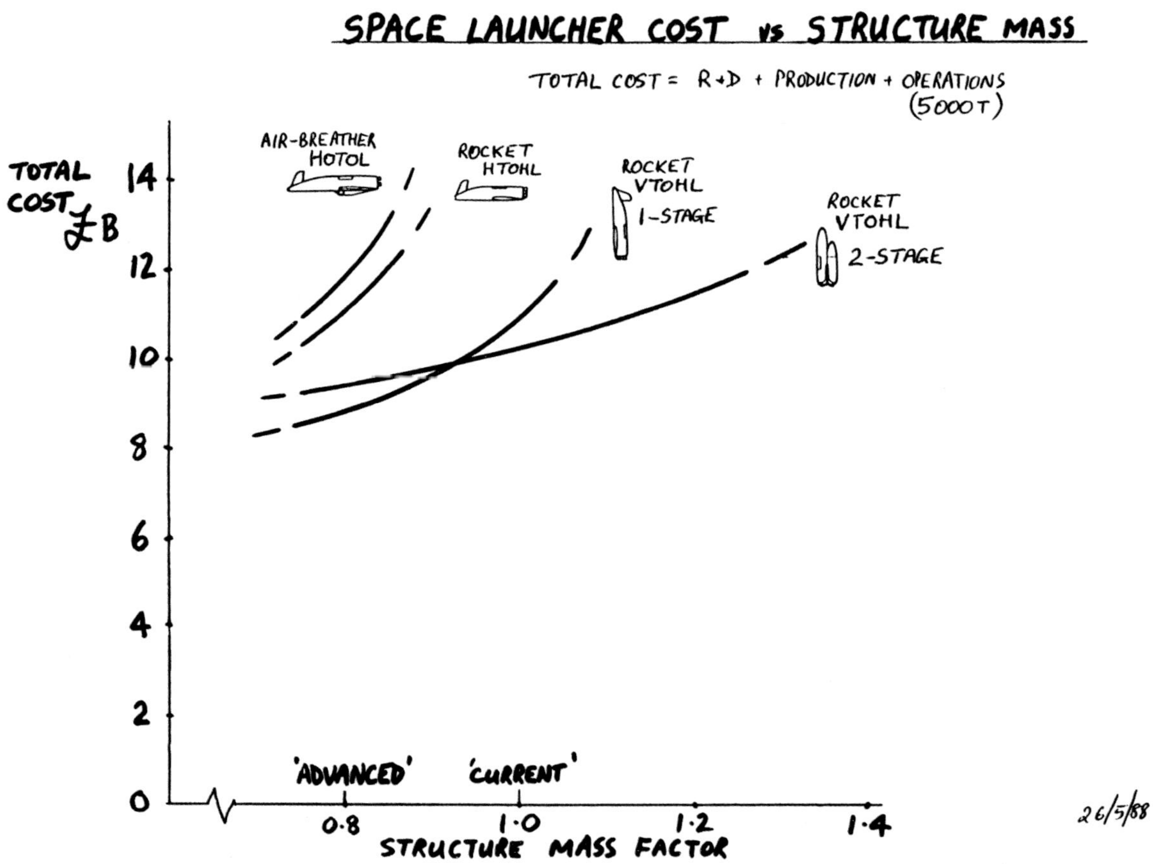

ALV designs used to illustrate a BAe graph on space launcher cost versus structure mass, dated May 26, 1988.

other than that actioned by Mr Yates, immediately. It is an unnecessary drain on Hotol funding and is causing considerable friction within the company team.

"I realise we await replies from Space and Communications to many of the questions raised and have asked Mr Conchie to chase these. You can expect Dr Parkinson to respond soon and it may then be necessary to do a little more work. Please discuss this with me if it is likely to be substantial.

"The staff previously working on ALVs can now be transferred to Hotol work or returned to their parent departments as Mr Gardner wishes. I realise they previously were managed by Mr Walley but this was for the duration of the ALV study only. This is completed and Mr Walley has gone away to do other things—we should do the same!"

Burns then sent out a follow-up memo addressed solely to Gardner, marked 'private and confidential', which said: "Further to Mr Young's memo re: Alternative Launch Vehicle Activity dated March 7, 1988, I see the workload of the ALV team staff as follows:

1. All-rocket alternatives (ALV 30A, 30C). No further design work. Comparison with Hotol to be agreed with Stevenage on the basis of Mr E. Webb's report, as actioned by Mr I. R. Yates (December 16, 1987).
2. ALV 100 (RB.545 engines in wing). As actioned by Mr I. R. Yates, engineering study of wing structure, actuation etc. to be pursued to derive realistic mass figures. If favourable, propose wind tunnel model programme to substantiate estimates. Put project 'on ice' pending results of this programme.
3. ESA Sponsored WLV Study. Schematic design of Hotol-based and blended wing-body SSTO designs with alternative air-breathing powerplants, sized to the two alternative missions (i.e. 2 x 2 x 2 = 8 configurations). [Also,] critical assessment of MBB's TSTO (Sänger-like) designs."

Burns was willing to see one of the remaining ALV team members, designer Keith George, transferred to another department but wanted to keep the others together.

Rather than dismissing all ALV studies and concentrating what scant resources were available on the main Hotol project, Burns clearly saw merit in a handful of the alternative designs—specifically the horizontal take-off rocket-Hotol ALV 30A, the VTO rocket-Hotol ALV 30C and ALV 100 with its wing-mounted RB.545s. While the ALV Group had effectively been dissolved as a distinct unit, this was by no means the end for these concepts.

7

THE HUGELY EXPENSIVE CLUB: JUNE 11, 1987 TO DECEMBER 31, 1987

AT THE beginning of June 1987, nine months on from its completion, the BNSC's 15-year space plan remained unpublished. And Sir Robin Nicholson's report on it (see Chapter 4) had yet to be discussed by Thatcher's cabinet. Roy Gibson remembered: "I'd been given to understand by Nicholson … that what they wanted was a space plan which was proportional to the size of the UK and its gross national product, and they were not looking to cut corners: they really wanted a proper effect. The Nicholson report is quite clear on this.

"But it never got on the cabinet table, it used to go regularly to cabinet and it slipped off the agenda more times than I care to think of. And then they pulled the skids under the Secretary of State. He really was a wet. Not Pattie, Paul Channon [Secretary of State for Trade and Industry], I think. We had to kind of brief him like a rugby coach before he went in to see Thatcher. He used to come out trembling and we'd say, did you get it? Oh, it never came up on the agenda.

"But eventually it was clear that she wasn't interested, wasn't interested any more."

Britain went to the polls on June 11, 1987, and gave the Conservative Party its third successive election victory. Prime Minister Margaret Thatcher was returned to power and Pattie was returned as Member of Parliament for Chertsey and Walton just as comfortably as he had been during the previous General Election in 1983.

But two days later, when Thatcher reshuffled her cabinet, Pattie's Minister of State, Industry and Information Technology post was unceremoniously dissolved—consigning him to the back benches and effectively removing Hotol's greatest advocate from government. Channon remained on the front bench but was moved on to become Secretary of State for Transport.

Pattie's former responsibilities now fell under the remit of Kenneth Clarke, who had been made both Chancellor of the Duchy of Lancaster and Minister of State for Trade and Industry. Channon was replaced by Lord Young and John Butcher became Parliamentary Under-Secretary of State for Trade and Industry.

RR DOES SOME PR

Meanwhile, the 1987 Paris Air Show had begun on June 11 and on June 15 Rolls-Royce released an uncharacteristically optimistic press release under the headline 'Hotol's engine calculations confirmed'. It read: "Eighteen months of work has confirmed the original estimates for the weight

Hotol promotional model based on Configuration F.

Evidently the same Hotol model was used as the basis for this period promotional art.

and performance of Rolls-Royce's revolutionary aerospace engine proposal ... the preliminary design and proof-of-concept programme began in February 1986 and included the examination of a number of alternative propulsion concepts in addition to the engine for British Aerospace's Hotol spaceplane.

"Rig testing of critical components of the Hotol engine, designated the RB.545, has been carried out in as realistic conditions as possible by a small team of specialists at Rolls-Royce's Ansty plant, near Coventry. Stewart Miller, Rolls-Royce director of corporate engineering, said: 'The test programme has produced some exciting and positive results. We have made significant progress in the last 18 months towards confirming the original ideas for such a propulsion system, which seized everyone's imagination three years ago. The rig testing and project design studies, which are being carried out at Rolls-Royce's Bristol plant, are proceeding to schedule, enabling us currently to define follow-on technology and associated programmes. We have been in discussion with European industry and remain committed to the extension of the programme into Europe.'"

This press release then formed the basis of an article in *The Times* the following day.

For most of Hotol's existence, Rolls-Royce had been a government-owned concern—but it was privatised on May 20, 1987. The Government raised £1.4bn from the sale of its shares and the new shareholders were doubtless wondering whether they had made the right decision to invest. As such, it was evidently now important that the company's ongoing research and development activities should be publicly viewed in a more positive light.

HOTOL DOWN UNDER

Wilson returned to Paris on June 25 for a two-day series of presentations on airbreathing propulsion by SNECMA, Fiat Aviazione, SEP and SNIA-BPD to ESA. These companies had been given a joint contract to study different combinations of turbojets, rockets, ramjets and scramjets and the technology needed to make such systems feasible.

Five days later, on June 30, Wake gave a Hotol presentation at the Australian Space Symposium. The main purpose of her trip down under was, however, to test Hotol model SB3 in the hypersonic shock tube, known as T3, at the Australian National University (ANU) in Canberra.

In a 1988 article for British Aerospace's in-house magazine, *Intercom*, she wrote: "The hypersonic shock tube at the university produces a flow of air at speeds up to 46,000mph at representative re-entry temperatures, but only for a fraction of a second. The power required to maintain such an airflow would light and heat a city the size of Manchester or Sydney ... A 1/250 scale Hotol model (about 8in long) was manufactured at Warton in

The enormous 1:5 scale model of Hotol Configuration F on display at the BAe stand during the 1987 Paris Air Show.

The white SB3 model undergoing tests in the T3 Stalker hypersonic shock tube at ANU in Canberra. ALISON WAKE

ANU's Dr Neil Mudford, left, Vince Capizzi of BAe Australia and Alison Wake discuss the black SB3 Hotol model on the desk (the dark object below Wake's pencil) at ANU. ALISON WAKE

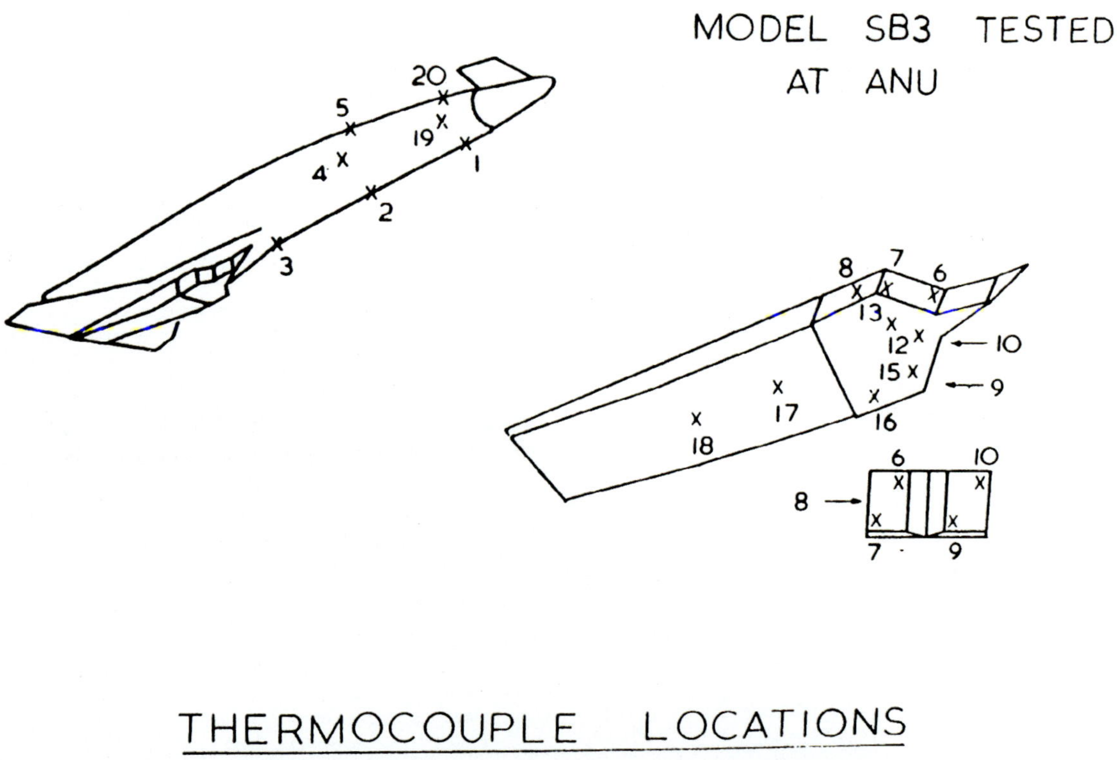

Diagram showing thermocouple locations within the SB3 model tested at ANU.

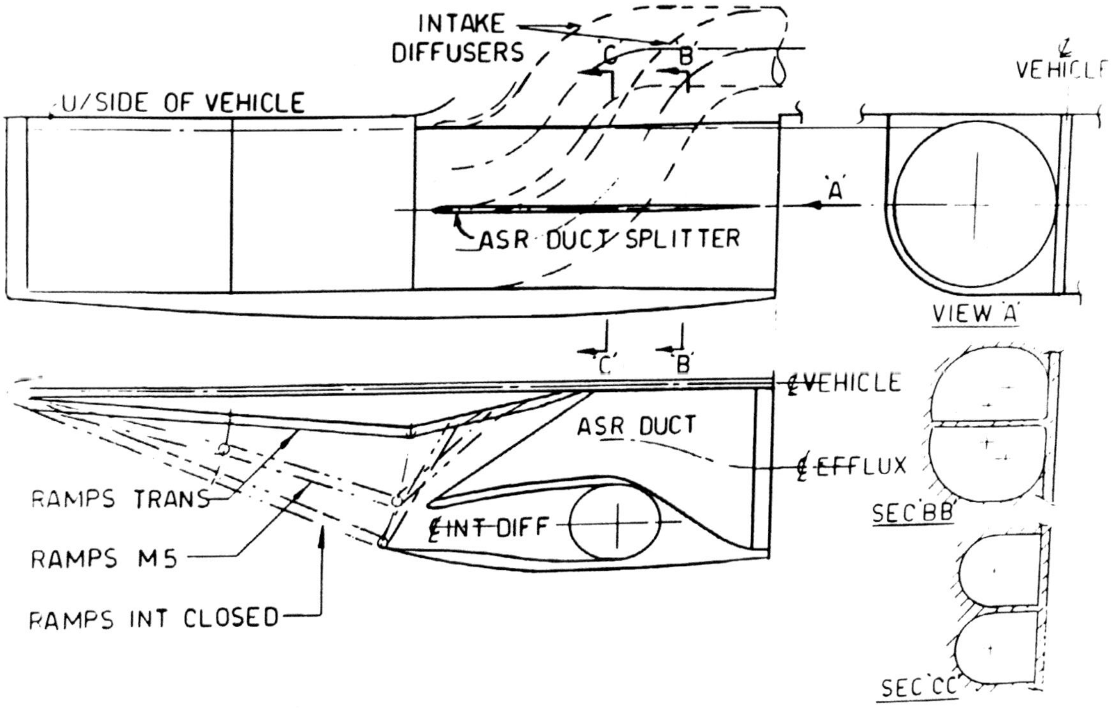

'Aft spill ramjet' proposal for making use of excess air from the intake.

our high-speed model shop and sent to Australia in April 1987, together with a wooden publicity model.

"On receipt of the model, 18 thermocouples were installed ... to give heat transfer rate information ... Testing took place during June ... which was Australia's winter, so no sunbathing on Bondi Beach! Test conditions were chosen to give a good database for the current re-entry trajectory and to enable different trajectories to be assessed. We carried out a total of 80 runs, covering speeds from 3.5km/s to 7.5km/s and angles of incidence from 15° to 45°."

In his summary for Yates issued on July 1, 1987, Burns noted that preliminary results of these tests "indicate that the highest heating rates occur on the intake (closed) face, as expected, being about four times the rate on the fuselage lower centre line".

Concerning Wilson's trip to Paris, he wrote: "It is believed that ESA will issue a request for proposals for a continuation study ... Propulsion companies, RR plus MBB being the front runners, wish to see airframe companies involved in this next stage. It is recommended that BAe should participate in this activity".

GOODBYE HOTOL 'F'

Burns' January update gave the strongest indications yet that Hotol Configuration F had been consigned to history and that the team at Warton were reshaping the vehicle into something altogether sleeker, just as Parkinson and Bond had hoped they would. Burns wrote: "Mass and aerodynamics estimates are being refined to enable a confident definition of Configuration G when final propulsion data is received. Aerodynamic refinements will include reduction of nose droop, reduced nose blunting and reduced wing leading edge radius inboard.

"Detailed liquid hydrogen tank structural investigations have shown that a lighter structure may be achieved with some internal stiffening, also reducing the penalty for a longer/smaller diameter tank. Consideration of 'tropical only' operation and sizing the fin for 2% probability crosswind leads to a reduction of about 45% in fin area."

If an 8,000psi hydraulics system could be introduced, a further 3.5% mass saving was feasible, but "development risks are high and no precursor programme is planned, in Europe, as far as is known".

Where the engine was concerned, "burning some of the hydrogen exhaust in the intake spill duct as a 'spill ramjet' is very beneficial". Final estimates of just how beneficial were in preparation at Filton. The 'spill' in question was excess air which had entered the vehicle's intake but which, being surplus to requirements, was being allowed to 'spill' out unused. In addition, data from Rolls-Royce on liquid oxygen pre-injection had yet to be delivered.

Hopes remained high for the enabling technology programme and "five teams have been set up at Warton to deal with development programmes on advanced materials and associated test facilities. Initial proposals for a software and artificial intelligence 'club' have [also] been agreed with the Technical Director, M.A.D., [Brian Young, Technical Director of BAe's Military Aircraft Division] and a kick-off meeting is planned".

THATCHER VS. EUROPEAN SPENDING

While all this was going on, Prime Minister Margaret Thatcher was engaging in an increasingly bitter conflict with Britain's European partners over the budget for the European research and development programme — Framework — which would have severe consequences for both British space science in general and Hotol in particular.

On July 9, 1987, *Nature* reported that Britain had vetoed approval for Framework's budget on the basis that major reforms were needed. The journal's Bill Johnstone wrote that "at the heart of the conflict is Thatcher's view that much of the EEC budget is misspent and that too much — now 70% — is used to subsidise the Community's farming, a policy that greatly benefits France".

The veto had "surprised many in the UK high-technology industries who were convinced that the third administration of Thatcher's government would approve the research and development budget without question. Such confidence seemed to be confirmed by the sacking of the previous information technology minister Geoffrey Pattie — a new team has been installed at the DTI led by Lord Young, a 'political heavyweight' and a confidant of the Prime Minister".

Johnstone noted that "Thatcher's government ... has been notorious in its opposition to increased public expenditure". As a footnote to the article, he added that "officials at the BNSC have met Lord Young and are confident that the Government will respond positively to their proposals by the end of this month. Unless it receives approval then, claims BNSC, Britain will be unable to take part in the immediate research projects planned by ESA. These include programmes for the Ariane space rocket and the Hermes space plane."

With hindsight, given Thatcher's stance on absolutely anything else which involved spending increases, particularly where Europe was concerned, and her black and white approach to policy in general, it seems clear that such confidence was badly misplaced.

NO MORE MONEY FOR SPACE

During Prime Minister's Questions in the House of Commons on July 23, 1987, Conservative MP Michael Marshall asked Thatcher: "Is my right honourable friend aware of the growing anxiety about reports that Her Majesty's Government have failed to reach agreement on an interdepartmental basis on the budget for space expenditure and that the proposal of the BNSC for increased space activities will therefore be rejected? Does that not call into question our future commitment to ESA and to the BNSC?"

Thatcher responded: "I do not believe that it does. It is quite correct that we have not been able to find the considerable amount of extra expenditure that was requested. As my honourable friend is aware, we spend through the taxpayer some £4.5bn on research and development. We are not able to find any more resources. Therefore, it would mean a switch of resources from one research or technology development to another. My colleagues felt that they could not make that switch and therefore we shall continue our subscription to ESA, but at present we are not able to find more money. I hope that the private sector, if it is interested in the results from such research, will come forward with considerable resources."

Gibson said that the space plan "didn't go through and they decided [the matter] out of cabinet ... that, really, we don't need to put any more money into space, we just go on as we are. So this was never pushed. I think this is probably why they've been a bit pernickety about publishing the space plan because I don't think, though I'm not sure, I don't think it was ever put onto the [cabinet] table ... I was informed, because I wasn't there, it was a deal between Kenneth Clarke, Lord Young and Margaret Thatcher."

He said he thought the space plan had suffered because Thatcher just didn't like Channon: "That was the genesis of it. If we'd had a minister who was in favour then I think a month or two after the plan was ready then he would have got it through. Because judged as impartially as I can, and obviously I'm not impartial, it wasn't a bad report and the choices were so wide that it was difficult to understand why the lowest wouldn't have been accepted, otherwise what the hell are you doing the exercise for? I think the lowest of them was something like a 40% increase. And it was not at all revolutionary in terms of areas ... A pity, some good work went into it. And industry, as I say, was devastated ... they'd invested, not very much but they'd invested something ... it meant a continuation of their long march through the desert as far as ESA programmes are concerned. Because a lot of the technology that they were using in ESA programmes was wearing a bit thin at the edges and needed either in-house investment or a national programme to support it or both, of course."

As far as Hotol's part in this was concerned, Gibson said: "Well, there never was a programme as such but it was inside industry. We put a little bit of money into it but our contribution was mainly in terms of getting it onto the agenda and sort of getting presentations and then wheeling a minister out to talk to the Germans. But industry put quite a lot of money into it, British Aerospace particularly."

Asked if Thatcher supported Hotol, he said: "No, I don't think so. She went absolutely cold on anything to do with space."

Thatcher's response to Marshall's question during PMQs on July 23 was quite clear as a statement of policy: "We shall continue our subscription to ESA, but at present we are not able to find more money." The space plan was dead in the water. And without the extra cash bound up in the space plan, there could be no further government funding for Hotol. Thatcher had made the decision but her announcement was so offhand—and so unexpected by the scientific community—that many did not immediately grasp its implications.

BABY HOTOL

Despite these ominous rumblings from on high, it continued to be business as usual for the Hotol team as they wrapped up the PoC Study. Parkinson, Wake and Dobie from Filton gave presentations to the director and department heads at RAE Farnborough on July 29, with Burns noting that "RAE will be able to offer only advisory support, due to absence of funds and inadequate staffing. However, actual support might be possible with funding from BNSC and staff support from BAe, e.g. for wind tunnel testing".

The next day Parkinson, who had been giving some thought to what the previously discussed Hotol sub-scale demonstrator vehicle might look like, handed a research paper to Burns and Wilson on the subject. He wrote: "It is desirable that any demonstrator vehicle be able to demonstrate the performance of a full-scale RB.545 engine over the airbreathing flight regime, although it would not necessarily have to fly up a full 'ascent corridor'.

"The presence of such a vehicle could be expected to impact the programme by requiring that full-scale vehicle development would be delayed until after flight test data was available from the demonstrator. The costs associated with such a demonstrator can be expected to depend on the size of the vehicle proposed, but it is desirable that the vehicle has aerodynamic characteristics not too dissimilar to the full-scale vehicle in order to get representative flight data on intake performance etc.

"The need to supply the engine with significant quantities of liquid hydrogen tends to preclude the use of an available manned airframe in any case."

In other words, there would be no suspending an RB.545 beneath the wing of an existing commercial airliner—it would need a dedicated test vehicle.

When it came to sizing this little Hotol, he said he was working on the assumption that the full-scale four-engine Hotol would have an all-up take-off mass of 260 tonnes, with a fuselage diameter of 6m and a wing area of 180sqm. On the basis that the demonstrator would only need one engine, "the thrust of a single RB.545 is 319kN. If we allow the vehicle a higher take-off acceleration it would simplify operations and allow us to avoid developing a special launch trolley for the vehicle. Since the launch mass will reduce as we increase the launch acceleration, this is obviously a good thing".

He determined that take-off mass would be about 16.25 tonnes. Fuselage diameter would be 2.6m, length would be 25m and wing area would be 33.75sqm. This would make it a little longer than an F-111 but a little shorter than a TSR2. "The mass problems associated with vehicle construction are probably not excessive," he wrote. "The cost of building and test flying two sub-scale demonstrators is approximately 360 MAU. The programme could add approximately four years to the Hotol development."

On this 'slow-track' development timeline, work on designing and building the flight demonstrators would begin in 1992, with the first vehicle being completed in 1996. A year of rocket-propelled flight testing would then take place—followed by three years of airbreathing flight tests up to 2000. The full-scale Hotol would then begin flight testing in 2002. On a 'fast-track', without the flight demonstrator, Hotol would begin flight testing in 1998.

On the same day, July 30, the BAe team held a meeting with Rolls-Royce to ensure that both companies' future programmes were in synch ahead of a planned meeting with the BNSC on August 24. And the managing directors of the UK's leading materials suppliers gathered at BAe's London HQ for a presentation on what Hotol might require from them.

GIBSON GIVES NOTICE

Despite completely rejecting Gibson's space plan, Thatcher had conceded that "we shall continue our subscription to ESA". Yet the Government now refused to make a payment of £7m to tide over preparatory research for the Columbus programme and Ariane 5/Hermes, in which Britain was supposed to be participating—albeit at an already low level. This was too much for Gibson, who handed in his resignation on August 4, 1987. He would stay on until the end of that month when he would be replaced by Jack Leeming, his deputy, who would then retire at the end of the year and hand on the reins to someone else.

According to a report by Simon Hadlington in *Nature* on August 13: "ESA had intended to hold a ministerial meeting in June to seek approval to start development of the [Columbus and Ariane 5/Hermes] programmes. That meeting was postponed until November, partly because the British government had not decided how much money it would give BNSC. ESA therefore requested extra funding from member states [the £7m] to continue the preparatory studies on Ariane 5 and Columbus until the November meeting.

"The British government refused to provide the extra money so Gibson felt obliged to resign ... shortly after Gibson announced his resignation, he was visited by ESA's director general, Reimar Lüst, and the chairman of the ESA council, Heinrik Grage, ostensibly to discuss ESA's long-term programmes, but they also asked Gibson to reconsider his decision to resign. Afterwards Lüst made it clear that ESA would push on with its space programme regardless of Britain's participation.

"Thatcher's suggestion that the private sector should put up more cash for research has infuriated industrialists, who say that many of the space-exploiting technologies are at such an early stage of development that it will be several years before financial returns permit substantial investment in basic research."

Evidently Pattie, who had been given the consolation of a knighthood in the meantime to become Sir Geoffrey, commented that Britain had "abdicated from space".

The day after Gibson's resignation, Burns reported to Yates that "a letter has been sent to MoD Contracts Department quoting the cost of the proposed Concept Validation Phase of nine months duration (October 1987 to June 1988) as £1.74m. It has previously been proposed that this phase should be funded 100% by the Government". It is unclear just how likely Burns thought this was — but Thatcher's fairly unambiguous statements on being unable to find more money for space and hopes that the private sector would come forward to pay for everything must have given rise to at least a twinge of doubt.

Conversely, there was cause for optimism where the still-fluid design of Hotol Configuration G was concerned: "The rigorous review of mass and aerodynamics models is nearing completion ... incorporation of the spill ramjet has been shown to increase payload by four tonnes on a fixed scale vehicle, equivalent 'roughly' to 80 tonnes reduction in gross lift-off mass on a scaled vehicle.

"The revised intake design has resulted in a significant increase in structure mass, alleviated partially by adoption of higher altitude trajectory. Further optimisation, including the heat exchangers, is in progress. The spill ramjet also allows some reduction in engine scale."

Things were looking up on materials too: "Further investigations of liquid hydrogen tank design have led to the adoption of double skinned carbon-PEEK structure with the cryogenic insulation in the sandwich. This allows the tank to be depressurised for servicing without external stiffening. It also offers a 'fail safe' structure in the event of penetration of the tank by space debris; this would result in loss of pressure but not structural collapse."

And not only that: "Some data has been obtained on titanium aluminides. This material offers no increase in strength/weight ratio at moderate temperatures but retains its strength to temperatures in the region of 1,000°K and is stated to be free from oxidation up to 1,300°K. It may well prove to be the optimum material for the thermal protection system on Hotol."

On the national stage, by the end of July the Government had grudgingly agreed to meet its ESA obligation on Columbus/Ariane 5/Hermes — though it had only handed over £4m of the requested £7m.

GIBSON'S PARTING ADVICE

The meeting between BAe/RR and the BNSC took place as planned on August 24 at Millbank Tower in London, with Conchie, Wilson (deputising for Burns, who was on holiday) and Parkin attending from BAe, Hillier, Denning and Brian Lowrie from RR, and Gibson, Leeming, A. C. Nicholas, Alan Hicks and Ms G. M. Kaspers from the BNSC.

According to the minutes, taken by Kaspers: "Mr Gibson described the UK funding position and the release of £4m by UK Government. This will keep the Ariane 5 and Columbus options open until the autumn when the Advisory Council on Science and Technology (ACOST) R&D review will take place."

ACOST had been formed the previous month as a restructuring of the Advisory Council on Applied Research and Development (ACARD) which had been in existence since 1976. However, ACARD's chairman, Rolls-Royce's Sir Francis Tombs, remained in post in ACOST, as did most other ACARD members.

Kaspers went on: "Mr Gibson anticipated that the results would be available by the end of October and in time for the ESA Ministerial Conference in November. November will also be the time when the BNSC will sort out its priorities and direction. Mr Conchie pointed out that it was difficult to estimate what should be spent on

Hotol in this phase with the funding for the next phase uncertain. Mr Conchie noted that BAe and RR were the only UK companies to respond so far to the Government request for industry investment and pointed out that the money provided in effect covered BAe and RR involvement in RADARSAT [Earth-imaging radar satellites being developed by the Canadian Space Agency] and Hotol."

The meeting then moved on to FESTIP and Kaspers recorded that "the ESA programme to be presented to Ministers is still undecided. The meeting discussed the advantages of pressing for FESTIP versus national funding on Hotol. Mr Conchie emphasised that German industry is currently unenthusiastic about FESTIP, preferring to concentrate on a national effort. This stems from a lack of confidence in the ESA Executive to manage such a programme and a desire not to see the French dominate again in launchers.

"Mr Leeming and Mr Gibson argued that it was important to have a line in the presentation to Ministers in November that gave a justification for FESTIP and some figures. Mr Gibson envisaged that even with a national spend on Hotol there would still be a need for an ESA programme to act as an anchor and a European focal point. This was a view that Mr Hillier supported. All agreed that this would still leave room for bilateral or multilateral arrangements. It was agreed that BNSC would draw up a draft description with figures and circulate it."

Despite Hillier nodding along with support for FESTIP, the Rolls-Royce team apparently indicated an ongoing reluctance to continue the company's involvement in Hotol, confirming "that they would keep working to the end of the year on company money but would not be able to step up their activities in the way originally foreseen. Both Rolls-Royce and British Aerospace agreed that the plans of work shown in their recent proposals were still valid but were hampered by the uncertainty over funding. Mr Gibson said there was no option but to proceed on the assumption that there would be no money from ESA or BNSC until the end of the year".

Throughout the meeting Gibson repeatedly stressed "the importance of showing ... the relevance of the Hotol technology to other areas of industry e.g. structures, materials and software". He evidently believed that the project's survival depended on its perceived potential for generating lucrative tech spinoffs that could benefit other areas of industry.

When it came to declassifying the RB.545, Kaspers wrote: "MoD has not contacted the BNSC about any change of position. Mr Hicks will check with Mr Armstrong (MoD) whether the MoD can be persuaded to rethink. RR have not pushed hard for declassification and have found it reasonably convenient to live with so far. BAe thought it would be necessary to have achieved declassification by spring '88."

Interviewed by Russell J. Hannigan in the early 1990s, Pattie recalled: "I think we could probably have mounted a major campaign to get [the engine] declassified without too much difficulty. These things are not completely immovable. You've got to be able to go to the PM and explain the situation. The problem was that Rolls-Royce were not particularly interested in actually doing it. They didn't want to get involved, so who would be campaigning for it? If a government department comes along and says 'we would like to have that engine declassified and, mark you, the engine makers don't want to have anything to do with it' they would say 'go away, stop wasting my time'. So it wasn't worth the effort, and we didn't seriously try. Rolls-Royce had their own reasons for not wanting to do it."

The BNSC meeting concluded with both BAe and RR outlining their priorities for the immediate future. BAe mainly wanted to continue modelling the air intake and finish work on Configuration G—with aerodynamics work being delayed into 1988. Rolls-Royce wanted to continue attempts to resolve heat exchanger frosting and keep on with basic design work but "RR would need to know by the beginning of December the status of the funding ... Plans by RR to place external technology contracts will now have to be delayed, probably until next year".

Lastly, it was noted that Butcher was to receive a Hotol presentation in three weeks, on September 14; the ESA Council of Ministers meeting would be on November 9-10; Prince Charles would receive his Hotol presentation, coordinated by BAe, on November 18, and it was suggested that BAe, RR and BNSC should meet again around December 10-20 "to discuss the future in the light of the review decisions".

MEETING OF MINDS

Two days after the meeting, Wilson issued his own set of notes on the meeting, reporting that it was "conducted as a 'meeting of minds' with a minimum of solid information put forward". Among the noteworthy points arising from it, he wrote, was the fact that BAe and RR would continue Hotol on a private venture basis until the end of 1987—though RR had indicated that they were now 'on hold' for the rest of the year.

He believed that BNSC were "strongly inclined to the next phase of Hotol being a three-year Feasibility Study starting on January 1, 1988" but "BNSC funding for 1988 and subsequent years has yet to go through a number

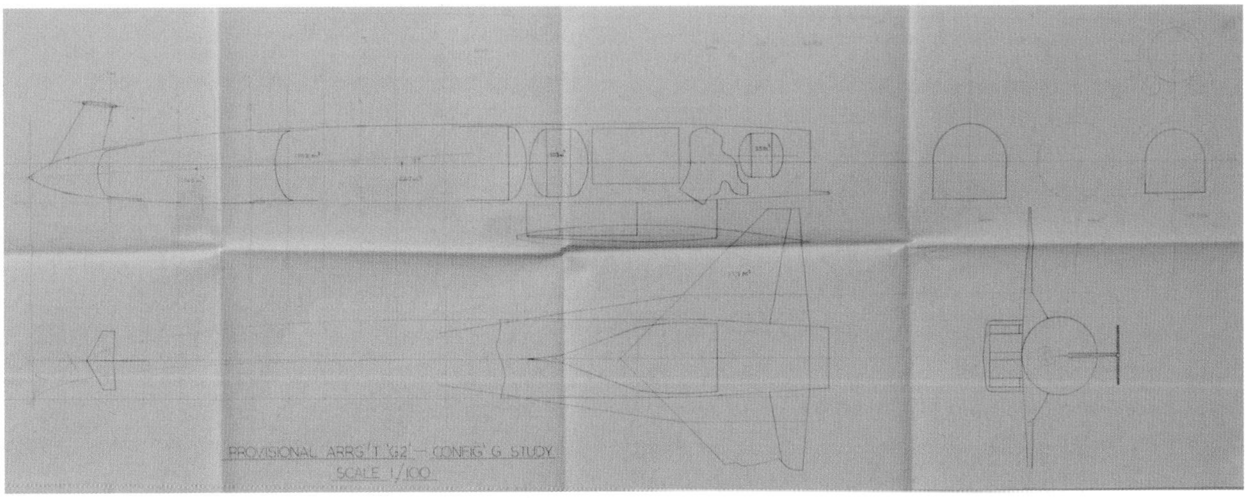

Hotol Configuration G2 was a provisional design featuring an unusual T-fin on its nose.

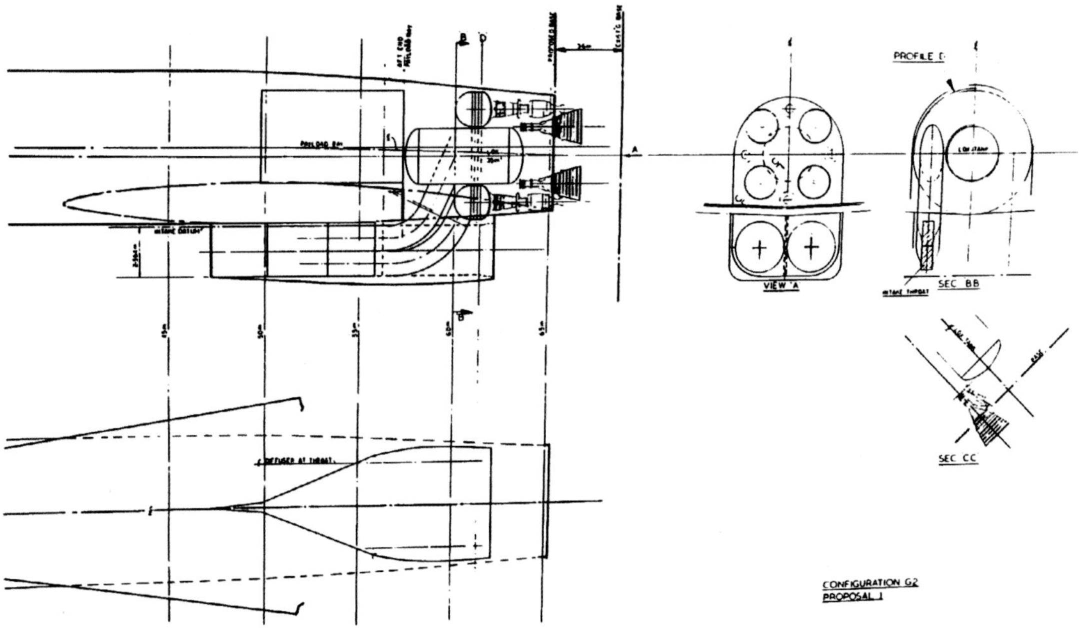

Proposed rear fuselage design for Configuration G2.

of stages". The first was consideration of "general space budget levels" by ACOST, second was getting the Cabinet Committee to agree to ACOST's recommendations, third was Ministerial agreement and lastly there was the ESA Council of Ministers discussion in November.

He also felt the BNSC anticipated "that the new government arrangements (ACOST etc.) will mean that a longer-term view will be possible i.e. it should be possible to secure a three-year programme starting on January 1, 1988". However, "neither BAe nor RR were prepared to commit themselves in detail to work programmes for the remainder of the year 'since this depended on further consideration' and depends to a great extent on our individual perceptions of the future".

In summary, "it is recommended that we write to BNSC pointing out the funding situation at the end of PoC (30.9.87, BNSC £1.06m, BAe £2.08m) and requesting a three-year programme of feasibility and enabling technology commencing January 1, 1988. Indicative figures for such a programme are £4.2m, £5.1m, £8.6m for each year. BNSC should be asked to correct the industry/HMG funding imbalance in 1988, which will have been exacerbated between the end of PoC and January 1, 1988".

Without the space plan, however, the BNSC's teeth had been pulled—it now had neither the money to pay for a three-year programme of feasibility and enabling technology, nor the political support to obtain it. Gibson and Leeming had attempted to steer BAe in the direction of spinoff technology, while Rolls-Royce had made it clear that without the extra money its resources would be directed elsewhere very shortly. Hotol's prospects were beginning to appear decidedly bleak.

Warton hosted a cryogenic tank materials workshop meeting on August 27, 1987, at which Essex-based composite materials manufacturer Pultrex had proposed internal filament winding of carbon reinforced thermoplastics, which Burns believed "reinforces the feasibility of the current carbon-PEEK sandwich tank scheme, with cryogenic insulation between the carbon-PEEK shells". Reporting on the meeting, he continued: "BP representatives, at the instigation of their managing director, were proposing bilateral agreements with BAe on development topics and had already taken steps to form partnerships with other materials companies. Reports on target material characteristics for all parts of the structure have been prepared, for issue to participating companies".

In his monthly report to Yates on September 8, 1987, Burns opined that "clearly the Concept Validation plan is shelved. BAe have estimated a requirement of £779,000 private venture funding to cover the remainder of the year beyond PoC."

Where Hotol's performance was concerned, all "deliberate optimisms" had now been removed from the figures for Configuration G, the numbers now reflecting the cold hard reality of what was achievable with the technology to hand: "With realistic refined drag figures, updated mass models with advanced materials, liquid oxygen pre-injection for anti-icing and without the (optimistic) instantaneous transition from airbreathing to optimum rocket climb, a payload of three tonnes is predicted for a 275-tonne (gross) vehicle.

"Note that the previous transition assumption would increase payload by about three tonnes and that no data has been received from Rolls-Royce on liquid oxygen pre-injection at high Mach/altitude for assisting transition. Clearly future effort must be concentrated on improving the thrust/weight ratio of the airbreathing propulsion and/or prolonging its usage."

A three-tonne payload/275-tonne vehicle was a perilously long way away from the seven-tonne payload/200-tonne vehicle so boldly envisioned back in 1984.

HOTOL CONFIGURATION G3

Butcher was given his Hotol briefing as scheduled on September 14, at which BAe were asked to provide further details on enabling technology, particularly advanced materials and software, with an emphasis on potential applications outside aerospace. Evidently this was another fishing exercise — seeking those money-making spinoffs — rather than evidence of a genuine interest in Hotol for its own sake.

During a planning meeting at Ansty on September 22, ostensibly to agree long-term plans for a Joint Propulsion Team (JPT) to work on optimising the engine, RR dropped the bombshell that the earliest date now anticipated for an RB.545 demonstrator engine run was mid-1996 — three full years later than previously planned. This would push Hotol's entry-into-service date back to no earlier than 2005.

While the final PoC Study report had not yet been completed, an 'executive summary' of it had been produced in draft form by the end of September 1987. This outlined the final form of what had now been designated Hotol Configuration G3. Based on realistic data, this was claimed to have a gross lift-off mass of 275 tonnes and a payload of 4.5 tonnes. It was 62m long with a maximum fuselage diameter of 7.7m and its wing area was 196sqm.

The executive summary, reference HPN 0012, opened with an account of the earlier work done on Hotol, reiterating and restating many points made previously elsewhere: "During Part 1 of the study, covering the first eight months... structure plus systems mass growth of 18% above the original project design, notably on the front fuselage and intake, was identified. The semi-circular intake with semi-conical centre-body was superseded by back-to-back rectangular intakes with vertical wedge compression surfaces, due to difficulty in ensuring satisfactory closure of the earlier design. The lifting foreplanes were deleted due to formidable aerodynamic heating problems predicted on re-entry."

This new variant, Configuration F, was scaled "at a target size appropriate to 230 tonnes gross lift-off mass, attainable with '80% structure', that is a figure which would be achievable by 20% reduction of structure mass below that estimated with conventional structural materials, and 100% estimated systems and propulsion mass figures.

"Early in the Study performance calculations revealed that airbreathing fuel was minimised by adopting a 'fast and low' climb profile. However, it was recognised that increased design pressures on the intake and engine would result in increased mass of some components".

Part 2 of the study, during the second half of 1986, had seen "the aerodynamic, structure and systems design of Configuration F... consolidated and refined with only small changes in [the] total mass estimate. A variety of front fuselage structural and thermal protection schemes were evaluated. Advanced materials investigations began. Wind tunnel models of the total configuration were tested in low- and high-speed tunnels and a broadly representative intake model was tested at RAE. Evaluation of the effects of advanced structural materials began.

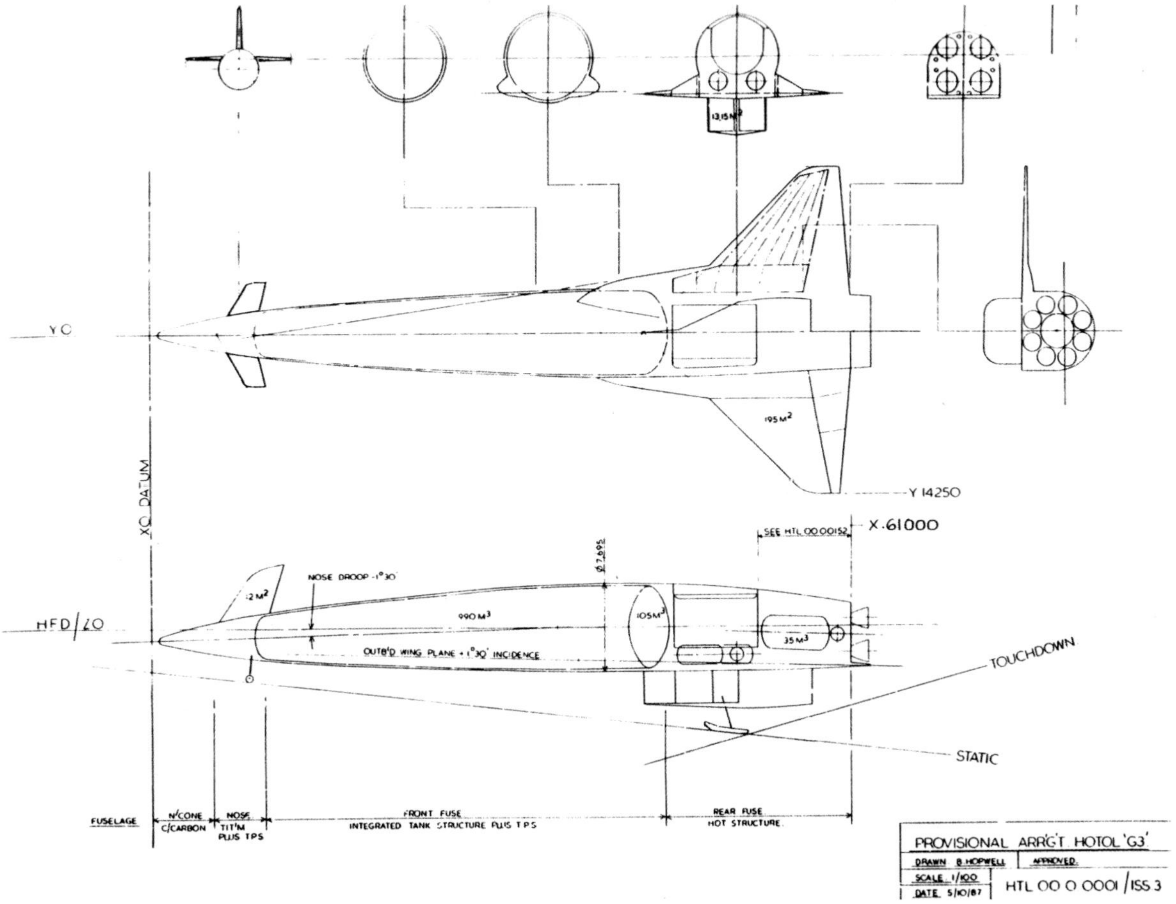

Hotol Configuration G3.

"A preliminary design of take-off trolley was schemed, leading to mass estimates and take-off performance calculations to define trolley propulsion and suspension requirements. Consideration of support loads on the trolley led to new fuselage structural design cases and confirmed the need for power-assisted rotation of Hotol to the take-off attitude.

"The PIG [Propulsion Integration Group] was formed in autumn 1986, with membership from BAe Divisions, Rolls-Royce and Reaction Engines. The aim of the group was to derive an optimum combination of vehicle configuration, intake, engine size and cycle, and ascent trajectory. This work necessitated the development and application of suitable 'rubberised' scaling models defining engine and intake performance and mass as well as close interaction with the Design Integration Group, a parallel group charged with propulsion installation aspects".

Part 3 of the study, the last part, had run from January to September 1987. During this period, work on advanced materials had led to a number of significant design changes. The nose cone had been designed as solid carbon-carbon at the front and titanium with TPS plates to the rear. Now it would be carbon-silicon carbide sandwich at the front and titanium and particulates with TPS plates to the rear. The nose fin remained unchanged: titanium with a carbon-carbon leading edge.

The liquid hydrogen tank was originally to be made from carbon-PEEK of uniform thickness with closed cell foam cryogenic insulation on the outside. Now it would be made from carbon-PEEK sandwich of graded thickness, with cryogenic insulation in the interspace. The TPS plates had gone from being 0.33m x 1m sliding titanium sandwich panels on the upper surfaces and nickel alloy on the lower surfaces to 0.33m x 4m carbon-silicon-carbide sandwich panels, each formed from four 0.33m x 1m plates bolted together, all over.

The centre fuselage, including the payload bay, had been plain titanium, now it would be titanium reinforced with particulates, ditto the wings. The wing strake, leading edge and flaps had gone from carbon-carbon to carbon-silicon carbide. The non-loading-bearing carbon-PEEK liquid oxygen tank was unchanged but the load-bearing rocket motor struts had gone from titanium to carbon-polyimide. The cryogenic engine pipes remained carbon-PEEK but the 400-700K temperature pipes went from titanium alloy to reinforced titanium and the 900K temperature nickel alloy pipes had been swapped for reinforced nickel alloy pipes.

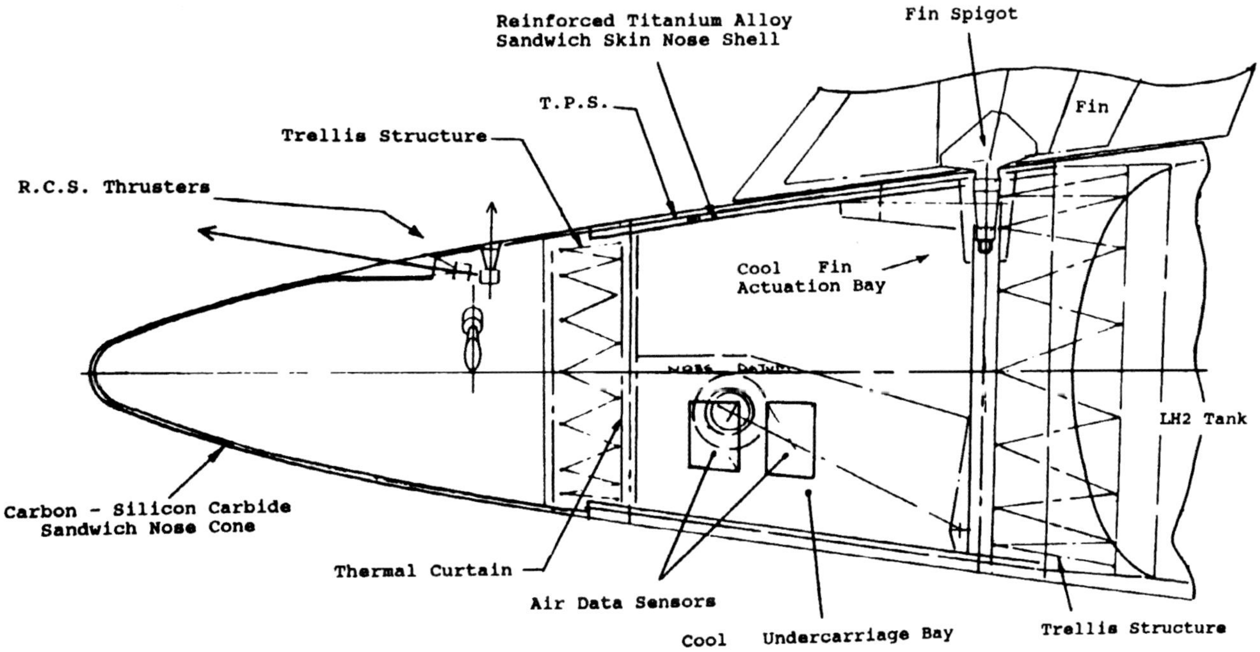

The nose cone for Configuration G was to be made from carbon-silicon carbide and reinforced titanium, rather than all carbon-carbon.

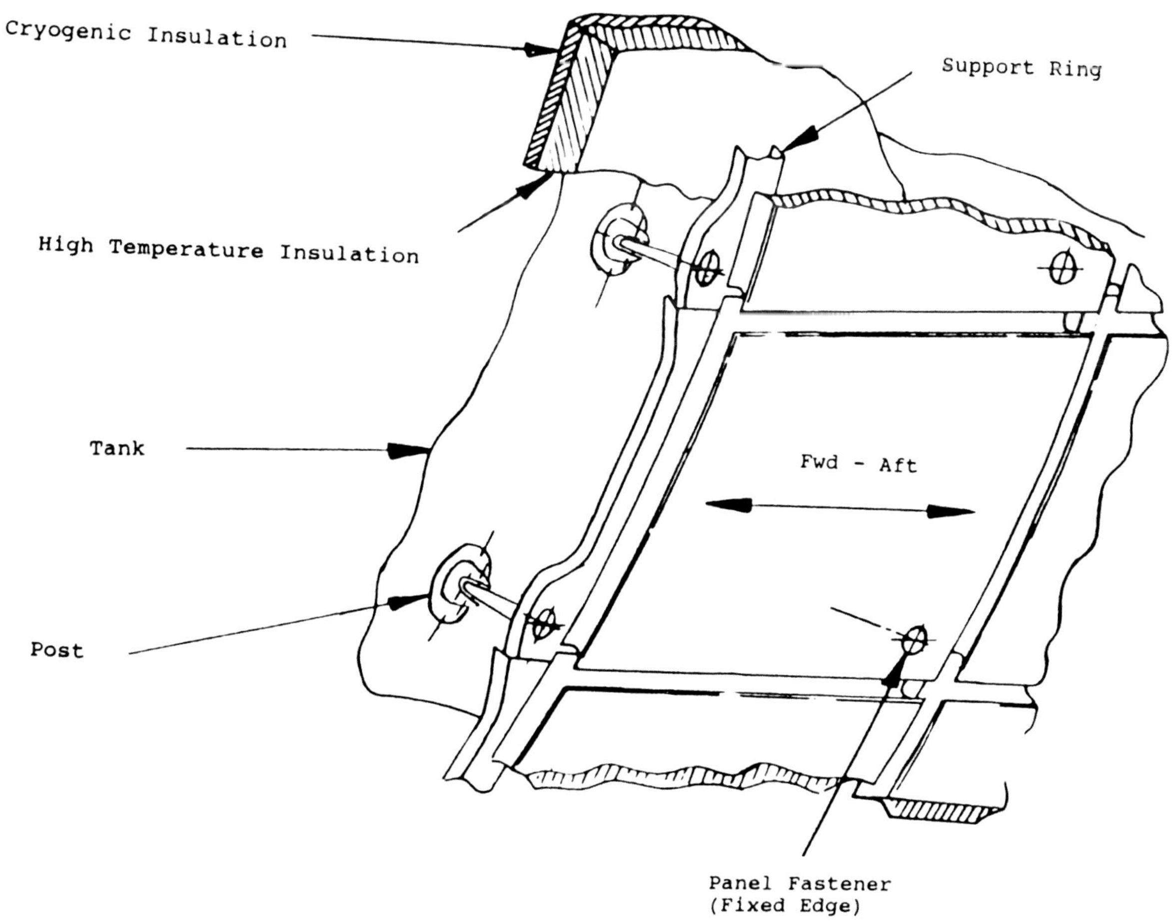

TPS panel diagram dated October 23, 1987. The design is largely unchanged from the earliest days of the project—although the posts attaching the panels to the tank are slimmer than before.

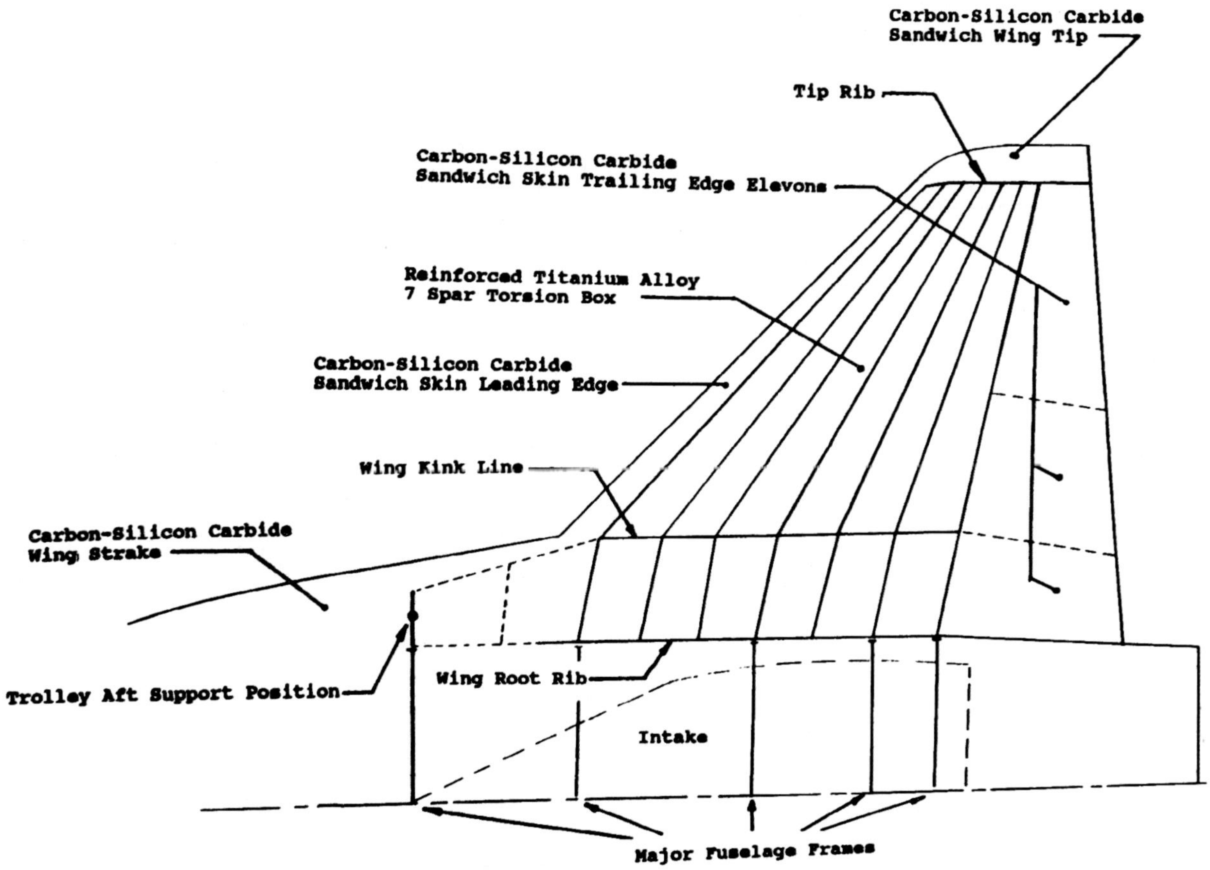

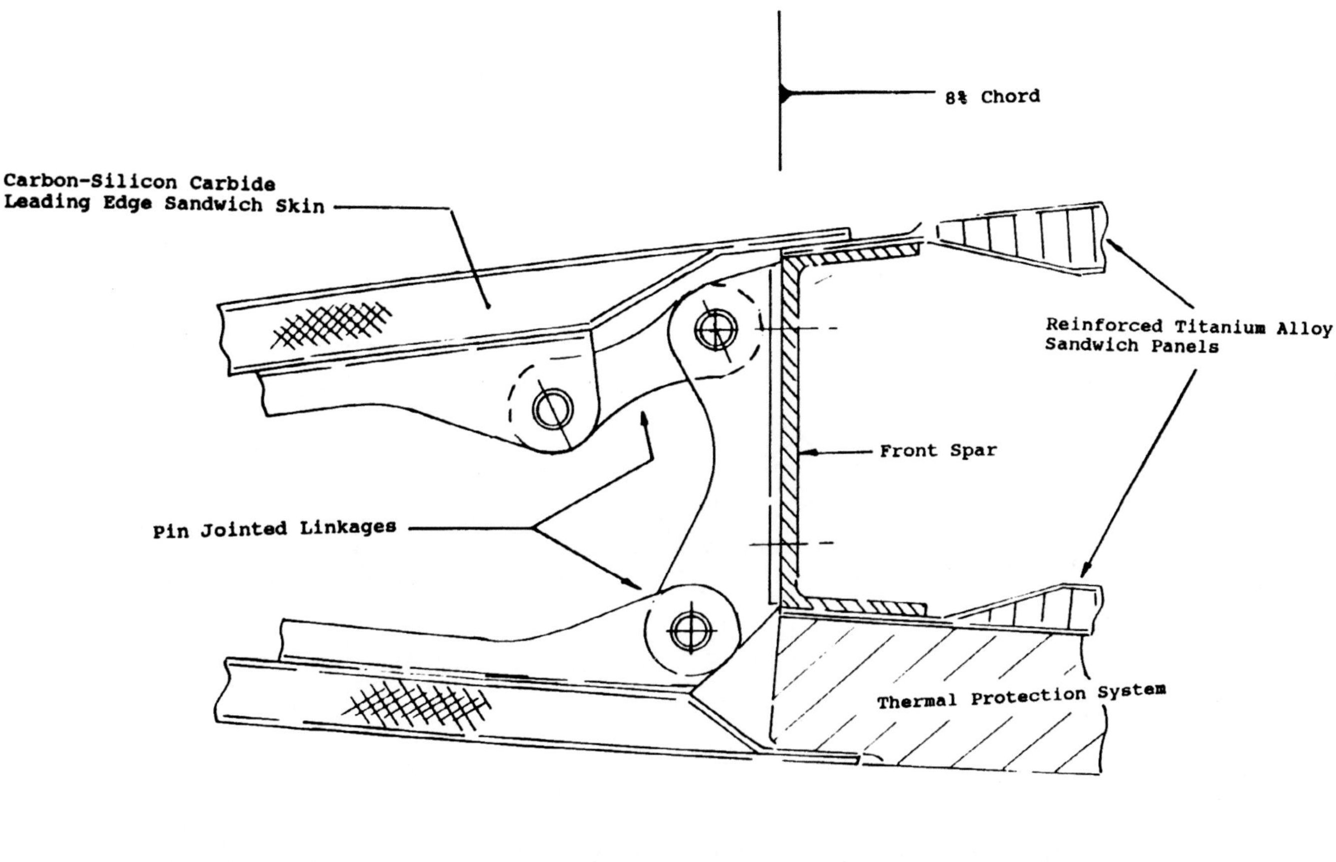

Wing design for Configuration G, showing the switch from carbon-carbon to carbon-silicon carbide for the leading edges.

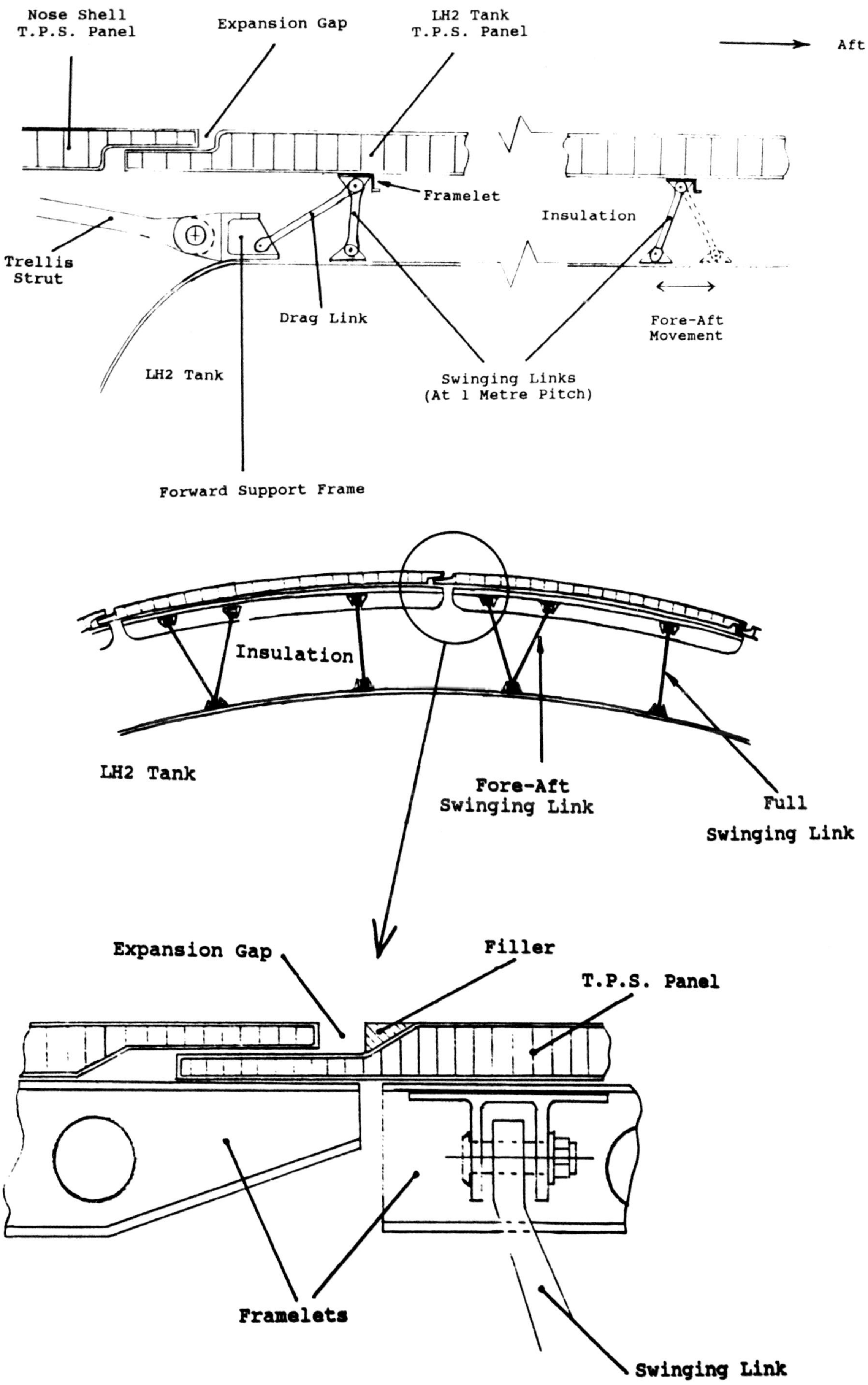

Longitudinal and circumferential views of the 'fail safe' TPS panel.

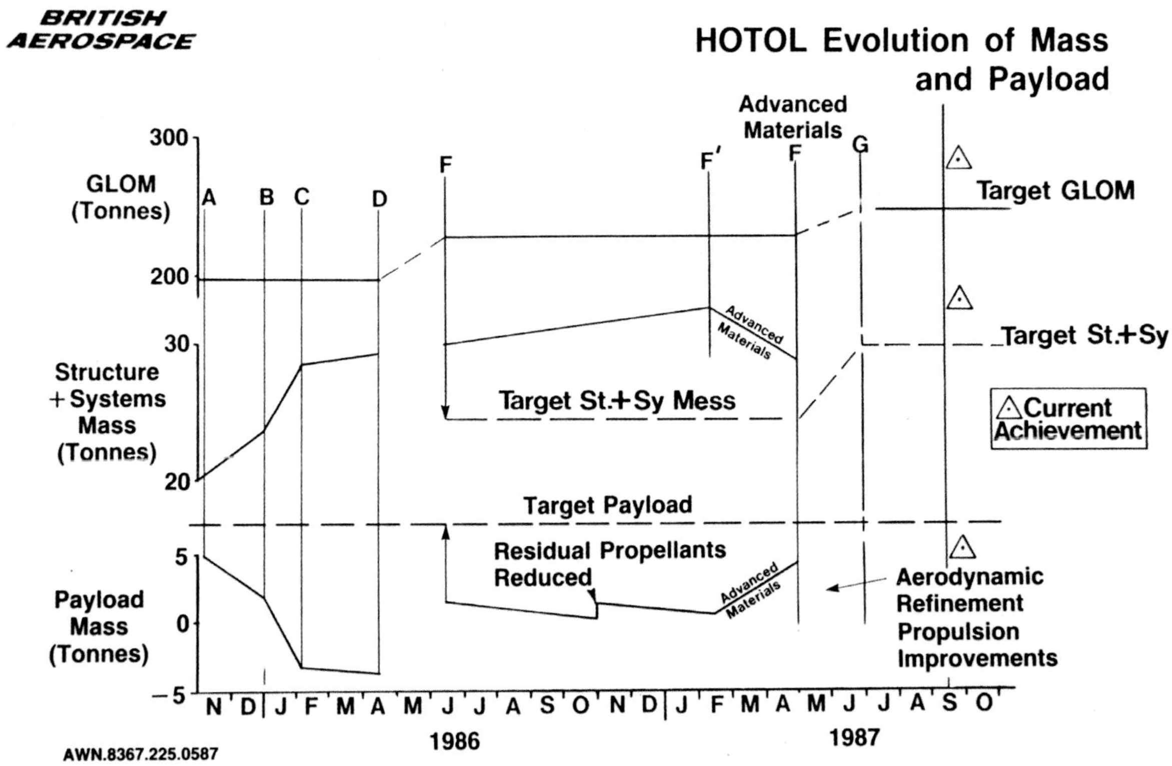

Chart showing the evolution of Hotol's mass and payload. It also shows the point at which each configuration succeeded the last—the briefest being Configuration B, which lasted just one month.

All of this had brought about a 14% structural mass reduction—about 4.5 tonnes all told.

Analysis of results from Warton's 1.2m and 0.45m wind tunnels, in the Mach 0.5 to 5.5 range, had revealed that induced drag was "somewhat higher than estimates at high supersonic speeds". Where stability and control were concerned, "lift, pitching moment and pitch control power vary smoothly with Mach number, confirming absence of shock stall effects at transonic speeds" but "diminished pitch control power at high supersonic speed requires large down deflection of controls to trim, due to aft centre of gravity at [the] top of [the] airbreathing ascent ([with the] liquid oxygen tank full), giving rise to large hinge moments and severe hydraulic power demands in countering gusts".

In other words, Hotol's centre of gravity shifted further and further rearwards as it climbed—since the liquid oxygen tank at the back remained full but the liquid hydrogen tank at the front was rapidly being depleted. The knock-on effect of this was serious control difficulties at the point where the airbreathing climb ended and the transition to pure rocket propulsion for the rest of the journey took place.

The re-entry heating rate tests in Australia with the 1:250 scale model had "confirmed that heating rates are highest on the intake; elsewhere they are broadly in agreement with estimates, detailed analysis still in progress in consultation with specialists". Tests to simulate Hotol's Autoland feature had enabled "control laws [to be] developed to give satisfactory performance in still air and constant headwinds. The effects of wind gradient, crosswind and turbulence are currently being assessed to determine touchdown scatter and limiting operating conditions".

WHAT THE PIG DID

The size and shape of the replacement for Configuration F had been determined by the PIG. The group had worked on defining engine models to investigate different ascent trajectories and engine sizes, with the overall size of the vehicle then being adjusted to suit.

Two conclusions had arisen from this, firstly: "The best performance was inferior to that previously assumed, due to proper recognition of component operating limits (mass penalties of exceedance) in the later modelling." And secondly: "The optimum trajectory involved a higher altitude/lower equivalent air speed ascent profile at the higher Mach numbers, leading to a larger intake, although lighter due to its lower design pressure."

According to the report: "The culmination of this work was the recognition of the need to place more emphasis on drag reduction, notably in the transonic/moderate

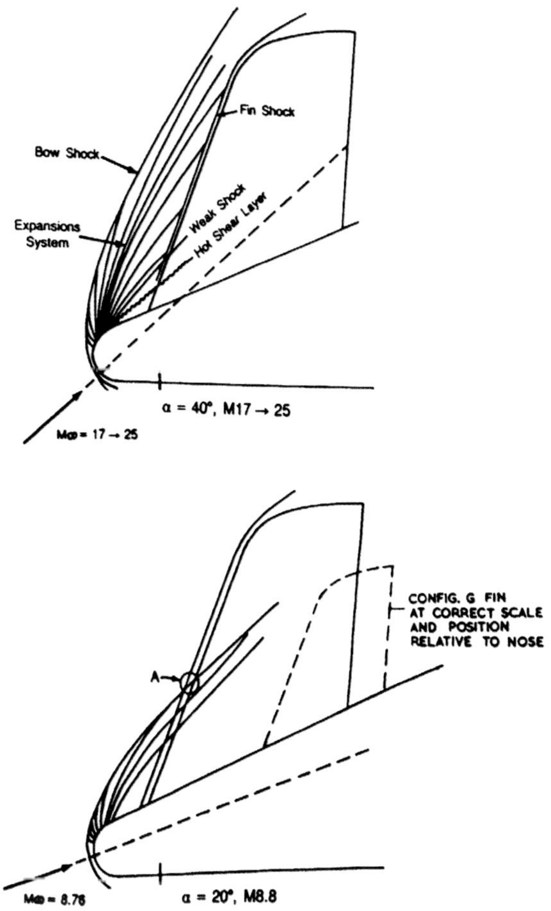

Configuration F had been notable for its large fin. By accepting a 1% probability of unmanageable crosswinds, it was determined that the fin for Configuration G could be shrunk to 60% of its original size.

supersonic speed range where spillage drag was high and excess thrust low. The best performance predicted at that time was a vehicle scaled at 300 tonnes gross lift-off mass, with the design seven-tonne payload, based on 15% reduction in structure mass from advanced materials; rocket chamber vacuum specific impulse—458 seconds (believed attainable); 'target' wave drag figures; idealised (minimum) intake drag (anticipating redesign); instantaneous transition from top of airbreathing climb to optimum rocket climb (optimistic)".

This was seen as unsatisfactory however, "particularly in view of the optimistic performance assumptions". So a new target was set for Configuration G: a 250-tonne vehicle with a seven-tonne payload, which "was to be achieved principally by refinement of aerodynamic, structural and propulsion system design".

During the same period, Scott-Scott's icing rig tests had yielded an interim solution to heat exchanger icing: feed liquid oxygen from the onboard tank into the intake during take-off and up to 25,000ft altitude. This required an extra 16 tonnes of liquid oxygen over and above what was actually needed to get into orbit.

The PIG next looked at drag reduction and ways of overcoming the penalties associated with having a long, slim, aerodynamic fuselage. Three different Hotol designs had been assessed during this phase—with 7m, 9m and 11m fuselage diameters. In addition, numerous different liquid hydrogen tank designs had been looked at—including compartmentalised tanks with differential pressurisation

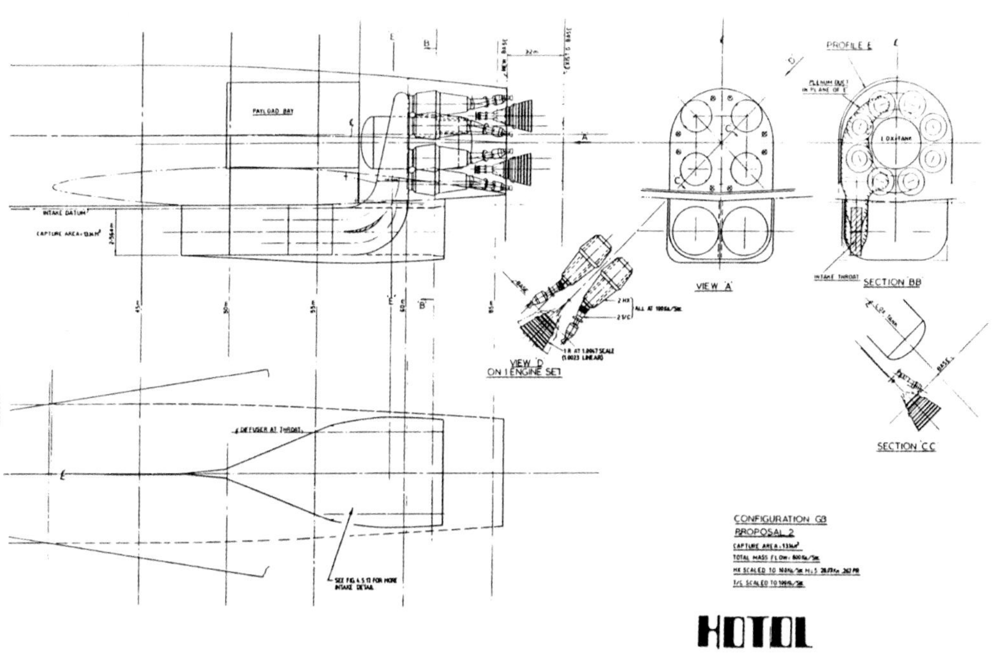

Configuration G3 rear fuselage design proposal, with the section view showing the new radial arrangement of the heat exchangers around the liquid oxygen tank.

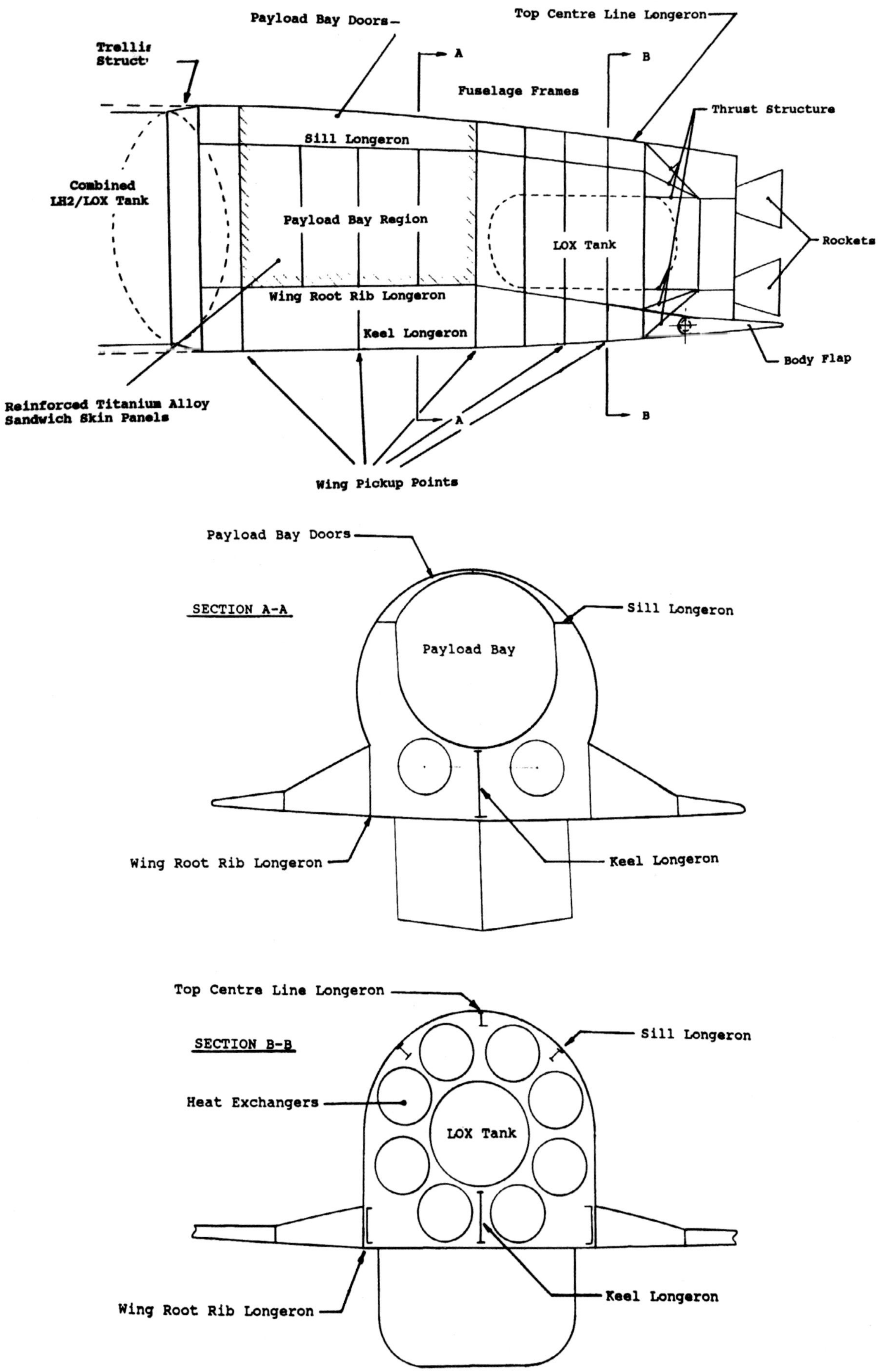

Rear fuselage structure for Configuration G.

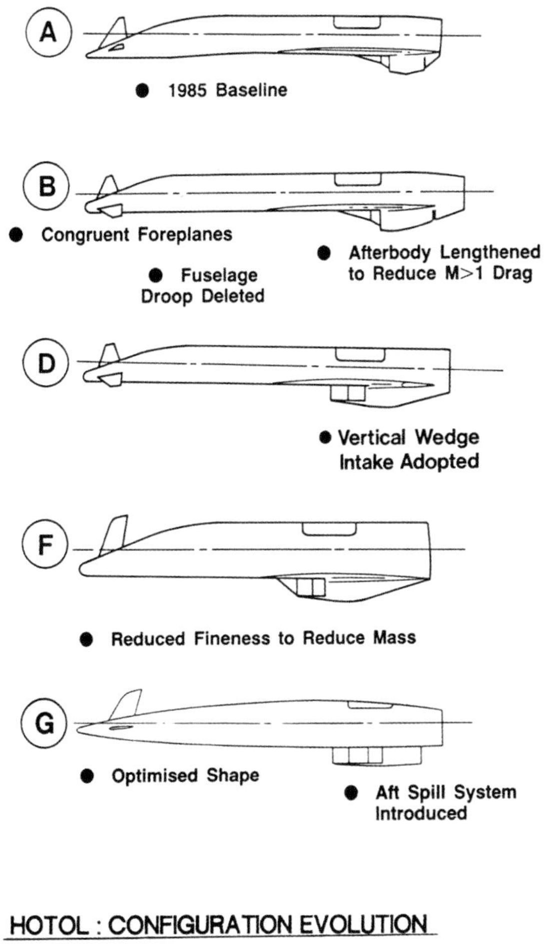

Hotol Configuration G (specifically G3) compared to earlier iterations. The overall shape has become longer and thinner, though not as long or thin as Configuration D, foreplanes have returned, the spill ramjet system has been introduced and the payload bay has moved further aft.

and sandwich-type tanks. Nose droop and wing leading edge radius were reduced, as was nose cone tip radius, even though the latter resulted in higher heating rates. The fin was shrunk to 60% of its original size by accepting a 1% probability of crosswinds that such a reduced fin would be unable to cope with when operating from an equatorial base. And bird strike resistance was designed out—accepting that any impact damage would have to result in a mission abort.

The liquid oxygen tank was divided in two, with one tank now attached onto the back end of the liquid hydrogen tank (to "avoid extra dished end domes") in front of the payload bay.

The intake was redesigned to lower drag and the spill ramjet had "been designed and adopted. This takes a large proportion of the hydrogen turbine exhaust and burns it in the intake spill duct, turning transonic intake spillage drag into 'spillage thrust' with an additional mass penalty".

The spill ramjet reduced space in the rear fuselage so the heat exchangers and turbo-compressors could no longer sit side by side and had to be repositioned radially around the rear liquid oxygen tank. Evidently "the preferred layout, currently being schemed, features paired heat exchangers and turbo-compressors (i.e. eight of each) for ease of installation, feeding four rocket chambers".

Another effect of adding the spill ramjet was to reduce the space available for a full wheeled main undercarriage, "so a central skid main undercarriage has been adopted, extending from the underside of the intake pod, with small twin stabilising wheels [outriggers], stowed in the rear corners of the pod". The nosewheel remained unchanged.

All of this amounted to Configuration G3.

END OF THE POC

Looking back over the course of the study, "it is recognised that there has been some imbalance between the intensive work devoted to airframe design and the comparatively low level of work on propulsion system optimisation. The latter is now believed to be the key to the success of the Hotol/RB.545 project.

"The airbreathing propulsion system consists of intake, ducting, heat exchangers, turbo-compressors and rocket chambers, in series, each upstream component having an influence on the pressure of the air delivered to the rocket chambers, while the mass and efficiency of each is dependent on its design pressure and airflow capacity. It is clear that there is a considerable scope for improvement in installed power plant efficiency by examining the trade-offs in component design.

"To this end BAe and Rolls-Royce have agreed to form a JPT [Joint Propulsion Team] to address this task and have agreed a work programme for the next six months. At the time of writing there is confident expectation that this work will result in attainment of the design payload at the current design scale."

The summary report ended by stating that, "at the conclusion of the two-year Proof of Concept Study the major objective of definition of the Hotol launch vehicle at an economically attractive size/mass has not yet been achieved but is believed to be attainable. Further intensive work in co-operation with Rolls-Royce is expected to lead to significant improvements in installed propulsion efficiency and achievement of the target performance.

"The studies have resulted in a clear understanding of the engineering challenges and technical risks involved in the design of a single stage to orbit launch vehicle. Enabling technology programmes have been proposed to bring the chosen design concepts to the required level of maturity in time to enter a full Development Programme. Test and Support facilities for such a programme have been defined".

THE 'HUGELY EXPENSIVE CLUB'

Space scientists from around the globe, members of the International Astronautical Federation (IAF), had gathered in Brighton on Saturday, October 10, 1987 to participate in the week-long 38th International Astronautical Congress (IAC)—with Wilson booked to give another presentation on Hotol. Running in parallel to this was Space '87, a BIS-organised exhibition at the Brighton Centre venue. The day before the exhibition opened, on Sunday, October 11, Kenneth Clarke visited it and was interviewed for national television news.

He told the interviewer that ESA was a "hugely expensive club" and that "at the moment we are paying a very great deal for the space programme—of the order of £100 million a year. We are not persuaded we should go beyond that on the plans of the European Space Agency. We have always said that the plans put forward by the European Space Agency are over-ambitious. We have to judge that against all the other claims for research and development in other areas that affect British industry."

He went on to say he believed that other, unspecified, European governments would support this view during the ESA Council of Ministers meeting in November.

While he was simply parroting Thatcher's previously stated policy, doing it so tactlessly right in front of the world's space science community finally caused the scales to fall from the eyes of all those who had hoped, somehow, that the Prime Minister would return to her previously supportive stance on space. Now there was no denying it: the full extent of the Government's rejection of any real space programme for Britain had been laid bare.

Pattie's immediate response to this was: "I think the Minister is going to be very disappointed if he thinks the other European nations are going to take the line that he has described. I remain of the view that it is literally inconceivable that Britain should continue at the same diminishing level of expenditure, which frankly boils down to us ceasing effective involvement in space."

According to a report by Chris Moncrieff in the *Western Daily Press* on October 13: "BAe were yesterday putting on a brave face about Mr Clarke's comments, which have hurt the company deeply. A company spokesman said: 'He has not really said anything different from Mrs Thatcher's statement back in July. He has just said it rather more forcibly.'"

While Thatcher had set the policy, and Butcher was technically the Minister directly responsible for space, Clarke's blunt comments effectively painted a target on his back—with many blaming him personally for the policy, though how much say he had ever had in its genesis is debatable. For his part, Clarke seems to have been happy to absorb the flak, pushing Butcher out of the picture and taking charge of the situation himself. Exactly how far it was really Thatcher, pulling his strings offstage, is unclear.

Parkinson was among those who blamed Clarke. He told Hannigan during the early 1990s: "I think Clarke came in feeling somewhat insecure and recognising that to make his political position more secure, he was going to have to be seen as a somewhat harder man than he had been previously. So he said no to space and discovered that gave him a political reputation. So he continued saying no to space, not that he was against space, not because it did his PR image any good, but because it did his political image good because he was seen by Maggie as someone who stood up to people and said no. It didn't matter what it was about, it just happened it was space that got it. Essentially, that left us rudderless."

Yet despite their hard-line stance on space generally, there is evidence to suggest that certainly Clarke and perhaps also Thatcher were willing to give Hotol specifically a chance—should its value to British industry prove undeniable.

BOND'S FIGHTING TALK

Alan Bond had been particularly appalled by Clarke's statements and on the evening of October 12 was interviewed by ITN News, standing in front of a large Hotol model at the IAC. He told the cameras he was prepared to take his engine designs abroad, even if it meant breaching the Official Secrets Act, in order to get the vehicle built: "My first step will be to Europe to try for support, probably from the French and Germans". He said he was "not going to stand by and watch the Government sit on something which is going to introduce a modern industrial revolution comparable to that of 150 years ago".

Asked what he thought of Butcher's imminent arrival at the IAC, he said: "I think they will probably nail him to a door." After confirming his willingness to sell his designs, in spite of their security classification, he said: "The rest of the world is going to move ahead. The British Government should be aware of that". And ESA was more than willing to move ahead with advanced launcher systems, "and we will get two fingers if we try to interfere after this".

Times science editor Pearce Wright, in an article on October 13, 1987, under the heading 'Top scientist in threat to quit space project', wrote: "Britain's top space scientist threatened to resign last night if the Government

Alan Bond at the IAC with Hotol model.

continues its refusal to fund research for the revolutionary space plane, Hotol ... Mr Bond said he had been approached with tentative offers of work abroad. He would prefer to work on the Continent but he would, if necessary, consider the United States. He said he was determined to ensure that the Hotol project went ahead even if it meant his risking imprisonment for breaching the Official Secrets Act. 'I have been in prison for the past five years with this project,' he told ITN news last night.

"Mr Bond could take his expertise abroad, but not his inventions. In theory, he owns the patents for the Hotol engine, but he could not share the technology with a foreign partner. When the patents were filed, Ministry of Defence experts referred them to Whitehall for a top [secret] security classification ... American and Japanese aerospace firms have already approached both Mr Bond, as the patent holder, and Rolls-Royce and British Aerospace for some form of partnership. But neither he nor the firms can accept because of the project's MoD classification.

"Mr Bond said: 'If we miss this opportunity, we will fade out of space technology totally. As happened in the field of military aircraft, we will end up buying space hardware from the United States. There are areas of space technology that have reached the stage where they should be self-financing. Telecommunications is the obvious one. Satellites are very expensive but the financial returns for communications and broadcasting have been huge.'

"Sir Raymond Lygo, chief executive of BAe, said yesterday that the space industry would become more viable if the Government did more to break harsh restrictive regulations, and changed its ambivalent attitude to military space and its stop-go policies on space technology. Sir Raymond attributed some of the Government's doubts about spending on space to a series of launch failures in 1985 and 1986. He said commercial customers for satellites were concerned about the impact of insurance costs and the lengthy delays in establishing operating systems, and the successful flight of the Ariane launch vehicle last month [presumably a reference to the launch of Ariane 3 V-19 on September 16, 1987] only marginally alleviated the problem.

"Sir Raymond told the meeting in Brighton that the Government felt on sounder political ground when concentrating on well-defined conventional projects which were easily understood by the electorate and had quicker and more certain returns."

Bond's protests made good copy and newspapers across Britain, both national and local, quickly picked up and ran with the story. Where the original announcement on space back in July had been greeted with barely a murmur, now it had become a hot topic—with the charismatic Bond pitted against Clarke in the public eye.

The *Daily Mirror* ran a piece by Frank Thorne on October 14 under the heading 'Mission Impossible' which included the earliest known appearance of the soon-to-be-popular pun 'Heartbreak Hotol', though it had little else new to offer. *Nature* ran an article by Simon Hadlington on October 15 which began: "The mood of cautious optimism within the British space community, which believed that there was a real chance of the Government increasing its investment in space research before next month's ministerial meeting of ESA, has been destroyed by the announcement by Mr Kenneth Clarke... that no more money will be forthcoming... the timing of Clarke's announcement has angered and puzzled the space community. It had been widely understood that the Government's newly created ACOST would review Britain's space programme before the ESA meeting and make recommendations to the Government." He wrote that "since the Prime Minister, Mrs Margaret Thatcher, announced in the House of Commons on July 23 that the Government would not increase its space budget 'for the time being', Britain's space community has been in turmoil" but "the space community seems to have been prompted by its own enthusiasm into believing that the Government was on the verge of reversing its earlier decision. Mr Clarke has put paid to that".

Wilson remembered the IAF congress both for Clarke's outburst and also because it coincided on its final night with the 1987 hurricane. He recalled: "I had given my paper entitled Hotol, Aerospaceplane for Europe during the morning session: it had gone well albeit there was some aggressive questioning. I could relax therefore and remember having a nice meal out with various BIS acquaintances. It was quite windy as I returned to my sea front hotel but, coming from the Fylde coast of Lancashire, it was nothing I wasn't used to.

"However, during the early hours I awoke to hear the shingle from the beach being rained from the heavens. I remember pulling the blankets well over my head, fearing the possibility of the large window next to the bed shattering. By the morning things had calmed down somewhat but the whole of the south of England was paralysed by unrooted trees and fallen power lines.

"Returning home by train was quite out of the question. In the end someone (I forget who) gave me a lift to Gatwick Airport, where I managed to catch the last flight to Manchester. My wife in Lancashire, which had escaped the storm, initially couldn't understand what all the fuss was about and was rather amused to think that all these folk meeting to discuss travelling through space couldn't even get home from Brighton.

"The seemingly cataclysmic atmosphere was further darkened over the weekend as one third was wiped off the value of the British and World Stock Markets on October 19, which came to be known as Black Monday."

In addition, on October 16, in the wake of the violent extratropical cyclone which had lashed the south of England and felled an estimated 15 million trees the night before, the Derbyshire-based *Ripley & Heanor News* ran the Hotol story on its front page, bookended by background pieces on 'local boy' Bond.

CLARKE DOUBLES DOWN

A meeting between BAe and Rolls-Royce was held at RR's London headquarters on October 22 to decide the content of the Hotol brochure that would be presented to Prince Charles the following month.

Six days later, on October 28, Clarke addressed the issue of BNSC funding in the House of Commons. It was clear from the outset that there remained some who just didn't realise that the BNSC's financial fortunes had been unequivocally declared more than three months earlier. Labour's Ernie Ross asked Clarke "when he expects to announce the level of financial support for the British Space Centre", only to get the standard reply: "The Government have decided not to increase public expenditure on space above the current level, which is already running at over £100 million a year."

Ross followed up with a reminder that the Japanese were now spending huge sums on space and "does he [Clarke] not consider it rather silly to go to the [ESA Council of Ministers] meeting [in November] with such a low spending plan for Britain?"

Clarke replied: "I shall go to the meeting of ESA at the Hague explaining that Britain wishes to play a constructive and useful role in the agency. However, we have argued repeatedly, and will continue to argue, that the ESA plan should be based on financial, scientific and commercial reality. We should judge carefully which targets to spend money on. I am sure that the Japanese have made a similar hard-nosed appraisal of their investment, and we believe that Europe should do the same in regard to its space effort."

Spencer Batiste asked him to reconfirm the Government's commitment to the success of the space industry and he invoked the familiar allusion to tech spinoffs: "I intend over the next few months to continue to hold discussions with British companies about the way in which we can obtain scientific and industrial value from our commitment to space. That is the message that I shall be taking to the ESA. It is no good arguing, however, that any money spent on any space programme is justifiable when it reaches the considerable sums arrived at by the European agency."

Conservative veteran Sir Trevor Skeet asked: "Should not my right honourable and learned friend bear in mind the advice of ACOST, which, as reported in the national press, has suggested that either we should give sufficient money to space or get out of it? Is it not bad for international collaboration if we cease to take a positive line on both space and research?"

Clarke told him: "I have an advantage over my honourable friend, because I have received the advice of ACOST, whereas he has to rely on newspaper reports. I shall be paying regard to the advice of ACOST. I agree entirely with my honourable friend's conclusion that we must make a positive contribution, but a positive contribution is to request the ESA seriously to reappraise its programmes and stop being led into grandiose, prestige projects that are of dubious scientific and economic value."

The following day Clarke and some of his underlings, including Butcher, received a personal briefing on Hotol at the DTI in London. The papers Butcher had requested on potential non-aerospace Hotol tech spinoffs had been sent to the BNSC, rather than being handed over at this meeting.

Meanwhile Wilson was once again standing in for Burns by giving Burns's paper The Design Challenge of Hotol at the Aerotech 87 Technology Conference organised by the Institute of Mechanical Engineers, which ran from October 27-30 at Birmingham's NEC.

HOTOL POC — TOTAL SPEND

In his report to Yates on November 5, Burns noted that HPN 0012, the executive summary of the final PoC report had now been issued but the full 300-page report remained a work in progress — its completion having "been hampered by insufficient typing staff at Warton". He noted that "Proof of Concept final spend is about £2.6m. Taking account of extra tasks, the actual overspend is about £130,000 (6%), largely due to promotional/presentation work. With no further funding from DTI, the actual financial split BAe/HMG comes out at 60%/40%, taking account of ALV and audit work, and will be 75%/25% by the end of 1987.

Engineering effort for October had been "directed mainly into production of the final report and preparation of associated presentation material" but there was still something to report on the latest Hotol design: "Close examination of the longitudinal balance of Configuration G using high-speed wind tunnel data, has revealed a mismatch between the trimmable centre of gravity range and the centre of gravity travel during the ascent. Measures to alleviate this problem for the next configuration iteration are being urgently pursued. Wing camber and twist are likely to be beneficial at high speed conditions. Jettisonable foreplanes assist take-off lift."

On the materials front, "carbon-PEEK samples have been tested at the Rubber and Plastics Research Association for permeability at room temperature; a report is expected soon. Samples have been delivered to Rutherford Appleton Laboratories for permeability tests in liquid hydrogen and testing is imminent. Discussions have been held with the Atomic Energy Research Establishment at Harwell on participation in collaborative programmes, with Rolls-Royce, on advanced ceramics for turbines, and with ICI on advanced fibre development for metal matrix and ceramic matrix materials".

In aerodynamics, it was "proposed to build a model of the US Space Shuttle orbiter for test in the Australian T4 hypersonic gun tunnel (free of charge) to calibrate heating rate measurements against flight data".

A SNOWBALL IN HADES

The ESA Council of Ministers meeting took place as planned at The Hague on November 9-10, 1987, and gave the go-ahead to Ariane 5 as well as approving three years of development work on Columbus and Hermes. Britain, represented by Clarke, was the only one of the 13 ESA member states failing to concur. Clarke told the assembly that Britain would continue to contribute 12.6% (about £85m) to ESA's overall programme but "will not give a penny more". He described Hermes as "expensive and unnecessary" and "an imitation of a 20-year-old American idea". He also exercised his right of veto to prevent a 5% increase in ESA's basic science programme for 1989.

In agreeing to press on with Ariane 5/Hermes without Britain, France, West Germany and Italy pledged to shoulder 80-90% of the cost between them. Columbus, being effectively an add-on to the American-led International Space Station, and the one element of the future programme that Britain remained interested in, would await the outcome of further negotiations with the Americans. Hotol was not on the agenda.

Clarke was not, however, wilfully concocting his strident dismissals of European projects in a vacuum. Perhaps surprisingly, his actions were strictly in accordance with the advice given to him by the experts — the BNSC. It was of course convenient that this advice complemented the Government's stated policy as of July 23.

Jack Leeming, writing in 2006, recalled that he had

written Clarke's speech for the ESA meeting: "As the then director general of BNSC, I certainly did not feel I could recommend Hermes and the very expensive proposals of ESA which were clearly too ambitious. As we approached the Ministerial conference in The Hague, I set about drafting a speech for Kenneth Clarke expressing our concern about the practicality of the programme, which I knew would find some sympathy amongst other ministers.

"I had hoped that Ken would read it out more in sorrow than in anger, but he read it in an aggressive tone when the German Minister, who was chairman, invited him to open the discussion. Far from placating other Ministers, he succeeded in antagonising them and as a reaction they went on to endorse the ESA proposals despite their own misgivings. Ken abstained from voting but isolated the UK and with it our hope of increasing our space expenditure. Within an increasing ESA expenditure we were left grappling to hold onto some of our existing commitments and the hope of funding a share of Hotol was destroyed."

The fact that Clarke had given a speech actually drafted by the director general of the BNSC, regardless of the manner in which he delivered it, does not seem to have been widely known at the time. Rather, as might be expected, Clarke was held personally responsible for his comments.

He appeared before the House of Commons on November 12, explaining that he "should like to make a statement on the outcome of the ESA council meeting that I attended". He told MPs Britain's commitment to European cooperation in space had not changed but "what has changed ... is the scale of ESA's aspirations. Overall, the total cost of the proposals put to us at The Hague would increase spending on space by more than two and half times over the next five years. For the United Kingdom, agreement to those programmes would have meant an increase to more than £200 million — the equivalent of more than a dozen new NHS hospitals — every year from now on.

"Our objection is, however, not solely that the bill is so huge. We recognise that space research is expensive, but we cannot see sufficient scientific, industrial or commercial benefits to justify such a huge increase. My approach at the council was therefore to press for a reassessment of priorities under present-day conditions, and to develop a strategy designed to achieve worthwhile aims which would yield solid and worthwhile returns."

After he had explained events in more detail, the Shadow Secretary of State for Trade and Industry, Bryan Gould, was first to chime in: "Will the Minister accept that what we have just heard is not so much a statement, more an admission of failure? ... He completely failed to bring about any reassessment of priorities within the European space programme, and found himself wholly isolated. He is reported as having said that he at least came back with his money still in his pocket. It might be nearer the truth to say that he came back with his tail between his legs and a flea in his ear."

He strongly criticized Clarke's approach in all areas and also asked: "Did the Government try to win ESA support for investment in the Hotol project?"

Clarke said: "The honourable gentleman asked about Hotol, the very ambitious programme put forward in particular by British Aerospace and Rolls-Royce for a reusable spacecraft ... There was never a snowball's chance in Hades that Hotol would be taken up by the European Space Agency at the Hague meeting. Sensibly, that was not put on the agenda."

There was a further debate on space spending on November 25, during which new Conservative MP Keith Mans asked: "Will my right honourable and learned friend ensure that, now that we are not providing extra funds for the ESA, extra money will be found from Government sources for the continuation of the Hotol project?"

Clarke replied noncommittally: "I have had yet another meeting to discuss the Hotol project with British Aerospace and Rolls-Royce. We must look for other international collaborators and see what the next step is if we are to continue to evaluate the project. This is a long-term matter, and it will have to be considered carefully once we have found what other industrial and governmental partners we might be able to collect for it."

That same day, BAe was concluding a two-day meeting with representatives of both the BNSC and RAE. On November 26, Burns wrote a short update article on Hotol for *Intercom*. Towards the end, it said: "The two agencies were very pleased with progress and there is confident expectation of additional funding from HMG in the new year. The rejection by HMG of the Space Plan and the lack of UK wholehearted commitment to European Space Agency programmes does not directly influence Hotol, at least in the short term.

"It is BAe's firm intention to go ahead with the project and encourage other UK and continental companies to join in cooperative technology activities in support of advanced space transport. Hotol is the spearhead of this technology."

Behind the scenes however, BNSC and RAE had in fact expressed reservations about the skid undercarriage and jettisonable foreplanes now included in the Hotol Configuration G design.

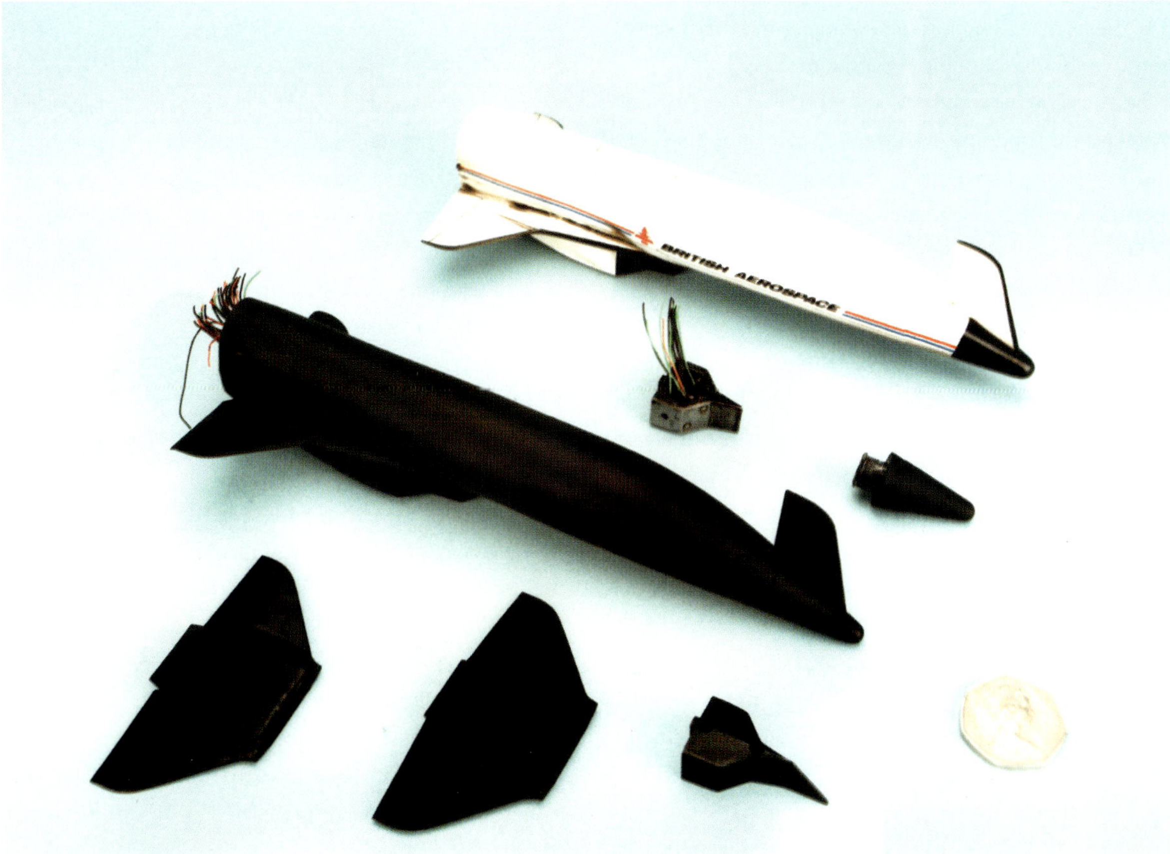

There were two SB3 hypersonic wind tunnel models—one made of steel, painted black, and another made of wood painted white.

AN EXCEPTION FOR HOTOL?

Despite the rejection of Gibson's space plan behind closed doors and the very public rejection of ESA's space programme—not to mention Clarke's overall general rigid adherence to Thatcher's ruling on space spending—there seems to have been a burgeoning sense of optimism at BAe that somehow an exception was about to be made for Hotol.

December 3, 1987, saw Parkinson sending a document entitled 'The Case for Hotol' to Burns and Parkin for comment. He attached a covering note which said: "Attached is a proposal currently being prepared for the Minister for the continuation of the Hotol programme. Peter [Conchie] is concerned that the proposal, when it is made, is successful and believes that the money from Government will be in a 50:50 match with BAe money."

The proposal itself outlined Hotol's background and anticipated performance before getting down to brass tacks: "To be able to proceed with confidence into a full development programme, it will be necessary to demonstrate the technical readiness in all key areas. In addition, it is expected that investment in key areas of technology would lead to substantial savings in development costs, either through improved productivity or through avoidance of cost overruns due to unexpected problems. As a consequence BAe proposed an enabling technology phase over the next four to six years as the next logical step for the Hotol programme. This would have to cover the following areas: propulsion; materials & structures; aerodynamics; command & control; certain sub-systems.

"It is expected that the investment in technology in this period will lead to technology advances of wider application than Hotol—driven by the focused requirements of the project. The enabling technology activities will have to be supported by continuing project studies to develop the concept and to act as a coordinating centre for the project."

Other UK companies had evidently indicated a willingness to invest in Hotol's enabling technology programme and it was anticipated that other nations without an aerospaceplane programme of their own would want to jump on board. In order to back all this, "for 1988 it is proposed that spending targets should be as follows (excluding propulsion): £1.9m for BAe continuing project studies; £1.6m at BAe for enabling technology; £1.2m for other UK enabling technology; up to £4m for non-UK project study and enabling technology participation. (Note: In addition to this, BAe has already invested over £1m during 1987 as post-Proof of Concept and initial enabling technology activity). It is suggested that UK Government funding be used to finance the project studies, and that

BAe use its matching funding to finance its participation in the enabling technology programme".

Furthermore, "for the period 1988-1990, the first estimates for the funding required to support Project Studies and Technology Development excluding propulsion were presented to BNSC as follows: project studies £1.9m in 1988, £2.4m in 1989 and £3m in 1990; technology development £12.3m in 1988, £21.3m in 1989 and £27.8m in 1990". A total of £68.7m over three years.

Perhaps surprisingly, given all the very pointed hints dropped by Gibson, Butcher and indeed Clarke himself, the proposal did not include a single tangible example of the potential tech spinoffs from Hotol that those holding the purse strings seem to have so avidly wanted to see. The vague mention of "technology advances of wider application than Hotol", when measured against a proposal that the Government invest at least £34.35m in the project, may not have been the most compelling case to set before Clarke.

Yet in his December 8 report to Yates, Burns evinced a quite remarkable optimism: "The climate is favourable for continued funding from DTI and an approach to the Minister is to be prepared following further discussions between BAe and BNSC. The latest information is that DTI may agree to not more than £2m for 1988 on a 50/50 basis. Additional funding may be forthcoming from continental European sources; the initiative for this latter activity is with industry. Rolls-Royce are likely to be funded to about half the level of BAe.

"Directives are being issued to continue work at the present rate until official funding is secured. It is considered important to ensure the commitment of Rolls-Royce at the required level of full-time staff through this period of uncertainty."

Beyond this, the full PoC Study report, coded HPN 0011, had now gone to print, and a visit to French company SEP had uncovered the existence of a new carbon matrix composite known as Cerasep which "is at a more advanced stage of development than carbon-carbon, has 40% better strength/weight ratio, undiminished up to 2,100K and in every other respect seems to be the most suitable material for the hottest parts of Hotol's structure".

Testing of the SB3 Hotol model had concluded in Australia and it was now on its way home in order to undergo tests up to Mach 10 in the RAE's low density high-speed wind tunnel. This was intended to generate longitudinal force and moment data. The Autoland simulator programme had also ended and "successful landings have been accomplished in headwinds up to 30 knots and crosswinds up to 20 knots with gusts up to 50% superimposed on the steady winds".

A meeting took place at BAe's London headquarters on December 16, at which it was decided that Warton should concentrate on both defining the structure and mass estimates of Configuration G and resolving the problem of mismatched centre of gravity and aerodynamic centre travel during ascent and recovery—as well as reducing hinge moments. Potential solutions tabled included wing camber revisions, in-flight liquid oxygen transfer and tabs on the vehicle's control surfaces.

THE PRINCE'S PLEA

Having by now received his personal briefing on Hotol from Brian Young, Prince Charles alluded to the vehicle's plight during a speech to the London Stock Exchange, which was reported by John Williams on the front page of the *Evening Standard* on December 17 under the heading 'Charles in Space Race Plea'.

While not mentioning Hotol by name, the Prince had apparently opined that, "we are in danger of losing another typical British and brilliantly simple aerospace concept to foreign interests unless we are extremely careful. Why is it that others see the commercial value in our ideas, but so often we do not?"

POC POSTMORTEM

By now the massive Hotol Final Report on Proof of Concept Study, HPN 0011, was being circulated. It reiterated the structural details outlined in the executive summary but in exhaustive detail.

Where it really fleshed out the project, however, was in areas such as the propulsion system. According to this section's introduction: "Within the PoC, much has been done to identify the critical issues and to refine the powerplant, but full airframe/intake/engine/flight profile optimisation has yet to be systematically undertaken.

"This is the principal task of the recently formed JPT ... following the definition of Configuration G, the aforementioned JPT optimisation study has commenced to a 12-month programme."

The incredible demands placed on the engine intake design, and the work done to meet those demands, was fully explained. The report listed a dozen design requirements for Configuration G's intake, with "the primary requirement [being] for a lightweight solution; the intake is designed for subcritical transient operation and for buzz but not for surge, it being argued that with the distortion ameliorating effect of the heat exchangers, surge will have a low probability; the intake is required to have adequate subcritical and supercritical mass flow margins for atmospheric/vehicle/engine rapid transients; [and]

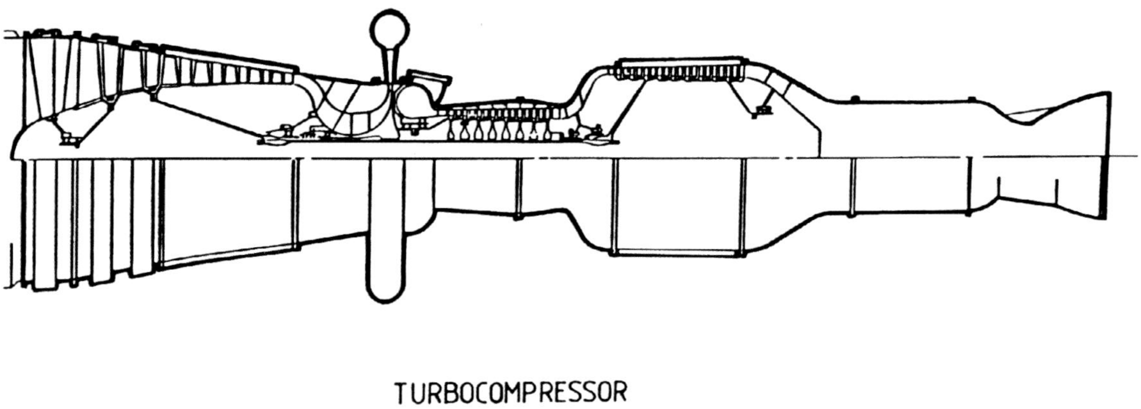

Turbocompressor design.

the installation is required to have acceptably low levels of installation drag bearing in mind the gross mismatch between intake supply and engine demand characteristic of this type of cycle at transonic conditions".

In addition, "the installation must be satisfactory for re-entry and the materials chosen accordingly; the intake must be fully closed for non-airbreathing flight; there is no airflow quality requirement identified for the engine; control of the intake must be maintained and design loads not exceeded following engine failure or shutdown in flight; the intake needs to be configured for high design point capture and minimum stability bleed to achieve minimum intake size; the installation must have adequate fuselage/wing boundary layer diverters; the probability of loss of vehicle must not exceed 1/500 flights. The powerplant should not directly contribute more than (say) 20% of such losses".

Configuration F had "placed heavy, almost exclusive emphasis on a simple, minimum mass approach". It had "a substantial engine nacelle which shrouded an over/under arrangement of four 'slimline' heat exchangers with associated turbocompressors. The intake was arranged to have the simplest possible three shock compression consistent with the recovery requirement and mass flow demand. Intake geometry was fixed during airbreathing ascent, the only variability being closure at Mach 5. Off-design matching was achieved via uncontrolled forespillage which was associated with high installation drag".

For re-entry it was to be closed off with a triangular guard and "all leading edges were radiused in accordance with kinetic heating rules generally adopted for the vehicle with consequent effect on high speed drag and spillage". However, "the overall length of the intake (and hence its weight) were compromised by aircraft balance considerations and the nacelle incorporated the main undercarriage gear. The result was a high drag solution (particularly at transonic conditions) which almost met the mass target".

The challenge for Configuration G was essentially to shave as much drag off the intake as possible. According to the report: "The approach adopted involved maximum use of bypass flow at Mach numbers less than 5.0. To keep bypass duct mass to an acceptable level, it was essential that the installation be kept as short as possible. The requirement for a large bypass exhaust area excluded the possibility of an 'in line' arrangement, the diffusers being curved upwards into the wing/fuselage while being kept as short as was consistent with a practical heat exchanger installation.

"During design evolution the heat exchangers became substantially larger (though not heavier) than the early slimline design and it became necessary to adopt a full S-duct diffuser locating the heat exchanger and turbocompressor totally within the fuselage and leading to reconfiguring of the oxygen tank. The compression geometry was revised to a four-shock system so as simultaneously to achieve maximum off-design recovery and intake maximum capture. With the new compression system (which involved two extra moving surfaces) it was possible to maintain high bypass ratio and to maximise low drag supersonic forespillage at intermediate Mach numbers without excessive recovery penalty."

Sharp leading edges had been adopted to minimise high-speed drag, the triangular re-entry guard was determined to be ineffective and so was deleted, "the lateral compression walls were extended to minimise high Mach number spillage and throat bleed at the design point was reduced to the minimum level shown acceptable by the high speed wind tunnel tests on RAE model 351. The diverter height was reduced to permit some outer boundary layer swallowing on the basis of Concorde experience, and lastly, but most importantly, a scheme was developed for burning turbine exhaust hydrogen in the bypass — the

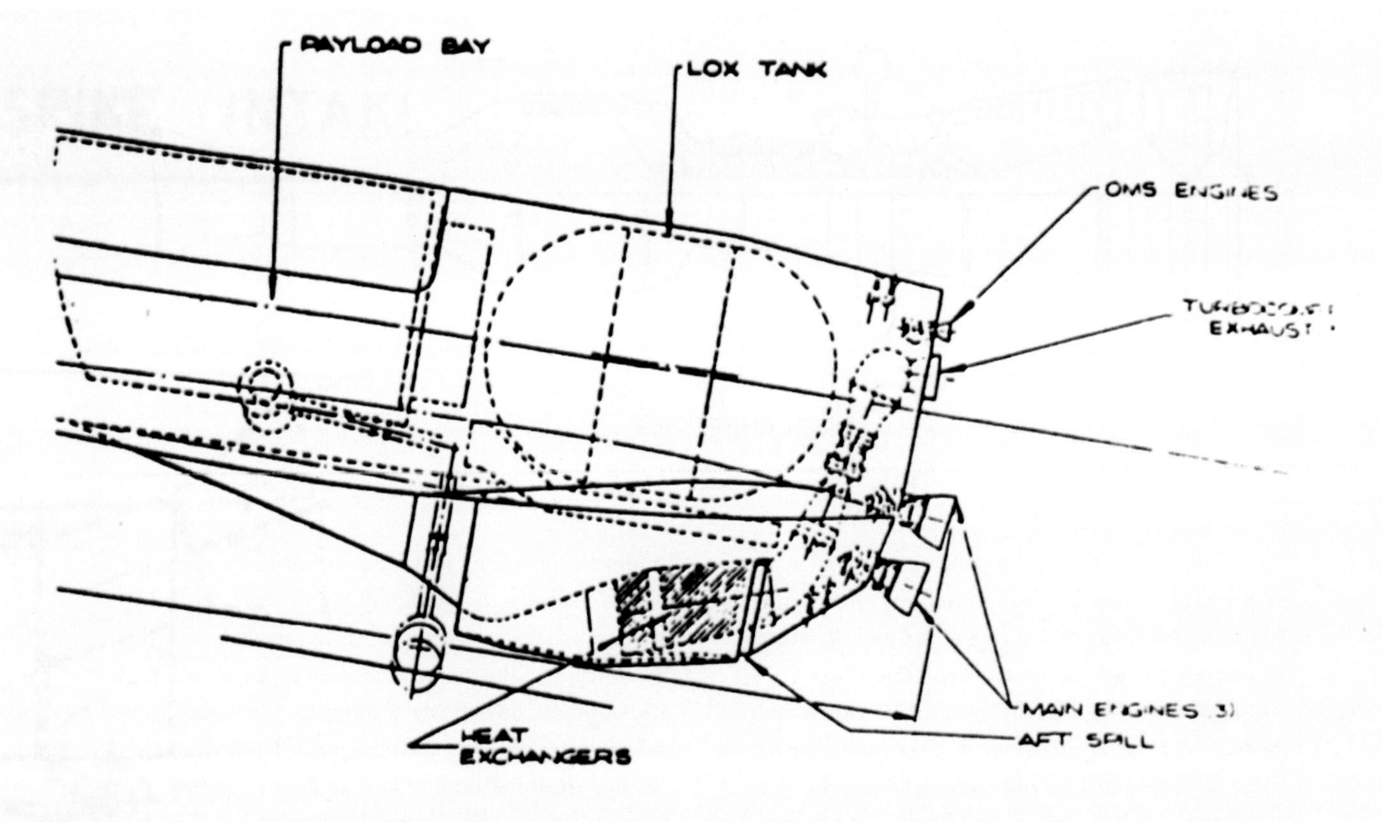

Expanding centrebody intake design for Hotol. This was described as a "very challenging engine installation" which was both "dimensionally large" and "impractical".

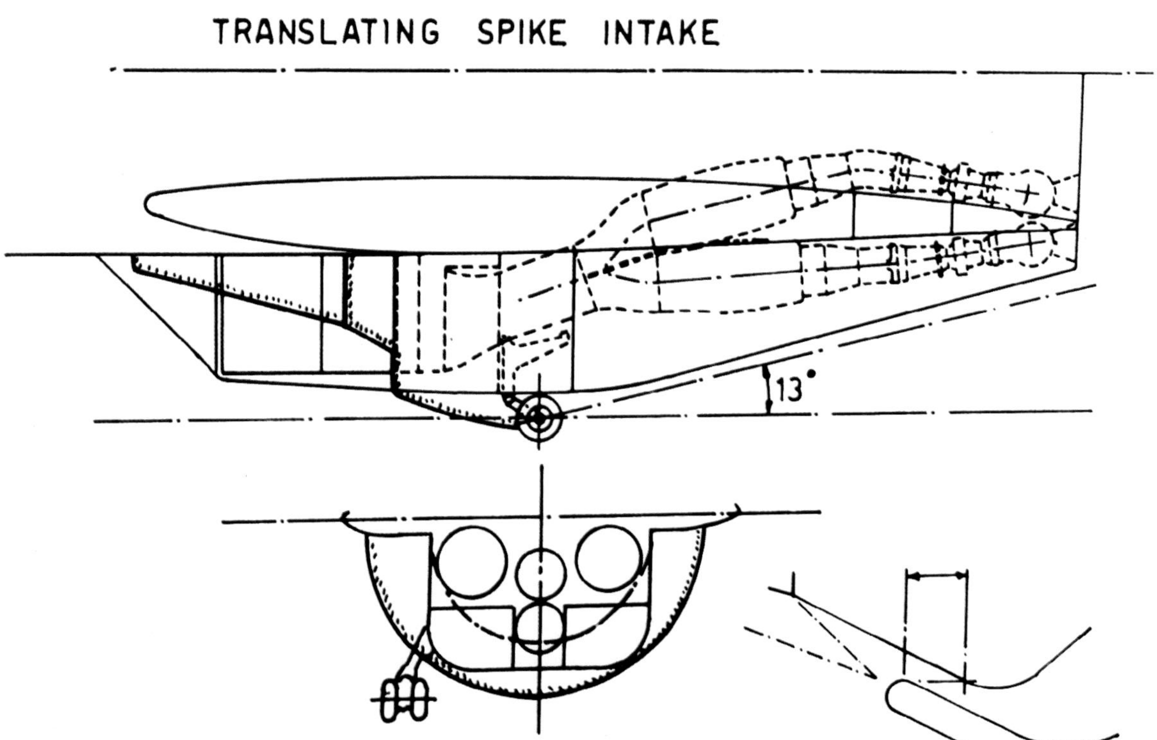

Translating cone intake.

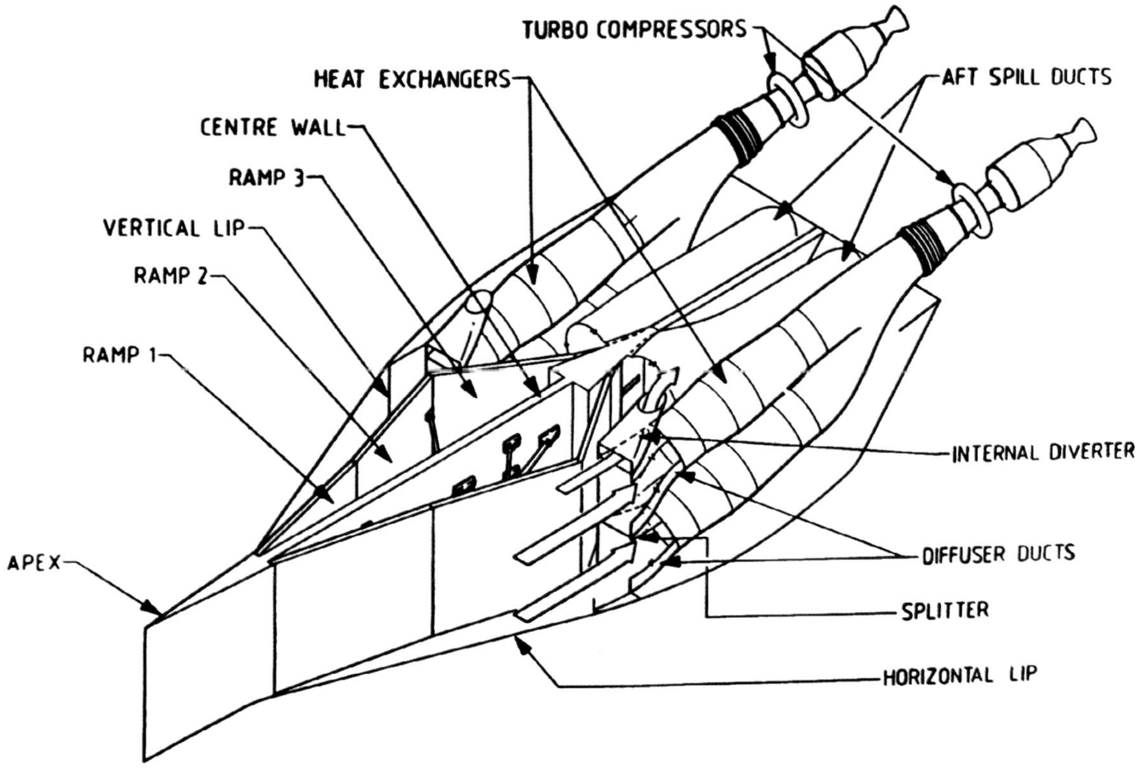

Intake cutaway showing heat exchangers and diffusers.

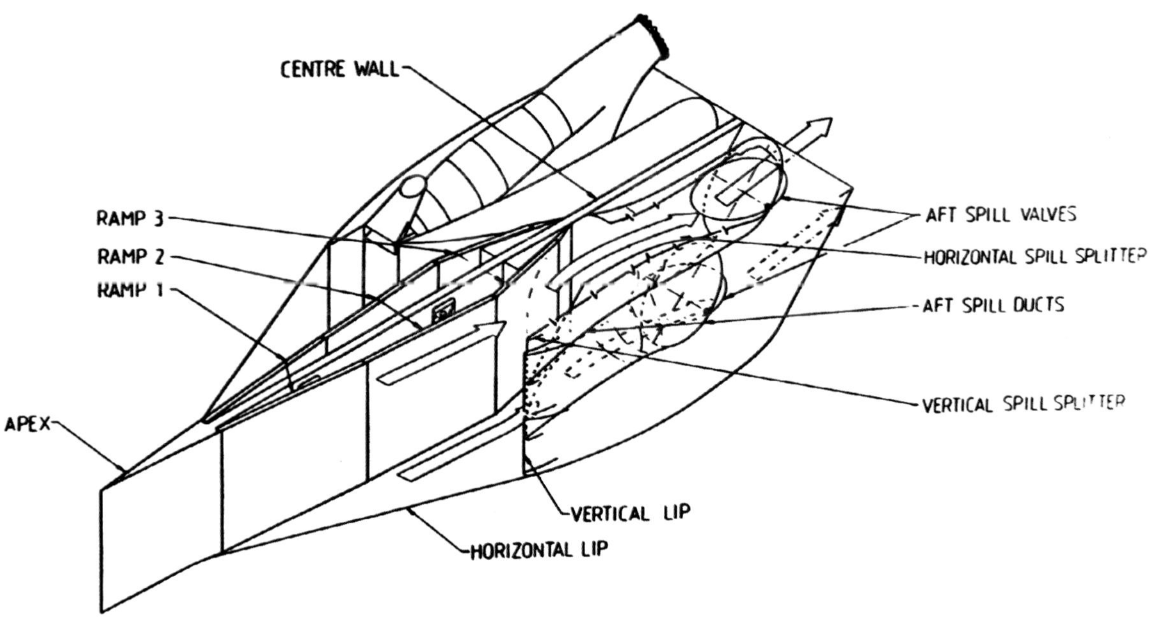

Intake cutaway showing cold aft spill ducts.

so-called Aft Spill Ramjet system (ASRJ). The resulting design met performance objectives though not without some attendant mass increase".

BICONE, CONE, NOSE AND S

Four alternative intake schemes had been investigated during the PoC—expanding bicone, translating cone, nose intake and top-mounted S-shape. The first of these "was the original arrangement from the pre-PoC studies, abandoned early during PoC because it was believed that a hot, pressurised, leak-proof, expanding centrebody could not be engineered, or at least could be engineered only at a weight which lost the potential weight advantage of a cylindrical structure".

The translating cone "was studied as a potential alternative for Configuration F. At the time of the study, when

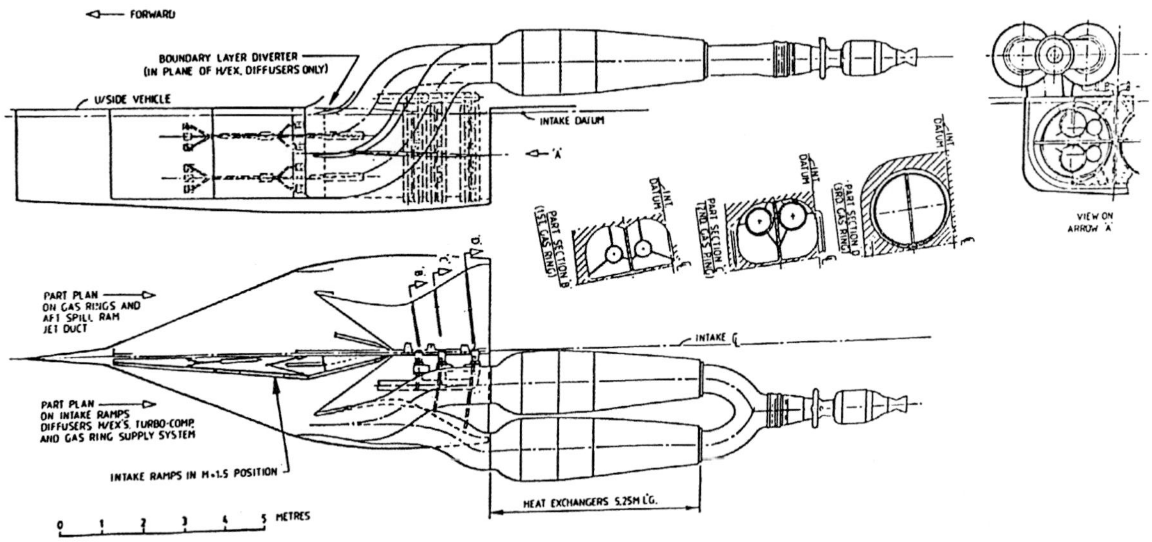

Low drag intake design.

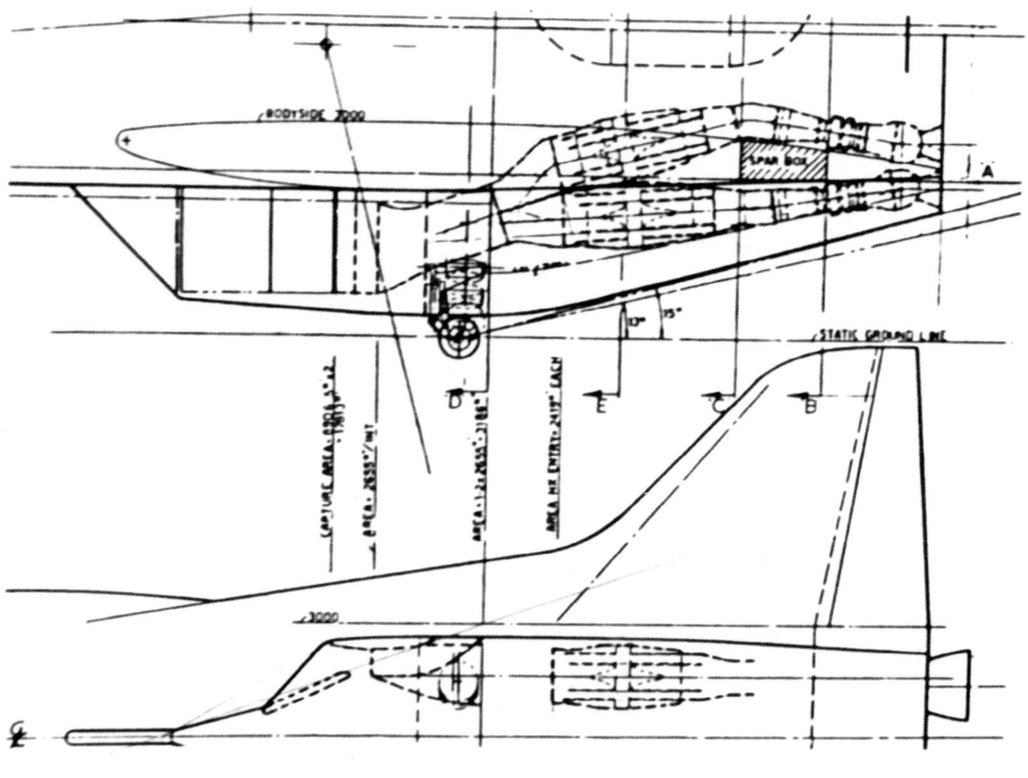

The intake design intended for Hotol Configuration F.

spillage drag considerations were secondary, this design foundered on the requirement for an extreme hooked cowl lip to facilitate full closure of the intake above Mach 5. The required lip angles produced very high levels of lip drag as well as large increases of nacelle cross sectional area. A translating cone version of the high bypass ratio intake was not attempted, but would clearly require some sort of telescoping cone arrangement".

The nose intake idea had come about as a result of designers realising that Configuration F's intake area and fuselage nose area were broadly similar—so why not delete the underbody intake and stick it on the fuselage nose instead? According to the report, "the possibility of a single large translating cone intake in the nose was examined in some detail. A preliminary structural analysis indicated however that this solution, in spite of having the advantage of cylindrical form, was extremely heavy.

"Three principal factors contributed to this heaviness: loss of pre-compression caused a 25% increase in intake area to supply the demanded airflow; the square-cubed mass rule makes single large structures substantially heavier than several smaller structures having the same total supply characteristic; the large surface area of the long duct would have required extensive, heavy insulation from the surrounding hydrogen tank skin."

The S-shaped intakes would have sat on top of the inner wings, on either side of the fuselage. The report stated: "This arrangement was briefly studied to ascertain whether a top mounted arrangement could be installed and to establish a preliminary mass estimate. The arrangement appeared practical on Configuration F with the then-slimline heat exchangers. Simple weight estimates suggested no significant mass change. Note that these intakes were sized on the assumption of an inverted airbreathing climb. This study was set aside pending a positive requirement to get the intake off the lower surface."

The new JPT would look to improve the 2D undersurface intake, with an alternative metallic cooled/thermal protected structure to be studied and a potential switch to a four-intake arrangement: "A four-abreast, undersurface, horizontal wedge arrangement holds some promise if a high bypass ratio configuration can be devised. It would also appear to represent the best re-entry option for undersurface mounting providing it is acceptable to delete the diverter. A twin shoulder-mounted arrangement sized for inverted airbreathing acceleration might be a practical solution if the intakes are found to be unacceptable on the lower surface during re-entry. Directional control in inverted flight might prove to be a difficult problem."

In addition: "A new study of conical intakes is proposed, as is a study of less conventional arrangements (for example, a multiple, in the wing, mouthorgan arrangement [i.e. the ALV 100 configuration]). Such studies are worthwhile only if carried through to a reliable performance/mass assessment which necessitates quite detailed design/structural analysis. It is therefore important to select winners."

HITTING THE SKIDS

Another particularly noteworthy aspect of the PoC final report was the new skid undercarriage: "A skid main undercarriage had previously been considered as an alternative to mainwheels but the side-study was not taken to

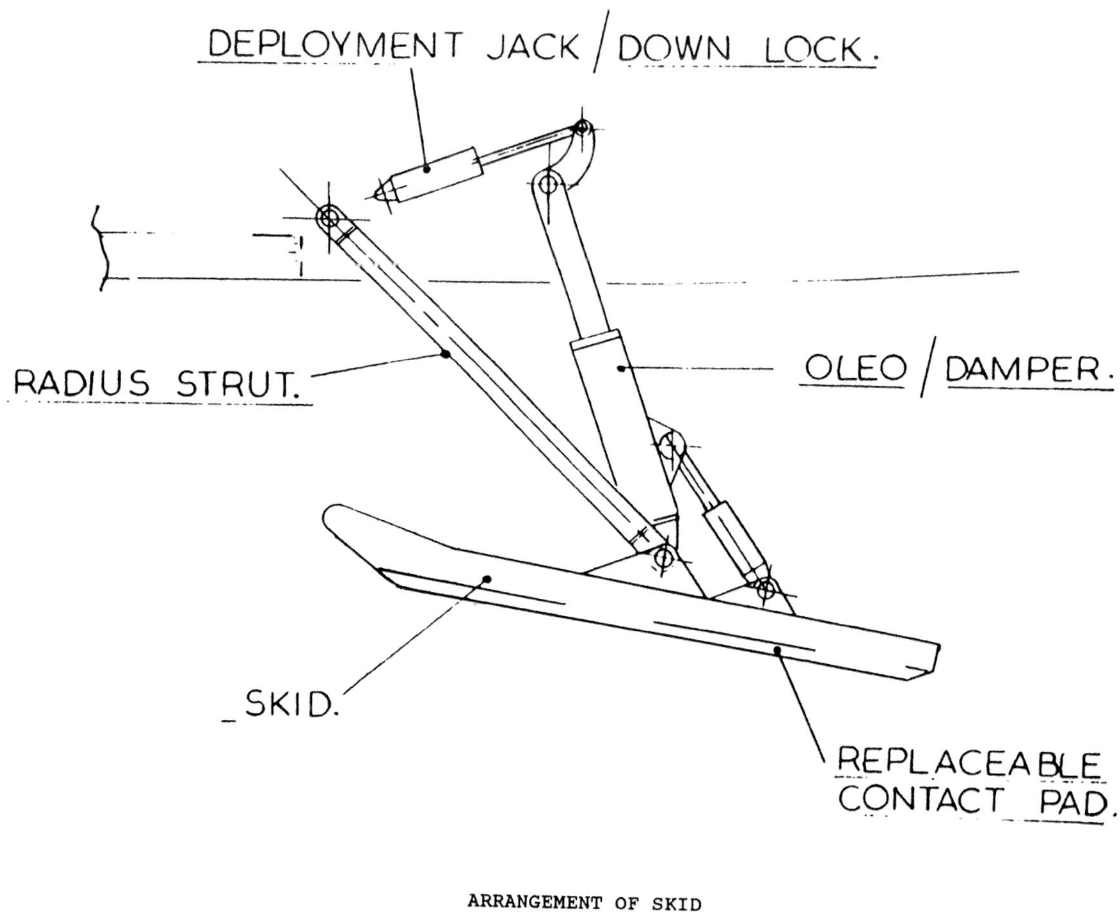

Detail of Configuration G3's skid undercarriage.

its final conclusion, since it appeared to offer no obvious advantage, nor was a quantitative mass comparison made.

"Incorporation of the aft spill duct in the intake pod has reduced the volume for mainwheel storage and moved any 'spare volume' aft of any suitable position which would allow controlled de-rotation after landing. The alternative of a stalky main undercarriage retracting into the wing roots would be undesirably heavy. So a skid main undercarriage has been adopted. It features a single main skid and twin small outrigged stabiliser skids." Each main skid would have a 'footprint' area of 2sqm with a crushable honeycomb shock absorber and a skid contact surface pad made of knotted 0.8mm wire, with 115 wires per knot, forming knots of 10mm diameter. This was expected to be eroded by 7.5mm during a landing.

The advantages of this were listed as "temperature constraints due to tyres removed; no brakes needed; no anti-skid system needed; fatigue cycle would be reduced; likely to be significantly lighter in weight". The disadvantages were: "No tyre to help absorb landing impact; no towing possible (would have to be loaded onto the trolley on the runway); skid wear would necessitate frequent replacement (but so do tyres); crushable struts would need replacement after every landing (acceptable)".

Noticeable by the absence from the report were the jettisonable foreplanes — presumably since their addition had only come about after the PoC Study had ended.

HOW TO MAKE IT

BAe had been determined throughout the PoC period to view the Hotol project as the basis for a practical real-world vehicle, rather than a tech concept study. Therefore, consideration had been given to how exactly the vehicle's major component parts would be made. For example, "a large nose cone designed in carbon-silicon carbide cannot be manufactured as one unit, but must be manufactured in smaller units which must be joined together. Joints in carbon-silicon carbide are weak, but since the loads are small this presents no severe problem.

"Since a high temperature furnace is required this component will probably be manufactured by a specialist company. [It is suggested] that the nose cone should be a sandwich structure for minimum mass. For Hotol this should have a foam core since corrugated and honeycomb cores cannot be easily manufactured for double curvature structures."

As mentioned previously, the carbon-PEEK liquid hydrogen tank would now be "stable during manufacture, service and repair. The sandwich core would be manufactured from a polymethacrylimide foam, or alternatively a PEEK foam if this is found to have satisfactory insulation properties. The manufacturing route would be similar for both the sandwich tank and the alternative design tanks.

"To date large composite structures have been manufactured using the filament winding build method, e.g. the sandwich structure fuselage of the Beech Starship aircraft. Although the liquid hydrogen tank for Hotol is much larger, a similar build route is considered feasible, although considerable development will be necessary to fabricate both machine tool resources as well as the tank itself.

"The tank wall is of varying thickness to ensure minimum mass. The proposed fibre lay-up is approximately quasi-isotropic but ply drop-offs must be accommodated in the winding pattern. The end domes of the tank and the attachment skirts will be manufactured separately and bonded to the main part of the structure. Similarly the internal tank frames and external posts must be bonded to the tank structure.

"In view of the size of the tank, the possibility of winding the structure inside a fixed outer shell is being investigated: this may have advantages over the conventional method of winding on the outside of a mandrel. The structural shape and winding process lead to excessive thickness at the apex of the cone, at the inside of kinks and at the apex of domes, so this would be left as excessive mass or machined away or wound by a discontinuous process. Ply drop-off already requires a discontinuous process and so this is the preferred method."

The fin, wing, rear fuselage, payload bay door and aeroshell panels would all be manufactured as "conventional sandwich structures using advanced materials (carbon-silicon carbide, titanium containing whiskers, particulates or fibres; or titanium aluminide). The whiskers or particulates will be used when small thin sheets have to be diffusion bonded together to make larger, thin sheets. In the case of the wing, the thin skins will be incorporated into long sandwich panels, and attached together at the spar positions.

"The first Hotol will require intensive internal inspection so the upper skin may be bolted to a diffusion bonded lower skin, spars and ribs. The wing and fin leading edges will be built as segments, with expansion joints between them; similarly the aeroshell is manufactured from many panels with expansion joints between them".

The report included an extensive list of the material and structural test facilities that would be required, as well as specialised material and structural test rigs already in existence, plus the new plants that would be required to deal with rapid solidification of materials, fibre reinforcement, particulate reinforcement and whisker reinforcement.

AN AIRWORTHY HOTOL

The report went into detail in considering flight load predictions (i.e. gusts), trolley and undercarriage loads, safety factors, failure cases and hazards such as bird impact, space debris impact, lightning strike and rain erosion.

Birdstrikes had already been identified as a real and ongoing concern for Hotol, but the report offered some reassurances: "Statistics for UK registered civil aircraft indicate that 92% of impacts occurred at altitudes below 2,500ft. At this height, in the ascent, Hotol is scheduled to have a speed of 560kts which implies that even small birds would cause substantial damage. However, the probability of birdstrike is low.

"The average rate for the larger civil jet aircraft is five strikes per 10,000 movements, so with the projected Hotol fleet (five vehicles, each performing 120 missions — 1,200 movements) a strike is unlikely during the life of the fleet. Any penetrations of the TPS during the ascent could lead to catastrophic failure during re-entry, therefore it is intended to install an impact detection system to allow the mission to be aborted in the event of a strike. This offers a high probability of saving the vehicle and its payload since at least 40% of the birds impacting with civil aircraft were less than 250g mass.

"Provided that the internal structure and systems layout are such that serious damage due to bird debris will not occur, a successful recovery and landing should be possible. Past birdstrike testing has shown that brittle sandwich structures (e.g. radomes) are prone to unsustainable damage and it is recommended that impact tests are made on specimens of all the types of structure proposed for the vulnerable areas of the aeroshell to appraise the extent and criticality of the damage inflicted.

"Current practice in USA, [which will be] followed by Hotol, is not to incorporate any protection against micro-meteorite or space debris impact due to its very low probability. The hazards of rain erosion and lightning strike are recognised and appropriate design measures are being taken."

Certain areas of risk during Hotol operations would have to be given special consideration: "There may be leakage of hydrogen from the liquid hydrogen tank; this could cause a fire hazard with the oxygen in the atmosphere and hence it must be purged overboard with a helium purge. As there are no crew on board Hotol, all damage to the structure must be monitored by instruments, e.g. bird strike and space debris damage to the nose cone, leading edges, aeroshell panels and intake. Decisions must be taken to abort the flight or to repair the vehicle in orbit using another launch vehicle or to continue without repair.

"Crack propagation in a pressurised tank, which has tensile stresses in the skin, would lead to an increased leakage of hydrogen which may exceed the purging capability — thus leading to a fire when in the atmosphere. The maximum permissible crack size for these conditions must be evaluated to ensure that it is not exceeded in flight."

ARTIFICIAL INTELLIGENCE

The PoC report also went into enormous depth when reviewing Hotol's command and control systems, including software and the use of artificial intelligence. It said: "Hotol places a premium on minimising operations costs. Most flights will use an unmanned vehicle with high reliance on automatic control systems and data interpretation. The application of AI techniques to command and control has been studied as a key enabling technology for a cost-effective, automatic, recoverable launch system.

"Key features required are 'transparency' and 'educability'. Transparency is the ability of the system to help the human operator understand what is going on and to operate the system reliably and effectively. Educability is the long-term requirement that a system can be 'educated' and evolved without difficulty as the human controllers develop their own understanding.

"AI application areas include: planning and scheduling, diagnostics, rule-based control and simulation. Planning, scheduling and resource allocations are of importance to mission scheduling and ground turnaround operations management. Since the vehicle and its support system will be in a continuous state of modification, a planning and activity support system must handle this. AI planning systems require significant abstraction and inferential reasoning capabilities.

"Use of 'expert systems' for problem diagnosis and data analysis will be required during launch, orbital flight, re-entry and ground turnaround. Properly implemented, such systems can replace the extensive checklists widespread in current operations. Such systems can also be linked to a simulator, so that anomalies and procedural modifications can be tested and verified before being introduced into service.

"The Hotol launch phase is expected to be one in which flight control modes may change quickly and without warning if problems arise. Immediate flight control will require highly reliable restricted-instruction-set coding schemes and 'provable' processor hardware architectures. The role of AI will be to reduce this demanding software burden, both by providing assistance in development, and by providing the non-critical decision and organising overlay to the flight control function.

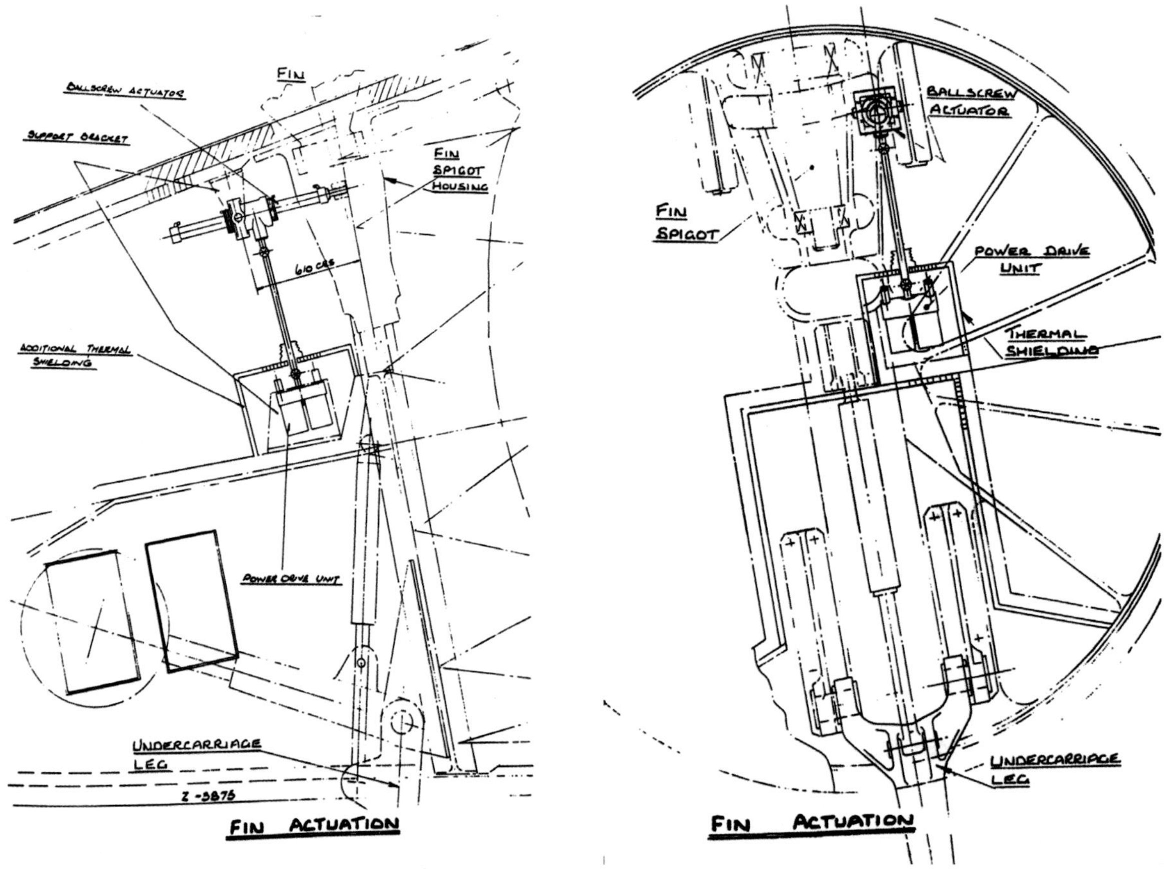

Fin actuation system, incorporating thermal shielding.

"System simulation has been a key tool in the development of automatic systems. The objective is to model the behaviour and interactions of the system components in a way which allows testing, failure mode simulation, and use of flight standard equipment. Simulation problems fall into two categories—those which involve intense numerical computation, for example of the dynamics of the vehicle, and those which represent the relational interactions within the system. AI based simulation tools such as the Xerox PARC 'Trillium' are now becoming available to allow a system developer to build and modify a relational model of his system at an early stage, and to test the system behaviours and human interface."

With hindsight it could be said that the development of artificial intelligence systems for Hotol certainly ought to have been an 'enabling technology' worth highlighting to the British Government as a spinoff with numerous potential applications. The 'internet' had existed in a very limited form since 1983 but would not become a true world wide web until around 1989-1990. Yet compact personal computers were becoming increasingly advanced and popular by 1987—the direction of travel was evident. Bond himself had quite audaciously demonstrated their capabilities in harnessing their power for his Hotol calculations. It might not have been such a stretch at this time, therefore, to suggest that the computer systems necessary for Hotol could have a far wider utility.

STAYING COOL

During a mission, Hotol would not only have to deal with massive external heating on re-entry and extremely cold fuel carried on board, but also internal systems which generated heat in their own right. These included the hydraulics, electronics, payload and fuel cells. Regulating the vehicle's internal temperature would require "duplex pumped freon loops to remove heat from the basically electrical sources for transportation to space radiators on orbit or to a water boiler at other times, leaving hydraulic rejected heat to be dissipated in separate dedicated water boilers".

These systems had been decided upon due to "the remoteness of the fin actuation systems from the electrical heat sources; the mass penalty arising from larger pipe bore, freon volume and heat exchanger size if the 80kw main hydraulic system heat load were to be needlessly circulated through the extensive freon loop together with the 7kw electrical load; [and] the extensive nature of the hydraulic systems, allowing relative freedom of boiler location with

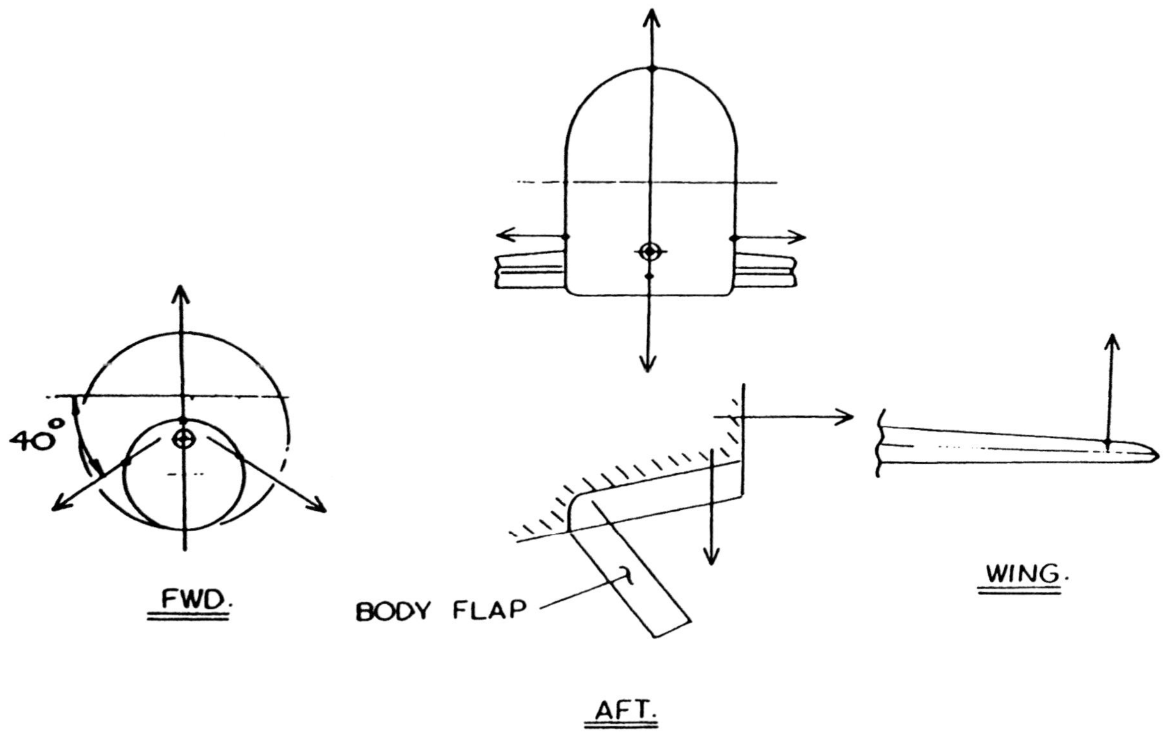

Diagram showing the RCS thruster locations for Hotol Configuration G.

a minimal heat transport penalty, the reverse being true of the other heat sources".

The freon system had been designed as two independent loops running closely in parallel, in such a way that "neither a single freon seal failure nor a single structural failure shall lead to loss of both loops". When Hotol was sitting on the runway or in a hangar, "a ground support heat exchanger allows for cooling of the systems ... without depletion of evaporant stock and, in addition, effects freezing of boiling water and chilling of the thermal control system generally to minimise the water required for the ascent. With the boiler isolated on orbit and flow switched to the surface radiators, the remaining water is allowed to freeze so as to enhance performance during the descent.

"Temperature control within the freon loops during ascent and descent, i.e. with the surface radiators bypassed, is effected by an intermittent spray onto tubes within the boiler carrying 'hot' freon in the same manner as on the Space Shuttle. Modulation is achieved by varying the duration of the spray. The surface radiators are fixed and are side located at the rear of the vehicle body. Being fixed, they are designed to withstand re-entry heating. Reservoirs absorb fluid thermal expansion and contraction, compensate for fluid loss and regulate pressure within the loops."

COLLECTING RESIDUALS

Hotol was to have an integrated propellant system, with hydrogen and oxygen used for the main engines, the OMS and the RCS. Three separate systems, operating independently of one another, would have resulted in "very significant mass penalties".

The report noted that "a major question throughout the design process has involved the propellant residual left after the main engine burn is complete. A significant part of this residual is present in the form of saturated liquid. Although unusable in the main engines (due to cavitation problems) there are crucial mass savings to be made if this propellant can be utilised in the OMS and/or RCS".

As such, Hotol had been designed with collector tanks to 'trap' saturated residual liquids from the main engine burn so they could be used for the OMS and RCS. Unfortunately, the low-density hydrogen needed a big cryogenic collector tank—another mass penalty. And then there was the question of heat leak into the collector tanks while in orbit, which "may prove to be one of the main limitations on orbital stay time".

It had earlier been determined "that storage of the re-entry propellant in the main tanks, in gaseous form, throughout the in-orbit mission, would have placed impossible requirements on the tank insulation".

Apparently, "design of the collector and auxiliary tanks is continuing at present. The aim is to produce tanks which are both mass efficient and effectively insulated. One option being investigated would involve replacing the liquid oxygen collector tank by a small compartment located over the outlet of the aft main oxygen tank. This

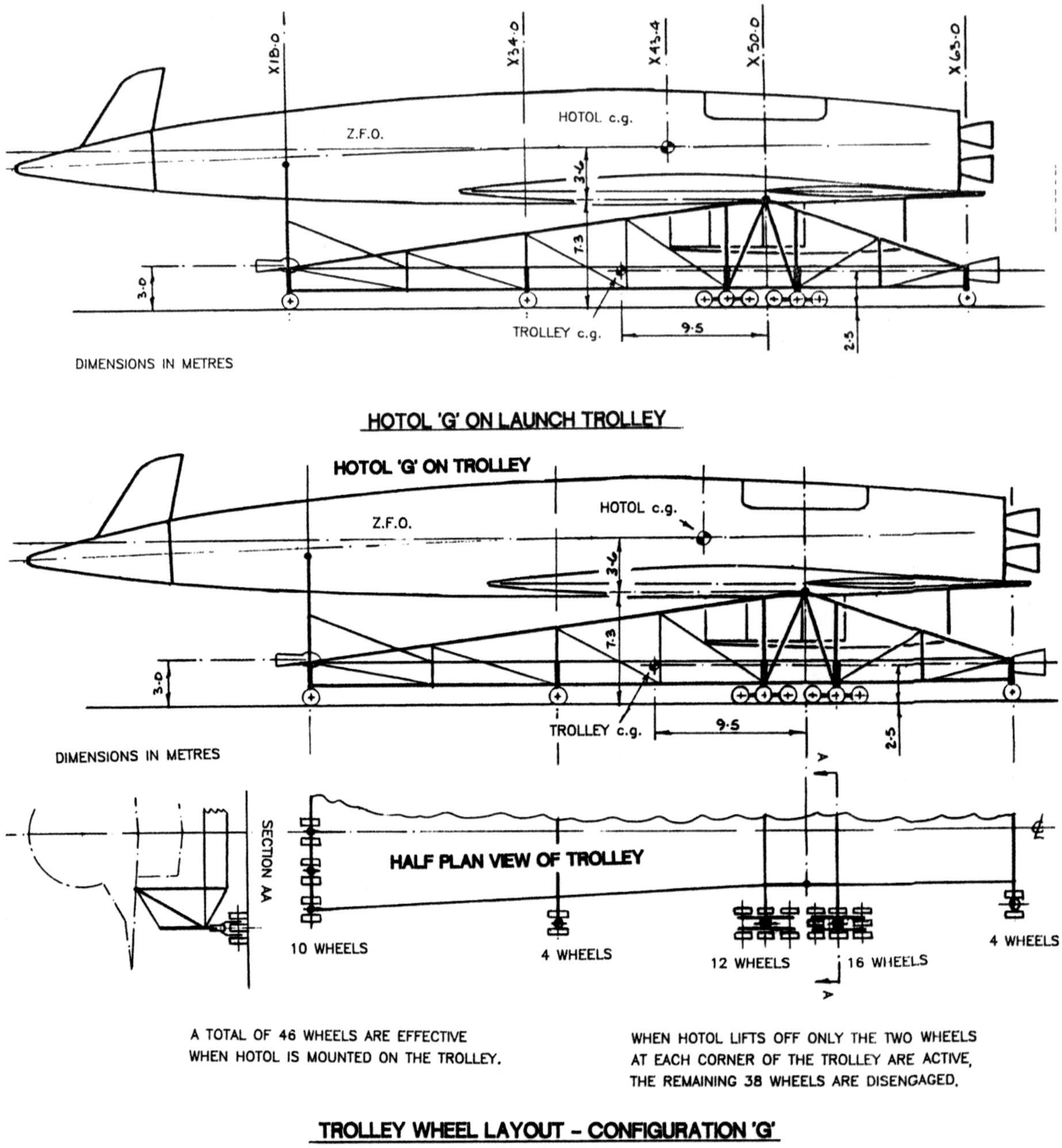

As a larger vehicle than its predecessor, Configuration G needed a sturdy 80-tonne welded steel trolley with a total of 46 wheels.

option would remove the need to install a separate tank in the main supply line, which in the case of the oxygen system, could otherwise impact on the overall length of the vehicle.

"Another important task currently underway is the simulation of the OMS operation for a wide range of different mission scenarios. Apart from verifying the design, this exercise should provide information on the capabilities and limitations of the system".

Beyond this, the BAe team had encountered four main issues when designing the fuel systems: "the division of propellant between tanks (e.g. the use of feeder tanks); the use of a single or multiple supply line (for either propellant or pressurant); the need to make provision for emergency dumping of propellant in flight; [and] the need to achieve necessary reliability levels".

Configuration F had been designed with one oxygen tank, one main hydrogen tank and two hydrogen feeder tanks. There would be two separate pipes running from the hydrogen tank into the feeder tanks, which would each then supply two engines. The "pressurant for each propellant system was supplied via a single duct. The pressurant gas consisted of 'hot' propellant vapour in both cases. Provision was made for in-flight dumping of both propellants via the two main fill lines. With regard to component redundancy, the decision was made that it was impractical in the main liquid supply system on the grounds of mass (it was also considered to be unnecessary to some extent in view of the very limited amount of component operation required).

"In the pressurant system, component redundancy was adopted. The consequences of either overpressuring or under-pressuring the tanks was considered sufficiently serious to merit the relatively small mass increase involved."

In Configuration G, the feeder tanks and their dual pipelines were deleted and there would be two main oxygen tanks instead of just one. This made it much easier to insert the OMS/RCS collector tanks into the system. The report included a detailed description of how the fuel supply system would operate from the tanks being filled on the ground up to main engine cut-off in space.

The precise details of Configuration G's fuel dumping system were still being considered as of November 1987 and "in an attempt to save inert mass, a proposal to pressurise the [up to this point unpressurised] main oxygen tanks with gaseous helium is being considered. The system proposed would use a gaseous helium tank submerged in the main hydrogen tank. Helium at about 21K would be passed through a heat exchanger (probably using the main engines as an enthalpy source) and then fed into the oxygen tanks. As a pressurant, helium would be far lighter than oxygen: however the mass of additional hardware required needs to be assessed".

TROLLEY EVOLUTION

The SSTO Hotol concept relied completely on the use of a launch trolley — a retractable undercarriage able to support the vehicle's mass during take-off would have had to weigh seven tonnes in its own right, effectively reducing the payload fraction to zero. Rescaling the vehicle to restore the seven-tonne payload resulted in something 150 tonnes heavier — "so the undercarriage is designed for landing only".

Switching from the 230-tonne Configuration F to the 275-tonne Configuration G, which also had a lower sea level thrust-to-weight ratio, had naturally resulted in the need for a bigger, sturdier trolley made from welded steel. Initially it was assumed that 26 wheels with Concorde tyres and three support points for the vehicle would be sufficient — that trolley weighing 65.6 tonnes. Configuration G, however, required an 80-tonne trolley with 46 wheels.

It was decided that during the take-off run the nose could be raised using full-up flap deflection "in conjunction with a suitable 'pusher' at the nose of the vehicle". At 240kts, the trolley's built-in 'pusher' would begin to elevate Hotol's nose, reaching "the end of its travel at 270kts, where the nose of the vehicle is released and continues to rotate to the lift-off speed of 280kts".

For a take-off distance of 3,000m, Configuration F needed a trolley incorporating 870kN of auxiliary thrust to be supplied by liquid hydrogen/liquid oxygen rockets — plus 1,200kN of retro thrust, to slow the trolley after take-off. With Configuration G, 1,850kN of auxiliary thrust was needed, plus 1,300kN of retro thrust, plus high energy brakes. In "an emergency case where all the braking system did not function correctly, for example assuming the unlikely case of all the retro rockets failing during a rejected take-off, then the vehicle/trolley would require 4,236m of runway, or the vehicle would hit an arrester system placed at 3,500m at around 150kts. Arrester systems capable of the energy required do exist e.g. AAI international Model 64 uses a tandem braking system and can arrest up to 360 tonnes. A special net would be required for Hotol simply due to the height of the vehicle/trolley (around 16m) and its associated high centre of gravity. Existing nets tend to be 6m or 7m high".

Under normal conditions, with the vehicle having taken off, the trolley would stop after 3,410m without retro rockets, so "obviously, the use of either parachutes or retro rockets brings the stopping distance well within 3,000m".

The PoC final report's overall conclusion was that "there is a high level of confidence that the objective of designing, at an economically attractive size, a single-stage-to-orbit vehicle powered by RB.545 propulsion units can be achieved".

And against all hope, it seemed as though the British government was minded to continue the project's funding too. In public, Clarke had given every possible indication that no further finance would be provided. Yet behind the scenes, his civil servants seem to have been encouraging BAe to forge ahead with hints that a softening of the Government's stance was just around the corner. Therefore, the Hotol team ended 1987 on a high note, confident that the project would continue on into its next phase during 1988.

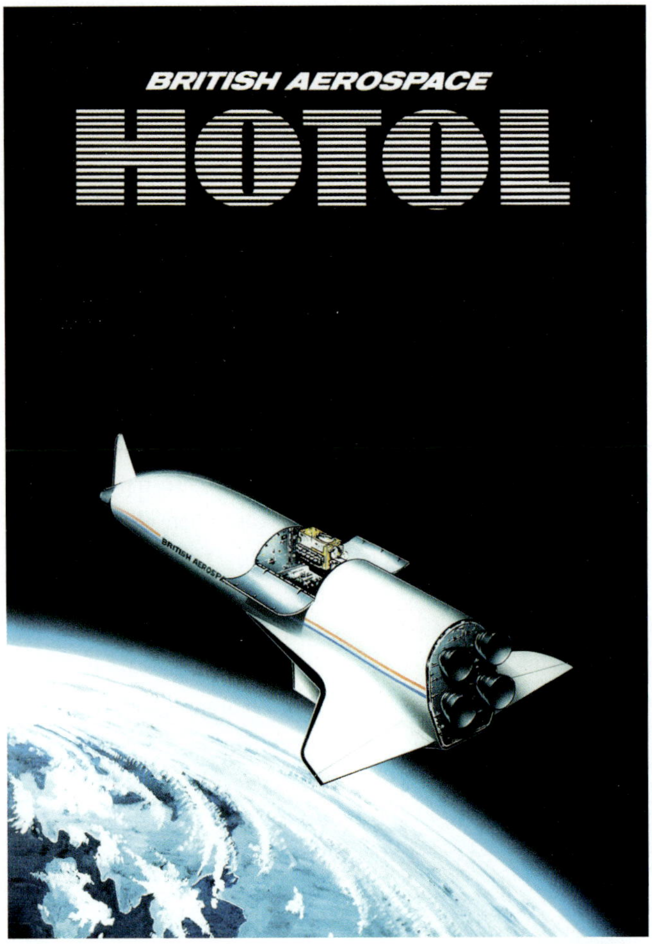

Proof-of-concept work on British Aerospace's horizontal take-off and landing, single-stage-to-orbit aerospaceplane continues to indicate that HOTOL is an entirely feasible concept for the world's first fully reusable and highly economic satellite launcher. Designed to place a 7–8 tonne payload in a 300 km orbit from an easterly equatorial launch, it is 52 m long, 20 m in wingspan and has a gross take-off weight of about 240 tonnes. Landing weight is less than 50 tonnes. Similar in size and weight to Concorde it has a payload bay diameter of 4.6 m to provide compatibility and interchangeability of payloads with the Shuttle Orbiter. At take-off it is eight times lighter than the Orbiter assembly but has double the payload/take-off mass fraction, ie 3.0% as opposed to 1.5%. The latter figure is typical for today's conventional and exceedingly expensive launchers.

The quantum improvement in performance has been achieved primarily by the use of a radically new hybrid rocket engine – the Rolls-Royce RB 545 – which breathes air while in the atmosphere and uses on-board oxygen in the vacuum of space. This halves the amount of dense liquid oxygen required to be carried on take-off. Performance is further enhanced because wings allow horizontal take-off with a much lower level of thrust, and therefore engine weight, than on a vertical take-off vehicle. HOTOL's thrust/weight ratio at take-off is less than 0.6 compared with Shuttle's 1.6 and it gets airborne with the ease and smoothness of a jet fighter, obviating stress on the payload.

By eliminating the need for launch towers and stacking procedures, horizontal operation saves substantially on launch preparation costs. A philosophy of 'one satellite one launch' reduces payload integration expense and the unmanned mode of operation in this primary role further reduces costs by dispensing with heavy and expensive life support systems and reducing ground control personnel to about 250 compared with the several thousands needed for Shuttle operations. The use of a separate trolley for take-off means that only a light-duty integral undercarriage is needed for landing. The resultant local mass saving leads to a 33% decrease in overall vehicle mass, and generates further substantial cost savings. Finally, the fact that HOTOL operates from a normal runway, that it is totally reusable, and that no parts are jettisoned in flight, brings the ambitious target of an 80% reduction in launch costs within reach. Only economies of this order, coupled with the inherent flexibility and high performance of HOTOL, will permit the true commercial development of Space.

The Design

The whole vehicle is based on a numerical optimization between mass, shape and drag parameters. The configuration is dominated by the large liquid hydrogen (LH2) fuel tank, which constitutes an integral part of the load carrying structure. An "aeroshell" is used to avoid LH2 boil-off (at 20°K, −253°C) and to withstand re-entry heating. The aeroshell consists of metal panels backed by high-temperature insulation and supported by the tank structure. Conventional nickel and titanium alloys could be used for the thermal protection panels, but advanced materials (metal matrix, carbon-carbon) are being studied for their performance advantages. The liquid oxygen (LOX) tank is ⅛ the volume of the LH2 tank but its contents account for over 50% of take-off mass. Of the 240 tonnes total, approximately 55% is LOX, 25% LH2, 10% airframe, 5% engines and 2% systems, leaving 3% as useful payload. The payload bay measures 7.5 m by 4.6 m and is capable of accommodating very large satellites, eg the Olympus class.

Work over the past 12 months has led to several changes from the original design:

- Modifications to fuselage shape.
- Deletion of the canard foreplanes.
- Modified air intake for better engine performance.
- Deletion of rear fins (insufficient moment arm relative to centre of gravity).
- Substitution of an active, all-moving forward fin.
- Change to an even number of engines (installational convenience).

The major engineering studies currently in hand are:

- Propulsion integration
- Structures and materials
- Aerodynamics
- Thermal design
- Command and control
- Sub-system design

Operations

Operations Base

HOTOL will operate from a standard airfield with facilities for transport aircraft flying-in the prepared payloads; fuel and pyrotechnics loading bays and a maintenance and loading hangar. The operational, technical and logistics organization will be geared to achieving a very rapid turnround from landing to take-off, as little as 48 hours if necessary.

HOTOL

Missions

HOTOL missions can include satellite launch and recovery; servicing of manned space stations and unmanned platforms; microgravity and scientific experiments; and military operations.

Take-off and Climb

Take-off at 280 knots is from a trolley and a conventional runway of approximately 3,500 m. Rotation is initiated by means of a mechanical pusher on the trolley and then aerodynamic controls take over. Provision if made to abort safely during the 1800 m take-off run or during the climb. In the latter case it is possible to divert back to base, to an alternate airfield down range, or to orbit.

After take-off the vehicle will accelerate to between 500 and 600 knots and then climb at constant airspeed during the airbreathing phase to Mach 5 at 26 km (85000') when the air intake closes. The engine then converts to pure rocketpower, using the on-board LOX. Thereafter acceleration continues to 90 km and a velocity of 7.9 km per second where, with an elliptical orbit established, the main engine is cut off and the vehicle coasts to operating altitude, typically 300 km. At this point the orbital manoeuvring engines initiate a circularization burn to establish the desired low earth orbit.

Re-entry

Mission duration can range from 12 to 100 hours with 24 hours fairly typical. Re-entry into the atmosphere is initiated by a de-orbit manoeuvre. The reaction control thrusters (RCS) turn HOTOL tail first, the OMS then fires to reduce forward speed and finally the RCS is used to set-up the correct re-entry attitude. For the re-entry phase a high angle of attack is maintained to maximize lift co-efficient. This enables re-entry to be achieved at high altitude to minimize peak velocity and aerodynamic heating. Once peak heating has been passed the vehicle is slowly pitched down to lower incidence to maximize lift-to-drag ratio and hence cross or down-range performance. In general, re-entry temperatures exceeding 1200°K will occur only under the nosecone, the leading edges and the lips and centre body of the intake. These "hot spots" are in the order of 1750°K.

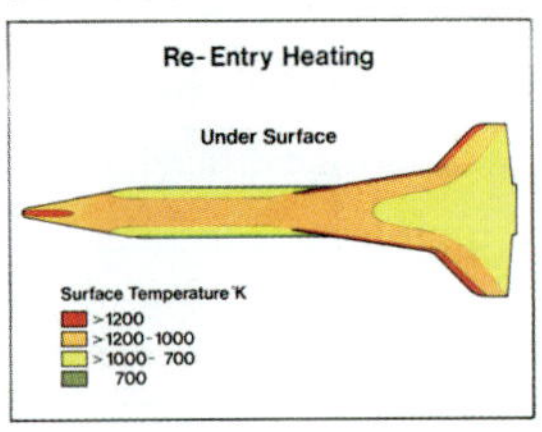

Approach and Landing

After re-entry the vehicle's position, speed and altitude are available from the global tracking network and from the Navstar global positioning system. For the final phase of the unpowered glide recovery the upper portion of the flightpath is lengthened or shortened to cater for tail or headwinds and an 18° glideslope is maintained by deploying and retracting the air brake. Descent is at 2.5° to 3°, touchdown is at 160 knots, and groundroll on a wet runway is 1500 m.

Development Programme

Following the Proof-of-Concept Study there will be sequential project definition and initial development phases over a period of about four years with Enabling Technology Programmes running in parallel. These programmes will investigate propulsion; structures, materials and manufacturing techniques; aerodynamics (notably hypersonics); advanced sub-systems; command and control; and unmanned flight operations. Successful completion should allow entry with confidence into a development phase beyond 1991, leading to flight trials in the final two years of the century and operational service at the turn of the century.

The costs of the development programme are currently estimated at a round figure of £5 billion. The programme is expected to involve experienced personnel and other resources of the member nations of ESA to ensure a timely and successful outcome to the overall programme for a European Spaceplane.

When the concept has been "proved" in the unmanned role, a dedicated manned version will be introduced to support the European man-in-space programme and, subsequently, to undertake manned missions as required on a world-wide basis.

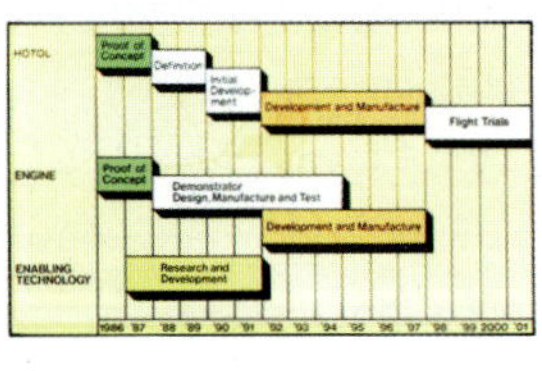

Conclusion

HOTOL has the potential not only to reduce launch costs dramatically and relax launch schedule constraints: it will also make in-orbit servicing and retrieval of spacecraft possible. The ease and smoothness of launch could change the design philosophy for future communications satellites. Perhaps most important of all, HOTOL is the key to Europe's attainment of total autonomy in Space.

Low speed aerodynamic characteristics were evaluated using a ¹⁄₂₀ scale model.

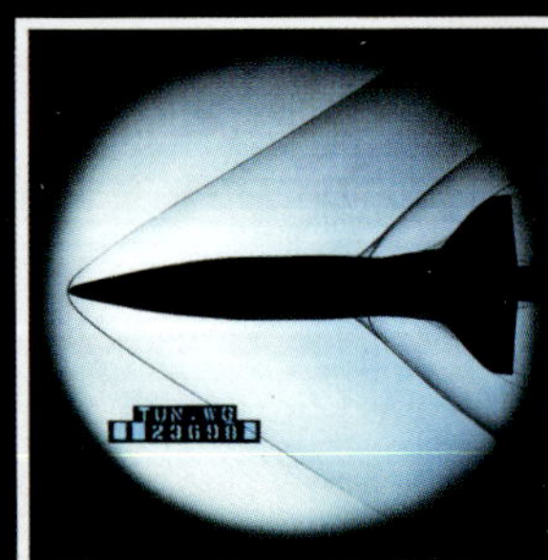

Schlieren is used to indicate shock patterns in high speed model tests up to Mach 5.5.

A ¹⁄₂₅₀ scale model for testing up to Mach 20 in the T3 free piston shock tunnel of the Australian National University, Canberra.

Alternative configurations for wind tunnel testing.

BRITISH AEROSPACE

Space & Communications Division

Argyle Way Stevenage Hertfordshire SG1 2AS
Telephone: National 0438 313456
International +44 438 313456
Telex: 82130 answerback BADSTE G

and

P.O. Box 5, Filton, Bristol, BS12 7QY.
Telephone: National 0272 693831
International +44 272 693831
Telex: 449452 answerback BACGW G

8

APPROACHING THE LIMIT: JANUARY 1, 1988 TO JULY 27, 1988

THROUGHOUT JANUARY 1988, the Hotol team continued to work on determining Configuration G's precise mass while attempting to resolve the vehicle's seemingly intractable centre of gravity issue.

By the end of the month, it seemed as though Hotol would indeed be made a special case where Government funding was concerned—defying the general prohibition on any further space spending. Burns reported to Yates on January 29 that "following negotiations between Space and Communications Division, Stevenage and BNSC, we are informed that HMG are likely to fund the Hotol programme to the level of £2.9m in 1988, £3.6m in 1989 and £4.9m in 1990. This is an average of £3.8m per annum over three years. These figures assume equal contributions from industry and are subject to satisfactory progress, with an annual review in the autumn of each year.

"Assuming two-thirds of the above funding goes to BAe, a third to other industry, the funding for BAe becomes £3.5m in 1988 (allowing for £0.3m BAe spend post PoC in 1987), £4.8m in 1989 and £6.4m in 1990. This falls somewhat short of the figures previously requested but is sufficient to continue project studies at the present level with an increasing level of spend on enabling technology.

"Staff levels, based on 1988 rates, will increase from the 1987 figure of 68 average to double that figure by 1990. A development cost programme for the three years is in an advanced stage of preparation."

Rolls-Royce was now becoming unusually active, which was taken as a positive sign: "A formal re-definition of the RB.545 performance, which will allow rigorous parametric investigations to proceed, has been received from RR. Following further work by BAe Filton and RR, an improved definition of the spill ramjet performance has [also] been defined. This definition is based on subsonic combustion over the whole operating range (i.e. not a scramjet). The figures yield a payload improvement in the region of two tonnes compared with the performance reported in HPN 0011".

Less positive was news of deputy technical manager Wilson's imminent departure from the project, scheduled for the end of February 1988, to take up a new position on Eurofighter in Munich. Burns ruefully noted that this "will cause some break in continuity of activity on propulsion" and "difficulty is being experienced in finding a suitable successor at Warton".

And the ALV studies went on, with "structural design of the wing on ALV 100 … underway [and] performance checks on the all-rocket version of Hotol, ALV 30, … underway at Stevenage."

This continuation of work on the all-rocket Hotol into February 1988 was very much against Bond's wishes however. He had written a letter to Burns on December 11, 1987, to say: "I thought it was implicit in the work done by Warton, Stevenage and myself that SSTO rockets [caps from the original text] DO NOT show enough promise within the foreseeable time frame to merit further investigation, being at their performance limit (actually beyond it in my optimistic calculations) and having little potential for growth in later generations.

"My understanding of the purpose of ALV studies was not to find an alternative to Hotol at any price, but to discover whether our target Hotol specification makes sense. Well, we know that it does—so why this nonsense about 'fully worked up all-rocket alternatives'? I love rockets as much as, and possibly more than, anyone at Warton. I also like steam engines and the grace of airships. I hope however that I can maintain adequate perspective to realise when their day is gone."

SSTO rockets were at their performance limit, he wrote, and required expensive launch pads for vertical launch or large ground assistance equipment for a horizontal launch. They also had "high noise levels for a given payload, giving no hope of future development to mainland UK operation and certainly would not allow high launch rates from anywhere".

He said he had "now given Warton claims for SSTO rockets a considerable amount of effort, all of which directly subtracts from my effort on Hotol". In doing so, he had "ignored problems of thrust buildup rate and efflux noise pressure field on the structure" and even then "I FIND NO JUSTIFICATION TO PURSUE ROCKETS FURTHER EVEN WITH SUCH ASSUMPTIONS SINCE ITS PERFORMANCE IS POOR AND ITS CHARACTERISTICS UNACCEPTABLE FOR FUTURE DEVELOPMENTS".

Back in lower case again, he continued: "I am not... prepared to invest any more time on this 'red herring' as it is much easier for others to make optimistic claims than for me to disprove them. If BAe wish to pursue a SSTO rocket as a separate project, clear and distinct from Hotol, that is their prerogative as long as I am not expected or requested to contribute further to it... I must further add that I believe that to follow such an alternative would be playing with political dynamite, and that there exists the high probability of conveying a lack of faith in the Hotol route, and potentially ending up without a project of this nature in the UK at all."

BLOCKED RADIATORS

There was a meeting on 'Hotol—Thermal Joint Team Activities' at Warton on February 5 which examined a Stevenage report on the vehicle's external radiators, either side of the payload bay. It had been decided that two radiator panels were needed in order to maintain an acceptable freon temperature in the cooling system since at least one panel would always be in shadow. Furthermore, the panels had to be "as far forward as possible to avoid both reflection from and blockage of the view of space by the wings.

"The minimum required total area is 14sqm assuming one panel sun-facing (with wing reflection) and the other space facing. Problems might arise with one panel sun-facing and the other earth facing, so that this attitude has to be either avoided or limited in duration."

It was eventually decided that rather than having two payload bay doors, hinged on either side, there would be a single door or hatch, hinged at the rear, which would swing up and back to then lie flat on the rear fuselage when open.

In the House of Commons on February 10, 1988, Conservative MP David Atkinson asked Clarke "if he has received any further proposals from British Aerospace and Rolls-Royce on Hotol". Clarke responded: "I have recently received a proposal from Rolls-Royce for a further year's work on the Hotol propulsion concept. I expect to receive a related proposal from British Aerospace shortly and I will consider them both with care."

This proposal, for a single year's continuation only, appears to have taken BAe by surprise. The agreed plan was to pursue a three-year extension—and BAe had been hard at work on a fully costed Hotol development programme to put before Clarke—but RR had abruptly blown that out of the water. Now BAe was forced to boil its three-year plan down to just a one-year feasibility study, since to do otherwise would expose an unacceptable degree of disunity between the two partner firms.

The following day, Burns wrote a memo to Young about an increasingly disillusioned Bond: "Alan Bond, in private conversation with Gerald Wilson ... has stated that he has decided not to pursue renewal of his consultancy contract with RR, which expires in mid-March 1988. I am not sure whether this contractually restricts RR's continued development of the RB.545, but the stimulus of his presence will be missing. Perhaps BAe should consider taking him on in a consultancy role."

February 15 saw Dr Jim Reynolds from the Space and Communications team at Bristol giving a presentation in Warton on a computer program he had developed to simulate Hotol's trolley take-off run as well as the rejected take-off scenario. Evidently "output from the program was to consist of the displacement, velocity, acceleration and force at various points on the vehicle and trolley. This would indicate the severity of any loadings induced by runway surface roughness, flap deployment, nose jacking, trolley wheel jacking, parachute deployment, braking and retro thrust application".

According to a meeting report issued two days later, "the program is now running satisfactorily at Bristol and output plots from four runs have been provided to the Hotol team at Warton. One outstanding query is the action of the flaps which do not appear to be operating correctly in the program. This is the subject of investigation by Dr Reynolds and Mr [David] Wood to determine whether the program or the data is at fault... A tape of the program has been loaded successfully on the Warton mainframe... once the program has successfully reproduced the Bristol results on the Warton mainframe, we will have a tool available which can be used for a number of different studies".

On the same day, February 17, Burns, Furniss and Parkinson met to discuss a new ESA-sponsored study on Winged Launcher Configurations (WLC). It had formally begun on February 1, would last until February 28, 1989, and followed the earlier propulsion studies. It would be led by MBB in association with BAe and RR, with Stevenage having negotiated BAe's involvement, which was viewed as politically desirable. Even though the funding from ESA only covered "0.7 men at each of the main companies... all companies involved have agreed to add private venture funding in order to bring this number up to 1.5 men".

General comments on the study arising from the meeting were: "The MBB study proposed defines mission requirements which are more suitable to TSTO [two-stage-to-orbit] than SSTO. The TSTO is less sensitive to design assumptions and so will pay a smaller penalty for non-optimisation. We must be very careful not to give away the knowledge and experience gained on Hotol, for instance, only basic data on materials must be provided. The only merit in this study appears to be in forming closer working relationships with MBB and gaining some front-line knowledge of ESA's working practices."

Wilson, still in-post as of February 18, sent a memo to senior weights engineer Ray Pickett to say that "a new engine (RB.545-02D) has been defined by Rolls-Royce for Configuration G3. This engine is roughly similar in overall performance to the scaled PS350 engine actually used in the G3 definition, but differs considerably in detail. Calculation of actual performance with this engine is in hand".

From a breakdown of component weights it appeared at first glance that the new engine was 363kg lighter than the one assumed for Configuration G3 but "these figures are now to be taken as basic components rather than installed items. A separate account is therefore required for: heat exchanger support links, turbo-compressor support links, TVC actuators (70kg per chamber), gaiters (26kg per chamber) and helium pressurisation/purge".

FIRST G3 SUMMIT

A two-day meeting was held from February 24-25 at Warton to discuss Configuration G3. The first day's discussions took place in the Defence Systems Conference Room, the second in the Jaguar Projects Conference Room and on both days there was lunch at The Villa, Wrea Green, a country hotel just up the road from Warton.

Wilson later recalled: "These were still the days when visitors, even those from another BAe site, were treated to a 'proper' lunch."

Those present included Burns, Wilson, Furniss, Wake, Hopwell, Pickett, Walmsley and Arthur Stead from Warton, Geoff Statham from Stevenage, Lock and Dobie from Filton, a representative from Brough, Bond, Scott-Scott and Varvill.

The post-meeting summary was blunt and to the point: "The original objective had been to complete the definition of Configuration G3, its mass statement and performance with updated propulsion data by the end of February 1988.

"In the event, due to ascent and re-entry control problems, unacceptability of the skid main undercarriage and excessive hydraulic system mass growth, G3 will be superseded. The actions were set to define G3 structure, systems and performance as a basis for extrapolation to a new configuration and to provide solutions to the known problems."

Among the actions to be taken were: optimise and simplify intake lines/ramp angles; define component masses for engine ducting; shift the intake pod rearward; redefine propellant system for higher flow rates, larger pipes, reduced dumping, reduce weight; delete OMS engines; shrink auxiliary and collector tanks; relocate RCS exhaust; reduce nose droop; reinstate wheeled main undercarriage; implement liquid oxygen transfer aft-forward of payload bay; add tabs to flaperons; revised 53-degree leading edge sweep delta wing planform with negative camber; flatten fuselage lines ahead of intake; Euler calculations on a 'banana' shaped fuselage.

The introduction of the RB.545-02D apparently increased the amount of oxygen that would come from the atmosphere significantly, which reduced the hydrogen requirement, which in turn meant the fuselage could be reduced in length by 6m.

Burns wrote to Yates about Bond again on February 26: "I have discussed with Alan Bond the latest situation regarding his consultancy contract with Rolls-Royce. Following a recent interview with Dr B. W. [Brian] Lowrie, head of high-speed propulsion at Rolls-Royce, Mr Bond reports that he is now more satisfied that Rolls-Royce are going to put the required effort into RB.545 development.

"He is therefore proposing to renew his contract with Rolls-Royce, subject to assurance that they will put in the required manning at Ansty on design and development of the pre-cooler. I have therefore not raised this matter with Hugh Hillier, nor is it necessary to consider any consultancy arrangement between BAe and Mr Bond. However, should his relations with Rolls-Royce break down, he could be a useful adjunct to the JPT to spur things along."

Three days later, Burns recorded in his monthly report: "A short test programme using the 1:250 scale model SB3 has been carried out in the RAE low density high-speed wind tunnel at Mach 10 to measure forces and moments. These results will be used to bridge the gap between previous high-speed wind tunnel results and Newtonian predictions."

Efforts to progress Hotol's enabling technology were also ongoing. Rutherford Appleton Laboratories testing of carbon-PEEK samples for hydrogen permeability had proven "very satisfactory" but no firm had yet come forward to develop the titanium reinforced with particulates that Hotol required.

At the end of February 1988, it was announced that Leeming had retired as director of the BNSC, having stayed on two months longer than originally planned, and it was not clear who his successor might be.

TAKING TAIG TO TASK

Work going into March concentrated on Hotol's flight control system, recalculations of mass, rear fuselage thermal design and structural and materials research.

On March 15, 1988, Burns felt compelled to send a memo upbraiding Warton's divisional research manager Ian C. Taig: "I understand that at your R&D meeting on March 14, you made a statement to the effect that Hotol was not a feasible project but merely an enabling technology study vehicle.

"This is certainly not the true situation. The Hotol project has strong, high-level backing from Headquarters, notably from the chief executive. While we recognise that in the European international forum we would not expect the Hotol project to be adopted without any changes, it is gaining status as time proceeds. It is true to say that it relies heavily on the successful outcome of enabling technology programmes, but so does any other contender for advanced space transport.

"I would be grateful if you would correct your mistaken impression at any future meetings."

From March 18-19, Hotol team member Alec Davies was at the University of Southampton to assess Hotol wind tunnel tests being carried out in the institution's isentropic light piston tunnel using thermochromatic liquid crystal paint. Two days later, on March 21, Davies, Wake and Phil Varty sat down with Ian Poll, professor of aeronautical engineering and director of the Goldstein Aeronautical Engineering Research Laboratory, from the University of Manchester, at Warton. This was to review a paper produced by Poll on "a preliminary analysis of the bow shock/dorsal fin shock interaction on the Hotol fin". Following on from this, Poll "submitted two costed proposals for consideration for funding under the Hotol Aerodynamic Enabling Technology programme".

The first was the development of a hypersonic shock tunnel at the Goldstein lab which would "produce a facility which would operate at two Mach numbers between 10 and 15, depending on nozzle geometry, with a usable core flow of 0.15m ... measurements would include pressures, surface heating, schlieren and interferometry. Prof. Poll was asked what the chances were of getting funding from the university. He said that it may be possible to get some, for items such as instrumentation ... but certainly nothing like the £77k required".

Poll's second proposal was for an "investigation of real gas behaviour in the interaction between a plane shock wave and an inclined cylinder. This subject would be addressed using pressure and surface heating measurements, flow visualisation and laser holography. The total cost for this is £133k over three years".

Wood met Dr L. Bernstein of the aeronautical engineering department of the University of London's Queen Mary College on March 23 to discuss "Dr Bernstein's prototype laser tracking technique for models in the college's shock tunnel with a view to developing it for use in providing real-time tracking data for our autoland free-flight models for Hotol". Unfortunately, "the conclusion reached was that there would be a number of difficulties associated with the use of a laser but that a microwave-based technique might be more appropriate and should be investigated further".

Another two-day configuration meeting was held on March 23-24 and all aspects of the vehicle's physical layout were examined, starting with the intake. It had been decided that double-hinged ramps would be retained as a baseline because the "single-hinged ramp, superficially simpler, has many disadvantages, additional closure flap, more severe re-entry heating etc." Mass was 5,540kg

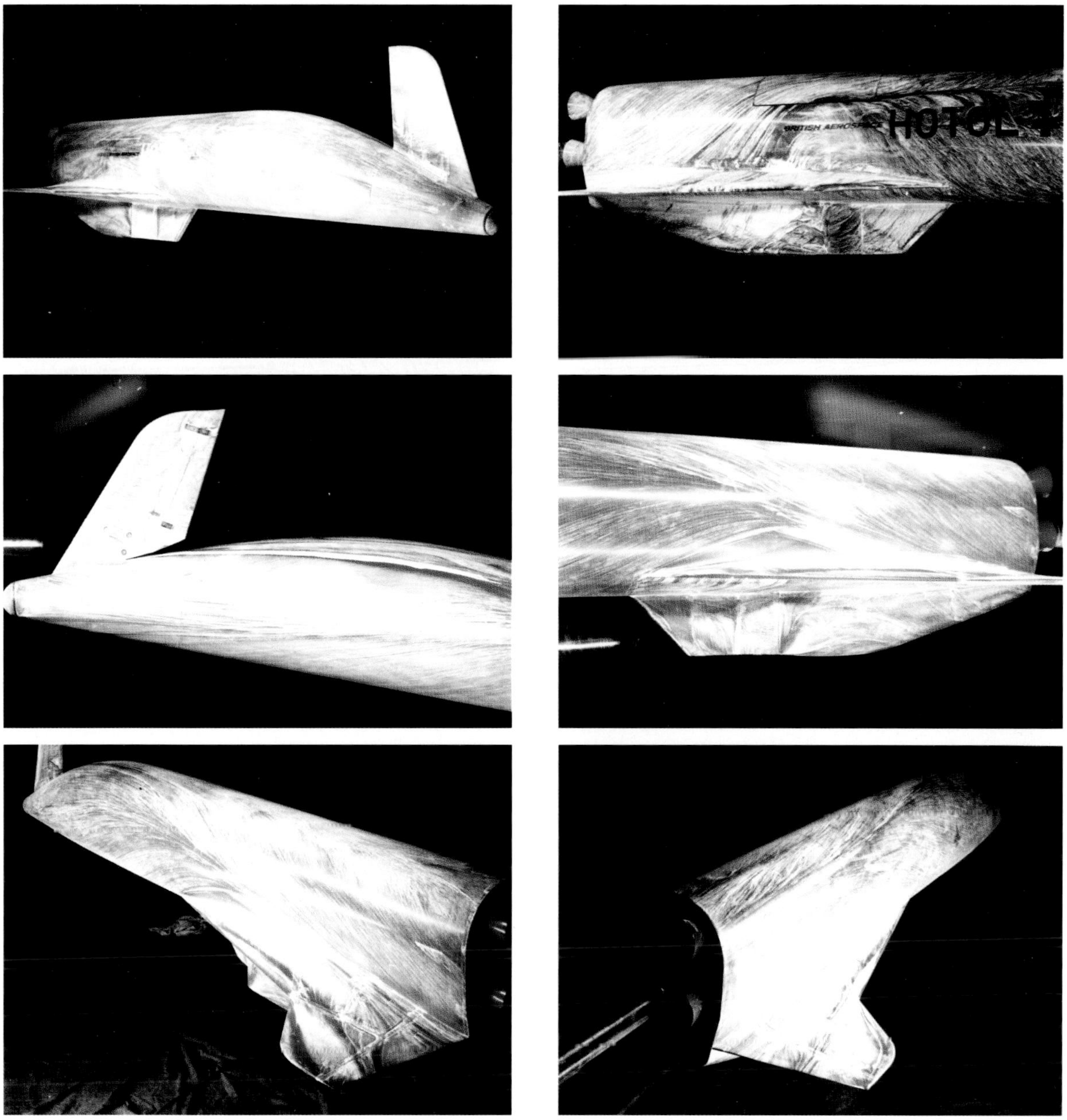

These images are believed to show the SB1 subsonic model, based on Configuration F, being tested at the University of Southampton's isentropic light piston tunnel using thermochromatic liquid crystal paint.

including actuation and gearbox—but not the power units, which were located within the fuselage near the payload bay—with a 13.1sqm capture area. BAe Brough was now developing the intake "seeking improved mechanical linkages and improved pressure balance to reduce actuation mass and ramp loading". A variable divider between the spill ramjet and heat exchanger flows was "deemed to be necessary, to be schemed and weighed".

With the rejection of a skid main undercarriage, Hotol's landing gear had been reimagined: "Warton reported that mainwheel undercarriage located outside intake pod adds at least 3.5 tonnes (250%) to undercarriage mass ... Alternative schemes were tabled with '[BAe] 146-style' undercarriage in intake pod located forward. These involved significant mass penalties elsewhere, either with long piping from relocated propulsion units to rocket motors, or long intake ducting."

Another issue being considered was controlled de-rotation on landing—getting Hotol's long nose down in a steady and controlled way, rather than allowing it to slam down into the runway. The solution proposed by Filton was "to control de-rotation by means of nose-mounted solid fuel rockets". These would be triggered according to pitch rate and it was agreed that they would be adopted with the specifics in terms of impulse and timings to be worked out via simulation.

A provisional Hotol Configuration G4 was to be worked out which would feature a liquid oxygen transfer

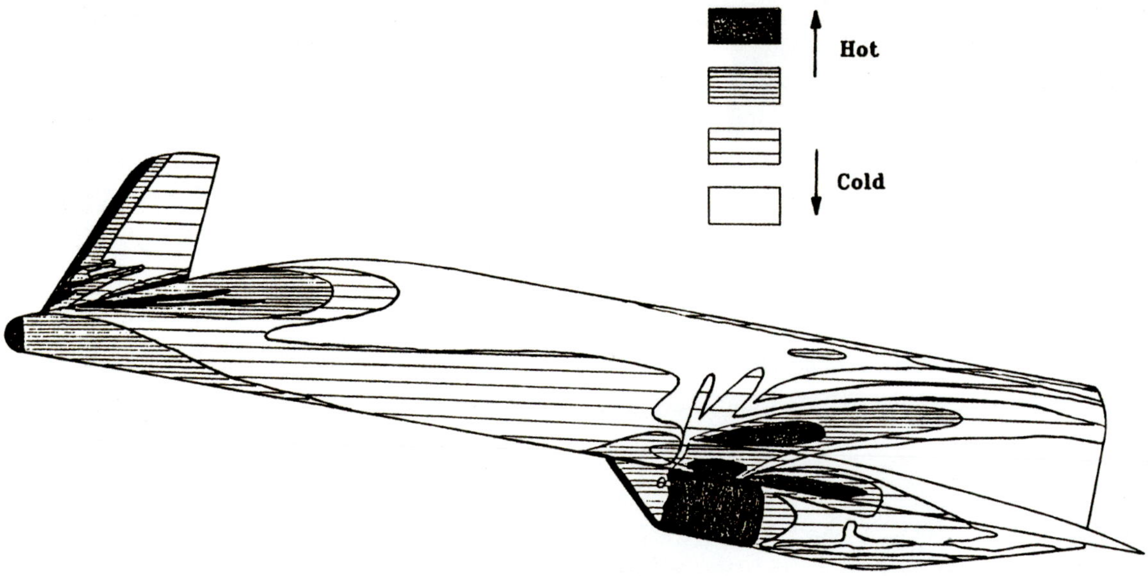

Example of Liquid Crystal Thermograph Results $\alpha = 10^{\circ}$

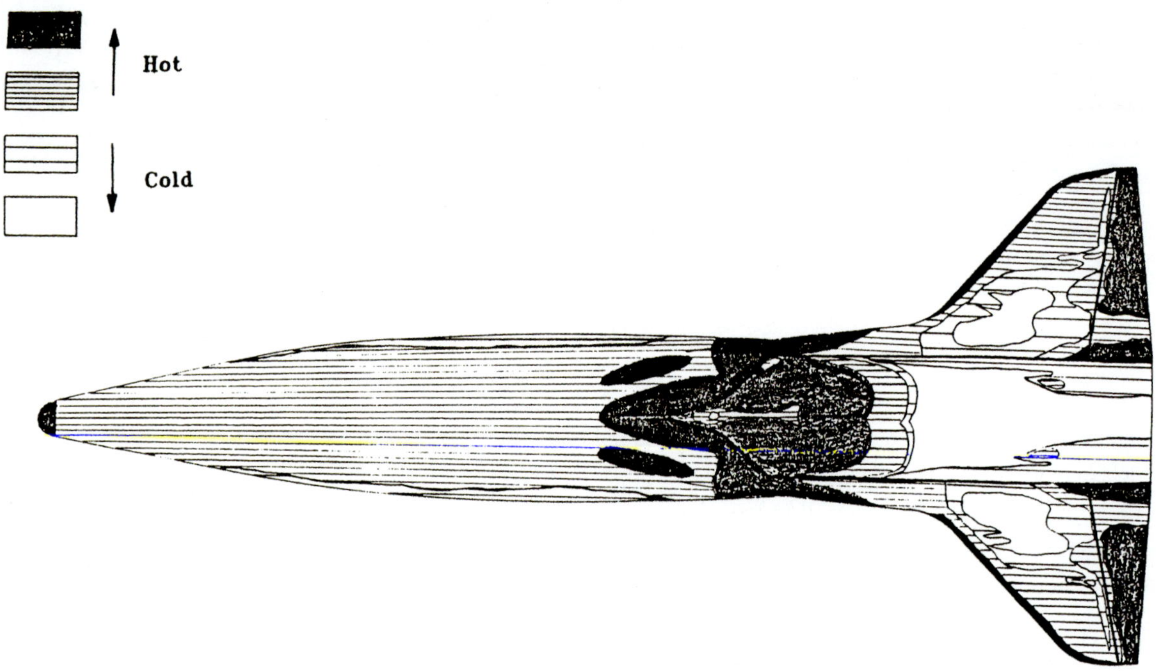

Example of Liquid Crystal Thermograph Results $\alpha = 15^{\circ}$, Flaps = 30°

Diagrams showing example results from tests on SB1 using liquid crystal paint.

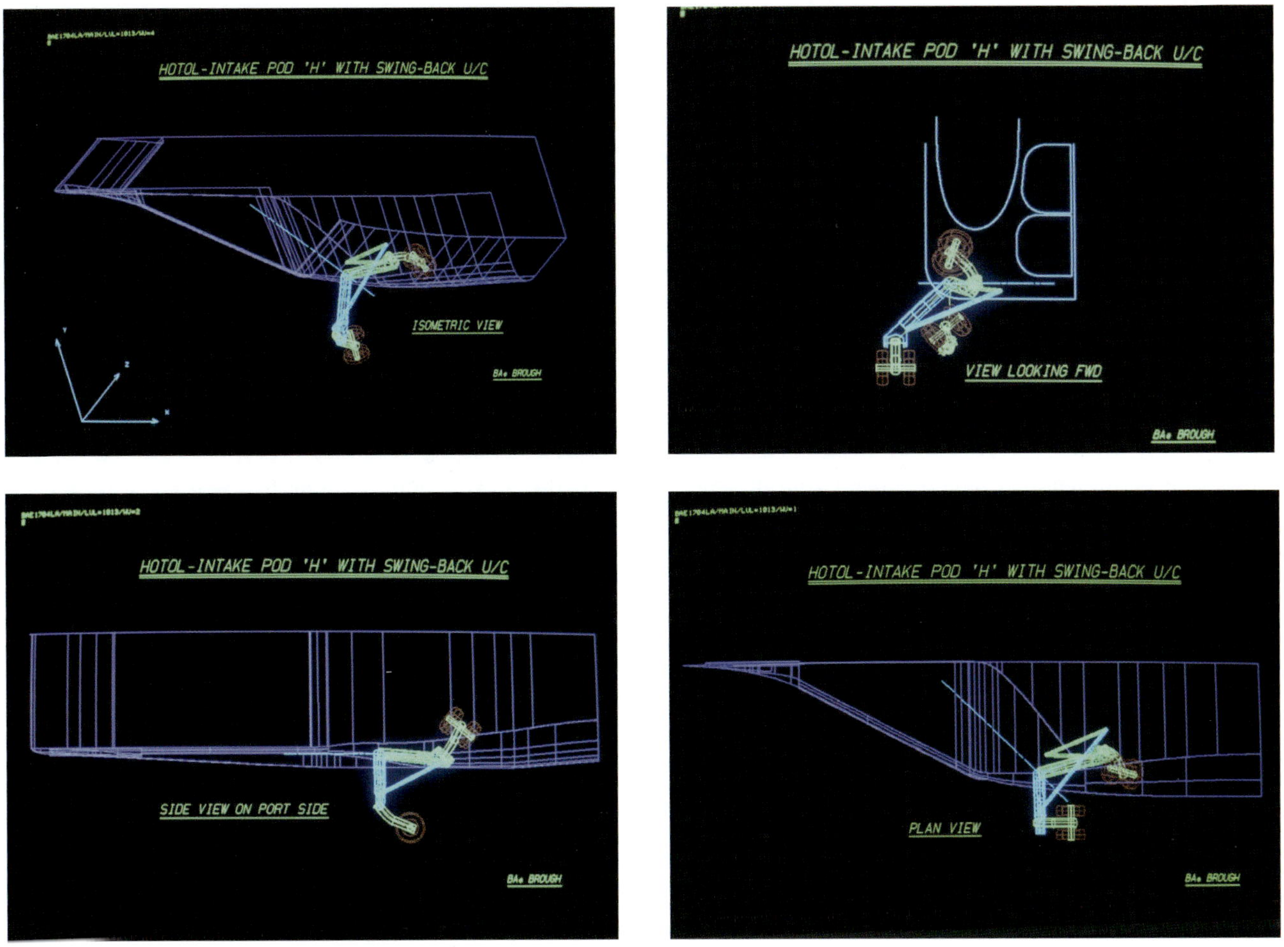

Screenshots showing work done at BAe Brough on Hotol's intake pod and main undercarriage housing.

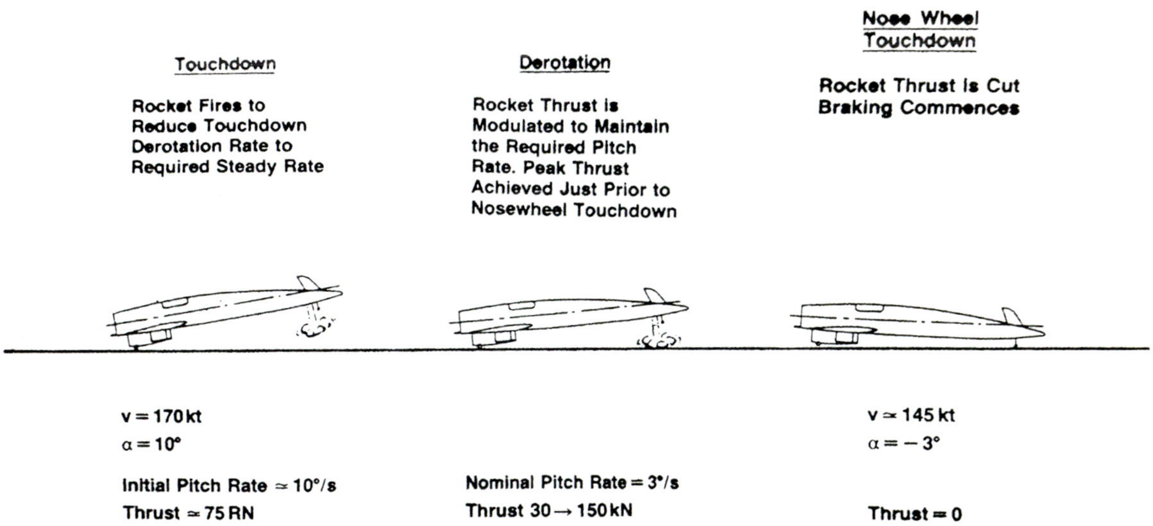

Solid fuel rockets were proposed as a means of getting Hotol's long nose gently down onto the runway during landing.

tank in its nose, 18 tonnes of liquid oxygen specifically for de-icing use, the revised RB.545-02D engine and nose rockets. Warton would also continue to investigate alternative propulsion/intake/tankage layouts. Rolls-Royce, meanwhile, was apparently now adopting an RB.545-03 variant with 12 compressors for reduced development risk. According to the meeting summary this would have "no significant effect on performance or weight. Design installation to be updated but this may be after the end of April [configuration] 'freeze'".

In aerodynamics, Hotol's wing area would be rechecked from a standpoint of controllability, hinge moments and ascent performance. Evidently "flight control system design estimates indicate that levels of lateral/directional instability at ascent speeds are excessive, resulting in insufficient gain or phase margins". It was noted that "turned-up wing tips to be investigated (area/dihedral) to improve both stability terms; should result in reduced fin area requirement, relieving actuation mass also".

The increase in wing leading edge sweep to 53 degrees had now been adopted to reduce aerodynamic centre travel and preserve transonic controllability.

On those same two days a much smaller gathering, Stead, Davies and Puttrell from Stevenage, held a meeting on Hotol Thermal Joint Team Activities at Warton. Among other things, sub-contracting of thermal analysis work on Hotol's nose cone to Hunting Engineering was discussed. Evidently, "Hunting's formal proposal for thermal analysis of the nose area has been received at Warton. The total exercise is divided into two phases of which only the first phase has been costed and defined in detail. This first phase, of three months duration, is concerned with the physical definition of the nose area and deciding upon the methods of heating rate prediction and techniques for the actual thermo-structural analysis".

MODELS GALORE

Wake wrote a memo on March 28 which outlined the full Hotol wind tunnel model programme proposed for 1988 to 1990 including both 'project' and 'enabling technology' models. The former included existing and new scale Hotol models.

Of these, SB2 had nearly reached the end of its usefulness in measuring drag and flow, with SB3 set to continue in use until the end of 1988. SC1 would enter service in mid-1988, followed by SC2—to be used for drag, pressure and intake flow testing before the end of the year. SC3, would then be used to measure heating from around May 1989. For next configuration freeze was due for late summer 1989 and would see the introduction of SD1, which would be used to study the attributes of Hotol's trolley, while SD2 would enter service at the beginning of 1990 for drag, pressure and intake flow work.

The 'enabling technology' models comprised five scale versions of specific parts and sections, particularly the rear fuselage and engines: R122, R123, R124, R125 and R126.

R122 was "multiple cold jets" and would be used starting in February 1989. R123 was "multiple warm jets", starting in January 1989, and R124 was "multiple hot jets (rockets)". R125 was also "multiple hot jets" while R126 was a model of the American Space Shuttle, and would be used for heating tests.

Earlier in the month, Young had written to Burns asking why a Space Shuttle model was needed. Burns had replied on March 17 to say that "the US Space Shuttle is the only [comparable] vehicle for which flight data are available, but of course we have access to limited published information only. So theoretical predictions (for model/wind tunnel conditions) may be validated primarily by wind tunnel results and the same theory used to predict for flight conditions where Shuttle data are available. Up to now we have had no success in obtaining geometric data for the Shuttle. USA seems to be trying to make it difficult for Europe to catch up".

Meanwhile, Walmsley and N. Barker had travelled to the European headquarters of private nonprofit applied science and technology development company Battelle in Geneva, Switzerland, to see what contribution it could make to developing advanced materials for Hotol.

Apparently, "Battelle are involved in testing of the SEP rocket components for Ariane/Hermes, the Columbus space station, development of materials operating in hydrogen and oxygen environments, hydrogen embrittlement, thermomechanical testing of composite and ceramic materials, development of aligned long whiskers in ceramic materials, fracture mechanics of Nicalon fibre yarns, and thermal stress failure of ceramics".

Walmsley gave a presentation on Hotol's structural design, followed by a presentation from Barker on materials for Hotol. The result was Battelle pledging to draft proposals for hydrogen embrittlement testing of carbon-PEEK and for high temperature ceramics testing. Walmsley noted: "They will also give a statement about their service for carrying out probability calculations on Hotol components to give a check for similar calculation carried out by BAe."

Following some discussion "it was noted that PTFE, Teflon and Mylar were very stable plastics in the presence of liquid oxygen, and could therefore be used as liners for the Hotol liquid oxygen tanks".

When it came to ceramic composites, Battelle were already working with Rolls-Royce and evidently "envisage a 'British Club' with the following membership: BAe and RR as users, Courtaulds as fibre and whisker manufacturer, ICI or BP as composite manufacturer and Battelle for carrying out the research on aligned whiskers". This would cost BAe £70,000 a year for three to four years.

Burns met the technical and sales directors of another advanced materials organisation, Materials Engineering and Testing Ltd (MET), in his office at Warton on March 31, 1988, along with Walmsley and Derek Caborn from the Hotol team. MET had facilities able to test materials "for tension compression bending impact, fatigue, fracture toughness, crack propagation and stiffness" up to 1,100°K, soon to be 1,300°K. This would allow them to conduct "standard material tests [which] have a lower priority than the effect of liquid oxygen on carbon-PEEK, permeability of carbon-PEEK to hydrogen and thermal micro-cracking of reinforced materials".

SHACKLETON'S SUPPORT

A day earlier, on March 30, Lord Shackleton had made a lengthy speech on the Government's space policy in the House of Lords. In it, he'd said: "With regard to our own programme, we took the view that we should not contribute to Hermes and we supported the Government in that. For the foreseeable future, space offers enough opportunity for tele-controlled craft for the involvement with man in space to be—at least for the Europeans—an expensive and hazardous diversion. There are scientists who say that they do not want astronauts putting their sticky fingers on their beautiful instruments at this stage.

"Anyhow, it is not necessary to put a European into space. Given that the Americans are to build a space station, Europe is right to participate in that through the Columbus programme. We argued that British participation should be confined to the advanced pressurised module and, subject to certain qualifications, the polar platform.

"We also take the view that Hotol is a long way in the future. The proof-of-concept stage is now nearly complete [sic] and if that is satisfactory, we should press on. The fact that it is a classified patent should not restrain us from allowing our European allies access to it, but I certainly hope that the British will develop this aspect. For these and other reasons we recommended that total national expenditure over a period of five years should rise to £200 million, of which about £25 million and no more would probably come from industry."

Later he bemoaned the "somewhat dry language of the DTI White Paper of last January on spending: 'No increase is proposed'. The DTI is taking a fresh look at the distribution of support for individual European and domestic programmes. There is not much excitement to be found there. And this would be the last criterion that I would add—excitement. From the evidence given to your Lordships' Committee there is one project which commanded tremendous enthusiasm—the Hotol programme. One witness described it as the touchstone to a range of new technologies for Britain in the 21st century. Another witness, no less than the chairman of Rolls-Royce, said that it would require substantial government funding and a positive and long-term UK commitment to space vehicle development.

"That is what we want and need—enthusiasm, excitement and long-term commitment—for even if there is no detectable and tangible commercial justification for Government to make long-term commitments to space research spending, there are other reasons. Simply put, we believe that it is exciting to extend the sum of human knowledge and push out the frontiers of our experience. I know that will be dismissed in some quarters as being old-fashioned romanticism, but I do not think it is the worse for that." Shackleton, however, was a Labour peer and had no power to influence policy.

RELYING ON THE RAMJET

Burns had issued his monthly report to Yates on March 25 but reissued it on April 11 with a note that a number of corrections had been made—and that the earlier version should be destroyed. It largely reiterated the points raised during the configuration meeting and stated that "the configuration is due to be 'frozen' at the end of April for the next study phase. This will embody the ... revised 53-degree delta wing, liquid oxygen transfer tank in the nose for centre of gravity control and turned-up wing tips".

Where propulsion was concerned, which fell outside the remit of the configuration study: "Investigations of increasing airbreathing Mach number beyond 5 indicate significant payload benefits. The investigation will continue, including a transition manoeuvre, effects of hydrogen over-fuelling and liquid oxygen pre-injection to maintain compressor inlet temperature and boost thrust.

"Although payload performance has been significantly improved and is still increasing, it relies heavily on the spill ramjet. Concern has been expressed by Rolls-Royce on having two critical powerplants. The spill ramjet would require special expensive test facilities to prove it on the ground and it will be necessary to show that it is safe to undertake flight proving of this feature."

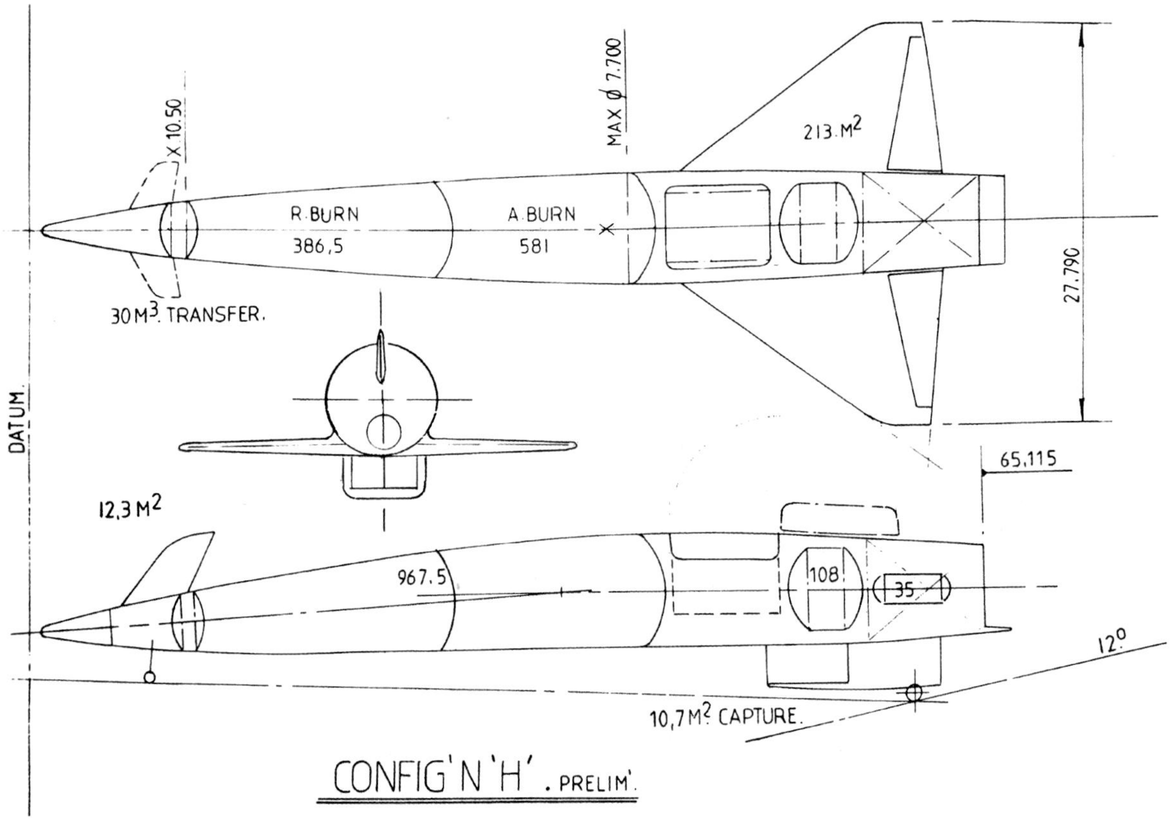

Drawing showing preliminary design for Hotol Configuration H.

The Alternative Launch Vehicle Group had now finally reached the end of the road as a semi-autonomous entity: "Structural definition of ALV 100 wing... is complete and weight estimation is in progress. A wind tunnel programme is being costed. A draft report on the Hotol/all-rocket (ALV 30) comparisons has been received from Stevenage. Some technical disagreements have been registered and these need to be resolved by discussion. The staff working on ALV studies are being transferred to work on the ESA-sponsored Winged Launcher Configuration (WLC) study."

April 18 saw the announcement, finally, of a replacement for Leeming as the BNSC's director—with career civil servant Arthur Pryor now taking the reins.

Three days later, on April 21, Burns wrote to C. N. Cox at Hunting Engineering to say that "we have had doubts about whether your proposal represents the best approach to the problem". In short, Hunting's proposed 'phase one' study of nose cone heating was deemed to be of little value on its own, since it only defined the nose cone shape to be studied and how heating would be measured. No costing had been given for phase two—the study itself. Therefore, Burns requested a new cost estimate covering both phases.

Aerodynamicist Nick Dale produced a draft specification for the SC2 wind tunnel model on April 25, 1988, with the summary stating: "Development of Configuration H has been based on testing carried out on SB2 (Configuration F). Confirmation of the estimated performance will be obtained with model SC2. Validation is required of drag estimates, stability levels, control powers, computational fluid mechanics codes and intake performance. In particular, more detailed information is required on the component contributions to lift, drag and stability than was possible on the earlier model SB2."

The SC2 model was to be tested between Mach 0.5 and Mach 6 in either Warton's 1.2m tunnel or the Sowerby guided weapons wind tunnel. It was to have optional wingtip fins, fixed foreplanes, the capability of mounting an all-moving front fin and a rear mounting point for an optional all-moving rear fin. Three different intake options were needed: closed, open but with fixed ramp position and open with variable ramp position. There would also be a 'body flap', at the rear of the vehicle below the engine nozzles, with four possible settings: closed or angled at 10, 30 or 50 degrees.

This also appears to be the earliest mention of the next major Hotol layout under the designation 'Configuration H'. The following day, Dale produced a second specification—this time for SC1, which would be the low-speed version of SC2. It would also be based on Configuration H but would be bigger, sized for use in Warton's 2.7m and 5.5m wind tunnels. It was also simpler, with only two

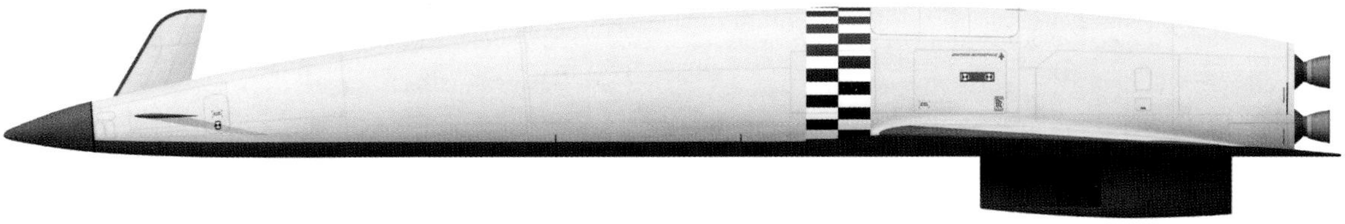

Hotol Configuration H. Chris Sandham-Bailey

intake options: open and closed. In addition, "testing with an undercarriage attached to the model may be required at a later date".

Burns wrote to C. R. Ross, a sales, marketing and PR consultant based in Leighton Buzzard on the same day to commission a very different sort of Hotol: "I understand that you have been concerned, in the past, with the supply of large-scale plastic models to the RAF. We have a possible requirement for a large-scale (about 1:10) model of Hotol to be suspended from the ceiling of a building." Attached to the full letter was a preliminary drawing of Configuration H.

RETURN OF THE FOREPLANES

The next two-day Hotol configuration meeting took place on April 27-28. In terms of performance and payload, Furniss reported that the optimum wing area for ascent had been calculated as 150sqm "but controllability requires additional area (213sqm)". The intake capture area had been optimised at 80% of its earlier 13.1sqm—10.7sqm.

AP Precision Hydraulics in Speke, Liverpool, had apparently offered to undertake undercarriage design free of charge, with slimline wheels and high-pressure tyres being considered to make storage easier. In aerodynamics, the wing planform had been adjusted from a 53-degree sweep to 54 degrees with -1% camber. Nose droop now ranged from 3-5 degrees.

Jettisonable foreplanes, to be dropped at Mach 2.5, had been reintroduced and the size of the forward liquid oxygen tank had been increased to reduce instability at Mach 5. Work continued on the de-rotation rockets in the nose as did work on reducing lateral instability. The meeting summary tersely stated "tip fins nbg"—no bloody good! However, "dihedral from [wing] root possibly to be adopted" and "rear fin study to continue".

Walmsley reported that "the need for ablative leading edges on intake beak and lips needs to be agreed and development included, if necessary, in enabling technology programme".

In his update for Yates on May 3, 1988, Burns wrote: "BNSC state that the Minister for Trade and Industry has requested a Hotol update briefing in the near future. The date has not yet been confirmed." He also described the characteristic features of Hotol Configuration H, now with 54-degree wing sweepback. Another change concerned the airbreathing phase of the ascent, which had been extended to Mach 5.5 with additional liquid hydrogen used to maintain the intake temperature.

With all this, "the predicted payload of Configuration H ... with a full transition manoeuvre incorporated is five tonnes (275t gross lift-off mass)".

Materials programmes had by now been agreed with ICI and Courtaulds for carbon-PEEK; IMI, BP and Alcan for reinforced titanium, and Dunlop, Ciba-Geigy, BP, ICI and Courtaulds for reinforced ceramics. The predicted total spend on this programme for 1988-90 was expected to be around £9m.

Five companies had been visited with regard to artificial intelligence work and three more were yet to be visited, though none were named specifically. Even though the ALV team had been transferred to WLC work by now, "agreement has been reached between Warton and Stevenage on the calculated performance of the all-rocket version of Hotol, ALV 30A". And a possible high-speed wind tunnel programme was being costed for study of ALV 100's wing structure.

On the same day, Burns held a 'materials for Hotol' meeting in his office with representatives of Warton's materials, stress and structural testing departments. This regular briefing was intended to keep those departments up to speed with what was happening with the project overall and this time Burns addressed the issue of finance.

According to the meeting summary, he explained that "DTI funding of £7.5m to BAe for three years for Hotol is the planning assumption. No DTI money has yet been formally agreed, but BAe has been spending its own money since January 1988. BAe will contribute £7.5m over three years to match the DTI funds. In addition, DTI are expected to provide £7.5m over three years to Rolls-Royce and the material supply companies such as ICI, BP etc. and this must be matched by company funds.

"However, present estimates indicate that £9m over

three years will be required for material development with £5.5m contributed by BP, ICI etc. and £3.5m contributed by BAe. There will be further costs after three years."

May 5 saw Burns in contact with Boeing's Lowell Richmond. In a memo, he said he had talked to Richmond about potential subcontracting on advanced materials and structures, computational fluid mechanics, advanced software/AI and lightweight on-board power and actuation system. Evidently though, "the overall impression given was that it would be difficult to find a formula for working".

DEATHS OF BROWN AND WILLMER

In mid-May Terry Brown, head of the Advanced Projects Group at Filton, who had led the effort to integrate Hotol's propulsion system into the airframe, died aged 52 after a brief and courageous battle with lung cancer. This came hard on the heels of another death in the Filton team, Tony Willmer having died suddenly and unexpectedly on March 31 aged 50. Willmer was a specialist in propulsion aerodynamics, compressible flow and thermodynamics.

In a paper to the BIS Spaceplanes History Conference at Cosford in 2005, Wilson said: "Tony's grasp of physics and mathematics was really fundamental to so much that we did in the integration of the propulsion system." Referring to Brown, he said: "Terry's consummate skill was as an Integrator. He could meld all the inputs from a diverse group of specialists and put it together as a solution. His grasp of the technicalities was superb and his ability to take the whole team along with him was second to none."

He went on to recall that "Hotol was a unique project in that the core team across the different sites was quite small and close knit and close friendships developed. As we all travelled around to each other's sites a day's work was often concluded with a meeting in a hotel or pub and other get togethers at Christmas and other times would involve wives as well. The loss of not just one but two members of the team within the space of a month or so was a deeply personal blow as well as a major loss of technical expertise."

Wrapping up, he said: "I would like to close this presentation on the birth and death of Hotol by recalling the tremendous excitement there was in working on it, in fact by recalling the life there was in the project. Hardly a week went by without there being some article in the newspapers, in the technical press or on television (e.g. Tomorrow's World).

"As I said before, several of us were engaged in quite an intensive round of presentations to various groups such as the BIS and branches of the Royal Aeronautical Society, and there was even a private presentation given by Brian Young and Peter Conchie to the Prince of Wales. At its heart, however, it was a small team, fewer than 50 people across the various sites, but work went on around the clock.

"One or two of us used to burn the midnight oil I know and then there was Alan Bond who was always up with the lark cranking away at what in those days was termed a computer, but was probably little more than an electrified slide rule. And then we would be on the road to wherever for one of our frequent meetings, often at RR Ansty which was the most convenient central meeting point from our diverse site locations.

"When meetings required overnight stays, this often led to technical ideas being tossed around until late into the night, stimulated of course by a suitable liquid propellant. Yes, there was certainly life in Hotol and it was the people who put it there."

A PLEA TO KEN

Bond wrote to Clarke on May 23: "Dear Mr Clarke, we are both, I am sure, well aware via the media of our mutual stands with respect to space activity. However, circumstances are such that it is necessary to write to you directly in order that I may be sure that the gravity of the situation of the Hotol project is fully understood by you.

"I have returned today from the funeral of Terry Brown of BAe Filton. He represented probably 50% of the hypersonic air intake expertise available in the UK, having been a veteran of Concorde and other long past projects. Six weeks ago Tony Willmer, also an intake aerodynamicist and Concorde veteran, died in his sleep. He probably represented 30% of our nationally available expertise.

"At the end of February this year Gerald Wilson, the deputy project leader at BAe Warton, demotivated by the lack of prospect for the Hotol project, moved to the European fighter project. He was the only available person with a unique combination of expertise in both airframe and engine technology.

"In April John Scott-Scott, the Rolls-Royce engineer in charge of the RB.545 and probably our last expert on rocket turbopumps asked for early retirement through frustration with indecision. This has been refused I am pleased to say.

"Over the next six years almost all of the people who ever worked on rocket propulsion in this country will retire. It will take 12 years to put the first Hotol vehicle on the runway. Engineers learn their trade by continuity with other engineers. Once that continuity is broken the cost of re-establishing it becomes impractically high and so the expertise is effectively lost.

"By now you should be beginning to see my anxiety. This nation, as I have repeatedly stated in public, is running out of the sort of expertise invested in the people I have cited. When I began the Hotol exercise six years ago, it was horrifying to discover the disaster that 15 years of negative government policy had left. We were rescuing the situation until last year, but we are now losing expertise faster than it can be built up.

"I am informing you of this, not from the viewpoint of a chairman massaging company statistics at the end of a (too) long reporting chain, but as an engineer working with the key people at the creative level. Our current position on Hotol is that we have a completely demotivated ageing team, sat on a vehicle concept which is well ahead of any competition from other nations and which could eventually result in the UK leading Europe into a dominating position in commercial access to space.

"I am attempting to raise capital from private enterprise and I believe there is a reasonable possibility that it can be done. It will, however, take time. If we are to succeed, the project must have government input in the short term. You already have the RR and BAe proposals for the next year and the next three years enabling technology programmes.

"Your approval and release of funding for the first year at least would give the breathing space needed to pursue the commercial routes. Unless this happens within a few weeks, I believe the project will effectively be dead in the United Kingdom.

"I recently saw you in a television interview in which you said words to the effect 'just because somebody invents something, it doesn't mean that you have to go and do it now'. You may be right. I believe in Hotol's case, if you want any British role in the vast returns yet to come from space, you could hardly be further wrong, if only for the reasons which I stated at the beginning of this letter."

Two days later, Bond copied the Clarke letter to Pattie on May 25, 1988, with a covering note which said: "Recently the Hotol project team had a number of ties produced to enhance team spirit. Some of these are being passed to people who have made contributions to the Hotol endeavour and I have therefore enclosed one for you, which I hope you will accept with my gratitude. You are the only politician in the past 25 years who has had the vision to see what those of us working on 'opening up' space are trying to do and who has attempted to enable us to get on an do the job. You have a great many friends in the space business and your retirement from the Cabinet was a blow to us all."

He also copied the Clarke letter to Lord Shackleton with a different covering note: "I am sorry that the Lords debate on March 30 did not yield more fruit but this was certainly not from lack of effort by yourselves. My own life has been chaotic. At the end of March Rolls-Royce exercised an option which they have had for two years to purchase the patent rights to the Hotol engine. Since this was a binding agreement I was powerless to prevent the purchase taking place although I advised RR that I had private funding almost ready. Of course, their purchase stopped that prospect as it was contingent on myself retaining the patent.

"Since then I have been following a new route which may yield private funding to develop the vehicle. I will have more detail of this after the early part of June and will inform you forthwith. Meanwhile the project is in a very serious state..."

Rolls-Royce's purchase of the RB.545 patent could be regarded, at this junction, as the company's first concrete step towards withdrawing itself from the Hotol project, having finally been able to extract this valuable asset from Bond's possession.

ROCKET-HOTOL REVISIONS

Interest in the all rocket Hotol, ALV 30A, from outside the Hotol team at BAe, up to and including Divisional Technical Director Gardner, appears to have increased significantly by late May 1988.

Evidently aware of this, and referring to Burns' statement that agreement had been "reached between Warton and Stevenage on the calculated performance of the all-rocket version of Hotol, ALV 30A", Eric Webb sent a memo to Burns, Parkinson and head of future concepts Tom Smith on May 26 headlined 'Hotol/ALV 30A comparisons'. He wrote: "My report dealing with the above topic was issued in December 1987. Since then... there have been no further studies of the alternative all-rocket vehicle ALV 30A... Consequently the attempts by Mr Burns and Dr Parkinson to revise the ALV 30A mass estimates must be viewed with extreme caution.

"However, I believe that both attempts have overestimated the size of ALV 30A relative to the current Hotol standard—in the latter case by a very considerable margin. The assumption that the Hotol mass increases can be applied to ALV 30A needs considerably more justification... I cannot accept the statement made... that ALV 30A would require an extra 2,000kg to allow for a 'stalky' main undercarriage. This implies that ALV 30A's undercarriage would be three times heavier than that of the equivalent Hotol. In fact, the cleaner underbody structure of ALV 30A (no intakes) simplifies the undercarriage design and is likely to result in a mass reduction relative to Hotol."

After providing further arguments, be concluded: "ALV 30A has an empty mass between 3.5% and 6.5% less than that of the equivalent Hotol—even after accepting mass increases which I believe are not wholly applicable."

A Hotol/ALV review then took place on May 27, presumably with Yates in attendance, and according to a memo sent by Burns to Wake, Walmsley, Stead, Furniss and Hopwell immediately afterwards: "We are instructed to prepare valid engineering comparisons of ALV 30A (HTOL) and ALV 30C (VTO HL) with Hotol. This requires work on aero/centre of gravity balance, hinge moments, drag, stressing and mass estimation. This will inevitably slow mainstream Hotol work; this is accepted." A deadline of June 3 was set for this effort.

Burns wrote a curious memo in Q&A form to Gardner on June 1, critiquing the conclusions of a report on the Hotol/all-rocket comparison. The Qs and As included: "Q: UK has convinced the world-wide aerospace community that airbreathing launch vehicles are the route to the future... A: I agree with the sentiment, but I believe they would be doing it anyway. I am sure NASP does not owe its origin to the existence of Hotol." And "Q: Rocket system has little or no (operational) flexibility... A: Yes (probably). The airbreather ought to have more potential—atmospheric ferry etc. but we have not explored it yet."

On the same day, a meeting was held at BAe's headquarters in The Strand, London, between Yates and Rolls-Royce representatives. Yates "expressed concern over the complexity of the RB.545 + spill ramjet asking: are RR happy with the current design and is an interactive (engine/spill ramjet) optimisation necessary". To which Hugh Hillier apparently replied: "Generally yes, and no." A presentation on the spill ramjet followed, after which it was noted that RR was "asking DTI for £ [in] July '88—one year programme. Heat exchanger rig (de-icing etc.) at Ansty; spill ramjet verification—theory—experiment (at Pyestock 1989-90); support involvement in BAe afterbody wind tunnel tests".

During the discussion which followed, Hillier said that the "RB.545/spill ramjet [is] no more complex than other airbreathers for TSTO/SSTO, e.g. Sänger". Yates drew attention to RR having wrong-footed BAe by asking for only a year-long programme in January 1988, stating that "BAe did one in a hurry to match RR March '88. BAe three-year programme (BNSC request) nearing completion, submit June '88". RR agreed to match this with its own three-year programme "including cross-feed technology programmes 'bigger box' after 1988 to attract greater £ ex DTI. No more RR £ into RB.545". Rolls-Royce's wallet was closed.

HOTOL CONFIGURATION H

Dale and Furniss from BAe Warton visited AP Precision Hydraulics in Liverpool, on June 3, 1988. As mentioned earlier AP, responsible for undercarriage design work on the BAe Hawk, McDonnell Douglas MD.11 and Saab Gripen, had expressed an interest in working on Hotol and during the meeting "their technical and sales director Mr K. Hayter... stated that AP were prepared to commit their own design resources to a preliminary study but would like to be considered in future Hotol funding".

After the Warton team had given a brief presentation on Hotol, a discussion ensued concerning differential braking rather than nosewheel steering to reduce nosegear complexity and weight, likely undercarriage fatigue, whether Hotol could be towed backwards on its undercarriage, how braking during landing could cause heavy loading on the noseleg, and how subsequent noseleg recoil might cause a second period of peak loading on the main legs.

At around this time the full project definition of Hotol Configuration H was published as report HPN 0014. The key propulsion improvements over Configuration G were listed as the RB.545-02D engine with liquid oxygen pre-injection for de-icing, improved thrust and reduced total propellant volume requirement; the spill ramjet with combustion temperature raised from 1,600K to 2,000K; and reduced intake size from 13.4sqm to 10.7sqm capture area.

In aerodynamics, Configuration H had a new cropped delta wing planform with 54-degree leading edge sweep, -1° camber across the total span and 213sqn area. There was also the 28 cubic metre volume liquid oxygen transfer tank in the nose which "allows the centre of gravity to be moved forward during the ascent between Mach 1.2 and Mach 5, 'chasing' the aerodynamic centre shift". In addition, the liquid hydrogen tank was compartmentalised so that the propellant in the rear compartment could be used up first during ascent "reinforcing the forward centre of gravity shift due to liquid oxygen transfer".

The 'droop' of Hotol's forward fuselage had been increased "to alleviate trim at high supersonic speed" although this was "relatively ineffective (detrimental) at transonic speed where wing lift is dominant". The jettisonable foreplanes would be retained "throughout the speed range where they are beneficial to trim, that is up to about Mach 2.5 or Mach 3".

The vehicle's ascent profile had also been changed.

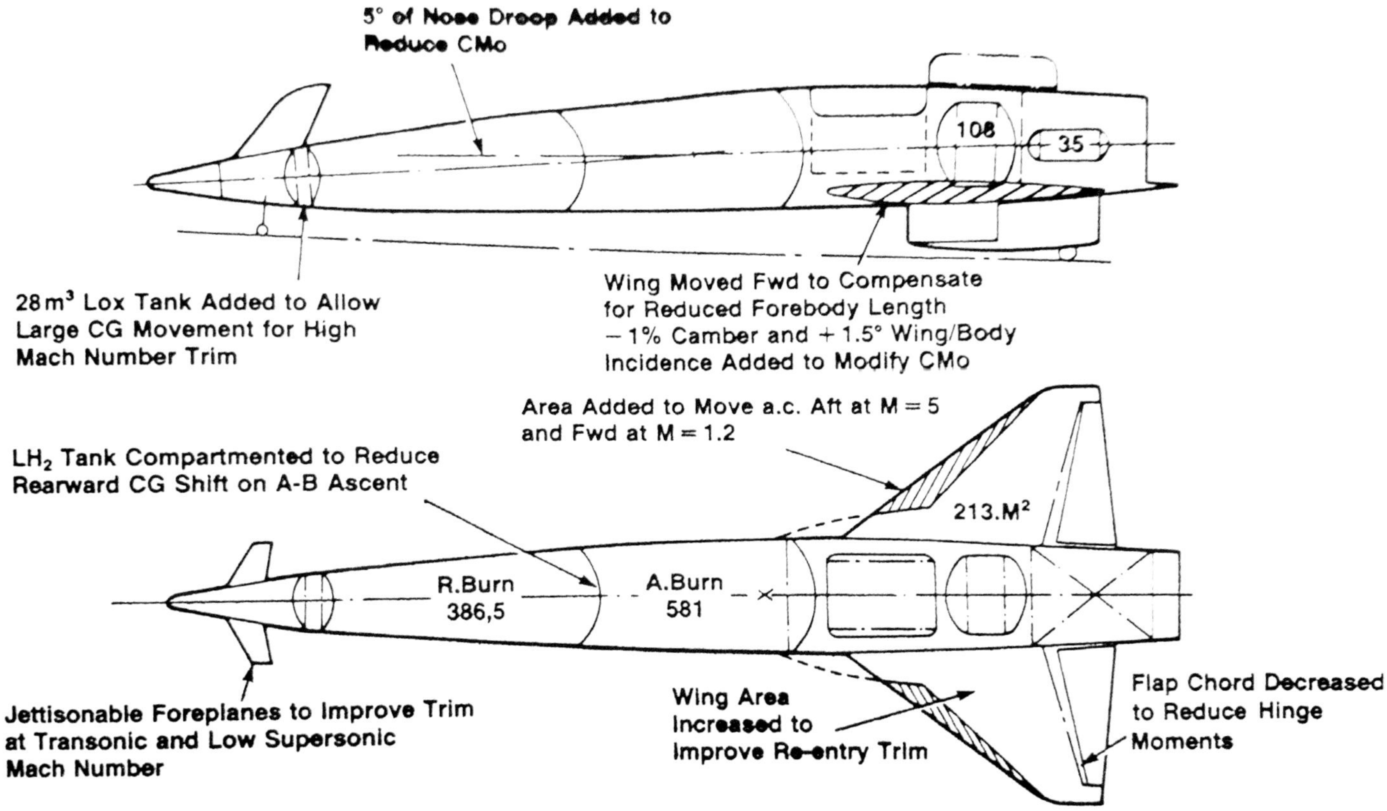

Diagram showing the aerodynamic changes incorporated into the Configuration H design.

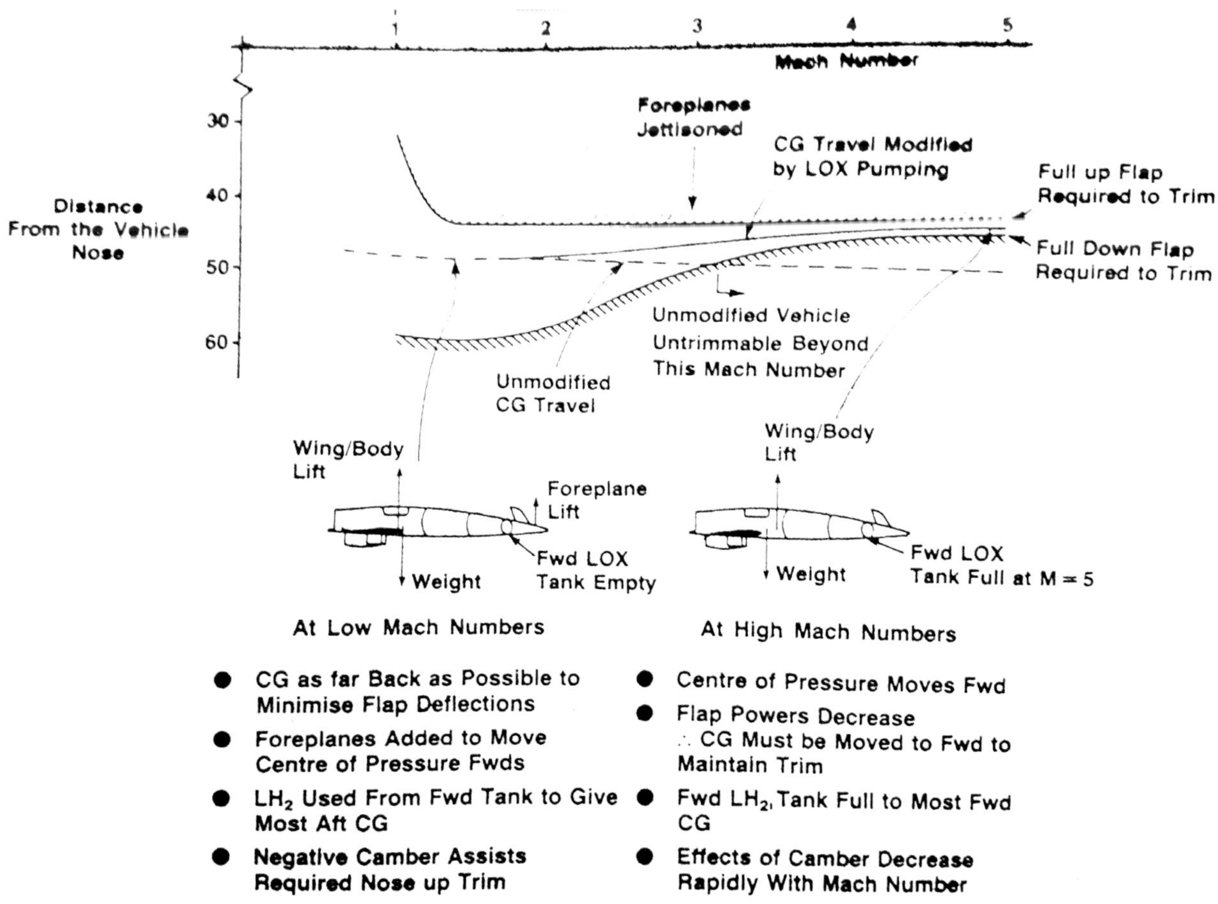

Hotol longitudinal trim characteristics.

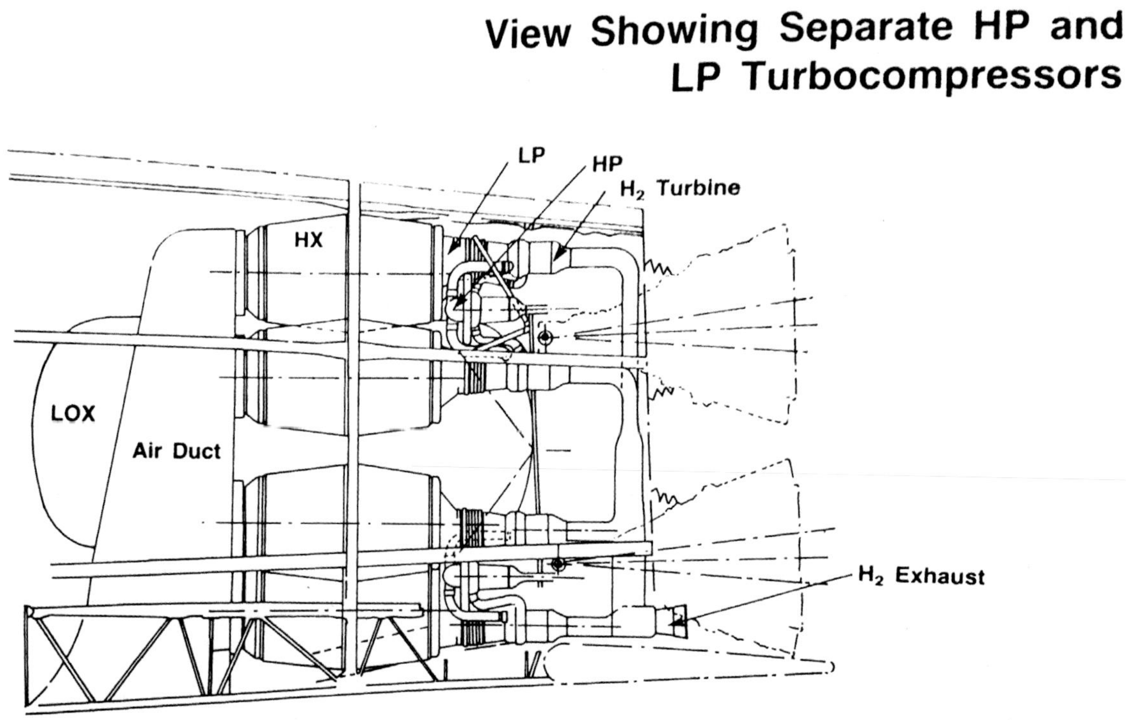

High-pressure and low-pressure turbo-compressor locations. The introduction of the spill ramjet had necessitated a dispersal of both heat exchangers and turbo-compressors.

According to the report: "A subsonic climb through the icing levels was the basis for the reported performance of Configuration G in the interests of minimising liquid oxygen use for de-icing. For 'H', the climb profile has been redefined, going supersonic at low altitude for two reasons: the reduced lift coefficient at the lower altitude in transonic flight, where stability in pitch is excessive, reduces control deflections and hinge moments, [and secondly] the propellant penalty for such a profile is greatly reduced using the 02D engine data. These measures result in greatly reduced control deflections and hinge moments."

Another crucial difference between Configurations G and H was the introduction of the nose rockets: "The current location of the '146-style' main undercarriage is some 10m behind the centre of gravity on landing. This would result in a 'slam down' de-rotation with very high nosewheel and fuselage loads, if unopposed. The proposed solution is to control de-rotation by means of downward firing rockets in the nose, triggered by the landing manoeuvre. The system is to be simulated."

In structural design, the introduction of the spill ramjet and subsequent relocation of the heat exchangers and turbo-compressors was outlined. It was noted that "a diffuser plenum distributes intake air to the eight heat exchangers and inline turbo-compressors. Hydrogen turbine exhaust is ducted into a collector ring with alternative outlets to the spill ramjet and two rear exhaust nozzles. Each propulsion component is self-suspended and self-aligned to its neighbour to avoid transmission of structural loads from one to another, and for ease of individual removal. Each of the liquid oxygen tanks is supported from the surrounding frames by pin-jointed struts which will allow translation and rotation of the tanks relative to structure to allow for differential expansion".

Actuation of the intake was also described. When it came to the undercarriage: "A skid main undercarriage was adopted, provisionally, for Configuration G . . . for ease of stowage and to minimise mass. More detailed studies revealed severe difficulties of stowage and mass penalties, so it was discarded. Investigation of main undercarriage units located outside the intake pod, retracting into the wing roots, indicated unacceptable mass penalties due to the very long legs required. The '146-style' undercarriage has therefore been reintroduced."

With all factors taken into account, Configuration H's realistic payload was 5,000kg. The report concluded saying: "The new Configuration H has been defined with essentially the same payload performance as its predecessor G, but with a much sounder engineering basis. Solutions have been defined to all the problems which had been identified previously and approximations in the performance calculations have been removed."

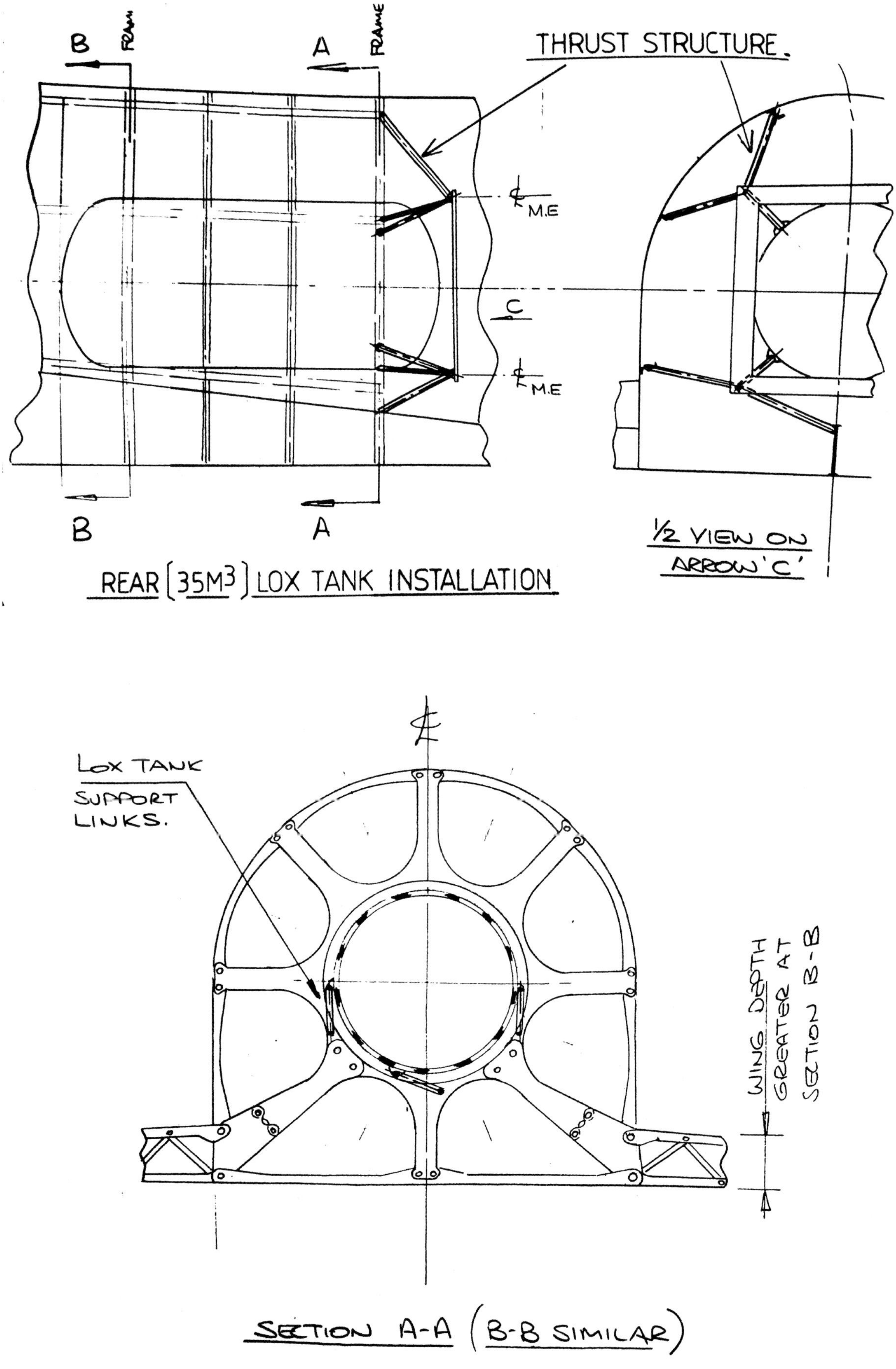

Configuration H rear fuselage structure.

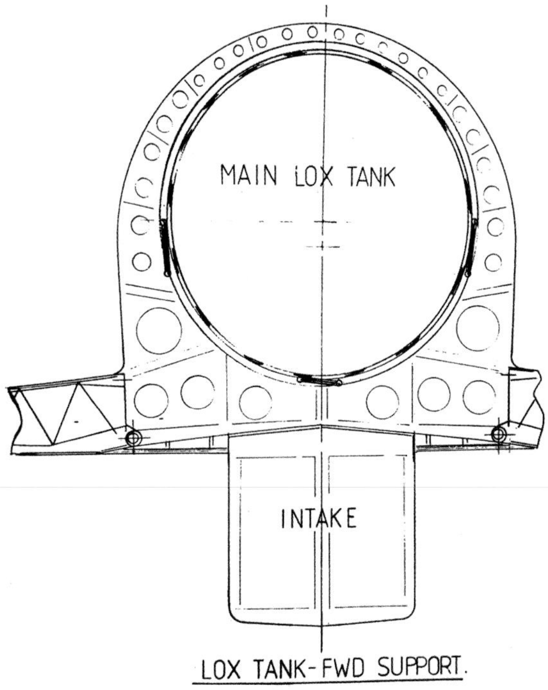

Main liquid oxygen tank forward support above the intake.

ECONOMY MEASURES

Burns sent his regular monthly update to Yates on June 6, noting that "a meeting with the Minister of Trade and Industry has been arranged for June 27, 1988. A paper summarising the commercial and technical case for development of the Hotol project is to be prepared jointly by Warton and Stevenage".

To the rest of the Hotol team he sent a memo headlined 'Economy measures'. This said: "We are instructed to cut peripheral costs by 30%. The question is how?" The answer was to reduce attendance at external courses, conferences and lectures, asking "sponsors for expenses to give lectures at remote (UK) locations". The team were also to "defer long distance calls (external to BAe) until the afternoon [to take advantage of the cheaper tariff] unless urgent. Most things can afford to wait half-a-day. Minimise the length of calls; making notes before a call can help". Distribution lists for reports were to be pruned to save paper, stationery requests "should be for the absolute minimum quantity" and where business trips were concerned, "minimise numbers attending meetings. Avoid overnight stays. Lavish meal expenses will be refused even if supported by bills".

To Young, he sent another memo headlined 'Hotol funding 1988': "Expenditure is approaching the limit of available British Aerospace P.D. funding for 1988, and directives will shortly require reissue to cover the second half of the year. Please confirm that Hotol work can proceed 'at risk' until BNSC/DTI funding is made available."

Francis Tombs and Ralph Robins from Rolls-Royce met with Clarke on June 7 and according to a report on it by Yates for Lygo, "there are conflicting reports". He wrote: "BNSC, Arthur Pryor, indicated that a clear invitation was given to Rolls-Royce, and will be extended to BAe, to look to the US for partnership. This comes from advice given by William Graham, scientific adviser to the US President, during meetings with Kenneth Clarke when it was indicated that there was a perceived window of opportunity before President Reagan departs in October/November [Reagan's two terms were up and the presidential election in November 1988 would see Republican George H. W. Bush facing Democrat Michael Dukakis].

"Ralph Robins said that he was not given much guidance by Clarke, he had heard the message about US

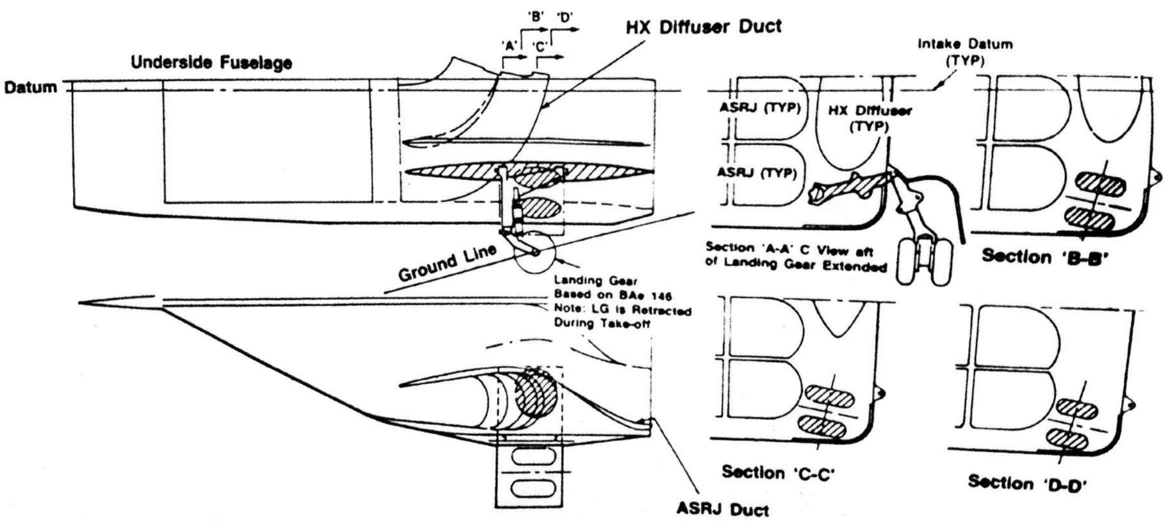

Landing gear housing within the intake pod of Configuration H.

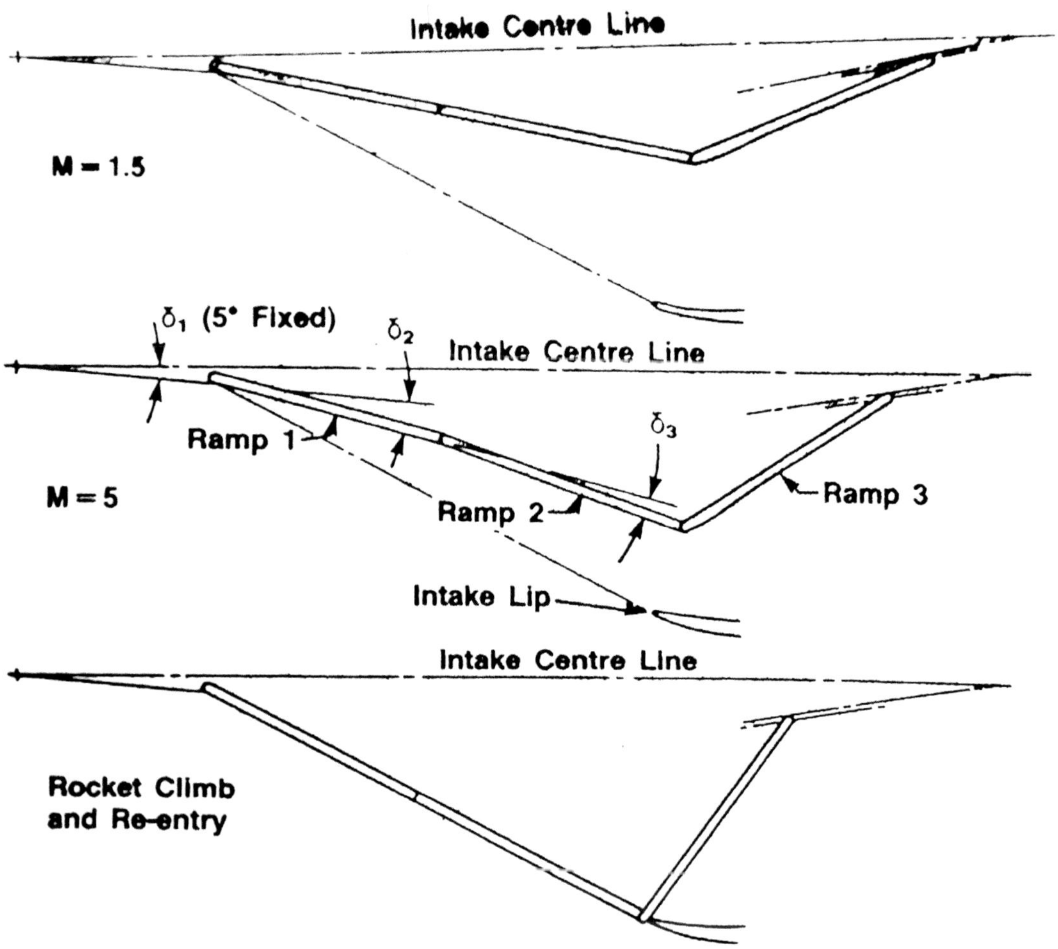

Intake ramp angles schedule—position at Mach 1.5, then at Mach 5, then closed during post-airbreathing rocket-powered climb and re-entry.

partnerships before, and was not taking much action. However, he agreed that declassification of the RB.545 engine would be pursued on a step-by-step basis as being the precondition for any sensible discussions with potential partners.

"Stewart Miller, Rolls-Royce technical director, indicated that Rolls-Royce prefer to work with Pratt & Whitney, and have said so to DTI. Working level activities within Rolls-Royce suggest they are preparing to talk about the total Hotol propulsion package, including intake. I warned Miller that they should be careful as much of the work was joint with BAe and the intake and spill ramjet etc. included our own IPR etc."

While solutions had been defined to all previously identified Hotol problems, there remained plenty of potential for new problems to emerge and such was the case at the configuration meeting on June 9, 1988. The meeting opened with discussion of the intake before moving on to propellant and "Mr G. Statham stated that a further mass increase in the propellant system is expected, although the weight of individual components had not been determined. The problem of the formation of saturated liquid oxygen was not precisely identified due to the lack of a suitable calculation programme, which would require three months to produce.

"The problem could be solved by increase of liquid oxygen tank pressure, incurring a mass penalty on the tank. It was stated also that the propellant system has not been critically examined from the point of reliability and integrity." Statham would now have to go away and investigate to see just how much of a mass penalty this was going to impose.

In aerodynamics, Bond had come up with an ingenious scheme which simultaneously addressed both the need to jettison the foreplanes and the need for a forward liquid oxygen tank for centre of gravity control: swap the tank for 200kg of water which could then be used to actively cool the foreplanes. The drawback was "there would be a mass increase for actuation and power generation which would need to be assessed. Warton agreed to study the proposal … [but] it was noted that this action could not be done immediately owing to pressure of work on the mainstream design and the requirement to study rocket-powered alternatives".

Burns sat down with Yates to discuss ALV 30A and ALV 30C on June 10, outlining a shared Warton/Stevenage study programme which would lead to a full report in September 1988. In a memo resulting from the meeting, he wrote: "It is required that we include the effect on operating costs of main base operations only without down-range diversions, which Stevenage now believe may be feasible. This will allow use of a trolley on rails for take-off instead of a steered trolley. A preliminary design study will be made."

PERSUADING KEN

The Hotol ministerial briefing paper for June 27, prepared by Burns and Parkinson, was submitted to Yates on June 16. Four of its six pages were devoted to a history of the project and extolling the benefits of cheaper satellite launches. Just four rather non-specific paragraphs were given over to the enabling technology, citing "advanced materials and structures for high strength/weight ratio at extremes of temperature; advanced aerodynamics: development of theoretical methods and test techniques notably for the prediction of hypersonic flows; command and control: the production of high integrity software and AI applied to autonomous control of unmanned vehicles; advanced systems: lightweight power and actuation".

The remaining two pages were headed 'recommendations' but rather than presenting bullet point recommendations, comprised instead a lengthy exhortation. It began: "The European Space Industry will not reach its full commercial potential unless a reliable... low-cost European launcher is available. Such a vehicle will require the development of various technologies and, as such, would act as a spearhead, a focus for R&D which could result in important commercial gains for other industries.

"Some examples—advanced materials for cryogenic fuel tanks would have widespread application to bulk fuel carriage and storage. Other materials, developed for high strength/weight ratio at high temperatures, would greatly improve the efficiency of reciprocating machinery. In another field, high integrity software will greatly improve the control of complex industrial operations such as nuclear power stations or oil rigs.

"It is important that the UK participates in these technology gains and we are fortunate that in the Hotol concept we have a potential solution which could be a catalyst for the development of a European vehicle. It is probably unrealistic to expect the UK to play a leading role in such a European programme. Rather we should be seen as good Europeans, providing the guiding innovative approach to a European solution.

"Clearly, the UK should not prematurely limit its horizons; areas which currently may not appear to have significant long term wealth creation possibilities may after a few years be seen clearly to be of great importance. Therefore, it would be prudent to continue to cover a wide field with the intention, after some years, of selling or licensing various technologies which could not be accommodated within a realistic UK contribution. However, for this approach to be successful, other European countries and industries must be brought into the Hotol programme as soon as possible."

Suggested likely partners included Italy, Sweden, Spain and Belgium; "the USA continues to display interest in the programme, but this is probably only to extract information, not really likely to be a genuine two-way collaboration possibility". The same was true of Japan.

The bottom line was, BAe wanted a three-year feasibility programme jointly funded by Government and industry. This 'recommendations' text was the furthest Burns and Parkinson had yet gone towards saying what Clarke seemingly wanted to hear: that there was money to be made from Hotol which didn't depend on the satellite business. But would the cited spin-off possibilities be enough to tempt Clarke, persuading him to approach Thatcher for a reversal of government policy, albeit a relatively minor one, in order to back Hotol?

DARK THOUGHTS AT BAE

Yates wrote a memo to Lygo with precisely that thought in mind on June 18: "A number of sources, BNSC, DTI, Rolls-Royce, seem to indicate that Kenneth Clarke will say that he has no inclination to fund any more work on Hotol, unless we can find some partnership arrangement or come up with a convincing strategy which will change his mind."

He said he had arranged a meeting between himself, Burns, Lygo and Bond, in Lygo's office, for Monday, June 27—hours before the crunch meeting with Clarke was due to take place. He wrote: "We know that Bond sold out his patent rights to Rolls-Royce earlier this year when Rolls-Royce exercised their option. I understand that working level discussions with Bond indicate that he may some time ago have come to terms with lack of HMG support and is beginning to turn his mind to other things, although this is not reflected in his public utterances. The meeting on the 27th should clarify. I also understand that Bond will be prepared to continue as a consultant to Rolls-Royce but on a much reduced basis from his previous 2-3 days per week.

"Internal studies have confirmed that we have a feasible configuration although some more work is still required. Studies of alternative launch configurations indicate that an all-rocket Hotol, although requiring significantly more fuel, is reasonably competitive because propulsion and systems are simpler. I have asked Warton and Stevenage to reconsider the cost of operations and to come up with relative ranking based on latest studies: study probably complete by September. Meantime work continues on the mainstream proposal.

"In preparation for the Ministerial meeting on the June 27, not knowing what was in Kenneth Clarke's mind, I asked Stevenage and Warton to produce a briefing paper addressing the market, the solution, and the way ahead. A copy is attached. Attached to the brief is an outline of the funding level I had planned to go forward to DTI prior to the recent negative messages after our meeting with Rolls-Royce on June 7. Over the next couple of days I will establish what a reasonable minimum 'keep Hotol alive' programme will cost (probably about £1m per year, not included in the current forecast).

"It now seems clear that Rolls-Royce are not prepared to put any more R&D money into the test and experimental programmes, but have agreed to keep theoretical engineering work going. I believe that BAe should continue with the basic configuration work and some hypersonic aerodynamics. I also believe that we can get DTI support for the Advanced Materials Initiative which I presented to the DTI today, June 17.

"On the whole it makes technical as well as political sense to continue 'as we are' until after the SBAC Show [Society of British Aerospace Companies—aka Farnborough International Airshow]. Clearly, we need to discuss this before we see Kenneth Clarke on the afternoon of June 27, and afterwards to think how we may wish to consider European, US and possibly Japanese partnerships with/without the Alan Bond airbreathing engine, or possibly alternative all-rocket Hotol devices."

Clarke finally answered Bond's letter of May 23 on June 22, offering his condolences for the death of Brown. He followed this up with: "I can understand your concern about the lack of experienced engineers available for the Hotol project, but your own fundamental contribution to the Hotol propulsion concept underlines that there are younger and equally enthusiastic engineers always coming along who can bring their own particular contributions. More generally, you will appreciate that I have to take a wider view and make hard decisions between many interesting and innovative projects, so as to achieve the greatest benefit to UK industry as a whole.

"In the case of Hotol, I am in the midst of discussions with the two major companies concerned. In view of what you say about private sector funding I would suggest that you might meet soon with Arthur Pryor, the new director general of the BNSC, so that he can be well briefed on the possibilities as you see them."

QUIZZING BOND

The meeting between Yates, Burns, Lygo and Bond took place as planned on June 27—even though the meeting with Clarke was postponed until Monday, July 18. Rather than there being a dialogue, Bond was essentially interrogated. Afterwards Burns summarised what the BAe team had learned: RR would keep funding engine design and performance estimation but not practical testing; Bond estimated the required enabling technology cost to be £120m and believed "that financial institutions will provide substantial funding if and when the enabling technology gap has been 'bridged'; Clarke was believed to have encouraged RR to sell the RB.545 abroad; oddly, it was suggested that "there is a lack of awareness in Government circles that Hotol is designed primarily for low cost to orbit. The 'Australia in 45 minutes' tag has probably done more harm than good".

Bond wasn't daunted by RR effectively swiping the RB.545 patent since "there are alternative propulsion cycles which could be exploited with another engine company abroad, without infringing the patent" but "the main difficulty in the immediate future is the lack of a heat exchanger rig programme. Alan Bond and John Scott-Scott had proposed a future rig test using a scaled-down heat exchanger with a Viper compressor, driven by a steam turbine as a stepping-stone between the heat exchanger sample tests and the full-scale engine".

In summary it was agreed that Hotol's "prospects [are] as good as ever", that materials and structures enabling technology should continue to be pushed, that DTI funding was still needed "to encourage commercial funding for bridging enabling technology phase" and BAe and Bond could "go elsewhere for [the] engine if RR will not cooperate (Japan favoured)".

July 5 found Conchie, Parkinson and Leeming, the latter in a consultancy role, giving a Hotol presentation to Italian government officials and representatives of Aeritalia, Fiat, Agusta and other Italian agencies in Rome. Evidently this was well-received and "it appears ... that Italian government funding may be available to Italian industry to participate in cooperative tasks with BAe". The next day an ESA WLC study review took place at MBB Ottobrunn in Bavaria, Germany, and "ESA representatives were pleased with the extent and depth of work done by BAe on the SSTO variants. The main conclusion so far is that the rocket/ramjet powerplant is superior to the pre-cooled turbojet in the specified missions and that a payload of about 7t is feasible with a 350t vehicle operating from Kourou in the space-platform rendezvous mission. By comparison, MBB's work on the TSTO vehicles revealed certain inconsistencies and it is felt that BAe gained useful prestige from this review".

LAST CHANCE WITH CLARKE

On Friday, July 15, ahead of the meeting with Clarke scheduled for the following Monday, Yates wrote to Lygo: "It is not clear what line the Minister will take, or indeed why he has asked for the meeting, but there is evidence that he is seeking to disengage DTI from any possible long-term commitment to support the programme. It is possible however, that he will be more sympathetic to a view that we have a game plan which seeks the maximum advantage for UK Ltd but accepts that if we get nowhere after a couple of years, we pull out."

He appended a list of 'fundamentals' for the meeting: that the need for satellite launchers would continue undiminished for the foreseeable future; that studies had shown Hotol was feasible; that Hotol-like vehicles would happen regardless of what the UK did; that new materials, new propulsion systems and new software would arise from Hotol, with the materials in particular offering "good prospects for eventual application outside aerospace"; that international collaboration was needed to make Hotol work; and that the UK Government needed to at least be seen to be supportive of Hotol in order to encourage international collaboration.

Six proposals were suggested: continue feasibility work on configuration and operating costs; confirm enabling technology programme over 2-3 years; continue seeking European partners; keep in close contact with Germany and France ("very likely that France will be looking for a way of escape [from Hermes] within two years due to growth in complexity and costs"); keep watch on US scene i.e. NASP; keep going till the end of 1990 ("BAe £2.8m per year"). And "if a way ahead is not clear by end 1990 undertake fundamental review and if necessary abandon".

The meeting on July 18, 1988, went ahead as planned. Lygo noted: "I met with the Chancellor [of the Duchy of Lancaster—Ken Clarke] on July 18 primarily to discuss Hotol. The Chancellor started by saying that he did not see a great future in his lifetime for Hotol! He was, therefore, doubtful about continuing Government funding but they had had approaches from the United States expressing interest in an exchange of ideas.

"I queried whether this would involve Rolls-Royce alone and he said no, it was intended to be an approach on the whole Hotol project. I said that I thought that the way ahead was in two parts: first we had to continue with the enabling technology so that we were in a position to make a substantial contribution to what had to be an international approach to the market.

"Second we needed somebody to fan this spark of an idea into a flame and I went over the reason why we had invented Hotol in the first place. In conclusion, it was agreed that we would lead an approach with Rolls-Royce, via the Ministry of Defence, for clearance to give a presentation to the Americans which I understand had come out of the Oval Office itself. I warned him that we would need to proceed with some caution and that British Aerospace, through me in particular, would wish to be involved since I had a worry that unless there was sufficient emphasis from the top we might lose the initiative altogether. He agreed."

The only Hotol-related actions arising from the meeting on the BAe side were for "Yates to pursue the Hotol requirement with regard to the MoD clearance and the acceptance of an invitation to make a presentation to the Americans and he should also expedite conversations with our potential Italian and German partners, while I discuss the matter with H. Matre [presumably Aérospatiale president and director general Henri Martre] when he visits later this week."

Yates produced a brief post-meeting memo for Young and Burns on July 21. Under the title 'Hotol The Way Ahead', it said: "Sir Raymond Lygo and I met with Kenneth Clarke on Monday, July 18, Roy Williams, DTI and Arthur Pryor, BNSC were present. We agreed to the Minister's proposal that an approach should be made to the Americans, in response to an earlier approach as indicated in my memo of June 18.

"I agreed with Sir Raymond that I will be responsible for organising the approach to the US, and lead the team. I have approached Rolls-Royce, speaking to Stewart Miller this morning, and in principle they will a) support declassification of the powerplant, b) come along in partnership to discuss Hotol.

"We agreed that we expected to brief NASA and DARPA, but do not wish US industry to be present. I anticipate that we need to achieve this briefing during the period mid-September/end of the first week in October. Ralph Robins/Stewart Miller will feed back any information after a visit by Kenneth Clarke to Rolls-Royce on July 22."

He requested "any technical points (including aeroelastics) covered by various/recent (reviews); ALV study; the operating costs model; any comments from Alan Bond to form a presentation we think might be appropriate for NASA/DARPA. I leave it to you to make the necessary arrangements with Rolls-Royce, you decide if separate or joint meetings are best.

"I will continue to head up the European initiative, having raised the matter with Dr [Erich] Riedl [German Secretary of State to the Federal Ministry for Economic Affairs and Energy] during his recent visit. Dr Riedl agreed he would contact [Heinz] Reisenhüber on his return to Bonn. However, I would be grateful for any early summary of contacts with MBB, Dornier etc. as well as AIT (who could be significant players in an early initiative) also recent work on relevant EFA contacts".

Lygo wrote to Clarke on July 21, saying: "Since our meeting to discuss Hotol, I have taken the following actions: I have raised with Dr Riedl the question of German participation and this he is going to take up in Bonn. Mr Yates has had preliminary discussions with Rolls-Royce with a view to opening discussions in the United States along the lines you suggested. We will be approaching our Italian partners, Aeritalia to seek their views on joining with us in pursuing the next stage of Hotol development.

"Until we have a clearer view of the possibilities of extending an opportunity to European partners to collaborate, and before we have a clearer idea of what the American objective might be, I believe it important that we continue to preserve our interests in Hotol and, for our part, we are prepared to continue the funding arrangements which have been in place. Certainly, I do not believe that any decision should be made other than to proceed, pending the reaction we get from the moves we are now making. Any weakness that we were to display now, as regards our resolution for carrying this thing forward, would be a bad basis upon which to seek collaborative partners."

AND THIS DECISION IS FINAL

Lygo received his response from Clarke in the form of a written reply to a question in the House of Commons on Monday, July 25, 1988, asking "the Chancellor of the Duchy of Lancaster when he expects to come to a decision on prospects for Hotol; and if he will make a statement". Clarke wrote: "The Government provided 50 per cent funding to enable proof of concept studies of Hotol to be carried out. These studies were completed earlier this year since when the two main companies involved, Rolls-Royce and British Aerospace, have been analysing the results. I have since held further talks with the companies.

"The scale of funding required to develop Hotol or any similar concept to eventual production would be far too great for the United Kingdom to contemplate on a national basis, particularly since only a relatively small number of such launch vehicles are likely to be required. I have, therefore, concluded that any further development must take place on the basis of international collaboration.

"The Government will be supporting efforts by United Kingdom companies to find suitable collaborators, but will not be providing any further financial support for the foreseeable future. In the meantime, I expect the United Kingdom, as an ESA member and a participant in earlier Ariane programmes, to have reliable access to ESA launchers which promise to be competitive throughout the 1990s."

This was Clarke's last day before being reshuffled away from Trade and Industry, to become Secretary of State for Health. Condemning Hotol was essentially his last act as Chancellor of the Duchy of Lancaster.

Lygo wrote to Lord Young two days later: "I am writing to you given Kenneth Clarke's movement from the Department and because of your knowledge of Hotol that will not as yet be shared by Kenneth's successor. It will come as no surprise to you to learn that British Aerospace is very disappointed at the statement made in the House of Commons on Monday, particularly since I had written to Kenneth Clarke last Thursday asking that no final decision be made pending the agreed attempt we were to make to look for partners, which I had discussed with him.

"The announcement, coming as it does before Farnborough [Airshow, taking place from September 4-11, 1988], could not have been worse timed. It is bound to attract a great deal of unpleasant publicity since our plans for promoting Hotol at Farnborough are too far advanced to be cancelled. I would welcome an opportunity to run over our plans with you—if necessary you could receive a small presentation. Our problem is simply that, without some indication that the Government would be prepared to support us within a collaborative venture with another company—which will almost certainly be supported by its government—we are in an extremely weak position. There has never been any suggestion that the UK should fund this enterprise alone. All we were seeking was continuing seedcorn to get us to a position where we could attract satisfactory partners."

In making such a definitive decision on Government funding for Hotol on his way out, Clarke had dealt the project a severe blow. Quite why he chose to stick the knife in at this late stage remains unclear to this day but without financial support from the British Government, the chances of BAe and RR attracting international partners for the project suddenly became exceedingly slim. Yet painful as it was, this was not the end.

9

OUTSTANDING ITEMS OF WORK: JULY 28, 1988 TO JUNE 11, 1989

A MYSTERIOUS ARTICLE appeared in the *Daily Express* of August 17, 1988, under the headline 'The 10,000mph dream is cleared for take-off'. The piece, attributed to Compton Miller, began: "For British inventor Alan Bond it is the grand obsession that has wrecked his marriage and almost given him a nervous breakdown. But now his plan to revolutionise space travel in the 21st century has been rescued by a City consortium.

"A vital £120 million will be injected by the consortium to enable Bond to go ahead with Hotol, his horizontal take-off-and-landing space launcher that he has developed with British Aerospace and Rolls-Royce. It is an amazing triumph against all the odds for the brilliant 44-year-old Bond..."

No further details of this unidentified 'consortium' were revealed. Bond himself was quoted in the piece, describing Thatcher as "unspeakable" and saying that "the British government is abysmally poor at providing funding for brilliant inventions. I don't think that it will help now. It's up to the private sector".

In fact, variants of the same story had appeared in more than a dozen local newspapers across Britain the day before.

Burns had clearly been unaware of any private sector funding when he wrote his July briefing notes for Yates, sent on August 10: "Following the statement by the Minister of Trade and Industry on July 25, reassessment of future programme priorities is in progress ... the major worry concerning the future of the project is the extent to which Rolls-Royce will continue to support engineering and performance studies. It is possible that this support could be withdrawn after completion of mass and performance definition of the current variant of the RB.545."

This was the RB.545-03 and it apparently had a firmer engineering basis than its predecessor, Burns writing that "there has been some minor deterioration in performance attributed to 'injection of reality' and this also involves increased liquid oxygen usage. The influence on payload for Hotol has not yet been assessed due to concentration of effort on the ESA WLC study".

Tests on the SB3 model at the University of Southampton had been completed and assessment of the rocket-powered Hotol alternatives was nearing completion.

THE CARROLL CONNECTION

Bond's prospective Hotol financial backers would turn out to be Carroll Group, a family-owned property development organisation run by wealthy 37-year-old businessman Gerald Carroll. An initial meeting between Carroll's front man Derrick Collier, who was the ex-managing director of Plessey Airports and a current board member

British Aerospace publicity artwork featuring Hotol Configuration H—which lacked the wing strakes of Configuration G but retained its upper rear fuselage curve, a feature deleted from the subsequent Configuration J.

of Carroll-owned FADC, and representatives of BAe and RR took place on August 24.

However, according to an unpublished paper written by Bond in November 1988, "Carroll [himself] chose to remain anonymous until 'in principle' interest had been expressed by the aerospace companies".

In his paper, Bond explained that Hotol had come to Carroll's attention as a result of the media coverage surrounding Bond himself and Clarke during October 1987 around the time of the IAF Conference in Brighton.

Subsequently, "in November 1987 a meeting took place between Gerald Carroll and Alan Bond at Carroll's invitation to explore the possibility of Carroll helping the Hotol project through its current problems by providing some private funding. Carroll had made BAe aware of this approach.

"The conclusion at that time was that private funding, even on a limited scale, would weaken the case being made for strong government support which was the aerospace industry's traditional funding source. It was agreed to await the outcome of negotiations between BAe, RR and the UK Government.

"During the first quarter of 1988 Alan Bond became convinced through his own information sources that Government funding for Hotol was unlikely and after convincing himself by analysis and dialogue with a range of financial groups that privately funded development of the project was a possibility, he contacted Gerald Carroll in March 1988 to re-explore his potential contribution to a private sector venture. A meeting subsequently took place between Carroll and Bond in June 1988 to examine several options.

"The announcement in the Commons by Clarke on July 25, of the Government's decision not to find further resources for Hotol led to a further meeting between Carroll and Bond in early August 1988. It was decided to attempt to interest BAe and RR in a joint venture activity with the Carroll Group, in which the Carroll Group would play the role of establishing the private sector funding from UK sources."

This was the origin of the £120m figure quoted by the *Daily Express*. As a result of the August 24 meeting, "cautious expressions of interest were received from all parties" but nothing happened and "the follow-on meetings … failed to take place, for various reasons". This was not quite the last that would be heard of Bond's Carroll Group investment plan, however.

AMERICAN DISINTEREST

Perhaps in line with Clarke's directive to seek partners in the US, Conchie, Burns and Nicholas from the BNSC met with a 'US contingent' on September 8, 1988. The Americans were NASP Wright-Patterson project manager Dr Bart Barthelemy, NASP Joint Program Office NASA deputy director Howard T. Wright, Paul Czysz from McDonnell Douglas, Robert Gulcher from Rockwell International and Colonel T. J. Bishop from the USAF.

Summarising the meeting, Conchie wrote: "This team, it transpired, was making a quick visit to Europe to explore common interests in aerospaceplanes and possibilities of collaboration in research programmes (one day in the UK, France and Germany). I arranged the meeting with A. D. Zinn and Gulcher (Rockwell) following contacts I made with them in LA earlier this year. Their travel arrangements, and therefore the meeting, were uncertain up to the last moment, indicating I believe, some uncertainty in Washington as to the value of the visit.

"A very extensive discussion took place on the position of UK and Europe to possible cooperation on an aerospaceplane. This is driven by the uncertainty of funding for the NASP and the thought that each could help the other, 'they are doing it—so should we?' and saving cost by shared research programmes. Some time was spent in bringing them up to speed on Space in Europe (Bishop and Czysz wondering why Europe could not rely on the US, as they do for civil aircraft! Barthelemy and Gulcher were much more realistic).

"I was surprised to learn that Dr [William R.] Graham, President Reagan's science advisor had already mentioned collaboration when last in London, presumably with John Fairclough [chief scientific advisor to the UK government], and they had some expectation of useful discussions during the visit of Robert Atkins [MP] in late October. I advised the need for staff work and (to C. Nicholas) for HMG to signal their interest in Hotol before the visit. We discussed the possible areas of collaboration … i.e. tank design and test including materials and special systems, heat exchangers, which would involve RR.

"In further discussion an aspect was touched on that I had raised last year with the Office of Science and Technology Policy (Dr Tom Rona) of the US putting money into Hotol as an insurance and in return receiving a vehicle as payment. No enthusiasm, but not perhaps forgotten."

ZERO PAYLOAD

Two days later, Burns sent his latest briefing to Yates and failed to mention the Americans. He similarly made no mention of Bond and his private sector consortium. What he did have to say, however, was quite shocking.

After acknowledging that BAe had agreed to fund Hotol work for the second half of 1988 to the tune of £1.9m, he recounted a meeting on September 2, 1988, at BAe HQ in front of Yates and senior directors where diagrams had been used to illustrate the payload performance of Hotol versus the rocket-powered alternatives. He wrote: "Whereas the predicted payload of Hotol G3 (Dec 1987) and H (May 1988) was about five tonnes at the nominal gross lift-off mass of 275 tonnes, significant mass growth has resulted in near zero payload on the current prediction".

In other words, the five tonnes previously available for use in carrying payload into space had just been almost completely swallowed up because recalculations had shown that the vehicle would be heavier than predicted in five areas: the rear fuselage was 2.5 tonnes heavier, the wing 0.5t, front fuselage 0.9t, cryogenic insulation 0.4t and propellant supply 0.3t. A total of 4.6 tonnes.

This mass growth had resulted from structural and engineering studies which updated earlier computer-generated data.

Additionally, under 'rocket-powered alternatives', he wrote: "Whereas the data presented at the December 1987 review on ALV 30A and 30C showed similar payload performance to Hotol at the same gross lift-off mass, and superior performance … the current predictions show inferior payload at the same gross lift-off mass … i.e. a bigger deterioration for the rocket-powered variants by comparison with Hotol. This is due to more realistic mass estimates, based on detailed engineering studies over the past three months. No further work on the rocket-powered alternatives is to be undertaken during the remainder of 1988, all effort being devoted to recovery of payload on Hotol."

Whether Bond derived any sense of satisfaction from the realisation that he had been right all along about the rocket-only SSTOs is unrecorded. Indeed, Burns went on to write: "A report on the study of SSTO vehicles designed to the ESA [WLC study] specified space platform rendezvous missions shows that a 350t vehicle, essentially a 'stretched' Hotol, powered by rocket ramjet, will accomplish the mission operating from Kourou with a payload of 7t …

HOTOL H CONFIGURATION

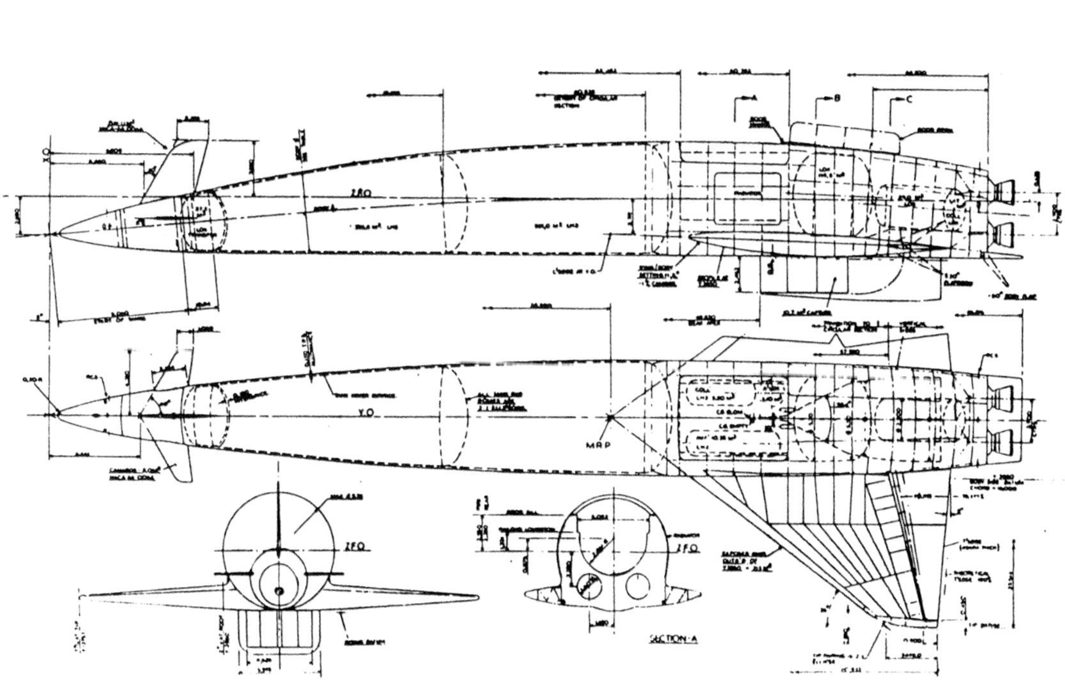

Fully detailed drawing of Hotol Configuration H.

"Substitution of the RB.545 in place of the rocket ramjet resulted in reduction of about 25t gross lift-off mass for the Kourou mission with a 7t payload. The latter figures do not form part of the contractual obligation and will not be reported but serve to illustrate the superiority of the RB.545..." He qualified this, however, by pointing out that the figures were based on the same computer data used in creating the 'five-tonne payload' Hotol Configuration H.

Meanwhile, a meeting had been held at Warton with representatives of French company Le Carbone who were "offering to supply sample panels and leading-edge components in carbon-carbon, carbon-silicon carbide and silicon carbide-silicon carbide for a total of £100,000. This represents a change of attitude by the French, but no order is being placed at present until the funding situation is clarified".

Following on from this, representatives of another French company, SEP, had now also visited Warton. They offered to share details of their advanced materials—as long as BAe would sign a confidentiality agreement. They "also mentioned that they had recently visited Japan and that the Japanese are gaining a lead over Europe in the field of advanced materials development".

THE WLC 'HOTOL'

Phase 1 of ESA's WLC study concluded with a presentation by 30 specialists at Noordwijk in the Netherlands on September 22-23. Furniss reported in a memo to Young that "the BAe presentation was generally well received. ESA/ESTEC had two reservations. The first was that the vehicle was not a trimmed vehicle. Since ESA/ESTEC were not aware of the difficulties in trimming these vehicles and the resolution of this problem has become a major configuration driver, a brief discussion was included in the BAe presentation.

"It was explained that this was a difficult task which at the beginning of Phase 1 had been agreed could not be addressed in the time scale and funding level of this study. Although in their presentation, MBB claimed their vehicle to be a trimmed vehicle, two questions (by the writer) showed this not to be the case.

"The second reservation was on the simulated representation of the vehicle ground track to meet the launch window constraint. The current CAPS system cannot directly model the ground track. The reservation was justified and an ESA-sponsored rider study (= £12,000) was accepted to identify the optimum ground track."

ESA had stated that BAe's SSTO design "appeared comprehensive" but that MBB's TSTO vehicle was "'woolly' at best". Furniss went on: "In a private conversation with [Heinz] Pfeffer (head of ESA Future Launcher Office) he indicated that his main concern was to ensure that MBB and BAe had sufficient technical capability to present an independent opinion to counter any future 'steam rolling' by the French on the optimum solution

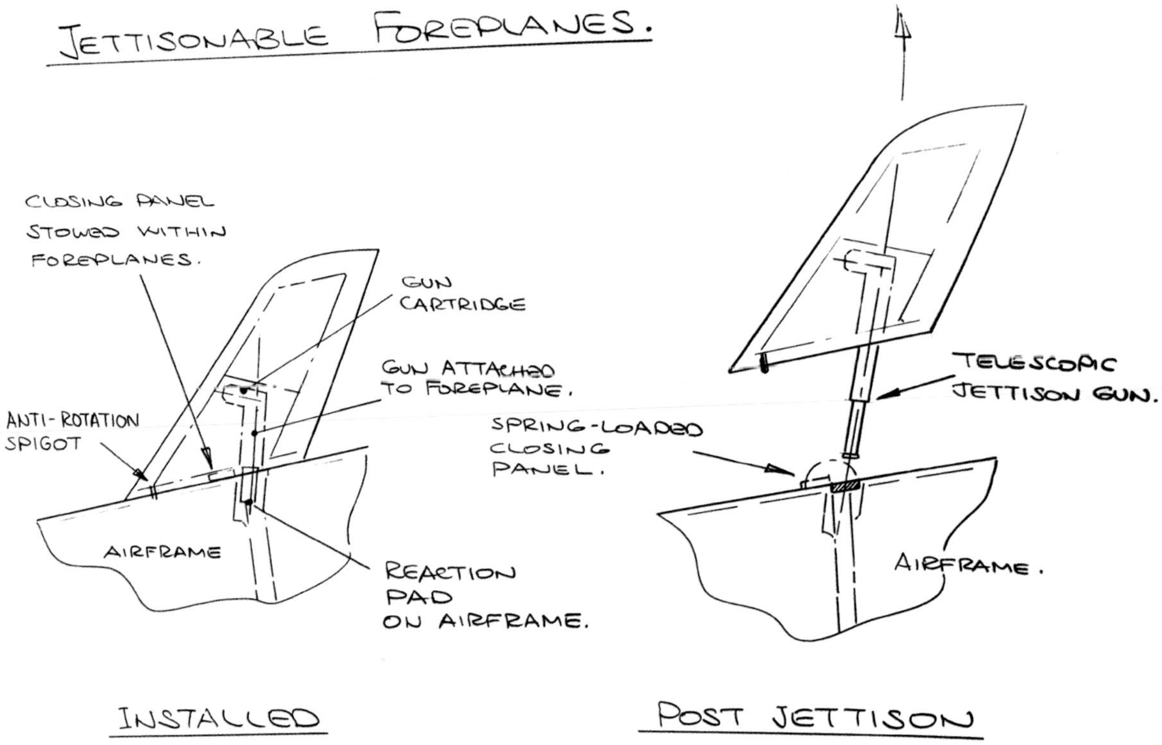

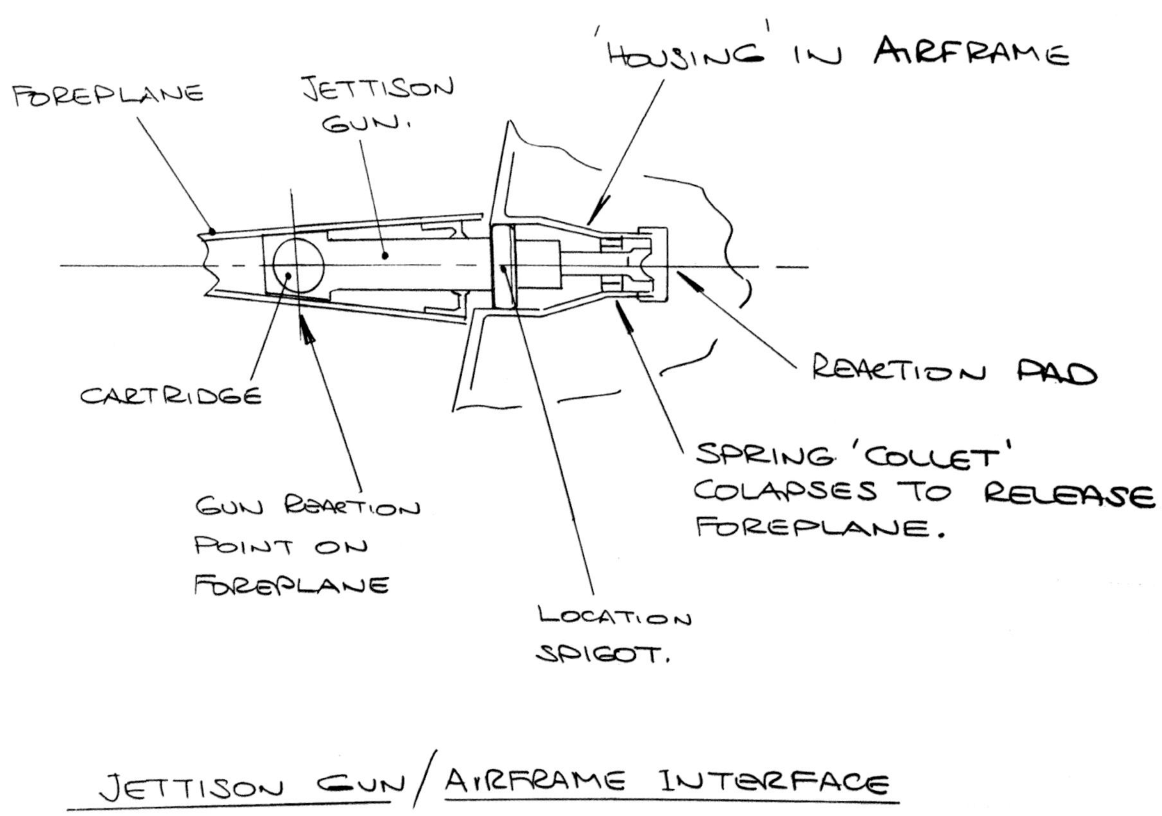

Design for jettisonable foreplanes—including cartridge-operated 'jettison gun'.

for future launch vehicles (i.e. he did not want another Hermes!)."

Pfeffer had wondered whether BAe and MBB could "come to some form of agreement as to the way forward (Hotol vs Sänger) and if BAe and MBB could pool their efforts".

It was evidently suggested that "ESA should pursue a European programme to meet these challenges (i.e. revive the proposed FESTIP programme)".

The subject of finance was brought to the fore again on October 4 when South Fylde's Conservative MP Michael Jack visited Warton. Jack "suggested that proposals might be put forward for enabling technology programmes for advanced aerospace and non-aerospace applications, dissociating these from the name 'Hotol'. It was also suggested by Mr Jack that a presentation to appropriate MPs by BAe, Rolls-Royce and any other companies involved could help the case".

In his update report of October 10, Burns noted that the £1.9m funding to tide the Hotol project over till the end of 1988 had not yet been approved by BAe's financial director, a delay which was causing difficulties in placing orders for advanced material samples.

He outlined four measures being taken to get some payload capacity back for Hotol. The first was liquid oxygen tanks made from fibre-reinforced titanium aluminide in the inner wings and centre section. Apparently, "this material has similar strength/weight properties to titanium with particulates but retains these properties to much higher temperatures. Some insulation will be necessary in the tank regions. 10mm thick approx. to minimise liquid oxygen boil-off on the ground and on ascent but structural material will survive re-entry temperatures without TPS".

The second measure was sub-cooling of propellants—reducing the temperature of the liquid hydrogen and liquid oxygen well below their boiling point to increase their density. This "enables a significant reduction in tank volume, notably on the hydrogen tank, saving about 2m length. Its practicality has been reasonably assured by discussion with [US gases and chemicals company] Air Products who are doing work for application to NASP, and also with Rolls-Royce".

Thirdly, Hotol's fuselage lines were being "totally optimised" from end to end based on revised CAPS modelling. And lastly, the RB.545-03 had been revised with improved propellant characteristics, revised de-icing figures thanks to the sub-cooled liquid oxygen and 180:1 expansion ratio rocket nozzles.

On October 12, Burns, Hopwell and Dale submitted a patent application for jettisonable foreplanes to BAe's patents officer, J. Eastmond. The mechanism would apparently be "based on that of the Lightning overwing tank jettison mechanism". It comprised "a cartridge-operated jettison gun housed within each foreplane and forming part of the load-bearing structure (resisting bending) in its unfired condition ... firing of each jettison cartridge is energised electrically by a pre-programmed signal from the flight control system. On firing, the explosive gases force the inner telescopic piston of the jettison gun to extend. The piston end load is reacted by a pad within the fuselage.

"After a predetermined travel, the outer piston extends and a spring collet releases the foreplane. Immediately after release, a spring-loaded cover plate closes over the spigot socket. This is primarily to prevent local cavity heating on re-entry".

WET WING BENEFITS

Burns recorded in his update report for Yates on November 10, 1988, that the £1.9m funding had now finally been signed off by BAe's financial director. The 'wet wing' design had allowed a reduction in Hotol's overall length from 66.5m to 60m, with beneficial side effects for both centre of gravity control and de-rotation on landing—it now being possible to control the latter without nose rockets.

Using titanium aluminide for the wing tanks allowed a reduction in other aspects of wing structure, resulting in a 1,500kg reduction in wing mass overall. RR had now determined that using densified liquid oxygen for de-icing, combined with the use of parahydrogen and the 180:1 nozzles, had "resulted in recovery of 03D engine performance to a better standard than the early 02 datum. Further improvements, to be identified shortly, include reduced liquid oxygen for de-icing with partial cooled air recirculation".

The Configuration H-based SC1 model was now being tested in Warton's 5.5m low speed wind tunnel and "preliminary results show satisfactory linear lift and pitching moments up to 20 degrees incidence, an adequate margin from normal operating limits".

RAL's final report on the hydrogen permeability of carbon-PEEK had finally been issued, indicating that "the amount of hydrogen lost through permeability in the Hotol mission will be very small, about 1g. Discussions with Air Products have shown that permeability of carbon-PEEK to hydrogen and degradation due to gaseous oxygen can be eliminated by a fluorination process. This involves gaseous infiltration and appears to offer a 'once and for all' protection against harmful effects".

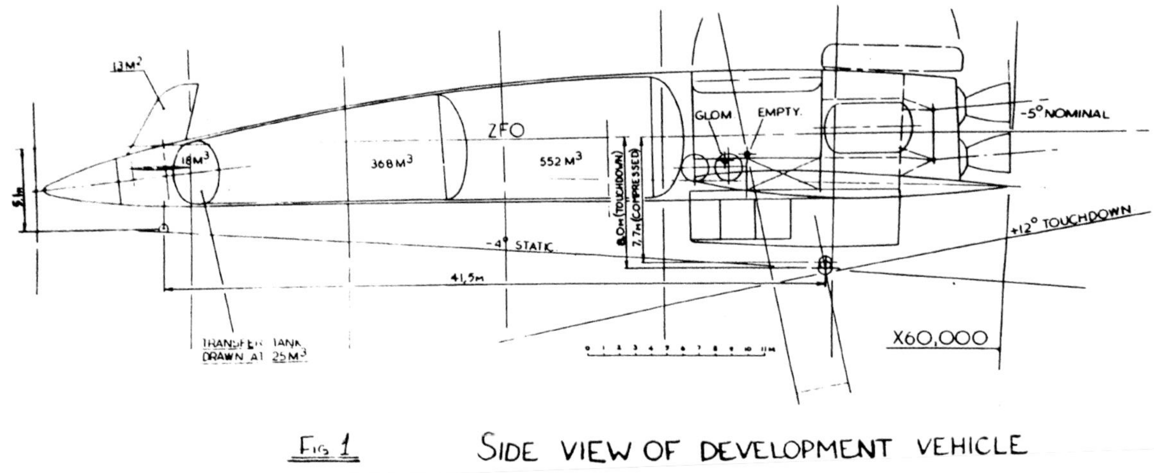

General arrangement of development vehicle for the wet wing Configuration H.

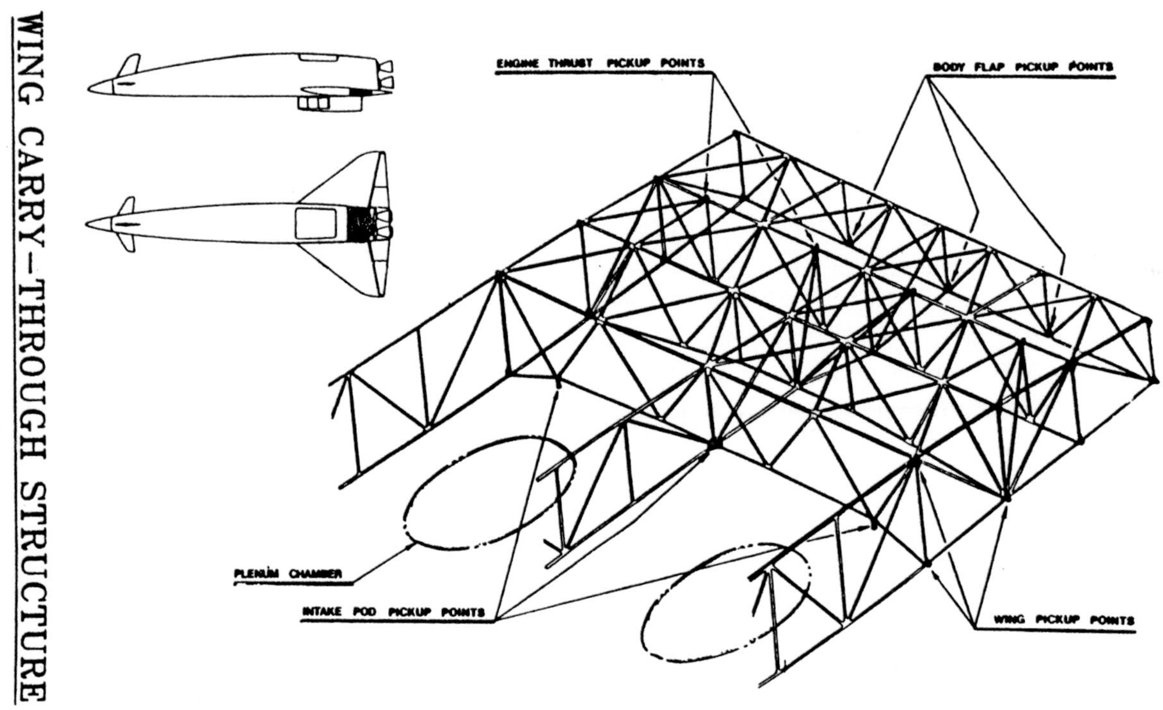

Wing carry-through structure within the rear fuselage.

Burns also noted that Wake had now left the Hotol team to join the wind tunnel department. She had "attended the bicentennial exhibition in Sydney [Wake had in fact presented a Hotol paper at Aerospace 88—a conference hosted by RAeS Australia, from October 10-11, 1988, which was timed to coincide with the Bicentennial Air Show, before attending the show itself at RAAF Richmond, 50km north-west of Sydney, to present Hotol information at the BAe stand]. She had reported that there was great interest in Hotol, both from well informed public and aerospace employees and some industrial contacts were made".

Wake herself later recalled that while she was there "someone tried to pay me to reserve a seat on the first Sydney to London flight!"

Meanwhile, back in the UK, Furniss had been appointed as Wilson's successor in the Hotol Deputy Technical Manager position.

During a discussion in the House of Commons on December 7, 1988, Michael Jack asked "the Chancellor of the Duchy of Lancaster what measures he has taken to promote and encourage overseas participation in the Hotol project". Rather than answering himself, the Chancellor, Tony Newton, fielded Robert Atkins MP who, as Conchie had mentioned previously, had visited the US in October in his capacity as DTI Parliamentary Under-Secretary.

Atkins said: "It is for Rolls-Royce and British Aerospace

Hotol Configuration J. CHRIS SANDHAM-BAILEY

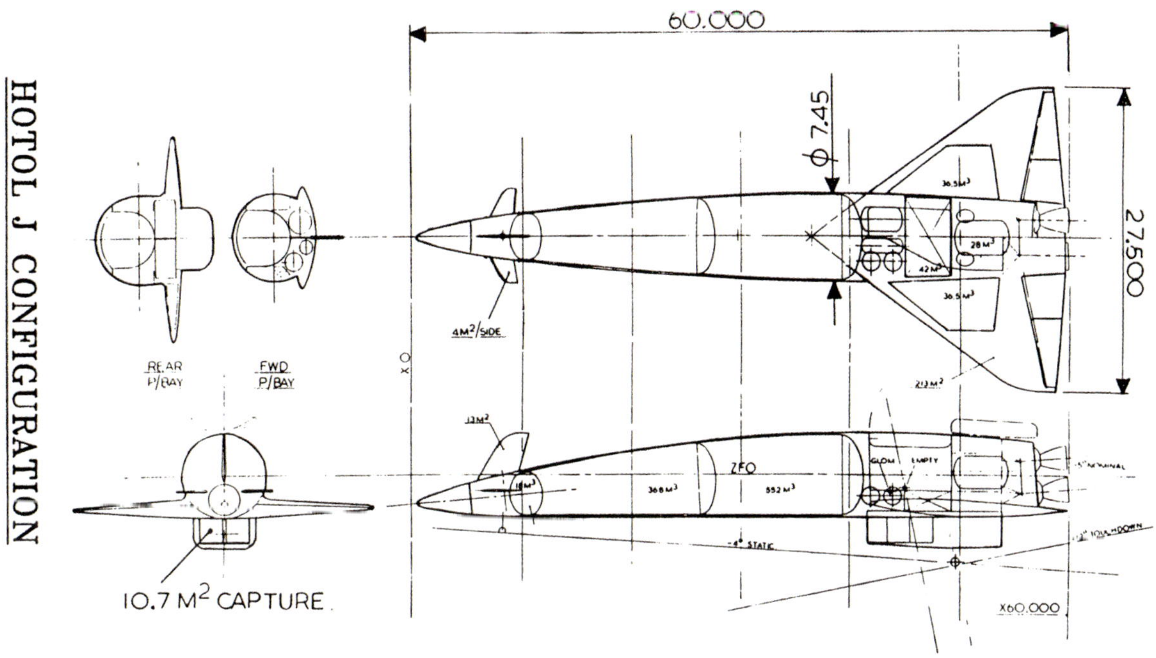

Configuration J — the 'wet wing' Hotol — was the last iteration to be fully worked through.

to determine jointly which pattern of international collaboration they wish to explore and we will support them in that endeavour. Following a visit that I made recently to Washington, where I met Dr Graham, the President's scientific advisor at the White House, I am pleased to tell the House that avenues have been established for the companies to pursue discussions with American counterparts."

Jack replied: "In welcoming my honourable friend's positive statement about future developments in respect of Hotol, may I ask him to confirm that the only real future for the project depends upon putting together international consortia with a vested interest in launching satellites? While he encourages that development, will he ensure that the companies participating in the materials development, technology and avionics associated with the project have sufficient encouragement from his department to continue the work? We must not allow the project to wither on the vine."

Atkins: "My honourable friend is right. I can do no better than quote from a report in the United States published recently by a group of people from the United States and other nations. It concluded that it was 'economically and technologically impossible for any single country or company to develop an HSCT [High Speed Civil Transport] aircraft'. Collaboration must be the order of the day."

Conservative MP for Stevenage Timothy Wood asked: "Bearing in mind the fact that Hotol holds the prospect of a reduction by a factor of four in the cost of satellite launches, which would benefit broadcasters, telecommunications networks and defence departments, is it not extremely important that the industries involved should cooperate internationally in this venture?"

Atkins: "As my honourable friend knows, it will cost many billions of pounds to develop Hotol. The early stages of such activity will require relatively small sums of about £2m to £3m a year, which it is well within the capability of the companies involved to provide. My honourable friend is right to say that this is an innovative project that deserves consideration, and we are doing just that."

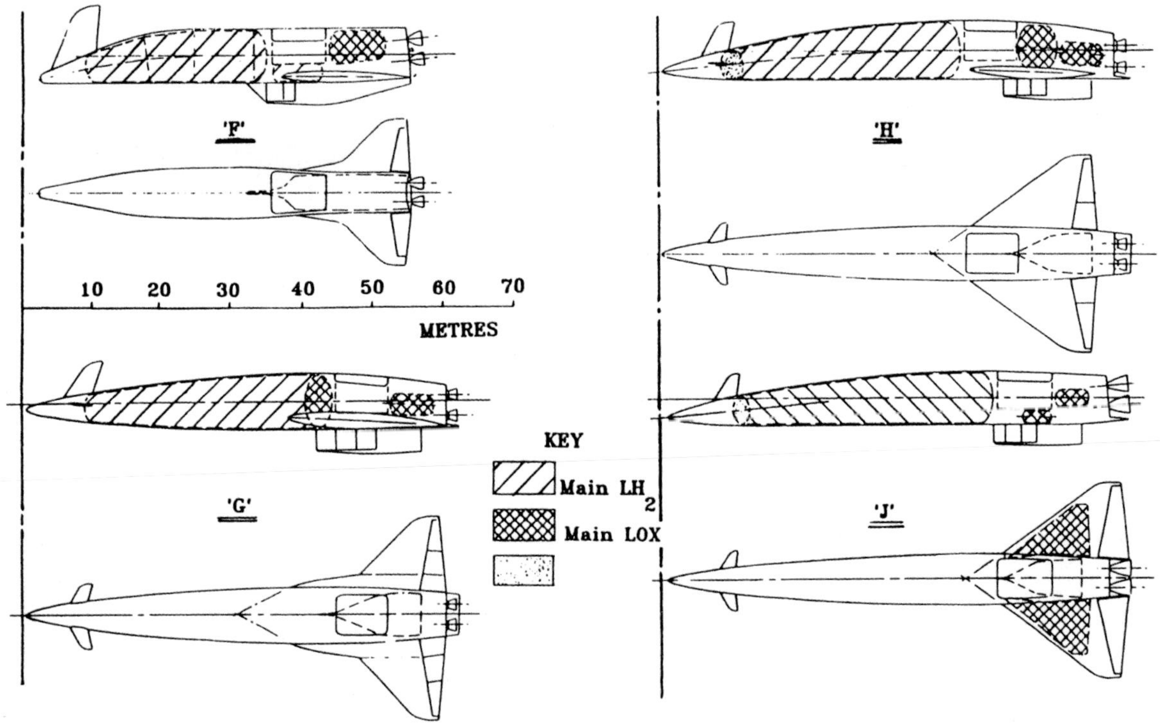

The evolution of Hotol from Configuration F, through Configurations G and H, to Configuration J.

ENGINEERING SLOW-DOWN

By the time of Burns' update on December 11, 1988, the 'wet wing' Hotol had been officially designated Configuration J. The detailed design of this new variant had not been as rapid as hoped however. Burns wrote: "There have been some delays due to staff retirements, illness and transfer of work on the intake from Brough to Filton due to overriding priority work at Brough. Completion of the design, notably on the rear fuselage at Warton and intake at Filton, is expected by the end of 1988.

"Optimisation of Configuration J is commencing; this will refine the fuselage lines, engine scale and ascent profile to maximise payload."

Things were not looking great at Rolls-Royce either: "Support from RR on RB.545 engineering and performance has now dwindled to effectively two people full-time at Patchway. Although those concerned are working effectively and enthusiastically, they are concerned about long-term support of the RB.545 by Rolls-Royce management."

Hunting Engineering's report on Hotol nose cone heating, prepared by B. R. Waine, J. A. Armstrong and N. R. Forman, had by now been completed and was delivered to Warton in December 1988. This indicated that thermal stresses on the nose cone during re-entry would be within the material limits of the already-selected carbon-silicon carbide—which was a relief since it meant that no further changes in this area were required.

Weeks now passed with work on Hotol reduced to a crawl. On January 12, 1989, Bond wrote to Timothy Wood to "correct two misimpressions conveyed by [Atkins'] reply" to his question on December 7: "Firstly Hotol, unlike any other spaceplane project is not constrained by having to carry out huge programmes of basic research. Whilst technology development is needed, this is relatively small and the speed at which the project can proceed is entirely dependent at the present time on its rate of funding.

"This would remain true up to about ten times the above rates of expenditure, when the speed at which the programme could be performed would then limit the rate of progress. Secondly, the implication was that both Rolls-Royce and British Aerospace were spending private resources at about the above rate. Whilst this is the case for British Aerospace, it is not true for Rolls-Royce. Rolls-Royce have never spent more than about £300,000 in any year of the project from their own resources and, since the acquisition of the patent rights to the engine from myself under a long-standing prior agreement in April 1988, have run down effectively to zero. No technology development occurred in 1988 and all design effort was disbanded in December 1988. The propulsion aspect of the Hotol project is therefore now ceased entirely to all intents and purposes. I believe this to be rather different to the situation stated in the House."

Wood replied a week later, saying: "I have carefully

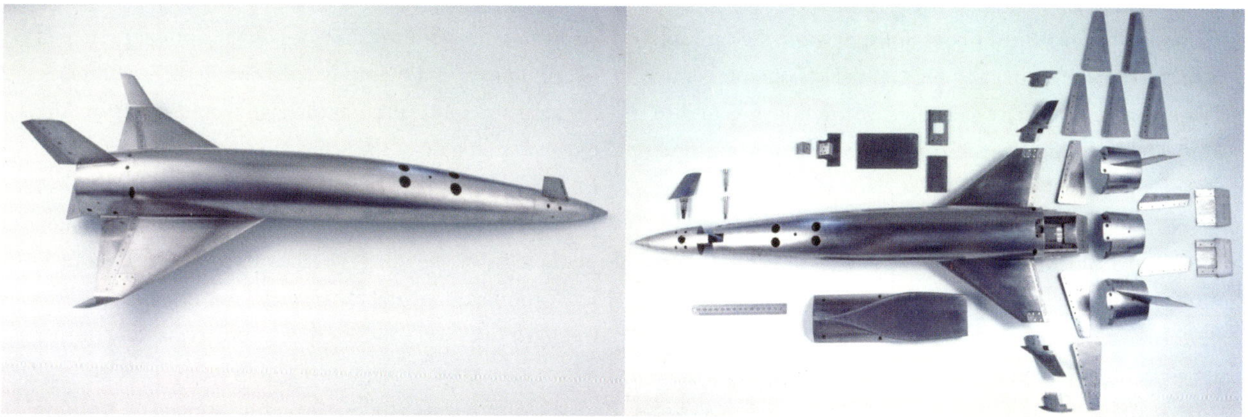

Hotol wind tunnel model SC2, based on Configuration H and intended for transonic/supersonic testing

noted your somewhat depressing comment in relation to technology development of the propulsion aspect of the Hotol project. I am taking the liberty of writing to the Minister concerned and the Space and Communications Division of British Aerospace to seek their comments on your points."

On January 30, Conchie responded to Wood's enquiry: "I think generally Alan is correct, Rolls-Royce have to our regret stopped development work. However, we are in discussion with Rolls-Royce on the way ahead and some design work has been proceeding. There are some signs that we can make progress in Europe and this will be helped by a low (but positive) profile in the UK. We are also in discussion with Alan and hope we can maintain a joint position on the way ahead."

CLAWING BACK PAYLOAD

Meanwhile, a Hotol review meeting had been held at Warton on January 16, 1989 and according to Burns, "the proportion of funding allocated to Hotol development has been reduced and that devoted to international activities, including assessment of MBB's two-stage vehicle, has been increased. Manning figures remain to be agreed with the technical director." At the same meeting, "it was shown that improvements from Configuration H (reported in September 1988) to the current datum Configuration J resulted in about 15% (6,300kg) reduction in structures plus systems mass. This had not resulted directly in an equivalent increase in payload due to minor changes in the aerodynamic assumptions and a number of updates of the propulsion data.

"The payload of Configuration J datum was defined as 4,880kg; optimisation studies indicated a possible improvement to 6,340kg for a more slender shape. Subsequent investigations of the latter vehicle have indicated some difficulties in accommodating auxiliary tanks and a small increase in hydraulic systems mass due to the increase centre of gravity/aerodynamic centre offset. However, incidence-dependent propulsion data is now available from Filton.

"This takes formal account of the pre-compression ahead of the intake, as a function of incidence as well as Mach number, affecting intake size, drag and propulsive thrust. Previously only a single crude Mach function with assumed incidence was used. This will influence the optimisation of the ascent trajectory and pull-up manoeuvre as well as affecting optimum fuselage shape. A further round of vehicle optimisation is therefore being undertaken before 'freezing' the configuration. The target date for completion of a full engineering design is end of March 1989 and compilation of a report by the end of April."

On the WLC study front, a meeting had been held with MBB on January 25, 1989, to discuss Phase 2. Evidently, "BAe requested a significant workshare for the Propulsion Team headed by Rolls-Royce but MBB, the study leaders, were adamant that the follow-on study should be devoted primarily to airframe work. The workshare percentages were agreed as follows: BAe 42%, MBB 40%, RR 15%, VDK (Belgian consultancy) 3%. RR are likely to refuse to participate in this study unless ESA provide additional funding or order the workshare to be revised.

"At the same meeting, agreement was secured that BAe and MBB would exchange technical data on a 1:1 basis between datum Hotol and Sänger designs. This will be treated carefully because it is believed that Hotol engineering is at a more advanced stage with a more confident basis of aerodynamics and structural data."

In his January 31, 1989, report to Yates, Burns recorded the completion of the SC2 high-speed model, another based on Configuration H, and noted that testing would begin during the first week of February.

Atkins was questioned about the Government's approach to Hotol in the House of Commons again on February 15, 1989, and in response to a point raised by

Labour MP for Wigan Roger Stott, he said: "We are still considering the matter although, as the honourable gentleman is aware, we have said that we are not prepared to provide the funding because we believe that it must come from a much wider collaboration. Nevertheless, the matter is constantly under review."

On the same day, Conchie led a team to Les Mureaux in France to give a presentation to Aérospatiale personnel. He later reported that they were "keenly interested in the Hotol project and particular questions concerned the intake. It was evident that their studies of airbreathers had highlighted this as a particularly difficult design".

The team moved on to Paris on February 16 to make a shorter presentation to ESA. Following on from this, Conchie reported that "both Aérospatiale and ESA expressed strong interest in the possibility of a European enabling technology programme but CNES might not be agreeable to the French participating at this stage. It was noted that CNES had prevented Aérospatiale and AMDBA from participating in the WLC study in 1988. A presentation to CNES is to be arranged in the near future".

TROLLEY TRIBULATIONS

Dale wrote a memo to Les Green, section leader for Warton's 5.5m wind tunnel, on February 22, 1989, on 'requirements for testing with a yawed ground belt'—effectively a moving surface, like a conveyor belt, used to simulate ground proximity during tests: "Hotol/trolley testing is at present programmed for March 1990. Testing is likely to comprise: mated testing with Hotol at various attitudes and with controls deflected; investigation of interference effects arising during Hotol/trolley separation; and evaluation of any trolley aerodynamic control devices." But "the longer-term requirement for testing with a yawed ground board depends upon: project status, problems encountered during the first phase defined above and international work shares. At present, therefore, the long-term requirement for using a yawed ground belt for Hotol project testing is unclear. Possession of such facility would, however, help strengthen BAe's position during negotiations on work shares".

Russell Hannigan at Stevenage had meanwhile produced a report on 'Hotol launch assist system requirements', assessing different potential options for take-off. These included the use of a heavy-duty integral undercarriage, jettisonable undercarriage, unpowered trolley, rocket-powered trolley, air cushion trolley, ground effect winged trolley, wheeled on rails, rail-guided air cushion vehicle, ground effect on rail, magnetic levitation and subsonic air-launch.

Burns sent Parkinson his views on the options presented by Hannigan in a memo dated February 27, 1988. He thought the integral undercarriage would result in "the massive scaling up of the vehicle to take the heavier undercarriage into orbit". A study had already been carried out on the jettisonable undercarriage and "the 'dollies' became pretty massive, they slug the take-off so require some auxiliary propulsion + parachutes, they have to be stressed for the abort case, and you have only to proceed a little further before they have merged into a trolley".

The unpowered trolley was a non-starter: "Overlong runway, additional on board fuel due to slugging the take-off, and no abort capability rule this out". The rocket-powered trolley was of course "our basic concept"; the air cushion trolley—effectively a hovercraft—wouldn't work because "it offers no resistance to side force so crosswind has to be precisely countered by lateral velocity. Wheels and brakes, as for other trolley concepts, are required for the abort case, so it can only become much more complex than a wheeled trolley".

The ground effect winged trolley would require a longer runway and "once you have a vehicle which leaves the ground a new set of hazards arises, requiring increased safety precautions and inevitably higher costs". Burns didn't have any strong objections to 'wheeled on rails'—"the fundamental benefits are absence of a guidance system and a smoother (presumably) ride. The operational restriction is that rails will be required at diversion sites (if any)". Even better was a rail-guided air cushion vehicle: "Quite a promising concept but would require a lot of development and proving". Ground effect on rail had the same issues as winged ground effect. Magnetic levitation would require expensive infrastructure.

However, for subsonic air-launch Burns wrote: "Our ALV studies showed that 747 and C-5A were too small. A 747-based six-engined canard was studied but ruled out at the December 1987 HQ review as being too costly to develop. But the new Antonov transport... if Glasnost continues to blossom, who knows?" The new Antonov transport he was referring to was the An-225, which had made its first flight just over two months earlier on December 21, 1988.

HOTOL ON PAUSE

Engineering work on Hotol was largely suspended during February 1989 while the team concentrated on the WLC study ahead of the next reporting date in April but was expected to recommence after Easter. Burns reported to Yates at the end of February that "testing of the wind tunnel model SC2, with blocked intake, in the Warton

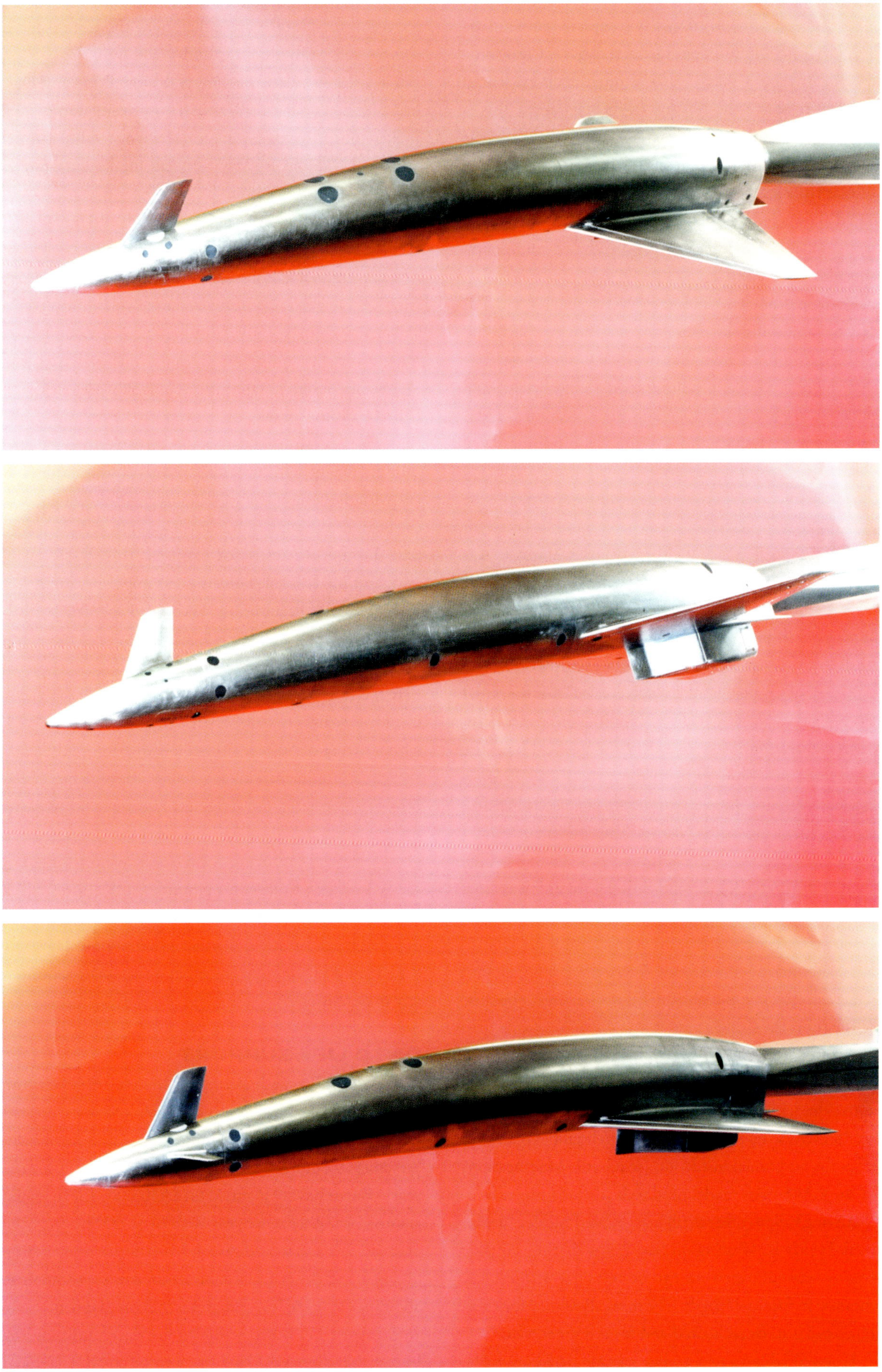

The SC2 model mounted and ready for testing.

1.2m high speed wind tunnel is complete. Some unsatisfactory pitching moment characteristics, at transonic speeds, have been noted. A local pitch-up is evident at incidences above the normal operating range; this is undesirable but not unacceptable. The total shift of the aerodynamic centre from 1.2m (rear) to 3m (forward) is substantially less than estimated. This is a good result and could allow a reduction in the control hinge moments to trim and/or a reduction in wing area based on re-entry and recovery control".

Under a heading of 'publicity' he wrote: "Lines definition for a new display model for the Paris Air Show has been based on a Configuration J4.5 in the knowledge that the long slender Configuration J5 has been found to be somewhat impractical and the optimum is likely to be between J4 and J5. The same definition has been passed to *Flight International* for their detailed cutaway drawing which is expected to be published in their issue dated March 25, 1989."

A design review was held on March 7 and it was reported that "it is still intended to complete the engineering definition and optimisation of Configuration J as near as possible to the end of March and to report by end of April 1989". Yates would then review progress on May 8.

Review of Configuration J5 had revealed "that the liquid oxygen tanks could not be accommodated in the slim [fuselage] section in the region of the payload bay. The 'J4.5' lines, provisionally defined for the Paris Air Show model represent a practical minimum cross-sectional area in this region (diameter 7.45m). This constraint should be applied in future CAPS optimisation". The now much smaller than expected aerodynamic centre shift was cited and it was "necessary urgently to assess the implications on liquid oxygen transfer, wing area and location, control hinge moment and foreplanes. A revised set of... relevant data... needs to be assembled. This work is urgent because of the short timescale".

Further work on the wet wings had determined that "the lightest solution [is] maximum liquid oxygen in wing with cylindrical tanks, placed longitudinally in the centre section. The wing loading relief due to liquid oxygen overrides the additional insulation [required]. Modifications of the CAPS mass model need to be defined urgently".

Among various other small mass-related tweaks, "design work by Mr R. Warrington has shown that the [intake/engine-related] pipework can be installed without any increase in fuselage length. The mass allowance for these pipes needs to be rechecked and revised if necessary".

Hopwell tabled a new trolley scheme based on earlier work done by Reg Langmead which "should make provision for Hotol to be rolled onto the trolley on its own wheels". Davies, Stead and Wood were working on gap heating and active cooling of the foreplanes and Dale had planned a visit to Westcott to investigate possible rocket motor installations for afterbody wind tunnel models R124 and R125. Lastly, an intake duct model was being tested at Filton.

On March 10, Burns send Gardner the draft of an article on general Hotol progress intended for publication in BAe's in-house magazine, now renamed from *Intercom* to *Interlink*. He wrote: "It is intended to dispel the impression at Warton that Hotol is fading away and to boost the morale of the team who are in need of a 'shot in the arm'."

Another design progress meeting took place on March 17 with Hotol's intake at the top of the agenda. Rolls-Royce had confirmed "that it is acceptable to allow flow through the intake at transonic and lower speeds on recovery, with the compressor 'windmilling'. This will not harm the engine, although only a small amount of flow would pass through the restricted passages. This should alleviate transonic control problems and might be useful as a drag control". In addition, Filton was looking at alternative schemes for pneumatic alleviation of intake ramp pressures.

A revision of the centre section fuel tanks had seen cylindrical tanks replace "a structurally rectangular tank" with a saving of 500kg, although owing to other factors the net improvement was only 300kg. The SC2 model was now being used to test drag and Hopwell was working on generating longitudinal trim data for Configuration J4.5. Dale was preparing a low-speed wind tunnel test for SC1 "with a trolley on a ground board". Burns noted that the "basic [trolley] design scheme is satisfactory but detailed work on the dynamics of separation from the trolley must be undertaken before we could reveal this in any presentation".

ONTO LIFE SUPPORT

Young sat down with Burns on March 28 to tell him what funding he could expect from BAe's Military Aircraft budget for the Hotol project during the remainder of 1989. Stevenage would get £200,000 to cover all work for the year—Burns having planned for £530,000. Filton would get just £45,000 for the year, with £132,000 having been planned. Warton would get £1.5m, compared to £2.34m planned, and the external contractor/enabling technology allowance was £0.7m, compared to £1m planned.

On April 11, Burns wrote to Gardner outlining the impact that this would have on the project. Stevenage and Filton would no longer be able to support the completion

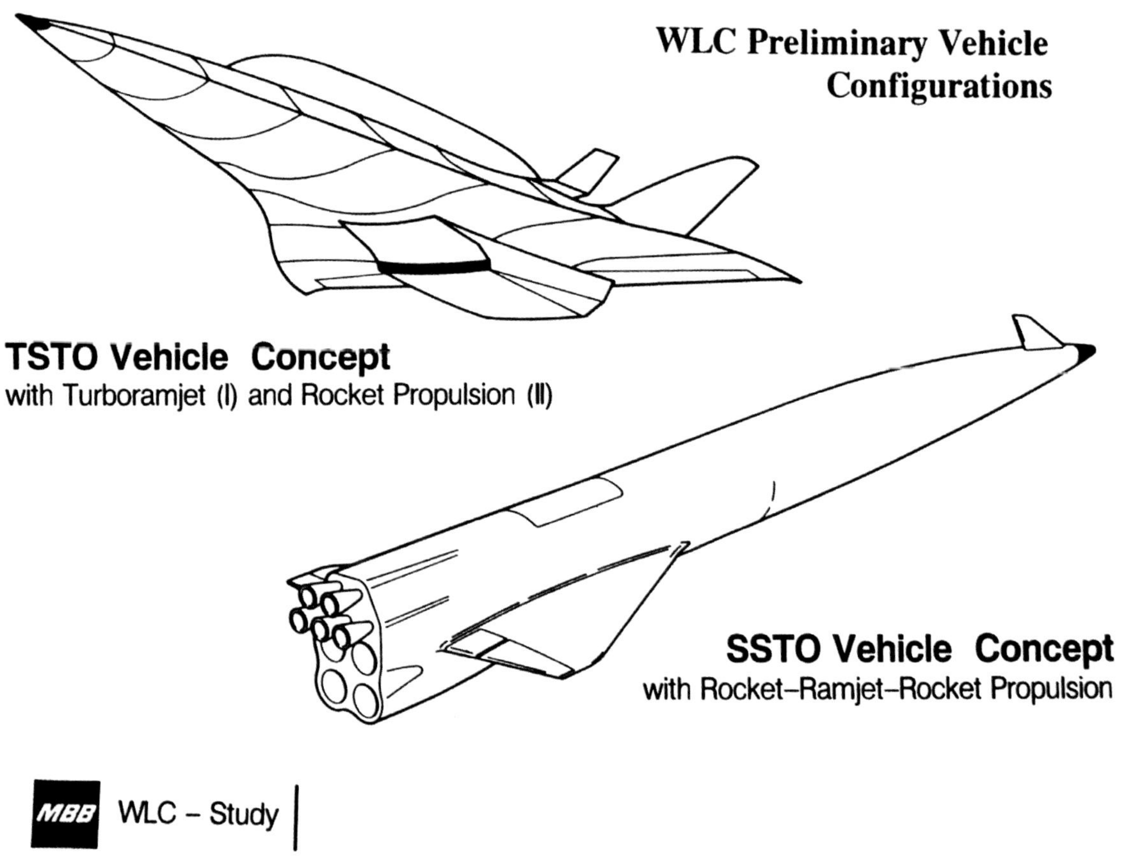

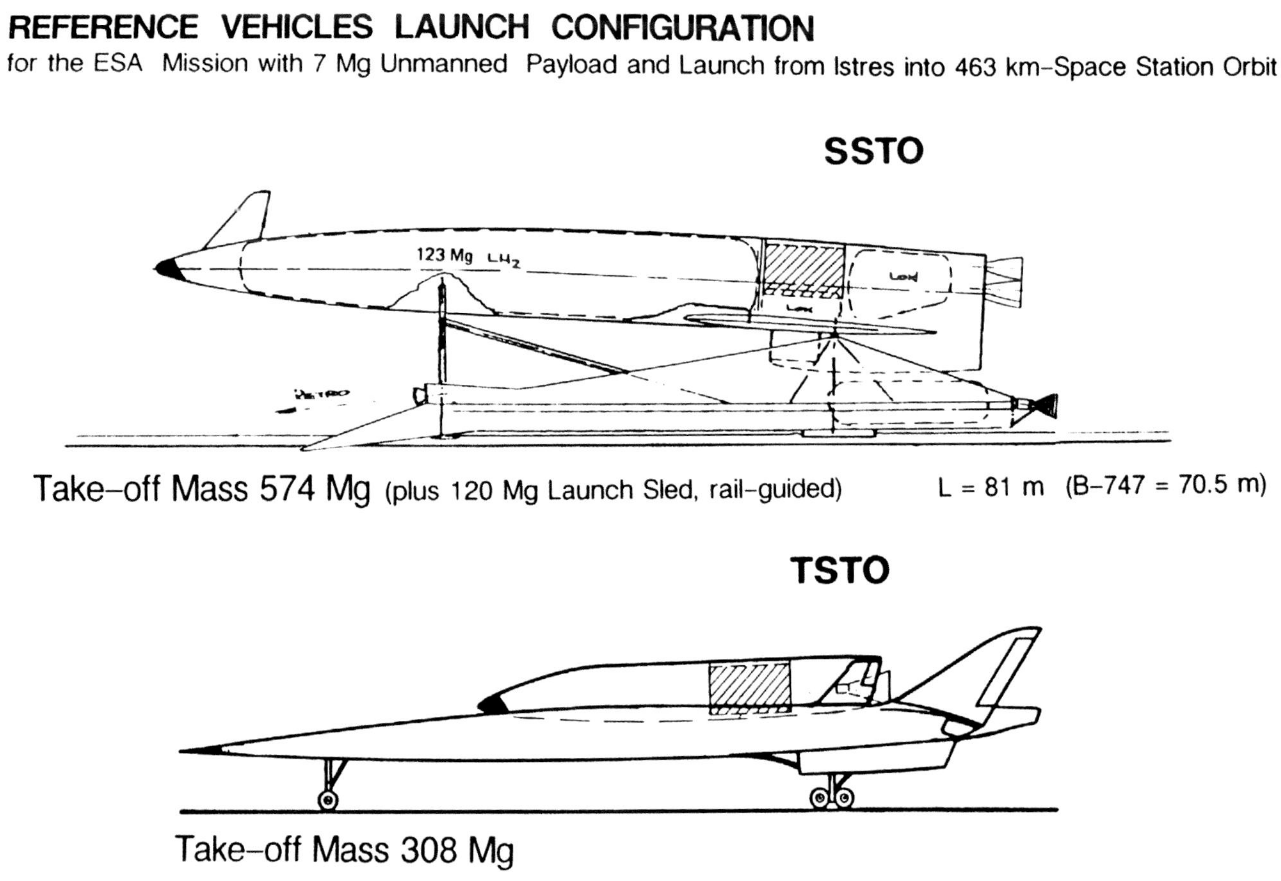

The WLC Study designs—a TSTO vehicle designed by MBB, which was essentially Sänger, and a SSTO vehicle from BAe which was a deliberately underdeveloped Hotol.

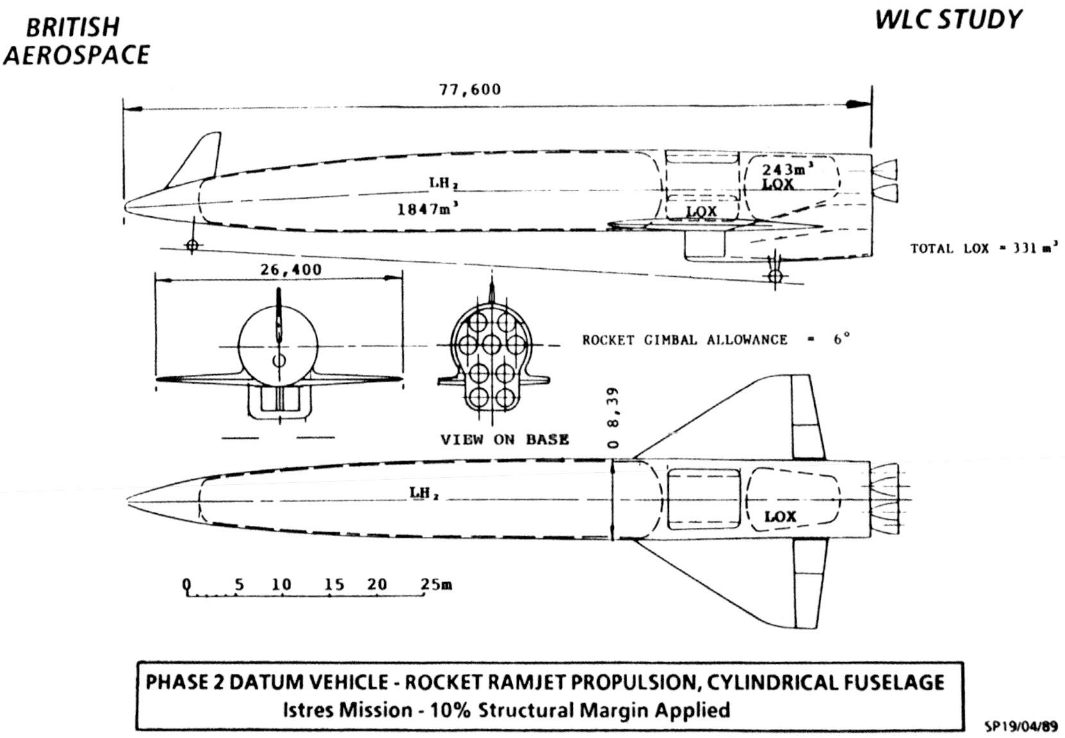

BAe's WLC Study phase 2 datum vehicle design, based heavily on Hotol—albeit significantly larger and without the RB.545.

of Configuration J design work; a full assessment of MBB's TSTO design would not be possible without involving Stevenage and Filton; "command and control enabling technology work will virtually stop unless Space Systems fund it themselves" and "the morale of the Hotol team will be seriously impaired. Most of them are already looking around for alternative jobs. It is their enthusiasm that has sustained Hotol over the past three-and-a-half years".

Under the heading 'comment', Burns wrote: "The logic of Mr Young's latest instructions is not understood. While we are acutely aware of the manpower shortage in Technical Directorate of Military Aircraft, there is not any problem of implementing the planned levels of support at Stevenage or Filton. If limitation of spend outside Military Aircraft is the problem then it would seem more logical to restrict spend outside BAe (which has escaped unscathed) rather than that planned for other BAe companies."

In his monthly report covering March, undated but certainly issued after April 5, Burns stated that "budgetary estimates for 1989 are being revised, taking account of: 1) Termination of Hotol work on completion of reporting and review. Team strength will be reduced and staff redeployed. 2) Self-financing by BAe companies involved in European activities, including Sänger assessment. 3) Reduced effort on enabling technology".

He went on: "Staff shortages at Warton (Advanced Studies) have caused some slippage in performance work, due to the inability to run ESA WLC study and Hotol work simultaneously. Staff shortages in Materials Development and Aerodynamics are restricting progress on enabling technology."

Yet even in the face of all this, engineering work continued. Configuration J performance estimates were being prepared ahead of the May 8 review and "further analysis of... SC2 results has shown that the desired change in zero lift pitching moment from positive at transonic Mach to negative at hypersonic Mach has been achieved but the negative moment is excessive. This would require a reduction in fuselage camber if design refinement were to continue... a short programme of tests on SC2 with open intakes is planned... it is hoped that undesirable pitch characteristics at transonic speeds are eliminated or alleviated with flow through the intakes".

Presentations to the European Space Research and Technology Centre in Noordwijk and to CNES in Paris had been planned for May 1989 and a progress meeting for Phase 2 of the WLC Study had taken place at Ottobrunn on April 5.

During the Ottobrunn event, Parkinson and Furniss had given presentations on SSTO studies and "while these were generally well received, considerable scepticism was evident within ESA concerning the viability of SSTO and its sensitivity. The case for SSTO has to be made on cost advantages by comparison with TSTO. The final presentations for Phases 1 and 2 are due to be made at a meeting at Noordwijk on May 10".

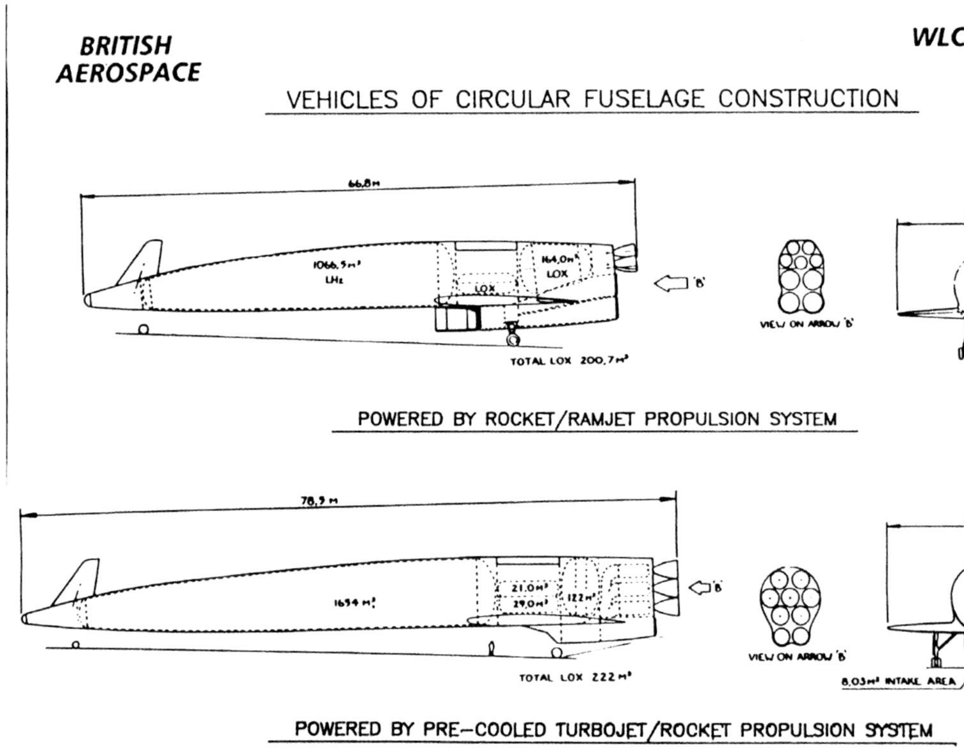

The pre-cooled turbojet/rocket propelled vehicle designed by BAe for the WLC Study was an enormous vehicle—longer than a modern Airbus A380, though still not as long as an An-225.

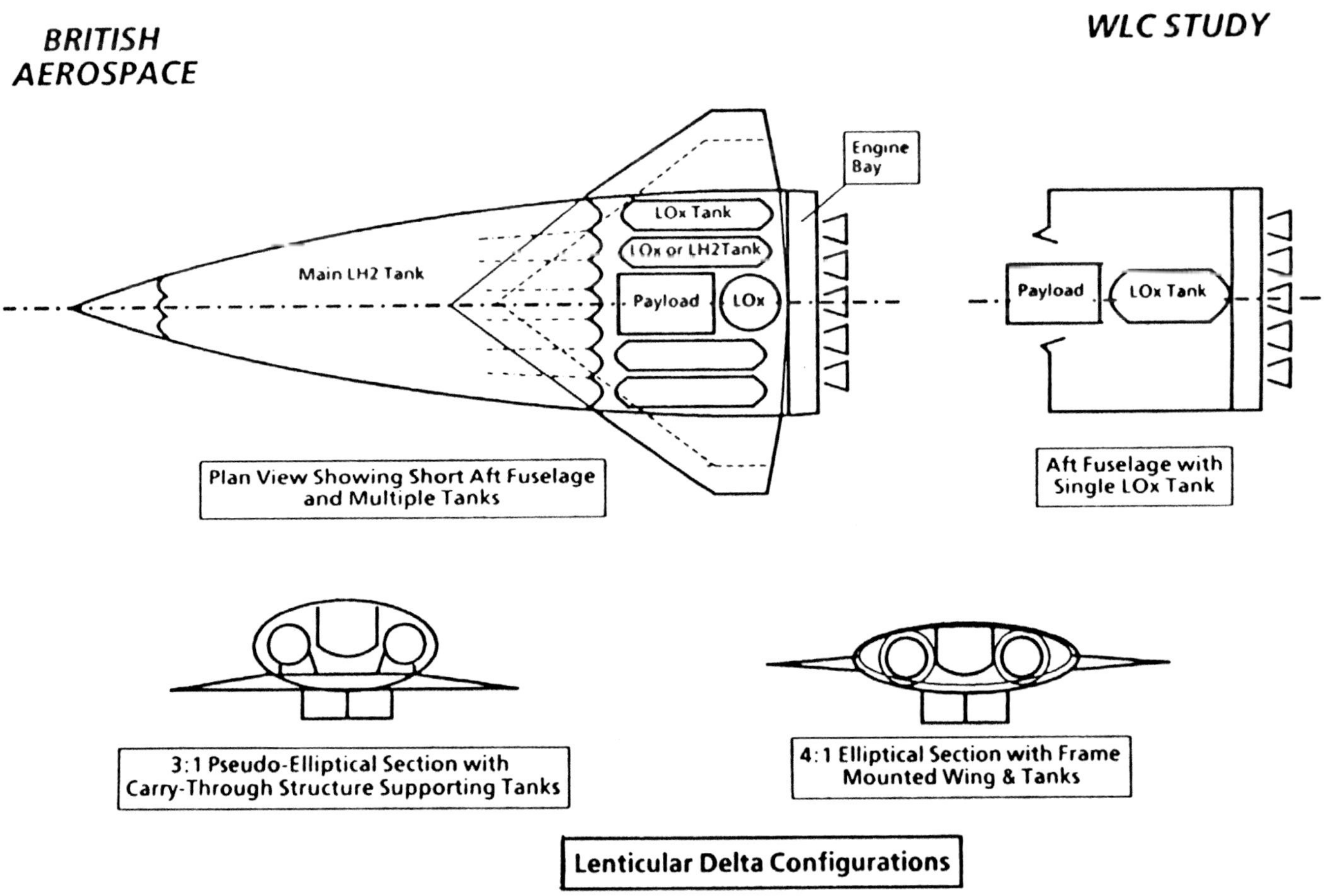

BAe lenticular delta or 'lifting body' design presented as part of the WLC Study. This shape would offer more lift and improved aerodynamics during supersonic cruise, compared to a cylindrical fuselage, at the expense of structural performance.

In the meantime, MBB had published some technical notes which "BAe have strong criticisms of... [and] which reflect the bias of MBB, for example: MBB, who have an agreed check function on performance calculations, allege that the payload of the SSTO reference vehicle is only 32% of BAe's figure" and "development costs for TSTO lower stage are based on an 'existing technology' correlation (despite a structure generally as hot as that of SSTO, cryogenic fuel carriage, novel power units etc.). They would rise by at least 50% if based on the same formula as SSTO". Even more surprisingly, "airframe production costs of TSTO lower stage, based on unreferenced formulae, are quoted as a mere 20% of those of SSTO, despite the heavier structure of the TSTO stage... [also] MBB's method of calculating recurring costs omits a number of important items, such as the influence of mission aborts and vehicle losses".

Burns said BAe would "protest strongly to ESA and require that the reports be withdrawn. It is recommended that BAe should threaten to withdraw from Phase 3 of the study unless the reports are withdrawn and revised. However, it is in BAe's interest to participate, to obtain access to MBB's design estimates and methods and as an agreed route into European cooperation".

SCOTT-SCOTT'S PEBBLE-BED

While Rolls-Royce had, by all accounts, stopped most of the meagre funding it had made available for RB.545 research by the end of 1988, Scott-Scott had continued to work on it at Ansty. On April 10, 1989, he issued an official Rolls-Royce report under the title 'demonstrator scheme for air handling and pre-cooler systems in RB.545-type engines'. The summary read: "A significant appreciation of the problems associated with ice deposition in pre-cooler assemblies for RB.545-type engines was obtained from small-scale testing of representative pre-cooler matrices. To progress beyond that stage and generate confidence in the total air-handling system, a demonstrator was devised, using existing components wherever possible.

"The associated rig was designed to achieve correct representation of flight conditions for the complete airbreathing trajectory, using a pebble-bed heat store for the tests at high Mach number."

The rig itself was to use a Viper turbojet compressor assembly linked to a Bristol Proteus gas turbine. Driven at a constant 5,000rpm, this would provide "adequate matching of flows for demonstration purposes... in addition, by suitable operation of the pebble-bed bypass system, correct reproduction of the pre-cooler inlet temperatures could be arranged. Details of the control of water content of the induced 'air' would have been developed along the lines of the previous test programme at No. 69 Test House, probably injecting steam instead of water to achieve better distribution and eliminate residual deposits. As a final demonstration of the compatibilities of the ice-control system (which is only needed in the lower atmosphere), the rig could have been operated on natural air by suitable valving, humidifying with steam to suit. Thus the complete spectrum of an RB.545 trajectory could have been reproducible."

It is clear from these last lines of the report ("could have been") that Scott-Scott knew his demonstrator would never be built, at least not at Rolls-Royce.

Burns wrote to Sid Swadling, director of engineering at what was now effectively a separate company, Airbus Division, British Aerospace, (Commercial Aircraft) Limited aka CAL, on April 12 to tell him that "the following rules [now] apply: finish reporting work on Hotol Configuration J at Week 17 [week beginning April 24]; no further work to refine Hotol design; no further wind tunnel work beyond reporting recent test results; any involvement in European activities (e.g. Sänger assessment) to be funded by CAL; agreed enabling technology activities focused on Hotol (e.g. core team work) will be funded by MAL [Military Aircraft Ltd. i.e. Warton]".

Herbert Grallert from MBB sent a fax to BAe on April 13 requesting a "refined sketch on the launch trolley proposal by BAe (correct scaling relative to the SSTO devices) and trolley mass assumption/installed thrust level" as part of the WLC Study. Furniss passed the fax to Parkinson, along with a sketch of Hopwell's trolley design, with a note saying: "Grallert request for these trolley data, to be put in the Executive Summary, are outside our contractual obligations. This work has been completed by ERNO. I don't think MBB liked ERNO results and are trying to set us up by asking us to put in some very preliminary BAe numbers. MBB are aware that ESA are concerned about the trolley and we should be very careful here. I do not believe we should give MBB any trolley description, we should also point out that the work was done by ERNO to complete the contractual requirements and no MBB estimates should be put in the Executive Summary."

BOND'S SATAN ENGINE

Burns wrote a memo to Young on April 18 with the heading 'Satan' Engine for Hotol. As previously hinted during his June 27, 1988, meeting with Burns, Yates and Lygo: "Alan Bond has defined an alternative to the

RB.545, named Satan, which he says does not infringe the patents sold to Rolls-Royce. He has informed the press and references to it have appeared in the daily papers and aerospace magazines. We had planned to assess the effects of substituting Satan for RB.545 on Hotol's performance. This would have involved Filton in some work to prepare installed performance data. A meeting had been planned for April 20, 1989, to receive the data and agree the work.

"In the light of current funding restrictions I have cancelled that meeting and informed A. Bond. He is considering whether he can raise funds to pay Filton to do the necessary work. We at Warton could then assess the performance effects with a small expenditure of effort. I am informing you of this situation because it is quite touchy politically. Alan Bond has the ear of the Press and it would look bad if they got hold of the story that BAe have refused to assess his new engine.

"I therefore ask: should we assess Satan in Hotol if A. Bond offers funds to Filton to do the installation estimates? Or should we fund Filton to do that work? Or should we leave it entirely alone?"

While Bond may or may not have informed the press of Satan's existence at this point, it is unclear which, if any, publications had chosen to run the story—perhaps because the details Bond was prepared to release were so scant. Certainly, a piece appeared in the *South Wales Echo* on August 3, 1989, which quoted Bond as saying that he had indeed invented a new engine and "it's called Satan ... it's significantly more efficient than the original Hotol engine, but I'm not revealing the details to anyone unless I can sell it. I can't even reveal what Satan stands for". He explained that he would not be patenting the design to avoid the risk of it being classified. According to the report, "Bond hopes funds will be available soon, allowing an 18-month trial. He hasn't named his prospective backer. He says he may offer the design to British Aerospace. BAe have said they'd like to hear more details of the engine."

Speaking in 2018, Bond explained that 'Satan' was not an acronym: "After the Hotol project came to an end and Richard Varvill and myself started looking at what we got wrong, it was clear that we needed a more efficient engine. So I devised this cycle which had an intermediate helium loop and we were looking for a name to distinguish it from the RB.545. I thought, well, we want a god in terms of a very hot place and I'd got a bit tired of all the Greek stuff with Hades and things like that—it didn't sound good. And there's a rather curious thing, that's not come about by design, that almost all British rocket engines which have had a name started with an 'S': the Sprite, the Spectre, the Stentor... for reasons that are not obvious—it just happened. I asked John Scott-Scott, of course he'd been around a lot longer than I had, and he said he was aware of it but it's just one of those things that came about. So I thought, well, we'll try to maintain this tradition and keep an 'S' so... Satan.

"I have personally no religious views and to me Satan is just another mythological character in charge of a very hot place. So that's how it came about but... first of all I did step on some toes of colleagues that did have religious sensibilities, which surprised me to be honest. But also I'd started to try to find private finance and one of the places we wanted to approach was the Kuwaiti investment office. Three weeks before we were about to approach them, Saddam Hussein invaded [on August 2, 1990]. And so it became obvious that the Satan name couldn't survive.

"One of my friends who's an archaeologist [Egyptologist Diane Holmes] went away and had a think about it and came back with the Sabre name [as a replacement for Satan]. All these rocket people get hung up on Greek mythology and things like that—the Atlases and the Titans—so I needed somebody that would have a lateral view of it. So she came up with that, which was also an acronym, which was nice. We still don't know whether the right name is Synergetic or Synergistic Air Breathing and Rocket Engine."

STAFF REDEPLOYMENT

Back in April 1989, on the 19th Burns wrote a memo to Gardner and Mick Mansell, Warton's recently appointed Director of Advanced Technology, to confirm the project changes already outlined and to make recommendations for staff redeployment. He proposed that Furniss should head a small team to "tackle the WLC study and Sänger TSTO audit. The former task, performance/scaling based on Hotol work, requires about three staff, of which ESA funding will pay for two". Supporting Furniss, he thought, should be Stead on systems and thermal studies, S. L. E. Gilkes on performance, Kevin Hargreaves on structural design to be assisted by 'A. N. Other'. He proposed Parkin for redeployment and promotion, Hopwell and Davies for redeployment to Advanced Systems and Dale to Aerodynamics. For Wood, he suggested a move into CAD/CAM, which was "his personal preference".

In his April full-month update to Yates—his final full-month update of the Hotol project, undated but apparently issued around May 15, Burns noted that BAe Military Aircraft funding to Stevenage had been terminated on April 13, 1989. Under 'engineering', he wrote: "Performance studies with the new incidence-dependent

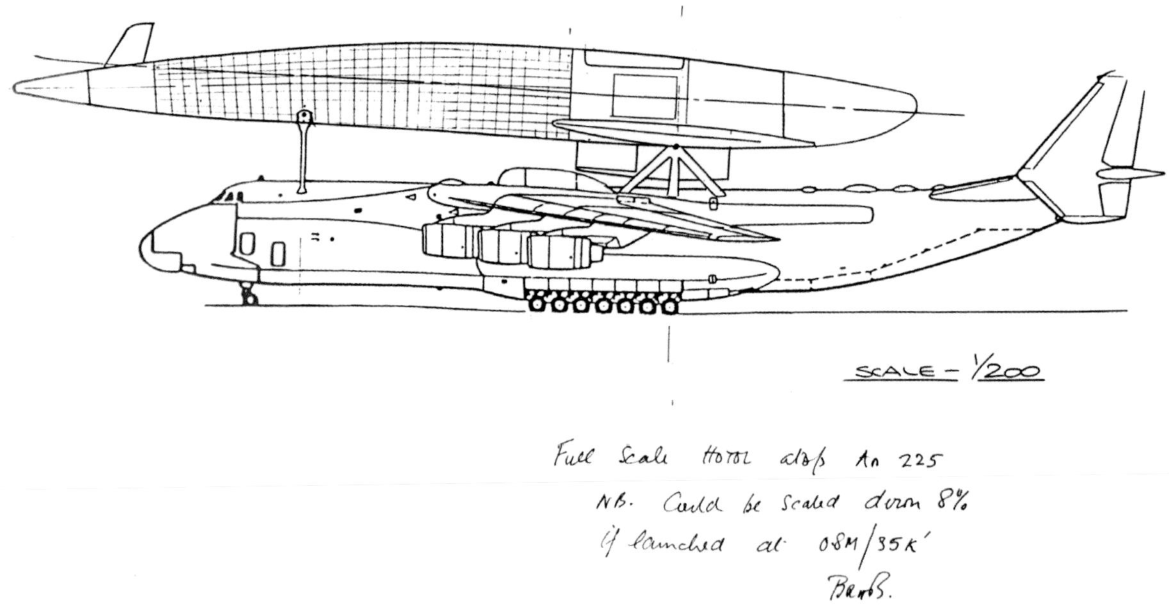

The drawing attached to Burns' May 25 annotated copy of Conchie's typed message.

propulsion data have shown a deterioration in performance. This is because pre-compression is reduced at the lower incidence associated with the increased wing area (necessary for re-entry control); consequently a lower/faster ascent profile involving higher drag is necessary to restore engine intake pressure.

"For similar reasons extending airbreathing beyond Mach 5 is not now beneficial. The outcome of this is that payload (4.8t) is unchanged from the figure reported at the review on January 16, 1989, despite significant savings in structure mass due to more efficient internal liquid oxygen tankage."

ANTONOV'S INVITATION

The long-anticipated May 8 review meeting was pushed back to June 30 and Conchie sent Burns a memo on May 19, 1989, to say: "Dr R. Parkinson has been approached to talk to the Antonov Design Bureau at the Paris Air Show on the possibility of An-225 (Dream) as a potential carrier vehicle for Hotol. I trust this will not embarrass you in any way."

Burns was unable to respond immediately since he had travelled to Bonn in Germany to give a presentation on Hotol at the Second European Aerospace Conference on Progress in Space Transportation, which took place from May 22-24, 1989. Conchie himself had also gone, along with Parkinson and Furniss.

Back at Warton the day after the conference ended, Burns responded with a handwritten annotation to Conchie's original typed message: "Brian Hopwell has already looked at this—see attached drawing. If the proposed meeting is to include a serious design discussion, then a Warton representative ought to be in on it. If it is about the 'business case', then we'll leave it to you."

The attached drawing showed a Hotol Configuration J-type vehicle, with an aerodynamic fairing covering the engine nozzles, mounted on the back of an An-225.

CONFIGURATION G TO H

The final Hotol review meeting eventually did take place on June 30, 1989, with a report detailing the last Hotol configuration 'freeze' being delivered in July. This document, coded HPN 0016, British Aerospace Hotol Feasibility—Report on Configuration Design Evolution Oct 1987-June 1989, would eventually run to more than 200 pages.

In addition to offering a basic history of the project and a development timeline for individual parts of the vehicle's structure (see Appendix II), it provided a detailed summary of exactly why and how Hotol had been evolved into Configuration J and then, ultimately, to Configuration K since the end of the PoC Study.

While this naturally repeated some of what Burns had previously explained in his monthly updates, it provided greater detail uninterrupted by other occurrences and is worth recapping here for the sake of clarity. Readers who feel they are already sufficiently familiar with this development may wish to skip ahead to the end of this chapter where the chronological account of events resumes.

The post-PoC period started with Configuration G, which "had a payload of 4.5t at a gross lift-off mass of 275t… the design of the wing strake was [then] modified to reflect a change in the capacity to resist a birdstrike. Previously the wing strake was designed to have sufficient structural integrity to continue the mission after a birdstrike. This capability was provided at a significant structural penalty.

"Because of the relatively low birdstrike risk anticipated for Hotol it was decided that the nose cone and leading edges should be designed such that no major structural damage would occur but on the detection of a birdstrike the mission would be aborted. The revised wing strake design resulted in a mass saving of 600kg." In its most advanced form, therefore, Configuration G had a calculated payload capability of 5.1t. Its engine was a PS350 standard RB.545, which used US Standard Atmosphere, 1976, data as the basis for the air it would be utilising. Its spill ramjet was designated Standard A and it used liquid oxygen for de-icing below 7.5km altitude. Indeed, the ascent profile called for the climb to 7.5km to be subsonic. Rocket specific impulse was 458 seconds with a nozzle area ratio of 100:1.

Unfortunately, "the longitudinal trim characteristics of Configuration G were unacceptable. The use of jettisonable foreplanes resolved the take-off trim problem but the vehicle could not be trimmed at high Mach numbers on the ascent nor during re-entry".

Configuration H then "resulted mainly from propulsion studies" using CAPS. It was "engineered to produce the first trimmable vehicle. The engine performance standard was updated by Rolls-Royce [to the RB.545-02D version] and intake sizing and spill ramjet performance optimisation studies were conducted. This time air data relating to an exclusively tropical atmosphere was used [from MIL-STD-210A, 1958] since "it was considered to be inappropriate to use a standard atmosphere for a vehicle launched from Kourou".

In addition, "to ensure that the heat exchangers do not ice up it was felt necessary to extend the liquid oxygen pre-injection cut-off altitude from 7.5km to 10km". The payload penalty for carrying this extra liquid oxygen was 350kg. But tests now showed that previous assumptions of intake diffusor duct efficiency had been too low and adding improved efficiency values to the calculations resulted in a whopping 1.9t payload increase.

The RB.545-02D's performance was achieved using "forced separation nozzles, giving an effective area ratio of 27.5:1 [up] to Mach 1.8, [then] 60:1 to Mach 3.6 and [finally] 100:1 above Mach 3.6. Taking the use of liquid oxygen injection for de-icing up to 10km altered the optimum ascent trajectory, allowing acceleration up to airframe structural limits—700kts—and "a climb at this limit until the intake design pressure is achieved".

The Standard A spill ramjet "was a simplified representation with some modified assumptions on lip and base drags. In this system the flow was allowed to choke at the bypass entry. This increases the internal pressure loss and reduces performance but produces a subsonic burning ramjet. Heat was added at the exit until the temperature reached a maximum of 1,600K". Payload with the RB.545-02D and Standard A ramjet was 6.6t.

Then the ramjet was updated to Standard B, with "the basic spill ramjet model... updated to represent more realistic internal pressure losses and, in agreement with Rolls-Royce, the maximum combustion temperature was allowed to increase to 2,000K. The revised performance... led to an increase in payload from 6.6t to 7.6t". The intake was then scaled to match the RB.545-02D's demands—reducing its area from 15sqm to 12sqm and increasing payload by a further 1.3t.

Having worked through these propulsion studies, the wings and fuselage were looked at next—as was the optimum point of transition from airbreathing to pure rocket power. As a result of these studies "the transition Mach number was increased from Mach 5 to 5.5 and a consistent transition pullup manoeuvre (i.e. one in which the assumed vehicle climb angle for the calculation of the rocket mass ratio matched that at the end of the airbreathing ascent) was assumed".

Configuration G had assumed an "instantaneous change of vehicle climb angle to 6.5°. The optimum climb angle achieved with Configuration H was 3.2°. The payload of this vehicle was calculated to be 9t".

CONFIGURATION H TO J

A payload of 9t was more than enough for Hotol but, as mentioned earlier, Configuration H was then comprehensively assessed during the summer of 1988 and "from the engineering study it was evident that the achievement of a controllable vehicle resulted in excessive mass penalties, not included in the CAPS model; optimisation of the front fuselage with 'Eminton' lines resulted in excess girth/volume/mass in the rear fuselage.

"As a result of this engineering assessment the basic mass empty of the CAPS Configuration H increased by 10.6t, leaving the vehicle with a payload of -1.6t. The changes in wing planform to the 54° cropped delta and the increase in wing thickness-to-chord ratio from 8-6-6% to 8%-7% in order to accommodate the outboard flap actuators increased the wing wave drag by a factor of 2.2. When the performance of the vehicle with the modified aerodynamics (particularly the above-mentioned wing wave drag) was assessed, the payload of the vehicle was further reduced to -4.5t."

This situation had evidently arisen because "the CAPS model used for the derivation of Configurations G and H was based on Configuration F structural design and layout. The model incorporated the performance benefits of the aft spill ramjet and the associated update in intake/engine mass model but the basic fuselage structural layout was unaltered from Configuration F.

"The discrepancy in the estimate for the basic mass empty between the CAPS and engineered Configuration H showed the model to be unrepresentative of the current vehicle design and totally inadequate for further vehicle optimisation studies. The engineering assessment of Configuration H showed the performance to be unacceptable."

This was the point at which the 'wet wing' had been introduced: "It was proposed that liquid oxygen be placed in the wing and with the provision of additional small liquid oxygen tanks beneath the payload bay it was possible to remove the large liquid oxygen tank just aft of the payload bay, and thus reduce the overall length of the fuselage by 5-6m."

In addition, the rear fuselage was redesigned to accommodate radial positioning of the heat exchangers and turbocompressors, with a liquid oxygen tank in the middle—a layout which the report aptly described as a "doughnut arrangement". The design also had a liquid oxygen trim tank in the nose and more liquid oxygen tanks below the payload bay. The large rear liquid oxygen tank was deleted.

Having already been given a change of planform, it was now decided that the wings could also be made from a different material—titanium with particulates being replaced by titanium aluminide. This allowed the lower surface re-entry insulation to be removed. The wing tanks still needed cryogenic insulation but this was now included as the core material of the skin panels' 'sandwich' structure.

The CAPS model was then given a major overhaul to account for all these changes, as well as jettisonable foreplanes.

RB.545-02D TO -04B

Early assessment of the 54° cropped delta wing with thickness to chord ratio of 8%-7% indicated that it "had a severe effect on the vehicle performance... as a result of this and a structural assessment to ensure adequate wing stiffness and hence aeroelastic properties, a wing of constant 7% thickness/chord was adopted. The improved vehicle performance resulting from the reduced wing wave drag outweighed the structural penalty from the increased skin thickness required (with the reduced wing depth) to maintain adequate stiffness properties".

With CAPS now using the latest mass data, calculations showed a payload increase of 7.95t—although this still only took the total up to 3.45t. And "at this stage the vehicle was considered to have a fineness ratio and wing area inconsistent with the requirements for re-entry trim".

Rolls-Royce had in the meantime swapped the RB.545-02D for the RB.545-03C. This represented an improved engineering standard, with "a more realistic representation of efficiencies and pressure losses. The low-pressure and high-pressure compressor efficiencies were reduced from 85% to 82%; the pre-burner and rocket chamber injector and the pipe pressure losses were included. The chamber and nozzle air film coolant allowance was increased from 5 to 9%. The liquid oxygen/air ratio required for heat exchanger de-icing was recalculated and increased by 25% (RR initial calculations were in error)".

The overall effect was to reduce payload again however, back down to 2.17t. According to the report, "it was obvious at this stage that the performance was inadequate and the vehicle was not fully optimised. Through the Joint Propulsion Team, ways of improving the engine performance were identified which led to the -03D engine". The RB.545-03D had basically the same cycle as the -03C engine with 180:1 area ratio nozzles but performance was improved by using pre-chilled propellants. Payload rose again, this time to 2.7t.

Studies had shown that for every four tonnes of liquid oxygen tankage that could be deleted, payload would increase by one tonne. So the RB.545-03D was re-examined to see if a way of reducing the quantity of liquid oxygen needed for de-icing could be found. The solution seemed to be the recirculation of cooled air using a larger low-pressure compressor. This incurred a mass penalty of 80kg per engine but significantly reduced the amount of liquid oxygen that had to be carried, taking the payload up to 3.76t and resulting in a new engine variant designated RB.545-04A. There was always a fly in the ointment however, and now it was found that "the fuselage fineness ratio of this vehicle was higher than that of vehicles shown to have satisfactory pitch control. Reducing the fineness ratio to that of a 'trimmed vehicle' reduced the payload to -0.85t". The team were back to square one again.

Next, they looked at engine chamber pressure and determined that increasing it using a 25% larger turbocompressor gave a thrust boost below Mach 2 of 18%, with about the same specific impulse. As always, using bigger

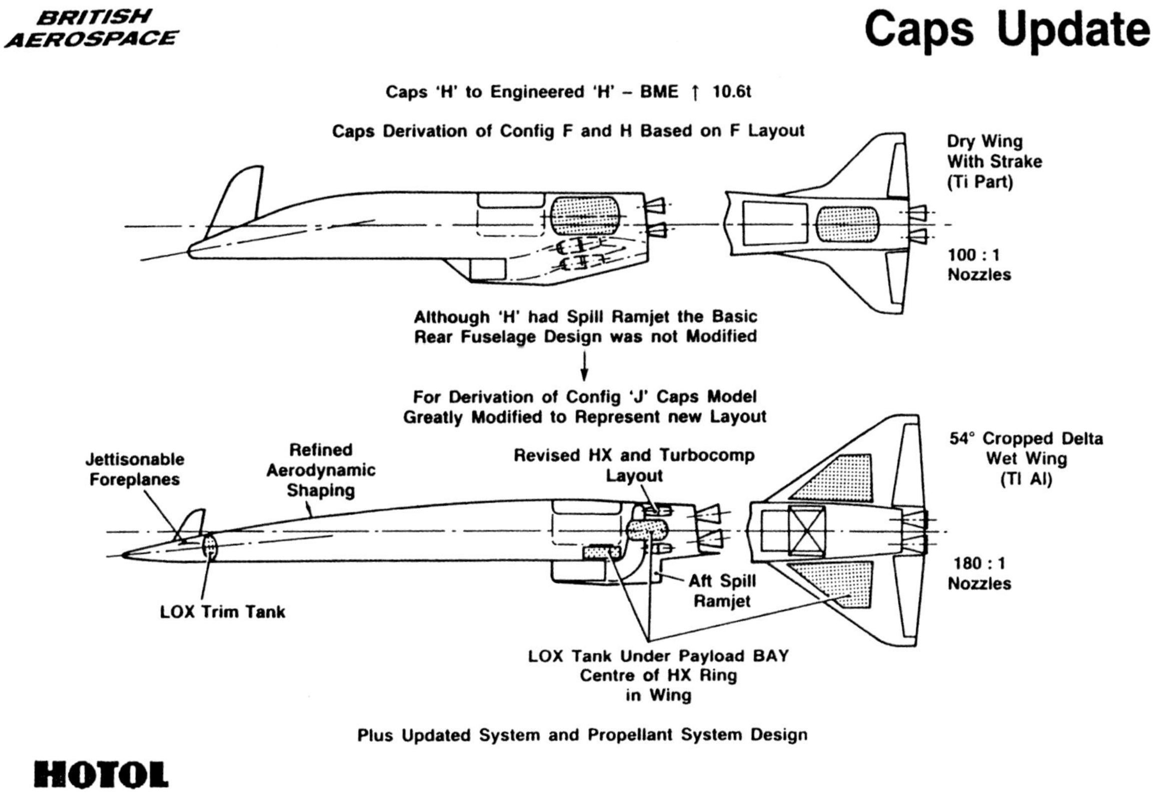

CAPS updates from Configuration F through to Configuration J—the latter bearing only a superficial resemblance to the former.

components brought with it another mass penalty—this time another 120kg per engine. This arrangement was designated RB.545-04B and it increased payload from -0.85t to 1.49t.

CONFIGURATION J4½ TO K

The vehicle was now given another round of optimisation, looking at the effects of varying ascent trajectory, transition Mach number, airbreathing and rocket engine sizes, and vehicle fineness ratio. This resulted in Configuration J4—with the maximum intake design pressure increased from 260Kpa to 280Kpa and the transition moved from Mach 5.5 to Mach 6. Payload rose accordingly to 4.88t.

It was then found that making the vehicle more slender, as Configuration J5, increased payload still further to 6.34t—but a question mark remained over that design's trim characteristics. Once again, "during the engineering assessment of these vehicles, a number of discrepancies were identified. The change in exposed wing area from the performance optimised 106sqm (exposed) for Configuration F, to the large wing of Configuration H, sized to provide adequate re-entry trim characteristics, introduced errors in both the low supersonic fuselage wave drag estimates and the high Mach number wing induced drag. The net result of these errors was to drive the vehicle to a slender [form] ... and increase the optimum transition [to] Mach 6.

"A further check on the vehicle propellant tank capacities showed that the amount of liquid oxygen assumed to fit in the wing tanks was optimistic. To fit all the liquid oxygen into the vehicle would require a larger wing. At this stage full incidence-dependent propulsion data were provided by Filton. Previously only Mach-dependent data, with an assumed Mach/incidence relationship had been available. The CAPS model was updated to correct the drag prediction errors, the updated engine standard was installed and Configuration J was reassessed."

Subsequently, exposed wing area was increased to 222sqm, the engine data was revised based on new test results and the ascent trajectory was optimised—resulting in what was now designated Configuration J4½, with a predicted payload of 3.67t.

But there were still further steps that could be taken. Making Configuration J4½ slenderer and increasing its wing area to 252sqm "was shown to give optimum performance". This design was then designated Configuration K.

At the time of the report, "adequate trim characteristics of Configuration K have not been confirmed, although it is anticipated that with this much larger wing, this slightly more slender vehicle can be adequately controlled. The possible benefits that may result from this larger wing on the control system (reduced hinge moments with reduced chord flaperons), and on the centre of gravity control

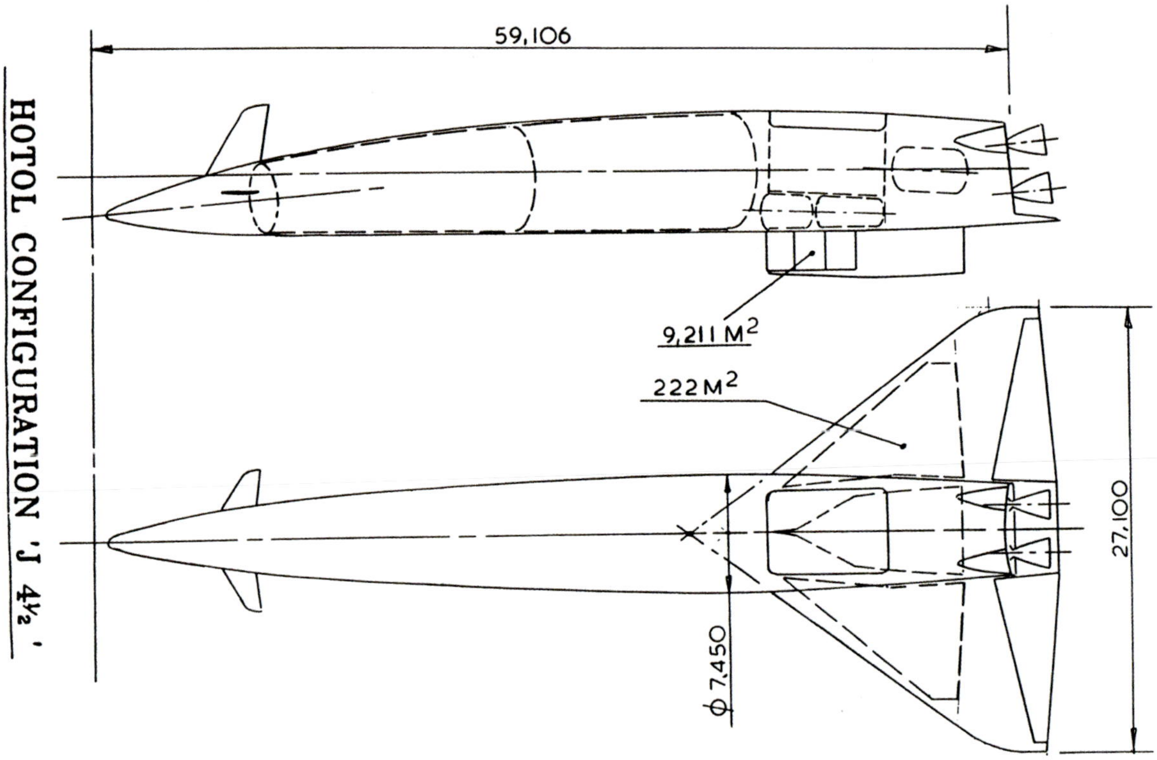

The Hotol Configuration J4½ with 222sqm wing area.

Hotol Configuration K. CHRIS SANDHAM-BAILEY

(smaller nose liquid oxygen transfer tank) have not been assessed. This work must be completed before the performance of Configuration K is confirmed".

The predicted payload for this design was 4.99t.

WHAT WAS IT MADE OF?

Efforts to find the best materials available for each element of Hotol's design had been ongoing throughout the project. The July 1989 report stated that "the present design of Hotol relies heavily on the development of advanced materials. These materials can be separated into four categories: high temperature materials, medium temperature materials, low temperature materials and insulation.

High temperature materials were needed for "components such as the nose cone, intake, TPS panels and wing/fin leading edges. These components are required to retain their strength at the temperatures encountered at the stagnation regions of the vehicle during atmospheric re-entry (approaching 2,000K) and survive the lifetime of the vehicle without undue erosion".

Candidate materials for these areas were carbon-carbon (with oxidation protection), carbon-silicon carbine and silicon carbide-silicon carbide.

Configuration J, the last variant for which full details were produced, had a carbon-silicon carbide nose cone, a fin made of titanium and particulates with a carbon-silicon carbide leading edge and a rear nose structure made of titanium and particulates with TPS panels on its lower surface.

The vehicle's TPS panels were made of carbon-silicon carbide. The forward fuselage, containing the liquid hydrogen tank, was entirely covered with TPS panels, underneath which was a layer of Protecalor high temperature insulation, then a layer of TG 15000 low temperature insulation, then an air gap, then the hydrogen tank itself made from carbon-PEEK sandwich.

HOTOL K CONFIGURATION

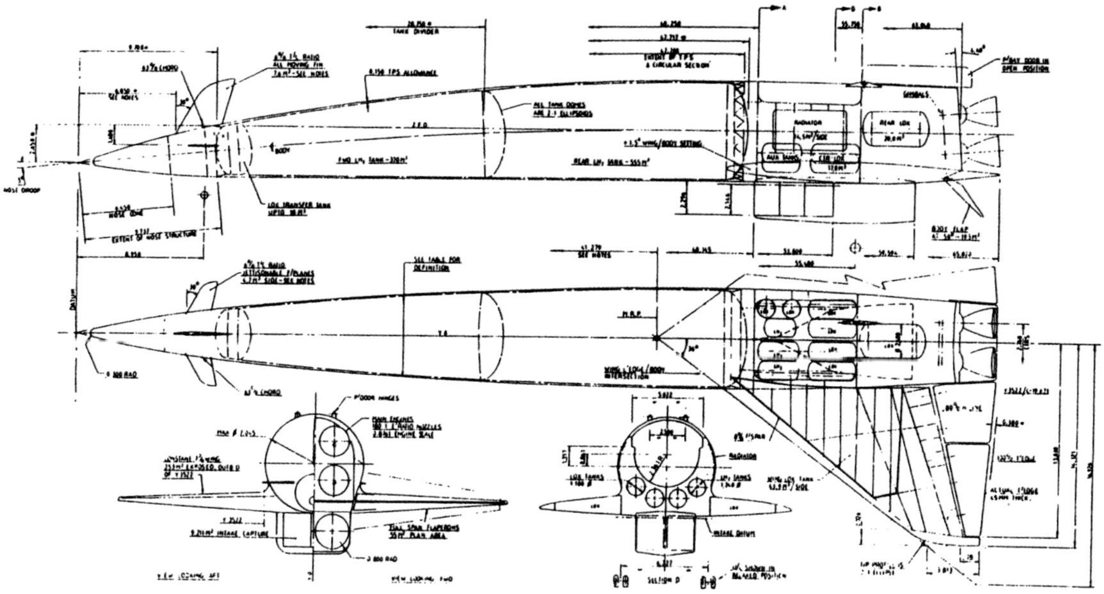

The final iteration of the airbreathing Hotol was Configuration K—although work on this design was never fully completed. Compared to Configuration J4½ it had an increased wing area and a slightly slimmer fuselage.

HOTOL J DATUM MATERIALS

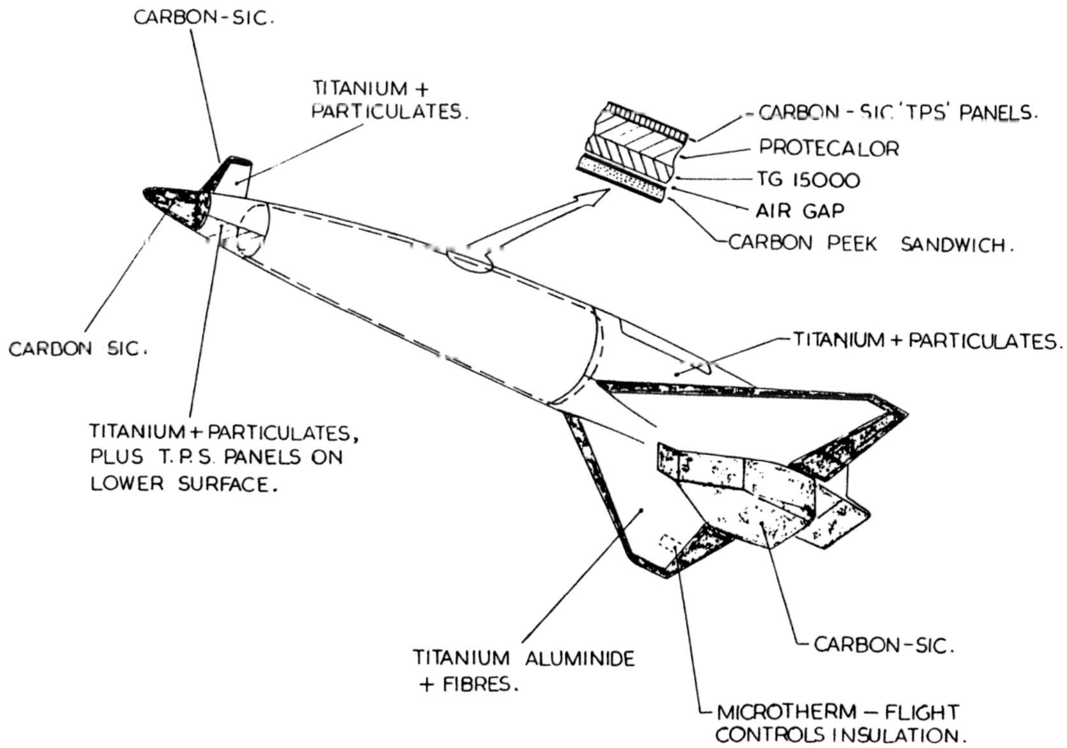

The materials chosen for Configuration J—with carbon-silicon carbide being favoured for the hottest regions.

The rear fuselage was made of titanium and particulates and the engine intake pod was made of carbon-silicon carbide.

When it came to Hotol's hot wing structure, "titanium aluminide reinforced by silicon carbide fibres is favoured because of its ability to retain its strength at temperatures up to 1,200K. This eliminates the requirement for insulation on the lower wing surface.

"The development of this material is still at an early stage and much work is required in order to verify the target properties used in the Hotol design stage. Also, since one of the main applications of this material will be thin gauge sandwich panels, the development of fine, small diameter silicon carbide fibres is also very important".

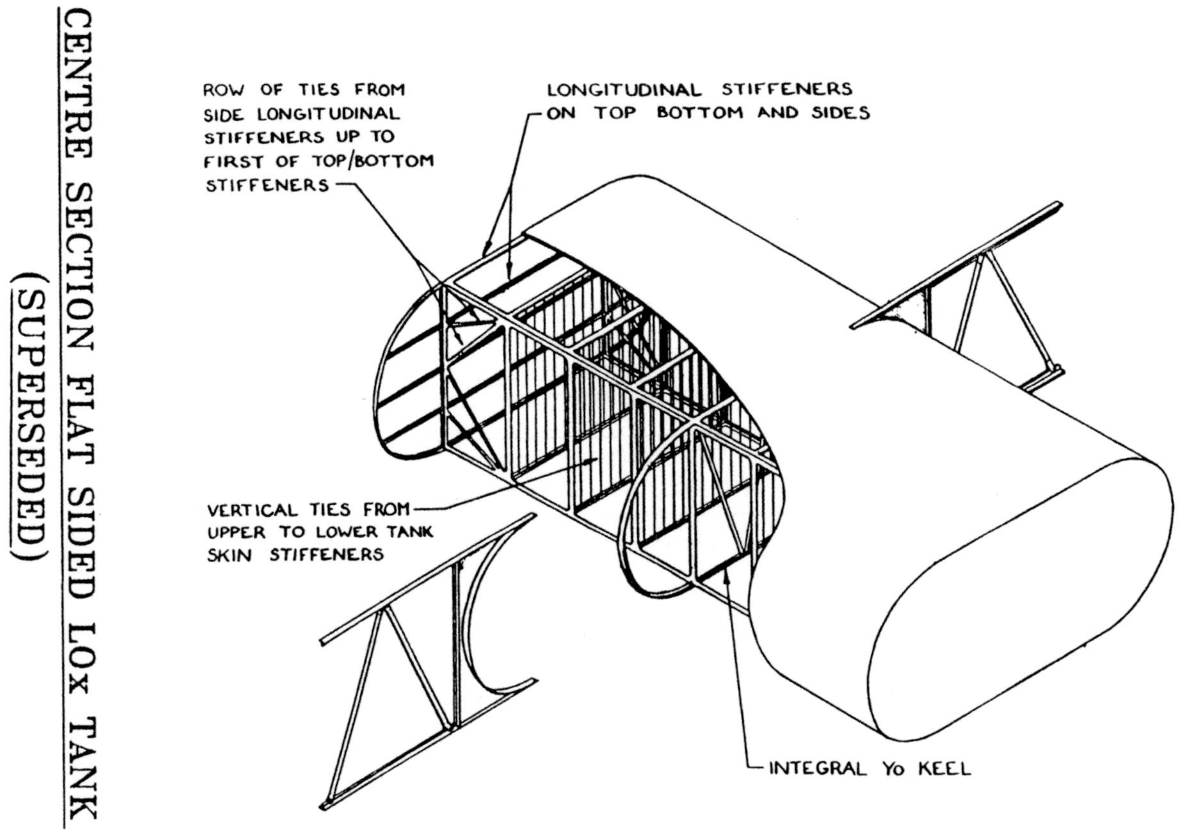

Arrangement of the liquid oxygen tank compartment below the payload bay.

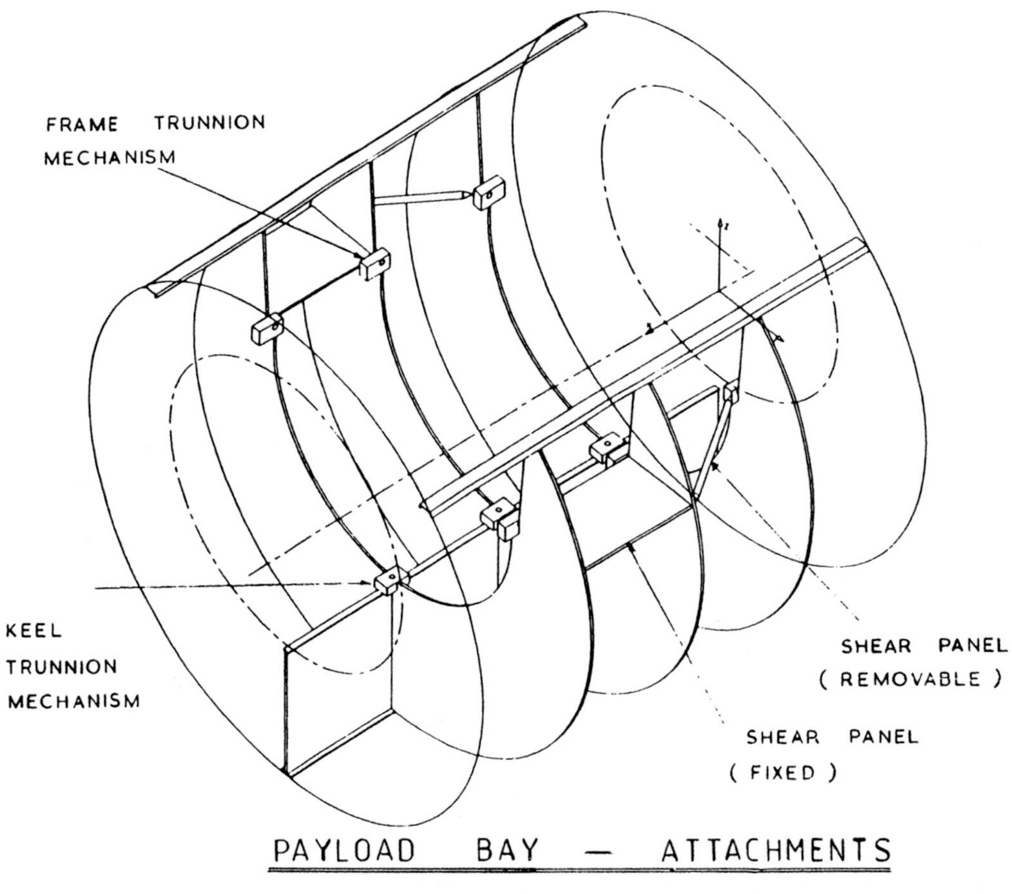

Payload bay attachment points.

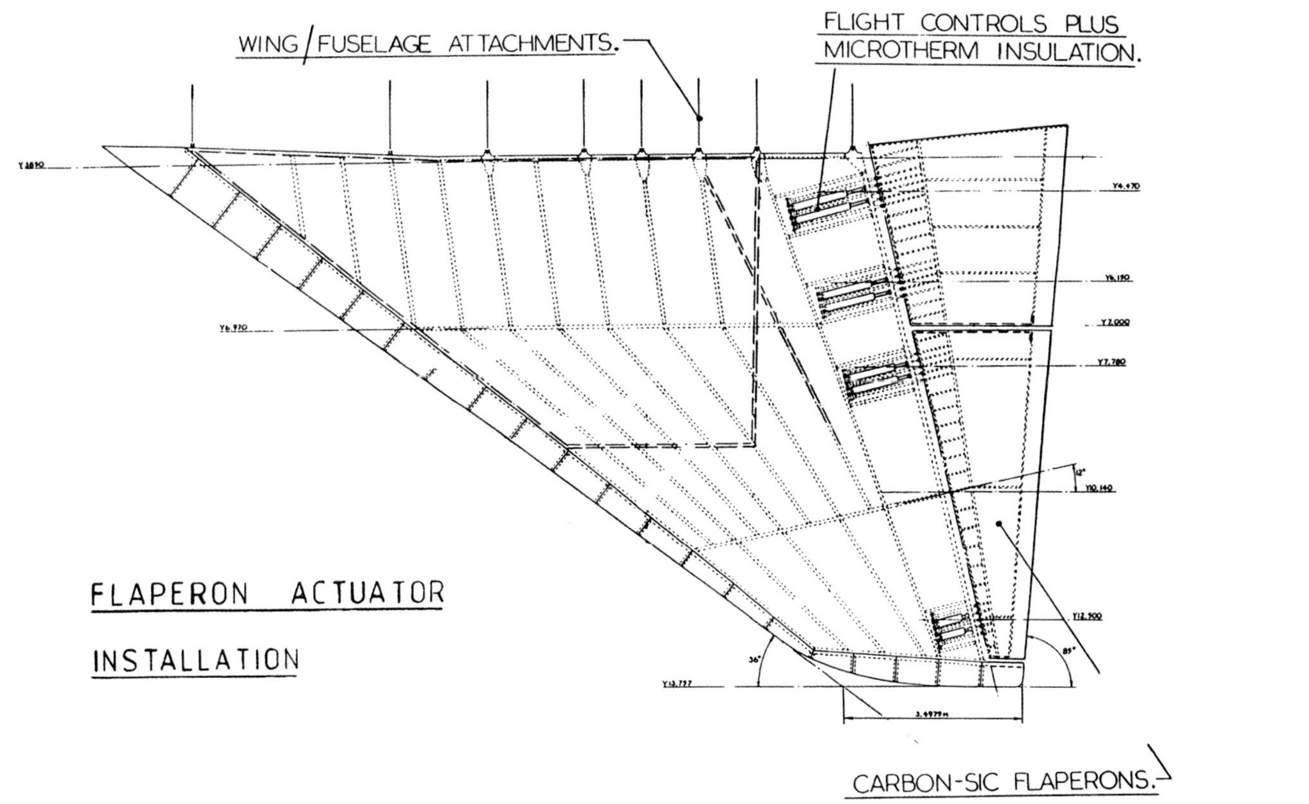

Hotol Configuration J flaperon design.

DESIGN FEATURES

Throughout the course of Hotol's rapid airframe/engine evolution, individual aspects of the design had themselves been regularly examined, re-examined and updated. For example, the July 1989 report said that four different foreplane arrangements had been examined post-PoC; first up being active foreplanes with ailerons on Configuration H: "The required foreplane area would be 9sqm each side, which is too large to avoid a gap appearing between the root rib and the fuselage side when deflected to a large negative angle on re-entry and would consequently give rise to unacceptably high heating rates and hence temperatures in this region."

Second was the same thing but for Configuration J5—which had the same problems. Third was J5 with active foreplanes and full-span flaperons. This entailed foreplanes that were 3sqm each side "the largest acceptable for avoiding a gap, with full-span flaperons retained to supplement the foreplanes as required".

Finally, there was Configuration J5 with active foreplanes/nosecone and ailerons. This unusual arrangement involved fixing "the foreplanes rigidly to the forward nosecone, thereby avoiding a gap appearing, and hinging the whole [nose] unit at the foreplane trailing edge". This apparently "looked promising but further, more detailed work is required before a definite conclusion can be reached as to its viability".

Nose 'blunting' was considered for Configuration J but "shortening the nose in the interests of mass saving was far outweighed by the drag increase. Nose bluntness for H and J was therefore left at 0.3m radius. It should be noted that re-entry trajectories which have low nose stagnation temperatures arising from other considerations would permit the use of a sharper nose and hence a small performance benefit".

When it came to the engine intake, "the basic design and structural materials of the twin-ramp vertical wedge air intakes and the layout of the propulsion units, circumferentially around a centre liquid oxygen tank in the rear fuselage, have not altered from those of Configuration G. Detailed structural and mechanical design have proceeded at Brough and Filton, leading to updated mass estimates and a higher level of confidence in the soundness of the design".

A key part of the system aboard Configuration J was the aft spill deflector vanes: "These (one per side) will be used to proportion the airflow between engine demand and the aft spill system, responding rapidly (200 degrees per second) to signals from the engine control system. Actuation will be by means of pneumatic motors in the rear fuselage, via worm gears".

Hotol's extensive and often massive engine pipework,

British Aerospace HOTOL

1 Nosecone – carbon silicone carbide (C/Sic)
2 Air data sensors
3 Nose reaction control system (RCS) thrusters (7)
4 Frames – titanium plus particulates (Ti+ part)
5 Truss structures of Ti+ part
6 Nosewheel doors of Ti+ part with thermal protection panels
7 Nosegear – steerable, forward-folding, and gravity operated on down operation. Tyre pressure 600lb/in^2
8 Forward systems bay
9 Undercarriage sheer webs of Ti+ part
10 Access door to forward systems bay
11 Water boilers
12 APUs (4)
13 Hydraulic reservoirs (4)
14 Hydraulic accumulators (4)
15 Hydrazine tanks (4)
16 Nitrogen tanks (6)
17 All-moving fin, torsion box of Ti+ part leading edges and tip C/Sic, trailing edge C/Sic sandwich
18 Hydraulically-actuated jacks for fin
19 Jettisonable titanium foreplanes
36 Aft dome to LH$_2$ tank
37 Rear truss structure – Ti+ part
38 Sandwich skin of Ti+ part
39 Spacionics bay
40 Payload bay
41 Rearward hingeing payload bay door
42 Space radiator
43 Payload bay trellis frames of Ti+ part
44 Reflective fabric liner in payload bay
45 Longerons of Ti+ part
46 Water boilers (4)
47 APUs (4)
48 Hydraulic reservoirs (4)
49 Hydraulic accumulators (4)
50 Water tanks (4)
51 Nitrogen tanks (6)
52 Hydrazine tanks (4)
53 Auxiliary LH$_2$ tank, capacity 7.17m^3
54 Auxiliary LH$_2$ tank, capacity 2.52m^3
55 Auxiliary LOX tanks (2), each with a capacity of 0.7m^3
56 Centre LOX tank, capacity 19m^3
57 Rear fuselage
58 Rear fuselage frames of Ti+ part
59 Rear thermal bulkhead of C/Sic
60 Upper keel structure
61 Lower keel structure
62 Body flap – C/Sic
63 Hinges for bodyflap (5)
64 Actuator for bodyflap
65 Intake structure
66 Replaceable leading edge
67 Intake ramp 1 – C/Sic
68 Intake ramp 2
69 Intake ramp 3
70 Keel – C/Sic
71 Forward spigot
72 Thrust spigot
73 Aft spigot
74 Swinging links
75 Screwjack actuators for ramps
76 Moveable vane
77 Boundary-layer bleed
78 Plenum intake
79 Diffuser in plenum
80 Intake lip
81 Spill system
82 Structure – C/Sic
83 Undercarriage doors – C/Sic
84 Main landing gear – gas actuated, carbon-carbon brakes; tyre pressures 600lb/in^2
85 Wing carry-through truss structure – Ti+ part
86 Rear LOX tank – Carbon PEEK
87 Engine thrust frame – Ti+ part
88 Thrust structure
89 Manifold
90 Heat exchangers (8)
91 Turbo compressors
92 Turbo compressor exhaust
93 Turbo pumps LH$_2$ (4)
94 Turbo pumps LOX (4)
95 Main engines (4)
96 Engine gimball actuators
97 RCS – rear
98 Leading edge of C/Sic panels
99 Tip of C/Sic
100 Inner flaperon C/Sic sandwich
101 Outer flaperon
102 Wing-to-fuselage attachments – titanium
103 Solid body side rib – titanium aluminide + Sic fibres
104 Solid front spar – titanium aluminide + Sic fibres
105 Wing LOX tank, capacity 2×38.5m^3
106 Rear solid spars – titanium aluminide + Sic fibres
107 Truss structure, spars and ribs – titanium aluminide

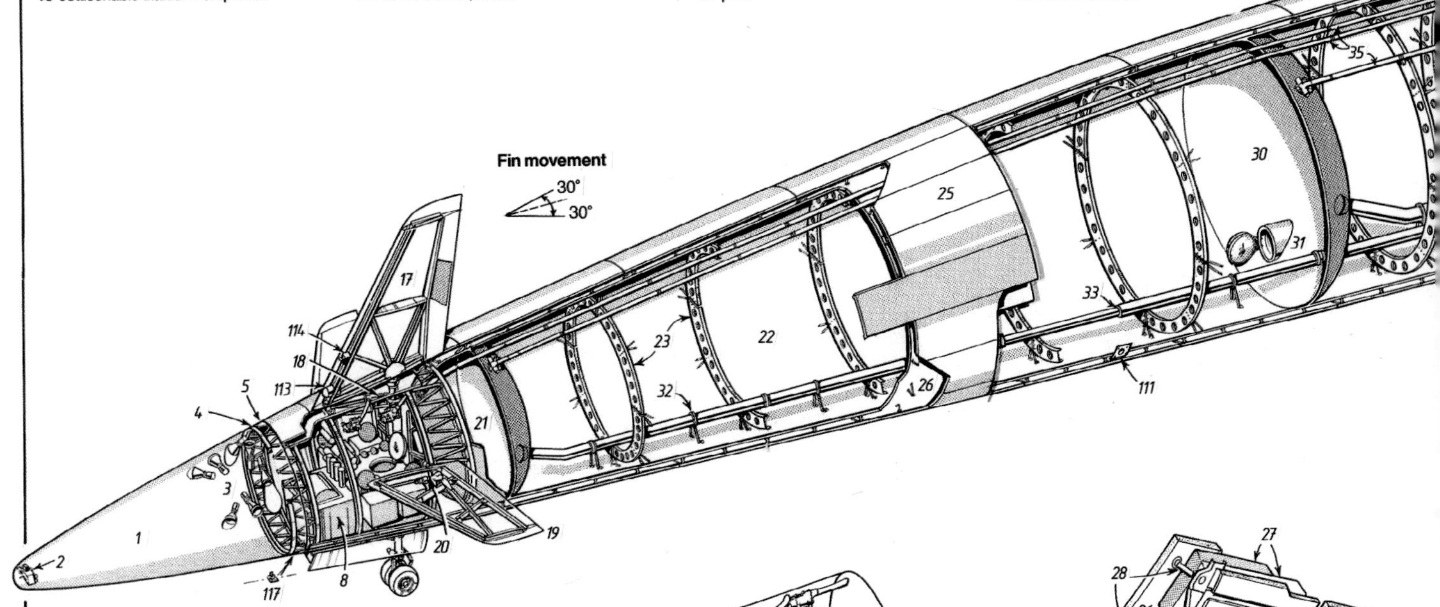

20 Jettison gun
21 Liquid Oxygen (LOX) transfer tank, Carbon-poly-ether-ketone sandwich (Carbon PEEK) capacity 18m^3
22 Liquid Hydrogen (LH$_2$) – forward tank – Carbon PEEK sandwich, capacity 398m^3
23 Baffles of Carbon PEEK
24 LH$_2$ aft tank – Carbon PEEK sandwich, capacity 597m^3
25 Thermal protection shield panel (TPS)
26 Tank wall
27 Tank insulation
28 Support posts
29 Segmented support frames
30 Tank divider
31 Access doors for tank inspection
32 LOX transfer pipe – Carbon PEEK
33 Helium purging on outside of LOX transfer pipe
34 LH$_2$ feed pipe – Carbon PEEK
35 Tank pressurisation lines – Carbon PEEK

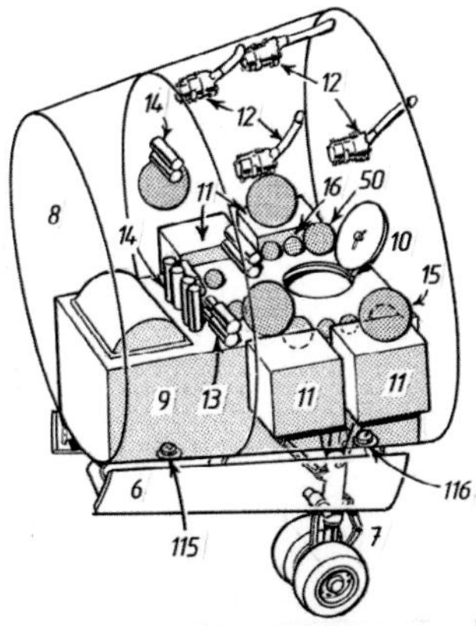

Detail of forward equipment bay (larger scale)

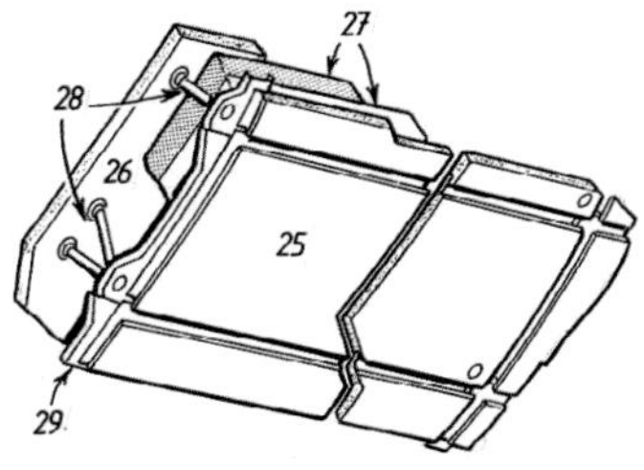

Detail of thermal protection shield panel

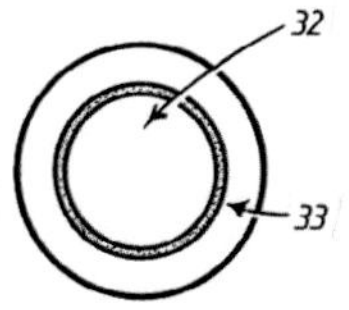

Detail of LOX transfer pipe

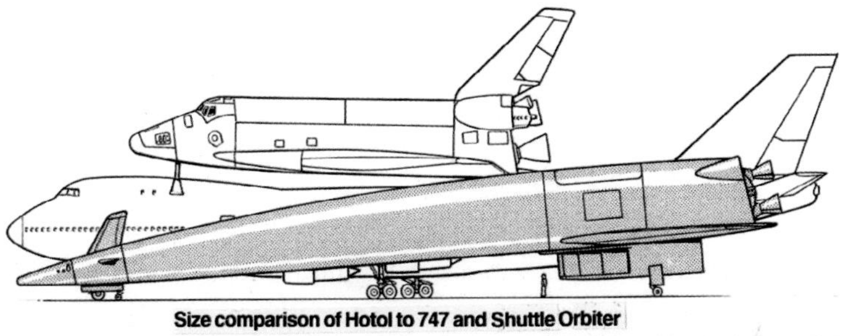

Size comparison of Hotol to 747 and Shuttle Orbiter

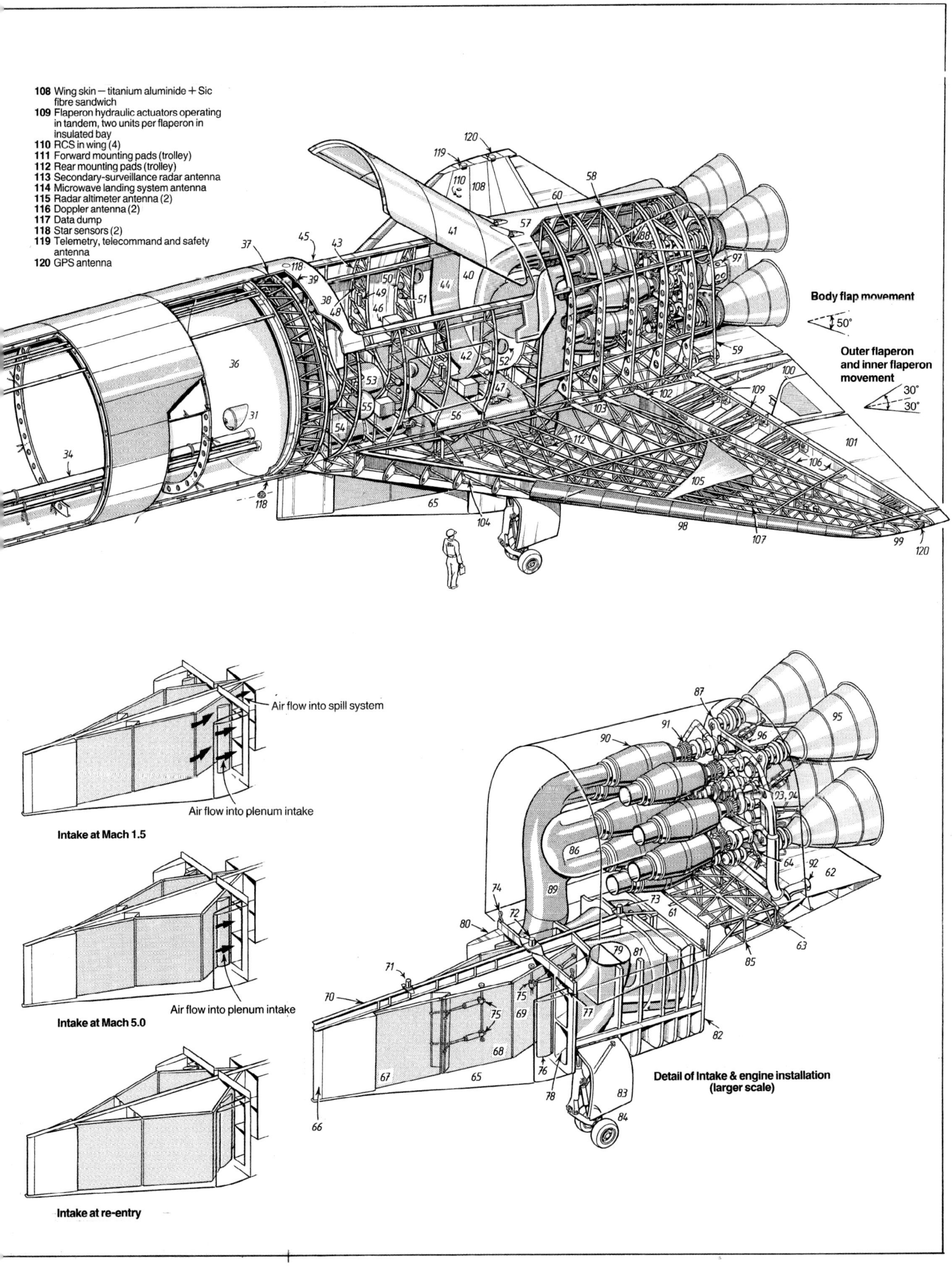

Hotol Configuration J4½ cutaway drawing by Tim Hall from Flight International's March 25, 1989, issue. The drawing was based on data supplied by the Hotol team at BAe and is regarded as highly accurate. FLIGHTGLOBAL

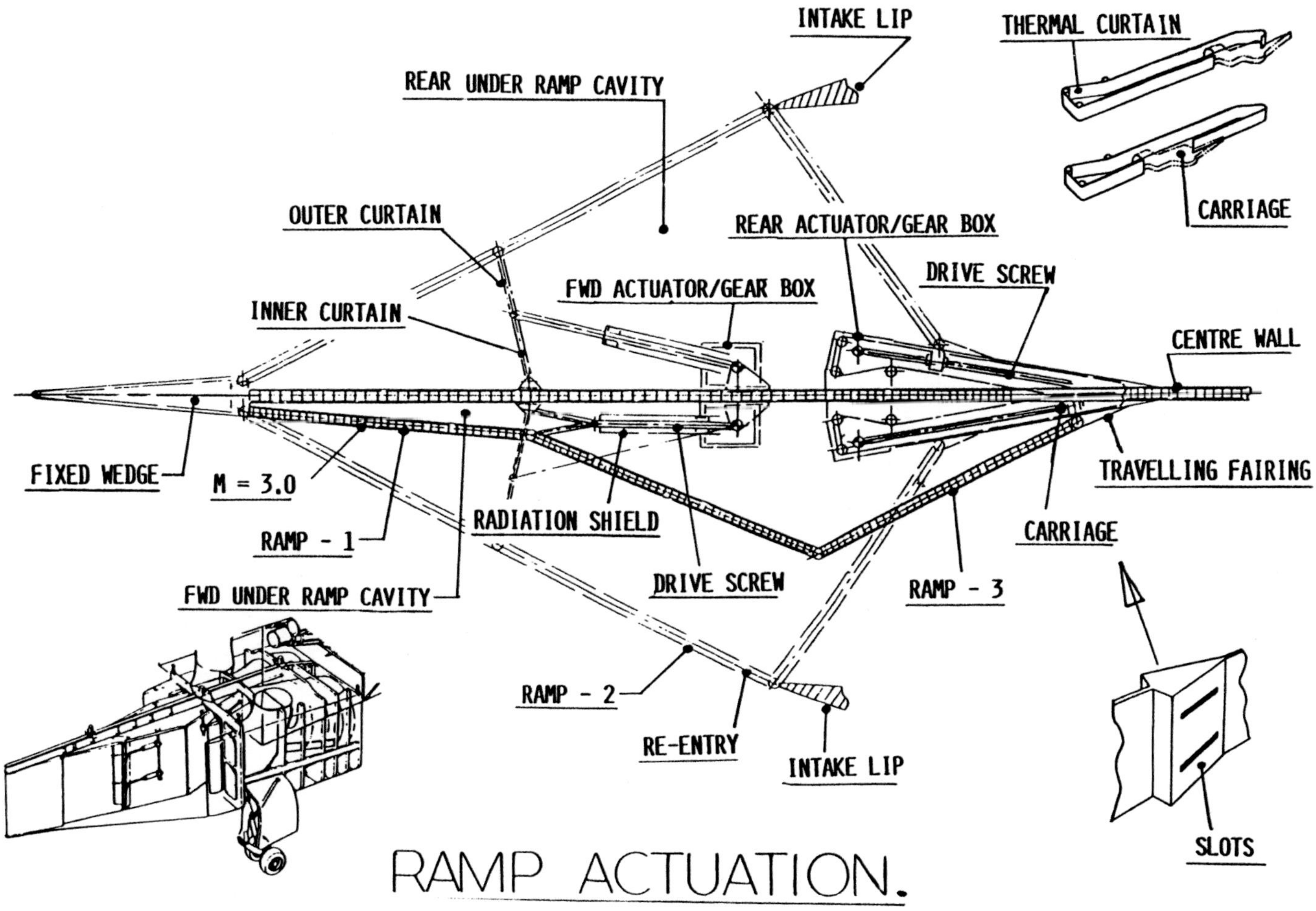

Intake ramp actuation diagram from the HPN0016 report—making this perhaps the final variant.

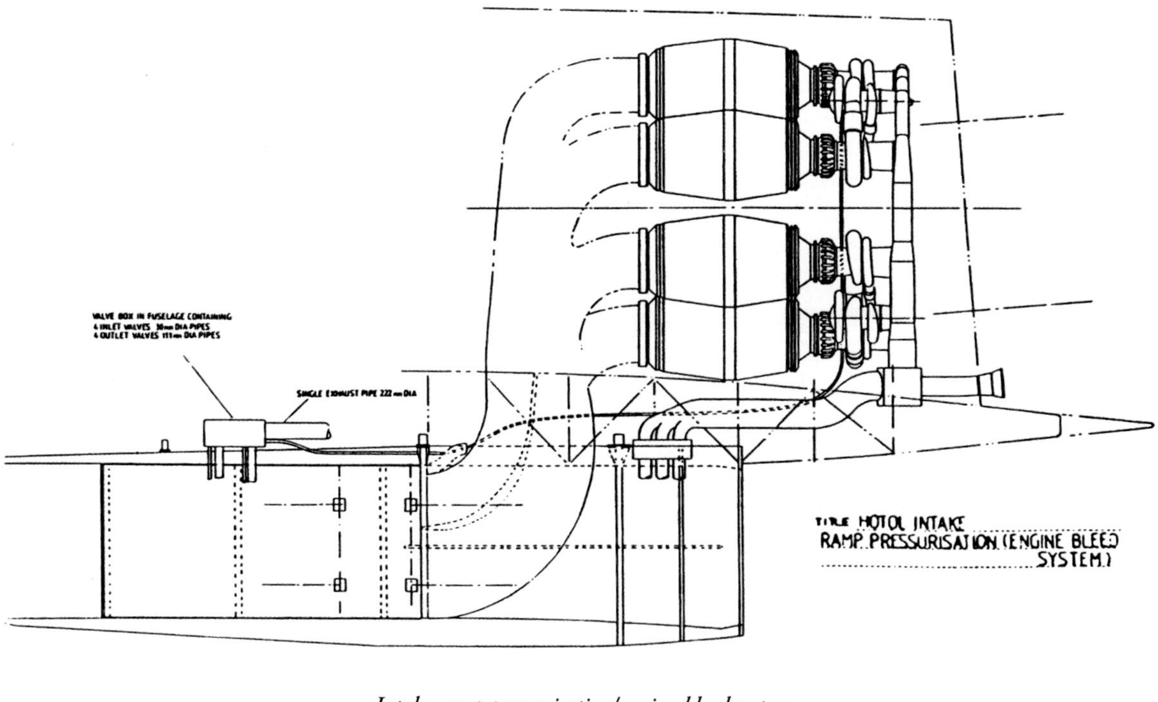

Intake ramp pressurisation/engine bleed system.

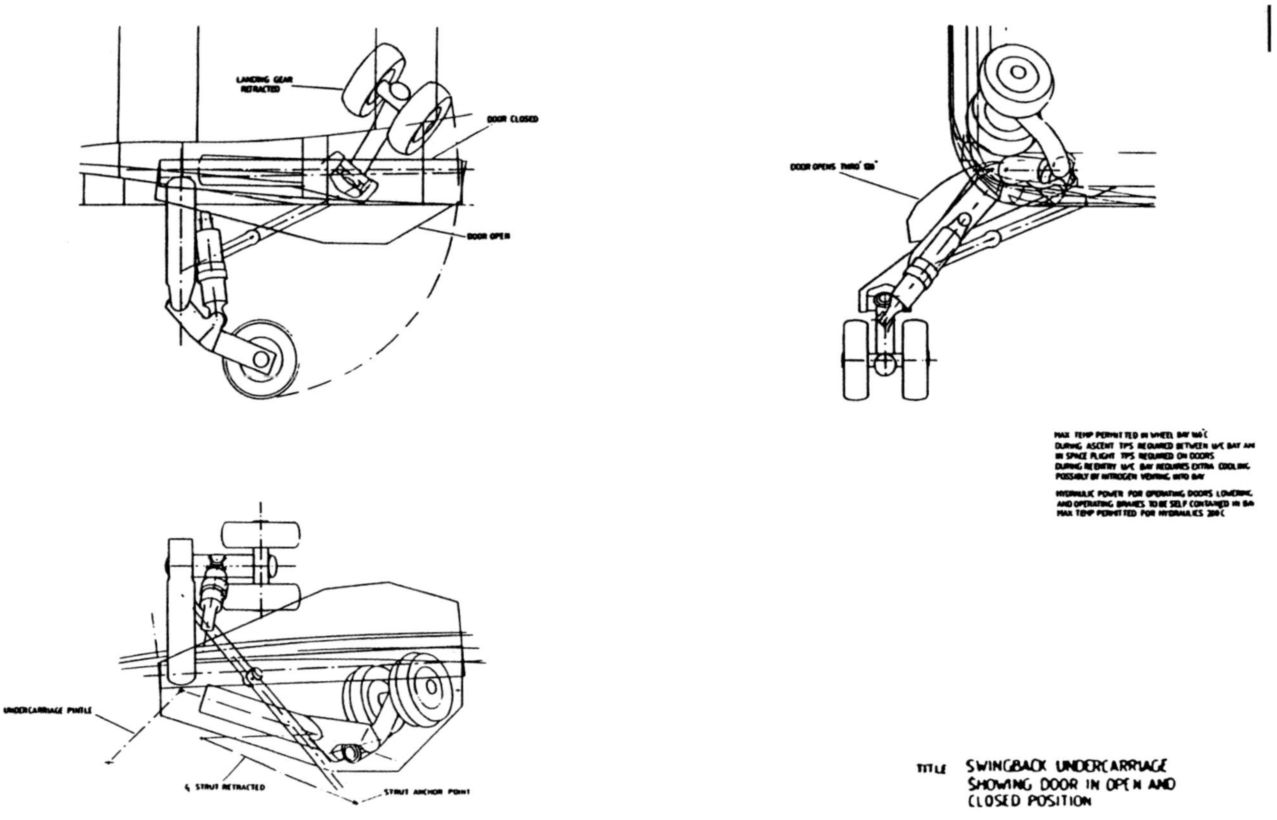

Revised undercarriage design — now bespoke rather than reusing existing BAe 146 components.

nicknamed 'the spaghetti' by the design team, had been a source of some difficulty throughout. According to the report: "The most significant development in this area has been to mount the turbopumps on the airframe rather than on the main engines, the latter being the conventional location. All the pipes from and to the liquid hydrogen, turbopumps feeding heat exchanger 1 and heat exchanger 2, the high-pressure turbocompressor, tank pressurisation and the de-icing pipe from the liquid oxygen turbopump can now be rigid. The number of flexible connections across each engine gimbal has therefore been reduced from 13 to five. Two of the remaining connections involve both high pressures and extreme temperatures outside the range of existing hose or bellows technology, and these have been identified as requiring inclusion under the heading of enabling technology". In other words, more development work was needed.

In the final equation, the BAe 146 undercarriage long assumed for Hotol had been dropped and in its place "a revised design has been adopted, mounted from a major component, saving in mass (275kg). The inside of the mainwheel bays and doors will be lined with insulation to protect the tyres from excessive temperatures (assumed limit 160°C), particularly during re-entry. Since drag loads will oppose lowering of the undercarriage, a 'one-shot' jack powered by a pressurised helium bottle will be employed".

TRIMMING HOTOL

One of the most difficult problems facing the Hotol team had been trimming the vehicle during its ascent. Crucial to this aspect of the design was the propellant supply system.

According to the report: "In addition to supplying propellants to the pumps at the correct flowrates and pressures, the supply subsystem is now also required to provide control of the vehicle centre of mass position. This trimming function is necessary during airbreathing ascent to counteract movement of the centre of pressure which takes place as the vehicle becomes hypersonic.

"Trimming is achieved in two ways. Firstly, single tanks have been replaced by multiple tanks which are carefully located in the vehicle and are used in strict sequence. In addition, it has been necessary, during airbreathing flight, to pump liquid oxygen from the rear of the vehicle up to a special nose tank."

The main liquid hydrogen tank had been divided into two compartments: "During take-off, liquid from the forward compartment is used to help lighten the nose. Shortly after take-off, the aft compartment is used. This helps to shift the centre of mass position forward, thus matching the centre of pressure movement. During rocket mode, the forward compartment is used. Each compartment has its own separate supply pipe with a stop valve in it. A single pressurisation system is used for both compartments."

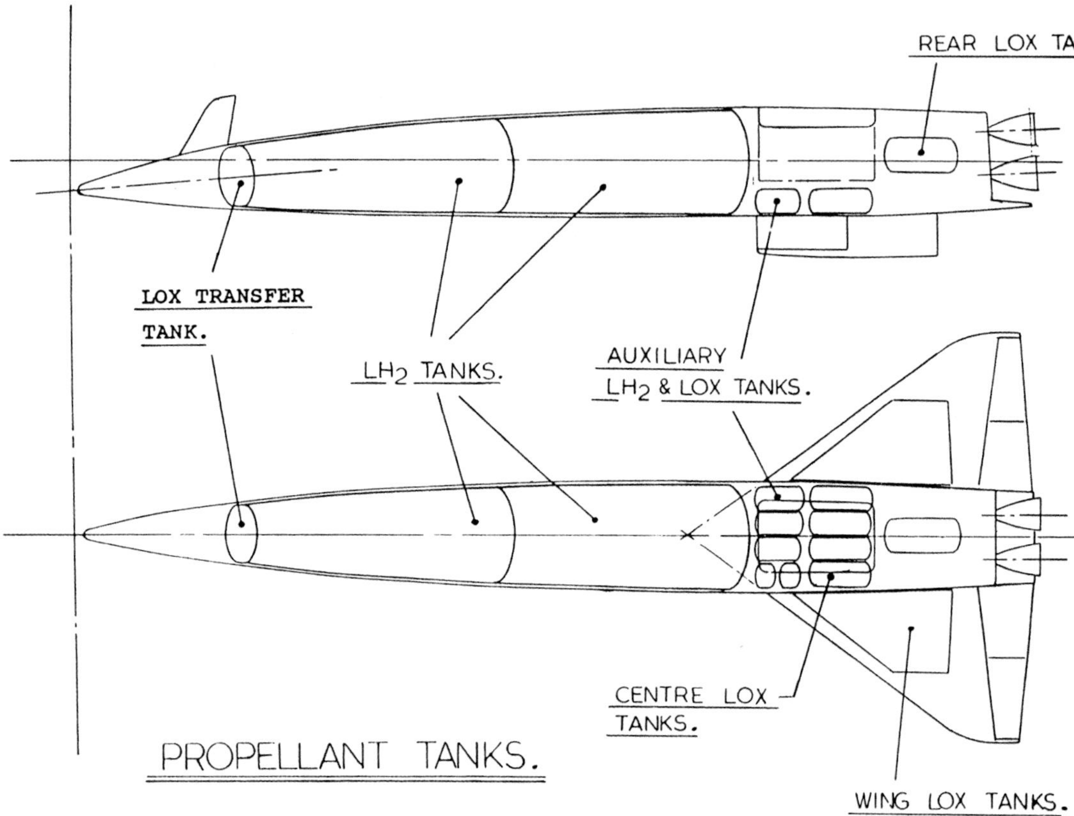

Hotol Configuration J with wet wing and liquid oxygen tanks positioned below the payload bay.

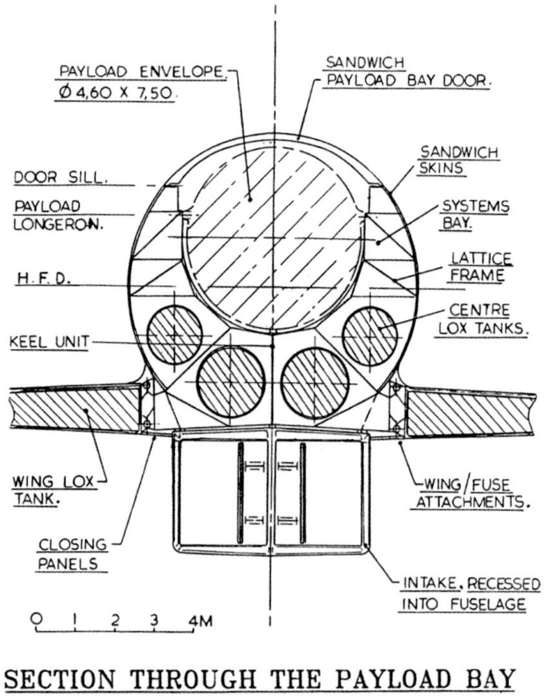

Section view showing the central liquid oxygen tanks.

For Configuration J/K, the vehicle had no fewer than eight liquid oxygen tanks—four cylindrical tanks linked together under the payload bay (the centre section tanks) with a common stop valve, the aft or 'doughnut' tank just forward of the rocket engines surrounded by turbocompressors, a non-cylindrical tank in each wing, and the nose tank.

The latter was empty at take-off but would need to have been chilled down to liquid oxygen temperatures prior to launch. According to the report: "At the appropriate time, liquid oxygen is pumped forward into it from the tanks at the rear. This has the effect of moving the centre of gravity position forward and consequently maintaining vehicle trim.

"The sequence of liquid oxygen tank usage is as follows. During take-off, liquid is drawn from the tanks beneath the payload bay. After take-off, the aft tank is used (it is from this tank that the bulk of the liquid oxygen is transferred to the nose). After depletion of the aft tank, the wing tanks are used together. Following transition, the wing tanks are used together with the nose tank. Finally, the centre section tanks (beneath the payload bay) are used.

"Transfer of liquid oxygen to the nose tank is accomplished in two stages. First, an air turbine-powered pump raises the pressure of a liquid oxygen bleed. Most of this liquid oxygen is used within the engines for de-icing during airbreathing flight. Another useful feature of this system is that it conditions the liquid oxygen supply lines during airbreathing ascent in preparation for the switch to rocket mode. Return of liquid oxygen from the nose is accomplished by using the considerable longitudinal static head which is available after transition."

PRE-CHILLED FUEL

Not only did the quantities of propellant in each of the eight tanks have to be correct at any given time, but the propellant itself had to be pre-chilled in order to reduce its volume: "The liquid hydrogen maximum bulk temperature during ascent has been reduced from 21.7K to 18K. Likewise the liquid oxygen temperature has been reduced from 93.7K to 67K. It must be emphasised that the propellants are still completely in liquid form (the use of 'slush' is not intended). Mass savings have been achieved by removing the recirculation pumps from the vehicle and instead placing them on the trolley. These pumps keep the supply systems cold prior to ignition by circulating propellants. They are not required after engine ignition."

The report noted that, "by using chilled liquid hydrogen, a 5% saving in tank volume has been made. In addition, the low fuel vapour pressure has enabled larger supply line pressure drops to be tolerated whilst still satisfying the engine pump NPSH requirement. Hence the supply line diameters (and masses) have been reduced ... As in the hydrogen system, the use of chilled oxygen enables savings in both tank volume (approximately 10%) and supply line mass. Against this however, the large number of tanks (each with its own stop valve) has itself led to a significant increase in the mass of the supply system. Despite this, the overall vehicle mass is minimised.

"High wing temperatures on re-entry have dictated the use of high temperature insulant in this area instead of the more efficient cryogenic foam. In addition, the wing tanks have a high surface area to volume ratio. This has led to larger rates of heat input during both ground hold and ascent. Under normal circumstances, the subsequent build-up of unusable saturated liquid would be unacceptable. However, it has been demonstrated that if the heat is distributed throughout a sufficient proportion of the liquid oxygen, then the resulting temperature increase will not be sufficient. Hence a recirculation (or 'stirring') system will be installed within each of the liquid oxygen tanks. This will consist of several small electric impellers. The details of this system still require some work, however it is already clear that even relatively inefficient recirculation (e.g. only 10% efficient) would be adequate."

The collector tanks intended to pick up residual saturated liquids from the main engines so they could be used in the orbital manoeuvring system had now been deleted (or at least repurposed)—since "in the hydrogen system, most saturated liquid can now be used in the main engines because of the static head available from the long supply line as main engine cut-off approaches. In the oxygen tanks, it has been decided to actively combat the build-up of saturated liquid by use of a mixing system. Removal of the collector tanks has led to dry mass savings and significant improvements in subsystem reliability.

"Pressurisation of the liquid oxygen tanks has been changed in two significant ways. Firstly, helium is used as the pressurant instead of gaseous oxygen. Secondly, a 'smart' pressurant system, which takes account of propellant static head, is used for the liquid oxygen wing tanks. This leads to reductions in tank design pressure, and hence mass."

OMS AND RCS

Now that saturated liquid residuals had been eliminated from the fuel supply system, and the collector tanks deleted from the fuel supply system, it was necessary to carry separate propellant for the OMS: "This propellant, required for the apogee firing, is contained in an additional set of auxiliary tanks (which have effectively replaced the collector tanks). The second major change in the OMS concerns the engines. In Configuration G, there was provision for a separate set of two OMS engines. Apart from the mass of these engines, they presented installation problems as there was insufficient area on the base of the vehicle to accommodate them.

"Enlarging the base area would have incurred a drag penalty. As an alternative it has been decided to incorporate an OMS mode of operation into the main engine design. Depending on the mass penalty of this additional feature, either two, three or all four engines could be adapted."

The report noted that the only real change from the OMS system envisioned for Configuration G was the disconnection of the collector tanks from the main fuel supply lines and their redesignation as 'auxiliary' tanks. Rather than 'collecting' propellant, the tanks would be pre-loaded before take-off, and although they were separate from the main fuel supply system, they would still be feeding the main engines.

Where the reaction control system was concerned, "since Configuration G was reported, the main hydrogen tank operating pressure has been reduced due to the adoption of a partially stiffened design. This has necessitated a slight rescaling of the reaction control thrusters which have had to grow in order to maintain their thrust levels.

"In addition, more detailed thermal analysis of the tank in orbit shows that the equilibrium temperature which its contents reach may be somewhat less than previously estimated. This will, to a great extent, depend upon the surface colour of the vehicle. A black vehicle will absorb more heat and consequently reach a higher equilibrium

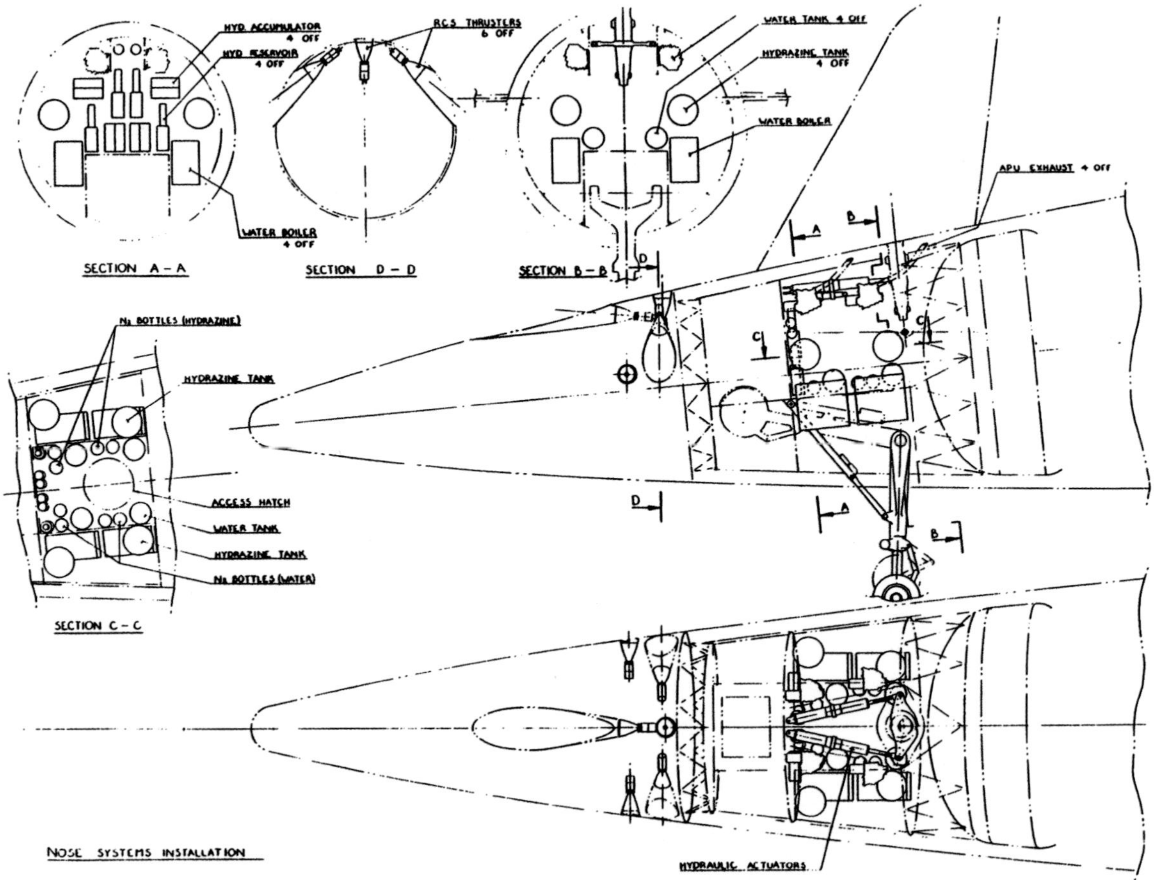

View of the late-series Hotol nose systems installation, including positioning of the RCS thrusters.

temperature than a white vehicle. The reaction control thruster specific impulse improves with increasing equilibrium temperature. In addition to vehicle outer surface emissivity, its attitude will also effect the temperature." In other words, if Hotol was black the RCS system would be more effective.

The position of Hotol's RCS thrusters had "been derived from consideration of a number of on-orbit manoeuvre scenarios. These scenarios fall into two categories; payload deployment and space station rendezvous. In addition to on-orbit requirements, the re-entry case has also been considered. However, the requirements for re-entry are not yet precisely defined".

SUBSONIC AIRLAUNCH

By July 1989, the elephant in the room for the airbreathing Hotol was the An-225. Towards the end of the report, a section headed 'Subsonic airlaunch of Hotol' recalled that "an assessment of the benefits of a subsonic airlaunch was conducted in 1986. The results showed a possible reduction in vehicle gross lift-off mass of 10%. However, there was no carrier aircraft in existence at the time that could be modified to be capable of carrying a fully-loaded Hotol. The expense of designing and building an aircraft specifically for the task was not justified for the performance gains.

"In the Antonov 225 an aircraft now exists which may be capable of carrying Hotol fully loaded. Also, the propulsion system has significantly changed since the early performance assessment. The use of de-icing liquid oxygen to 10km has greatly reduced the engine specific impulse, penalising the vehicle by approximately 1.5 tonnes of payload."

A preliminary study had been conducted to see what performance gains might be possible by launching the 4.99t payload Hotol Configuration K from the back of this new Soviet aircraft: "Two basic approaches to the airlaunch were considered: 1. Launch Hotol at Mach 0.8, and at altitudes at which the vehicle could be accelerated using the RB.545 in airbreathing mode. 2. Launch Hotol at Mach 0.8 at 10km. At this altitude and Mach number the airbreathing thrust of the RB.545 is insufficient to sustain level flight so the vehicle is to be powered initially by the rocket engines to flight conditions where airbreathing operation becomes acceptable. An altitude of 10km was chosen since this is the altitude at which de-icing liquid oxygen must be traded against the extra propellant used during the initial rocket boost."

AIRLAUNCH OF HOTOL FROM AN ANTONOV 225

ANTANOV 225 – MAXIMUM TAKE-OFF MASS 600t
MAXIMUM EXTERNAL PAYLOAD 250t
(CURRENTLY CLEARED TO 200t)

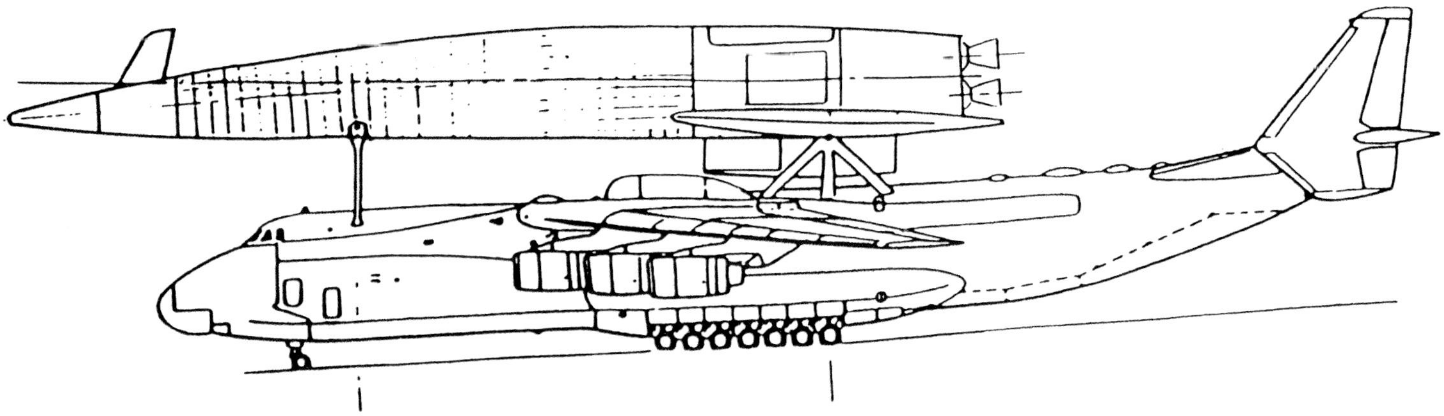

Variant of the Brian Hopwell's May 25 drawing from the HPN 0016 report of July 1989, showing an airbreathing Hotol mounted atop the An-225. This time there is no aerodynamic fairing over the engine nozzles.

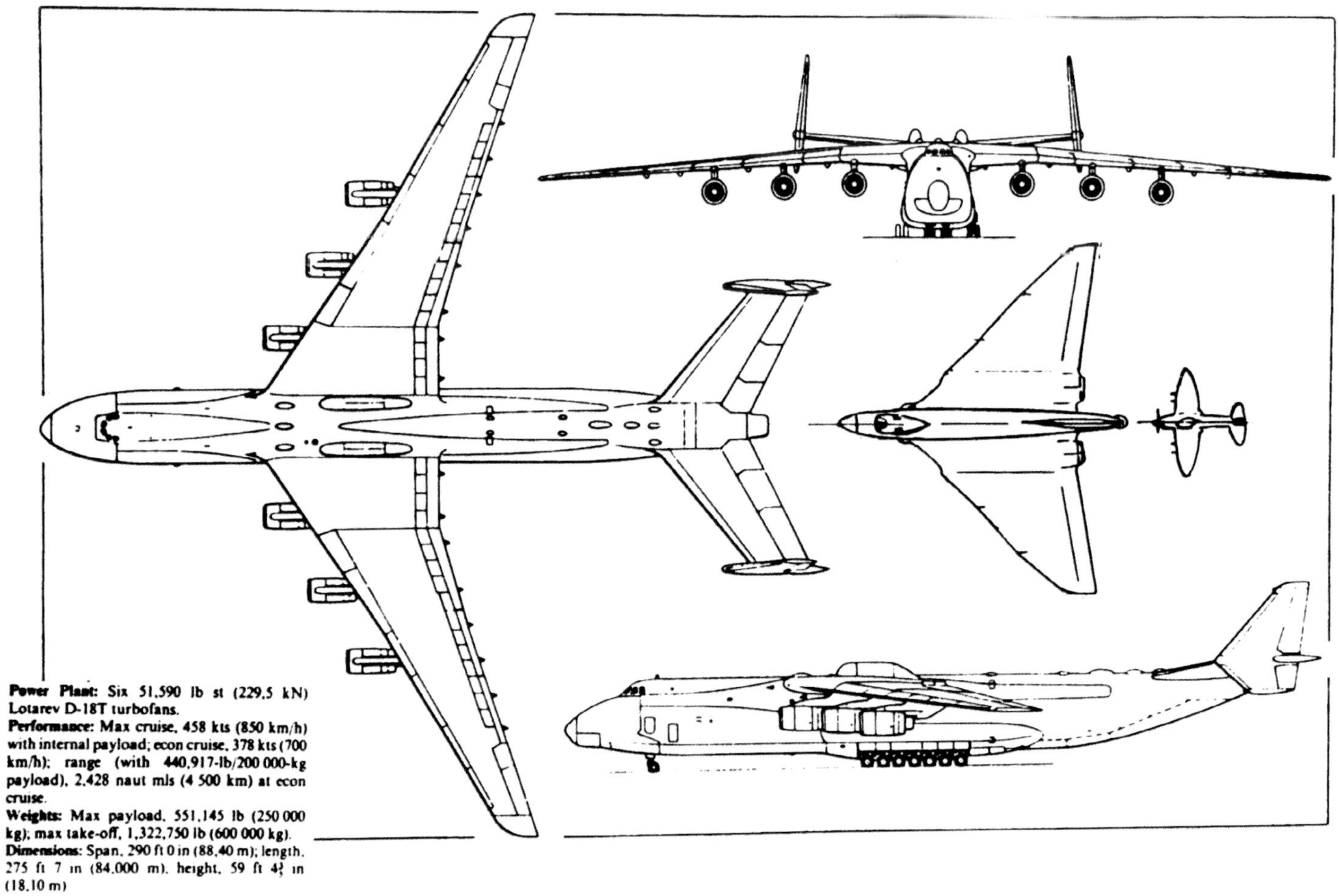

Size comparison of An-225, Avro Vulcan and Supermarine Spitfire. The top view of the An-225 also shows its load attachment points.

This determined that that optimum launch altitude was 6km at Mach 0.8. This produced a payload improvement of 2.71t—allowing Hotol Configuration K to carry 7.7t into orbit. Handily, "this launch point also coincides with the point of minimum de-icing liquid oxygen usage. The de-icing liquid oxygen is reduced from 19.26t to 12.85t".

However, it was emphasised that "the results from these studies must only be considered as preliminary. They do not represent an optimised configuration and therefore are believed to be pessimistic. The effect of the airlaunch on the propulsion system (intake sizing, heat exchanger and turbocompressor sizing, the reliance on the aft spill ramjet) and the vehicle fineness ratio must be properly assessed. It is anticipated that the performance will improve significantly with optimisation.

"However, the engineering implications must also be properly studied. The control characteristics of the paired vehicles and of Hotol itself with the new ascent trajectory must be assessed. The method of vehicle separation has to be defined and, in the case of using a rocket boost, the operational and 'reliability' aspects of this more complex method of engine operation must be considered.

"The ability of the Antonov 225 to carry Hotol at 275t must be confirmed. It is currently stated to be capable of carrying 250t externally. The use of such a carrier aircraft would give additional operational flexibility which is of interest to ESA and it would of course match that claimed for Sänger. The Antonov 225 would also provide a worldwide ferry capability."

NOT COMPLETELY SOLVED

The report concluded: "It is considered that the current Configuration K, based on a solid foundation of aerodynamic, structural, systems and propulsion design, is engineered in sufficient depth to be put forward as a candidate design in the proposed European Advanced Space Transport Study.

"The one known problem that can not claim to have been completely solved is controllability. In pitch, the 'corridor' of acceptable centre of gravity positions on the ascent is narrow and depends critically on our ability in future to design to the required pitching moment. Of similar concern is the control margin on re-entry. Small active foreplanes could alleviate the former problem but not the latter."

A brief list of "the problems that are not completely solved and outstanding items of work" was appended which included: "Trim drag, lateral/directional control, body flap effectiveness/spill ramjet, abort cases—control/propellant management, and foreplane jettison—acceptable trim change".

By the end of June 1989, the Hotol project was winding down. Rolls-Royce had long-since ceased to provide any meaningful financial support for the RB.545 on which it depended and even British Aerospace had drastically scaled back the support it was willing to give. Yet as Burns indicated in the HPN 0016 report, there remained a glimmer of hope for the future. The unexpected appearance of the An-225 with its remarkable payload-carrying capability and its physical layout—specifically tailored to allow the carriage of air-launched loads on its back—had opened up a host of new options for Hotol. It remained to be seen whether an agreement could be reached with the Soviets that would allow further development of this nascent concept. Ukraine-based Antonov had, however, already pushed the door ajar by inviting BAe to view the An-225 at the Paris Air Show on June 12, 1989...

10

INTERIM HOTOL: JUNE 12, 1989 TO JUNE 20, 1991

Dr Bob Parkinson had been contacted out of the blue in May 1989 as "the man responsible for Hotol" by Bruce Bird, commercial director of Luton-based Air Foyle Heavylift—newly appointed exclusive worldwide general sales agent of the Ukraine-based Antonov Design Bureau.

Bird had invited him, on behalf of Antonov, to view the An-225—a development of the An-124 and at this time the world's largest aircraft—at the Paris Air Show on June 12. The company was planning on bringing it to the show with the Buran shuttle mounted on its back and was aware, not only that the British were working on a space vehicle of their own, but also that airlaunch was likely to be beneficial for such a vehicle. It seemed like a potentially profitable arrangement for all concerned.

Speaking in 2010, Parkinson recalled that seeing both the An-225 and Buran up close was "an opportunity not to be missed. Steve Furniss from Warton, who was actually the engineer who'd been doing all the performance optimisation sums up there was also going to be in Paris, so we got invitations for the two of us to go and visit the 225 at Paris.

"We made ourselves known and were taken through the barrier and climbed into the aircraft, welcomed by the Russians, who said 'welcome to our dance hall', because it's that big inside, and in front of us, on the other wall, there was a poster the Russians had produced with a Hotol on top of the Antonov 225.

"And we had a very pleasant visit and got to climb up to the front office of the 225, which is sort of a ten-storey high building in the air... quite impressive... and you get to it by a loft ladder basically... because the main cargo bay is just a large empty space... and in the ceiling of this large empty space there's a door about the size of a loft access door, and you get through it... and you get up there and there's a whole world up there—the control cabin and a galley and sleeping quarters and goodness knows what.

"Anyway, we had a very pleasant visit, we enjoyed the visit and so forth and went away with comradely feelings I suppose, and that could have been that."

The Antonov An-225, with Buran attached, flying over Paris in 1989. RALF MANTEUFEL

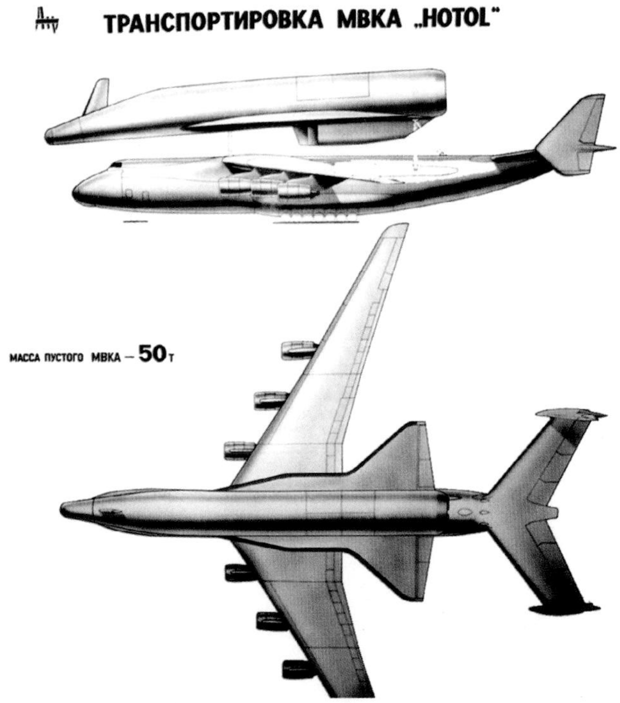

The image produced by the Soviets showing Hotol on top of the An-225. ANTONOV

In his post-air show report, Furniss wrote: "Dr Parkinson and myself met with P. V. [Petro Vasylovych] Balabuyev, the chief designer, and Anatoli Bulanenko (English speaking) the deputy chief designer of the An-225 ... We were shown around the aircraft and allowed to take photographs ... On entering the fuselage we saw a large poster of the An-225 with Hotol on its back. The Antonov team did not appear to know a great deal about the Hotol project.

"We were told that the An-225 is currently cleared to carry 200 tonnes externally (literature provided stated 250 tonnes). There was a very strong attitude of 'you tell me what you want and we will provide it'. They saw no problem with carrying Hotol on the vehicle at 275 tonnes and appeared very keen to sell us an aircraft, although they were sorry to say that an aircraft could not be provided for two-and-a-half years because of other aircraft production requirements.

"When told that if required, a carrier aircraft would not be needed before the year 2000 they were disappointed and after stating that they would all be retired by then, lost interest in the discussion."

He wrote that the An-225 had been specifically designed to carry payloads externally, with four attachment stations comprising a total of ten attachment points. Indeed, "the An-225 flew to Paris with Buran on top and the opportunity was taken to have a relatively close look at the vehicle. The main point of interest was the re-entry heating problem experienced in the gap between the flaps. This area was very badly burnt and some material had been lost. Repairs had not been carried out since Buran's flight [on November 15, 1988]. The severity of the aerothermal environment must not be underestimated and such lessons must not be forgotten in the Hotol design".

Furniss and Parkinson, along with Conchie and Lowrie from Rolls-Royce, then remained in Paris to give a Hotol presentation to CNES the following day. Furniss noted that "the aim was to show the detail in the Hotol design and to persuade them that such a project was feasible and that a coordinated European enabling technology programme should be undertaken urgently.

"It was emphasised that the programme need not be linked at this stage to a particular project since most of the technology is common to all the proposed European future launch vehicles. The reception was very friendly with no serious technical challenge. In fact, when the design process was described, for example the heating problems associated with active foreplanes, there were expressions of agreement in the audience.

"M. [Daniel] Mugnier (director, CNES) did believe we had been optimistic in our assessment of the expected satellite launch requirements, but such estimates are very difficult to forecast. In this and other discussions with French counterparts, it is quite obvious that they have a much better understanding of the design process which will lead to a future launch vehicle than MBB. The French appear to be extremely sceptical about the Sänger project."

SEEKING INVESTORS

Bond was at the Ritz Hotel in Mayfair, London, on Tuesday, July 25, 1989 to discuss private finance for Hotol with Lord Shackleton, Lord [Geoffrey] Rippon of Hexham, Richard Wilson and Michael B. Dodson.

He explained the project's current status and how much money was needed initially: £5m for Stage 1 'Proof of Concept' with the Satan engine. Then, according to his post-meeting notes, "after discussion, it was generally agreed that the best way of proceeding would be to have a launch seminar in a committee room at the House of Lords, hosted by Lord Rippon and Lord Shackleton, at which Alan Bond would explain the concept with photographs, drawings etc. to a carefully selected audience of perhaps about 20 top industrialists and investors, who could be interested in the project for one reason or another.

"There could be, say, as examples Robert Maxwell (space), Lord Weinstock (electronics for the space vehicle etc.), Sir John Cuckney (3i) [3i, formerly known as Investors in Industry Group, being a British multinational private equity and venture capital company]. The Carroll

Group had already expressed an interest and willingness to invest a sum of money, as yet unspecified, in Stage 1 of the project.

"Lord Shackleton felt this was probably the best way of launching the fund-raising effort and expressed his willingness to assist in any way possible; and Lord Rippon said that he could arrange for a committee room to be available at a particular date, but this would now have to wait until late October due to the ending of the current session of Parliament."

Once the lords had left, Bond, Wilson and Dodson discussed whether to bring in Charles Fry of Johnson Fry "who had access to a tremendous amount of funds through his fund-raising organisation under the BES [Business Expansion Schemes] schemes. Fry had expressed to Dodson a willingness to go with the scheme".

Dodson had brought two early BAe-produced Hotol brochures with him and said it would be important to generate some publicity materials to hand out to potential investors. Bond "said that this would provide no problem and he would supply these".

DEATH OF BURNS

Bryan Robert Alexander 'Sandy' Burns died suddenly on Sunday, September 24, aged 59, while still leading the Hotol team. In his paper to the BIS Spaceplanes Symposium at Cosford, Gerald Wilson described Sandy Burns as "quite simply a 'natural' aerodynamicist... he could size a tailplane or work out an elevator angle more or less in his head. His practical and down to earth leadership of the overall design of Hotol was fundamental to the success of the team." Steve Furniss, the senior remaining team member at Warton, remembers receiving a call on the Monday from Sandy's wife, Jean, advising that Sandy had died over the weekend. This came as a tremendous big shock as there was no warning and Sandy had appeared quite well the week before.

Parkinson later remembered: "Sandy died... in the summer... [and] there was a big aerospace engineering conference Aerotech 89 in Birmingham in October [October 31-November 3] and I had to go and give Sandy's paper to that and things and that was almost the farewell to Hotol, we thought."

Meanwhile, British Aerospace had continued to consider how Hotol Configuration K might be optimised for launch from an An-225. David Cundy from Advanced Studies at Warton sent Webb a memo on October 4, 1989, with the results of work he'd carried out on a pure-rocket variant of K. The original fuselage shape was retained but the computer model was adjusted to remove the engine intakes and foreplanes, with the RB.545s replaced with rocket engines and extra TPS added where the intake would have been under the payload bay. Wing area was reduced slightly to 218sqm as this was "the minimum wing area necessary on Hotol-K for trim and it was expected that performance improvements would only come from a reduction in area". Pre-chilled propellants were also assumed.

He concluded: "The maximum payload achieved during optimisation was 10.36 tonnes at a thrust-to-weight of 1.3 and an optimum pull-up normal acceleration of 1.2 'g'. Changes to thrust-to-weight only yield a payload change of 0.25 tonnes per 10% engine size."

Six potential avenues for future development were listed: "Variation of the launch conditions to check the effect of altitude and Mach number down to sea level static; variation in wing size to check on the wing size/liquid oxygen capacity trade-off (assuming no trim limits); improvement/audit of the mass scaling laws to represent the different design conditions; [gaining] some detailed knowledge of engine geometry to improve engine bay definition, required base areas, allowable cross sectional areas etc.; slight variations in the ascent trajectory (e.g. incidence vs climb angle) to increase efficiency; engine data covering different nozzle areas and mixture ratios over the full flight envelope."

YATES GOES TO MOSCOW

Burns was gone but Yates, the recipient of his 40-plus monthly updates on the Hotol project remained—and he was as keen to see Hotol succeed as ever. Parkinson recalled: "The Deputy Chief Executive of British Aerospace was Ivan Yates and he'd actually been looking after us and we'd been reporting to him on the progress of the thing and... this was in the era of Glasnost and opening up of the Soviet Union and... he went out to whatever the Soviet Union was there, out to Moscow, to talk about what collaboration there could be between British Aerospace and the Russian aerospace industry and the one thing they wanted to talk about was Hotol.

"And they had had a programme of their own... the Antonov 225 wasn't just for carrying Buran around—it was for doing all sorts of interesting things, but one of the things was for air-launching a reusable spaceplane called MAKS, which we didn't know about at the time, but anyway. And having come back from Moscow with this information Peter Conchie said have you thought about cutting down this, taking out the airbreathing bit, making it a pure rocket and launching it off the 225 as a sort of Interim measure?"

Yates had visited the Ministry of Aviation Industry in Moscow during the last week of October 1989 and met Radomir S. Korol, chief of the Ministry's General Department. In a draft letter written three months later, he recalled that Korol had told him he should "think about the possibility of some cooperative work on reusable space launchers" and "mentioned that as the USSR had already developed for [its] own programmes much of the technology necessary, it was a waste of… resources to develop it nationally, or on a European basis, for vehicles such as Hotol". Furthermore, Korol "suggested that I might consider setting up an international symposium, between USSR, UK, France and Germany, at which some of these issues could be addressed".

Yates had explained to him that "this would take some time to organise, and in any case I could not do anything until I had completed the review of the Hotol programme due at the end of the year".

Parkinson produced two separate reports in November 1989 on Bond's Satan engine—'The Impact of Alan Bond's 'Satan' Engine Proposals on the Commercial Case for Hotol' and 'The Potential Profitability of Alan Bond's 'Satan' Engine Applied to Hotol'. Neither gave any specific details of Satan itself, other than to state that installing it could improve Hotol's payload by 30%. The first paper used this figure to extrapolate the likely per tonne payload launch price for Hotol ("if Alan Bond's performance increase could be realised, the marginality of the commercial Hotol concept is improved") while the second looked primarily at different ways in which a Satan-powered Hotol could be financed.

December 13, 1989, saw Webb drawing up a list of "air-launched rocket study tasks"—most of which involved checking through Cundy's work, using his results to produce a baseline vehicle design, analysing that design, then completing the remainder of Cundy's work on optimisation. It would also be necessary to "briefly investigate ground-launched (VTO and HTO) vehicles to the same standard, look at sensitivities to rocket performance and mass estimates, investigate aerodynamic and structural problems related to separation and examine post-separation performance with some or all engines failed".

Just over a week later, on December 21, Yates wrote to Minister of State for Trade and Industry Douglas Hogg to suggest that the Government might like to fund limited studies on an air-launched rocket-only Hotol. And on December 28 the self-proclaimed 'father of Hotol', Sir Raymond Lygo, retired from British Aerospace. His replacement as chief executive was Dick Evans—formerly the deputy managing director at BAe Warton.

HOTOL-ROCKET

Cundy and Webb's work coalesced into a January-February 1990 report, unattributed except to Warton's Advanced Studies Department, entitled 'Hotol-Rocket—Initial Evolution and Performance'. According to the introduction: "Hotol-Rocket is essentially an all rocket-powered version of the airbreathing Hotol concept. Developed during the summer of 1989 for comparison with the Antonov An-225 launched Hotol, it appeared to have a significantly better payload fraction with less risk. Consequently, further work is now under way to verify the original result and further evaluate the concept."

The Hotol Configuration K design had been modified to remove the now redundant airbreathing systems—the intake, turbocompressors, heat exchangers and associated pipework—and as Cundy had previously mentioned, extra TPS panelling was added to cover the space where the intake had been. What had been the heat exchanger bay now became solely the aft liquid oxygen tank bay—with the tank that had been the 'hole' of the 'doughnut' expanded out to fill the space. It was noted that "research and development would be much easier than Hotol if the wet wing tanks were removed as well as the airbreathing components" but the wing tanks were retained for the time being.

More detailed assessment of this new design had now been carried out, and "the major effect of the new mission [i.e. airlaunch and no switch from airbreathing to pure rocket propulsion] was to change the relative amounts of liquid oxygen and liquid hydrogen used. Losing the large liquid hydrogen burn of the airbreather at low altitude resulted in a halving of the liquid hydrogen requirement for Hotol-Rocket.

"The result was a lower liquid hydrogen tank volume and hence a shorter forebody. The increased liquid oxygen usage inherent in the non-airbreathing ascent increased liquid oxygen tankage by 25%, however this was easily accommodated in the new large aft liquid oxygen bay… Wing size was reduced to the minimum required for Hotol-K trim requirements—increased wing loading is certainly beneficial to the payload fraction but trim requirements have not been recalculated for the new, shorter fuselage.

"Reduced fineness ratio was not addressed but might be expected to increase payload since the rocket ascent favours the shorter, fatter vehicle. Optimising vehicle thrust-to-weight ratio and the severity of the pull-up manoeuvre indicated a thrust to weight ratio of circa 1.35 at 1.25 'g'. Payload was over ten tonnes." Gross lift-off mass was reduced from 275 to 250 tonnes.

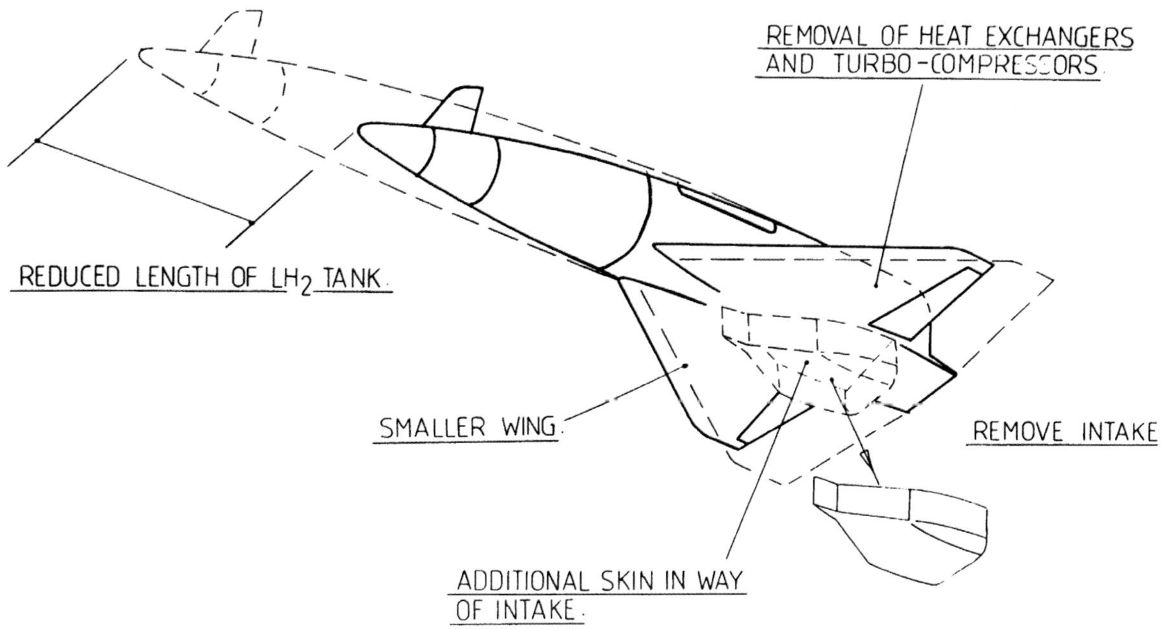

How does the Hotol vehicle change if you swap the airbreathing engines for a pure rocket alternative and introduce air-launch? Less liquid hydrogen fuel is required, so the fuselage shrinks, and wing area can be reduced.

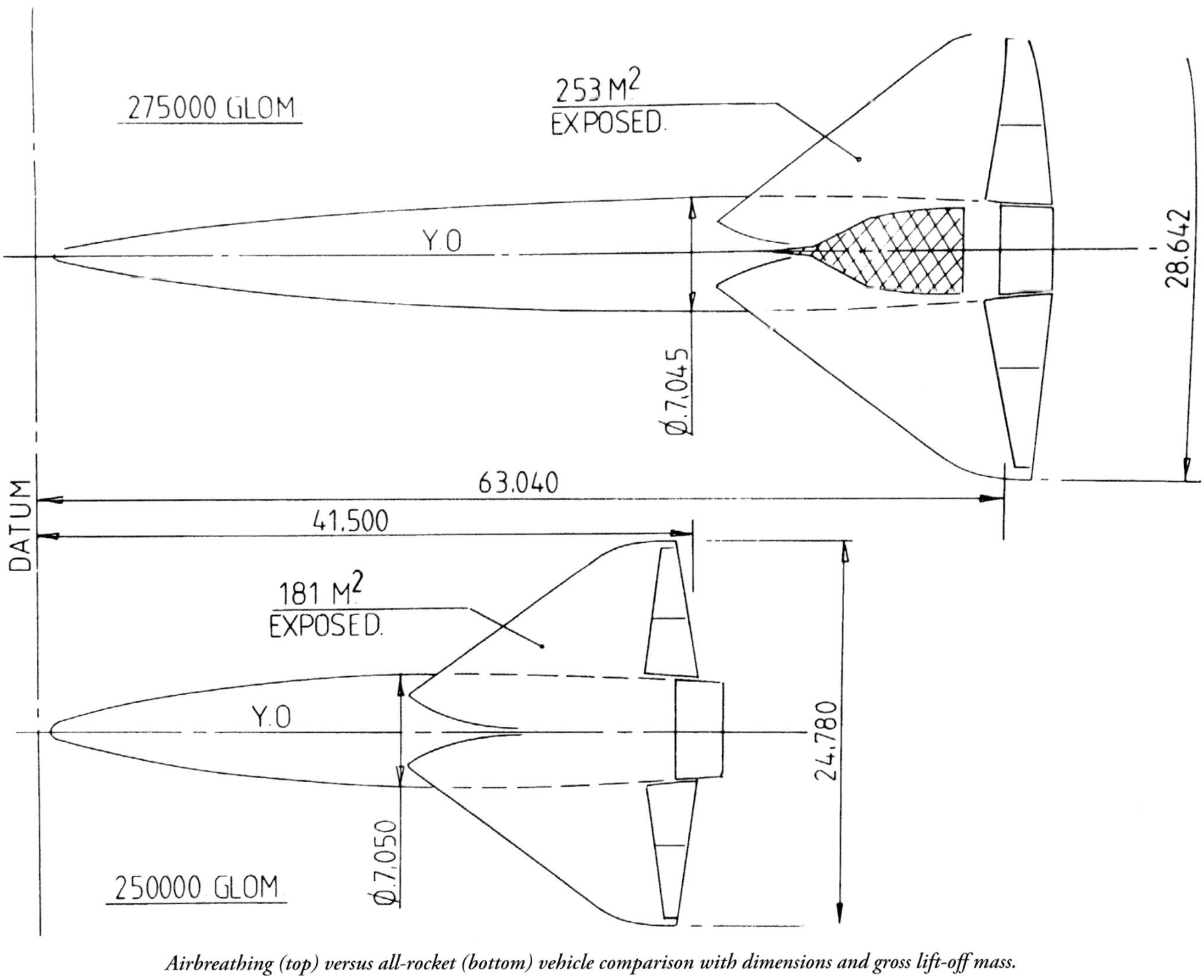

Airbreathing (top) versus all-rocket (bottom) vehicle comparison with dimensions and gross lift-off mass.

ORBITER 0061

Appended to the report was a 1:200 scale general arrangement drawing of the 'air-launched all-rocket vehicle with dry wing', coded HTL.00.0.0061 Issue 3. This would subsequently be referred to as Orbiter 0061 or just 'Orbiter 61' and was in effect the first variant of Interim Hotol.

The vehicle depicted was, as the report described, a clear derivative of Hotol Configuration K with, from nose to tail, the instantly recognisable nose fin, nosewheel, liquid oxygen trim tank, large liquid hydrogen tank, central liquid oxygen tank, payload bay with lid-type door plus four more liquid oxygen tanks and two auxiliary liquid hydrogen tanks below it, then another liquid oxygen tank to the rear and four rocket engines right at the back. The delta wings were low-set, as usual, and there was a body flap below the rocket nozzles.

Overall length was given as 42.65m, wingspan was 24.78m and exposed wing area was 181sqm. Nose fin area was 10.7sqm. Maximum fuselage diameter was 7.05m. The undercarriage mainwheels, without an intake pod to retract into, were housed in the fuselage underside, below the payload bay, instead.

Confusingly, a second drawing was also appended, this time showing 'Orbiter-61' in 1:195 scale. While most other dimensions remained the same, length was given as 41.5m and wing area as 180.85sqm. The rear liquid oxygen tank was also shown as being significantly smaller than the one in the 1:200 scale drawing.

Geoff Statham at BAe Stevenage also produced a report at this time which gave basic preliminary data on liquid oxygen/liquid hydrogen rocket engine options. The list included HM7 A from Ariane (H8)'s third stage, HM7 B from Ariane (H10)'s third stage, Ariane 5's HM60, RL10 from Centaur and Saturn I's second stage, J2 from Saturn IB's second stage, J2S (not actually used in anything up to this point), the Space Shuttle's RS-25 main engine, LE-5 from the Japanese H-I launch vehicle second stage, the LE-5 with nozzle expander from the also-Japanese H-II launch vehicle, LE-7 from the H-II's second stage and the Russian Energia Core Stage Engine about which "virtually no information [is] available".

DEAR KOROL

Yates wrote to Korol on January 30, 1990, reminding him of what they had discussed the previous October and saying "I think that a discussion at this stage between USSR, UK, France and Germany would be a little premature because their positions (Hotol, Sänger, Hermes/

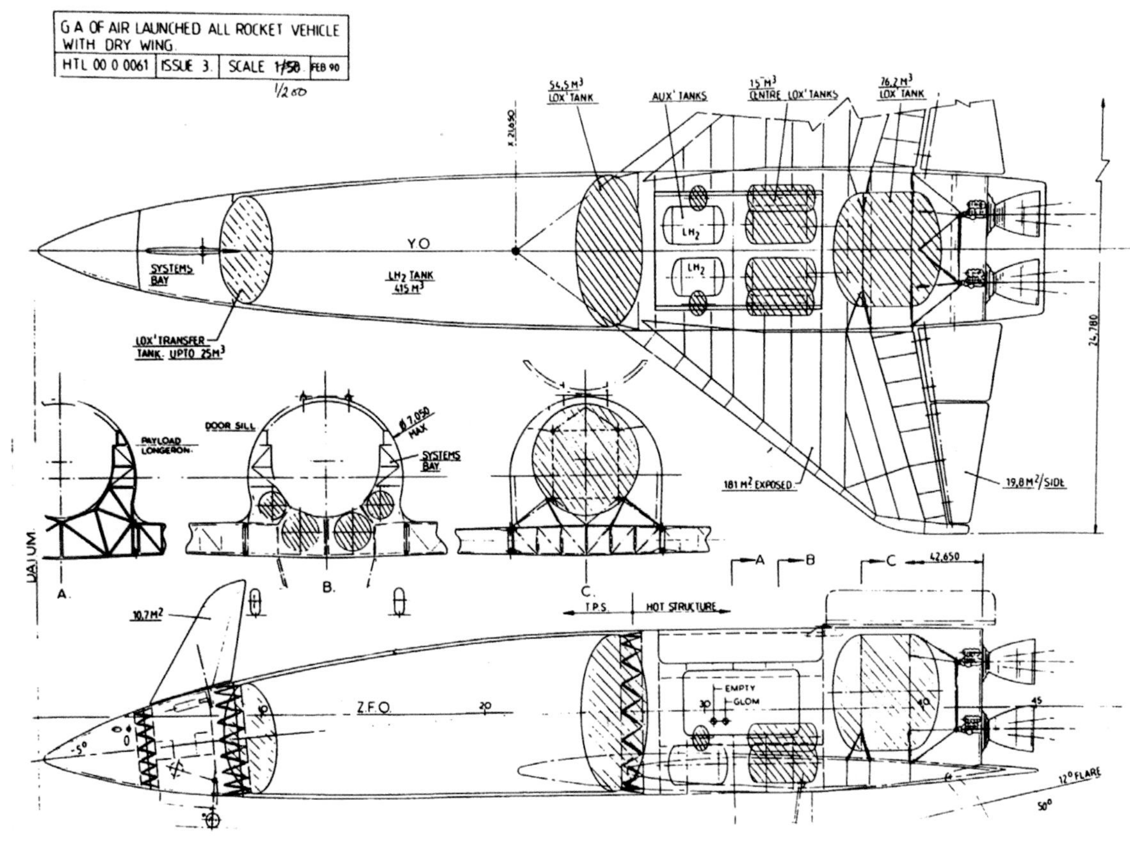

The 1:200 scale general arrangement drawing of the 'air-launched all-rocket vehicle with dry wing', coded HTL.00.0.0061 Issue 3, dated February 1990.

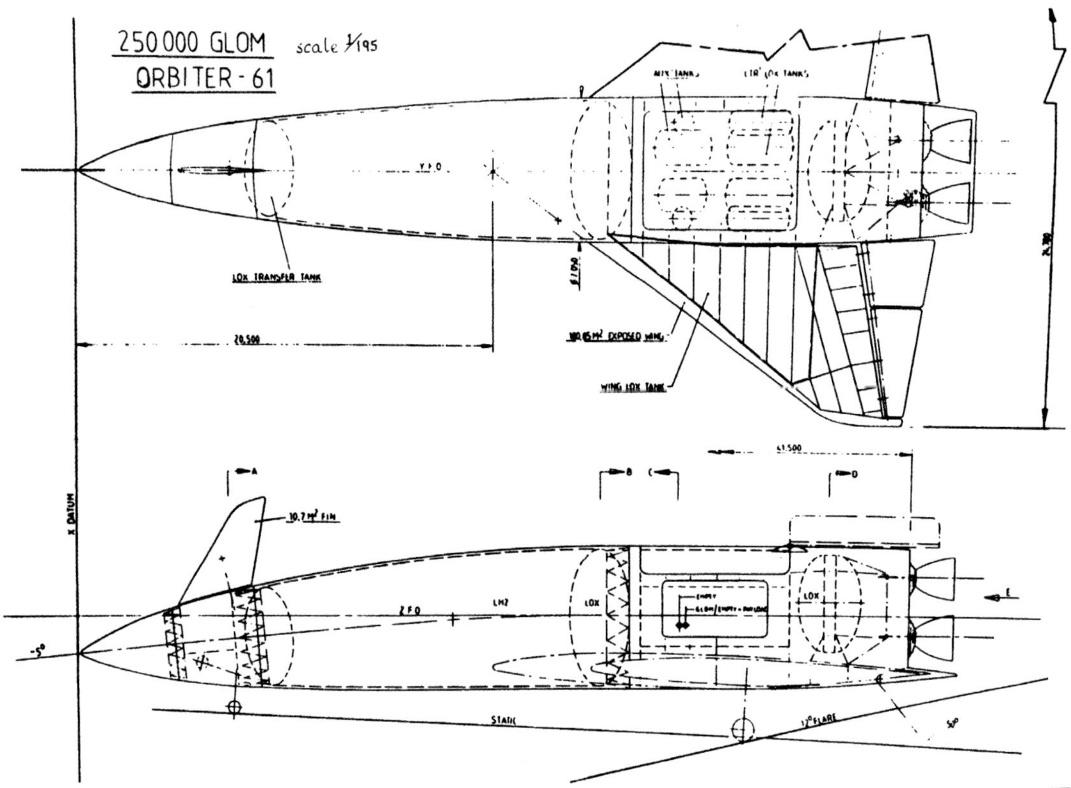

Orbiter-61 in 1:195 scale, which had slightly different dimensions to the HTL.00.0.0061 design and a noticeably smaller liquid oxygen tank at the rear.

Ariane V) and funding status are different in each case. Thus, I think such discussions would have to be in late 1990 or in 1991 to be constructive.

"However, we need to find a way to make progress and I see considerable merit in some USSR-UK discussions to follow up the points concerning technology and to explore opportunities. A useful and potentially attractive basis for such discussions is the concept of an air-launched vehicle using the Antonov 225 in conjunction with a version of Hotol (possibly powered only by rocket engines).

"The performance and the economics of such a proposal depend critically upon the level of technology assumed. Therefore, it would be well worthwhile arranging some meetings for a few of our experts to explore these ideas further. I think we should aim to reach a preliminary conclusion by mid-1990, and, if it shows promise, the proposal could be included with others at a later joint European meeting.

"We believe there is considerable merit in the Antonov 225/Hotol proposition. I have written to explain these proposals to the UK Department of Trade and Industry and will have a meeting with Minister Hogg soon. Meantime, I would be pleased to receive your reactions to this proposal."

'Soon' turned out to be very soon indeed, since Yates met Hogg on February 5. In a post-meeting memo, he wrote: "He [Hogg] was accompanied by his Private Secretary Ms K. Phillips, his Parliamentary Private Secretary Mr Michael Brown MP and Mr C. Nicholas from BNSC. Mr D. J. Brookman was with me.

"His reaction to my letter of December 21, 1989 ... was somewhat defensive (clearly smelling a rat!). After discussion he asked me to let him have in writing a short proposal which he promised quickly to 'staff' around other Ministers (MoD, FCO) and let me have an HMG view."

Margaret Thatcher was still the British Prime Minister in February 1990 and evidently continued to be just as ill-disposed towards Hotol as she had been in 1987.

By February 23, 1990, the head of Advanced Studies at Warton, Liddell, was growing concerned that Yates was about to embark on an ambitious course of collaboration with the Soviets without putting the necessary resources in place to do the job. He wrote a memo to Gardner, saying: "As I noted following Yates' January review, he is still effectively ignoring our messages re: the absence of space in our business plan and consequent funding and priority obstacles to significant commitment to space studies. I keep pointing out to him that we are only working at the conceptual study/parametric level. Whilst this is sufficient to support general reviews of system possibility, should Yates succeed in establishing a dialogue with the Soviets we will be drawn into a real engineering debate.

"To support such a debate we should have designed, as opposed to merely sketched as is currently the case, the air-launched rocket-powered option. To do this would require a significantly increased commitment to the activity than we are currently making, both in terms of men and money. Such a commitment would be inconsistent with out previous agreements on this topic."

QUESTIONS FROM BOTH SIDES

As had previously been the case, Liddell's concerns seemed to carry little weight and negotiations between BAe and the Russian Ministry of Aviation Industry progressed and a date was set for a British team to travel out to Moscow for a meeting—July 2, 1990.

Well in advance of this, on March 12, 1990, Parkinson drew up a list of 17 first-thoughts 'Questions for Russians'. Among other things he wondered what the An-225's actual maximum payload was, what altitude it could achieve and what speed. What were its manoeuvring limits? Would there be a problem with starting one rocket engine while Hotol was still attached to the aircraft? Were there particular constraints on hardpoint loadings or centre of gravity positions? What would it cost to maintain, including support infrastructure? What was its likely turnaround time? What Russian engines would be available for the orbiter? What were their features and what would they cost?

He also began to make preparations for the meeting itself and the likely discussions to be had. On May 22 he sent John Platt, head of the Advanced Studies Group at Warton, "an overview of the work that I believe is required for the An-225 study". The actual list was headed 'What we are expected to do' and included four main categories: performance, operations, economics and technology/marketing. For performance, it was necessary to "design/engineer a launch vehicle consistent with the carriage capability of the An-225; evaluate the inputs provided by the USSR; carry out an engineering and structural assessment of the reference vehicle covering aerodynamics, structure, materials, systems etc; evaluate the launch vehicle separation (sequencing and flight dynamics); provide thermal analysis for the vehicle up to separation to assess propellant quality, and check thermal history re: baseline Hotol data throughout mission for substantial changes".

The operations tasks were: "Analyse the propellant dumping problem with the orbiter attached to the An-225; perform operational timelining, facilities and effort for vehicle turnaround and launch; evaluate and size airborne support equipment required in support of An-225 carriage; examine maintainability & reliability budgets for vehicle." The economics tasks were essentially working out programme costs and workshare between Britain and the Russians, and technology/marketing involved assessing technological requirements and raising awareness of the project.

Also on May 22, Conchie sent a specification document headed 'An-225/Interim Hotol Study Proposal' to Yates for comment ahead of sending it to the Russians. It outlined the basic system, the desired payload to orbit (seven tonnes, as usual), expected take-off conditions (equatorial), separation conditions (Mach 0.8 at 9,000m in level flight), orbiter dimensions (41.5m long, 24.8m wingspan, 180.9sqm wing area—evidently the details of the second Orbiter 0061 drawing) and all-up mass at separation (250 tonnes). There were also launch abort constraints (the need to dump propellants) and ferry conditions (empty orbiter 32t, internal payload 4.5t—ferry range still to be determined).

Eight days later, on May 30, 1990, the Russians sent back a telex with 16 questions of their own, on topics ranging from Interim Hotol's weight and centre of gravity to where the attachment points would need to go on the An-225 and whether some cargo would need to go inside the aircraft, and if so, what? Would it be possible to equip the An-225 with Rolls-Royce RB.211 (Trent) engines? What materials would Hotol be made of? What were Hotol's aerodynamic characteristics at hypersonic and at landing speed? What were its overload limits? Would it be crewed? What were its flight path parameters? What communication links would be required between the An-225 and Hotol?

BAE GOES TO MOSCOW

The long-anticipated BAe/Soviet meeting took place as planned on July 2-3, 1990. Parkinson later recalled: "A little team of us went out... to Moscow, of which I was the junior member because it was Ivan Yates leading the delegation because he'd been the one who'd contacted me... Peter Conchie and his replacement [as business development director], because Peter was about to retire, who was Peter Finch. And we had a translator... and Jack Leeming, who was the government contact. And myself who was the sort of junior engineer... because everybody else was a director or something.

"It was an interesting meeting because we all sat on one side of a long table and the Russians all sat on the other side of the long table with the head of the Russian... whatever it was... [presumably Korol] in front of Ivan

Yates and there was a sort of empty seat opposite me. And then... pleasantries were exchanged but little more, and then after a few minutes the door opened and an elderly gentleman, I think even at that time he had to be assisted to get to it, came and sat in the seat opposite me, looked me in the eye and started asking technical questions.

"They weren't actually very difficult technical questions but they were technical questions that were 'have you thought about...' [and] 'do you know...' and I could answer these questions, but clearly they were a sort of test, an exam, and I passed the exam. And it was that I was the guy who knew how things worked and all the others were bureaucrats.

"I was the guy who knew how things worked and if I didn't know how things worked they weren't going to talk to me about things. This guy was the chief designer of Buran, [Gleb] Lozino-Lozinskiy, and a lot of other things as well, including some of the MiGs... because he was ex Mikoyan design bureau. As a consequence of this we set up the Interim Hotol/Antonov programme as a joint programme between us."

A post-meeting 'protocol' document, signed by Conchie and Korol, was then produced which noted the points of agreement between BAe and the Ministry of Aviation Industry.

In short, a joint six-month feasibility study would run from July to December 31, 1990, with each party paying for their own costs. This would cover the technical feasibility of the project specification, the availability of a Soviet rocket engine for the orbiter, the operational costs of the system and revenue potential, projected timescales and division of tasks between the two parties.

A pledge was made that "each party will make available such information about An-225/orbiter systems as is required to complete the feasibility study". The aim was to present it to ESA but "the final results... will not be presented to ESA without the prior agreement of both parties". Information about the project would be released to the public for the first time at the Farnborough air show—due to take place from September 2-9, 1990.

ORBITER SPECIFICATION

Parkinson got started on working out which side should do which tasks immediately after returning home and on July 4 produced a new version of the specification document. This now gave payload requirements for the orbiter: 7,000kg mass delivered, 275km orbital altitude, 4.55m payload bay diameter, 7.5m payload bay length, and 63 hours maximum stay time in orbit.

An "assumed launch operations sequence" was also set out: "Payload will be loaded into the orbiter vehicle, [this] will be mated with the An-225 and pre-flight checks carried out. Adjacent to the take-off runway, cryogen propellants will be loaded into the orbiter vehicle. The composite vehicle will take off, climb to the operational altitude, turn onto the launch track and wait until the proper moment of launch arrives. The orbiter will light one engine... [and] will then be released from the An-225, and the two vehicles manoeuvre to give an adequate separation distance. The orbiter... will light its remaining engines and accelerate to orbital injection conditions. The An-225 will return to the take-off site."

Evidently, "the take-off point currently being considered is at or close to Kourou, French Guiana, with the following worst-case take-off (and landing conditions: orbiter fully loaded, altitude sea level, surface temperature 18°C to 34°C, winds (1% max) 10m/s westerly, 5m/s crosswind, relative humidity 82.8-89.3%, runway length 3,000m, wet".

The orbiter's vital statistics remained the same as they had been in the May 22 specification except for length, which had increased from 41.5m to 45m. It would have four liquid oxygen/liquid hydrogen main rocket engines of unspecified type and two orbital manoeuvring engines. Most of the detail on these systems was 'to be determined'. Whether this variant—with the 45m fuselage—was actually drawn and whether this drawing was then passed to the Soviets is unclear.

Detail was now given, however, on the physical interfaces between the An-225 and the orbiter: main structural support and release mechanisms next to the orbiter's main undercarriage bay; forward structural support and release mechanism below the orbiter's liquid hydrogen tank; emergency propellant dump and tank pressurisation line (routed through the main support); electrical power and command interface (also through the main support) and insulation gas interface (routed through the forward support).

There would also be a radio telemetry link between the two vehicles after separation. On board the An-225 would be six tonnes of airborne support equipment comprising the orbiter internal insulation purging system, emergency propellant dump pressurisation equipment, on-board checkout and monitoring equipment for launch, and fire detection/firefighting gear.

A minimum fleet size of two An-225s and four orbiters was envisioned and it was intended "that the system will be capable of supporting between 24 and 48 launches per year. Under exceptional conditions it is desirable to be able to launch two (different) orbiters within 48 hours of one another. There will be a closedown period coincident with the annual storm season of approximately six weeks during which European overhauls will have to be undertaken".

Cost per launch was expected to be 13.6 MAU in 1990 ESA Accounting Units—about a third of the projected cost of an Ariane 5 launch.

PERESTROIKA

Stevenage was visited on July 13, 1990, by the financial director of liaison company Anglo-Soviet Materials Ltd, Paul Allen, plus Valery A. Biryukov the general director of SAPEM, the Soviet association for advanced materials, and Alexander V. Eliutin, deputy director of Institute Giredmet, a research and design organisation. There to meet them were David Friston and Conchie—with a brief appearance from Parkinson. In his post-meeting report, Friston wrote: "Mr V. Biryokov explained that with perestroika it was hoped that cooperation between the Soviet Union and the west would improve. To this end a materials exchange presentation was being arranged with the DTI and was to be chaired by Rolls-Royce."

Biryokov and Eluitin outlined the range of materials and technology they could offer, then "Bob Parkinson ran through and gave them a copy of a list of high-tech materials that we would be interested in. We were invited to visit them in the USSR, if need be. They said that they would be in touch."

Finch met Mansell from Warton to discuss Hotol on July 17, 1990, and sent him a letter the following day outlining plans for another meeting in the USSR. He added: "I was a little concerned at John [Platt]'s insistence that Antonov should be pressed to provide evidence of their aircraft's capability. I understand fully the danger of proceeding as far as a presentation to ESA without establishing a degree of confidence in our total proposal. However, we must not treat the Soviets as a 'junior partner'.

"Their engineers have said, in the presence of very senior Soviet officials, that with the RB.211 engines they can achieve the necessary flight parameters. We will seek confirmation of this but when it arrives we should accept it. We would not expect the Soviets to challenge our competence; we should not (overtly) challenge theirs."

On July 19, BAe Stevenage business manager Dave Helas produced the first draft of an An-225/Interim Hotol programme description which outlined three parallel strands of development: the orbiter programme, orbiter enabling technology and the An-225 programme. Each was then subdivided into various phases from initial study through to full production. Where the orbiter was concerned, "production ... should be paced such that the second vehicle is available within six months of the first operational flight and a production rate maintained of one every six months thereafter".

However, in his introduction Helas made it clear that all his milestones and timetables had "been produced with little consultation and [are] intended to be used as a starting point for discussion".

SOVIETS TO FARNBOROUGH

Arrangements had been made for the BAe team to return to Moscow on August 8-10 but Finch sent Mansell a telex on August 1 to say: "For several internal reasons I now find it inconvenient to go to Russia on August 8-10. I know John Platt would prefer not to go as well. I propose to suggest that if they are coming to Farnborough we should meet with them then. We would not be able to see their facilities but we could hold the opening discussions on Antonov feasibility." Mansell agreed and Finch sent Korol a telex on August 3 which blamed "illness" for the cancellation. This was presumably a reference to Conchie, who had recently suffered a stroke—hastening his retirement and propelling Finch into the driving seat at Stevenage without the requisite handover period. Finch also asked Korol to resend a telex which had apparently never arrived.

Korol responded on August 13 with a copy of the missing telex, the gist of which was that the Ministry of Aviation Industry had "got the government's permission to perform works on research of feasibility of the An-225/Interim Hotol system". In the meantime, the Farnborough meeting had expanded into a five-day tour from September 3-7, taking in Stevenage, Warton and Farnborough. Nine Soviets would attend—four 'specialists' and five 'others'. The specialists were Anatoly G. Vovnyanko from Antonov, Valery R. Gavrilov from the Ministry of Aviation Industry, A. S. Rudakov and Vladimir A. Skorodelov from NPO Molniya. The 'others' were Korol, Balabuyev, CIAM director D. Ogorodnikov, G. Pavlovets from CAGI and Deputy Minister V. T. Ivanov.

At Warton, Liddell was unhappy with the continuation of Hotol work and with plans to have Russians visiting the site, where work was under way on other, potentially sensitive, advanced military projects. He wrote a memo to Gardner on August 16: "A recent planned visit to Moscow was postponed due to Peter Conchie's illness and current plans are based on discussions with the Soviets during Farnborough Air Show. Space Ltd [i.e. Space Systems at BAe Stevenage] are keen to promote visits to BAe during this period, but we have advised them that visits to Warton will not be possible with the implication that visits should therefore be centred at Stevenage.

"Unless you see any other reasons for wishing to meet with and have discussions with members of the proposed Russian party here at Warton, I will continue to take the above line, for example, at the Hotol Review scheduled to be run by Ivan Yates next Tuesday."

Gardner stamped the hard copy of Liddell's memo as received on August 17 and added a handwritten note: "Agreed [underlined]. Also we will not [underlined] discuss advanced projects." On an appended draft itinerary of the visit, Gardner underlined the part of the trip intended to encompass Warton and wrote "Not Warton" next to it.

Given ongoing world events at the time of writing, excluding the Russians from one of Britain's most sensitive defence technology sites seems not only prudent but entirely the right thing to have done.

A new itinerary was issued thereafter which did not include Warton. Instead, the Russians would be spending more time at Stevenage that day, with an evening dinner at Redcoats, a restaurant in Redcoats Green, Hertfordshire, just outside Stevenage.

On Monday, September 3, the day before the Soviets were due to arrive, and with Finch already installed in the BAe chalet at Farnborough, a fax arrived from Russia requesting a host of additional information. Among the 12 sets of data requested were "more precise definition of liquid-fuel rocket engine locations" and "detailed weight breakdown of the orbiter and its main systems, inertia moments at the take-off point and during landing".

Finch faxed the list on to Warton and Stevenage, who both then answered as best they could, though much of the requested detail had not yet been firmly decided upon.

A press release went out on September 5, announcing that "British Aerospace Space Systems and the Soviet Ministry of Aviation Industry have signed a Protocol for a six-month joint study programme for a new low-cost satellite launch system. The protocol calls for full cooperation between the parties, with study data and analyses being shared throughout the programme.

"The study, to be carried out simultaneously in the UK and the USSR, will consider the feasibility of an 'Interim Hotol' which would be launched at an altitude of 9,000m from the Soviet Antonov An-225 super transport aircraft. The Hotol Proof of Concept studies carried out by British Aerospace demonstrated that by using an airbreathing engine for the initial phases of flight, carefully optimising the vehicle design and using advanced structural technology, the performance required for such a vehicle was possible.

"The production of the Antonov An-225 with its heavy lift capacity provided British Aerospace with the possibility to design an 'Interim Hotol' capable of meeting some of the objectives of the Hotol programme at reduced development cost. By removing the requirement for the vehicle to take off from a runway and by launching from

Publicity stills showing an An-225 model with the Orbiter 61 variant of Hotol mounted on its back for launch. Two images show the model depicting a launch in progress, though the engineering work required to make this a feasible process had yet to be done.

a flying aircraft, the airbreathing propulsion system can be replaced by high performance rocket propulsion. The vehicle would have the capability of placing a payload of seven tonnes into a 300km near equatorial orbit from an operating site close to the equator."

SOVIETS TO STEVENAGE

The meeting on September 6 at Stevenage was attended by Finch, Parkinson, Helas and A. D. Couchman from Space Systems plus Liddell, Platt, Wake and George Appleyard from Warton. The Soviets were Korol, Pavlovets, Gavrilov, Rudakov, Skorodelov, I. S. Seleznyov from Raduga and E. A. Fedosov from SRIAS—with Ivanov, Balabuyev and Ogorodnikov being apparently unable to attend.

After a BAe video and slideshow, Finch explained how BAe's business operated across different sites and "on the question of a visit to Warton during the next visit to the UK, Mr Liddell said it would be decided later". There was a discussion on how to avoid crossed wires during communications—with reference to the missing telex—and it was agreed that telexes should be followed by confirmation phonecalls. Then "it was agreed that project leaders for both sides should be nominated and these were as follows: BAe—Dr Parkinson, Soviets—Prof. [Vladimir Yakovlevich] Neiland (deputy director TsAGI [the Soviet central aerohydrodynamic institute])".

There was a discussion about the request for additional data made prior to the Soviets' arrival—and the inability of BAe to supply much of it. "Mr Korol said that all this information was required for the first approach in the calculation of trajectory data. Mr Finch replied that the study would give new characteristics and therefore, not all of the Hotol data was applicable."

Further slides were presented and one "showed the extent to which the air-launched rocket-powered Interim Hotol differed from the Configuration K Hotol; the Soviets acknowledged that there were significant changes." Talks then focused on the rocket engines and systems that the Soviets could potentially supply, particularly a two-position nozzle.

The Soviets gave a presentation on a simulated launch and "Mr Skorodalov explained that this simulation showed how the proposed [An-225/Interim Hotol] launch system could be used for the inspection of orbiting spacecraft i.e. in respect of nuclear threat." Korol then went on to say "that this type of launch system enabled a far greater degree of flexibility than present systems which could be very vulnerable to delays caused by adverse weather conditions, and more important, the proposed system was not tied to specific launch sites. Mr Finch agreed that these were the selling points that would help our case and should be listed by both sides in parallel to the economic justification".

Parkinson explained that the dimensions of the payload bay in the orbiter "were determined by the original intention to be compatible with the STS, and the requirement to carry pressurised containers to the space station. It was agreed that these requirements could be reviewed during the study phase and possibly changed if strong alternative cases were put forward".

Evidently the Soviets had conducted their own mass calculations based on the data supplied by BAe and reached the conclusion that the orbiter's structure would be 3.5 tonnes heavier than BAe's predictions. Platt replied that "one would get this result using conventional structures. For instance, the pressurised liquid hydrogen tank forms a major part of the orbiter structure. Mr Pavlovets commented that it was this sort of initial information that their experts required together with mass breakdowns".

Eventually another protocol document was drawn up summarising the agreements made during the meeting, including the naming of the two project leaders; responsibility for setting the work breakdown structure being given to BAe; the need to "prepare an agreed list of possible missions capable of being served by the An-225/Interim Hotol vehicle" since the Soviets evidently did not view it as a pure commercial satellite launcher; the need for BAe to visit TsAGI's wind tunnel facilities as soon as possible with the cost of testing being shared 50:50; and that "aerodynamic information on Hotol and the An-225 would be exchanged by October 15, 1990".

Over the next three weeks, BAe tried to work out how the project tasks would be divided up between the British centres and the Soviets. This proved to be no easy feat and had resulted by October 5 in a complex flow chart showing how the many different work packages fed into one another.

The October 1990 issue of *Engineering News* newspaper featured an article headlined 'New 'lift' for BAe's spaceplane' illustrated with a photograph of an An-225/Interim Hotol display model positioned to show the point of separation. The article began: "The presence of the world's largest and heaviest aircraft—the Antonov An-225—added just the right 'show' element to an otherwise low-key Farnborough 90 International in September. But it required the not inconsiderable financial help of the Soviet Ministry of Aviation Industry's new found partner British Aerospace to enable fuel to be bought for the leviathan's second and final display of the show's week.

"So keen is the USSR to encourage cooperation with the West—and thus generate much-needed hard currency—that it has signed an agreement for a six-month joint study programme for a low-cost satellite launch system, through which study data and analyses will be shared fully. The study will consider the feasibility of what is being termed an 'Interim Hotol', to be launched at 30,000ft from a dorsal position on an An-225."

TRIP TO TSAGI

Two Warton men, high-speed wind tunnel testing specialist Russ Whitaker and wind tunnel model specialist Brian Eccles, visited TsAGI in Moscow with Helas from October 10-12. Whitaker's post-visit report stated: "On arrival at Moscow airport two suitcases had not arrived. The resulting three-hour delay in the airport was also suffered by the two TsAGI and one Antonov representatives as well as our interpreter. In the TsAGI main lecture hall, Professor Pavlovets spoke about TsAGI and introduced many TsAGI professors, academicians and doctors ... The BAe visitors introduced themselves making it clear that they were from two separate company operating divisions and sites within BAe. These proceedings and the arrival at TsAGI (and departure) were video-taped by the security representative."

TsAGI was apparently vast, accommodating 10,000 workers and around 50 wind tunnels. The report went on: "Organisation of the tour was excellent with presenters joining and leaving the party throughout. All the presenters were keen, knowledgeable and quite willing to answer questions. Control rooms, data acquisition systems and instrumentation were not shown and little could be gathered by questioning. The quality of interpretation varied greatly between the three interpreters present. On occasions it was not possible to obtain satisfactory answers to questions because of time and interpretation difficulties."

First up was a low-speed wind tunnel, designated T101, with a full-scale MiG-29 model suspended within it. Evidently this was "used for aircraft model, helicopter model with powered motors, automobile and statue testing. The general impression of TsAGI was of older facilities, with many probably under-utilised. The size of the facilities indicated that massive electrical and compressed air supplies were available."

The party then moved on to a high-speed tunnel with a 2.25 x 2.25m working section—T109. This had been "built in 1953 and is situated underground because of the fear of bomb damage 'following Hiroshima'". Evidently "a twin-finned, twin-engined combat aircraft model (MiG-29?) was being rigged in the working section whilst the visit was taking place. The front part of the model was concealed by a security cover". A sub-transonic wind tunnel was next, then "the showpiece facility"—the 10-year-old high-speed T128 tunnel.

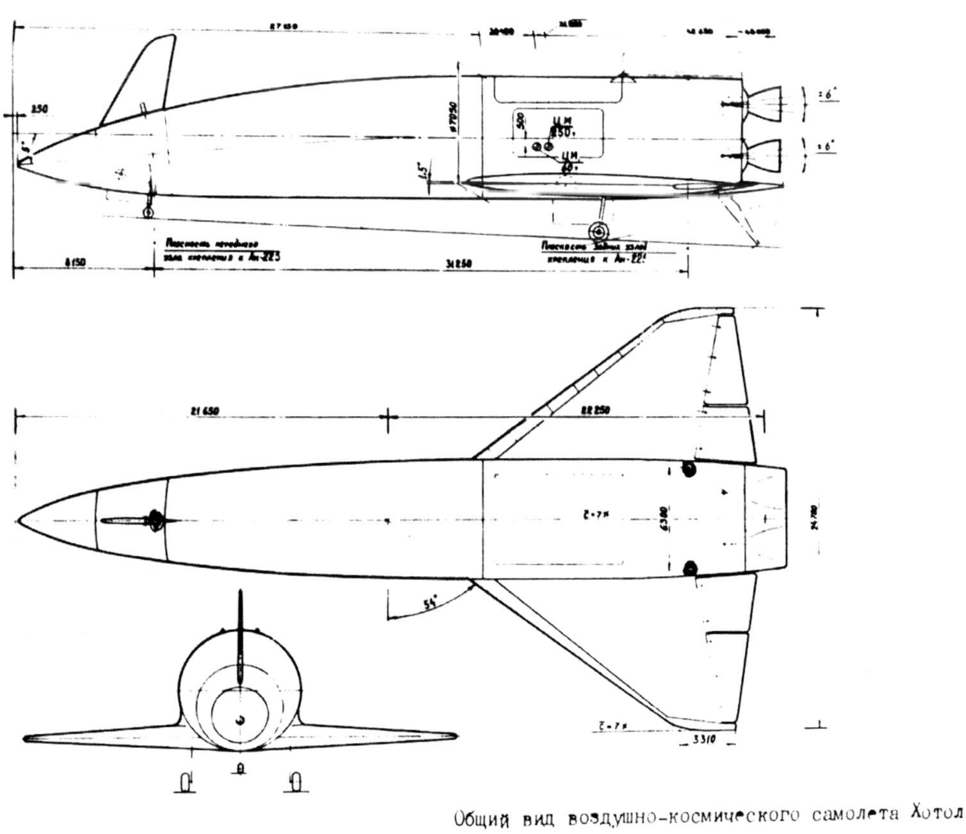

Drawing from Russian report published in 1991 showing the design from HTL.00.0.0061—including a forward view which is missing from the BAe version. AUTHOR'S COLLECTION

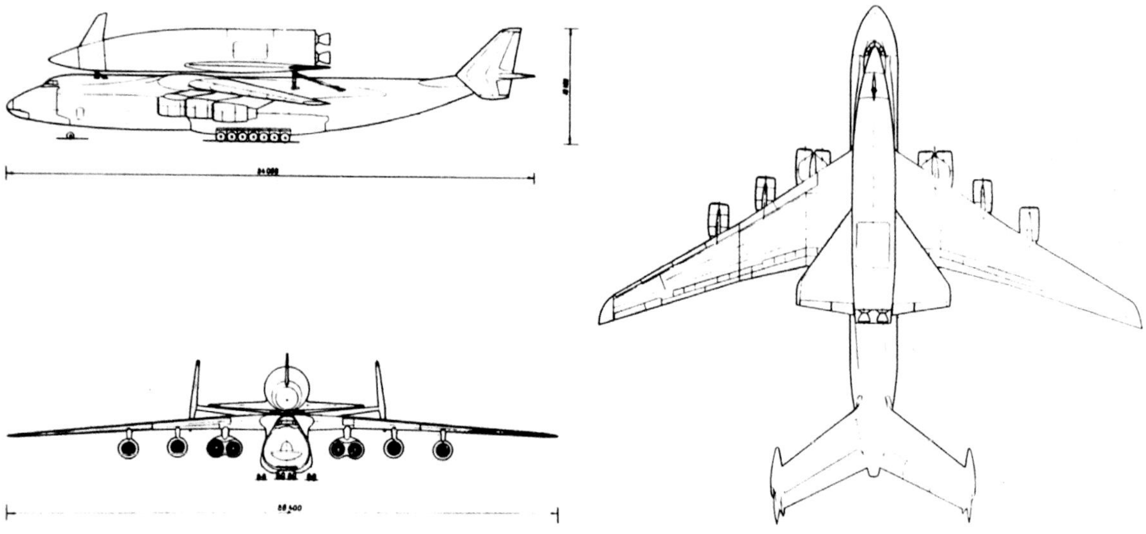

Общий вид авиационно-космической системы АН-225/Хотол с 8 двигателями Д18Т

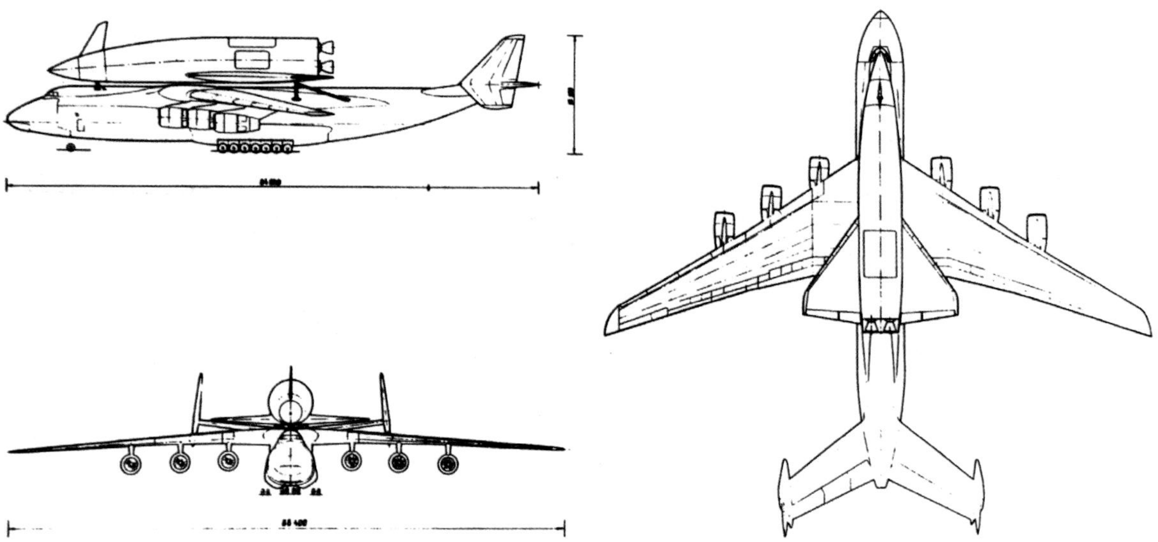

Общий вид авиационно-космической системы АН-225/Хотол с 6 двигателями

Early on, Antonov acknowledged that a modified An-225 with either more engines, or more powerful engines, would be needed to reach the speed and altitude required to launch Hotol. AUTHOR'S COLLECTION

The report noted that "the tour did not include viewing of design and manufacture facilities. However, all drawings presented were hand-drawn on tracing paper. When the possibility of TsAGI accepting CATIA [Computer-Aided Three-dimensional Interactive Application—a suite of design software systems developed by Dassault in 1982 and still used today] Hotol geometric data on floppy disc was mentioned they thought they would be able to decode it.

"BAe explained that all design was done on computer terminals, from which all the surface definitions were transferred on to CNC machines. TsAGI agreed that this was the way they also worked but showed no evidence of this."

Apparently "no computers were shown but some computer output of tunnel data was shown. TsAGI claimed to use a pressure sensitive paint which is not responsive to temperature change in wind tunnel testing. However, when asked if samples were available for return to BAe, Professor Pavlovets told the author that he 'should have brought a bigger suitcase'... In spite of the author's request, the tour did not include hypersonic facilities. In spite of questioning, no information on these was given."

In his notes on the trip, Helas reported that, "the Soviets

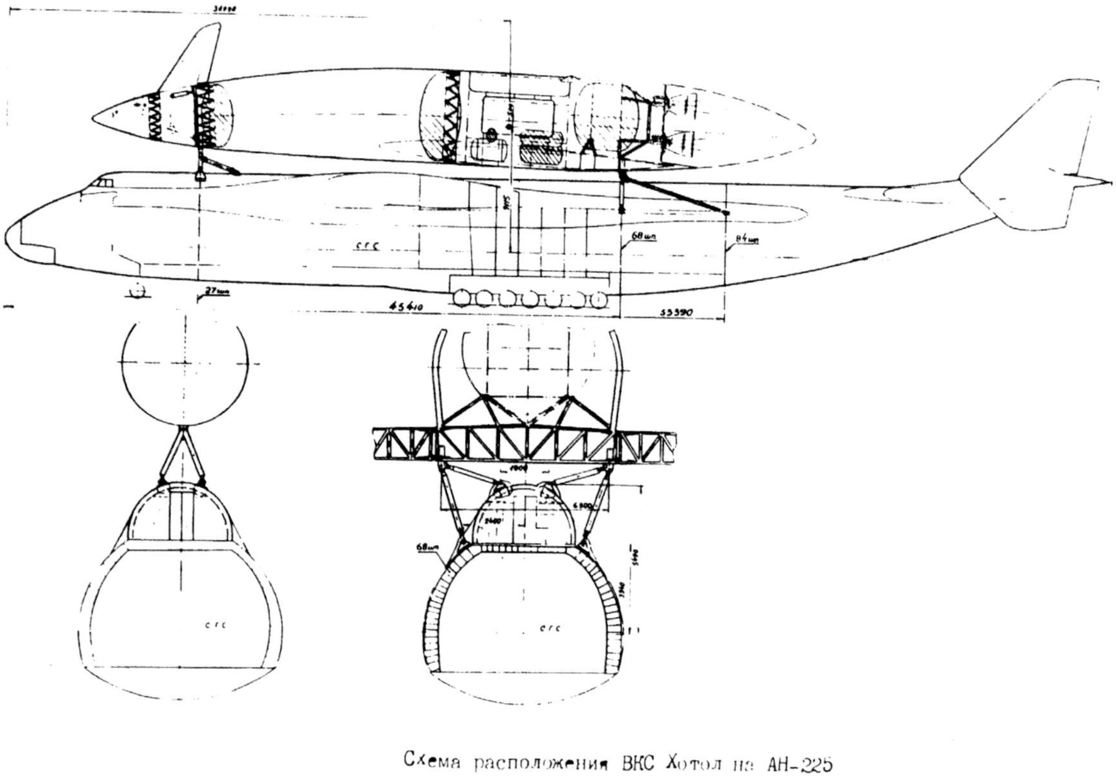

Tentative design for the attachment points required to carry Hotol on the An-225. AUTHOR'S COLLECTION

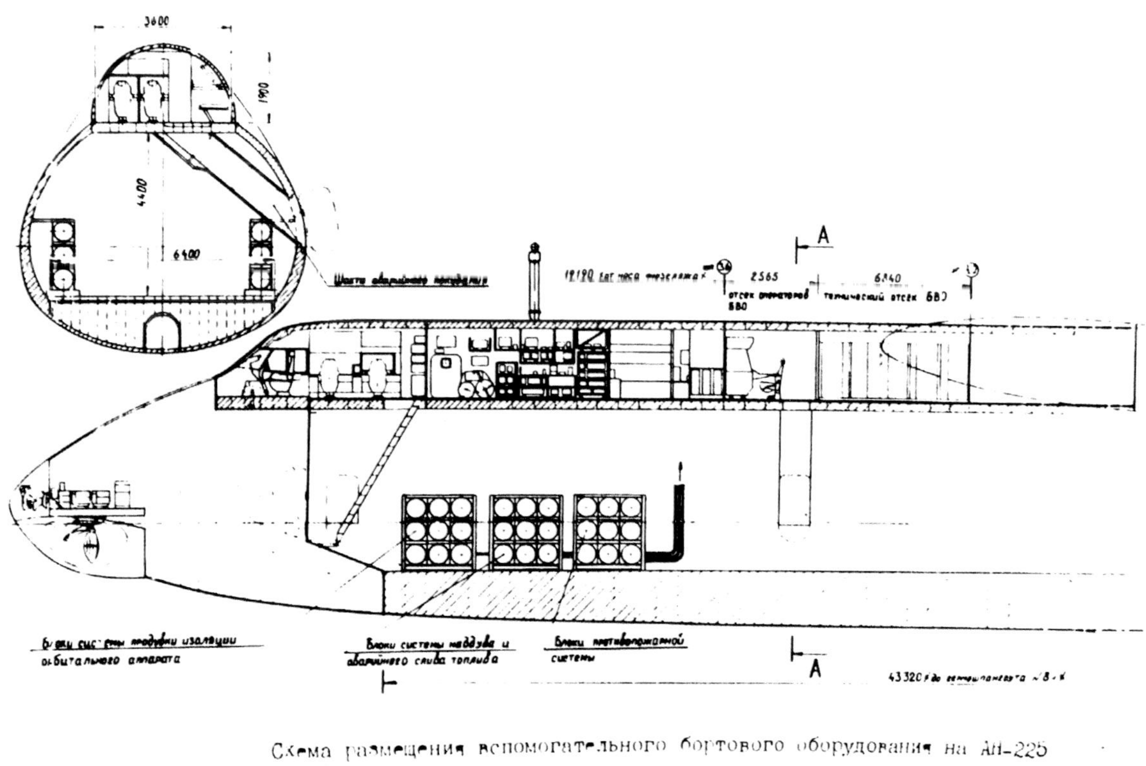

How the interior of the An-225 might be configured for the Hotol launch mission. AUTHOR'S COLLECTION

had received general arrangement drawings of the orbiter with conflicting dimensions; I said that the latest one was probably the one to use but this would be confirmed by Warton". This suggests that the Russians were working from the two slightly different drawings of Orbiter 0061 produced at the beginning of the year—or possibly the January-February 0061 and the 45m fuselage version outlined by Parkinson in May. Either way, it appears that little further design and engineering work had been carried out on the vehicle since that point.

According to Whitaker's summary: "A proposal for the delivery date (March 27, 1991) of the Hotol [wind tunnel] model from BAe Warton to TsAGI was made and an An-225/Hotol interface agreed. A proposal for the costing of wind tunnel testing... at $1,000 per polar was made by TsAGI and agreed. A draft wind tunnel programme was also agreed. Protocol work package details were also discussed.

"On the second day, the Antonov representative proposed that his company should build the model. The approximate costs and timescales given were considerably less than BAe estimates (delivery: about Dec '90: cost £20,000-£30,000 at the most disadvantageous exchange rates). A flutter model and test was also proposed. BAe must decide... whether they require Antonov to design and manufacture the model."

EDUCATING ESA AND SDIO

By this time, MBB had got in touch to request that BAe take part in the next round of the WLC study—Phase 4. BAe Stevenage, coordinating the two companies' space vehicle efforts, wasn't sure if this was worthwhile and called a meeting at Warton to discuss it. Helas, Longstaff, Steve Kemble and Dave Salt travelled up to see Platt, Webb, Appleyard, Stead, Cundy, Hargreaves, Whitaker and Eccles on October 18-19, 1990.

At this point, BAe Warton was already actively participating in two entirely separate Hotol-related projects: An-225/Interim Hotol plus efforts by McDonnell Douglas and Rockwell International to develop an SSTO for the US Department of Defense's Strategic Defense Initiative Organisation (SDIO). The McDonnell Douglas project was the Delta Clipper, aka DC-X.

When it came to WLC Phase 4, according to Helas's post-meeting report, "the general opinion both at Stevenage and Warton was that no useful purpose was being served by continued detailed study into SSTO subsystems apart from educating ESA". Therefore, BAe would only continue into WLC Phase 4 if "the An-225/Interim Hotol concept is accepted by ESA as an integral part of this future work, i.e. replacing SSTO".

On the McDonnell Douglas study, "there was agreement that further support on airbreathing vehicles should be curtailed, and work should concentrate only on rocket powered concepts. Warton said this would greatly assist in maximising their limited resources which was essential with the very short timescales for this work. Also, because Warton's funding for this work was said to be barely sufficient, any cross-fertilisation/commonality between the Hotol projects would help this situation.

"On the question of the outcome of the down-selection process, i.e. winged versus vertical take-off rocket, McDonnell Douglas had asked BAe if they would still like to participate if a non-winged solution was chosen. Stevenage said that in this event they might wish to continue whereas Warton were unsure at this stage".

Looking back on this period, former BAe Stevenage engineer Mark Hempsell recalled: "The McDonnell Douglas study was quite separate from Interim Hotol. I was located at Huntingdon Beach to support their team and provide liaison with BAe (I still have my California driving licence as a souvenir)... The Delta Clipper was championed by Max Hunter (by then retired) and championed in McDonnell Douglas by William (Bill) Gaubatz. They wanted always an SSTO vertical take off but wanted to prove it is a best with a trade off. One guy in the team was given the task of producing a vertical launched winged vehicle and BAe produced a horizontal launched winged vehicle.

"They wanted us and MBB to provide an international element to the supporting choir. They were only interested in Hotol as it gave authority to the horizontal launched winged option. They were not interested in airbreathing because their thinking was more in line with Eric Webb and they didn't see the need and of course it would not make sense for the vertical take off option that was supposed to win... The key point here is that the vehicle produced used technology assumptions provided by McDonnell Douglas, not those that came out of the Hotol studies.

"It was argued this was so the trade off options could be seen as like for like comparisons. As I recall they had precious little interest in what technology BAe had to offer and ignored all the suggestions we made. Including using sub-cooled propellent to avoid venting—which given the subsequent history of the DC-X demonstrator was perhaps unwise.

"Eric Webb loved it as he felt it proved his point, but the rest of us thought the technology assumptions behind it were unrealistic (which they had to be to make the vertical launched option work). Making the judgement this was not going anywhere, BAe quietly withdrew from the next stage; MBB stayed in I think because [Dietrich] Koelle saw in the Delta Clipper his own Beta concept".

During the October 1990 meeting, it was also noted that at Rockwell, "there was intense interest... in the An-225/Interim Hotol concept but it was agreed that though discussions with Rockwell International on 'air-launched rockets' should continue, explicit discussions of the An-225 concept and possible US involvement, should be kept at bay until the conclusion of the six-month study".

When discussion turned to the An-225/Interim Hotol project itself, "Warton were in agreement with Antonov producing the wind tunnel test model for the main composite testing... it was thought that BAe could lay claim to this model after testing, having paid for its manufacture".

BANNED FROM WARTON

Whitaker wrote to F. W. Armstrong at RAE Farnborough on October 26, 1990, to see whether a delegation of Soviet engineers could visit the RAE Bedford wind tunnel facilities. He outlined his trip to TsAGI, then said: "NATO rules prohibit the entry of personnel from the Warsaw Pact countries to the Warton site. The Soviets were very keen to come to Warton to see the wind tunnels in which Hotol had been developed. Unfortunately, their entry to the Warton site would not be allowed... I was hoping that we could offer a tour of the RAE Bedford facilities as the best possible compromise".

The Soviets duly arrived for the next round of meetings, at Stevenage, on Monday, November 19, 1990. They stayed at the Blakemore Hotel, Little Wymondley, near Stevenage, and were shuttled back and forth throughout the week, finally departing on the Friday. Discussions continued to centre on wind tunnel testing but also covered potential engine failure cases, installed equipment, launch trajectories, mass calculations and potential configuration changes to Orbiter 0061.

Work on refining 0061's design was now well under way, with Hopwell running through a number of iterations. One of the Soviets' comments during the meetings had concerned "low volume utilisation" at the rear of the vehicle—a criticism that had been accepted—and efforts were now being made to remedy this. It was also noted that "propulsion considerations are leading to a big base area and stubby wings. This is also the trend in the USA. The effect in the aerodynamic area needs assessment".

While the agreed BAe/Soviet six-month study period had been due to end on December 31, 1990, it was apparently agreed by both parties that the work should now continue into 1991.

In the meantime, British Prime Minister Margaret Thatcher, arguably Hotol's greatest opponent, had announced her resignation on November 22, 1990, prompting a leadership battle which saw John Major taking her place with effect from November 28.

ORBITERS 0062-0065

With the next BAe/Soviet meeting set to take place in Moscow on January 21-24, 1991, in early 1991 Hopwell produced a report entitled 'Notes for Moscow Meeting, Jan '91—Orbiter Configuration'. This said: "The orbiter configuration shown at the November meeting was derived from earlier Hotol work with airbreathing engines. Only first order changes had been made to incorporate rocket propulsion and to optimise for air launch. Since then, various modifications to the configuration have been explored."

Baseline requirements for all designs were: gross mass at separation of not more than 250 tonnes; payload of seven tonnes or above; payload bay dimensions of 7.5m long and 4.6m diameter; advanced materials to be used where appropriate; potential for high cross-range mission; wings with just enough lift for re-entry and landing; engine size and nozzle area ratio optimised for maximum payload.

The report went on: "Initial configuration (HTL.00.0.0061). At the November meeting the main drawbacks of this configuration were correctly identified... the wing was almost certainly too big [and] the volume utilisation of the rear fuselage was very low. The wing selected for this initial configuration was an arbitrary choice based on Hotol experience. For the preliminary studies of the air launch concept, optimisation of wing area was not regarded as a first priority task. These studies did, however, indicate that the wing was probably oversized.

"The low volume utilisation of the rear fuselage was also a direct consequence of the derivation of the configuration from a Hotol design. The optimum body shape for an airbreathing configuration is much more slender than that for a rocket powered vehicle and there is of course the need to accommodate intakes and turbomachinery in the rear fuselage. In converting the Hotol design to rocket propulsion the rear fuselage became significantly fatter and shorter. Clearly there is now a need to redesign this part of the vehicle since low volume utilisation inevitably results in excess structure mass."

Orbiter 0062 (HTL.00.0.0062), described by Hopwell as "original lifting body vehicle" does not seem to have gone very far and appears to have been a very short, fat, vehicle—precise dimensions being unavailable. Orbiter 0063, a "new CAPS vehicle", was slightly more fleshed out. It retained most of the original Configuration K layout but squashed up into a stubbier, fatter fuselage.

Hopwell described Orbiters 0064 and 0065 in a little more detail: "Configuration HTL.00.0.0064... has a broadened fuselage so that liquid oxygen tanks can be

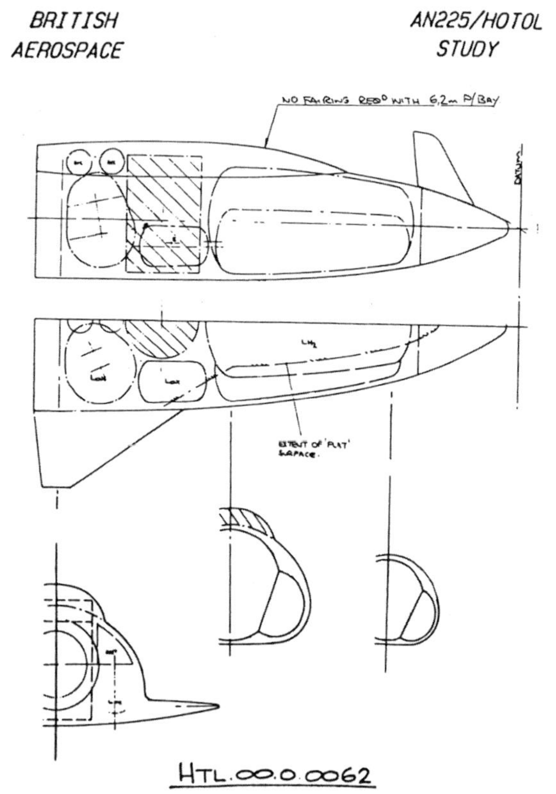

Hopwell's Orbiter 0062 (HTL.00.0.0062) lifting body design.

arranged alongside the payload bay. The latter has been rotated through 90 degrees to make more efficient use of the rear fuselage space [making it effectively 'vertical' rather than 'horizontal']. The liquid hydrogen tank is a twin lobe design. This is heavier than a circular section tank but results in more body lift and hence a reduction in wing size. The broad rear fuselage also has the effect of reducing the exposed area of the wing and hence wing mass. It must be emphasised that the detailed analysis of this configuration has not been completed so the advantages postulated above cannot be quantified.

"Configuration HTL.00.0.0065 … represents an attempt to achieve the advantages of a broad fuselage whilst avoiding the penalties of a twin lobe liquid hydrogen tank. Again, no detailed analysis results are available."

In handwritten notes, he added: "-0064 and -0065 are preliminary arrangements only and the fuel volumes are based on the CAPS output for -0061. They also incorporate a vertical payload bay. Because of the large base areas (+80sqm) the engine arrangement shown uses seven main engines in order to fill the base area and also the Soviets seem to use multiple small engines rather than 2/3 large ones themselves. The configurations have been roughly balanced about the payload bay and the hypersonic centre of pressure [cp] of -0065 has been checked and found to be aft of the payload bay."

OUTNUMBERED TEN TO ONE

For the third time, a delegation from BAe travelled to Moscow, on January 21, 1991. The participants were Helas, Parkinson, Kemble, Webb, Appleyard, Hargreaves and Whitaker. According to the post-meeting summary written by Helas: "The BAe party was met at Moscow airport by TsAGI personnel and taken to the Intourist Hotel [a hotel exclusively for foreign tourists]. Meetings commenced the following day … at times the Soviets outnumbered BAe representatives by almost ten to one, illustrating the importance they are attaching to this project."

During the four days of discussions, Antonov raised "concern about Hotol engine ignition whilst still attached to the An-225. However, BAe is seriously considering changing this requirement for ignition to take place after release from the An-225. Construction of the low-speed wind tunnel mode is proceeding satisfactorily with testing due to take place in March 1991.

"BAe presented the latest ideas on Hotol configuration evolution which proved to be very similar to TsAGI proposals tabled for the first time. TsAGI have completed two independent mass analyses of the first configuration which, although differing in some of the detail, overall showed reasonable agreement".

The Soviets' propulsion specialists had said they were "confident they can produce a rocket engine with the required performance using proven technology" but contrary to expectations, "their preference is for larger rather than smaller engines i.e. three or four".

There had been some discussion about a jettisonable fairing for the orbiter's engine nozzles during take-off and climb but "BAe were concerned about the cost penalties for this throwaway structure and therefore [it] should only be adopted if absolutely necessary".

When it came to the An-225, "the basic assumption used was the availability of a 3km runway at Kourou and a take-off mass of 620 tonnes for the eight D-18T engine version and 600 tonnes for the Rolls-Royce Trent engine version. [Notwithstanding the engine ignition question] there were no major obstacles in achieving the separation conditions; Antonov had devised a special manoeuvre comprising a shallow dive to attain Mach 0.8 followed by a steep climb with orbiter separation occurring at that point".

HOTOL VERSUS STAR WARS

Although it had been hinted at by Skorodalov in September, Parkinson then circulated a separate 'executive summary' which laid bare what he considered to be the primary reason for the Soviets' interest in Hotol:

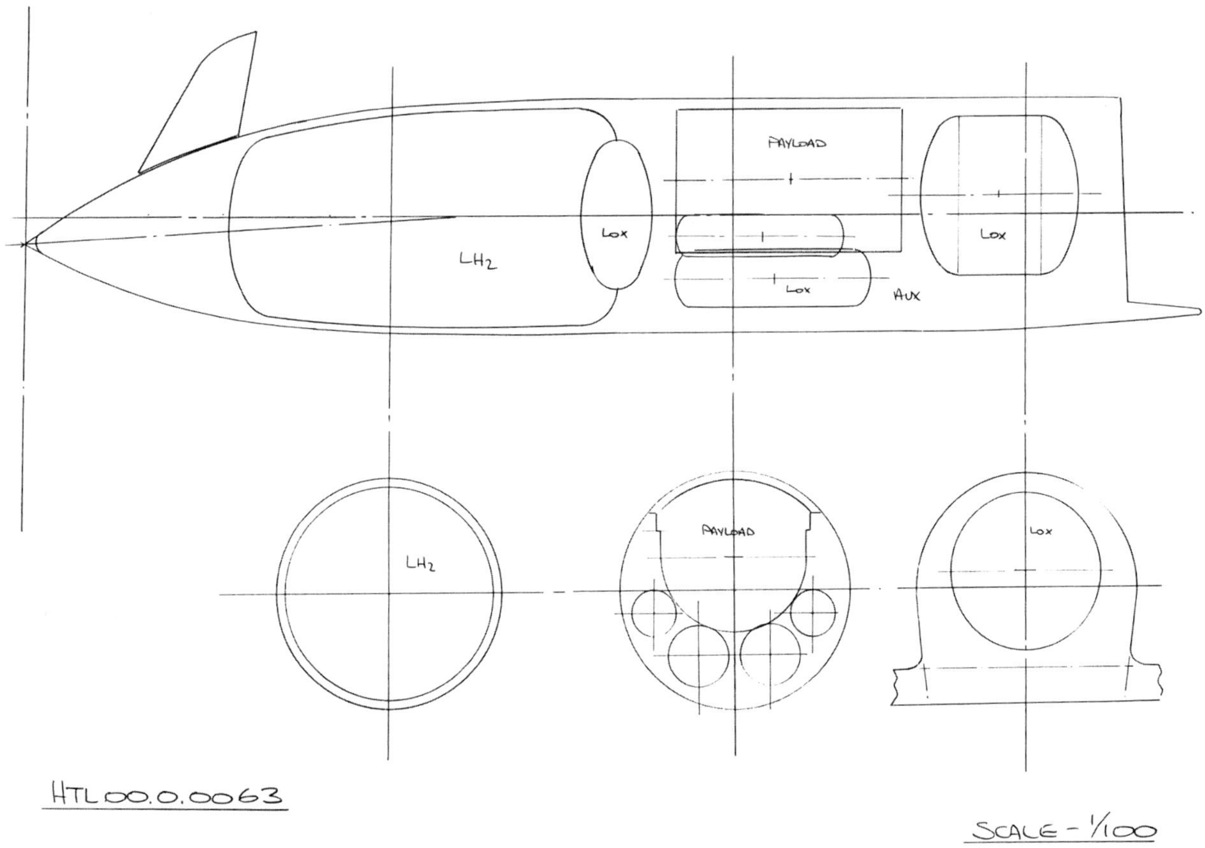

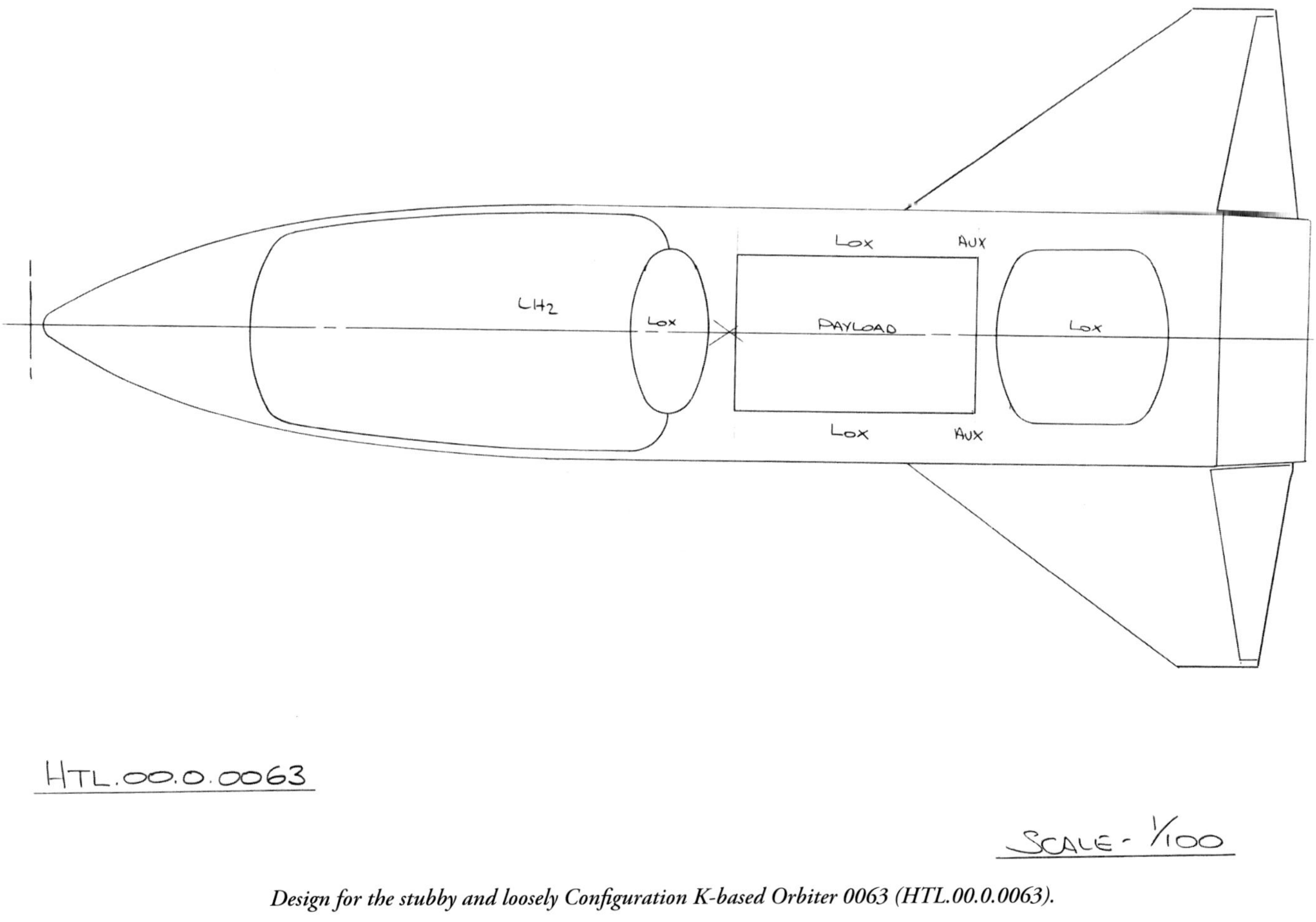

Design for the stubby and loosely Configuration K-based Orbiter 0063 (HTL.00.0.0063).

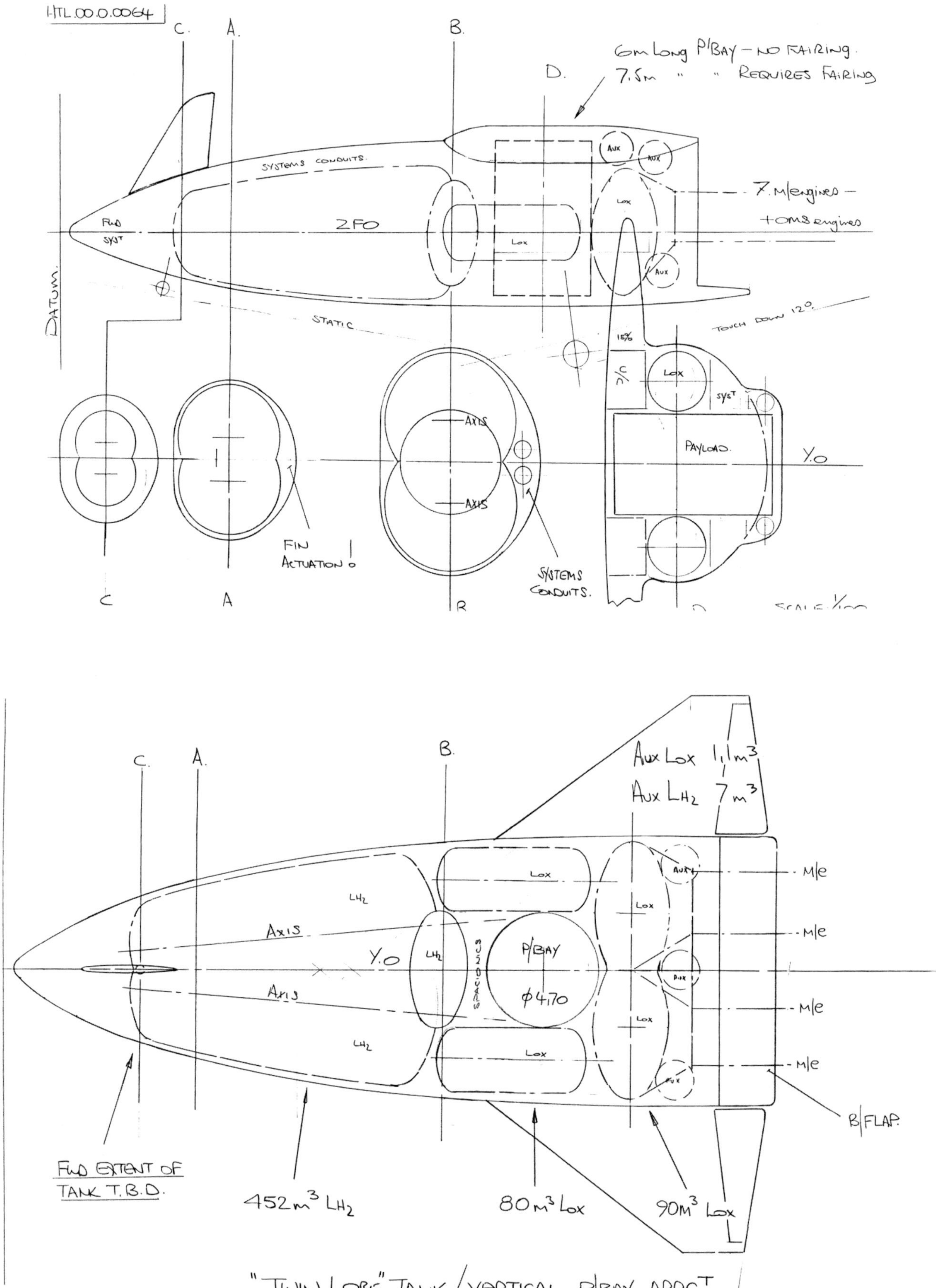

The broader, flatter Orbiter 0064 with unusual 'vertical' payload bay.

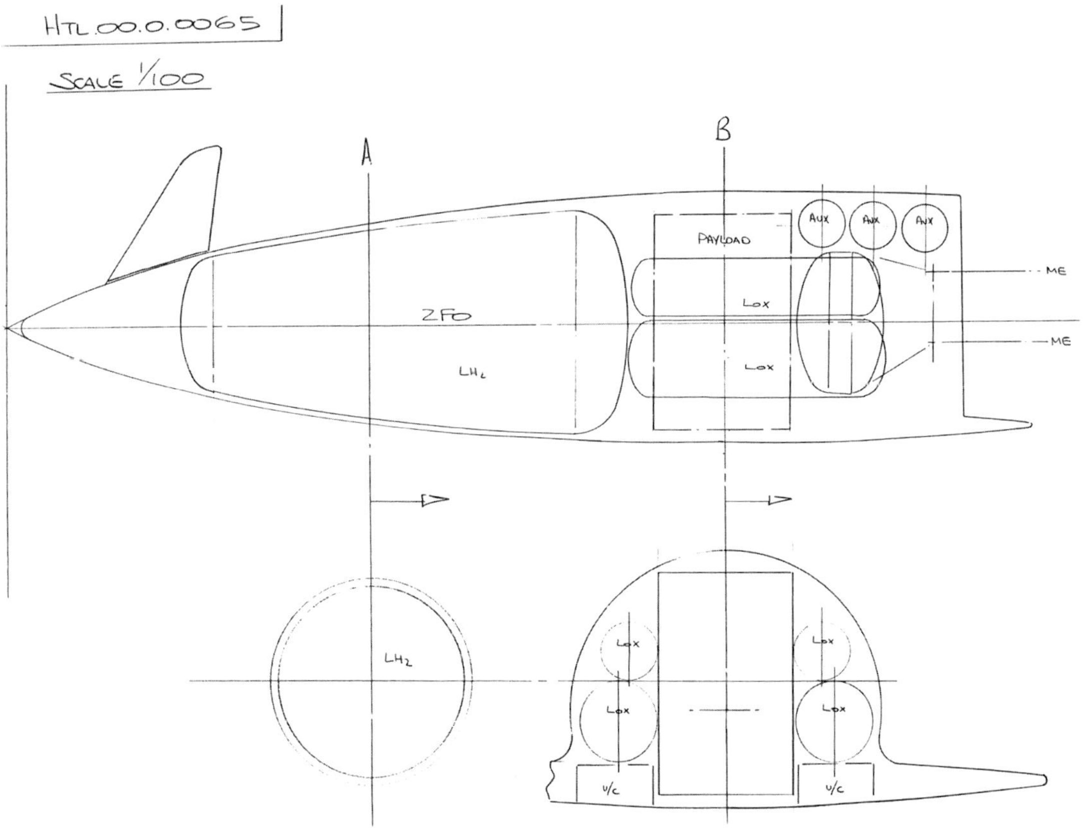

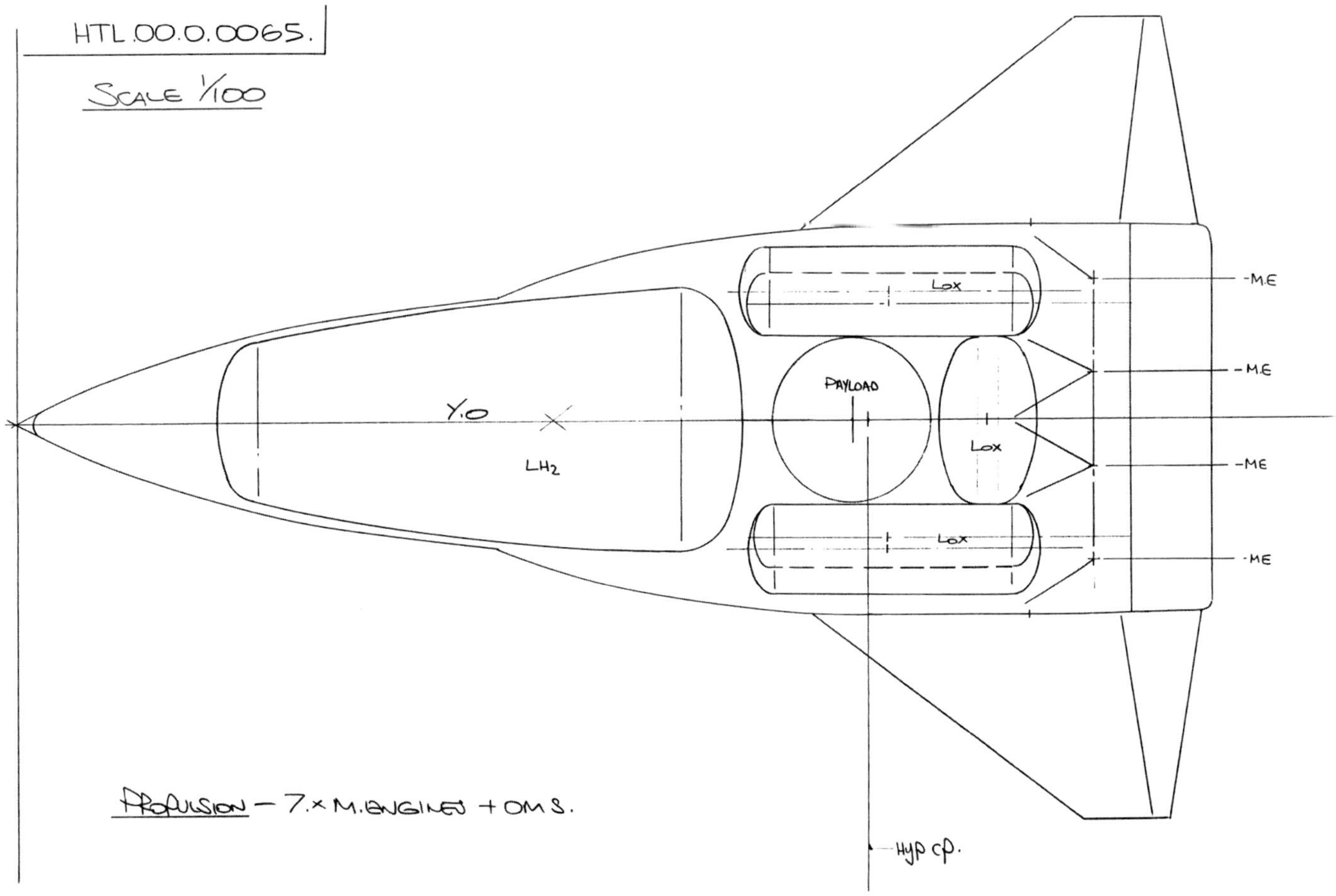

Similar to Orbiter 0064, Orbiter 0065 was a preliminary design only.

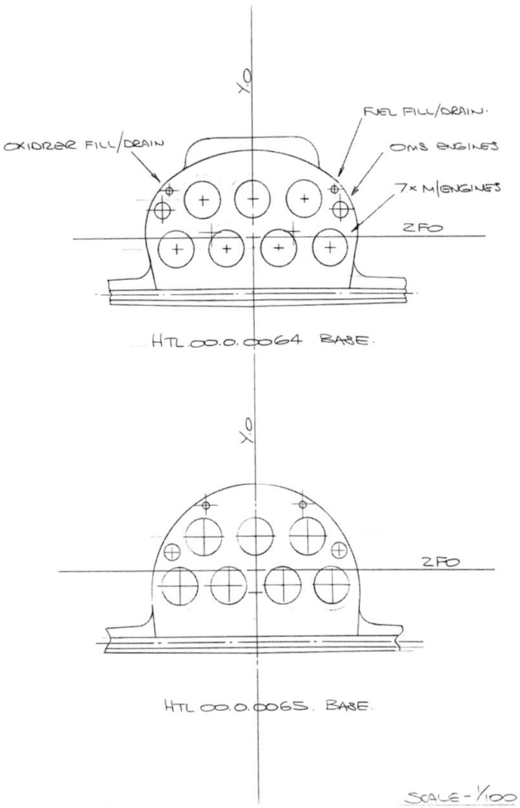

Orbiter 0064 and Orbiter 0065 rear end comparison. Each was to have seven main engines.

"The Soviet side are obviously taking the proposal very seriously. They fielded in excess of 30 specialists as well as [German Ivanovich] Zagaynov—director of TsAGI, Korol—Ministry of Aviation Industry and Lozino-Lozinskiy of Molniya Design. They expected me to talk with senior officials about our proposals for presenting this to ESA and progress beyond that point.

"While the Soviets are interested in the commercial possibilities of the vehicle (and hard currency return), their mission studies show great interest in 'uncooperative rendezvous on demand' for inspection in low Earth orbit which they quote as 'being under United Nations auspices' to ensure non-military activities in Outer Space. This appears to be a counter to SDI (they said as much). As a consequence, the Soviets considered up to four operational bases spread across Europe and the Soviet Union."

The Strategic Defense Initiative (SDI) was a proposed space-based system intended to protect the USA from nuclear missile attack. Announced in 1983 by President Ronald Reagan, by 1986 it had acquired the popular nickname 'Star Wars'. While orbiting laser and particle-beam weapons had initially been considered as means by which to knock out incoming Soviet missiles shortly after launch, by 1990 the most promising concept was 'Brilliant Pebbles'. This system would consist of thousands of small satellites, the 'pebbles', each equipped with missiles. If an ICBM launch was detected, the pebbles would pick up the missiles' rocket motors using infrared seekers then launch their own projectiles in an attempt to collide with and detonate the ICBMs in the air.

Evidently the Soviets were very concerned about these plans and wanted a means by which to inspect otherwise unidentified satellites in space. While any orbiting objects could be tracked from the ground, knowing what those objects actually were was a different matter; it was necessary to get up close and physically look at them. Interim Hotol, with its emphasis on low cost and early availability, seems to have fit the bill for this mission.

Parkinson went on to say that there were two 'scenarios' for USSR/European cooperation—'narrow' and 'broad'. The 'narrow' scenario involved Europe simply buying specific bits of equipment from the Soviets, essentially the specially equipped An-225s, for hard currency and nothing more. The 'broad' scenario would involve a partnership between ESA and the USSR with each side funding development of "appropriate items". Evidently the Soviets were keen to know, "for the 'broad scenario', would there be a guarantee that the Soviet Union could buy its own orbiter to operate independently within the Soviet Union at the end of development (as well as participating in the commercial revenues of a joint operating organisation). It was made quite clear that this was a prerequisite for Soviet participation in the programme".

Not only that, "the Soviets made it clear that they have a lot of technology which they would like to put into this project, and I was asked why we did not simply use the expertise of Lozino-Lozinskiy's Molniya Design Bureau. It was also clear that the Soviets have conducted their own studies of vehicles of this type and believe that they know better ways of doing it but will not table their proposals because they believe that BAe is responsible for the orbiter design and they cannot make an input unless the rules for cooperation are fully defined".

AIRBREATHER'S LAST GASP

February 20 saw the final presentation of the ESA WLC Study Phase 3, with Appleyard, Hargreaves, Stead, Webb and Parkinson from BAe all travelling to ESTEC in Noordwijk to take part.

The vehicle presented by BAe as the Phase 3 datum was an incredible 85m long with a 29.6m wingspan and 242sqm wing area. Maximum fuselage diameter was 8.357m. It had a 17sqm area fin and canards that were 4.7sqm each. Overall, this made it the largest and most extreme Hotol-like vehicle ever considered—longer and

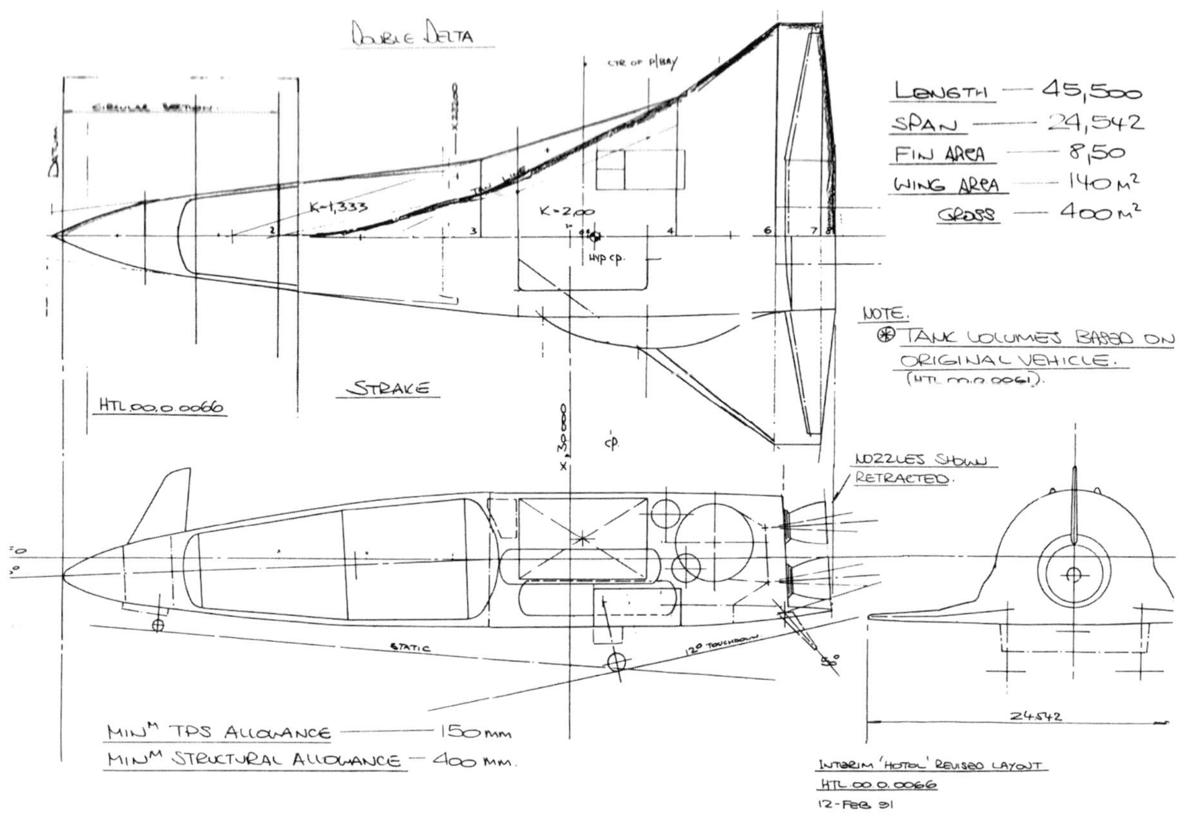

Orbiter 0066 as a work in progress on February 12, 1991.

larger even than Reaction Engines' Skylon D1 spaceplane.

A series of seven design changes were listed: increased wing size (180sqm to 242sqm exposed area) and changed planform (leading edge sweep 58-degrees to 54-degrees); repositioned wing (further aft); liquid oxygen transfer tank incorporated into front end of liquid hydrogen tank; jettisonable foreplanes; auxiliary fuel tank location defined; partitioned liquid hydrogen tank; incorporation of liquid oxygen tank in wing structure". The first four had been "carried out for controllability reasons". A chart included in the presentation showed that when subsystems were factored into the design's payload equation, it came out at minus 4.46 tonnes.

This presentation appears to have represented BAe's last work on an airbreathing Hotol-derived vehicle.

ORBITER 0066

Hopwell's latest Interim Hotol orbiter configuration, Orbiter 0066, was outlined in a handwritten report accompanied by a variety of sketches dated February 26, 1991. He wrote: "The enclosed revised Interim Hotol vehicle is based on the original (HTL.00.0.0061) CAPS output propellant quantities. I have retained a circular liquid hydrogen tank rather than use a multi-lobed one... the centre portion of the fuselage has been flattened out in section to give a semi-lifting body type shape in order to package the centre and balance the vehicle without the need for a liquid oxygen tank forward of the payload bay.

"As can be seen from the calculations—the hypersonic cp is aft of the payload bay centre point and both the gross lift-off mass and the empty centre of gravity are close together and very near to the centre point of the payload bay. The wing has been positioned aft in order to achieve the correct hypersonic cp position and as a result of this when positioning the main undercarriage it was found that part of the undercarriage bay was forward of the wing—therefore the wing planform has been amended a) with a small strake, b) made into a double-delta planform.

"The double delta is favoured as it gives a greater depth for stowage of the undercarriage because of its greater chord length and it also minimises the size of fairing required above the wing. The rear liquid oxygen tank has been shown as a sphere in order to achieve minimum mass and also to give the best fuel balance! If an ellipsoid tank was used it would have had a shorter arm relative to the centre of the payload bay and therefore would have to have a greater capacity in order to achieve the same fuel balance.

"By using a spherical tank it gives plenty of space to run all of the systems—pipes etc. When all of the fuel pipes/valves etc. have been installed in the aft bay of the vehicle I don't think there will be all that much free space. This vehicle has not been optimised via CAPS yet. When done so, we can

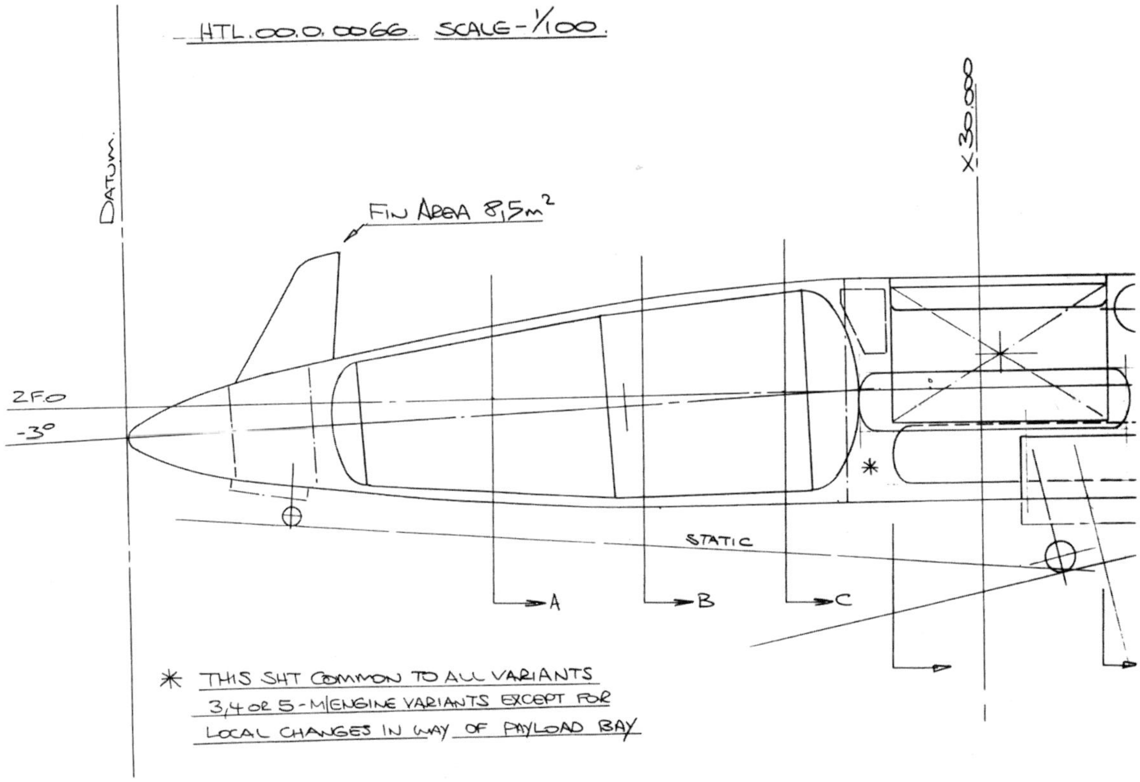

Orbiter 0066 as a work in progress on February 12, 1991.

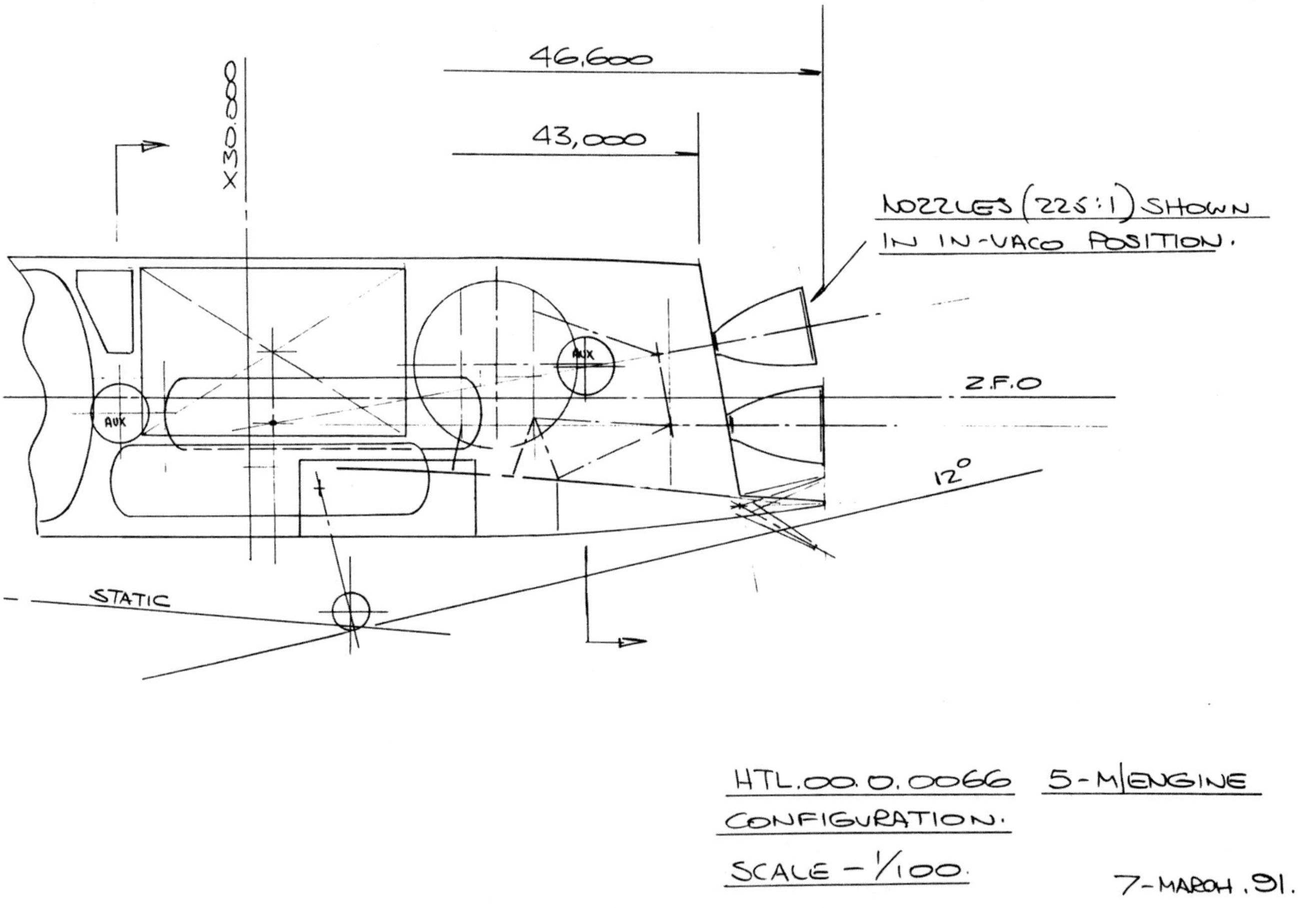

Orbiter 0066 rear end in five-engine configuration, dated March 7, 1991.

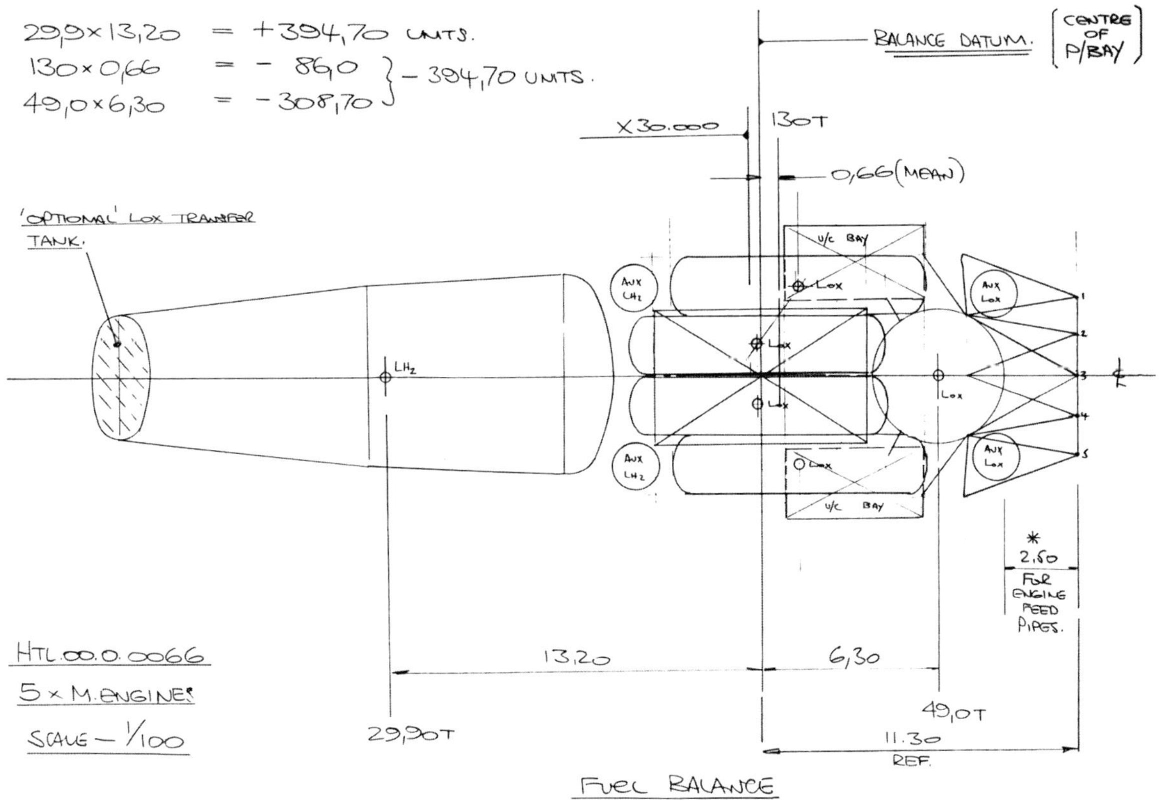

Tankage layout for the five-engine Orbiter 0066.

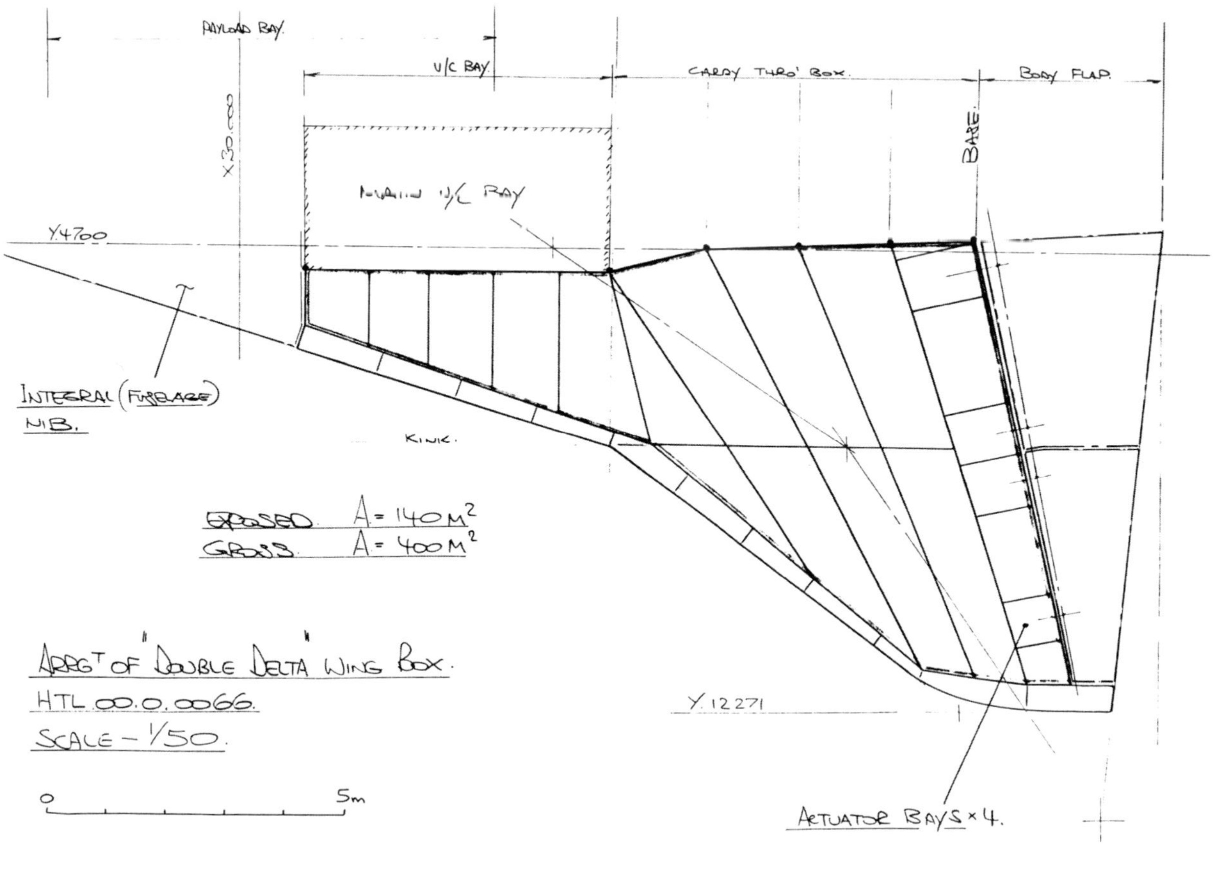

Wing arrangement for Orbiter 0066.

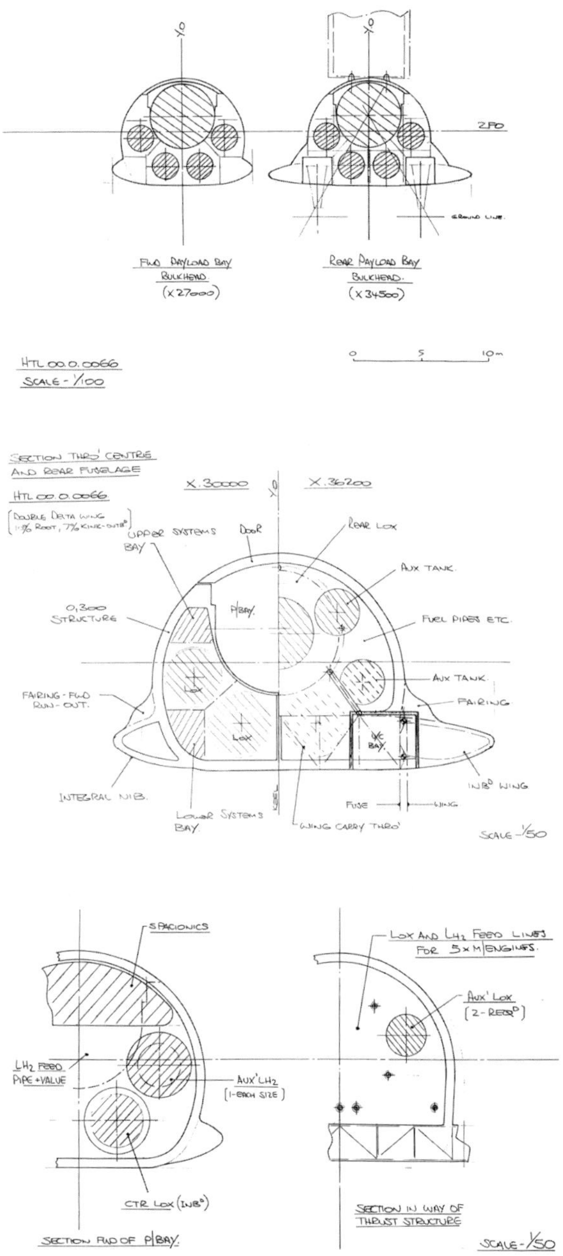

Section views of Orbiter 0066.

probably get more liquid oxygen and liquid hydrogen into the same external profile—or we can scale down the whole vehicle. I have made provision for a liquid oxygen transfer tank as until aero department have done a lot of work on the controllability we won't know if we can do without it."

PAYMENT IN PCs

Helas and Whitaker were invited to watch the beginning of low-speed wind tunnel tests on the newly completed Interim Hotol model, combined with an existing An-225 model, at Antonov's headquarters in Kiev, Ukraine, from March 4-7, 1991.

Reporting on the visit, Whitaker wrote: "The wind tunnel tests were witnessed—but only briefly. Much time

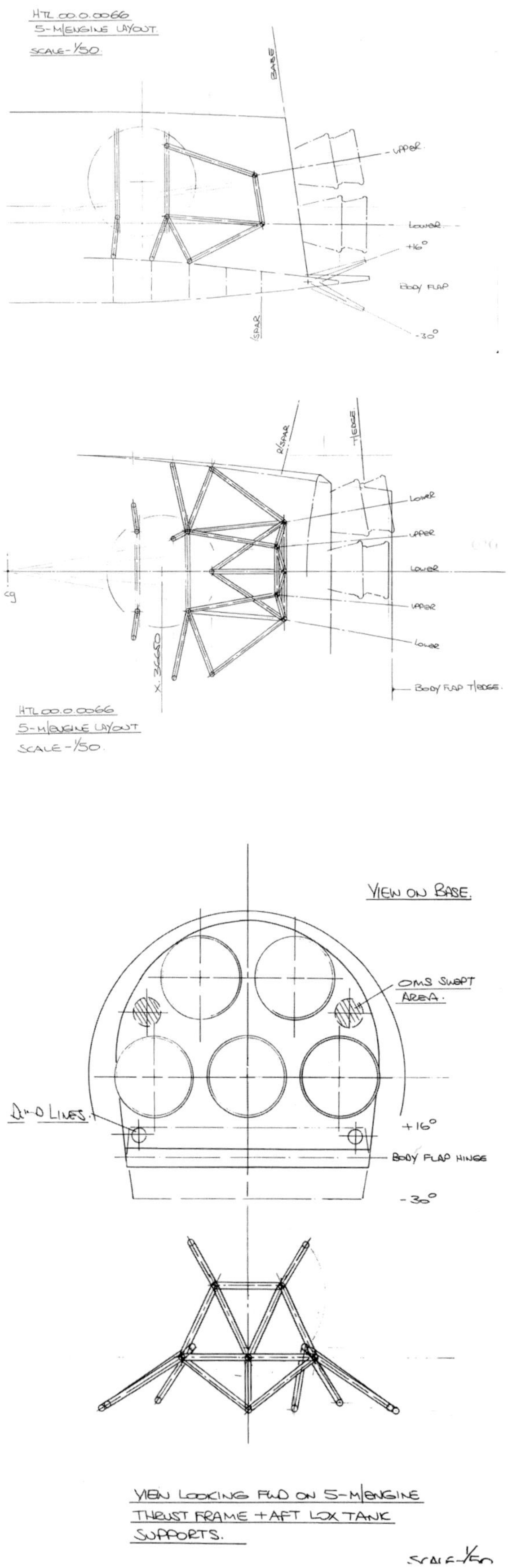

Orbiter 0066 rear fuselage structure.

was spent in meetings and formalities. The model was of better standard than initially specified and the wind tunnel tests were being handled competently. Early results showed no unexpected or undesirable characteristics."

However, he also noted: "There appears to be a certain lack of accord between Antonov and TsAGI which is, at least partially, attributable to Ukraine's independent political stance. Antonov appears keen to establish a development facility independent of the Moscow-based TsAGI organisation."

The cost to BAe of conducting this work was $57,350: $32,500 for the model, $10,000 for modifications and $14,850 for half the cost of the actual tests with TsAGI picking up the other 50%. But the Ukrainians didn't want payment in cash, rather "the costs will be paid in hardware which is required by the departments associated with the project... a list of requirements was provided. It appears that Antonov receive payment for all work from elsewhere, thus the above materials are a 'bonus' for the department involved. They include PCs, copiers, computer consumables and some minor 'model shop' consumables. It is unlikely that these will be subject to... export restrictions but this will be checked by Space Systems Ltd."

More generally, "Antonov believe that transport and launch of the orbiter can be achieved without the use of the proposed jettisonable rear fairing. The main problem will be unsteady aerodynamic loads on the An-225 tail from the bluff orbiter base. Only a two-minute engine warm-up is currently required for the An-225 Lotarev engines (previously understood to be 20 minutes)... Antonov maintain that it may be feasible to ignite the orbiter rockets on the An-225. A very preliminary test has shown a heat transfer rate to an equivalent proximity plate of 120kW/sqm."

Antonov were, however, concerned about how liquid oxygen would be drained from the orbiter in an emergency situation. Whitaker went on: "Modifications to allow the An-225 to carry the orbiter would include the replacement of the single inner-pylon engine with a twin engine pylon i.e. eight TD-18s or re-engining with six RR Trent engines. On the return journey, Prof. Pavlovets from TsAGI, Moscow, requested a brief meeting with Mr Helas. The subject was the method of delivery of the computer hardware with which BAe will pay TSAGI for the impending transonic wind tunnel tests." Evidently both Antonov and TsAGI wanted payment in PCs and other equipment, rather than money.

Finally, Whitaker reiterated: "There appear to be political issues between... TsAGI and Antonov, possibly involving Ukraine's aspirations for independence, which must be handled with care by BAe."

HOTROCK

At a Space Studies progress meeting on March 14 at Stevenage, it was noted that "work on base area has resulted in a change to five engines. Cost is reduced (Parkinson recommendation), a better match with base shape is achieved ... The latest bell diameter/required spacing estimates leave the base area (i.e. size) unchanged. The engines gimbal outwards only and separate OMS engines are necessary. Wing area stands at 140sqm exposed. This should be checked against the vehicle definition within Stevenage's re-entry programme... A scheme was tabled for retractable foreplanes which were not subject to rotation (i.e. in a horizontal plane) during deployment. Area is limited and an assessment is required of their effectiveness as well as hinge moments".

R. M. Hodgkins travelled to Moscow on April 5 to spend a whole week observing wind tunnel tests. At another progress meeting on the same day, efforts to work out what sort of systems mass Interim Hotol might need, based on information from existing aircraft, were discussed. It was recorded that "systems mass data have been collated for BAe 111, Super VC10, Airbus A330, Concorde and Hermes. When hydraulic system masses are plotted against installed power, a good correlation is obtained except for Concorde which looks about 30% light. The feeling is that this could be due to the compact installation, i.e. shorter pipes and less fluid of the highly swept delta configuration. Unfortunately, all totals include functions not found on Hotrock. These can only be separated, with available data, for Concorde in which case they account for about 30% of the total. After this step, correlation with Hotrock is very good."

The Hotrock name for Interim Hotol seems to have first emerged with the issuing of a document entitled 'HOTROCK Controllability Study', produced by Webb, towards the end of March 25, 1991, and began appearing in other documents shortly thereafter.

Parkinson met with Jörg Feustel-Büechl and Heinz Pfeffer in Paris on April 11 to discuss a joint UK/Soviet presentation of the project to ESA. In a memo to Finch the following day, he wrote: "We gave some presentation material to ESA to show how much we had done... Feustel-Büechl was impressed by the extent of the investigations and the extent of our cooperation with the Soviets. It is worth having 'identifiably Soviet' material in the presentation. The use of the estimate for the delta V gains made possible by use of the An-225, and the comparative mass estimates made him think that we were being realistic."

Clearly, when ESA learned that the Russians were involved with this new iteration of Hotol they sat up and paid attention as never before. As Parkinson would later explain to author Russell J. Hannigan, "it's a bit like being the smallest boy in the playground, but you have this great big brother! It's no longer 'Bob Parkinson' talking about it, it's the Russians talking about it. This is no longer a vehicle that is designed by someone who has only designed things using pieces of paper. It's actually been approved by the people who designed Buran."

On the same day, Webb sent Helas an agenda for the Soviets' next visit to Stevenage on April 15-19, under the heading 'Suggested agenda for An-225/"Hotrock" meeting', and the orbiter was referred to as 'Hotrock' throughout.

NOSE FIN DOUBTS

The post-meeting report was written by Paul Murray, who reported to Appleyard, and stated that Antonov's low speed wind tunnel tests had now been completed and that the results were fully in alignment with predictions. Transonic tests at TsAGI were not yet finished but stability characteristics had been found to be satisfactory over the required range of parameters.

Helas had agreed to continue funding tests and "both sides understand that Hotol model geometry is not quite accurate (new configuration now)". Orbiter 0067 was discussed, with Webb pointing out that it offered "better lift at separation" and that five engines were preferable to the two other options on the table: three or four engines. Nose radius had increased from 0.3 to 0.5m and 0067's payload was 4,663kg with a 2,500kg contingency. The Russians had argued that in its current position, the "fin will burn off", with Webb countering that "payload changes if fin location changes".

Murray recorded Parkinson saying that he had started work on a draft presentation for ESA. TsAGI's Professor Valerii Vladimirovich Lazarev said they would be able to give ESA a list of predictions to guarantee mass properties—"In Russia, no project can proceed without approval from TsAGI, CIAM [Central Institute of Aviation Motors] etc." Parkinson said they should tell ESA that the configuration had been thoroughly analysed and "prove that any changes will be better than previous Hermes configuration".

During the 'missions' section of the debate, Lazarev had listed four "uses of Hotrock: urgent reconnaissance of natural catastrophes; supply of long duration space missions; rescue of space station personnel and international inspection of undeclared launches".

He had then asked "why was [the] seven-tonne payload selected? 80% of requirements for payloads are ten not seven tonnes".

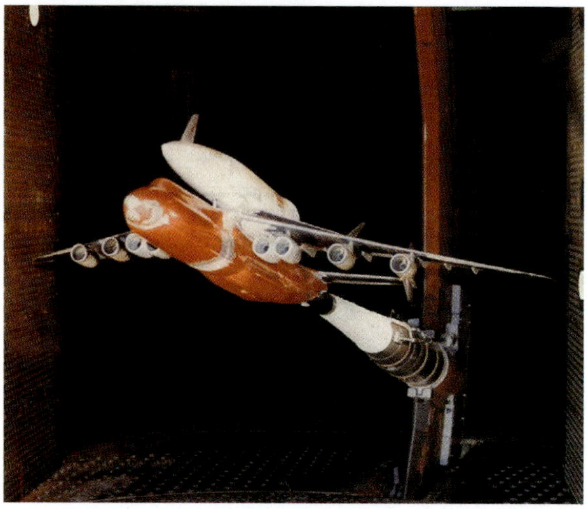

Testing with An-225 and Interim Hotol wind tunnel models at TsAGI. AUTHOR'S COLLECTION

Parkinson had responded that the "mass of payload [is] difficult to define exactly, as users would like larger masses (ten tonnes) but could fly with smaller masses. [We] believe [the] 'best' is ten tonnes but if we can provide a vehicle of this sort with a smaller payload, [it] would still attract [a] considerable number of users. [We] looked at [the] volume and shape of payloads as well as their mass. Wide payloads do not have long length and vice versa … some payloads associated with manned space stations could well occupy [the] full payload bay … believe we need 7.5m long payload bay but 4.5m diameter, on basis of Shuttle compatibility".

Lazarev asked, "what if [the] payload [is] only 4.5 tonnes? Parkinson responded: "[We] need to talk to users before continuing with the programme but [it's probably] okay if [it is] 4.5 tonnes with possibility of future increase".

Later on, discussion turned once again to the nose fin. Neiland said that heating above the vehicle's bow shock would be "much worse lower down". Lazarev said a forward fin would require a 90-degree sweepback. Webb said he had been "advised during Hotol research that [a] forefin would work (further aft of nose)". Neiland had said TsAGI could test the nose and fin section in their high-speed T117 wind tunnel, then "goodbye fin!" A rear fin, he said, would mean a reduction in TPS mass, fin mass and actuator loads, as well as improved reliability.

Much time was spent discussing the launch procedure and trajectories. Korol said there was a "need to relate trajectory to attainment of a fixed point of separation. Radio electronics specialists see [a] major problem [with this]. Need great degree of accuracy if considering rendezvous in orbit. Need accuracy geographically and in timing. One second late and you are 8km behind." Extra fuel might be required for corrections and 'joining units' might be necessary for a rendezvous—resulting in "quite considerable reduction in payload".

Neiland said that "at [the] ESA presentation, these problems need not be raised. Could name a few dozen! Leave these questions for ESA to ask. At this stage adopt concepts to present to ESA—perhaps two. Accept one as a base." He went on to say it would be necessary to "rigidly limit the number of questions to be solved for [the] ESA presentation".

SWITCH TO REAR FIN

The April 29 Space Studies progress meeting heard that the BAe/Soviet presentation to ESA was now set to take place on June 21 and the next scheduled BAe trip to the USSR, due in May, was now unnecessary. Appleyard would, however, give a presentation on Hotrock to an ESTEC-sponsored symposium on aerothermodynamics in Noordwijk on May 28.

All wind tunnel tests had now been completed and Appleyard had received a full report. Apparently "only minor problems have been revealed. However, further analysis is still required". As far as the launch was concerned, "work has been done on the energy/height and pre-release manoeuvring study, but not enough to arrive at a conclusion".

Work on two different orbiter wing configurations had been carried out and it had been determined that 500kg of payload could be gained by increasing the thickness/chord ratio—though "more work is required to find the optimum after accounting for drag". Two different wing surface areas—the original 140sqm plus a new 100sqm layout—were being studied.

Four engines with thrust vector control would now be assumed, "in line with the Soviet engine scale" and on the issue of fin heating, "Stevenage are inclined to support Prof. Neiland's view on conditions behind the bow shock/ Mach wave and ahead of the fin leading edge".

Following on from that, "because of Soviet doubts as to the feasibility of the forefin, a rear located fin/fin and rudder should be reviewed. Although a recent estimate has indicated a threefold increase in structure mass, use of recovery alone should have a beneficial effect on reducing lateral loads. Revised fin size(s) and peak hinge moment(s) are required".

Parkinson produced a 'Proposal for a UK Infrastructure Preparatory Programme' document in May 1991 which outlined the by-now-familiar advantages of investing in enabling technology and infrastructure programmes, though this time based on work supporting the An-225/ Interim Hotol concept. He gave examples of how much other countries were spending on space infrastructure and suggested, as before, that the UK should be working primarily on advanced materials and structures.

By the time of the next Space Studies progress meeting, on May 14, 1991, no further work had been done on analysing the wind tunnel test results, nor on the energy/ height and pre-release manoeuvring study. The configuration had changed a little though: "Separate OMS engines are not required since a separate propellant supply system is provided for the main engines in OMS mode" and "to bring the centre of gravity further forward, the liquid hydrogen auxiliary tank has been split. The section containing the RCS allocation has been moved forward of the main liquid hydrogen tank".

It had been concluded that "a wing of 100sqm exposed area is considered adequate for re-entry and touchdown. Touchdown speed is around 150/160kts. The optimum thickness/chord ratio is 12% when ascent equivalent airspeed is reduced to 500kts". Smaller wings posed their own problems though: "To partly compensate for the loss of flap effectiveness with the small, 100sqm wing, and to allow a more rearward wing location, a 28% flap chord has been assumed with an unswept trailing edge. The feasibility of the consequently more highly swept flap hinge line remains to be investigated.

Despite agreeing with the Soviets that a rear-set fin was probably best, "a forward fin should be assumed for the purposes of the ESA presentation". This was no doubt because work on adding a rear fin to the orbiter was still at an early stage: "The cross-wind landing case, the only criterion applied so far, requires a fin and rudder area, when located at the rear, of 25.6sqm. Other design cases must be considered".

The next Space Studies meeting was on May 20 and was mostly concerned with preparations for the ESA presentation. It appears that around this time the name 'Hotrock' was dropped—just two months after its first appearance.

MAINTAINING MOMENTUM

On May 22, 1991, Helas faxed Webb a draft proposal for continued BAe support going into the second half of the year. The introduction said: "There is a need to maintain the present momentum of work through the second half of 1991 in parallel to the efforts to attract support from BNSC, ESA, and perhaps other quarters. This will also help to ensure our continued collaboration with the Soviets, thus giving us the all-important access to their expertise and facilities.

"Ideally, the level of support at both Stevenage and

Warton should remain constant with a similar level of expenditure on wind tunnel models and testing to be performed within the Soviet Union. Testing would, in part, repeat a few of the test polars of the first phase but with the latest Interim Hotol configuration.

"New separation tests would then be performed using a twin sting [i.e. two separate mounting points within the wind tunnel—one for the orbiter and one for the An-225] which was originally developed for Buran testing. In addition, it would be desirable to perform further flutter tests for the eight-engined version of the An-225 and to conduct relatively simple Interim Hotol 'front end' hypersonic tests to explore forward fin heating problems.

"In practice, present budget constraints at both Stevenage and Warton will not permit all of the above test proposals but it might be just possible to fund the new model configuration and perform combined separation testing in the TsAGI T128 tunnel."

He then listed "proposed An-225/Interim Hotol activities for the second half of 1991". Handwritten beneath this on the file copy was an additional first item: "Agree a name for 'Interim Hotol'!!"

BAe press officer John Humby circulated a press release, presumably on Thursday, June 20, which was under embargo until Friday, June 21, 1991. It was headlined: 'Joint British-Soviet Study of the 'Interim Hotol' Air Launched Space Vehicle Completed' and it said: "The study of 'Interim Hotol', a new air-launched, reusable space vehicle announced jointly by British Aerospace Space Systems Ltd. and the Soviet Ministry of Aviation Industry at the Farnborough Air Show in September 1990, has been completed.

"The study considered the feasibility of launching Interim Hotol at an altitude of 9,000m from the Soviet Antonov An-225 super transport aircraft. The study has demonstrated that the An-225 is capable of providing an airborne launch platform for Interim Hotol and that using conventional rocket propulsion after separation, the orbiter would be capable of lifting 6-8 tonnes into low Earth orbit.

"The study not only included design work and technical interchanges between the two groups, but also wind tunnel tests of the composite vehicle carried out using Soviet transonic facilities. The study, extended from its planned duration of six months because of the good progress made, has proved the feasibility of the combined vehicle and demonstrated that a joint Soviet-British team of some 50 engineers and scientists can work productively and harmoniously together on a high technology project.

"Development and operational costs were analysed and it was confirmed that launch costs could be reduced to approximately 20% of those of current expendable launchers. This coupled with the wide choice of orbits accessible from a conventional launch/retrieval site provides a highly credible commercial potential for the system. The results of the study have, today, been presented to the European Space Agency and similar presentations will be made to other European national governments, space agencies and space engineering companies.

"A full development programme would require international participation and it is hoped that partners would be found from within Europe, as there is considerable commonality between this work and work currently being carried out on programmes such as the German Sänger and the French PREPHA [national Research and Technology Programme for Advanced Hypersonic Propulsion].

"The immediate priority for both partners is to initiate enabling technology programmes to meet specific requirements in area such as materials, structures, avionics, thermal protection and propulsion systems. The combination of this technology development and the Soviet capability and facilities for hypersonic research will take this proposal for an economic, reliable and reusable launch vehicle one stage further, with an anticipated first flight test in 2005."

Much had changed since the first presentation of Hotol to ESA in January 1985—six and a half years earlier. Interim Hotol offered two compelling new attractions: a pre-existing first stage in the form of the massive An-225 and the opportunity to engage with the formidable scientific and engineering might of the USSR, long the deadly opponent of ESA's member countries. Would this be enough to tempt the Europeans into a new partnership?

11

HOTOL-M, P150, RADEM AND SKYLON: JUNE 21, 1991 TO OCTOBER 14, 1994

PARKINSON AND Finch arrived in Paris for the presentation to ESA on the day itself—Friday, June 21, 1991. Helas, Webb, Platt and the Soviets were already there, having arrived the day before. The team had been given three hours in the afternoon to make their pitch and had chosen to divide this up into 140 minutes' talking time, with 10 minutes allowed for different speakers to swap places on the podium and 30 minutes for discussion with the audience at the end.

The presentation itself was further subdivided into seven sections: 20 minutes on joint BAe/Soviet statements of intent, 15 minutes of introduction to the system, 20 minutes on the main engines from CIAM, 30 minutes on the orbiter design from BAe Warton, 25 minutes on the An-225 from TsAGI and Antonov, 15 minutes on operations from BAe Stevenage and lastly 10 minutes on the development programme, also from BAe Stevenage. This left five minutes of wiggle room for overruns or other delays.

The introduction outlined the origin of the project back in 1989 and how it followed on from the airbreathing Hotol, stating: "Technically the vehicle we are going to present is a two-stage, not a single-stage vehicle. The advantage we have is that the first stage is already flying!"

A highly simplified version of the workshare arrangement was also given—a European orbiter with Soviet engines; a Soviet carrier with European on-board systems—before the Soviets stepped up to give their introduction, outlining the commercial possibilities of the system. They also cited 'ecological cleanliness' as an advantage, with "elimination of alienation zones for dropping used expendable units, launch area noise at start, the absence of air pollution by unusual fuel and combustion products, as well as the absence of discarded launcher components in low altitude orbits".

They even went so far as to strongly hint at the anti-SDI operation: "It is important to emphasize the special kind of mission the future system may have to perform—namely, matching the injection trajectory and the orbit plane with an arbitrary inclination for rendezvous with a satellite residing there. These missions are needed when it is necessary to rescue the crew in a dangerous situation, or to inspect satellites with undeclared purposes of mission."

The cover of the booklet produced to accompany the Interim Hotol/An-225 presentation to ESA on June 21, 1991—featuring artwork based on a photo from the set of publicity stills produced around nine months earlier.

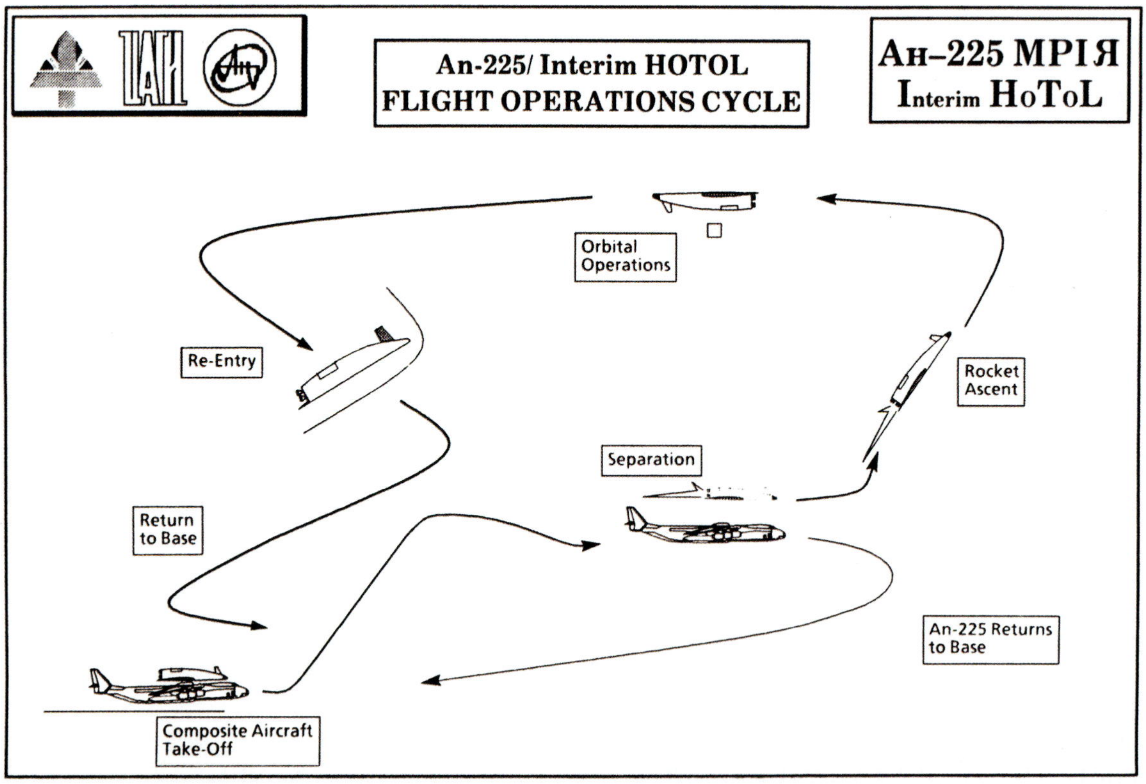

The An-225/Interim Hotol flight operations cycle, as discussed by Parkinson.

It was pointed out too that using the An-225 meant Hotol could fulfil its original promise of launch from a conventional runway, and without the troublesome requirement for a trolley. The wide range of facilities offered by TsAGI was outlined and it was explained that "the year of joint work with BAe on the assessment of the An-225/Interim Hotol project feasibility has demonstrated the fruitfulness of such a cooperation. In particular, the Soviet side has carried out the analysis of system mission opportunities, trajectories, performed the estimation of aerodynamic heating and weight of the orbiter, separation dynamics etc."

Parkinson then took the podium to outline the basics of the system, including the flight operations cycle: loading the orbiter onto the aircraft, ascent to 9km and Mach 0.8 before release, rocket propulsion into orbit, completion of mission, then return via gliding re-entry. Orbiter details as presented were: all-up mass 250 tonnes, empty mass 31.4 tonnes, payload mass 5.5 to eight tonnes, length 36.45m, wingspan 21.6m and thrust-to-weight ratio at launch 1.3.

Next up were TsIAM, the main USSR research institute for aero and space engines, and the Soviet Chemical Automatics Design Bureau (CADB) to talk about the orbiter's main engines. Interim Hotol would be powered by four liquid-fuelled rocket engines derived from the RD-0120—the type used by the second stage of the super-heavy Energia launch vehicle. These would be fitted with two-position nozzles, the moving part of which would slide into the extended position at an altitude of 13km.

The total cost of 40 engines, each capable of five missions, was $1bn and it would take eight years to get the first examples ready for service.

ORBITER DESIGN

BAe Warton representatives then presented a section on the orbiter, explaining how it had initially been based on Hotol Configuration K but with the airbreathing engine components removed—allowing a reduction both in length and wingspan. The text of the speech said: "The design retained many features in the airbreathing Hotol system—such as a forward liquid oxygen 'transfer tank' to allow the vehicle centre of gravity to be matched with the aerodynamic centre of pressure as the vehicle accelerated between Mach 0.8 and Mach 5. Some of these features proved to be unnecessary with the vehicle concept being considered in this study, and disappeared later. You will find -0061 as the reference configuration for the study, but at the end of the study we re-optimised the design by putting back all the data we had obtained into the computer, to provide an updated design known as -0068. There are intermediate concepts generated to analyse particular aspects of the problem, which account for the missing numbers.

"A mass statement was generated for -0061. This was not only a mass output from the CAPS computer model, but also a mass analysis from detailed engineering analysis. In parallel, the Soviet engineers did a similar exercise, giving the vehicle configuration to two of their design teams to assess. One team was at TsAGI, and one at NPO Molniya. As a consequence of these studies, we generated three separate opinions of the mass of Orbiter -0061. From these we can work out a 'variability' for each area of the design.

"After discussions on the major divergencies, this indicated that overall differences of opinion of about 7% existed ... because of the uncertainties in mass estimation shown, an additional contingency allowance or global margin of 2.5 tonnes has been agreed for these studies. This reduces the computer's seven-tonne payload for this configuration to four-and-a-half tonnes, but Orbiter -0061 has to be re-optimised before we can use its payload results."

From Orbiter 0061, efforts had focused on increasing payload and a key means of doing this was reducing wing size: "The effect of reducing wing exposed area is to increase the payload but to decrease the re-entry cross-range and increase the landing speed. Currently we are proposing an exposed wing of 100sqm. The cross-range now amounts to 28 degrees and the landing speed to 165kts, both of which are considered adequate."

In addition, "the use of lobed tanks—particularly with the liquid oxygen tank to improve geometric packing in the rearbody area—could save mass. Changes to the nose geometry improve re-entry characteristics, capitalising on the reduced importance of drag on ascent. We also considered turning the payload bay through 90 degrees to reduce overall vehicle length—although this would restrict the total length available for the payload bay. We considered changes to the wing planform, and the number of engines. In configuration -0068 we have not taken all those factors into effect, but it represents a 'partial' optimisation ... basically the vehicle has become shorter and fatter, with a blunter nose and wing leading edge, and a smaller wing".

The audience were treated to slides showing Orbiter 0068's internal and external layout, with the unnamed speaker continuing: "One feature is the need to provide afterbody fairings to accommodate the main undercarriage. Note the large flap areas for control during re-entry and recovery. A deployable foreplane has been added to assist control. The liquid oxygen tank arrangement has been designed to maximise volume utilisation while

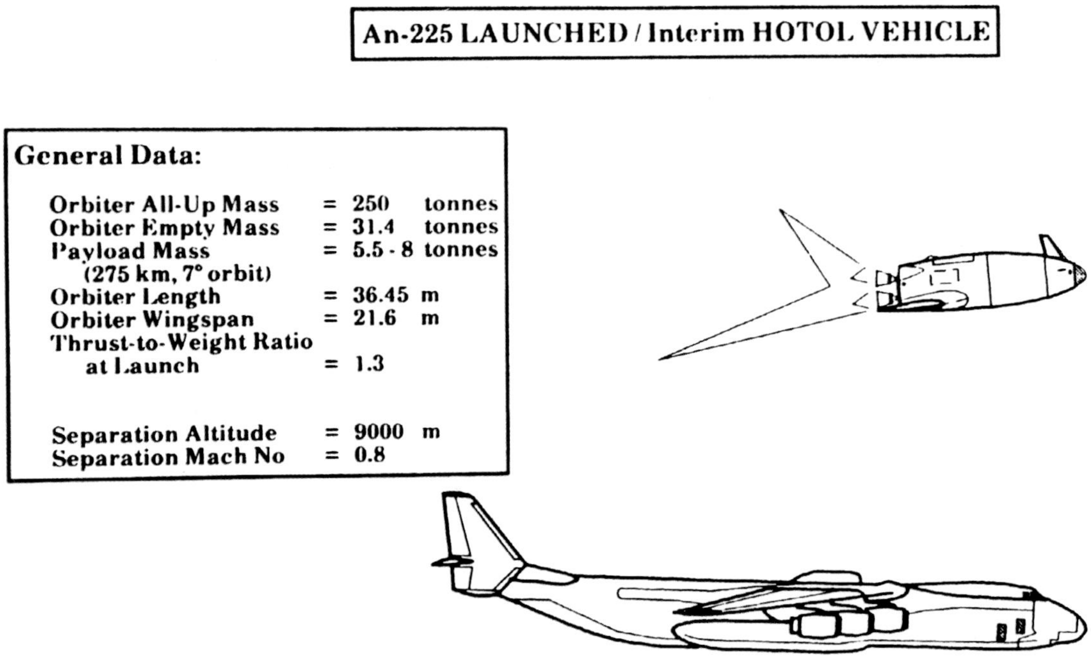

Basic data on the Interim Hotol orbiter accompanied by line art.

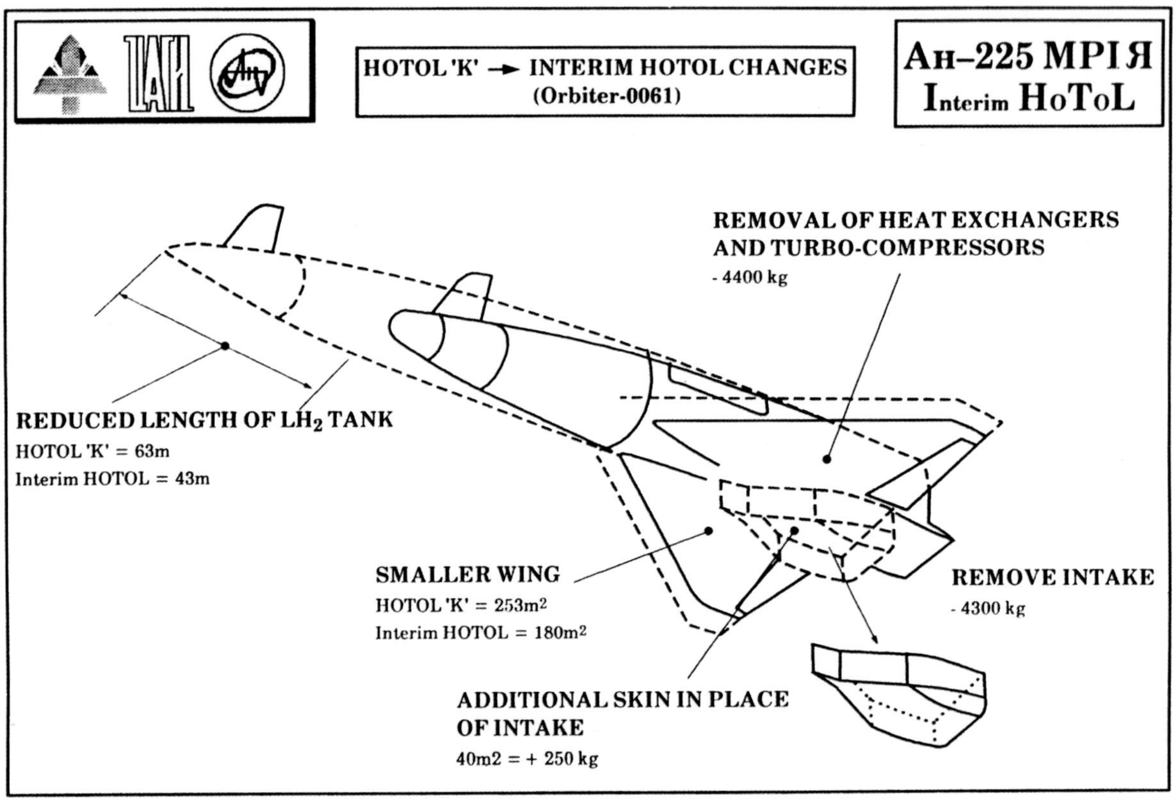

Recycled artwork showing the key changes resulting from the switch to all-rocket propulsion—but now with dimensions and weight savings shown.

keeping acceptable centre of gravity control."

Payload for Orbiter 0068 came out at 5,485kg—plus the 2,500kg contingency, hence Parkinson's earlier description of the payload being between 5.5 and eight tonnes. In terms of materials, the nose cone, forefin leading edge, wing leading edges and control surfaces were to be made of carbon-silicon carbide, the upper fuselage was titanium with particulates and the lower fuselage was covered in sandwich-type TPS panels made of carbon-silicon carbide on the exterior then, Protecalor, TG15000 and finally

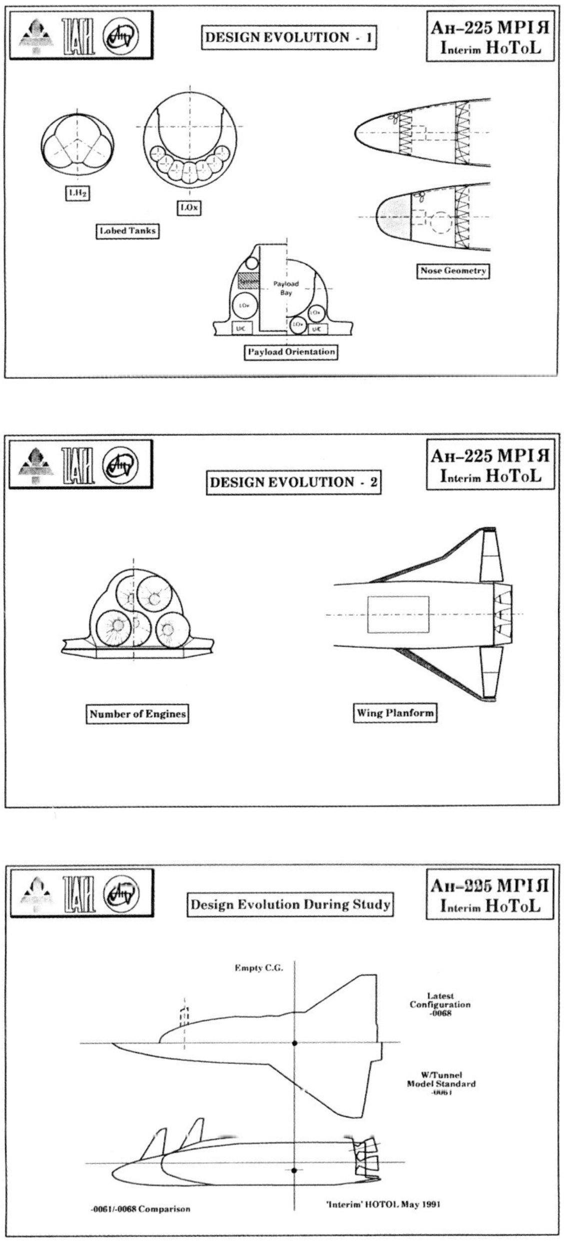

Diagrams showing the design evolution of the Interim Hotol orbiter, from the beginning of the study up to the latest iteration, Orbiter 0068.

carbon-PEEK on the interior. The wings would be made of titanium aluminide with fibres. Inside the cargo bay door there would be flexible insulation made from carbon-bismaleimide resin panels.

The vehicle's sub-systems were outlined too: "Auxiliary propulsion would use oxygen and hydrogen propellants stored in separate tanks and pressure fed either to OMS engines or to the main engine in OMS mode. RCS would largely be by cold gas thrusters from the residual hydrogen. Flying control actuation uses a 2x2 redundancy hydraulics system. For electrical power we have basedlined one-shot batteries for the short flight duration (circa 63 hours) although fuel cells would be a possibility if their reliability were proven.

"Thermal control proposes to use external panel radiators on orbit, and thermal storage/ammonia boilers for ascent and recovery. Avionics would use quadruplex safety critical systems, with navigation by inertial measurement and GPS. It is intended that the vehicle would continue to fly through the first loss of avionics redundancy, and initiate aborts at a two-lane failure."

AERODYNAMIC CONTROL

Engine thrust vectoring was key to keeping Interim Hotol under control during the ascent: "In the period immediately following separation the centre of lift moves forward quite dramatically as the vehicle accelerates through Mach 4, due to the transfer of lift from the wings to the vehicle body. During ascent the principal control forces will be generated by engine thrust vectoring, with the flaps assisting pitch trim (principally during the pull-up manoeuvre).

"This avoids having to size the hydraulics for full authority control of a fully loaded vehicle with one lane of hydraulics failed. The centre of lift shifts considerably as the vehicle accelerates, but trim can be achieved at all Mach numbers by a combination of centre of gravity control (draining liquid oxygen tanks in sequence), flap deflection and engine thrust vector control. The forward fin is locked during ascent to limit the control powers required of the forward hydraulics system."

During re-entry "the vehicle will be trimmed for high lift by using the body and wing flaps, with roll control using the RCS to achieve the cross range requirements. Finally, the vehicle becomes a true aerodynamic glider as it moves to recovery and landing. At this stage the forward fin becomes active and foreplanes are deployed to assist in pitch control. Once again the centre of lift shifts significantly as the vehicle slows from Mach 5, but the vehicle mass is considerably reduced, making the control forces more handleable".

It was noted that "there has been particular discussion about the heating of the forward fin, but with this shortened vehicle rear fins become a possibility. Early experimental work would help clear this point". Other "problem areas" identified were the ongoing need for advanced materials development, demonstration of structural components, pitching moment prediction, trim and control during re-entry and recovery, and sub-system definition. The use of chilling to increase propellant density was still foreseen but "the effect of this has not been included in the current design".

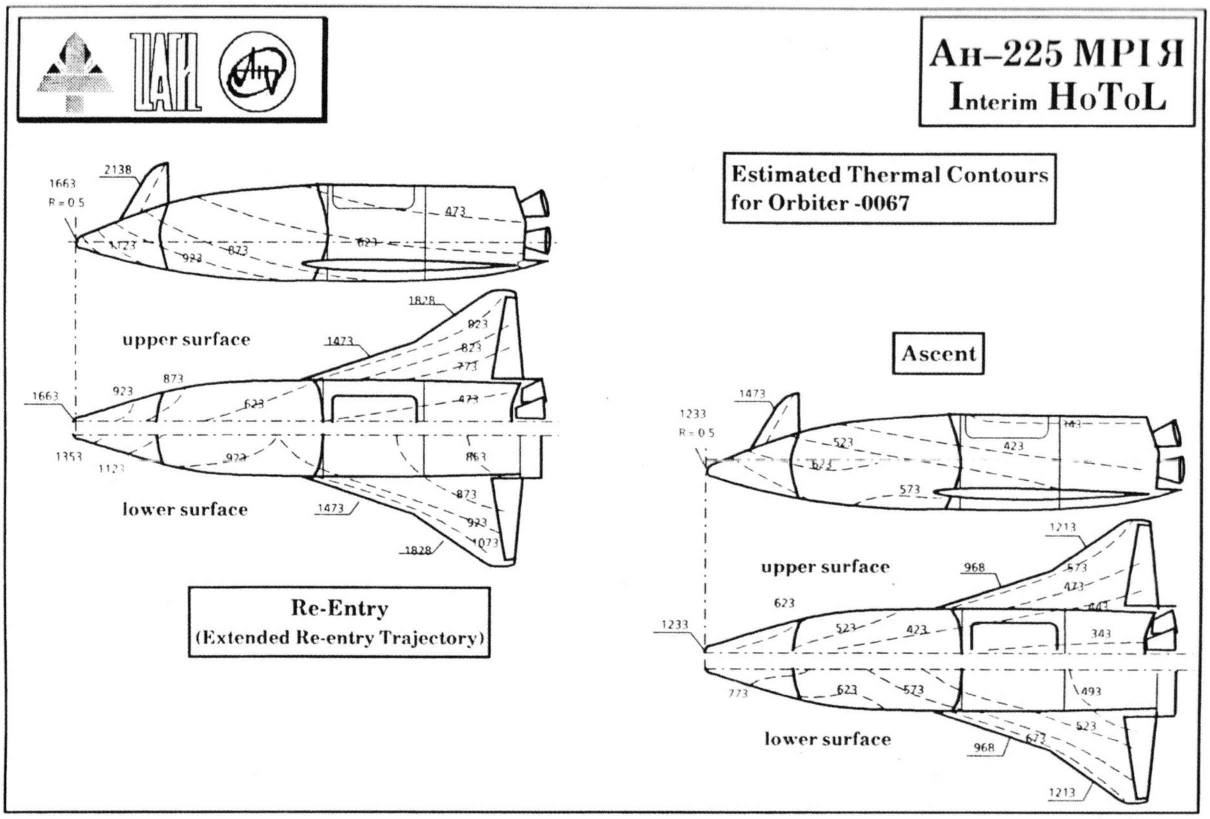

A rare view of Orbiter 0067, utilised here to show thermal contours for ascent and re-entry.

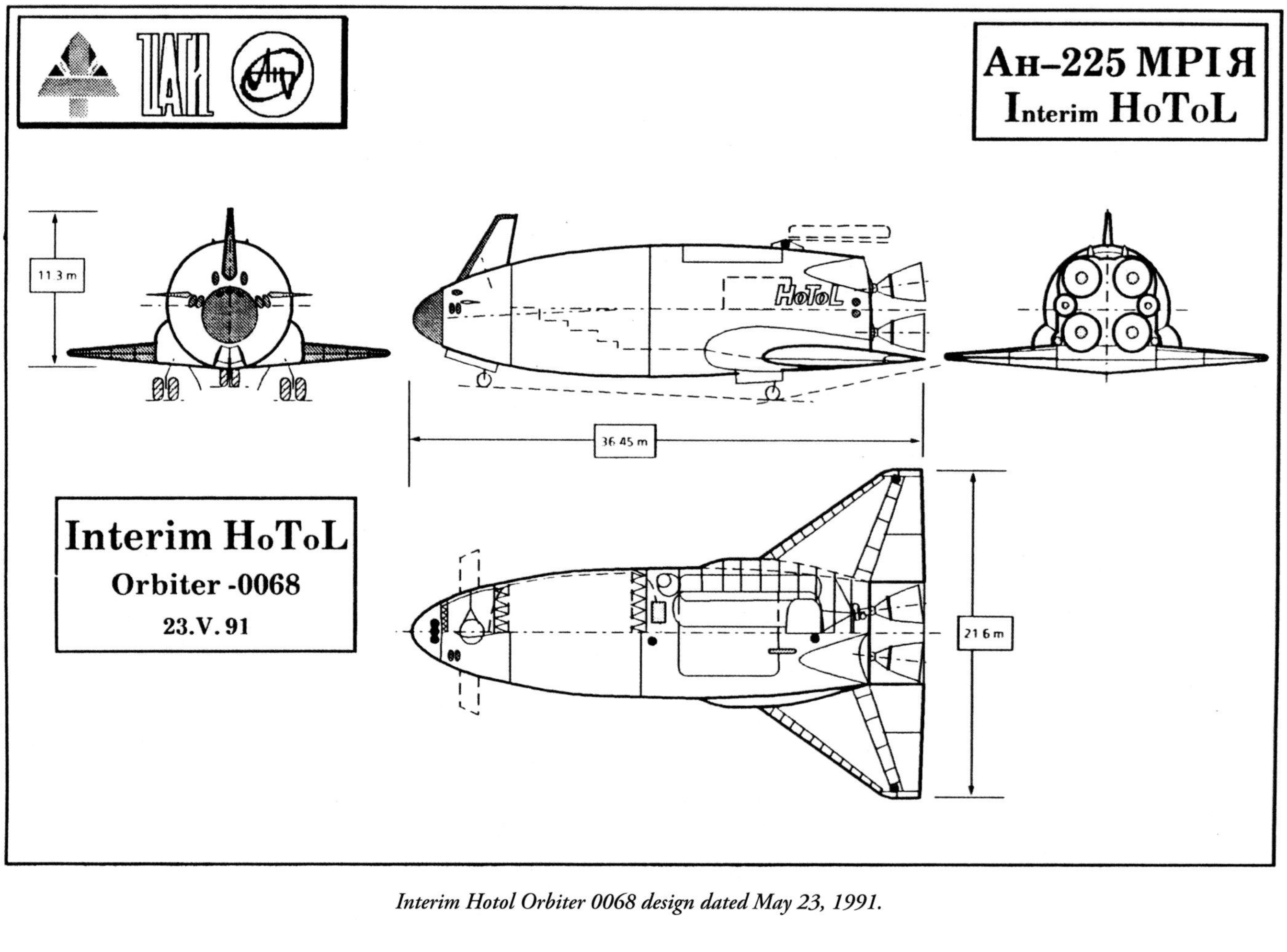

Interim Hotol Orbiter 0068 design dated May 23, 1991.

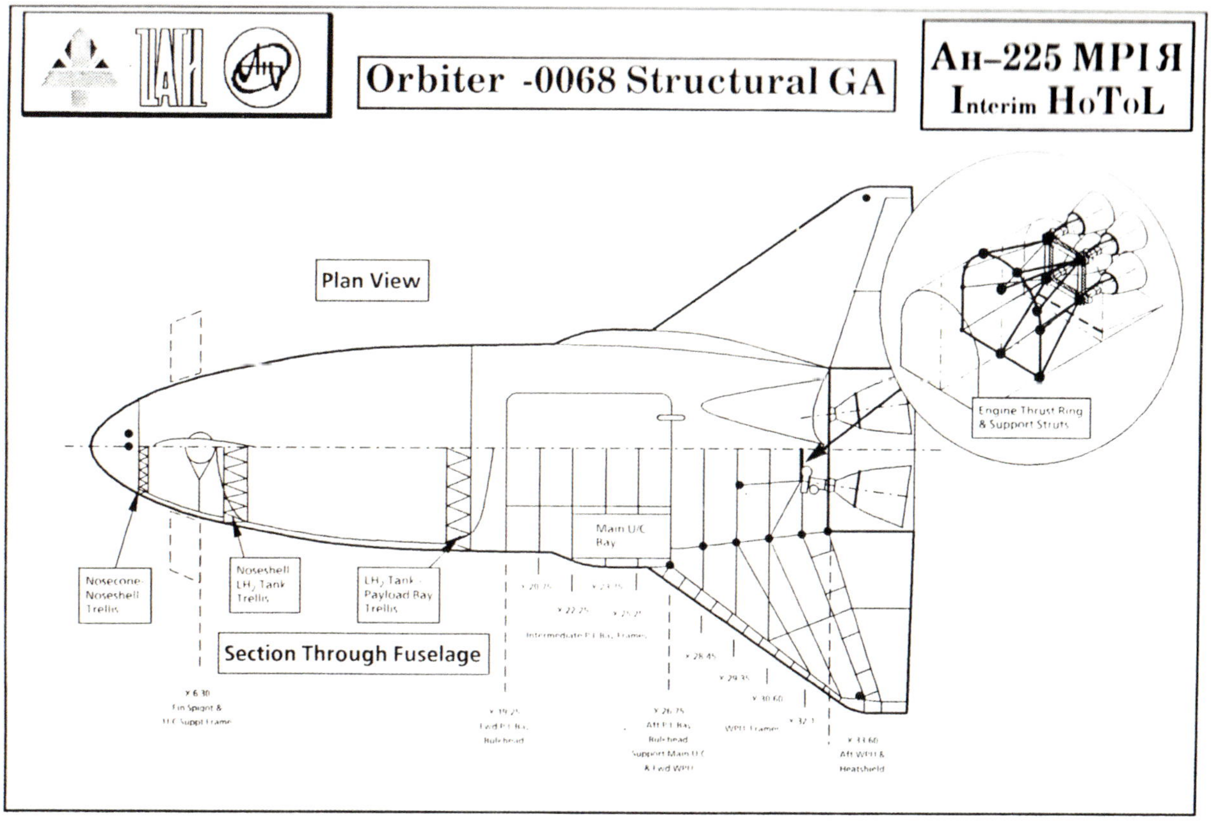

Plan view showing the structure of Orbiter 0068.

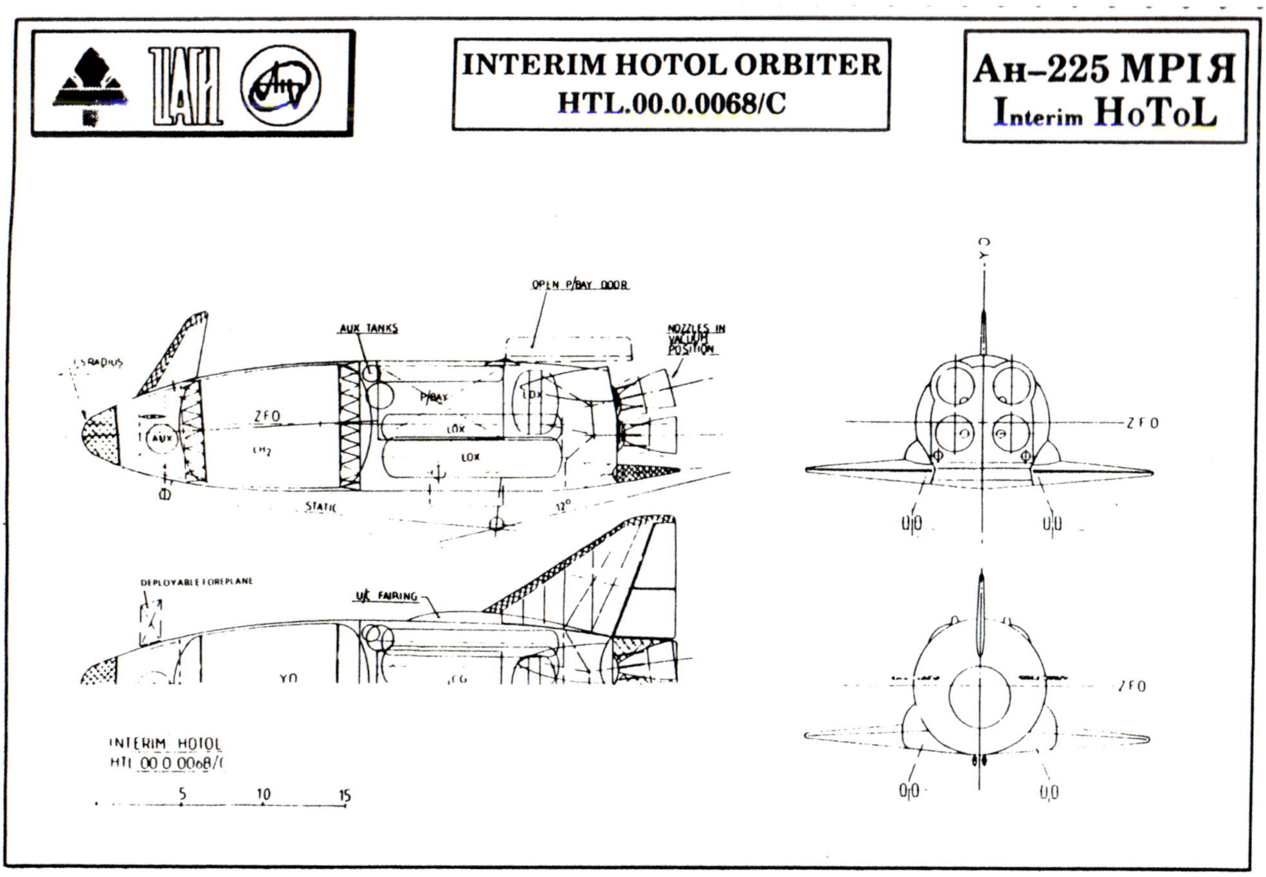

The newest version of Interim Hotol at the time of the June 21, 1991, presentation: Orbiter 0068c. One of the most obvious differences between 0068 and 0068c was the latter's much longer main undercarriage legs.

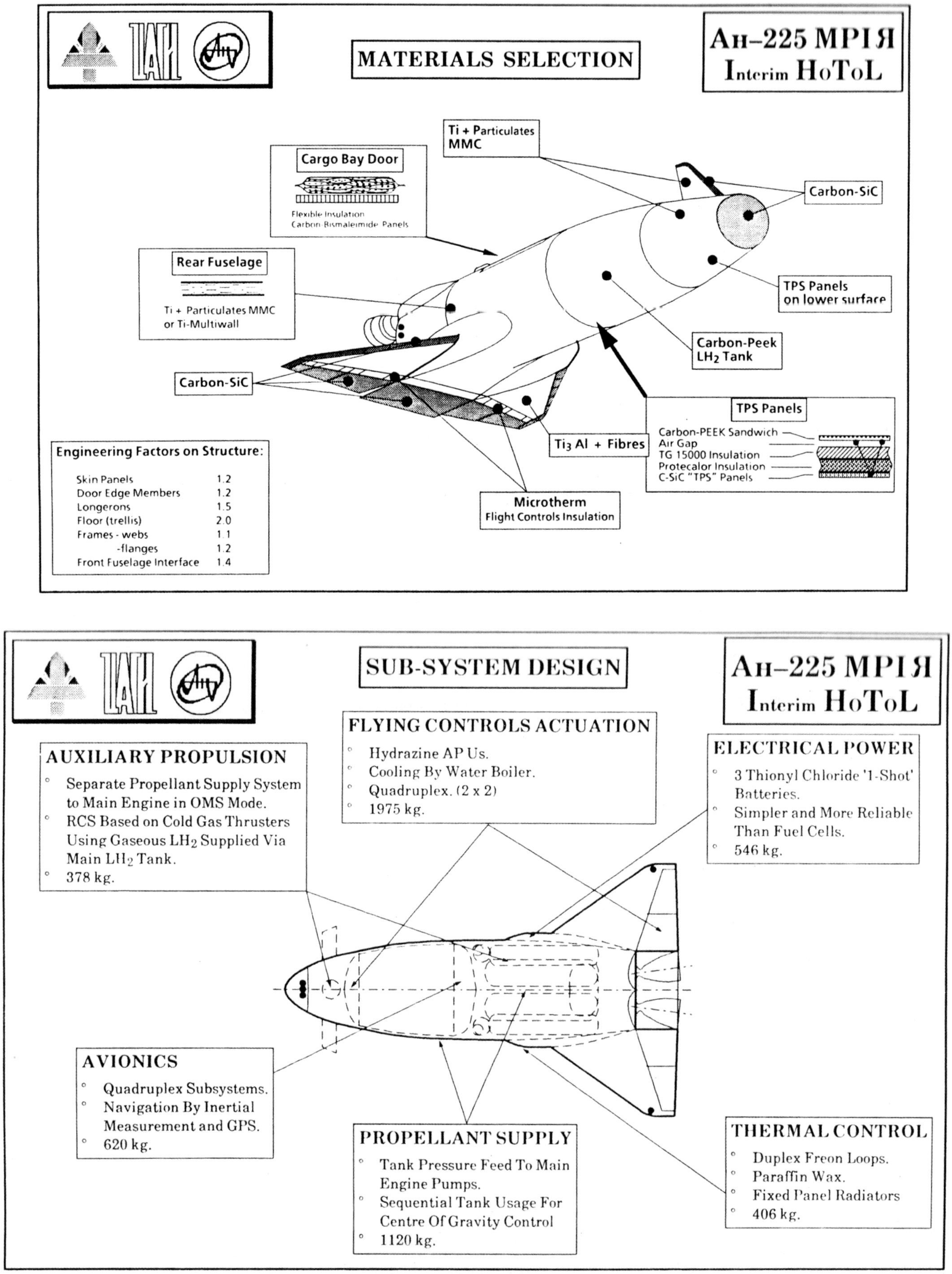

Materials and subsystem design for the Interim Hotol orbiter.

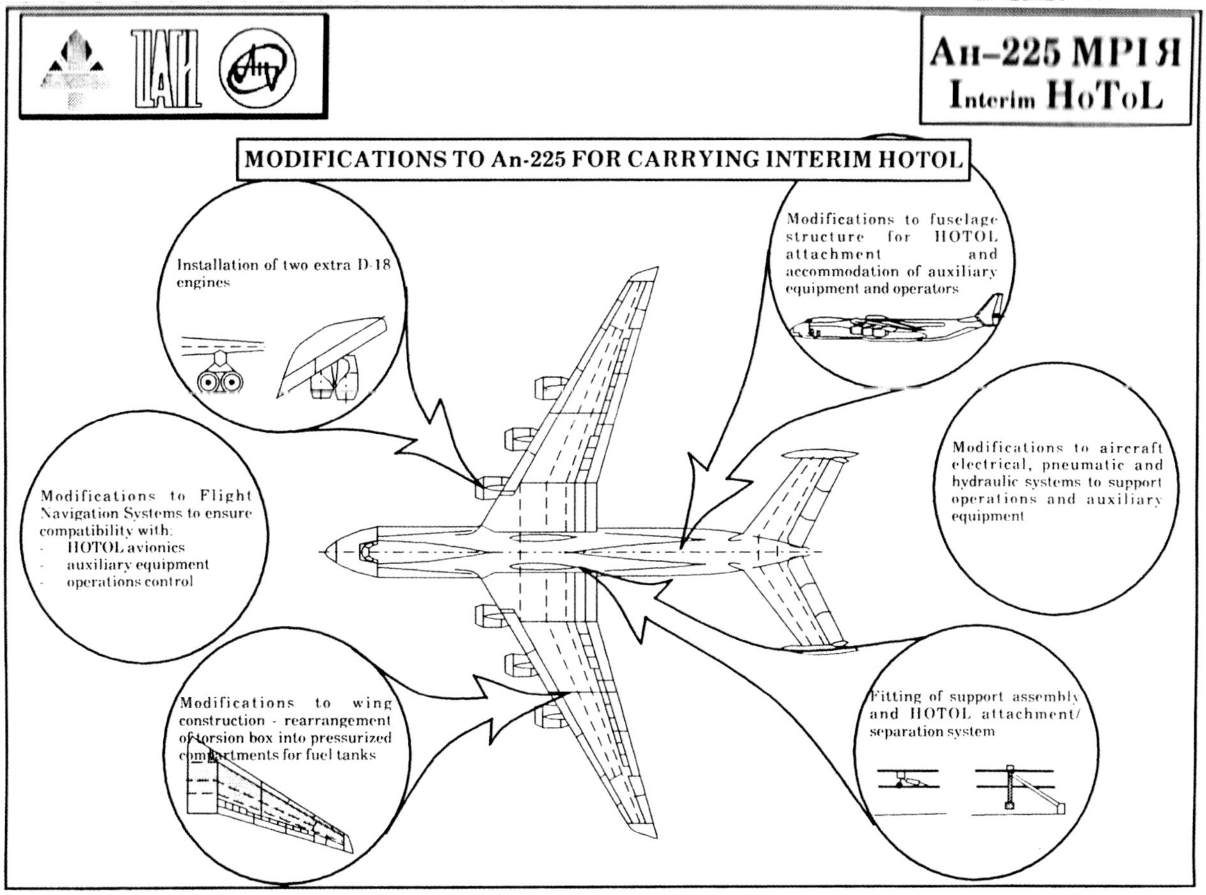

The adaptations that would be required to convert the An-225 into a first-stage for the Interim Hotol system.

AN-225 AS A CARRIER

Antonov and TsAGI then took up the baton to discuss adaptation of the An-225 for the launcher mission. Work had been carried out in five areas: "Determining weight and balance data for the system; the parameters of dynamic separation before and after release; the attachment and release fittings; the internal airborne support equipment required; and estimating the development phases and costs of the An-225".

As such, "the following changes were envisaged to the An-225: to provide the required take-off and landing characteristics, flight speed and altitude of operation, the An-225 thrust-weight ratio needs to be increased. This can be done by changing to Rolls-Royce Trent engines, or installing eight Lotarev D-18T engines. Installation of the six Trent engines is more costly but would allow, if needed, an expansion of the flight radius of the aircraft.

"Strengthening of the fuselage structure is required to provide for installation and attachment of the Hotol orbiter and onboard support equipment. We need to design the load carrying assemblies and attachment/ separation system. The aircraft integrated flight-navigation system needs to be integrated with the orbiter radio system, the integrated support equipment and the airborne support equipment operators".

If eight D-18T engines were to be fitted, "the extra engines [would be] installed by podding the inboard pylon to take twin engines—like the Boeing B-52".

The orbiter would be attached at three points: "one to the orbiter nose, and two main supports to the aft fuselage. The front assembly load-carrying struts take up loads in the plane perpendicular to the aircraft centre line. Front assembly rods are attached by means of spherical support hinges to fuselage frames. Attachment, installation and separation of the orbiter from the aircraft is carried out by means of lock-retainer devices located on attachment fittings. In addition, there is provided disconnection of service lines, mating and demating electrical connectors and pipelines needed for normal functioning of the orbiter in flight".

The An-225 would have to carry equipment for a variety of tasks, including functional and parametric checking of the orbiter, electrical power supply, inert gas supply for purging the thermal insulation of the liquid hydrogen tank, helium gas as a pressurant for emergency propellant dumping, fire warning and suppression systems, navigation, and airborne support equipment workstations—all of which had been defined by BAe.

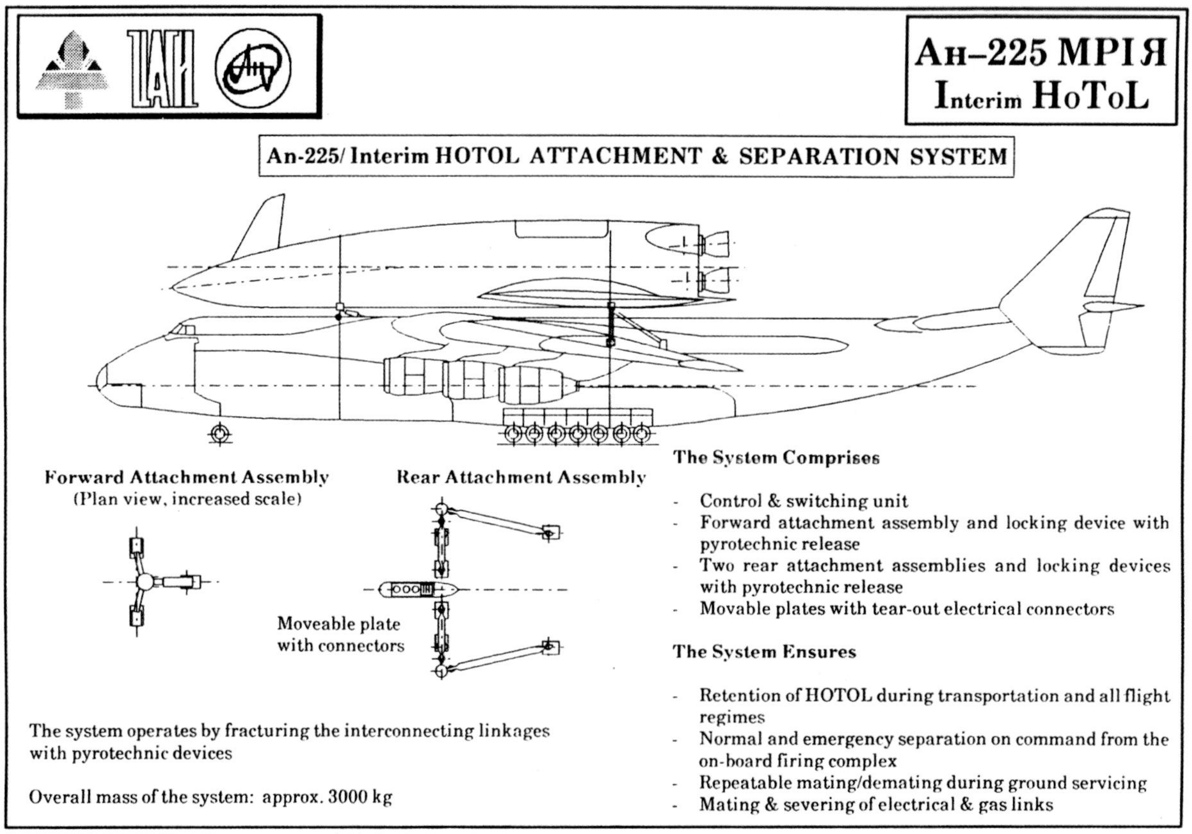

The attachment and separation system—illustrated with the old Orbiter 0061 design.

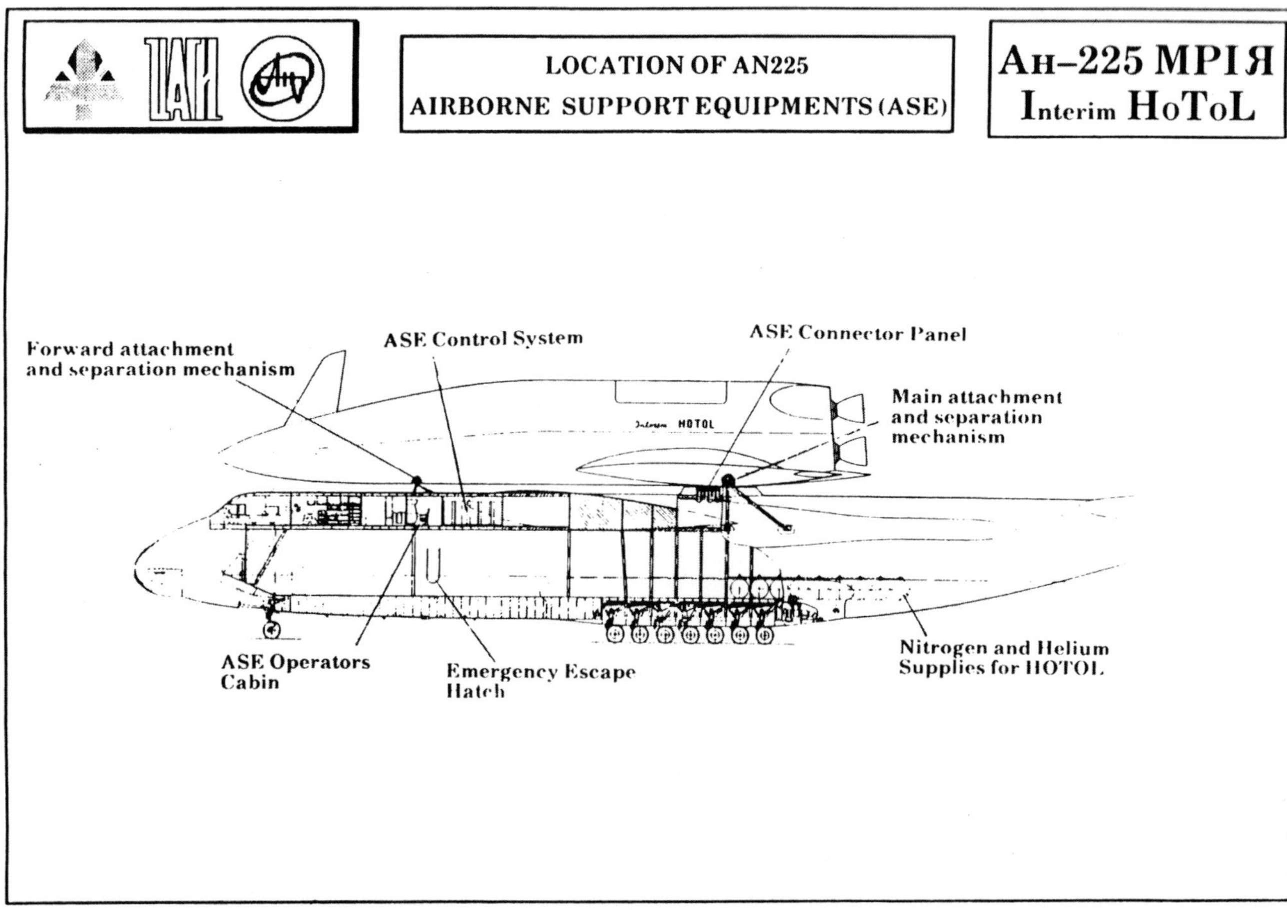

Diagram showing the airborne support equipment that would be installed in the An-225 launcher.

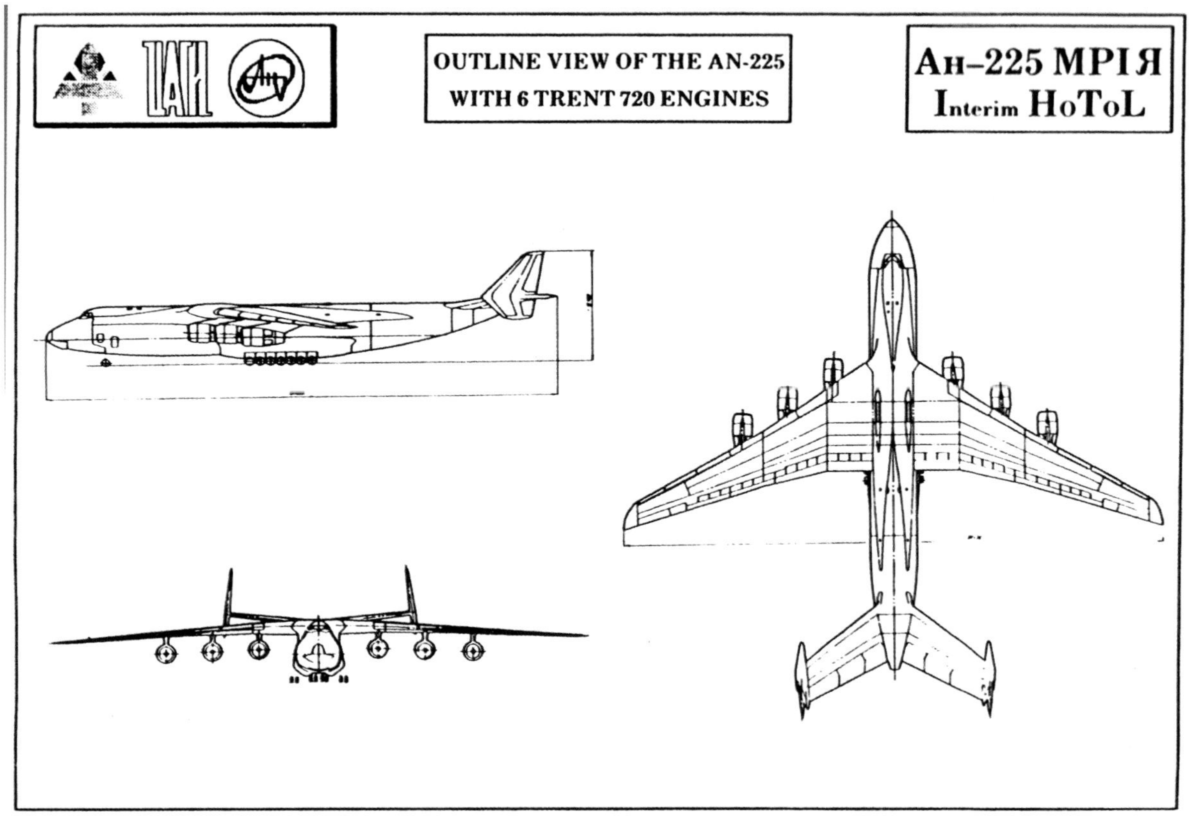

An-225 with six Rolls-Royce Trent engines—one of two ways to improve the aircraft's thrust-weight ratio.

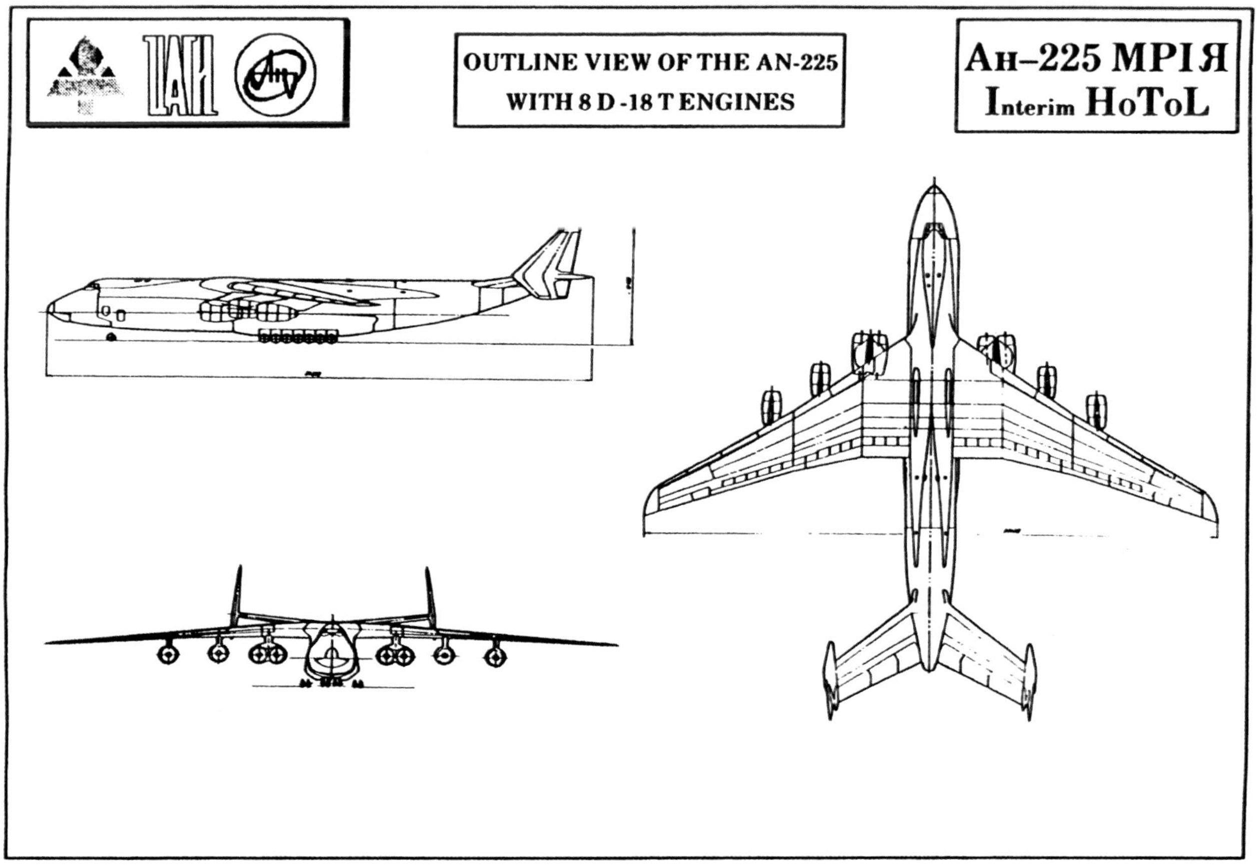

The other re-engining alternative for the An-225 when carrying Interim Hotol was to fit eight D-18T engines—by using each inner wing pylon to hold two engines instead of one.

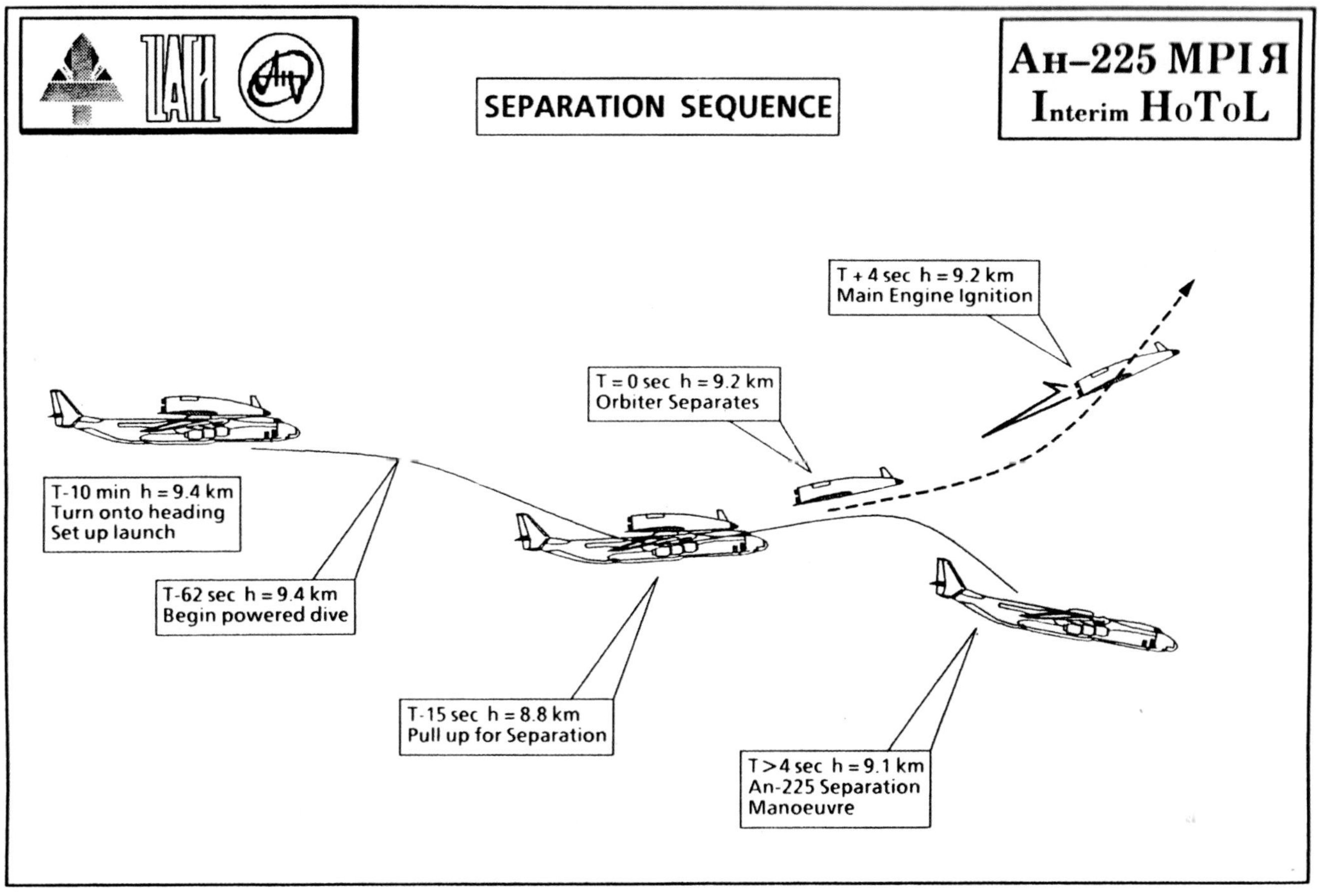

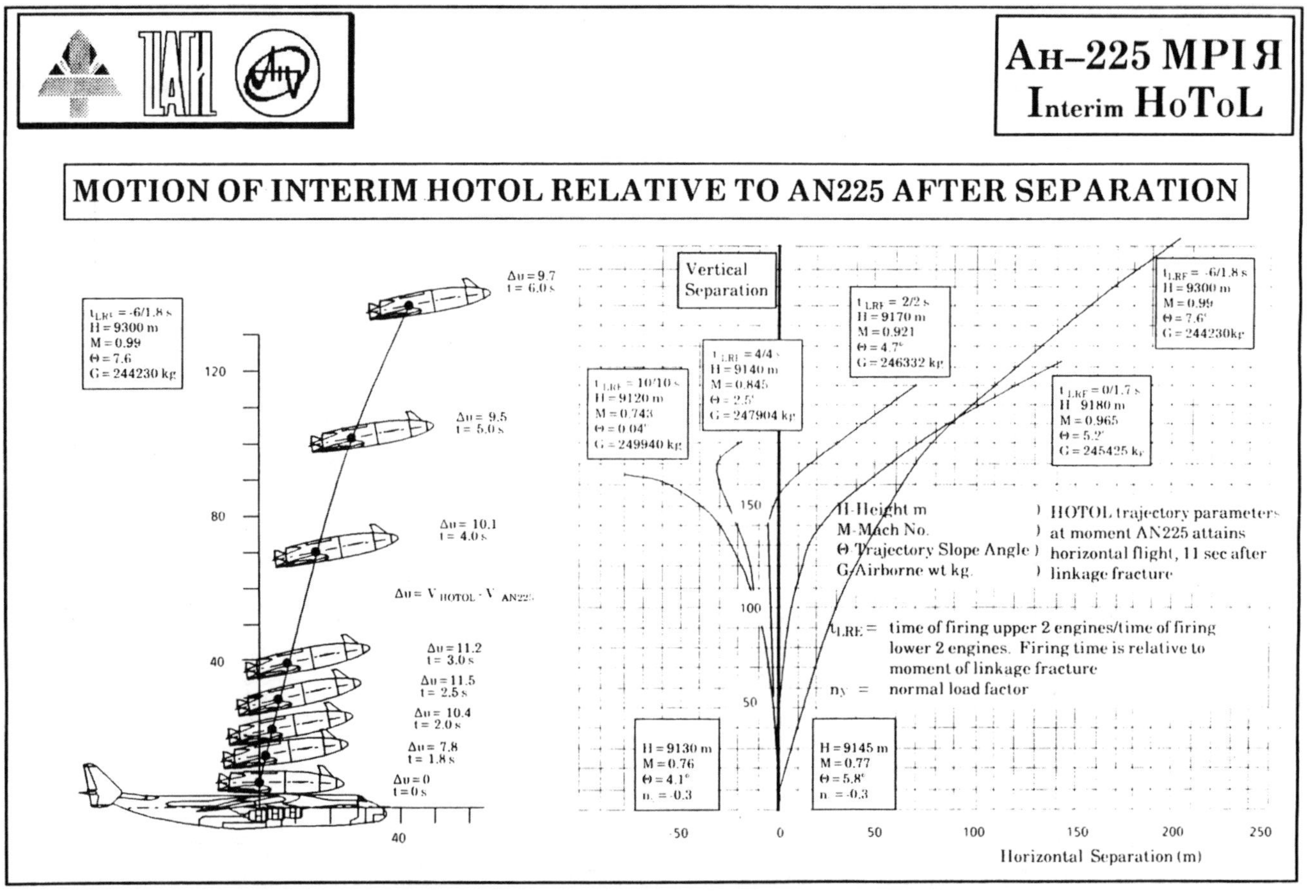

Details of the An-225/Interim Hotol separation sequence.

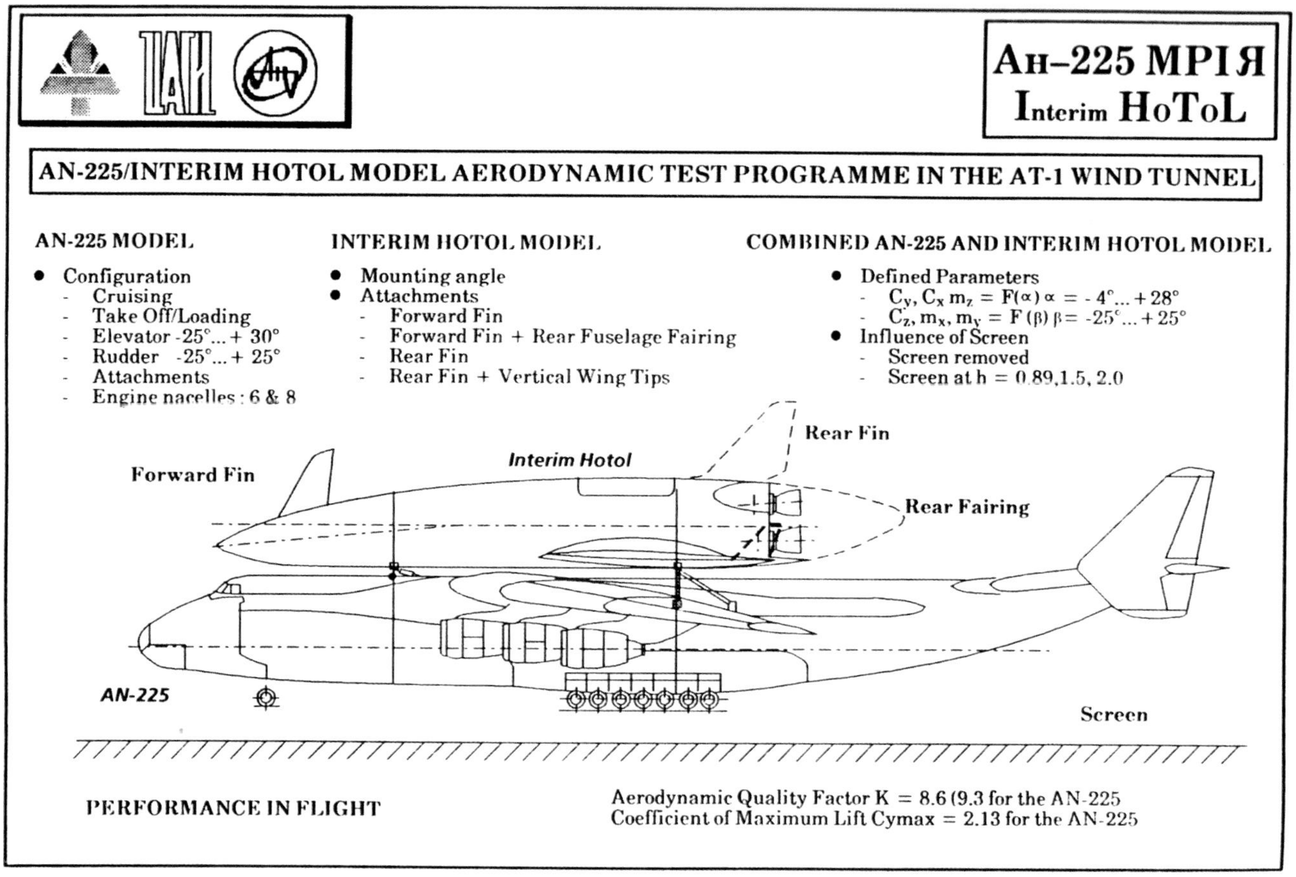

Details of the An-225/Interim Hotol test programme carried out in Antonov's AT-1 wind tunnel—including tests with a tailfin.

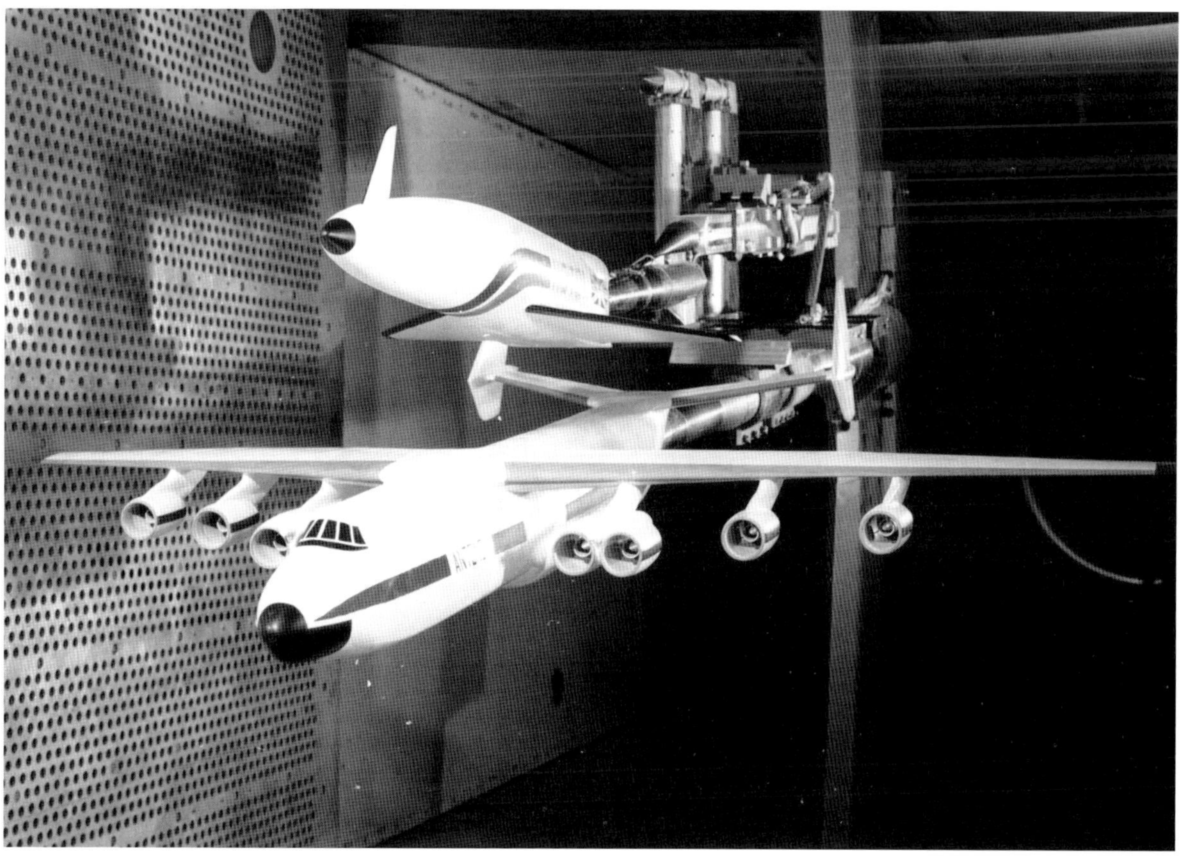

The An-225/Interim Hotol wind tunnel models at TsAGI—but painted up for presentation purposes. AUTHOR'S COLLECTION

The aircraft's take-off weight at the beginning of the mission would be 616 tonnes, requiring a 3,000m runway. The launch sequence was: reach 9.4km altitude and turn onto correct heading for launch; power dive to Mach 0.8 and 8.8km altitude; pull-up within g-load limitations to reach negative normal g-loading; break the An-225/orbiter connections; orbiter separation at 9.2km altitude; ignition of the orbiter's main engines and lateral evasion manoeuvre by the An-225; the latter dropping to 9.1km altitude, with return to level flight around 11 seconds after breaking connection.

The audience then heard all about the Antonov-made Interim Hotol wind tunnel model and the low-speed tests carried out in the company's wind tunnel, known as AT-1, followed by details of testing for flutter in TsAGI's T-104 tunnel.

OPERATIONS AND WRAP-UP

Stevenage were back on the podium for the penultimate subject: operations. Some discussion on emergency procedures and abort cases was followed by a look at how long the orbiter could carry cryogenic fuel prior to launch. Evidently, "the specification was that airborne carriage should last up to an hour after take-off, which itself could be up to 40 minutes after loading the liquid hydrogen. We expect to load the propellants in a sub-cooled [chilled] state, with the liquid hydrogen at about 18K, to inhibit boil-off before launch. In these circumstances propellant boil-off losses would start to occur about 40 minutes into the flight if we left the tank at its loading pressure.

"However, if we allow the tank pressure to gradually rise towards its full operational pressure it is possible to have flights of up to 140 minutes' length before boil-off losses start to occur. Some of the advantage is that we have a tank not only wrapped in cryogenic insulation, but surrounded by an efficient thermal protection system as well".

The proposed ground turnaround sequence was then described, followed by an operations timetable and a discussion of the facilities required for orbiter servicing, payload integration and vehicle integration. When it came to the road ahead for the An-225/Interim Hotol combination, the audience were told that "there is a clear need for a technology programme—at least an airframe technology programme—before we can reasonably commit to full development. There are already relevant European national technology programmes underway… although

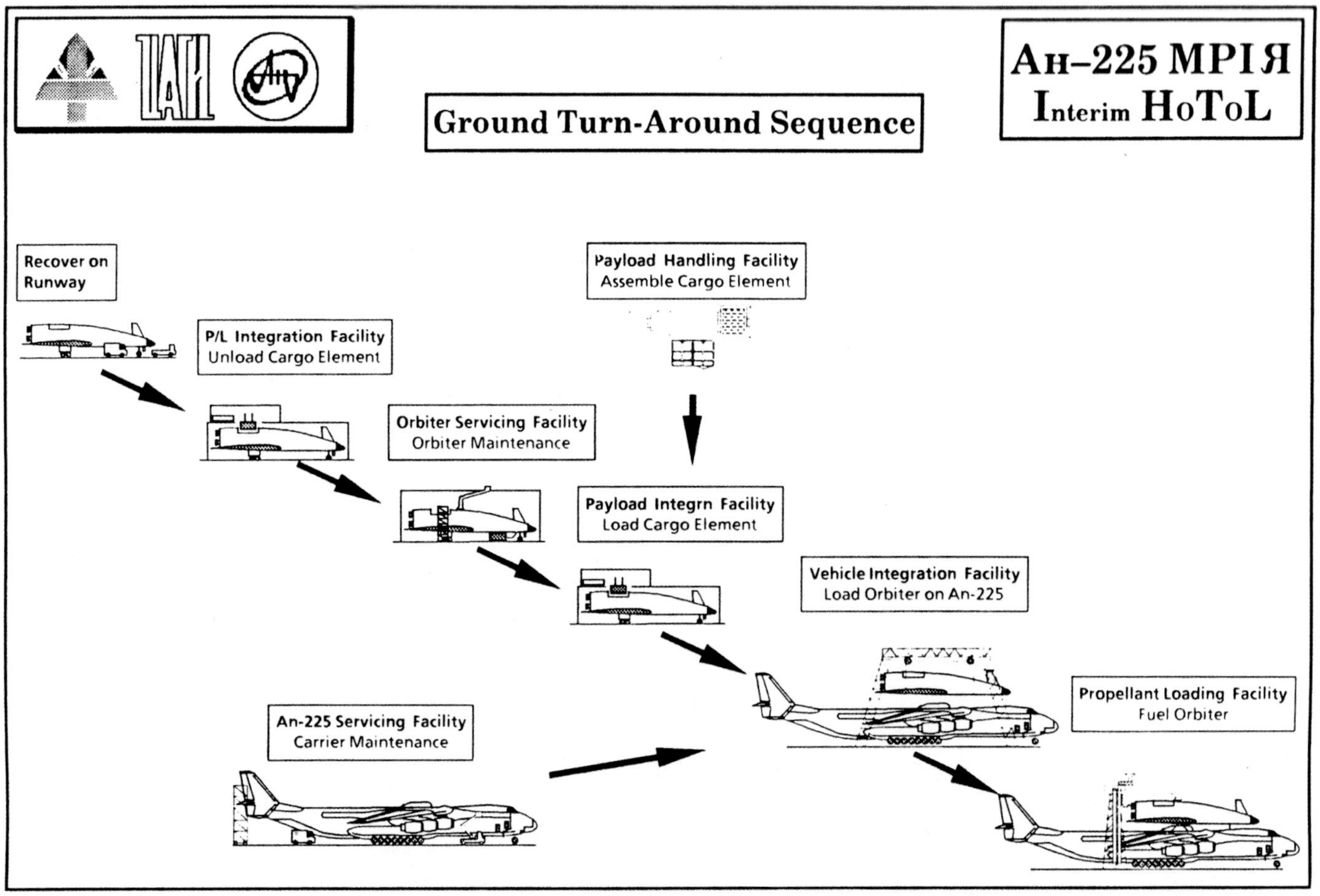

Proposed ground turnaround sequence for the launch system.

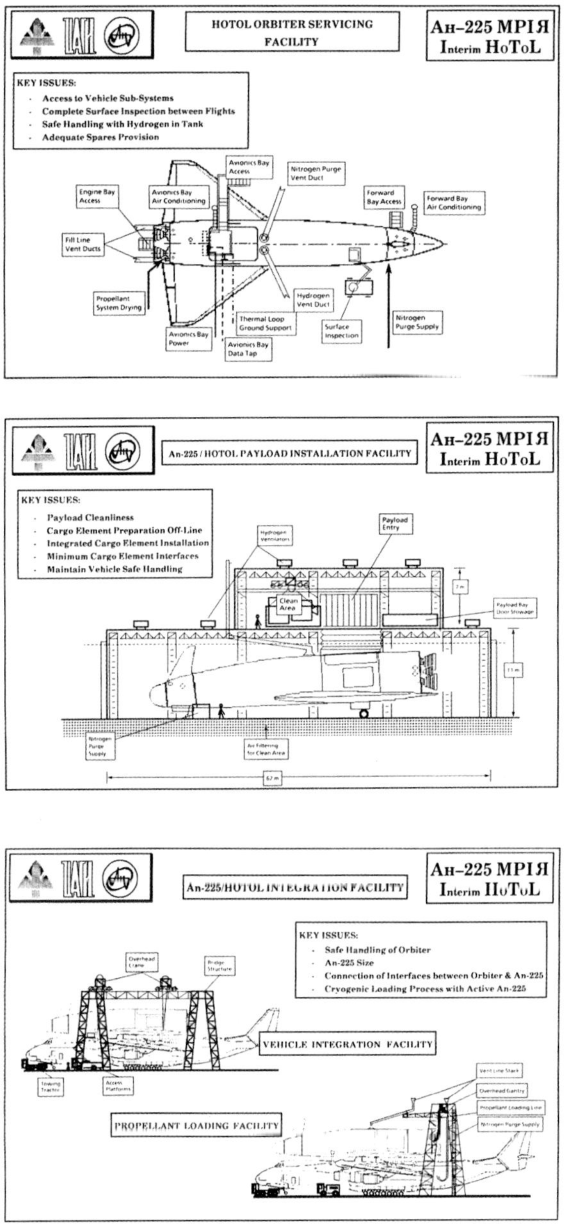

Orbiter servicing, payload installation and An-225/Hotol integration.

they are not directed towards this particular vehicle. I have deliberately left the extent of the enabling technology undefined, because this is partly a political problem. However, with the right coordination a decision in the next three years or so might be possible".

The cost per launch to LEO was expected to be about 1.5 MAU per tonne, compared to 5.5 MAU per tonne for Ariane 5, and the presentation finally ended with recommendations: "Our first recommendation is that ESA should look further at the concept presented, since it not only appears to have the potential to work, but could lead to a share between ESA and the Soviet Union. But in addition we (British Aerospace) would remind the ESA nations that the Soviet facilities and capabilities represent a valuable resource which Europe can and should tap into.

"These facilities are under some threat, and need Western support to be sustained, but a degree of support could well benefit Europe as much as the USSR. Europe will be investing something like 92 MAU per year in hypersonic research in the next few years. If only 5% of that expenditure were used to buy services from the relevant facilities in the USSR the immediate returns would be far in excess of those that could be gained through spending the money at home. This might require some modification to ESA standard practices of geographical return, but in addition, it would confirm to the Soviet Union our willingness to collaborate, and would tap the undoubted expertise available to ensure our mutual success."

SO HOW DID IT GO?

Webb wrote to Mansell on the following Tuesday, June 25, to give a summary of how events had unfolded at the presentation and afterwards: "The presentation was well received by the ESA representatives present . . . The meeting was followed by a press conference at Le Bourget. This was not well attended primarily because it was the last Friday of the airshow and most press correspondents had left for home. In fact, most interest was shown by the Soviet press. Brief reports did appear in the national press on Saturday and a short item was shown on the end of Friday's ITN News at Ten.

"The final event of the day was a meeting between the BAe and Soviet representatives. At this meeting, the leader of the Soviet delegation, R. S. Korol of the Ministry of Aviation Industries, announced the Soviet intention of including this programme in a list of collaborative technical programmes to be proposed by Gorbachev at the G7 meeting to be held in July. Peter Finch replied that he did not think this was a good idea for two reasons: 1) We don't want to get the USA involved at this stage; 2) It would probably embarrass the UK Government.

"Peter Finch then suggested that it would be better for President Gorbachev to discuss this programme during his private meeting with Mr Major following the G7 meeting. Korol agreed with this proposal but was not convinced that the programme should be entirely excluded from the G7 package. BAe Space Systems are taking steps to ensure that HMG are advised of these developments. Clearly it is the intention of the Soviets to take every opportunity to raise the profile of this programme. It is therefore vitally important that there should be no confusion with regard to BAe's and in particular MAL's [BAe Military Aircraft Limited's—i.e. BAe Warton's] policy."

The 17th G7 summit was hosted by British Prime

Hotol-M. CHRIS SANDHAM-BAILEY

Minister John Major in London on July 15-17, 1991, with Gorbachev as the guest of the G7 nations: Canada, France, Germany, Italy, Japan, the UK and the USA. The Soviet President set out plans to reform the Soviet economy but whether Interim Hotol was mentioned at all is unclear. Certainly, Gorbachev did not succeed in galvanising the sort of financial support from the others that had been hoped for.

HOTOL-M

In August 1991, BAe representatives visited Molniya's office in Moscow and "were presented with the results of Molniya's own analysis of the An-225/Hotol concept. The Molniya analysis indicated that using kerosene to augment the thrust of a liquid oxygen/liquid hydrogen engine would increase Hotol's payload by four tonnes".

The Molniya report detailed two air-launched spaceplanes: Hotol-2M, which was essentially Orbiter 68d with a rear fin, and Hotol-M, which was largely the same as Hotol-2M but using a 'three-component' engine design (liquid oxygen, liquid hydrogen and kerosene). The engines would burn liquid hydrogen and kerosene for higher thrust during the boost phase but revert back to more efficient liquid hydrogen burning later on.

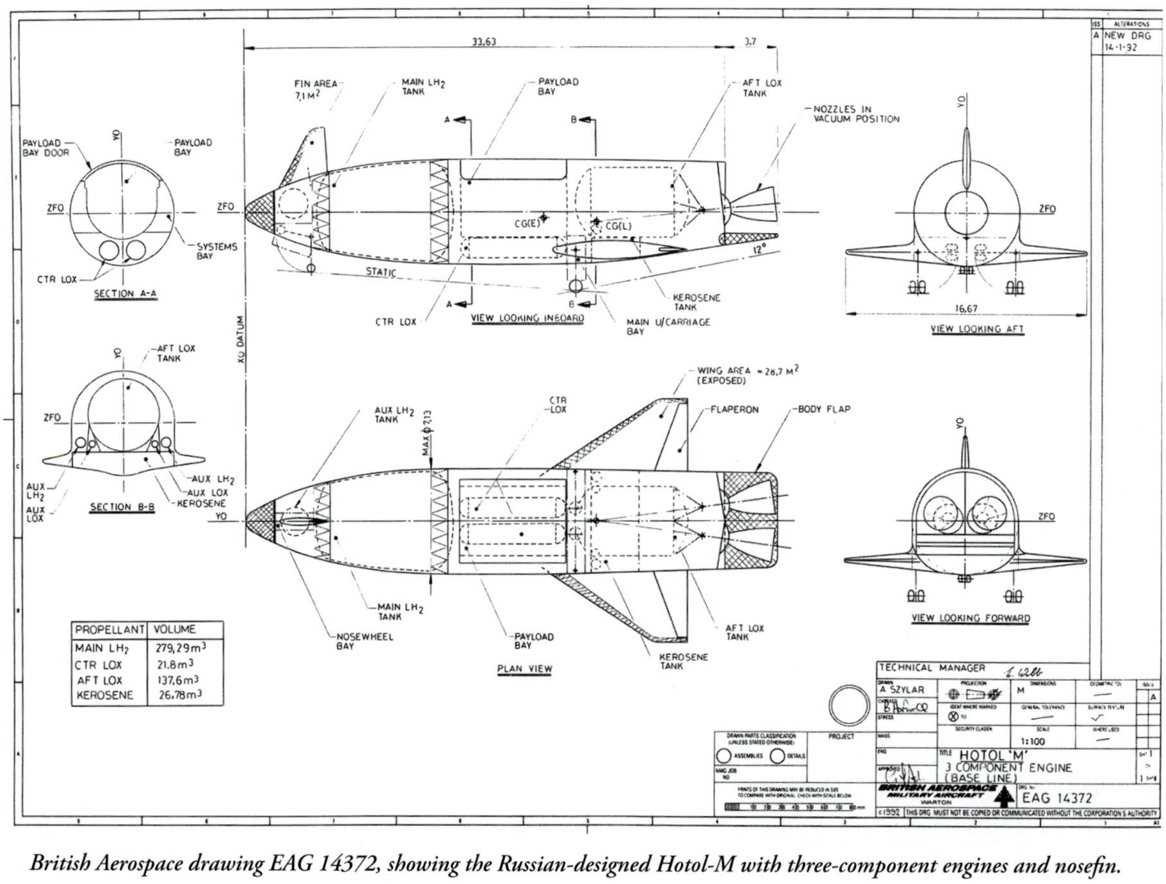

British Aerospace drawing EAG 14372, showing the Russian-designed Hotol-M with three-component engines and nosefin.

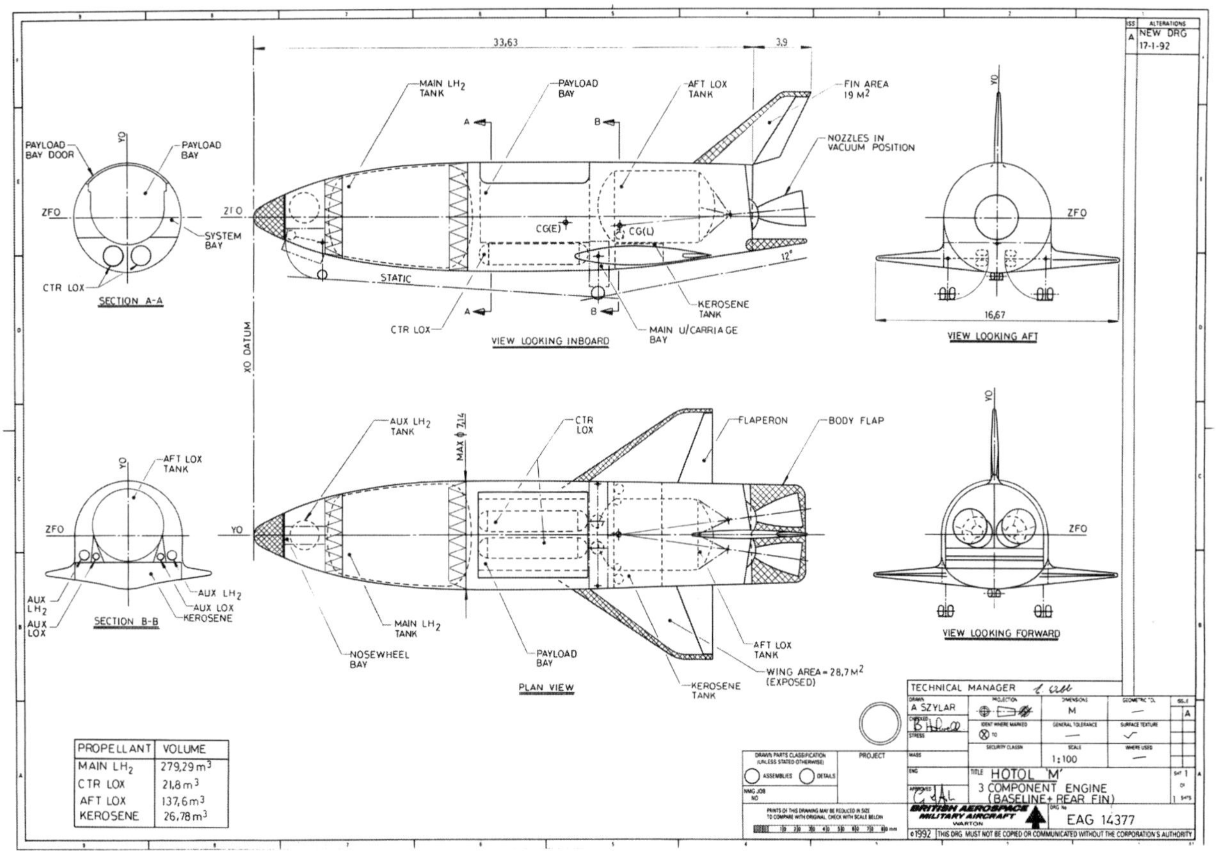

Drawing EAG 14377 showing Hotol-M with tailfin.

Shortly after this visit, Moscow was rocked by the 1991 Soviet coup d'état attempt, with communist hardliners attempting to forcibly seize control of the country from Gorbachev. The Soviet Union was in a state of collapse, with Estonia, Latvia, Lithuania and Armenia having already declared independence in 1990. Food, medicine and other consumables had become scarce and inflation was exceeding 300%. As the coup unfolded on August 19, 1991, there were tanks on the streets and newly appointed President Boris Yeltsin famously addressed the crowds while standing on one of them. It seems unlikely that the An-225/Interim Hotol project was at the forefront of any Russian's mind during this time.

Five days later, on August 24, 1991, Ukraine declared independence from the Soviet Union, making Antonov officially a Ukrainian company.

ORBITER 0068E

The upheaval resulting from these momentous events caused a lengthy pause in the collaborative effort between BAe and their formerly Soviet partners. In the meantime, BAe continued to work on the orbiter with Parkinson producing a document entitled 'Review of An-225/ Interim Hotol Mass' on February 19, 1992—though it was distributed only to Webb and Cundy at Warton plus Jonathan Schulster at Stevenage. The stated goal was to "review the CAPS mass estimate for Orbiter -68d with the intention of identifying where mismatches may exist between the current CAPS model and current thinking".

Features he thought were not accounted for by CAPS included changes in the vehicle's dimensions resulting from the use of chilled propellants, the availability of new insulants, "particularly flexible external insulation" from the Hermes programme, "the possible use of carbon-bismaleimide sandwich panels for the skin structure of the rear fuselage" and "the use of glass-ceramic undersurface and titanium upper surface for a 'warm wing' instead of the currently assumed titanium aluminides". Appended to the report was a drawing showing a vehicle labelled Orbiter -0068e, which illustrated the revised, slightly smaller, structure.

DISASTER AT STEVENAGE

While this work had been going on, British Aerospace Space and Communications had begun to struggle financially. The situation had gone from bad to worse and recalling what happened, Parkinson said: "A big thing that affects my career at this stage is that in [February] 1992, the Space and Communications group ... basically ran out of money. And they ran out of money on the one thing

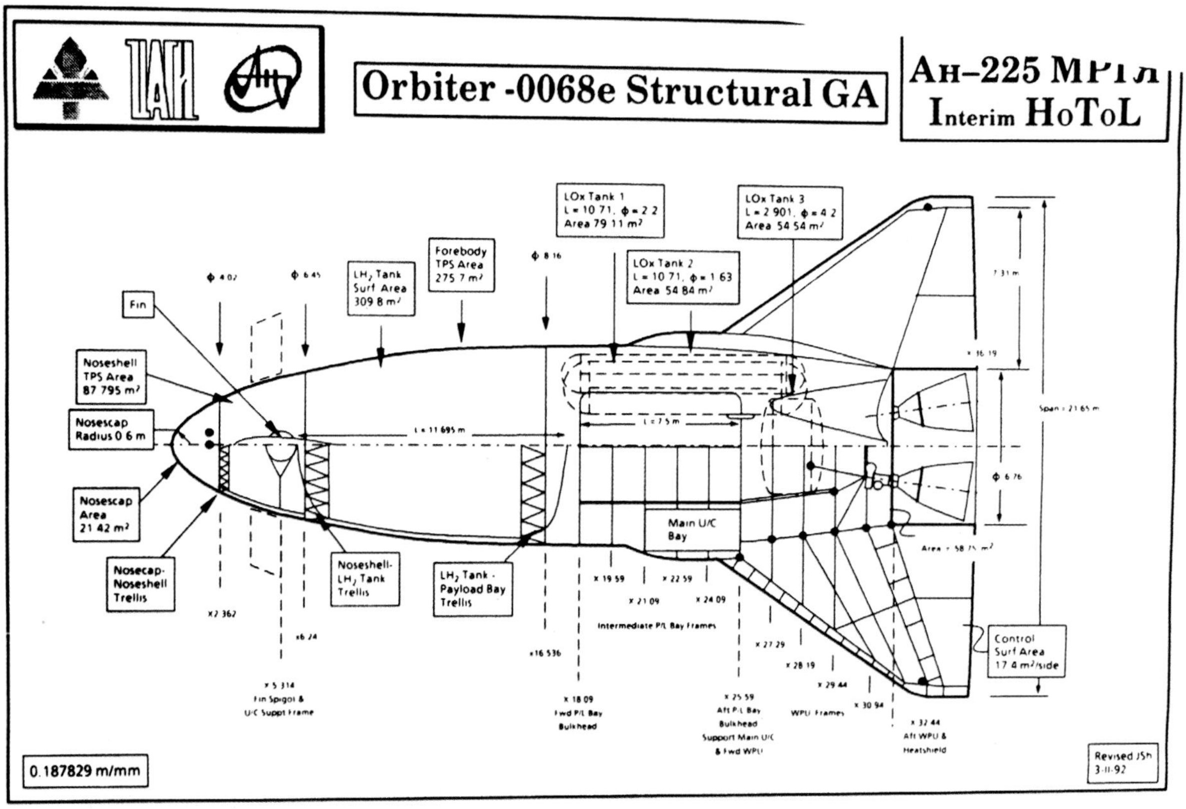

Top view showing the structural arrangement of Interim Hotol Orbiter -0068e.

they should have been good at, which was communication satellites. And they ran out of money on communication satellites because all communication satellites were basically commercial bids to customers and they were losing the bids regularly and that was the major part of their business and ... suddenly they made everybody redundant. And they made all the 'headquarters' people redundant and my group was part of headquarters.

"And the guy who came to wield the axe had this thing—he wanted to eliminate everybody at that level. And I escaped this for an odd reason ... the rule was, if you didn't have enough money to support people for 18 months they had to go. Now I had been taking little contracts from ESA, not because we needed them but because headquarters people were on overheads—they didn't cost the firm directly, they cost them indirectly so I didn't have to have money to support my group but I'd been taking contracts from ESA, mainly to keep track of what ESA were doing. And to keep my foot in with ESA.

"So I actually had money, and it was enough money to keep two of us going. It was myself and Steve Kemble who did the trajectory work that nobody else understood. He had to stay as far as I was concerned. The guy with the axe got very frustrated by this but ... nobody was going to help him and wouldn't actually tell him the reason why he couldn't fire me, because I appeared to be self-supporting as it were. What he actually missed completely for ages and ages—in fact through this entire period, and that nobody was telling him, was that not only did I have money, but it wasn't being used. He'd not spotted that I was still an overhead charge and not part of this. But what it meant was I lost most of my team. And that was quite upsetting. We kind of continued working, I lost Dave Helas, among other things, my guy with the Russians."

Elaborating a little further on the backdrop to this calamity, he said: "The reason they were losing jobs was that Hughes [Electronics Corporation—one of the world's largest satellite manufacturers at that time] would come in late and underbid us. We felt that we couldn't do that because we had to give the right price as it were. At any stage we could have known that Hughes were going to do this and deliberately underbid them when they came in and they would've only done it once. So it would've only had to happen once. We wouldn't have had to lose every time.

"They [BAe Space and Communications management] wouldn't take this approach and eventually they just ran out of money. And the company had to be reorganised, reconstituted. We lost a lot of good people. And we slowly staggered back to our feet and most of the people who'd been responsible for this went ... But 1992 was effectively an end of an era even though the Hotol and launch vehicle work continued for a while afterwards."

Engineer Mark Hempsell, who had worked at BAe Stevenage until 1992, noted that "it was starving in a sea of plenty. For example, they rejected an opportunity to put BAe kit on Hughes satellites on the grounds it would make Hughes more competitive—but Hughes were winning 95% of the market anyway and we could have had a piece of that action".

TECHNICAL AUDIT

Even as the axe was falling on Stevenage, though the cuts had not yet been made public, March 1992 saw the publication of a document entitled 'Technical Audit of the I-Hotol Proof of Concept Study', edited by R. G. [Richard] Bavin of the Defence Research Agency's (DRA) Command and Maritime System Group. The DRA had been formed less than a year earlier as an amalgamation of the five defence research establishments—including the RAE. Indeed, its headquarters had been created at the RAE's Farnborough site.

Bavin's introduction summed up the system's history as far as the June 21, 1991, presentation then went on: "The presentation was well attended and the audience included the director general of ESA, the director of space transportation, and members of the Ariane Programme Board. BNSC have now asked RAE to carry out an independent assessment of the work to date."

After going through all aspects of the system, he concluded: "There is obviously a technical risk associated with the programme, but it is much less than the original Hotol concept, and will be less than the Sänger programme, which involves development of two vehicles. Also, having the Soviets as partners with their extensive knowledge and good development record of building space launchers will be a considerable advantage—their influence has already been noted at BAe/Soviet meetings. The Soviets can be innovative but are better known for low-tech reliable engineering solutions.

"To summarise, there will be a technical risk but it should be acceptable compared to other programmes... the joint BAe/Soviet study on the Interim Hotol/Antonov concept has been of a very high standard and has demonstrated the ability of the UK and USSR to work together regardless of language, communications, political and economic difficulties to evaluate the concept of a novel space launcher. An outline design with an acceptable payload has been produced, and development and recurring flight costs have been established.

"The payload for version 0068 has been calculated to be approximately 5.5 tonnes with a contingency mass of 2.5 tonnes based on a fully fuelled orbiter mass of 250 tonnes... the mass budget, a critical area of the project, has been checked independently by two Russian groups and would appear to be realistic. The payload mass of approximately eight tonnes will complement the 16 tonne LEO capacity of Ariane 5.

"The Russians have shown great enthusiasm for the project and have probably spent considerably more effort on the study than BAe. All Russian effort was government funded and they obviously had high level support for the work, probably up to Mr Gorbachev. There has essentially been no change in the working relationship now that contacts are Russian and Ukrainian. The situation does however need to be handled with care and a clear understanding of the difficult period Ukraine and Russia are facing.

"The greatest area of risk is probably in the use of some of the new materials which have never been made in the sizes and shapes required. This would lead to mass penalties if alternative back-up materials were selected. Risk areas in the aerodynamics field are separation of the orbiter from the Antonov, and uncertainty of the CFD code validations for calculation of drag and heating of the orbiter. However, in both these areas the Soviets have either practical knowledge or sufficient large and high speed wind tunnels to validate the codes and models."

P150 – DROPPING THE INTERIM

A report was produced by Cundy at Warton on April 16, 1992, which reviewed the Soviets' work of eight months earlier on three-component engines for Interim Hotol—resulting in Hotol-2M and Hotol-M—and assessed its impact on the system's payload.

He noted that "in favour of a three-component vehicle is its higher overall propellant density yielding a small, lighter structure. However, the lower specific impulse of liquid oxygen/kerosene combustion requires an increased propellant fraction to reach orbit. The Molniya work claims to show that the penalties of the less efficient ascent are more than outweighed by the benefits of lower structural mass".

In working through this concept, it had apparently been decided that another attempt should be made to rename the vehicle. Consequently, "a new designation has been agreed for BAe's air-launched reusable rocket. The designation Interim Hotol reverts to Hotol and carries the project number P150. Consequently, the different orbiter designs described in this report are:

Orbiter 68d—optimised liquid oxygen/liquid hydrogen design (June 1991). Shown to BNSC, ESA, USSR. Designation to remain unchanged.

P150-202—a modified, rear finned Orbiter 68d. The baseline liquid oxygen/liquid hydrogen design for this study.

P150-302—optimised vehicle using NPO Molniya's '3-component' engine".

While P150-202 retained the now-familiar short and rotund appearance of Interim Hotol, redesigning Orbiter 68d to take advantage of the three-component engine had resulted in a significant change in appearance for P150-302. Cundy explained that "optimisation of the configuration and major changes to the propellant volumes and ascent trajectory have yielded a longer, slimmer vehicle".

To be more specific, "the fuselage differs from Orbiter 68d in the following areas:

a) The foreplanes have been removed and the nosecone shortened from 7m to 5m length for consistency with Molniya's Hotol-M.
b) The upper centre section liquid oxygen tanks have been removed because of their minimal storage capacity. The lower centre section liquid oxygen tanks have been shortened to 7.5m to fit underneath the payload bay. The aft liquid oxygen tank diameter is enlarged to fill the space between the upper fuselage and the wing carry-through box.
c) The liquid hydrogen tank mass equations have been revised while the aft liquid oxygen tank mass equations have been simplified pending further review.
d) The kerosene tank is buried in the wing carry-through box. Tank and supply system masses are order of magnitude estimates only.
e) The propellant supply system mass estimate is revised to reflect the change from two to three propellants.
f) The actuation and hydraulic system mass have been changed to incorporate the effects of changes to control surface areas. Hinge moments are assumed to vary in proportion to area to the power 1.5".

And that was just the fuselage. P150-302 had the same 'hot structure' titanium aluminide wings as Orbiter 68d. Their aspect ratio, sweepback angle and taper had similarly been retained, but "exposed wing area and thickness/chord have been optimised. Resulting wing details are: reference gross area: 133.5sqm, exposed area 56sqm, flap area 15sqm, aspect ratio 1.93, leading edge sweep 57 degrees. Nominal strakes are featured to minimise high local heating rates at the wing/fuselage junction during re-entry. However, they have not been included in wing area or mass calculations".

Given that there had initially been doubts over the 100sqm wing area, 56sqm was a significant leap forward in reducing structural mass, made possible by the overall reduction in the vehicle's size.

Naturally, a fin was still needed for lateral control during unpowered flight and Cundy noted that in P150-302 it had been "sized by the landing approach. In view of the switch from a forward to a rear fin on P150, P150-302 is shown with a rear fin. Fin area has only been crudely estimated (based on the US shuttle geometry) since no lateral control work has been done to date. Exposed area: 19sqm, aspect ratio 3.7, leading edge sweep 45 degrees, taper ratio 0.4".

As noted, the flip-out foreplanes designed into Orbiter 68d had been deleted "for better comparison with the Molniya design" but the 24sqm body flap at the rear was retained since it "has the combined function of protecting the engine nozzles from high re-entry temperatures as well as augmenting the control power of the wing flaps".

Naturally, liquid oxygen was required as normal as the oxidiser "but the ascent fuel consists of both liquid hydrogen and kerosene. Liquid oxygen and liquid hydrogen are still used for OMS burns. The main engines are based on BAe's understanding of the RD-701 three-component engine featured in Hotol-M. Like the baseline two-component engine, the nozzle features a retractable high expansion ratio section for increased efficiency at high altitude".

In 'Mode-1' the engines would burn 79% liquid oxygen, 15% kerosene and 6% liquid hydrogen, before switching to 'Mode-2' at high altitude for a 6:1 ratio of liquid oxygen and liquid hydrogen. As with Orbiter 68, there would be no separate OMS engines—just OMS propellant fed to the main engines from separate tanks dedicated to the purpose. However, "the Molniya vehicle does show two separate OMS engines and TsIAM have also recently indicated (Moscow, January 1992) that the three-component engine could not be used for OMS burns. A 35kN thrust OMS engine would have a mass of approximately 90kg". The RCS remained unchanged.

Cundy concluded with a point-by-point comparison between the P150-302 and Hotol-M. The latter had its liquid oxygen divided between tanks in front of the payload bay and behind it which "will allow much better control of the centre of gravity during ascent and may well be lighter too". This feature had not been incorporated into P150-302 however, "because of the need to provide associated mass estimation". Hotol-M's fuselage was two tonnes lighter but it had proven difficult to work out why this should have been the case since Molniya had

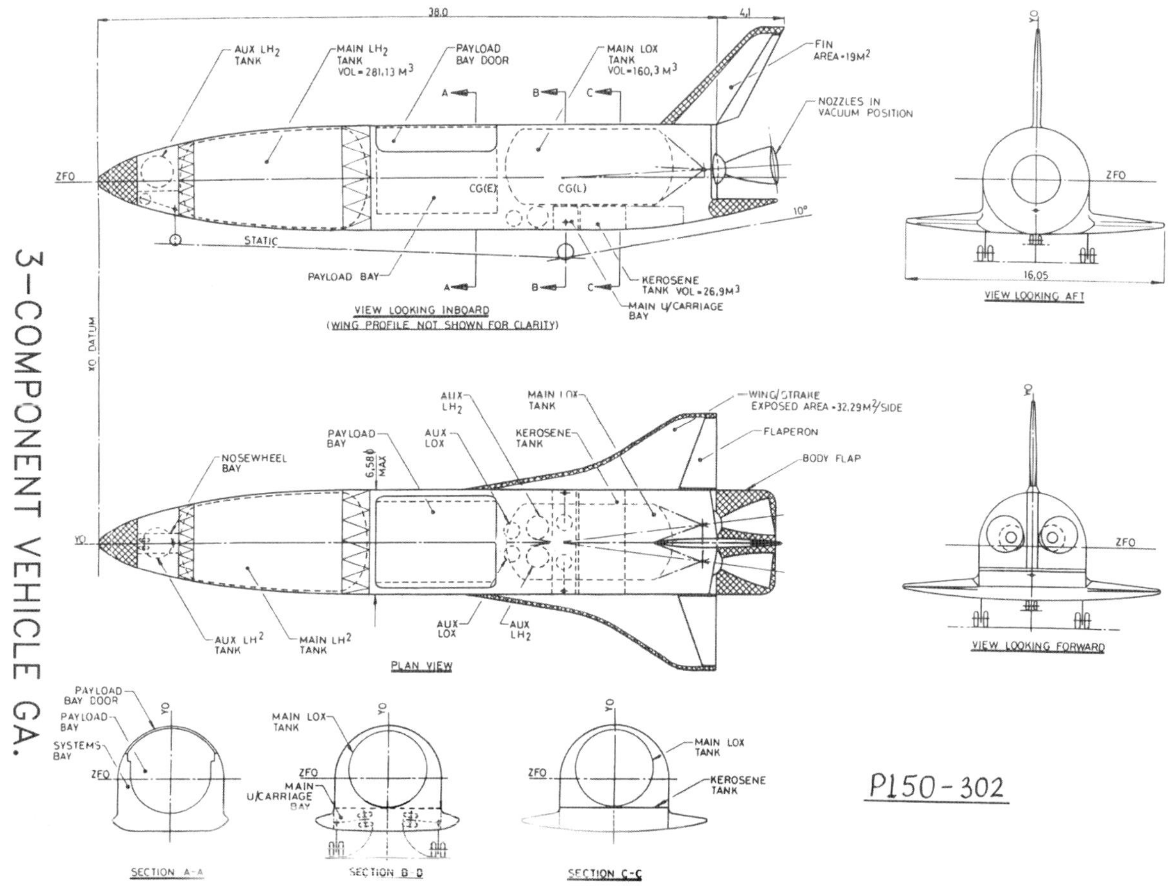

General arrangement view of the twin rocket engine air-launched P150-302, perhaps the very last iteration of Hotol.

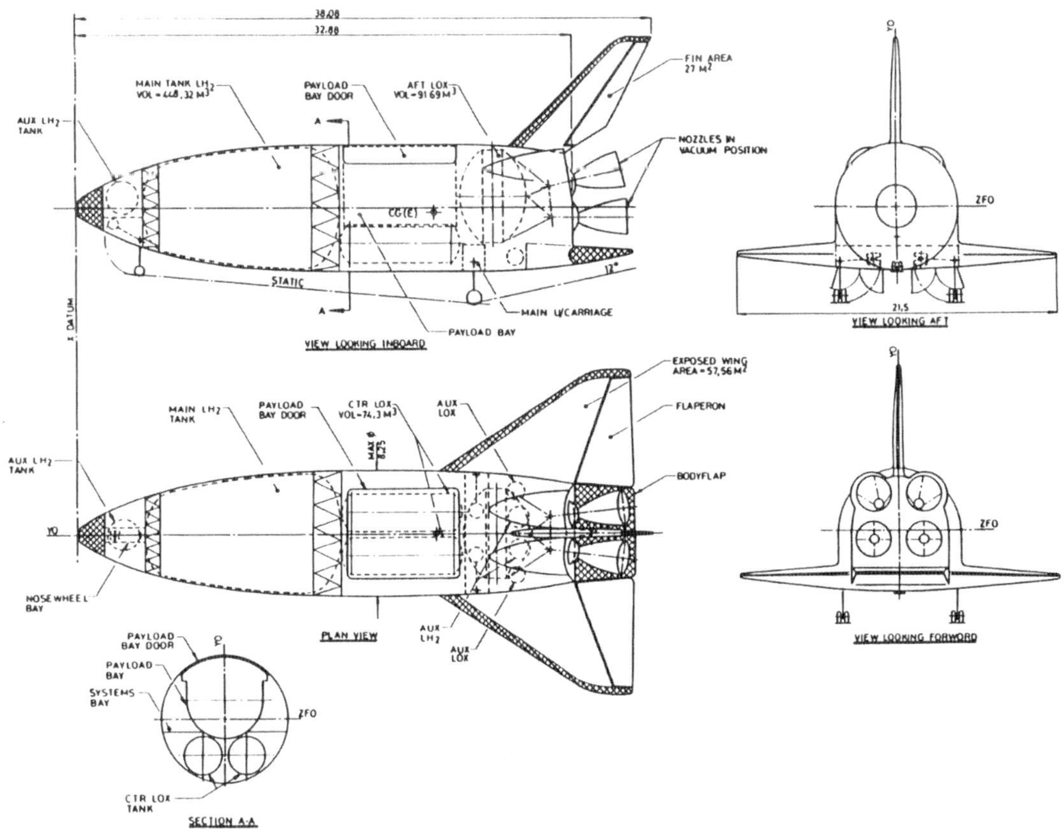

General arrangement view of the shorter, fatter P150-202.

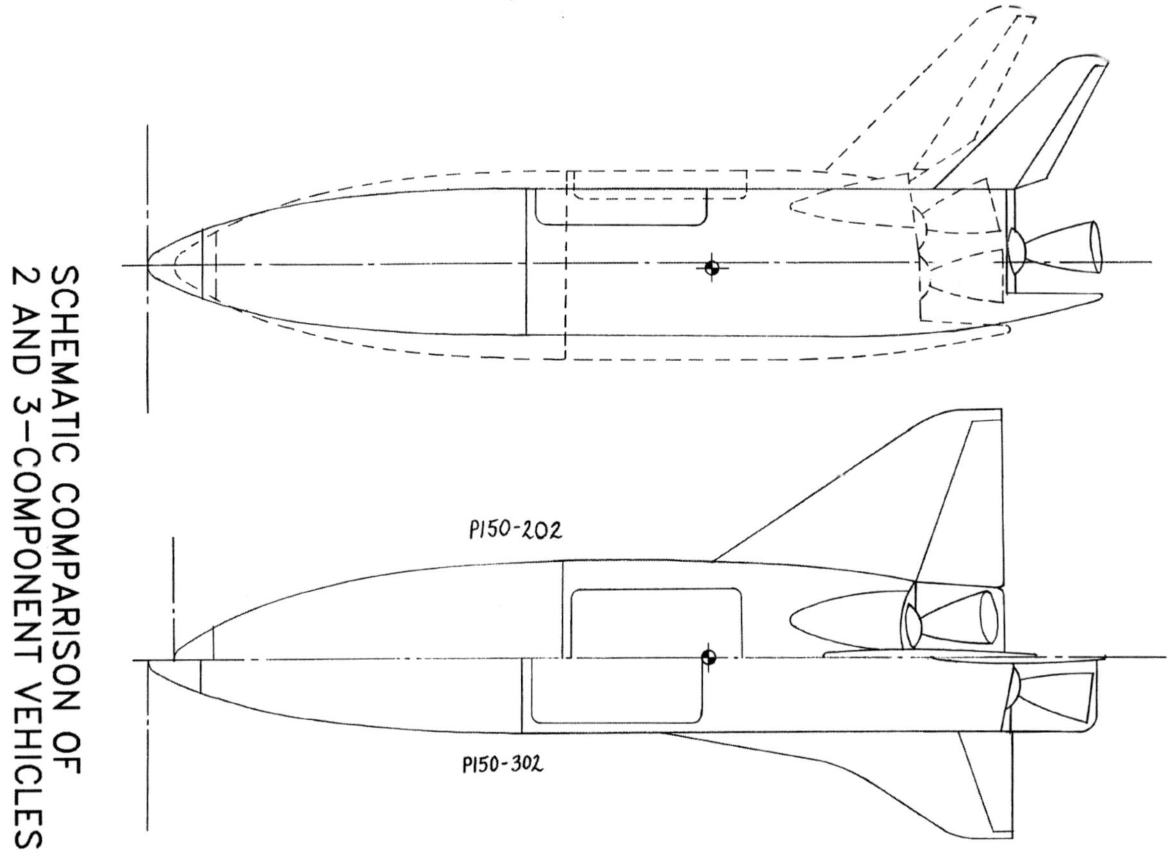

Comparison of the P150-202 against the longer and more slender P150-302.

BRITISH
AEROSPACE

An-225/HoToL Future Launch System

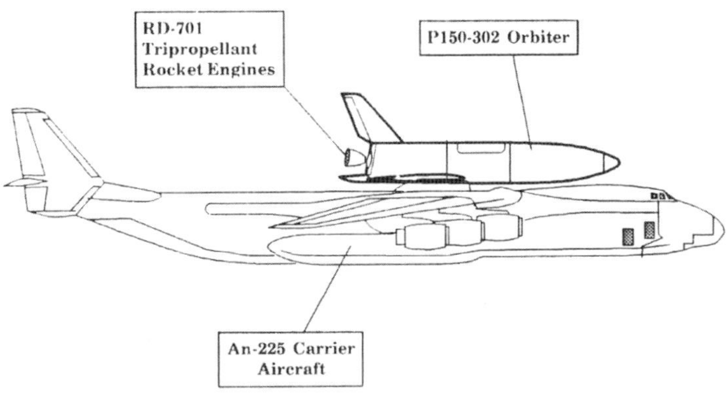

Mass Analysis		
Dry Mass		**26077 kg**
Body Structure	13810 kg	
Wings	3075 kg	
Equipment	3880 kg	
Propulsion	5312 kg	
Propellant		**213498 kg**
Liquid Hydrogen	18434 kg	
Kerosene	21302 kg	
Liquid Oxygen	171400 kg	
Aux Propellant	1577 kg	
Residuals	785 kg	
Payload		**8523 kg**
Contingency Margin		**2500 kg**
TOTAL		**250598 kg**

P150-302 orbiter—still under the Hotol banner—with An-225 carrier aircraft.

not provided a detailed mass breakdown. Another major difference was the quantity of propellant that Molniya believed would be unusable: 1,975kg, compared to BAe's much more optimistic allowance of 417kg.

It may not have been obvious at the time, but Hotol-M and P150-302 would prove to be the final iterations of the Hotol launcher lineage. The Hotol project remained to be concluded—but no further payload-carrying vehicles bearing the Hotol name are known to have been designed past this point.

SKORODELOV'S RETURN

Less than two weeks later, Skorodelov was at Stevenage for two days of meetings during which the differences between British and Russian—now referred to as CIS (Commonwealth of Independent States)—mass calculations for the two- and three-component propellant systems were discussed. According to post-meeting notes from BAe, it was explained to him that "Geoff Statham's systems [for the orbiter] used stop-valves which were servo-operated using the up-stream pressure of the liquid propellant within the line. This method promises low mass, but is very unconventional and possibly unrealistic, if only due to the very low pressures involved. Skorodelov had assumed operation by high pressure helium, which would have a storage penalty.

"It was agreed that a separate specialist meeting was required to identify the basis of the discrepancies. Skorodelov pointed out that there would be a smaller penalty for thrust vector control [TVC] in the case of the three-component vehicle with just two engines. He spoke of TVC actuation (for three-component) using high pressure kerosene. This brings to mind the 'fueldraulic' system, which is a feature of the Lightning aircraft, for driving low pressure fuel turbopumps using some of the output of the high pressure fuel pumps on the engines. This is not strictly actuation but most of the elements are present.

"Having recently looked at the feasibility of using 'big' hydraulic accumulators to minimise installed power in the actuation system, it was interesting to have our actuation mass estimate supported by the CIS figure. However, it was not possible to discover either what reliance Skorodelov's specialists would place on accumulators or what continuous surface rates were available. There was no opportunity to discover whether [TsAGI's] Lazarev had estimates of his own".

By now the redundancy programme at Stevenage was stepping up into high gear and the Hotol team were losing their jobs—with the exception of Parkinson and Kemble. Newspapers across Britain announced on Wednesday, June 3, 1992, that 640 jobs were to be axed from British Aerospace's satellite production factory since "BAe Space Systems, a British Aerospace subsidiary, has been unsuccessful in winning contracts over the past six months in a highly competitive market".

With many of the team gone and with little budget available for continued work at Warton, the project once again entered a state of near-dormancy. Months passed.

INTEREST REKINDLED?

Longstaff, now having left BAe Stevenage to become managing director of Guest Associates (Europe)—a division of a much larger American company specialising in helping aerospace firms secure government contracts—wrote to Edward Leigh MP, recently appointed Parliamentary Under-Secretary of State for Technology and the de facto British Space Minister, on October 29 with the goal of encouraging him to take an interest in Hotol.

On November 9, 1992, the *Telegraph* newspaper ran a story by Steven Young headlined 'Euro spacemen look to east and west' which noted that "Britain has established a leading role in Earth observation since it opted out of the expensive manned programmes in 1987. That decision has been vindicated by recent events, says Edward Leigh MP, the British Space Minister, who is now signalling a small shift in British space policy.

"The minister says he wants to put some 'zest' into the British space programme by taking part in a project to develop the next generation of European launch vehicles. He believes that experience gained by BAe during its work on the Hotol spaceplane will prove invaluable to ESA. 'Until we get some sort of reusable launcher it is going to be difficult to bring down the costs of space, which at the moment are far too high,' he said. 'That is why I think the whole Hotol concept is very exciting.'"

Eight days after the story went to press, Leigh finally responded to Longstaff's original letter, saying: "I am aware of the potential of Hotol and of Hotol/Antonov 225 in reducing the cost of access to space, and I hope that it will be possible for the European Space Agency's Future European Space Transportation Investigation Programme (FESTIP) to commence in early 1993.

"When the programme has been fully defined, the Government will make a decision as to whether the UK will participate, and at what level. The FESTIP programme will enable Hotol and other concepts to be studied thoroughly on a European basis in collaboration with industry within the CIS. As you imply in your letter, it is essential that there should be international collaboration on the

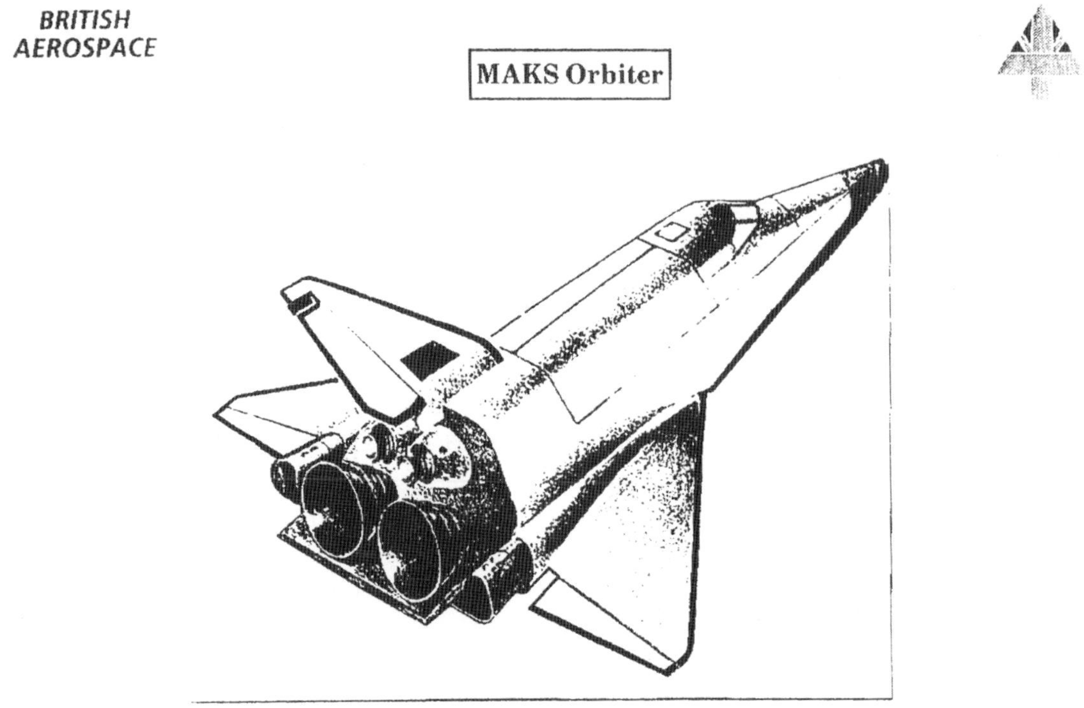

The Russian MAKS orbiter.

development of aerospaceplane projects such as Hotol if the high development costs are to be afforded. The obvious forum for such collaboration is ESA, which now has a firm mandate to explore collaboration with the CIS."

Meanwhile, Parkinson had successfully managed to return one former Hotol team member to BAe; he remembered: "We did eventually after six months manage to drag [Dave Helas] back onto the team as a part timer, really because of his special expertise with the Russians, and he carried on for some time."

At the ESA Ministerial Council meeting in Granada, Spain, on November 9-10, 1992, the decision was made to finally abandon the Hermes space vehicle after several years of difficulties. The activities of its developer, Euro-Hermespace, would be wound down over the coming months and the company put into a dormant state in mid-1993.

RADEM... AND SKYLON

Webb and Helas flew out to Kiev, Ukraine, on November 22, 1992, for a meeting at Antonov the following day. According to the protocol issued afterwards: "At the meeting, BAe informed Antonov about work carried out by BAe on the An-225/Hotol aerospace system within the scope of ESA tasks on this system and handed over documentation on this work. BAe specialists acquainted themselves with the An-77 prototype [proposed Westernised version of the An-70, redesignated An-7-X in 1999] and strength test facilities at Antonov. Antonov informed BAe that the An-225/Hotol design was considered both by Russia and Ukraine as the design for international cooperation of the countries within ESA."

It was agreed that BAe would ask Leigh to write to the Ukrainian Prime Minister Leonid Kuchma and the Vice-Premier of Russia, Yegor Gaidar, "relating to cooperation on the programme". Furthermore, "during November 1992, Antonov will analyse the documents on the separation process of the An-225 carrier and Hotol spacecraft, and will inform BAe of the results".

Perhaps most importantly, "during December 1992 and January 1993, BAe, NPO Molniya and Antonov plan to carry out preliminary studies on the configuration and technical problems associated with the RADEM space technology demonstrator, taking into account the availability of existing CIS knowledge and hardware".

RADEM, which stood for Rocket Ascent DEMonstrator—or Rocket Ascent DEmonstration Mission depending on context, was effectively an uncrewed subscale air-launched technology demonstrator capable of reaching Mach 12. It was intended to trial and showcase systems and materials that could later appear on the full-size An-225/Hotol or MAKS launchers.

The British team then travelled on to Moscow for discussions with TsAGI and Molniya. They were also shown a Buran static test vehicle in the Molniya factory. A day after returning home, Webb joined Parkinson and Longstaff in Orlando, Florida, for the four-day American Institute of Aeronautics and Astronautics' Fourth International

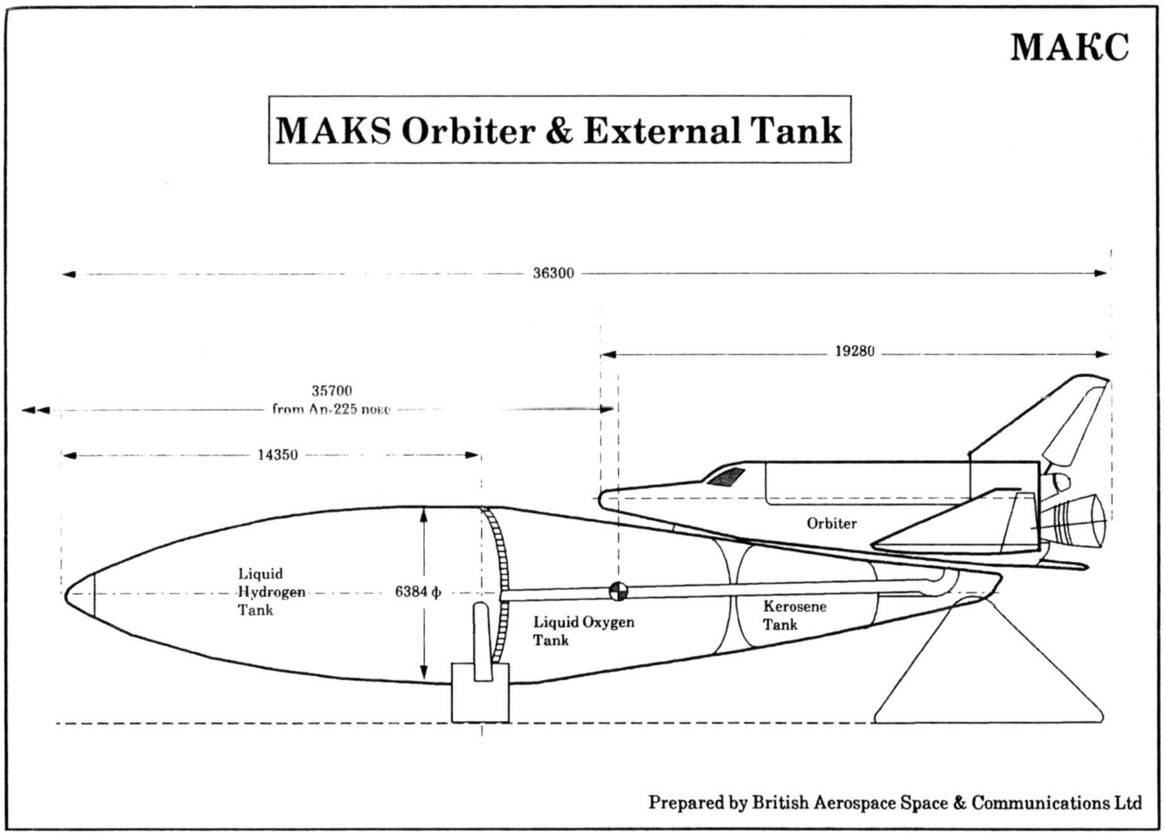

The MAKS orbiter with external tank—containing liquid hydrogen, liquid oxygen and kerosene.

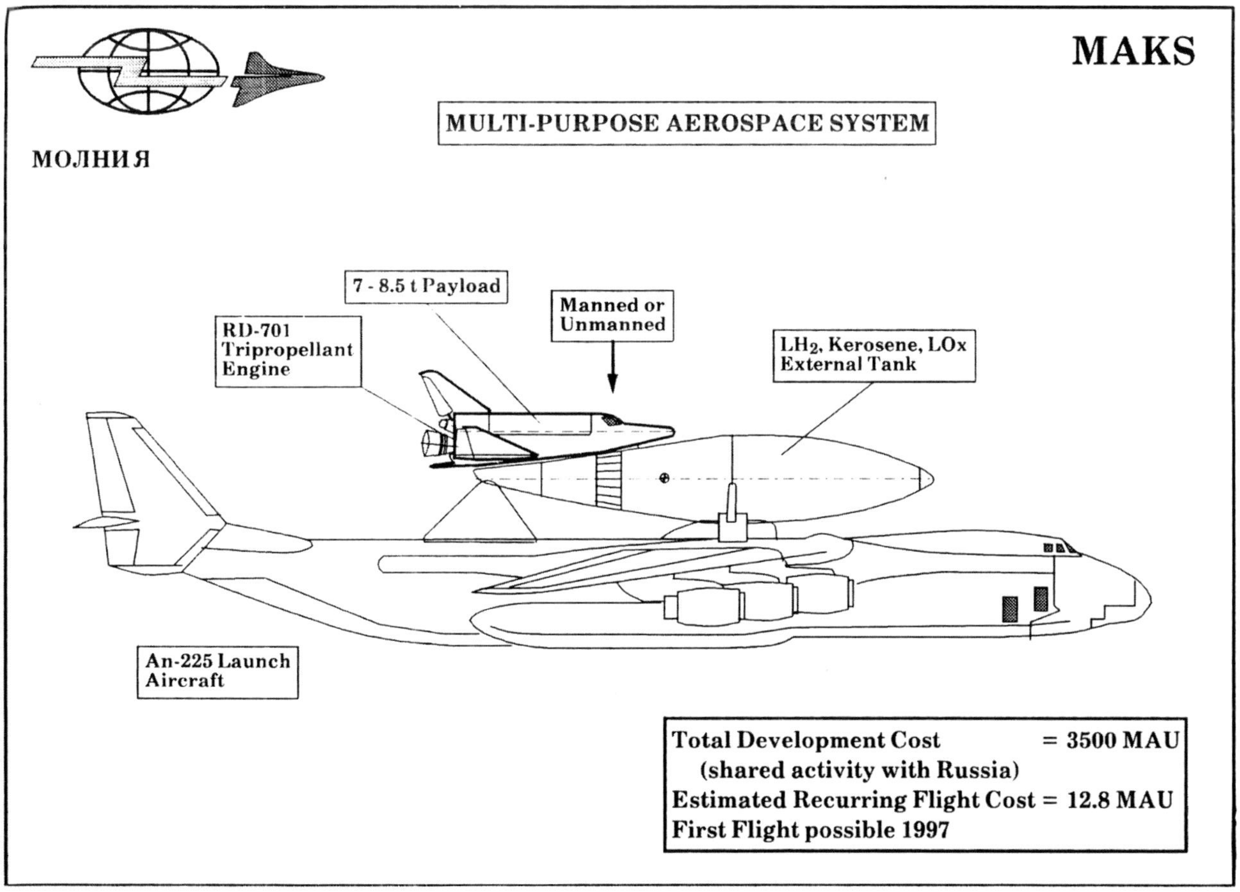

MAKS was also a candidate for air-launch from the An-225.

Aerospace Planes Conference which started on December 1. A paper authored by Parkinson and himself, entitled 'The Status of Aerospaceplane Research in the UK', was presented at the conference.

This briefly recounted the whole Hotol saga, all the way up to Molniya's unveiling of the RD-701 tripropellant engine. The paper noted that, "since installed engine thrust is a major design driver, the RD-701 allows a reduction in the engine mass. It also reduces the amount of liquid hydrogen carried, and hence vehicle volume. Our studies indicated that there was a 1-2 tonne payload gain through the use of such an engine.

"Optimisation of the tripropellant vehicle design resulted in a slimmer (and longer) vehicle than the pure liquid oxygen/liquid hydrogen vehicle. Both these vehicles now have a tail fin. Configuration refinement has moved the centre of gravity further forward, thereby reducing the advantage of the nose fin to the extent that the additional actuation required overwhelms its potential advantage".

And that was as far as work had progressed. The paper went on to discuss ESA's WLC studies and NPO Molniya's MAKS (Multipurpose Aerospace System) concept, which was similar to the An-225/Interim Hotol combination but involved a much smaller orbiter and a large expendable 'drop tank' carrying all its propellants.

The discussion now turned to something new—a concept that was being developed by Alan Bond, whose Reaction Engines consultancy business, with the addition of Richard Varvill and John Scott-Scott from Rolls-Royce, had become an aerospace company in its own right as of August 1989. The paper said: "While BAe switched attention to the An-225 concept, the problem of designing an airbreathing engine with the right compromise of performance and mass, and integrating it with an airframe, has been pursued in the UK by A. Bond's company Reaction Engines.

"With the experience gained from the airbreathing Hotol studies it is possible to improve the engine cycle in a way that would increase the payload fraction by about 30%. Reaction Engines has also looked at innovative ways of integrating engine and airframe to overcome some of the problems encountered with airbreathing Hotol Configuration K. The result is the Skylon concept—named after an obelisk erected at the Festival of Britain, which it resembles.

"Although Skylon has not been subjected to the same rigorous engineering analysis as Hotol K, there is good reason to think that a successful SSTO using an airbreathing engine of this sort can be constructed. The estimate for the payload is 8-10 tonnes with a 275-tonne take-off mass. In addition, Reaction Engines have suggested that the take-off trolley can be eliminated by using a rocket-assisted take off [RATO] that unloads the undercarriage during this critical manoeuvre.

Publicity photo showing Reaction Engines founders Richard Varvill, left, and Alan Bond at work—with Skylon artworks both on the wall behind and on the desk in front of Bond. REACTION ENGINES

"The Skylon studies indicate that subsonic combustion airbreathing engines may still be able to give an attractive performance for a single stage to orbit vehicle, and should not be ignored in future activities."

A diagram included with the paper showed the 'Skylon Vehicle Concept'. It was a slender vehicle, 81.95m long, with short low-set wings positioned halfway along the fuselage—each tipped with a large engine nacelle. It was vaguely reminiscent of the ALV 100C but had a Hotol-type nosefin and foreplanes rather than a tail fin.

An initial paper featuring Skylon, entitled 'Application Potential of the SABRE Jet Engine for Propulsion of Single Stage to Orbit Reusable Launchers', which outlined a very early version of Skylon, had in fact been produced by Reaction Engines more than a year earlier on November 29, 1991.

As had become customary by now, Parkinson's report to the AIAA drew the conclusion that a collaborative approach to vehicle development was the way forward and "the initial stages of such a collaborative programme would be a coordination of the available technology within Europe, and an enabling technology programme to put the missing pieces into place before commitment to full development.

"ESA now has plans for a Future European Space Transportation Investigations Programme (FESTIP) which is intended to fulfil this role, and the UK is preparing to

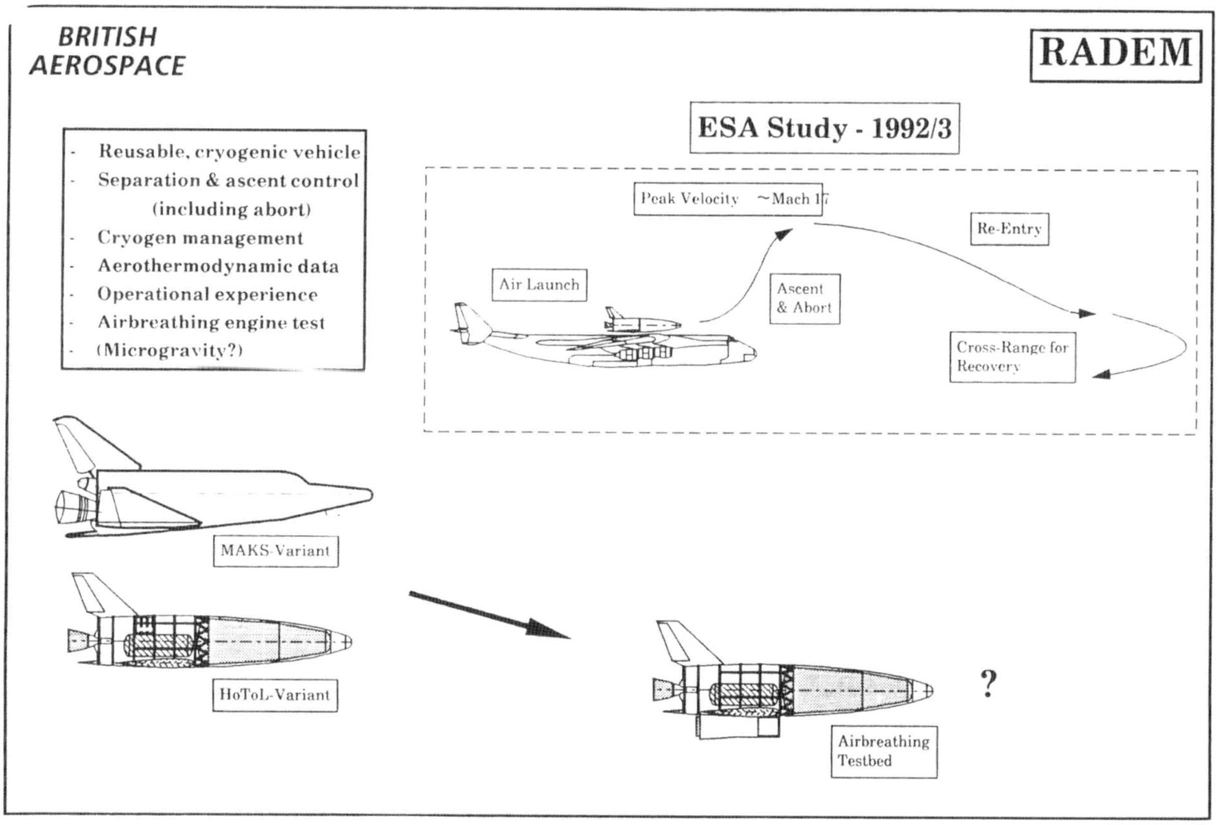

Brief illustrated outline of goals set for the proposed RADEM project.

participate in this."

The report ended by stating that "the current conclusions of the UK aerospaceplane studies are: reduced operating cost vehicles are possible, using near-term achievable technology; the most immediately achievable vehicles use pure rocket propulsion using the An-225 carried as a launch platform (MAKS & An-225/Hotol); subsonic combustion airbreathing cycles may provide higher performance and economically attractive SSTOs in the longer term, but involve development of a new engine type; two-stage (supersonic separation) TSTOs and scramjet SSTO vehicles have inferior cost/performance to any of the above".

On the second day of the conference at 8.24am, before proceedings recommenced, Webb and Longstaff were able to watch NASA Space Shuttle *Discovery* embark on STS-53 from Kennedy Space Center, carrying the classified DoD-1 satellite for the US Department of Defense.

WORKING FOR ESA

FESTIP had first been discussed six years earlier but now, finally, it was about to become a reality. The joint BAe/CIS RADEM project could, it was proposed, be conducted under the auspices of the wider FESTIP programme.

Parkinson would later report that, "at the beginning of 1993, ESA asked British Aerospace, in collaboration with NPO Molniya, TsAGI and Antonov, to investigate the design of a rocket-powered, air-launched, hypersonic demonstrator to act as a test bed for technologies associated with future reusable, low operating cost launch systems. RADEM would demonstrate operational reusability in a winged vehicle together with structural and engine technologies for future launch systems".

Numerous different layouts were considered in two broad aerodynamic forms—the RADEM MAKS-Variant and the RADEM Hotol-Variant. On April 6, Parkinson himself had drawn RADEM Configuration 1201, an example of the latter. This 21.27m long, 11.63m wingspan vehicle featured the familiar large liquid hydrogen tank up front with twin liquid oxygen tanks to the rear. At the very back was a single Russian D-57M engine—a powerplant apparently designed in 1975 and since mothballed.

In a presentation to the BNSC on April 22, 1993, entitled 'The UK & FESTIP—The Hotol Background', Parkinson outlined both variants with the MAKS-Variant shown as a forerunner for the full MAKS system, complete with disposable fuel tanks, and the Hotol-Variant shown as a potential demonstrator for both Interim Hotol's rocket systems and the airbreathing systems of Skylon.

SKYLON REVEALED

Coincidentally, the May 1993 issue of the British

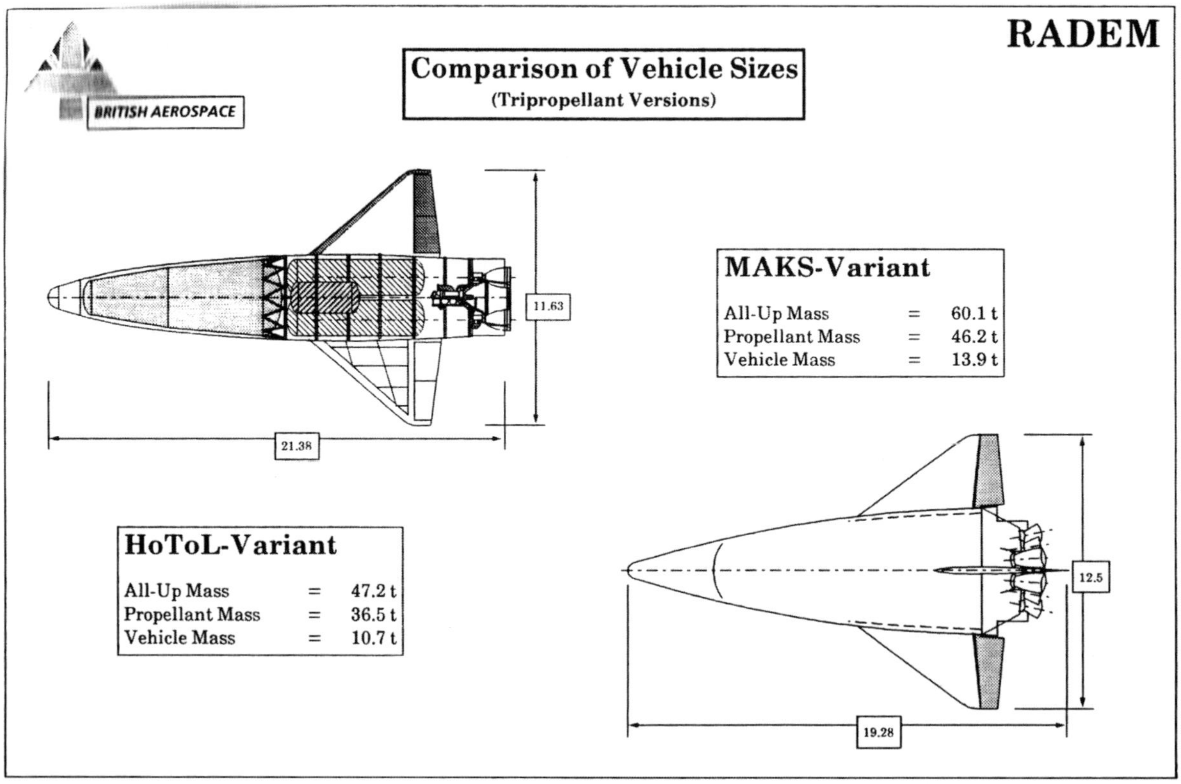

The tripropellant RADEM Hotol-Variant and MAKS-Variant.

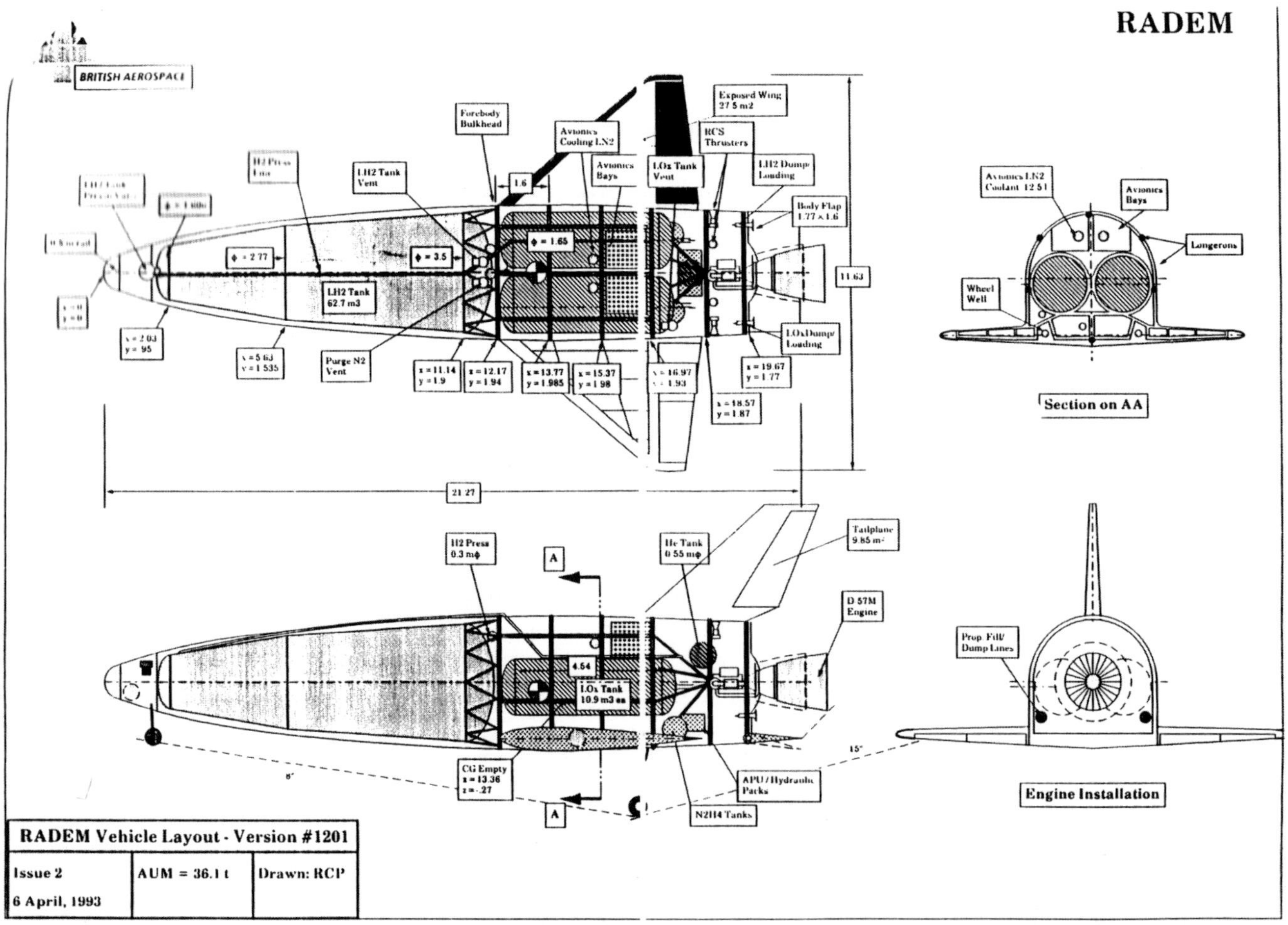

RADEM Configuration 1201, as drawn by Parkinson.

Interplanetary Society's *Spaceflight* magazine included an article jointly written by Varvill and Bond which divulged many more details of the Skylon vehicle and its SABRE engines than had previously been publicly available.

It explained that "the Skylon/SABRE concept developed from a design review of the BAe Hotol/RB.545 vehicle. Skylon is designed to launch a ten tonne payload into a 300km due east orbit from Kourou (or any other near equatorial launch site). The payload into a 460km 28.5 degree (space station) orbit is 7.7 tonnes. The fuselage contains a central payload bay and liquid oxygen tankage plus two hydrogen tanks occupying the tapered ends of the fuselage.

"The swept delta wing is located roughly midway along the fuselage and carries an integrated intake/engine nacelle on each wingtip. Aerodynamic control is achieved by active foreplanes in pitch, an active forward fin in yaw and ailerons in roll. Thrust vector control takes over progressively during the rocket ascent by collective gimballing of the rocket chambers within each nacelle."

Skylon dealt with the centre of pressure shift problem by managing fuel usage between the enormous front and rear hydrogen tanks and "residual centre of gravity/centre of pressure mismatches are trimmed out by the active foreplanes which, due to their large moment arm about the centre of gravity, result in negligible trim drag penalties".

Also, "by locating the engine nacelles on the wingtips rather than on the fuselage base, considerable freedom is gained to position the dry centre of gravity close to the hypersonic centre of pressure, thereby achieving a trimmable vehicle during re-entry".

The article also elaborated on Parkinson's brief mention of RATO: "One of the most unsatisfactory features of Hotol was the need to develop a high speed (300kts) launch trolley to save the weight of a take-off undercarriage. Due to the fuel savings of the SABRE engine, it has been possible to replace this feature with an integrated RATO unit in Skylon. Such systems have a good precedent in the 1950s cruise missiles which employed expendable RATOs in order to achieve a 'zero length launch'. Using this system, Skylon would become airborne after only seven seconds and in a distance of 650m".

The SABRE engine was described as similar to Hotol's "simple" RB.545 which "has traded simplicity for better performance. The SABRE engine differs from the RB.545 in that the air compressors are driven by a separate power loop rather than employing the work capacity of the hydrogen stream directly.

"The SABRE performs its start transient in rocket mode, transferring to airbreathing mode immediately that mainstage combustion is initiated. The engine operates in airbreathing mode during an optimum ascent to an altitude of 26km at Mach 5. The vehicle then performs a programmed dive followed by a pull up in order maximise the climb angle at the start of the rocket ascent. At this point, the engine transitions to rocket mode, while continuing to operate, in order to complete the ascent to transfer orbit injection at about 80km.

"The air inlets are closed on transition to rocket operation and remain closed throughout the rest of the mission including re-entry. In order to match the captured airflow to the engine demand, a bypass duct is included with a reheat burner. This is in effect a subsonic combustion ramjet which operates in parallel with the main engines. The thrust of this system peaks around transonic flight and contributes considerably to the vehicle performance for this reason. At higher Mach numbers, this system is ineffective and all propulsion is derived from the main engines." Like Hotol, Skylon benefitted significantly from 'spill ramjets'.

A data panel appended to the article gave Skylon's mass at launch as 275t, with mass at RATO cut-off as 262t. Mass at the point of transition to pure rocket power was 224t and mass at transfer orbit was 55.7t. Payload was 10t, length was 82m, maximum fuselage diameter was 6.25m and wingspan, across the nacelles, was 27m—with this variant being referred to as Configuration A4.

THE RB.545'S FATE

The decision to publish details of the SABRE may well have been influenced by the declassification of the RB.545 following a change in government policy. Indeed, the same issue of *Spaceflight* contained an article by Hempsell entitled 'Hotol's Secret Engines Revealed'.

With assistance from Varvill, Hempsell, who had become a lecturer in space technology at the University of Bristol after leaving BAe, outlined the RB.545's background, its cycle and its application in Hotol. He then posed the question: "So what does the future hold for the RB.545? The data presented in the article represent the engine status as in 1989. By that time Rolls-Royce [had] decided that the investment required to take the engine through its development phase and produce an operational engine in terms of company manpower, money and political capital was too large given the eventual market in terms of the number of engines required by the Hotol project (even on the most optimistic assumptions), and has not supported any further work on the RB.545.

"It is difficult to fault Rolls-Royce's decision. It is a very commercial company operating in a very tough marketplace and it must husband its investments wisely for the benefit of its employees and shareholders. However, one must question why a British firm should be operating in an environment where this is the correct decision. Its main competitors in the USA, Pratt & Whitney and General Electric, are likely to have come to a very different decision, probably to the long-term benefit of both company and nation."

LEIGH GETS THE BOOT

Hotol's new would-be political champion, Edward Leigh, was unceremoniously ejected from the Government by John Major on May 27, 1993, during a Cabinet reshuffle—casting the project once again into the political void from which it had barely begun to clamber.

More months passed. The July 13, 1993, issue of *Flight International* included a report by Graham Warwick on the imminent demise of the NASP programme. Evidently design work had come to a grinding halt in May, Warwick quoting acting NASP programme director Colonel Philip Bruce as saying: "In the past, the plan was to [build] two X-30 flight vehicles... Two things happened over the last 18 months which made [the decision to proceed with that] difficult. Firstly, we costed out the X-30 programme and found that it was very expensive. In today's budget climate, the programme was deemed unaffordable." The second thing had been a mid-1992 Defense Science Board review, which had raised major technical concerns about the X-30's likely performance and its transition to hypersonic flight. While further NASP-related work was still planned, this was the beginning of the end for the ambitious and lavishly funded project.

Parkinson gave a presentation to Michael Paillon, head of the Commission of the European Communities' (CEC) Space Unit, on August 26, 1993, which outlined the "objectives of the Hotol programme", assessed the "threats to [the] European position" (USAF Spacelifter, US SSTO Delta Clipper, Lockheed/Krunichev/Energia Proton, Pegasus launcher) and urged the CEC to "encourage appropriate technology developments, outside nationalistic 'technology for technology's sake' programmes" but made no mention of RADEM.

And in September 1993, Parkinson produced a new presentation entitled 'The An-225/Hotol Option'. This once again reiterated the history of Hotol as an airbreathing system and went so far as to detail the P150-302 orbiter configuration. The D-57 powered RADEM Configuration 1201 drawing was included alongside a comparison of a tripropellant RADEM Hotol-Variant and MAKS-Variant. These configurations went unnumbered but each had multiple engines.

HEARTBREAK HOTOL REVISITED

What was now referred to simply as An-225/Hotol remained a viable prospect for development going into and throughout 1994, with RADEM as the proposed technology demonstrator. Little if any progress was made on the former but work on the latter continued—culminating in a presentation to ESTEC in Noordwijk on June 30, 1994, in front of a large audience.

In its final form, RADEM would use an existing rocket engine or engines in order to minimise costs. The single D-57 option had by now been rejected in favour of multiple smaller engines: European HM-7Bs, Russian KRDs or American RL-10s. Another option was the Energomash RD-120, which could be used in conjunction with two or more HM-7Bs as a three-component system.

Two vehicle concepts were put forward—Configuration 1603, using six HM-7Bs with an integral hydrogen tank, and the tripropellant Configuration 2802, which used installed propellant tanks with two HM-7Bs and one RD-120.

Thermal protection on both would initially be via Russian TZMK-10 tiles as used on Buran, and "advanced TPS concepts could then be demonstrated as they became available on selected test areas of the vehicle".

The propellant tanks would be made of aluminium-lithium "since NPO Molniya have already done test tank demonstration work on this system. Alternative tank structures (e.g. carbon-PEEK) could be substituted later if required".

The carrier aircraft would, of course, be the An-225 since "the nearest alternative would be to modify an Airbus A300B to carry up to 55 tonnes in air launch mode. This would require extensive conversion to be able to perform the carriage and separation required".

It was concluded that the RADEM system would be relatively cheap, since it mostly relied on off-the-shelf technology, and effective both in demonstrating the technology required for future launcher systems and the collaborative working processes necessary for a successful collaboration between ESA and the CIS.

July 19, 1994, saw British Aerospace Space Systems being acquired by Matra Marconi Space (MMS) for £56m, further divorcing Parkinson and his small team from Webb and those still able to contribute to Hotol work at Warton—on paper at least.

The *Observer* newspaper of August 28, 1994, published an article by Nicholas Booth with the by-now ubiquitous 'Heartbreak Hotol' headline. Based largely on a new

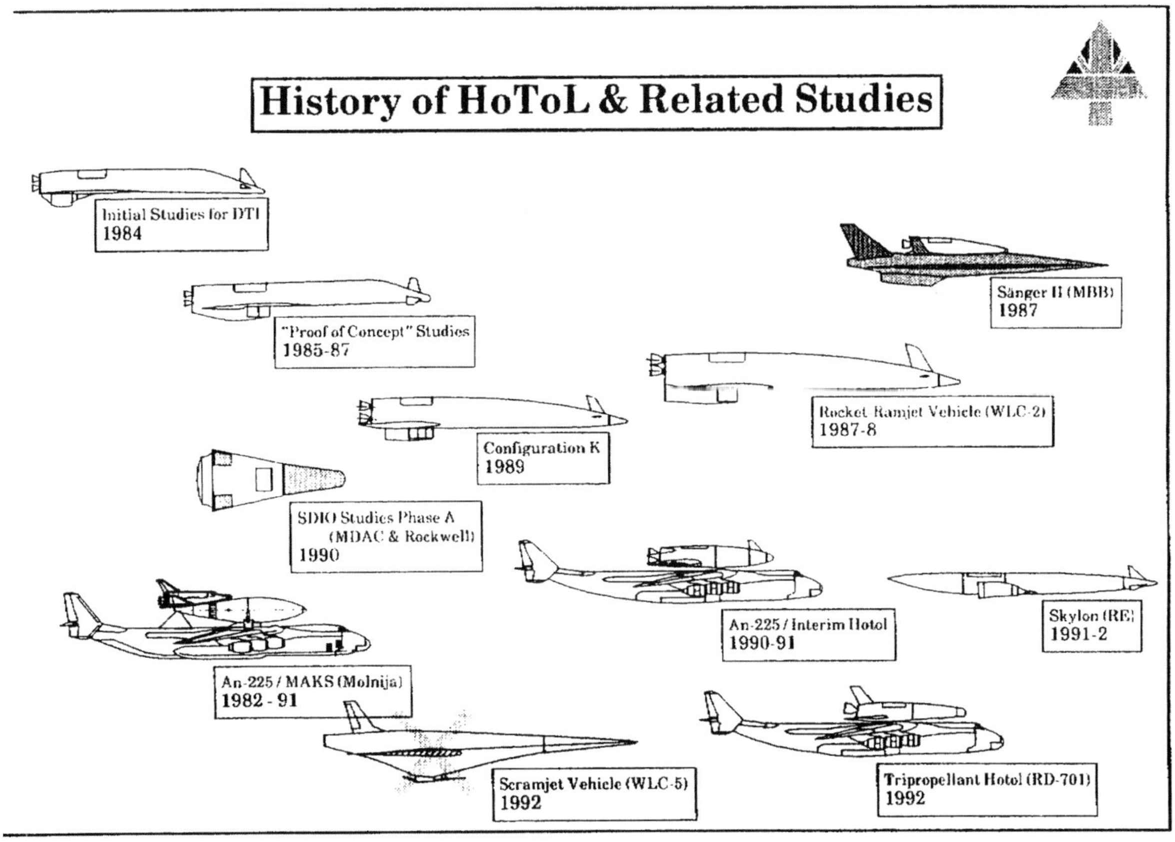

Graphic showing the 'history of Hotol and related studies' from a paper by Parkinson dated August 24, 1993.

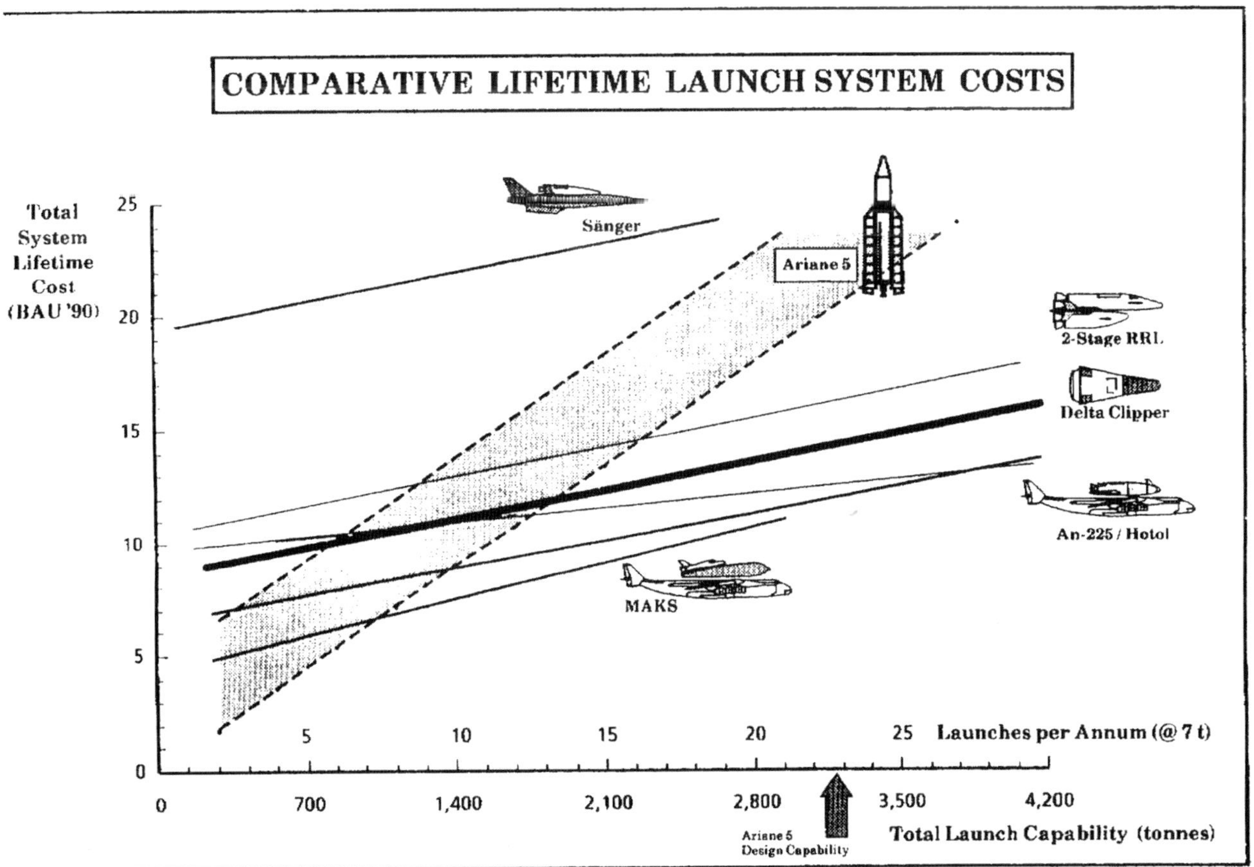

An-225/Interim Hotol and MAKS were both presented as far more cost effective options than Sänger or Ariane 5.

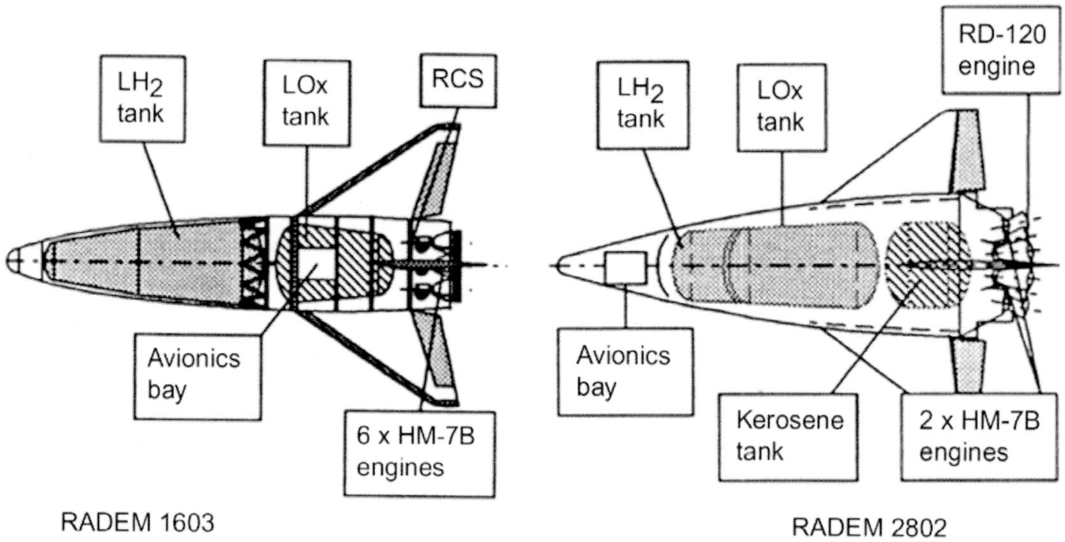

RADEM 1603, powered by six HM-7Bs, and the tripropellant 2802.

interview with Bond, this sought to commemorate the ten-year anniversary of the project's initial unveiling and commiserate over its lack of success. Bond had told Booth that Hotol "captured the public imagination quite vividly" but "we could never satisfactorily accommodate the landing gear. [With Skylon] we can now do that, because of weight savings thanks to improved technology. And by placing the engines over the wings, we also increase efficiency".

It was noted that, after months of prevarication, the UK Government had pledged just £50,000 to ESA, Bond commenting: "I cannot express the level of insult I feel to those of us who have put body and soul into keeping Britain in this field. I really wish ESA would kick us out for penny-pinching".

Two days later, Skorodelov sent Webb a fax saying: "I remember with pleasure our collaboration on the An-225/Hotol and RADEM projects. I regret that you could not attend at the RADEM presentation in Noordwijk. We hope to continue our collaboration on the development of the advanced reusable space transportation systems. We consider experimental aerospace system RADEM to be a real step in this direction. The RADEM can satisfy to a considerable extent the interests of different European concepts of the future reusable space transportation system. We hope for active participation of your BAe department in these works."

He said he hoped to meet Webb again at the 1994 Farnborough Air Show, which was due to take place from September 5-11.

FARNBOROUGH 1994

BAe liaison consultant Abdul H. Mahir wrote to Parkinson on September 1, 1994, to confirm that a meeting had indeed been arranged to take place at Farnborough on September 7. Attending from the British side were the BNSC's Derek Gould, Parkinson who was now representing MMS Space Systems, Webb from BAe Defence and Mahir. The Russians in attendance were Anatoly Bratukhin from the State Committee of the Defence Industry plus Skorodelov, Mikhail Gofin (commercial director) and Alexander Sergeevich Bashilov (general director) from NPO Molniya. Ukraine fielded two representatives: O. Urussky from the Ukrainian National Space Agency and Dr Ivan Serdijk from Antonov.

The resulting protocol noted five points of agreement: that the collaboration on An-225/Hotol and RADEM had "made a valuable contribution to the problem of creating a reusable space transportation system"; that the strong commonality between An-225/Hotol and MAKS could allow further developments "capable of supporting the long-term European programmes as well as serving the interests of future Russian and Ukrainian programmes"; that RADEM could itself serve as the precursor to a new reusable space transportation system "similar to MAKS or An-225/Hotol"; that BNSC, the Russian State Committee on the Defence Industry and the Ukrainian National Space Agency believed RADEM should be continued; and lastly, that those three organisations "agree to continue to encourage ESA to open negotiations regarding continuing joint studies on the development and creation of the RADEM system".

Parkinson, Skorodelov, Serdijk and Neiland produced a paper for the 45th IAF Congress at Jerusalem, Israel, on October 9-14, 1994, entitled 'RADEM: An Air Launched, Rocket Demonstrator for Future Advanced Launched

Systems' which reiterated much of what had already been said at Noordwijk in June. The Russians would return to Farnborough again in 1996 for a final meet-up with BAe personnel, including Webb, but this would prove to be the very last gasp for Hotol.

Asked in 2010 when the Hotol project was cancelled, Parkinson said: "Well it didn't—it just didn't get continued. We did our work, we'd reported it to ESA, the ESA people had at that point a continuing investigation of possible [systems]... largely led by the Germans who were actually prepared to put money into the thing but we were part of it... we did quite a good job [of RADEM]... but once again there wasn't a take-up of the thing, it wasn't that it was cancelled, it was that nobody bought the product as it were."

RIGGED FROM THE START?

Parkinson had come to the view, over time, that throughout the period of Hotol's existence—when considerable effort was being made to impress ESA and persuade it to invest both politically and financially in Hotol—the agency had in fact been far less able to influence the course of events than most had suspected owing to powerful vested interests.

As Hempsell would later explain, "ESA had next to no say in the future of European launchers, which was entirely in the hands of CNES. So, all the ESA studies and work was so much wasted time and paper, it was always going to be ignored... basically I think in hindsight ESA was much weaker than we thought at the time".

Parkinson said that "...nobody would take the idea of reusable launchers forwards at that stage [during the 1980s and 1990s]. Politics again. The French weren't in favour, they had their own problems with Ariane 5 and... [with reusable launchers] you're actually talking about turning the world upside down a bit.

"You're upsetting the way that the European launch vehicle business was organised. And to some extent the European launcher vehicle business is paced by a little group in Vernon in France... The way it works is that you've got an operational vehicle like Ariane and you therefore need a support staff of engineers who know how the thing works and in particular how the engine works, so you've got to keep them employed, but you don't really want to expand that, or contract it.

"So that group develops a new engine and then looks after it and as their workload drops off they can look at the next engine. So it's paced by how often that group can produce a new engine. It's the way the French keep the thing going. They don't want to expand that and do different things.

"If they're in the middle of developing Ariane 5, they're not going to take on anything new ... And this was explained to me by one of the ESA guys on one occasion and that drives the whole of the European launch vehicle schedule. You can't have a new launch vehicle more often than a certain amount, dependent basically on the engine people in Vernon.

"It's not unusual for things to come down to a fairly closed dependence on a particular group. Somewhere there's going to be a pinch point in the case of the launch vehicle business as it's currently set up. It sits in this group in Vernon. It could be somewhere else... [another example is] the number of launches a year that Space Shuttle [could] do was limited by their ability to produce external tanks at Michoud and if you wanted more than eight launches a year, or five to eight launches a year, you basically had to build a whole new facility so that was the pinch point you see, it's not the engines it's another component, but there's something that limits your flow-through and that's normal in engineering."

Interim Hotol had been feasible but had not been chosen for development simply because the money had to go elsewhere and because the Europeans had been unwilling to share the technology they had developed, even if it meant getting something valuable back in return. Parkinson said: "It's always a bit frustrating because we knew that in this particular case there wasn't any technical reason for [An-225/Hotol not being taken forward], it was just that there wasn't funding to do it. It was slightly disappointing because... there was an opportunity being missed.

"The Russians had a lot of things that if we got the right sort of deal going would have benefitted European space and so forth and it looked like the Europeans... didn't really want Russians taking part of their technology. If we'd have done the deal with the Russians, then we'd have to give the Russians things to do and the Europeans really wanted to hold onto those things. The fact that it would have been cost-effective and we'd move towards better launch vehicles and so forth was ignored because it was not their objective.

"Their objective was to keep the technology in place. It didn't matter... to some extent it didn't matter about the final objective, it was the local things that were always the problem. It was only us who dreamt of cheap launches into space, that wanted the end product. The rest wanted something else."

ARIANE WINS

The original aim of Hotol, back in 1982, had been to

replace the costly and wasteful Ariane 5 launcher with a cheaper reusable system. But few appreciated that the Ariane programme had already become, effectively, too big to challenge by this point. The French CNES oversaw the Ariane programme and maintained the spaceport it relied on, and the lead contractor responsible for manufacturing it was French, but other European nations including Germany, Italy, Spain, Belgium, Switzerland and Sweden all had a massive financial stake in its success.

And the money invested didn't just go to France—carefully measured portions of it were distributed across hundreds of subcontractors in those investor nations. Replacing Ariane with a new reusable launcher system would have required the wholesale dismantling of this painstakingly assembled and politically sensitive structure. Establishing a new structure in its place, with all the political wrangling, horse-trading and cost that this would entail, was hard to contemplate.

Had Hotol been a dead cert for success, with no one able to deny its advantages and feasibility, it might have stood a better chance of—as Parkinson put it—turning the world of European launchers upside down. But the classification of Bond's engine patent right at the beginning had generated doubt and scepticism even as the project was unveiled which would, ultimately, prove insurmountable.

The An-225/Interim Hotol concept moved the goalposts, making it that much more difficult to deny the benefits of a 'HOrizontal Take-Off and Landing' vehicle, but by then Ariane had become even more deeply entrenched and immovable. And the involvement of the Russians, as attractive and intriguing as their technological prowess was, proved to be a fresh source of doubt.

All that aside, could Hotol have been developed into a physical vehicle that worked? The airbreathing Hotol relied on cutting edge technology which required significant investment to realise. And the British government, for reasons already discussed, declined to make that investment. The actual sum spent on Hotol over the years was undeniably miniscule in comparison to the vast quantities of cash routinely spent on other projects by the British government. Bond and Parkinson have regularly cited £10m (about £24m today, allowing for inflation) as the likely spend by all concerned, certainly on the airbreathing portion of the project, with less than half of that actually coming from the government.

It is often argued—and indeed was often argued at the time—that the cost of developing an SSTO launcher was too much for any one nation to bear, making international collaboration essential and putting Hotol on a collision course with Ariane and everything that went with it. But that isn't, and wasn't, entirely true since the UK had money to invest in large-scale infrastructure projects even then. It was a matter of political will as much as economic circumstances. Money can be transferred from one budget to another, with one area of spending diminished in order to provide the funds for something else, as long as those controlling the purse strings have sufficient political clout to make it happen.

In 2019, the latest cost estimate for the London to Birmingham stretch of the HS2 railway line was between £49bn and £56.6bn—with some estimates placing the final total at closer to £65bn (equivalent to about £22.4bn in 1986 money). Would £22.4bn have been sufficient to get Hotol built circa 1985-2000, assuming ongoing confidence in the underpinning technology throughout that period? *Flight International* reported on an estimated £0.5bn total development cost for Hotol in 1984. By February 1986, the magazine was reporting an estimate of £4bn.

In December 1986, Burns had estimated the cost of building a Hotol demonstrator at £0.5bn and in March of the following year he repeated *Flight International's* figure for the full development programme: £4bn.

Even assuming explosive growth in the cost of developing Hotol, with the delays, overruns and uncontrolled additional expenditure which tend to characterise such enormous aerospace projects, could the project have been successfully completed with an equivalent price-tag smaller than that of the London to Birmingham stretch of the HS2 railway line? We will sadly never know for certain but the end product of a determined attempt to develop Hotol might well have been more interesting.

12

HOTOL'S MAJOR CONTEMPORARIES

The mid-1980s to early 1990s was truly the era of the reusable launch system. The French were hell-bent on securing support for their Hermes spaceplane and the Americans had their own reasons for wanting a cheap launcher, resulting in NASP. The Germans, partners in Hermes, created Sänger II because they wanted something for themselves.

And then there was Skylon, Reaction Engines' shot at devising a horizontal take-off and landing vehicle which resolved the configuration-related problems that had plagued the airbreathing SSTO Hotol.

While there were still more contemporary designs, such as the Japanese HOPE-X, India's Hyperplane, Dassault's STAR-H and McDonnell Douglas's Delta Clipper, it is Hermes, NASP, Sänger II and latterly Skylon, which loom largest in the Hotol story and which are thus worth a cursory review.

HERMES 1976-1986

The Ariane 5/Hermes combination was the spark that ignited the Hotol project. The Ariane rocket came first, with Ariane 1-4 being developed by CNES and French industry. The project had begun in January 1973 under the designation L3S, with Aérospatiale as the prime contractor with Société Européenne de Propulsion (SEP) producing the first and second stage engines.

The third stage engines were to be produced by Air Liquide and MBB and other companies involved were Dornier Flugzeugwerke, Swedish firm Volvo, French electronics giant Matra, plus Ferranti and Marconi in Britain. Launches would take place at the Guiana Space Centre at Kourou, French Guiana, on the northern coast of South America.

Even before the official go-ahead had been given to build Ariane 1, a whole family of Ariane developments had been planned—Arianes 2-4. The possibility of using Ariane 4 to launch a manned capsule was discussed in October 1975 and in the autumn of 1976 Frédéric d'Allest, CNES director of launch vehicles, suggested a mini shuttle with a mass of just five to six tons as a potential payload for Ariane 4.

CNES then commissioned Aérospatiale to study a manned Ariane-launched space vehicle, with a mass not exceeding 6.5 tonnes, in April 1977. By December 1977, a vehicle had been defined that would be capable of carrying three crew with 120kg of supplies and equipment each, plus 400kg of cargo for a mission lasting seven days. That same month, ESA committed to the production of ten Ariane 1 launchers.

The Hermes name was apparently already in place by that point, having been suggested by d'Allest's son. Hermes was the messenger of the gods and the shuttle would bring 'messages', or payload, to the 'modern-day gods', astronauts aboard a space station. D'Allest was evidently told some time later, by a German colleague, that Hermes was also the patron god of thieves as a result of stealing from Apollo.

By December 1978 it had been realised that an allowance of 6.5t was nowhere near enough for a shuttle-type vehicle and the nascent Hermes' mass quickly grew to ten tonnes—making it too heavy for Ariane 4. However, CNES was already planning a heavier variant of Ariane 4 that would be able to manage a 10t payload, naturally to be designated Ariane 5. Hermes at this point was a 12.55m long hypersonic glider with delta wings, vaguely reminiscent of the Space Shuttle orbiter in appearance.

The concept—now with enough room for five astronauts in space suits or two plus 1.5t of cargo—was first shown to the public at the Paris Air Show in June 1979. The vehicle was to be fully automated, though the crew would have the ability to take control at any point. The TPS was carbon-carbon and the overall programme cost was expected to be below $1.2bn. The first successful launch of Ariane 1 was on Christmas Eve, 1979—the firing button having been personally pressed by French President Valéry Giscard d'Estaing. CNES and ESA then created a new company for managing Ariane operations: Arianespace.

During 1980, a Hermes-like vehicle was considered as part of the French Minos project for an orbital materials processing factory, which would eventually evolve into a proposed orbital laboratory called Solaris. Then, during 1983, CNES decided to proceed with a more ambitious Hermes programme intended to produce a fully viable vehicle—acknowledging that international investment would be required to help fund it.

A specification was issued by CNES in 1984 which required a vehicle with a mass of 16.7t—with the still-being-designed Ariane 5's payload requirement, formerly 15t, being correspondingly bumped up to 17t. The new operational Hermes would need to be 15-18m long and around 6m tall, with a 35 cubic metre payload bay 3m in diameter. Cargo capacity had to be 4.5t plus two pilots and two passengers. It needed to be possible, as an alternative, to carry two extra passengers in place of the cargo. Autonomous operation was required on flights that were expected to last between 10 and 90 days. Mission over, Hermes would then land on a 4,000m runway at around 300km/h. Each vehicle, however many there ended up being, would be required to perform ten missions a year for a decade—a total of 100 missions.

CNES thought Aérospatiale's aircraft division would be the ideal contractor to build Hermes, but the company was initially reluctant, preferring to concentrate on its Airbus programme. Consequently, CNES made an approach to Dassault instead. Both firms would be invited to tender for the project in March 1984, with a deadline of March 31, 1985 for project submissions.

CNES next began the process of ensuring that ESA adopted Hermes, thereby drawing in funds from other European nations. The proposal was made in June 1984 and ESA officials apparently had to be told twice to include it on the agenda for the Council of Ministers meeting in Rome on January 30-31, 1985, before they acquiesced and did it.

Next, French President Francois Mitterrand badgered German Chancellor Helmut Kohl to back Hermes during a Franco-German summit in October 1984. Kohl eventually agreed but the Germans evidently harboured serious doubts about the project. When push came to shove, as noted in Chapter 2, the Council of Ministers at Rome declined the opportunity to install Hermes in its long-term plan and instead asked "France to keep the Agency informed of progress on the Hermes manned spaceplane programme". Not the desired result—but if anything it redoubled French resolve to get what they wanted.

The Aérospatiale and Dassault proposals were duly handed in to CNES on time. The former described a vehicle known as Hermes 122 which looked like a little Space Shuttle, with a cranked delta wing and single rear fuselage fin. The latter described Hermes 5D aka Hermes 35, featured a pure delta with wingtip fin control surfaces rather than a tail fin.

Aérospatiale's Hermes 122 was 15.5m long and 7m tall with a wingspan of 11m. The flight deck was based on the Airbus A320 cockpit and the 5m x 3m cargo bay had a volume of 43 cubic metres. The programme cost estimate was $2bn.

Dassault's Hermes 5D/35 was 17.9m long and 5.1m tall with a wingspan of 10.2m. The cargo bay had a 35 cubic metre capacity and the estimated price tag was $1.6bn.

Designing the vehicle had proven taxing for both sides since Ariane 5, large and powerful as it was, could only lift 15t at the start of Hermes development—rising to just over 20t. This severely limited the size of Hermes—and due to the required launch configuration atop the rocket, wing area had to be kept below 85sqm. This in turn made it difficult to provide an acceptable landing speed. Perhaps worst of all, Hermes was a small manned vehicle and the crew needed a windscreen. But windscreen materials of the time could only withstand up to 500°C—so Hermes would need a long nose to provide passive protection for it during re-entry.

While it was generally agreed that Dassault had

Concept art showing the Aérospatiale Hermes, with single rear fin and integral engines. CNES

provided a superior bid, Mitterrand and French Prime Minister Laurant Fabius preferred Aérospatiale for political reasons. As such, it was decided that the two companies should share the prime contractor role—Aérospatiale with overall responsibility and Dassault with responsibility for the vehicle's aerodynamics.

A joint ESA/CNES working group was then set up in April 1985 to liaise with the contractors. The other member states of ESA were invited to participate and almost all took up the invitation. In October, a provisional work share was established with France taking 50% and retaining control of the project, Germany getting 15%; Italy 13%; Belgium 7%; the Netherlands 5%; the UK, Spain and Sweden had 4% each; Switzerland 2%, Austria 1.5%, Denmark 1%, Ireland 0.6% and Norway was included but it's share undecided—for an oversubscribed total of 107.1%. At this point, CNES only really wanted to build two Hermes vehicles, each carrying out 30 missions spread across 15 years for a total of 60 missions from 1995 to 2010.

With Dassault in charge of aerodynamics, the Hermes 5D/35 design now became the baseline configuration and development commenced. There was a sizeable snag however. The Germans had not yet firmly agreed to their participation—and made this clear in January 1986—resulting in much anxiety about the resulting funding gap should they eventually decide against paying for a stake in Hermes.

At the same time, Dassault progressed Hermes 5D to Hermes 5L3, which was 1.82m shorter. This in turn was superseded by Hermes 5M1 in March 1986, which retained the 5L3 dimensions but introduced aerodynamic refinements to its shape. The *Challenger* Shuttle disaster of January 28, 1986, had also resulted in calls for a crew escape system to be included in the vehicle's design—such as making a quartet of solid fuel boosters available to power Hermes, or even just a part of Hermes, away from danger if required. This, however, added substantially to the weight of a vehicle that was already on the margin of acceptable payload for Ariane 5.

In April 1986, the Germans said they would not make a final decision on participation until the summer of 1987. It was clear that Germany wanted greater participation in the design and construction of the vehicle in exchange for their financial contribution.

As mentioned in Chapter 4, the 74th ESA Council meeting from June 25-27, 1986, passed an enabling resolution for a Hermes preparatory programme to run from October 1986 to mid-June 1987. A breakdown of work was also pencilled in, with French companies

Concept art showing the Dassault Hermes, with twin fins. CNES

The Dassault version of Hermes as it was intended to operate atop Ariane 5, compared to Ariane 5 without Hermes. CNES

Aérospatiale, Dassault-Breguet, Matra, Alcatel-Thompson and SEP responsible for the overall programme, aeronautics and TPS, data management, telecommunications and hot structures respectively. German firms MBB-ERNO and Dornier would handle propulsion/aft section and life support, while Belgian ECTA and Elenco were responsible for the electrical system and fuel cells. Dutch firm Fokker would work on the vehicle's robotic arm, named Hera, and Italian Aeritalia would design the thermal control systems.

ESA also rebalanced the overall industrial share percentages, with France now on 40%, Germany 30%, the UK 15% and Italy on 13%—even though Germany had yet to fully commit.

Kohl did eventually announce, in October 1986, that Germany would indeed be taking a 30% stake in the project. The French Prime Minister, Jacques Chirac, simultaneously approved an increase of the French commitment, back up to 45%. *Air & Cosmos* magazine of November 1, 1986, quoted Aérospatiale space and ballistics division chief Jean-Charles Poggi as saying: "We don't necessarily need German ingenuity. We need the German money."

The Hermes preparatory programme began officially on November 30—a month later than originally planned.

HERMES 1987-1990

Technical issues were beginning to mount up for Hermes by early 1987. The vehicle's mass estimate in March 1986 had been around 17t—just within Ariane 5's capability. But by February 1987, thanks to the new escape system and other factors, this had ballooned to nearly 26t. The capacity of Ariane 5 had increased too, to 18.6t, but that was plainly nowhere near enough.

The baseline design was now Hermes 5M2. Earlier variants had featured an opening Space Shuttle-style cargo bay with two doors, but this was now scrapped and replaced with a closed, pressurised, bay—reducing capacity from 4.45t to 3t. Overall vehicle length had decreased again from the 5M1's 16.08m to 15.43m. Height was reduced from 5.1m to 3.4m and wingspan from 10.2m to 10.07m.

Perhaps the most important change was the introduction of the expendable HPM—Hermes Propulsion Module. This was an adapter that would sit between Hermes and Ariane 5 but it also contained two orbital insertion thrusters and 7t of fuel. These engines would increase the vehicle's velocity even after the burnout of the rocket's central core. The HPM would then remain attached during the first part of the mission, allowing Hermes to correct its trajectory and rendezvous with its target space station. It would then be ditched, allowing Hermes to shed critical mass prior to re-entry. Ariane 5 would now be required to lift 21t into LEO—13.9t for Hermes including the HPM, 3t payload and 1.5t mission fuel with a 2.6t mass margin.

Two months later, ESA was forecasting a first flight by the end of 1997. Work continued into the summer and autumn of 1987. In October, *Flight International* reported Roy Gibson as saying that Hermes' payload would be so small it would effectively be "a taxi for two people and a ham sandwich".

At the ESA Council of Ministers meeting on November 9-10, 1987, the cost of developing Hermes to a point of operational readiness was set at \$5.4bn—\$619m for Phase 1, from 1988 to 1990, and \$4.78bn for Phase 2. The former would define Hermes' systems, purpose and safety requirements as well as reducing technological risk, ensuring compatibility with the space stations Hermes would serve and establishing the industrial and financial underpinnings for Phase 2.

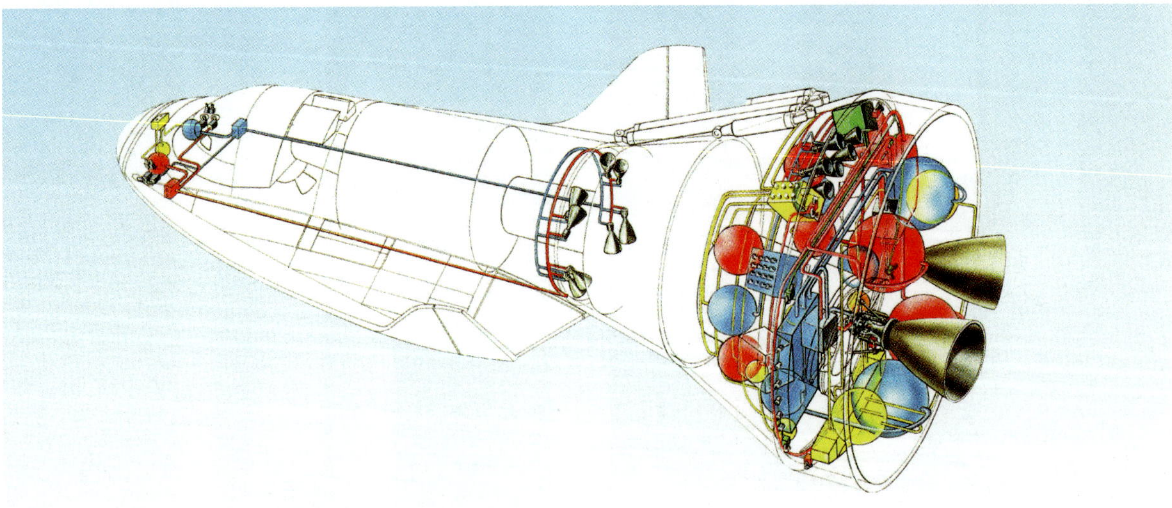

Later variants of Hermes shifted the vehicle's engines to an expendable module known as the HPM. CNES

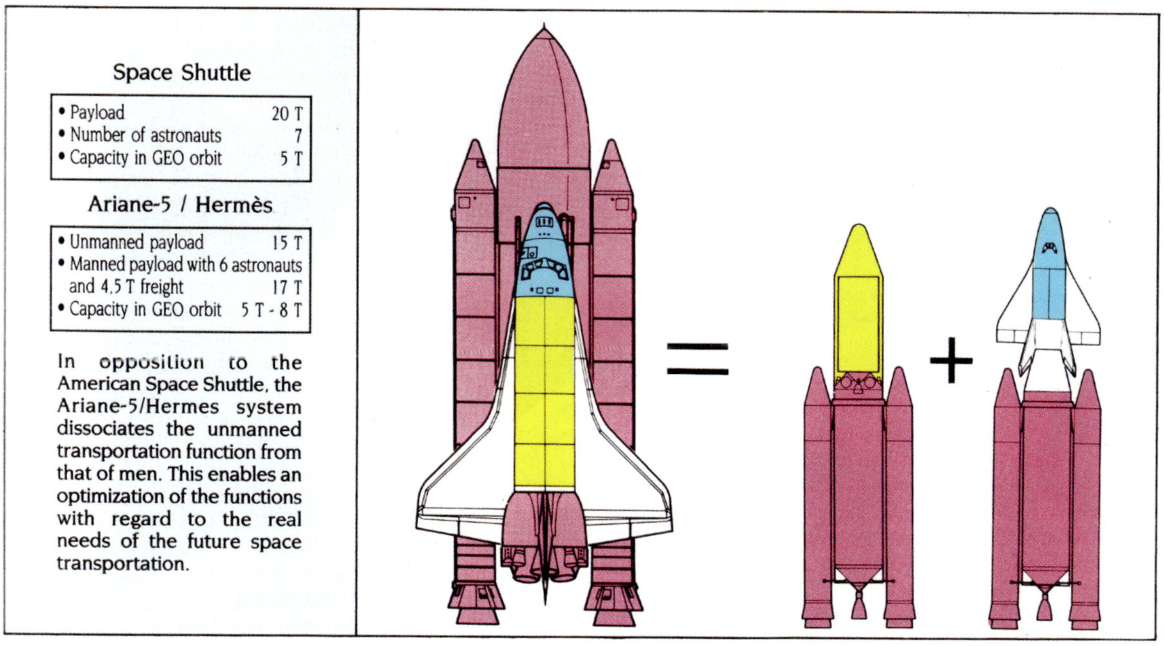

Graphic comparing Ariane 5/Hermes to the Space Shuttle, with some interesting claims made for the former's capabilities. CNES

There would then be a nine-month interim period in 1991 before the commencement of Phase 2 itself—which would see the two Hermes vehicles built and test-flown.

Negative reports about Hermes began to circulate in the French press during early 1988—with many in the scientific community feeling that a manned presence in space was largely unnecessary, even undesirable. ESA argued that there were still some tasks that could not be automated and that there was still plenty to be gained from observing the effects of low gravity on human beings. Moreover, it was suggested that since the Americans and Soviets had already been doing this for some time, Europe ought to be doing it too.

Three new potential configurations for Hermes had been proposed by May 1988: 5MX-A, 5MX-B and 5MX-C—all making use of an enlarged HPM adapter, now dubbed HRM (Hermes Resource Module).

5MX-A featured an HRM that carried not only the usual thrusters but 1.5t of cargo too. 5MX-B had an unpressurised HRM housing the thrusters plus radiators, oxygen tanks and fuel tanks. The HRM for 5MX-C even had a pressurised cargo bay, plus space suit storage and could be accessed by the crew via a tunnel. None of these met requirements and a host of new options were subsequently formulated, including 5MX-E which prioritised space for cargo.

At the same time, it was becoming apparent that if Hermes was going to dock with a space station designed to be compatible with US vehicles, it would need a larger, heavier, docking unit. And all the existing configuration options already had significantly greater mass than Ariane 5 was capable of lifting.

By January 1989, huge effort was being expended on the HRM's design—what it would contain, how its thrusters would be positioned, how it would accommodate the vehicle's radiators, how those radiators could be protected during launch and so on. At this point, the Hermes-HRM payload capacity had shrunk significantly: it would be able to take 1.6t into orbit but could only bring 0.58t back down.

Crew escape options hadn't been forgotten either. The favoured system was a rocket-powered ejectable cabin module, but it proved extremely difficult both to design in its own right and to integrate into the design of Hermes.

A new aerodynamic baseline design, Hermes 8M1, was defined at this time—early 1989—and combined with the HRM design from 5MX-E, resulting in Hermes 8M1-E. This had a combined length of 18.3m. Height was 2.95m and wingspan was 9.01m. By now it was hoped that Ariane 5 would be able to cope with a payload of 23.7t. 8M1-E was expected to weigh 21t without cargo.

The industrial stakes had been further refined by this point too, with France on 42.65%, Germany on 26.7%, Italy 12.47%, Belgium 5.86%, Spain 4.4%, Netherlands 2.4%, Switzerland 1.9%, Austria 0.5%, Denmark 0.4% and Norway 0.2%. Canada had also got in on the action to the tune of 0.45%.

The Berlin Wall came down on November 9, 1989, heralding the beginning of German reunification—which would prove to be an expensive, budget-sapping process

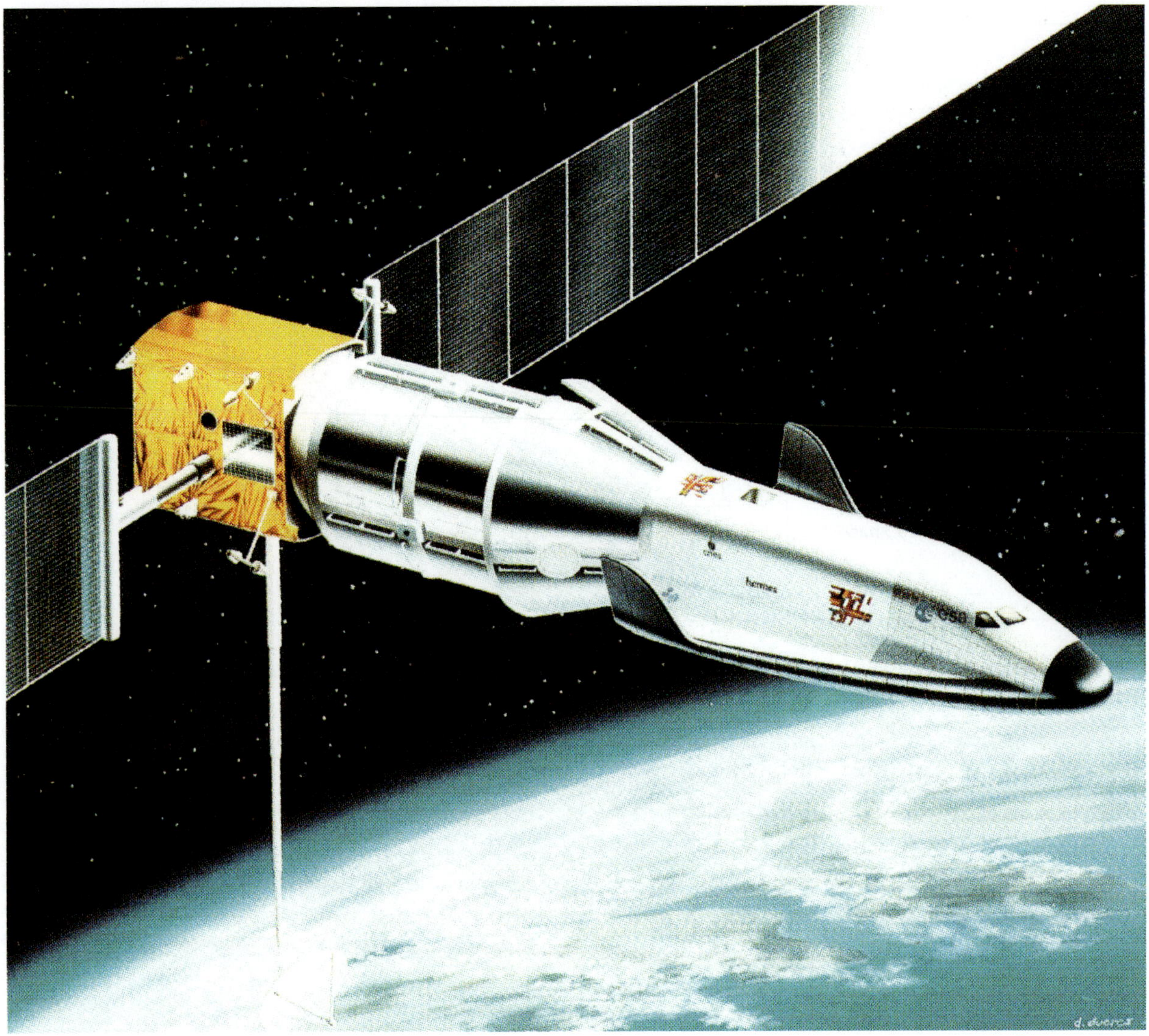

Concept art showing Hermes with the enlarged HRM adapter. CNES

for Germany. At the end of 1989, it was recommended by the Ariane Programme Board that the switch from Hermes Phase 1 to Phase 2 should be delayed until June 1991. And in February 1990 it would be pushed back still further, to July 1, 1991.

Consideration was now being given to deleting the propulsion part of the HRM—with extra fuel being put into Ariane 5 instead to free up space. This resulted in an extensive redesign and a thorough revision of the configuration. Numerous further potential iterations were sketched out until, by the middle of 1990, a new layout known as Hermes 8P8 had been reached. This was slightly longer overall than the 8M1-E at 18.6m, with Hermes itself being 12.7m in length and the HRM being 5.9m. This proved to be yet another interim design however, with Dassault processing dozens of further iterations in an attempt to establish Hermes Shape 1—a fixed baseline for the physical vehicle.

Just as BAe was by this time exploring options with the Soviets, an ESA delegation visited Moscow on March 22-24, 1990, to discuss potential collaborative working on European projects including Hermes.

At the same time, the decision to delay the beginning of Hermes Phase 2 was having serious knock-on consequences. Many participating nations had been working to the original timetable, building up teams of experienced, and expensive, engineers in readiness to get started on what promised to be a challenging endeavour. Now those engineers would have to remain idle for longer than expected, with more than a suspicion that this delay might stretch out even further. Who would pay for those teams to remain together? If no additional funding was forthcoming, they might have to be disbanded.

The president of CNES, Jacques Louis Lion, announced in October 1990 that technical difficulties encountered during development had resulted in a cost increase for Hermes—25% more money was needed from programme leader France and 20% more for each of the other stakeholders. An extremely bitter pill to swallow for all concerned, particularly when the programme was already looking increasingly shaky.

On November 6, 1990, it was decided that Aérospatiale and Dassault, rather than continuing to operate as separate prime contractors, would finally form a joint entity, EuroHermespace, to become a single prime contractor—based in Toulouse, where the French planned to build Hermes. While the decision to form EuroHermespace was nominally taken by ESA, many of the member states were apparently not consulted before it was a done deal—causing more ill will towards the French and fostering a growing atmosphere of mistrust, compounded by the sense that Hermes was rapidly becoming a money pit.

HERMES 1991-1992

There remained a gaping hole on the Hermes Phase 1 balance sheet going into January 1991—with Germany delaying a decision on payment of its share until February 28.

A special meeting of the ESA Council took place on February 7-8, 1991, at Santa Margherita Ligure, near Genoa in northern Italy, to establish a new plan for Europe's space projects, including Hermes, which was now clearly struggling to make progress. It was decided in the end to delay Hermes' first test flight until the end of 2000, providing more breathing room for engineering work but once again driving up costs, and now only a single vehicle would be completed. Initial maximum payload would be just 1t, even if Ariane 5's launch capacity could be brought up to 22.4t.

The first operational mission with a projected three-tonne cargo would only be possible if an Ariane 5 Mk.2 capable of lifting 24.4t could be developed. And this was pushed back to 2004, incurring yet more costs.

The amount of money needed just to get to the point of having an operational vehicle ready to carry out missions, set at $5.4bn in November 1987, had by now risen to $8.86bn. Then, in March, the Germans decided they would only be willing to stump up $66.42m for 1991 and lengthy further negotiations over funding ensued.

Nevertheless, the Hermes engineering team continued to refine the vehicle throughout 1991, resulting in a series of configurations labelled 8R1. Compared to 8P8, 8R1-A was 16cm longer at 18.76m for the Hermes/HRM combination—all of this growth being accounted for by the HRM. Fuselage diameter was 2.77m, wingspan 9.4m and wing area 83.6sqm. And it was acknowledged that this would not be the final shape either, since a number of problems remained to be addressed. It was hoped instead that a true final form would be reached by the first quarter of 1993.

April 1991 saw the beginning of a seven-week Ariane 5-Hermes feasibility review. This concluded that the 4% mass margin that had been allowed for operational flights wasn't enough—overweight as it was, Hermes still needed to allow for greater mass margins. Not only that, it was now decided that the vehicle had to have some form of protection from orbital debris: another factor likely to drive up weight. On top of even this, it was deemed that the manoeuvre required to separate Hermes from the HRM prior to re-entry presented an unacceptable risk. If the complex automated uncoupling process failed, there would be dire consequences and no manual separation option had been considered.

Even as the vehicle's engineers and designers were attempting to address these issues, another special meeting of the ESA council was held—this time at Darmstadt, near Frankfurt in Germany, from August 31-September 1—which saw yet more haggling over funding and payment plans. Then came the next full ESA Council of Ministers meeting on November 18-20, 1991, at the Alte Residenz in Munich. Less than a week beforehand, Norway decided to pull out of the Hermes project on the grounds that it was unlikely to see any economic benefits from its investment any time soon. During the three-day meeting itself, no firm decision could be reached on any aspect of the programme. Instead, further decision-making was deferred for a year; until the next scheduled meeting at the end of 1992. At this point, Europe had apparently already spent some $1.2bn on the Hermes programme—perhaps 70 times as much as the total spent on Hotol.

In order to protect the vehicle from meteors and space debris, Hermes was redesigned with a triple skin on its underside and a double skin on its upper forward section. In addition, a full-scale mock-up of the flight deck was constructed and installed in a Caravelle aircraft for zero gravity testing.

EuroHermespace's 130 staff finally moved into their new offices in Colomiers, near Toulouse in the south of France, on January 23, 1992. Having already spent $241m in 1991, the company was committed to spending $376m for 1992. However, it would only receive $246m during the year. In the meantime, work had been taking place on a project dubbed Hermes X-2000, which essentially removed the only worthwhile aspect of the system—its crew—and made it a fully automated uncrewed vehicle. It would weigh 16-18t, which at least put it within Ariane 5's launch capability.

Hermes X-2000 continued on into 1992 and by June its

cost was estimated at $3.9bn, which was a great deal less than the crewed variant but still incredibly expensive for an uncrewed demonstrator. Also in June 1992, German Research and Technology Minister Heinz Riesenhuber, perhaps to no-one's surprise, announced that Germany would be unable to make a financial commitment to Hermes for at least ten years.

The engineering team continued to produce a bewildering array of new potential configurations for the crewed Hermes throughout this period and a full-scale test piece Hermes carbon-carbon nose cone was delivered to Dassault by Aérospatiale on July 9, 1992. It did not, of course, reflect whatever the final shape was going to end up as.

However, six days earlier, on July 3, 1992, it had already been agreed between French Minister of Research and Space Hubert Curien and Riesenhuber that the Hermes programme would be scrapped. The decision was formally approved at an ESA Council meeting on September 8, 1992—finally ending the project that prompted the genesis of Hotol.

NASP

Prior to Frank Miles' August 23, 1984, ITN News at Ten briefing on Hotol, the Americans had already quietly begun work on their own horizontal take-off and landing SSTO under a classified programme codenamed Copper Canyon. Initiated by the Defense Advanced Research Projects Agency (DARPA), this secretive study had a more militaristic character than that of Hotol.

In a speech to the AIAA Second International Aero-Space Planes Conference in Orlando, Florida, during late October 1990, Bruce Abell described attending a Copper Canyon briefing given to President Reagan's science advisor George 'Jay' Keyworth II. He said: "Imagine our shock, and delight, in [April] 1984 to have someone walk in and describe a programme that could offer a flexible, lower-cost alternative for space access ... it was NASP's potential for space access, far and away above any other possible uses, that prompted our strong support for creating a highly visible national programme".

All concerned must have been even more shocked and not necessarily delighted to discover some months later that the British were, coincidentally, already working on an apparently similar system. It was clearly a hot enough topic to be debated by Congress on July 24, 1985 (see Chapter 2). Defense Secretary Caspar Weinberger then gave the formal go-ahead for the project in December 1985 and Reagan himself announced it to the public in his 'new Orient Express' speech on February 4, 1986.

It seems entirely possible, however, that the 'new Orient Express' line was public relations fluff. After all, Reagan's pet project, the Strategic Defense Initiative (SDI) aka 'Star Wars' programme—putting numerous small missile or laser-armed satellites into orbit for anti-Soviet ICBM operations—required a cheap launch system capable of making lots of flights within a short time period. There were other potential military use cases too, such as reconnaissance-strike.

Whatever its ultimate purpose, the American SSTO vehicle was intended to use a combined ramjet/scramjet airbreathing propulsion system for much of the journey between take-off and orbit—with a supplemental propulsion system, most likely pure rockets, for take-off and for the latter high-Mach part of the trip. When under ramjet/scramjet power, it would use liquid or slush hydrogen as its fuel and air as the oxidiser.

Copper Canyon was now regarded as having been 'Phase 1' of the new National Aero-Space Plane programme—NASP. Phase 2 was where the real project began—the design of the X-30, a technology demonstrator for the concept. Seven contracts were awarded to the American aviation industry on April 7, 1986: a pair worth $175m each to General Electric/Aerojet TechSystems and Pratt & Whitney for the engines and five worth $32m each to Boeing, General Dynamics, Lockheed, McDonnell Douglas and Rockwell International for the airframe. Rocketdyne later joined the engine side using its own money to buy in.

Between them, the airframe companies produced a wide variety of different aerodynamic concepts which were in some cases presented to the public in the form of colourful fully-painted artworks and photographs of models.

General Electric was eliminated on September 15, 1987. Meanwhile, the airframe manufacturers turned in their conceptual projects, complete with estimated weights, and the two companies with the heaviest estimates, Lockheed and Boeing, were dropped from the programme on October 20, 1987.

This left a total of five 'prime contractors' progressing on to the next part of Phase 2: Pratt & Whitney and Rocketdyne on propulsion and General Dynamics, McDonnell Douglas and Rockwell International on the airframe side. This rather unlikely quintet would remain involved until the end of the programme. The US Government's NASP budget for the 1988 fiscal year was $254m, rising to $316m for 1989. Between them, the contractors also chipped in around $700m of their own money.

Reagan then left office in 1989 and his successor, President George H. W. Bush, commenced a programme of

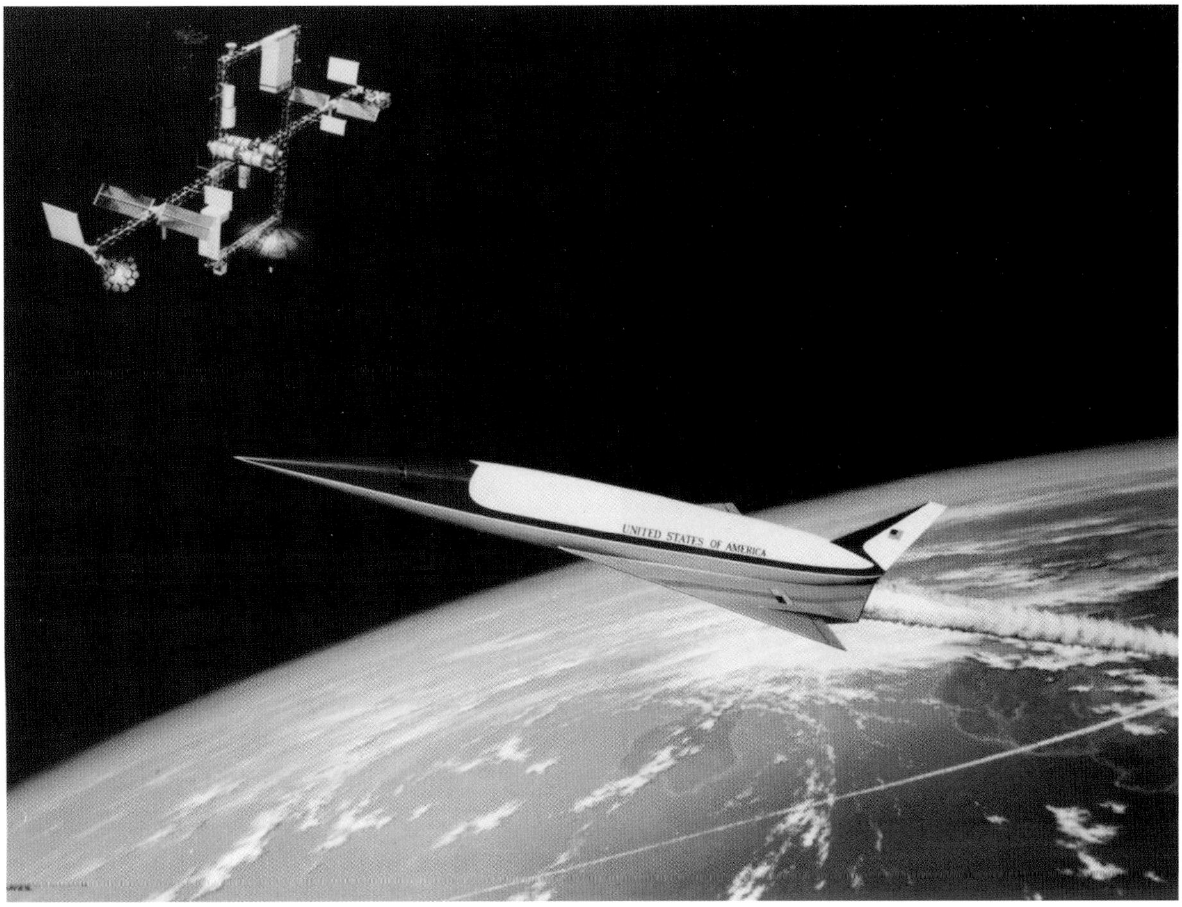

NASA baseline design for NASP, from 1985. NASA

Unattributed NASP design circa 1986. NASA

General Dynamics NASP design concept. NASA

defence spending cuts. The SDI programme was re-aligned and downgraded as the perceived threat from a fragmenting and disintegrating Soviet Union diminished. Within a relatively short time, the Department of Defense lost its likely major reason for wanting NASP.

The project continued nonetheless and in October 1990 it was announced that a single design configuration for the X-30 had been chosen—described in an *Aviation Week & Space Technology* article on the subject, published on October 29, 1990, as a "directionally stable lifting body that incorporates short wings, dual stabilizers, and a two-man, dorsal crew compartment. Propulsion for the vehicle is expected to be provided by three to five scramjet engines and by a single 50,000-70,000lb-thrust rocket integrated into the airframe.

"The SSTO X-30 aircraft, which will take off and make powered landings like a conventional airplane, is expected to be 150-200ft [45.72-60.96m] long and have a take-off gross weight of about 250,000-300,000lb [113.4-136 tonnes]. The two-man crew will sit side-by-side in a small 'blister' located just aft of the hypersonic vehicle's nose".

Evidently, up to May 1990, "only the government's Joint Program Office, headed by USAF civilian scientist Robert Barthelemy, had access to each contractor's data.

McDonnell Douglas NASP design concept. NASA

Rockwell International NASP design concept. NASA

Concept art showing the unified X-30 NASP configuration. NASA

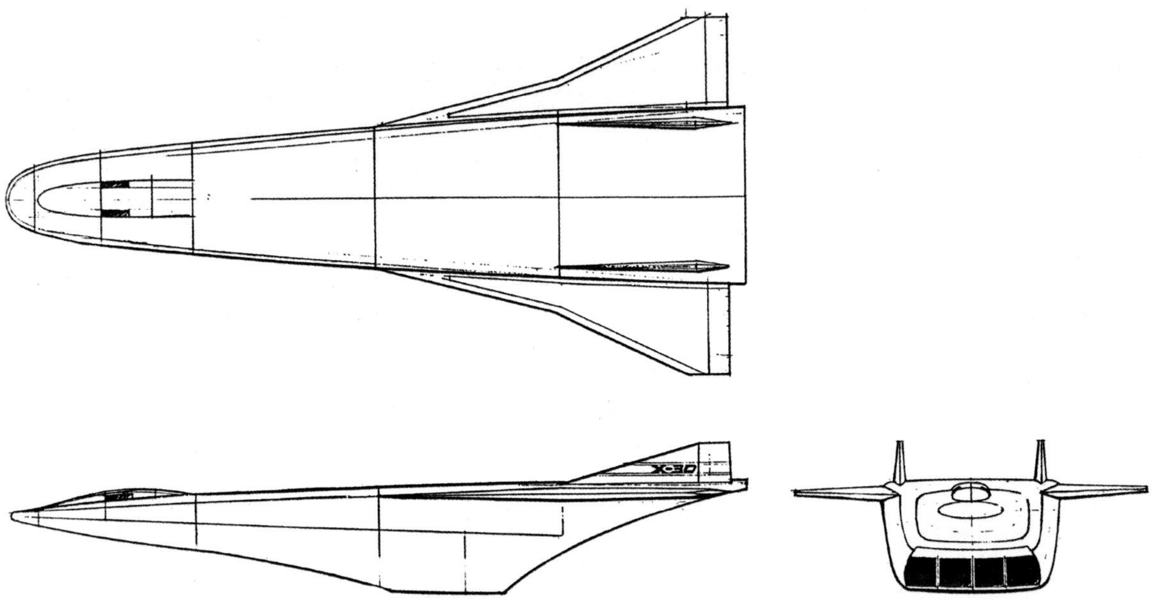

X-30 NASP general arrangement circa October 1990. NASA

After the teaming arrangement was approved, however, the contractors were allowed to share data and to examine the existing designs. Much of this mutual technology exploration work was performed in June and July of this year".

In other words, throughout the four years between the contracts being awarded in April 1986 and the point at which the contractors were 'teamed up' in May 1990, NASP had existed as five, and then three, entirely separate lines of airframe development. All the vast sums of money spent had been divided up between the competing teams for their separate efforts, rather than being put towards a common goal. The *AW&ST* article went on: "Following this work, [Rockwell corporate vice-president Barry J. Waldman said] 'we set up an ad hoc engineering staff and used teams consisting of members from the five contractors to make technology comparisons. We looked at the original six designs [five from the contractors and a 'baseline' design drawn up by NASA in 1985] then we laid out some new candidate designs that embodied features from all the old designs. Much of the groundwork for developing these new designs was provided by the government. The government had performed extensive evaluations of the old designs and was able to brief the contractor team on the strengths and weaknesses of each one. This allowed the team to capture the strengths of the previous designs when the new ones were developed'."

During this process, two fundamentally different layouts had emerged: lifting body versus winged aircraft. On balance, the former was preferred "because of the propulsion advantages it provided". Waldman had explained that "at high speeds, the only way to compress air for the propulsion system is by using the forebody of the vehicle. And, the aft body of the aircraft needs to be used as an expansion nozzle for the engines. The wider the body, the more air you can compress and feed into the engines. So, even though the wide body may add some drag, it also helps provide the aircraft with greater thrust".

Evidently, "with all that lift available, we found we didn't need much of a wing. The main purpose of the wing now seems to be to provide control surfaces". It had been determined that two smaller tailfins provided better directional stability than one large one.

As far as the propulsion system was concerned, *AW&ST* said the designs of Pratt & Whitney and Rocketdyne would be combined, though the process of actually doing that had barely begun. The airframe-integrated rocket would basically be used to cover all the areas of the flight regime that the scramjets couldn't.

The five prime contractors on NASP, now bound by the 'teaming agreement' of May 1990 into a National Contractor Team, were to be equal partners—albeit led by Waldman. He told the magazine: "By equally dividing the contract fee, all the contractors will recognise that the only way to earn any money is to do what's best for the programme. No single company can earn very much if everyone isn't earning the same. The only way a company can succeed is if the whole team does". It was agreed that McDonnell Douglas would handle fuselage development, vehicle thermal controls, aerodynamic stability and control. General Dynamics would concentrate on integration of airframe subassemblies and integration of the airframe and engines. Rockwell's North American

Aircraft division would develop the vehicle management system and subsystems. Pratt & Whitney would look at engine flow path integration and controls while Rocketdyne would lead on engine systems integration, propulsion structures and materials.

Naturally, the whole thing was being backed by NASA plus an enormous supporting cast of expert consultants, research organisations and smaller companies specialising in space technology.

But the wind had shifted. SDI, which had already been putting a great deal of work into finding an alternative to NASP as its launch system, such as Delta Clipper, was being wound down and its remains transmuted into other projects.

It had initially been hoped that the X-30 would be about the same size as a Lockheed SR-71 Blackbird but after two further years of work, in 1992, the X-30 had a gross weight of 400,000lb and the engineers were still struggling to get it to the point where it would be able to achieve orbital velocity. The projected programme cost was creeping towards $15bn and it was thought that even if its engineering difficulties were conclusively overcome, the X-30 would not be ready to fly for another eight to ten years.

As noted in Chapter 11, NASP eventually died a slow death with *Flight International* reporting on July 13, 1993, that "work on the X-30 has stopped for the time being, its goal 'unobtainable'".

SÄNGER 1986

MBB's Sänger II, or simply 'Sänger', was Germany's two-stage-to-orbit system consisting of a very large hypersonic first stage with a smaller orbiter carried on, and launched from, its back. It was named after a German TSTO project of 1967 which itself was named after Austrian spaceplane pioneer Eugen Sänger, who had died in 1964 aged just 59.

The precise origins of the Sänger II system itself, however, are slightly unclear. In 1994, MBB hypersonic technology programme manager Heribert Kuczera told Russell J. Hannigan: "The British came up with Hotol and submitted this proposal to ESA. We knew a little about this concept—maybe not everything—but at this time our Ministry said 'what is your reply, what is your suggestion?' We said we would think about it. So we did some work over a weekend and on Monday we sat together, discussed our ideas, and then we made a few pictures and we gave it to our Ministry and they said, 'okay, we have your ideas—fine'.

"We did not make a proposal, but just a brochure with a few pictures and just a few comments on it. We were saying it shouldn't be a single stage, it should be a two-stage-to-orbit. We were surprised that they took this brochure, a few pages, and submitted it to ESA and said 'that's the German proposal'. We didn't know this. I have only heard that Dr J-B [Jan-Baldem] Mennicken [the German Bundesministerium für Forschung und Technologie (BMFT) or Ministry of Research and Technology's Director General for Aerospace and Transportation Technology, among other things] was happy to have a very beautiful colour brochure and I think it was, maybe, his first visit to ESA HQ. He turned up and said 'here is our proposal'."

It was MBB's Space Group under Ernst Högenauer that had been given the job and specifically Dietrich E. Koelle at MBB Ottobrunn who was tasked with leading the team that would develop the company's Hotol-competitor spaceplane. The colour brochure referenced by Kuczera is undated and extremely thin on content, beginning: "In order to continue its space exploration and growing utilisation activities in space Europe needs a cost-effective Space Transport System which reduces the space transportation cost to some 10% of the present high values, which allows low Earth orbits to be reached from European airports.

"The answer to the European needs in global and orbital passenger transport as well as small cargo transport into orbit is Sänger II. Sänger is a two-stage winged space transportation system for crew transfer, supply and serving functions, complementing a ballistic unmanned launcher for larger payloads. The first stage is a derivative or forerunner of a future hypersonic global transport plane, carrying the second stage—a rocket plane—to its separation speed of Mach 6 at some 35km altitude. The second stage uses lightweight high-performance rocket engines, thus avoiding the development of new combinations of airbreathing rocket engines.

"For launch and landing conventional airport facilities are foreseen without any special launch assist installations. The first stage [unnamed in the text but referred to as the EHTV—later revealed to stand for European Hypersonic Transport Vehicle—in one of the illustrations] should have as much as possible design commonality with a global hypersonic transport plane in order to reduce development cost. The second stage design concept has been studied by MBB under the designation Horus [Hypersonic Orbital Research and Utilisation System] since 1984. The total launch mass is less than 500 tons (Boeing 747 class). The payload mass and volume is designed for convenient transport of up to 12 people and a small payload to the LEO space station.

The cover of MBB's initial proposal brochure for Sänger II from 1986. AIRBUS

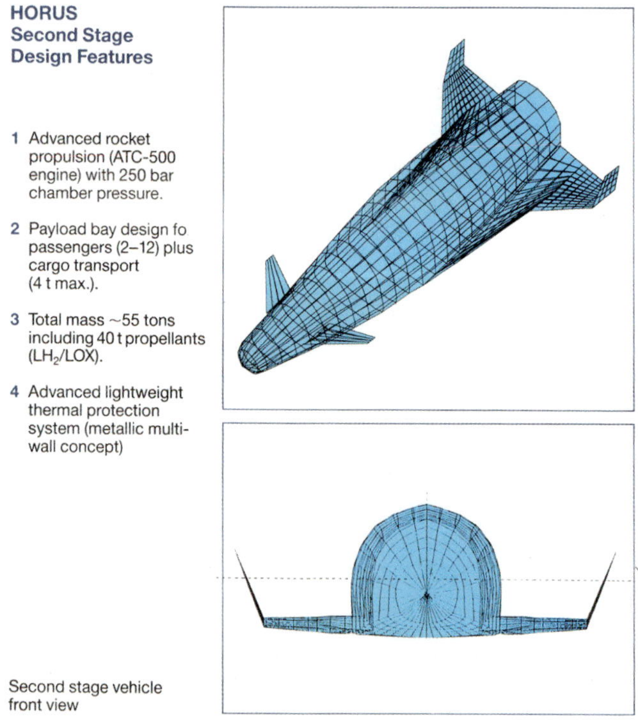

Full page from the brochure showing the second stage, Horus, looking rather different from how it appears on the cover. AIRBUS

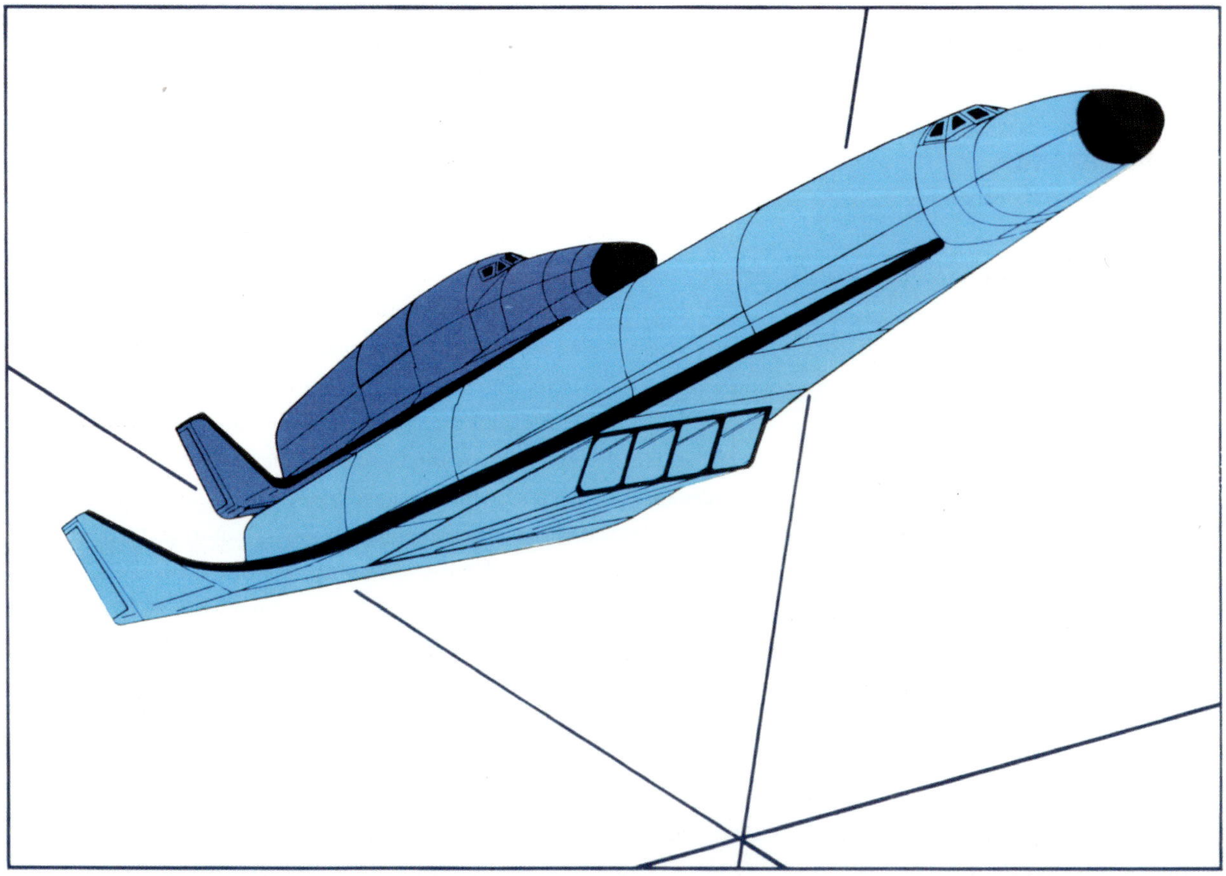

Illustration from the Sänger II brochure showing the air intakes of the first stage vehicle. AIRBUS

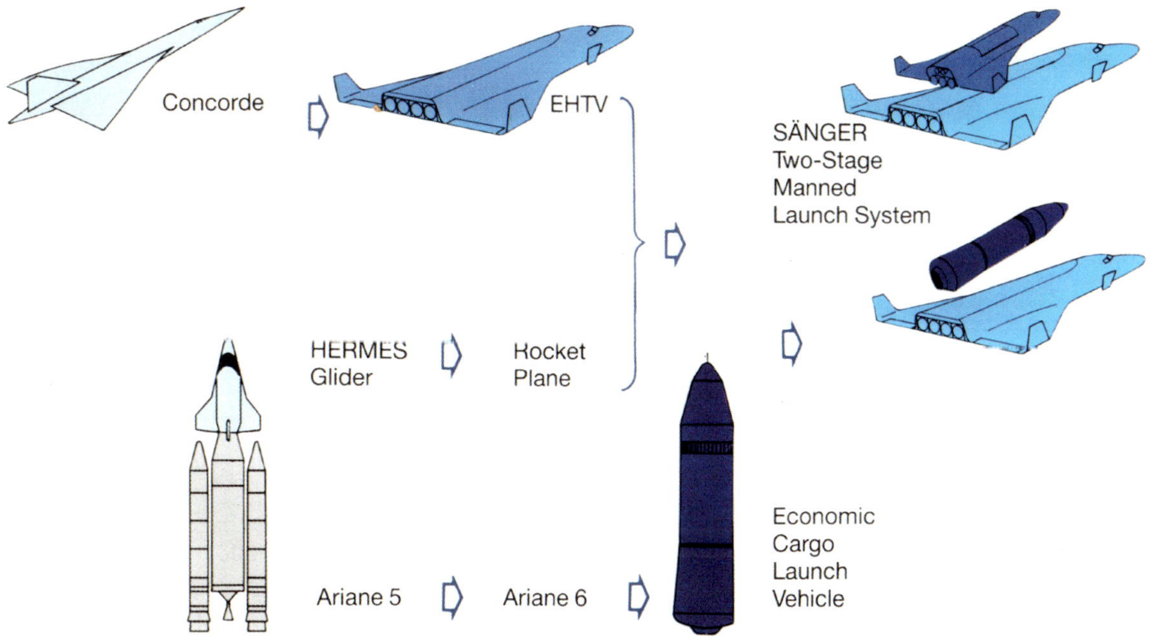

Artwork from the 1986 brochure showing a rather stilted progression from Concorde and Ariane 5/Hermes to the Sänger II system. This also appears to be the earliest mention of 'EHTV' as the name of the hypersonic first stage. AIRBUS

"Two-stage Sänger transport system allows maximum operational flexibility—the only system to allow launches from European airports into all orbit planes."

In their book, Deutsche Raketenflugzeuge und Raumtransporter-Projekte, Dietrich Koelle, Peter Sacher and Herbert Grallert stated that Horus's "configuration and … name come from an MBB proposal from 1985 for an unmanned winged upper stage for Ariane 5 with a total mass of 54t, which finally became the upper stage for Sänger II with a total mass of 96t in 1987/88".

Whether Horus had originated as a massively overweight uncrewed Hermes analogue in 1984 or 1985, the TSTO was revealed to the world in September 1986—appearing in the September 20 issue of *Flight International*. Högenauer himself penned an article on Sänger for the German December 1986 edition of *Fusion* magazine. He wrote: "In 1984, Messerschmitt-Bölkow-Blohm … began work—on its own initiative and with its own funds—on winged and reusable spacecraft. These investigations led to a German space transport concept that was presented to the ESA board at the beginning of 1986 … the first stage, the basis for the new space transporter, is a hypersonic aircraft equipped with six airbreathing engines … the required turbojet engines, of course, do not as yet exist, but can be developed as an extension of existing technologies … [the engine, known as the TRA-400] runs on liquid hydrogen as fuel and uses atmospheric air as the oxidiser. The weight of one motor is three tons; with the help of the turbine and an effective intake area of 2.5sqm, 200kg of air per second can be sucked in.

"In supersonic flight, the adiabatically compressed air will, of course, reach a high entry temperature. It must therefore flow through an entry cooler, thus increasing the efficiency of combustion. The volumes of ambient air from which the engine obtains the necessary flow-through of 200kg per second varies, of course, with altitude. Close to the ground, it is 150 cubic metres; at an altitude of 15km, however, it is 1,000 cubic metres. Under these conditions, attaining uniform combustion, and thus uniform thrust, presents a tremendous technological challenge."

In outlining the project, Högenauer did not shy away from the Mach 5+ airliner concept which had been floated in connection with both Hotol and NASP: "Sänger's first stage will also form the technological basis for a future European hypersonic passenger aircraft. There are therefore technological similarities with the 'Orient Express', a hypersonic passenger plane planned by the United States to which President Reagan ascribed so much importance in his speech before Congress.

"The development of Sänger therefore embraces two projects: a fundamental advantage of having two stages. The technology for a future hypersonic passenger plane is produced as a 'byproduct', so that Sänger not only offers the possibility of securing technological competitiveness of the Federal Republic (and Western Europe) in astronautics, but in aeronautics as well."

He pointed out that Horus, which had a mass of around 60t, was fitted with a regular rocket engine fuelled by liquid hydrogen and oxygen from on board tanks. Another second stage had also been designed, known as Cargus. This would be a fully-automated uncrewed vehicle designed purely for carrying payloads of up to ten tonnes. Indeed its name, rather than being a clever acronym, was straightforwardly derived from the word 'cargo' with the U and S on the end possibly standing for Upper Stage.

Högenauer thought Horus represented "a further development of the US Space Shuttle Orbiter and the space glider Hermes, and is provided with an active drive and return system. Within the fuselage of the vehicle, located beneath the cargo area, is a long tank with liquid hydrogen. Depending on the size of the cargo to be carried, there will be room for between two and ten astronauts. Behind the hydrogen tank and the cargo bay, which accommodates up to two tons, is a spherical tank for liquid oxygen".

Horus, or Cargus, would be brought to an altitude of 30km and a speed of 2km per second. It would then fire its engine, separate from the first stage, and accelerate up to 8km per second on a trajectory ending in LEO. The fuel required for this feat amounted to six tonnes of hydrogen and 30 tonnes of oxygen.

If preparatory work began in 1987, Högenauer wrote, "the operational employment of the space transport system can be expected in 2004-2008". And "with the space transporter depicted here, Europe will, after a development period of 15 years, have available a system that will appear on the market at the right time with the right technology at the right price. This 'timing' will secure Europe's competitive ability against the United States and Japan".

Högenauer also used his article as a platform to cast doubt on the claims being made for Hotol, saying: "Hotol, which is ... viewed by the British as a successor of Hermes, is quite otherwise. Of course, there are many experts who hold the opinion that the very optimistic claims about Hotol cannot yet be realised. Thus, the value of 7:200 for the payload/launch mass that is specified stands in clear contradiction to American investigations of one- and two-stage space transporters. According to these investigations, a one-stage transporter must, for a payload of seven tons, have 800 tons (and not 200 tons, as assumed for Hotol) at launch. Also, the developmental risk with futuristic combination engines, which many conceivable drive types involve, can hardly be estimated at present.

"Therefore, Hotol may rather be the basis for a space transporter of the fourth generation. It is thus not to be considered an alternative to Sänger but rather a successor, if we consider an extrapolation of the technological development."

SÄNGER 1987

The BMFT funded a comprehensive concept study of Sänger in 1987. Koelle and Kuczera then presented a paper on the system in Brighton at the 38th Congress of the International Astronautical Federation in October 1987—the same event during which Kenneth Clarke made his famous 'hugely expensive club' remarks (see Chapter 7).

Both Horus and Cargus were now better defined, with the latter being a relatively simple expendable ballistic stage capable of launching payloads of up to 15t into LEO. Some vital statistics were also given for the EHTV, which looked far sleeker than it had before. It would be 92m long with a wingspan of 46m, a wing area of 880sqm and a fuel tank volume of 2,500 cubic metres. Propulsion was by six 400kN turboramjets using liquid hydrogen. Vehicle net mass was 112t with a propellant mass of 150t. Payload mass, the upper stage, was 66-91t—with 91t being the maximum mass for a fully-loaded Horus. Take-off mass was therefore 300-350t.

In order to launch Horus, the EHTV would need to be capable of a Mach 4 cruise plus a dash up to Mach 7 prior to separation. In this mode, range was 5,000km. The authors noted that "stage separation is a specific problem of the two-stage launcher, especially at Mach 7 at 31km altitude. However, calculations have shown positive aerodynamic forces for a separation of the upper stage under its own power".

Early on, the paper still notes that "a major design driver and requirement for the first stage design was the maximum commonality with a hypersonic passenger aircraft. Such an aircraft with a flight range of over 10,000km can transfer some 250 business class passengers within three hours 15 minutes between the major traffic hubs (Frankfurt—Los Angeles—Tokyo) probably for the same seat-km-cost as a Boeing 747, depending mainly on the price of liquid hydrogen in quantity production".

In "passenger plane" form, the EHTV had the same physical dimensions as the launcher variant but with fuel tankage reduced to 1,800 cubic metres. Vehicle net mass was given as "95t + 26t (Cabin, Equipm.)". Propellant mass was 120t and the payload, 250 passengers plus cargo, was 35-40t for a total take-off mass of 270-280t. There would still be six engines but at a reduced standard of 350kN. Cruising speed was Mach 4.5 with no hypersonic dash and flight range was 10,360km.

Operational lifetime was the same for both launcher and passenger aircraft variants: 15 years.

Two missions were defined for Sänger: Sänger with Horus for crewed space operations and space station

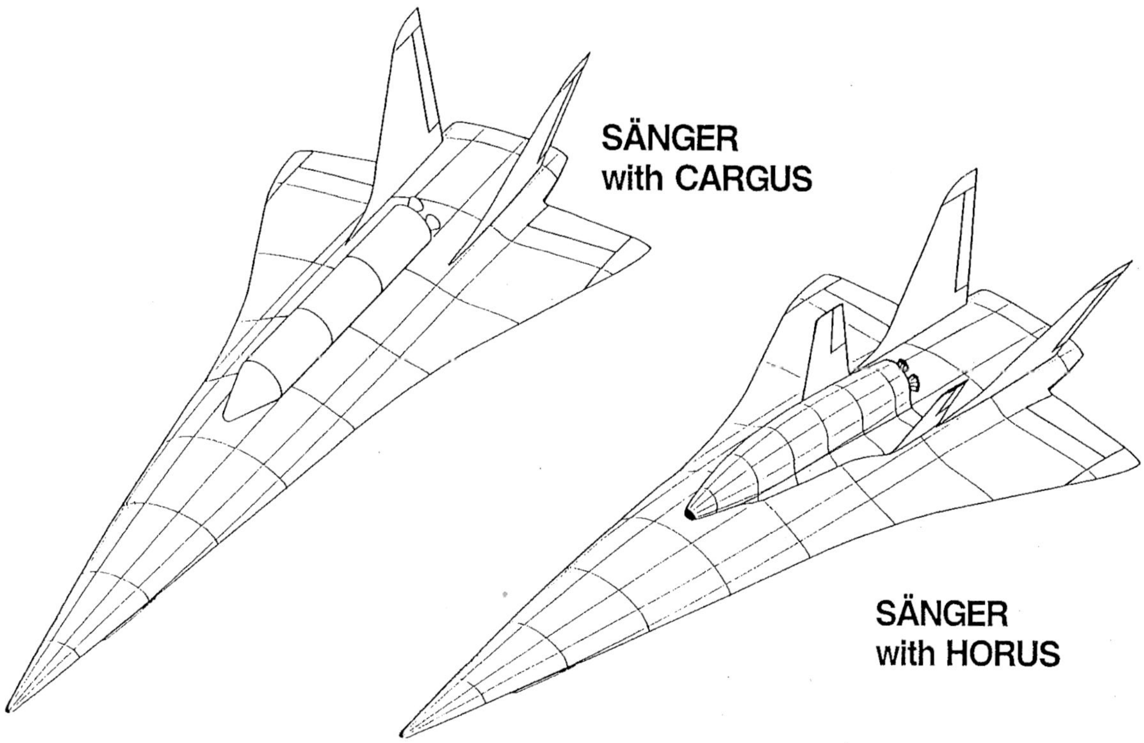

Comparison of the Sänger EHTV with Cargus and with Horus, from 1987. AIRBUS

support or Sänger with Cargus "for all heavy payload launch operations into LEO, polar orbits, GEO and lunar/planetary missions". For the crewed operations, there would be room in Horus for two pilots and four passengers plus 2-3t of cargo. Alternatively, "for a potential later space tourism, the cabin can accommodate 36 passengers for an orbital flight of some hours (300km orbit, 60-degree inclination for maximum area coverage)". The vehicle would be configured to spend a maximum of one day in orbit before returning and the cost per launch had been calculated at $18m assuming 12 launches per year—or $12.3m per launch if 30 launches per year could be managed.

Horus would be powered by a pair of MBB-designed rocket engines "based on the high-pressure technology pioneered by MBB. The engine size is comparable to the HM60 Vulcain and the SSME … This is, however, only due to the large expansion ratio of 300 which is feasible for a second stage application".

Cargus "can be a shortened version of Ariane 5 core stage H.155, modified for attachment to the EHTV first stage … this stage uses the HM60 engine which—in spite of its relatively low performance—is a cost-effective solution for this expendable vehicle".

Cargus launch costs would be significantly greater than those for Horus, due to its expendable nature: $40m per launch for a 12-launch year or $37m-a-go for 30 launches in a year.

LART 1987

As an alternative to Sänger, the DASA-ERNO Orbital Systems and Launcher Division in Bremen had a team led by engineer Johann Spies working on another spaceplane project in parallel at this point: LART (LuftAtmender RaumTransporter or Airbreathing Space Vehicle). An SSTO horizontal take-off and landing vehicle, LART included an airbreathing rocket engine somewhat similar in concept to the RB.545 and described in a brochure dated May 1987.

It would not be going too far to suggest that LART was the German attempt to create a Hotol analogue. The brochure began by setting out the essential requirements underpinning the system—it had to be simple, reusable and capable of crewed or alternatively fully automated operations. Turnaround time needed to be short and inherent reliability was deemed essential.

It had to be "as environmentally friendly as possible" and it was proposed that a pure rocket-powered test vehicle could be flown by 1995, with the fully developed vehicle being operationally available from 2005 for a lifetime of 200 flights over the course of a decade. The automated version would be LART A and the crewed version would be LART B—with the former's maximum payload being a whopping 14t in a cylindrical 4.5m x 15m bay.

The vehicle would need to be able to return and land whether empty or fully loaded, would "be able to survive mission abort at any time through a safe [powered]

Artwork from the cover of the LART brochure. VIA MARTIN BAYER

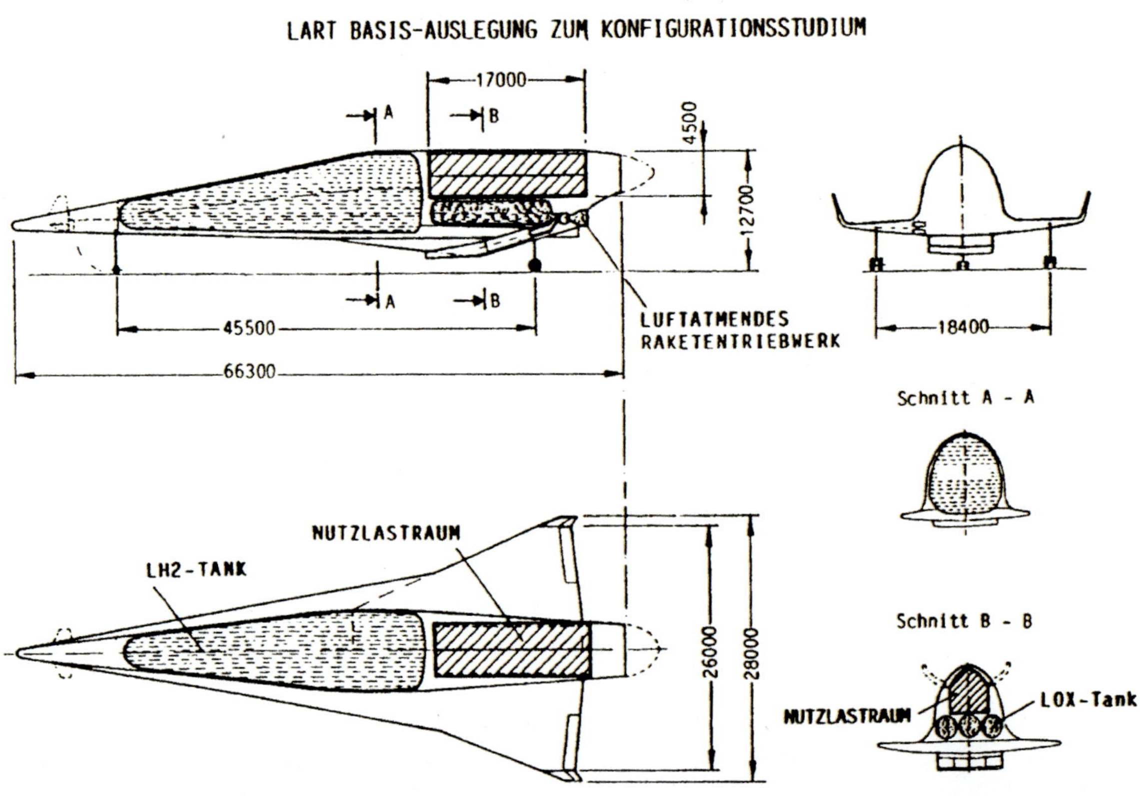

General arrangement of LART—LuftAtmender RaumTransporter—the 'German Hotol'. VIA MARTIN BAYER

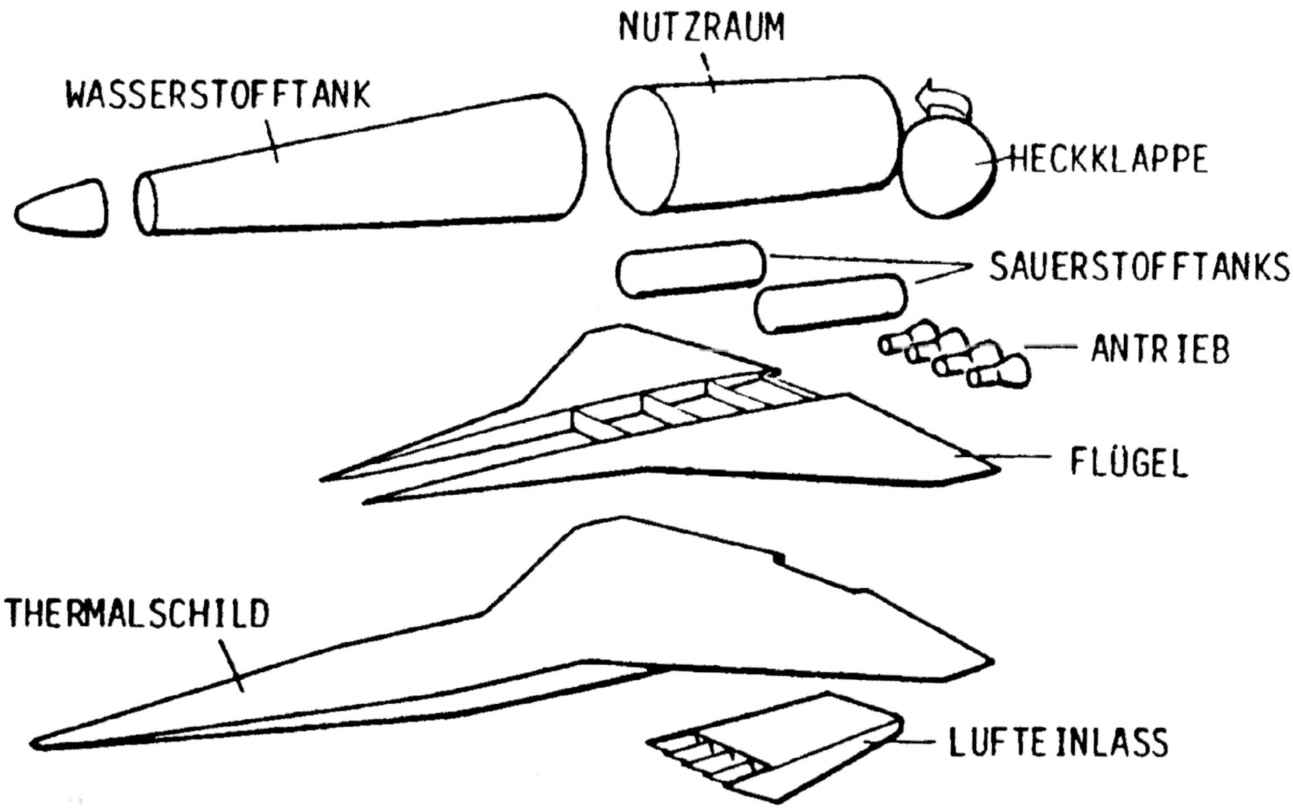

Diagram showing LART's major components in a style very reminiscent of the first Hotol brochure. VIA MARTIN BAYER

landing" and "be capable of ferry flights without take-off aids when empty".

In the version depicted in the brochure, LART would be 66.3m long with a 28m wingspan. Its forward fuselage would contain the liquid hydrogen tank, with the payload bay behind it. Here the figures indicated on the drawing differed from those in the text, showing a 17m long bay. Three cylindrical liquid oxygen tanks would be positioned below that with four rocket nozzles immediately behind them. Like Hotol, LART was to have a large ventral intake.

Empty mass would be 46.5t and 261.3t of fuel would be carried in the main tanks plus another 4.2t of fuel for orbital manoeuvring. With the addition of the 14t payload, take-off weight was 326t.

The actual take-off procedure would involve LART being mounted on a trolley before being accelerated down a 3,800m mag-lev track—a system that would later be entirely ruled out as an option for Hotol on the grounds of sheer cost.

LART's engine was a rather ill-defined "propulsion concept" known as LARA (LuftAtmender RaketenAntrieb or Airbreathing Rocket Propulsion). This would have three operating modes: pure airbreathing operation, mixed operation and pure rocket operation. The first was basically, albeit vaguely, similar to the way the RB.545 operated; the second involved injecting liquid oxygen into the hot ram air flow and increasing the compressor flowthrough, and the third was again the same as the RB.545 in rocket mode. The transition point was Mach 6 at 28km altitude.

The brochure suggested that LART could cover a wide range of orbital altitudes, taking payloads into LEO and/or retrieving them for a return trip back down to Earth as required. It could also linger in LEO to wait for and recover stages from GEO.

A whole host of bullet-pointed "socio-political" arguments were said to stand in LART's favour, including: "General technology boost and 'spin-offs'; catching up on American technology advance; new transport options; more commercialisation and less taxpayer burden by reducing transport costs; environmentally friendly propulsion; jobs in the aerospace industry; international cooperation; aerospace industry cooperation; improved negotiation position in the space station scenario; European taking of the initiative; gaining political prestige; raising national awareness; 'Made in Europe'—reputation on the global market".

As far as those 'spin-offs' were concerned, potential wider applications for LART technologies were said to include "advanced atmospheric flights, manoeuvrable re-entry devices, transatmospheric vehicles, military 'aerospace' vehicles and 'aero-assisted orbital transfer vehicles".

The overall development cost was expected to be around

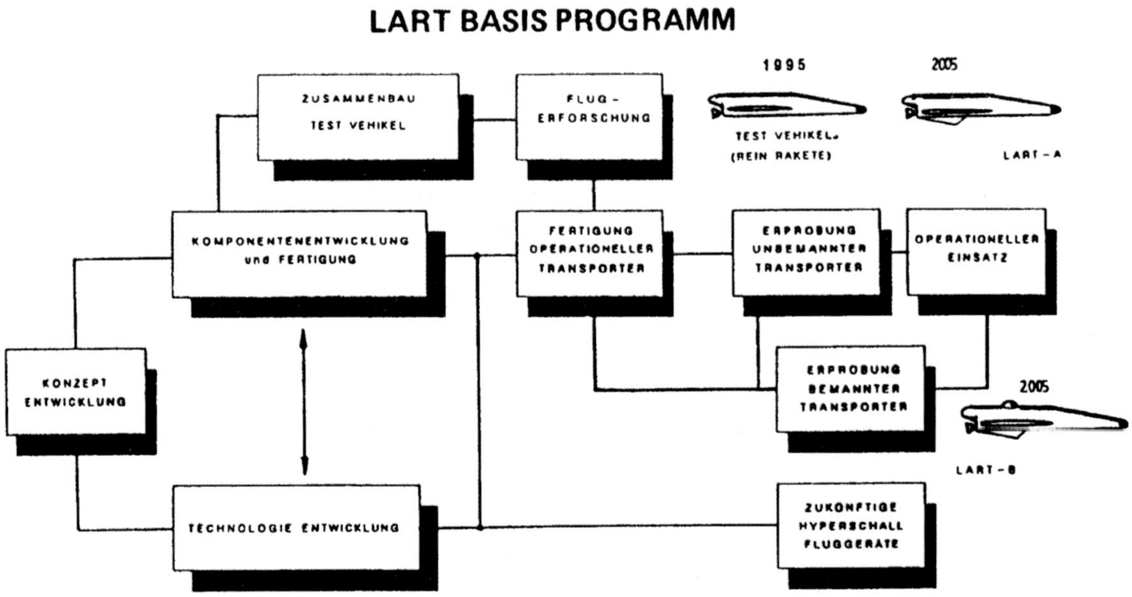

Proposed LART programme show the automated LART A and the crewed version, LART B. VIA MARTIN BAYER

Concept art showing a variant of LART with overwing side intakes. AIRBUS

$9.2bn, with the cost of each individual LART vehicle being $492m.

Kuczera told Russell J. Hannigan in 1994: "We had a working group led by the BMFT discussing potential concepts, [including] Sänger and LART, and the final result was that Sänger was selected as the reference concept. It was a vote of many experts that the Sänger concept was the most convincing concept. There were some activities [on LART] for a short period of time, and then everything was dead, because the weight was given to Sänger."

SÄNGER 1988

By the time of Koelle and Kuczera's next update to the Congress of the International Astronautical Federation, the 39th held at Bangalore, India, in October 1988, the BMFT had launched the German National Hypersonics

Technology Program. Running from 1988 to 1992, this \$210m five-year "dedicated technology programme comprises selected developments in the area of airbreathing propulsion, hypersonic aerothermodynamics and materials/structures which will be complemented later by activities in the area of flight control and subsystems".

In addition, "in parallel ... a two-and-a-half-year System Definition Study is performed by MBB together with other German companies (Dornier, MAN and Linde). [Also] in parallel, a two-year propulsion system study is performed by MTU Munich together with MBB".

Sänger, which had previously been presented as a real project intended to create real physical Hermes-successor vehicles, was now being referred to as "the reference vehicle concept" for this programme. Nevertheless, the report continued to treat Sänger as a project that could—perhaps would—result in a real vehicle comparable to the X-30 or Hotol.

In some respects, little had changed over the course of the year. Sänger still consisted of the EHTV, Horus and Cargus. The EHTV first stage was still "optimised and configured such that maximum commonality exists with a later hypersonic passenger plane". It had, however, been shrunk. Fuselage length was reduced from 92m to 81m and wingspan was shortened from 46m to 41.4m. This was "made feasible by a reduction of propellant mass from 130t to 100t [the 1987 report had given propellant mass as 150t, rather than 130t]. Otherwise the vehicle net mass has been increased to 149t in order to have a more robust design with mass margin".

This "involved a reduction in flight range from 5,000km (one leg) to 3,700km which is considered still to be sufficient". Separation speed had been reduced from Mach 7 to Mach 6.8 because "the practical limit of ramjet propulsion is considered to be Mach 7". There had been no discussion in the 1987 report concerning choice of materials for the EHTV but the 1988 report described a basic structure made of titanium alloys with leading edges made of silicon carbide-silicon carbide.

There would now be only five engines, rather than six, and three options were being considered: "1) turbojet-ramjet engine combination in parallel arrangement with common air inlet and partially shared nozzle configuration; 2) turbojet-ramjet engine in coaxial arrangement with plug nozzle (gas generator or expander cycle); 3) turbofan-ramjet in coaxial arrangement with adjustable and cooled fan blades (windmilling fan, type hyper-crisp)". Evidently the most suitable of the three would be picked in early 1989.

In terms of operational details, the EHTV would cruise

Concept art for the Sänger system circa 1988. AIRBUS

at Mach 0.8 or Mach 4.4, rather than Mach 4, and would have an operational lifetime of 25 years. The airliner variant would cruise at Mach 4.4 but other details, including 10,500km range and 15-year lifespan, remained the same.

When it came to the 1988 Horus, apparently "in the 1987/88 period studies ... concentrated on the propulsion system optimisation, the thermal protection system and the experimental analysis of different tail/wingtip fins at low speed". A complete redesign was "under way in the second part of 1988". The work done to date had resulted in a change from two engines to just one, supplemented by a pair of 40kN orbital manoeuvre engines. Doing this reduced both the initial engine cost and ongoing maintenance costs. As for the thermal side, "an advanced metallic multi-wall TPS is under development at MBB which promises lower specific mass than systems with ceramic tiles".

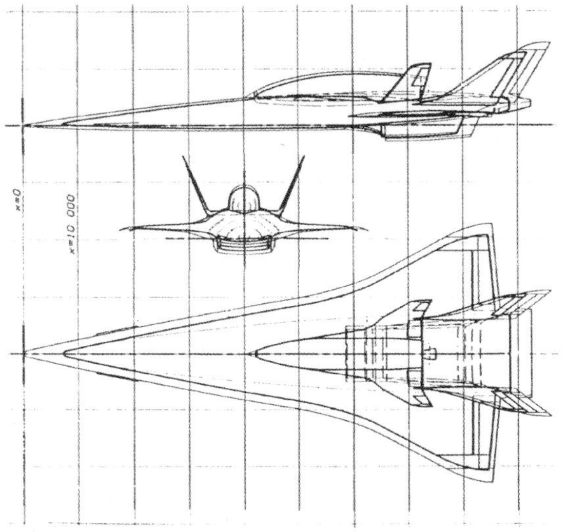

Drawing showing how the EHTV's overall size could be reduced as a result of lowering propellant mass from 130t to 100t. AIRBUS

Little work had evidently been done on the Ariane 5 core stage-based Cargus but "the expendable … stage will be analysed in more detail in 1988/89 at MBB-UO (ERNO) in Bremen".

The authors thought that "the Sänger EHTV and Horus development could begin as an ESA programme in the mid-1990s when the funding demand for Ariane 5 and Hermes is reducing, allowing for the start of the new programme. The time until the mid-1990s is required and will be utilised for technological and organisational preparations. On the other hand, the project start should not be later, since each year delay will cost Europe an additional expense for transportation of more than $1.23bn per year. [The] reason for this is the cost difference between Ariane 5/Hermes and Sänger/Horus/Cargus launch cost".

SÄNGER 1989

The Koelle and Kuczera double act returned for another update at the 40th IAF Congress in Spain in October 1989. They opened their paper by saying that Sänger "has reached by now the status of a matured design concept" and listed six major achievements over the preceding year: a design review by the BMFT in January 1989; CAD redesign of Horus; construction of a 10m Sänger model for exhibition at the Le Bourget Air Show; verification of aerodynamic design data in a series of wind tunnel tests; simulation of the separation procedure; and lastly ascent trajectory/propulsion optimisation.

Furthermore, "a special study has been initiated in 1989 for the task definition and analysis of concept alternatives for a hypersonic flight demonstrator". The essential requirements for this experimental aircraft were the ability to take off and land in Germany, avoidance of any

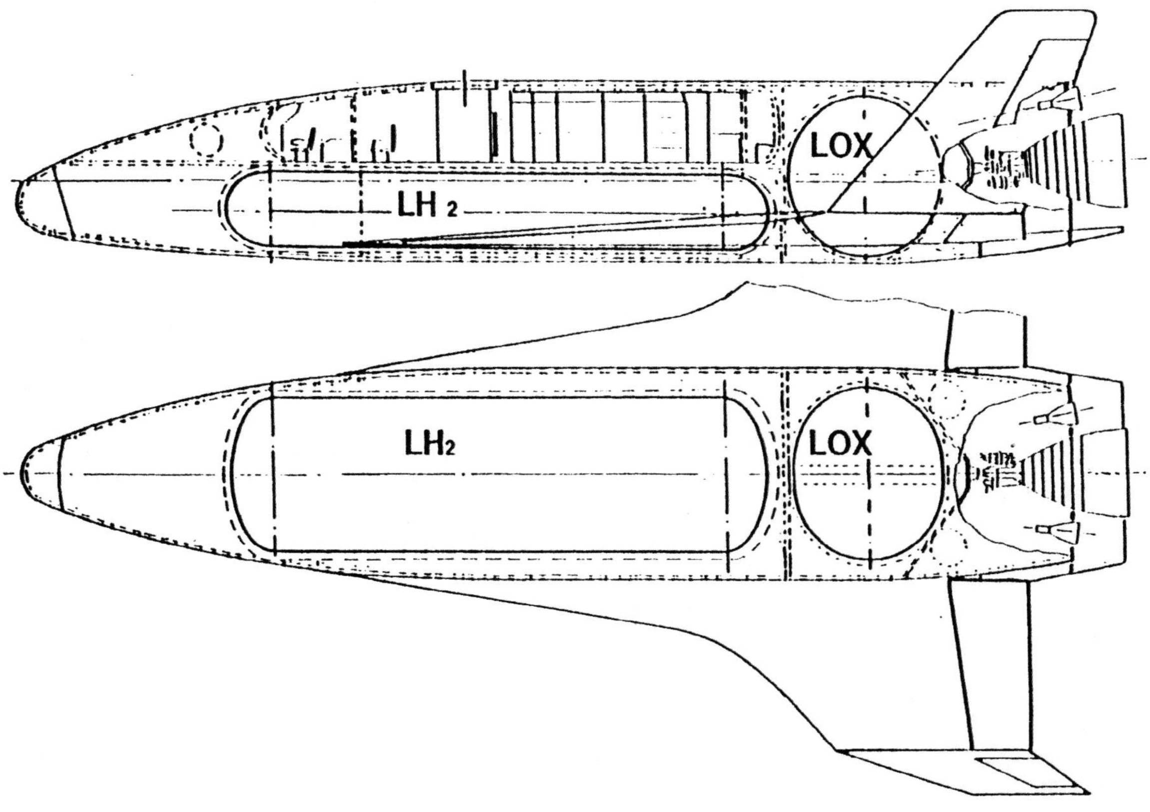

Cargus layout as of 1988. AIRBUS

Concept art showing the Sänger system as it appeared in 1989. AIRBUS

environmental or noise pollution, first flight before the year 2000 and development of technologies relevant to Sänger.

More specifically, it would have to take off and land on a conventional runway and be powered by a turbo-ramjet engine. The switchover from turbojet to ramjet operation would take place between Mach 2.2 and Mach 2.8 and maximum speed would need to be Mach 5.6 for one minute at 25,000m altitude.

By now all mentions of the hypersonic passenger plane and space tourism had been dropped from the report.

Sänger continued to consist of the EHTV, Horus and Cargus but the EHTV's fuel mass had been reduced still further—from 100t to 95t—and its forward fuselage shape had been revised in order to increase precompression at the air inlet. Dornier had been working on a "quasi-cylindrical" or 'bubble' tank concept for the EHTV and the hot areas would now be made from carbon-carbon. The number of engines had increased back to six, though drawings appended to the paper continued to show only five intakes.

As to the engines themselves, the paper reported that the MTU/MBB study had been successful in "reducing the engine configuration options from six to three (integrated turboramjet with and without high-temperature fan and parallel engine arrangement". But given that the original remit of the study had been to reduce the engine configuration options from three to just one, it is unclear whether this could really be regarded as a success.

Evidently the redesigned Horus had now been reduced in size—though dimensions had not previously been given. This new variant, known as Horus 3C, would be 28.3m long, with a wingspan of 15.7m. Dry mass was 21.85t and total mass at stage separation had risen to 96t. The cockpit could accommodate two pilots plus three passengers and nominal gross payload was given as 3.1t. There would be no airlock "since no EVA manoeuvres are expected to be required from Horus".

There had now been some further work on Cargus since it had "increased in size in order to keep the desired LEO payload mass of up to 14t. According to the analyses made by MBB-ERNO Bremen, aerodynamic stabilisers are required for the critical phase of stage separation, increasing the total net mass to some 11.5t, including the payload fairing of 1.5t".

With Sänger consisting of three separate and unique vehicles, the total system development cost by the end of 1989 was estimated at $20bn.

SÄNGER 1990

The 41st IAF Congress in October 1990 saw Koelle and Kuczera giving their latest Sänger update a bit closer to home: in Dresden, Germany. During the preceding year,

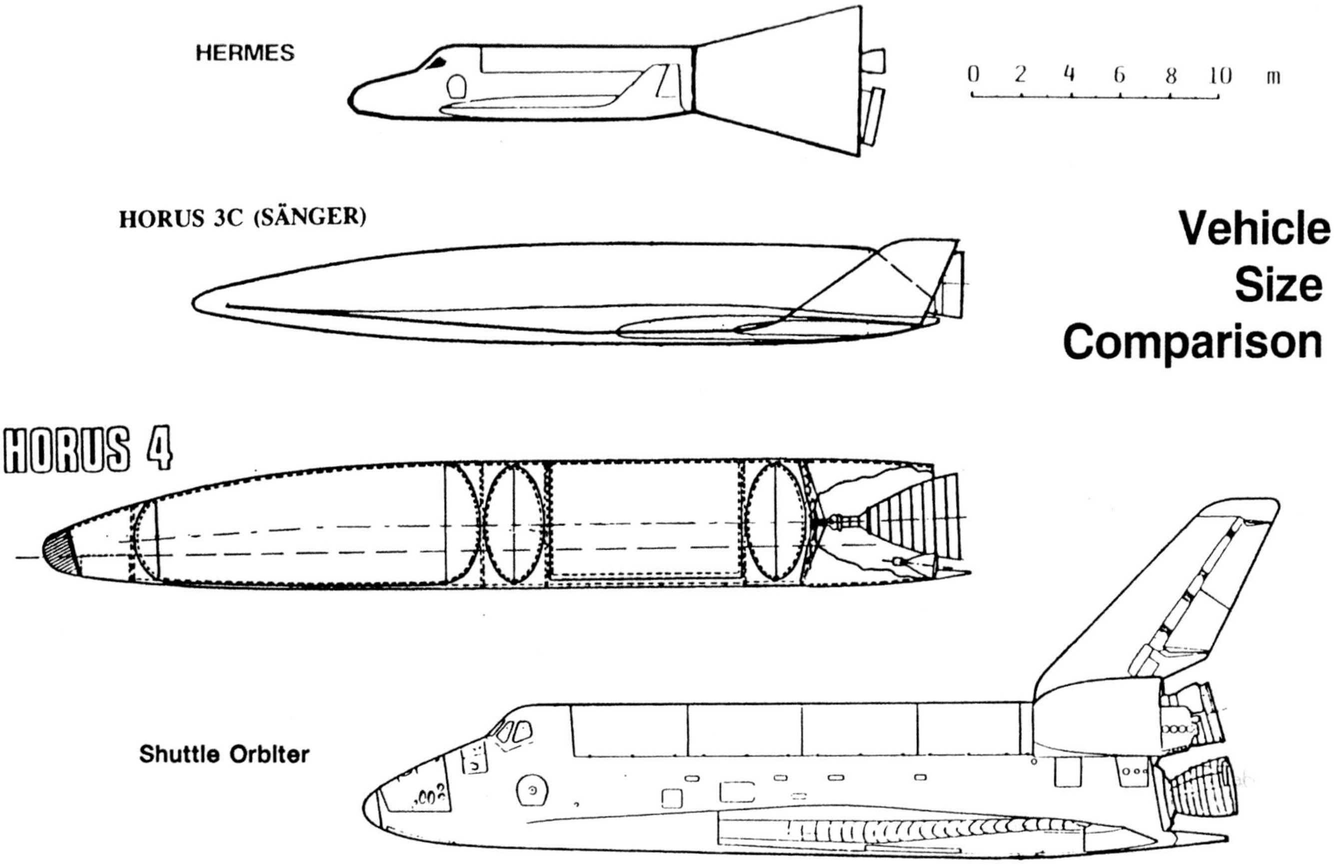

Drawing from the WLC studies, showing a size comparison between Hermes, Horus, Horus 4 (a WLC studies design) and the Space Shuttle. AIRBUS

Cargus had been dropped—replaced with an uncrewed variant of Horus with a capacious cargo bay known as Horus-C (the 'C' standing for Cargo), "mainly for economic reasons" but "the disadvantage of a reduced payload capability is more than balanced by the new payload retrieval capability (up to seven tonnes) which is important for reusable platforms like Eureca [the EUropean REtrievable CArrier—an uncrewed 4.5-tonne satellite which would eventually be launched by Space Shuttle *Atlantis* on July 31, 1992, and retrieved on July 1, 1993, by Space Shuttle *Endeavor*]".

The vehicle for crewed missions was now designated Horus-M ('M' for Manned). Basing both upper stages on essentially the same airframe was expected to massively reduced the overall development cost of the programme. The report noted that "the upper stage total mass has been increased somewhat [to 112t] in order to achieve the desired external commonality of both Horus versions, and to increase the mass margin ... With the new Horus requirements the ascent propellant mass has grown from 68.5t to 80.9t. The resulting tank volume, however, needed only to be increased from 193 to 200 cubic metres, leaving the external [EHTV] vehicle dimensions almost unchanged". This was because the MBB team had cottoned on to the advantages of sub-cooling liquid hydrogen to increase its density—reducing the tank volume requirement.

More thermal studies had been carried out as well as more wind tunnel experiments, further fine-tuning the aerodynamics of both the EHTV and Horus. A detailed financial analysis had also been conducted, concluding that the cost of a single Sänger Horus-M launch was now $24.8m compared to the 1987 figure of $18m, on the basis of 12 flights per year. However, where the expendable Cargus had been costed at $40m per launch, Horus-C was expected to cost just $22.5m per launch.

During 1990, a team consisting of Dornier, MBB and MTU personnel had been formed to come up with proposals for the hypersonic demonstrator aircraft commissioned the year before. They initially focused on an engine arrangement with the turbojet and ramjet combustion chambers running in parallel but with a common intake. The turbojet would be based on the Eurofighter's EJ200 power plant and the overall airframe design was

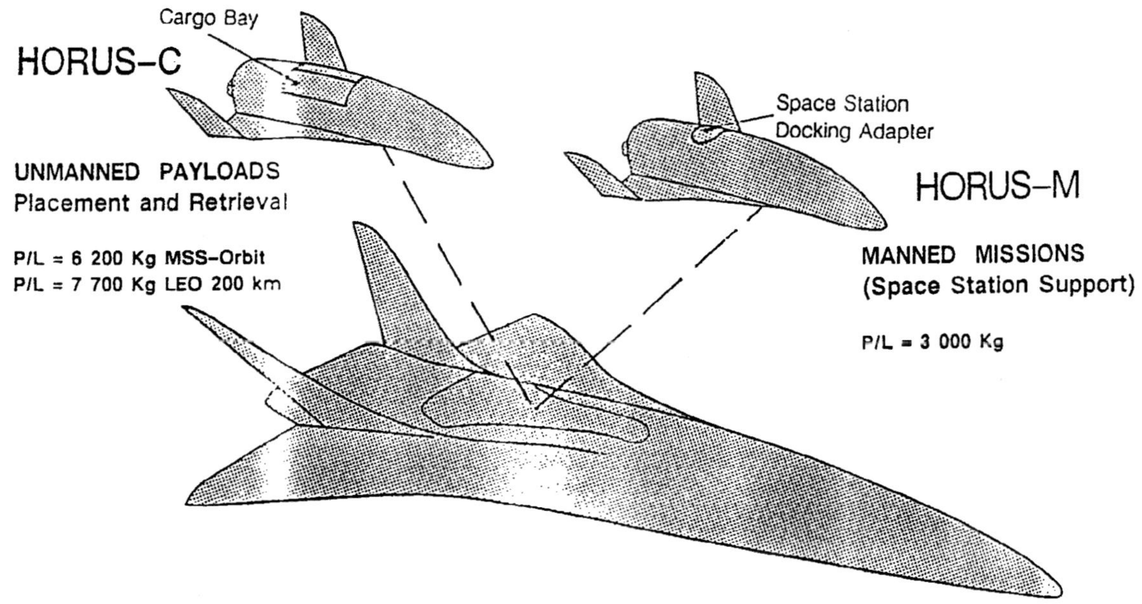

Cargus was dead by 1990, with Sänger's second stage now consisting of either an autonomous Horus-C or crewed Horus-M—the common airframe resulting in significant savings. AIRBUS

derived from an earlier MBB concept known as HYPAC, from HYPersonic AirCraft, which had been designed to reach Mach 5.

SÄNGER 1991-1992

In a report delivered to the AIAA Fourth International Aerospace Planes Conference in Orlando, Florida, on December 1-4, 1992, Kuczera and Helmuth Hauck explained that Phase I of the BMFT's German Hypersonics Technology Programme would last until the end of that year and an extension up to 1995 was planned.

Those three years would be spent "increasing international collaboration as well as supporting the creation of a dedicated ESA technology programme", as opposed to concentrating on the further development of the Sänger system. Indeed, the report went on: "The main goal of this extension phase and a subsequent Phase II is to establish a well-founded technological basis for the next generation of space transportation systems. Of particular importance is the definition of a comprehensive technology verification concept for ground and flight tests including the implementation of an appropriate hypersonic experimental vehicle".

The hypersonic demonstrator aircraft programme begun in 1989 had by now evolved a design known as HYTEX, from HYpersonic Technology EXperiment. The first iteration of this was relatively small, with a take-off weight of 15.9t, and a top speed of Mach 5.6. However, it was clear that this would be insufficient to fully explore the performance expected from Sänger. Therefore, this initial configuration was dubbed HYTEX-5.6 and another design with a take-off weight of 41.6t was devised in 1991 that could go all the way up to Mach 6.8, the appropriately-named HYTEX-6.8.

HYTEX-5.6 was 27m long with a wingspan of 9.05m and a wing area of 69sqm. HYTEX-6.8 was 30.06m long with a wingspan of 12.25m and a wing area of 107sqm.

These details were not presented in the December 1992 report, rather they were outlined in Koelle, Sacher and Grallert's Deutsche Raketenflugzeuge und Raumtransporter-Projekte book. The report instead says that "Sänger is still in its conceptual phase, it is not yet a project. Being a reference concept it is easily and flexibly adaptable to changing requirements. In its role as reference concept for the Hypersonics Technology Programme it acts as focal point for all activities and governs all technology developments".

Despite five years of what, to the casual observer, had very much appeared to be project work, the Sänger team maintained that it had never been more than a concept. However, with Hermes having already died by this point, with Interim Hotol 'completed' and with NASP foundering on the rocks of post-SDI official disinterest, the likelihood of Sänger ever becoming more than whatever it had become up to this point was rapidly diminishing.

Even then, work on Sänger continued at a low level and as part of ESA's FESTIP until the German Hypersonic Programme finally concluded in 1995.

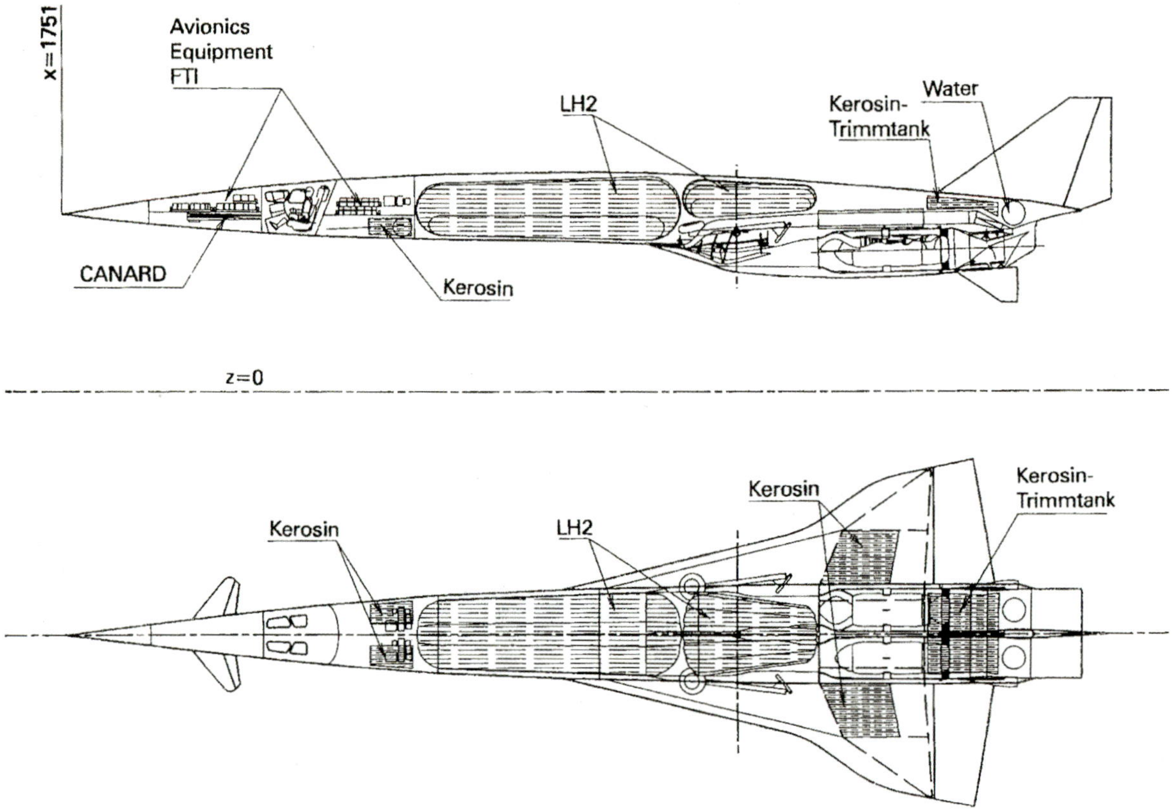

MBB design for the HYTEX experimental hypersonic vehicle from 1991. AIRBUS

SKYLON CONFIGURATION A4 TO B1

RB.545 inventor Alan Bond's association with Hotol ended in 1989. Rolls-Royce had bought the patent rights to RB.545 in 1988 and he had already devised a more viable alternative, known at this point as Satan. With the Hotol team at BAe substantially reduced and with the thoughts of those who remained turning to an air-launched pure rocket variant, Bond decided to take matters into his own hands.

According to the article by Bond and Richard Varvill in *Spaceflight* magazine of May 1993: "Rolls-Royce's acquisition of the Hotol powerplant patents in April 1988 and its official notification to ESA of its intention to withdraw from spaceplane work in January 1989 meant that a hard-won technology lead on the rest of the world was in danger of being lost. It was against this background that Reaction Engines Ltd was formed.

"Reaction Engines Ltd is a propulsion engineering company with the main objective of developing engines for highly economic space transportation. The company was formed in August 1989 [the date of its official incorporation was August 15], and was developed from Alan Bond's consultancy 'Reaction Engines', which played a significant role in determining the design of the Hotol engines. Reaction Engines Ltd has drawn together a small team of propulsion expertise within the UK whose experience ranges from the earliest days of British post-war rocketry including Blue Streak, Black Knight, Black Arrow and the experimental liquid oxygen/hydrogen programme to modern gas turbines and the Hotol studies. Currently the company is engaged in the design of Sabre, a very advanced engine to propel the Skylon spaceplane, which is also a Reaction Engines design."

The Reaction Engines founders, from left, Alan Bond, Richard Varvill and John Scott-Scott. REACTION ENGINES

The origin of the Sabre name can be found in Chapter 9 and an outline of the vehicle described in the *Spaceflight* article is in Chapter 11.

Reaction Engines Ltd founders Bond, Varvill and Scott-Scott had worked out a configuration for an unpiloted

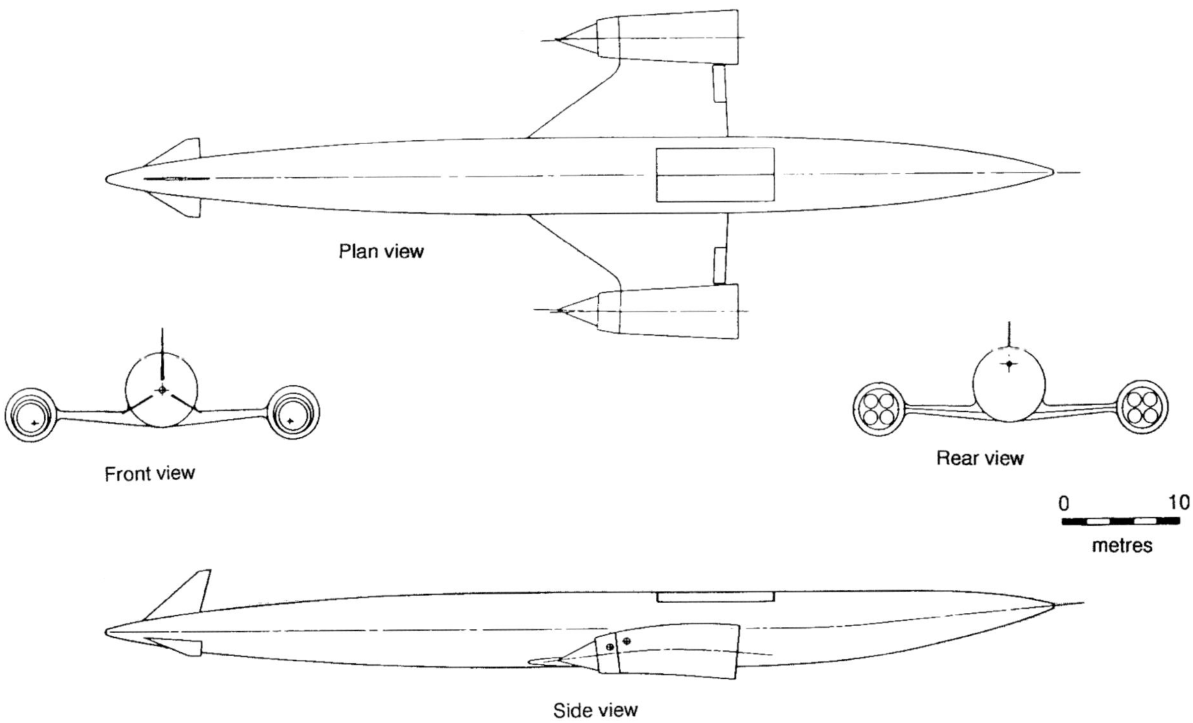

Skylon Configuration A4. REACTION ENGINES

horizontal take-off and landing SSTO vehicle specifically intended to address and resolve Hotol's problems. As mentioned before, the article included a drawing of Skylon Configuration A4, which had a long slender fuselage reminiscent of both the earliest Hotol configurations and the ALV 100—with stubby low-set wings at the fuselage mid-point and wingtip engine nacelles. The nose had both a fin and canards, like those of early Hotols, and the payload bay was set slightly to the rear. The take-off procedure involved an integrated RATO system.

Following on from Skylon Configuration A4 was the short-lived Skylon Configuration B1. Mark Hempsell, a former director of Reaction Engines, explained: "Configuration B1 had a vertical take-off rocket in the belly (I don't think there was a B2). Skylon would jump off a stand and be accelerated to flight speed. Rockets do not weigh much and it reduced the undercarriage mass to compensate, it also meant it did not need a special long runway.

"The problem was that in the few seconds the take-off engine was operating there was no abort option and that broke one of the rules Alan and Richard had set. It was abandoned once they embraced the water-cooled undercarriage in Configuration C. I would have lived with the no-abort, as losses would be statistically very small, as in many respects it is the best approach. I do not think any artwork was ever produced; I certainly have only ever had a verbal description so I do not know how the fins were arranged."

Certainly, by 1995 Configuration B1 had been superseded by Configuration C1. In a presumably unpublished and undated paper, which appears to have been drafted during the mid-1990s, Bond noted that, "while Skylon builds on the experience of Hotol, no way is it simply a Hotol Mark II. Skylon is named after the tower-like centrepiece set up at the 1951 Festival of Britain Exhibition [held on London's South Bank]. It looks somewhat like the 1951 tower and Bond likes to think that Skylon recaptures some of the spirit of the technology that the 1951 monument represented.

"Skylon has been designed as a purely commercial vehicle with the goal of putting payloads into LEO as cheaply as possible. It is a concept incorporating operational flexibility and high reliability, and it is expected to operate under commercial conditions like cargo-carrying aircraft. Its designers say that they have deliberately chosen the design so that its development does not depend on any major technological breakthroughs or research into new materials. Like Hotol, its engines can be developed on simple testbeds rather than in massive wind tunnels typical of most advanced airbreathing engines.

"The Skylon design has already gone through many changes of configuration. The latest version is designated C1."

SKYLON CONFIGURATION C1

Certainly the longest-lived variant of Skylon—perhaps the longest lived single variant of any spaceplane—was

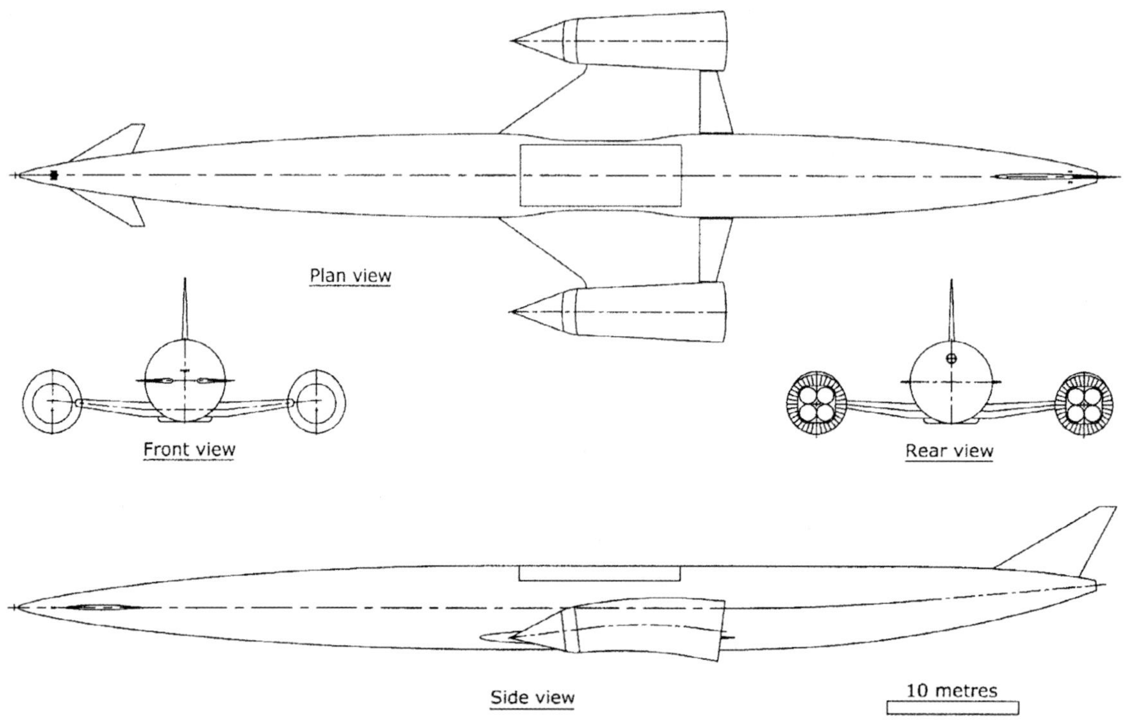

Skylon Configuration C1. REACTION ENGINES

Configuration C1, which remained largely unchanged for 13 years from 1995 to around 2008.

Even at a glance, the differences between Configurations A4 and C1 were quite clear. The latter had a tail fin rather than a nose fin, and the canards were now positioned horizontally rather than diagonally. The wings were reshaped with much larger control surfaces along their trailing edges and the fuselage had been given an area rule 'wasp waist'. And the payload bay had been moved forwards to sit neatly between the wings.

According to Bond's undated description of it: "Skylon looks like some kind of advanced supersonic aircraft. For an aircraft-like vehicle, it's an impressive 82m in length (Concorde is approximately 62m long) with the engine nacelles mounted on the tips of a delta wing giving a total wingspan of 25m. This arrangement represents one of many improvements over the earlier Hotol design.

"Hotol's engines were housed in the back of the fuselage which would have meant that the vehicle's aerodynamic lift would have tracked forward at supersonic speeds while its centre of gravity remained at the rear, leading to problems in balance and control of the vehicle. By mounting the engines on the wing and moving the wing forward, Skylon has greater aerodynamic stability as the centre of gravity travels forward with the forward movement of the aerodynamic lift. Final adjustments to achieve aerodynamic balance are made using a pair of active foreplanes.

"Skylon would take off and land horizontally using its own undercarriage just like an airplane. While the basic vehicle, empty of propellants and payload, would weigh only 40 tonnes, its total mass would be 275 tonnes. The diameter of the fuselage at 6.25m is comparable to that of a Boeing 747 (6.1m). The liquid hydrogen and oxygen propellants are contained in pairs of tanks that are located to the front and rear of the payload bay. Access to the payload compartment is via a pair of doors in the top of the fuselage as in the US Space Shuttle. The payload bay also has the same diameter as the Space Shuttle's, 4.6m, but is about two-thirds as long at 12.3m. This length has been deliberately chosen to correspond to a standard 40ft long cargo container as used in air and road transport.

"For routine missions, containerised payloads would be loaded into the payload bay without the need for extensive interfacing activities in a clean room. This would significantly cut down the time and manpower needed to turn around the vehicle for its next launch. Taking off from an equatorial launch site, Skylon would be capable of placing 12 tonnes into a 300km orbit, or 9.5 tonnes into a 460km, 28.5-degree space station orbit.

"Skylon has deliberately not been planned as a piloted vehicle like the American Shuttle. However, Skylon could carry a special 'passenger container' with room for 60 people. Eventually, a special passenger version of Skylon could be built with a more convenient side ingress."

The vehicle's Sabre engines "represent a considerable advance of the earlier RB.545 design. When Skylon takes

Studio photo of a Skylon Configuration C1 model. REACTION ENGINES

off and flies through the atmosphere, the engines operate in airbreathing mode, taking in air through a pre-cooled turbo-compressor and feeding the resultant high-pressure air into pairs of rocket nozzles where the atmospheric oxygen is burned with liquid hydrogen from one of the main propellant tanks. Once the vehicle has climbed to an altitude of 30km and attained a speed of Mach 5.5, the air inlets are closed, the pre-cooled turbo-compressor is isolated, and the engines operate as pure rockets, burning on-board supplies of liquid hydrogen and liquid oxygen".

According to a paper presented at the 46th IAF Congress in Oslo, Norway, on October 2-6, 1995: "The Sabre engine has traded simplicity for a lower fuel flow by interposing a Brayton cycle power loop in between the 'hot' airstream and the 'cold' hydrogen stream. The closed power loop requires a working fluid that remains gaseous at temperatures as low as 30K, restricting the choice to hydrogen or helium. Helium was chosen … [due to reduced] loop pressure ratio; helium's higher molecular weight results in lighter turbines with fewer stages; helium's inert nature permits a wider choice of precooler alloys.

"The air enters the cycle via the air intake where it is cooled to low temperature prior to entry into the air compressor. Following compression the airflow is divided, part flowing to the main combustion chamber and the remainder passing to the fuel rich preburner. The hot gas from the preburner passes through a heat exchanger to raise the helium outlet temperature from the precooler to a constant turbine entry temperature.

"The preburner gas then flows to the main combustion chamber to complete its combustion with the remaining air prior to expansion through the exhaust nozzle. From the heat exchanger, the helium is expanded through the main drive turbines to drive the air compressor, and then to another heat exchanger where it is cooled by hydrogen delivered from the hydrogen pump. The cold helium then flows to the circulator and thence to the precooler to pass around the cycle once more. The warm hydrogen emerging from the second heat exchanger drives the hydrogen turbopump and then the helium circulator before passing into the preburner."

When Skylon switched from airbreathing mode to pure rocket power, the engines' inlet would close and "the turbocompressor is run down while simultaneously the liquid oxygen turbopump is run up. The preburner temperature is reduced in rocket mode reflecting the reduced power demand of the liquid oxygen turbopump. The high pressure liquid oxygen is evaporated in the main chamber cooling jacket in order to allow the same oxidiser injectors to be used in both modes".

Each engine nacelle was 16.5m long and 4.5m in diameter, weighing 6.5 tonnes. Their odd curving shape, with their intakes drooped seven degrees downwards, relative to the fuselage centreline, was in order "to minimise the effects of the vehicle incidence". During the switchover from airbreathing to rocket modes, "the intake centrebody is translated forward while picking up three conical frustrums, thereby sealing the nacelle for the rocket ascent and re-entry".

The description noted: "By comparison, Hotol's engines

were much heavier because of the massive air intakes. The Skylon nacelles are lighter since they are mostly occupied by massive/extensive pre-coolers which extract heat at a rate of 400 megawatts per nacelle (a rate equivalent to the power generated by a small power station) and lack Hotol-style air intakes."

The system did rely on its heat exchangers but "similar [ones] were proved feasible during the Hotol project, though this is one area where much more work needs to be done if Skylon is to fly. Still, Bond and his colleagues are confident that there will be no fundamental difficulties in developing the heat exchangers".

Skylon would have a pair of OMS engines at the rear of the fuselage plus 38 RCS thrusters "distributed at various points over the vehicle". The fuselage itself would have a 0.5mm thick corrugated aeroshell made of carbon fibre reinforced glass-ceramic. Reaction Engines was said to be working with AEA Technology to develop this material. The wing leading edges and nose cone would be made from silicon carbide.

In spite of the various very noticeable visual changes, perhaps the biggest difference between Configuration C1 and the earlier iterations was in its mode of take-off—not depicted in the drawings. The RATO system was gone. Instead, Skylon would rely on the use of a 5.6km-long reinforced runway plus high-pressure carrier-fighter style tyres and water-cooled brakes for the abort case.

The Oslo paper stated: "Conventional undercarriages for large jets weigh 3-4% of the take-off mass, which would be unacceptable for an SSTO (9.6 tonnes for a 275-tonne gross take-off weight). For this reason, Hotol was designed to take off from a specially designed launch trolley in order to lighten the undercarriage for landings only.

"Early Skylon designs retained the landing undercarriage but rejected the trolley in favour of a 'hotlift' (rocket boost) take-off system. However, review of the hotlift system led to the conclusion that this method was operationally undesirable, expensive and represented seven seconds of the ascent in which there were no abort options ... Following analysis it was found that a take-off/landing capable undercarriage for Skylon could be engineered for a mass of 1.5% of gross take-off weight providing attention was paid to the tyres/wheels, oleos and the brakes.

"The mass of the wheels and tyres can be reduced on the condition that spaceports are built with stronger pavements than usual, thereby overriding current runway loading limitations. Consequently, a highly-loaded tightly-spaced wheel assembly can be specified, consisting of two oleos with four wheels per oleo. The tyre width and diameter are determined by stowage requirements necessitating a tyre pressure of 26.5 bar (385psi) which is similar to carrier-based fighters. The high take-off speed (155m/s) is not considered unduly severe since unmodified Concorde tyres have been satisfactorily tested up to these speeds on a rolling road facility."

The undated description outlined a typical Skylon take-off: "The spaceplane would need a ground crew of between 150 and 200 at most to prepare it for take-off. Its containerised payload would be loaded in a cargo building in a matter of hours. The vehicle would then be towed by a standard aircraft tractor to a fuelling apron and its tanks filled with liquid oxygen and hydrogen ... To avoid the problem of propellant vapours being vented near the vehicle, a problem which resulted in an [in-flight] explosion on board the DC-X in June 1994, the propellants will be heavily subcooled to keep them well below their boiling temperatures.

"After fuelling, the tractor would tow Skylon to the head of an aircraft-style runway, where it could wait up to two hours for its launch window to open. Once the engines are turned on, Skylon would remain stationary on the runway for seven seconds while the thrust increased. It would then accelerate down the runway as thrust approached maximum. It would attain its full airbreathing thrust of about 200 tonnes at take-off. Take-off would occur 45 seconds after engine start when the vehicle would be travelling at 350mph."

If the vehicle suffered an engine failure while accelerating down the runway, particularly just before rotation, this would represent "an exceptionally severe braking problem", according to the IAF Congress report. Solving it by conventional means would require carbon-carbon brakes weighing "over four tonnes based on allowable temperature rise. Having examined a number of options including deceleration rockets, trip wires and parachutes etc. it was concluded that by far the best solution was a water-cooled braking system". In this instance, a braking assembly mass of just 415kg would be required—plus 1.2 tonnes of water. When the abort command was issued, the water would be blasted down onto the brakes "via a one-shot pyrotechnic pressurisation device. Assuming a successful take-off, the water is simply dumped overboard. Therefore, the effective mass of the cooling system carried into orbit is approximately 100kg representing the tanks, plumbing, valves and pyrotechnic".

The undated description noted that Skylon would need 4.1km of runway to take off, plus 1.5km in order to stop in the event of a last second abort. It said: "In the event that one of the engines shuts down after take-off, then the liquid oxygen would be dumped to lighten the vehicle, which would be able to fly back to the launch site. With one engine out of action, Skylon is still capable of stable flight. Just before returning to the launching ground, the vehicle would dump the liquid hydrogen and then do a normal landing.

"If Skylon has to abort while ascending in rocket mode, the engines would shut down and the vehicle would effect a re-entry and head for a downrange landing site. On the other hand, if it has to abort near the end of its rocket ascent, then Skylon would continue into LEO and abort from there back to the take-off site. The aerodynamic surfaces of Skylon are sized to control the vehicle in all abort situations."

If there was no abort, Skylon would "continue to accelerate to reach Mach 5 at an altitude of 26km. At this point, to enable the vehicle to be oriented correctly for the rocket ascent, the spaceplane dives to achieve Mach 5.4 at an altitude of 23.5km and then does a 1.9g pull-up. After climbing to 30km, the engines would switch to rocket mode when they would attain a thrust of up to 300 tonnes.

"After accelerating under rocket power and reaching an altitude of between 80 and 90km, the engines would be turned off and the vehicle would enter a transfer orbit to reach the desired LEO altitude. Skylon will be able to stay for up to a week in orbit, but it is seldom likely to remain in space that long. Unlike the US Shuttle for example, Skylon is not intended to be a platform for experiments. It is simply designed to deliver satellites and other payloads into space, and to retrieve hardware if required. It's a bus to get from Earth to LEO and back, not a luxury caravan.

"To de-orbit, the RCS thrusters would be used to manoeuvre the vehicle into a tail-first, upside-down position, and the OMS engines will slow the vehicle by around 60m/sec. The RCS thrusters will then pitch the spaceplane over so that it is right-side up but an angle of about 70 degrees. Re-entry begins at an altitude of around 120km. The re-entry flight path is determined by the goal of keeping the temperature of the underside of the vehicle below 1,100K. The vehicle glides down, continually decelerating to touch down on the runway at the relatively slow speed of about 150mph.

"Skylon's aerodynamic characteristics mean that it has a 3,000km cross-range capability. It is also capable of landing in a 40mph crosswind. Upon return from orbit, Skylon could be readied for flight again in approximately two days."

Bond's, and his company's, attitude towards programmes backed by fickle penny-pinching governments was hinted at by his closing paragraph: "Reaction Engines maintains that Skylon is a near-term project capable of entering service after a nine-and-a-half year development programme which would be funded by commercial finance. They estimate the programme cost to be £5bn (at 1992 prices)."

SKYLON CONFIGURATION C2

A new variant of Skylon was finally revealed in September 2009—Configuration C2. According to the Reaction Engines Skylon Users' Manual, "this configuration ... has been mostly created by a direct scaling of C1, with the mass scaled by 1.25 and linear dimensions scaled by 1.08. It is intended as a starting point for a major redesign exercise that will revise the Skylon design to create Configuration D1.

"One area in which the C2 is not a direct scaling of C1 is the payload bay interfaces. These have been revised in light of a series of market and future application studies".

As such, the vehicle's length was increased from 82m to 83.3m, fuselage diameter from 6.25m to 6.75m and wingspan from 25m to 25.4m. Empty mass was 53t, propellant mass was 277t and nominal take-off mass was 345t—compared to the oft-stated 275t of Configuration C1. Payload capability was increased from 12t to 15t.

The vehicle's materials and basic structure remained largely the same, as did its take-off procedure—except it would now carry three tonnes of water for the brakes in case of an abort.

During ascent, C2 would accelerate to Mach 5.14, rather than Mach 5.4, and switch to pure rocket mode at 28.5km altitude, rather than 23.5km.

As far as that payload bay was concerned, "the bay has two payload interfaces, one in the front and the other at the rear. The front location has provisions to load cryogenic oxygen, hydrogen and helium, but in all other respects the two interfaces are identical and mirror each other. A payload can, therefore be placed at either end without alteration".

The Users' Manual also included some details of Skylon ground operations: "Skylon operates like an aircraft. Its integration and servicing occur in a hangar, it is supported horizontally on its undercarriage and for flight it is towed out to a runway for fuelling and take-off. The location and detailed design of the launch site or sites have not yet been established". It was stated, however, that Skylon needed a 5.5km runway for its exclusive use.

SKYLON CONFIGURATION D1

The last known variant of Skylon at the time of writing was Configuration D1, as outlined in the Skylon Users' Manual Revision 2 of June 2014, compiled by Hempsell. Dimensionally, D1 represented a compromise between C1

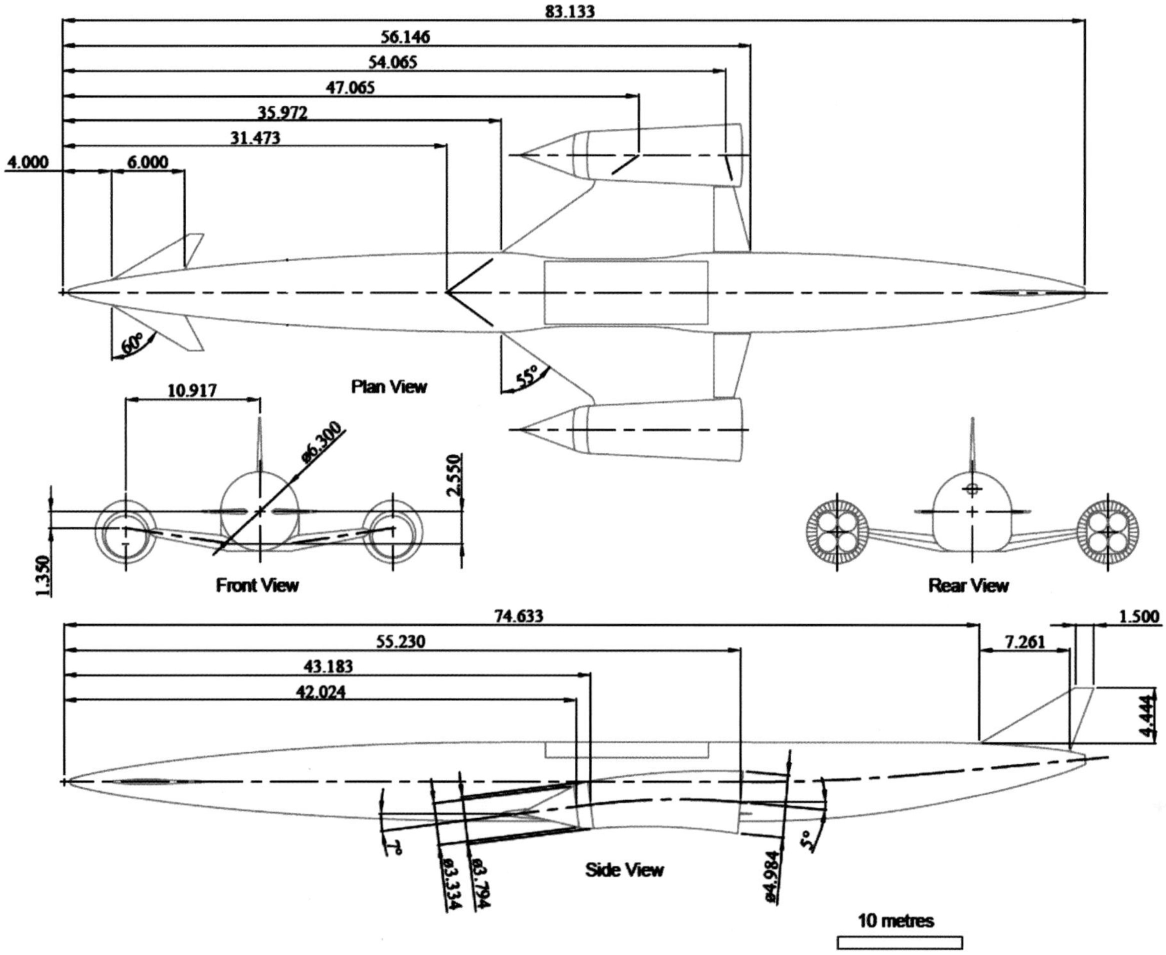

Skylon Configuration D1. REACTION ENGINES

and C2. It was a little larger than the former and a little smaller than the latter at 83.113m long with a fuselage diameter of 6.3m, although the wingspan was greater than either at 26.818m.

A feature of D1 that was not present in either C-type was the inclusion of more specific details of the OMS: "In addition to the main propulsion system tanks there are a set of secondary cryogenic tanks which feed the orbital manoeuvring engines, the reaction control thrusters and the fuel cell power supply. The Skylon Orbital Manoeuvring Assembly (SOMA) engines on the D1 configuration use a design concept produced by Airbus Defence and Space.

"The SOMA is an expander cycle with a single turbine powering both the oxygen and hydrogen pumps, and a gearbox to account for their different speed requirements. In order to meet the Skylon ... packaging requirements the pumps feed two thrust chambers. The overall configuration is designed so that two SOMAs can be mounted to produce a four-nozzle cluster."

The empty mass of Configuration D1 was 53.4t, plus 6.5t for 'consumables' including residual liquids and auxiliary propellants. Usable ascent propellant mass was 250.1t, nominal payload was 15t and gross take-off mass was 325t.

Skylon kept the memory of the airbreathing Hotol alive for nearly three decades before Reaction Engines finally went into administration at the end of October 2024. John Lanfear Scott-Scott died on December 12, 2015, aged 81 and Alan Bond had retired from Reaction Engines in October 2017.

Hotol reunion during the BIS UK Spaceplanes Symposium over the weekend of September 17/18, 2005, at RAF Museum, Cosford. Pictured left to right, in front of an Avro Blue Steel missile, are Roger Longstaff, Gerald Wilson, Eric Webb, Alan Bond, John Scott-Scott, Bob Parkinson, Mark Hempsell and Dave Salt.

ABBREVIATIONS

ACARD Advisory Council on Applied Research and Development
ACOST Advisory Council on Science and Technology
AI Artificial Intelligence
AIAA American Institute of Aeronautics and Astronautics
ALV Alternative Launch Vehicles
BAC British Aircraft Corporation
BAe British Aerospace
BBC British Broadcasting Corporation
BMFT Bundesministerium für Forschung und Technologie
BNSC British National Space Centre
BP British Petroleum
CADB Chemical Automatics Design Bureau
CAPS Computer Aided Project Studies
CATIA Computer-Aided Three-dimensional Interactive Application
CEC Commission of the European Communities
CFM Carbon Fibre Matrix
CFRP Carbon Fibre Reinforced Plastic
CIAM Central Institute of Aviation Motors
CIS Commonwealth of Independent States
CIT Cranfield Institute of Technology
CNES Centre National d'Études Spatiales
CRACE Combined Rocket and Air Cycle Engine
DARPA Defense Advanced Research Projects Agency
DIG Design Integration Group
DRA Defence Research Agency
DTI/DoI Department of Trade and Industry
EEC European Economic Community
EFA European Fighter Aircraft, later Eurofighter Typhoon
EHTV European Hypersonic Transport Vehicle
ELDO European Launcher Development Organisation
EOARD European Office of Aerospace Research and Development
ESA European Space Agency
ESRO European Space Research Organisation
ESTEC European Space Research and Technology Centre
ET Enabling Technology
FESTIP Future European Space Transportation Investigations Programme
GEO Geosynchronous Orbit
GLOW Gross Lift-Off Weight
H2 Hydrogen
HMG Her Majesty's Government
HORUS Hypersonic Orbital Research and Utilisation System
HOTOL HOrizontal Take-Off and Landing
HPM Hermes Propulsion Module
HRM Hermes Resource Module
HSCT High Speed Civil Transport
HTOHL Horizontal Take-Off, Horizontal Landing
HYPAC Hypersonic Aircraft
HYTEX Hypersonic Technology Experiment
IAF International Astronautical Federation
IPR Intellectual Property Rights
ISS International Space Station
JPT Joint Propulsion Team
ICBM Intercontinental Ballistic Missile
ICI Imperial Chemical Industries
IMI Imperial Metal Industries
ITN Independent Television News
ITV Independent Television
LACE Liquid Air Cycle Engine
LART Luftatmender Raumtransporter
LCN LSAR Control Number
LEO Low Earth Orbit
LOX Liquid oxygen
LSAR Logistics Support Analysis Record
MAKS Multipurpose Aerospace System
MAP propyl methacrylate
MBB Messerschmitt Bölkow Blohm
MECO Main Engine Cut-Off
MET Materials Engineering and Testing Ltd
MGPEV Mobile Ground Preparation and Erection Vehicle
MMS Matra Marconi Space
MoD Ministry of Defence
NASA National Aeronautics and Space Administration
NASP National Aero-Space Plane
NGTE National Gas Turbine Establishment
NPSH Net Positive Suction Head
ODW Oblique Detonation Wave
OG Originators Group
OMS Orbital Manoeuvring System
PEEK polyetheretherketone
PIG Performance Integration Group

PLM	Propulsion Liaison Meeting
PMQs	Prime Minister's Questions
PoC	Proof-of-Concept
PPS	Parliamentary Private Secretary
PV	Private Venture
RADEM	Rocket Ascent Demonstration Mission / Rocket Ascent Demonstrator
RAE	Royal Aircraft Establishment
RAeS	Royal Aeronautical Society
RAL	Rutherford Appleton Laboratories, Chilton
RATO	Rocket Assisted Take-Off
RCS	Reaction Control System
RR	Rolls-Royce
SABRE	Synergetic Air Breathing Rocket Engine
SBAC	Society of British Aerospace Companies
SDI	Strategic Defense Initiative
SDIO	Strategic Defense Initiative Organisation
SEP	Société Européene de Propulsion
SI	Specific Impulse
SLS	Space Launch System
SOMA	Skylon Orbital Manoeuvring Assembly
SSME	Space Shuttle Main Engine
SSTO	Single Stage To Orbit
STS	Space Transportation System
TPS	Thermal Protection System
TSTO	Two Stage To Orbit
TVC	Thrust Vector Control
USAF	US Air Force
VTO	Vertical Take-Off
VTOHL	Vertical Take-Off, Horizontal Landing
WLC	Winged Launcher Configurations

VEHICLE DATA TABLE

Type	Intake area	Length	Max diameter	Wingspan	Wing area
Hotel 1984 (BAe press release)	N/A	54.376m	N/A	17.101m	N/A
Hotol A (1.2.86 Hotol presentation)	N/A	62m	5.7m	19.7m	173sqm
Hotol B	N/A	70m	5.7m	20m	N/A
Hotol C	N/A	62m	5.6m	19.66m	171.96sqm/ 296.55sqm
Hotol D	N/A	62.2m	5.6m	N/A	172sqm
Hotol F	N/A	56.89m	N/A	~21m	106sqm
Hotol G2 (undated, Bond collection)	13.16sqn	68.837m	N/A	N/A	177sqm
Hotol G3	13.15sqm	66m	7.695m	~28.5m	195sqm
Hotol H	10.7sqm	65.115m	7.7m	27.79m	213sqm
Hotol J	10.7sqm	60m	7.45m	27.5m	213sqm
Hotol J4.5	9.211sqm	59.106m	7.45m	27.1m	222sqm
Hotol K	9.211sqm	63.04m	7.04m	N/A	253sqm
Interim Hotol (Feb '90)	-	42.65m	7.05m	24.78m	181sqm
Interim Hotol Orbiter 61	-	41.5m	7.05m	24.78m	180.85sqm
Interim Hotol Orbiter 61 (Soviet)	-	43.9m	7.05m	24.78m	N/A
Interim Hotol Orbiter 66 (12.2.91)	-	45.5m	N/A	24.542m	140sqm
Interim Hotol Orbiter 66 (7.3.91)	-	46.6m	N/A	24.542m	140sqm
Interim Hotol Orbiter 68 (23.5.91)	-	36.45m	N/A	21.6m	N/A
Interim Hotol Orbiter 68d	-	33m	8.4m	N/A	N/A
Interim Hotol Orbiter 68e (3.11.92)	-	N/A	8.16m	21.65m	58.75sqm
Hotol M (14.1.92)	-	33.63m	7.13m	16.67m	57.4sqm
Hotol M (17.1.92)	-	33.63m	7.14m	16.67m	57.4sqm
P150-302 (16.2.92)	-	38m	6.58m	16.05m	64.58sqm
WLC-2 rocket/ramjet	N/A	66.8m	N/A	22.1m	N/A
WLC-2 pre-cooled turbojet/rocket	8.03sqm	78.5m	N/A	23.8m	N/A
WLC-2 SSTO	N/A	77.6m	8.39m	26.4m	N/A
WLC-3 SSTO	9.245sqm	85m	8.357m	29.6m	242sqm
RADEM Hotol-Variant	-	21.27m	N/A	11.63m	55sqm
RADEM Hotol-Variant (Tripropellant)	-	21.38m	N/A	11.63m	55sqm
RADEM MAKS-Variant	-	19.28m	N/A	12.5m	N/A
Skylon 1992	N/A	81.95m	N/A	N/A	N/A
Skylon C1	N/A	82m (84m, 2011)	6.25m	25m	N/A
Skylon C2 (scaled C1)	N/A	83.3m	6.75m	25.4m	N/A
Skylon D1	N/A	83.113m	6.3m	26.818m	N/A
Note: Some there was sometimes a degree of variation within individual configurations. For example, the length of Configuration H was given as 66.5m in one report.					

APPENDIX II

HOTOL HISTORY OF STRUCTURAL DEVELOPMENT

The following extract from period reports details the evolution of the airbreathing Hotol's individual components during the lifetime of the project.

NOSE STRUCTURE

Feb 86 **Carbon-carbon monolithic structure, designed to aerodynamic and birdstrike criteria. Remarks:** The nose structure incorporated all the fuselage structure ahead of the liquid hydrogen tank.

Oct 86 **Reduced length carbon-carbon sandwich structure (nose cone) ahead of an insulated titanium ally sandwich structure (nose shell); the nose shell TPS consists of carbon-carbon TPS panels and protecalor insulation. Remarks:** A titanium nose shell was necessary for compatibility with a titanium fin spigot and spigot housing, avoiding differential thermal expansion problems of dissimilar materials in the presence of severe temperature gradient. A carbon-carbon spigot and housing were not practical due to low bearing strength of the material.

Mar 87 **Nose shell only:** titanium alloy replaced by reinforced titanium alloy. Remarks: Mass saving due to improved specific strength.

Sep 87 **Nose cone only:** birdstrike requirement deleted and impact detection system introduced. Remarks: Mass saving justified by low probability of impact.

Oct 87 **Carbon-carbon replaced by carbon-silicon carbide. Remarks:** Carbon-silicon carbide requires no oxidation protection and has a high specific strength.

Dec 88 **Full thermal analysis of nose structure conducted by Huntings. No design change. Material still carbon reinforced silicon carbide (C/SiC) for nose cone and particulate reinforced titanium for nose structure with TPS on lower surface. Remarks:** Thermal stresses within material limits – no redesign required.

LIQUID HYDROGEN TANK

Dec 85 **Carbon-PEEK uniform thickness (membrane) pressure stabilised tank protected by TPS. Remarks:** Carbon-PEEK has a higher specific strength than alternative materials and less susceptible to thermal micro-cracking.

Jun 86 **Alternative tank designs with and without hot load carrying structures were investigated. Remarks:** None of these produced a lighter structure therefore not incorporated.

Mar 87 **Carbon-PEEK tailored thickness tank skin. Remarks:** Mass saving by thinning the tank where possible.

Apr 87 **A non-circular section, flat bottomed, load-carrying tank was examined as part of an investigation into lifting body fuselages. Remarks:** This was found to be prohibitively heavy since the membrane tank structure had to be replaced by a stiffened structure.

Jun 87 **Investigation into partially stiffened and compartmentalised tanks. Remarks:** Mass saving dependent on front fuselage fineness ratio.

Jul 87 **Investigation into sandwich skin tank incorporating the cryogenic insulation into the core. Remarks:** Because this tank requires the membrane skin to be split into two equal directionally balanced skins there is no increase in overall mass over the optimised thickness achieved with a single skin except for any balancing requirement.

May 88 **Main Liquid oxygen tank moved from aft end of liquid hydrogen tank to rear fuselage. Small liquid oxygen trim tank incorporated at front of liquid hydrogen tank. Remarks:** Vehicle trim requirement at high Mach numbers.

Nov 88 **Carbon-PEEK liquid oxygen transfer pipe designed.**

Feb 89 **Liquid hydrogen sandwich skin sizes reassessed in light of foreplane and trim tank loads and configuration change.**

TPS PANELS

Jan 86 **The thermal protection system panels consisted of 1/3m x 1m sliding sandwich panels, supported rigidly by one post on one corner and by the adjacent panels around its periphery. These were designed in titanium alloy on the upper 2/3 of the fuselage and nickel alloy on the lower 1/3 due to higher temperatures. Remarks:** The TPS system is designed to be non-load carrying and to allow relative thermal expansion to occur without producing any thermal stresses in the tank or TPS panel. Panels were sized to avoid panel flutter at the design EAS.

Jun 86 **The material for the TPS panels was changed to carbon-carbon on both upper and lower surfaces. Remarks:** This gave a mass saving and reduced the thermal expansion of the TPS panels, with wider temperature limits.

Apr 87 **The longitudinal length of the panels was increased and each panel was supported by a number of swinging links. Remarks:** This produced a fail safe panel attachment.

Oct 87 **The length of the TPS panels was reduced to approximately 4m and the material changed to carbon-silicon carbide. Remarks:** Carbon-silicon carbide requires no oxidisation protection. The 4m panel might have to consist of 4 x 1m panels bolted together because of manufacturing limitations.

May 89 **Panel sizes reassessed for increase aerodynamic pressures. No significant changes in panel size or fixation design. Remarks:** New ascent trajectory (700kts EAS).

TRELLIS STRUCTURES

Oct 86 **Titanium alloy trellis structure designed to connect the nose structure and the centre/rear fuselage to the liquid hydrogen tank. Remarks:** Permits relative thermal expansion and minimises axial heat conduction between the components.

Mar 88 **The three trellis connections between a) nosecone-nose structure (carbon-silicon carbide); b) nose structure-liquid hydrogen tank (titanium + particulates); c) liquid hydrogen tank-main fuselage (titanium + particulates) have been sized.**

FOREPLANES

Feb 86 **Carbon-carbon structure same as the fin. Remarks:** The foreplanes were deleted for Configuration F due to severe heating and aerodynamic problems.

Sep 87 **Jettisonable foreplanes for use on take-off and ascent are being reconsidered.**

Apr 89 **Jettisonable foreplanes incorporated. Material changed to carbon-fibre. Remarks:** Foreplanes required at take-off and low altitude only. Jettisoning alleviates hypersonic control and avoids high temperatures associated with ascent and re-entry.

FIN

Feb 86 **Carbon-carbon sandwich skins on multi-spar internal structure. Remarks:** 12sqm fin.

Feb 87 **Various torsion box materials, with and without TPS investigated. Reinforced titanium without TPS chosen. Carbon-carbon leading edge, trailing edge and tip. Leading edge designed by birdstrike requirement. Remarks:** 33sqm fin. The fin spigot is unsuitable in carbon-carbon because of low bearing strength. Necessary to avoid dissimilar materials for the spigot and fin structure in presence of severe temperature gradients. Final choice of material is dependent on fin temperatures.

Sep 87 **Birdstrike requirement removed from leading edge. Remarks:** Mass saving. Justified by low probability of impact.

Oct 87 **Carbon-silicon carbide leading edge, trailing edge and tip. Remarks:** Carbon-silicon carbide requires no oxidation protection and has a high specific strength.
Only design change is the size. Material still titanium + particulates for the torsion box and carbon-silicon carbide for the leading edge, tip and trailing edge.

PAYLOAD BAY

Mar 86 **Payload bay doors:** titanium alloy sandwich structure designed to carry fuselage end load and shear and aerodynamic loading.

Feb 87 **Payload bay doors:** material changed to carbon-PEEK with external TPS using carbon-carbon aeroshell panels. Remarks: Changed to be compatible with the surrounding carbon-PEEK structure.

Mar 87 **Payload bay doors:** Material changed to reinforced titanium. Remarks: Mass saving due to improved specific strength.

May 88 **Design remains unchanged except for the payload bay door – now hinged along its aft edge. Material still titanium + particulates. Remarks:** Rearward hinged door avoids covering the radiators when open and provides a base for a docking hatch.

Dec 88 **Additional rectangular liquid oxygen tank incorporated beneath payload bay. Remarks:** Redistribution of liquid oxygen from rear fuselage saves fuselage length/mass.

Apr 89 **Rectangular liquid oxygen tank replaced by four cylindrical tanks. Remarks:** Mass saving.

REAR FUSELAGE

Apr 86 **Original design was a combination of frames, longerons and sandwich skins manufactured in titanium alloy.**

Feb 87 **Design changed to insulated carbon-PEEK structure with carbon-carbon TPS panels. Remarks:** Small mass saving over initial design.

Mar 87 **Reverted back to original non-insulated design using reinforced titanium alloy. Remarks:** Larger mass saving over initial design, due to improved specific strength.

Sep 87 **Rear fuselage changed to accommodate revised powerplant installation and split liquid oxygen tanks. Payload bay and wing carry-through box incorporated into rear fuselage definition. Remarks:** Vehicle layout changed to obtain better centre of gravity balance.

Oct 87 **Rear fuselage shortened. Remarks:** Achieved by joining the forward liquid oxygen tank to the liquid hydrogen tank.

Apr 88 **Possible use of glass reinforced composites investigated. Remarks:** No clear benefit.

May 88 **Rear fuselage lengthened to accommodate main liquid oxygen tank – repositioned from aft end of liquid hydrogen tank. Remarks:** Vehicle trim requirement.

Apr 89 **Rear fuselage shortened with redistribution of liquid oxygen to payload bay and wing; frame design optimised. Remarks:** Mass saving.

WING CARRY-THROUGH STRUCTURE

Feb 88 **Distinct carry through structure not possible in rear fuselage. Loads made to pass around engine components. Remarks:** Revised engine installation.

Apr 89 **Distinct carry through structure reintroduced; number of wing carry through frameworks optimised – four in rear fuselage, one in payload bay. Remarks:** Engine installation optimised and wing root thickness reduced; wing loading changed due to introduction of wing liquid oxygen tank.

LIQUID OXYGEN TANKAGE

Mar 86 **Carbon-PEEK single skinned liquid oxygen tank with end stiffening rings.**

Sep 87 **Single liquid oxygen tank replaced by two tanks. One forward and one after of the payload bay. Remarks:** Vehicle balance requirement.

Oct 87 **Integration of forward liquid oxygen tank with liquid hydrogen tank. Forward liquid oxygen tank becomes a pressure-stabilised membrane structure making up part of the forward fuselage; structure changed to sandwich tank. Remarks:** The liquid oxygen tank is separated from the liquid hydrogen tank by a purged curved bulkhead; improved safety and servicing with no mass penalty.

May 88 **Main liquid oxygen tank moved from aft of liquid hydrogen tank to rear fuselage; trim tank added to front of liquid hydrogen tank. Remarks:** Vehicle trim requirements.

Nov 88 **Main rear fuselage liquid oxygen tank deleted—liquid oxygen redistributed to payload bay and wing. Remarks:** Mass saving.

AFT LIQUID OXYGEN TANK SUPPORT STRUCTURE

Jan 87 **Liquid oxygen supported from wing carry-through box by four supports (a rigid tripod, two swinging A-frames and one pin-jointed strut). These supports were titanium alloy. Remarks:** This type of support structure allows differential expansion of tank and surrounding structure.

Mar 87 **Material changed to reinforced titanium alloy. Remarks:** Mass saving due to improved specific strength.

Sep 87 **Support arrangement changed for smaller tank. Remarks:** Fore/aft loads now reacted by thrust structure.

ENGINE PIPEWORK

Apr 89 **Pipework layout detailed. Reassessment of pipe materials and flexible joint design. Remarks:** Updated Rolls-Royce data. Reduced number of flexible couplings.

THRUST STRUCTURE

Apr 86 **Originally three struts coming from each of the rockets linked by a thrust ring. Half of the thrust load was reacted by the full liquid oxygen tank and half by the fuselage longerons. This was designed in titanium alloy. Remarks:** Approximately 50% of the maximum thrust is initially reacted by the liquid oxygen tank. The percentage split changes during flight.

Mar 87 **Material changed to reinforced titanium alloy; potential use of carbon-polyimide. Remarks:** Mass saving due to improved specific strength; potential mass saving with carbon-polyimide dependent upon temperature of bay. Not incorporated.

Sep 87 **More of thrust load reacted by fuselage longerons instead of liquid oxygen tank. Remarks:** Split liquid oxygen tank has changed requirements. 87% of max thrust load goes into the fuselage longerons.

Apr 89 **Design unchanged except for resizing. Material still titanium + particulates.**

WING TORSION BOX

Jan 86 **Initial design of sandwich skins and multi-spars. Titanium alloy upper skin and nickel alloy upper skin and nickel alloy lower skin; lower skin changed to titanium with high density (minimum thickness) insulation with nickel alloy TPS panels. Remarks:** To reduce mass and relative thermal expansion of the structure.

Apr 86 **Thickness/chord ratio was set at 6% outboard of the kink and 8% at the root. Remarks:** To reduce mass limited by maximum thickness/chord allowed for aerodynamic performance.

Jan 87 **Material changed to carbon-carbon; carbon-PEEK wing with insulation on both surfaces, using carbon-carbon TPS panels. Remarks:** Mass saving with carbon-carbon; no mass saving with carbon-PEEK wing due to reduction in effective depth of torsion box. Not incorporated.

Mar 87 **Material changed to reinforced titanium alloy with insulation on the lower surface, using carbon-carbon TPS panels. Remarks:** Mass saving over previous designs. Adopted for Configuration G.

Oct 87 **Changing the lower surface insulated skin to a non-insulated reinforced nickel or titanium-aluminide skin thereby saving the insulation mass. Remarks:** To be investigated when more material data becomes available.

Apr 88 **54° leading edge delta planform adopted (strake deleted). Remarks:** Aerodynamic redesign.

Nov 88 **Titanium aluminide reinforced by silicon carbide fibres adopted as datum wing material; integral wing liquid oxygen tank incorporated. Remarks:** Eliminates requirement for lower wing skin insulation (mass saving); rear fuselage shortened (mass saving).

Feb 89 **Constant 7% thickness to chord wing design adopted with increased wing skin thicknesses to maintain previous wing stiffness. Remarks:** Mass/drag optimum (CAPS).

Apr 89 **Trellis wing spar construction assessed. Remarks:** No mass benefit – production and fuel movement advantages.

May 89 **Wing planform area increased to 222sqm. Remarks:** Liquid oxygen tankage requirement.

WING STRAKE, LEADING EDGE AND TRAILING EDGE/FLAPS

Jan 86 **Initially these components were included as mass estimates in the basic wing, using carbon-carbon material.**

Aug 87 **These items were structurally analysed as individual items in carbon-carbon. Remarks:** New mass scaling rules supplied for vehicle optimisation.

Apr 88 **54° leading edge delta planform adopted (strake deleted). Remarks:** Aerodynamic redesign.

Oct 88 **Reassessed due to changes in wing design. Material still carbon-silicon carbide.**

UNDERCARRIAGE

Oct 85 **Nosewheel:** a conventional oleo pneumatic steerable nosewheel. The original main undercarriage design was a conventional wheel undercarriage stored in the wing strake. Remarks: Conical intake has insufficient space for stowage of the main undercarriage.

Mar 86 **Wheel undercarriage stored in a rectangular intake pod. Remarks:** Reduces length of leg thereby reducing mass of undercarriage. Made possible by revised intake shape.

Oct 87 **The design was changed to a central skid undercarriage stored beneath the air intake with two outriggers stored further aft inside the air intake pod. Remarks:** The skid design was necessary to minimise the mass and locate the undercarriage slightly aft of the aircraft centre of gravity during landing.

May 88 **Intake-mounted '146' type undercarriage adopted replacing skid undercarriage. Remarks:** Packaging problems solved.

Dec 88 **Application of new materials assessed. Remarks:** Mass saving.

Mar 89 **Intake-mounted 'swingback' undercarriage adopted. Remarks:** Improved geometry eliminates requirement for de-rotation rockets.

INTAKE/FUSELAGE INTERFACE

Oct 85 **Carbon-carbon intake structure attached to the rear fuselage by seven links. These links are designed to allow for relative thermal expansion but carry, thrust/drag/undercarriage/inertia forces in the axial direction and undercarriage and inertia forces in the vertical and lateral directions. The temperature of the links has not been evaluated but the link material is probably nickel alloy.**

Oct 87 **The position, size, configuration and mass**

of intake has varied. The wheel undercarriage has been replaced by a central skid, thus modifying the interface forces. The nickel links will probably incorporate particulates, whiskers or fibres. Remarks: There has been a gradual tendency for the heat exchangers and turbocompressors to be located higher in the rear fuselage with a reduction in the interface loads. However, there is now s spill ramjet in the pod. The mass has reduced and the strength increased at temperature to increase the specific strength and reduce the link mass.

Oct 88 **No design change except for the location of the intake/fuselage attachments on the fuselage. Remarks:** Configuration changes.

TROLLEY INTERFACE

Oct 85 **The original concept was a front support cradle near the aft end of the liquid hydrogen tank and twin main supports at the wing front spar, but this front support position gave an excessive fuselage bending moment for trolley mounted case. Remarks:** Heavy mass for Hotol fuselage.

Aug 86 **Forward support moved to front end of liquid hydrogen tank. Remarks:** Reduced mass for Hotol fuselage, and improved stability in take-off run.

Oct 86 **Forward support moved back to mid-length of liquid hydrogen tank to optimise front fuselage bending moment distributions. Remarks:** Further mass reduction for Hotol fuselage.

Nov 86 **Proposed to move main support to spar 2 to reduce rear fuselage bending moments. Remarks:** Not adopted since it would have reduced the effectiveness of the wing flaps in rotating Hotol to the lift-off attitude and thus have required a higher forward pusher load.

Nov 86 **A rear end tension link introduced for rejected take-off case only, to limit front fuselage bending moment. Remarks:** Avoiding significant increase in Hotol fuselage mass which would otherwise have been necessary due to the high retardation in the RTO case.

Oct 87 **Due to a reduction in the specified retardation, RTO case bending moments are no longer critical for Configuration G, allowing the rear link to be dispensed with. Remarks:** Mass of rear link is deleted.

Apr 89 **Preliminary interface design details assessed.**

BODY FLAP

Oct 87 **No design change. Material still carbon-silicon carbide.**

APPENDIX III

WHO WAS WHO

Name	Affiliation	Role and Notes
Abell, Bruce	US Government	Assistant Director of Public Affairs, White House Office of Science and Technology Policy
Abrahams, T.	DTI	Secretary to the Minister
Allen, John	BAe Kingston	Kingston Advanced Projects Group Chief Engineer
Allen, Paul	Anglo-Soviet Materials Ltd	Financial Director
Andrews, David	-	-
Andrews, S. G.	S. G. Andrews Consultants	-
Appleyard, George	BAe Warton	Advanced Projects Engineer
Aries, Ian	BAe Stevenage	Stevenage Programme & Costs Lead
Armstrong, Frank	RAE Farnborough	-
Armstrong, J. A.	Hunting Engineering	-
Arnall, John	BAe HQ	Head of Research and Development
Atkins, Robert	House of Commons	MP for South Ribble
Atkinson, David	House of Commons	MP for Bournemouth East
Baker, Richard	BAe Warton	Alternative Launch Vehicle (ALV) Engineering
Balabuyev, Petro Vasylovych	Antonov Design Bureau	Chief Designer
Barker, N.	BAe Warton	Materials Specialist
Barnes, James	Ministry of Defence	Research and Development Dept. Deputy Controller
Barthelemy, Robert R. 'Bart'	NASP Wright-Patterson	Project Manager
Bashilov, Alexander Sergeevich	NPO Molniya	General Director
Batiste, Spencer	UK Government	MP for Elmet and PPS to Geoffrey Pattie
Bavin, Richard	Defence Research Agency	Engineer
Bernstein, Dr L.	University of London	Member of the Aeronautical Engineering Department
Bird, Bruce	Air Foyle Heavylift	Commercial Director
Biryukov, Valery A.	SAPEM	General Director
Bishop, Colonel T. J.	USAF	-
Blonstein, Larry	BAe Stevenage	Sales Manager
Bond, Alan	Reaction Engines	Hotol Originator and Engine Inventor
Booth, Nicholas	*The Observer* newspaper	Journalist
Bouillot, Jean-Claude	CNES	-
Bratukhin, Anatoly	Soviet State Committee of the Defence Industry	-
Briggs, Gordon	BAe Australia	Space Systems Manager
Broddle, K.	BAe Brough	Chief Stressman
Brookman, D. J.	BAe HQ	-
Brown, Bob	BAe Warton	Alternative Launch Vehicle Designer
Brown, Terry	BAe Filton	Head of Advanced Projects, Filton Lead for Propulsion System & Intake Installation

Name	Affiliation	Role and Notes
Brown, Michael	UK Government	MP for Brigg and Cleethorpes and PPS to Douglas Hogg
Brubaker, Harold	US Congress	North Carolina Representative
Bruce, Colonel Philip	NASP	Programme Director
Bulanenko, Anatoli	Antonov Design Bureau	Deputy Chief Designer
Burns, Sandy	BAe Warton Core Team	Project & Technical Manager, Hotol Project Leader
Burns, Jean	-	Wife of Sandy Burns
Bush, George H. W.	US Government	41st US President
Butcher, John	UK Government	MP for Coventry South West and Under-Secretary of State for Trade and Industry
Caborn, Derek	BAe Warton Core Team	Structures & Materials
Capizzi, Vince	BAe Australia	-
Carroll, Gerald	Carroll Group	Entrepreneur and Businessman
Cayley, Sir George	British Association for the Advancement of Science	Victorian Engineer, Inventor and Aviator
Channon, Paul	UK Government	MP for Southend West and Secretary of State for Trade and Industry
Charles, Prince of Wales	British Royal Family	Heir to the Throne
Childs, Bill	BAe Stevenage	Chief Engineer
Chirac, Jacques	French Government	Prime Minister
Clarke, Kenneth	UK Government	MP for Rushcliffe and Chancellor of the Duchy of Lancaster
Cleaver, Val	RR Rocket Engine Division	Chief Rocket Propulsion Engineer
Coleman, Herbert J.	*Aviation Week & Space Technology* magazine	Journalist
Collier, Derrick	Carroll Group	Board Member of Carroll-owned FADC
Conchie, Peter	BAe Stevenage	Space & Comms Division Business Development Director
Cook, J. A. E. A.	RAE Farnborough	Materials and Structures Specialist
Cook, T. A.	RAE Farnborough	Aerodynamics Specialist
Cooper, Robert F.	USAF Aero Propulsion Laboratory, Wright-Patterson	Researcher
Corfield, Frederick	UK Government	Minister of State for Trade and Industry
Couchman, A. D.	BAE Stevenage	-
Covault, Craig	*Aviation Week & Space Technology* magazine	Journalist
Cox, C. N.	Hunting Engineering	-
Creasey, Ray	BAe Warton	Director of Engineering ca. 1964
Crowfoot, Frank	BAe Filton	Aerodynamicist and Hotol Vehicle Designer
Cuckney, John	Investors in Industry (3i)	Industrialist
Cundy, David	BAe Warton	Advanced Studies Team Engineer
Curien, Hubert	French Government	Minister of Research and Space
Czysz, Paul	McDonnell Douglas	Fellow in Hypersonic Aircraft Concepts
Dale, Nick	BAe Warton Core Team	Aerodynamics
D'Allest, Frédéric	CNES	Director of Launch Vehicles
Davies, Alec	BAe Warton Core Team	Systems & Thermal Analysis
Deller, Maurice	RAE Farnborough	Head of Space Department
Deloffre, Bernard	Aérospatiale	-

Name	Affiliation	Role and Notes
Denning, Ralph	RR Patchway	Head of Future Concepts
D'Estaing, Valéry Giscard	French Government	President
Dobie, Bill	BAe Filton	Filton Lead for Vehicle Performance & Aerodynamics
Dryell, Dave	RR Patchway	Propulsion Design Lead
Dodson, Michael B.	-	-
Dommett	RAE Farnborough	Specialist
Dukakis, Michael	US Democratic Party	Presidential Candidate
Duncan, Sir William	RR HQ	Chairman and Chief Executive
Eastmond, John	BAe	Patents Officer
Eccles, Brian	BAe Warton	Wind Tunnel Model Specialist
Eliutin, Alexander V.	Institute Giredmet	Deputy Director
Escher, William J. D.	Astronautics Corporation of America	-
Evans, Dick	BAe HQ	Lygo's Replacement as Chief Executive
Fabius, Laurent	French Government	Prime Minister
Fairclough, John	UK Civil Service	Chief Scientific Advisor
Fedosov, E. A.	SRIAS	-
Feustel-Büechl, Jörg	ESA	-
Field, Stan	BAe Brough	Technical Director
Finch, Peter	BAe Stevenage	Business Development Director
Forman, N. R.	Hunting Engineering	-
Friston, David	BAe Stevenage	-
Fry, Charles	Johnson Fry	Investment Entrepreneur
Furniss, Steve	BAe Warton Core Team	Performance Lead
Gaidar, Yegor	Russian Government	Vice-Premier
Gardner, Dave	BAe Warton	Technical Director, Military Aircraft (succeeding Brian Young)
Gaubatz, Bill	McDonnell Douglas	-
Gavaghan, Helen	*New Scientist*	Journalist
Gavrilov, Valery R.	Ministry of Aviation Industry	-
George, Keith	BAe Warton	Alternative Launch Vehicle (ALV) Design
George, Peter	RR Patchway	Propulsion Designer
Gibson, Roy	BNSC	Director
Gilkes, Steve	BAe Warton Core Team	Performance Engineer
Gofin, Mikhail	NPO Molniya	Commercial Director
Gorbachev, Mikhail	Soviet Government	President
Gould, Bryan	House of Commons	MP for Dagenham and Shadow Secretary of State for Trade and Industry
Gould, Derek	RAE Farnborough	Space Department
Grage, Heinrick	ESA	Council Chairman
Graham, Dr William R.	US Government	Science Advisor to President Reagan
Grallert, Herbert	MBB Ottobrunn	MBB Lead on Winged Launcher Configuration Study for ESA
Greeley, Brendan M. Jr.	*Aviation Week & Space Technology* magazine	Journalist
Green, Les	BAe Warton	Wind Tunnel Section Leader

Name	Affiliation	Role and Notes
Green, Willard J.	Aerojet TechSystems	Engineer
Greenhalgh, Mark	BAe Warton Core Team	Structures & Materials
Grimwade, John	*The Times*	Artist
Gulcher, Robert	Rockwell International	-
Hadlington, Simon	*Nature* journal	Journalist
Hall, Dr Ian	BAe HQ	Corporate Technical Director
Hannigan, Russell J.	-	Author and Consultant
Hargreaves, Kevin	BAe Warton Core Team	Structures & Materials
Hayter, K.	AP Precision Hydraulics	Technical and Sales Director
Heath, Ted	UK Government	Prime Minister
Helas, Dave	BAe Stevenage	Business Manager
Hempsell, Mark	BAe Stevenage	Engineer and later Reaction Engines Director
Heseltine, Michael	UK Government	MP for Henley and Secretary of State for Defence
Hewitt, Tony	RR Patchway	RR Propulsion Performance Lead
Hicks, Alan	BNSC	-
Hillier, Hugh	RR Patchway	RR Technical Director
Hindley, Keith	*The Times*	Journalist
Hodges, Geoff	RR Patchway	RR Propulsion Performance
Hodgkins, R. M.	BAe	Wind Tunnell Specialist
Högenauer, Dr Ernst	MBB Munich Space Group	Vice President
Hogg, Douglas	UK Government	MP for Grantham and Minister of State for Trade and Industry
Holmes, Diane	-	Archaeologist and Egyptologist
Holt, John	BAe Stevenage	Managing Director
Hopmann, Helmut	MBB	Propulsion Specialist
Hopwell, Brian	BAe Warton Core Team	Design Lead
Howe, Geoffrey	UK Government	MP for East Surrey and Foreign Secretary
Humby, John	BAe Stevenage	Public Relations Manager
Hunter, Max	-	Aerospace Engineer
Ince, Martin	*The Engineer* magazine	Journalist
Ingamells, Mike	BAe Warton	Alternative Launch Vehicle (ALV) Engineering
Inskip, Robin	BAC	Deputy Managing Director ca. 1966
Ivanov, V. T.	Soviet Ministry of Aviation Industry	Deputy Minister
Jack, Michael	House of Commons	MP for South Fylde
Jackson, N.	BAe Brough	Chief Designer
Jenkins, James	Boeing	-
Johnson, M.	RR	-
Kaspers, G. M.	BNSC	-
Kemble, Steve	BAe Stevenage	Launch Trajectory Specialist
Keyworth, George 'Jay'	US Government	Science Advisor to President Reagan
Kleinau, Wolfgang	MBB	-
Koelle, Dietrich E.	MBB Ottobrunn	Sänger Project Leader
Kohl, Helmut	German Government	Chancellor
Korol, Radomir S.	Soviet Ministry of Aviation Industry	General Department Chief

Name	Affiliation	Role and Notes
Kuchma, Leonid	Ukrainian Government	Prime Minister
Kuczera, Heribert	MBB	Hypersonic Technology Programme Manager
Langmead, Reg	BAe Warton Core Team	Structures & Materials
Lazarev, Valerii Vladimirovich	TsAGI	-
Leeming, Jack	BNSC	Director
Leigh, Edward	UK Government	MP for Gainsborough
Lester, Don	BAe Stevenage	Spacecraft Systems
Lewis, Gordon	RR	Technical Director
Lewis, Tom	US Congress	Florida Representative
Leyman, Clive	BAe Filton	Chief Aerodynamicist and Hotol Vehicle Designer
Liebherr	-	-
Liddell, Peter	BAe Warton	Head of Advanced Projects
Lion, Jacques Louis	CNES	President
Lo, Hsu	-	-
Lock, Stan	BAe Filton	Design Lead for Propulsion System & Intake Installation
Longstaff, Roger	BAe Stevenage	Space Operations and Vehicle Systems Lead, Stevenage
Lowrie, Brian	RR Patchway	Project Lead
Lüst, Reimar	ESA	Director General
Lygo, Sir Raymond	BAe HQ	Corporate Chief Executive
Mahir, Abdul H.	BAe	Liaison Consultant
Major, John	UK Government	Prime Minister
Mans, Keith	House of Commons	MP for Wyre
Mansell, Mick	BAe Warton	Director of Advanced Technology
Marshall, Michael	House of Commons	MP for Arundel
Martre, Henri	Aérospatiale	President and Director General
Martin, Charles	BAe Stevenage	Assistant Chief Engineer
Maxwell, Robert	Maxwell Communications Corporation	Businessman (and Fraudster)
McNally, Richard	BAe Warton	Chief Cost Estimator for New Projects
Mennicken, Jan-Baldem	BMFT	Director General for Aerospace and Transportation Technology
Metcalfe, Hugh	BAe HQ	Deputy Chief Executive (Operations)
Mews, Humphrey	Clarence House	Deputy Private Secretary to the Prince of Wales
Miles, Frank	Independent Television News	Science Correspondent
Miller, Brian A.	Martin-Baker Aircraft	Head of Marketing
Miller, Compton	*Daily Express*	Journalist
Miller, Stewart	RR	Director of Corporate Engineering
Mitterrand, Francois	French Government	President
Moncrieff, Chris	*Western Daily Press*	Journalist
Morris, A. T. J.	RR	Engineer
Moss, Barrie	CIT	-
Mowbray, Dr	RAE Farnborough	Specialist
Mugnier, Daniel	CNES	Director
Mudford, Dr Neil	Australian National University	-
Murray, Paul	BAe Warton	Advanced Projects Engineer

Name	Affiliation	Role and Notes
Natenbruk, Dr Peter	ERNO	-
Neiland, Vladimir Yakovlevich	TsAGI	Deputy Director
Newton, Tony	UK Government	MP for Braintree and Chancellor of the Duchy of Lancaster
Nicholas, Cliff	BNSC	Head of Space Department
Nicholson, Sir Robin	UK Civil Service	Chief Scientific Advisor
Ogorodnikov, D.	CIAM	Director
Ohlsen, Ulf	Volvo	-
Paillon, Michael	Commission of the European Communities	Head of the Space Unit
Parkin, Mike	BAe Warton Core Team	Deputy Project Manager, Programme & Costs Lead
Parkinson, Colin	BAe Filton	Structures & Stress Lead for Propulsion System & Intake Installation
Parkinson, Dr Bob	BAe Stevenage	Hotol Originator, Stevenage & Space Operations Lead
Parry, Dave	BAe Warton	Divisional Projects Director
Pattie, Geoffrey	UK Government	MP for Chertsey and Walton and Minister of State, Industry and Information Technology
Pavlovets, G.	CAGI	-
Pfeffer, Heinz	ESA Paris	ESA Lead for Future Launcher Concepts
Phillips, K.	UK Government	Private Secretary to Douglas Hogg MP
Pickett, Ray	BAe Warton Core Team	Weights Dept Engineer
Platt, John	BAe Warton	Head of the Advanced Studies Group
Poggi, Jean-Charles	Aérospatiale	Space and Ballistics Division Chief
Poll, Dr/Prof Ian	CIT then Manchester University	Re-entry Heating Consultant
Pope, Geoffrey	RAE Farnborough	Director
Pryor, Arthur	BNSC	Director
Quistgaard, Eric	ESA	Former Director General
Reagan, Ronald	US Government	40th US President
Reeh, Derek	BAe Warton	Hotol Project Pilot, Flight Operations
Rees, Peter	UK Civil Service	Treasury Chief Secretary
Reynolds, Dr Jim	BAe Filton (S&C)	Lead for Trolley Studies
Richmond, Lowell	Boeing	Aeronautical Engineer
Riedl, Erich	German Government	Secretary of State to the Federal Ministry for Economic Affairs and Energy
Riesenhuber, Heinz	German Government	Research and Technology Minister
Rippon, Lord Geoffrey	House of Lords	-
Robins, Ralph	RR	Chief Executive Officer
Robinson, L. J.	UK Civil Service	DTI Space Department Deputy Director
Roe, Frank	BAe Warton	Managing Director
Rona, Dr Tom	US Government	Science Advisor
Ross, C. R.	-	Sales, Marketing and PR Consultant
Ross, Ernie	House of Commons	MP for Dundee West
Rudakov, A. S.	NPO Molniya	-
Ruppe, Harry	Munich Technical University	Professor of Rocket Technology
Sacher, Peter	MBB	Aerospace Engineer

Name	Affiliation	Role and Notes
Saddam Hussein	Iraqi Government	Dictator
Salt, Dave.	BAe Stevenage	System Safety and Operations
Sänger, Eugen	-	Aerospace Engineer and Spaceplane Pioneer
Schaeffer, Johan	Dornier Flugzeugwerke	President
Schulster, Jonathan	BAe Stevenage	-
Scott, Alistair	BAe Stevenage	Space Sales
Scott-Scott, John	RR Anstey	Hotol Originator, RR Rocket Technology Lead
Seleznyov, I. S.	Raduga	-
Serdijk, Dr Ivan	Antonov Design Bureau	-
Seyfang, George	BAe Warton	Future Defence Systems Department Engineer
Shackleton, Lord Edward	House of Lords	-
Skeet, Sir Trevor	House of Commons	MP for North Bedfordshire
Skorodelov, Vladimir A.	NPO Molniya	-
Smith, Ian	CIT	-
Smith, Tom	BAe Warton	Head of Research (Aerodynamics) Department ca. 1964
Spies, Johann	ERNO	Aerospace Engineer
Stalker, Ray	University of Queensland	Professor of Mechanical Engineering
Statham, Geoff	BAe Stevenage	Propellant Supply and RCS Engineer
Stead, Arthur	BAe Warton Core Team	Vehicle Systems Lead
Swadling, Sid	BAe Filton	Technical Director, Commercial Aircraft
Swinerd, Dr Graham	BAe Stevenage	Orbital Dynamics Lead
Taig, Ian C.	BAe Warton	Divisional Research Manager
Tayler, Mike	BAe Filton (Space & Comms)	-
Tebbit, Norman	UK Government	MP for Chingford and Chancellor of the Duchy of Lancaster
Thatcher, Margaret	UK Government	Prime Minister
Thomson, John	Ministry of Defence	Director of Defence Concepts Staff
Thorne, Frank	*Daily Mirror*	Journalist
Tombs, Sir Francis	RR	Chairman
Toussaint, Marcel	Eurospace	-
Tranter	DTI	-
Turcat, André	Académie nationale de l'air et de l'espace	Academy Founder and Retired Test Pilot
Urussky, O.	Ukrainian National Space Agency	-
Vandenkerckhove, Jean	ESA	Assistant Technical Director and later Consultant
Varty, Phil	BAe Warton Core Team	Aerodynamics
Varvill, Richard	RR Patchway	RR Propulsion Designer
Villain, Michel	Aérospatiale	-
Von Braun, Wernher	NASA	Aerospace Engineer and Space Architect
Vovnyanko, Anatoly G.	Antonov Design Bureau	-
Wade	RAE Farnborough	Specialist
Wake, Alison	BAe Warton Core Team	Aerodynamics Lead
Waine, B. R.	BAe Brough	-
Waldman, Barry J.	Rockwell International	Corporate Vice President
Walgate, Robert	*Nature* journal	Journalist

Name	Affiliation	Role and Notes
Walley, Dave	BAe Warton	Alternative Launch Vehicle (ALV) Team Leader
Wallis, Barnes	Vickers Armstrongs	Engineer and Inventor
Walmsley, Sid	BAe Warton Core Team	Structures & Materials Lead
Walters, Ian	BAe Stevenage	-
Warrington, R.	BAe	Engineer
Warwick, Graham	*Flight International* magazine	Journalist
Way, David	NGTE Pyestock	National Gas Turbine Establishment
Webb, Eric	BAe Warton	Advanced Projects Dept CAPS Architect
Weinberger, Caspar	US Government	Defense Secretary
Weinstock, Lord Arnold	General Electric Company	Industrialist
Whitaker, Russ	BAe Warton	Wind Tunnel Testing Specialist
Williams, John	*Evening Standard* newspaper	Journalist
Williams, Roy	DTI	-
Willmer, Tony	BAe Filton	Lead for Propulsion & Intake Installation Aerodynamics
Wilson, Gerald	BAe Warton Core Team	Deputy Technical Manager, Propulsion Lead
Wilson, Richard	-	-
Wood, David	BAe Warton Core Team	Performance
Wood, Timothy	House of Commons	MP for Stevenage
Wright, Howard T.	NASP Joint Program Office/ NASA	NASA Deputy Director for NASP
Wright, Pearce	*The Times* newspaper	Science Editor
Xuan, Xie Guang	-	-
Yates, Ivan	BAe HQ	Deputy Chief Executive
Yeltsin, Boris	Russian Government	President
Young, Brian	BAe Warton	Sometime Technical Director, Military Aircraft
Young, Lord David	House of Lords	-
Young, Steven	*The Telegraph* newspaper	Journalist
Zagaynov, German Ivanovich	TsAGI	Director
Zinn, A. D.	Rockwell International	-

BIBLIOGRAPHY

BOOKS

Carbonel, J-C; French Secret Projects 3: French and European Spaceplane Designs 1964-1994, Crécy Publishing, 2021.
Hallion, Richard P.; The Hypersonic Revolution Volume II, Aeronautical Systems Center, 1995.
Hannigan, Russell J.; Spaceflight in the Era of Aero-Space Planes, Krieger Publishing Company, 1994.
Heppenheimer, T. A.; Facing the Heat Barrier: A History of Hypersonics, NASA History Division, 2007.
Koelle, Dietrich E.; Sacher, Peter; Grallert, Herbert; Deutsche Raketen-flugzeuge und Raumtransporter-Projekte, Bernard & Graefe, 2007.
Kuczera, H. and Sacher, P. W.; Reusable Space Transportation Systems, Springer Praxis Books, 2011.
Sharp, Dan; British Secret Projects 5: Britain's Space Shuttle, Crécy Publishing, 2016
Van den Abeelen, Luc; Spaceplane Hermes: Europe's Dream of Independent Manned Spaceflight, Springer-Praxis, 2017.

MISCELLANEOUS SOURCES

Anon; Skylon Assessment Report, ESA, 2011.
Anon; LART Zusammenfassung, May 1987.
Anon; Space Transportation of the Future, Spaceflight magazine, Vol. 23, October 8, 1981.
Anon; Sänger II The Two-Stage Space Transport System, MBB, 1986.
Barthelemy, Robert R.; The National Aerospace Plane Program: A Revolutionary Concept, John Hopkins APL Technical Digest, Volume 11, Numbers 3 and 4, 1990.
Bond, A.; An Update on SKYLON, 10th Appleton Space Conference, 2014.
Buffo, M.; Technical Comparison of Seven Nations' Space Plane Programs, AIAA Space Programs and Technologies Conference, 1990.
Burns, B. R. A.; HOTOL... Some Questions Answered, Intercom magazine, April 1986.
Burns, B. R. A.; The Design Challenge of Hotol, Aero Tech 87, Birmingham, October 27-30, 1987.
Burns, B. R. A.; HOTOL: An Advanced European Space Transporter, Aerospace Vehicle Conference, Washington, DC, 1987.
Burns, B. R. A.; HOTOL: Space Transport for the 21st Century, Aerotech 1989.
Conchie, P. J.; The Hotol Space Transportation System, AIAA 11th Communication Satellite Systems Conference, 1986.
Conchie, P. J.; Hotol—A Future Launcher for Europe, AIAA First National Aero-Space Plane Conference, 1989.
Coppinger, Rob; Secret Files Reveal US Interest in UK HOTOL Spaceplane, Fight International, February 23, 2009.
Cox, Nicholas P. G.; Ideas and Action... The Emergence of the Hotol Project, Master of Philosophy thesis for the University of Oxford (unpublished), 1989.
Czysz, P. and Little, M.; Rocket Based Combined Cycle Engine (RBCC)—A Propulsion System for the 21st Century, AIAA/DGLR Fifth International Aerospace Planes and Hypersonics Technologies Conference, 1993.
Dorrington, G. E.; Optimum Directions for Air-Breathing Launch Vehicle Design, AIAA, 1987.
Dorrington, G. E.; Comparisons of Rocket and Air-Breathing Vehicle Concepts for Earth-to-Orbit Transportation, AIAA 26th Joint Propulsion Conference, 1990.
Dujarric, C.; Possible Future European Launchers—A Process of Convergence, Third European Symposium on Aerothermodynamics for Space Vehicles, ESTEC, 1998.
Hannigan, R. and Sved, J.; True Space Transportation: The Key to a New Era in Space Operations, AIAA Fourth International Aerospace Planes Conference, 1992.
Harriott, Maj. Arthur V.; Space Activities of Western Europe, USAF, April 1986.
Hempsell, M.; HOTOL's Secret Engines Revealed, Spaceflight magazine, pp.168-172, May 1993.
Hempsell, M. and Longstaff, R.; SKYLON User Manual Revision 1, Reaction Engines, 2009.

Hempsell, M. and Longstaff, R.; SKYLON User Manual Revision 1.1, Reaction Engines, 2010.

Hempsell, M. et al.; Progress on the SKYLON and SABRE Development Programme, 62nd International Astronautical Congress, 2011.

Hempsell, M. and Longstaff, R.; SKYLON User Manual Revision 2, Reaction Engines, 2014.

Högenauer, Ernst; A Space Transport for the Year 2000, EIR Science & Technology, Vol. 14, Number 8, February 20, 1987.

Kikukawa, H.; Weight Reduction Technology for Space Plane Structures, AIAA Third International Aerospace Planes Conference, 1991.

Koelle, Dietrich E. and Kuczera, H.; Sänger—An Advanced Launcher System for Europe, 38th Congress of the International Astronautical Federation, 1987.

Koelle, Dietrich E. and Kuczera, H.; Sänger—Space Transportation System—Status Report 1988, 39th Congress of the International Astronautical Federation, 1988.

Koelle, Dietrich E.; Sänger II, A Hypersonic Flight and Space Transportation System, AIAA, 1988.

Koelle, Dietrich E. and Kuczera, H.; Sänger—Space Transportation System, 40th Congress of the International Astronautical Federation, 1989.

Koelle, Dietrich E. and Kuczera, H.; Sänger—Space Transportation System—Progress Report 1990, 41st Congress of the International Astronautical Federation, 1990.

Koelle, Dietrich; Options for a Next Generation European Launch System, AIAA Space Programs and Technologies Conference and Exhibit, 1993.

Kuczera, H. and Hauck, H.; The German Hypersonics Technology Programme—Status Report 1992, AIAA Fourth International Aerospace Planes Conference, 1992.

Lanshin, A.; Analysis of Some SSTO Aerospace Plane Propulsion Effectiveness, AIAA/DGLR Fifth International Aerospace Planes and Hypersonics Technologies Conference, 1993.

Lean, Thomas; An Oral History of British Science—Dr Bob Parkinson, National Life Stories, British Library, 2010/11.

Lean, Thomas; An Oral History of British Science—John Scott-Scott, National Life Stories, British Library, 2010/11.

Leeming, Jack; HOTOL—The Political Issues, Space Chronicle: JBIS, Vol. 59, Suppl. 2, pp/122-124, 2006.

Lenorovitz, J. M.; New Hotol Version Emerges Following British/Soviet Study, Aviation Week & Space Technology, September 9, 1991.

Longstaff, Roger and Bond, Alan; The SKYLON Project, 17th AIAA International Space Planes and Hypersonic Systems and Technologies Conference, 2011.

Longstaff, Roger; From HOTOL to SKYLON British Spaceplane Programmes: Past, Present and Future, 18th AIAA International Space Planes and Hypersonic Systems and Technologies Conference, 2012.

Lozino-Lozinsky, G. and Skorodelov, V.; International Reusable Aerospace System MAKS Present State of the Art and Perspectives, AIAA/DGLR Fifth International Aerospace Planes and Hypersonics Technologies Conference, 1993.

Lygo, Sir Raymond; Picking Winners to Safeguard Competitiveness in Manufacturing, IMechE, Proc Instn Mech Engrs Vol. 201, No B2, 1989.

Marshall, J.B. and Statham, G.; Design and Operational Analysis of the HOTOL Auxiliary Propulsion Subsystems, AIAA, 1991.

Millard, Douglas; An Overview of United Kingdom Space Activity 1957-1987, ESA HSR-36, 2005.

Montpellier, Matthew Godwin; Oral History of Europe in Space—Interview with Roy Gibson, ESA, 2007.

Parkinson, R. C. and Neiland, V. Ya.; The An-225/Interim Hotol Launch Vehicle, 42nd International Astronautical Congress, 1991.

Parkinson, R. C.; The An-225/Interim Hotol Launch Vehicle, AIAA Third International Aerospace Planes Conference, 1991.

Parkinson, R. C. and Longstaff, R.; The United Kingdom Perspective on the Applications of Aerospace Planes in the 21st Century, AIAA Third International Aerospace Planes Conference, 1991.

Parkinson, R. C.; Project 'Interim Hotol' Update, Space Technology International, pp.127-128, 1992.

Parkinson, R. C. and Webb, E.; The Status of Aerospaceplane Research in the UK, AIAA Fourth International Aerospace Planes Conference, 1992.

Parkinson, R. C. and Webb, E.; An-225/HOTOL, AIAA/DGLR Fifth International Aerospace Planes and Hypersonics Technologies Conference, 1993.

Parkinson, R. C., Skorodelov, V. A., Serdijk, I. I. and Neiland, V. Ya.; RADEM—An Air Launched, Rocket Demonstrator for Future Advanced Launch Systems, 45th International Astronautical Congress, 1994.

Parkinson, R. C.; Cost Sensitivity as a Selection Issue for Future Economic Space Transportation Systems, 45th International Astronautical Congress, 1994.

Parkinson, R. C.; Interim Hotol—Air Launch to Orbit, Space Chronicle: JBIS, Vol. 59, Suppl. 2, pp.125-132, 2006.

Rowley, J. D.; HOTOL Command & Control Systems, Aerospace Vehicle Conference, Annapolis, Maryland, 1988.

Scott, Alistair; Peter Conchie OBE, FRAeS (1928-2015), Spaceflight, Vol. 57, November 2015.

Speer, Maj. T. E. and Hoyt, Capt. A. R.; European Hypersonic Technology 1988-1993; European Office of Aerospace Research and Development, London, 1993.

Townend, L. H., Pike, J., Nonweiler, T. R. F. and Parker, E. Ann; Forebody Design for the Aerospaceplane, AIAA 26th Joint Propulsion Conference, 1990.

Trevino, Cdr. Robert C., European Space Developments and Programs at the 29th Farnborough International Aerospace Exhibition, Office of Naval Research European Office, February 1991.

Various; National Aero-Space Plane Team Selects Design, Aviation Week & Space Technology, October 29, 1990.

Various; Space Chronicle: UK Spaceplanes, JBIS, Vo. 59, Suppl. 2, 2006.

Varvill, R. and Bond, A.; Skylon: A Key Element of a Future Space Transportation System, Spaceflight magazine, pp.162-166, May 1993.

Varvill, R. and Bond, A.; The Skylon Spaceplane, 46th International Astronautical Congress, October 2-6, 1995.

Varvill, R. and Bond, A.; A Comparison of Propulsion Concepts for SSTO Reusable Launchers, JBIS, Vol. 56, pp.108-117, 2003.

Varvill, R. and Bond, A.; The SKYLON Spaceplane, JBIS, Vol. 57, pp.22-32, 2004.

Varvill, R. and Bond, A.; The SKYLON Spaceplane—Progress to Realisation, JBIS, Vol. 61, pp.412-418, 2008.

Wake, A. J.; Aerothermodynamics—The Required Tools, Aerospace Vehicle Conference, Annapolis, Maryland, 1988.

Webb, E. and Cundy, D.; The Effect of Launch Conditions on the Design of Winged Re-Usable Rockets, AIAA/DGLR Fifth International Aerospace Planes and Hypersonics Technologies Conference, 1993.

Webber, H., Bond, A. and Hempsell, M.; The Sensitivity of Precooled Air-Breathing Engine Performance to Heat Exchanger Design Parameters, JBIS 60.5, 2007.

Wilson, Gerald; HOTOL: Aerospaceplane for Europe, Space Technology Vol. 9, No. 3, pp221-232, 1989.

Wilson, Gerald; HOTOL the Reality: Birth & Death of the Project, BIS UK Spaceplanes Symposium, RAF Museum, Cosford, September 17-18, 2005.

Yamanaka, T.; 'Spaceplanes' R&D Status of Japan, AIAA Third International Aerospace Planes Conference, 1991.

Yates, I.; Innovation and Investment for Survival and Prosperity: The New Battle of Britain, AIAA/AHS/ASEE Aircraft Design, Systems and Operations Conference, 1990.

Young, S.; Soviet Cooperation Gives Hotol a New Lease of Life, Spaceflight magazine, pp.326-327, October 1990.

All other sources—particularly company reports—are referenced within the text and are deliberately not included here.

INDEX